# UNIX® System Administration Handbook

## THIRD EDITION

Evi Nemeth
Garth Snyder
Scott Seebass
Trent R. Hein

*with*
*Adam Boggs, Rob Braun, Dan Crawl,*
*Ned McClain, Lynda McGinley,*
*and Todd Miller*

**Prentice Hall PTR**
Upper Saddle River, NJ 07458
www.phptr.com

ISBN 0-13-020601-6

90000

9 780130 206015

Editorial/production supervisor: *Patti Guerrieri*
Acquisitions editor: *Mary Franz*
Marketing manager: *Bryan Gambrel*
Manufacturing manager: *Maura Zaldivar*
Editorial assistant: *Noreen Regina*
Cover design director: *Jerry Votta*
Cover designers: *Garth Snyder and Tyler Curtain*

Prentice Hall books are widely used by corporations and government agencies for training,
marketing, and resale. Volume discounts are available. For more information, contact the corporate sales department:

Prentice Hall PTR                  Phone:  (800) 382-3419
Corporate sales department         Fax:    (201) 236-7141
One Lake Street                    Email:  corpsales@prenhall.com
Upper Saddle River, NJ 07458

The names of all products and services mentioned in this book are the trademarks or service
marks of their respective companies or organizations.

Printed in the United States of America
10 9 8 7 6 5 4 3 2 1

**ISBN 0-13-020601-6**

Prentice-Hall International (UK) Limited, *London*
Prentice-Hall of Australia Pty. Limited, *Sydney*
Prentice-Hall Canada Inc., *Toronto*
Prentice-Hall Hispanoamericana, S.A., *Mexico*
Prentice-Hall of India Private Limited, *New Delhi*
Prentice-Hall of Japan, Inc., *Tokyo*
Pearson Education Asia Pte. Ltd.
Editora Prentice-Hall do Brasil, Ltda., *Rio de Janeiro*

We dedicate this edition
of *UNIX System Administration Handbook*
to the memory of three giants in the UNIX and Internet worlds:
John Lions, Jon Postel, and Rich Stevens.

**John Lions**, a professor at the University of New South Wales, wrote a wonderful commentary on the UNIX source code in the mid-1970s. It explained the 10,000 lines of code that made up UNIX in those days; John's book was used in operating systems classes around the world. A copyright dispute forced the book out of print, but it circulated among students for years in the form of photocopies of photocopies. Ours is hardly readable. John died in December, 1998.

❧

**Jon Postel** was the editor of the RFC series (as well as the author of many RFCs), the benevolent dictator of Internet names and numbers, and the technical conscience of the Internet. For years he led the way as the Internet was transformed from a playground of geeks and university students to perhaps the most significant social and economic force since the industrial revolution. Jon died in October, 1998. (www.postel.org)

❧

**Rich Stevens** is well known in academia for his wonderful books on networking and UNIX programming. Students love these books because Rich's examples always show exactly how to do something or just how to find out what the network protocols are really doing. Rich's generous contributions to the Internet community often took the form of answers to TCP questions raised on network-related mailing lists. It's hard to imagine a more accessible or more authoritative source; the second volume of Rich's *TCP/IP Illustrated* series was effectively the definition of TCP. Rich died in September, 1999. (www.kohala.com)

# Table of Contents

i

**CHAPTER 2    BOOTING AND SHUTTING DOWN**                                    **12**

## CHAPTER 3  ROOTLY POWERS                                                                    37

## CHAPTER 4  CONTROLLING PROCESSES                                                      45

## CHAPTER 5  THE FILESYSTEM                                                                   60

## CHAPTER 9   PERIODIC PROCESSES        157

## CHAPTER 10   BACKUPS        164

**CHAPTER 11  SYSLOG AND LOG FILES**

**CHAPTER 12   DRIVERS AND THE KERNEL**                                                **224**

## NETWORKING

## CHAPTER 13  TCP/IP NETWORKING                                                          261

## CHAPTER 14    ROUTING                                                                            342

## BUNCH O' STUFF

# *Foreword*

I am pleased to welcome Linux to the UNIX System Administration Handbook! The previous edition of this book described six variants of UNIX, all of which were proprietary. Reflecting real-world use, this edition covers only four systems, of which two (half!) are free. The UNIX scene has changed a lot in just five years.

Systems like Linux and FreeBSD have established beyond doubt the credibility of the open source model. These systems are as stable and full-featured as their commercial counterparts; better yet, their developer communities move quickly to fix bugs and to add support for popular features. How many traditional vendors can say that?

As this book shows, system administrators have often been ill-served by the traditional development model. Vendors do what they want (often for reasons that are less than clear), and admins adapt. They have to, since the software is designed as one large, integrated system. Touch one component, and several others break.

As we gain experience with the process of assembling complete systems from many separate components, this situation will improve. There's really no reason why an administrator shouldn't choose, say, an authentication system in the same way that a secretary chooses a word processor. Experience shows that the opportunity for comparison and choice is all that's needed for good software to triumph over bad.

Looking through this new edition of the Handbook, it's clear that we still have a way to go towards making UNIX administration graceful, easy, and pure. If the last decade is any indication, however, we will see rapid progress in the years ahead. In the meantime, enjoy this book. To infinity and beyond!

Linus Torvalds
June, 2000

# Foreword to the Second Edition

There are a lot of books about system administration out there. Why is this one special? We can think of two reasons.

First, it's good. The authors do real system administration on real systems with a lot of users, a lot of networking, and a lot of special connectivity. They've been at it long enough that they can still recall what a Unibus adaptor was and what was wrong with the DZ11 (no interrupts). They've lived in a "dirty" world with lots of different systems from lots of different vendors and lots of different versions of the operating system. They've been bitten by alligators of every type and persuasion. This is not a nice, neat book written for a nice, clean world. It's a nasty book written for a nasty world.

Second, it's comprehensive. There are a lot of good books about specific UNIX® topics (we know of a great book on **sendmail**, for example), but few books on the general problem of system administration that are worth their weight in dead trees.[1] The initial draft of the first edition of this book was called *UNIX System Administration Made Difficult*, which seemed appropriate: the "… Made Simple" style of books always seemed to gloss over so many details that they actually made the job harder.

The fact is that system administration is difficult. UNIX systems are tremendously powerful, and with power comes some measure of complexity. PCs get complicated, too, when you start connecting them to networks, modems, printers, and third-party disks, and when you realize that you need to worry about topics such as backups and security. Suddenly, managing a PC starts to look a lot like administering a UNIX box: "It's easy! Just click here, then you have to turn off the printer to use the network (select here, pull down this menu, and click on "Disable" and "Apply"), then pull down this menu, then select the selector, type in your hostname here, then click here,

---

1. UNIX is a registered trademark of The Open Group in the United States and other countries.

here, and double-click here (dismiss that dialog box, it always gives that, I don't know why…), then pop up here, select that menu, enable the network, then go over there to start up the TCP/IP application, then—Whoops! We forgot to set the network mask; no problem, just go back to the third menu selection and change the mask— Drat, that disabled the network, just fix that (click, drag, click)… Great, now start up the TCP/IP application again (click), and now you can use **telnet**! See, easy!"

By contrast, UNIX boxes have the network installed by default. It is set up once, and most users never see how the configuration is done. Unfortunately, system administrators are not "most users" and so we get to go through the messy process of setting it up.

The authors also have something to offer for those rare, calm moments when you have the chance to reflect on how to improve your environment to make your life a bit easier. For example, this book will help you tune your network to maximize throughput, minimize delay, and avoid single points of failure. It will also give you hints on how to let the good guys in while keeping the bad guys out.

Some people do have isolated UNIX boxes without networks, printers, modems, or maybe even third-party disk drives. If you are one of these rare birds, or you feel that your vendor's point-and-click graphical interface fills all your needs (and you aren't curious about what goes on behind the curtain), you may not need this book. It goes into detail about obscure things you may never need to know.

However, such simple environments make up a tiny and dwindling fraction of the real world. This is a book for the rest of us.


Eric Allman
Marshall Kirk McKusick
August, 1994

# *Foreword to the First Edition*

The administration of UNIX systems has always been a somewhat neglected subject. I think this happened for several reasons, all connected to various aspects of its unusual history.

First, the creation and early spread of the system took place among devotees, people who soon became knowledgeable of its nooks and crannies. These groups were often irritated by the formalities and procedures common in the big computer centers that were the chief computational resources during the 1970s, and they were ingenious in developing their own wizardly administrative recipes instead of relying on cookbooks.

Second, a typical UNIX system inhabits a computing niche unusual until recently. Most commonly, such systems are either medium-size machines serving a single department in a company or university, or workstations used by a single person but connected by a network to many other systems. For the most part—though there are now exceptions—UNIX systems are not big machines with professional, on-site staff from the manufacturer or a big computer center, nor personal computers owned by isolated individuals.

For a large machine, it is expected that professionals will provide the support. For the personal computer, the manufacturer is expected to write the administrative cookbook for the limited range of uses to which the machine will be put. The purchasers of a midrange machine may find themselves suddenly nominated to be the staff; this can make them feel nearly as much on their own as if they had bought a personal computer, but they must face the complexities of keeping an eye on multiple users, dealing with one or more networks, and handling all the other daunting conundrums that turn up.

Finally, UNIX systems come from a variety of sources. Although there is a common core of useful administrative tools and procedures, not all suppliers provide a useful degree of support. Also, many sites import substantial amounts of software from university distributions, Usenet, or other places that provide the programs, but little else.

Despite the problems, many of the purveyors of UNIX systems do a good job of telling their customers how to run them. Nevertheless, a comprehensive book discussing administration is clearly needed. The manufacturer's theory of what you want to do is not necessarily your own, and the documentation may be scattered; your supplier may be more talented at building hardware than at generating useful manuals; or you may be using popular software that didn't come in the box.

Therefore, this book is most welcome.

Dennis Ritchie
October, 1988

# *Preface*

When we were writing the first edition of this book in the mid-1980s, we were eager to compare our manuscript with other books about UNIX system administration. To our delight, we could find only three. These days, you have your choice of at least fifty. Here are the features that distinguish our book:

- We take a practical approach. Our purpose is not to restate the contents of your manuals but rather to give you the benefit of our collective experience in system administration. This book contains numerous war stories and a wealth of pragmatic advice.

- We cover UNIX networking in detail. It is the most difficult aspect of UNIX system administration, and the area in which we think we can most likely be of help to you.

- We do not oversimplify the material. Our examples reflect true-life situations, with all their warts and unsightly complications. In most cases, the examples have been taken directly from production systems.

- We emphasize the use of software tools. Every piece of software mentioned in the text is either a standard UNIX tool or is freely available from the Internet—sometimes both, since many vendors don't do a perfect job of keeping up with new releases.

- We cover all the major variants of UNIX.

## OUR FOUR EXAMPLE SYSTEMS

There have historically been two main flavors of UNIX: one from AT&T (known generically as System V) and one from the University of California, Berkeley (known as BSD). Neither AT&T nor Berkeley is still active in the UNIX marketplace, but the terms "AT&T UNIX" and "Berkeley UNIX" live on.

This book covers four different operating systems:

- Solaris™ 2.7
- HP-UX® 11.00
- Red Hat® Linux 6.2
- FreeBSD® 3.4 (and bits of 4.0)

We chose these systems because they are among the most popular and because they illustrate a broad range of approaches to UNIX administration. The first two systems are similar to AT&T UNIX, FreeBSD is a direct descendant of Berkeley UNIX, and Red Hat Linux is something of a mix.

We provide detailed information about each of these example systems for every topic that we discuss. Comments specific to a particular operating system are marked with the manufacturer's logo.

There are many other versions of UNIX. Most fall within the range of variation defined by these four systems, but a few (such as AIX and SCO) are so beautifully strange that they must be taken on their own terms.

## THE ORGANIZATION OF THIS BOOK

This book is divided into three large chunks: Basic Administration, Networking, and Bunch o' Stuff.

Basic Administration provides a broad overview of UNIX from a system administrator's perspective. The chapters in this section cover most of the facts and techniques needed to run a stand-alone UNIX system.

The Networking section describes the protocols used on UNIX systems and the techniques used to set up, extend, and maintain networks. High-level network software is also covered here. Among the featured topics are the Domain Name System, the Network File System, routing, **sendmail**, and network management.

Bunch o' Stuff includes a variety of supplemental information. Some chapters discuss optional software packages such as the UNIX printing system (or more accurately, systems). Others give advice on topics ranging from hardware maintenance to the politics of running a UNIX installation.

## CONTACT INFORMATION

In this edition, we're pleased to welcome Adam Boggs, Rob Braun, Dan Crawl, Ned McClain, Lynda McGinley, and Todd Miller as contributing authors. We've turned to them for their deep knowledge in a variety of areas (and also for their ability to function amid the shifting sands of this book and its temperamental parents). Their contributions have greatly enriched the overall content of the book and the collective experience that we're able to share with you.

Please send suggestions, comments, typos, and bug reports to sa-book@admin.com. We answer all mail, but please be patient; it is sometimes a few days before one of us is able to respond. To get a copy of our current bug list and other late-breaking information, visit our web site at www.admin.com.

We hope you enjoy this book, and we wish you the best of luck with your adventures in system administration!


Evi Nemeth
Garth Snyder
Scott Seebass
Trent R. Hein


June, 2000

# *Acknowledgments*

Hundreds of readers have sent us bug fixes, comments, and criticisms on the first and second editions of this book. We would like to thank everyone who took the time to write us, and we hope that we've successfully incorporated the feedback we received.

System administration for UNIX has become more complex over the last eleven years, and the breadth of this text has grown proportionately. Many folks have helped with this edition in one way or another, assisting with everything from technical reviews to overall moral support. These people deserve special thanks for hanging in there with us and helping us get this edition out the door:

| | | |
|---|---|---|
| Eric Allman | Steve Gaede | Jeff Moe |
| Pete Barber | Andrew Gollan | Herb Morreale |
| Dave Barr | Bob Gray | Laszlo Nemeth |
| Dave Clements | Andreas Gustafsson | Tobi Oetiker |
| David Conrad | Geoff Halprin | Ray Plzak |
| Drew Eckhardt | Daniel Karrenberg | Andy Rudoff |
| Randy Else | Cricket Liu | Greg Shapiro |
| Bill Fenner | Bill Manning | Daniel Sully |
| Peggy Fenner | Lynda McGinley | Paul Vixie |
| Jeff Forys | Hal Miller | |

We give special thanks to Barb Dijker for all the extra effort she put into reviewing this edition, and to Pat Parseghian for her extra efforts on the second edition and her continued moral support on this edition.

Mary Franz, the editor of this edition, is deserving not only of special thanks but also an award for successfully dealing with temperamental authors. Mary was infinitely patient with us, even when we didn't deserve it, and she did everything possible to encourage our continued focus on quality in this edition.

Thanks also to the editor of the first edition, John Wait.

Many thanks go to Tyler Curtain, our copy editor for the first and second editions. Tyler also remained onboard as our staff cartoonist.

Mary Lou Nohr did an outstanding job as copy editor of this edition; we greatly appreciate her efforts and flexibility.

Danny Savard at Hewlett-Packard and Andy Rudoff at Sun Microsystems deserve a round of thanks for coercing their respective organizations into providing us with reference hardware.

Finally, the computer science department at the University of Colorado deserves many thanks for providing computing resources and numerous "test subjects."

# SECTION ONE

## BASIC ADMINISTRATION

# 1 Where to Start

We set out to write a book that could be a system administrator's trusty companion, providing the practical advice, comfort, and basic system administration theory that you can't get from reading manual pages. As a result, this book is designed to complement—not replace—your system's documentation.

We think this book will help you in five ways:

- It will give you an overview of the major administrative systems, identifying the different pieces of each and explaining how they work together.

- It will introduce general administrative techniques that we have found, through experience, to be worthwhile.

- It will help you choose solutions that continue to work well as your site grows in size and complexity.

- It will help you sort good ideas from bad and educate you about various atrocities of taste committed by operating system developers.

- It will summarize common procedures so that you don't have to dig through the excessive detail of the manuals to accomplish simple tasks.

It's impossible to perform these functions with perfect objectivity, but we think we've made our biases fairly clear throughout the text. One of the interesting things about system administration is the fact that reasonable people can have dramatically different notions of what constitute the most appropriate policies and procedures. We offer our subjective opinions to you as raw data. You'll have to decide for yourself how much to accept and to what extent our comments apply to your environment.

## 1.1 SUGGESTED BACKGROUND

We assume in this book that you have a certain amount of UNIX experience. In particular, you should have a general concept of how UNIX looks and feels from the user's perspective before jumping into administration. There are several good books that can get you up to speed; see the reading list on page 11.

You perform most administrative tasks by editing configuration files and writing scripts, so you must be familiar with a text editor. We strongly recommend that you learn **vi**. It is standard on all UNIX systems, and though it may appear a bit pale when compared with glitzier offerings such as **emacs**, it is perfectly usable. If you become addicted to another editor, you may soon tire of dragging it along with you to install on every new system. To the dismay of many, using Microsoft Word as one's only text editor is a significant impediment to effective system administration.

One of the mainstays of UNIX administration (and a theme that runs throughout this book) is the use of scripts to automate administrative tasks. To be an effective administrator, you must be able to read and modify **sh** scripts. Scripts that you write from scratch can be written in the shell or scripting language of your choice.

For new scripting projects, we recommend Perl. As a programming language, it is a little strange (OK, more than a little). However, it does include many features that are indispensable for administrators. The O'Reilly book *Programming Perl* by Larry Wall et al. is the standard text; it's also a model of good technical writing. A full citation is given on page 11.

We also recommend that you learn **expect**, which is discussed in a bit more detail starting on page 519. You will most likely pick up **expect** quite rapidly.

## 1.2 THE SORDID HISTORY OF UNIX

UNIX originated as a research project at AT&T Bell Labs in 1969. In 1976, it was made available at no charge to universities and thus became the basis of many operating systems classes and academic research projects.

In the late 1970s, AT&T created its UNIX Support Group (USG, later spun off as Unix System Laboratories, USL) to deploy UNIX as a commercial product. Bell Labs and USG both continued the development of UNIX, but the two groups' efforts diverged. USL's releases, System III and System V, were widely distributed and have had a proportionately greater impact on modern systems.

Berkeley UNIX began in 1977 when the Computer Systems Research Group (CSRG) at the University of California, Berkeley, licensed code from AT&T. Berkeley's releases (called BSD, for Berkeley Software Distribution) began in 1977 with 1BSD for the PDP-11 and culminated in 1993 with 4.4BSD.

Source licenses for AT&T releases were always expensive for nonacademic users. At first, the licenses were cheap or free for universities, but as UNIX gained commercial acceptance, the price rose rapidly. Eventually, Berkeley set the long-term goal of removing AT&T's code from BSD, a tedious and time-consuming process. Before the work could be completed, Berkeley lost funding for operating systems research and the CSRG was disbanded.

Before collapsing, the CSRG released its final collection of AT&T-free code, known as 4.4BSD-Lite. Most current versions of BSD UNIX (including BSD/OS, FreeBSD, NetBSD, and OpenBSD) claim the 4.4BSD-Lite package as their grandparent.

Although BSD and System V are the core systems from which most other versions of UNIX are derived, neither of these "pure" systems was ever much of a force in the commercial market. Typically, a vendor would start with a vanilla AT&T or BSD system and proceed to develop it independently. Some vendors didn't want to commit to one flavor of UNIX and supported both or developed hybrids that combined both sets of features. Not surprisingly, these UNIX variants tended to diverge from one another over time.

The most recent major development in the UNIX world has been the advent of the Linux kernel and the many UNIX systems that are now based upon it. Linux is a soup-to-nuts reimplementation of the UNIX kernel that was begun in 1991 as a personal project of Linus Torvalds, a Finnish graduate student. Over the years, the Linux project accumulated many developers, users, and enthusiasts. It has grown into a full-featured, production-quality kernel that many vendors support as their primary operating system. Many big-ticket commercial software packages (such as Oracle) have also been ported to Linux.

## 1.3  EXAMPLE UNIX SYSTEMS

In this book, we have chosen four popular UNIX variants as our examples: Solaris 2.7, HP-UX 11.00, Red Hat Linux 6.2, and FreeBSD 3.4. These systems are representative of the overall UNIX marketplace, and they're all so common that it's hard to find a UNIX site that doesn't use at least one of them.

Sun Microsystems' Solaris is a System V derivative with many extensions. Sun UNIX (yes, that's what it was called in the mid-80s) was originally the progeny of Berkeley UNIX, but a (now historic) corporate partnership between Sun and AT&T forced a change of platform.

HP's HP-UX is a hybrid of the System V and Berkeley UNIX trees, but with odd surprises of its own.

Several free UNIX systems are available for Intel hardware, and of these Linux is currently the most popular.[1] Linux itself is just a kernel; you must add on a full comple-

---

1. Linux has been ported to a variety of other hardware platforms, including the Nintendo64 video game system. Who says Nintendo doesn't make real computers?

ment of commands, utilities, and daemons to form a complete UNIX system. The various Linux "distributions" bundle the kernel with the other components needed for a full installation. Linux distributors make many choices while assembling their products, so versions of Linux can be quite different from one another. A few companies (including Red Hat, SuSE, and Corel) provide production-grade distributions with full support.

FreeBSD is a system based on Berkeley's 4.4BSD-Lite release. Like Linux, it runs on a variety of Intel platforms. A commercially supported version is available from BSDI.

## 1.4  NOTATION AND TYPOGRAPHICAL CONVENTIONS

In this book, filenames, commands, and literal arguments to commands are shown in boldface. Placeholders (e.g., command arguments that should not be taken literally) are in italics. For example, in the command

**cp** *file directory*

you're supposed to replace *file* and *directory* with the names of an actual file and an actual directory.

Excerpts from configuration files and terminal sessions are shown in a fixed-width font.[2] Sometimes, we annotate interactive sessions with italic text. For example:

```
% grep Bob /pub/phonelist        /* Look up Bob's phone # */
Bob Knowles 555-2834
Bob Smith 555-2311
```

Outside of these specific cases, we have tried to keep special fonts and formatting conventions to a minimum so long as we could do so without compromising intelligibility. For example, we often talk about entities such as the UNIX group daemon and the printer anchor-lw with no special formatting at all.

In general, we use the same conventions as the UNIX manual pages for indicating the syntax of commands:

- Anything between square brackets ("[" and "]") is optional.
- Anything followed by an ellipsis ("…") can be repeated.
- Curly braces ("{" and "}") indicate that you should select one of the items separated by vertical bars ("|").

For example, the specification

**bork** [**-x**] {**on**|**off**} *filename* …

would match any of the following commands:

```
bork on /etc/passwd
bork -x off /etc/passwd /etc/termcap
bork off /usr/lib/tmac
```

---

2. Actually, it's not really a fixed-width font, but it looks like one. We liked it better than the real fixed-width fonts that we tried. That's why the columns in some examples may not all line up perfectly.

We use shell-style globbing characters for pattern matching:

- A star (*) matches zero or more characters.
- A question mark (?) matches one character.
- A tilde or "twiddle" (~) means the home directory of the current user.
- ~*user* means the home directory of *user*.

For example, we sometimes refer to the BSD startup scripts **/etc/rc**, **/etc/rc.boot**, and **/etc/rc.local** with the shorthand pattern **/etc/rc\***.

Text within quotation marks often has a precise technical meaning. In these cases, we ignore the normal rules of English and put punctuation outside the quotation marks so that there can be no confusion about what's included and what's not.

### System-specific information

Information in this book generally applies to all four of our example systems unless a specific attribution is given. Details particular to one system are marked with the vendor's logo:

Solaris 2.7                    HP-UX 11.00

Red Hat Linux 6.2             FreeBSD 3.4

These logos are used with the permission of their respective owners. However, the vendors have neither reviewed nor endorsed the contents of this book.

## 1.5 HOW TO USE YOUR MANUALS

The UNIX manuals contain all the information needed to keep the system running, yet that information is sometimes hard to find and often cryptic. You *must* have access to a complete set of manuals for your version of UNIX. However, that does not necessarily mean that you need to buy printed books. Most documentation is available in electronic form, either as part of the system installation procedure or from the vendor's web site.

UNIX systems typically come with two types of documentation: "man pages" and supplemental documents. Man pages (so called because they are designed for use with the **man** command) are concise descriptions of individual commands, file formats, or library routines. They are usually kept on-line but may also be supplied in printed form.

Supplemental documents can include both individual articles and book or pamphlet-length treatments of particular topics. The supplemental materials are not limited to describing just one command, so they can adopt a tutorial or procedural approach. Many pieces of software have both a man page and an article. For example, the man page for **vi** tells you about the command-line arguments that **vi** understands, but you have to go to the supplement to learn how to actually edit a file.

Since the man pages are closely tied to the software they describe, vendors tend not to change them very much unless they modify the software itself.[3] Not so with the supplements—many vendors have entirely replaced the traditional manuals with new books and documents.

Many of the most important parts of UNIX are maintained by neutral third parties such as the Internet Software Consortium and the Apache Software Foundation. These groups typically provide adequate documentation for the packages they distribute. Vendors sometimes ship the software but skimp on the documentation, so it's often useful to check back with the original source to see if additional materials are available.

Another useful source of information about the design of many UNIX software packages is the "Request for Comments" document series, which describes the protocols and procedures used on the Internet. See page 263 for more information.

### Organization of the man pages

All UNIX systems divide the man pages into sections. However, the exact definition of each section varies among systems. The basic organization of the man pages is shown in Table 1.1.

**Table 1.1   Sections of the UNIX man pages**

| Solaris HP-UX | Linux FreeBSD | Contents |
| --- | --- | --- |
| 1 | 1 | User-level commands and applications |
| 2 | 2 | System calls and kernel error codes |
| 3 | 3 | Library calls |
| 4 | 5 | Standard file formats |
| 5 | 7 | Miscellaneous files and documents |
| 6 | 6 | Games and demonstrations |
| 7 | 4 | Device drivers and network protocols |
| 1m | 8 | System administration commands |
| 9 | 9 | Obscure kernel specs and interfaces |

Many systems further subdivide the man pages in each section. For example, section 3m often contains man pages about the system's math library. There is also considerable variation in the exact distribution of pages; some systems leave section 8 empty and lump the system administration commands into section 1. A lot of systems have discontinued games and demos, leaving nothing in section 6.

Most systems allow you to create a section of the manuals called "l" for local man pages. Another common convention is section "n" for software that isn't strictly local but isn't standard, either.

---

3. But this is not always the case. HP has done an excellent job of editing the man pages.

**troff** input for man pages is traditionally kept in the directories **/usr/man/man***X*, where *X* is a digit **1** through **9**, or **l** or **n**. Formatted versions of the manuals are kept in **/usr/man/cat***X*. The **man** command will format man pages on the fly; if the **cat** directories are writable, **man** will also deposit the formatted pages as they are created, generating a cache of commonly read man pages. You can preformat all man pages at once with the **catman** command if space permits. On some systems, such as FreeBSD, the man pages have been moved to **/usr/share/man**. Many systems compress their man pages with **compress** or **gzip** to save space.

 Solaris now uses SGML as the formatting language for most man pages instead of the traditional **troff**. Man pages in **troff** format are still supported, but they are kept in separate directories.

### man: read manual pages

**man** *title* formats a specific manual page and sends it to your terminal via **more** (or whatever program is specified in your PAGER environment variable). *title* is usually a command, device, or filename. The sections of the manual are searched in roughly numeric order, although sections that describe commands (sections 1, 8, and 6) are usually searched first.

The form **man** *section title* gets you a man page from a particular section. Thus, **man tty** gets you the man page for the **tty** command and **man 4 tty** gets you the man page for the serial driver.

 Under Solaris, you must preface the section number with the **-s** flag, for example, **man -s 4 tty**.

Almost all versions of **man** check to see if you have defined the MANPATH environment variable, which should contain a colon-separated list of directories if it exists. MANPATH overrides or extends the list of directories that **man** searches. For example, the command

```
setenv MANPATH /home/share/localman:/usr/share/man
```

in your **.login** file would cause **man** to search a hierarchy of local man pages before **/usr/man**. The **sh** version would be

```
MANPATH=/home/share/localman:/usr/share/man
export MANPATH
```

On some systems, MANPATH completely overrides the default search path, so you must explicitly include the default directory if you want to continue to see your vendor's man pages.

**man -k** *keyword* prints a list of man pages that have *keyword* in their one-line synopses. For example:

```
% man -k translate
gftype (1L)  - translate a font file for humans to read
pktype (1L)  - translate a packed font file
tr (1)       - translate characters
```

The keywords database is normally kept in a file called **whatis** in the root of the man page hierarchy (**/usr/man** or **/usr/share/man**). If you add additional man pages to your system, you may need to rebuild this file with **catman -w**.

## 1.6 ESSENTIAL TASKS OF THE SYSTEM ADMINISTRATOR

The sections below give an overview of some tasks that system administrators are typically expected to perform. These duties need not necessarily be performed by one person, and at many sites the work is distributed among several people. However, there does need to be at least one person who understands all of the chores and makes sure that someone is doing them.

### Adding and removing users

*See Chapter 6 for more information about adding new users.*

The system administrator adds accounts for new users and removes the accounts of users that are no longer active. The process of adding and removing users can be automated, but certain administrative decisions (where to put the user's home directory, on which machines to create the account, etc.) must still be made before a new user can be added.

When a user should no longer have access to the system, the user's account must be disabled. All of the files owned by the account must be backed up to tape and disposed of so that the system does not accumulate unwanted baggage over time.

### Adding and removing hardware

*See Chapters 8, 12, and 23 for more information about these topics.*

When new hardware is purchased or when hardware is moved from one machine to another, the system must be configured to recognize and use that hardware. Hardware-support chores can range from the simple task of adding a printer to the more complex job of adding a disk drive.

### Performing backups

*See Chapter 10 for more information about backups.*

Performing backups is perhaps the most important job of the system administrator, and it is also the job that is most often ignored or sloppily done. Backups are time-consuming and boring, but they are absolutely necessary. Backups can be automated and delegated to an underling, but it is still the system administrator's job to make sure that backups are executed correctly and on schedule.

### Installing new software

When new software is acquired, it must be installed and tested, often under several versions of UNIX and on several types of hardware. Once the software is working correctly, users must be informed of its availability and location. Local software should be installed in a place that makes it easy to differentiate from the system software. This organization simplifies the task of upgrading the operating system since the local software won't be overwritten by the upgrade procedure.

### Monitoring the system

Large UNIX installations require vigilant supervision. Daily activities include making sure that email and web service are working correctly, watching log files for early signs of trouble, ensuring that local networks are all properly connected, and keeping an eye on the availability of system resources such as disk space.

### Troubleshooting

UNIX systems and the hardware they run on occasionally break down. It is the administrator's job to play mechanic by diagnosing problems and calling in experts if needed. Finding the problem is often harder than fixing it.

### Maintaining local documentation

*See page 809 for suggestions regarding documentation.*

As the system is changed to suit an organization's needs, it begins to differ from the plain-vanilla system described by the documentation. It is the system administrator's duty to document aspects of the system that are specific to the local environment. This chore includes documenting any software that is installed but did not come with the operating system, documenting where cables are run and how they are constructed, keeping maintenance records for all hardware, recording the status of backups, and documenting local procedures and policies.

### Auditing security

*See Chapter 21 for more information about security.*

The system administrator must implement a security policy and periodically check to be sure that the security of the system has not been violated. On low-security systems, this chore might only involve only a few cursory checks for unauthorized access. On a high-security system, it can include an elaborate network of traps and auditing programs.

### Helping users

Although helping users with their various problems is rarely included in a system administrator's job description, it claims a significant portion of most administrators' workdays. System administrators are bombarded with problems ranging from "My program worked yesterday and now it doesn't! What did you change?" to "I spilled coffee on my keyboard! Should I pour water on it to wash it out?"

## 1.7  HOW TO FIND FILES ON THE INTERNET

A wealth of information about system administration is available, in many forms. A list of "starter" resources can be found in Chapter 27, *Policy and Politics*.

The Internet is by far the richest deposit of information. You can type questions about system administration topics into any of the popular search engines, such as www.yahoo.com, www.altavista.com, www.google.com, and www.webopedia.com.

Many sites cater directly to the needs of system administrators. Here are a few that we especially like:

- freshmeat.com – a huge collection of Linux software
- www.ugu.com – the Unix Guru Universe; lots of stuff for sysadmins
- www.stokely.com – a good collection of links to sysadmin resources
- www.tucows.com – Windows and Mac software, filtered for quality
- slashdot.org – "the place" for geek news
- www.cpan.org – a central source for Perl scripts and libraries
- securityfocus.com – security info; huge searchable vulnerability database

## 1.8  SYSTEM ADMINISTRATION UNDER DURESS

System administrators wear many hats. In the real world, they are often people with other jobs who have been asked to look after a few computers on the side. If you are in this situation, you may want to think a bit about where it might eventually lead.

The more you learn about UNIX, the more the user community will come to depend on you. Networks invariably grow, and you may be pressured to spend an increasing portion of your time on administration. You will soon find that you are the only person in your organization who knows how to perform a variety of important tasks.

Once coworkers come to think of you as the local system administrator, it is difficult to extricate yourself from this role. We know several people that have changed jobs to escape it. Since many administrative tasks are intangible, you may also find that you're expected to be both a full-time administrator and a full-time engineer, writer, or secretary.

Some unwilling administrators try to fend off requests by adopting an ornery attitude and providing poor service. We do not recommend this approach; it makes you look bad and creates additional problems.

Instead, we suggest that you document the time you spend on system administration. Your goal should be to keep the work at a manageable level and to assemble evidence that you can use when you ask to be relieved of administrative duties. In most organizations, you will need to lobby the management from six months to a year to get yourself replaced, so plan ahead.

On the other hand, you may find that you enjoy system administration and that you yearn to be a full-time administrator. You will have no problem finding a job. Unfortunately, your political problems will probably intensify. Refer to Chapter 27, *Policy and Politics*, for a preview of the horrors in store.

### System Administration Personality Syndrome

One unfortunate but common clinical condition resulting from working as a system administrator is System Administration Personality Syndrome. The onset of this condition usually begins early in the third year of a system administrator's career and the syndrome can last well into retirement. Characteristic symptoms include but are not limited to:

- Acute phantom pagerphobia: the disturbing feeling that your pager has gone off (when it really hasn't) and that your peaceful evening with your significant other is about to abruptly end, resulting in a 72-hour work marathon without food

- User voodoographia: the compulsive creation of voodoo-doll representations of the subset of your user population that doesn't seem to understand that their persistent lack of planning doesn't constitute an emergency in your world

- Idiopathic anal tapereadaplexia: the sudden, late-night urge to mount backup tapes to see if they're actually readable and labeled correctly

- Scientifica inapplicia: the strong desire to violently shake fellow system administrators who seem never to have encountered the scientific method

Many curative therapies can be used to treat this unfortunate condition. The most effective are a well-developed sense of humor and the construction of a small but well-endowed office wine cellar. You might also consider the more meditative approach of silently staring off into space and clicking your heels together whenever the words "Is the server down again?" are spoken in your vicinity. If all else fails, take a vacation.

## 1.9 RECOMMENDED READING

ANDERSON, GAIL, AND PAUL ANDERSON. *The UNIX C Shell Field Guide.* Englewood Cliffs, NJ: Prentice Hall. 1986.

HEWLETT-PACKARD COMPANY. *The Ultimate Guide to the VI and EX Text Editors.* Redwood City, CA: Benjamin/Cummings. 1990.

ABRAHAMS, PAUL W., AND BRUCE A. LARSON. *UNIX for the Impatient, 2nd Edition.* Reading, MA: Addison-Wesley. 1995.

PEEK, JERRY, TIM O'REILLY, AND MIKE LOUKIDES. *UNIX Power Tools, 2nd Edition.* Sebastopol, CA: O'Reilly & Associates. 1997.

MONTGOMERY, JOHN, AND WOODY LEONHARD. *The Underground Guide to Unix: Slightly Askew Advice from a Unix Guru.* Reading, MA: Addison-Wesley. 1995.

REICHARD, KEVIN, AND ERIC FOSTER-JOHNSON. *Unix in Plain English, 3rd Edition.* Foster City, CA: IDG Books Worldwide. 1999.

RANKIN, BOB. *The No BS Guide to Linux.* No Starch Press. 1997.

WALL, LARRY, TOM CHRISTIANSEN, AND RANDAL L. SCHWARTZ. *Programming Perl, 2nd Edition.* Sebastopol, CA: O'Reilly & Associates. 1997.

# 2 *Booting and Shutting Down*

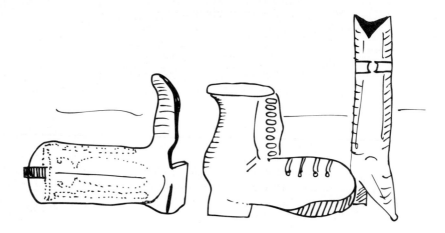

UNIX is a complex operating system, and turning UNIX systems on and off is more complicated than just flipping the power switch. Both operations must be performed correctly if the system is to stay healthy.

Although the boostrapping process has always been somewhat mysterious, it was simpler in the days when one manufacturer controlled all of the system's hardware and software. Now that UNIX runs on PCs, the boot procedure has to play by Microsoft's rules and deal with a large variety of potential configurations. Although we discuss the boot procedure for all our example systems, you'll see that we have quite a bit more to say about the PC-based versions of UNIX than about the "captive" systems.

Although this chapter appears early in the book, it refers to material that is not discussed in detail until many hundreds of pages later. In particular, familiarity with the material in Chapter 5, *The Filesystem*, Chapter 12, *Drivers and the Kernel*, and Chapter 28, *Daemons*, will prove helpful. If your system already boots without any problem, you may want to skip this chapter and come back to it later.

An additional caveat: the booting process is hardware dependent. The information that follows is generically true but may differ from reality for your system.

## 2.1 BOOTSTRAPPING

Bootstrapping is the nerd word for "starting up a computer." The normal facilities provided by the operating system are not available during the startup process, so the computer must "pull itself up by its own bootstraps." During bootstrapping, the kernel is loaded into memory and begins to execute. A variety of initialization tasks are performed, and the system is then made available to users.

Boot time is a period of special vulnerability. Errors in configuration files, missing or unreliable equipment, and damaged filesystems can all prevent a computer from coming up. Boot configuration is often one of the first tasks an administrator must perform on a new system. Unfortunately, it is also one of the most difficult, and it requires some familiarity with many other aspects of UNIX.

When a computer is turned on, it executes boot code that is stored in ROM. That code in turn attempts to figure out how to load and start your kernel. The kernel probes the system's hardware, then spawns the system's **init** process, which is always PID 1.

Several things must happen before a login prompt can appear. Filesystems must be checked and mounted, and system daemons started. These procedures are managed by a series of shell scripts that are run in sequence by **init**. The startup scripts are often referred to as "rc files" because of the way they are named; the "rc" stands for "runcom" or "run command," a historical remnant of the CTSS operating system circa 1965. The exact layout of the startup scripts and the manner in which they are executed vary among systems. We cover the details later in this chapter.

### Automatic and manual booting

Most UNIX systems can boot in either automatic mode or manual mode. In automatic mode, the system performs the complete boot procedure on its own, without any external assistance. In manual mode, the system follows the automatic procedure up to a point but then turns control over to an operator before most initialization scripts have been run. At this point, the computer is in "single-user mode." Most system processes are not running, and other users cannot log in.

In day-to-day operation, automatic booting is used almost exclusively. A typical boot procedure for a modern machine is to turn on the power and wait (and wait ...) for the system to come on-line. Nevertheless, it's important to understand your automatic boot procedure and to know how to perform a manual boot. You'll usually have to boot manually when some problem breaks automatic booting, for example, a corrupted filesystem or an improperly configured network interface.

### Steps in the boot process

A typical bootstrapping process consists of six distinct phases:

- Loading and initialization of the kernel
- Device detection and configuration
- Creation of spontaneous system processes
- Operator intervention (manual boot only)
- Execution of system startup scripts
- Multiuser operation

Administrators have little control over most of these steps. We effect most bootstrap configuration by editing the system startup scripts.

### Kernel initialization

*See Chapter 12 for
more information
about the kernel.*

The UNIX kernel is itself a program, and the first bootstrapping task is to get this program into memory so that it can be executed. The pathname of the kernel is vendor dependent, but it has traditionally been something like **/unix** or **/vmunix**. These days, every vendor calls its kernel something different.

Most systems implement a two-stage loading process. During the first stage, the system's ROM loads a small boot program into memory from disk. This program then arranges for the kernel to be loaded. This procedure occurs outside the domain of UNIX and so is not standardized among systems.

The kernel performs memory tests to find out how much RAM is available. Many of the kernel's internal data structures are statically sized, so the kernel sets aside a fixed amount of real memory for itself when it starts. This memory is reserved for the kernel and cannot be used by user-level processes. On most systems, the kernel prints a message on the console that reports the total amount of physical memory and the amount available to user processes.

### Hardware configuration

One of the kernel's first chores is to check out the machine's environment to see what hardware is present. When you construct a kernel for your system, you tell it what hardware devices it should expect to find; when the kernel begins to execute, it tries to locate and initialize each device that you have told it about. Most kernels print out a line of cryptic information about each device they find.

The device information provided at kernel configuration time is often underspecified. In these cases, the kernel tries to determine the other information it needs by probing the bus for devices and asking the appropriate drivers for information. The drivers for devices that are missing or that do not respond to a probe will be disabled. Even if a device is later connected to the system, it will not be accessible to UNIX processes until the machine has been rebooted.[1]

### System processes

Once basic initialization is complete, the kernel creates several "spontaneous" processes in user space. They're called spontaneous processes because they are not created by the normal UNIX **fork** mechanism; see page 47 for more details.

The number and nature of the spontaneous processes vary from system to system. On BSD systems, there are three:

- **swapper** – process 0
- **init** – process 1
- **pagedaemon** – process 2

---

1. Some modern "high availability" systems can have hardware added as the system is running. Although this feature is becoming more common as time goes on, most systems still need to be shut down in order for new hardware to be added safely and recognized correctly.

The exact number of spontaneous processes varies on System V-ish machines:

- **sched** – process 0
- **init** – process 1
- Various memory and kernel process handlers

Under Linux, there is no visible PID 0. There are several handler processes in addition to **init**; the exact complement varies depending on the version of the kernel:

- **init** – process 1
- Various memory and kernel handlers (**kflushd**, **kupdate**, **kpiod**, **kswapd**)

Of all of these processes, only **init** is really a full-fledged user process. The others are actually portions of the kernel that have been dressed up to look like processes for scheduling or architectural reasons.

Once the spontaneous processes have been created, the kernel's role in bootstrapping is complete. However, none of the processes that handle basic operations (such as accepting logins) have been created, nor have most of the UNIX daemons been started. All of these tasks are taken care of (indirectly, in some cases) by **init**.

### Operator intervention (manual boot only)

*See Chapter 3 for more information about the root account.*

If the system is to be brought up in single-user mode, a command-line flag passed in by the kernel notifies **init** of this fact as it starts up. During a single-user boot, you are normally prompted to enter the root password. If you enter the right password, the system will spawn a root shell. You can type <Control-D> instead of a password to bypass single-user mode and continue to multiuser mode. Red Hat just drops you to a shell without asking for a password.

*See Chapter 5 for more information about filesystems and mounting.*

From the single-user shell, you can execute commands in much the same way as when logged in on a fully booted system. However, only the root partition is usually mounted; you must mount other filesystems by hand in order to use programs that don't live in **/bin**, **/sbin**, or **/etc**.[2] Daemons do not normally run in single-user mode, so commands that depend on server processes (e.g., **mail**) will not work correctly.

In many single-user environments, the filesystem root directory starts off being mounted read-only. If **/tmp** is part of the root filesystem, a lot of commands that use temporary files (such as **vi**) will refuse to run. To fix this problem, you'll have to begin your single-user session by remounting **/** in read/write mode. The exact way that this is done varies by system. On most systems, you can run **mount /** to make **mount** consult the **fstab** or **vfstab** file and determine how the filesystem should be mounted.

 Red Hat's single-user mode is a bit more aggressive than normal. By the time you reach the shell prompt, it will have tried to mount all local filesystems. Although this seems helpful at first, it can prove problematic if you have a sick filesystem.

2.  Some systems will also have **/usr** mounted.

The **fsck** command is normally run during an automatic boot to check and repair filesystems. When you bring the system up in single-user mode, you must run **fsck** by hand. See page 136 for more information about **fsck**.

When the single-user shell exits, the system will attempt to continue booting into multiuser mode.

### Execution of startup scripts

By the time the system is ready to run its startup scripts, it is recognizably UNIX. Even though it doesn't quite look like a fully booted system yet, there are no more "magic" steps in the boot process. The startup scripts are just normal shell scripts, and they're selected and run by **init** according to an algorithm that, though sometimes tortuous, is eminently comprehensible.

The care, feeding, and taxonomy of startup scripts merits a major section of its own. It's taken up in more detail starting on page 24.

### Multiuser operation

See page 105 for more information about the login process.

After the initialization scripts have run, the system is fully operational, except that no one can log in. For logins to be accepted on a particular terminal (including the console), a **getty** process must be listening on it.[3] **init** spawns these **getty** processes directly, completing the boot process. **init** is also responsible for spawning graphical login systems such as **xdm**, **gdm**, or **dtlogin** if the system is set up to use them.

Keep in mind that **init** continues to perform an important role even after bootstrapping is complete. On BSD-based systems, **init** has only two states: single-user and multiuser. On other systems, **init** has one single-user and several multiuser "run levels" that determine which of the system's resources are enabled. Run levels are described later in this chapter, starting on page 25.

## 2.2  BOOTING PCs

At this point we've seen the general outline of the boot process. We now revisit several of the more important (and complicated) steps, filling in some additional details and describing the specific behavior of our example systems.

We start our grand tour once again with the initial power-on sequence and the loading of the kernel. On traditional hardware, this is a straightforward process that merits only a few lines of description.

PC booting, on the other hand, is a lengthy ordeal that requires quite a bit of background information to understand. If you don't need to deal with PCs, you might want to jump ahead to page 22.

---

3. Except under Solaris, which uses a more complex system.

### How a PC is different from proprietary hardware

When a machine boots, it begins by executing code stored in ROMs. The exact location and nature of this code varies, depending on the type of machine you have. On a machine designed explicitly for UNIX, the code is typically firmware that knows how to use the devices connected to the machine, how to talk to the network on a basic level, and how to understand disk-based filesystems. Such omniscient firmware is very convenient for system administrators. For example, you can just type in the filename of a new kernel, and the firmware will know how to locate and read that file.

On PCs, this initial boot code is generally called a BIOS (Basic Input/Output System), and it is extremely simplistic compared to the firmware of a UNIX machine. Actually, a PC has several levels of BIOS: one for the machine itself, one for the video card, and one for the SCSI card if the system has one.

The built-in BIOS knows about some of the devices that live on the motherboard, typically the IDE controller (and disks), keyboard, serial ports, and parallel ports. SCSI cards are usually only aware of the devices that are connected to them. Working out the conflicts and interactions among all these various BIOSes can be a real nightmare. In many cases, mass confusion reigns supreme over which BIOS gets to choose what device to try to boot from.

### The PC boot process

Modern BIOSes are a little smarter than they used to be. They usually allow you to enter a configuration mode at boot time by holding down one or two special keys; better BIOSes have even hit upon the innovation of telling you what those special keys are so you don't have to look them up in the manual.

The BIOS will normally let you select which devices you want to try to boot from, which sounds more promising than it actually is. You can usually specify something like, "Try to boot off the floppy, then try to boot off the CD-ROM, then try to boot off the hard disk." Unfortunately, the BIOS is generally limited to booting from the first IDE CD-ROM drive or the first IDE hard disk. If you have been very, very good over the previous year, Santa might even provide you with a BIOS that acknowledges the existence of SCSI cards.

We would like to offer you some useful guidance for negotiating this quagmire. Alas, it is impossible; this phase of the boot process is entirely under the control of the hardware manufacturers and their wretched BIOSes. You will have to negotiate with them for succor.

Once your machine has figured out what device to boot from, it will try to load the first 512 bytes of the disk. This 512-byte segment is known as the Master Boot Record or MBR. The MBR contains a program that tells the computer from which disk partition to load a secondary boot program (the "boot loader"). For more information on PC-style disk partitions and the MBR, refer to Chapter 8, *Adding a Disk*.

The default MBR is a simple program that tells the computer to get its boot loader from the first partition on the disk. Both Linux and FreeBSD provide a more sophisticated MBR that knows how to deal with multiple operating systems and kernels.

Once the MBR has chosen the partition to boot from, it tries to load the boot loader specific to that partition. The boot loader is then responsible for loading the kernel.

### LILO: the Linux boot loader

LILO is both incredibly complex and incredibly stupid. It provides many advanced facilities that most other boot loaders lack, but it's also missing some simple features.

LILO comes with almost all Linux distributions, including Red Hat. When you first install the system, Red Hat's installation scripts will plonk down a copy of LILO with the generic options; you'll have very little say in the process. LILO isn't strictly required for booting Linux, but it should be considered a fact of life. Learn to love it.

LILO can either be installed into the MBR of the disk or it can be installed into the boot record of the Linux root partition.

LILO is configured and installed with the **lilo** command. **lilo** bases the installed configuration on the contents of the **/etc/lilo.conf** file. To change your boot configuration, you simply update **/etc/lilo.conf** and rerun **lilo**. LILO must be reconfigured every time the boot process changes—in particular, every time you want to add a new boot partition and every time you have a new kernel to boot.

### Configuring LILO

Here's a basic **lilo.conf** file for a Linux system that has both a production kernel and a backup kernel:

```
boot=/dev/hda            # Put boot loader on MBR
root=/dev/hda1           # Specify root partition
install=/boot/boot.b
map=/boot/map
delay=20                 # 2sec for user interrupt
image=/vmlinuz           # Kernel to boot
    label=linux          # Label to refer to this entry
    read-only
image=/vmlinuz-backup # Backup entry
    label=backup
    read-only
```

Each possible boot scenario has a label. At boot time, you can tell LILO which one to use by entering the appropriate label. The first label to appear in **lilo.conf** becomes the default.

The default scenario (named linux) boots the file **/vmlinuz**. The read-only tag specifies that the kernel should mount its root filesystem read-only. This option should always be present; the startup scripts will take care of remounting the partition read-write at the appropriate time. This system is also configured to boot a backup kernel, **/vmlinuz-backup**. It's always a good idea to have such an alternate.

Running **lilo** without any arguments will generate and install the boot loader and tell you which entries are available. It puts a star next to the default image. However, if you have made an error in the **lilo.conf** file, **lilo** usually won't discover the problem until halfway through the installation of the boot loader. When this happens, the boot loader is in a confused state. *Do not reboot* until you've run **lilo** successfully. To avoid getting into this situation, you can run **lilo -t** to test the configuration without really installing it. If everything looks kosher, you can then run **lilo** for real. It is something of a mystery why **lilo** does not run this pretest for you by default.

**lilo**'s output when run with the config file above is:

```
# lilo
Added linux*
Added backup
```

When the system boots, LILO prints the following prompt:

```
LILO:
```

It then waits 2 seconds (20 tenths of a second, set with the delay tag), then boots the **/vmlinuz** kernel and mounts the first partition of the first IDE disk as the root partition. You can see a list of defined boot scenarios by pressing the <Tab> key:

```
LILO: <Tab>
linux   backup
LILO:
```

To boot using an alternate scenario, just enter its label at the prompt.

### The FreeBSD boot loader

The FreeBSD boot loader is simple and efficient. It's divided into two parts: one that lives in the MBR and one that lives in the FreeBSD root partition. The two segments must be installed separately.

You install the MBR-resident portion of the boot loader with the **boot0cfg** command. For example, the command

```
# boot0cfg -B /dev/wd0
```

installs the first-stage boot loader into the MBR of the first IDE disk on the system. Very little configuration of the first-stage boot loader is necessary or possible. At boot time, it scans the list of available drives (which it obtains from the BIOS) and looks for partitions that it thinks are bootable. It presents the list of bootable partitions in a little menu:

```
F1  FreeBSD
F2  Windows

Default: F1
```

For more information about fine-tuning the installation of the first-stage boot loader, refer to the **boot0cfg** man page.

Booting

The second part of the boot loader is the one that actually boots FreeBSD and lets you pass special options to the kernel. It's installed into the FreeBSD root partition with **disklabel -B**. **disklabel** is used for almost all disk configuration, so it's a robust program with many features. You can specify many different options when installing the boot loader, but the defaults are usually fine. For example,

```
# disklabel -B /dev/wd0s1
```

installs the default boot loader on the first partition of the first IDE disk.

This second-stage boot loader refers to the following files to obtain its configuration:

> **/boot/loader.conf**
> **/boot/loader.conf.local**
> **/boot/defaults/loader.conf**

The last of these files contains the default settings for the boot loader and should never be modified—the options it specifies can be overridden in the **loader.conf** and **loader.conf.local** files, as well as on the boot loader command line at boot time. The **boot**(8) and **loader**(8) man pages provide the dirt on all the boot loader options.

### Multibooting on PCs

Since many operating systems run on PCs, it is fairly common to set up a machine to be able to boot several different systems. To make this work, you need to configure a boot loader to recognize all of the different operating systems on your disks. In the next few sections, we cover some common multiboot stumbling blocks and then review example configurations for Linux and FreeBSD.

Every disk partition can have its own second-stage boot loader. However, there is only one MBR. When setting up a multiboot configuration, you must decide which boot loader is going to be the "master." For better or worse, your choice will often be dictated by the vagaries of the operating systems involved. Linux pretty much has to be booted by LILO, so that's generally the best MBR option for any system that has a Linux partition. The one exception to this rule is Windows NT/2000, which *must* have its boot loader installed in the MBR.

### Multibooting gotchas

Installing a multiboot system can make you tear your hair out. This section is meant to prevent you from going bald.

If you're installing a multiboot system that includes a consumer version of Windows (95, 98, or Me), always install Windows before you install anything else. The consumer versions of Windows are very stupid and have no idea that other operating systems may exist on the same machine. They will always want to take partition 1 on your first hard disk and will overwrite other boot loaders during installation.

The same rule applies to Windows NT/2000: always install Windows first. The reasons are slightly different, but the upshot is the same. The NT/2000 boot loader really,

really wants to be installed in the MBR and be the One True Boot Loader for the system. Resistance is futile.

To get the NT/2000 boot loader to boot a UNIX partition, install UNIX and then boot to it using a floppy or CD-ROM. You'll need to peel off the first 512 bytes of the UNIX partition (this is the partition boot record), and write them to a file. You can do this with the **dd** command. Here is an example from Linux:

```
# dd if=/dev/hda2 of=linux.bin bs=512 count=1
```

You must then copy this file to the NT/2000 partition and add an entry to the NT boot loader configuration that tells it how to boot using this file. We don't describe the NT boot loader in this book, but all you really have to do is add a line to **C:\boot.ini** that contains the file's path along with a label. For the Linux case, the line would look something like this:

```
C:\linux.bin="Linux"
```

For more information about the format of the **boot.ini** file, see the on-line Microsoft Knowledge Base at support.microsoft.com.

If Linux and Windows NT/2000 are cohabitating, LILO will need to be installed onto Linux's disk partition, since the MBR is already spoken for. To do this, have the boot line in **lilo.conf** point to your Linux partition. For example, if Linux is on the second partition on the first IDE hard disk, the line would be

```
boot=/dev/hda2
```

You'll need to make this change *before* you copy the second-stage boot loader to a file and transfer it to the NT partition. In fact, you will need to repeat the entire process whenever you rerun **lilo**.

### LILO multiboot configuration

To configure a multiboot system that uses LILO in the MBR (e.g., Linux with Windows 98), begin with the standard LILO configuration as outlined on page 18. You can then go back and add entries for the other operating systems to **/etc/lilo.conf**.

Here's the **lilo.conf** entry you need to boot Windows from the first partition of your first IDE disk:

```
other = /dev/hda1
label = windows
table = /dev/hda
```

A complete **lilo.conf** file that boots Windows from partition 1, Linux from partition 2, and FreeBSD from partition 3 would look something like this:

```
boot = /dev/hda          # install on the MBR of 1st IDE drive
delay = 20               # Wait 2 sec. for user's boot choice
default = linux          # If no input, boot linux from 2nd partition
image = /boot/vmlinuz-2.3.41
    root = /dev/hda2
```

```
        label = linux
        read-only
other = /dev/hda1        # boot from 1st partition
        label = windows
        table = /dev/hda
other = /dev/hda3        # boot from 3rd partition
        label = freebsd
        table = /dev/hda
```

You'll need to rerun **lilo** after putting these entries into **lilo.conf**. Remember to run **lilo -t** first to test the config file.

### FreeBSD multiboot configuration

FreeBSD's boot loader automatically tries to detect bootable partitions. However, you can also declare the bootable partitions explicitly with **boot0cfg**'s **-m** *mask* option. The *mask* should be a bitmask of the partitions you would like to be able to boot from. The first partition is represented by binary 0001 (hex 0x1), the second partition is binary 0010 (0x2), and so on. For example, the command

```
# boot0cfg -B -m 0x7
```

installs a new first-stage boot loader and tells it that partitions 1, 2, and 3 are bootable (binary 0111 = hex 0x7). When the system starts up, the boot menu will include at least three options, one for each bootable partition you specified.

## 2.3  BOOTING IN SINGLE-USER MODE

The following sections give the nitty-gritty details of single-user booting on each of our example operating systems.

### Solaris single-user mode

To interrupt the boot procedure and enter the boot PROM on Sun hardware, press the L1 and 'a' keys simultaneously. L1 is sometimes labeled STOP on modern Sun keyboards. From the boot PROM, you can type **boot -s** to boot to single-user mode.

To boot an alternate kernel under Solaris, you usually have to type the full Solaris name of the device and the file. The Solaris device name is the long, bizarre string of characters you see when you do an **ls -l** on the **/dev** file:

```
% ls -l /dev/rdsk/c0t0d0s0
lrwxrwxrwx   1 root     root        55 Jan 15  1998 /dev/rdsk/c0t0d0s0 ->
    ../../devices/sbus@1f,0/SUNW,fas@e,8800000/sd@0,0:a,raw
```

To boot the kernel stored as **/kernel/backup** on this disk, you'd need to enter the following command at the boot PROM monitor:

**boot /devices/sbus@1f,0/SUNW,fas@e,8800000/sd@0,0:a,raw/kernel/backup**

Table 2.1 lists some of the more useful commands you can enter from Sun's boot PROM and a brief description of their functions.

**Table 2.1   Boot PROM commands on Sun hardware**

| Command | Function |
|---|---|
| **boot** /path_to_kernel | Boots an alternate kernel |
| **boot -s** | Boots into single-user mode |
| **boot -r** | Reconfigures the kernel and probes for new devices |
| **boot -a /etc/system.bak** | Makes kernel read **/etc/system.bak** instead of **/etc/system** |
| **probe-scsi** | Shows a list of all attached SCSI devices |

### HP-UX single-user mode

The procedure for booting single-user on an HP-UX machine seems to depend on the exact type of machine. The following example is from an HP 9000/735.

First, interrupt the boot process when prompted to do so. You'll receive a prompt. At that prompt, type **boot pri isl** to get to a smarter prompt that will let you boot single-user. This prompt should look something like this:

```
ISL> prompt:
```

The following command selects a kernel and boots the system into single-user mode:

```
ISL> prompt: hpux -iS /stand/vmunix
```

### Linux single-user mode

You'll usually enter Linux's single-user mode through LILO. At the LILO prompt, enter the label of the configuration you want to boot (as specified in **lilo.conf**), followed by **-s** or **single**. For example, the default configuration shipped with Red Hat is called "linux", so to boot that configuration into single-user mode, you'd use

```
LILO: linux single
```

LILO accepts a variety of other command-line options; Table 2.2 shows examples.

**Table 2.2   Examples of LILO's boot time options**

| Option | Meaning |
|---|---|
| **root=/dev/foo** | Tells the kernel to use **/dev/foo** as the root device |
| **single** | Boots to single-user mode |
| **init=/sbin/init** | Tells the kernel to use **/sbin/init** as its **init** program |
| **ether=0,0,eth1** | Makes the kernel probe for a second Ethernet card |

Red Hat's single-user mode is particularly fragile. Red Hat tries to **fsck** and mount every local filesystem before it enters single-user mode, and almost none of its commands are statically linked. If your shared libraries are not mounted or are not functioning properly, commands that are not statically linked will not run. Even Red Hat's basic file manipulation commands, networking utilities, and text editors require the presence of a functioning set of shared libraries.

For these reasons, trying to deal with Red Hat's single-user mode is often a waste of time. If you have broken your libraries or your linker, you'll need to have a Red Hat rescue floppy handy. Instead of entering single-user mode, it's almost always more convenient to use Red Hat's "confirmation" boot mode for minor problems or to go directly to the rescue floppy.

### FreeBSD single-user mode

To enter single-user mode, first select FreeBSD from the first-stage boot loader:

```
F1      FreeBSD
Default: F1
```

Then, interrupt the boot loader when prompted and type **boot -s**:

```
Hit [Enter] to boot immediately, or any other key for the command prompt.
Booting [kernel] in 9 seconds...
<Spacebar>
Type '?' for a list of commands, 'help' for more detailed help.
disk1s1a:> boot -s
```

The system continues booting up to the point at which you are prompted for the path to a shell. You can just press <Enter> for **/bin/sh**.

The second-stage boot prompt understands a variety of commands. For example, to locate and boot an alternate kernel, you'd use a sequence of commands such as this:

```
disk1s1a:> ls
d  var
d  stand
d  etc
...
kernel.SYNACK
kernel.LMC
kernel
...
disk1s1a:> unload
disk1s1a:> load kernel.SYNACK
disk1s1a:> boot
```

This transcript shows the operator obtaining a directory listing of the default root filesystem, unloading the default kernel (**/kernel**), loading a replacement kernel (**/kernel.SYNACK**), and then continuing the boot process.

## 2.4 STARTUP SCRIPTS

After you exit from single-user mode (or, in the automated boot sequence, at the point at which the single-user shell would have run), **init** executes the system startup scripts. These scripts are really just garden-variety shell scripts that are interpreted by **sh**. The exact location, content, and organization of the scripts vary considerably from system to system.

Startup scripts can be organized in two principal ways, each deeply rooted in ancient history. On systems descended from BSD, the scripts are kept in the **/etc** directory and have names starting with the letters **rc**. On SystemV-derived systems, the scripts are kept in the **/etc/init.d** directory and links to them are made in the directories **/etc/rc0.d**, **/etc/rc1.d**, and so on. SysV's organization is cleaner, and since each script can be used to either start or stop a facility, it allows the system to be shut down in an orderly manner.

Some tasks that are often performed in the startup scripts are:

- Setting the name of the computer
- Setting the time zone
- Checking the disks with **fsck** (only in automatic mode)
- Mounting the system's disks
- Removing old files from the **/tmp** directory
- Configuring network interfaces
- Starting up daemons and network services

Most startup scripts are quite verbose and print out a description of everything they are doing. This loquacity can be a tremendous help if the system hangs midway through booting or if you are trying to locate an error in one of the scripts.

On systems of yore, it was common practice to modify startup scripts to make them do the right thing for a particular environment. These days, the scripts supplied by your vendor should be general enough to handle most any configuration. Instead of putting the details of your local configuration in the code of the scripts, you put them in a separate configuration file (or set of files) that the scripts consult. The config files are normally just mini **sh** scripts that the startup scripts include to define the values of certain shell variables.

### SystemV-style startup scripts

SystemV-ish scripts are the most common today; they are used by three of our four example operating systems. We will first describe the general idea of the system, then cover each OS's individual quirks.

The SystemV **init** defines 7 "run levels," each of which represents a particular complement of services that the system should be running:

- Level 0 is the level in which the system is completely shut down.
- Level 1 or S represents single-user mode.
- Levels 2 through 5 are multiuser levels.
- Level 6 is a "reboot" level.

Levels 0 and 6 are special in that the system can't actually remain in them; it shuts down or reboots as a side effect of entering them. On most systems, the normal multiuser run level is 2 or 3. Run levels 4 and 5 are rarely used, and run levels 1 and S are different on each system.

Single-user mode was traditionally **init** level 1. It brought down all multiuser and remote login processes and made sure the system was running a minimal complement of software. Since single-user mode provides root access to the system, however, administrators wanted the system to prompt for the root password whenever it was booted into single-user mode. The S run level was created to address this need: it spawns a process that prompts for the root password. On Solaris, S is the "real" single-user run level, but on Linux, it serves only to prompt for the root password and is not a destination in itself.

There seem to be more run levels defined than are strictly necessary or useful. The usual explanation for this is that a phone switch had 7 run levels, so it was thought that a UNIX system should have at least that many. Red Hat actually supports up to 10 run levels, but levels 7 through 9 are undefined.

The **/etc/inittab** file tells **init** what to do at each of its run levels. Its format varies from system to system, but the basic idea is that **inittab** defines commands that are to be run (or kept running) when the system enters each level.

As the machine boots, **init** ratchets its way up from run level 0 to the default run level set in **/etc/inittab**. To accomplish the transition between each pair of adjacent run levels, **init** runs the actions spelled out for that transition in **/etc/inittab**. The same progression is made in reverse order when the machine is shut down.

Unfortunately, the semantics of the **inittab** file are fairly crude, and they don't mesh well with the way that services are actually started and stopped on UNIX systems. To map the facilities of the **inittab** file into something a bit more usable, descendants of SystemV implement an additional layer of abstraction. This layer usually takes the form of a "change run levels" command that's run out of **inittab**. It executes scripts from a run-level-dependent directory to bring the system to its new state.

It's usually not necessary for system administrators to deal directly with **/etc/inittab** because the script-based interface is adequate for almost any application. In the remainder of this chapter, we will tacitly ignore the **inittab** file and the other glue that attaches **init** to the execution of startup scripts. Just keep in mind that when we say that **init** runs such-and-such a script, the connection may not be quite so direct.

The master copies of the startup scripts live in a directory called **init.d**. The **init.d** directory is usually in **/etc**, but that is not always the case. Each script is responsible for one daemon or one particular aspect of the system. The scripts understand the arguments **start** and **stop** to mean that the service they deal with should be initialized or halted. Most also understand **restart**, which is typically the same as a **stop** followed by a **start**. As a system administrator, you can manually start and stop individual services by running the associated **init.d** script with an appropriate argument.

For example, here's a simple startup script that can start, stop, or restart **sshd**:

```
#! /bin/sh
test -f /usr/local/sbin/sshd || exit 0
case "$1" in
    start)
            echo -n "Starting sshd: sshd"
            /usr/local/sbin/sshd
            echo "."
            ;;
    stop)
            echo -n "Stopping sshd: sshd"
            kill `cat /var/run/sshd.pid`
            echo "."
            ;;
    restart)
            echo -n "Stopping sshd: sshd"
            kill `cat /var/run/sshd.pid`
            echo "."
            echo -n "Starting sshd: sshd"
            /usr/local/sbin/sshd
            echo "."
            ;;
    *)
            echo "Usage: /etc/init.d/sshd start|stop|restart"
            exit 1
            ;;
esac
```

Although the scripts in **init.d** can start and stop individual services, **init** needs additional information about which scripts to run (and with what arguments) to enter any given run level. Instead of looking directly at the **init.d** directory when it takes the system to a new run level, **init** looks at a directory called **rc**_level_**.d**, where _level_ is the run level to be entered (e.g., **rc0.d**, **rc1.d**, and so on)

These **rc**_level_**.d** directories typically contain symbolic links that point back to the scripts in the **init.d** directory. The names of these symbolic links all start with **S** or **K** followed by a number and the name of the service that the script controls (e.g., **S34named**). When **init** transitions from a lower run level to a higher one, it runs all the scripts that start with **S** in ascending numerical order with the argument **start**. When **init** transitions from a higher run level to a lower one, it runs all the scripts that start with **K** (for "kill") in descending numerical order with the argument **stop**. Depending on the system, **init** may look only at the **rc**_level_**.d** directory appropriate for the new run level, or it may look at every **rc**_level_**.d** directory between the current run level and the new run level.

To tell the system when to start a daemon, we need to make symbolic links into the appropriate directory. Most systems seem to start the majority of their networking daemons during run level 2. For example, to tell the system to start **sshd** during run level 2 and to stop the daemon nicely before shutting down, we could make the following pair of links:

```
# ln -s /etc/init.d/sshd /etc/rc2.d/S99sshd
# ln -s /etc/init.d/sshd /etc/rc0.d/K25sshd
```

The first line tells the system to run the **/etc/init.d/sshd** startup script as one of the last things to do when entering run level 2 and to run the script with the **start** argument. The second line tells the system to run **/etc/init.d/sshd** relatively early when shutting down the system and to run the script with the **stop** argument. Some systems treat shutdown and reboot differently, so we will have to put a symlink in the **/etc/rc6.d/** directory as well, to make sure the daemon shuts down properly when the system is rebooted.

### Solaris startup scripts

Solaris, HP-UX, and Red Hat all use SystemV-style startup scripts that are kept in an **init.d** directory. Under Solaris, both the **init.d** and **rc**_level_**.d** directories are in **/etc**.

In the past, Solaris's **init.d** scripts referred to configuration files that were scattered all over the system, forming a huge, indecipherable mess. In recent releases, Sun has fixed a lot of this confusion. The startup scripts are much improved and are now relatively self-contained.

Several config files can be found in the **/etc/defaults** directory, although there aren't a huge number of options there to tweak. Other config files are still somewhat scattered. Table 2.3 lists several important ones.

**Table 2.3   Solaris startup configuration files**

| File | Purpose |
| --- | --- |
| **/etc/.UNCONFIGURED** | Tells the startup scripts to attempt to reconfigure the system from scratch (typically used only during installation) |
| **/etc/hostname.**_interface_ | Contains the hostname to be assigned to a network interface |
| **/etc/dhcp.**_interface_ | Requests that an interface be configured with DHCP |
| **/etc/defaultrouter** | Contains the hostname or address of the default gateway |

### HP-UX startup scripts

Under HP-UX, the actual startup scripts are kept in **/sbin/init.d**. The run-level directories are also in **/sbin**. Config files that change the behavior of the startup scripts generally live in **/etc/rc.config.d**. Their names correspond to the names of the startup scripts in **/sbin/init.d**. For example, the script

```
/sbin/init.d/SnmpMaster
```

gets its configuration information from

```
/etc/rc.config.d/SnmpMaster
```

and is actually invoked from **init** by way of the links

```
/sbin/rc2.d/S560SnmpMaster
/sbin/rc1.d/K440SnmpMaster
```

HP-UX saves the output of startup scripts in **/etc/rc.log**. If one of your startup scripts fails, check **/etc/rc.log** to see if it contains any relevant error messages or hints as to the source of the problem. This saving of startup script output is a most useful and excellent feature, and it's simple to implement, too. It's surprising that other vendors haven't caught on to it.

The config files in **/etc/rc.config.d** can be rather confusing, although they are generally well commented. Table 2.4 gives a short explanation of some of the more commonly modified files.

**Table 2.4    Commonly modified HP-UX config files in /etc/rc.config.d**

| File(s) | Purpose |
| --- | --- |
| **SnmpMaster** | A master switch that turns all SNMP support on or off |
| **Snmp*** | Other SNMP-related options |
| **acct** | Turns process accounting on or off. See **acct**(1M) |
| **auditing** | Configures system auditing. See **audsys**(1M) and **audevent**(1M) |
| **cde** | Holds CDE (Common Desktop Environment) settings |
| **clean*** | Control various boot time cleanup operations |
| **desktop** | Configures which desktop environment is to be the default |
| **hpbase100conf** | Configures 100 Mb/s interfaces |
| **hpetherconf** | Configures Ethernet interfaces. See **lanadmin**(1M) |
| **list_mode** | Configures startup presentation options |
| **lp** | Turns the print spooler on or off |
| **mailservs** | Starts **sendmail** or specifies a mail server |
| **nameservs** | Configures/starts the name server daemon |
| **nddconf** | Sets tunable kernel parameters at startup time, using **ndd** |
| **netconf** | Specifies network device configuration (IP address, etc.) |
| **netdaemons** | Tells which networking daemons to start |
| **nettl** | Configures network tracing and logging[a] |
| **nfsconf** | Sets NFS configuration options |
| **pd** | Configures the HP Distributed Print Service |
| **vt** | Starts **vtdaemon**. Depends on **ptydaemon** |
| **xfs** | Turns the X Windows font server on or off |

a. See **nettl**(1M), **nettlconf**(1M), and **nettlgen.conf**(4) for more information.

For most of these files, the default values are usually OK. The most common files that you might need to touch are probably **netconf**, **netdaemons**, and perhaps **nddconf**.

### Red Hat startup scripts

Startup scripts are one of the things that distinguish Linux distributions from each other. Debian uses startup scripts that are very similar to Solaris's, and Slackware uses scripts that are similar to FreeBSD's. Red Hat uses a hybrid of the SystemV and BSD systems, with a few twists thrown in just to make life difficult for everyone.

Red Hat's scripts are a complicated mess; they contain many comments such as

```
# stupid hack, but it should work
```

and

```
# this is broken!
```

Red Hat's **init** is fundamentally of the SysV ilk. At each run level, **init** invokes the script **/etc/rc.d/rc** with the current run level as an argument. **/etc/rc.d/rc** usually runs in "normal" mode, in which it just does its thing, but it can also run in "confirmation" mode, in which it asks you before it runs each individual startup script. Use the **chkconfig** command to manage the links in the run-level directories.

Red Hat also has an **rc.local** script much like that found on FreeBSD. **rc.local** is the last script run as part of the startup process. It's best to avoid adding your own customizations to **rc.local**; use the SystemV-style facilities instead.

Here's an example of a Red Hat startup session:

```
[kernel information]
INIT: version 2.77 booting
                Welcome to Red Hat Linux
         Press 'I' to enter interactive startup.
Mounting proc filesystem                                  [ OK ]
Setting clock  (utc): Fri Mar 10 07:16:41 MST 2000        [ OK ]
Loading default keymap                                    [ OK ]
Activating swap partitions                                [ OK ]
   ...
```

Once you see the "Welcome to Red Hat Linux" message, you can press the 'i' key to enter confirmation mode. Unfortunately, Red Hat gives you no confirmation that you have pressed the right key. It blithely continues to mount local filesystems, activate swap partitions, load keymaps, and locate its kernel modules. Only after it switches to run level 3 will it actually start to prompt you for confirmation:

```
                Welcome to Red Hat Linux
         Press 'I' to enter interactive startup.
Mounting proc filesystem                                  [ OK ]
Setting clock  (utc): Fri Mar 10 07:16:41 MST 2000        [ OK ]
Loading default keymap                                    [ OK ]
Activating swap partitions                                [ OK ]
Setting hostname redhat.synack.net                        [ OK ]
Checking root filesystem
/dev/hda1: clean, 73355/191616 files, 214536/383032 blocks [ OK ]
Remounting root filesystem in read-write mode             [ OK ]
```

```
Finding module dependencies                                 [ OK ]
Checking filesystems                                        [ OK ]
Mounting local filesystems                                  [ OK ]
Turning on user and group quotas for local filesystems      [ OK ]
Enabling swap space                                         [ OK ]
INIT: Entering runlevel: 3
Entering interactive startup
Start service kudzu (Y)es/(N)o/(C)ontinue? [Y]
```

Interactive startup and single-user mode both begin at the same spot in the booting process. When the startup process is so broken that you cannot reach this point safely, you can use a rescue floppy to boot.

You can also pass the argument **init=/bin/sh** to LILO to trick it into running a single-user shell before **init** even starts.[4] If you take this latter tack, you will have to do all the startup housekeeping by hand, including manually **fsck**ing and mounting the local filesystems.

Most configuration of Red Hat's boot process should be achieved through manipulation of the config files in **/etc/sysconfig**. These files are similar in concept and execution to those found in **/etc/rc.config.d** in HP-UX, though there are fewer files and more options in each file. Table 2.5 summarizes the function of the items in the **/etc/sysconfig** directory.

**Table 2.5    Files and subdirectories of Red Hat's /etc/sysconfig directory**

| File/Dir | Function or contents |
| --- | --- |
| **apmd** | Lists arguments for the Advanced Power Management Daemon |
| **clock** | Specifies the type of clock that the system has (almost always UTC) |
| **console** | A mysterious directory that is always empty |
| **hwconf** | Contains all of the system's hardware info. Used by Kudzu. |
| **i18n** | Contains the system's local settings (date formats, languages, etc.) |
| **init** | Configures the way messages from the startup scripts are displayed |
| **keyboard** | Sets keyboard type (use "us" for the standard 101-key U.S. keyboard) |
| **mouse** | Sets the mouse type. Used by X Windows and **gpm**. |
| **network** | Sets global network options (hostname, gateway, forwarding, etc.) |
| **network-scripts** | A directory that contains accessory scripts and network config files |
| **pcmcia** | Tells whether to start PCMCIA daemons and specifies options |
| **sendmail** | Sets options for **sendmail** |

Several of these items merit additional comments:

- The **hwconf** file contains all of your hardware information. The obnoxious Kudzu service checks it to see if you have added or removed any hardware

---

4. We once had a corrupted keymap file, and since Red Hat loads the keymap file even in single-user mode, single-user was useless. Setting **init=/bin/sh** was the only way to boot the system to a usable single-user state to fix the problem.

and asks you what to do about changes. You will probably want to disable this service on a production system because it delays the boot process whenever it detects a change to the hardware configuration, resulting in an extra 30 seconds of downtime for every hardware change made.

- The **network-scripts** directory contains additional material related to network configuration. The only things you should ever need to change are the files named **ifcfg-***interface*. For example, **network-scripts/ifcfg-eth0** contains the configuration parameters for the interface eth0. It sets the interface's IP address and networking options. See page 300 for more information about configuring network interfaces.

- The **sendmail** file contains two variables: DAEMON and QUEUE. If the DAEMON variable is set to yes, the system will start **sendmail** when the system boots. QUEUE tells how long after an error **sendmail** should queue mail before trying to redeliver it.

### FreeBSD startup scripts

This section is specifically about FreeBSD, but the general outline of the startup process applies to most other BSD systems.

FreeBSD's **init** runs only a single startup script, **/etc/rc**. This master script then runs the system's other **rc** scripts, all of which live in **/etc** and are called **rc.***something*. Scripts are run in a predefined order, with no concept of run levels.

**/etc/rc** starts off by reading (executing, really) three files that specify configuration information:

- **/etc/defaults/rc.conf**
- **/etc/rc.conf**
- **/etc/rc.conf.local**

The **rc.conf** files can also specify other directories in which to look for startup files. You specify the other directories by setting the value of the local_startup variable.

These config files work their magic by defining the values of shell variables. The **rc** scripts later check these variables to determine how to behave. **/etc/rc** uses the shell's **source** command (or more accurately, its not-very-intuitive alias, ".") to interpolate the config files and subsidiary scripts into its own execution stream; in effect, this procedure concatenates all the config files and startup scripts into one big script.

**/etc/defaults/rc.conf** is a huge file that lists all the configuration parameters and their default settings. This file should never be edited; the startup script bogeyman will hunt you down. To change the contents of a variable, just override its default value by setting it again in **/etc/rc.conf** or **/etc/rc.conf.local**. The **rc.conf** man page has an extensive list of the variables you can specify.

As you can see from looking at **/etc**, there are quite a few different **rc** scripts.

```
% ls /etc/rc*
rc             rc.diskless1    rc.isdn       rc.pccard
rc.atm         rc.diskless2    rc.local      rc.resume
rc.conf        rc.firewall     rc.serial     rc.devfs
rc.i386        rc.network      rc.shutdown   rc.suspend
```

**/etc/rc** starts by calling **rc.diskless1** if the kernel is configured to be a diskless client. It next calls **rc.sysctl**, **rc.serial**, **rc.pccard**, and **rc.network**, then goes on to perform some housekeeping functions. As one of its final acts, it runs the **rc.local** script. If a script does not exist, **rc** just skips it. (In the listing above, **rc.sysctl** doesn't exist.)

The default **rc.serial** script does nothing, but it defines a set of functions that can be used to initialize serial ports and devices at boot time.

If PCMCIA/CardBus support was specified in one of the **rc.conf** files, **rc.pccard** loads kernel modules relating to the PCMCIA controller and starts **pccardd**, the daemon that controls the configuration and deconfiguration of PCMCIA cards as they are inserted and removed.

**rc.network** is a long and involved script that sets up the machine's networking environment. It uses variables specified in **rc.conf** to configure interfaces and deal with DHCP, PPP, routing, and firewalls. You don't normally need to touch the script since all configuration is done in **rc.conf**. The **rc.network** script calls several other network-related **rc** scripts: **rc.atm**, **rc.isdn**, and **rc.firewall**.

To configure a network interface under FreeBSD, set the variables called hostname, defaultrouter, and ifconfig_*if* (where *if* is the name of the interface). The ifconfig_*if* variable should contain a string of options to be passed to **ifconfig** for that interface.

For example, these lines

```
hostname="my.fullyqualified.name"
ifconfig_de0="inet 192.168.1.2 netmask 0xffffff00"
defaultrouter="192.168.1.1"
```

configure the host with an address of 192.168.1.2 and a default route to 192.168.1.1. To use DHCP to configure the interface, use a line like this:

```
ifconfig_de0="DHCP"
```

Here, DHCP will set the hostname (based on the returned IP address), the IP address, and the default route for the interface all at once.

## 2.5  REBOOTING AND SHUTTING DOWN

UNIX filesystems buffer changes in memory and write them back to disk only sporadically. This scheme makes disk I/O faster, but it also makes the filesystem more susceptible to data loss when the system is rudely halted.

Traditional UNIX machines were very touchy about how they were shut down. Modern systems have become less sensitive, but it is always a good idea to shut down the machine nicely when possible. Improper shutdown can result in anything from subtle, insidious problems to a major catastrophe.

On non-UNIX operating systems, rebooting the operating system is an appropriate first course of treatment for almost any problem. On a UNIX system, it's better to think first and reboot second. UNIX problems tend to be subtler and more complex, so blindly rebooting is effective in a smaller percentage of cases. UNIX systems also take a long time to boot, and multiple users may be inconvenienced.

You usually need to reboot when you add a new piece of hardware or when existing hardware becomes so confused that it cannot be reset. If you modify a configuration file that's used only at boot time, you must reboot to make your changes take effect. If the system is so wedged that you cannot log in to make a proper diagnosis of the problem, you obviously have no alternative but to reboot.

Some things can be changed and fixed without rebooting, but whenever you modify a startup script, you should reboot just to make sure that the system will come back up successfully.

Unlike bootstrapping, which can be done in essentially only one way, there are a number of ways to shut down or reboot. They are:

- Turning off the power
- Using the **shutdown** command
- Using the **halt** and **reboot** commands (BSD, Linux)
- Sending **init** a TERM signal
- Using **telinit** to change **init**'s run level (SystemV-ish systems)
- Killing **init**

### Turning off the power

Even on a small UNIX system, turning off the power is not a good way to shut down. You can potentially lose data and leave the system's files in an inconsistent state.

Some machines (e.g., HPs) have a "soft power switch," which means that when you press the power button, the machine actually runs some commands to perform a proper shutdown sequence. If you're not sure whether your machine provides this feature, don't poke the power button to find out! It's better to perform the shutdown sequence yourself.

That said, however, powering off is not the end of the world. In the event of a flood or fire, it's OK to turn off the power if you can't afford the time to bring machines down gracefully. Old-style machine rooms often had a panic button that turned everything off at once.

### shutdown: the genteel way to halt the system

**shutdown** is the safest, most considerate, and most thorough way to initiate a halt or reboot or to return to single-user mode. Unfortunately, almost every vendor has decided to tamper with its arguments. We discuss the command in general, then provide a table listing the syntax and arguments you will need on each platform.

You can ask **shutdown** to wait a while before bringing down the system. During the waiting period, **shutdown** sends messages (a la **wall**) to logged-in users at progressively shorter intervals, warning them of the impending downtime. By default, the warnings simply say that the system is being shut down and give the time remaining until the event; you can also supply a short message of your own. Your message should tell why the system is being brought down and should estimate how long it will be before users can log in again. On most systems, users cannot log in when a **shutdown** is imminent, but they will see your message if you specified one.

Most versions of **shutdown** let you specify whether the machine should halt, go to single-user mode, or reboot. Sometimes, you can also specify whether you want to **fsck** the disks after a reboot. On modern systems with large disks, a complete **fsck** can take a long time; you can generally skip the checks if you shut the system down cleanly. Some systems automatically skip the **fsck** checks whenever the filesystems were properly unmounted.

Table 2.6 outlines the **shutdown** command-line arguments on our example systems.

**Table 2.6    The many faces of shutdown**

| System | Pathname | Time | Rᵃ | H | S | F |
|--------|----------|------|----|----|----|----|
| Solaris | **/usr/sbin/shutdown** | -g*secs* | **-i6** | **-i0** | **-iS** | – |
| HP-UX | **/etc/shutdown** | *secs* | **-r** | **-h** | – | – |
| Red Hat | **/sbin/shutdown** | *time* | **-r** | **-h** | – | **-f** |
| FreeBSD | **/sbin/shutdown** | +*mins* | **-r** | **-h** | – | – |

a. R = Reboot, H = Halt, S = Enter single-user mode, F = Skip **fsck**

### halt: a simpler way to shut down

The **halt** command performs the essential duties required to bring the system down. It is called by **shutdown -h** but can also be used by itself. **halt** logs the shutdown, kills nonessential processes, executes the **sync** system call (called by and equivalent to the **sync** command), waits for filesystem writes to complete, and then halts the kernel.

**halt -n** prevents the **sync** call; it's used after **fsck** repairs the root partition, to prevent the kernel from overwriting repairs with old versions of the superblock that have been cached in memory. **halt -q** causes an almost immediate halt, without synchronization, killing of processes, or writing of logs. This flag is rarely appropriate.

### reboot: quick and dirty restart

**reboot** is almost identical to **halt**, but it causes the machine to reboot from scratch rather than halting. **reboot** is called by **shutdown -r**. Like **halt**, it supports the **-n** and **-q** flags.

### Sending init a TERM signal

The results of killing **init** are unpredictable and often nasty. Consult your documentation before sending any signals. When the BSD version of **init** receives a TERM signal, it usually kills all user processes, daemons, and **getty**s and returns the system to single-user mode. This facility is used by **shutdown**.

*See page 51 for more information about kill.*
To send a signal to a process, you normally need to look up its process ID number with **ps**; however, **init** is always process 1. Use the **kill** command to send the signal:

```
# sync; sync
# kill -TERM 1
```

More information about signals is given in Chapter 4.

### telinit: change init's run level

On systems with the beefy multilevel **init**, you can use the **telinit** command to direct **init** to go to a specific run level. For example,

```
# telinit S
```

takes the system to single-user mode on Solaris and HP-UX. Under Red Hat, you need to change to run level 1; otherwise, you'll just start a root shell without actually changing the run level:

```
# telinit 1
```

When you use **telinit**, you do not get the nice warning messages or grace period that you get with **shutdown**. The command

```
# shutdown -i1
```

brings the system to the same state with more grace. **telinit** is most useful for testing changes to the **inittab** file. **telinit -q** makes **init** reread the **inittab** file.

### Killing init

**init** is so important to the operation of the system that if it is killed with **kill -KILL** or **kill -9**, most computers will reboot automatically (some kernels just panic). This is a rough way to reboot; use **shutdown** or **reboot** instead.

# 3 *Rootly Powers*

Every file and process on a UNIX system is owned by a particular user account. Other users can't access these objects without the owner's permission, so this convention helps to protect users against each other's misdeeds, both intentional and accidental.

System files and processes are owned by a fictitious user called "root", also known as the superuser. As with any account, root's property is protected against interference from other users. To make administrative changes, you'll need to use one of the methods of accessing the root account described in this chapter.

The root account has several "magic" properties. Root can act as the owner of any file or process. Root can also perform several special operations that are off-limits to other users. The account is both very powerful and, in untrained or malicious hands, very dangerous.

This chapter introduces the basics of superuser access for administrators. Chapter 21, *Security*, describes how to avoid unwanted and embarrassing superuser access by others. Chapter 27, *Policy and Politics* covers the relevant political and administrative aspects.

## 3.1 OWNERSHIP OF FILES AND PROCESSES

Every UNIX file has both an owner and a "group owner." The owner of the file enjoys one special privilege that is not shared with everyone on the system: the ability to modify the permissions of the file. In particular, the owner can set the permissions on a file so restrictively that no one else can access it.[1] We take up the subject of file permissions in Chapter 5, *The Filesystem*.

*See page 79 for more information about groups.*

While the owner of a file is always a single person, many people may be group owners of the file, so long as they are all part of a single UNIX group. Groups are defined in the **/etc/group** file.

The owner of a file gets to specify what the group owners can do with it. This scheme allows files to be shared among members of the same project. For example, we used a UNIX group to control access to the source files for the first edition of this book.

Both ownerships of a file can be determined with **ls -l** *filename*. For example:

```
% ls -l /staff/scott/todo
-rw-------  1  scott  staff  1258 Jun 4 18:15  /staff/scott/todo
```

This file is owned by the user "scott" and the group "staff."

UNIX actually keeps track of owners and groups as numbers rather than as text names. User identification numbers (UIDs for short) are mapped to user names in the **/etc/passwd** file, and group identification numbers (GIDs) are mapped to group names in **/etc/group**.[2] The text names that correspond to UIDs and GIDs are defined only for the convenience of the system's human users. When commands such as **ls** want to display ownership information in a human-readable format, they must look up each name in the appropriate file or database.

Processes have not two but four identities associated with them: a real and effective UID and a real and effective GID. The "real" numbers are used for accounting, and the "effective" numbers are used for the determination of access permissions. Normally, the real and effective numbers are the same. The owner of a process can send the process signals (see page 48) and can also reduce (degrade) the process's scheduling priority.

*See page 70 for more information about permission bits.*

While it is not normally possible for a process to alter its four ownership credentials, there is a special situation in which the effective user and group IDs may be changed. When a command is executed that has its "setuid" or "setgid" permissions bit set, the effective UID or GID of the resulting process may be set to the UID or GID of the file containing the program image rather than the UID and GID of the user that ran the command. The identity of the process is thus "promoted" for that specific command only.

UNIX's setuid facility allows programs run by ordinary users to make use of the root account in a limited and tightly controlled way. For example, the **passwd** command that users run to change their login password is a setuid program. It modifies the **/etc/passwd** file in a well-defined way and then terminates. Of course, even this lim-

---

1. In fact, the permissions can be set so restrictively that even the owner of a file cannot access it, a feature that is actually more useful than it may seem.
2. Some systems no longer store this information in text files. See Chapter 18, *Sharing System Files*, for more information.

ited task has potential for abuse, so **passwd** requires users to prove that they know the current account password before it agrees to make the requested change.

## 3.2  THE SUPERUSER

The defining characteristic of the root account is its UID of 0. UNIX does not prevent you from changing the username on this account or from creating additional accounts whose UIDs are 0, but both actions are very bad ideas. Such changes have a tendency to create inadvertent breaches of system security. They also engender confusion and scorn when other people have to deal with the strange way you've configured your system.

UNIX permits the superuser (that is, any process whose effective UID is 0) to perform any valid operation on any file or process.[3] In addition, some system calls (requests to the kernel) may be executed only by the superuser. Some examples of such restricted operations are:

- Changing the root directory of a process with **chroot**
- Creating device files
- Setting the system clock
- Raising resource usage limits and process priorities
- Setting the system's hostname
- Configuring network interfaces
- Shutting down the system

An example of superuser powers is the ability of a process owned by root to change its UID and GID. The **login** program is a case in point; the process that prompts you for your password when you log in to the system initially runs as root. If the password and username that you enter are legitimate, **login** changes its UID and GID to your UID and GID and executes your shell. Once a root process has changed its ownerships to become a normal user process, it can't recover its former privileged state.

## 3.3  CHOOSING A ROOT PASSWORD

*See page 666 for more information about password cracking.*

The root password should be at least eight characters in length; seven-character passwords can be cracked quite easily. On some systems, it doesn't help to use a password longer than eight characters because only the first eight are significant.

It's important that the root password be selected so as not to be easily guessed or discovered by trial and error. In theory, the most secure type of password consists of a random sequence of letters, punctuation, and digits. But because this type of password is hard to remember and usually difficult to type, it may not be optimally secure if administrators write it down or type it slowly.

---

3. "Valid" is an important weasel word here. Certain operations (such as executing a file on which the execute permission bit is not set) are forbidden even to the superuser.

Until recently, a password consisting of two randomly selected words separated by a punctuation mark was a pretty good compromise between security and memorability. Unfortunately, such passwords can now be cracked pretty quickly; we now advise against this scheme.

These days, we suggest that you form a root password by boiling down a phrase of "shocking nonsense," defined by Grady Ward in an earlier version of the PGP Passphrase FAQ:

> *"Shocking nonsense" means to make up a short phrase or sentence that is both nonsensical and shocking in the culture of the user. That is, it contains grossly obscene, racist, impossible or otherwise extreme juxtapositions of ideas. This technique is permissible because the passphrase, by its nature, is never revealed to anyone with sensibilities to offend.*
>
> *Shocking nonsense is unlikely to be duplicated anywhere because it does not describe a matter of fact that could be accidentally rediscovered by someone else. The emotional evocation makes it difficult for the creator to forget. A mild example of such shocking nonsense might be, "Mollusks peck my galloping genitals." The reader can undoubtedly make up many far more shocking or entertaining examples for him or herself.*

You can reduce such a phrase to an eight-character password by recording only the first letter of each word or by some similar transformation. Password security will be increased enormously if you include numbers, punctuation marks, and capital letters. (Some systems now require this.)

You should change the root password

- At least every three months or so
- Every time someone who knows the password leaves your site
- Whenever you think security may have been compromised
- On a day you're not planning to party so hard in the evening that you will have forgotten the password the next morning

## 3.4 BECOMING ROOT

Since root is just another user, you can log in directly to the root account. However, this turns out to be a pretty bad idea. To begin with, it leaves no record of what operations were performed as root. That's bad enough when you realize that you broke something last night at 3:00 a.m. and can't remember what you changed; it's even worse when the access was unauthorized and you are trying to figure out what an intruder has done to your system. Another disadvantage is that the log-in-as-root scenario leaves no record of who was really doing the work. If several people have access to the root account, you won't be able to tell who used it when.

For these reasons, most systems allow root logins to be disabled on terminals and across the network—everywhere but on the system console. We suggest that you use these features. See *Secure terminals* on page 660 to find out what file you need to edit on your particular system.

### su: substitute user identity

A slightly better way to access the root account is to use the **su** command. If invoked without any arguments, **su** will prompt you for the root password and then start up a root shell. The privileges of this shell remain in effect until the shell terminates (via <Control-D> or the **exit** command). **su** doesn't record the commands executed as root, but it does create a log entry that states who became root and when.

The **su** command can also substitute identities other than root. Sometimes, the only way to reproduce or debug a user's problem is to **su** to their account so that you reproduce the environment in which the problem occurs.

If you know someone's password, you can access that person's account directly by executing **su** *username*. As with an **su** to root, you will be prompted for the password for *username*. On some systems, the root password will allow an **su** or **login** to any account. On others, you must first **su** explicitly to root before **su**ing to another account; root may **su** to any account without providing a password.

It's a good idea to get in the habit of typing the full pathname to the **su** command (e.g., **/bin/su** or **/usr/bin/su**) rather than relying on the shell to find the command for you. This will give you some protection against programs called **su** that may have been slipped into your search path with the intention of harvesting passwords.[4]

On many systems, you must be a member of the group "wheel" in order to use **su**.

### sudo: a limited su

Since the privileges of the superuser account cannot be subdivided, it is hard to give someone the ability to do one task (backups, for example) without giving that person free run of the system. And if the root account is used by several administrators, you really have only a vague idea who's using it or what they've done.

Our solution to these problems is a program called **sudo** that is currently maintained by Todd Miller (who was also a contributor to this book). It's available from www.courtesan.com.

**sudo** takes as its argument a command line to be executed as root (or as another restricted user). **sudo** consults the file **/etc/sudoers**, which lists the people who are authorized to use **sudo** and the commands they are allowed to run on each host. If the proposed command is permitted, **sudo** prompts for the *user's own* password and executes the command.

---

4. For the same reason, we highly recommend that you *not* include "." (the current directory) in your shell's search path. While convenient, this configuration makes it easy to inadvertently run "special" versions of system commands that a user or intruder has left lying around for you as a trap. Naturally, this advice goes double for root.

Additional **sudo** commands may be executed without the "sudoer" having to type a password until a five-minute period (configurable) has elapsed with no further **sudo** activity. This timeout serves as a modest protection against users with **sudo** privileges who leave terminals unattended.

**sudo** keeps a log of the command lines that were executed, the people who requested them, the directory from which they were run, and the times at which they were invoked. This information can be logged via syslog or placed in the file of your choice. We recommend using syslog to forward the log entries to a "secure" central host.

A log entry for randy executing **sudo /bin/cat /etc/sudoers** might look like this:

```
Dec 7 10:57:19 tigger sudo: randy: TTY=ttyp0 TTY=ttyp0 ;
    PWD=/tigger/users/randy; USER=root ; COMMAND=/bin/cat /etc/sudoers
```

The **sudoers** file is designed so that a single version can be used on many different hosts at once. Here's a typical example:

```
# Define aliases for machines in CS & Physics departments
Host_Alias   CS = tigger, anchor, piper, moet, sigi
Host_Alias   PHYSICS = eprince, pprince, icarus

# Define collections of commands
Cmnd_Alias  DUMP = /usr/sbin/dump, /usr/sbin/restore
Cmnd_Alias  PRINTING = /usr/sbin/lpc, /usr/bin/lprm
Cmnd_Alias  SHELLS = /bin/sh, /bin/tcsh, /bin/csh

# Permissions
mark, ed    PHYSICS = ALL
herb        CS = /usr/local/bin/tcpdump : PHYSICS = (operator) DUMP
lynda       ALL = (ALL) ALL, !SHELLS
%wheel      ALL, !PHYSICS = NOPASSWD: PRINTING
```

The first five noncomment lines define groups of hosts and commands that are referred to in the permission specifications later in the file. The lists could be included literally in the specs, but the use of aliases makes the **sudoers** file easier to read and understand; it also makes the file easier to update in the future. It's also possible to define aliases for sets of users and for sets of users as whom commands may be run.

Each permission specification line includes information about

- The users to whom the line applies
- The hosts on which the line should be heeded
- The commands that the specified users may run
- The users as whom they may be executed

The first permission line applies to the users mark and ed on the machines in the PHYSICS group (eprince, pprince, and icarus). The built-in command alias ALL allows them to run any command. Since no list of users is specified in parentheses, **sudo** will only run commands as root.

The second permission line allows herb to run **tcpdump** on CS machines and dump-related commands on PHYSICS machines. However, the dump commands can only be run as operator, not as root. The actual command line that herb would type would be something like

```
% sudo -u operator /usr/sbin/dump 0u /dev/rsd0a
```

The user lynda can run commands as any user on any machine, except that she can't run several common shells. Does this mean that lynda really can't get a root shell? Of course not:

```
% cp -p /bin/csh /tmp/csh
% sudo /tmp/csh
```

Generally speaking, any attempt to allow "all commands except..." is doomed to failure, at least in a technical sense. However, it may still be worthwhile to set up the **sudoers** file this way as a reminder that root shells are frowned upon. It may discourage casual use.

The final line allows users in the UNIX group wheel to run **lpc** and **lprm** as root on all machines except eprince, pprince, and icarus. Furthermore, no password is required to run the commands.

Note that commands in **/etc/sudoers** are specified with full pathnames to prevent people from executing their own programs and scripts as root. Though no examples are shown above, it is possible to specify the arguments that are permissible for each command as well. In fact, this simple configuration only scratches the surface of the beauty and splendor that is the **sudoers** file.

To modify **/etc/sudoers**, you use the **visudo** command, which checks to be sure no one else is editing the file, invokes an editor on it, and then verifies the syntax of the edited file before installing it. This last step is particularly important because an invalid **sudoers** file might prevent you from **sudo**ing again to fix it.

The use of **sudo** has the following advantages:

- Accountability is much improved because of command logging.
- Operators can do chores without unlimited root privileges.
- The real root password can be known to only one or two people.
- It's faster to use **sudo** than to run **su** or to log in as root.
- Privileges can be revoked without the need to change the root password.
- A canonical list of all users with root privileges is maintained.
- There is less chance of a root shell being left unattended.
- A single file can be used to control access for an entire network.

There are a couple of disadvantages as well. The worst of these is that any breach in the security of a sudoer's personal account can be equivalent to breaching the root account itself. There is not much you can do to counter this threat other than to caution your sudoers to protect their own accounts as they would the root account.

**sudo**'s command logging can be subverted by tricks such as shell escapes from within an allowed program or by **sudo csh** and **sudo su** if you allow them.

## 3.5 OTHER PSEUDO-USERS

Root is the only user that has special status in the eyes of the UNIX kernel, but several other pseudo-users are defined by the system. It's customary to replace the encrypted password field of these special users in **/etc/passwd** with a star so that their accounts cannot be logged in to.

### daemon: owner of unprivileged system software

The daemon account usually has UID 1. Files and processes that are part of the operating system but that need not be owned by root are often given to daemon. This convention helps to avoid the security hazards associated with ownership by root. There is also a UNIX group called "daemon" that exists for similar reasons.

### bin: owner of system commands

On some systems, the bin user owns the directories that contain the system's commands and most of the commands themselves as well. Dedicating a special user account to this task is often regarded as superfluous (or perhaps even slightly insecure), so modern systems generally just use the root account.

### sys: owner of the kernel and memory images

On some systems, the user sys owns special files such as **/dev/kmem**, **/dev/mem**, and **/dev/drum** or /dev/swap, which are, respectively, the kernel's address space, the physical memory of the system, and an image of the system's swap space. Few programs access these files, but those that do run setuid to sys if this ownership convention is in use. On some systems, a group called "kmem" or "sys" is used instead of a "sys" user account.

### nobody: the generic NFS user

Most versions of UNIX define a user called "nobody" with UID -1 or -2. The architects of Solaris were moved to select UID 60,001 (and to add the user "noaccess" at UID 60,002), which just shows how difficult it can be to kick the habit of gratuitous changes.

See page 491 for more information about the nobody account.

The Network File System (NFS) uses the nobody account to represent root users on other systems for purposes of file sharing. To strip remote roots of their rootly powers, the remote UID 0 has to be mapped to something other than the local UID 0. The nobody account acts as the generic alter ego for these remote roots.

Since the nobody account is supposed to represent a generic and relatively powerless user, it shouldn't own any files. If nobody does own files, remote roots will be able to take control of them. Nobody shouldn't own no files!

Some daemons, such as **fingerd**, run as nobody.

UIDs are often represented as short integers and thus -1 might appear as 32,767. This wrapping can thwart the scheme for determining the next available UID that is used by many **adduser** programs.

# *4* *Controlling Processes*

A process is the abstraction used by UNIX to represent a running program. It's the object through which a program's use of memory, processor time, and I/O resources can be managed and monitored.

It is part of the UNIX philosophy that as much work as possible be done within the context of processes, rather than handled specially by the kernel. Although portions of the kernel cannot be made to fit this model, it is used by most system software. System and user processes all follow the same rules, so you can use a single set of tools to control them both.

## 4.1 COMPONENTS OF A PROCESS

A process consists of an address space and a set of data structures within the kernel. The address space is a set of memory pages[1] that the kernel has marked for the process's use. It contains the code and libraries that the process is executing, the process's variables, its stacks, and various extra information needed by the kernel while the process is running. Because UNIX supports virtual memory, there is not necessarily a correlation between a page's location within an address space and its location inside the machine's physical memory or swap space.

The kernel's internal data structures record various pieces of information about each process. Some of the more important of these are:

---

1. Pages are the units in which memory is managed, usually 1K to 8K in size.

- The process's address space map
- The current status of the process (sleeping, stopped, runnable, etc.)
- The execution priority of the process
- Information about the resources the process has used (for accounting)
- The process's signal mask (a record of which signals are blocked)
- The owner of the process

In traditional UNIX, a process also keeps track of which instructions the CPU is currently executing on its behalf. Some modern systems allow more than one "processor" to execute code within a process at the same time (the extra processors may be real or simulated, depending on the hardware and system load). In these systems, information about each execution context is contained in an object called a thread.

In concept, two threads can be scheduled and prioritized independently despite being contained within a single process. In practice, the thread API used by most vendors doesn't encourage such fine-grained scheduling. Most scheduling issues are still handled at the process level, and thus far, multithreading has had little impact on system administration.

Many of the parameters associated with a process directly affect its execution: the amount of processor time it gets, the files it can access, and so on. In the following sections, we discuss the meaning and significance of the parameters that are most interesting from a system administrator's point of view. These attributes are common to all versions of UNIX.

### PID: process ID number

The kernel assigns a unique ID number to every process. Most commands and system calls that manipulate processes require you to specify a PID to identify the target of the operation. PIDs are assigned in order as processes are created. When the kernel runs out of PIDs, it starts again at 1, skipping over any PIDs that are still in use.

### PPID: parent PID

UNIX does not supply a system call that creates a new process running a particular program. Instead, an existing process must clone itself to create a new process. The clone can then exchange the program it is running for a different one.

When a process is cloned, the original process is referred to as the parent, and the copy is called the child. The PPID attribute of a process is the PID of the parent from which it was cloned.[2]

### UID and EUID: real and effective user ID

*See page 79 for more information about UIDs.*

A process's UID is the user identification number of the person who created it, or more accurately, it is a copy of the EUID value of the parent process. Usually, only the creator (aka the "owner") and the superuser are permitted to manipulate a process.

---

2. At least initially. If the original parent dies, **init** (process 1) becomes the new parent. See page 48.

The EUID is the "effective" user ID, an extra UID used to determine what resources and files a process has permission to access at any given moment. For most processes, the UID and EUID are the same, the usual exception being programs that are setuid.

Why have both a UID and an EUID? Simply because it's useful to maintain a distinction between identity and permission, and because a setuid program may not wish to operate with expanded permissions all of the time. On most systems, the effective UID can be set and reset to enable or restrict the additional permissions it grants.

### GID and EGID: real and effective group ID

*See page 79 for more information about groups.*

The GID is the group identification number of a process. The EGID is related to the GID in the same way that the EUID is related to the UID. If a process tries to access a file for which it does not have owner permission, the kernel will automatically check to see if permission may be granted on the basis of the EGID.

On some systems, a process can be in more than one group at a time. In this case, the GID and EGID are actually a list of group numbers. When the process attempts to access a resource, the entire list is checked to see if it belongs to an appropriate group.

### Niceness

A process's scheduling priority determines how much CPU time it receives. The kernel uses a dynamic algorithm to compute priorities, taking into account the amount of CPU time that a process has recently consumed and the length of time it has been waiting to run. The kernel also pays attention to an administratively set value that's usually called the "nice value" or "niceness," so called because it tells how nice you are planning to be to other users of the system. We take up the subject of niceness in detail on page 52.

### Control terminal

Most processes have a control terminal associated with them. The control terminal determines default linkages for the standard input, standard output, and standard error channels. When you start a command from the shell, your terminal normally becomes the process's control terminal. The concept of a control terminal also affects the distribution of signals, which are discussed starting on page 48.

## 4.2  THE LIFE CYCLE OF A PROCESS

To create a new process, a process copies itself with the **fork** system call. **fork** creates a copy of the original process that is largely identical to the parent. The new process has a distinct PID and has its own accounting information.

**fork** has the unique property of returning two different values. From the child's point of view, it returns zero. The parent, on the other hand, is returned the PID of the newly created child. Since the two processes are otherwise identical, they must both examine the return value to figure out which role they are supposed to play.

Controlling Processes

After a **fork**, the child process will often use one of the **exec** family of system calls to begin execution of a new program.[3] These calls change the program text that the process is executing and reset the data and stack segments to a predefined initial state. The various forms of **exec** differ only in the ways that they specify the command-line arguments and environment to be given to the new program.

*See Chapter 2 for more information about booting and the **init** daemon.*

When the system boots, the kernel autonomously creates and installs several processes. The most notable of these is **init**, which is always process number 1. **init** is responsible for forking a shell to execute the **rc** startup scripts, if your system uses them. All processes other than the ones the kernel creates are descendants of **init**.

**init** also plays another important role in process management. When a process completes, it calls a routine named **_exit** to notify the kernel that it is ready to die. It supplies an exit code (an integer) that tells why it's exiting. By convention, 0 is used to indicate a normal or "successful" termination.

Before a process can be allowed to disappear completely, UNIX requires that its death be acknowledged by the process's parent, which the parent does with a call to **wait**. The parent receives a copy of the child's exit code (or an indication of why the child was killed, if the child did not exit voluntarily) and can also obtain a summary of the child's use of resources if it wishes.

This scheme works fine if parents outlive their children and are conscientious about calling **wait** so that dead processes can be disposed of. If the parent dies first, however, the kernel recognizes that no **wait** will be forthcoming and adjusts the process to make the orphan a child of **init**. **init** is supposed to accept these orphaned processes and perform the **wait** needed to get rid of them when they die.

In the past, **init** occasionally did not do its job properly and zombies—processes that are no longer actually running but are still listed by the kernel—were left around. We have not seen this behavior recently, however.

## 4.3  SIGNALS

Signals are process-level interrupt requests. About thirty different kinds are defined, and they're used in a variety of ways:

- They can be sent among processes as a means of communication.

- They can be sent by the terminal driver to kill, interrupt, or suspend processes when special keys such as <Control-C> and <Control-Z> are typed.[4]

- They can be sent by the administrator (with **kill**) to achieve various results.

- They can be sent by the kernel when a process commits an infraction such as division by zero.

---

3. Actually, they're not all system calls. Usually, all but one are library routines.

4. The functions of <Control-Z> and <Control-C> can be reassigned to other keys with the **stty** command, but this is rare in practice. In this chapter we refer to them by their conventional bindings. See page 111 for more information.

*A core dump is a memory image of a process that can be used for debugging.*

When a signal is received, one of two things can happen. If the receiving process has designated a handler routine for that particular signal, the handler is called with information about the context in which the signal was delivered. Otherwise, the kernel takes some default action on behalf of the process. The default action varies from signal to signal. Many signals terminate the process; some also generate a core dump.

Specifying a handler routine for a signal within a program is referred to as "catching" the signal. When the handler completes, execution restarts from the point at which the signal was received.

To prevent signals from arriving, programs can request that they be either ignored or blocked. A signal that is ignored is simply discarded and has no effect on the process. A blocked signal is queued for delivery, but the kernel doesn't require the process to act on it until the signal has been explicitly unblocked. The handler for a newly unblocked signal is called only once, even if the signal was received several times while reception was blocked.

Table 4.1 lists the signals that all administrators should know. The uppercase convention for signal names derives from C language tradition. You might also sometimes see signal names written with a SIG prefix (e.g., SIGHUP) for similar reasons.

**Table 4.1    UNIX signals that every administrator should know**

| # | Name | Description | Default | Can catch? | Can block? | Dump core? |
|---|------|-------------|---------|------------|------------|------------|
| 1 | HUP | Hangup | Terminate | Yes | Yes | No |
| 2 | INT | Interrupt | Terminate | Yes | Yes | No |
| 3 | QUIT | Quit | Terminate | Yes | Yes | Yes |
| 9 | KILL | Kill | Terminate | No | No | No |
| a | BUS | Bus error | Terminate | Yes | Yes | Yes |
| a | SEGV | Segmentation fault | Terminate | Yes | Yes | Yes |
| 15 | TERM | Software termination | Terminate | Yes | Yes | No |
| a | STOP | Stop | Stop | No | No | No |
| a | TSTP | Keyboard stop | Stop | Yes | Yes | No |
| a | CONT | Continue after stop | Ignore | Yes | No | No |
| a | WINCH | Window changed | Ignore | Yes | Yes | No |
| a | USR1 | User-defined | Terminate | Yes | Yes | No |
| a | USR2 | User-defined | Terminate | Yes | Yes | No |

a. Varies among systems. See **/usr/include/signal.h** or **man signal** for more specific information.

There are other signals not shown in Table 4.1, most of which are used to report obscure errors such as "illegal instruction." The default handling for signals like that is to terminate with a core dump. Catching and blocking are generally allowed because some programs may be smart enough to try to clean up whatever problem caused the error before continuing.

Controlling Processes

The BUS and SEGV signals are also error signals. We've included them in the table because they're so common: 99% of the time that a program crashes, it's ultimately one of these two signals that finally brings it down. By themselves, the signals are of no specific diagnostic value. Both of them indicate an attempt to use or access memory improperly.

Most terminal emulators will send a WINCH signal when their configuration parameters (such as the number of lines in the virtual terminal) change. This convention allows emulator-savvy programs (text editors, mostly) to reconfigure themselves automatically in response to changes. If you can't get windows to resize properly, make sure that WINCH is being generated and propagated correctly.

The signals named KILL and STOP cannot be caught, blocked, or ignored. The KILL signal destroys the receiving process, and STOP suspends its execution until a CONT signal is received. CONT may be caught or ignored, but not blocked.

TSTP is a "soft" version of STOP that might be best described as a request to stop. It's the signal generated by the terminal driver when you type a <Control-Z> on the keyboard. Programs that catch this signal usually clean up their state, then send themselves a STOP signal to complete the stop operation. Alternatively, TSTP may simply be ignored, to prevent the program from being stopped from the keyboard.

The signals KILL, INT, HUP, QUIT, and TERM may all sound as if they mean about the same thing, but their uses are actually quite different. It's unfortunate that such vague terminology was selected for them. Here's a decoding guide:

- KILL is unblockable and terminates a process at the OS level. A process can never actually "receive" this signal.

- INT is the signal sent by the terminal driver when you type <Control-C>. It's a request to terminate the current operation. Simple programs should quit (if they catch the signal) or simply allow themselves to be killed, which is the default if the signal is not caught. Programs that have a command line or input mode should stop what they're doing, clean up, and wait for user input again.

- TERM is a request to terminate execution completely. It's expected that the receiving process will clean up its state and exit.

- HUP has two common interpretations. First, it's understood as a reset request by many daemons. If a daemon is capable of rereading its configuration file and adjusting to changes without restarting, a HUP can generally be used to trigger this behavior.

  Second, HUP signals are sometimes generated by the terminal driver in an attempt to "clean up" (i.e., kill) the processes attached to a particular terminal. This can happen, for example, when a terminal session is concluded or when a modem connection is inadvertently dropped (hence the name "hangup"). The details vary by system.

Shells in the C shell family (**csh**, **tcsh**, et al.) usually make background processes immune to HUP signals so that they can continue to run after the user logs out. Users of Bourne-ish shells (**sh**, **ksh**, **bash**, etc.) can emulate this behavior with the **nohup** command.

- QUIT is similar to TERM, except that it defaults to producing a core dump if not caught. A few programs cannibalize this signal and interpret it to mean something else.

The signals USR1 and USR2 have no set meaning. They're available for programs to use in whatever way they'd like. For example, **named** interprets these signals as a request to set its debugging level.

## 4.4   KILL: SEND SIGNALS

As its name implies, the **kill** command is most often used to terminate a process. **kill** can send any signal, but by default it sends a TERM. **kill** can be used by normal users on their own processes or by the superuser on any process. The syntax is

kill [-signal] pid

where *signal* is the number or symbolic name of the signal to be sent (as shown in Table 4.1) and *pid* is the process identification number of the target process. On some systems, a *pid* of -1 broadcasts the signal to all processes except system processes and the current shell.

A **kill** without a signal number does not guarantee that the process will die because the TERM signal can be caught, blocked, or ignored. The command

kill **-9** pid

will "guarantee" that the process will die because signal 9, KILL, cannot be caught. We put quotes around "guarantee" because processes can sometimes become so wedged that even KILL does not affect them (usually because of some degenerate I/O vapor lock such as waiting for a disk that has stopped spinning). Rebooting is usually the only way to get rid of these naughty processes.

## 4.5   PROCESS STATES

A process is not automatically eligible to receive CPU time just because it exists. There are essentially four execution states that you need to be aware of; they are listed in Table 4.2 on the next page.

A runnable process is ready to execute whenever CPU time is available. It has acquired all the resources it needs and is just waiting for CPU time to process its data. As soon as the process makes a system call that cannot be immediately completed (such as a request to read part of a file), UNIX will put it to sleep.

Sleeping processes are waiting for a specific event to occur. Interactive shells and system daemons spend most of their time sleeping, waiting for terminal input or net-

**Table 4.2    Process states**

| State | Meaning |
| --- | --- |
| Runnable | The process can be executed. |
| Sleeping | The process is waiting for some resource. |
| Zombie | The process is trying to die. |
| Stopped | The process is suspended (not allowed to execute). |

work connections. Since a sleeping process is effectively blocked until its request has been satisfied, it will get no CPU time unless it receives a signal.

Stopped processes are administratively forbidden to run. Processes are stopped on receipt of a STOP or TSTP signal and are restarted with CONT. Being stopped is similar to sleeping, but there's no way to get out of the stopped state other than having some other process wake you up (or kill you).

## 4.6  NICE AND RENICE: INFLUENCE SCHEDULING PRIORITY

The "niceness" of a process is a numeric hint to the kernel about how the process should be treated in relationship to other processes contending for the CPU. The strange name is derived from the fact that it determines how nice you are going to be to other users of the system. A high nice value means a low priority for your process: you are going to be nice. A low or negative value means high priority: you are not very nice.

The range of allowable niceness values varies among systems. The most common range is -20 to +19. Some systems use a range of a similar size beginning at 0 instead of a negative number (typically 0 to 39). The ranges used on our example systems are shown in Table 4.3.

Despite their numeric differences, all systems handle nice values in much the same way. Unless the user takes special action, a newly created process inherits the nice value of its parent process. The owner of the process can increase its nice value but cannot lower it, even to return the process to the default niceness. This restriction prevents processes with low priority from bearing high-priority children. The superuser has complete freedom in setting nice values and may even set a processes's niceness so low that no other process can run.

On some systems, the kernel will automatically boost the nice value of processes that have accumulated "excessive" CPU time or that have been put in the background.

*See Chapter 25 for more information about performance.*

Manually setting process priorities is quickly becoming a thing of the past. When UNIX ran on the puny systems of the 1970s and 80s, performance was most significantly affected by which process was on the CPU. Today, with more than adequate CPU power on most desktops, the scheduler usually does a good job of servicing all processes. Unfortunately, I/O performance has not kept up with increasingly fast CPUs, and the major bottleneck on most systems has become the disk drives.

A process's nice value can be set at the time of creation with the **nice** command and can be adjusted during execution with the **renice** command. **nice** takes a command line as an argument, while **renice** takes a PID or (sometimes) a username.

Some examples:

```
% nice +10 ~/bin/longtask
% renice -5 8829
```

Unfortunately, there is little agreement among systems about how the desired priorities should be specified; in fact, even **nice** and **renice** from the same system usually don't agree. Some commands want a nice value increment, whereas others want an absolute nice value. Some want their nice values preceded by a dash. Others want a flag (**-n**), and some just want a value.

To complicate things, there is a version of **nice** built into the C shell and some other common shells (but not **sh**). If you don't type the full path to the **nice** command, you'll get the shell's version rather than the operating system's. This can be confusing because shell-**nice** and OS-**nice** almost always use different syntax (and sometimes different ranges of values as well).

Table 4.3 summarizes all these variations. A *prio* is an absolute nice value, while an *incr* is relative to the niceness of the shell from which **nice** or **renice** is run. Wherever an *-incr* or a *-prio* is called for, you can use a double dash to enter negative values (e.g., *--***10**). Only the shell **nice** understands plus signs (in fact, it requires them); leave them out in all other circumstances.

**Table 4.3     How to express priorities for various versions of nice and renice**

| System | Range | OS nice | csh nice | renice |
|--------|-------|---------|----------|--------|
| Solaris | 0 to 39 | *-incr* or **-n** *incr* | *+incr* or *-incr* | *incr* or **-n** *incr* |
| HP-UX | 0 to 39 | *-prio* or **-n** *prio* | *+incr* or *-incr* | **-n** *prio*[a] |
| Red Hat | -20 to 20 | *-incr* or **-n** *incr* | *+incr* or *-incr* | *prio* |
| FreeBSD | -20 to 20 | *-prio* | *+incr* or *-incr* | *prio* |

a. Uses absolute priority, but adds 20 to the value you specify.

The most commonly **nice**d process in the modern world is **xntpd**, the clock synchronization daemon. Since CPU promptness is critical to its mission, it usually runs at a nice value about 12 below the default (that is, at a higher priority than normal).

If a process goes berserk and drives the system's load average to 65, you may need to use **nice** to start a high-priority shell before you can run commands to investigate the problem. Otherwise, your commands may never get a chance to run.

## 4.7   PS: MONITOR PROCESSES

**ps** is the system administrator's main tool for monitoring processes. While versions of **ps** differ in their arguments and display, they all provide essentially the same information. Part of the enormous variation among versions of **ps** can be traced back to the wide gap between **ps** versions that originated in System V (Solaris, HP-UX) and those that descended from BSD (Red Hat, FreeBSD). However, **ps** is also a command that vendors tend to customize for other reasons. It's closely tied to the kernel's handling of processes, so it tends to reflect vendors' underlying kernel changes.

**ps** can be used to show the PID, UID, priority, and control terminal of processes. It can also give information about how much memory a process is using, how much CPU time it has consumed, and its current status (running, stopped, sleeping, etc.). Zombies show up in a **ps** listing as <exiting> or <defunct>.

Understanding **ps** output is an important administrative skill. Looking at a **ps** listing, you can determine (among other things) what processes are running on your system, how much CPU time and memory they're using, and who owns each one.

Implementations of **ps** have become hopelessly complex over the last few years. Several vendors have abandoned the attempt to define meaningful displays and made their **ps**es completely configurable. With a little customization work, almost any desired output can be produced. The **ps** used by Red Hat is a trisexual and hermaphroditic version that understands several other **ps**'s option sets and uses an environment variable to tell it what universe it's living in.

Do not be alarmed by all of this complexity: it's there mainly for kernel developers, not for system administrators. Although you will use **ps** frequently, you only need to know a few specific incantations.

 On Red Hat and FreeBSD, a useful overview of all the processes running on the system can be obtained with **ps aux**. Here's an example of a **ps aux** on a machine running FreeBSD (the Red Hat output is slightly different):

```
% ps aux
USER     PID  %CPU %MEM  VSZ  RSS  TT STAT STARTED TIME    COMMAND
root       0   0.0  0.0    0    0  ?? DLs  8:35PM  0:00.06 (swapper)
root       1   0.0  0.0  208  120  ?? Ss   8:35PM  0:00.20 init-s
root       2   0.0  0.0    0   12  ?? DL   8:35PM  0:00.03 (pagedaemon)
root      46   0.0  0.0  160  112  ?? Ss   8:37PM  0:01.45 syslogd
root      66   0.0  0.0  228  152  ?? I    8:37PM  0:00.23 cron
root      75   0.0  0.0  236  104  ?? IWs  8:37PM  0:00.02 lpd
root     100   0.0  0.0  204   92  ?? Is   8:37PM  0:00.19 inetd
evi     1251   0.0  0.0  320  256  p8 Is+  1:50PM  0:00.47 -csh(csh)
evi     1517   0.0  0.0  128   64  p8 S+   3:17PM  0:00.03 manlogger
evi     1520   0.0  0.0  332  224  pa R+   3:17PM  0:00.04 ps-aux
...
```

The meaning of each field is explained in Table 4.4.

Another useful set of arguments for Red Hat and FreeBSD is **lax**, which provides more technical information. It is also faster to run because it doesn't have to translate every UID to a username—efficiency can be important if the system is already bogged down by some other process. **ps** is generally quite expensive to run.

**Table 4.4   Explanation of ps -aux output (FreeBSD)**

| Field | Contents |
|---|---|
| USER | Username of the process's owner |
| PID | Process ID |
| %CPU | Percentage of the CPU this process is using |
| %MEM | Percentage of real memory this process is using |
| VSZ | Virtual size of the process, in kilobytes |
| RSS | Resident set size (number of 1K pages in memory) |
| TT | Control terminal ID |
| STAT | Current process status: |
| | R = Runnable                        D = In disk (or short-term) wait |
| | I = Sleeping (> 20 sec)    S = Sleeping (< 20 sec) |
| | T = Stopped                         Z = Zombie |
| | Additional Flags: |
| | > = Process has higher than normal priority |
| | N = Process has lower than normal priority |
| | < = Process is exceeding soft limit on memory use |
| | A = Process has requested random page replacement |
| | S = Process has asked for FIFO page replacement |
| | V = Process is suspended during a **vfork** |
| | E = Process is trying to **exit** |
| | L = Some pages are locked in core |
| | X = Process is being traced or debugged |
| | s = Process is a session leader (head of control terminal) |
| | W = Process is swapped out |
| | + = Process is in the foreground of its control terminal |
| STARTED | Time the process was started |
| TIME | CPU time the process has consumed |
| COMMAND | Command name and arguments[a] |

a. Arguments can be truncated; add the **ww** argument to prevent this. Programs can modify
   this info, so it's not necessarily an accurate representation of the actual command line.

Shown here in an abbreviated example, **ps lax** includes fields such as the parent process ID (PPID), nice value (NI), and resource the process is waiting for (WCHAN).

```
% ps lax
UID PID  PPID CPU PRI NI VSZ  RSS  WCHAN STAT  TT TIME    COMMAND
  0   0    0   0  -18 0   0    0   a5e6c  DLs   ?? 0:00.06 (swapper)
  0   1    0   0   10 0  208  120  wait    Is   ?? 0:00.20 init-s
  0   2    0   0  -18 0   0   12   a203c  DL    ?? 0:00.06 pagedaemon
  0  46    1   0    2 0  160  112  select  Ss   ?? 0:01.47 syslogd
  0  77    1   0    2 0  160   88  select  IWs  ?? 0:00.07 portmap
  0  84    1   0    2 0  260  204  select  IWs  ?? 0:00.23 mountd
...
```

 Under Solaris and HP-UX, **ps -ef** is a good place to start (it also works on Red Hat).

```
% ps -ef
 UID    PID  PPID   C    STIME   TTY   TIME   COMD
 root     0     0  80   Dec 21    ?    0:02   sched
 root     1     0   2   Dec 21    ?    4:32   /etc/init-
 root     2     0   8   Dec 21    ?    0:00   pageout
 root   171     1  80   Dec 21    ?    0:02   /usr/lib/sendmail-bd
 trent  8482  8444  35  14:34:10  pts/7  0:00  ps-ef
 trent  8444  8442 203  14:32:50  pts/7  0:01  -csh
 ...
```

The columns are explained in Table 4.5.

**Table 4.5  Explanation of ps -ef output (Solaris, HP-UX, and Red Hat)**

| Field | Content | Field | Content |
|-------|---------|-------|---------|
| UID | Username of the owner | STIME | Time the process was started |
| PID | Process ID | TTY | Control terminal |
| PPID | PID of the parent process | TIME | CPU time consumed |
| C | CPU use/scheduling info | COMD | Command and arguments |

Like **ps -lax** in the Red Hat and FreeBSD worlds, **ps -elf** shows additional gory details on SysV-ish systems:

```
% ps -elf
  F  S  UID  PID  PPID   C  P  NI   ADDR   SZ  WCHAN   TIME  COMD
 19  T  root    0     0  80  0  SY  f00c2fd8   0          0:02  sched
  8  S  root    1     0  65  1  20  ff26a800  88  ff2632c8  4:32  init-
  8  S  root  142     1  41  1  20  ff2e8000 176  f00cb69   0:00  syslogd
 ...
```

The STIME and TTY columns have been omitted to fit this page; they are identical to those produced with **ps -ef**. Nonobvious fields are described in Table 4.6.

**Table 4.6  Explanation of ps -elf output (Solaris, HP-UX, IRIX, and Red Hat)**

| Field | Contents |
|-------|----------|
| F | Process flags; possible values vary by system (rarely useful for sysadmins) |
| S | Process status:<br>O = Currently running    S = Sleeping (waiting for event)<br>R = Eligible to run     T = Stopped or being traced<br>Z = Zombie          D = Uninterruptible sleep (disk, usually) |
| C | Process CPU utilization/scheduling info |
| P | Scheduling priority (internal to the kernel, different from nice value) |
| NI | Nice value or SY for system processes |
| ADDR | Memory address of the process |
| SZ | Size (in pages) of the process in main memory |
| WCHAN | Address of the object the process is waiting for |

## 4.8  TOP: MONITOR PROCESSES EVEN BETTER

*top is available from*
*www.groupsys.com.*

Since commands like **ps** offer only a one-time snapshot of your system, it is often difficult to grasp the "big picture" of what's really happening. **top** is a free utility by William LeFebvre that runs on many systems and provides a regularly updated summary of active processes and their use of resources.

For example:

```
last pid: 21314; load averages: 2.97, 2.95, 2.89  15:51:51
75 processes: 71 sleeping, 3 running, 1 zombie
cpu states: 44.5% user, 0% nice, 23.9% system, 31.6% idle
Memory: 113M avail, 108M in use, 4972K free, 6232K locked

  PID  USER  PRI  NICE   SIZE    RES  STATE   TIME  WCPU  CPU   COMMAND
 1313  root    1   -19   292K   148K  sleep   0:00  9.3%  0.7%  erpcd
 2858  root    1     0  1564K   676K  sleep   0:20  5.4%  0.7%  sendma
 1310  root   27     0   812K   488K  run     0:00  7.6%  0.3%  sendma
  981  root   29     0  2152K  2324K  run     0:03  0.0%  0.0%  top
  192  root    1     0    44K   276K  sleep   0:48  0.0%  0.0%  in.rlo
  778  uucp   27     0   244K   508K  run     0:04  0.0%  0.0%  uucico
 5298  randy  15     0   228K   176K  sleep   0:00  0.0%  0.0%  csh
  151  root   15     0    12K     8K  sleep  54:40  0.0%  0.0%  update
 0962  trent  15     0   212K     0K  sleep   0:00  0.0%  0.0%  csh
 5843  beth   15     0   208K     0K  sleep   0:00  0.0%  0.0%  csh
  167  root   15     0   100K     0K  sleep   0:00  0.0%  0.0%  lpd
 1311  randy   5     0   224K   408K  sleep   0:00  0.0%  0.0%  prev
```

By default, the display is updated every 10 seconds. The most active processes appear at the top. **top** also accepts input from the keyboard and allows you to send signals and **renice** processes, so you can observe how your actions affect the overall condition of the machine.

**top** must consume a small portion of the CPU to show an update every 10 seconds. It should generally be used only for diagnostic purposes, not as a "Hey, look what neat tools I run in my spare windows" toy.

Root can run **top** with the **-q** option to goose it up to the highest possible priority. This can be very useful when you are trying to track down a process that has already brought the system to its knees.

## 4.9  RUNAWAY PROCESSES

*See page 766 for more*
*information about*
*runaway processes.*

Runaway processes come in two flavors: user processes that use up excessive amounts of a system resource such as CPU time or disk space, and system processes that suddenly go berserk and exhibit wild behavior. The first type of runaway is not necessarily malfunctioning; it might simply be a resource hog. System processes are always supposed to behave reasonably.

You can identify processes that use excessive CPU time by looking at the output of **ps**. If it is obvious that a user process is consuming more CPU than can reasonably be expected, investigate the process. Step one is to contact the process's owner and ask what's going on. If the owner can't be found, you will have to do some poking around of your own. Although you should normally avoid looking into users' home directories, it is acceptable when you are trying to track down the source code of a runaway process to find out what it's doing.

There are two reasons to find out what a process is trying to do before tampering with it. First, the process may be both legitimate and important to the user. It's unreasonable to kill processes at random just because they happen to use a lot of CPU. Second, the process may be malicious or destructive. In this case, you've got to know what the process was doing (e.g., cracking passwords) so you can fix the damage.

If the reason for a runaway process's existence can't be determined, suspend it with a STOP signal and send email to the owner explaining what has happened. The process can be restarted later with a CONT signal. Be aware that some processes can be ruined by a long sleep, so this procedure is not always entirely benign. For example, a process may wake to find that some of its network connections have been broken.

If a process is using an excessive amount of CPU but appears to be doing something reasonable and working correctly, you should **renice** it to a higher nice value (lower priority) and ask the owner to do the nicing in the future.

Runaway processes that produce output can fill up an entire filesystem, causing numerous problems. When a filesystem fills up, lots of messages will be logged to the console and attempts to write to the filesystem will produce error messages.

The first thing to do in this situation is to stop the process that was filling up the disk. If you have been keeping a reasonable amount of breathing room on the disk, you can be fairly sure that something is amiss when it suddenly fills up. There's no command analogous to **ps** that will tell you who's consuming disk space at the fastest rate, but there are several tools that can identify files that are currently open and the processes that are using them. See the information on **fuser** and **lsof** starting on page 63 for more information.

You may want to suspend all suspicious-looking processes until you find the one that's causing the problem, but remember to restart the innocents when you are done. When you find the offending process, remove the files it was creating.

An old and well-known prank is to start an infinite loop from the shell that does:

```
while 1
    mkdir adir
    cd adir
    touch afile
end
```

This program occasionally shows up running from an unprotected login or from a terminal that was left logged in. It does not consume much actual disk space, but it fills up the filesystem's inode table and prevents other users from creating new files. There is not much you can do except clean up the aftermath and warn users to protect their accounts. Because the directory tree that is left behind by this little jewel is usually too large for **rm -r** to handle, you may have to write a script that descends to the bottom of the tree and then removes directories as it backs out.

If the problem occurs in **/tmp** and you have set up **/tmp** as a separate filesystem, you can reinitialize **/tmp** with **newfs** instead of attempting to delete individual files. See Chapter 8 for more information about the management of filesystems.

Controlling Processes

# 5 *The Filesystem*

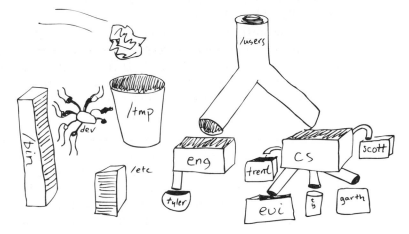

Quick: which of the following would you expect to find in a "filesystem"?

- Processes
- Serial ports
- Interprocess communication channels
- Shared memory segments

If the system is UNIX, the answer is "all of the above." And yes, you might find some files in there, too.

While the basic purpose of a filesystem is to represent and organize the system's storage resources, programmers have been eager to avoid reinventing the wheel when it comes to managing other types of objects. Frequently, it has proven to be natural and convenient to map such objects into the filesystem namespace. There are some advantages to this unification (consistent programming interface, easy access from the shell) and some disadvantages (Frankenstein-like filesystem implementations), but like it or not, this has become the UNIX way.

The filesystem can be thought of as comprising four main components:

- A namespace – a way of naming things and arranging them in a hierarchy
- An API[1] – a set of system calls for navigating and manipulating nodes
- A security model – a scheme for protecting, hiding, and sharing things
- An implementation – code that ties the logical model to an actual disk

1. Application Programming Interface, a generic term for the set of routines that a library, operating system, or software package provides for programmers to call.

*NFS, the Network File System, is described in Chapter 17.*

Modern UNIX filesystems define an abstract kernel-level interface that accommodates several different back ends. Some portions of the file tree are handled by the traditional disk-based implementation; others are fielded by separate drivers within the kernel. For example, NFS filesystems are handled by a driver that forwards the requested operations to a server on another computer.

Unfortunately, the architectural boundaries are not clearly drawn, and there are quite a few special cases. For example, device files provide a way for programs to communicate with drivers inside the kernel. They are not really data files, but they're handled by the basic filesystem driver and their characteristics are stored on disk. Perhaps the details would be somewhat different if the filesystem were reimplemented in light of the last few decades' experience.

Another complicating factor is that modern versions of UNIX tend to support more than one type of disk-based filesystem. In addition to the tried-and-true 4.3BSD-based filesystem that serves as most systems' default, there may be alternatives that feature higher reliability or easier fault recovery (such as HP-UX's VXFS), filesystems that support substantially mutated semantics (such as the Solaris and HP-UX access control list extensions), and filesystems that accommodate other systems' media (such as DOS disks or ISO-9660 CD-ROMs). Those filesystems may vary in their particulars from the standard UNIX filesystem we describe in this chapter.

## 5.1 PATHNAMES

The filesystem is presented as a single hierarchy that starts at the directory **/** and continues downward through an arbitrary number of subdirectories. **/** is also called the root directory.

The list of directories that must be traversed to locate a particular file, together with its filename, form a "pathname." Pathnames can be either absolute (**/tmp/foo**) or relative (**book3/filesystem**). Relative pathnames are interpreted starting at the current directory. You might be accustomed to thinking of the current directory as a feature of the shell, but every process has a current directory.

The terms *file, filename, pathname,* and *path* are more or less interchangeable (or at least, we use them interchangeably in this book). *Filename* and *path* can be used for both absolute and relative paths; *pathname* generally suggests an absolute path.

The filesystem can be arbitrarily deep. However, each component of a pathname must have a name no more than 255 characters long, and a single path may not contain more than 1,023 characters. To access a file with a pathname longer than this, you must **cd** to an intermediate directory and use a relative pathname.[2]

There are essentially no restrictions on the naming of files and directories, except that names are limited in length and must not contain the "/" character or nulls. In

---

2. In case this isn't clear: most filesystem disk formats do not themselves impose a limit on the total length of pathnames. However, the system calls that access the filesystem do not allow their string arguments to be longer than 1,023 characters.

particular, spaces are permitted ... kind of. Because of UNIX's long tradition of separating command-line arguments at whitespace, legacy software tends to break when spaces appear within filenames.

Given the amount of file sharing among different types of systems these days, it's no longer safe to assume that filenames will not contain spaces. Even if you don't share files with Macs and PCs, there are plenty of users in the habit of typing them. Any scripts you write that deal with the filesystem must be prepared to deal with spaces.

In general, spaceful filenames just need to be quoted to keep their pieces together. For example, the command

```
% more "My excellent file.txt"
```

Would preserve **My excellent file.txt** as a single argument to **more**.

## 5.2 MOUNTING AND UNMOUNTING FILESYSTEMS

The filesystem is composed of smaller chunks—also called filesystems—each of which consists of one directory and its subdirectories and files. It's normally apparent from context which type of "filesystem" is being discussed, but for clarity, we will use the term "file tree" to refer to the overall layout of the filesystem and reserve the word "filesystem" for the chunks attached to the tree.

Most filesystems are disk partitions, but as we mentioned earlier, they can be anything that obeys the proper API: network file servers, kernel components, memory-based disk emulators, etc.

Filesystems are attached to the tree with the **mount** command. **mount** maps a directory within the existing file tree, called the mount point, to the root of the newly attached filesystem. The previous contents of the mount point become inaccessible as long as another filesystem is mounted there. Mount points are usually empty directories, however.

For example,

```
# mount /dev/sd1c /users
```

would install the filesystem stored on the disk partition represented by **/dev/sd1c** under the path **/users**. You could then use **ls /users** to see the filesystem's contents.

A list of the filesystems that are customarily mounted on a particular system is kept in the **/etc/fstab**, **/etc/vfstab**, or **/etc/checklist** file, depending on the OS. The information contained in this file allows filesystems to be checked (**fsck -p**) and mounted (**mount -a**) automatically at boot time. It also serves as documentation for the layout of the filesystems on disk and enables short commands such as **mount /usr**; the location of the filesystem to mount is looked up in **fstab**. See page 133 for a complete discussion of the **fstab** file and its brethren.

Filesystems are detached with the **umount** command. On most systems, you cannot unmount a filesystem that is busy. There must not be any open files or processes whose current directories are there, and if the filesystem contains executable programs, they cannot be running.

 FreeBSD allows **umount -f**, which forces a busy filesystem to be unmounted. This is not usually a good idea because the programs that are using it may become quite confused (and crash). Use the **-f** option at your own risk.

 Solaris 8 also provides **umount -f**, although it's possible to achieve the same effect under earlier Solaris releases through a two-step process. First, run **lockfs -h** *dir* on the mount point to "hard lock" the filesystem. You can then **umount** it normally.

If the kernel complains that a filesystem you are trying to unmount is busy, you can run the **fuser** command on most systems to find out why. When invoked in the form **fuser -c** *mountpoint*, **fuser** prints out the PID of every process that's using a file or directory on that filesystem, plus a series of letter codes that show what's being done with the files. For example,

```
% fuser -c /usr
/usr:    157tm   315ctom  474tom   5049tom   84tm   496ctom
490tm   16938c   16902ctm 358ctom   484tm
```

The exact number of possible letter codes varies from system to system. The most common codes are c for a process that has its current directory on the filesystem, o for an open file, t for a running program, m for a mapped file (shared libraries, usually), and r for a process whose root directory is on the filesystem (set with **chroot**).

To determine exactly what the offending processes are, just run **ps** with the list of PIDs returned by **fuser**. For example,

```
% ps -fp "157 315 5049"
  UID   PID   PPID  C  STIME  TTY  TIME  CMD
  root  5049  490   0  Oct 14 ?    0:00  /usr/bin/X11/xdm
  root  157   1     0  Jun 27 ?    5:26  /usr/sbin/named
   lp   315   1     0  Jun 27 ?    0:00  /usr/lib/lpsched
```

The quotation marks force the shell to pass the list of PIDs to **ps** as a single argument.

**fuser** can also report on the use of specific files (as opposed to entire filesystems); the syntax is **fuser -f** *filename*. **fuser** also allows **-k** to kill (or send a signal to) each of the offending processes. Dangerous—and you must be root (or use **sudo**).

 Red Hat's **fuser**, by Werner Almesberger, uses **-m** instead of **-c**. To report on individual files, just omit the **-m** option. Red Hat's **fuser** also has a nifty **-v** option that gives **ps**-like output:

```
% fuser -mv /usr
        USER  PID  ACCESS  COMMAND
/usr    root  1    ....m   init
        root  125  ....m   apmd
        root  274  ....m   portmap
        root  321  ....m   syslogd
```

FreeBSD does not have the **fuser** command, but it does provide **fstat**, which has similar capabilities.

Another alternative to **fuser** is the free **lsof** utility by Vic Abell of Purdue University. In fact, **lsof**'s output is rather more informative and usable than that of **fuser**. **lsof** is available from

> ftp://vic.cc.purdue.edu/pub/tools/unix/lsof/

It works on all of our example systems.

## 5.3  THE ORGANIZATION OF THE FILE TREE

The UNIX filesystem has never been very well organized. Various incompatible naming conventions are used simultaneously, and different types of files are scattered randomly around the namespace. In many cases, files are divided up by function and not by how likely they are to change, making it difficult to upgrade the operating system. The **/etc** directory, for example, contains some files that are never customized and some that are entirely local.

Innovations such as **/var** have helped to solve a few problems, but most systems are still a disorganized mess. Nevertheless, there's a culturally correct place for everything. Most UNIX software can be installed with little reconfiguration if your system is set up in a standard way. If you try to improve upon the default structure, you are asking for trouble.

*See Chapter 12 for more information about configuring the kernel.*

The root filesystem includes the root directory and a minimal set of files and subdirectories. The file containing the kernel lives in the root filesystem. It's usually called **unix** or **vmunix**; it can be right in the root directory or secreted in a subdirectory such as **/kernel** or **/stand**. Also part of the root filesystem are **/dev** for device files, **/etc** for critical system files, **/sbin** and **/bin** for important utilities, and sometimes **/tmp** for temporary files.

Some systems keep shared library files and a few other odd things such as the C preprocessor in the **/lib** directory. Others have moved these items into **/usr/lib**, sometimes leaving **/lib** as a symbolic link.

The directories **/usr** and **/var** are also of great importance. **/usr** is where most standard programs are kept, along with various other booty such as on-line manuals and libraries. It is not strictly necessary that **/usr** be a separate filesystem, but for convenience in administration it almost always is. Both **/usr** and **/var** must be available in order for the system to come up all the way to multiuser mode.

**/var** provides a home for spool directories, log files, accounting information, and various other items that grow or change rapidly and vary on each host. Since **/var** contains log files, which are apt to grow in times of trouble, it is a good idea to put it on its own filesystem if that is practical.

Most of the contents of **/var** originally lived in **/usr**; on your system, you may still find symbolic link fossils from the usrzoic era.

Home directories of users should be kept on a separate filesystem, usually mounted in the root directory or occasionally beneath **/usr**. Separate filesystems can also be used to store bulky items such as source code libraries and databases.

Some of the more important standard directories are listed in Table 5.1 (some rows have been shaded to improve readability).

**Table 5.1    Standard directories and their contents**

| Pathname | Contents |
| --- | --- |
| **/bin** or /sbin | Commands needed for minimal system operability[a] |
| **/dev** | Device entries for terminals, disks, modems, etc. |
| /etc | Critical startup and configuration files |
| **/lib** | Libraries for the C compiler |
| /tmp | Temporary files that disappear between reboots |
| /sys | Kernel-building work area, configuration files (BSD) |
| /proc | Images of all running processes (some newer systems) |
| /stand | Stand-alone utilities, disk formatters, diagnostics, etc. |
| /usr/bin | Executable files |
| /usr/games | Games and diversions (most are not much fun) |
| /usr/include | Header files for C programs |
| /usr/5bin | System V compatibility commands on BSD systems |
| /usr/sbin | Even more system maintenance commands |
| /usr/lib | Support files for standard UNIX programs |
| /usr/man | On-line manual pages |
| /usr/share | Items common to multiple systems (often includes man pages) |
| /var/adm | Accounting files and records of resource usage |
| /var/log | Various system log files (on some systems) |
| /var/spool | Spooling directories for printers, UUCP, mail, etc. |
| /var/tmp | Temporary space (files don't disappear after reboots) |
| /usr/ucb | Berkeley utilities and programs |
| /usr/local | Local software (stuff you install) |
| /usr/local/adm | Local accounting and log files |
| /usr/local/bin | Local executables |
| /usr/local/etc | Local system configuration files and commands |
| /usr/local/lib | Local support files |
| /usr/local/sbin | Local system maintenance commands |
| /usr/local/src | Source code for **/usr/local/\*** |
| /kernel | Files needed to load the kernel (Solaris) |

a. Where **/sbin** is present, **/bin** is usually a symbolic link to **/usr/bin**.

The Filesystem

## 5.4  FILE TYPES

Most filesystem implementations define seven types of files. Even if you are adding something new and wonderful to the file tree (such as the process information listed under **/proc**), it must still be made to look like a collection of these seven types:

- Regular files
- Directories
- Character device files
- Block device files
- UNIX domain sockets
- Named pipes (FIFOs)
- Symbolic links

A few systems do not support UNIX domain sockets or named pipes.

### Regular files

A regular file is just a bag o' bytes; UNIX imposes no structure on its contents. Text files, data files, executable programs, and shared libraries are all stored as regular files. Both sequential and random access are allowed.

### Directories

A directory contains named references to other files. You can create directories with **mkdir** and delete them with **rmdir** if empty. You can delete nonempty directories with **rm -r**.

The special entries "." and ".." refer to the directory itself and to its parent directory; they may not be removed. Since the root directory has no parent directory, ".." there is the same as ".".

A file's name is actually stored within its parent directory, not with the file itself. In fact, more than one directory (or more than one entry in a single directory) can refer to a file at one time, and the references can have different names. Such an arrangement creates the illusion that a file exists in more than one place at the same time.

These additional references ("links") are indistinguishable from the original file; as far as UNIX is concerned, they are equivalent. UNIX maintains a count of the number of links that point to each file and does not release the file's data blocks until its last link has been deleted. Links cannot cross filesystem boundaries.

References of this sort are usually called "hard links" these days to distinguish them from symbolic links, which are described below. You create hard links with **ln** and remove them with **rm**.

It's easy to remember the syntax of **ln** if you keep in mind that it mirrors that of **cp**. The command **cp oldfile newfile** creates a copy of **oldfile** called **newfile**, and **ln oldfile newfile** makes the name **newfile** an additional reference to **oldfile**.

It is important to understand that hard links are not a distinct type of file. Instead of defining a separate "thing" called a hard link, the filesystem simply allows more than one directory entry to point to a particular file. The underlying attributes of the file, such as ownerships and permissions, are shared among all links.

### Character and block device files

*See Chapter 12 for more information about devices and drivers.*

Device files allow UNIX programs to communicate with the system's hardware and peripherals. When the kernel is configured, modules that know how to communicate with each of the system's devices are linked in.[3] The module for a particular device, called a device driver, takes care of the messy details of managing the device.

Device drivers present a standard communication interface that looks like a regular file. When the kernel is given a request that refers to a character or block device file, it simply passes the request to the appropriate device driver. It's important to distinguish device *files* from device *drivers*, however. The files are just rendezvous points that are used to communicate with the drivers. They are not the drivers themselves.

Character device files allow their associated drivers to do their own input and output buffering. Block device files are used by drivers that handle I/O in large chunks and want the kernel to perform buffering for them. Some types of hardware, such as hard disks and tape drives, can be represented by both block and character device files. (How do you know which version to use for a given purpose? Unfortunately, there is no rule of thumb—you have to either memorize the common cases or look them up.)

Device files are characterized by two numbers, called the major and minor device numbers. The major device number tells the kernel which driver the file refers to, and the minor device number tells the driver which physical unit to address. For example, major device number 6 on a Linux system indicates the parallel port driver. The first parallel port (**/dev/lp0**) would have major device number 6 and minor device number 0.

Some device drivers use the minor device number in a nonstandard way. For example, tape drivers often use the minor device number to select a density at which to write tapes and to determine whether the tape should be rewound when the device file is closed. On some systems, the "terminal driver" (which actually handles all serial devices) uses minor device numbers to distinguish modems used as outgoing dialers from modems used on dial-in ports.

You can create device files with **mknod** and remove them with **rm**. Most systems provide a shell script called **MAKEDEV** (usually found in **/dev**) that creates the appropriate sets of device files for common devices. Be sure to read the **MAKEDEV** script to see what it will do before blindly invoking it.

---

3. On many systems, these modules can also be loaded dynamically by the kernel.

The Filesystem

### UNIX domain sockets

Sockets are connections between processes that allow them to communicate in a hygienic manner. UNIX provides several different kinds of sockets, most of which involve the use of a network. UNIX domain sockets are local to a particular host and are referenced through a filesystem object rather than a network port. The POSIX standard refers to them as "local domain sockets."

*See Chapter 11 for more information about syslog.*

Although socket files are visible to other processes as directory entries, they cannot be read from or written to by processes not involved in the connection. Some standard facilities that use UNIX domain sockets are the printing system, the X Windows system, and syslog.

UNIX domain sockets are created with the **socket**() system call and can be removed with the **rm** command or the **unlink**() system call when the socket no longer has any users.

### Named pipes

Like UNIX domain sockets, named pipes allow communication between two unrelated processes running on the same host. They're also known as "FIFO files" (FIFO is short for the phrase "first in, first out"). You can create named pipes with **mknod** and remove them with **rm**.

As with UNIX domain sockets, real-world instances of named pipes are few and far between. They rarely, if ever, require administrative intervention.

### Symbolic links

A symbolic or "soft" link points to a file by name. When the kernel comes upon a symbolic link in the course of looking up a pathname, it redirects its attention to the pathname stored as the contents of the link. The difference between hard links and symbolic links is that a hard link is a direct reference, whereas a symbolic link is a reference by name; symbolic links are distinct from the files they point to.

You create symbolic links with **ln -s** and remove them with **rm**. Since they can contain arbitrary paths, they can refer to files on other filesystems or to nonexistent files. Several symbolic links can also form a loop.

A symbolic link can contain either an absolute or a relative path. For example,

```
# ln -s ../../ufs /usr/include/bsd/sys/ufs
```

links **/usr/include/bsd/sys/ufs** to **/usr/include/ufs** with a relative path. The entire **/usr/include** directory could be moved somewhere else without causing the symbolic link to stop working.

Beware of using ".." in pathnames that travel through symbolic links, since symbolic links can't be followed in reverse. ".." always refers to a directory's true parent. For example, with the link above, the path

```
/usr/include/bsd/sys/ufs/../param.h
```

resolves to

> /usr/include/param.h

not to

> /usr/include/bsd/sys/param.h

It is a common mistake to think that the first argument to **ln -s** has something to do with your current working directory. It is *not* resolved as a filename by **ln**; it's simply used verbatim as the target of the symbolic link.

## 5.5  FILE ATTRIBUTES

Every file has a set of nine permission bits that control who can read, write, and execute the contents of the file. Together with three other bits that affect the operation of executable programs, these bits constitute the file's "mode." The twelve mode bits are stored together with four bits of file-type information in a 16-bit word.

The four file-type bits are set when the file is created and can't be changed, but the twelve mode bits can be modified by the file's owner or the superuser using the **chmod** (change mode) command. Use **ls** to inspect the values of these bits. An example is given on page 71.

### The setuid and setgid bits

The bits with octal values 4000 and 2000 are the setuid and setgid bits. These bits allow programs to access files and processes that would otherwise be off-limits to the user that runs them. The setuid/setgid mechanism for executables is described on page 38.

When set on a directory, the setgid bit causes newly created files within the directory to take on the group ownership of the directory rather than the default group of the user that created the file. This convention makes it easier to share a directory of files among several users, as long as they all belong to a common group. Check your system before relying on this feature, since not all versions of UNIX provide it (though our example systems all do). This interpretation of the setgid bit is unrelated to its meaning when set on an executable file, but there is never any ambiguity as to which meaning is appropriate.

A few systems allow the setgid bit to be set on nonexecutable plain files to request special locking behavior when the file is opened.

### The sticky bit

The bit with octal value 1000 is called the sticky bit. The sticky bit is an example of UNIX outgrowing something but not being able to keep it from tagging along anyway. Small-memory systems like the PDP-11/70s where UNIX spent its preteen years needed some programs to stay in memory or on the swap device continuously. The sticky bit was very important then. In today's world of $25 memory modules and fast disk drives, the sticky bit on an executable is obsolete and modern kernels silently ignore it.

If the sticky bit is set on a directory, most versions of UNIX (including our example OSes) don't allow you to delete or rename a file unless you are the owner of the directory, the owner of the file, or the superuser. Having write permission on the directory is not enough. This convention is an attempt to make directories like **/tmp** a little more private and secure.

 Solaris and HP-UX are slightly less stringent in their handling of sticky directories: you can delete a file in a sticky directory if you have write permission on it, even if you aren't the owner. This actually makes a lot of sense, though it makes little practical difference.

### The permission bits

The nine permission bits are used to determine what operations may be performed on a file, and by whom. UNIX does not allow permissions to be set on a per-user basis.[4] Instead, there are sets of permissions for the owner of the file, the group owners of the file, and everyone else. Each set has three bits: a read bit, a write bit, and an execute bit.

It's convenient to discuss file permissions in terms of octal (base 8) numbers, because each digit of an octal number represents 3 bits and there are 3 bits in each group of permission bits. The topmost three bits (with octal values of 400, 200, and 100) control access for the owner. The second three (40, 20, and 10) control access for the group. The last three (4, 2, and 1) control access for everyone else ("the world"). In each triplet, the high bit is the read bit, the middle bit is the write bit, and the low bit is the execute bit.

Each user fits into only one of the three permission sets. The permissions used are those that are most specific. For example, the owner of a file always has access determined by the owner permission bits and never the group permission bits. It is possible for the "other" and "group" categories to have more access than the owner, although this configuration is rarely used.

On a regular file, the read bit allows the file to be opened and read. The write bit allows the contents of the file to be modified or truncated; however, the ability to delete or rename the file is controlled by the permissions on its parent directory (because that is where the name-to-dataspace mapping is actually stored).

The execute bit allows the file to be executed. There are two types of executable files: binaries, which the CPU runs directly, and scripts, which must be interpreted by a shell or some other program. By convention, scripts begin with a line of the form

```
#!/bin/csh -f
```

---

4. More accurately, the traditional UNIX security model does not allow this. Solaris and HP-UX can be configured with enhancements that alter many aspects of the traditional UNIX security model. Among other things, they support access control lists. However, those extensions are not described here.

that specifies an appropriate interpreter. Nonbinary executable files that do not spec-ify an interpreter are assumed (by your shell) to be **sh** scripts.[5]

For a directory, the execute bit (often called the "search" or "scan" bit in this context) allows the directory to be entered or passed through while evaluating a pathname, but not to have its contents listed. The combination of read and execute bits allows the contents of the directory to be listed. The combination of write and execute bits allows files to be created, deleted, and renamed within the directory.

### Viewing file attributes

The filesystem maintains about forty separate pieces of information for each file, but most of them are useful only to the filesystem itself. As a system administrator you will be concerned mostly with the link count, owner, group, mode, size, last access time, last modification time, and type. You can inspect all of these with **ls -l**.

An attribute change time is also maintained for each file. The conventional UNIX name for this time (the "ctime") leads some people to believe that it is the file's cre-ation time. Unfortunately, it is not; it just records the time that the attributes of the file (owner, mode, etc.) were last changed (as opposed to the time at which the file's contents were modified).

Consider the following example:

```
% ls -l /bin/sh
-rwxr-xr-x   1 root    bin    85924 Sep 27  1997 /bin/sh
```

The first field specifies the file's type and mode. The first character is a dash, so the file is a regular file. The codes shown in Table 5.2 represent the various types of files.

**Table 5.2  File-type encoding used by ls**

| File type | Symbol | Created by | Removed by |
|---|---|---|---|
| Regular file | - | editors, **cp**, etc. | **rm** |
| Directory | d | **mkdir** | **rmdir**, **rm -r** |
| Character device file | c | **mknod** | **rm** |
| Block device file | b | **mknod** | **rm** |
| UNIX domain socket | s | **socket**(2) | **rm** |
| Named pipe | p | **mknod** | **rm** |
| Symbolic link | l | **ln -s** | **rm** |

The next nine characters in this field are the three sets of permission bits. Although these bits have only binary values, **ls** shows them symbolically with the letters r, w, and x for read, write, and execute. In this case, the owner has all permissions on the file and everyone else has only read and execute permission.

---

5. The kernel understands the #! ("shebang") syntax and acts on it directly. However, if the interpreter is not specified completely and correctly, the kernel will refuse to execute the file. The shell then makes a second attempt to execute the script by calling **sh**.

If the setuid bit had been set, the x representing the owner's execute permission would have been replaced with an s, and if the setgid bit had been set, the x for the group would also have been replaced with an s. The last character of the permissions (execute permission for "other") is shown as t if the sticky bit of the file is turned on. If either the setuid/setgid bit or the sticky bit is set but the corresponding execute bit is not, these bits appear as S or T.

The next field in the listing is the link count for the file. In this case it is 1, indicating that **/bin/sh** is the only name by which this file is known. Every time a hard link is made to a file, the count is incremented by 1.

All directories will have at least two hard links: the link from the parent directory and the link from the special file "." inside the directory itself. Symbolic links do not affect the link count.

The next two fields in **ls**'s output are the owner and group owner of the file. In this example, the file's owner is root, and the file belongs to the group bin. The filesystem actually stores these as the user and group ID numbers rather than as strings. If the text versions can't be determined, these fields will contain numbers. This might happen if the user or group that owns the file has been deleted from the **/etc/passwd** or **/etc/group** file. It could also indicate a problem with your network administrative database; see Chapter 18.

The next field is the size of the file in bytes. This file is 85,924 bytes long, almost 84K.[6] Next comes the date of last modification: September 27, 1997. The last field in the listing is the name of the file, **/bin/sh**.

**ls** output is slightly different for a device file. For example:

```
% ls -l /dev/ttya
crw-rw-rw- 1 root daemon   12, 0 Dec 20  1998 /dev/ttya
```

Most fields are the same, but instead of a size in bytes, the major and minor device numbers are shown. **/dev/ttya** is the first unit controlled by device driver 12 (on this system, the terminal driver).

One **ls** option that's useful for scoping out hard links is **-i**, which makes **ls** show each file's "inode number." Without going into too much detail about the implementation of the filesystem, we'll just say that the inode number is an index into a table that enumerates all the files in the filesystem. Inodes are the "things" that are pointed to by directory entries; entries that are hard links to the same file will have the same inode number. To figure out a complex web of links, you'll need **ls -l** to show link counts, **ls -i** to show inode numbers, and **ls -R** to list files recursively. Of course, you can use these options together in any combination.

---

6. K stands for kilo, a metric prefix meaning 1,000; however, computer types have bastardized it into meaning $2^{10}$ or 1,024. Similarly, a computer megabyte is not really a million bytes but rather $2^{20}$ or 1,048,576 bytes. The International Electrotechnical Commission is promoting a new set of numeric prefixes (such as kibi- and mebi-) that are based explicitly on powers of 2. At this point, it seems unlikely that common usage will change.

The system keeps track of modification timestamps, link counts, and file size information automatically. Conversely, the permission bits, ownership, and group ownership change only when they are specifically altered with the **chmod**, **chown**, and **chgrp** commands.

### FreeBSD bonus flags

FreeBSD and other 4.4BSD-based systems define a variety of "bonus" flags that can be set on files. These flags generally invoke additional filesystem semantics. For example, the sappnd flag makes a file append-only (useful for log files) and the schg flag makes it immutable and undeletable. Use **ls -lo** to see the flags attached to a file:

```
% ls -lo /kernel
-r-xr-xr-x  1 root  wheel  schg 2498230 Nov 30 23:51 /kernel
```

Use the **chflags** command to change them:

```
# chflags noschg /kernel
# ls -lo /kernel
-r-xr-xr-x  1 root  wheel  - 2498230 Nov 30 23:51 /kernel
```

See the **chflags**(1) man page for a list of the available flags.

### chmod: change permissions

The **chmod** command changes the permissions on a file. Only the owner of the file and the superuser can change its permissions. To use the command on early UNIX systems, you had to learn a bit of binary or octal notation, but current versions accept either octal notation or a more cryptic mnemonic syntax. The octal syntax is generally more convenient for system administrators, but it can only be used to specify an absolute value for the permission bits. The mnemonic syntax can modify some bits while leaving others alone.

The first argument to **chmod** is a specification of the permissions to be assigned, and the second and subsequent arguments are names of files on which permissions should be changed. In the octal case, the first octal digit of the specification is for the owner, the second is for the group, and the third is for everyone else. If you want to turn on the setuid, setgid, or sticky bits, you use four octal digits rather than three, with the three special bits forming the first digit.

Table 5.3 illustrates the eight possible combinations for each set of three bits, where r, w, and x stand for read, write, and execute.

**Table 5.3    Permission encoding for chmod**

| Octal | Binary | Perms | Octal | Binary | Perms |
|-------|--------|-------|-------|--------|-------|
| 0 | 000 | - - - | 4 | 100 | r - - |
| 1 | 001 | - - x | 5 | 101 | r - x |
| 2 | 010 | - w - | 6 | 110 | r w - |
| 3 | 011 | - w x | 7 | 111 | r w x |

For example, **chmod 711 myprog** gives all permissions to the owner and execute-only permission to everyone else.[7]

The full details of **chmod**'s mnemonic syntax can be found in the **chmod** man page. Some examples of mnemonic specifications are shown in Table 5.4.

**Table 5.4    Examples of chmod's mnemonic syntax**

| Spec | Meaning |
| --- | --- |
| **u+w** | Adds write permission for the owner of the file |
| **ug=rw,o=r** | Gives r/w permission to owner and group, and read permission to others |
| **a-x** | Removes execute permission for all 3 categories (owner/group/other) |
| **ug=srx,o=** | Makes the file setuid and gives r/x permission to owner and group only |
| **g=u** | Makes the group permissions be the same as the owner permissions |

The hard part about using the mnemonic syntax is remembering whether **o** stands for "owner" or "other" ("other" is correct). Just remember **u** and **g** by analogy to UID and GID; only one possibility will be left.

### chown and chgrp: change ownerships

The **chown** command changes a file's ownership, and the **chgrp** command changes its group ownership. The syntax of **chown** and **chgrp** mirrors that of **chmod**, except that the first argument is the new owner or group, respectively. To use **chgrp**, you must either be the owner of the file and belong to the group you're changing to or be the superuser.

Most versions of **chown** and **chgrp** offer the recursive **-R** flag, which changes the settings of a directory and all the files underneath it. For example, the sequence

```
# chmod 755 ~matt
# chown -R matt ~matt
# chgrp -R staff ~matt
```

might be used to set up the home directory of a new user after you had copied in the default startup files. Make sure that you don't try to **chown** the new user's dot files with a command such as

```
# chown -R matt ~matt/.*
```

The pattern will match **~matt/..** and will therefore end up changing the ownership of the parent directory and probably the home directories of other users.

On some systems, **chown** can change both the owner and group of a file at once, usually with the syntax

**chown** *user:group file* ...

---

7. If **myprog** were a shell script, it would need both read and execute permission turned on. In order for the script to be run by an interpreter, it must be opened and read like a text file. Binary files are executed directly by the kernel and therefore do not need read permission turned on.

For example,

```
# chown -R matt:staff ~matt
```

Older systems use a dot to separate the user and group instead of a colon.

Versions of UNIX that derive from System V often allow users to give away their files with **chown**, whereas BSD-based systems normally restrict the use of **chown** to the superuser. Real-world experience has shown that the System V convention leads to a variety of unintended and unwanted consequences, ranging from users being able to evade disk quotas to significant lapses in system security. If your system allows the promiscuous behavior to be turned off, we suggest you do that.

### umask: assign default permissions

You can use the built-in shell command **umask** to influence the default permissions given to the files you create. The **umask** is specified as a three-digit octal value that represents the permissions to take away. When a file is created, its permissions are set to whatever the creating program asks for minus whatever the **umask** forbids. Thus, the digits allow the permissions shown in Table 5.5.

**Table 5.5   Permission encoding for umask**

| Octal | Binary | Perms | Octal | Binary | Perms |
|-------|--------|-------|-------|--------|-------|
| 0 | 000 | rwx | 4 | 100 | –wx |
| 1 | 001 | rw– | 5 | 101 | –w– |
| 2 | 010 | r–x | 6 | 110 | ––x |
| 3 | 011 | r–– | 7 | 111 | ––– |

For example, **umask 027** allows all permissions for the owner but forbids write permission to the group and allows no permissions for anyone else. The default **umask** value is often 022, which denies write permission to the group and world.

*See Chapter 6 for more information about startup files.* There is no way you can force users to have a particular **umask** value, since they can always reset it to whatever they want. However, you can provide a suitable default in the sample **.cshrc** and **.profile** files that you give to new users.

# 6 *Adding New Users*

Adding and removing users is a routine chore on most systems. These tasks are simple, but they are also boring; most administrators build tools to automate the process and then delegate the actual work to an assistant or operator.

Account hygiene is a key determinant of system security. Infrequently used accounts are prime targets for hackers, as are accounts with easily guessed passwords. Even if you use your system's default tools to add and remove users, it's important to understand the underlying changes the tools are making.

## 6.1 THE /ETC/PASSWD FILE

The **/etc/passwd** file is a list of users recognized by the system. The system consults the file at login time to determine a user's UID and to verify the user's password. Each line in the file represents one user and contains seven fields separated by colons:

- Login name
- Encrypted password (unless a shadow password file is used; see below)
- UID number
- Default GID number
- "GECOS" information: full name, office, extension, home phone
- Home directory
- Login shell

For example, the following lines are all valid **/etc/passwd** entries.

```
root:jsg8Y.1p6uWMo:0:0:The System,,x6096,:/:/bin/csh
jl:Hwex6bM8cT3/E:100:0:Jim Lane,ECT8-3,,:/staff/jl:/bin/sh
dotty:oP0vdZ/s93ZiY:101:20::/home/korbel/dotty:/bin/csh
```

The contents of **/etc/passwd** are often shared among systems with a database system such as NIS or NIS+. See Chapter 18, *Sharing System Files*, for more information.

The following sections discuss the **/etc/passwd** fields in more detail.

### Login name

Login names (also known as usernames) must be unique and, depending on the operating system, usually no more than 8 characters long.[1] If you use NIS or NIS+, login names are limited to 8 characters, regardless of the operating system.

In the past, login names were traditionally limited to alphanumeric characters. Modern systems allow them to contain any characters except colons and newlines. However, it's probably wise to stick to alphanumerics and to limit login names to 8 characters. This policy will avert potential conflicts with email systems and older software and will guarantee that users can have the same login name on every machine. Remember, the fact that you have a homogeneous environment today doesn't mean that this will be the case tomorrow.

Login names are case sensitive; however, most mail systems (including **sendmail**) expect login names to be lower case. For this reason, we suggest avoiding uppercase characters in login names unless the user is not expected to receive any mail. Lowercase names are traditional, and they are also easier to type.

Login names should be easy to remember, so random sequences of letters do not make good login names. Avoid "handles" and cutesy nicknames. Since login names are often used as email addresses, it's useful to establish a standard way of forming them. It should be possible for users to make educated guesses about each other's login names. First names, last names, initials, or some combination of these all make reasonable naming schemes.

*See page 550 for more information about mail aliases.* Any fixed scheme for choosing login names eventually results in duplicate names or names that are too long, so you will sometimes have to make exceptions. In the case of a long name, you can use the **/etc/mail/aliases** file to equate two versions of the name, at least as far as mail is concerned.

For example, suppose you use an employee's first initial and last name as a paradigm. Brent Browning would therefore be "bbrowning", which is 9 characters and therefore too long. Instead, you could assign the user the login "brentb", leaving "bbrowning" as an **aliases** file entry:

```
bbrowning: brentb
```

If your site has a global mail alias file, each new login name must be distinct from any alias in this file. If it is not, mail will be delivered to the alias rather than the new user.

---

1. FreeBSD allows login names to be up to 16 characters long, and Red Hat allows 32 characters.

If you have more than one machine, login names should be unique in two senses. First, a user should have the same login name on every machine. This rule is mostly for convenience, both yours and the user's.

*See page 660 for a discussion of login equivalence issues.*

Second, a particular login name should always refer to the same person. Some UNIX commands (e.g., **rlogin** and **ssh**) can be set up to validate remote users based on their login names. Even if scott@boulder and scott@refuge were two different people, one might be able to log into the other's account without providing a password if the systems were not set up properly.

Experience also shows that duplicate names can lead to email confusion. The mail system might be perfectly clear about which scott is which, but users will often send mail to the wrong address.

### Encrypted password

**/etc/passwd** stores passwords in an encrypted form. Unless you can perform DES encryption in your head (we want to meet you), you must either set the contents of this field by using the **passwd** command (**yppasswd** if you use NIS) or by copying an encrypted password string from another account.[2]

When you edit **/etc/passwd** to create a new account, put a star (*) in the encrypted password field. The star prevents unauthorized use of the account until you have set a real password. Never leave this field empty—that introduces a jumbo-sized security hole because no password is required to access the account.

On systems that use standard DES passwords, the unencrypted password is limited to 8 characters. Longer passwords are accepted, but only the first 8 characters are significant. The encrypted DES password will be 13 characters long, regardless of the length of the unencrypted password. DES passwords are encrypted with a random 2-character "salt" so that a given password can correspond to many different encrypted forms. If two users happen to select the same password, this fact usually cannot be discovered by inspection of the **passwd** file.

 HP-UX systems in "trusted mode" allow and use passwords of any length. They accomplish this feat by running multiple iterations of the DES algorithm, one for each 8-character segment.

Red Hat Linux and FreeBSD include support for MD5-based passwords, which can also be of any length. Encrypted MD5 passwords are easy to spot because they are 31 characters long and the first 3 characters are always "$1$".

As computing hardware has become faster, it has become increasingly dangerous to leave encrypted passwords in plain view. Today, most systems allow you to hide the encrypted passwords by placing them in a separate file that is not world-readable. This is known as a shadow password mechanism. See page 656 for a more general discussion of shadow passwords.

---

2. Most, but not all, systems use DES to encrypt passwords. You can only copy encrypted passwords among machines that use the same encryption algorithm.

On Solaris, shadow passwords are required. You must modify the shadow password file when adding and removing users to keep it consistent with **/etc/passwd**. The Solaris **shadow** file is described on page 82.

## UID number

On most modern systems, UIDs are 32-bit integers that can represent the values 0 to 2,147,483,647. However, because of interoperability issues with older systems, we suggest limiting the largest UID at your site to 32,767 if possible. Current versions of Linux have a maximum UID of 65,535 due to the size of a UID field in the default filesystem; this state of affairs will certainly change in the future.

By definition, root has UID 0. Most systems also define pseudo-users bin, daemon, and perhaps some others. It is customary to put such fake logins at the beginning of the **/etc/passwd** file and to give them low UIDs. To allow plenty of room for any non-human users you might want to add in the future, we recommend that you assign UIDs to real users starting at 100.

*See page 41 for more information about **sudo**.*

It is never a good idea to have multiple accounts with UID 0. While it might seem convenient to have multiple root logins with different shells and/or passwords, this setup just creates more potential security holes and gives you multiple logins to secure. If people need to have alternate ways to log in as root, you are better off if they use a program like **sudo**.

Avoid recycling UIDs for as long as possible, even the UIDs of people that have left your organization and had their accounts permanently removed. This precaution prevents confusion if files are later restored from backups, in which users are identified by UID rather than by login name.

*See Chapter 17 for more information about NFS.*

UIDs should be kept unique across your entire organization. That is, a particular UID should refer to the same login name and the same person on every machine. Failure to maintain distinct UIDs can result in security problems with systems such as NFS and can also result in confusion when a user moves from one workgroup to another.

It can be hard to maintain unique UIDs when groups of machines are administered by different people or organizations. The problems are both technical and political. The best solution is to have a central database that contains a record for each user and enforces uniqueness. We use a home-grown database called Uniquid.[3] A simpler scheme is to assign each group within an organization a range of UIDs and let each group manage its own set. This solution keeps the UID spaces separate (a requirement if you are going to use NFS to share filesystems) but does not address the parallel issue of unique login names.

## Default GID number

*"wheel" was analogous to the root account in the TOPS-20 OS.*

Like a UID, a group ID number is a 16 or 32-bit integer which might be signed or unsigned. GID 0 is reserved for the group called "root" or "wheel". GID 1 is usually the group "daemon".

---

3. Uniquid is available from ftp://ftp.colorado.edu/its/unix/src/uniquid.tar.gz.

Groups are defined in the **/etc/group** file, with the GID field in **/etc/passwd** providing the effective GID at login time. Modern versions of UNIX allow a user to be in up to 16 groups at a time, so the effective GID is never used to determine access. The GID field in **/etc/passwd** is therefore something of a historical legacy, although its value is still included in the user's group list.

On HP-UX, the user's group list is initialized at login time from **/etc/logingroup**, not from **/etc/group**. We suggest that you make **/etc/logingroup** a symbolic link to **/etc/group** so that HP-UX behaves like most other systems with respect to its handling of multiple groups.

The only time at which the effective GID is of any relevance is during the creation of new files and directories. When BSD semantics are in effect, new files inherit the GID of their parent directory. When BSD semantics are not in effect, new files are assigned the user's current effective GID; to change this GID, users run the **newgrp** command.

Most operating systems do not default to the BSD semantics, but they support BSD semantics as an option, either through a **grpid** option to **mount** or through use of the setgid bit (02000) on individual directories. BSD semantics are always in effect on FreeBSD, which lacks the **newgrp** command (this is considered a feature).

### GECOS field[4]

The GECOS field has no well-defined syntax. It originally held the login information needed to transfer batch jobs from UNIX systems at Bell Labs to a mainframe running GECOS; these days, only the name remains.

The GECOS field is commonly used to record personal information about each user. A few programs will expand an '&' in the GECOS field to the user's login name, which saves a bit of typing. Both **finger** and **sendmail** perform this expansion, but many programs do not. It's best not to rely on this feature.

Although you can use any formatting conventions you like, **finger** interprets comma-separated GECOS entries in the following order:

- Full name (often the only field used)
- Office number and building
- Office telephone extension
- Home phone number

The **chfn** command (**passwd -g** on Solaris) lets users change their own GECOS information. **chfn** is useful for keeping things like phone numbers up to date, but it can be misused: a user can change the information to be either obscene or incorrect. Our academic computing center, which caters to hordes of undergraduates, has disabled the **chfn** command.

---

4. When Honeywell took over the computer division of GE, GECOS was changed to GCOS; both spellings survive today.

### Home directory

Users are placed in their home directories when they log in. If a user's home directory is missing at login time, the system prints a message such as "no home directory." Some systems allow the login to proceed and put the user in the root directory. Others do not allow logins without a valid home directory.

Be aware that if home directories are mounted over NFS, they may be unavailable in the event of server or network problems.

### Login shell

*We recommend **tcsh** as the default shell for new users.*

The login shell is normally a command interpreter such as the Bourne shell or the C shell (**/bin/sh** or **/bin/csh**), but it can be any program. **sh** is the default on most systems and is used if **/etc/passwd** does not specify a login shell. Other common shells include **ksh** (the Korn shell), **bash** (the GNU Bourne again shell), and **tcsh** (a fancy C shell with command editing).

On most systems, users can change their shells with the **chsh** command. On Solaris, only the superuser can change a user's shell (using **passwd -e**) unless NIS or NIS+ is in use. The file **/etc/shells** contains a list of shells that **chsh** will permit users to select; root can use **chsh** without restrictions. If you add entries to **/etc/shells**, be sure to use absolute paths since **chsh** and other programs expect them.

## 6.2  THE FREEBSD /ETC/MASTER.PASSWD FILE

On FreeBSD, the "real" password file is **/etc/master.passwd**. The **/etc/passwd** file exists for backward compatibility, but it is generated from the **master.passwd** file and is never edited directly. Whenever you modify **/etc/master.passwd** by running **vipw**, **passwd**, **chfn**, **chsh**, or **chpass**, **/etc/passwd** is generated for you along with a hashed representation of **/etc/master.passwd** created by the **pwd_mkdb** utility.

The **master.passwd** file functions as a shadow password file in that it is readable only by root (the derived **/etc/passwd** file does not contain any passwords). The **master.passwd** file also contains three additional fields not found in **passwd**:

- Login class
- Password change time
- Expiration time

The login class (if one is specified) refers to an entry in the **/etc/login.conf** file. Login classes determine user resource limits and control other login settings. See the next section for specifics.

The password change time field implements a policy known as "password aging." It contains the time (in seconds since the UNIX epoch) after which the user will be forced to change his or her password. You can leave the field blank, indicating that the password never expires. We are not very enthusiastic about password aging; see page 657 for a more complete discussion.

**Adding New Users**

The account expiration time gives the time and date (in seconds, as for password expiration) at which the user's account will expire. The user cannot log in after this date unless the field is reset by an administrator. If this field is left blank, the account will not expire.

## 6.3  THE FREEBSD /ETC/LOGIN.CONF FILE

FreeBSD's **/etc/login.conf** file sets account-related parameters for users and groups of users. Its format is similar to that of the **termcap** and **printcap** files and consists of colon-delimited key/value pairs and Boolean flags.

When a user logs in, the login class field of **/etc/master.passwd** determines which entry in **/etc/login.conf** to apply. If no login class has been specified by the user's **master.passwd** entry, the default class is used.

A **login.conf** entry can set any of the following:

- Resource limits (maximum process size, number of open files, etc.)
- Session accounting limits (when logins are allowed, and for how long)
- Default environment variables
- Default paths (PATH, MANPATH, etc.)
- Location of the message of the day file
- Host and TTY-based access control
- Default **umask**
- Account controls (minimum password length, password aging)

In this example, intended for a sysadmin, some of the default values are overridden:

```
sysadmin:\
      :ignorenologin:\
      :requirehome@:\
      :maxproc=unlimited:\
      :openfiles=unlimited:\
      :tc=default:
```

Users in the sysadmin login class are allowed to log in even when **/var/run/nologin** exists, and they need not have a working home directory (this option allows logins when NFS is not working). Sysadmin users may start any number of processes and open any number of files.[5] The last line pulls in the contents of the default entry.

## 6.4  THE SOLARIS AND RED HAT /ETC/SHADOW FILE

The use of a shadow password file is mandatory under Solaris. You can also use it under Red Hat Linux if you install the **shadow** package.

The **/etc/shadow** file is readable only by the superuser and serves to keep encrypted passwords safe from prying eyes. It also provides account information that's not

---

5. There is still a hard limit on the total number of processes and open files that the kernel can support, but no artificial limit is imposed.

available from **/etc/passwd**. Unlike the FreeBSD **master.passwd** file, the **shadow** file is not a superset of the **passwd** file, and the **passwd** file is not generated from it; you must maintain both files by hand.

Like **/etc/passwd**, **/etc/shadow** contains one line for each user. Each line contains nine fields, separated by colons:

- Login name
- Encrypted password
- Date of last password change
- Minimum number of days between password changes
- Maximum number of days between password changes
- Number of days in advance to warn users about password expiration
- Number of inactive days before account expiration (Solaris)
- Account expiration date
- Flags

*See page 92 for more information about **usermod**.* The only fields that are required to be nonempty are the username and password. Absolute date fields in **/etc/shadow** are specified in terms of days (*not* seconds) since Jan 1, 1970, which is not a standard way of reckoning time on UNIX systems. Fortunately, you can use the **usermod** program to set the expiration field.

A typical **shadow** entry looks like this:

```
millert:inN0.VAsc1Wn.:11031::180:14::18627:
```

Here is a more complete description of each field:

- The login name is the same as in **/etc/passwd**. This field simply connects a user's **passwd** and **shadow** entries.

- The encrypted password is identical in concept and execution to the one previously stored in **/etc/passwd**.

- The last change field indicates the time at which the user's password was last changed. This field is generally filled in by **/bin/passwd**.

- The fourth field sets the number of days that must elapse between password changes. Once users change their password, they cannot change it again until the specified period has elapsed. This feature seems useless, and we think it could be somewhat dangerous when a security intrusion has occurred. We recommend against setting a value for this field.

- The fifth field sets the maximum number of days allowed between password changes. This feature allows the administrator to enforce password aging; see page 657 for more information. Under Linux, the actual maximum number of days is the sum of the maximum field and the inactive (seventh) field.

- The sixth field sets the number of days before password expiration that the **login** program should begin to warn the user of the impending expiration.

- Solaris and Linux differ in their interpretation of the seventh field. The Solaris behavior is as follows: If a user has not logged in to his or her account within the number of days specified in the seventh field, the account will be disabled. Disused accounts are a favorite target of hackers, and this feature attempts to give you a way to take such accounts "off the market." However, it only works if the user can be found in the **/var/adm/lastlog** file; users that have never logged in will not be automatically disabled. This feature does not work very well in a networked environment because each host has its own **lastlog** file.

  Under Linux, the seventh field has a completely different meaning: it specifies how many days after the maximum password age has been reached to wait before treating the login as expired. This seems a rather gratuitous difference, and the Solaris behavior is much more useful. To make matters worse, the Linux documentation is extremely vague with respect to the meaning of this field. We had to read the source code to find out what it did.

- The eighth field specifies the day (in days since Jan 1, 1970) on which the user's account will expire. The user may not log in after this date until the field has been reset by an administrator. If the field is left blank, the account will never expire.

- The ninth field (the "flags" field) is currently always empty and is reserved for future use.

Now that we know what each of the fields means, let's look at our example line again:

```
millert:inN0.VAsc1Wn.:11031::180:14::18627:
```

In this example, the user millert last changed his password on March 14, 2000. The password must be changed again within 180 days, and millert will receive warnings that the password needs to be changed for the last two weeks of this period. The account expires on December 31, 2001.

## 6.5 THE /ETC/GROUP FILE

The **/etc/group** file contains the names of UNIX groups and a list of each group's members. For example:

```
wheel:*:0:root,evi,garth,scott,trent
csstaff:*:100:lloyd,evi
student:*:200:dotty
```

Each line represents one group and contains four fields:

- Group name
- Encrypted password (vestigial and rarely used)
- GID number
- List of members, separated by commas

As in **/etc/passwd**, fields are separated by colons. On some systems, group names must be 8 or fewer characters long. While it is possible to enter a group password (to allow users not belonging to a group to change to it by using the **newgrp** command), this is rarely done. Most sites put stars in the password field, but it is safe to leave the password field blank if you wish. The **newgrp** command will not change to a group without a password unless the user is already listed as being a member of that group.

Be careful not to inadvertently add spaces between the names of group members. Most systems will ignore everything after the first space.

As with usernames and UIDs, group names and GIDs should be kept consistent among machines that share files using NFS. Consistency can be tricky to maintain in a heterogeneous environment, since different operating systems use different GIDs for the same group names. We've found that the best way to deal with this issue is to avoid using a system group as the default login group for a user. This principle also applies to vendor-supplied groups such as "staff".

To avoid collisions with vendor-supplied GIDs, we suggest starting local groups at GID 100, or after the vendor-supplied groups end, whichever is greater.

## 6.6  ADDING USERS

Before you create an account for a new user, it's very important that the user sign and date a copy of your local user agreement and policy statement. (What?! You don't have a user agreement and policy statement? See page 782 for more information about why you need one and what to put in it.)

Users have no particular reason to want to sign a policy agreement, so it's to your advantage to secure their signatures while you still have some leverage. We find that it takes more effort to secure a signed agreement after an account has been released. If your process allows for it, it's best to have the paperwork precede the creation of the account.

Mechanically, the process of adding a new user consists of three steps required by the system, two steps that establish a useful environment for the new user, and several extra steps for your own convenience as an administrator.

Required:

- Edit the **passwd** and **shadow** files to define the user's account.
- Set an initial password.
- Create the user's home directory.

For the user:

- Copy default startup files to the user's home directory.
- Set the user's mail home and establish mail aliases.

For you:

- Add the user to the **/etc/group** file.
- Configure disk quotas.
- Verify that the account is set up correctly.

*See page 41 for more information about **sudo**.*

Each vendor provides tools that can do some of these steps for you, but in the next few sections we'll go over the steps as you'd do them by hand. You must perform each step as root or use a program such as **sudo** that allows you to run commands as root.

### Editing the passwd and shadow files

To safely edit the **passwd** file, run **vipw** to invoke a text editor on a copy of it. The default editor is **vi**, but you can specify a different one by setting the value of the EDITOR environment variable. The existence of the temporary edit file serves as a lock; **vipw** allows only one person to edit the **passwd** file at a time. When the editor terminates, **vipw** replaces the original **passwd** file with your edited copy.

On Solaris systems, **vipw** asks if you want to edit the **shadow** file after you have edited the **passwd** file. You should say yes.

Under FreeBSD, **vipw** edits the **master.passwd** file instead of **/etc/passwd**. After installing your changes, **vipw** runs **pwd_mkdb** to generate the derived **passwd** file and two hashed versions of **master.passwd** (one that contains the encrypted passwords and is readable only by root, and another that lacks the passwords and is world-readable).

For example, adding the following line to **/etc/passwd** would define an account called "tyler":

```
tyler:*:103:100:Tyler Stevens, ECEE 3-27, x7919,:/home/staff/tyler:/bin/csh
```

Note the lack of an encrypted password. If the system were using a **shadow** file, we'd set the encrypted password field to "x" and add a matching entry to **/etc/shadow**:

```
tyler:*::::::18627:
```

This **shadow** line for "tyler" has no encrypted password and sets the account to expire on December 31, 2001.

### Setting an initial password

Root can change any user's password with the **passwd** command:

```
# passwd user
```

*Rules for selecting good passwords are given on page 655.*

**passwd** prompts you to enter a new password and asks you to repeat it. If you choose a short, all-lowercase password, **passwd** will complain and ask you to use something longer. FreeBSD will grudgingly accept the password if you insist on it about 3 times, but most other versions of UNIX require you to use a password that contains mixed case or more characters. **passwd** might let you know what the rules are for your particular UNIX if it doesn't like your initial attempt.

Your password-picking skills are probably well developed, but users sometimes need help. We suggest replacing your system's **passwd** command with an updated version that checks prospective passwords for guessability before accepting them. Several **passwd** replacements are in common use. We like **npasswd**, which is available from

> http://www.utexas.edu/cc/unix/software/npasswd

 The **passwd** program that comes with Red Hat checks prospective passwords to make sure they are not in the system dictionary. This precaution is not quite as thorough as the checks performed by **npasswd**, but it helps.

Never leave a new account—or any account that has access to a shell—without a password.

### Creating the user's home directory

Any directory you create is initially owned by root, so you must change its owner and group with the **chown** and **chgrp** commands. The following sequence of commands would create a home directory appropriate for our example user:

```
# mkdir /home/staff/tyler
# chown tyler /home/staff/tyler
# chgrp staff /home/staff/tyler
# chmod 700 /home/staff/tyler
```

### Copying in the default startup files

You can customize some commands and utilities by placing configuration files in a user's home directory. Startup files traditionally begin with a dot and end with the letters **rc**, short for "run command," a relic of the CTSS operating system. The initial dot causes **ls** to elide these files from directory listings unless the **-a** option is used; the files are considered "uninteresting." Table 6.1 on the next page lists some common startup files.

If you don't already have a set of good default startup files, **/usr/local/lib/skel** is a reasonable place to put them. Copy in some files to use as a starting point and modify them with a text editor. You may wish to start with vendor-supplied files from the **/etc/skel** directory, if your system provides them (**/usr/share/skel** on FreeBSD).

Make sure the startup files contain defaults that are reasonable for unsophisticated users. However, don't confuse users by "protecting" them from UNIX; entries such as

```
alias dir ls -l
alias rm rm -i
alias cp cp -i
```

are in poor taste.

Depending on the user's shell, **/etc** may contain system-wide startup files that are processed before the user's own startup files. For example, all of our example systems' Bourne shells (**sh**) read **/etc/profile** before processing ~/**.profile**. For other shells, see the man page for the shell in question for details.

**Table 6.1    Common startup files and their uses**

| Command | Filename | Typical uses |
|---------|----------|--------------|
| **csh/tcsh** | **.login** | Sets the terminal type (if needed)<br>Sets up environment variables<br>Sets **biff** and **mesg** switches |
|  | **.cshrc** | Sets command aliases<br>Sets the search path<br>Sets the **umask** value to control permissions<br>Sets cdpath for filename searches<br>Sets the prompt, history, and savehist variables |
|  | **.logout** | Prints "to do" reminders<br>Clears the screen |
| **sh** | **.profile** | Similar to **.login** and **.cshrc** for **sh** |
| **vi** | **.exrc** | Sets **vi** editor options |
| **emacs** | **.emacs_pro** | Sets **emacs** editor options<br>Sets **emacs** key bindings |
| **mailx** | **.mailrc** | Defines personal mail aliases<br>Sets mail reader options |
| **tin** | **.newsrc** | Specifies newsgroups of interest |
| **xrdb** | **.Xdefaults** | Specifies X11 configuration: fonts, color, etc. |
| **startx** | **.xinitrc** | Specifies the initial X11 environment |
| **xdm** | **.xsession** | Specifies the initial X11 environment |

The command sequence for installing startup files for the new user tyler would look something like this:

```
# cp /usr/local/lib/skel/.[a-zA-Z]* ~/tyler
# chmod 644 ~tyler/.[a-zA-Z]*
# chown tyler ~tyler/.[a-zA-Z]*
# chgrp staff ~tyler/.[a-zA-Z]*
```

Note that we cannot use

```
# chown tyler ~tyler/.*
```

because tyler would then own not only his own files but also the parent directory ".." (**/home/staff**) as well. This is a very common and dangerous sysadmin mistake.

### Setting the user's mail home

It is convenient for each user to receive email on only one machine. This scheme is often implemented with an entry in the global aliases file **/etc/mail/aliases** or the **sendmail** userDB. See Chapter 19 for general information about email; the various ways to implement mail homes are discussed starting on page 549.

### Editing the /etc/group file

To continue the processing of the new user tyler, we should add his login name to the list of users in group 100, since that was the default group to which we assigned him in the **/etc/passwd** file. Strictly speaking, tyler will be in group 100 whether he is listed in **/etc/group** or not, because his **passwd** entry has already given him this membership. However, this information should be entered in **/etc/group** so that you always know exactly which users belong to which groups.[6]

Suppose we also wanted to put tyler in the group "wheel". On some systems, users must be in this group to use the **su** command. We would simply make the following changes to **/etc/group**:

```
wheel:*:0:root,evi,garth,scott,trent,tyler
csstaff::100:lloyd,evi,tyler
```

### Setting disk quotas

If your site uses disk quotas, you should set quota limits for each new account with the **edquota** command. **edquota** can be used interactively, but it is more commonly used in "prototype" mode to model the quotas of the new user after those of someone else. For example, the command

```
# edquota -p proto-user new-user
```

sets *new-user*'s quotas to be the same as *proto-user*'s. This way of using **edquota** is especially useful in **adduser** scripts.

Since disk space is cheap these days, we're not big proponents of disk quotas. They often seem to cause more problems than they solve, and they impose an additional support burden on administrators. Back when we used quotas (many years ago), we maintained several accounts that existed only to serve as user quota prototypes.

### Verifying the new login

To verify that a new account has been properly configured, first log out, then log in as the new user and execute the following commands:

```
% pwd       /* To verify the home directory */
% ls -la     /* Check owner/group of startup files */
```

You will need to notify new users of their login names and initial passwords. This is also a good time to point users towards additional documentation on local customs if you have any.

*See page 782 for more information about written user contracts.* If your site requires users to sign a written contract, be sure this step has been completed before releasing the account. This check will prevent oversights and strengthen the legal basis of any sanctions you might later need to impose.

Be sure to remind new users to change their passwords immediately.

---

6. The kernel doesn't actually care what's in **/etc/passwd** or **/etc/group**; it only cares about raw UID and GID numbers. **passwd** and **group** store account information for use by high-level software such as **login**. See page 105 for details about the login process.

## 6.7  REMOVING USERS

When a user leaves your organization, that user's login account and files must be re-moved from the system. This procedure involves removing all references to the login name that were added by you or your **adduser** program. You may want to use the following checklist:

- Set the user's disk quota to zero, if quotas are in use.
- Remove the user from any local user databases or phone lists.
- Remove the user from the **aliases** file or add a forwarding address.
- Remove the user's crontab file and any pending **at** jobs.
- Kill any of the user's processes that are still running.
- Remove any temporary files owned by the user in **/var/tmp** or **/tmp**.
- Remove the user from the **passwd** and **group** files.
- Remove the user's home directory.
- Remove the user's mail spool.

Before you remove a user's home directory, be sure to relocate any files that are needed by other users. Since you often can't be sure which files those might be, it's always a good idea to make an extra tape backup of the user's home directory and mail spool before deleting them.

*See page 490 for more information about quotas and NFS.*

Once you have removed a user, you should verify that the user's old UID owns no more files on the system. A fast way to perform this check is to use the **quot** com-mand. For example, to see which users are taking up space on **/home**, we could run the following command:

```
# quot /home
```

```
/dev/rdsk/c0t3d0s6:
156254   millert
34520    hilbert
 5572    #1161
  683    #1069
```

In addition to telling us the number of disk blocks consumed by each user, **quot** tells us that two UIDs that are not listed in **/etc/passwd** own files. To find the exact paths to these orphaned files, we'd have to use

```
# find -x /home -nouser -print
```

This command takes considerably longer to run than **quot**.

Despite its name, **quot** does not require that disk quotas be active. However, because it accesses raw disk partitions, it only works on local disks. It cannot be used to ana-lyze filesystems mounted over NFS.

## 6.8  DISABLING LOGINS

On occasion, a user's login must be temporarily disabled. Before networking invaded the UNIX world, we would just put a star in front of the encrypted password, making it impossible for the user to log in. However, users could still log in across the network without entering a password, so this technique no longer works very well.

These days, we replace the user's shell with a program that prints a message explaining why the login has been disabled and provides instructions for rectifying the situation. This pseudo-shell should not be listed in **/etc/shells**; many daemons that provide nonlogin access to the system (e.g., **ftpd**) check to see if a user's login shell is listed in **/etc/shells** and will deny access if it is not (which is the behavior you want).

There is one problem with this method of disabling logins, however. By default, **sendmail** will not deliver mail to a user whose shell does not appear in **/etc/shells**. It's generally a bad idea to interfere with the flow of mail, even if the recipient is not able to read it immediately. You can defeat **sendmail**'s default behavior by adding a fake shell named **/SENDMAIL/ANY/SHELL/** to the **/etc/shells** file.

## 6.9  VENDOR-SUPPLIED ACCOUNT MANAGEMENT UTILITIES

Solaris, HP-UX, and Red Hat Linux provide a similar set of utilities that help to automate the creation, deletion, and modification of users and groups. FreeBSD has a separate set of utilities, which we describe briefly on the next page.

The **useradd** command adds users to the **passwd** file (and to the **shadow** file, if applicable). It provides a command-line-driven interface that is easy to run by hand or to call from a home-grown **adduser** script. The **usermod** command changes the **passwd** entries of existing users. The **userdel** command removes a user from the system, optionally deleting the user's home directory. **groupadd**, **groupmod**, and **groupdel** commands also operate on the **/etc/group** file.

Although these commands are convenient, they are rarely sufficient to implement all of a site's local policies. We recommend that you write your own **adduser** and **rmuser** scripts (which may or may not call the vendor utilities). Perl is great for this.

For example, to create a new user "hilbert" with **useradd** (using the system defaults), you could simply run:

```
# useradd hilbert
```

This command would create the following entry in **/etc/passwd**. Note that **useradd** puts a star in the password field, effectively disabling the account until you assign a real password.

```
hilbert:*:105:20::/home/hilbert:/bin/sh
```

**useradd** is generally more useful when given additional arguments. In the next example, we specify that hilbert's primary group should be "faculty" and that he should also be added to the "famous" group. We also override the default home directory location and ask **useradd** to create the home directory if it does not already exist:

```
# useradd -c "David Hilbert" -d /home/math/hilbert -g faculty -G famous -m
    -s /bin/tcsh hilbert
```

This command creates the following **passwd** entry:

```
hilbert:*:105:30:David Hilbert:/home/math/hilbert:bin/tcsh
```

It also adds hilbert to the "faculty" and "famous" groups in **/etc/group**, creates the directory **/home/math/hilbert**, and populates it based on the contents of **/etc/skel**. On Solaris (and Linux, if shadow passwords are in use), an entry for hilbert would also be created in **/etc/shadow**.

You can determine the default **useradd** settings with **useradd -D**; with HP-UX and Red Hat Linux, you can set those defaults in the **/etc/default/useradd** file.

**usermod** modifies an account that already exists and takes many of the same flags as **useradd**. For example, we could use the following command to set an expiration date of July 4, 2002 on hilbert's account:[7]

```
# usermod -e "July 4, 2002" hilbert
```

The **userdel** command deletes user accounts, effectively undoing all the changes made by **useradd**. To remove hilbert, we would use the following command:

```
# userdel hilbert
```

This command removes references to hilbert in the **passwd**, **shadow** (if it is in use), and **group** files. By default, it would not remove hilbert's home directory. (At our site, we generally keep deleted users' home directories around for a few weeks anyway to avoid having to restore requested data from a backup tape.)

 FreeBSD comes with **adduser** and **rmuser** scripts written in Perl that you can either use as supplied or modify to fit your local needs. FreeBSD's **rmuser** script does a good job of removing instances of the user's files and processes (a task that other vendors' **userdel** programs do not even attempt).

Unlike **useradd** and **userdel**, **adduser** and **rmuser** are interactive programs that prompt you for information about each account to be created. You can set site-wide defaults in **/etc/adduser.conf**. By default, **adduser** copies startup files from the directory **/usr/share/skel**.

---

7. HP-UX only supports this style of account expiration when the system is configured in "trusted mode."

# 7 *Serial Devices*

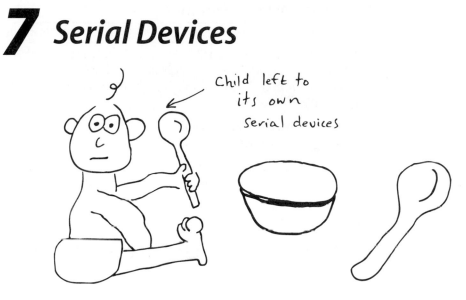

Child left to its own serial devices

Serial ports are one of the handiest I/O facilities available on UNIX systems. Although they are not especially fast, they are quite flexible and can be found on everything from PCs to mainframes.

Serial ports can be used with a variety of devices, including printers, terminals, and other computers. They're also found on a lot of custom-made, hobbyist, and low-volume equipment (media changers, temperature sensors, even sewing machines). A device can be attached to the system either directly (with a cable) or via a telephone line with modems at each end.

This chapter describes how to attach serial devices to your system and explains how to configure your software to take advantage of them. We will often use terminals, modems, and printers as specific examples, but other devices are essentially similar.

The first few sections address serial hardware and cabling considerations. Then, starting on page 103, we talk about the software infrastructure that has historically been used to support hardware terminals. Few sites use terminals anymore, but their ghosts live on in UNIX's handling of pseudo-terminals and window systems. The remainder of the chapter (starting on page 113) provides some general background on modems, serial debugging, and newer standards such as the Universal Serial Bus.

## 7.1 SERIAL STANDARDS

Most serial ports obey some variant of the standard known as RS-232. This standard specifies the electrical characteristics and meaning of each signal wire, as well as pin assignments on the traditional 25-pin (DB-25) serial connector shown in Exhibit A.

**Exhibit A     A male DB-25 connector**

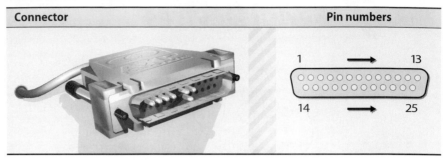

| Connector | Pin numbers |
| --- | --- |

Full RS-232[1] is overkill for all real-world situations, as it defines numerous signals that are unnecessary for basic communication. DB-25 connectors are also inappropriately large for use on patch panels and laptop computers. As a result, a number of alternative connectors have come into widespread use. These are described in the section titled *Alternative connectors* starting on page 97.

Traditional RS-232 uses shielded, twisted-pair cable, usually stranded 22-gauge wire. The original RS-232 signal voltages were ±12 volts DC, but ±5 volts is more common these days. Sometimes, ±3 volts is used. Higher voltages are less susceptible to interference. All of these voltages comply with the RS-232 specification, so it's perfectly OK to connect devices that use different voltage standards.

RS-232 is not an electrically "balanced" system; it uses a single conductor for the data traveling in each direction. Ergo, there is actually no good reason to use twisted pairs. The benefit of STP cabling is all in the shield, which may (or may not) help to reduce external interference. In fact, the use of twisted-pair cable can actually reduce the reliability and range of serial cables if the two data lines (TD and RD) are placed together on a single pair. So don't do that.

There is no commonly agreed-upon standard for which RS-232 signals should be run together on a twisted-pair cable. Some sources recommend pairing signal grounds with both TD and RD, but this pairing costs an extra conductor and provides multiple paths for the signal ground. As far as we know, there is no compelling reason to use this convention.

DB-25 connectors are either male (with pins sticking out, called DB25P) or female (with matching holes, DB25S). There are tiny invisible numbers near the pins or holes which label them from 1 to 25. You can see the numbers best by holding the connector up to the light and viewing it at an angle. Sometimes only pins 1, 13, 14, and 25 are numbered.

---

1. To be technically correct, this standard should now be referred to as EIA-232-E. However, no one will have the slightest idea what you are talking about.

Exhibit A shows a male DB-25. As with all serial connectors, the pin numbers on a female connector are a mirror image of those on a male connector, so that like-numbered pins mate. The diagram is drawn from the orientation shown (as if you were facing the end of the cable, about to plug the connector into your forehead).

Note that in Exhibit A, only seven pins are actually installed. This is typical for the real world. The RS-232 signals and their pin assignments on a DB-25 connector are shown in Table 7.1. Only the shaded signals are ever used in practice; all others can be ignored.

**Table 7.1    RS-232 signals and pin assignments on a DB-25**

| Pin | Name | Function | Pin | Name | Function |
|-----|------|----------|-----|------|----------|
| 1 | FG | Frame ground | 14 | STD | Secondary TD |
| 2 | TD | Transmitted data | 15 | TC | Transmit clock |
| 3 | RD | Received data | 16 | SRD | Secondary RD |
| 4 | RTS | Request to send | 17 | RC | Receive clock |
| 5 | CTS | Clear to send | 18 | – | Not assigned |
| 6 | DSR | Data set ready | 19 | SRTS | Secondary RTS |
| 7 | SG | Signal ground | 20 | DTR | Data terminal ready |
| 8 | DCD | Data carrier detect | 21 | SQ | Signal quality detector |
| 9 | – | Positive voltage | 22 | RI | Ring indicator |
| 10 | – | Negative voltage | 23 | DRS | Data rate selector |
| 11 | – | Not assigned | 24 | SCTE | Clock transmit external |
| 12 | SDCD | Secondary DCD | 25 | BUSY | Busy |
| 13 | SCTS | Secondary CTS | | | |

There are two interface configurations for serial equipment: DTE (Data Terminal Equipment) and DCE (Data Communications Equipment). DTE and DCE share the same pinouts, but they specify different interpretations of the RS-232 signals.

Every device is configured as either DTE or DCE; a few support both, but not simultaneously. Computers, terminals, and printers are generally DTE, and most modems are DCE. DTE and DCE serial ports can communicate with each other in any combination, but different combinations require different cabling.

There is no sensible reason for both DTE and DCE to exist; all equipment could use the same wiring scheme. The existence of two conventions is merely one of the many pointless historical legacies of RS-232.

DTE and DCE can be quite confusing if you let yourself think about the implications too much. When that happens, just take a deep breath and reread these points:

- The RS-232 pinout for a given connector type is always the same, regardless of whether the connector is male or female (matching pin numbers

Serial Devices

always mate) and regardless of whether the connector is on a cable, a DTE device, or a DCE device.

- All RS-232 terminology is based on the model of a straight-through connection from a DTE device to a DCE device. (By "straight through," we mean that TD on the DTE end is connected to TD on the DCE end, and so on. Each pin connects to the same-numbered pin on the other end.)

- Signals are named relative to the perspective of the DTE device. For example, the name TD (transmitted data) really means "data transmitted from DTE to DCE." Despite the name, the TD pin is an input on a DCE device. Similarly, RD is an input for DTE and an output for DCE.

- When you wire DTE equipment to DTE equipment (computer-to-terminal or computer-to-computer), you must trick each device into thinking that the other is DCE. For example, both DTE devices will expect to transmit on TD and receive on RD; you must cross-connect the wires so that one device's transmit pin goes to the other's receive pin, and vice versa.

- Three sets of signals must be crossed in this fashion for DTE-to-DTE communication (if you choose to connect them at all). TD and RD must be crossed. RTS and CTS must be crossed. And each side's DTR pin must be connected to both the DCD and DSR pins of the peer.

- To add to the confusion, a cable crossed for DTE-to-DTE communication is often called a "null modem" cable. You might be tempted to use a null modem cable to hook up a modem, but since modems are DCE, that won't work! A cable for a modem is called a "modem cable" or a "straight cable."

Because the issue of DTE vs. DCE is so confusing, you may occasionally see well-intentioned but ill-advised attempts to bring some sanity to the nomenclature by defining DTE and DCE as if they had separate pinouts (e.g., renaming DCE's TD pin to be RD, and vice versa). In this alternate universe, pinouts vary but cable connections (by signal name) do not. We suggest that you ignore any material that talks about a "DTE pinout" or a "DCE pinout"; it is unlikely to be a reliable source of information.

Originally, DTE devices were supposed to have male connectors and DCE devices were supposed to have female. Eventually, hardware designers realized that male connectors are more fragile. Expensive computing hardware now usually has female connectors, and most cables are male on both ends.[2]

Exhibit B shows pin assignments and connections for both null-modem and straight-through cables. Only signals used in the real world are shown.

---

2. At Qwest, the terms "male" and "female" are considered inappropriate. Employees are encouraged to use the words "plug" and "receptacle." Heh heh, they said "receptacle."

**Exhibit B    Pin assignments and connections for DB-25 cables**

| Legend | Straight | Null modem |
|---|---|---|
| Frame ground FG<br>Transmitted data TD<br>Received data RD<br>Request to send RTS<br>Clear to send CTS<br>Data set ready DSR<br>Signal ground SG<br>Data carrier detect DCD<br>Data terminal ready DTR | 1 —— 1<br>2 —— 2<br>3 —— 3<br>4 —— 4<br>5 —— 5<br>6 —— 6<br>7 —— 7<br>8 —— 8<br>20 —— 20 | 1 —— 1<br>2 ✕ 2<br>3 3<br>4 ✕ 4<br>5 5<br>6 ✕ 6<br>7 —— 7<br>8 ✕ 8<br>20 20 |

## 7.2    ALTERNATIVE CONNECTORS

The following sections describe the most common alternative connector systems: mini DIN-8, DB-9, and RJ-45. Despite their physical differences, these connectors all provide access to the same electrical signals as a DB-25. Devices that use different connectors are always compatible if the right kind of converter cable is used.

### The mini DIN-8 variant

Mini DIN-8s are found on Macs and on some laptops and workstations. This almost circular and extremely compact connector provides connections for seven signals. It is illustrated in Exhibit C.

**Exhibit C    A male mini DIN-8 connector**

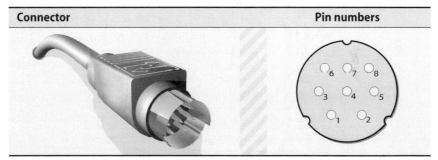

Neighborhood computer dealers usually carry injection-molded DB-25 to mini DIN-8 converter cables. Don't try to make them yourself because a mini DIN-8 is so tiny that it defies attempts to secure connections with human fingers. Pin assignments are shown in Table 7.2.

Serial Devices

**Table 7.2    Pins for a mini DIN-8 to DB-25 straight cable**

| DIN-8 | DB-25 | Signal | Function |
|-------|-------|--------|----------|
| 3 | 2 | TD | Transmitted data |
| 5 | 3 | RD | Received data |
| 6 | 4 | RTS | Request to send |
| 2 | 5 | CTS | Clear to send |
| 4,8 | 7 | SG | Signal ground |
| 7 | 8 | DCD | Data carrier detect |
| 1 | 20 | DTR | Data terminal ready |

### The DB-9 variant

Commonly found on PCs, this nine-pin connector (which looks like a DB-25 "junior") provides the eight most commonly used signals.

**Exhibit D    A male DB-9 connector**

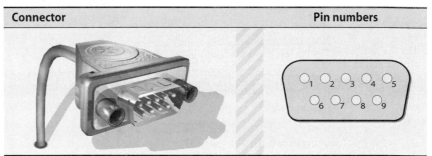

| Connector | Pin numbers |
|-----------|-------------|

PC dealers in your area should carry prefab DB-9 to DB-25 converter cables. Table 7.3 shows the pin assignments.

**Table 7.3    Pins for a DB-9 to DB-25 straight cable**

| DB-9 | DB-25 | Signal | Function |
|------|-------|--------|----------|
| 3 | 2 | TD | Transmitted data |
| 2 | 3 | RD | Received data |
| 7 | 4 | RTS | Request to send |
| 8 | 5 | CTS | Clear to send |
| 6 | 6 | DSR | Data set ready |
| 5 | 7 | SG | Signal ground |
| 1 | 8 | DCD | Data carrier detect |
| 4 | 20 | DTR | Data terminal ready |

### The RJ-45 variant

An RJ-45 is an eight-wire modular telephone connector. It's similar to the standard RJ-11 connector used for telephone wiring in the United States, but an RJ-45 has 8 pins (an RJ-11 has only 4). RJ-45 connectors are most commonly used for Ethernet wiring, but they work fine for serial communication, too.

**Exhibit E    A male RJ-45 connector**

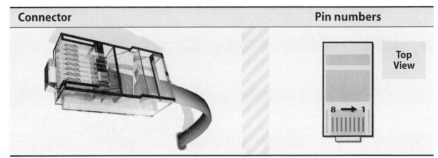

RJ-45 jacks are usually not found on computers or garden-variety serial equipment, but they are often used as intermediate connectors when routing serial lines through patch panels. They can sometimes be found on devices that have many ports in close proximity, such as terminal servers. RJ-45s are often used with flat telephone cable rather than stranded twisted-pair; either is acceptable for serial connections.

RJ-45s are compact, self-securing, and cheap. They are crimped onto the cable with a special tool. It takes less than a minute to attach one. If you are designing a large cabling system from scratch, RJ-45s are a good choice for intermediate connectors.

There are several systems for mapping the pins on an RJ-45 connector to a DB-25. We like Dave Yost's system, which adds an RJ-45 socket to every device and uses standardized RJ-45 connector cables to allow communion with either DCE or DTE equipment. Dave's standard is presented in the next section.

### The Yost standard for RJ-45 wiring

*This specification was written by Dave Yost (Dave@Yost.com). He updated it for this book.*

Here is a scheme that offers solutions to several RS-232 hassles:

- All cable connectors are of the same sex and type (male RJ-45).
- There is no distinction between DTE and DCE.
- You need only one kind of connector cable.
- You can mass-produce cables quickly, using only a crimping tool.

Each serial port on every piece of equipment gets its own appropriately wired DB-25 or DB-9 to RJ-45 adaptor. This adaptor is permanently screwed onto the port. The port now presents the same connector interface, female RJ-45, regardless of whether its underlying connector is DB-25 or DB-9, DTE or DCE, male or female. Furthermore, every serial port now transmits and receives data on the same pins.

Serial Devices

Once you have put these adaptors on your RS-232 ports, you can connect anything to anything without using null-modems or null-terminals, changing pins on cable connectors, or building special cables. You can connect modem to computer, modem to terminal, terminal to computer, terminal to terminal, computer to computer, etc., all with one kind of cable.

The cables are jacketed, eight-wire ribbon cable. The connectors on each end are squeezed onto the cable with a crimping tool, so there is no soldering or messing with pins.

There are three signal wires (one data and two control) going in each direction, plus a pair of signal grounds. The cables are not wired normally (i.e., with each connector pin connected to the corresponding pin at the other end of the cable). They are wired "with a twist," or "mirror image," or "side-to-side reversed," or whatever you want to call it. That is, pin 1 at one end of the cable goes to pin 8 on the other end, etc. (This meaning of "twist" is distinct from its use in the term "twisted pair.") This scheme works because the layout of the signals on the ribbon cable is symmetrical. That is, each transmit pin has its corresponding receive pin at the mirror-image wire position across the flat cable.[3]

Ready-made RJ-45 cables are usually wired straight through. To use them, you will have to remove the connector from one end and crimp on a new one with the wires reversed. Female-to-female RJ-45 connectors ("butt blocks") are available for extending cable lengths, but remember: two twisted cables joined with such a coupler make a straight-through cable.

Many vendors make DB-25 to RJ-45 adaptors. Their internal color coding does not match the cable colors. The adaptors, wire connectors, and wire have become available at electronics stores, sadly without any help on using them for RS-232.

*See page 375 for more information about Category 5 cable.*

This scheme was intended for use with jacketed ribbon cable, in which all the wires are side by side. Twisted-pair cable, by contrast, has four pairs of wire, each pair twisted against itself along the cable's length. If you use twisted-pair cable (such as Category 5 cable) you should not wire your cables as you normally would for RJ-45 (e.g., for 10BaseT, telephone, etc.). Rather, you should wire them so that wires 3:4 and wires 5:6 make pairs. Other pairings will be susceptible to data signal crosstalk. The pairing of the remaining wires is not important, but 1:2 and 7:8 will be about as good as any.

Inside an adaptor is an RJ-45 socket with 8 wires coming out of it. These wires have RS-232 pins (or pin sockets, as appropriate) crimped onto them. You simply push these pins into the proper holes in the RS-232 connector and then snap the adaptor housing on.

---

3. Dave doesn't say this explicitly, but you must in fact wire the cable without a physical twist to achieve the "with a twist" effect. Because the connectors at the ends of a cable point away from each other, their pin numbering is automatically reversed.

**Table 7.4    Wiring for a Yost RJ-45 to DB-25 or DB-9 adaptor**

| RJ-45 Cable | | Adaptor | Connect to DCE pins | | | Connect to DTE pins | | |
|---|---|---|---|---|---|---|---|---|
| | | | DB-25 | DB-9 | Signal | DB-25 | DB-9 | Signal |
| 1  Brown | (to Gray) | Blue | 4 | 7 | RTS | 5 | 8 | CTS |
| 2  Blue | (to Orange) | Orange | 20 | 4 | DTR | 8 | 1 | DCD |
| 3  Yellow | (to Black) | Black | 2 | 3 | TD | 3 | 2 | RD |
| 4  Green | (to Red) | Red | 7 | 5 | GND | 7 | 5 | GND |
| 5  Red | (to Green) | Green | 7 | 5 | GND | 7 | 5 | GND |
| 6  Black | (to Yellow) | Yellow | 3 | 2 | RD | 2 | 3 | TD |
| 7  Orange | (to Blue) | Brown | 8 | 1 | DCD | 20 | 4 | DTR |
| 8  Gray | (to Brown) | White | 5 | 8 | CTS | 4 | 7 | RTS |

There is one problem, however: both ground pins have to go into the same DB-25 or DB-9 hole (pin 7 or 5, respectively). You can crimp these wires together so they come out to one pin with a tiny plastic thingy made by AMP called a "Tel-splice connector ½ tap dry," part number 553017-4. So far, this part seems to be available only in quantity 1,000 for $80 or so. Believe me, you want them if you're going to wire more than a few adaptors.

Some DTE devices require the DSR signal to be active before they will send data. This signal is usually provided by the DCE device, but you can fake it by wiring together pins 20 and 6 (4 and 6 on a DB-9 connector). This way, the DTE device will receive the DSR signal from itself whenever it asserts DTR.

On some DCE printers, pin 7 of the RJ-45 adaptor (the brown wire) should be connected to the DSR line (pin 6 on both DB-25 and DB-9). Read your printer documentation to find out if it provides useful handshaking signals on DSR instead of DCD.

*Dave Yost*
*Los Altos, CA*
*July 1999*

Thanks to folks at Berkeley for this idea. Their wiring is slightly different, I gather for historical reasons, but the basic idea was there. If I can find out who really originated this scheme, I'd like to credit him or her by name.

## 7.3  HARD AND SOFT CARRIER

UNIX expects to see the DCD signal, carrier detect, go high (positive voltage) when a device is attached and turned on. This signal is carried on pin 8 of the standard DB-25 connector. If your serial cable has a DCD line and your computer really pays attention to it, you are using what is known as hard carrier. Most systems also allow soft carrier, where the computer pretends that DCD is always asserted.

For certain devices (particularly terminals), soft carrier is a great blessing. It allows you to get away with using only three lines for each serial connection: transmit, receive, and signal ground. However, modem connections really need the DCD signal. If a terminal is connected through a modem and the carrier signal is lost, the modem should hang up, especially on a long distance connection. There are numerous war stories about astronomical phone bills incurred when a modem became wedged and did not drop carrier for days.

Different versions of UNIX deal with soft carrier in different ways. Early versions required a patch to the terminal driver, but that was cumbersome and silly. Most modern systems have solved this problem by setting a default carrier mode for serial ports in the system configuration files. In addition, **stty -CLOCAL** can be used to force a terminal to assume soft carrier on a running system. For example,

```
# stty -CLOCAL < /dev/tty03
```

would enable soft carrier for the port **tty03**.

Some systems will need a ">" instead of a "<" in this command; see the section on **stty** starting on page 111 for more information.

## 7.4  HARDWARE FLOW CONTROL

The CTS and RTS signals are used to make sure that a device does not send data faster than the receiver can process it. For example, if a modem is in danger of running out of buffer space (perhaps because the connection to the remote site is slower than the serial link between the local machine and the modem), it can tell the computer to shut up until more room has become available in the buffer.

Flow control is essential for high-speed modems and is also very useful for printers. On systems that do not support hardware flow control (either because the serial ports do not understand it or because the serial cable leaves CTS and RTS disconnected), flow control can sometimes be simulated in software using the ASCII characters XON and XOFF. However, software flow control must be explicitly supported by high-level software, and even then it does not work very well.[4]

 On Sun hardware, flow control must be set up with the **eeprom** command.

Most terminals ignore the CTS and RTS signals. By jumpering pins 4 and 5 together at the terminal end of the cable, you can fool the few terminals that require a handshake across these pins before they will communicate. When the terminal sends out a signal on pin 4 saying "I'm ready," it gets the same signal back on pin 5 saying "Go ahead." You can also jumper the DTR/DSR/DCD handshake in this way.

## 7.5  CABLE LENGTH

The RS-232 standard specifies a maximum cable length of 75 feet at 9,600 bps. Standards are usually conservative, and RS-232 is no exception. We have routinely run RS-232 cables much greater distances, up to about 1,000 feet. We have hit the limit somewhere between 800 and 1,000 feet but have found that the particular brand of devices on each end makes quite a difference.

---

4. XON and XOFF are <Control-Q> and <Control-S>, respectively. This is a problem for **emacs** users because <Control-S> is the default key binding for the **emacs** search command. To fix the problem, bind the search command to some other key.

## 7.6 SERIAL DEVICE FILES

Serial ports are represented by device files in or under **/dev**. Most computers have two serial ports built in. In the past they were usually known as **/dev/ttya** and **/dev/ttyb**, but naming conventions have diverged over time.

Sometimes, more than one device file refers to the same serial port. For example, **/dev/cua/a** on a Solaris system refers to the same port as **/dev/term/a**. However, the minor device number for **/dev/cua/a** is different:

```
% ls -lL /dev/term/a /dev/cua/a
crw-rw-rw- 1 root  sys   29, 0      Jan 15  1998/dev/term/a
crw------- 1 uucp uucp  29, 131072 Jan 15  1998/dev/cua/a
```

 Multiple device files are primarily used to support modems that handle both incoming and outgoing calls. In the Solaris scheme, the driver allows **/dev/term/a** to be opened only when DCD has been asserted by the modem, indicating the presence of an active (inbound) connection (assuming that soft carrier is not enabled on the port). **/dev/cua/a** can be opened regardless of the state of DCD; it's used when connecting to the modem to instruct it to place a call. Access to each device file is blocked while the other is in use.

 FreeBSD lets you specify initial and locked states for ports in **/etc/rc.serial**. This feature is handy when you want to override the behavior of poorly written programs that don't configure the ports correctly. If you set the port parameters (flow control, baud rate, etc.) of the locked device and then open it with a program, the kernel will ignore attempts to reconfigure the port. See **sio**(4) for more details.

As always, the names of the device files do not really matter. Behavior is determined by the major and minor device numbers, and the names of device files are merely conventional.[5]

Table 7.5 on the next page shows the standard naming conventions for serial port device files on our example systems. Filenames are shown for the first two ports; additional ports are named similarly.

## 7.7 SOFTWARE CONFIGURATION FOR SERIAL DEVICES

Once a device has been connected with the proper cable, software on the host machine must be configured to take advantage of it. Unlike devices that connect directly to the host's bus, serial devices do not require configuration at the kernel level.[6] High-level software must still be told about the new devices, however.

---

5. Which is not to say that you can pick your own names; most software assumes that you will use the standard naming conventions.

6. Actually, the serial ports themselves do require kernel-level configuration, but this is always done for you by the vendor.

**Table 7.5  Device files for the first two serial ports**

| System | Standard files | Auxiliary files | |
|---|---|---|---|
| Solaris | **/dev/term/[a,b]** | **/dev/cua/[a,b]** | (dial-out) |
| HP-UX[a] | **/dev/tty0p[0,1]** | **/dev/cul0p[0,1]** | (dial-out modem) |
|  |  | **/dev/cua0p[0,1]** | (direct-connect dial-out) |
|  |  | **/dev/ttyd0p[0,1]** | (dial-in modem) |
|  |  | **/dev/c0p[0,1]_lp** | (serial printer) |
| Red Hat | **/dev/ttyS[0,1]** | **/dev/cua[0,1]** | (dial-out, historical compatibility only) |
| FreeBSD | **/dev/ttyd[0,1]** | **/dev/cuaa[0,1]** | (dial-out modem) |
|  |  | **/dev/cuala[0,1]** | (dial-out modem, locked state) |
|  |  | **/dev/cuaia[0,1]** | (dial-out modem, initial state) |

a. See the **mksf**(1M) manual page for a full explanation of the many exciting options.

The configuration chores for a new device depend on the type of device and the uses to which it will be put:

- For a hardwired terminal, you must tell the system to listen for logins on the terminal's port. You specify the speed and parameters of the serial connection. Configuration for terminals is described in the next section.

- Dial-in modems are configured similarly to hardwired terminals. However, the exact procedure may be slightly different on some systems.

- To configure a dial-out modem for use by humans, you must put entries in **/etc/remote** for use by the **tip** and **cu** commands. This procedure is described on page 114.

- To use a modem to connect to a remote network using PPP, see page 291. You may need additional software.

- See Chapter 23, *Printing,* for information about how to set up a serial printer. Some printers only receive data; others are bidirectional and can return status information to the host computer.

- A custom serial device that you will use only from your own software needs no special configuration. You can simply open the device file to access the device. Refer to the **termio** man page or the man page for the **tty** driver to learn about the **ioctl** calls that set the speed, flag bits, and buffering mode of the serial port.

## 7.8  CONFIGURATION OF HARDWIRED TERMINALS

Over the last decade, cheap computers have almost entirely replaced ASCII terminals. However, even the "terminal" windows on a graphical display use the same drivers and configuration files as real terminals, so system administrators still need to understand how they work.

Terminal configuration involves two main tasks: making sure that a process is attached to a terminal to accept logins, and making sure that information about the terminal is available once a user has logged in.

### The login process

The login process involves several different programs.

The **init** daemon is started at boot time. One of its jobs is to spawn a process, usually **getty** (but not on Solaris), on each terminal port that is turned on in the **/etc/ttys** or **/etc/inittab** file (depending on the system). **getty** sets the port's initial characteristics (such as speed and parity) and prints a login prompt.

The sequence of events in a complete login is as follows:

- A user enters a login name at **getty**'s prompt.
- **getty** executes the **login** program with the specified name as an argument.
- **login** requests a password and validates it against **/etc/passwd**.[7]
- **login** prints the message of the day from **/etc/motd**.
- **login** sets up the TERM environment variable and runs a shell.
- The shell executes the appropriate startup files.[8]
- The shell prints a prompt and waits for input.

When the user logs out, control returns to **init**, which wakes up and spawns a new **getty** on the terminal port.

Files in **/etc** control the characteristics associated with each terminal port. These characteristics include the presence of a login prompt and **getty** process on the port, the baud rate to expect, and the terminal type (among other things).

Unfortunately, terminal configuration is one area where there is little agreement among vendors. Table 7.6 lists the files used by each system.

**Table 7.6    Terminal configuration files**

| System | On/off | Term type | Parameters | Monitor |
|--------|--------|-----------|------------|---------|
| Solaris[a] | _sactab | _sactab | zsmon/_pmtab | ttymon |
| HP-UX | /etc/inittab | /etc/ttytype | /etc/gettydefs | getty |
| Red Hat | /etc/inittab | /etc/ttytype | /etc/gettydefs | getty |
| FreeBSD | /etc/ttys | /etc/ttys | /etc/gettytab | getty |

a. Solaris configuration files are in **/etc/saf** and should be managed with **sacadm**.

---

7. On some systems, **/etc/passwd** is superseded or complemented by an administrative database system such as NIS. See Chapter 18 for more information.

8. **.profile** for **sh**, **ksh**, and **bash**; **.cshrc** and **.login** for **csh** and **tcsh**.

### The /etc/ttys and /etc/ttytab files

Systems based on 4.3BSD or later have both the port and terminal type information merged into a single file, sometimes called **ttytab** and sometimes called **ttys** (Free-BSD). The format is:

```
device program termtype {on|off} [secure]
```

Fields are separated by whitespace. *program* is the monitor process that **init** should start if the port is turned on. **getty**, the usual entry in this field, takes an argument that indicates the speed and configuration parameters of the serial port.

*termtype* is the terminal type; it names an entry in **termcap** or **terminfo** (see page 109). When you log in, the TERM environment variable is set to the value of this field.

The keywords "on" and "off" enable or disable logins on the port (that is, they specify whether or not *program* should be executed). If the "secure" keyword is present, root may log in on this terminal. Many sites do not allow root logins from public terminal rooms or dial-ins.

Here are some sample entries from an **/etc/ttys** file:

```
console  none                            unknown  off  secure
ttyd0    "/usr/libexec/getty std.9600"   dialup   off  secure
ttyd1    "/usr/libexec/getty std.9600"   dialup   off  secure
ttyd2    "/usr/libexec/getty std.9600"   dialup   off  secure
```

The argument to **getty** refers to an entry in the **inittab**, **gettytab**, or **gettydefs** file, depending on the system.

**init** reads the **ttys** or **ttytab** file only once. If you change the configuration file, you must explicitly tell **init** to reread the file by sending it a hangup signal. **init** is always process number 1, so the command

```
# kill -1 1
```

executed as root will usually work. Don't mistype and leave out the dash!

### The /etc/ttytype file

On some systems, terminal type information is separated from **/etc/ttys** and kept in a file called **/etc/ttytype**. The format of an entry in **ttytype** is:

```
termtype device
```

*device* is the short name of the device file representing the port, and *termtype* is as described above for the new-style **/etc/ttys**. Here is a sample **ttytype** file:

```
wyse     console
dialup   ttyi0
dialup   ttyi1
vt320    ttyi2
h19      ttyi3
dialout  ttyi4
```

## The /etc/gettytab file

The **gettytab** file associates symbolic names (such as std.9600, used in the examples above) with port configuration information such as speed, parity, and desired login prompt. Here is a sample:

```
# The default entry, used to set defaults for other entries, and in cases
# where getty is called with no specific entry name.

default:\
    :ap:lm=\r\n%h login\72 :sp#9600:

# Fixed-speed entries

2|std.9600|9600-baud:\
    :sp#9600:
h|std.38400|38400-baud:\
    :sp#38400:
```

The format is the same as that of **/etc/printcap** and **/etc/termcap**. The lines with names separated by a vertical bar (|) list the names by which each configuration is known. The other fields in an entry set the options to be used with the serial port.

Most systems come with preset **gettytab** entries appropriate for a variety of terminals. See page 712 for a description of the general file format; refer to your manuals for information about specific variables.

## The /etc/inittab file

The Solaris, HP-UX, and Red Hat versions of **init** support various "run levels" that determine which system resources are enabled. There are eight run levels: 0 to 6, plus "s" for single-user operation. When you leave single-user mode, **init** prompts you to enter a run level unless an initdefault field exists in **/etc/inittab** as described below. **init** then scans the **inittab** file for all lines that match the specified run level.

Run levels are usually set up so that you have one level where only the console is enabled and another level that enables all terminals. You can define the run levels in whatever way is appropriate for your system; however, we recommend that you not stray too far from the defaults.

Entries in **inittab** are of the form

> *id:run-levels:action:process*

Here's a simple example of an **inittab** file:

```
::sysinit:/etc/setclk </dev/console >/dev/console 2>&1
co:234:respawn:/etc/getty console console
11:234:respawn:/etc/getty tty11 9600
12:234:off:/etc/getty tty12 9600
```

In this format, *id* is a one or two-character string used to identify the entry. *id* can be null, as in the first line. For terminal entries, it is customary to use the terminal number as the *id*.

Serial Devices

*run-levels* enumerates the run levels to which the entry pertains. If no levels are specified (as in the first line), then the entry is valid for all run levels. The *action* field tells how to handle the *process* field; some universally understood values are listed in Table 7.7. Some systems support additional options.

**Table 7.7**   **Common values for the /etc/inittab *action* field**

| Value | Wait? | Meaning |
|---|---|---|
| initdefault | – | Sets the initial run level |
| boot | No | Runs when **inittab** is read for the first time |
| bootwait | Yes | Runs when **inittab** is read for the first time |
| once | No | Starts the process once |
| wait | Yes | Starts the process once |
| respawn | No | Always keeps the process running |
| powerfail | No | Runs when **init** receives a power fail signal |
| powerwait | Yes | Runs when **init** receives a power fail signal |
| sysinit | Yes | Runs before accessing the console |
| off | – | Terminates the process if it is running, on some systems |

If one of the *run-levels* matches the current run level and the *action* field indicates that the entry is relevant, **init** uses **sh** to execute (or terminate) the command specified in the *process* field. The Wait? column in Table 7.7 tells whether **init** waits for the command to complete before continuing.

In the example **inittab** file above, the first line sets the clock, the middle lines spawn **getty** processes, and the last line ensures that there is no **getty** on **tty12**.

The command **telinit -q** makes **init** reread the **inittab** file.

### The /etc/gettydefs file

Like the **gettytab** file, **gettydefs** defines port configurations used by **getty**. A system will usually have one or the other, never both. The **gettydefs** file looks like this:

```
console# B9600 HUPCL # B9600 SANE IXANY #login: #console
19200# B19200 HUPCL # B19200 SANE IXANY #login: #9600
9600# B9600 HUPCL # B9600 SANE IXANY HUPCL #login: #4800
4800# B4800 HUPCL # B4800 SANE IXANY HUPCL #login: #2400
2400# B2400 HUPCL # B2400 SANE IXANY HUPCL #login: #1200
1200# B1200 HUPCL # B1200 SANE IXANY HUPCL #login: #300
300# B300 HUPCL # B300 SANE IXANY TAB3 HUPCL #login: #9600
```

The format of an entry is

```
label# initflags # finalflags # prompt #next
```

**getty** tries to match its second argument with a *label* entry. If it is called without a second argument, the first entry in the file is used. The *initflags* field lists **ioctl** flags that should be set on a port until **login** is executed. The *finalflags* field sets flags that should be used thereafter.

There must be an entry that sets the speed of the connection in both the *initflags* and the *finalflags*. The flags available vary by system; check the **gettydefs** man page for authoritative information (usually, the flag names are the same ones used when setting the options from a C program).

The *prompt* field defines the login prompt, which may include tabs and newlines in backslash notation. The *next* field gives the label of an **inittab** entry that should be substituted for the current one if a break is received. This was useful decades ago when modems didn't negotiate a speed automatically and you had to match speeds by hand with a series of breaks. Today, it's an anachronism. For a hardwired terminal, *next* should refer to the label of the current entry.

Each time you change the **gettydefs** file, you should run **getty -c gettydefs**, which checks the syntax of the file to make sure that all entries are valid.

### Solaris and sacadm

Rather than traditional UNIX **getty**s that watch each port for activity and provide a login prompt, Solaris has a convoluted hierarchy called the Service Access Facility that controls TTY monitors, port monitors, and many other things that provide a lot of complexity but little added functionality.

To set up a serial port to provide a login prompt, you must first configure a "monitor" that watches the status of the port (**ttymon**). You then configure a port monitor that watches the TTY monitor. For example, to set up a 9,600 baud monitor on **ttyb** to print a login prompt with terminal type VT100, you'd use the following commands.

```
# sacadm -a -p myttymon -t ttymon -c /usr/lib/saf/ttymon -v 1
# pmadm -a -p myttymon -s b -i root -fu -v 1 -m "`ttyadm -d /dev/term/b -l
    9600 -T vt100 -s /usr/bin/login`"
```

The **/etc/ttydefs** file is used much like **gettydefs** on other systems to set speed and parity parameters.

See the manual pages for **saf**, **pacadm**, **pmadm**, **ttyadm**, and **ttymon** as well as the terminals chapter in the Solaris AnswerBook for more information about setting up these monitors. Have fun.

### Terminal support: the termcap and terminfo databases

UNIX has always supported many different terminal types, as opposed to some large vendors whose software only worked with their own brand of terminals. UNIX provides this support through a database of terminal capabilities that specifies the features and programming quirks of each brand of terminal.

Some systems call this database **termcap**; others use a different format that's called **terminfo**. A few provide both terminal databases for maximum compatibility. The databases are usually found in **/etc** or **/usr/share**.

As shipped, both databases contains entries for hundreds of different terminals. It's highly unlikely that you would ever need to write your own terminal description. However, some vendors insist on renaming the "xterm" terminal type, so you might have to add a new and improved name for an existing entry.

*See page 112 for more information about configuring terminals at login time.*

UNIX programs look at the TERM environment variable to determine what kind of terminal you are using. The terminal can then be looked up in **termcap** or **terminfo**. Alternatively, the terminal's **termcap** entry can be placed directly in the environment under the TERMCAP environment variable. Users normally arrange to have their TERMCAP and TERM variables set up at login time.

Now that physical terminals are no longer much used, only a handful of terminal types are relevant to daily life. A good rule of thumb is that everything emulates a DEC VT100 until proven otherwise.

## 7.9  SPECIAL CHARACTERS AND THE TERMINAL DRIVER

The terminal driver supports several special functions that you access by typing particular keys (usually control keys) on the keyboard. The exact binding of functions to keys can be set with the **tset** and **stty** commands. Table 7.8 lists some of these functions, along with their default key bindings.

**Table 7.8  Special characters for the terminal driver**

| Name | Default | Function |
|------|---------|----------|
| ERASE | ^H | Erases one character of input |
| WERASE | ^W | Erases one word of input |
| KILL | ^U | Erases the entire line of input |
| EOF | ^D | Sends an "end of file" indication |
| INTR | ^C | Interrupts the currently running process |
| QUIT | ^\ | Kills the current process with a core dump |
| STOP | ^S | Stops output to the screen |
| START | ^Q | Restarts output to the screen |
| DISCARD | ^O | Throws away pending output |
| SUSPEND | ^Z | Suspends the current process |
| LNEXT | ^V | Interprets the next character literally |

Depending on what a vendor's keyboards look like, the default for ERASE might also be the delete character, for which different OSes have different text representations. It's indicative of the disastrous fragmentation of the UNIX industry that vendors cannot even agree on what code the backspace key should generate.

On very early systems, the characters #, @, and delete were the defaults for ERASE, KILL, and INTR. A few systems still secretly use those defaults before you log in, so don't use these characters in passwords.

## 7.10  STTY: SET TERMINAL OPTIONS

**stty** lets you directly change and query the various settings of the terminal driver. There are about a zillion options; these are documented in the man page for the **tty** driver (usually **tty**(4) or **tty**(5), not **tty**(1), which is a simple program that tells you which terminal or pseudo-terminal you've logged in on).

In most cases, the option names used in the **tty** man page are the same names used by **stty**, but sometimes there are slight differences. Many options are the same among systems, but there are enough discrepancies, even among related variants, that you should consult the man page for your local system.

Options to **stty** can be placed on the command line in any order and in any combination. A dash before an option negates it. For example, to configure a terminal for 9,600 bps operation with even parity and without hardware tabs, use the command

```
% stty 9600 even -tabs
```

A good combination of options to use for a plain-vanilla terminal is

```
% stty intr ^C kill ^U erase ^H -tabs
```

Here, **-tabs** prevents the terminal driver from taking advantage of the terminal's built-in tabulation mechanism, which is useful because many terminals are not very smart about tabs. The other options set the interrupt, kill, and erase characters to <Control-C>, <Control-U>, and <Control-H> (backspace), respectively.

You can use **stty** to examine the current modes of the terminal driver as well as to set them. **stty** with no arguments produces output like this:

```
% stty
speed 9600 baud; -parity hupcl
rows = 24; columns = 80
erase = ^h; swtch = <undef>;
brkint -inpck -istrip icrnl -ixany imaxbel onlcr
echo echoe echok echoctl echoke iexten
```

For a more verbose status report, run **stty everything**, **stty -a**, or **stty all**, depending on your system. The output in this case is something like:

```
% stty -a
speed 9600 baud;
rows = 24; columns = 80; ypixels = 364; xpixels = 739;
eucw 1:0:0:0, scrw 1:0:0:0
intr = ^c; quit = ^|; erase = ^h; kill = ^u; eof = ^d; eol = <undef>;
eol2 = <undef>; swtch = <undef>; start = ^q; stop = ^s; susp = ^z;
dsusp = ^y; rprnt = ^r; flush = ^o; werase = ^w; lnext = ^v;
-parenb -parodd cs8 -cstopb hupcl cread -clocal -loblk -crtscts
-parext -ignbrk brkint ignpar -parmrk -inpck -istrip -inlcr
-igncr icrnl -iuclc ixon -ixany -ixoff imaxbel isig icanon -xcase
echo echoe echok -echonl -noflsh -tostop echoctl -echoprt echoke
-defecho -flusho -pendin iexten opost -olcuc onlcr -ocrnl -onocr
-onlret -ofill -ofdel
```

Serial Devices

The format of the output is similar but lists more information. The meaning of the output should be intuitively obvious (if you've written a terminal driver recently).

**stty** operates on the file descriptor of its standard input or standard output (depending on your system), so it is possible to set and query the modes of a terminal other than the current one by using the shell redirection characters ">" and "<". On most systems, you must be the superuser to change the modes on someone else's terminal.

## 7.11 TSET: SET OPTIONS AUTOMATICALLY

**tset** initializes the terminal driver to a mode appropriate for a given terminal type. The type can be specified on the command line; if it is left out, **tset** uses the value of the TERM environment variable.

**tset** supports a syntax for mapping certain values of the TERM environment variable into other values. This feature is useful if you often log in through a modem or data switch and would like to have the terminal driver configured correctly for the terminal you are really using on the other end of the connection rather than something generic and unhelpful such as "dialup."

## 7.12 HOW TO UNWEDGE A TERMINAL

Some programs (such as **vi**) make drastic changes to the state of the terminal driver while they are running. This meddling is normally invisible to the user, since the terminal state is carefully restored whenever the program exits or is suspended. However, it is possible for a program to crash or be killed without performing this housekeeping. When this happens, your terminal may behave very strangely: it might fail to handle newlines correctly, to echo characters that you type, or to execute commands properly.

Another common way to confuse a terminal is to accidentally run **cat** or **more** on a binary file. Most binaries contain a delicious mix of special characters that is guaranteed to send some of the less-robust terminals and emulators into outer space.

To fix this situation, you can use **reset** or **stty sane**. **reset** is actually just a link to **tset** on most systems, and it can accept most of **tset**'s arguments. However, it is usually run without arguments. Both **reset** and **stty sane** restore the correctitude of the terminal driver and send out an appropriate reset code from **termcap** or **terminfo**, if one is available.

In many cases where a reset is appropriate, the terminal has been left in a mode in which no processing is done on the characters you type. Most terminals generate carriage returns rather than newlines when the Return or Enter key is pressed; without input processing, this key generates <Control-M> characters instead of sending the current command off to be executed. To enter newlines directly, use <Control-J> or the line feed key (if there is one) instead of the Return key.

## 7.13  MODEMS

A modem converts the digital serial signal produced by a computer into an analog signal suitable for transmission on a standard phone line. Modems are used for a variety of applications. See page 291 for a typical example.

External modems have an RJ-11 jack on the analog side and an RS-232 interface of some type on the digital side—usually a female DB-25. They usually have a series of lights on the front that display the modem's current state and level of activity. These lights are incredibly useful for debugging, so modems should generally be located somewhere in plain sight.

Internal modems are usually seen only on PCs. They plug into an ISA, PCI, or PCM-CIA slot and have an RJ-11 jack that sticks out the back of the computer's case once the modem has been installed. They are cheaper than external modems but more troublesome to configure, and they generally lack indicator lights.

If you are considering an internal modem, you must check to be sure it's specifically supported by your version of UNIX. Fast CPUs have made it possible to simplify modem hardware by performing some signal processing tasks on the host processor. Unfortunately, modems that work this way require sophisticated drivers and aren't likely to be compatible with PC-based versions of UNIX.

Modems vary somewhat in general robustness, but this characteristic is hard to judge without direct experience. In the past, we have found some modems to be significantly more tolerant of line noise than others. These days, most designs use a standard chipset from one of several large manufacturers, so it's likely that the variations among modems are not so great as they once were.

High-speed modems require complex firmware, and this firmware is occasionally buggy. Manufacturers share firmware among models when possible, so good or bad firmware tends to run in product lines. For this reason, we still recommend sticking with well-known brands. We've had good luck with 3Com products.

### Modulation, error correction, and data compression protocols

Long ago, it was important to check the exact protocols supported by a modem because standards were continually changing and modem manufacturers did not always implement a complete suite of protocols. These days, modems of a given speed all support pretty much the same standards. The only real difference between them is the quality of the firmware, electronics, and support.

A protocol's baud rate is the rate at which the carrier signal is modulated. If there are more than two signal levels, then more than one bit of information can be sent per transition and the speed in bits per second will be higher than the baud rate. Historically, the data speed and signaling speed of modems were the same, leading to a casual conflation of the terms "baud" and "bps" (bits per second).

The fastest modems available today use the "56K" V.90 standard, which doesn't actually provide 56 Kb/s of throughput. At best, it allows 33.6 Kb/s from computer to

ISP and 53 Kb/s in the other direction. Nevertheless, V.90 achieves speeds that are very close to the theoretical and legal limits of signaling over ordinary voice telephone lines, and it's not expected to be superseded any time soon.

Two earlier "56K" systems, X2 and 56Kflex, were attempts by manufacturers (US Robotics—now part of 3Com—and Rockwell, respectively) to get V.90-class modems to market before a proper standard existed. Although they are still supported by some ISPs, these systems are expected to die out very soon. Many X2 and 56Kflex modems can be upgraded to V.90, so don't throw them out.

A few modems with top speeds of 28.8 Kb/s and 14.4 Kb/s are still available, but they are becoming rare. You can pick up V.90 modems quite cheaply at sales and at on-line auctions, so there is no reason to compromise.

Line noise can introduce a significant number of errors into a modem connection. Various error correction protocols have been developed to packetize the transmitted data and provide checksum-based correction for errors, insulating the user or application from line faults. You used to have to know something about this to configure your modem correctly, but these days it usually just works.

Data compression algorithms can be used to shrink the number of bits that must be transmitted between analog endpoints. The amount of compression varies from worse than none (when transmitting data that has already been compressed) to at most about 4:1. A more typical value is 1.5:1. In general, the average configuration does better with one of these compression algorithms turned on.

### Dial-out configuration: /etc/phones and /etc/remote

The **tip** and **cu** commands provide a basic keyboard interface to serial devices. They are most often used with modems but can also be used to talk to printers and terminals. **tip** and **cu** use two config files that record phone numbers (**/etc/phones**) and serial port information (**/etc/remote**).

The **/etc/remote** file looks like this:

```
# /etc/remote:  Dialer definitions

dial19200|19200 Baud:dv=/dev/cul0:br#19200:\
    cu=/dev/cul0:at=hayes:du:
dial38400|dialer|38400 Baud:dv=/dev/cul0:br#38400:\
    cu=/dev/cul0:at=hayes:du:

# Commonly dialed hosts

ucc:pn=3338118:tc=dial38400
cc:pn=@:tc=dial38400
dca:dv=/dev/ttyh1,/dev/ttyh2:br#9600:pa=none
```

The first two entries describe dialer configurations. The next section provides shortcuts for dialing particular hosts. Note that in the cc entry, the phone number is written as pn=@, which means to look for the phone number(s) in **/etc/phones**.

```
# /etc/phones: This file can contain long distance
# billing numbers and unpublished telephone numbers,
# so it's not usually world-readable.

cc      5552530
monet  8,,510,555-4567,,,,xxxx-xxx
```

The **phones** file contains symbolic definitions of phone numbers. In this example, xxxx-xxx could represent a long distance billing number. Punctuation is used to signify delays or to wait for a second dial tone. The characters depend on the brand of modem: commas, equal signs, and stars all commonly have special meanings.

### Bidirectional modems

It is occasionally handy to use a single modem for both dial-in and dial-out services. This configuration requires special treatment of the serial port, since **getty** normally takes full control of serial ports at boot time. Other processes that want to use the modem are shut out, unable to open the port even when the modem is not actually in use. Unfortunately, there is little standardization among systems for the management of bidirectional modems.

Solaris requires you to take the following steps to make a port bidirectional:

- Include the **-b** flag to **ttyadm** when attaching the port monitor.
- Use **/dev/cua/a** (not **/dev/term/a**) as the argument to **ttyadm**.
- Edit **/etc/uucp/Devices** to list the bidirectional service name.

See *How to Set Up Bidirectional Modem Service* in the Solaris AnswerBook for explicit examples and details.

Under HP-UX and Red Hat, a special **getty** called **uugetty** can be used on bidirectional ports. **uugetty** shares lock files with **cu**, **tip**, and **uucico** to avoid conflicts.

## 7.14  DEBUGGING A SERIAL LINE

Debugging serial lines is not difficult. Some typical errors are:

- Forgetting to tell **init** to reread its configuration files
- Forgetting to set soft carrier when using three-wire cables
- Using a cable with the wrong nullness
- Soldering or crimping DB-25 connectors upside down
- Connecting a device to the wrong wire due to bad or nonexistent wire maps
- Setting the terminal options incorrectly

A breakout box is an indispensable tool for debugging cabling problems. It is patched into the serial line and shows the signals on each pin as they pass through the cable. The better breakout boxes have both male and female connectors on each side and so are totally flexible and bisexual in their positioning. LEDs associated with each "interesting" pin (pins 2, 3, 4, 5, 6, 8, and 20) show when the pin is active.

Some breakout boxes are read-only and just allow you to monitor the signals; others let you rewire the connection and assert a voltage on a particular pin. For example, if you suspected that a cable needed to be nulled (crossed), you could use the breakout box to override the actual cable wiring and swap pins 2 and 3 and also pins 6 and 20.

*See page 391 for more information about Black Box.*

A cheap breakout box can be worse than no breakout box at all. Our favorite is the BOB-CAT-B made by Black Box. It is an easy-to-use box that costs around $250. You can reach them at (724) 746-5500 or www.blackbox.com.

## 7.15 OTHER COMMON I/O PORTS

Serial ports used to be the unchallenged standard for attaching low-speed peripherals to UNIX systems, but now that UNIX is increasingly seen on PC hardware, we have inherited several additional options from the PC world.

PC-style parallel ports are similar in concept to serial ports, but they transfer eight bits of data at once rather than just one. They're significantly faster than serial ports but require bulkier cabling and connectors. Parallel interfaces are most commonly found on printers, but in the Windows world they're also used to connect Zip and tape drives, which require more bandwidth than a serial port can deliver. UNIX support for parallel devices other than printers is scant, however.

USB, the Universal Serial Bus, is a more recent innovation that puts traditional serial and parallel ports to shame. It's fast, architecturally elegant, and uses standardized cables that are both simple and cheap. Unfortunately, it will take years for organizations to get rid of their existing serial and parallel devices. For now, we can only dream of living in the USB promised land (and hope that Microsoft doesn't build on all the good lots first).

### Parallel ports

PCs have had parallel ports for decades, but only recently have they started to make their way onto UNIX systems. Any UNIX system based on PC hardware will have a parallel port, of course, but some manufacturers have also begun to add them onto dedicated UNIX workstations so that UNIX wireheads can use printers made for the Windows market.

Parallel ports have adhered to five or six different protocol standards over the years, but contemporary parallel interfaces are compatible with all earlier versions. The best standard now available is IEEE-1284, which incorporates compatibility with most prior standards (both de facto and written).

To achieve the fastest throughput speeds, modern parallel ports can be set to operate in either EPP (Enhanced Parallel Port) mode or ECP (Extended Capability Port) mode, both allowing speeds of 2 MB/s and beyond. The two high-speed modes are more or less equivalent, except that ECP supports DMA. It's questionable whether this makes any difference in practice.

Computers usually provide a female DB-25 connector for the parallel port, and peripherals tend to have a female 36-pin Centronics connector. Therefore, most parallel cables are male DB-25 to male Centronics. A third connector type, mini-Centronics, is also permitted by IEEE-1284.

Parallel cables can be up to 10 meters long. Since cable lengths are limited and only two types of connectors are in common use, it's more cost-effective to buy prefabricated parallel cables than to make them yourself.

Although there are many Windows peripherals that can connect to a PC's parallel port, only printers are widely and generically supported under UNIX. Other peripherals, such as Zip drives and video cameras, need a device-specific driver to be usable. Drivers are available for a number of popular devices, but support varies by operating system, and the drivers must usually be installed by hand. As might be expected, Linux is miles ahead in this arena.

For better or worse, UNIX support for parallel devices will probably never get much better than it already is because development effort is likely to be concentrated on USB in the foreseeable future.

For a useful list of parallel port FAQs and related parallel port information, see the entry under "parallel port" at www.webopedia.com.

### USB: the Universal Serial Bus

*For more information about USB, see the site www.usb.org.*

USB is a generic peripheral interconnect system designed by Compaq, DEC, IBM, Intel, Microsoft, NEC, and Northern Telecom. The first USB standard was published in 1995. Acceptance of USB in the Windows world has snowballed rapidly over the last couple of years, to the point that almost all new PCs now come with USB ports. Most new computer peripherals are available in USB versions as well.

USB is a great system. We think it's likely to gain wide acceptance in the UNIX world and to stay in use for many years to come. It has almost all the properties and features one could wish for in a low-speed bus:

- Up to 127 devices can be connected.
- Cables have only four wires: power, ground, and two signal wires.
- Connectors and connector genders are standardized.
- The connectors are small, and the cables are thin and flexible.
- Devices can be connected and disconnected without powering down.
- Signaling speeds up to 12 Mb/s are possible.
- Legacy serial and parallel devices can be connected with adaptors.

USB can even be used as a LAN technology, although it's really not designed for that.

Unfortunately, only HP-UX provides any form of USB support as of this writing: its newest workstations use USB keyboards and mice. Linux is close behind, but its USB support is not yet fully baked. It is beyond doubt, however, that USB will soon be fully mainstream on most UNIX systems.

Serial Devices

# *8* *Adding a Disk*

There is never enough disk space. The minute a new disk is added to the system, it is half full; or so it seems. Getting users to clean up their disk space is as difficult as getting a teenager to clean up his room. Therefore, an administrator will occasionally have to install new disk drives.

Most systems connect their disks through a standard peripheral bus called SCSI (the Small Computer Systems Interface, pronounced "scuzzy"). An alternative interface called Integrated Drive Electronics (IDE) is supported by PCs. We begin this chapter with a general discussion of the SCSI and IDE standards and the structure of modern hard disks. We then discuss the general mechanisms by which disks are formatted and partitioned and the procedure for initializing filesystems.

Although most vendors use standardized disk interfaces, they seem to have made a point of using proprietary commands to set up new disks; accordingly, you'll see a lot of vendor-specific details in this chapter. We try to cover each system in enough detail that you can at least understand the commands that are used and can locate the necessary documentation. We also illustrate each system's installation procedure for one particular disk.

## 8.1 DISK INTERFACES

In the beginning, computer manufacturers all defined their own proprietary interfaces for hard disks and other peripherals. This state of affairs was due in part to the immature state of interface technology, but it was also partly due to the manufacturers' desire to control the peripheral market for their machines. Eventually, third-party vendors started to make add-on disk systems that were cost effective and compatible. To add insult to injury, the third-party disk systems often yielded better performance than their officially sanctioned counterparts.

Computer vendors didn't much care for this turn of events. In several highly publicized lawsuits, they attempted to protect interface specifications as trade secrets or as patented technology. Ultimately, the question became moot as the industry migrated toward standard interface technologies.

These days only a few interface standards are in common use, although several new technologies are on the horizon. It's important to select disk drives that match the interfaces of the system on which they will be installed. If a system supports several different interfaces, you should use the one that best meets your requirements for speed, redundancy, mobility, and price.

- SCSI is one of the most common and widely supported disk interfaces. It comes in several flavors, all of which support multiple disks on a bus and various speeds and communication styles. SCSI is described in more detail in the next section.

- IDE was developed as a simple, low-cost interface for PCs. It was originally called "Integrated Drive Electronics" because it put the hardware controller in the same box as the disk platters and used a relatively high-level protocol for communication between the computer and the disks. This is now the standard architecture for all modern disks, but the name lives on. IDE disks are medium in speed, high in capacity, and unbelievably cheap. However, the interface design makes IDE a practical option only for workstations with four or fewer devices. See page 124 for more information about IDE.

- Fibre Channel is a serial interface that is gaining popularity in the enterprise environment due to its high bandwidth and to the large number of devices that can be attached to it at once. Fibre Channel devices connect together with a fiber optic or twinaxial copper cable. Current speeds are 100 MB/s and up. Common topologies include loops, called Fibre Channel Arbitrated Loop (FC-AL), and fabrics, which are constructed with Fibre Channel switches. Fibre Channel can speak several different protocols, including SCSI and even IP. Fibre Channel devices are identified by a hard-wired ID number called a World Wide Name that's similar to an Ethernet MAC address.

- The Universal Serial Bus (USB) has become popular for connecting devices such as keyboards and mice, but it has enough bandwidth to support slower disk devices such as removable hard disks and CD-ROM drives. USB is common on PCs and enables you to easily move a disk among systems.

SCSI and IDE are by far the dominant players in the disk drive arena. They are the only interfaces we will discuss in detail.

**Adding a Disk**

## The SCSI interface

Several chip sets implement the SCSI standard, so vendors sometimes put SCSI support right on the CPU or peripheral board. SCSI defines a generic data pipe that can be used by all kinds of peripherals. Most commonly, it's used for disks, tape drives, scanners, and printers. The SCSI standard does not specify how a disk is constructed or laid out, only the manner in which it communicates with other devices.

The SCSI standard has been through several revisions, with SCSI-3 being the current version. SCSI-1 was developed in 1986 as an ANSI standard based on the Shugart Associates System Interface (SASI), which was a commercially available system bus. SCSI-2 was developed in 1990. It is backward compatible with SCSI-1 but adds several performance features. These features include command queuing, which allows devices to reorder I/O requests to optimize throughput, and scatter-gather I/O, which permits Direct Memory Access (DMA) from discontiguous memory regions.

You might see the terms "fast" and "wide" applied to SCSI-2 devices, which means that the bus speed is doubled or that the number of bits transferred simultaneously is larger, typically 16 or 32 bits instead of the usual 8.[1] Wide SCSI chains can also support up to 16 devices; narrow SCSI allows only 8. Fastness and wideness are separate features that are commonly used together for synergistic increases.

SCSI-3 is actually a family of standards. It includes specifications for various physical media, including the traditional parallel buses and high-speed serial media such as Fibre Channel and IEEE 1394 ("FireWire"). It also defines the SCSI command sets and introduces enhancements to support device autoconfiguration, multimedia applications, and new types of devices.

Although the SCSI-3 specification has not yet been finalized, many of its features have already made their way to the marketplace, often under the name "Ultra SCSI." SCSI-3 encompasses SCSI-2, so a certain degree of backward compatibility is built in. Keep in mind, however, that putting an older device on a newer bus can slow down the entire bus. It will also affect the maximum cable length.

Another feature that is sometimes used in SCSI systems is "differential SCSI." In normal ("single-ended") SCSI, every other pin is grounded to help reduce crosstalk among signals.[2] This construction limits the cable length to 6 meters for SCSI-1 and 3 meters for SCSI-2. Ultra SCSI reduces the total bus length even further, to 1.5 meters. Differential signalling puts an inverted signal next to each pin instead of a ground, making the net voltage zero and reducing noise significantly.

Differential signalling increases the cable length limit to 25 meters for SCSI-2 and to 12 meters for Ultra SCSI. The extra length is a big win when all of your disks (or tape libraries) are in a distant external cabinet. However, since differential signalling is

---

1. 32-bit SCSI buses are not very common. Some may require multiple cables, referred to as the A cable and the B cable.
2. Crosstalk is most significant on a parallel electrical bus. It is not a concern for serial and fiber optic transports such as Fibre Channel, which have a much longer maximum cable length.

completely incompatible with nondifferential devices, you *must* make sure you have
a differential controller, disk, cable, and terminator. Label these well to ensure that
you do not accidentally mix them up with your single-ended devices, or things will
not work at all.

Table 8.1 summarizes the different SCSI versions and their associated bus bandwidths
and cable lengths.

**Table 8.1    The evolution of SCSI**

| Version | Freq. | Width | Speed | Length | Diff. length |
|---|---|---|---|---|---|
| SCSI-1 | 5 MHz | 8 bits | 5 MB/s | 6m | 25m |
| SCSI-2 | 5 MHz | 8 bits | 5 MB/s | 6m | 25m |
| Fast SCSI-2 | 10 MHz | 8 bits | 10 MB/s | 3m | 25m |
| Fast/wide SCSI-2 | 10 MHz | 16 bits | 20 MB/s | 3m | 25m |
| Ultra SCSI | 20 MHz | 8 bits | 20 MB/s | 1.5m[a] | 25m |
| Wide Ultra SCSI[b] | 20 MHz | 16 bits | 40 MB/s | 1.5m[a] | 25m |
| Wide Ultra2 SCSI[b] | 40 MHz | 16 bits | 80 MB/s | –[c] | 25m (HVD)[d]<br>12m (LVD) |
| Wide Ultra3 SCSI[e] | 80 MHz | 16 bits | 160 MB/s | –[c] | 12m (LVD) |

a. Varies; see the comments in the text below.

b. Wide Ultra SCSI and wide Ultra2 SCSI are sometimes called Fast-20 wide SCSI and Fast-40
wide SCSI, respectively.

c. These versions of SCSI use only differential signalling.

d. HVD is High Voltage Differential and LVD is Low Voltage Differential. HVD is used for the earlier SCSI versions and is not defined above Ultra2 SCSI.

e. Wide Ultra3 SCSI is sometimes called Ultra-160.

The maximum cable length for single-ended Ultra and wide Ultra SCSI depends on
the number of devices in use. For 8 devices, 1.5 meters is the maximum; if only 4
devices are used, the bus can be extended to 3 meters. Wide Ultra SCSI only supports
all 16 devices in differential mode.

Many types of connectors are used for SCSI devices. They vary, depending on the
version of SCSI in use and type of connection: internal or external. Narrow SCSI devices have 50 pins, and wide SCSI devices have 68 pins. Internal devices typically
accept a 50-pin header or a 68-pin male mini-micro connector attached to a ribbon
cable. External drives usually connect to the computer with a high density 50 or 68-
pin mini-micro connector. Apple reduced the 50 pins to 25 by tying all of the ground
lines together and shoehorning the bus onto a DB-25 connector.

An interesting variant that's especially useful for hot-swappable drive arrays is the
Single Connector Attachment (SCA) plug. It's an 80-pin connector that includes the
bus connections, power, and SCSI configuration, allowing a single connector to provide all of the drives' needs.

Adding a Disk

Exhibit A shows pictures of the most common connectors. Each connector is shown from the front, as if you were about to plug it into your forehead.

**Exhibit A**    **Common SCSI connectors (front view, male except where noted)**

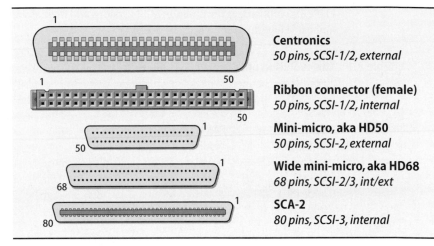

**Centronics**
*50 pins, SCSI-1/2, external*

**Ribbon connector (female)**
*50 pins, SCSI-1/2, internal*

**Mini-micro, aka HD50**
*50 pins, SCSI-2, external*

**Wide mini-micro, aka HD68**
*68 pins, SCSI-2/3, int/ext*

**SCA-2**
*80 pins, SCSI-3, internal*

The connectors on SCSI devices are almost always female, and the ends of SCSI cables are male. SCSI buses use a daisy chain configuration, so most external devices have two SCSI ports. The ports are identical and interchangeable, so either one can be the input. For some reason, scanner vendors seem to consider themselves exempt from the normal laws of physics and sometimes provide only one SCSI port. If not internally terminated, these devices require a special type of terminator.

Internal SCSI devices are usually attached to a ribbon cable; only one port is needed on the actual SCSI device because connectors can be clamped onto the middle of the ribbon cable. When using a ribbon cable, make sure pin 1 on the SCSI bus is connected to pin 1 on the hard drive.[3]

Each end of the SCSI bus must have a terminating resistor ("terminator"). These resistors absorb signals as they reach the end of the bus and prevent noise from reflecting back onto the bus. Terminators take several forms, from small external plugs that you snap onto a regular port to sets of tiny resistor packs that install onto a device's circuit boards. Some devices are even autoterminating.

SCSI-1 used a different terminator design from that of later versions of SCSI ("passive" rather than "active"), so very old terminators (and old self-terminating devices) can cause problems on a newer SCSI bus. In practice, we have rarely found such old terminators to be an issue.

One end of the bus normally terminates inside the host computer, either on the SCSI controller or on an internal SCSI drive. The other end usually terminates on an exter-

---

3. Pin 1 on a ribbon cable is usually marked with a red stripe.

nal device, or on the SCSI controller if there are no external devices. If you experience seemingly random hardware problems on your SCSI bus, first check that both ends of the bus are properly terminated. Improper termination is one of the most common SCSI configuration mistakes, and the errors it produces can be obscure and intermittent.

Each device has a SCSI address or "target number" that distinguishes it from the other devices on the bus. Target numbers start at 0 and go up to 7 or 15, depending on whether the bus is narrow or wide. The SCSI controller itself counts as a device and is usually target 7 (even on a wide bus, for backward compatibility). All other devices must have their target numbers set to unique values. It is a common error to forget that the SCSI controller has a target number and to set a device to the same target number as the controller.

A SCSI address is essentially arbitrary. Technically, it determines the device's priority on the bus, but in practice the exact priorities don't make much difference. Some systems pick the disk with the lowest target number to be the default boot disk, and some require the boot disk to be target 0.

If you're lucky, a device will have an external thumbwheel with which the target number can be set. Other common ways of setting the target number are DIP switches and jumpers. If it is not obvious how to set the target number on a device, consult the hardware manual. Most hardware specifications can be found on the manufacturer's web site these days; trying to set up a random disk used to involve quite a lot of trial and error.

The SCSI standard supports a form of subaddressing called a "logical unit number." Each target can have several logical units inside it. A plausible example might be a drive array with several disks but only one SCSI controller. However, logical units are seldom used in real life. When you hear "SCSI unit number," you should assume that it is really a target number that's being discussed until proven otherwise. If a SCSI device contains only one logical unit, the LUN usually defaults to 0.

SCSI buses are generally quite easy to configure, but a variety of things can go wrong:

- Many workstations have internal SCSI devices. Check the listing of current devices before you reboot to add a new device. Remember that most tape systems and some floppy drives (most notably, HP's) are SCSI.

- Make sure that a differential SCSI controller has only differential devices and differential terminators connected to it, and make sure that a single-ended SCSI chain does not contain any differential devices. The single-ended and differential signaling techniques are incompatible.

- After you have added a new SCSI device, check the listing of devices discovered by the OS when it reboots to make sure that everything you expect is there. Most SCSI drivers will not detect multiple devices that have the same SCSI address, which is an illegal configuration. SCSI address conflicts can lead to very strange behavior.

- Some expansion boxes (enclosures with a power supply and one or more SCSI devices) terminate the bus inside the box. If devices are attached after the expansion box, you can have reliability problems with any of the devices on the SCSI chain. Always double-check that you have exactly two terminators and that they are both at the ends of the bus.

- The thumbwheel used to set a device's SCSI address is sometimes connected backwards. When this happens, the thumbwheel will change the SCSI address, but not to the displayed value.

- When figuring the length of your SCSI-2 bus, make sure you count the cables inside devices and expansion boxes. They can be quite long. Also remember that the maximum length can be reduced if older SCSI devices are added to a newer SCSI bus.

- Never forget that your SCSI controller uses one of the SCSI addresses!

### The IDE interface

IDE, also called ATA (for AT Attachment), was designed to be simple and inexpensive. It is most often found on PCs or low-cost workstations. The controller is built into the disk, which reduces interface costs and simplifies the firmware. IDE became popular in the late 1980s. Shortly thereafter, ATA-2 was developed to satisfy the increasing demands of consumers and hard drive vendors.

ATA-2 adds faster Programmed I/O (PIO) and Direct Memory Access (DMA) modes and extends the bus's Plug and Play features. It also adds a feature called Logical Block Addressing (LBA), which (in combination with an enhanced PC BIOS) overcomes a problem that prevented BIOSes from accessing more than the first 1024 cylinders of a disk. This constraint formerly limited disk sizes to 504MB. Who would have thought a disk could get that big!

Since the BIOS manages part of the bootstrapping process, it is sometimes necessary to create a small bootable partition within the first 1024 cylinders to ensure that the kernel can be loaded by an old BIOS. Once the kernel is up and running, the BIOS is not needed and you can access the rest of your disk. This silly maneuver is unnecessary on modern hardware since LBA gets rid of cylinder-head-sector (CHS) addressing in favor of a linear addressing scheme.

ATA-3 adds additional reliability, more sophisticated power management, and self-monitoring capabilities. ATA-4 is still being developed. Ultra-ATA is an attempt to bridge the gap between ATA-3 and ATA-4, adding high-performance modes, called Ultra DMA/33 and Ultra DMA/66, that extend the bus bandwidth from 16 MB/s to 33 MB/s and 66 MB/s, respectively. ATA-4 is also a much-needed attempt to merge ATA-3 with the ATA Packet Interface (ATAPI), a protocol that allows CD-ROM and tape drives to work on an IDE bus.

IDE disks are almost always used internally (unless you consider a disk hanging out the side of the computer for testing purposes "external"). The maximum cable length for an ATA-2 bus is a mere 18 inches, which can make it difficult even to reach your system's top drive bay. In addition to the short cable length, an IDE bus can accommodate only two devices. To compensate for these shortcomings, most manufacturers provide more than one IDE bus on their motherboards.

IDE devices are accessed in a connected manner, which means that only one device can be active at a time. Therefore, performance is best if you spread the devices out over multiple buses. Put fast devices such as hard drives on one bus and tapes or CD-ROMs on another to prevent the slower devices from hindering the faster ones. SCSI handles multiple devices on a bus much better than does IDE.[4]

The IDE connector is a 40-pin header that connects the drive to the interface card with a ribbon cable. Newer IDE standards such as Ultra DMA/66 use a different cable that provides more ground pins and therefore reduces electrical noise. If a cable or drive is not keyed, be sure that pin 1 on the drive goes to pin 1 on the interface card. Pin 1 is usually marked with a small "1" on one side of the connector. If it is not marked, a rule of thumb is that pin 1 is usually the one closest to the power connector. Pin 1 on a ribbon cable is usually marked in red. If there is no red stripe on one edge of your cable, just make sure you have the cable oriented so that pin 1 is connected to pin 1, and mark it clearly for next time.

If you have more than one device on an IDE bus, you must designate one as the master and the other as the slave. Some older IDE drives do not like to be slaves, so if you are having trouble getting one configuration to work, try reversing their roles and make the other device the slave. If things are still not working out, you might be better off making each device a master of its own IDE bus.

When considering IDE hardware, keep in mind the following points:

- New IDE drives work on older cards, and old IDE drives work on newer cards. Naturally, only the features common to both devices are supported.

- The cable length is exceedingly short, which can make adding an extra device to the bus a stretch. If you experience random flakiness, check the cable length. A custom cable can make all the difference.

- Dealing with an old BIOS that does not see past the first 500MB of a disk is a bona fide nightmare. Check to see if the manufacturer has issued a firmware update to fix the problem. If not, you can replace the system's motherboard for $100 or less; it's worth it. Fortunately, BIOSes that old are rarely seen today.

- Well-designed drivers can significantly increase performance and reliability, especially when they support the most recent standards. Find out which features your driver supports (e.g., DMA and PIO modes) and compare those features to the range of options available in the marketplace. This is also good advice when you are shopping for disks.

---

4. SCSI supports overlapping commands, command queuing, scatter-gather I/O, and higher transfer rates. These features allow it to perform better than IDE in a multiuser environment such as UNIX.

Adding a Disk

### Which is better, SCSI or IDE?

This is a frequently asked question that's often waved away with talk about how each standard has its own advantages. However, we'll go out on a limb and give you a straight answer: SCSI is better. Usually.

A more accurate answer would be that SCSI beats IDE in every possible technical sense, but SCSI equipment may not be worth the enormous price premium it now commands. For a single-user workstation, a good IDE disk is a simple, high-capacity, dirt-cheap solution that provides 85% of the performance of a SCSI setup. In most cases, upgrading a single-user workstation to SCSI will not increase the system's perceived performance.

However, in some situations SCSI is advisable or even mandatory:

- If you absolutely must have the best possible performance, go SCSI. Part of the increased performance will come from SCSI's technical superiority, but an even larger part will come from the fact that disk drive manufacturers use the IDE/SCSI divide to help them stratify the disk drive market. For business reasons, they simply don't put IDE interfaces on the latest and greatest disk mechanisms.

- Servers and multiuser systems require SCSI. The SCSI protocol is unparalleled in its ability to manage multiple simultaneous requests in an efficient manner. On a busy system, you'll see a concrete and measurable improvement in performance.

- If you want to connect many devices, SCSI wins again. SCSI devices play well with others; IDE devices hog and fight over the bus.

- You might need some particular feature that only SCSI provides. For example, it's impossible to build a hot-pluggable disk array out of IDE drives.

## 8.2 DISK GEOMETRY

The geometry of a hard disk and the terminology used to refer to its various parts are shown in Exhibit B. This information is provided mainly to improve your general knowledge. Modern disk drives are still based on this same basic design, but the software no longer knows (or needs to know) much about the physical construction of the drive.

A typical hard drive consists of spinning platters coated with a magnetic film. Data is read and written by a small head that changes the orientation of the magnetic particles on the surface of the platters. The data platters are completely sealed so that no dust or dirt can get in. This feature makes fixed hard disks far more reliable than removable media.

In the very early days of computer hardware, disk drives usually had one platter. An increase in storage capacity was provided by an increase in the diameter of the platter. On the wall of one of our user areas is an ancient disk over four feet in diameter that held approximately 280K of data. That's less than 10% of the capacity of a modern extended density floppy.

**Exhibit B    Disk geometry lesson**

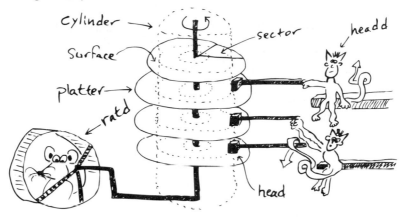

Today, hard disks usually have several small platters stacked on top of one another rather than having a single large platter. Both sides of the platters are used to store data, although one side of one platter usually contains positioning information and cannot be used for storage. Single-platter densities are currently up around 10GB, with no end to Moore's Law[5] in sight.

Platters rotate at a constant speed. They are read from and written to by little skating heads that move back and forth like the needle on a record player. The heads float very close to the surface of the platters but do not actually touch them. The distance between the head and the spinning platter can be compared to an F-16 fighter jet flying at full speed 10 feet above the ground. If a head does touch a platter, this event is called a head crash; it can be very destructive.

Rotational speeds have increased dramatically over time. Older disks ran at 3,600 RPM or 5,400 RPM. 7,200 RPM is currently the upper-mass-market standard, and 10,000 RPM and 15,000 RPM drives are becoming popular at the high end. Higher rotational speeds decrease latency and increase the bandwidth of data transfers but may potentially introduce thermal problems stemming from increased heat production. Be sure you have adequate air circulation if you plan to purchase a cutting-edge drive.

At least one head is required for each surface. The heads on early drives had to move huge distances, but the modern geometry of small, stacked platters is more efficient. The diameter of disks continues to decrease, from a standard of 14 inches 20 years ago, to 5 1/4 inches 10 years ago, to 3 1/2 inches and smaller today.

---

5. Moore's Law states that technology (CPU speed, disk sizes, etc.) will double about every 18 months.

Moving the head to the correct position to read a particular piece of data is called seeking. Each position that a head can occupy as the disk spins under it is called a track. Tracks are further divided into sectors, which are usually 512 bytes long.

A set of tracks on different platters that are the same distance from the spindle is called a cylinder. If all the heads move together, as is typical on most mass-market drives, the data stored in a single cylinder can be read without any additional movement. Although heads move amazingly fast, they still move much slower than the disks spin around. Therefore, any disk access that does not require the heads to seek to a new position will be faster.

The UNIX filesystem attempts to exploit this fact to improve efficiency. Unfortunately, the original BSD filesystem code is thwarted by a now-universal practice known as zone sectoring, in which tracks on the outside of a platter contain more sectors than inner tracks. To fully optimize the internal workings of the drive, the layout information is not shared with the software. Instead, an artificial cylinder-head-sector (CHS) addressing scheme is made up to fit the size of the disk. Even today, many filesystem optimizations are based on complete fiction.

Although almost any CHS values that multiply out to match the size of the disk can be used, the manufacturer will typically have some suggested values. Some configurations—such as those with more than 1,024 cylinders or more than 255 heads—may cause problems with some operating systems or boot loaders. This is usually only a concern on PCs running old hardware or multiple operating systems.

## 8.3  AN OVERVIEW OF THE DISK INSTALLATION PROCEDURE

The procedure for adding a new disk involves the following steps:

- Connecting the disk to the computer
- Creating device files through which the disk can be accessed
- Formatting the disk
- Labeling and partitioning the disk
- Establishing logical volumes
- Creating UNIX filesystems within disk partitions
- Setting up automatic mounting
- Setting up swapping on swap partitions

The following sections describe the process in general, without reference to any particular vendor's peculiarities. Starting on page 138, we describe the exact procedure for our four example systems.

### Connecting the disk

The way a disk is attached to the system depends mostly on the interface that is used. The rest is all mounting brackets and cabling. If the disk is IDE, try to configure the system with only one IDE disk per bus. Double-check your cable orientation and the master/slave settings on each disk. If the disk is SCSI, double-check that you have properly terminated both ends of the SCSI bus, that the cable length is less than the maximum appropriate for the SCSI variant you are using, and that the new SCSI target does not conflict with the controller or another device on the bus. Fore more details, see the system-specific sections toward the end of this chapter.

### Creating device entries

*See Chapter 12 for more information about device files.*

Before you can access a new disk, you need device files in **/dev** that point to it. You will need both block device files (generally used for mounting filesystems) and character device files (used for backing up and checking the integrity of filesystems). Many versions of UNIX automatically create files for all possible SCSI devices; details start on page 138.

It is possible to destroy a filesystem in seconds by writing randomly on the disk, so you should set the permissions on disk device files quite restrictively. We allow read and write access for the owner (root) and read access for the group owner (operator); this setup allows **dump** to be run by operators without superuser privileges but prevents mere mortals from reading from the raw device.

### Formatting the disk

Overeager vendors often quote disk capacities in terms of the number of unformatted bytes. About 10% of that capacity is typically used up to mark the disk surfaces so that the hardware and software can find the data that is written there. When purchasing disks, always think in terms of formatted size and compare prices accordingly.

Another common trick is to quote disk sizes in "megabytes" that are really millions of bytes. In the context of computer systems, a megabyte is actually $2^{20}$ or 1,048,576 bytes. Using the $1\,\text{MB} = 1,000,000$ byte convention overstates the capacity of a disk drive by almost 5%.[6] Be sure to check your units when comparing disk capacities.

The formatting process writes address information and timing marks on the platters to delineate each sector. It also identifies "bad blocks," imperfections in the media that result in areas that cannot be reliably read or written. On older disks (including SMD disks), the UNIX device driver is responsible for understanding bad blocks and mapping them to replacement blocks elsewhere on the disk. SCSI disks have bad block management built in, so neither you nor the driver need to worry about it.[7]

All hard disks come preformatted, and the factory formatting is often more precise than any formatting you can do in the field. It is best to avoid doing a low-level format if it is not required. If you encounter read or write errors on a disk, first check for cabling, termination, and address problems, which can cause symptoms similar to those of a bad block. If after this procedure you are still convinced that the disk is bad, you might be better off to replace it with a new one rather than waiting long hours for a format to complete.

---

6. Of course, the prefix "mega" really does mean "million," so the practice is not entirely indefensible.
7. However, any bad blocks that appear after a disk has been formatted will not be "handled"; they can manifest themselves in the form of read and write errors and lost data.

IDE disks are usually not designed to be formatted outside of the factory. However, you may be able to get special formatting software from the manufacturer, usually for Windows. Make sure the software matches the drive you plan to format and follow the manufacturer's directions carefully.

SCSI disks format themselves in response to a command that you send from the host computer. The procedure for sending this command varies from system to system. On PCs, you can often send the command from the SCSI controller's BIOS. Use the **format** command on Solaris and the **mediainit** command on HP-UX.

Some systems let you verify the integrity of a disk by writing random patterns onto it and then reading them back. This process is very time consuming, so unless you suspect that the disk is bad or you bill by the hour, you may want to skip it. Barring that, let the tests run overnight. Don't be concerned about "wearing out" a disk with overuse or aggressive testing. Disks are designed to withstand constant activity.

### Labeling and partitioning the disk

After a disk has been formatted and its bad sectors remapped, it must be divided into chunks called *partitions* or *slices*. Partitioning allows the disk to be treated as a group of independent data areas rather than as one vast expanse of blocks. Partitioning also allows "bonus" items such as the boot blocks and the partition table itself to be hidden from high-level software (e.g., the filesystem). Only the device driver knows about the layout of the entire disk; other software works with the cleaned-up abstraction of partitions.

Partitions make backups easier, prevent users from poaching each other's disk space, improve performance, and confine potential damage from runaway programs. On most operating systems, the partition table is kept on the disk in a record called the label. The label usually occupies the first few blocks of the disk. Its exact contents vary, but it generally contains enough information to get the system booting.

Partitions are, in concept, distinct and separate from one another. However, almost all systems define one partition to be an image of the entire disk. That way, user-level commands can access the disk "directly" through a normal device file. For example, a user-level process could write the disk's label or duplicate its contents to a backup disk by using the **dd** command. Of course, this special partition must be used carefully, since it allows every partition on the disk to be screwed up at once.

Some systems go even farther down this treacherous path and allow you to define multiple overlapping sets of partitions. For example, partitions 0, 1, and 2 might divide up the disk one way, while partitions 3 and 4 do it another way. You're expected to use one set of self-consistent partitions and simply ignore the others. In real life, such overlapping partitions invite operator errors and are a common cause of random data corruption.

Modern systems tend to use fewer partitions than their predecessors, but on most systems you will have at least the following three.

- **The root partition:** Everything needed to bring the system up to single-user mode is kept here. A second copy of this partition is often stored on another disk for emergencies.

- **The swap partition:** A swap area stores pages of virtual memory when not enough physical memory is available to hold them. Every system should have at least one swap partition. See page 760 for more information about virtual memory.

- **The user partition:** Home directories, data files, source code libraries, and other random data files find a home here.

Opinions differ on the best way to split disks into partitions. Here are some hints:

- If you have multiple disks, make a copy of the root filesystem on one of them and verify that you can boot from it.

- As you add memory to your machine, you should also add swap space. For normal use, you should have at least as much swap space as real memory. This amount of swap allows a kernel crash dump to fit in the swap area in the event of a system panic.

- Splitting swap space among several disks increases performance. This technique works for filesystems, too; put the busy ones on different disks. See page 764 for notes on this subject.

- If you intend to back up a partition, don't make it bigger than the capacity of your backup device. See page 167.

- Try to cluster information that changes quickly on a few partitions that are backed up frequently.

- It's a good idea to create a separate filesystem (**/tmp**) for temporary files because it limits the files to a finite size and saves you from having to back them up.

- If your system keeps log files in **/var**, it's a good idea for **/var** to be a separate disk partition. Many systems ship with **/var** as part of a very small root partition, making it easy to fill the root and bring the machine to a halt.

### Establishing logical volumes

Some systems have a "logical volume manager" that provides a sort of supercharged version of disk partitioning. We can't cover the details of all the different volume managers and their features here, but they have some characteristics in common that are worth noting. (However, we do show the use of the Veritas LVM in our HP-UX example; see page 143.)

Most volume managers let you group multiple disks or partitions into a logical volume, or metadisk, that appears to the user as a single virtual disk. The components of a logical volume can be put together in various ways. Concatenation keeps each device's physical blocks together and lines the devices up one after another. Striping interleaves the components so that adjacent virtual blocks are actually spread over multiple physical disks. By reducing single-disk bottlenecks, striping can often provide higher bandwidth and lower latency.

Some volume managers support RAID5 (Redundant Array of Inexpensive Disks), which is striping with an extra checksum. The checksum provides enough redundancy that the logical volume's data can be reconstructed if one of the disks goes bad. This feature can also be found in smart disk arrays, which are sometimes referred to as hardware RAID.

Mirroring is another common feature of volume managers. A mirrored volume is associated with another volume of the same size. Whenever data is written to one side of the mirror, it is duplicated on the other side. If one of the mirrored volumes experiences a hardware failure, the system automatically starts using ("fails over to") the other with no interruption in service. Once the original problem has been fixed, the two sides of the mirror must be resynchronized.

Veritas is a logical volume manager that's supported on both Solaris and HP-UX. Sun also sells a volume manager of its own called Solstice DiskSuite. Vinum is an open source volume manager for FreeBSD; it was inspired by Veritas. Linux has an implementation of kernel RAID support and a separate open source volume manager known as Linux LVM.

### Creating UNIX filesystems

Even after a hard disk has been conceptually divided into partitions, it is still not ready to hold UNIX files. The filesystem needs to add a little of its own overhead before the disk is ready for use.

To install a filesystem within a disk partition, you use either **newfs** or **mkfs**. **newfs** is actually just a friendly front end for **mkfs**. Under old versions of UNIX you had to know a lot about the characteristics of the disk, but this is no longer the case. Unless you are doing something strange, you should be able to build the filesystem by specifying nothing but the **newfs** command and the partition name.

We will cover the exact procedure in more detail later. The rest of this section discusses how files are placed on the disk when you build the filesystem. If you are not interested, just skip ahead to the next section and revel in blissful ignorance.

Here, we describe the Berkeley Fast File System implemented by McKusick, Joy, and Leffler for 4.2BSD. It's used by most modern versions of UNIX. A BSD filesystem consists of five structural components:

- A set of inode storage cells
- A set of scattered "superblocks"
- A map of the disk blocks in the filesystem
- A block usage summary
- A set of data blocks

Each filesystem partition is divided into cylinder groups of from 1 to 32 cylinders each. Structures such as inode tables are allocated among the cylinder groups so that blocks that are accessed together can be stored close to each other on the disk. This grouping reduces the need to seek all over the disk when accessing blocks in the same file.

Inodes are fixed-length table entries that each hold information about one file. Since space for inodes must be set aside when UNIX does its initial structuring of the filesystem, you must decide in advance how many of them to create. It is impossible to predict exactly how many files (inodes) will someday be needed; UNIX uses an empirical formula to guesstimate an appropriate number, based on the size of the partition and an average file size.

You can adjust the number of inodes either up or down when you create the filesystem: more inodes for filesystems with lots of small files (such as Usenet news partitions or source code repositories), and fewer inodes for filesystems with a few large files (such as a filesystem containing a database). The default value provides enough inodes to fill the disk with 2KB files, which is usually plenty.

See page 136 for more information about **fsck**.

A superblock is a record that describes the characteristics of the filesystem. It contains information about the length of a disk block, the size and location of the inode tables, the disk block map and usage information, the size of the cylinder groups, and a few other important parameters of the filesystem. Because damage to the superblock could erase some extremely crucial information, several copies of it are maintained in scattered locations. This was not always true: early filesystems were totally destroyed if the superblock became corrupted. If necessary, you can tell **fsck** to use an alternative superblock when rebuilding a damaged filesystem. **newfs -N** will show the locations of backup superblocks. Block 32 always holds a backup.

For each mounted filesystem, UNIX keeps both an in-memory copy of the superblock and several on-disk copies. The **sync** system call flushes the cached superblocks to their permanent homes on disk, making the filesystem consistent for a split second. This periodic save minimizes the amount of damage that would occur if the machine were to crash when the filesystem had not updated the superblocks. **sync** also flushes modified inodes and cached data blocks. Most systems perform a **sync** every 30 seconds to minimize the amount of data lost in the event of a crash.

A filesystem's disk block map is a table of the free blocks it contains. When new files are written, this map is examined to devise an efficient layout scheme.

The block usage summary records basic information about the blocks that are already in use.

### Setting up automatic mounting

A filesystem must be mounted before it becomes available to UNIX processes. The mount point for a filesystem can be any directory, but the files and subdirectories beneath it will not be accessible while a filesystem is mounted there. See page 62 for more information about mounting filesystems. Be sure that the partition you are mounting or checking has a valid filesystem on it—if you try to **mount** or **fsck** your swap partition, you can really mess things up.

After installing a new disk, you should mount new filesystems by hand to test that everything is working correctly. For example,

```
# mount /dev/sd1a /mnt
```

would mount the filesystem in the partition represented by the device file **/dev/sd1a** (device names will vary among systems) on the directory **/mnt**. If the filesystem is brand new, its contents should look something like this:

```
# ls /mnt
lost+found
```

The **lost+found** directory is automatically created when you build a filesystem. It is used by **fsck** in emergencies; do not delete it. The **lost+found** directory has some extra space preallocated so that **fsck** can store "unlinked" files there without having to allocate additional directory entries on an unstable filesystem. Some systems provide a **mklost+found** command that can recreate this special directory if it is accidentally deleted.

You can verify the size of a filesystem with the **df** command. Here's a BSD example:

```
# df /usr
Filesystem    1K-blocks   Used     Avail    Capacity  Mounted on
/dev/wd0s1f   810495      509516   236140   68%       /usr
```

The units reported by **df** are 1K or 512-byte blocks, depending on the OS. **df -k** will force 1K blocks to be displayed on some systems.

 On HP-UX, the **df** command is quite different. You can use the **bdf** command ("Berkeley **df**") to get output like that shown above.

 You will generally want to configure the system to mount local filesystems at boot time. A configuration file in **/etc** lists the device names and mount points of all the system's disks (among other things). On most systems this file is called **/etc/fstab** (for "filesystem table"), but under older versions of HP-UX it is called **/etc/checklist**, and on Solaris it has been reformatted and renamed **/etc/vfstab**. For the rest of this section, we will refer to the file as "the **fstab** file" even though it might actually be named something different on your system.

An **fstab** file that included the filesystem above might look something like this:[8]

```
# Device        Mountpoint  FStype  Options    Dump  Pass#
/dev/wd0s1b     none        swap    sw         0     0
/dev/wd0s1a     /           ufs     rw         1     1
/dev/wd0s1f     /usr        ufs     rw         2     2
/dev/acd0c      /cdrom      cd9660  ro,noauto  0     0
proc            /proc       procfs  rw         0     0
server:/export  /server     nfs     rw         0     0
```

8. This example is from FreeBSD. All but Solaris will be similar.

There are six fields per line, separated by whitespace. Each line describes a single filesystem. The fields are traditionally aligned for readability, but this is not required.

*See Chapter 17 for more information about NFS.*

The first field gives the device name. The **fstab** file can include mounts from remote systems, in which case the first field contains an NFS path, as in the last line. The notation *server:/export* indicates the **/export** directory on the machine named *server.*

In some cases, the first field can specify a virtual filesystem type instead of a device name. The proc filesystem above is an example; it exports kernel process information to user utilities. You might also see swap listed as the device for memory filesystems that use swap as a backing store, such as tmpfs on Solaris.

The second field specifies the mount point, and the third field indicates the type of filesystem. The exact type name used to identify local filesystems varies among machines: Solaris and FreeBSD use ufs; HP-UX uses vxfs or hfs; Linux uses ext2.

The fourth field lists the mount options (rw, for read/write, is the default). The fifth field specifies a "dump frequency" value which can theoretically be used by backup products but usually isn't.

*fsck is described on page 136.*

The sixth field specifies the pass in which **fsck** should check the filesystem. Filesystems with the same value in this field are checked concurrently, if possible. Do not set two filesystems on the same disk to the same value or you will cause the disk head to seek back and forth so much that performance will be significantly degraded. Only filesystems on separate disks should be checked in parallel.

**mount**, **umount**, **swapon**, and **fsck** all read the **fstab** file, so it is important that the data presented there be correct and complete. **mount** and **umount** use the **fstab** file to figure out what you want done if you specify only a partition name or mount point on the command line. For example, using the **fstab** file just shown, the command

```
# mount /cdrom
```

would be the same as typing

```
# mount -t cd9660 -o ro,noauto /dev/acd0c /cdrom
```

The command **mount -a** mounts all regular filesystems listed in the **fstab** file; it is usually executed from the startup scripts at boot time. The **-t** or **-F** flag (**-t** for Red Hat and FreeBSD, **-F** for Solaris and HP-UX) constrains the operation to filesystems of a certain type. For example,

```
# mount -at ufs
```

would mount all local disk filesystems on a FreeBSD system. The **mount** command reads **fstab** sequentially; therefore, filesystems that are mounted beneath other filesystems must follow their parent partitions in the **fstab** file. For example, the line for **/usr/local** must follow the line for **/usr** if **/usr** is a separate filesystem.

The **umount** command for unmounting filesystems accepts a similar syntax. On most systems, you cannot unmount a filesystem that a process is using as its current directory or one on which files are open. There are ways of getting around this constraint; see page 62.

### Enabling swapping

One of the early advantages of UNIX was its implementation of virtual memory. This feature allows the operating system to pretend that the machine has more memory than it actually does. If processes try to use this "extra" memory, the system's disks are brought into use as a kind of ultra-slow RAM. Juggling the contents of memory to and from disk is known as swapping or paging.[9]

To make swapping efficient, raw partitions (partitions without filesystems) are normally used as the backing store. Instead of using a filesystem structure to keep track of the swap area's contents, the kernel maintains its own simplified mapping from memory blocks to disk blocks. It's also possible to swap to a file in a filesystem partition, but this configuration is slower than using a dedicated partition.

*See page 764 for more information about splitting swap areas.*
The more swap space you have, the more virtual memory your processes can allocate. The best swapping performance is achieved when the swap area is split among several drives (or better yet, among several SCSI buses).

You can manually enable swapping to a particular device, but you will generally want to have this function performed automatically at boot time. On most systems, swap areas can be listed in the **fstab** file, the same file that's used to enumerate mountable filesystems. A swap entry looks something like:[10]

```
/dev/da0b      none        swap       sw        0      0
```

During startup, a command (often **swapon** or **swap**) is run to enable swapping on all partitions listed in the **fstab** file. The vendor-specific sections starting on page 138 identify the particular command and syntax used by each system.

## 8.4  FSCK: CHECK AND REPAIR FILESYSTEMS

The UNIX filesystem is surprisingly reliable, and it does a remarkable job of coping with unexpected system crashes and flaky hardware. However, filesystems can become damaged or inconsistent in a number of ways.

Any time the kernel panics or the power fails, small inconsistencies may be introduced into the filesystems that were active immediately preceding the crash. Since the kernel buffers both data blocks and summary information, the most recent image of the filesystem is split between disk and memory. During a crash, the memory portion of the image is lost. The buffered blocks are effectively "overwritten" with the versions that were most recently saved to disk.

---

9.  Swapping and paging are technically distinct. For now, we will group them together and call the combination "swapping," as the UNIX manuals do. For a more detailed description of virtual memory under UNIX, see page 760.

10. From FreeBSD; other systems will vary.

There are a couple of approaches to fixing this problem. Minor damage can usually be fixed with the **fsck** command ("filesystem consistency check," spelled aloud or pronounced "fs check" or "fisk"). This isn't a very architecturally elegant way of approaching the issue, but it works pretty well for all the common inconsistencies.

Journaling filesystems (aka logging filesystems) write metadata out to a sequential log file that is flushed to disk before each command returns. The metadata eventually migrates from the log to its permanent home within the filesystem. If the system crashes, the log can be rolled up to the most recent consistency point; a full filesystem cross-check is not required. This feature can save you many hours of boot time on a system with large filesystems.

 Journaling is available on Solaris's UFS filesystem and on VXFS for HP-UX. See the HP-UX example starting on page 143 for an explanation of how to enable journaling.

If some form of journaling is not available, you must wait for **fsck** to work its magic. The five most common types of damage are:

- Unreferenced inodes
- Inexplicably large link counts
- Unused data blocks not recorded in the block maps
- Data blocks listed as free that are also used in a file
- Incorrect summary information in the superblock

**fsck** can safely and automatically fix these five problems. If **fsck** makes corrections to a filesystem, you should rerun it until the filesystem comes up completely clean.

Disks are normally checked at boot time with **fsck -p**, which examines all local filesystems listed in **/etc/fstab** and corrects the five errors listed above. Recent operating systems keep track of which filesystems were unmounted cleanly and check only the "dirty" ones. If some form of journaling is enabled, **fsck** simply tells you that the filesystem is journaled and rolls up the log to the last consistent state.

**fsck -p** can also be run on a particular filesystem. For example:

```
# fsck -p /dev/rsd0g
```

**fsck** accepts both block and character (raw) devices; it usually runs faster on the raw device. Some systems will use the raw device regardless of which one you specify.

When **fsck -p** reads the **fstab** file to find out which filesystems to check, it obeys the sequence indicated by the last field of each entry. Filesystems are checked in increasing numeric order. If two filesystems are on different disks, they can be given the same sequence number; this configuration makes **fsck** check them simultaneously, minimizing the time spent waiting for disk I/O. Always check the root partition first.

Errors that do not fall into one of the five categories above are potentially serious. They cause **fsck -p** to ask for help and then quit. In this case, run **fsck** without the **-p** option. When run in manual mode, **fsck** asks you to confirm each of the repairs that it wants to make. The following list shows some of the errors that **fsck** considers dangerous enough to warrant human intervention.

- Blocks claimed by more than one file
- Blocks claimed outside the range of the filesystem
- Link counts that are too small
- Blocks that are not accounted for
- Directories that refer to unallocated inodes
- Various format errors

Unfortunately, it is difficult to patch a disk by hand without extensive knowledge of the implementation of the filesystem. Unless you are attempting to establish yourself as a cult leader in a small town in Texas, you should never attempt to write directly to the filesystem through the device files.

Many operating systems supply a filesystem debugger (often called **fsdb**) that can help you examine and change low-level filesystem data, but you will still need a detailed understanding of what you are doing to use this tool effectively. As long as you stick to reading the filesystem and do not try to modify it, however, you don't risk compounding the corruption.

In practice, this state of affairs means that you have little choice but to accept the fixes proposed by **fsck**. You can minimize problems by carefully recording the messages that **fsck** produces, since they will sometimes provide a clue about the file or files that are causing problems. If **fsck** asks for permission to delete a file, you should try to copy it to a different filesystem before allowing **fsck** to proceed. Be aware that any time you attempt to access a damaged filesystem, you risk panicking the system.

If a damaged filesystem (one that **fsck** cannot repair automatically) contains valuable data, *do not* experiment with it before making an ironclad backup. You can try to **dump** the disk, but since **dump** expects to be reading an undamaged filesystem, the resulting image may be missing data (or **dump** may crash). The best insurance policy is to **dd** the entire disk to a backup file or backup disk.

If **fsck** knows only the inode number of a file, you can use the **ncheck** command on some systems to discover the file's pathname. To zero out a bad inode that **fsck** isn't able to fix, use the **clri** command (the data will, of course, be lost).

If **fsck** finds a file whose parent directory cannot be determined, it will put the file in the **lost+found** directory in the top level of the filesystem. Since the name given to a file is recorded only in the file's parent directory, names for orphan files will not be available and the files placed in **lost+found** will be named with their inode numbers.

## 8.5  VENDOR SPECIFICS

Unfortunately, the installation of new disks is a task that every UNIX vendor has decided to handle differently. For each vendor, we list the commands needed to add a disk and then present a bloody, blow-by-blow example of the procedure. Even a single vendor's commands may vary among hardware architectures and OS releases.

Each example shows the addition of a SCSI disk with several partitions: one partition is a backup root partition (mounted on **/bkroot**), one is a swap partition, and one stores user files (mounted on **/new**). The disk we add is a Seagate ST446452W wide Ultra SCSI disk with an unformatted capacity of 63GB and a formatted capacity of about 47GB.

In many cases, seemingly arbitrary values are passed to the formatting programs. The reason is that many of the arguments are not meaningful for SCSI disks.[11] In the olden days, you really had to know the exact layout of each disk; now, you just use the numbers made up by the manufacturer or the software.

### Adding a disk to Solaris

In this section we review the process used to add a disk to a SPARC-based Solaris system. The procedure is similar for Solaris on Intel hardware, but the device names differ and the tasks vary somewhat. If you are using the Veritas volume manager on Solaris, you can refer to the HP-UX section on page 143, since HP also uses Veritas.

After you connect the new disk (with the power off), run the **probe-scsi** command from the PROM monitor to check the target numbers of all SCSI devices.[12] If your system continuously auto-reboots with no message but

```
rebooting...
```

you have an address conflict or a termination problem. If the system boots, you can look at the console messages to be sure the disk was found.

Our **probe-scsi** output looked like this:

```
ok probe-scsi
...
Target 3
  Unit 0   Disk     SEAGATE ST446452W       0001
ok boot -r
```

Specifying the **-r** flag when booting tells Solaris to reconfigure itself by scanning for new hardware and creating the appropriate device files for you. Once the system is booted, look in the output of **dmesg** to find the kernel messages relating to the new disk. In our case, the kernel complains because we have not yet written a Solaris label on the disk. However, that's actually a good sign, because it means that the kernel is aware that the disk is present.

```
sd3 at esp0: target 3 lun 0
sd3 is /sbus@1f,0/espdma@e,8400000/esp@e,8800000/sd@3,0
WARNING: /sbus@1f,0/espdma@e,8400000/esp@e,8800000/sd@3,0 (sd3):
        corrupt label - wrong magic number
        Vendor 'SEAGATE', product 'ST446452W', 91923356
        512 byte blocks
```

---

11. Although it is still sometimes possible to adjust geometry specifications to improve the performance of your disk, that topic is beyond the scope of this book.

12. If your PROM monitor does not seem to understand **probe-scsi**, try typing **n** to get to the new-style monitor. The new-style monitor's prompt is "ok".

The block and character (raw) device files for the disk will appear under **/dev/dsk** and **/dev/rdsk**, respectively. The names of device files for disks are of the form

**/dev/[r]dsk/c**W**t**X**d**Y**s**Z

where W is the controller number, X is the SCSI target number, Y is the SCSI logical unit number (or LUN, almost always 0), and Z is the partition (slice) number. These device files are actually just symbolic links into the **/devices** tree, where the real device files live. You should use always use the links located in **/dev**, however, as the files in **/devices** are hard to type and subject to change.

Whenever you add new hardware, you should run **boot -r** from the boot monitor to make sure that links for the new devices are set up properly. You can also create the appropriate links for disks with the **drvconfig** and **disks** commands (which actually run **devfsadm**). They take no arguments:

```
# drvconfig; disks
```

Under Solaris, partition 2 typically refers to the entire disk. We'll use that partition when formatting and labeling the disk. Since our disk is SCSI target 3, the raw device file we will use to refer to the entire disk is **/dev/rdsk/c0t3d0s2**.

The **format** program formats and partitions disks. It is menu driven:

```
# format /dev/rdsk/c0t3d0s2
/dev/rdsk/c0t3d0s2: configured with capacity of 43.77GB
selecting /dev/rdsk/c0t3d0s2
[disk formatted]

FORMAT MENU:
...
```

If the disk was not previously labeled or if it was formerly used on another operating system, **format** might ask if you want to label the disk immediately. If you say yes, **format** installs a generic Solaris label. Otherwise, you can write the label manually with **format**'s **label** command. We suggest starting with a default label and checking to see if the partitions are reasonable:

```
format> label
Ready to label disk, continue? y
format> partition
PARTITION MENU:
...
partition> print
Current partition table (default):
Total cylinders available: 9994+2 (reserved cylinders)
  Part  Tag     Flag  Cylinders   Size          Blocks
   0    root    wm      0-28    130.05MB    (29/0/0)     266336
   1    swap    wu     29-57    130.05MB    (29/0/0)     266336
   2    backup  wu      0-9993   43.77GB    (9994/0/0)  91784896
   ...
   6    home    wm     58-9993   43.51GB    (9936/0/0)  91252224
```

The default label is not very useful for our purposes, so we will increase the size of the backup root partition, increase the size of the swap partition, and decrease the size of the new home partition. The flags for the root and home partitions should be "wm" (writable and mountable), and the flags for the swap partition should be "wu" (writable and *not* mountable). The following excerpt shows how to do one partition; the others are configured similarly.

```
partition> 0
  Part  Tag     Flag  Cylinders    Size           Blocks
    0   root    wm       0-28    130.05MB   (29/0/0)    266336

Enter partition id tag[root]: root
Enter partition permission flags[wm]: wm
Enter new starting cyl[0]: 0
Enter partition size[266336b, 29c, 130.05mb, 0.13gb]: 2gb
```

Once you have sized all the partitions, print out the partition table again to verify that it looks OK. Make sure that no partitions overlap (or at least, no partitions that you plan to use); filesystem corruption will almost certainly result. When you're sure everything is right, type **label** again to rewrite the new partition information. In our example:

```
partition> print
Current partition table (unnamed):
Total cylinders available: 9994 + 2 (reserved cylinders)
  Part  Tag     Flag  Cylinders    Size           Blocks
    0   root    wm       0-456    2.00GB   (457/0/0)   4197088
    1   swap    wu    457-2283    8.00GB   (1827/0/0)  16779168
    2   backup  wu      0-9993   43.77GB   (9994/0/0)  91784896
    6   home    wm   2284-9993   33.76GB   (7710/0/0)  70808640

partition> label
Ready to label disk, continue? yes
```

To exit **format**, enter the **quit** command twice: once to get out of partition mode, and once to leave **format**.

```
partition> quit
format> quit
```

Now that we've labeled the disk, we're ready to create filesystems for the backup root and user filesystems.

```
# newfs /dev/rdsk/c0t3d0s0
newfs: construct file system /dev/rdsk/c0t3d0s0: (y/n)? y
/dev/rdsk/c0t3d0s0: 4197088 sectors in 457 cylinders of 28 tracks, 328 sectors
2049.4MB in 42 cyl groups (11 c/g, 49.33MB/g, 8000 i/g)
super-block backups (for fsck -F ufs -o b=#) at:
 32, 101392, 202752, 304112, 405472, 506832, 608192, 709552, 810912,
 912272, 1013632, 1114992, 1216352, 1317712, 1419072, 1520432, 1621792,
 ...
```

We then check our newly created filesystems with **fsck**.

```
# fsck /dev/rdsk/c0t3d0s0
** /dev/rdsk/c0t3d0s0
** Phase 1 - Check Blocks and Sizes
** Phase 2 - Check Pathnames
** Phase 3 - Check Connectivity
** Phase 4 - Check Reference Counts
** Phase 5 - Check Cyl groups
2 files, 9 used, 2055846 free (14 frags, 256979 blocks,  0.0% fragmentation)
```

We would also run **newfs** and **fsck** on partition 6, but that's not shown here.

Once the filesystems have been created, we can go ahead and mount them. **mount** uses block device files (in **/dev/dsk**) rather than character device files (in **/dev/rdsk**) to access the partition.

Newer versions of Solaris support journaling on UFS filesystems (the default filesystem type). By writing metadata changes to a separate part of the disk known as the log before copying them out to their permanent home, you can guarantee filesystem consistency. This feature is especially handy for large filesystems that take a long time to **fsck** after a system crash.

To enable journaling (aka logging), pass the **-o logging** flag to **mount** (or put it in your **/etc/vfstab** file). When the system comes back up, **fsck** will simply roll the log instead of performing a complete check. It's normally a good idea to use this option; however, we omit it from our testing below in the interest of clarity.

We're finally ready to mount the new partitions:

```
# mkdir /bkroot
# mkdir /new
# mount /dev/dsk/c0t3d0s0 /bkroot
# mount /dev/dsk/c0t3d0s6 /new
# df -k /bkroot
Filesystem          kbytes    used    avail    capacity  Mounted on
/dev/dsk/c0t3d0s0   2055855   9       1994171  1%        /bkroot
```

**df** shows that the backup root partition has been correctly mounted.

We next inform the kernel, by using **swap -a**, of the new swap space on partition 1; then, with **swap -l**, we make sure it is being used:

```
# swap -a /dev/dsk/c0t3d0s1
# swap -l
swapfile            dev    swaplo  blocks    free
...
/dev/dsk/c0t3d0s1   32,25  16      4194272   4194272
```

**swap -l** lists all the currently active swap areas. Since the new swap partition is included in its output, we know that everything is hunky dory.

You must add entries to the **/etc/vfstab** file if you want your new filesystems to be mounted automatically when the system boots. The Solaris **/etc/vfstab** file is a little bit different from other systems' **/etc/fstab** files. It contains both the block device and the raw device (used by **mount** and **fsck**, respectively), as well as the mount point. It then specifies the type of the filesystem and the pass number for parallel **fsck**ing. Next is a yes or a no that tells the boot process whether that filesystem should be mounted at boot time. The last field specifies options such as logging. If the information is not relevant to that filesystem type, use a dash as a place holder.

Here are the lines we would add for our new filesystems and swap space:

```
#device            device             mount   FS     mount
#to mount          to fsck            point   Type   at boot
/dev/dsk/c0t3d0s0  /dev/rdsk/c0t3d0s0 /bkroot ufs    1   yes  -
/dev/dsk/c0t3d0s6  /dev/rdsk/c0t3d0s6 /new    ufs    2   yes  -
/dev/dsk/c0t3d0s1  -                  -       swap   -   no   -
...
```

To turn the **/bkroot** filesystem into a useful backup of the root partition, we need to copy over the contents of the standard root. **ufsdump** and **ufsrestore** are the proper tools for the job:

```
# cd /bkroot
# ufsdump 0uf - / | ufsrestore -rf -
DUMP: Date of this level 0 dump: Tue Jun  7 19:11:44 1994
...
```

The **bkroot** partition will not be bootable until **installboot** has been run on the new disk to copy a small boot program to the beginning of the disk. When the system is powered on, the PROM monitor loads the boot program, and the boot program then loads the kernel from the root filesystem. **installboot** needs to be pointed both at the disk and at a file containing the boot block to be written:

```
# /usr/sbin/installboot /usr/lib/fs/ufs/bootblk /dev/rdsk/c0t3d0s0
```

The final step of the installation process is to reboot and verify that all filesystems mount correctly and that swapping is enabled on the new swap partition. You must also ensure that you can boot from the **/bkroot** partition once all of the files have been copied over—don't wait until your main root partition is blown to find out that there's a problem.

## Adding a disk to HP-UX

As of HP-UX 10.20, the Veritas logical volume manager was shipped with HP-UX, and as of HP-UX 11.00, Veritas is the default filesystem. It's a nice addition, especially when you consider that HP-UX formerly did not even support the notion of disk partitions. Veritas is also available on Solaris, Windows NT, and other operating systems.

A logical volume manager gives you a lot of flexibility, but it also makes disk management somewhat more complex. We will use the volume manager commands to set up a backup root, a large free space partition, and some swap space; however, coverage of the advanced features provided by the logical volume manager is beyond the scope of this book. See the man pages and the user guide for more information.

Before you boot UNIX, you can obtain a listing of the system's SCSI devices from the PROM monitor. Unfortunately, the exact way in which this is done varies quite a bit among machines. After you boot, you can verify that the kernel has recognized your device by looking at the output of the **dmesg** or **ioscan** commands. Our disk engenders the following **ioscan** output, which verifies that the new disk is target 3:

```
# ioscan -fn -C disk
Class    I   H/W Path   Driver  S/W State   Description
=========================================================
...
disk     2   8/16/5.3.0   sdisk   CLAIMED     SEAGATE ST446452W
                          /dev/dsk/c0t3d0   /dev/rdsk/c0t3d0
disk     1   8/16/5.6.0   sdisk   CLAIMED     SEAGATE ST34573N
                          /dev/dsk/c0t6d0   /dev/rdsk/c0t6d0
```

After you have verified that the disk is visible to the hardware and the kernel, you are ready to begin software configuration. The volume manager specifies three tiers of abstraction. First, you must identify *physical volumes*, such as the new disk we are about to install. Second, you group physical volumes into *volume groups*, which are treated as a single large pool of disk space. Finally, you divide a volume group into *logical volumes*, which are treated as separate disks. In essence, logical volumes serve the same function as disk partitions on other systems.

The **pvcreate** command identifies physical volumes. Physical volumes are referred to by their device files, which can be found in **/dev/dsk** and **/dev/rdsk** (for the block and character devices, respectively). These files are created automatically by the **insf** command at boot time. The naming convention is

> **/dev/[r]dsk/cItDdN[sP]**

where I is the controller bus instance number of the interface, D is the disk's SCSI address (target number), N is the logical unit number (LUN, normally 0), and P is an optional partition number. For our example, the devices we use for our new disk are **/dev/rdsk/c0t3d0** and **/dev/dsk/c0t3d0** for the character and block devices, respectively. See the man page for **disk** in section 7 of the manual for the complete scoop on naming.

Under normal circumstances you really shouldn't low-level format a modern hard drive. However, if you're determined to do it, now's the time; use the **mediainit** command. Once a low-level format operation has been started, it cannot be interrupted or the disk will be corrupt and you will have to format it again. Formatting can take a very long time.

For this example, we skip low-level formatting and simply identify the physical volume with **pvcreate**. The -**B** option leaves space for booting information, which is added with the **mkboot** command:

```
# /usr/sbin/pvcreate -B /dev/rdsk/c0t3d0
Physical volume "/dev/rdsk/c0t3d0" has been created.
# mkboot /dev/rdsk/c0t3d0
```

After defining the disk as a physical volume, you must add it to a new volume group with the **vgcreate** command. You can add additional disks to a volume group with **vgextend**, but our example volume group will contain only a single disk.

*See Chapter 12 for more information about kernel parameters.*

Before you create a volume group, you must manually create a directory for it (typically **/dev/vg**XX, where XX is the volume group number) and create a device file called **group** in that directory to represent it. The minor device number of the device file must be unique among all the volume groups on the system. It has the format 0xNN0000, where NN is a hexadecimal (base 16) number that ranges from a minimum of 00 to a maximum number of groups controlled by the tunable kernel parameter called maxvgs. The default maximum is 14 in hex (20 in decimal), allowing values for NN to be between 00 and 13 hex. You can increase the value of maxvgs if you need more than 20 volume groups.

You may also need to adjust the physical extent size of the volume group if your disk is very large. The physical extent size is the basic allocation unit, and the sizes of logical volumes (described later) will be rounded up to a multiple of this value. The physical extent size is specified in megabytes and defaults to 4MB. If when configuring your logical volumes you see an error message such as "File too big" or "No such device," try specifying a larger physical extent size with the -**s** flag to **vgcreate**. We suggest starting at 8MB and working your way up; we used 16MB for our 47GB disk.

```
# mkdir /dev/vg01
# mknod /dev/vg01/group c 64 0x010000
# vgcreate -s 16 /dev/vg01 /dev/dsk/c0t3d0
Increased the number of physical extents per physical volume to 2805.
Volume group "/dev/vg01" has been successfully created.
Volume Group configuration for /dev/vg01 has been saved in
    /etc/lvmconf/vg01.conf
```

```
# vgdisplay /dev/vg01
--- Volume groups ---
VG Name              /dev/vg01
VG Write Access      read/write
VG Status            available
...
```

Once your disks have all been added to a convenient volume group, you can split the volume group's pool of disk space back into logical volumes. The **lvcreate** command creates a new logical volume. Specify the size of the volume in megabytes with the -**L** flag or in logical extents with the -**l** flag. The logical extent size is the same as the physical extent size described above and is typically 4MB per extent unless you specified a different value to **vgcreate**. Sizes specified in megabytes will be rounded up to the nearest multiple of the logical extent size.

In the sequence below, we specify the size of the backup root (1GB) and swap space (1GB) in megabytes.[13] We obtain the remaining number of logical extents from the **vgdisplay** command and assign them to the third logical volume. The default name for a logical volume is **/dev/vg**XX**/lvol**N, where XX is the volume group number and

N is an increasing number. You can change the name of the logical volume to something more descriptive with the **-n** flag, but we just used the default names.

If you plan to use a logical volume as a boot or swap device or to store system core dumps, you must specify contiguous allocation and turn off bad block remapping with the **-C** and **-r** flags to **lvcreate**, as we do below.

```
# lvcreate -C y -r n -L 1024 /dev/vg01
Logical volume "/dev/vg01/lvol1" has been successfully created with character
      device "/dev/vg01/rlvol1".
Logical volume "/dev/vg01/lvol1" has been successfully extended.
Volume Group configuration for /dev/vg01 has been saved in
      /etc/lvmconf/vg01.conf
# lvcreate -C y -r n -L 1024 /dev/vg01
Logical volume "/dev/vg01/lvol2" has been successfully created with character
      device "/dev/vg01/rlvol2".
...
# lvcreate -l 2676 /dev/vg01
Logical volume "/dev/vg01/lvol3" has been successfully created with character
      device "/dev/vg01/rlvol3".
...
```

We must run the **lvlnboot** command to notify the system of the new root and swap volumes. See the man page for **lvlnboot** for more information about the special procedures for creating boot, swap, and dump volumes.

```
# lvlnboot -r /dev/vg01/lvol1
Volume Group configuration for /dev/vg01 has been saved in
      /etc/lvmconf/vg01.conf
# lvlnboot -s /dev/vg01/lvol2
Volume Group configuration for /dev/vg01 has been saved in
      /etc/lvmconf/vg01.conf
```

Another common way to create a logical volume is to use **lvcreate** to create a zero-length volume and then use **lvextend** to add storage to it. That way, you can specify exactly which physical volumes in the volume group should compose the logical volume. If you use **lvcreate** to allocate space, it simply uses free extents from any physical volumes in the volume group, which is good enough for most situations.

Once the logical volumes have been created, verify them by running **vgdisplay -v /dev/vg01** to double-check their sizes and make sure they were set up correctly. At this point, you can also determine which logical volumes a particular physical volume belongs to with **pvdisplay -v /dev/dsk/c0t3d0**. The output of **pvdisplay** in verbose mode can be very long, so pipe it through a pager such as **more**.

After you have defined the logical volumes, you can create filesystems within them with the **newfs** command. The default filesystem type is specified in **/etc/default/fs** and is typically **vxfs**, the Veritas filesystem. You can override the filesystem type with

---

13. HP-UX limitations require swap space to reside in the first 2GB of the physical disk and the boot volume to be the first logical volume. The 1GB root and 1GB swap were chosen carefully to work around this constraint. See the man page for **lvlnboot** for more details on this subject.

the -F option to most filesystem-related commands. Another option is **hfs**, which is HP-UX's version of the Berkeley Fast File System (the default on most versions of UNIX). HFS is mostly there for backward compatibility; VXFS is a better choice for new installations.

**newfs** takes the character (raw) device associated with the target logical volume as a command-line argument. In our example:

```
# newfs -F vxfs /dev/vg01/rlvol1
version 3 layout
1048576 sectors, 1048576 blocks of size 1024, log size
1024 blocks
unlimited inodes, 1048576 data blocks, 1047224 free data blocks
32 allocation units of 32768 blocks, 32768 data blocks
first allocation unit starts at block 0
overhead per allocation unit is 0 blocks
```

```
# newfs -F vxfs /dev/vg01/rlvol3
version 3 layout
43843584 sectors, 5480448 blocks of size 8192, log size 256 blocks
...
```

Since VXFS is a journaled filesystem (similar to Solaris with its **-o logging** mount option), **fsck** is always quick and usually has little to do.

```
# fsck /dev/vg01/rlvol1
file system is clean - log replay is not required
```

We are now ready to mount our new filesystems. As always, **mount** requires a block device. To verify that the mount operation worked correctly, we run the **bdf** command (the Berkeley version of **df**, which some folks find easier to understand):

```
# mkdir /new
# mount /dev/vg01/lvol3 /new
# bdf /new
Filesystem        kbytes     used   avail      %used   Mounted on
/dev/vg01/lvol3   43843584   3616   43497480   0%      /new
```

Next, we add entries for the disk to the **/etc/fstab** file, formerly called **/etc/checklist** on HP-UX 10 and earlier. The **/etc/fstab** file lists the block device, mount point, filesystem type, options, backup frequency, and **fsck** pass for each filesystem; you can also add an optional comment. The delaylog option used below sacrifices some reliability for speed. See the **mount_vxfs** man page for more information about this and other VXFS mount options. Our two new filesystems are entered like this:

```
/dev/vg01/lvol1      /bkroot  vxfs  delaylog  0  2
/dev/vg01/lvol3      /new     vxfs  delaylog  0  2
```

*See Chapter 12 for more information about kernel parameters.*

All that's left to do is to enable swapping on our second logical volume. The **swapon** command specifies a device for swapping and should be given the block device name. You may have to modify the kernel parameter called maxswapchunks if you are trying to add a lot of swap areas; the **swapon** command will warn you if there is a problem. After running **swapon**, it's a good idea to run **swapinfo**, as we do here, to make sure the new swap area was added properly.

```
# swapon /dev/vg01/lvol2
# swapinfo
               Kb        Kb        Kb   START/        Kb
TYPE        AVAIL      USED      FREE   LIMIT   RESERVE  PRI   NAME
dev        262144         0    262144       0         -    1   /dev/vg00/lvol2
dev       1048576         0   1048576       0         -    1   /dev/vg01/lvol2
reserve         -     50876    -50876
```

Everything looks good. Don't forget to add an entry for the swap device to **/etc/fstab**, or the system will forget you have the extra space the next time you reboot. A swap entry looks like this:

```
/dev/vg01/lvol2        /          swap defaults  0  0 # swap device
```

That's all there is to it! We'd now reboot the system to verify that the entries added to **/etc/fstab** are correct and that everything comes up as expected. If you omit this step, the system will doubtless break several weeks later when the reboot occurs for some other reason. Check things out now to save someone else a big headache.

### Adding a disk to Red Hat Linux

After installing your new disk, it's a good idea to make sure the system can see the new device before booting up the kernel. If it's an IDE disk, check to be sure the disk is recognized in the BIOS setup display, which you usually access by typing a magic key sequence before the system boots. Consult the manuals that came with your computer or motherboard for specific information on BIOS configuration for IDE devices. In most cases, no special configuration is necessary.

Many SCSI cards also have a BIOS setup screen that you can invoke before the system boots. If this option is available, you scan the SCSI bus to make sure the new device appears. If this procedure hangs or produces a warning message, it's possible that you picked a SCSI ID that was already in use or that you did not install terminators in the right places.

You can also use the SCSI BIOS to low-level format a disk. This operation takes a long time on some disks and cannot be interrupted, so plan ahead.

*See page 246 for more information about installing device drivers.*

If your SCSI card does not provide its own user interface, you can always just try to boot the system and note the messages displayed by the kernel. If you do not see any messages from a SCSI driver, it is possible that you need to install the driver before the disk can be recognized by the kernel.

In our case, we saw the following messages from our BusLogic SCSI host adaptor:

```
scsi0 : BusLogic BT-948
scsi : 1 host.
  Vendor: SEAGATE   Model: ST446452W        Rev: 0001
  Type:   Direct-Access              ANSI SCSI revision: 02
Detected scsi disk sda at scsi0, channel 0, id 3, lun 0
```

```
scsi0: Target 3: Queue Depth 28, Asynchronous
SCSI device sda: hdwr sector=512 bytes. Sectors=91923356 [44884 MB] [44.9 GB]
sda: unknown partition table
```

Ignore warnings about the partition table, since this is the first time the disk has been used. Once the system has finished booting, you can move on to partitioning the disk.

You must first check to see if device files for the disk already exist. In Linux, the names for SCSI disk device files are of the form **/dev/sd**XN, where X is a lowercase letter that identifies the drive ('a' is the lowest numbered SCSI disk, 'b' is the second lowest, and so on[14]) and N is the partition number, starting at 1. When referring to the whole disk, simply omit the partition number. There are no character (raw) disk devices in Linux.

In this example, our disk is the first one on the SCSI chain. The first partition is therefore **/dev/sda1**, and the disk as a whole is referred to as **/dev/sda**. If these device files do not exist, we can create them with the **/dev/MAKEDEV** script:

```
# cd /dev
# ./MAKEDEV sda
```

The disk is now ready to be partitioned. As in most PC operating systems, the tool used for partitioning under Red Hat is called **fdisk**. Though all versions of **fdisk** do approximately the same thing (they implement Microsoft's standard partitioning system), there are many variations among them. You would be wise to read the man page for your particular system to be sure it matches what we show here.

```
# fdisk /dev/sda
The number of cylinders for this disk is set to 5721.
There is nothing wrong with that, but this is larger than 1024,
and could in certain setups cause problems with:
1) software that runs at boot time (e.g., LILO)
2) booting and partitioning software from other OSs
   (e.g., DOS FDISK, OS/2 FDISK)
```

Since we will be using this disk only on our Linux system, we will ignore the helpful warning. As stated in the geometry discussion on page 124, it is sometimes important to make the first partition small to ensure that it will work with an old BIOS and will work with other operating systems that might be installed on the system.

The **fdisk** program is interactive; pressing **m** displays a list of all its commands. The ones we will use here are:

- **n** to create a new partition
- **t** to change the type of a partition
- **p** to print the partition table
- **w** to write the partition table to disk

---

14. Note that this letter refers to the *order* of the target numbers of the SCSI devices, not to the target numbers themselves. If you add or remove a disk, all the drive letters change!

Since our disk does not yet have partitions, we start by creating a new one. If there are old partitions from a disk's former life, you may have to remove them with **fdisk**'s **delete** command before you can create new ones. The **fdisk** program will not change anything on disk until you tell it to write the partition table.

The partition table has room for four "primary" partitions which can be used to hold data. Alternatively, you can create an "extended" partition, which is a primary partition that points to another partition table, giving you another four "logical" partitions. Although the use of extended partitions can overcome the normal four-partition restriction, it is simplest to stick with primary partitions if only a few will be needed, and that's what we'll do in this case:

```
Command (m for help): new
Command action
   e     extended
   p     primary partition (1-4): p
Partition number (1-4): 1
First cylinder (1-5721, default 1): 1
Last cylinder or +size or +sizeM or +sizeK (1-5721, default 5721): +2G

Command (m for help): print
Disk /dev/sda: 255 heads, 63 sectors, 5721 cylinders
Units = cylinders of 16065 * 512 bytes

   Device  Boot  Start   End    Blocks   Id  System
/dev/sda1              1   255   2048256   83  Linux
```

We create a swap partition similarly, except that we change the type from Linux to Linux Swap. Although the kernel does not care about the partition type, some programs or scripts try to use the type to figure out what each partition is. Linux swap areas cannot currently exceed 2GB, so we specify the maximum size. This is probably overkill for most PC applications, but since we have disk space to spare, we might as well be generous. **mkswap** will warn us if it cannot use all of the space we have allocated.

```
Command (m for help): new
   e   extended
   p   primary partition (1-4): p
Partition number (1-4): 2
First cylinder (256-5721, default 256): 256
Last cylinder or +size or +sizeM or +sizeK (256-1275, default 1275): 511

Command (m for help): type
Partition number (1-4): 2
Hex code (type L to list codes): 82
Changed system type of partition 2 to 82 (Linux swap)
```

The third partition, which contains the rest of the disk, is defined in a similar manner. We review the partition table one last time before writing it.

```
Command (m for help): print
Disk /dev/sda: 255 heads, 63 sectors, 5721 cylinders
Units = cylinders of 16065 * 512 bytes
   Device Boot  Start   End     Blocks   Id  System
/dev/sda1              1   255    2048256   83  Linux
/dev/sda2            256   511    2056320   82  Swap
/dev/sda3            512  5721   41849325   83  Linux
```

A star appears next to the number of blocks if the partition does not end on a cylinder boundary. You can either delete the partition and recreate it by entering a number of cylinders (as above), or live with the fact that a small bit of disk space may be unusable. We are happy with the new partition table, so we write the label out to disk:

```
Command (m for help): write
The partition table has been altered!
Calling ioctl() to re-read partition table.
SCSI device sda: hdwr sector=512 bytes. Sectors=91923356 [44884 MB] [44.9 GB]
sda: sda1 sda2 sda3
Syncing disks.
```

Some administrators like to reboot after writing the partition table to make sure everything is stable and consistent before they create the filesystems. It probably isn't really necessary these days, but if you are used to installing Windows, you may feel more comfortable rebooting.

We're now ready to create filesystems. The current de facto filesystem type for Linux is the Extended 2 filesystem ("ext2fs"), which is based on the Berkeley Fast File System (FFS). A variety of filesystem types are available for Linux, of which several appear to be potential future replacements for ext2fs. The procedure for creating new filesystems is roughly the same for most other types; however, very few filesystems provide a **mkfs** program.

To create an ext2fs filesystem, run **mke2fs** with the device and size of the partition on the command line. (The size can be found in the **fdisk** output above.)

```
# mke2fs /dev/sda1 2048256
mke2fs 1.14, 9-Jan-1999 for EXT2 FS 0.5b, 95/08/09
Linux ext2 filesystem format
514000 inodes, 2048001 blocks
102412 blocks (5.00%) reserved for the super user
First data block=1
Block size=1024 (log=0)
Fragment size=1024 (log=0)
250 block groups
8192 blocks per group, 8192 fragments per group
2056 inodes per group
Superblock backups stored on blocks:
8193, 16385, 24577, 32769, 40961, 49153, 57345, 65537,
...
Writing inode tables:  250/250 done
Writing superblocks and filesystem accounting information:
done
```

The process for creating the larger filesystem is the same, but it takes significantly longer. If you know that you will not need all of the inodes that **mke2fs** allocates by default, you can reduce the number of inodes per group, speeding up the **mke2fs** and giving you more space for real data. However, it's much better to have too many inodes than too few, since running out of inodes will prevent you from creating any more files. You cannot add more inodes after the filesystem has been created.

We run **fsck** on our filesystems to make sure they were created properly. The **-f** flag forces **fsck** to check new filesystems rather than assuming that they are clean.

```
# fsck -f /dev/sda1
Parallelizing fsck version 1.14 (9-Jan-1999)
e2fsck 1.14, 9-Jan-1999 for EXT2 FS 0.5b, 95/08/09
Pass 1: Checking inodes, blocks, and sizes
Pass 2: Checking directory structure
Pass 3: Checking directory connectivity
Pass 4: Checking reference counts
Pass 5: Checking group summary information
/dev/sda1: 11/514000 files (0.0% non-contiguous), 67014/2048001 blocks
```

New filesystems can be mounted as soon as their mount points are created:

```
# mkdir /bkroot
# mount /dev/sda1 /bkroot
# df -k /bkroot
Filesystem   1k-blocks  Used  Available  Use%  Mounted on
/dev/sda1    1981000    13    1878575    0%    /bkroot
```

To ensure that the system mounts the new filesystems at boot time, we add a line for each one to the **/etc/fstab** file. Each line should list the name of the device, the mount point, the filesystem type, the mount options, the backup frequency, and the pass number for **fsck**:

```
/dev/sda1       /bkroot ext2  defaults  0  2
/dev/sda3       /new    ext2  defaults  0  2
```

The Linux boot loader, LILO, must be written to the disk device to make it bootable. The **lilo** command does the actual installation. It takes its configuration (what the kernel is called, which other OSes exist on the machine, etc.) from the **/etc/lilo.conf** file. See page 18 for more information about configuring and installing LILO.

The final step is to create the swap space and add it to the system. Swap partitions must be initialized with **mkswap**, which takes as arguments the device name and the size of the swap partition in sectors. The size can be obtained from **fdisk**, as shown above. You can also pass **mkswap** the **-c** flag, which tells it to clear the sectors before using them. This takes a long time, however, and it isn't really necessary.

With the swap area created, we enable it with the **swapon** command. **swapon** also verifies that the swap area was properly added.

```
# mkswap -c /dev/sda2 2056320
Setting up swapspace version 1, size = 2105667584 bytes
```

```
# swapon /dev/sda2
# swapon -s
Filename     Type        Size       Used   Priority
/dev/hda5    partition   133020     688    -1
/dev/sda2    partition   2056316    0      -2
```

As with regular filesystems, you must add the new swap partition to the **/etc/fstab** file if you want the system to remember it the next time you reboot. The following entry would be appropriate for our example disk:

```
/dev/sda2        swap      swap defaults  0   0
```

Make sure you reboot to test the changes that were made to the **/etc/fstab** file and to make sure that the new filesystems and swap space come on-line correctly.

### Adding a disk to FreeBSD

Getting our 47GB example disk to work on a FreeBSD system proved to be a challenge. The **disklabel** partitioning tool repeatedly gave us a confusing "no space left on device" message. After spending quite a bit of time checking for off-by-one errors, trying different parameters, and taking blind shots in the dark, we gave up and used a much smaller disk for our example (a Seagate ST32550W, which is a 2GB wide SCSI-2 disk). The underlying problem will probably be fixed by the time you read this, but if you run into similar issues, you might try to make use of the installation utility **/stand/sysinstall**.

As on other systems, you should try to verify the installation of the new disk at as low a level as possible. Modern SCSI controllers have a BIOS setup screen that you can access by hitting a magic key sequence during the power-on self-test before booting. The BIOS may let you scan the SCSI bus for devices and warn you of possible conflicts or problems. The SCSI BIOS often lets you low-level format the disk as well.

When you boot the system, look for messages that indicate that the kernel has seen the new drive:

```
da0 at bt0 bus 0 target 3 lun 0
da0: <SEAGATE ST32550W SUN2.1G 0418> Fixed Direct Access SCSI-2 device
da0: 3.300MB/s transfers, Tagged Queueing Enabled
da0: 2048MB (4194995 512 byte sectors: 255H 63S/T 261C)
```

Partitioning in FreeBSD is typically a two-stage process: first you create a *slice* to contain the FreeBSD data, then you *partition* it by placing a BSD label on that slice. A FreeBSD slice is identical to what other operating systems call a partition, and it is stored in the same **fdisk** partition table used by Red Hat, Windows, and other PC operating systems. Just try to remember that in FreeBSD a slice is really an **fdisk** partition, and a partition is really a logical unit inside a slice that is specified by the BSD volume label.[15] Unfortunately, as with other systems, the terms slice and partition are sometimes used interchangeably.

---

15. Note that the FreeBSD terminology is the opposite of that used by Solaris on Intel systems. In Solaris, volumes in the **fdisk** label are called partitions, and volumes in the Solaris label are called slices.

We refer to our disk by the device files **/dev/da0** and **/dev/rda0**, which are, respectively, the block and character (raw) devices for the entire disk. These names followed by a letter (e.g., **/dev/da0a**) specify a BSD partition (a-h) on the first FreeBSD slice. The four slices can be accessed separately through the files **/dev/[r]da0s[1-4]**. Your device names may vary depending on your disk controller, so double-check that you are referring to the right device for your disk before you go and format it.

As with other operating systems, the utility to edit slices is called **fdisk**. **fdisk** can be run in automatic mode or in interactive mode. Until you have added a few disks by hand, the interactive mode is simplest. You can edit the current slice table with the **-e** flag or create a new one with the **-i** flag.

```
# fdisk -i da0
```

The default with **-i** is to make the entire disk a FreeBSD slice and to make it slice 4. Since FreeBSD is the only operating system that we are going to use on this disk, we'll just accept the defaults (the session is not shown). You may need to experiment if you are editing an existing partition table. **fdisk** will try to warn you if you are doing anything that might affect other operating systems. Remember that nothing is saved until you allow **fdisk** to write out the new slice table, so you can always start over.

After the new slices have been written out, we run **fdisk** again to make sure everything looks good:

```
# fdisk da0
******* Working on device /dev/rda0 *******
parameters extracted from in-core disklabel are:
cylinders=261 heads=255 sectors/track=63 (16065 blks/cyl)
parameters to be used for BIOS calculations are:
cylinders=261 heads=255 sectors/track=63 (16065 blks/cyl)

Media sector size is 512
Warning: BIOS sector numbering starts with sector 1
Information from DOS bootblock is:
The data for partition 1 is:
<UNUSED>
The data for partition 2 is:
<UNUSED>
The data for partition 3 is:
<UNUSED>
The data for partition 4 is:
sysid 165,(FreeBSD/NetBSD/386BSD)
    start 1,  size 4192964 (2047 Meg), flag 80 (active)
        beg:  cyl 0/ sector 2/ head 0;
        end:  cyl 260/ sector 63/ head 254
```

Our new slice is now ready to be labeled. A BSD disk label (partition label, really) allows up to 8 partitions, named a through h. Partition a is normally used for the root partition, b for swap, and c for the whole slice. To write the label, you use **disklabel** with the **-r** and **-w** flags. The **-r** flag tells **disklabel** to access the disk directly rather than using the device driver's notion of what the disk label is, which is likely to be wrong when you are dealing with a new disk. The **-w** flag takes as arguments the disk device name and the type of disk as specified in **/etc/disktab**. For most disks, you can specify the disk type as **auto**; **disklabel** uses autodetected parameters to write a basic label. For example:

```
# disklabel -r -w da0 auto
```

If automatic detection does not work, you will have to create a new entry for your disk in **/etc/disktab**.

Once a label has been written, you can edit it with **disklabel -e**. This command converts the disk label to a nice human-readable format and starts a **vi** session on the results. If the numbers do not look right, you can change them within the editor. The partition information appears at the bottom of the file.

If you did not specify an **/etc/disktab** entry when labeling the disk, you will probably start with a single partition that contains the entire slice. You can copy that line to use as the basis for other partitions. Update the partition letter, the size in sectors, the offset, the filesystem type (4.2BSD or swap), and the fragment and block sizes to be used by **newfs**.

We partitioned our disk with a 1GB root partition and a 1GB swap partition, as shown below. The device passed to **disklabel**, **/dev/rda0c**, specifies the raw FreeBSD slice that we want to partition.

```
# disklabel -r -e /dev/rda0c
type: SCSI
disk: SEAGATE
sectors/track: 63
tracks/cylinder: 255
sectors/cylinder: 16065
cylinders: 261
sectors/unit: 4194995

...
8 partitions:
#        size     offset    fstype   [fsize  bsize  bps/cpg]
  a:  2097153          0    4.2BSD    1024   8192      16
  b:  2097841    2097154     swap
  c:  4194995          0    4.2BSD    1024   8192      16
```

Filesystems are created with the **newfs** command. Remember to specify the raw device name of the partition on which to create the new filesystem.

```
# newfs /dev/rda0a
/dev/rda0a:
2097152 sectors in 512 cylinders of 1 tracks, 4096 sectors
1024.0MB in 32 cyl groups (16 c/g, 32.00MB/g, 7744 i/g)
super-block backups (for fsck -b #) at:
 32, 65568, 131104, 196640, 262176, 327712, 393248,
 458784, 524320, 589856, 655392, 720928, 786464, 852000,
 ...
```

Adding a Disk

Once the filesystem is created, we run a quick **fsck** to make sure that **newfs** produced a usable filesystem. **fsck** requires the raw device, too.

```
# fsck /dev/rda0a
** /dev/rda0a
** Last Mounted on /bkroot
** Phase 1 - Check Blocks and Sizes
** Phase 2 - Check Pathnames
** Phase 3 - Check Connectivity
** Phase 4 - Check Reference Counts
** Phase 5 - Check Cyl groups
1 files, 1 used, 1017070 free (14 frags, 127132 blocks, 0.0% fragmentation)
```

The **swapon** command enables swapping on a partition. The partition type must be swap in the disk label. The **swapinfo** command, which is identical to **pstat -s**, reports on the devices that are currently being used for swapping. In our example:

```
# swapon /dev/da0b
# swapinfo
Device         1K-blocks   Used    Avail    Capacity   Type
/dev/wd0s1b       70784      0     70656       0%      Interleaved
/dev/da0b       1048920      0   1048792       0%      Interleaved
Total           1119448      0   1119448       0%
```

To have the new partitions automatically mounted and swapped on at startup, we add the appropriate lines to the **/etc/fstab** file:

```
# Device         Mountpoint  FStype  Options  Dump  Pass#
...
/dev/da0a        /new        ufs     rw       2     2
/dev/da0b        none        swap    sw       0     0
```

Test the **fstab** configuration by unmounting the filesystem and running **mount -a** to mount all the filesystems it lists. If the new filesystem is mounted correctly, reboot to make sure that the configuration really works.

# 9 Periodic Processes

The key to staying in control of your system is to automate as many tasks as possible. For example, an **adduser** program can add new users faster than you can, with a smaller chance of making mistakes. Almost any task can be encoded in a shell, Perl, or **expect** script.

It's often useful to have a script or command executed without any human intervention. For example, you might want to have a script verify (say, every half-hour) that your network routers and bridges are working correctly and have it send you email when problems are discovered.[1]

## 9.1 CRON: SCHEDULE COMMANDS

Under UNIX, periodic execution is handled by the **cron** daemon. **cron** starts when the system boots and remains running as long as the system is up. **cron** reads one or more configuration files containing lists of command lines and times at which they are to be invoked. The command lines are executed by **sh**, so almost anything you can do by hand from the shell can also be done via **cron**.[2]

A **cron** configuration file is called a "crontab," short for "cron table." All crontab files are stored in a single system directory, where cron knows to look for them. The **crontab** command transfers crontab files to and from this directory.

---

1. Many sites go further than this and dial a pager with a modem, so that an administrator can be summoned as soon as a problem is detected.
2. Some versions of **cron** permit shells other than **sh** to be used as well.

Typically, there is (at most) one crontab file per user: one for root, one for jsmith, and so on. Crontab files are named with the login names of the users they belong to, and **cron** uses these filenames to figure out which UID to use when running the commands that each file contains.

Old versions of **cron** scan their crontabs periodically and execute all commands that should have been run since the last scan. Modern versions parse the crontabs, figure out which of the listed commands needs to be run soonest, and go to sleep until the command's execution time has arrived.

On some systems, sending **cron** a hangup signal forces it to reread the crontabs. However, it is usually not necessary to send the signal by hand because **crontab** automatically tells **cron** to update itself whenever it changes a configuration file.

*See Chapter 11 for more information about syslog.*

**cron** normally does its work silently, but some versions can keep a log file (usually **/var/cron/log** or **/var/adm/cron/log**) that lists the commands that were executed and the times at which they ran. On some systems, creating the log file enables logging, and removing the log file turns logging off. On other systems, the log is turned on or off in a configuration file. Yet another variation is for **cron** to use syslog. The log file grows quickly and is rarely useful; leave logging turned off unless you're debugging a specific problem.

Most **cron**s do not compensate for commands that are missed while the system is down. In addition, some versions of **cron** do not understand daylight saving time, causing commands to be skipped or run twice when time changes occur. If you use **cron** for time-sensitive tasks (such as accounting), keep an eye open for these situations. You can forestall potential problems by avoiding times of day that may be affected by transitions (times between 1:00 and 3:00 a.m. in the U.S., for example).

## 9.2 THE FORMAT OF CRONTAB FILES

All the crontab files on a system share a common format. Comments are introduced with a pound sign in the first column of a line. Each noncomment line contains six fields and represents one command:

*minute hour day month weekday command*

The first five fields are separated by whitespace, but within the *command* field whitespace is taken literally.

*minute, hour, day, month,* and *weekday* give information about the times at which the command should be run. Their interpretations are shown in Table 9.1.

Each of the time-related fields may contain

- A star, which matches everything
- A single integer, which matches exactly
- Two integers separated by a dash, matching a range of values
- A comma-separated series of integers or ranges, matching any listed value

**Table 9.1    Crontab time specifications**

| Field | Description | Range |
|---|---|---|
| *minute* | Minute of the hour | 0 to 59 |
| *hour* | Hour of the day | 0 to 23 |
| *day* | Day of the month | 1 to 31 |
| *month* | Month of the year | 1 to 12 |
| *weekday* | Day of the week | 0 to 6 (0 = Sunday) |

For example, the time specification

```
45  10  *  *  1-5
```

means "10:45 a.m., Monday through Friday." A hint: never put a star in the first field unless you want the command to be run every minute.

There is a potential ambiguity to watch out for with the *weekday* and *day* fields. Every day is both a day of the week and a day of the month. If both *weekday* and *day* are specified, a day need satisfy only one of the two conditions in order to be selected. For example,

```
0,30  *  13  *  5
```

means "every half-hour on Friday, and every half-hour on the 13$^{th}$ of the month," not "every half-hour on Friday the 13$^{th}$."

*See page 40 for more information about su.* The *command* is the **sh** command line to be executed. It can be any valid shell command and should not be quoted. *command* is considered to continue to the end of the line and may contain blanks or tabs. The superuser's crontab can run commands as an arbitrary user by prefacing them with **/bin/su** *username* **-c**. (You will need to put the actual command in quotes.)

Most versions of **cron** allow the use of percent signs (%) to indicate newlines within the *command* field. Only the text up to the first percent sign is included in the actual command; the remaining lines are given to the command as standard input.

Here are some examples of legal crontab commands:

```
echo The time is now `date` > /dev/console
write garth % Hi Garth. % Remember to get a job.
cd /etc; /bin/mail -s "Password file" evi < passwd
```

And here are some complete examples of crontab entries:

```
30  2  *  *  1    (cd /users/joe/project; make)
```

This entry will be activated at 2:30 each Monday morning. It will run **make** in the directory **/users/joe/project**. An entry like this might be used to start a long compilation at a time when other users would not be using the system. Usually, any output produced by a **cron** command is mailed to the "owner" of the crontab.[3]

---

3. That is, the user after whom the crontab file is named. The actual owner of crontab files is generally root.

```
20  1  *  *  *      find /tmp -atime +3 -exec rm -f {} ';'
```

This command will run at 1:20 each morning. It removes all files in the **/tmp** directory that have not been accessed in 3 days.

```
55  23  *  *  0-3,6 /staff/trent/bin/acct-script
```

This line runs **acct-script** at 11:55 p.m. every day except Thursdays and Fridays.

## 9.3  CRONTAB MANAGEMENT

**crontab** *filename* installs *filename* as your crontab, replacing any previous version. **crontab -e** checks out a copy of your crontab, invokes your editor on it (as specified by the EDITOR environment variable), and then resubmits it to the crontab directory. **crontab -l** lists the contents of your crontab to standard output, and **crontab -r** removes it, leaving you with no crontab file at all.

Most systems allow root to supply a *username* argument so that other users' crontabs can be viewed or edited. For example, **crontab -r jsmith** erases the crontab belonging to the user jsmith. Under Red Hat and FreeBSD, which allow both a *username* and a *filename* argument in the same command, the username must be prefixed with **-u** to disambiguate (e.g., **crontab -u jsmith crontab.new**).

Without command-line arguments, **crontab** will try to read a crontab from its standard input. If you enter this mode by accident, don't try to exit with <Control-D>; doing so will erase your entire crontab. Use <Control-C> instead.

By default, all users can submit crontab files to **cron**. Two configuration files, usually called **cron.allow** and **cron.deny**, allow you to override this policy. These files can be rather hard to find. Check the directories **/etc/cron.d**, **/usr/lib**, **/usr/lib/cron**, and **/var/spool/cron**. Under FreeBSD, the files are located in **/var/cron** and are called simply **allow** and **deny**. (Table 9.2 on page 163 lists the standard location of **cron**-related files on our four example systems.)

If the allow file exists, then it contains a list of all users that may submit crontabs, one per line. Anyone not listed can't invoke the **crontab** command. If the allow file doesn't exist, then the deny file is checked. It, too, is just a list of users, but the meaning is reversed: everyone except the listed users is allowed access. If neither the allow file nor the deny file exists, only root can submit crontabs.

It's important to note that access control is implemented by **crontab**, not by **cron**. If a user is able to sneak a crontab file into the appropriate directory by other means, **cron** will blindly execute the commands that it contains.

## 9.4  SOME COMMON USES FOR CRON

A number of standard tasks are especially suited for invocation by **cron**, and these usually make up the bulk of the material in root's crontab. In this section we'll look at a variety of such tasks and the crontab lines used to implement them.

UNIX systems often come with some crontab entries preinstalled for you. If you want to deactivate the standard entries, comment them out by inserting a pound sign at the beginning of each line. Don't delete them completely; you might want to refer to them later.

### Cleaning the filesystem

Some of the files on any UNIX system are worthless junk (no, not the system files). For example, whenever a program crashes, the kernel writes out a file that contains an image of the program's address space. These files used to be named **core**, but some systems now include the program name or PID in the name of the core file (for example, **netscape.core** or **core.7288**).[4] Core files are useful for software developers, but for administrators they are usually a waste of space. Users often don't know about core files, so they tend not to delete them on their own.

*NFS, the Network File System, is described in Chapter 17.*

NFS is another source of extra files. Because NFS servers are stateless, they have to use a special convention to preserve files that have been deleted locally but are still in use by a remote machine. Most implementations rename such files to **.nfs***xxx* where *xxx* is a number. Various situations can result in these files being forgotten and left around after they are supposed to have been deleted.

Many programs create temporary files in **/tmp** or **/var/tmp** that aren't erased for one reason or another. Some programs, especially editors, like to make backup copies of each file they work with.

A partial solution to the junk file problem is to institute some sort of nightly disk space reclamation out of **cron**. Modern systems usually come with something of this sort set up for you, but it's a good idea to review your system's default behavior to make sure it's appropriate for your situation. Below are several common idioms implemented with the **find** command.

```
find / -xdev -name core -atime +7 -exec rm -f {} ';'
```

This command removes core images that have not been accessed in a week. The **-xdev** argument makes sure that **find** won't cross over to filesystems other than the root; this restraint is important on networks where many filesystems may be cross-mounted.[5] If you want to clean up more than one filesystem, use a separate command for each (note that **/var** is often a separate filesystem).

```
find / -xdev -atime +3 '(' -name '#*' -o -name '.#*' -o -name '*.CKP' -o
    -name '*~' -o -name '.nfs*' ')' -exec rm -f {} ';'
```

This command deletes files that begin with # or .# or .nfs, or end with ~ or .CKP, and that have not been accessed in three days. These patterns are typical of various sorts of temporary and editor backup files.

---

4. The word "core" means "memory." This term originated on early computer systems, which used little ferrite donuts mounted on a woven mesh as memory elements.

5. Not all versions of **find** support the **-xdev** argument. On some systems, it's called **-x**.

```
find /var/preserve -mtime +14 -exec rm -f {} ';'
```

This command removes files in **/var/preserve** two weeks after they were last modified. This directory is used by **vi** to store copies of files that users were editing when the system crashed. These files are never removed unless they are claimed by their owners with **vi -r** *filename*.

```
cd /tmp; find . ! -name . ! -name lost+found -type d -mtime +3
    -exec /bin/rm -rf {} ';'
```

This command recursively removes all subdirectories of **/tmp** not modified in 72 hours. Plain files in **/tmp** are removed at boot time by the system startup scripts, but some systems do not remove directories. If a directory named **lost+found** exists, it is treated specially and is not removed. This is important if **/tmp** is a separate filesystem. See page 138 for more information about **lost+found**.

If you use any of these commands, you should make sure that users are aware of your cleanup policies.

### Network distribution of configuration files

*See Chapter 18 for more information about sharing configuration files.*

If you are running a network of machines, it's often convenient to maintain a single, network-wide version of configuration files such as the mail aliases database (usually **/etc/mail/aliases**). Master versions of these files can be distributed every night with **rdist** or an **expect** script.

Sometimes, postprocessing is required. For example, many systems require you to run **newaliases** to convert a text file of mail aliases to the hashed format used by **sendmail**. You might also need to load files into an administrative database such as NIS or NIS+.

### Rotating log files

UNIX log files generally grow without bound until they are manually reset. There are various ways to prevent logs from overflowing, the simplest being to simply truncate them at periodic intervals.

A more conservative strategy is to "rotate" log files by keeping several older versions of each one. This scheme prevents log files from getting out of control but never leaves you without any recent log information. Since log rotation is a recurrent and regularly scheduled event, it's an ideal task for **cron**. See *Rotating log files* on page 205 for more details.

## 9.5 VENDOR SPECIFICS

The locations of the various files and directories related to **cron** are summarized in Table 9.2, and system-specific details follow.

**Table 9.2    Cron-related files and directories by system**

| System | Crontab directory | Allow/deny dir | Log file |
|---|---|---|---|
| Solaris | **/var/spool/cron/crontabs** | **/etc/cron.d** | **/var/cron/log** |
| HP-UX | **/var/spool/cron/crontabs** | **/usr/lib/cron** | **/var/adm/cron/log** |
| Red Hat | **/var/spool/cron** | **/etc** | **/var/log/cron** |
| FreeBSD | **/var/cron/tabs** | **/var/cron** | Uses syslog[a] |

a. The default configuration routes **cron**-related messages to **/var/cron/log.***.

 To turn on logging under Solaris, edit **/etc/default/cron** and set CRONLOG=YES. This configuration file also allows you to set the value of the PATH environment variable passed to commands.

 Red Hat and FreeBSD use "Vixie-cron," a freely available implementation of **cron** written by Paul Vixie. It provides several enhancements over most standard **cron**s. For example, Vixie-cron allows you to specify the values of environment variables within a crontab file.

One especially useful feature of Vixie-cron is that it allows step values in crontab time specifications. For example, the series 0,3,6,9,12,15,18,21 can be written more concisely in Vixie-cron as 0-21/3.

See the man pages for **cron** and **crontab** for more information.

Periodic Processes

# 10 Backups

At most sites, the information stored on computers is worth more than the computers themselves. It is also much harder to replace. Protecting this information is one of the system administrator's most important (and, unfortunately, most tedious) tasks.

There are hundreds of creative and not-so-creative ways to lose data. Software bugs routinely corrupt data files. Users accidentally delete their life's work. Hackers and disgruntled employees erase disks. Hardware problems and natural disasters take out entire machine rooms.

If executed correctly, backups allow the administrator to restore a filesystem (or any portion of a filesystem) to the condition it was in at the time of the last backup. Backups must be done carefully and on a strict schedule. The backup system and backup media must also be tested regularly to verify that they are working correctly.

The security of dump tapes directly affects your company's bottom line. Senior management needs to understand what the backups are actually supposed to do, as opposed to what they *want* the backups to do. It may be okay to lose a day's work at a university computer science department, but it probably isn't okay at a commodity trading firm.

We begin this chapter with some general backup philosophy, followed by a discussion of the most commonly used backup devices and media (their strengths, weaknesses, and costs). Next, we discuss the standard UNIX backup and archiving commands and give some suggestions as to which commands are best for which situations. We then talk about how to design a backup scheme and review the mechanics of the

UNIX commands **dump** and **restore**. Finally, we take a look at Amanda, a free network backup package and offer some comments about its commercial alternatives.

## 10.1  MOTHERHOOD AND APPLE PIE

Before we get into the meat and potatoes of backups, we want to pass on some general hints that we have learned over time (usually, the hard way). None of these suggestions is an absolute rule, but you will find that the more of them you follow, the smoother your dump process will be.

### Perform all dumps from one machine

**rdump** allows you to perform dumps over the network. Although there is some performance penalty for doing this, the ease of administration makes it worthwhile. We have found that the best method is to run a script from a central location that executes **rdump** (by way of **rsh** or **ssh**) on each machine that needs to be dumped, or to use a software package (commercial or free) that automates this process. All dumps should go to the same backup device (nonrewinding, of course).

If your network is too large to be backed up by a single tape drive, you should still try to keep your backup system as centralized as possible. Centralization makes administration easier and allows you to verify that all machines were dumped correctly. Depending on the backup media you are using, you can often put more than one tape drive on a server without affecting performance. With today's high-performance (6 MB/s and up) tape drives, however, it may be impractical to do this.

Dumps created with **rdump** can only be restored on machines that have the same byte order as the dump host (and in most cases, only on machines running the same OS). You can sometimes use **dd** to take care of byte swapping problems, but this simple fix won't help resolve differences among incompatible versions of **rdump**.

### Label your tapes

It is essential that you label each dump tape clearly and completely. An unlabeled tape is a scratch tape.

The tapes themselves should be labeled to uniquely identify their contents. Detailed information such as lists of filesystems and dump dates can be written on the cases.

You must be able to restore the root and **/usr** filesystems without looking at dump scripts. Label the dump tapes for these filesystems with their format, the exact syntax of the **dump** command used to create them, and any other information you would need to restore from them without referring to on-line documentation.

Free and commercial labeling programs abound. Save yourself a major headache and invest in one. If you purchase labels for your laser printer, the label vendor can usually provide (Windows) software that generates labels. For the economy-minded, a quick **troff** program will do the trick.

Backups

### Pick a reasonable backup interval

The more often backups are done, the smaller the amount of data that can be lost in a crash. However, backups use system resources and an operator's time. The sysadmin must provide adequate data security at a reasonable cost of time and materials.

On busy systems, it is generally appropriate to back up filesystems with home directories every workday. On systems that are used less heavily or on which the data is less volatile, you might decide that performing backups several times a week is sufficient. On a small system with only one user, performing backups once a week is probably adequate. How much data are your users willing to lose?

### Choose filesystems carefully

Filesystems that are rarely modified do not need to be backed up as frequently as users' home directories. If only a few files change on an otherwise static filesystem (such as **/etc/passwd** in the root filesystem), these files can be copied every day to another partition that is backed up regularly.

The Usenet spool directory on a news server is a good example of a filesystem that should not be backed up; don't waste the time and tape. News is volatile and could never be restored to its exact state in the past. That's why web sites like www.deja.com are popular with Usenet junkies.

If **/tmp** is a separate filesystem, it should not be backed up. The **/tmp** directory should not contain anything essential, so there is no reason to preserve it. In case this seems obvious, we know of one large site that does daily backups of **/tmp**.

### Make daily dumps fit on one tape

*See Chapter 9 for more information about **cron**.*

In a perfect world, you could do daily dumps of all your user filesystems onto a single tape. High-density media such as DLT and AIT make this goal practical for some sites. You can mount a tape every day before you leave work and run the dumps late at night from **cron**. That way, dumps occur at a time when files are not likely to be changing, and the dumps have minimal impact on users.

Unfortunately, this goal is becoming less and less realistic. When users can purchase 40GB disks for $240, there's not much of an economic barrier to the escalation of disk space. Why clean up your disks and enforce quotas when you can just throw a little money at the problem?

If you can't fit your daily backups on one tape, you have several options:

- Buy a higher-capacity tape device.
- Buy a stacker or library and feed multiple pieces of media to one device.
- Change your dump sequence.
- Write a smarter script.
- Use multiple backup devices.

Your automated dump system should always record the name of each filesystem it has dumped. Good record keeping allows you to quickly skip forward to the correct filesystem when you want to restore a file. It is also a good idea to record the order of the filesystems on the outside of the tape. (We've said it before, but it bears repeating: be sure to use the nonrewinding tape device to write tapes with multiple dumps.)

### Make filesystems smaller than your dump device

**dump** is perfectly capable of dumping filesystems to multiple tapes. But if a dump spans multiple tapes, an operator must be present to change tapes[1] and the tapes must be carefully labeled to allow restores to be performed easily. Unless you have a good reason to create a really large filesystem, don't do it.

### Keep tapes off-site

Most organizations keep backups off-site so that a disaster such as a fire cannot destroy both the original data and the backups. "Off-site" can be anything from a safe deposit box at a bank to the President's or CEO's home. Companies that specialize in the secure storage of backup media guarantee a secure and climate controlled environment for your archives. Always make sure your off-site storage provider is reputable, bonded, and insured.

The speed with which tapes are moved off-site should depend on how often you need to restore files and on how much latency you can accept. Some sites avoid making this decision by performing two dumps a day (to different tape devices): one that stays on-site and one that is moved immediately.[2]

### Protect your backups

Dan Geer, a security consultant, said, "What does a backup do? It reliably violates file permissions at a distance." Hmmm.

Secure your backup tapes. They contain all of your organization's data and can be read by anyone who has physical access to them. Not only should you keep your tapes off-site, but you should also keep them under lock and key. If you use a commercial storage facility for this purpose, the company you deal with should guarantee the confidentiality of the tapes in their care.

Some companies feel so strongly about the importance of backups that they make duplicates, which is really not a bad idea at all.

### Limit activity during dumps

Filesystem activity should be limited during dumps because changes can cause **dump** to make mistakes. You can limit activity either by doing the dumps when few active users are around (at night or on weekends) or by making the filesystem accessible only to **dump**.

---

1. That is, unless you have a stacker, jukebox, or library, and your version of **dump** supports it.
2. A large financial institution located in the World Trade Center kept its "off-site" backups one or two floors below their offices. When the building was bombed, the backup tapes (as well as the computers) were destroyed. Make sure "off-site" really is.

This precaution sounds fine in theory, but it is rarely practiced. Users want 24/7 access to all filesystems. These days it is impossible to do a backup with no disk activity.

*See page 503 for more information about filers.*
Filers such as Network Appliance's F700 series provide on-line backups with snapshots of the filesystem at regular, tunable intervals. This feature enables safe backups to be made of an active filesystem and is one of the important advantages of using a dedicated filer.

### Check your tapes

We've heard many horror stories about system administrators that did not discover problems with their dump regime until after a serious system failure. It is essential that you continually monitor your backup procedure and verify that it is functioning correctly. Operator error ruins more dumps than any other problem.

The first check is to have your dump software attempt to reread tapes immediately after it has finished dumping. Scanning a tape to verify that it contains the expected number of files is a good check. It's best if every tape is scanned, but this no longer seems practical for a large organization that uses hundreds of tapes per day. A random sample would be most prudent in this environment.

*See page 180 for more information about **restore**.*
It is often useful to run **restore t** to generate a table of contents for each filesystem and to store the results on disk. These catalogs should be named in a way that relates them to the appropriate tape; for example, **ocean:usr.Jan.13**. A week's worth of these records make it easy to discover what tape a lost file is on. You just **grep** for the filename and pick the newest instance.

In addition to providing a catalog of tapes, a successful **restore t** indicates that the dump is OK and that you will probably be able to read the tape when you need to. A quick attempt to restore a random file will give you even more confidence in your ability to restore from that tape.[3]

You should periodically attempt to restore from various tapes to make sure that it is still possible to do so. Every so often, try to restore from an old (months or years) dump tape. Drives have been known to wander out of alignment over time and to become unable to read their old tapes. The tapes can be recovered by a company that specializes in this service, but it will be expensive.

A related check is to verify that you can read the tapes on hardware other than your own. If your machine room burns, it does not do much good to know that the dump tapes could have been read on a tape drive that has now been destroyed.

Consider the following story, which circulated through the grapevine a couple of years ago: *A major research firm in California had an operator who was too busy hacking to do dumps. He opened tapes, labeled them, and filed them without ever putting any data on them. This charade went on for two or three months until someone insisted on having a file restored. What happened to him? Fired? No, he was trans-*

---

3. **restore t** reads the directory for the dump, which is stored at the beginning of the tape. When you actually go out and restore a file, you are testing a more extensive region of the medium.

*ferred internally, but was eventually arrested and convicted on unrelated electronic fraud charges. Rumor has it he got 40 years.*

### Develop a tape life cycle

Tapes have a finite life. It's great to recycle your media, but be sure to abide by the manufacturer's recommendations regarding the life of tapes. Most manufacturers quantify this life in terms of the number of passes that a tape can stand: a backup, a restore, and an **mt fsf** (file skip forward) each represent one pass.

### Design your data for backups

With disks so cheap and new storage architectures so reliable, it's tempting not to back up all your data. A sensible storage architecture—designed rather than grown willy nilly as disk needs increase—can do a lot to make backups more tractable. Start by taking an inventory of your storage needs:

- The various kinds of data your site will deal with
- The expected volatility of each type of data
- The backup frequency you require to feel comfortable with potential losses
- The political boundaries over which the data will be spread

Use this information to design your site's storage architecture with backups and potential growth in mind. Most sites are not ready to place complete trust in snazzy "black boxes" such as RAID systems or Network Appliance snapshots. Keeping project directories and users' home directories on a dedicated file server can make it easier to manage your data and ensure its safety.

### Prepare for the worst

After you have established a backup procedure, explore the worst case scenario: your site is completely destroyed. Determine how much data would be lost and how long it would take to get your system back to life (include the time it would take to acquire new hardware). Then determine if you can live with your answers.

## 10.2  BACKUP DEVICES AND MEDIA

Since many types of failure can damage several pieces of hardware at once, backups should be written to some sort of removable media. For example, backing up one hard disk to another (although better than no backup at all) provides little protection against a controller failure. Companies that back up your data over the Internet have entered the scene over the last few years, but most backups are still stored locally.

Many kinds of media store data by using magnetic particles. These media are subject to damage by electrical and magnetic fields. Here are some specific hazards to avoid:

- Audio speakers contain large electromagnets; it's not a good idea to store tapes on or near them. Even small speakers designed for use with computers can be hazardous.

- Transformers and power supplies (including UPS boxes) generate electro-magnetic fields. The "wall warts" used to power many peripherals contain transformers.

- Hard disks and tape drives have motors and magnetic heads, and their cases are often unshielded. Drives in metal cases are probably safe.

- Monitors use transformers and high voltages. Many monitors retain an electrical charge even after being turned off. Color monitors are the worst. Never store tapes on top of a monitor.

- Prolonged exposure to the Earth's background radiation affects the data on magnetic media, limiting its life span. All tapes will become unreadable over a period of years. Most media will keep for three years, but if you plan to store data longer than that, you should either use optical media or re-record the data.

The following sections describe some of the media that can be used for backups. The media are presented roughly in order of increasing capacity.

Many tape drives compress data before writing it to tape, allowing more data to be stored than the tape's nominal capacity would suggest. Manufacturers like to quote tape capacities in terms of compressed data; they often optimistically assume a compression ratio of 2:1 or more. In the sections below, we ignore compression and cite the actual number of bytes that can physically be stored on each piece of media.

The assumed compression ratio of a drive also affects its throughput rating. If a drive can physically write 1 MB/s to tape but the manufacturer assumes 2:1 compression, the throughput magically rises to 2 MB/s. As with capacity figures, we have ignored throughput inflation below.

Although cost and media capacity are both important considerations, it's important to consider throughput as well. Fast media are more pleasant to deal with, and they allow more flexibility in the scheduling of dumps.

### Floppy disks

Floppies are the most inconvenient way to store backups. They are slow and do not hold much data (up to 2.8MB, currently). Although the individual disks are cheap, they hold so little data that they are in fact the most expensive backup medium over-all. Floppy disks only last for a couple of years; *never* use them for long-term storage. On the other hand, floppy drives are inexpensive and often come with the system.

### Super floppies

Iomega Zip drives are now ubiquitous, and they are often the default external me-dium on home PCs. The storage capacity of these drives has increased from 100MB to 250MB. The drives are available with parallel, serial, SCSI, and USB connectors.

Imation markets a SuperDisk product that can write both traditional floppy disks and special 120MB media.

Although these products are useful for exchanging data, their high media costs make them a poor choice for backups.

### CD-R and CD-RW

The recent decreases in the price of recordable and read/write CDs makes them a far more attractive medium for backups than they were a few years ago. Both forms hold about 650MB. Drives that write these CDs are available in as many varieties as your favorite hard disk: SCSI, IDE, parallel, USB, etc.

CDs are written with a laser through a photochemical process. Although hard data has been elusive, it is widely believed that CDs have a substantially longer shelf life than magnetic media. Write-once CDs, known as CD-Rs, are not quite as durable as normal (stamped) CDs. CD-R is not a particularly good choice for normal backups, but it's good for archiving data you might want to recover a long time in the future.

Recordable DVD technology is not yet widely available, but we look forward to its debut in the next couple of years. The capacity should be somewhere around 10GB.

### Removable hard disks

A series of high-capacity removable disks have come onto the market over the last few years. Castlewood Industries has a 2.2GB product called an Orb drive. It comes in internal and external Ultra SCSI, EIDE, and USB varieties. For the gory details, see www.castlewood.com.

Another popular drive is the Iomega Jaz, which holds 2GB and claims an average transfer rate of 8.7 MB/s. The Jaz also claims a data shelf life of 10 years, whereas the Orb sets a more realistic target of 5 years. More information about the Jaz drive can be obtained from www.iomega.com.

The removable disk drive market is becoming very competitive, and prices vary daily. The main advantage of these products is speed: they achieve transfer rates comparable to normal disk drives. They are attractive as backup devices for small systems and home machines, although the disks themselves are somewhat pricey.

### 8mm cartridge tapes

Several brands of tape drive record to standard 8mm (small-format) videotapes. The drives are often referred to as "Exabytes drives," after the first company that produced them. The original format held 2GB, and the newer formats hold up to 7GB. The hardware compression built into some drives pushes the capacity even higher.

The size of 8mm tapes makes off-site storage very convenient. Originally, the drive mechanisms were somewhat problematic in that they would fall out of alignment every 6-12 months and require a costly repair from the manufacturer. This is no longer the case.

8mm tapes come in both video and data grades. Some manufacturers insist on data grade and void your warranty if you use unapproved media. We have found video

Backups

grade to be quite acceptable if it does not jeopardize the warranty. Be aware that both grades of tape are susceptible to heat damage.

### DAT (4mm) cartridge tapes

DAT (Digital Audio Tape) drives are helical scan devices that use 4mm cartridges. Although these drives are usually referred to as DAT drives, they are really DDS (Digital Data Storage) drives; the exact distinction is unimportant. The original format held about 2GB, but successive generations have improved DDS's capacity significantly. The current generation (DDS-4) holds up to 20GB.

DAT drives seek rapidly and transfer data at up to about 2.5 MB/s (for DDS-4), making the systems relatively fast. Their large capacity allows a complete backup to be performed without operator intervention at many sites. The 4mm tapes are compact, reducing the need for storage space and making off-site storage easy. DAT drives do not have a history of alignment problems.

### Travan tapes

Worth a brief mention here is the next generation of QIC tape technology, known as Travan. Travan drives use a linear recording technology and support media from 2.5GB to 10GB. The drives are inexpensive, but the tapes cost slightly more than those of other high-capacity tape systems, about $3/GB. The marketing hype claims a sustained transfer rate of approximately 1 MB/s.

Many manufacturers make Travan drives, but UNIX support is patchy. As of this writing, UNIX drivers are available for drives from HP, Tandberg, and Tecmar.

### OnStream ADR

A relative newcomer to the tape drive scene is OnStream's Advanced Digital Recording system. ADR is based on a linear recording technology and currently supports media sizes of 15GB and 25GB. The drives are cheap, and the cost of media is in line with other tape systems of similar capacities. The drives are pretty quick, too, with the 25GB model serving up 2 MB/s of throughput.

OnStream has had a few startup hiccups, which is probably to be expected from a new company using new technology to deploy a completely new product line. Current indications are that the early bugs have pretty much been worked out. However, the UNIX drivers for these devices are still somewhat new and are rumored to have some problems.

Currently, no autoloaders, jukeboxes, or stackers of any sort are available for the OnStream system, but that will probably change over the next year or so.

### DLT

Digital Linear Tapes are a popular backup device. These drives are reliable, affordable, and hold large amounts of data. They evolved from DEC's TK-50 and TK-70 cartridge tape drives, which were popular peripherals on the DEC VAXstation. The first generation of DLT drives could read the old TK-70 tapes. DEC sold the technology to Quantum, which popularized the drives by increasing their speed and capacity and by dropping their price.

DLT tapes hold a lot of data, up to 40GB. Transfer rates run about 6 MB/s. Manufacturers boast that the tapes will last 20 to 30 years; that is, if the hardware to read them still exists. How many 9-track tape drives are still functioning and on-line these days?

The downside of DLT is the price of media, which runs about $65 per tape, although the prices are decreasing. For a university, this is a huge expense; for a Wall Street investment firm, it might be OK.

### AIT

Advanced Intelligent Tape is Sony's own 8mm product on steroids. In 1996, Sony dissolved its relationship with Exabyte and introduced the AIT-1, an 8mm helical scan device with twice the capacity of 8mm drives from Exabyte. Since the original product release, Sony has introduced two new products: a higher-capacity AIT-1 with an extended tape length, and a new AIT-2 drive. Sony plans to release AIT-3 in the near future.

The Advanced Metal Evaporated (AME) tapes used in AIT drives have a long life cycle. They also contain a built-in EEPROM that gives the media itself some smarts. Software support is needed to make any actual use of the EEPROM, however. AIT-2 claims a 6 MB/s native transfer rate with a media capacity of 50GB. Drive and tape prices are both on a par with DLT.

### Mammoth

Exabyte's Mammoth is an improved version of the 8mm tape system. Exabyte chose to develop and manufacture its own mechanism after its falling out with Sony. The Mammoth products still rely on Sony for the AME media, but the tapes do not contain a memory chip.

The first generations of the Mammoth line had reliability problems. However, Exabyte listened to their customers and improved the products. They now claim a failure rate of only 1%.

The original tiff between Exabyte and Sony was based on Sony's poor manufacturing quality. Sony ran only one production line for both consumer products and data drives, so your Exabyte was essentially identical to your camcorder in Sony's eyes. However, Sony seems to be ahead of the curve right now.

Mammoth-2 drives offer a blindingly fast 12 MB/s native transfer rate, far faster than other tape drives in this price range.

### Jukeboxes, stackers, and tape libraries

With the low cost of disks these days, most sites have so much disk space that a full backup requires multiple tapes, even at 20GB per tape. One solution for these sites is a stacker, jukebox, or tape library.

Backups

A stacker is a simple tape changer that is used with a standard tape drive. It has a hopper that you load with tapes; it unloads full tapes as they are ejected from the drive and replaces them with blank tapes from the hopper. Most stackers hold about ten tapes.

A jukebox is a hardware device that can automatically change removable media in a limited number of drives, much like an old-style music jukebox that changed records on a single turntable. Jukeboxes are available for several types of media, including DAT, DLT, AIT, and CD. Jukeboxes are often bundled with special backup software that understands how to manipulate the changer. Storage Technologies and Sony are two manufacturers of these products.

Tape libraries are a hardware backup solution for large data sets—terabytes, usually. They are closet-sized mechanisms with multiple tape drives (or CDs) and a robotic arm that retrieves and files media on the library's many shelves. As you can imagine, they are quite expensive to purchase and maintain, and they have special power, space, and air conditioning requirements. Most purchasers of tape libraries also purchase an operations contract from the manufacturer to optimize and run the device. The libraries have a software component, of course, which is what really runs the device. Storage Technology is a leading manufacturer of tape libraries.

### Hard disks

We would be remiss if we did not mention the decreasing cost of hard drives as a reason to consider disk-to-disk backups. Although we suggest that you not duplicate one disk to another within the same physical machine, hard disks can be a good, low-cost solution for storage over a network.

One obvious problem is that hard disk storage space is finite and must eventually be reused. However, disk-to-disk backups are an excellent way to protect against the accidental deletion of files. If you maintain a day-old disk image in a well-known place that's shared over NFS, users can recover from their own mistakes without involving an administrator.

### Summary of media types

Whew! That's a lot of possibilities. Table 10.1 summarizes the characteristics of the media discussed in the previous sections.

W. Curtis Preston has compiled an excellent reference list of backup devices by manufacturer. It's available from www.backupcentral.com/hardware-drives.html.

### What to buy

When you buy a backup system, you pretty much get exactly what you see in Table 10.1. All of the media work pretty well, and among the technologies that are close in price, there generally isn't a compelling reason to prefer one over another. Buy a system that meets your specifications and your budget.

**Table 10.1    Backup media compared**

| Medium | Capacity[a] | Speed[a] | Drive | Media | Cost/GB | Reuse? | Random? |
|---|---|---|---|---|---|---|---|
| Floppy disk | 2.8MB | < 100 KB/s | $15 | 25¢ | $91.43 | Yes | Yes |
| SuperDisk | 120MB | 1.1 MB/s[b] | $200 | $8 | $68.27 | Yes | Yes |
| Zip 250 | 250MB | 900 KB/s | $200 | $15 | $61.44 | Yes | Yes |
| CD-R | 650MB | 2.4 MB/s | $200 | 75¢ | $1.18 | No | Yes |
| CD-RW | 650MB | 2.4 MB/s | $200 | $2 | $3.15 | Yes | Yes |
| Jaz | 2GB | 7.4 MB/s | $350 | $100 | $50.00 | Yes | Yes |
| Orb | 2.2GB | 12.2 MB/s[b] | $200 | $40 | $18.18 | Yes | Yes |
| Exabyte (8mm) | 7GB | 1 MB/s | $1,200 | $8 | $1.14 | Yes | No |
| Travan | 10GB | 1 MB/s | $200 | $34 | $3.40 | Yes | No |
| DDS-4 (4mm) | 20GB | 2.5 MB/s | $1,000 | $30 | $1.50 | Yes | No |
| ADR | 25GB | 2 MB/s | $700 | $40 | $1.60 | Yes | No |
| DLT (1/2 in.) | 40GB | 6 MB/s | $4,000 | $60 | $1.50 | Yes | No |
| AIT-2 (8mm) | 50GB | 6 MB/s | $3,500 | $95 | $1.90 | Yes | No |
| Mammoth-2 | 60GB | 12 MB/s | $3,500 | $80 | $1.33 | Yes | No |

a. Uncompressed capacity and speed
b. Maximum burst transfer rate; the manufacturer does not disclose the true average throughput.

DAT and Exabyte drives are excellent solutions for small workgroups and for individual machines with a lot of storage. The startup costs are relatively modest, the media are widely available, and several manufacturers are using each standard. Both systems are fast enough to back up a buttload of data in a finite amount of time.

ADR may well deserve to be listed along with DAT and Exabyte, but the newness of the technology and the fact that there is currently only one supplier make it slightly less desirable in our opinion.

DLT, AIT, and Mammoth-2 are all roughly comparable. There isn't a clear winner among the three, and even if there were, the situation would no doubt change within a few months as new versions of the formats were deployed. All of these formats work well, and they all address the same market: university and corporate environments that need serious backup hardware (which is to say, pretty much all university and corporate environments).

In the following sections, we use the generic term "tape" to refer to the media chosen for backups. Examples of backup commands are phrased in terms of tape devices.

## 10.3  SETTING UP AN INCREMENTAL BACKUP REGIME

The **dump** and **restore** commands are the most common way to create and restore from backups. These programs have been part of UNIX for a very long time, and their behavior is well known. At most sites, **dump** and **restore** are the underlying commands used by automated backup software.

Backups

### Dumping filesystems

The **dump** command builds a list of files that have been modified since a previous dump, then packs those files into a single large file to archive to an external device. **dump** has several advantages over the other utilities described later in this chapter:

- Backups can span multiple tapes.
- Files of any type (even devices) can be backed up and restored.
- Permissions, ownerships, and modification times are preserved.
- Files with holes are handled correctly.[4]
- Backups can be performed incrementally (with only recently modified files being written out to tape).

The **dump** command understands the layout of raw filesystems, and it reads a filesystem's inode tables directly to decide which files must be backed up. This knowledge of the filesystem allows **dump** to be very efficient, but it also imposes a few limitations.[5]

*See Chapter 17 for more information about NFS.*

The first limitation is that every filesystem must be dumped individually. If you have a disk that is partitioned, you must dump each partition separately. The other limitation is that only filesystems on the local machine can be dumped; you cannot dump an NFS filesystem mounted from a remote machine. However, you can dump a local filesystem to a remote tape drive with **dump**'s evil twin, **rdump**.

The most important feature of **dump** is its support for the concept of an "incremental" backup. Although it is possible to back up the entire system each day, it is usually not practical. Incremental dumps make it possible to back up only files that have changed since the last backup.

When you do a dump, you assign it a backup level, which is an integer from 0 to 9. A level N dump backs up all files that have changed since the last dump of level less than N. A level 0 backup places the entire filesystem on the tape. With an incremental backup system, you may have to restore files from several sets of backup tapes to reset a filesystem to the state it was in during the last backup.[6]

Another nice feature of **dump** is that it does not care about the length of filenames. Hierarchies can be arbitrarily deep, and long names are handled correctly.

**dump** accepts many arguments, but they do not vary too much from platform to platform. We briefly describe the flags you will probably need to dump a network of machines. However, you *must* check these flags against the man pages on the machine where you are dumping because most vendors have tampered with the meaning of at least one flag.

---

4. Holes are blocks that have never contained data. If you open a file, write one byte, seek 1MB into the file, then write another byte, the resulting file will take up only two disk blocks even though its logical size is much bigger. Files created by **dbm** or **ndbm** contain many holes.

5. **dump** requires access to raw disk partitions. Anyone allowed to do dumps can read all the files on the system with a little work.

6. Actually, most versions of **dump** do not keep track of files that have been deleted. If you restore from incremental backups, deleted files will be recreated.

**dump** parses its arguments differently from most other UNIX commands. It expects all the flags to be contained in the first argument, and the flags' arguments to follow in order. For example, where most commands would want **-a 5 -b -c 10**, **dump** would want **abc 5 10**.

The first argument to **dump** must be the incremental dump level. **dump** uses the **/etc/dumpdates** file to determine how far back an incremental dump must go. The **u** flag causes **dump** to automatically update **/etc/dumpdates** when the dump completes. The date, dump level, and filesystem name are recorded. If you never specify the **u** flag, all dumps become level 0s because no record of having previously dumped the filesystem will ever be created. If you change a filesystem's name, you can edit the **/etc/dumpdates** file by hand.

*See page 247 for information about device numbers.*

**dump** sends its output to some default device, usually the primary tape drive. If you want to use a different device, use the **f** flag to tell **dump** to send its output elsewhere. If you are placing multiple dumps on a single tape, make sure you specify a nonrewinding tape device (a device file that does not cause the tape to be rewound when it is closed—most tape drives have both a standard and a nonrewinding device entry). Read the man page for the tape device to determine the exact name of the appropriate device file.[7] Table 10.2 gives some hints for our four example systems.

**Table 10.2    Device files for the default SCSI tape drive**

| System | Rewinding | Nonrewinding |
|--------|-----------|--------------|
| Solaris | **/dev/rmt/0** | **/dev/rmt/0n** |
| HP-UX | **/dev/rmt/0m** | **/dev/rmt/0mn** |
| Red Hat | **/dev/st0** | **/dev/nst0** |
| FreeBSD | **/dev/rsa0** | **/dev/nrsa0** |

If you choose the rewinding device by accident, you will end up saving only the last filesystem dumped. Since **dump** does not have any idea where the tape is positioned, this mistake does not cause errors. The situation only becomes apparent when you try to restore files.

When you use **rdump** to dump to a remote system, you specify the identity of the remote tape drive as *hostname:device*; for example,

```
# rdump 0uf anchor:/dev/nst0 /spare
```

Permission to access remote tape drives is controlled by the **.rhosts** mechanism. We recommend that you use an SSH tunnel instead. See page 672 for more information.

In the past, you had to tell **dump** exactly how long your tapes were so that it could stop writing before it ran off the end of a tape. Most modern tape drives can tell when they have reached the end of a tape and can report that fact back to **dump**, which

---

7. All the entries for a tape unit use the same major device number. The minor device number tells the driver about special behaviors (rewinding, byte swapping, etc.).

then rewinds and ejects the current tape and requests a new one. Since the variability of hardware compression makes the "virtual length" of each tape somewhat indeterminate, it's always best to rely on the end-of-tape indication if your hardware and your version of **dump** support it.

Unfortunately, the nifty end-of-tape detection became available long after the various versions of UNIX had split apart from one another, so different **dump**s handle the end of the tape in different ways. Some assume that tape drives are capable of generating an EOT unless you tell them otherwise; they place no default limit on the size of a tape. Others assume a tape length of 2,300 feet and a density of 1,600 bpi, which are perfectly good defaults for the 9-track tapes of 15 years ago but not reasonable for today's media. These versions of **dump** will usually honor an EOT if it occurs before the expected end of the tape, so the right thing to do in these cases is to lie to **dump** and tell it that the tape is much longer than it really is.

All versions of **dump** understand the **d** and **s** options, which specify the tape density in bytes per inch and the tape length in cubits, respectively. (OK, OK, it's actually feet.) A few more-sensible versions let you specify sizes in kilobytes. For those versions that don't, you must do a little bit of arithmetic to express the size you want.

For example, let's suppose we want to do a level 5 dump of **/work** to a DDS-1 (DAT) drive whose native capacity is 1GB and whose typical compressed capacity is about 1.5GB. DAT drives can report EOT, so we need to lie to **dump** and set the tape size to a value that's much bigger than 1.5GB, say 4GB. That works out to about 60 kilofeet at 6,250 bpi:

```
# dump 5usdf 60000 6250 /dev/rst0 /work
DUMP: Date of this level 5 dump: Mon May  8 16:59:45 2000
DUMP: Date of last level 0 dump: the epoch
DUMP: Dumping /dev/hda2 (/work) to /dev/rst0
DUMP: mapping (Pass I) [regular files]
DUMP: mapping (Pass II) [directories]
DUMP: estimated 942223 tape blocks on 0.23 tape(s).
...
```

The flags **5usdf** are followed by the parameters to **s** (size: 60,000), **d** (density: 6,250), and **f** (tape device: **/dev/rst0**). Finally, the filesystem name (**/work**), which is always present, is given. Most versions of **dump** allow you to specify the filesystem by its mount point, as in the example above. Some require you to specify the raw device file.

The last line of output shown above verifies that **dump** will not attempt to switch tapes on its own initiative, since it believes that only about a quarter of a tape is needed for this dump. It is fine if the number of estimated tapes is more than 1, as long as the specified tape size is larger than the actual tape size. **dump** will reach the actual EOT before it reaches its own computed limit.

 The Solaris **dump** command has nothing to do with backups; it's a tool for examining object files. Whenever Sun's engineering team is feeling blue, one of the managers tells a joke about some ignorant hick trying to back up his disks with **dump**, and they all have a good laugh. The actual dump command is **/usr/sbin/ufsdump**. Fortunately, **ufsdump** accepts the same flags and arguments as other systems' traditional **dump**. For example, the command

```
# ufsdump 0uf /dev/rmt/2 /dev/rdsk/c0t3d0s5
```

dumps partition 5 of the drive at SCSI target 3 onto tape drive 2.

 You will probably have to explicitly install **dump** and **restore** on your Linux systems. The default is to not install these commands. An **rpm** (Red Hat Package Manager) file is available for easy installation. Under Linux, nothing is statically linked, so you need the shared libraries in **/lib** to do anything useful (yuck). The **restore** commands in FreeBSD, OpenBSD, and NetBSD are statically linked. Static linking makes it easier to recover from a disaster because **restore** is then completely self-contained.

## Dump sequences

Because dump levels are arbitrary (they have meaning only in relation to other levels), dumps can be performed on various schedules. The schedule that is right for you depends on:

- The activity of your filesystems
- The capacity of your dump device
- The amount of redundancy you want
- The number of tapes you want to buy

In the days when it took many tapes to back up a filesystem, complicated dump sequences were useful for minimizing the number of tapes consumed by each day's backups. As tape capacities have grown, it has become less useful to make fine distinctions among dump levels.

Because most files never change, even the simplest incremental schedule eliminates many files from the daily dumps. As you add additional levels to your dump schedule, you divide the relatively few active files into smaller and smaller segments.

A complex dump schedule provides the following three benefits:

- You can back up data more often, limiting your potential losses.
- You can use fewer daily tapes (or fit everything on one tape).
- You can keep multiple copies of each file, to protect against tape errors.

In general, the way to select a sequence is to determine your needs in each of these areas. Given these constraints, you can design a schedule at the appropriate level of sophistication. We describe a couple of possible sequences and the motivation behind them. One of them might be right for your site—or, your needs might dictate a completely different schedule.

### A simple schedule

If your total amount of disk space is smaller than the capacity of your tape device, you can use a completely trivial dump schedule. Do level zero dumps of every filesystem each day. Reuse a group of tapes, but every N days (where N is determined by your site's needs), keep the tape forever. This scheme will cost you

$$(365/N) * (\text{price of tape})$$

per year. Don't reuse the exact same tape for every night's dump. It's better to rotate among a set of tapes so that even if one night's dump is blown, you can still fall back to the previous night.

This schedule provides massive redundancy and makes data recovery very easy. It's a good solution for a site with lots of money but limited operator time (or skill). From a safety and convenience perspective, this schedule is the ideal. Don't stray from it without a specific reason (e.g., to conserve tapes or labor).

### A moderate schedule

A more reasonable schedule for most sites is to assign a tape to each day of the week, each week of the month (you'll need 5), and each month of the year. Every day, do a level 9 dump to the daily tape. Every week, do a level 5 dump to the weekly tape. And every month, do a level 3 dump to the monthly tape. Do a level 0 dump whenever the incrementals get too big to fit on one tape, which is most likely to happen on a monthly tape. Do a level 0 dump at least once a year.

The choice of levels 3, 5, and 9 is arbitrary. You could use levels 1, 2, and 3 with the same effect. However, the gaps between dump levels give you some breathing room if you later decide you want to add another level of dumps.

This schedule requires 24 tapes plus however many tapes are needed to perform the level 0 dumps. Although it does not require too many tapes, it also does not provide much redundancy.

## 10.4 RESTORING FROM DUMPS

Most of the many variations of the program that extracts data from dump tapes are called **restore**. We first discuss restoring individual files (or a small set of files), then explain how to restore entire filesystems.

### Restoring individual files

The first step to take when you are notified of a lost file is to determine which tapes contain versions of the file. Users often want the most recent version of a file, but that is not always the case. For example, a user who loses a file by inadvertently copying another file on top of it would want the version that existed before the incident occurred. It's helpful if you can browbeat users into telling you not only what files are missing, but also when they were lost and when they were last modified.

If you do not keep on-line catalogs, you must mount tapes and repeatedly attempt to restore the missing files until you find the correct tape. If the user remembers when the files were last changed, you may be able to make an educated guess about which tapes the files might be on.

After determining which tapes you want to extract from, create and **cd** to a temporary directory such as **/var/restore** where a large directory hierarchy can be created;
most versions of **restore** must create all of the directories leading to a particular file
before that file can be restored. Do not use **/tmp**—your work could be wiped out if
the machine crashes and reboots before the restored data has been moved to its original location.

The **restore** command has many options. Most useful are **i** for interactive restores of
individual files and directories and **r** for a complete restore of an entire filesystem.
You might also need **x**, which requests a noninteractive restore of specified files—be
careful not to overwrite existing files.

**restore i** reads the catalog from the tape and then lets you navigate through the directory of the dump as you would a normal directory tree, using commands called
**ls**, **cd**, and **pwd**. You mark the files that you want to restore with the **add** command.
When you are done selecting, type **extract** to pull the files off the tape.

*See page 186 for a*
*description of* **mt**.

If you placed multiple files on a single tape, you must use the **mt** command to position the tape at the correct dump file before running **restore**. Remember to use the
nonrewinding device!

For example, to restore the file **/users/janet/iamlost** on a FreeBSD system from a
remote tape drive, you might issue the following commands. Let's assume that you
have found the right tape, mounted it on **tapehost:/dev/nst0**, and determined that
the filesystem containing janet's home directory is the fourth one on the tape.

```
# mkdir /var/restore
# cd /var/restore
# rsh⁸ tapehost mt -f /dev/nst0 fsf 3
# rrestore if tapehost:/dev/nst0
restore> ls
.:
janet/  garth/  lost+found/ lynda/
restore> cd janet
restore> ls
afile bfile cfile iamlost
restore> add iamlost
restore> ls⁹
afile bfile cfile iamlost*
restore> extract
You have not read any volumes yet.
Unless you know which volume your files are on you should
start with the last volume and work towards the first.
Specify next volume #: 1
set owner/mode for '.'? [yn] n
```

8. You could instead use the **ssh** command here for added security.

9. The star next to **iamlost** indicates that it has been marked for extraction.

Volumes (tapes) are enumerated starting at 1, not 0, so for a dump that fits on a single tape, you specify 1. When **restore** asks if you want to set the owner and mode for ".", it's asking if it should set the current directory to match the root of the tape. Unless you are restoring an entire filesystem, you probably do not want to do this.

Once the **restore** has completed, you need to give the file to janet:

```
# cd /var/restore
# ls users/janet
iamlost
# ls ~janet
afile bfile cfile
# cp -p users/janet/iamlost ~janet/iamlost.restored
# chown janet ~janet/iamlost.restored
# chgrp student ~janet/iamlost.restored
# rm -rf /var/restore
# mail janet
Your file iamlost has been restored as requested and has
been placed in /users/janet/iamlost.restored.

Your name, Humble System Administrator
```

Some administrators prefer to restore files into a special directory, allowing users to copy their files out by hand. In that scheme, the administrator must protect the privacy of the restored files by verifying their ownership and permissions. If you choose to use such a system, remember to clean out the directory every so often.

If you created a backup with **rdump** and are unable to restore files from it with **restore**, try running **rrestore** instead. To minimize the chance of problems, use the same host to read the tape as was used to write it.

In general, **restore i** is the easiest way to restore a few files or directories from a dump. However, it will not work if the tape device cannot be moved backward a record at a time (a problem with some 8mm drives). If **restore i** fails, try **restore x** before jumping out the window. **restore x** requires you to specify the complete path of the file you want to restore (relative to the root of the dump) on the command line. The following sequence of commands repeats the previous example, using **restore x**:

```
# mkdir /var/restore
# cd /var/restore
# rsh tapehost mt -f /dev/nst0 fsf 3
# rrestore xf tapehost:/dev/nst0 /users/janet/iamlost
```

### Restoring entire filesystems

With luck, you will never have to restore an entire filesystem after a system failure. However, the situation does occasionally arise. Before attempting to restore the filesystem, you must make sure that whatever problem caused the filesystem to be destroyed in the first place has been taken care of. It's pointless to spend numerous hours spinning tapes only to lose the filesystem once again.

Before you begin a full restore, you must create and mount the target filesystem. See Chapter 8, *Adding a Disk*, for more information about how to prepare the filesystem. To start the restore, **cd** to the mount point of the new filesystem, put the first tape of the most recent level 0 dump in the tape drive, and type **restore r**.

**restore** will prompt for each tape in the dump. After the level 0 dump has been restored, mount and restore the incremental dumps. Restore incremental dumps in the order they were created. Because of redundancy among dumps, it may not be necessary to restore every incremental. Here's the algorithm for determining which dumps to restore:

**Step 1:**  Restore the most recent level 0 dump.

**Step 2:**  Restore the lowest-level dump of all dumps made subsequent to the dump you just restored. If multiple dumps were made at that level, restore the most recent one.

**Step 3:**  If that was the last dump that was ever made, you are done.

**Step 4:**  Otherwise, go back to step 2.

Here are some examples of dump sequences. You would only need to restore the levels shown in boldface.

```
0 0 0 0 0 0
0 5 5 5 5
0 3 2 5 4 5
0 9 9 5 9 9 3 9 9 5 9 9
0 3 5 9 3 5 9
```

*See Chapter 8 for more information about **newfs** and mount.*
Let's take a look at a complete command sequence. If the most recent dump was the first monthly after the annual level 0 in the "moderate" schedule on page 180, the commands to restore **/home**, residing on the physical device **/dev/dsk/c201d6s0**, would look like this (the device names and **newfs** command are OS dependent):

```
# /etc/newfs /dev/dsk/c201d6s0 QUANTUM_PD1050S
# /etc/mount /dev/dsk/c201d6s0 /home
# cd /home
/* Mount first tape of level 0 dump of /home. */
# restore r
/* Mount the tapes requested by restore. */
/* Mount first tape of level 5 monthly dump. */
# restore r
```

If you had multiple filesystems on one dump tape, you would have to use the **mt** command to skip forward to the correct filesystem before running each **restore**. See page 186 for a description of **mt**.

This sequence would restore the filesystem to the state it was in when the level five dump was done, except that all deleted files would be ghoulishly resurrected. This problem can be especially nasty when you are restoring an active filesystem or are

restoring to a disk that is nearly full. It is quite possible for a **restore** to fail because
the filesystem has been filled up with ghost files.[10]

## 10.5  DUMPING AND RESTORING FOR UPGRADES

When you perform an OS upgrade, you must back up all filesystems with a level 0
dump and, possibly, restore them. The restore is needed only if the new OS uses a
different filesystem format or if you change the partitioning of your disks. However,
you *must* do backups as insurance against any problems that might occur during the
upgrade. A complete set of backups also gives you the option of reinstalling the old
OS if the new version does not prove satisfactory.

Be sure to back up and restore any system-specific files that are in **/** or **/usr**, such as
**/etc/passwd**, **/etc/shadow**, or **/usr/local**. UNIX's brain-dead directory organization
mixes local files with vendor-distributed files, making it quite difficult to pick out
your local customizations.

You should do a complete set of level 0 dumps immediately after an upgrade, too.
Most vendors' upgrade procedures set the modification dates of system files to the
time when they were mastered rather than to the current time. Ergo, incremental
dumps made relative to the pre-upgrade level 0 will not be sufficient to restore your
system to its post-upgrade state in the event of a crash.

## 10.6  USING OTHER ARCHIVING PROGRAMS

**dump** is not the only program you can use to archive files to tapes; however, it is
usually the most efficient way to back up an entire system. **tar**, **cpio**, and **dd** can also
move files from one medium to another.

### tar: package files

**tar** reads multiple files or directories and packages them into one file, often a tape
file. **tar** is a useful way to back up any files whose near-term recovery you anticipate.
For instance, if a user is leaving for six months and the system is short of disk space,
you can use **tar** to put the user's files on a tape and then remove them from the disk.

**tar** is also very useful for moving directory trees from place to place, especially if
your system's **cp** does not support recursive copying or you are copying files as root
(**tar** preserves ownership information). For example, the command

```
    tar cf - fromdir | ( cd todir ; tar xfp - )
```

creates a copy of the directory tree *fromdir* in *todir*. Avoid using ".." in the *todir* argument, since symbolic links and automounters can make it mean something different
from what you expect. We've been bitten several times.

---

10. Some versions of **dump** and **restore** are rumored to keep track of deletions. We believe Solaris and
Linux to be among these.

Most versions of **tar** do not follow symbolic links by default, but they can be told to do so. Consult your **tar** manual for the correct flag; it varies from system to system.

The biggest drawback of **tar** is that most versions do not allow multiple tape volumes. If the data you want to archive will not fit on one tape, you cannot use **tar**. If your **tar** does claim to support multiple volumes, be very skeptical. Most multivolume implementations of **tar** are broken.

Another problem with many versions of **tar** is that pathnames are limited to 100 characters. This limitation prevents **tar** from being used to archive deep hierarchies. If your version of **tar** supports an option to use longer pathnames (as does GNU's **tar**) and you use that option, remember that people with the standard **tar** may not be able to read the tapes you write.[11]

**tar**'s **b** option lets you specify a "blocking factor" to use when writing a tape. The blocking factor is specified in 512-byte blocks; it determines how much data **tar** buffers internally before performing a write operation. Some DAT devices do not work correctly unless the blocking factor is set to a special value, but other drives do not require this setting.

On some systems, certain blocking factors may yield better performance than others. The optimal blocking factor varies widely, depending on the computer and tape drive. In many cases, you will not notice any difference in speed. When in doubt, try a blocking factor of 20.

**tar** expands holes in files and is intolerant of tape errors.

### cpio: SysV-ish archiving

**cpio** is similar to **tar** in functionality. It dates from the beginning of time and is rarely used today. Like **tar**, **cpio** can be used to move directory trees. The command

> **find** *fromdir* **-depth -print | cpio -pdm** *todir*

would make a copy of the directory tree *fromdir* in *todir*. Most versions of **cpio** do not allow multiple tape volumes. Some versions of **cpio** do not handle pipes gracefully, and only the superuser can copy special files. When using **cpio**, read your man pages carefully; the options vary greatly among systems.

### dd: twiddle bits

**dd** is a file copying and conversion program. Unless it is told to do some sort of conversion, **dd** just copies from its input file to its output file. If a user brings you a tape that was written on some non-UNIX system, **dd** may be the only way to read it.

*See Chapter 8 for more information about **newfs**.*

One historical use for **dd** was to create a copy of an entire filesystem. However, a better option these days is to **newfs** the destination filesystem and then run **dump** piped to **restore**. **dd** can sometimes clobber partitioning information if used incorrectly. It can only copy filesystems between partitions of exactly the same size.

---

11. The GNU implementation includes a filename mapping table as one of the files in the archive. Users of the standard **tar** can extract the contents of the archive and fix it up by hand, but the process is tedious.

Backups

**dd** can also be used to make a copy of a magnetic tape. With two tape drives, say, **/dev/rmt8** and **/dev/rmt9**, you'd use the command

```
% dd if=/dev/rmt8 of=/dev/rmt9 cbs=16b
```

With one drive (**/dev/rmt8**), you'd use the following sequence:

```
% dd if=/dev/rmt8 of=tfile cbs=16b
/* Change tapes. */
% dd if=tfile of=/dev/rmt8 cbs=16b
% rm tfile
```

Of course, if you have only one tape drive, you must have enough disk space to store an image of the entire tape.

Another historical use of **dd** was to convert between various flavors of QIC tape that differed only in their byte order. For example, to read on a Sun machine a **tar** tape written on an SGI machine, you could use

```
% dd if=/dev/rst8 conv=swab | tar xf -
```

The name of the tape device is system dependent.

### volcopy: duplicate filesystems

**volcopy** makes an exact copy of a filesystem on another device, changing the block size as appropriate. It is available on Solaris, HP-UX, and Linux systems. You can use **volcopy** to back up a filesystem to a removable disk pack or to make a complete copy of a filesystem on tape. Consult the man page on your system for the appropriate options and syntax.

## 10.7 USING MULTIPLE FILES ON A SINGLE TAPE

In reality, a magnetic tape contains one long string of data. However, it's often useful to store more than one "thing" on a tape, so tape drives and their UNIX drivers conspire to provide you with a bit more structure. When **dump** or some other command writes a stream of bytes out to a tape device and then closes the device file, an "end of file" marker is automatically placed on the tape. This marker separates the stream from other streams that are written subsequently. When the stream is read back in, reading stops automatically at the EOF.

You can use the **mt** command to position a tape at a particular stream or "file set," as **mt** calls them. **mt** is especially useful if you put multiple files (for example, multiple dumps) on a single tape. It also has some of the most interesting error messages of any UNIX utility. The basic format of the command is

```
mt [-f tapename] command [count]
```

*tapename* is the device name of the tape (nonrewinding if you want to do any sort of file operations). HP-UX uses **-t** instead of **-f**.

There are numerous choices for *command*. They vary from platform to platform, so we discuss only the ones that are essential for doing backups and restores:

**rew**    rewinds the tape to the beginning.

**offl**    puts the tape off-line. On some tape drives, this command causes the tape to pop out of the drive. Most dump scripts use this command to eject the tape when they are done, giving a clear indication that everything finished correctly.

**status**    prints information about the current state of the tape drive (whether a tape is loaded, etc.).

**fsf** [*count*]    fast-forwards the tape. If no *count* is given, **fsf** skips forward one file. With a numeric argument, it skips the specified number of files. Use this command to skip forward to the correct filesystem on a tape with multiple dumps.

**bsf** [*count*]    should backspace *count* files. On some systems, the current file is counted. On others, it is not. On some systems, **bsf** does nothing (silently). If you go too far forward on a tape, your best bet is to **rew** it and start again from the beginning.

Consult your manuals for an exact list of commands supported by **mt**.

## 10.8 AMANDA

The Advanced Maryland Automatic Network Disk Archiver, Amanda, is a sophisticated network backup system that can replace the home-grown scripts used by many sites. It can back up all the machines on a LAN to a single server's tape drive. It supports most flavors of UNIX and many different kinds of backup media.

Amanda was originally written by James da Silva of the University of Maryland in 1991. It's now supported by a team of sysadmins from around the world. The latest information and source code are available from www.amanda.org.

Amanda is not itself a backup program, but rather a wrapper that manages other backup software. Most sites will have Amanda use their systems' native **dump** and **restore** commands as the underlying backup software, but Amanda can also drive **gnutar** and even Samba's **smbtar** for those pesky NT machines.

Amanda supports a wide variety of tape drives, and it also takes advantage of jukeboxes and stackers. Amanda can use your tape drives' hardware compression facilities, or it can compress backup images with **compress** or **gzip** on client machines before the data goes over the network.

Another great feature of Amanda is tape management. Amanda writes a header on each tape it uses and so will never overwrite the wrong tape. In addition, Amanda manages dump levels based on configuration parameters and the fullness of tapes. Amanda keeps records of which backups are on which tapes, and it can print out

Backups

sticky labels showing the contents of each tape. (These labels become very useful when the disk that holds Amanda's database crashes.)

Amanda is one of the most popular free backup solutions in common use. It boasts implementation at about 1,500 sites worldwide. It seems to scale well and is constantly being enhanced to support the latest and greatest backup devices.

### The architecture of Amanda

In the Amanda model, tape drives and holding disks are attached to a central server. The server also hosts all the Amanda config files, log files, and databases. Amanda can only write one backup image to tape at a time, but it can spool multiple dumps to its holding disks simultaneously and then stream them out to tape.

Amanda supports multiple "configurations" on the same server machine. For example, one configuration might perform only level 0s of clients, while another does only incrementals. Each configuration generates its own log files and databases.

The Amanda server looks at its configuration files to determine which filesystems need to be backed up, which tape devices are available, and how much of the system's resources (network bandwidth, tapes, CPU load, etc.) it is allowed to use. It then contacts client machines and asks them to estimate the size of their backup files. Using this information, Amanda schedules the backups.

The Amanda server is actually a collection of programs that implement the various parts of the system. It is best to run the server programs on a fast machine that is not generally busy. If you are backing up large amounts of data, the server should have the best connectivity your network architecture permits. Since the holding disk is used to spool dump images from the network to the tape drive, it should be at least as large as the largest partition you want to back up. Amanda also needs some disk space (< 75MB) for its own logs and databases.

As of this writing, the latest stable release of Amanda is 2.4.1p1; the examples, configuration files, and commands shown in this chapter are taken from that version.

### Amanda setup

When you download Amanda, take the latest stable version, not the current development snapshot. We are talking about backups, so you want something stable!

After unpacking the source code, read the **README, docs/SYSTEM.NOTES**, and **docs/INSTALL** files. Any architecture-specific gotchas are documented in the file **SYSTEM.NOTES**. The **INSTALL** file gives step-by-step instructions for installation.

Before running **configure**, run **configure --help** to see the complete list of options. In addition to deciding where the software should be installed, you must decide what user and group Amanda should run as. For each partition you intend to back up with **dump**, the corresponding raw device needs to be readable by this user. Often, you can handle access by **chgrp**ing the device files to a specially created group and setting Amanda to run as that group.

After running **configure**, run **make** and **make install** to complete the installation.

Every Amanda client needs to have access to the Amanda binaries. However, it's not a good idea to have every client access the binaries through NFS, since there are times at which all the clients will need to run simultaneously (in particular, at the beginning of the backup procedure, when Amanda asks the clients to estimate their dump sizes). It's best to install the binaries on each client's local disks, usually somewhere under **/usr/local**.

The following programs should be installed on every client. They should never be run by hand.

| | |
|---|---|
| **amandad** | handles all communication between the client and the central server; runs all the other client programs. |
| **selfcheck** | checks that the client is set up for Amanda: has correct device permissions, can find **gzip**, can write to **/etc/dumpdates**, etc. |
| **sendbackup** | performs the backups. |
| **sendsize** | estimates backup sizes at different dump levels. |

Client machines need some other configuration as well. Both **/etc/inetd.conf** and **/etc/services** need to have a new line added for Amanda. Each device that you want to back up must be readable by Amanda's group, and the **/etc/dumpdates** file must be writable by this group as well. Once you think everything has been set up correctly, use **amcheck** to verify the configuration.

The appropriate line for the **inetd.conf** file is shown below (assuming you choose "amanda" as the Amanda user and group when you installed the software).

```
amanda dgram  udp wait   amanda /usr/local/sbin/amandad amandad
```

This line can be used on both server and client. You may wish to further protect the backup system by calling Wietse Venema's TCP wrappers package from **inetd.conf**; see page 666 for more information.

Here is the line for **/etc/services**:

```
amanda     10080/udp
```

A list of the Amanda server commands follows. Most take a command-line argument that tells them which Amanda configuration to use.

| | |
|---|---|
| **amdump** | does the nightly dumps; usually run by **cron**. |
| **amflush** | flushes the holding disk to tape if there were problems. |
| **amcleanup** | cleans up if the master host crashed during dumps. |
| **amrestore** | handles restore operations from Amanda dumps. |
| **amlabel** | writes Amanda labels on tape; used to avoid mistakes with overwriting wrong tapes, etc. |

| amadmin | finds the right tape to restore from and performs various other administrative chores. |
|---|---|
| amcheck | verifies that you are using the correct (expected) tape, that there is enough free space on the holding disk, and that client hosts are set up properly. |
| amtape | manages stackers and tape changers. |
| amplot | draws graphs of Amanda activity (e.g., holding disk and network usage) for each dump run. |

Each configuration is kept in a separate directory and needs the files **amanda.conf** and **disklist**. The **amanda.conf** file specifies the server's general configuration, and the **disklist** file specifies which clients and filesystems to back up. These files live only on the server.

### The amanda.conf file

**amanda.conf** is quite a large file, so we discuss it in four logical pieces: local information, dump strategy, resource parameters, and dump type definitions. These pieces are purely our invention; neither Amanda nor the Amanda documentation distinguishes the parts of the **amanda.conf** file in this way.

The file format is fairly self-explanatory, so we present it in the form of a long example with commentary on each section. We begin with the local information section, which identifies your organization and dumpmeister, defines log files and other configuration files, and specifies the format of tape labels (the logical labels recorded on the tapes themselves, not sticky labels).

```
############################################################
# Local parameters
############################################################

org "Podunk Univ."      # your organization name for reports
mailto "amanda"         # space-separated list of operators at your site
dumpuser "amanda"       # the user to run dumps as

runtapes 1              # number of tapes to use in a single run of amdump
tpchanger "chg-manual"  # tape changer glue script (provided with Amanda)
tapedev "/dev/rmt/0bn"  # the no-rewind tape device to be used

labelstr "^Podunk-[0-9][0-9]*$"  # label constraint regex: all tapes must match

infofile "/usr/adm/amanda/podunk/curinfo"  # database directory
logdir "/usr/adm/amanda/podunk"            # log directory
indexdir "/usr/adm/amanda/podunk/index"    # index directory
```

Amanda reads the label from each piece of media and will not use a tape unless its label matches the regular expression specified in labelstr. Therefore, all tapes must be labeled by **amlabel** before they can be used to store backups. Labels cannot contain whitespace characters.

It is up to the system administrator to define a meaningful naming scheme. For example, you might want to have the * in the regex match as a hint to the compression used or the type of machine backed up. In the example above, tapes would have labels Podunk-01, Podunk-02, and so on.

If you try to reuse a tape before the normal rotation cycle has been completed, the server will reject it. This feature prevents you from accidentally overwriting a tape that is still of historical importance in the backup scheme you have defined.

The parameters of that scheme (how often a particular tape can be used, how often each filesystem should get a level 0 dump, when to increase the dump level, etc.) are defined in the second section of **amanda.conf**.

```
###########################################################
# Strategy parameters
###########################################################

dumpcycle 4 weeks # the number of days in the normal dump cycle
bumpdays 2        # minimum days at each level
bumpsize 20 Mb    # minimum savings (threshold) to bump level 1 -> 2
bumpmult 2        # threshold = bumpsize * bumpmult^(level-1)
runspercycle 20   # the number of amdump runs in dumpcycle days
                  # 4 weeks * 5 amdump runs per week (weekdays)
tapecycle 25 tapes # the number of tapes in rotation
                  # 4 weeks (dumpcycle) * 5 tapes per week (weekdays)
                  # plus a few to handle errors that need amflush and
                  # so we do not overwrite the full backups performed
                  # at the beginning of the previous cycle
```

In the Amanda system, dumps are not rigidly scheduled by calendar date. Instead, you give Amanda general information about how much redundancy you want it to maintain. Amanda then tries to spread the work out across the entire dump cycle so that tapes are used efficiently and protection is maximized. Amanda recalculates its daily schedule each night, using real-time information about each client filesystem. It's really not possible to predict the exact dump agenda in advance.

A "dump cycle" is a period in which level 0 dumps will be done at least once on every client filesystem. Long cycles increase Amanda's scheduling flexibility, but they may also increase the average number of tapes that must be read to complete a restore. Amanda might perform level 0 dumps more frequently than the cycle time requires if tape is available.

The Amanda model assumes that dumps will be done every day. If this isn't true, you should set the runspercycle parameter to the actual number of dump days in a cycle. This example configuration does dumps only on weekdays, which is reasonable if someone must be physically present to change tapes.

Another assumption that's made by default is that one dump tape will be written per day (or per "run," in Amanda terminology). If you're using a stacker or jukebox, you can write multiple tapes per run. Additional configuration is required.

The tapecycle parameter tells how many tapes you plan to use in regular rotation. A minimal value is the number of runs per dump cycle times the number of tapes per run, plus a few extra to handle edge conditions and tape problems. If you allocate at least twice the minimal number of tapes, you are always guaranteed to have on hand at least two level 0 dumps of each filesystem.

The "bump" parameters let you exercise some control over how large an incremental dump must become before Amanda shifts up to the next level of dump. The parameters are specified in a rather mathematical and nonintuitive way. Fortunately, you can use the **bumpsize** option of **amadmin** to make sure that you've really implemented the strategy you intended.

For example, with the parameters shown above and assuming the configuration files are stored in a directory called **podunk**, **amadmin** would report:

```
# amadmin podunk bumpsize
Current bump parameters:
bumpsize 20480 KB    - minimum savings (threshold) to bump level 1 -> 2
bumpdays 2           - minimum days at each level
bumpmult 2           - threshold = bumpsize * (level-1)**bumpmult

Bump ->  To      Threshold
   1   ->  2       20480 KB
   2   ->  3       40960 KB
   3   ->  4       81920 KB
   4   ->  5      163840 KB
   5   ->  6      327680 KB
   6   ->  7      655360 KB
   7   ->  8     1310720 KB
   8   ->  9     2621440 KB
```

After an initial level 0, Amanda will start by doing level 1 dumps. Once the level 1 dumps become larger than 20MB, Amanda will shift to level 2 dumps. Once the level 2 dumps get larger than 40MB, Amanda will move up to level 3, and so on.

You should carefully tune these parameters to balance your desire for redundancy against the cost of tapes. Too much redundancy will result in high operating costs, and too little redundancy may result in lost data.

The rest of **amanda.conf** is devoted to parameters that specify how much network bandwidth, CPU, and disk space (on the server) to use; the type of tape drive to back up to; and the types of client partitions to be backed up.

```
############################################################
# Resource parameters
############################################################

tapetype EXB-8500    # what kind of tape it is (see tapetypes below)
inparallel 4         # maximum client dumpers that will run in parallel
netusage 600 Kbps    # maximum net bandwidth for Amanda, in KB per sec
etimeout 300         # number of seconds to wait for estimate per filesystem
```

```
holdingdisk hd1 {
    comment "main holding disk"
    directory "/dumps/amanda"        # mount point of holding disk
    use 8196 Mb                      # how much space we can use on it
}

define tapetype EXB-8500 {
    comment "Exabyte EXB-8500 drive on decent machine"
    length 4200 mbytes
    filemark 48 kbytes
    speed 474 kbytes
}
```

This example shows the configuration for an Exabyte 8500 tape drive. The tape type parameters are extremely important and should never be guessed. If your tape drive isn't listed in the sample **amanda.conf** file that comes with the distribution, you can probably find it in the **docs/TAPETYPES** file or at

> http://www.cs.columbia.edu/~sdossick/amanda

You might also try asking for an appropriate configuration on one of the amanda mailing lists. If all else fails, you can use the **tapetype** program that comes with Amanda. It determines the correct parameters for your tape drive by filling a tape with 32KB blocks. However, regard this procedure as a last resort—it can take a very long time (1 or 2 days!) on some tape drives.

The final resource parameters are the dump types, which represent the different types of data (e.g., volatile, important, static, etc.) that filesystems might contain. Each file-system on a client must be assigned a particular dump type. The dump type also specifies what kind of compression (if any) should be applied when the data is archived. Here are some examples:

```
############################################################
# Dump type definitions
############################################################

define dumptype comp-user {
    comment "partitions on reasonably fast machines"
    compress client fast
    priority medium
}

define dumptype comp-root {
    comment "root partitions on reasonably fast machines"
    compress client fast
    priority low
}

define dumptype nocomp-user {
    comment "partitions on slow machines"
    compress none
    priority medium
}
```

```
define dumptype clone-user {
    comment "partitions which should only get incrementals"
    compress client fast
    skip-incr
    priority medium
}

define dumptype comp-high-samba {
    comment "used for NT filesystems"
    program "GNUTAR"
    compress server fast
}

define dumptype dos-user {
    comment "used for dos partitions that are always mounted"
    program "GNUTAR"
    compress client fast
}
```

These particular dump types are all predefined by Amanda. You can use them directly, customize them for your own purposes, or write your own specifications from scratch. The comment field hints at what each dump type does.

The compress parameter specifies where dump data is to be compressed: on the client, on the server, or nowhere. You specify the compression program (e.g., **compress** or **gzip**) when you initially install Amanda. The possible values for the compress option are none, client best, client fast, server best, and server fast. The default is client fast.

compress none turns compression off. You might want to choose this option if the server's tape drive implements compression in hardware. The client options compress the dumps before they are sent over the network to the server, and the server options compress the dumps once they have reached the server's holding disk. If you want to use software compression, it generally makes more sense to perform the compression on the clients.

The best and fast modifiers tell the compressor how hard to work at squeezing the data; compare with **gzip --best** and **gzip --fast**. We only use fast; best can take much longer, and the compression is not significantly better.

The holdingdisk parameter has two possible values: yes and no. It specifies whether the holding disk should be used to spool this backup. You would want to turn this option off when archiving the holding disk itself. The default value is yes.

The maxdumps parameter specifies the maximum number of concurrent dumps that can be run on a client. The default value is 1, but you could increase it for better performance on beefy file servers that have lots of CPU and network bandwidth.

The priority parameter tells how important the backup is. The possible values are low, medium, and high. The default is medium. If there is not enough tape to store all the dumps that have been scheduled, the lower-priority dumps are skipped. In the event of a tape error, Amanda tries to marshall the higher-priority backups onto the holding disk; if there is room, the lower-priority dumps are put there as well.

We recommend defining a different dump type for each priority. Home directories should be dumped at high priority. Medium priority is good for local software packages (e.g., **/usr/local**), and low priority is appropriate for system files that do not change very often.

The program parameter specifies whether to use **dump** or **gnutar**. **dump** is the default and is usually a better choice.

The skip-full option instructs Amanda to skip the filesystem when a level 0 dump is due. You would generally select this option when level 0 dumps are performed outside of Amanda. For example, you might choose to do level 0s only when the machine is in single-user mode.

The skip-incr option makes Amanda skip all dumps except level 0s. You'd choose this option for archive configurations in which only full dumps are done and the tapes are saved indefinitely.

### The disklist file

The **amanda.conf** file tells how to do dumps without actually specifying any clients or filesystems to dump. That information is recorded in the **disklist** file. Each client filesystem is assigned one of the dump types defined in **amanda.conf**.

```
######################################################################
# client    partition    dumptype         # mountpoint
######################################################################

# the dump server
ocean      sd0a          comp-root        # /
ocean      sd0g          comp-user        # /usr
ocean      sd0d          comp-user        # /var
ocean      sd0h          comp-high        # /amanda

# lorien's NT partition mounted via Samba on ocean
ocean      //lorien/c$   comp-high-samba  # c:\

# prototype
squish     yc0t0d0s0     comp-high        # /
squish     yc0t0d0s6     comp-high        # /usr
squish     yc0t0d0s3     comp-high        # /var
squish     yc0t0d0s7     comp-high        # /local

# clone
zamboni    c0t0d0s0      clone-user       # /
zamboni    c0t0d0s6      clone-user       # /usr
zamboni    c0t0d0s3      comp-root        # /var
zamboni    c0t0d0s7      comp-user        # /local
```

```
# slow PC
fuzz        sd1a        nocomp-high     # /
fuzz        sd1f        nocomp-high     # /local
fuzz        sd1e        nocomp-high     # /usr
fuzz        sd1d        nocomp-high     # /var
fuzz        /dos        dos-user        # /dos
```

The first column is the hostname of the client machine to back up. The second column lists the target disk partition. You can use either the device name (as above) or the mount point.

Note that the dump server's (ocean's) holding disk, **/dumps/amanda**, is not mentioned in the **disklist** file. In our case it is not necessary to back up this partition because its contents are limited to dump images stored during Amanda runs. If you keep Amanda logs or other important information on the holding disk, you should back it up by using the holdingdisk dump type parameter.

The skip-incr option (included in the clone-user type defined above) is handy for backing up clones of a prototype machine. At our site, we have one prototype machine for each architecture that's cloned onto other machines of the same architecture. Since the root partitions of the clones are the same as that of their prototype, we don't need to waste tape space backing them up every night.

However, every clone has a few unique files (e.g., config files in **/etc**), so we still do a level 0 once during the dump cycle. If you have a similar setup and choose not to perform nightly backups of certain filesystems, make sure that they are indeed identical to something that does get archived every night. In our example, zamboni's **/var** partition holds users' email, so it has to be backed up every night.

*See Chapter 26 for more information about Samba.*

We've installed the Samba program **smbtar** on our dump server so that we can back up NT filesystems. In this example configuration, we back up lorien's C: drive. Notice that the client host listed in the **disklist** file is ocean, not lorien. If you're using Samba to access a filesystem, the Amanda client must be the UNIX host on which **smbtar** is located rather than the NT machine. (We don't specify fuzz's **/dos** partition this way because it is always mounted and is not accessed through Samba.) Amanda distinguishes between Samba partitions and regular mount points (e.g., **/usr** or **/dos**) by the number of slashes at the beginning: two for Samba and one for regular mounts.

### Amanda log files

Amanda creates two log files on the server for each run. The first is **amdump.**$n$, where $n$ is the number of additional Amanda runs that have occurred since the log file was created. This file contains a verbose description of the scheduling decisions that Amanda has made. The other log file is **log.***date.n*, where *date* is the date of the run and $n$ is the number of runs already made on that day.

### Amanda debugging

After every run, Amanda generates a summary report of the run's activities and emails it to the dumpmeister. This report includes information about the amount of tape used, the filesystems that were successfully backed up, and any errors that were encountered. Here is an example from a configuration using a different **disklist** than that shown above:

```
To: amanda@ocean
Subject: Podunk Univ. AMANDA MAIL REPORT FOR September 1, 1999

These dumps were to tape Podunk-481.
Tonight's dumps should go onto 1 tape: Podunk-482.

FAILURE AND STRANGE DUMP SUMMARY:
  fuzz   sd1a   lev 0    FAILED    [no estimate or historical data]
  ...
    taper: FATAL syncpipe_get: w: unexpected EOF

STATISTICS:                   Total    Full     Daily
                              -------- -------- --------
Dump Time (hrs:min)           3:02     0:36     0:04     (0:34 start, 1:49 idle)
Output Size (meg)             2954.6   2666.8   287.8
Original Size (meg)           7428.1   6292.5   1135.5
Avg Compressed Size (%)       39.8     42.4     25.3
Tape Used (%)                 70.5     63.5     7.0      (level:#disks ...)
Filesystems Dumped            18       8        10       (1:8 2:2)
Avg Dump Rate (k/s)           105.3    124.5    43.4
Avg Tp Write Rate (k/s)       1254.2   1251.8   1276.9

NOTES:
    planner: Adding new disk zamboni:c0t0d0s7.
    driver: WARNING: /dumps/amanda: 8550400 KB requested, but only 1035113
       KB available.
    planner: Forcing full dump of squishy.c0t0d0s0 as directed.
    planner: Request to fuzz timed out.
    planner: Incremental of ocean:sd0h bumped to level 2.
  ...
    driver: going into degraded mode because of tape error.
  ...
```

One common problem is for Amanda to be unable to write backups onto a tape. This problem can occur when there isn't a valid tape in the drive or when some kind of tape error occurs during writing (as in the example with host fuzz above). In either case, Amanda still spools the backups to the holding disk. To write these buffered dumps to tape, insert the proper tape in the drive and run **amflush**.

To diagnose other problems, you can investigate either the log files on the server or the debug files on the client. The location of log files on the server is specified in the **amanda.conf** file. The debug files are located in each client's **/tmp/amanda** directory, that is, if you compiled Amanda with **--with-debugging** (the default).

Amanda generates the email report from the log file. For example, here's the log file (**amdump.**$n$) from which the email above was derived.

Backups

```
SETTING UP FOR ESTIMATES...
dumper: pid 18199 executable dumper version 2.4.1p1, using port 791
...
driver: started dumpersetup_estimates: ocean:sd0d: command 0, options:
   last_level 1 next_level0 6 level_days 16
   getting estimates 0 (20023) 1 (2735) -1 (-1)
...
zamboni:c0t0d0s0 lev 1 skipped due to skip-incr flag
planner: SKIPPED zamboni c0t0d0s0 1 [skip-incr]
...
GETTING ESTIMATES...
got result for host ocean disk sd0a: 0 -> 53797K, 1 -> 1797K, -1 -> -1K
got result for host ocean disk sd0d: 0 -> 19695K, 1 -> 2696K, -1 -> -1K
...
ANALYZING ESTIMATES...
...
pondering ocean:sd0d... next_level0 6 last_level 1 (not due for a full dump,
   picking an incr level)
...
```

Here is the other log file, **log.19990901.0,** that corresponds to the original email:

```
START planner date 19990901
START driver date 19990901
INFO planner Adding new disk depot:dsk/d1.
SUCCESS planner zamboni c0t0d0s0 1 [skipped: skip-incr]
WARNING driver WARNING: /dumps/amanda: 8550400 KB requested, but only
   1035113 KB available.
...
START taper datestamp 19990901 label Podunk-481 tape 0
FAIL planner fuzz sd1a 0 [no estimate or historical data]
...
STATS driver startup time 2019.456
SUCCESS dumper ocean sd0a 0 [sec 418.311 kb 25088 kps 59.97 orig-kb 58087 ]
SUCCESS dumper ocean sd0d 1 [sec 15.867 kb 800 kps 50.42 orig-kb 2719 ]
...
SUCCESS taper ocean sd0a 0 [sec 53.366 kb 25088 kps 474.612 {wr: writes 2
   rdwait 0.000 wrwait 0.032 filemark 38.332 }]
SUCCESS taper ocean sd0d 1 [sec 6.345 kb 800 kps 133.3 {wr: writes 1 rdwait
   1.470 wrwait 0.356 filemark 2.637 }]
...
STRANGE dumper ocean sd0h 1 [sec 82.435 kb 33.4 kps 0.4 orig-kb 155.0 ]
   sendbackup: start [ocean:sd0h level 1 datestamp 19990901]
   | DUMP: Date of this level 1 dump: Wed Sep 01 23:47:54 1999
   | DUMP: Date of last level 0 dump: Mon Aug 30 23:43:23 1999
   | DUMP: Dumping /dev/rsd0h (/amanda) to standard output
   | DUMP: mapping (Pass I) [regular files]
   | DUMP: mapping (Pass II) [directories]
   ? DUMP: (This should not happen) bread from /dev/rsd0h [block 64]:
   count=8192, got=-1
   | DUMP: estimated 38 blocks (19KB) on 0.00 tape(s).
   | DUMP: dumping (Pass III) [directories]
```

```
| DUMP: dumping (Pass IV) [regular files]
| DUMP: level 1 dump on Wed Sep 01 23:47:54 1999
| DUMP: 310 blocks (155KB) on 1 volume
| DUMP: DUMP IS DONE
sendbackup: size 158720
sendbackup: end
...
```

Each SUCCESS dumper line means that a dump was written to the holding disk, and each SUCCESS taper line means a dump was written to tape. A STRANGE dumper means that Amanda saw error output while running **dump**. When dump errors occur, Amanda saves the output in this log file (it puts a "?" in front of the offending lines) and also includes it in the email summary.

Another common problem occurs when Amanda cannot get an estimate of the dump sizes for a client's filesystems. The first things to check in this situation are that the client is reachable over the network and that its copy of Amanda is set up properly. You can also check the debug files in the client's **/tmp/amanda** directory. Each of Amanda client programs writes debugging output here every time it runs.

When Amanda can't obtain a size estimate, look at **sendsize**'s debug file. **sendsize** parses the output of **dump** and looks for the estimated size line. If it doesn't see it, Amanda reports [no estimate]. Here's an example of a **sendsize.debug** file:

```
sendsize: getting size via dump for c0t0d0s3 level 1
sendsize: running "/usr/ccs/bin/dump 1sf 100000 - /dev/dsk/c0t0d0s3"
   DUMP: Date of this level 1 dump: Wed Sep 01 21:59:36 1999
   DUMP: Date of last level 0 dump: Mon Aug 30 05:08:33 1999
   DUMP: Dumping /dev/dsk/c0t0d0s3 (/var) to standard output
   DUMP: mapping (Pass I) [regular files]
   DUMP: mapping (Pass II) [directories]
   DUMP: mapping (Pass II) [directories]
   DUMP: mapping (Pass II) [directories]
   DUMP: estimated 7150 tape blocks on 0.00 tape(s).
   DUMP: dumping (Pass III) [directories]
   ....
calculating for amname 'c0t0d0s7', dirname '/local'
sendsize: getting size via dump for c0t0d0s7 level 0
sendsize: running "/usr/ccs/bin/dump 0sf 100000 - /dev/dsk/c0t0d0s7"
   DUMP: Cannot open/stat /dev/rdsk/c0t0d0s7, Permission denied
   ....
(no size line match in above dump output)
```

In this case, it's obvious that we need to fix the permissions on **/dev/rdsk/c0t0d0s7**.

If you can't solve your problem by looking in the log files or the Amanda documentation, you may want to look over the archives of the Amanda mailing lists. You can search them at

http://www.egroups.com/list/amanda-users
http://www.egroups.com/list/amanda-hackers

Backups

### File restoration from an Amanda backup

To restore from Amanda backups, use the **amadmin** and **amrestore** programs. Let's walk through a complete example.

Suppose we have a user who deleted a whole directory and wants it restored. The first step is to find the tapes on which the directory was backed up. To do this, you need the following information:

- The name of the machine and partition on which the directory resided
- The full path to the directory
- The date the directory was lost or corrupted
- The date the directory was last modified

The dates will determine a range of tapes that contain the directory in a state we might want to restore. Let's suppose the directory we want to restore is in zamboni's **/local** partition, and that it was modified on October 5 and deleted on October 12. **amadmin** will determine which tapes we need:

```
% amadmin podunk find zamboni c0t0d0s7
date          host      disk      lv  tape         file  status
2000-01-26    zamboni   c0t0d0s7  1   Podunk-795   33    OK
2000-01-25    zamboni   c0t0d0s7  1   Podunk-794   41    OK
2000-01-23    zamboni   c0t0d0s7  0   Podunk-792   9     OK
2000-01-22    zamboni   c0t0d0s7  1   Podunk-791   32    OK
...
1999-10-13    zamboni   c0t0d0s7  1   Podunk-685   38    OK
1999-10-12    zamboni   c0t0d0s7  1   Podunk-684   37    OK
1999-10-11    zamboni   c0t0d0s7  1   Podunk-683   39    OK
1999-10-10    zamboni   c0t0d0s7  1   Podunk-682   72    OK
1999-10-09    zamboni   c0t0d0s7  1   Podunk-681   44    OK
1999-10-08    zamboni   c0t0d0s7  1   Podunk-680   88    OK
1999-10-07    zamboni   c0t0d0s7  1   Podunk-518   35    OK
1999-10-06    zamboni   c0t0d0s7  1   Podunk-517   33    OK
1999-10-05    zamboni   c0t0d0s7  1   Podunk-516   33    OK
1999-10-04    zamboni   c0t0d0s7  1   Podunk-515   51    OK
1999-10-03    zamboni   c0t0d0s7  1   Podunk-514   16    OK
1999-10-02    zamboni   c0t0d0s7  1   Podunk-513   19    OK
1999-10-01    zamboni   c0t0d0s7  1   Podunk-512   36    OK
1999-09-30    zamboni   c0t0d0s7  1   Podunk-511   15    OK
1999-09-29    zamboni   c0t0d0s7  1   Podunk-510   78    OK
1999-09-28    zamboni   c0t0d0s7  0   Podunk-509   99    OK
...
```

The **find** option causes **amadmin** to go through each log file in the **amanda.conf** configuration, searching for the machine and partition we supplied as arguments. To do our restore, we need the level 0 tape Podunk-509 and the level 1 tape Podunk-683 from the day before the deletion. For the level 1, we could theoretically use any tape written after the 5th, since the user claims the directory wasn't modified between the 5th and the 12th. In the absence of a reason to do otherwise, however, it's best to use the latest available tape. Users don't always have perfect memories.

Next, we use **amrestore** to actually restore the data. We'd start with the tape Podunk-509, since it's the level 0. After inserting the tape into the tape drive, we could run

```
% amrestore -p /dev/rmt/0bn zamboni c0t0d0s7 | restore if -
```

to locate the appropriate record and start an interactive restore. **amrestore** looks at each dump image on the tape until it finds the one we're looking for, then splurts that dump image to its standard output to be read by the **restore** command. The actual restore procedure works just as described starting on page 180. After extracting from the level 0 tape, we'd repeat the process with the level 1 tape.

**amrestore** can recognize the appropriate dump because Amanda put a 32K header in front of each dump that records where it came from and how it was compressed. If compression was used, **amrestore** automatically pipes the tape image through the appropriate decompressor.

Searching all the headers can take quite a long time, since **amrestore** might have to skip over hundreds of filesystems. The output of **amadmin** shows which file set we're looking for, so it is not really necessary to let **amrestore** do all this work. We can simply run **mt fsf** to fast-forward the tape before running **amrestore**.

You must run the **restore** process on the same operating system and architecture that generated the original dump. Amanda doesn't know anything about the actual contents of the dump, and it can't shield you from cross-platform compatibility issues.

If the Amanda logs are deleted, we can always look at the tape labels to find the tapes we need. But what if **amrestore** itself has been deleted? Fear not: **amrestore** doesn't really do anything more than **dd**. If you look at the 32K header of the backup you want to restore, you'll see instructions for restoring it. For example, here's the header from the level 0 tape:

```
# mt -f /dev/rmt/0bn fsf 99
# dd if=/dev/rmt/0bn bs=32k count=1
AMANDA: FILE 19990928 zamboni c0t0d0s7 lev 0 comp .gz
To restore, position tape at start of file and run:
dd if=<tape> bs=32k skip=1 | gzcat | restore ...f -

1+0 records in
1+0 records out
```

### Alternatives to Amanda: other open source backup packages

Several other free backup tools are available on the Internet for download. A few worth mentioning are:

- BURT – a backup and recovery utility based on Tcl/TK 8.0
- CD Backup Linux – an automated utility designed specifically for CD-Rs
- **hostdump.sh** – a quick and dirty backup utility
- KBackup – a GUI-based backup tool for UNIX. Nice features.
- **star** – a faster implementation of **tar**. Has some additional features such as automatic byte swapping. Won't clobber existing files on restore.

## 10.9 COMMERCIAL BACKUP PRODUCTS

We would all like to think that UNIX is the only OS in the world, but unfortunately, that is not the case. When looking at commercial backup solutions, you should consider their ability to handle any other operating systems that you are responsible for backing up. Most contemporary products take cross-platform issues into consideration and enable you to include Windows and Macintosh workstations in your UNIX backup scheme. You must also consider non-UNIX storage arrays and file servers.

Users' laptops and other machines that are not consistently connected to your network should also be protected from failure. When looking at commercial products, you may want to ask if each product is smart enough not to back up identical files from every laptop. How many copies of **command.com** do you really need?

Since we find that Amanda works well for us, we don't have much experience with commercial products. We asked some of our big-bucks buddies at commercial sites for quick impressions of the systems they use. Their comments are reproduced below.

### ADSM/TSM

This product was developed by IBM and later purchased by Tivoli. It is marketed today as the Tivoli Storage Manager (TSM). TSM is a data management tool that also handles backups. More information can be found at www.tivoli.com.

Pros:

- Backed by IBM; it's here to stay
- Attractive pricing and leasing options
- Very low failure rate
- Uses disk cache; useful for backing up slow clients
- Deals with Windows clients
- Excellent documentation (priced separately)

Cons:

- Poorly designed GUI interface
- Every 2 files =1K in the database.
- The design is incremental forever

### Veritas

Veritas sells backup solutions for a variety of systems. When you visit their web site (www.veritas.com), make sure you select the product that's appropriate for you.

Pros:

- Decent GUI interface
- Connects directly to Network Appliance filers
- Push install for UNIX
- Can write tapes in **gnutar** format
- Centralized database, but can support a distributed backup system

Cons:

- Some bugs
- Didn't support DHCP clients (may have changed by now)
- Pricing is confusing and annoying
- NT support was spotty

### Legato

Legato backup software is sold directly from Legato, but it's also bundled by some major computer manufacturers, such as Compaq. More information can be found at www.legato.com.

Pros:

- Nice GUI
- Very reasonably priced
- Automatic mail to users informing them of backup status

Cons:

- Some problems with a corrupted index file
- Not recommended for 100+ clients
- Didn't support heterogeneity of clients (even though advertised to do so)
- Couldn't handle a large filesystem
- Poor support

### Other alternatives

W. Curtis Preston, author of the O'Reilly backup book, maintains a very useful web page about backup-related topics (disk mirroring products, advanced filesystem products, remote system backup products, off-site data-vaulting products, etc.). Among other resources, it includes an extensive table of just about every piece of commercial backup software known to mankind. We recommend both the book and the web site highly. The address is www.backupcentral.com.

## 10.10  RECOMMENDED READING

PRESTON, CURTIS W. *Unix Backup and Recovery.* O'Reilly, 1999.

# 11 *Syslog and Log Files*

The accounting system, the kernel, and various utilities all emit data that is logged and eventually ends up on your finite-sized disks. Most of that data has a limited useful lifetime and needs to be summarized, compressed, archived, and eventually thrown away.

## 11.1 LOGGING POLICIES

Logging policies vary from site to site. Common schemes include the following:

- Throw away all data immediately.
- Reset log files at periodic intervals.
- Rotate log files, keeping data for a fixed time.
- Compress and archive logs to tape or other permanent media.

The correct choice for your site depends on how much disk space you have and how security conscious you are. Even sites with an abundance of disk space must deal with the cancerous growth of log files.

Whatever scheme you select, maintenance of log files should be automated with **cron**. See Chapter 9, *Periodic Processes*, for more information about this daemon.

### Throwing away log files

We do not recommend throwing away all logging information. Sites that are subject to security problems routinely find that accounting data and log files provide important evidence of break-ins. Log files are also helpful for alerting you to hardware and software problems. In general, given a comfortable amount of disk space, data should be kept for at least a month and then discarded. In the real world, it may take this long for you to realize that your site has been compromised by a hacker and that you need to review the logs. If you need to go back further into the past, you can recover older log files from your backup tapes.

Some administrators allow log files to grow until they become bothersome, then restart them from zero. This plan is better than keeping no data at all, but it does not guarantee that log entries will be retained for any particular length of time. Average disk usage may also be higher than with other management schemes.

### Rotating log files

Most sites store each day's log information on disk, sometimes in a compressed format. These daily files are kept for a specific period of time and then deleted. If you have sufficient disk space, it is handy to keep the log files uncompressed so that they can be easily searched with **grep**.

At our site we dedicate a disk partition on a central logging host (**/var/log**) to log files. We compress data that's more than a week old with **gzip**.

One common way of implementing this policy is called "rotation." In a rotation system, you keep backup files that are one day old, two days old, and so on. Each day, a script renames the files to push older data toward the end of the chain.

If a log file is called **logfile**, for example, the backup copies might be called **logfile.1**, **logfile.2**, and so on. If you keep a week's worth of data, there will be a **logfile.7** but no **logfile.8**. Every day, the data in **logfile.7** is lost as **logfile.6** overwrites it.

Suppose a file needs daily attention and you want to archive its contents for three days (to keep the example short). The following script would implement an appropriate rotation policy:

```
#!/bin/sh
cd /var/log
mv logfile.2 logfile.3
mv logfile.1 logfile.2
mv logfile logfile.1
cat /dev/null > logfile
chmod 600 logfile
```

Ownership information is important for some log files. You may need to run your rotation script from **cron** as the log files' owner rather than as root, or you may need to add a **chown** command to the sequence.

Some sites identify log files by date rather than by sequence number; for example, **logfile.tues** or **logfile.aug26**. This system is a little harder to implement, but it can be worth the effort if you frequently refer to old log files. It's much easier to set up in Perl than in **sh**. One useful idiom that doesn't require any programming is

```
mv logfile logfile.`date +%Y.%m.%d`
```

This scheme has the advantage of making **ls** sort the log files chronologically.

Some daemons keep their log files open all the time. Because of the way the filesystem works, our example script cannot be used with such daemons. Instead of flowing to the recreated **logfile**, log data will start to mysteriously disappear; the active reference to the original file keeps it alive even after you delete the directory entry and create a new file with the same name. The file doesn't disappear (and its disk space is not reclaimed) until every reference has been closed. To install a new log file, you must either signal the daemon or kill and restart it.

Here is an updated example that uses both compression and signals:

```
#!/bin/sh
cd /var/log
mv logfile.2.gz logfile.3.gz
mv logfile.1.gz logfile.2.gz
mv logfile logfile.1
cat /dev/null > logfile
kill -signal pid
gzip logfile.1
```

*signal* represents the appropriate signal for the program writing the log file; *pid* is its process ID. The signal can be hardcoded into the script, but you must determine the PID of the daemon dynamically, either by reading a file that the daemon has left around for you (e.g., **/etc/syslog.pid**, described below) or by filtering the output of **ps**. Some systems provide a standard command (such as Albert Cahalan's **skill** or Werner Almesberger's **killall**, both supplied with Red Hat) that simplifies the stereotypical **ps**-**grep**-**kill** sequence.[1]

Each program behaves differently with respect to logging. Consult the appropriate chapter in this book (or your manuals) to determine what procedures are necessary in each case.

Many systems supply an off-the-shelf log rotation script that is run out of **cron**. By all means, use the standard script if it does what you want. See the vendor-specific sections starting on page 209 for details.

If your system doesn't supply a rotation system, we suggest that you use a Perl script called **rotz** written by Matt Segur and Michael Bernstein for this purpose. It's available from www.admin.com.

### Archiving log files

Some sites must archive all accounting data and log files as a matter of policy, perhaps to provide data for a potential audit. In this situation, log files should be first rotated on disk and then written to tape or other permanent media. This scheme reduces the frequency of tape backups and gives you fast access to recent data.

---

1. Beware: Solaris and HP-UX also have a **killall** command, but it does something completely different. Use **pkill** on Solaris to get a **killall**-like effect.

*See Chapter 10 for more information about backups.*

Log files should always be included in your regular backup sequence. They may also be archived to a separate tape series. Separate tapes are more cumbersome, but they impose less of a documentation burden and won't interfere with your ability to recycle dump tapes. If you use separate tapes, we suggest that you use **tar** format and write a script to automate your backup scheme.

## 11.2  FINDING LOG FILES

UNIX is often criticized for being inconsistent, and indeed it is. Just take a look at a directory of log files and you're sure to find some with names like **maillog**, some like **ftp.log**, and maybe even some like **lpNet**, **lpd-errs**, or **console_log**. In addition to having random names, log files are often scattered across directories and filesystems.

This section attempts to help you find all the files that are quietly taking over your disk and to suggest a granularity for dealing with each. We also note the "usual place" for log files on our four example systems.

*The format of the **syslog.conf** file is described on page 211.*

To locate your log files, read your system's startup scripts (**/etc/rc\***, **/etc/rc.d/\***, or **/etc/init.d/\***) to see if logging is turned on when daemons are run. You may have to read the man pages for individual daemons to see where the log data actually goes. Most programs these days handle logging via syslog, which is described later in this chapter. Check syslog's configuration file, **/etc/syslog.conf**, to find out what happens to the messages.

Table 11.1 compiles information about some of the more common log files on our example systems. Specifically, it lists

- The log files to archive, summarize, or truncate
- The program that creates each
- An indication of how each filename is specified
- The frequency of attention that we consider reasonable
- The required owner and group of the log file
- A description of the file's contents

Table 11.1 on the next page lists logs under their generic names; vendor-specific deviations begin on page 209. Not all files appear on all systems.

Filenames are relative to **/var/adm** or **/var/log** unless otherwise noted (however, files in the group called "extras" are locally installed and would follow your local conventions).

The character in the Where column tells how the log file is specified: S for programs that use syslog, C if logging options are set on the command line at boot time, F for programs that use a configuration file, and H if the filename is hardwired in code. Actual filenames may vary widely, especially for files maintained via syslog. The names listed in Table 11.1 are typical examples only.

The Freq column indicates our suggested cleanup frequency.

**Table 11.1  Log files on parade**

|  | File | Program | Where[a] | Freq[a] | Owner[a] | Contents |
|---|---|---|---|---|---|---|
| Vendor-supplied files | messages | various | S | M | R | Often the main system log file |
| | syslog | various | S | M | R | Often the main system log file |
| | shutdownlog | shutdown | S | M | R | Reasons for shutdown |
| | sulog | su | H | M | R | Root access via su |
| | authlog | su[b] | S | M | R | Authorizations |
| | mqueue/syslog | sendmail | F | W | R | Email handling log |
| | ftp.log | ftpd | S | W | R | FTP connection log |
| | gatedlog | gated | CS[c] | W | R | Network routing daemon log |
| Accounting files | acct | kernel | C | D | R | BSD process accounting (binary) |
| | pacct | kernel | C | D | R | SysV process accounting (binary) |
| | wtmp[d] | login | H | M | R | Connect-time accounting (binary) |
| | lpacct | lpd | F | M | D | BSD printer accounting |
| | lpd-errs | lpd | F | W | D | BSD printer errors |
| | aculog | tip, uucp | H | M | U | Dial-out accounting |
| | fd2log | runacct | F | M | R | System V accounting errors |
| Extras | news/news | innd | H | D | N | News transactions and errors |
| | news/*log | nnrpd | S | W | N | News readers' activity |
| | majordomo.log | Majordomo | F | M | R | Mailing list manager log |
| | sudo.log | sudo | S | M | R | Log of root access via sudo |
| | tcp.log | tcpd | S | W | R | TCP connections |
| | X0msgs | X11 | H | M | R | X Windows server log |
| | xdm-errors | xdm | F | M | R | X Windows display manager errors |
| | httpd/*_log | httpd | F | W | R | Web server logs |

a. Where:  S = Syslog, H = Hardwired, F = Configuration file, C = Command line
   Freq:    D = Daily, W = Weekly, M = Monthly
   Owner:  R = root/system, U = uucp/daemon, N = news/news, D = daemon/daemon

b. **passwd**, **login**, and **shutdown** also write to the authorization log.

c. Specified on the command line in version 2.1; later versions use syslog.

d. Sometimes also maintained in a revised format as **wtmpx**.

Log files usually have mode 644. Some sites reduce permissions to 640 or to 600; never give write permission to anyone but the owner. **sulog**, **authlog**, and **sudo.log** should have mode 600. **mqueue/syslog** and **pacct** are also good candidates for restrictive permissions.

## 11.3  FILES **NOT** TO MANAGE

You might be tempted to manage all log files with a rotation and archiving scheme. But there are two files that you should not touch: **/var/adm/lastlog** and **/etc/utmp**.

*See the footnote on page 176 for more info about sparse files.*

**lastlog** records each user's last login and is a sparse file indexed by UID. It stays smaller if your UIDs are assigned in some kind of numeric sequence. Don't copy **lastlog** or it will really use all the disk space that **ls -l** reports.

**utmp** attempts to keep a record of each user that is currently logged in. It is sometimes wrong, usually because a user's shell was killed with an inappropriate signal and the parent of the shell did not clean up properly. **utmp** is often world-writable.

## 11.4  VENDOR SPECIFICS

Vendors seem to have hidden log files all over the disk. Careful detective work with your daemons' config files and your syslog configuration file will find many of them. This section details some of the more obscure nooks and crannies in which log files have been hidden.

 Solaris has the most disorganized collection of log files ever. With a directory called **/var/log** it shouldn't be so hard. A few pointers:

- **/var/log/***
- **/var/cron/log**
- **/var/lp/logs/***
- **/var/saf/_log**
- **/var/saf/zsmon/log**
- **/var/adm/{messages, aculog, sulog, vold.log, wtmpx}**
- **/var/adm/log/asppp.log**

*See page 291 for more information about PPP.* This last file is for the PPP protocol for dial-up network connections. Solaris 2.4 seemed to ship with logging to it turned on, even if you did not have the PPP software installed or in use. It filled with messages about the lack of connection paths.

You can run the vendor-supplied **/usr/lib/newsyslog** script out of **cron** to rotate the main log files, **/var/adm/messages** and **/var/log/syslog**.

 HP-UX log files are in **/var/adm**. There are a lot of odd little mystery files in this directory, many of which are not log files, so be careful what you touch. The file **nettl.LOG00** is a network control and statistics file; see **man nettl** for details. By default, all log entries submitted via syslog go into the **/var/adm/syslog** directory.

 Red Hat gets a gold star for logging sanity. Not only are logs clearly named and consistently stored in **/var/log**, but Red Hat also provides a superior tool, **logrotate**, for rotating, truncating, and managing them. New software packages can drop a configuration file into the **/etc/logrotate.d** directory to set up a management strategy for their logs. What are you trying to do, Red Hat, put us all out of a job?

 FreeBSD is another prize winner in the realm of logging. Log files are generally found in **/var/log**, although **cron**'s log is kept in **/var/cron** and accounting files are kept in **/var/account**. The **newsyslog** utility is responsible for managing and rotating logs. It runs out of **cron** and takes its marching orders from **/etc/newsyslog.conf**.

FreeBSD also runs the **periodic** command from **cron** on a daily, weekly, and monthly basis to execute scripts stored under **/etc/periodic**. Log maintenance can be done from these scripts if you find that **newsyslog** doesn't meet your needs.

## 11.5  SYSLOG: THE SYSTEM EVENT LOGGER

Syslog, originally written by Eric Allman, is a comprehensive logging system. Many vendors use syslog to manage the information generated by the kernel and the system utilities.

Syslog has two important functions: to liberate programmers from the tedious mechanics of writing log files and to put administrators in control of logging. Before syslog, every program was free to make up its own logging policy. System administrators had no control over what information was kept or where it was stored.

Syslog is quite flexible. It allows messages to be sorted by their source and importance ("severity level") and routed to a variety of destinations: log files, users' terminals, or even other machines. Syslog's ability to centralize the logging for a network is one of its most valuable features.

Syslog consists of three parts:

- **syslogd**, the logging daemon (along with its config file, **/etc/syslog.conf**)
- **openlog** et al., library routines that submit messages to **syslogd**
- **logger**, a user-level command that submits log entries from the shell

In the following discussion, we first cover the configuration of **syslogd** and then briefly show how to use syslog from Perl scripts.

**syslogd** is started at boot time and runs continuously. Programs that are syslog-aware write log entries (using the **syslog** library routine) to the special file **/dev/log** (or, on some systems, **/var/run/log**), which is either a UNIX domain socket, a named pipe, or a STREAMS module, depending on the system. **syslogd** reads messages from this file, consults its configuration file, and dispatches each message to the appropriate destinations. On many systems, **syslogd** also reads kernel messages from the device **/dev/klog**.

A hangup signal (HUP, signal 1) causes **syslogd** to close its log files, reread its configuration file, and start logging again. If you modify **/etc/syslog.conf**, you must send a hangup signal to **syslogd** to make your changes take effect. A TERM signal causes **syslogd** to exit.

**syslogd** writes its process ID to the file **/var/run/syslog.pid** (or **/etc/syslog.pid**, on a few systems). This convention makes it easy to send signals to **syslogd** from a script. For example, the following command sends a hangup signal:

```
# kill -HUP `/bin/cat /var/run/syslog.pid`
```

Trying to compress or rotate a log file that **syslogd** has open for writing is not healthy and has unpredictable results. Some vendors provide you with a skeletal script, often

**/usr/lib/newsyslog**, that purports to rotate log files.[2] A better one, **rotz**, is available from www.admin.com.

### Configuring syslogd

The configuration file **/etc/syslog.conf** controls **syslogd**'s behavior. It is a text file with a relatively simple format. Blank lines and lines with a pound sign (#) in column one are ignored. The basic format is:[3]

```
selector <Tab> action
```

For example, the line

```
mail.info        /var/log/maillog
```

would cause messages from the email system to be saved in the file **/var/log/maillog**. The *selector* and *action* fields *must* be separated by one or more tabs; spaces don't work (in most versions) and become invisible errors that are very hard to track down. Cutting and pasting with your window system is one way to introduce such errors.

Selectors identify the program ("facility") that is sending a log message and the message's severity level with the syntax

```
facility.level
```

Both facility names and severity levels must be chosen from a short list of defined values; programs can't make up their own. Facilities are defined for the kernel, for common groups of utilities, and for locally written programs. Everything else is classified under the generic facility "user".

Selectors can contain the special keywords * and none, meaning all or nothing, respectively. A selector can include multiple facilities separated with commas. Multiple selectors can also be combined with semicolons.

In general, selectors are ORed together; a message matching any selector will be subject to the line's *action*. However, a selector with a level of none excludes the listed facilities regardless of what other selectors on the same line may say.

Here are some examples of ways to format and combine selectors:

```
facility.level                      action
facility1,facility2.level           action
facility1.level1;facility2.level2   action
*.level                             action
*.level;badfacility.none            action
```

Table 11.2 on the next page lists the valid facility names (some rows have been shaded to improve readability). Most versions of syslog define 18 different facilities, but 21 are defined in the latest release. The extra slots are reserved for future use.

---

2. This embryonic **newsyslog** script is different from (and inferior to) the FreeBSD **newsyslog** utility.

3. Very old versions of syslog use a different syntax that we will not describe here.

**Table 11.2  Syslog facility names**

| Facility | Programs that use it |
|----------|----------------------|
| kern | The kernel |
| user | User processes (the default if not specified) |
| mail | **sendmail** and other mail-related software |
| daemon | System daemons |
| auth | Security and authorization-related commands |
| lpr | The BSD line printer spooling system |
| news | The Usenet news system |
| uucp | Reserved for UUCP, which doesn't use it |
| cron | The **cron** daemon |
| mark | Timestamps generated at regular intervals |
| local0-7 | Eight flavors of local message |
| syslog[a] | **syslogd** internal messages |
| authpriv[a] | Private authorization messages (should all be private, really) |
| ftp[a] | The FTP daemon, **ftpd** |
| * | All facilities except "mark" |

a. Newer facilities in version 8.1 from Berkeley.

**syslogd** itself produces time stamp messages, which are logged if the "mark" facility appears in **syslog.conf** to specify a destination for them. Timestamps can help you figure out that your machine crashed between 3:00 and 3:20 a.m., not just "sometime last night." This information can be a big help when you are debugging problems that seem to occur on a regular basis. For example, many sites have experienced mysterious crashes when the housekeeping staff plugged in vacuum cleaners late at night, tripping the circuit breakers.

If your system is quite busy, other log messages often provide adequate time stamp information. But in the wee hours of the morning, that is not always the case.

Syslog's severity levels are listed in order of descending importance in Table 11.3.

**Table 11.3  Syslog severity levels (descending severity)**

| Level | Approximate meaning |
|-------|---------------------|
| emerg | Panic situations |
| alert | Urgent situations |
| crit | Critical conditions |
| err | Other error conditions |
| warning | Warning messages |
| notice | Things that might merit investigation |
| info | Informational messages |
| debug | For debugging only |

The severity level of a message specifies its importance. In the **syslog.conf** file, levels indicate the *minimum* importance that a message must have in order to be logged. For example, a message from the mail system at level warning would match the selector mail.warning as well as the selectors mail.notice, mail.info, mail.debug, *.warning, *.notice, *.info, and *.debug. If **syslog.conf** specifies that mail.info messages be logged to a file, then mail.warning messages will go there also.

The *action* field tells what to do with a message. The options are listed in Table 11.4.

**Table 11.4     Syslog actions**

| Action | Meaning |
|---|---|
| *filename* | Writes the message to a file on the local machine |
| *@hostname* | Forwards the message to the **syslogd** on *hostname* |
| *@ipaddress* | Forwards the message to the host at IP address *ipaddress* |
| *user1,user2,...* | Writes the message to users' screens if they are logged in |
| * | Writes the message to all users logged in |

*See page 523 for more information about how hostnames are translated to IP addresses.*
If a *filename* action is used, the filename should be an absolute path. On most systems, the file must exist; **syslogd** will not create it. If a *hostname* is used rather than an IP address, it must be resolvable through a translation mechanism such as DNS or NIS.

Some versions of syslog use the **m4** macro preprocessor on the configuration file. Check your manual pages and use quotes liberally so that your configuration means what you intend. For example, you must quote anything that is an **m4** keyword or contains a comma. Here is a typical **m4**-style entry:

```
auth.notice              ifdef(`LOGHOST', `/var/log/authlog', `@loghost')
```

Note that the quotes used are the back-tick and the single apostrophe. This line directs messages to the file **/var/log/authlog** if LOGHOST is defined. Otherwise, messages are forwarded to the machine loghost. **m4**'s ifdef statements are very powerful; they allow sysadmins to create a single **syslog.conf** that can be used on all machines.

Although multiple facilities and levels are allowed in a selector, there is no provision for multiple actions. To send a message to two places (such as to a local file and to a central logging host), two lines with the same selectors can be included in the configuration file.

### Red Hat enhancements to syslog

Red Hat ships a version of **syslogd** with several enhancements. It allows log messages to be sent to named pipes as well as to files, and it also allows spaces as separators in **syslog.conf**, eliminating a common source of confusion.

In **syslog.conf**, the characters = and ! can be prefixed to priority levels to indicate "this priority only" and "except this priority and higher." Table 11.5 shows examples.

**Table 11.5   Examples of priority level qualifiers in Red Hat's syslog.conf**

| Selector | Meaning |
|---|---|
| mail.info | Selects mail-related messages of info prio. and higher |
| mail.=info | Selects only messages at info priority |
| mail.info;mail.!err | Selects only priorities info, notice, and warning |
| mail.debug;mail.!=warning | Selects all priorities except warning |

Red Hat's **syslogd** is especially cautious in its handling of the network. Unless started with the **-r** flag, it will refuse to accept messages from other machines at all. By default, Red Hat's **syslogd** also refuses to act as a third-party message forwarder; messages that arrive from one network host cannot be sent on to another. Use the **-h** flag to override this behavior. (If you want these options turned on all the time, add the flags to the **/etc/rc.d/init.d/syslog** script.)

Red Hat uses a separate process, **klogd**, to obtain messages from the kernel and inject them into the syslog message stream. While it's possible to tweak this process, it's rarely necessary or appropriate.

### FreeBSD enhancements to syslog

Like Red Hat, FreeBSD provides some extra ways to specify priority levels in the **syslog.conf** file. They are illustrated in Table 11.6.

**Table 11.6   Examples of priority level qualifiers in FreeBSD's syslog.conf**

| Selector | Meaning |
|---|---|
| mail.info | Selects mail-related messages of info priority and higher |
| mail.>=info | Same meaning as mail.info |
| mail.=info | Selects only messages at info priority |
| mail.<=info | Selects messages at info priority and below |
| mail.<info | Selects all priorities lower than info |
| mail.>info | Selects all priorities higher than info |

In a defiant gesture against syslog's classification scheme, FreeBSD allows you to select messages based on the name of the program from which they originate rather than just the generic and more nebulously defined facility name. Unfortunately, since **syslogd** doesn't actually know this information, it has to guess by checking messages to see if they look like they start with a program name and a colon. For example, **syslogd** would interpret the message

```
named: starting.  named 4.9.7 Sat Sep  2 09:39:12 GMT 1998 PHNE_14618
```

as having come from **named**. In the **syslog.conf** file, sections that should apply only to messages from a particular program are introduced by an exclamation mark and the program name.

For example, the lines

```
!named
*.*        /var/log/named.log
```

send all messages that look like they came from **named** to **/var/log/named.log**.

While it's useful to be able to route log messages based on their program of origin, this feature is a hack. The message formatting convention that it relies upon is not universally enforced or even universally followed.

FreeBSD's **syslogd** must be told which remote hosts to accept log messages from with the **-a** option. Sets of remote hosts can be specified as network numbers with masks (e.g., **-a 128.138.192.0/20**) or as domain names (e.g., **-a \*.cs.colorado.edu**). If you do not want to accept any messages from the network, you can prevent **syslogd** from even opening its network port with the **-ss** option.

You can put **syslogd**'s command-line arguments in **/etc/rc.conf** so that they'll be used automatically at boot time. For example:

```
syslogd_flags="-a 128.138.192.0/20 -a *.cs.colorado.edu"
```

## Config file examples

Below are three sample **syslog.conf** files that correspond to a stand alone machine on a small network, a client machine on a larger network, and a central logging host on the same large network. The central logging host is called "netloghost".[4]

*Stand-alone machine*

A basic configuration for a stand-alone machine is shown below:

```
# Small network or stand-alone syslog.conf file

# emergencies: tell everyone who is logged on
*.emerg                                    *
#  important messages
*.warning;daemon,auth.info,user.none /var/adm/messages
#  printer errors
lpr.debug                          /var/adm/lpd-errs
```

The first noncomment line writes emergency messages to the screens of all current users. An example of emergency-level messages are those generated by **shutdown** when the system is about to be turned off.

The second line writes important messages to **/var/adm/messages**. The info level is below warning, so the daemon,auth.info clause includes additional logging from **passwd**, **su**, and daemon programs. The third line writes printer error messages to **/var/adm/lpd-errs**.

---

4. More accurately, it uses "netloghost" as one of its hostname aliases. This allows the identity of the log host to be modified with little reconfiguration. An alias can be added in **/etc/hosts** or set up with a CNAME record in DNS. See page 445 for more information about DNS CNAME records.

### Network client

A network client typically forwards serious messages to a central logging machine:

```
# CS Department syslog.conf file for non-master machines

# Emergencies: tell everyone who is logged on
*.emerg;user.none                              *

# Forward important messages to the central logger
*.warning;lpr,local1.none              @netloghost
daemon,auth.info                       @netloghost

# Send local stuff to the central logger too
local2.info;local0,local7.debug        @netloghost

# cardd logs through facility local1 -- send to boulder
local1.debug                           @boulder.colorado.edu

# Keep printer errors local
lpr.debug                              /var/adm/lpd-errs

# sudo logs to local2 - keep a copy here
local2.info                            /var/adm/sudolog

# Keep kernel messages local
kern.info                              /var/adm/kern.log
```

This configuration does not keep much log information locally. It's worth mentioning that if netloghost is down or unreachable, log messages will be irretrievably lost. You may want to keep some additional local duplicates of important messages to guard against this possibility.

At a site with lots of local software installed, lots of messages can be logged inappropriately to facility user, level emerg. In this example, user/emerg has been specifically excluded with the user.none clause in the first line.

See page 41 for more information about **sudo**.

The second and third lines forward all important messages to the central logging host; messages from the printing system and the campus-wide card access system are explicitly excluded. The fourth line forwards local logging information to netloghost as well. The fifth line forwards card access logging information to the campus-wide logging host, boulder. The last two entries keep local copies of printer errors and **sudo** log messages.

### Central logging host

This example is for netloghost, the central, secure logging host for a moderate-sized network of 400 to 500 hosts.

```
# CS Department syslog.conf file, master logging host

# Emergencies to the console and log file, with timing marks
*.emerg                          /dev/console
*.err;kern,mark.debug;auth.notice    /dev/console
*.err;kern,mark.debug;user.none    /var/adm/console.log
```

```
auth.notice                              /var/adm/console.log

# Send non-emergency messages to the usual log files
*.err;user.none;kern.debug               /var/adm/messages
daemon,auth.notice;mail.crit             /var/adm/messages
lpr.debug                                /var/adm/lpd-errs
mail.debug                               /var/adm/mail.log

# Local authorization stuff like sudo and npasswd
local2.debug                             /var/adm/sudo.log
local2.alert                             /var/adm/sudo-errs.log
auth.info                                /var/adm/auth.log

# Other local stuff
local0.info                              /var/adm/netblazer.log
local4.notice                            /var/adm/da.log
local6.debug                             /var/adm/annex-isn.log
local7.debug                             /var/adm/tcp.log

# User stuff (the default if no facility is specified)
user.info                                /var/adm/user.log
```

Logging data arriving from local programs and from **syslogd**s on the network is written to files. In some cases, the output from each facility is put into its own file.

The central logging host generates the time stamp for each message as it writes the message out. The timestamps do not reflect the time on the originating host. If you have machines in several time zones or your system clocks are not synchronized, the timestamps can be somewhat misleading.

### Sample syslog output

Below is a snippet from one of the log files on the master syslog host at the University of Colorado's computer science department. About 200 hosts log to this machine.

```
Dec 18 15:12:42 av18.cs.colorado.edu sbatchd[495]: sbatchd/main: ls_info()
    failed: LIM is down; try later; trying ...
Dec 18 15:14:28 proxy-1.cs.colorado.edu pop-proxy[27283]: Connection from
    128.138.198.84
Dec 18 15:14:30 mroe.cs.colorado.edu pingem[271]: maltese-
    office.cs.colorado.edu has not answered 42 times
Dec 18 15:15:05 schwarz.cs.colorado.edu vmunix: Multiple softerrors: Seen 100
    Corrected Softerrors from SIMM J0201
Dec 18 15:15:05 schwarz.cs.colorado.edu vmunix: AFSR = 0x4c21, AFAR0 =
    0x87ffdd30, AFAR1 = 0xb8f8a0
Dec 18 15:15:48 proxy-1.cs.colorado.edu pop-proxy[27285]: Connection from
    12.2.209.183
Dec 18 15:15:50 av18.cs.colorado.edu last message repeated 100 times
```

This example contains entries from several different hosts (av18, proxy-1, mroe, schwarz, and stall) and from several programs: **sbatchd**, **pop-proxy**, **pingem**, and the kernel (**vmunix**).

Syslog / Log Files

Note the last line of the excerpt, which complains of a message being repeated 100 times. To help keep the logs shorter, syslog generally attempts to coalesce duplicate messages and replace them with this type of summary. However, the machine from which this example was drawn accepts log entries from many other hosts, so this particular message is a bit misleading, It actually refers to the previous log entry from av18, not the entry immediately preceding it in the composite log.

It's a good idea to peruse your log files regularly. Determine what is normal so that when an anomaly occurs, you can recognize it. Better yet, set up a log postprocessor such as **swatch** to trap these cases automatically; see *Condensing log files to useful information* on page 222.

### Designing a logging scheme for your site

At a small site it is adequate to configure logging so that important system errors and warnings are kept in a file on each machine, much as was done before we had syslog. The **syslog.conf** file can be customized for each host.

On a large network, central logging is essential. It keeps the flood of information manageable and, with luck, makes auditing data unavailable to a person who violates the security of a machine on the network. Hackers often edit system logs to cover their tracks; if log information is whisked away as soon as it is generated, it is much harder to destroy. But be aware that anyone can call **syslog** and fake log entries from any daemon or utility. Syslog also uses the UDP protocol, which is not guaranteed to be reliable; messages can get lost. Your firewall should not allow external sites to submit messages to your **syslogd**.

*See Chapter 18 for more information about distributing files on a network.*

Choose a stable machine as your logging server, preferably one that is well secured and does not have many logins. Other machines can use a generic configuration file that is maintained in a central place. Thus, only two versions of the **syslog.conf** file need be maintained.[5] This approach allows logging to be complete but at the same time is not a nightmare to administer.

Some very large sites may want to add more levels to the logging hierarchy. Unfortunately the current version of syslog retains the name of the originating host for only one hop. If host "client" sends some log entries to host "server," which sends them on to host "master," master will see the data as coming from server, not from client.

### Software that uses syslog

Table 11.7 lists some of the programs that use syslog, the facilities and levels they log to, and a brief description of each program. Some rows have been shaded to improve readability.

With all this information, it should be perfectly clear which messages to keep and which to discard, right? Well, maybe not. In practice, you just have to learn what the useful logging levels are for your system. It's best to start with an excessive amount

---

5. On machines that preprocess the **syslog.conf** file with **m4**, you can even integrate these two configurations into a single file.

**Table 11.7    Software that uses syslog**

| Program | Facility | Levels | Description |
|---|---|---|---|
| amd | daemon | err-info | NFS automounter |
| date | auth | notice | Sets the time and date |
| ftpd | daemon | err-debug | FTP daemon |
| gated | daemon | alert-info | Routing daemon |
| halt/reboot | auth | crit | Shutdown programs |
| inetd | daemon | err, warning | Internet super-daemon |
| login/rlogind | auth | crit-info | Login programs |
| lpd | lpr | err-info | BSD line printer daemon |
| named | daemon | err-info | Name server (DNS) |
| nnrpd | news | crit-notice | INN news readers |
| ntpd | daemon, user | crit-info | Network time daemon |
| passwd | auth | err | Password-setting program |
| popper | local0 | notice, debug | Mac/PC mail system |
| sendmail | mail | alert-debug | Mail transport system |
| su | auth | crit, notice | Switches UIDs |
| sudo | local2 | alert, notice | Limited **su** program |
| syslogd | syslog, mark | err-info | Internal errors, timestamps |
| tcpd | local7 | err-debug | TCP wrapper for **inetd** |
| cron | cron, daemon | info | System task-scheduling daemon |
| vmunix | kern | *varies* | The kernel |

of logging and gradually winnow out the cases that you don't want. Stop winnowing when you feel comfortable with the average data rate.

### Debugging syslog

The **logger** command is useful for submitting log entries from shell scripts. You can also use it to test changes in **syslogd**'s configuration file. For example, if you have just added the line

```
local5.warning          /tmp/evi.log
```

and want to verify that it is working, run

```
% logger -p local5.warning "test message"
```

A line containing "test message" should be written to **/tmp/evi.log**. If this doesn't happen, perhaps you forgot to create the **evi.log** file, to give the file appropriate permissions, or to send **syslogd** a hangup signal.

Early versions of **syslogd** have a fixed constant, NLOGS, that determines the total number of actions that can be specified in the configuration file. It is usually set to 20. If you exceed this number, **syslogd** ignores the extra actions and quietly throws away the log messages that would have been sent to them.

Later versions of **syslogd** replace the fixed table with a linked list but still include another constant, MAXUNAMES (also 20), that limits the number of users who can be the destination of a message.

When invoked with the **-d** (debug) flag, **syslogd** displays a table of the facilities, levels, and actions specified in the **syslog.conf** file. Each incoming message is also echoed to the screen along with information about how it is being processed. Here are a few rows from such a table:

```
0 0 0 0 0 0 0 0 0 0 0 0 0 0 0 0 0 0 0 0 X WALL:
7 X 4 6 6 4 4 4 4 4 4 4 4 4 4 4 4 4 4 4 X FILE: /adm/msgs
X X X X X 7 X X X X X X X X X X X X X X X FILE: /adm/lperr
0 0 0 0 0 0 0 0 0 0 0 0 0 0 0 0 0 0 0 0 0 UNUSED:
0 0 0 0 0 0 0 0 0 0 0 0 0 0 0 0 0 0 0 0 0 UNUSED:
```

In this table, columns correspond to facilities and rows to actions. The values displayed are the priority levels as represented internally; an X means none.

If there are lines in the table that have the tag UNUSED and no action, you still have fewer than NLOGS destinations. If you don't see any such lines, make sure you have not exceeded the limit; check your configuration file by probing the last entry in your **syslog.conf** file with **logger**. Lines with both UNUSED and a filename mean that you have forgotten to create the log file.

Be careful about logging to the console device, **/dev/console**. If the console is an old VT100 terminal and someone has inadvertently typed <Control-S> on it, output to the console will stop. Each call to **syslog** will block, and your system will slow to a crawl. A good way to check for this degenerate condition is to send a syslog message to the console via **logger**. If **logger** hangs, you need to find the offending console, type a <Control-Q>, and rethink your logging strategy.

Another drawback to logging on the console is that the flood of messages sparked by a major problem can make the console unusable at precisely the moment that it is most needed. Depending on how your console is set up and managed (e.g., through a console server), console logging may also have some security implications.

### Using syslog from programs

The library routines **openlog**, **syslog**, and **closelog** allow programs to use the syslog system. Versions of these library routines are available for both C and Perl; we will describe only the Perl interface here. To import the definitions of the library routines, include the line

```
use Sys::Syslog;
```

at the beginning of your Perl script.

The **openlog** routine initializes logging, using the specified facility name:

```
openlog(ident, logopt, facility);
```

Messages are logged with the options specified by *logopt* and begin with the identification string *ident*. If **openlog** is not used, *ident* defaults to the current username, *logopt* to an empty string, and *facility* to "user". The *logopt* string should contain a comma-separated list of the options shown in Table 11.8.

**Table 11.8    Logging options for the openlog routine**

| Option | Meaning |
| --- | --- |
| pid | Include the current process's PID in each log message. |
| ndelay | Connect to **syslogd** immediately (don't wait until a message is submitted). |
| cons | Send messages to the system console if **syslogd** is unreachable. |
| nowait | Do not **wait**(3) for child processes forked to write console messages. |

For example, a reasonable invocation of **openlog** might be

```
openlog("adminscript", "pid,cons", "daemon");
```

The **syslog** routine sends a *message* to **syslogd**, which logs it at the specified *priority*:

```
syslog(priority, message, ...);
```

The date, time, hostname, and *ident* string from the **openlog** call are prepended to the message in the log file. *message* may be followed by various other parameters to form a **printf**-style output specification that can include text and the contents of other variables; for example,

```
syslog("info", "Delivery to '%s' failed after %d attempts.", $user, $nAttempts);
```

The special symbol %m expands to an error message derived from the current value of **errno** (the most recent UNIX error code).

A priority string of the form "*level|facility*" sets both the severity level and the facility name. If you did not call **openlog** and specify an *ident* string, the **syslog** routine also checks to see if your *message* has the form of a standard UNIX error message such as

```
adminscript: User "nobody" not found in /etc/passwd file.
```

If it does, the part before the colon is secretly adopted as your *ident* string. These helpful (but undocumented) features make it unnecessary to call **openlog** at all; however, it is still a good idea. It's better to specify the facility name in one place (the **openlog** call) than to repeat it throughout your code.

The **closelog** routine closes the logging channel:

```
closelog();
```

You must call this routine if you want to reopen the logging channel with different options. It's also good form to call **closelog** when your program exits.

Here's a complete example:

```
use Sys::Syslog;

openlog("adminscript", "cons,pid", "user");
syslog("warning","Those whom the gods would destroy, they first teach Basic.");
closelog();
```

This scriptlet produces the log entry:

```
Dec 28 22:56:24 moet.colorado.edu adminscript[191]: Those whom the gods
    would destroy, they first teach Basic.
```

## 11.6  CONDENSING LOG FILES TO USEFUL INFORMATION

Syslog is great for sorting and routing log messages, but when all is said and done, its end product is still a bunch of log files. While they may contain all kinds of useful information, those files aren't going to come and find you when something goes wrong. Another layer of software is needed to analyze the logs and make sure that important messages don't get lost amid the chatter.

A variety of free tools are available to fill this niche, and most of them are pretty similar: they scan recent log entries, match them against a database of regular expressions, and process the important messages in some attention-getting way. Some tools mail you a report; others can be configured to make noise, print log entries in different colors, or page you. Tools differ primarily in their degree of flexibility and in the size of their off-the-shelf database of patterns.

Two of the more commonly used log postprocessors are Todd Atkins' **swatch** and Craig Rowland's **logcheck. swatch** is available from

> ftp://ftp.stanford.edu/general/security-tools/swatch/

and **logcheck** from

> http://www.psionic.com/abacus/logcheck/

**swatch** is a Perl script that gets its marching orders from a configuration file. The configuration syntax is fairly flexible, and it also provides access to the full pattern-matching mojo of Perl. While **swatch** can process an entire file in a single bound, it's primarily intended to be left running so that it can review new messages as they arrive, a la **tail -f**. A disadvantage of **swatch** is that you must build your own configuration pretty much from scratch; it doesn't know about specific systems and the actual log messages they might generate.

**logcheck** is a more basic script written in **sh**; the distribution also includes a C program that **logcheck** uses to help it record its place within a log file. Since **logcheck** knows how far it has read in a log file, there is perhaps less chance of a message slipping by at startup or shutdown time; in addition, **logcheck** can run at intervals from **cron** rather than running continuously.

**logcheck** comes with sample databases for several different versions of UNIX. Even if you don't want to use the actual script, it's worth looking over the patterns to see if there are any you might want to steal for your own use.

Both of these tools have the disadvantage of working on only a single log file at a time. If your syslog configuration sorts messages into many different files, you might want to duplicate some of the messages into a central file that is frequently truncated, then use that summary file to feed a postprocessing script. That's easier than setting up a complicated network of scripts to handle multiple files.

No matter what system you use to scan log files, there are a couple of things you should be sure to look for and immediately bring to the attention of an administrator:

- Most security-related messages should receive a prompt review. It's often helpful to monitor failed login, **su**, and **sudo** attempts in order to catch potential break-ins before they happen. If someone has just forgotten his password (as is usually the case), a prompt and proactive offer of help will make a good impression and cement your reputation for clairvoyance.

- Messages about disks that have filled up should be flagged and acted on immediately. Full disks often bring all useful work to a standstill.

- Messages that are repeated many times deserve attention, if only in the name of hygiene.

# *12* *Drivers and the Kernel*

A UNIX system encompasses essentially three layers of abstraction:

- The hardware
- The operating system kernel
- The user-level programs

The kernel hides the system's hardware underneath an abstract, high-level programming interface. It is responsible for implementing many of the facilities that users and user-level programs take for granted. For example, the kernel assembles all of the following UNIX concepts from lower-level hardware features:

- Processes (time sharing, protected address spaces)
- Signals and semaphores
- Virtual memory (swapping, paging, mapping)
- The filesystem (files, directories, namespace)
- Interprocess communication (pipes and network connections)

The kernel contains device drivers that manage its interaction with specific pieces of hardware; the rest of the kernel is, to a large degree, device independent. The relationship between the kernel and its device drivers is similar to the relationship between user-level processes and the kernel. When a process asks the kernel to "Read the first 64 bytes of **/etc/passwd**," the kernel might translate this request into a device driver instruction such as "Fetch block 3,348 from device 3." The driver would further break this command down into sequences of bit patterns to be presented to the device's control registers.

The kernel is written mostly in C, with a little assembly language for low-level processing. Many years ago, a compiled UNIX kernel was quite modest in size, usually well under half a megabyte. Today, with fancy networking, network file systems, multithreading, and inexpensive memory, kernel sizes range from 400K to over 15MB.

## 12.1 KERNEL TYPES

All systems allow you to provide the kernel with explicit information about the hardware it should expect to find on your system (or pretend not to find, as the case may be). Some kernels can also prospect for devices on their own.

Solaris uses an almost completely modular kernel, and it can load device drivers as they are needed. You do not need to tell Solaris ahead of time what hardware is on the system, thanks largely to Sun's well-defined (compared with a PC), proprietary hardware architecture. When Solaris finds a new device connected to the system, it looks for and loads a corresponding driver module. Surprisingly, this scheme actually works fairly well most of the time.

Like Solaris, HP-UX supports a relatively small and well-defined hardware base. It can usually determine what's on your system without much hand-holding from you.

In general, FreeBSD and other BSD-derived systems must be told explicitly at kernel compilation time what devices might be found on the system. In some cases, you must also specify exactly where on the system you expect the kernel to find the devices. This requirement is often troublesome if you aren't sure exactly what hardware your system contains. PC manufacturers usually don't give you much technical information, so you must often take your system apart and visually inspect the pieces to answer questions such as, "What chipset does my Ethernet card use?"

Linux is a bit of a cross between Solaris and BSD. Like FreeBSD, Linux is crippled by the PC environment, in which it's difficult to take an accurate inventory of the system's hardware. You can configure a Linux kernel just as you configure a FreeBSD kernel, telling it all about your hardware beforehand and making one giant kernel. Or, you can configure Linux to behave more like Solaris and load most of its drivers only when needed. Linux's module support is limited compared to Solaris, but many of its limitations have been dictated by the restrictions of PC hardware.

Table 12.1 shows the location of the kernel build directory and the standard name of the installed kernel on each of our example systems.

**Table 12.1    Kernel build directory and location by system**

| System | Build directory | Kernel |
|--------|-----------------|--------|
| Solaris | – | **/kernel/unix** |
| HP-UX | **/stand** | **/stand/vmunix** |
| Linux | **/usr/src/linux** | **/vmlinuz** or **/boot/vmlinuz** |
| FreeBSD | **/usr/src/sys** | **/kernel** |

Drivers / Kernel

## 12.2  WHY CONFIGURE THE KERNEL?

When the system is installed, it comes with a generic kernel that's designed to run on most any hardware. The generic kernel includes many different device drivers and option packages. Since the kernel only needs to run on your particular system, it's a good idea to reconfigure it to get rid of the modules you won't be using and to turn off options that don't interest you.

Building a kernel tailored to the system is a good habit to get into. Your well-tuned configuration, once attained, can serve as a reference guide for the system's hardware. Although unused features and drivers might not interfere directly with the operation of the system, they can still consume memory.

Modern kernels are better than their predecessors at flushing unwanted drivers from memory, but compiled-in options will always be turned on. Although reconfiguring the kernel for efficiency reasons is less important than it used to be, a good case can still be made for doing so.

*Instructions for adding a new driver start on page 246.*

Another reason to reconfigure the kernel is to add support for new types of devices (i.e., to add new device drivers). The driver code can't just be mooshed onto the kernel like a gob of Play-Doh; it has to be integrated into the kernel's data structures and tables. On some systems, this procedure may require that you go back to the configuration files for the kernel and add in the new device, rebuilding the kernel from scratch. On other systems, you may only need to run a program designed to make these configuration changes for you.

Some systems include the concept of a "loadable" device driver, in most cases implying that new code can be loaded into the kernel while it is running. A good human analogy might be having brain surgery while operating heavy machinery.

Building a kernel is not difficult; it's just difficult to fix when you break it.

## 12.3  CONFIGURING A SOLARIS KERNEL

At boot time, the Solaris kernel probes the machine for devices and initializes a driver for each device it finds. It makes extensive use of loadable modules and loads code only for the devices that are actually present, unless forced to do otherwise.

Depending on your point of view, this automatic configuration makes configuring a custom kernel more or less of a necessity under Solaris than on other systems. In an ideal world, the kernel would correctly identify its hardware environment 100% of the time. Unfortunately, flaky, nonstandard, or just plain buggy hardware (or Solaris drivers) can turn this creature comfort into a torment.

That said, let's look at how to custom-configure a Solaris kernel, should you ever need to do so.

### The Solaris kernel area

To make on-demand module loading work correctly, Solaris relies heavily on a particular directory organization. Solaris expects to find certain directories in certain places, and these directories must contain specific types of modules:

- **/kernel** – modules common to machines that share an instruction set

- **/platform/**platform-name**/kernel** – modules specific to one type of machine, such as an Ultra Enterprise

- **/platform/**hardware-class-name**/kernel** – modules specific to one class of hardware; for example, all sun4u machines

- **/usr/kernel** – similar to **/kernel**

You can determine your platform-name and hardware-class-name with **uname -i** and **uname -m**, respectively. Here's an example:

```
% uname -i
SUNW,Ultra-Enterprise
% uname -m
sun4u
```

When Solaris boots, it searches the path

**/platform/**platform-name**/kernel:/kernel:/usr/kernel**

in an attempt to find a kernel. It first looks for files named **unix**, and then it looks for files named **genunix**. **genunix** is a generic kernel that represents the platform-independent portion of the base kernel.

Each of the directories listed above can contain several standard subdirectories, listed in Table 12.2. Since the subdirectories can exist within any of the kernel directories, we use the generic name **KERNEL** to symbolize any and all kernel directories.

**Table 12.2   Subdirectories of Solaris kernel directories**

| Subdir | What it contains |
|--------|------------------|
| **drv** | Loadable object files for device drivers |
| | Configuration files listing probe addresses for each device |
| **misc** | Loadable object files for miscellaneous kernel routines |
| **cpu** | CPU-specific module for the UltraSPARC |
| **strmod** | STREAMS modules |
| **sparcv9** | The 64-bit kernel |
| **fs** | Filesystem-related kernel modules |
| **exec** | Modules for decoding executable file formats |
| **sched** | Operating system schedulers |
| **sys** | Loadable system calls |
| **genunix** | Generic platform-independent kernel |
| **unix** | The base platform-specific kernel |

Drivers / Kernel

You should not normally have to change any files in these directories unless you install a new device driver. The one exception to this rule may be the **.conf** files in the **KERNEL/drv** directory, which specify device-specific configuration parameters. It's rarely necessary to change them, however, and you should really only do it if a device's manufacturer tells you to.

### Configuring the kernel with /etc/system

Solaris's **/etc/system** file serves as the master configuration file for the kernel. Table 12.3 shows the directives and variables that can appear in this file. Directives are keywords in their own right; variables must be assigned a value with the set directive.

**Table 12.3   Directives and variables used in /etc/system**

| Name | Type[a] | Meaning |
|------|------|---------|
| rootfs | D | Specifies the filesystem type of the root partition |
| rootdev | D | Specifies the location of the root partition |
| forceload | D | Specifies drivers ("modules") that should be loaded |
| exclude | D | Specifies modules that should NOT be loaded |
| moddir | D | Specifies a new path to modules |
| set | D | Sets kernel tuning variables (such as maxusers) |
| maxusers | V | Controls table sizes and various other parameters |
| pt_cnt | V | Sets the number of available PTYs |
| max_nproc | V | Sets the maximum number of processes |
| maxuprc | V | Sets the maximum number of user processes |

a. D = directive, V = variable

**/etc/system** is consulted at boot time and can be so badly mutilated that the system no longer boots. **boot -a** lets you specify the path to a backup copy of **/etc/system** if you made one (if you don't have a backup copy and your existing one doesn't work, you can use **/dev/null**).

### An example /etc/system file

Let's look at a sample **/etc/system** file for a simple kernel.

```
rootfs:ufs
rootdev:/sbus@1,f8000000/esp@0,800000/sd@3,0:a
```

These lines specify that the root filesystem will be of type UFS (Unix File System) and that it will reside on the sd3a disk partition. The syntax used to specify the root device is identical to that used by Sun's **openprom** monitor. It varies from platform to platform, so consult your hardware manual or follow the symlinks in **/dev** that map the weird names to sensible ones. An **ls -l** after following the link will show the exact long name.

```
moddir: /platform/SUNW,Ultra-Enterprise/kernel:/platform/sun4u/kernel:
    /kernel:/usr/kernel
```

This line (which has been wrapped to fit the page) specifies the search path for loadable modules. This value is suggested by the **kernel** man page; however, it is not the default, so you must specify it explicitly.

```
exclude: sys/shmsys
forceload: drv/superplotter
```

The first line excludes the shared memory system from the kernel, making it slightly leaner. (This is actually a bad idea in the general case. Things will break.) The second line forces the "superplotter" driver to be loaded.

```
set maxusers=64
```

This line sizes the kernel's tables appropriately for 64 simultaneous logins.

### Debugging a Solaris configuration

Since Solaris makes up its view of the world on the fly, debugging a troubled machine can be frustrating. Fortunately, Solaris provides several tools that display the machine's current configuration.

The **prtconf** command prints the machine's general configuration, including its machine type, model number, amount of memory, and some information about the configured hardware devices. Lines that describe devices (drivers, really) are indented to show the dependencies among them.

**sysdef** is **prtconf** on steroids. In addition to the information given by **prtconf**, it also lists pseudo-device drivers, tunable kernel parameters, and the filenames of loaded modules. If you modify the default kernel for an important machine, be sure to add a copy of the output of **sysdef** to your documentation for the machine.

The **modinfo** command reports information about dynamically loaded modules. Solaris dynamically loads device drivers, STREAMS modules, and filesystem drivers, among other things. Don't be surprised if **modinfo**'s output contains upwards of fifty entries. See page 253 for more information about **modinfo**.

## 12.4  BUILDING AN HP-UX KERNEL

HP-UX takes the older approach of building all of its drivers into one monolithic kernel. It also has a complex and confusing configuration file. However, HP-UX's SAM administration tool provides a way to bypass all the nasty configuration files.

You should definitely use SAM the first few times you build an HP-UX kernel. The interface is straightforward: just click and build. One major drawback of building your kernel this way is that when you click "Process new kernel," you must be prepared to reboot with the new kernel right then and there.

Drivers / Kernel

In this section we discuss building an HP-UX kernel by hand, since this procedure is generally undocumented by HP and is less obvious than using SAM. Building a kernel by hand gives you more control. You can configure the kernel, build it, and wait until the time is right to boot it. Also, you don't need to have an X display or waste time clicking and dragging when the alternative is to type a couple commands.

The HP-UX kernel is configured in the file **/stand/system**. You should copy this file to a different name; we'll use **system.example**. The **system** file is normally generated by SAM, so it is cryptic and uncommented. The only way to find out what all the bizarre commands and variables mean is to use SAM. Fortunately, you can load SAM and print out a copy of the configuration parameters screen. This procedure gives you a reference list of the names of configurable variables, a one-sentence description of their meanings, and their default values. We suggest keeping a copy around for reference.

Our **system.example** file is just a list of drivers, subsystems, and variables to be built into the kernel. In the file, devices are generally listed first, followed by subsystems. Variables and their values are listed last.

```
GSCtoPCI
asio0
c730
sdisk
sctl
cdfs
nfs_core
...
STRMSGSZ 65535
dump lvol
nstrpty 60
```

As you can see, deciphering this list can be difficult without the decoding guide from SAM. If a variable is set to the default value, it is left out of the configuration file. Table 12.4 lists some of the more frequently used variables and their default values.

**Table 12.4   Useful variables from the HP-UX system file**

| Variable | Default | Meaning |
|----------|---------|---------|
| maxfiles_lim | 1024 | Hard limit on open files per process |
| maxusers | 60 | Maximum number of simultaneous users |
| maxuprc | 75 | Maximum number of user processes |
| nproc | 276 | Maximum number of processes |
| nfile | 910 | Maximum number of open files |
| nflocks | 200 | Maximum number of file locks |
| ninode | 476 | Maximum number of open inodes |
| npty | 60 | Maximum number of PTYs |
| nstrtel | 60 | Maximum number of **telnet** session devices |
| nkthread | 499 | Maximum number of kernel threads |

Once you have built the **system.example** file, all that remains is to build the kernel with **mk_kernel**. By default, **mk_kernel** builds the kernel (using **/stand/system**) and puts it in **/stand/vmunix.test**. Use the **-s** flag to point **mk_kernel** at a different configuration file, and the **-o** flag to request a different target kernel name. For our example kernel, we'd use the following command:

```
# mk_kernel -s /stand/system.example -o /stand/vmunix.example
```

At this point, you can reboot any time you wish. If you want the new kernel to be booted automatically, copy your old **/stand/vmunix** somewhere else and put the new kernel in its place.

## 12.5  CONFIGURING A LINUX KERNEL

Linux kernel configuration has come a long way, but it still feels very primitive compared to most other systems. The process revolves around the **/usr/src/linux/.config** file. All of the kernel configuration information is specified in this file, but its format is pretty cryptic. To save folks from having to mess with the **.config** file, Linux has several **make** targets that let you configure the kernel with different interfaces.

If you are running X Windows, the prettiest configuration interface is provided by **make xconfig**. This command brings up a graphical configuration screen from which you can pick the devices you want added to your kernel (or compiled as a loadable module).

If you are not running X, you can use a **curses**-based[1] alternative invoked with **make menuconfig**. Finally, there is the older style **make config**, which prompts you to respond to every single configuration option available without letting you later go back and change your mind.

We recommend **make xconfig** if you are running X and **make menuconfig** if you aren't. Avoid **make config**.

These tools are straightforward as far as the options you can turn on, but unfortunately they are painful to use if you want to maintain several versions of the kernel for multiple architectures or hardware configurations.

The various configuration interfaces described above all generate a **.config** file that looks something like this:

```
# Automatically generated make config: don't edit
#
# Code maturity level options
#
CONFIG_EXPERIMENTAL=y
#
# Processor type and features
#
```

---

1. **curses** is a library used to create text-based GUIs that run in a terminal window.

```
# CONFIG_M386 is not set
# CONFIG_M486 is not set
# CONFIG_M586 is not set
# CONFIG_M586TSC is not set
CONFIG_M686=y
CONFIG_X86_WP_WORKS_OK=y
CONFIG_X86_INVLPG=y
CONFIG_X86_BSWAP=y
CONFIG_X86_POPAD_OK=y
CONFIG_X86_TSC=y
CONFIG_X86_GOOD_APIC=y
...
```

As you can see, the contents are rather cryptic and provide no descriptions of what the CONFIG tags mean. Sometimes you can figure out the meaning. Basically, each CONFIG line refers to a specific kernel configuration option. The value y compiles the option into the kernel; m enables it, but as a module.

Some things can be configured as modules and some can't. You just have to know which is which; it's not clear from the **.config** file. There is also no easy mapping of the CONFIG tags to meaningful information. However, you can usually extract this information from the **Config.in** file located in each driver directory. The **Config.in** files are difficult and inconvenient to track down, so it's best to just use **make xconfig** or **make menuconfig**.

Once you have a working, running kernel, you may need to pass special configuration options to it at boot time, such as the root device it should use or an instruction to probe for multiple Ethernet cards. LILO, the Linux boot loader, passes in these options. You add static configuration options to the **/etc/lilo.conf** file by using the append keyword; see page 18 for more information.

If it's not possible to edit the **lilo.conf** file (perhaps you broke something and the machine can't boot), you can pass the options in when LILO first loads. For example, at the LILO boot prompt, you could type

LILO: **linux root=/dev/hda1 ether=0,0,eth0 ether=0,0,eth1**

to tell LILO to load the kernel specified by the "linux" tag, to use the root device **/dev/hda1**, and to probe for two Ethernet cards.

### Building the Linux kernel binary

Setting up an appropriate **.config** file is the most important part of the Linux kernel configuration process, but you must jump through several more hoops to turn that file into a finished kernel. Here's an outline of the entire process:

- **cd** to **/usr/src/linux**.
- Run **make xconfig** or **make menuconfig**, depending on your preference.
- Run **make dep**.
- Run **make clean**.
- Run **make bzImage**.

- Run **make modules**.
- Run **make modules_install**.
- Copy **/usr/src/linux/arch/i386/boot/bzImage** to **/boot/vmlinuz**.
- Edit **/etc/lilo.conf** and add a configuration for the new kernel.
- Run **/sbin/lilo** to install the reconfigured boot loader.

The **make clean** step is not always strictly necessary, but it is generally a good idea to start with a clean build environment. In practice, many problems can be traced back to skipping this step.

### Tuning your Linux configuration

Unfortunately, the **.config** file does not provide a mechanism for tuning kernel parameters. However, Linux does provide an extensive kernel-to-userland interface through files in the **/proc** filesystem.

Several files and directories in **/proc** let you view and set kernel options at run time. These files mimic standard UNIX files, but they are really back doors into the kernel. If one of these files has a value you would like to change, you can try writing to it. Not all of the files can be written to (regardless of their apparent permissions), and no documentation tells you which ones can or cannot be written. (Hmm, do you see a theme developing here?)

For example, to change the maximum number of open files a process can have, try

```
# echo 32768 >> /proc/sys/fs/file-max
```

Once you get used to this unorthodox interface, you'll find it quite useful, especially for changing configuration options. A word of caution, however: changes are not remembered across reboots. If you want to make permanent changes, you must add **echo** commands to your startup scripts. Table 12.5 lists some useful options.

**Table 12.5    Files in /proc for commonly tuned kernel parameters**

| Dir[a] | File | Default | Function |
|---|---|---|---|
| F | **file-max** | 4096 | Sets max # of open files per process |
| F | **inode-max** | 16384 | Sets max # of open inodes per process |
| N | **ip_forward** | 0 | Allows IP forwarding when set to 1 |
| N | **icmp_echo_ignore_all** | 0 | Ignores ICMP pings when set to 1 |
| N | **icmp_echo_ignore_broadcasts** | 0 | Ignores broadcast pings when set to 1 |

a. F = **/proc/sys/fs**, N = **/proc/sys/net/ipv4**

## 12.6  BUILDING A FREEBSD KERNEL

Although the examples in this section are specifically from a FreeBSD machine, configuration for NetBSD, OpenBSD, and BSD/OS is similar.

Drivers / Kernel

BSD kernels each have a name that is used throughout the configuration process. The kernel name can be anything you like, but it should be descriptive of the system or systems on which the kernel is to run. If the kernel is being built for one particular machine, that machine's hostname makes a good kernel name.

To build a FreeBSD kernel, you first create a configuration file that lists that parameters of the new kernel. You then run the **config** command to build a kernel compilation directory as specified in your config file. The name you give the configuration file becomes the name of the compilation directory and ultimately of the kernel.

The files needed to build a BSD kernel reside in **/usr/src/sys**, which is usually symbolically linked to **/sys**. In the following discussion, we use the uppercase name **SYS** to refer to this directory, just to emphasize that it doesn't really matter where it's located. If you cannot find the kernel configuration directory for your machine, consult your manuals.

Here is an **ls -F** of the **SYS** directory for FreeBSD:

```
# ls -F
Makefile    ddb/       libkern/    netinet/    pccard/
alpha/      dev/       miscfs/     netipx/     pci/
boot/       gnu/       modules/    netkey/     posix4/
cam/        i386/      msdosfs/    netnatm/    sys/
coda/       i4b/       net/        netns/      ufs/
compile/    isa/       netatalk/   nfs/        vm/
conf/       isofs/     netatm/     ntfs/
contrib/    kern/      netgraph/   pc98/
```

The **i386** directory contains architecture-specific modules:

```
% ls -F i386
Makefile    boot/      eisa/       ibcs2/      isa/
apm/        conf/      i386/       include/    linux/
```

Another important directory in the **SYS** area is **SYS/**_arch_**/conf**, where the kernel configuration files are stored; each file corresponds to one kernel. In this book we assume that you are using the Intel i386 architecture, although FreeBSD also supports the Alpha architecture. **config** reads a configuration file from **SYS/**_arch_**/conf** and creates the corresponding compilation directory in **SYS/compile/**_KERNEL_NAME_.

For example, when the system is first installed, it comes with a generic kernel named GENERIC. The default kernel configuration file is **SYS/i386/conf/GENERIC**, so the default compilation directory would be **SYS/compile/GENERIC**.

The rest of the directories in **SYS** contain various parts of the kernel that are assembled to create the executable image. The exact files and subdirectories vary widely among BSD systems.

### The master recipe for building a kernel

The following list details the eight steps involved in building a kernel. We take up each of these steps in the subsequent sections.

- Audit the system's hardware.
- Create and edit the kernel's configuration file in **SYS/i386/conf**.
- Run the **config** program from the **conf** directory.
- Run **make depend** in the compilation directory.
- Build the kernel with **make**.
- Archive the old kernel and install the new one.
- Test and debug the new kernel.
- Document the new kernel.

### Audit the system's hardware

Before you can configure a kernel, you need to know what devices it must handle. Start by taking a hardware inventory of your system. Make a list of all the devices connected to the computer, including

- Disks and CD-ROM drives, and their controllers
- Network interfaces
- Specialty hardware
- The keyboard and mouse

This hardware audit can be a grueling task in the PC world. PC manufacturers often just give you a packaged machine and don't tell you what kind of hardware is inside; "an Ethernet card" is not enough. There are hundreds of different PC cards marketed under dozens of names. Frequently, the only way to do the audit is to open up your machine and look at what you've got. If you think you know the name of the device driver, you can look at the man page for that driver. Unfortunately, FreeBSD provides little documentation of the exact devices that a driver supports.

Remember to check what the generic kernel reports about your hardware at boot time; its output can give you hints as to which drivers you should keep in your kernel. You can check the current kernel's idea of your hardware with the **dmesg** command. You can also use the **SYS/i386/conf/LINT** file as an extra reference.

### Create a configuration file in SYS/i386/conf

Once you know how you want your kernel configured, you must put this information into a form that **config** can understand. To do this, you create a configuration file in **SYS/i386/conf**. The name can be any valid filename, but it should be descriptive enough that a stranger to your **SYS** directory can tell what each kernel is for.

Don't create the configuration file from scratch. Instead, copy the **GENERIC** configuration and delete the parts you don't want. If you get stuck on something related to the configuration file and can't figure it out from the material here, refer to the documentation for **config**. The man pages for individual device drivers are also a good source of information and usually show any kernel config lines you might need. For example, the man page for **de** begins with

```
SYNOPSIS

device de
```

which is the exact line you need to put in the kernel config file to include that device. (Of course, this method is still a bit backward because you need to know the name of the device driver before you can look up the man page. **man -k** is your friend.)

The format of a kernel configuration file requires quite a few pages to describe, so instead of interrupting our overview of the kernel building process with a complete discussion, we'll defer the details until page 237.

### Run config

You must **cd** to **SYS/i386/conf** before running **config**; it expects to find the configuration file specified on the command line in the current directory. Simple versions of **config** take the name of the configuration file as their only argument. Fancier versions support a number of options. To set up the compilation directory for the kernel described in **SYS/i386/conf/EXAMPLE**, we would use the following commands:

```
# cd SYS/i386/conf
# config EXAMPLE
```

If the **config** command produces error messages, you must go back and fix your configuration file before continuing. If you get through **config** without any errors, you can assume that your configuration was at least syntactically valid and that the kernel compilation can proceed.

### Run make depend

After **config** finishes, change your working directory to the new kernel's compilation directory (**cd ../../compile/EXAMPLE**) and do an **ls**. You should see lots and lots of files. Don't worry about their contents; **config** knows what it's doing.

Now run **make depend** inside the compilation directory. This command initializes the file dependency information used by **make**. **make depend** may produce voluminous output.

### Build the kernel

In the compilation directory, simply type **make**. You must watch carefully for error messages during the compilation. **make** will usually detect errors and abort the compilation, but it always helps to be alert. For extra protection, use the **tee** command to have **make** keep a record of everything that gets sent to your screen.

```
# make |& tee ERRS.LOG
```

The **&** behind the vertical bar ensures that both error messages and status messages will be directed through the pipe. Bourne shell users should use

```
# make 2>&1 | tee ERRS.LOG
```

to achieve similar results.

If an error occurs during compilation, you should first suspect your configuration file. If you get messages about missing files or undefined routines, you have probably left something out of the config file. If you get messages complaining about syntax errors, the fault may be with your configuration file or with the system, although the latter is not likely.

### Install the new kernel

Before you boot a new kernel, make sure you can recover your system if the new kernel doesn't work. Never replace the old kernel directly with a new one, because you will then have nothing to boot from in the event of a catastrophe. Traditionally, kernels have been called **/vmunix**, but every OS seems to call them something different these days. Under FreeBSD, the kernel is **/kernel**.

You should back up your old kernel by moving **/kernel** to **/kernel.works**. All systems provide some way to keep an old kernel bootable while you test a new one. Check the section on boot loaders in Chapter 2, *Booting and Shutting Down,* for more information, or consult your manuals.

**/kernel** can be a hard link to some other filename, so you can just make a link to your new kernel rather than copying it. If the kernel is not called **/kernel** and you don't make this link, the boot loader will have difficulty finding it.

### Test the new kernel

If the system boots successfully, you are probably in good shape. However, you should try a few checks just to make sure. Run **ls** on at least one directory in each filesystem. Success indicates that the filesystem is functioning correctly. **ping** another machine on your network to see if your network device is working properly.

### Document the new kernel

Before washing your hands of this whole sordid kernel business, go back to your original **SYS/i386/conf/***KERNEL_NAME* file and put in copious comments so that you will understand what you have done when you come back to read it six months or a year later.

If you have lots of free space, you can preserve the **SYS/compile/***KERNEL_NAME* directory to speed up subsequent alterations. If you're tight on space, just delete it; everything it contains can be regenerated with **config**.

## 12.7   CREATING A BSD CONFIGURATION FILE

Creating the configuration file (under **SYS/i386/conf**) is the hardest part of building a BSD kernel; the rest of the process is quite mechanical.

A configuration file is a list of control phrases, one per line. Any line beginning with a tab character is considered a continuation of the previous line. Anything between a pound sign (#) and the end of a line is considered a comment, and blank lines are ignored. Keywords must be separated by whitespace, but except for this and the special meaning of tabs as continuation characters, spaces and tabs are ignored.

Drivers / Kernel

Integers in the configuration file can be entered in hexadecimal, octal, or decimal form. Octal numbers are identified by a leading zero, and hexadecimal numbers by a leading 0x. Strings must be double quoted if they contain numbers used as text.

A control phrase begins with a single keyword that indicates how the remainder of the line is to be interpreted. The rest of the line provides the keyword's arguments. Some keywords can accept a list of arguments separated by spaces or commas, but it's wise to use only one argument per line. Most keywords that can accept multiple arguments can also have arbitrarily many control lines.

The order in which control phrases appear is usually not important; Table 12.6 shows the traditional order.

**Table 12.6    Keywords used in BSD configuration files**

| Keyword | Function |
|---|---|
| machine | Sets the machine type |
| cpu | Sets the CPU type |
| ident | Sets the name of the kernel |
| maxusers | Sets the kernel's table sizes |
| options | Sets various compile-time options |
| config | Assigns the root and swap areas |
| controller | Declares a disk or tape controller |
| disk | Declares a disk connected to a controller |
| tape | Declares a tape connected to a controller |
| device | Declares devices without controllers |
| pseudo-device | Declares pseudo-devices |

### The maxusers keyword

The maxusers keyword sets the sizes of several important system tables. As its name suggests, the argument to maxusers is roughly the maximum number of simultaneous users that the system is expected to support (though most versions of UNIX don't actually enforce a limit on the number of users per se). If you want to tune this value yourself, you should boost it by 1 for each expected simultaneous user and, if you are configuring the kernel for an NFS server, by 1 for each client machine. Add 8 for each frame buffer on which a window system can be run.

The maxusers number affects the values of several other kernel parameters, such as the maximum number of processes, the number of file table entries, and the number of buffers for terminal I/O. The most important of these is the maximum number of processes on the system. Here's the formula:

$$\text{Maximum processes} = 20 + 16 * \text{maxusers}$$

This maximum process count includes the 18 or so processes that start when the system is booted.

### The options keyword

Clauses asserted in an options directive become variables that are defined for the C preprocessor during compilation of the kernel. There are two different forms of the options statement.

In the first form, tokens are defined but given no particular value. Such tokens specify whether an option is on or off, using the preprocessor directives #ifdef and #ifndef. When a token is supplied as an argument to an options statement, the corresponding preprocessor symbol is defined and the option is enabled. For example, the phrase to include NFS in the kernel is

    options    NFS

Note that with FreeBSD, any string in the config file containing both letters and numbers needs to be quoted. For example the ISO-9660 filesystem used on CD-ROMs is enabled with the following line:

    options    "CD9660"

The second form of options statement not only defines a symbol but also gives it a specific value. The kernel code uses the symbol as if it were a constant, and the C preprocessor makes an appropriate substitution wherever the symbol appears. This type of symbol is declared with the syntax

    options    symbol="value"

For example, to modify the value of the MAXDSIZ option, which sets the maximum amount of virtual memory that can be allocated to the data segment of a single process, you would use a line such as

    options    MAXDSIZ="(64*1024*1024)"

This example sets the value to 64 megabytes.

The most common options are listed below. None of these options take a value. See your vendor's documentation for a complete list.

INET   This option includes networking support. Networking has become so pervasive that a lot of software is likely to break if you don't include it; it's an option in name only. When you enable INET, you should also include the pseudo-device loop. See page 242 for information about pseudo-devices. The INET option includes only software-side networking support. Network hardware is declared later in the config file.

FFS   This option allows local disks to be attached to the machine. It's omitted only when an extremely lean kernel for a diskless client or an embedded device is set up.

NFS   This option includes NFS support in the kernel. It's required for both NFS clients and servers.

GATEWAY     This option is for use on machines that have more than one
network interface and are intended to perform Internet routing and forwarding functions. This option currently has only
minor ramifications: it increases the sizes of some kernel data
structures to cope with the expected load and provides for
special network behavior if one of the interfaces goes down.

## The config keyword

The config keyword specifies the location of the root partition on the system's disks.

*See page 133 for
more information
about the **fstab** file.*

The root partition is the topmost component of the filesystem. It contains the directory **/** and several other important files and subdirectories. Information about how
to mount filesystems is normally kept in the **/etc/fstab** file, but UNIX can't get to this
file until the root partition has already been mounted.

To bootstrap the filesystem, information about the partition that holds the root must
either be compiled into the kernel or, on some systems, passed to the kernel by the
bootstrap loader. The situation for swapping is not as dire, since it's unlikely that any
swapping will occur until the **/etc/rc*** scripts run the **swapon** command.

A config line has the form

```
config kernel_name root on partition
```

The *kernel_name* parameter sets the filename under which the compiled kernel will
be stored. FreeBSD kernels are named **kernel**; alternates are often named to identify
the disk they use for the root partition (e.g., **dakernel**).

The *partition* parameter tells which partition the root filesystem is located on. The
partition is typically wd0 for IDE systems and da0 for SCSI systems.

Here's a complete example:

```
config kernel root on wd0
```

The ability to build variant kernels is useful for disaster planning. An alternate root
partition equipped with its own kernel can be of great help when your main root
partition is damaged. If the alternate root is on the same disk drive or controller as
the one that got trashed, be sure to verify the stability of the hardware before rebooting. Otherwise, you run the risk of destroying the alternate root, too.

On some systems, a floppy disk or CD-ROM controls the boot procedure. The floppy
disk knows the location of the kernel and can control its invocation. If you maintain
an alternate root partition, you may have to build a new boot floppy that uses it.

## Hardware devices

The syntax for declaring devices is confusing, and the basic entries required to make
the system run vary from machine to machine. Section 4 of the BSD manuals covers
devices. Most man pages for device drivers list an example config line you can include in the kernel.

Take the following instructions with a grain of salt. We discuss the general syntax, but since we expect that you will mostly be paring down your system's generic configuration, we don't talk about how to write your own device specifications from scratch.

The basic form of a declaration is:

*device-type device-name* at *connection-info* port *address* [*device-class*] irq *interrupt*

Not all clauses are applicable to all devices.

*device-type* is the type of device you are declaring. A few types of devices, such as controller and disk, have special keywords. Others use the generic keyword device.

*device-name* is the standard name of the device (or more accurately, the name of the device driver), plus the logical unit number. For example, the name for the first IDE controller is wdc0. As you wade through the generic configuration, you can look up each device in section 4 of the manuals to find out what it is and whether it applies to you. Note that the logical unit number has *no* relationship to any hardware-specified selection number of the device.

The *connection-info* for a device tells the kernel where to find the device and what kind of device it is. For disk and tape drives, this connection info is usually the name of a controller. For controllers and devices, it's the name of a bus or bus controller. For example, the following lines define the system's ISA bus, an IDE controller that's attached to it, and an IDE disk that's attached to the IDE controller:

```
controller      isa0
controller      wdc0    at isa? port "IO_WD1" bio irq 14
disk            wd0     at wdc0 drive 0
```

It is usually sufficient to state that a device is connected to a particular type of controller without specifying which one. For example, the location of the wdc0 IDE controller is indicated above not as isa0 or isa1, but as the more generic isa?.

The *address* parameter, the argument to the port keyword, represents the location of the device's command and status registers in the address space of the bus or backplane to which it is connected. Controllers and devices connected directly to a bus often have this parameter filled in. Each kind of device has a certain number of address locations that it occupies in the bus's address space. The values only need to be specified for ISA or EISA devices; PCI drivers can dynamically determine the address range a device is using.

Set the *interrupt* to the interrupt vector (IRQ) the device has been configured to use. This parameter only needs to be specified for ISA and EISA devices. PCI drivers can dynamically determine the interrupt a device is using.

For some device drivers, you must specify a *device-class*. This parameter is mainly used for network devices and some controllers. To see if a specific device needs a device class, refer to its man page.

Drivers / Kernel

Here's the config line for an ISA NE200 network card that uses most of these options:

```
device ed0 at isa? port 0x360 net irq 10
```

This line says to locate the device ed0 on the ISA bus at I/O address 0x360. It uses interrupt 10. It's more typical that some keywords can be left out. Here's another Ethernet card, this time on the PCI bus:

```
device de0
```

Thanks to the wonders of PCI, we are not required to specify all the gory details.

The most effective way to organize your declarations is to pair related devices. If you have a controller, put the devices attached to it nearby. For example, if you have an IDE controller, put your IDE disk and CD-ROM declarations right after it. That way it's easier to visualize the dependencies.

### The pseudo-device keyword

Theoretically, pseudo-device drivers are programs that act like device drivers but don't have any real hardware to back them up. We say "theoretically" because some kernel options that masquerade as pseudo-devices do not act like device drivers at all, at least from the user's point of view. The syntax for pseudo-device lines is

```
pseudo-device device-name number-of-instances
```

*device-name* is the name of the pseudo-device and *number-of-instances* is an optional integer telling how many of the imaginary devices the driver should pretend are present. Many drivers do not use the instance count.

There are only a few pseudo-devices, but most of them are obligatory for correct operation of the system. Some systems have a number of nonstandard pseudo-devices that support windowing systems, extra keyboards, or auxiliary displays. Consult the manuals of your system to learn how to deal with these, or just include all the pseudo-devices from your generic configuration file for a more festive atmosphere.

Some common pseudo-devices are:

pty     PTYs are pseudo-terminals. They mimic terminals, but instead of having an actual terminal on one end, they are connected to a UNIX process. PTYs are used heavily by programs such as **ssh**, **xterm**, **telnet**, and **rlogin**, and they are also used by a few standard utilities such as **script** to do input processing.

*See Chapter 13 for more information about interfaces and addressing.*

loop     The loop driver simulates an interface to a network that contains only the local host. It allows stand-alone machines to use network software, and it also provides a standard way for a machine to address packets to itself. It is required if you specify the INET option.

### A sample FreeBSD configuration file

Let's look at a configuration file for a simple kernel which we'll call EXAMPLE:

```
machine     "i386"
cpu         "I386_CPU"
cpu         "I486_CPU"
cpu         "I586_CPU"
cpu         "I686_CPU"
ident       EXAMPLE
maxusers    32
```

The first few lines specify that we are building a kernel for Intel PCs and that the kernel should support all the different CPU types specified. This section also identifies the configuration with the name EXAMPLE. The maxusers line sets the kernel tables up for approximately 32 simultaneous users and 532 simultaneous processes.

```
...
options     INET        # Internet: TCP/IP
options     "CD9660"    # ISO 9660 CD-ROM filesystem
options     FFS         # (FFS) Local filesystem
options     NFS         # Network filesystem
...
```

This is just a snippet from the options section of the configuration file. Our sample kernel is configured with support for Internet (IP) networking, local filesystems, the ISO-9660 filesystem (used most commonly on CD-ROMs), and NFS.

```
config kernel root on wd0
```

The default root device is the first IDE hard disk.

```
controller isa0
controller pnp0
controller eisa0
controller pci0
```

These lines declare the various buses supported by the system: ISA, EISA, and PCI. The second line declares Plug and Pray support for ISA devices (pnp0).

```
controller      atkbdc0 at isa? port IO_KBD tty
device          atkbd0  at isa? tty irq 1
device          psm0    at isa? tty irq 12
device          vga0    at isa? port ? conflicts
# splash screen/screen saver
pseudo-device   splash
# syscons is the default console driver, resembling a SCO console
device          sc0     at isa? tty
```

This section declares all items needed to get a console on your machine. It declares the keyboard and its controller, the mouse, the display card, and the console itself.

```
# Floppy drives
controller      fdc0    at isa? port "IO_FD1" bio irq 6 drq 2
disk            fd0     at fdc0 drive 0
```

```
disk            fd1         at fdc0 drive 1
# IDE controller and disks
controller      wdc0        at isa? port "IO_WD1" bio irq 14
disk            wd0         at wdc0 drive 0
disk            wd1         at wdc0 drive 1
controller      wdc1        at isa? port "IO_WD2" bio irq 15
disk            wd2         at wdc1 drive 0
disk            wd3         at wdc1 drive 1
```

Here we declare the controllers and disks for our example system: a floppy controller, two floppy drives (even though only one is used, declaring them both doesn't hurt), and two IDE controllers with corresponding disks.

```
options         ATAPI         # Enable ATAPI support for IDE bus
options         ATAPI_STATIC  # Don't do it as an LKM
device          acd0          # IDE CD-ROM
```

Under FreeBSD, we need to include these special options to enable IDE devices. Although IDE can be configured as a loadable kernel module (the "LKM" referred to in the comment), it must be statically configured if you're using an IDE disk as your root partition. Otherwise, the system cannot recognize your root disk at boot time.

```
pseudo-device   loop          # Network loopback
pseudo-device   ether         # Ethernet support
pseudo-device   bpfilter 4    # Berkeley packet filter
```

Of these pseudo-devices, only loop is mandatory. In general, you should retain all the pseudo-devices in the GENERIC configuration. Obviously, you need the ether pseudo-device to use Ethernet devices. You need the bpfilter pseudo-device to run **tcpdump** and DHCP clients, so keep it.

You may want to leave out bpfilter support to prevent people from sniffing the network. However, if you omit bpfilter, you won't be able to legitimately snoop to diagnose problems.

### Tuning the FreeBSD kernel

The GENERIC kernel is not tuned for high performance, as you will notice especially if you are building a high-volume web server. Here are some suggestions for building a better FreeBSD kernel.

To some extent, you can dynamically tune the FreeBSD kernel with the **sysctl** command, which provides a user-level interface to many of the kernel's internal data structures. **sysctl** lets you dynamically change selected kernel parameters; it's a powerful (and dangerous) command.

**sysctl -a** lists the kernel variables you can look at and possibly change. Almost all the parameters described in Table 12.7 can be changed dynamically. Documentation on what each variable does is typically meager, although the variable names usually give a hint. Be careful when tuning your kernel with **sysctl** because you can easily break things.

The changes that **sysctl** makes to kernel variables are not remembered across reboots. A useful paradigm is to first test changes by using **sysctl**, then make them permanent by changing the kernel config file and recompiling the kernel. This procedure has the advantage of safety, since you can simply reboot to reset the system no matter how much you've screwed things up.

Table 12.7 lists the most commonly tuned **sysctl** variables, their default values, and their meanings.

**Table 12.7    Interesting FreeBSD kernel variables accessible through sysctl**

| Variable | Default | Meaning |
|---|---|---|
| kern.maxfiles | 1064 | Maximum # of open files |
| kern.maxproc | 532 | Maximum # of processes |
| kern.maxfilesperproc | 1064 | Maximum # of open files per process |
| kern.maxprocperuid | 531 | Maximum # of processes per uid |
| kern.ipc.nmbclusters | 1024 | Maximum # of network buffers |
| kern.ipc.maxsockets | 1064 | Maximum # of available sockets |
| kern.ipc.somaxconn | 128 | Maximum # of simultaneous unaccepted sockets |

Note that in the default configuration, a single user can consume all but one of the system's process slots. Even if only one person will actually use the system, these defaults create a potential problem because no headroom is reserved for starting system processes. You should make the gap between maxproc and maxprocperuid much larger than the default.

Below, we describe some simple parameters you might change in your kernel config to get better performance out of the GENERIC kernel. These tweaks are designed specifically for use on a web server, although they should increase performance for most network servers.

```
maxusers 256
```

The maxusers keyword adjusts many other variables in the kernel, such as the maximum number of processes, the maximum number of processes per user, the system-wide limit on open files, the per-process limit on open files, and the maximum number of network buffers. Be generous when configuring a server.

```
options NMBCLUSTERS=4096
```

Here, we set the number of network buffers to a more reasonable value. The default is 256, which is laughably low for a medium or high-performance network server.

```
options CHILD_MAX=1024
```

This option sets the maximum number of child processes on the system. The number should be high on a network server. In general, network server daemons create a child process for each incoming request.

```
options OPEN_MAX=1024
```

This option sets the maximum number of file descriptors on the system. This number should generally be the same as CHILD_MAX, since each incoming network connection gets assigned its own file descriptor. Given the way that network servers generally work, if you have fewer file descriptors than child processes, you will be limited by the number of file descriptors; the converse is also true.

## 12.8  ADDING DEVICE DRIVERS

A device driver is a program that manages the system's interaction with a particular piece of hardware. The driver translates between the hardware commands understood by the device and the stylized programming interface used by the kernel. The existence of the driver layer helps keep UNIX reasonably device independent.

Device drivers are part of the kernel; they are not user processes. However, a driver can be accessed both from within the kernel and from the user space. User-level access to devices is usually provided through special device files that live in the **/dev** directory. The kernel transforms operations on these special files into calls to the code of the driver.

The old days were a time of chaos in which vendors shipped specialized boards for many of the devices connected to a machine. Eventually, the industry reached something closer to stability, with most systems supporting SCSI as their standard interface for disks, tapes, and CD-ROM drives. Vendors incorporated standard features such as Ethernet into their machines, and there was much rejoicing.

Then came the PC, which reintroduced chaos into the system administrator's world. Once again, proprietary interfaces reigned, multiple "standards" were introduced, and a dizzying array of hardware with varying levels of operating system support were available. Behold:

- Over 30 different PC SCSI chipsets are supported by Linux, and each is packaged and sold by at least twice that many vendors.

- Over 200 different PC network interfaces are out there, each being marketed by several different vendors under different names.

- Newer, better, cheaper types of hardware are being developed all the time. Each will require a device driver in order to work with your UNIX of choice.

With the remarkable pace at which new hardware is being developed, it is practically impossible to keep the mainline OS distributions up to date with the latest hardware. It is not at all uncommon to have to add a device driver to your kernel to support a new piece of hardware.

Vendors are becoming more aware of the UNIX market, and they even provide UNIX drivers on occasion. You may be lucky and find that your vendor will furnish you with drivers and installation instructions. More likely, you will only find the driver you need on some uncommented web page.

In either case, this section shows you what is really going on when you add a device driver. We assume that you are comfortable with basic kernel configuration as covered earlier in this chapter.

### Device numbers

Many devices have a corresponding file in **/dev**, the notable exceptions on modern operating systems being network devices. By virtue of being device files, the files in **/dev** each have a major and minor device number associated with them. The kernel uses these numbers to map references to a device file to the corresponding driver.

The major device number identifies the driver that the file is associated with (in other words, the type of device). The minor device number usually identifies which particular instance of a given device type is to be addressed. The minor device number is sometimes called the unit number.

You can see the major and minor number of a device file with **ls -l**:

```
% ls -l /dev/sda
brw-rw---- 1 root    disk    8,   0 Mar  3 1999 /dev/sda
```

This example shows the first SCSI disk on a Linux system. It has a major number of 8 and a minor number of 0.

The minor device number is sometimes used by the driver to select the particular characteristic of a device. For example, a single tape drive can have several files in **/dev** representing it in various configurations of recording density and rewind characteristics. In essence, the driver is free to interpret the minor device number in whatever way it wants. Look up the man page for the driver to determine what convention it's using.

There are actually two types of device files: block device files and character device files. A block device is read or written one block (a group of bytes, usually a multiple of 512) at a time; a character device can be read or written one byte at a time. Some devices support access through both block and character device files. Disks and tapes lead dual lives; terminals and printers do not.

Device drivers present a standard interface to the kernel. Each driver has routines for performing some or all of the following functions:

```
attach     close      dump       ioctl      open       probe
psize      read       receive    reset      select     stop
strategy   timout     transmit   write
```

It is sometimes convenient to implement an abstraction as a device driver even when it controls no actual device. Such phantom devices are known as pseudo-devices. For example, a user who logs in over the network is assigned a PTY (pseudo-TTY) that looks, feels, and smells like a serial port from the perspective of high-level software.

This trick allows programs written in the days when everyone used a TTY to continue to function in the world of windows and networks.

When a program performs an operation on a device file, the kernel automatically catches the reference, looks up the appropriate function name in a table, and transfers control to it. To perform an unusual operation that doesn't have a direct analog in the filesystem model (for example, ejecting a floppy disk), the **ioctl** system call can be used to pass a message directly from user space into the driver.

Drivers and their corresponding configuration files are typically stashed in a nonobvious location to prevent the uninitiated from mucking with them. Table 12.8 outlines the default locations of drivers and their config files.

**Table 12.8    Driver configuration files by system**

| System | Config location | Driver location |
|--------|-----------------|-----------------|
| Solaris | **/kernel/drv/*conf** | **/kernel/drv/*** |
| HP-UX | **/stand/system** | **/usr/conf/*** |
| Linux | **/usr/src/linux/.config** | **/usr/src/linux/drivers/*** |
| FreeBSD | **/usr/src/sys/i386/conf/**_KERNEL_ | **/sys/i386/conf/files*** |

In the sections below, we show three scenarios for adding a new driver to the kernel: for Solaris, Linux, and FreeBSD. We won't cover adding a driver to HP-UX because third-party devices are relatively rare in that environment (HP-UX comes with drivers for all HP hardware).

### Adding a Solaris device driver

Adding a device driver to Solaris is the easiest of all. Solaris drivers are usually distributed as a package. You can use **pkgadd** to automatically add the device driver to the system. When device drivers are not distributed as a package or when package addition fails, it's trivial to add the drivers by hand because they are all implemented as loadable kernel modules.

Solaris drivers are almost always distributed as object files, not as source code as is common on FreeBSD and Linux systems. In this example, we add the device "snarf" to Solaris. The snarf driver should come with at least two files, including **snarf.o** (the actual driver) and **snarf.conf** (a configuration file). Both files should go into the **/platform/sun4u/kernel/drv** directory.

Once the **.conf** file has been copied over, you can edit it to specify particular device parameters. You should not normally need to do this, but sometimes configuration options are available for fine-tuning the device for your application.

After the files have been copied into place, you'll need to load the module. You insert loadable kernel modules into the running kernel with the **add_drv** command. (More on loadable kernel modules later in this chapter.) In this case, we'll load snarf into the kernel by running the command **add_drv snarf**. That's it! This is definitely the least painful of our three examples.

### Adding a Linux device driver

On Linux systems, device drivers are typically distributed in one of three forms:

- A patch against a specific kernel version
- A loadable module
- An installation script that applies appropriate patches

The most common of all these is the patch against a specific kernel version. These patches can in most cases be applied with the following procedure:

```
# cd /usr/src/linux ; patch -p1 < driver.diff
```

Diffs made against a different minor version of the kernel may fail, but the driver should still work. Here, we cover how to manually add a network "snarf" driver to the kernel. It's a very complicated and tedious process, especially when compared to the other operating systems we've seen.

By convention, Linux kernel source is in **/usr/src/linux**. Within the **drivers** subdirectory, you'll need to find the subdirectory that corresponds to the type of device you have. A directory listing of **drivers** looks like this:

```
% ls -F /usr/src/linux/drivers
Makefile   cdrom/   i2o/          nubus/      sbus/     telephony/
acorn/     char/    isdn/         parport/    scsi/     usb/
ap1000/    dio/     macintosh/    pci/        sgi/      video/
atm/       fc4/     misc/         pcmcia/     sound/    zorro/
block/     i2c/     net/          pnp/        tc/
```

The most common directories to which drivers are added are **block**, **char**, **net**, **usb**, **sound**, and **scsi**. These directories contain drivers for block devices (such as IDE disk drives), character devices (such as serial ports), network devices, USB devices, sound cards, and SCSI cards, respectively. Some of the other directories contain drivers for the buses themselves (e.g., **pci**, **nubus**, and **zorro**); it's unlikely that you will need to add drivers to these directories. Some directories contain platform-specific drivers, such as **Macintosh**, **acorn**, and **ap1000**. Some directories contain specialty devices such as **atm**, **isdn**, and **telephony**.

Since our example device is a network-related device, we will add the driver to the directory **drivers/net**. We'll need to modify the following files:

- **drivers/net/Makefile**, so that our driver will be compiled
- **drivers/net/Config.in**, so that our device will appear in the config options
- **drivers/net/Space.c**, so that the device will be probed on startup

After putting the **.c** and **.h** files for the driver in **drivers/net**, we'll add the driver to **drivers/net/Makefile**. The lines we'd add (near the end of the file) follow.

Drivers / Kernel

```
ifeq ($(CONFIG_SNARF),y)
    L_OBJS += snarf.o
else
    ifeq ($(CONFIG_SNARF),m)
    M_OBJS += snarf.o
    endif
endif
```

This configuration adds the snarf driver so that it can be either configured as a module or built into the kernel.

After adding the device to the **Makefile**, we have to make sure we can configure the device when we configure the kernel. All network devices need to be listed in the file **drivers/net/Config.in**. To add the device so that it can be built either as a module or as part of the kernel (consistent with what we claimed in the **Makefile**), we add the following line:

```
tristate 'Snarf device support' CONFIG_SNARF
```

The tristate keyword means you can build the device as a module. If the device cannot be built as a module, use the keyword bool instead of tristate. The next token is the string to show to the user on the configuration screen. It can be any arbitrary text, but it should identify the device that is being configured. The final token is the configuration macro. This token needs to be the same as that tested for with the ifeq clause in the **Makefile**.

The last file we need to edit to add our device to the system is **devices/net/Space.c**. **Space.c** contains references to the probe routines for the device driver, and it also controls the device probe order. Here, we'll have to edit the file in two different places. First we'll add a reference to the probe function, then we'll add the device to the list of devices to probe for.

At the top of the **Space.c** file are a bunch of references to other probe functions. We'll add the following line to that list:

```
extern int snarf_probe(struct device *);
```

Next, to add the device to the actual probe list, we need to determine which list to add it to. A separate probe list is kept for each type of bus (PCI, EISA, SBUS, MCA, ISA, parallel port, etc.). The snarf device is a PCI device, so we'll add it to the list called pci_probes. The line that says

```
struct devprobe pci_probes[] __initdata = {
```

is followed by an ordered list of devices. The devices higher up in the list are probed first. Probe order does not usually matter for PCI devices, but some devices are sensitive. Just to be sure the snarf device is detected, we'll add it to the top of the list:

```
struct devprobe pci_probes[] __initdata = {
#ifdef CONFIG_SNARF
    snarf_probe, 0},
#endif
```

The device has now been added to the Linux kernel. When we next configure the kernel, the device should appear as a configuration option under "network devices."

### Adding a FreeBSD device driver

Adding a completely new device driver to a FreeBSD machine involves adding it to a couple of configuration files and editing the kernel source code to include references to the driver's routines. This procedure is not for the faint of heart!

We will use a FreeBSD system as our example, but all BSD systems (including NetBSD and OpenBSD) are essentially similar, except that the locations of files may differ. We will add a "snarf" device (a pseudo-network device) for our example.

First, we have to copy our source files to the proper location:

```
# cp ~bbraun/snarf.c /sys/pci/snarf.c
```

Since our device is a PCI device, we'll put the source files in **SYS/pci** with all the other PCI drivers. If your device doesn't fall into an existing category, you'll have to put it in a new directory and edit **SYS/i386/conf/files.i386**. As long as the driver belongs to an existing category, it will automatically be compiled and linked into the kernel.

Next, we add the device to the kernel configuration file. We put the following entry in our **EXAMPLE** configuration:

```
device snf0    # Snarf, our fake network device.
```

This line instructs the **config** program to include the files for the driver in the kernel. Since network devices do not have major and minor numbers, we do not need to tell the kernel what the numbers are. If we were adding a block device or a character device, we would have to tell the kernel which major and minor numbers to use.

If you are installing someone else's driver, the documentation should tell you the major and minor numbers to use. Use only the numbers in the documentation; otherwise, you might create conflicts with already-assigned numbers.

To tell the kernel which major number to use, edit **SYS/i386/conf/majors.i386** and add the appropriate entry. What "the appropriate entry" means varies from device to device. Refer to the driver's documentation.

The next steps include:

- Running **config** and building a new kernel
- Copying the old kernel aside and installing the new kernel
- Rebooting and testing the new kernel

These steps are all explained earlier in this chapter. Finally, you may need to create device files (see page 252) and test the device itself.

## 12.9  DEVICE FILES

By convention, device files are kept in the **/dev** directory.[2] Large systems, especially those with networking and pseudo-terminals, may support hundreds of devices. Solaris and HP-UX handle this complexity quite nicely by using a separate subdirectory of **/dev** for each type of device: **disk**, **cdrom**, **terminal**, etc.

Device files are created with the **mknod** command, which has the syntax

> **mknod** *filename type major minor*

where *filename* is the device file to be created, *type* is **c** for a character device or **b** for a block device, and *major* and *minor* are the major and minor device numbers. If you are creating a device file that refers to a driver that's already present in your kernel, check the man page for the driver to find the appropriate major and minor device numbers (in section 4 for FreeBSD or section 7 for Solaris and HP-UX; Linux doesn't have man pages for device drivers).

A shell script called **MAKEDEV** is sometimes provided (in **/dev**) to automatically supply default values to **mknod**. Study the script to find the arguments needed for your device. For example, to make PTY entries on a FreeBSD system, you'd use the following commands:

```
# cd /dev
# ./MAKEDEV pty
```

## 12.10  NAMING CONVENTIONS FOR DEVICES

Naming conventions for devices are somewhat random. They are often holdovers from the way things were done on a DEC PDP-11.

For devices that have both block and character identities, the character device name is usually prefaced with the letter **r** for "raw" (e.g., **/dev/da0** vs. **/dev/rda0**). An alternative convention is to store character device files in a subdirectory that has a name that starts with **r** (e.g., **/dev/dsk/dks0d3s0** vs. **/dev/rdsk/dks0d3s0**). However, an **r** does not always imply a raw device file.

*See Chapter 7 for more information about serial ports.*

Serial device files are usually named **tty** followed by a sequence of letters that identify the interface the port is attached to. Sometimes, a TTY is represented by more than one device file; the extra files usually provide access to alternative flow control methods or locking protocols.

BSD disk names often begin with a two-letter abbreviation for either the drive or the controller, followed by the drive number and partition name. For example, **da0a** is the block device that represents the **a** partition of the first disk drive on a SCSI controller; **rda0a** is the corresponding character device.

---

2. The primary device files in Solaris are kept in **/devices**, but links to **/dev** are maintained automatically.

The names of tape devices often include not only a reference to the drive itself but also an indication of whether the drive rewinds after each tape operation and the density at which it reads and writes. Each vendor has a different scheme.

Table 12.9 lists some typical names for common devices (disk and CD-ROM drives) on our example systems.

**Table 12.9    Device naming conventions for disks and tapes[a]**

| System | SCSI disk | SCSI CD-ROM | IDE disk |
|--------|-----------|-------------|----------|
| Solaris | **/dev/[r]dsk/c**AtBdNsP | **/dev/[r]dsk/c**AtBdNsP | **/dev/[r]dsk/c**AtBdNsP |
| HP-UX | **/dev/[r]dsk/c**AtBdN | **/dev/[r]dsk/c**AtBdN | – |
| Linux | **/dev/sd**LP | **/dev/scd**N | **/dev/hd**LP |
| FreeBSD | **/dev/da**NsP | **/dev/da**NsP{**lmh**} | **/dev/wd**NsP |

a. A = controller number, B = SCSI ID, L = unit letter, N = unit number, P = partition letter or number

## 12.11  LOADABLE KERNEL MODULES

Loadable kernel modules have come a long way since the last revision of this book. Among our example systems, Solaris, Linux, and FreeBSD all support kernel modules, although the degree of support varies widely. Solaris is a very modular kernel, Linux is pretty modular, and FreeBSD barely supports kernel modules at all.

LKM support allows a device driver—or any other kernel service—to be linked into and removed from the kernel while it is running. This facility makes the installation of drivers much easier, since the kernel binary does not need to be changed. It also allows the kernel to be smaller because drivers are not loaded unless they are needed.

Loadable modules are implemented by providing one or more documented "hooks" into the kernel that additional device drivers can grab onto. A user-level command communicates with the kernel and tells it to load new modules into memory. There is usually a command that unloads drivers as well.

Although loadable drivers are convenient, they are not entirely safe. Any time you load or unload a module, you risk causing a kernel panic. We don't recommend loading or unloading an untested module when you are not willing to crash the machine.

Like other aspects of device and driver management, the implementation of loadable modules is OS dependent. The sections below outline the commands and caveats appropriate for Solaris, Linux, and FreeBSD.

### Loadable kernel modules in Solaris

In Solaris, virtually everything is a loadable module. The **modinfo** command lists the modules that are currently loaded.

Drivers / Kernel

The output looks like this:

```
# modinfo
Id   Loadaddr   Size    Info   Rev   ModuleName
 1   ff07e000   3ba0    1      1     specfs (filesystem for specfs)
 2   ff086000   1340    -      1     swapgeneric (root/swap config)
 3   ff082000   1a56    1      1     TS (time sharing sched class)
 4   ff084000   49c     -      1     TS_DPTBL (Timesharing dispatch)
 5   ff095000   15248   2      1     ufs (filesystem for ufs)
 6   ff0b8000   20e0    1      1     rootnex (sun4c root nexus)
 7   ff084a00   170     57     1     options (options driver)
 8   ff08dc00   2f4     62     1     dma (Direct Memory Access)
 9   ff08c000   968     59     1     sbus (SBus nexus driver)
 ...
```

On our Solaris system, the list continued for 80-odd lines. Many elements that are hardwired into the kernel on other versions of UNIX (such as UFS, the local filesystem) are loadable drivers in Solaris. This organization should make it much easier for third parties to write packages that integrate easily and seamlessly into the kernel, at least in theory.

You can add a driver with the **add_drv** command. This command loads the driver into the kernel and makes the appropriate device links (all links are rebuilt each time the kernel boots). Once you **add_drv** a driver, it remains a part of the system until you actively remove it. You can unload drivers by hand with **rem_drv**.

Whenever you add a driver using **add_drv**, it is a good idea to also run **drvconfig**. This command reconfigures the **/devices** directory and adds any files that are appropriate for the newly loaded driver.

Loadable modules that are not accessed through device files can be loaded and unloaded with **modload** and **modunload**.

### Loadable kernel modules in Linux

Linux is both more and less sophisticated than Solaris in its handling of loadable kernel modules, at least from the system administrator's point of view. Under Linux, almost anything can be built as a loadable kernel module. The exceptions are the root filesystem type and the device on which the root filesystem resides.

Loadable kernel modules are conventionally stored under **/lib/modules/**version, where *version* is the version of your Linux kernel as returned by **uname -r**. You can inspect the currently loaded modules with the **lsmod** command:

```
# lsmod
Module          Size     Used by
ppp             21452    0
slhc            4236     0 [ppp]
ds              6344     1
i82365          26648    1
pcmcia_core     37024    0 [ds   i82365]
```

This machine has the PCMCIA controller modules, the PPP driver, and the PPP header compression modules loaded.

Linux LKMs can be manually loaded into the kernel with **insmod**. For example, we could manually insert our example snarf module with the command

> # **insmod /path/to/snarf.o**

Parameters can also be passed to loadable kernel modules; for example,

> # **insmod /path/to/snarf.o io=0x***XXX* **irq=***X*

Once a loadable kernel module has been manually inserted into the kernel, it will only be removed if you explicitly request its removal. We could use **rmmod snarf** to remove our snarf module.

You can use **rmmod** at any time, but it works only if the number of current references to the module (listed in the Used by column of **lsmod**'s output) is 0.

Linux LKMs can also be loaded semiautomatically by **modprobe**, which is like a souped-up **insmod** that understands dependencies, options, and installation and removal procedures. **modprobe** uses **/etc/conf.modules** to figure out how to handle each module.

You can dynamically generate an **/etc/conf.modules** file that corresponds to all your currently installed modules by running **modprobe -c**. This command generates a long file that looks like this:

```
#This file was generated by: modprobe -c (2.1.121)
path[pcmcia]=/lib/modules/preferred
path[pcmcia]=/lib/modules/default
path[pcmcia]=/lib/modules/2.3.39
path[misc]=/lib/modules/2.3.39
...
# Aliases
alias block-major-1 rd
alias block-major-2 floppy
...
alias char-major-4 serial
alias char-major-5 serial
alias char-major-6 lp
...
alias dos msdos
alias plip0 plip
alias ppp0 ppp
options ne io=x0340 irq=9
```

The path statements tell where a particular module can be found. You can modify or add entries of this type if you want to keep your modules in a nonstandard location.

The alias statement provides a mapping between block major device numbers, character major device numbers, filesystems, network devices, and network protocols and their corresponding module names. This facility supports dynamic loading as implemented by **kerneld** (discussed below).

The options lines are not dynamically generated. They specify options that should be passed to a module when it is loaded. For example, we could use the following line to tell the snarf module its proper I/O address and interrupt vector:

```
options snarf io=0xXXX irq=X
```

**modprobe** also understands the statements pre-install, post-install, pre-remove, post-remove, install, and remove. These statements allow commands to be executed when a specific module is inserted into or removed from the running kernel. They take the following forms

```
pre-install module command ...
install module command ...
post-install module command ...
pre-remove module command ...
remove module command ...
post-remove module command ...
```

and are run before insertion, simultaneously with insertion (if possible), after insertion, before removal, during removal (if possible), and after removal.

But wait, there's more! Loadable kernel modules can also be loaded and unloaded dynamically with the **kerneld** daemon. When **kerneld** is running, modules are automatically loaded when the devices they serve are referenced. **kerneld** gets its information from **/etc/conf.modules**, just as **modprobe** does; it uses the alias statements to determine which module goes with a given device.

For example, if someone tries to access a serial port and no serial driver has been loaded, **kerneld** examines the **conf.modules** file to see which module is associated with character major device number 4. **kerneld** does all the same fancy tricks as **modprobe**; it's just designed to be used as a daemon.

### Loadable kernel modules in FreeBSD

FreeBSD's module support is new compared to that of Solaris and Linux. Current versions of FreeBSD cannot insert a device driver into the running kernel, but they can add functionality on the fly. Actually, FreeBSD's module support is only slightly better than opening up **/dev/kmem** and dumping in some code. Perhaps for this reason, loadable module support is disabled in the GENERIC kernel.

The FreeBSD **modload**, **modstat**, and **modunload** commands manipulate kernel modules. You will no doubt be shocked to discover that these commands load a module, display module status, and unload a module, respectively. Each utility performs **ioctl**s on **/dev/lkm**.

By default, FreeBSD's kernel modules live in **/modules**. If something can be added as a kernel module, it will be found there. Any of the modules listed in **/modules** can be inserted using the aforementioned utilities.

## 12.12  RECOMMENDED READING

MCKUSICK, MARSHALL KIRK, ET AL. *The Design and Implementation of the 4.4BSD Operating System.* Reading, MA: Addison-Wesley. 1996.

This book is a good reference for detailed information about the configuration and internals of the BSD kernel. There is a new version in development that will be based on FreeBSD instead of 4.4BSD.

BECK, MICHAEL, ET AL. *Linux Kernel Internals, Second Edition.* Reading, MA: Addison-Wesley. 1997.

A few new books on the internals of the Linux kernel are available, but we still like this older one. It's a bit outdated, but it gives a very good explanation of the kernel's inner workings.

Drivers / Kernel

## 14.4.2 RECOMMENDED READINGS

# SECTION TWO

## NETWORKING

# 13 *TCP/IP Networking*

there is no need
for Microsoft to
support TCP/IP.

GATES
1994

Microsoft has invented
a new protocol. We're
calling it TCP/IP.

GATES
1995

It would be hard to overstate the importance of networks to modern computing, although that doesn't seem to stop people from trying. At many sites, web and email access are now the main activities for which computers are used. As of early 2000, the Internet is estimated to have 300 million users, and it still seems to be growing exponentially. Maintenance of local networks, Internet connections, web sites, and network-related software is a bread-and-butter portion of most sysadmins' jobs.

TCP/IP is the networking protocol suite most commonly used with UNIX, MacOS, Windows, Windows NT, and most other operating systems. It is also the native language of the Internet. IP stands for Internet Protocol and TCP for Transmission Control Protocol.

TCP/IP defines a uniform programming interface to different types of network hardware, guaranteeing that systems can exchange data ("interoperate") despite their many differences. IP, the suite's underlying delivery protocol, is the workhorse of the Internet. TCP and UDP (the User Datagram Protocol) are transport protocols that are built on top of IP to deliver packets to specific applications.

TCP is a connection-oriented protocol that facilitates a conversation between two programs. It works a lot like a phone call: the words you speak are delivered to the person you called, and vice versa. The connection persists even when neither party is speaking. TCP provides reliable delivery, flow control, and congestion control.

UDP is a packet-oriented service. It's analogous to sending a letter through the post office. It does not provide two-way connections and does not have any form of congestion control.

TCP/IP

TCP is a polite protocol that forces competing users to share bandwidth and generally behave in ways that are good for the productivity of the overall network. UDP, on the other hand, blasts packets out as fast as it can. Better behavior for UDP is being worked on, but it doesn't yet seem to have become a high priority.

As the Internet becomes more popular and more crowded, we need the traffic to be mostly TCP to avoid congestion and effectively share the available bandwidth. Measurements of protocol utilization over the past few years show UDP traffic increasing from about 5% of the bytes in 1997-98 to about 7% in 1999-00. Applications such as games, music, voice, and video are starting to make their presence felt.

This chapter introduces the TCP/IP protocols in the political and technical context of the Internet. Unfortunately, even basic networking is too big a topic to be covered in a single chapter. Other network-related chapters in this book include Chapter 14, *Routing*, Chapter 20, *Network Management and Debugging*, and Chapter 16, *The Domain Name System*.

The next few sections include background material on the protocols and politics of the Internet and are quite opinionated and fluffy. Skip ahead to page 271 to go directly to the gory details of IP, or to page 306 to jump to vendor-specific configuration information.

## 13.1  TCP/IP AND THE INTERNET

TCP/IP and the Internet share a history that goes back several decades. The technical success of the Internet is due largely to the elegant and flexible design of TCP/IP. In turn, the leverage provided by the Internet has helped TCP/IP prevail over several competing protocol suites that were favored at one time or another for political or commercial reasons.

### A brief history lesson

Contrary to popular belief, the Internet is not a Microsoft product that debuted in 1995, nor is it the creation of a U.S. vice president. The progenitor of the modern Internet was a network called ARPANET that was established in 1969 by DARPA (Defense Advanced Research Project Agency), the R&D arm of the U.S. Department of Defense. The ARPANET eventually became the NSFNET backbone, which connected supercomputer sites and regional networks.

By the end of the 1980s, the network was no longer a research project and it was time for the National Science Foundation to extract itself from the networking business. We transitioned to the commercial Internet over a period of several years; the NSF-NET was turned off in April of 1994. Today's backbone Internet is a collection of private networks owned by Internet service providers (ISPs) that interconnect at many so-called peering points.

In the mid-1980s, the Internet essentially consisted of the original ARPANET sites and a handful of universities with Digital Equipment Corporation's VAX computers running Berkeley UNIX on 10 Mb/s Ethernets connected by 56 Kb/s leased digital telephone lines. Every September, when students came back to school, the Internet would suffer what became known as congestion collapse. Van Jacobson, a researcher in the Network Research Group at Lawrence Berkeley Labs, would look at the protocols' behavior under load and "fix" them. The algorithms we now know as slow start, congestion avoidance, fast retransmit, and fast recovery all arose from this context.

Moore's law (the rule of thumb that hardware speeds double every 18 months) and market pressure have greatly accelerated the development of the net. Since the late 1980s when the current TCP algorithms were stabilized, the speed of network interfaces has increased by a factor of 1,000 (from 6% efficiency on early 10 Mb/s Ethernets to near 90% efficiency on gigabit Ethernets), the speed of leased circuits by a factor of 12,000, and the total number of hosts by a factor of 50,000.

Anyone who has designed a software system and seen it obsoleted by the next generation of hardware or the next release of an operating system knows how amazing it is that our Internet is still alive and kicking, running basically the same TCP/IP protocol suite that was designed 25 years ago for a very different Internet. Our hats are off to Bob Kahn, Vint Cerf, Jon Postel, Van Jacobson, and all the other people who made it happen.

## How the Internet is managed today

The development of the Internet has always been a cooperative and open effort. Now that it is a driving commercial force in the world economy, several sectors are worried that the Internet seems to be in the hands of a bunch of computer geeks, with perhaps a little direction from the U.S. government. Like it or not, Internet governance is coming.

Several organizations are involved:

- ICANN, the Internet Corporation for Assigned Names and Numbers: if anyone can be said to be in charge of the Internet, this group is it. (www.icann.org)

- IETF, the Internet Engineering Task Force: this group oversees the development and standardization of the technical aspects of the Internet. It is an open forum in which anyone can participate. (www.ietf.org)

- ISOC, the Internet Society: ISOC is a membership organization that represents Internet users. (www.isoc.org)

Of these groups, ICANN has the toughest job: establishing itself as the authority in charge of the Internet, undoing the mistakes of the past, and foreseeing the future.

## Network standards and documentation

The technical activities of the Internet community are summarized in documents known as RFCs; an RFC is a Request for Comments. Protocol standards, proposed changes, and informational bulletins all usually end up as RFCs. Sometimes the

TCP/IP

name is accurate and anyone who has comments on a proposal is encouraged to reply. Other times, the RFC mechanism simply documents or explains something about existing practice.

RFCs are numbered sequentially; currently, there are about 3,000. RFCs also have descriptive titles (e.g., *Algorithms for Synchronizing Network Clocks*), but to forestall ambiguity they are usually cited by number. Once distributed, the contents of an RFC are never changed. Updates are distributed as new RFCs with their own reference numbers. By convention, updated RFCs contain all the material that remains relevant, so the new RFCs completely replace the old ones, at least in theory.

The process by which RFCs are published is itself documented in the RFC titled *Internet Official Protocol Standards*. This RFC also includes pointers to the most current RFCs for various protocol standards. Since the information changes frequently, this RFC is reissued every 100 RFCs: the current version is RFC2600, the next version will be RFC2700, and so on. The Internet standards process itself is described in RFC2026. Another useful meta-RFC is RFC2555, *30 Years of RFCs*, which describes some of the cultural and technical context behind the RFC system.

Don't be scared away by the wealth of technical detail found in RFCs. Most contain introductions, summaries, and rationales that are useful for system administrators. Some are specifically written as overviews or general introductions. RFCs may not be the gentlest way to learn about a topic, but they are authoritative, concise, and free.

Not all RFCs are dry and full of boring technical details. Some of our favorites on the lighter side (some written on April 1st) are RFCs 1118, 1149, 2324, and 2795:

- RFC1118 – *The Hitchhiker's Guide to the Internet*
- RFC1149 – *A Standard for the Transmission of IP Datagrams on Avian Carriers*
- RFC2324 – *Hyper Text Coffee Pot Control Protocol (HTCPCP/1.0)*
- RFC2795 – *The Infinite Monkey Protocol Suite (IMPS)*

They are a good read and give a bit of insight into the people who are designing and building our Internet.

In addition to being assigned its own serial number, an RFC may also be assigned an FYI (For Your Information) number, a BCP (Best Current Practice) number, or a STD (Standard) number. FYIs, STDs, and BCPs are subseries of the RFCs that include documents of special interest or importance.

FYIs are introductory or informational documents intended for a broad audience. They are usually an excellent place to start research on an unfamiliar topic. STDs document Internet protocols that have completed the IETF's review and testing process and have been formally adopted as standards. BCPs document recommended procedures for Internet sites; they consist of administrative suggestions and for system administrators are often the most valuable of the RFC subseries.

RFCs, FYIs, STDs, and BCPs are numbered sequentially within their own series, so a document can bear several different identifying numbers. For example, RFC1635, *How to Use Anonymous FTP*, is also known as FYI0024.

RFCs are available from numerous sources. There's a list of actively maintained RFC mirrors at www.rfc-editor.org, which is dispatch central for RFC-related matters.

## 13.2  NETWORKING ROAD MAP

Now that we've provided a bit of context, let's take a look at the TCP/IP protocols themselves. TCP/IP is a "protocol suite," a set of network protocols designed to work smoothly together. It includes several components, each defined by a standards-track RFC or series of RFCs:

- IP, the Internet Protocol, which routes data packets from one machine to another (RFC791)

- ICMP, the Internet Control Message Protocol, which provides several kinds of low-level support for IP, including error messages, routing assistance, and debugging help (RFC792)

- ARP, the Address Resolution Protocol, which translates IP addresses to hardware addresses (RFC823)[1]

- UDP, the User Datagram Protocol, and TCP, the Transmission Control Protocol, which deliver data to specific applications on the destination machine. UDP provides unverified, "best effort" transport for individual messages, whereas TCP guarantees a reliable, full duplex, flow controlled, error corrected conversation between processes on two hosts. (RFCs 768 and 793)

TCP/IP is designed around the layering scheme shown in Table 13.1.

**Table 13.1   TCP/IP network model**

| Layer | Function |
| --- | --- |
| Application layer | End-user application programs |
| Transport layer | Delivery of data to applications[a] |
| Network layer | Basic communication, addressing, and routing |
| Link layer | Network hardware and device drivers |
| Physical layer | The cable or physical medium itself |

a. Optionally addressing reliability and flow control issues

After TCP/IP had been implemented and deployed, the International Organization for Standardization came up with its own seven-layer protocol suite called OSI. It was

TCP/IP

---

1. This is actually a little white lie. ARP is not really part of TCP/IP and can be used with other protocol suites. However, it's an integral part of the way TCP/IP works on most LAN media.

a consummate design-by-committee white elephant, and it never really caught on because of its complexity and inefficiency. Some think a financial layer and a political layer should have been added to the original seven OSI layers.[2]

Exhibit A shows how the various components and clients of TCP/IP fit into its general architecture and layering scheme.

**Exhibit A    One big happy TCP/IP family**

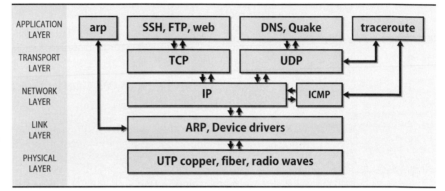

## 13.3  PACKETS AND ENCAPSULATION

UNIX can support a variety of physical networks, including Ethernet, FDDI, token ring, ATM (Asynchronous Transfer Mode), wireless Ethernet, and serial-line-based systems. Hardware is managed within the link layer of the TCP/IP architecture, and higher-level protocols do not know or care about the specific hardware being used.

Data travels on a network in the form of *packets*, bursts of data with a maximum length imposed by the link layer. Each packet consists of a header and a payload. The header tells where the packet came from and where it's going. It can also include checksums, protocol-specific information, or other handling instructions. The payload is the data to be transferred.

The name of the primitive data unit depends on the layer of the protocol. At the link layer it is called a *frame*, at the IP layer a *packet*, and at the TCP layer a *segment*. Here, we use "packet" as a generic term that encompasses all these cases.

As a packet travels down the protocol stack in preparation for being sent, each protocol adds its own header information. Each protocol's finished packet becomes the payload part of the packet generated by the next protocol. This nesting is known as encapsulation. On the receiving machine, the encapsulation is reversed as the packet travels back up the protocol stack.

2. In fact, a T-shirt showing this extended nine-layer model is available from the computer science department at the University of Colorado. Email tshirt@cs.colorado.edu for details.

For example, a UDP packet being transmitted over Ethernet contains three different wrappers or envelopes. On the Ethernet wire, it is "framed" with a simple header that lists the source and next-hop destination hardware addresses, the length of the frame, and the frame's checksum (CRC). The Ethernet frame's payload is an IP packet, the IP packet's payload is a UDP packet, and the UDP packet's payload is the actual data being transmitted. Exhibit B shows the components of such a frame.

**Exhibit B    A typical network packet**

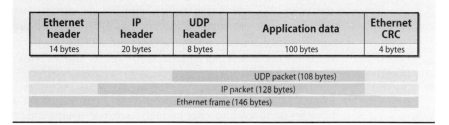

We use the term "byte" to refer to an 8-bit data unit. In days of yore, "byte" was a more general term, so you will often see the term "octet" used in RFCs instead.

**The link layer**

In this section, we cover several topics that bridge the gap between the lowest layers of the networking software and the network hardware itself.

*Ethernet framing standards*

One of the main chores of the link layer is to add headers to packets and to put separators between them. The headers contain the packets' link-layer addressing information and checksums, and the separators ensure that receivers can tell where one packet stops and the next one begins. The process of adding these extra bits is known generically as framing.

Two different standards for 10 Mb/s Ethernet framing are in common use: DIX Ethernet II and the IEEE 802.2 LLC SNAP.[3] UNIX hosts generally use Ethernet II, as do Cisco routers. Novell and IPX networks normally use 802.2. Ethernet and 802.2 differ in some fields of the frame header but do not conflict, so receivers can determine unambiguously which format is being used by each individual packet and decode the header appropriately.

The framing that a machine uses is determined both by its interface card and by the interface card's driver. On PCs running Windows you can choose which style of framing you want, but on UNIX you usually cannot. Both types of framing interoperate

---

3.  The link layer is actually divided into two parts: MAC, the Media Access Control sublayer and LLC, the Link Layer Control sublayer. The MAC layer deals with the media and gets packets onto the wire. The LLC layer handles the framing.

just fine from UNIX's perspective. On the other hand, Windows machines that use different framing on the same network cannot talk to each other. As a sysadmin, you usually don't need to worry about framing mismatches unless you are performing low-level debugging of a mixed network.

### Ethernet cabling and signalling standards

The cabling options for 10 Mb/s Ethernet are fairly straightforward, but things get somewhat more complicated in the 100 Mb/s arena. Years ago, there were three different standards for twisted-pair wire (TX, which uses two pairs of Category 5 wire, and T4 and VG, which each require four pairs of Category 3 wire) and one for fiber (FX, which uses multimode fiber optic cable). Hewlett-Packard championed the VG standard (which wasn't really Ethernet) and was the first to bring a product to market. Other manufacturers ignored the VG system and scurried to implement TX. TX is now used everywhere.

Refer to Chapter 15, *Network Hardware*, for more information about the various Ethernet standards. Another useful reference to the ins and outs of Ethernet is the web site wwwhost.ots.utexas.edu/ethernet, which is maintained by Charles Spurgeon.

### Wireless networking

The IEEE 802.11 standard attempts to define framing and signalling standards for wireless links. Unfortunately, it was originally rather vague and included several parameters and options that were not fully specified. One interoperability issue you may need to pay attention to is that of "translation" vs. "encapsulation."

Translation converts a packet from one format to another; encapsulation wraps the packet with the desired format. Windows systems tend to default to encapsulation and UNIX systems to translation; the wireless base stations must be explicitly configured. If you are deploying a wireless network, you must make sure that your base stations and the workstations they talk to are all operating in the same mode.

Laptop computer users encounter another problem caused by the ambiguity of the 802.11 specification. Wireless PCMCIA cards (which tend to be power hogs) have a power saving mode that is incompatible with some base stations. It is turned on by default, of course. If you are building a wireless network and find that users' laptops don't work on it, suggest that they try turning the power-saving feature off. A wireless home network that uses the Apple AirPort base station and Lucent cards is unbeatable. You can hack anywhere: in bed, by the pool, or even down the block.

### Maximum transfer units

The size of packets on a network may be limited both by hardware specifications and by protocol conventions. For example, the payload of an Ethernet frame can be no longer than 1,500 bytes. The size limit is associated with the link-layer protocol and is called the maximum transfer unit or MTU. Table 13.2 shows typical values for the MTU.

**Table 13.2    MTUs for various types of network link layer**

| Network type | Maximum transfer unit |
| --- | --- |
| Ethernet | 1,500 bytes (1,492 with 802.2 framing) |
| FDDI token ring | 4,500 bytes (4,352 for IP/FDDI) |
| PPP modem link | Configurable, often 512 or 576 bytes |
| PC stacks | Configurable, usually defaults to 512 |
| ATM | 53 bytes (see comments below) |
| Point-to-point WAN links (T1, T3) | Configurable, often 1,500 or 4,500 bytes |

For ATM, the term MTU doesn't quite apply; ATM lies somewhere in between the physical layer and the link layer. An ATM cell is normally 53 bytes with a 48-byte payload, but with AAL/5 framing, packets can be as large as $2^{16}$. The ATM community typically chooses and MTU of 9,180 for normal mode and 1,500 for LANE (Local Area Network Emulation) mode.

In the TCP/IP suite, the IP layer splits packets to conform to the MTU of a particular network link. If a packet is routed through several networks, one of the intermediate networks may have a smaller MTU than the network of origin. In this case, the router that forwards the packet onto the small-MTU network will further subdivide the packet in a process called fragmentation. Fragmentation is an unwelcome chore for a busy router. The TCP protocol can determine the smallest MTU along the path to the destination and use that size from the outset. UDP is not so nice and is happy to shunt extra work to the IP layer. In the IPv6 protocol, intermediate routers can no longer perform fragmentation—MTU discovery is required.

Fragmentation problems can be insidious. If you are using a tunneled architecture for a virtual private network, for example, you should look at the size of the packets that are traversing the tunnel. They are often 1,500 bytes to start with, but once the tunneling header is added, they become 1,540 bytes or so and must be fragmented. Setting the MTU of the link to a smaller value will avert fragmentation and increase the performance of the network. Consult the **ifconfig** man page to see how to set an interface's MTU.

### Packet addressing

Like letters or email messages, network packets must be properly addressed in order to reach their destinations. Several addressing schemes are used in combination:

- MAC (media access control) addresses for hardware
- IP addresses for software
- Hostnames for people

A host's network interface may have a link-layer MAC address that distinguishes it from other machines on the physical network, an IP address that identifies it on the global Internet, and a hostname that's used by humans.

TCP/IP

The lowest level of addressing is dictated by network hardware. For example, Ethernet devices are assigned a unique 6-byte hardware address at the time of manufacture. Token ring interfaces have a similar address that is also six bytes long. Some point-to-point networks (such as PPP, described on page 291) need no hardware addresses at all; the identity of the destination is specified as the link is established.

A six-byte Ethernet address is divided into two parts: the first three bytes identify the manufacturer of the hardware, and the last three bytes are a unique serial number that the manufacturer assigns. Sysadmins can often identify at least the brand of machine that is trashing the network by looking up the 3-byte identifier in a table of vendor IDs. A current vendor table is available from

http://www.isi.edu/in-notes/iana/assignments/ethernet-numbers

This information used to be published regularly in the RFC series, but it is no longer distributed that way. RFC1700 (1994) was the last *Assigned Numbers* RFC. The official repository of all the Internet's magic numbers is www.iana.org/numbers.htm.

Ethernet hardware addresses should be permanently assigned and immutable; unfortunately, some network interface cards let you specify the hardware address. Wireless cards are especially bad in this respect. Don't assign values in the multicast address range (odd second digit) or use other special values. Solaris and Red Hat let you change the hardware address of any interface, but please don't do that.

At the next level up from the hardware, Internet addressing (more commonly known as IP addressing) is used. One 4-byte IP address is assigned to each network interface. IP addresses are globally unique[4] and hardware independent. We ramble on for pages about IP addresses in the next section.

*See page 285 for more information about ARP.*
The mapping between IP addresses and hardware addresses is implemented at the link layer of the TCP/IP model. On networks that support broadcasting (i.e., networks that allow packets to be addressed to "all hosts on this physical network"), a protocol called ARP allows mappings to be discovered automatically, without assistance from a system administrator.

Since IP addresses are long, seemingly random numbers, they are hard for people to remember. UNIX systems allow one or more hostnames to be associated with an IP address so that users can type **telnet anchor** instead of **telnet 128.138.242.1**.

This mapping can be set up in several ways, ranging from a static file (**/etc/hosts**) to the NIS and NIS+ database systems to DNS, the world-wide Domain Name System. Keep in mind that hostnames are just a shorthand way of writing IP addresses.

### Ports

IP addresses identify machines, or more precisely, network interfaces on a machine. They are not specific enough to address particular processes or services. TCP and

---

4. This is a small lie that's true in most situations. See the discussion of NAT starting on page 279 for the straight dope on nonunique IP addresses.

UDP extend IP addresses with a concept known as a "port." A port is 16-bit number that supplements an IP address to specify a particular communication channel. Standard UNIX services such as email, FTP, and the remote login server all associate themselves with "well-known" ports defined in the file **/etc/services**. To help prevent impersonation of these services, UNIX systems restrict access to port numbers under 1,024 to root.

### Address types

At both the IP layer and the link layer, there are several different types of addresses:

- Unicast – addresses that refer to a single host (network interface, really)
- Multicast – addresses that identify a group of hosts
- Broadcast – addresses that include all hosts on the local network

Multicast addressing facilitates applications such as video conferencing in which the same set of packets must be sent to all participants. The Internet Group Management Protocol (IGMP) constructs and manages sets of hosts that are treated as one multicast destination. Multicasting is still somewhat experimental. However, the voice-over-IP and video-on-demand markets may speed up its deployment somewhat.

Multicast link-layer addresses have the low-order bit of their high-order byte (the first byte on the wire) set to 1; that is, any address with an odd first byte is a multicast address. These multicast addresses are used by various pieces of hardware for discovery protocols or for spanning tree algorithms. Lots of old crufty protocols also have reserved addresses in this range. The value assigned for IP multicast on the Internet is 01:00:5E.

The link-layer broadcast address is all 1s in binary or ff:ff:ff:ff:ff:ff in hexadecimal.

At the IP layer, multicast addresses begin with a byte in the range 224 to 239. Broadcast addresses have a host part that is all 1s.

## 13.4  IP ADDRESSES: THE GORY DETAILS

An IP address, also called an Internet address, is four bytes long and is divided into a network part and a host part. The network part identifies a logical network to which the address refers, and the host part identifies a machine on that network.

By convention, IP addresses are written as decimal numbers, one for each byte, separated by periods. For example, the IP address for our machine boulder is written as "128.138.240.1". The leftmost byte is the most significant and is always part of the network portion.

When 127 is the first byte of an address, it denotes the "loopback network," a fictitious network that has no real hardware interface and only one host. The loopback address 127.0.0.1 always refers to the current host. Its symbolic name is "localhost".

An interface's IP address and other parameters are set with the **ifconfig** command. Jump ahead to page 300 for a detailed description of **ifconfig**.

TCP/IP

## IP address classes

Historically, IP addresses were grouped into "classes," depending on the first bits of the leftmost byte. The class determined which bytes of the address were in the network portion and which were in the host portion. Today, routing systems use an explicit mask to specify the network portion and can draw the line between any two bits, not just on byte boundaries. However, the traditional classes are still used as defaults when no explicit division is provided.

Classes A, B, and C denote regular IP addresses. Classes D and E are used for multicasting and research purposes. Table 13.3 describes the characteristics of each class. The network portion of an address is denoted by N, and the host portion by H.

**Table 13.3    Historical Internet address classes**

| Class | 1st byte[a] | Format | Comments |
|---|---|---|---|
| A | 1-126 | N.H.H.H | Very early networks, or reserved for DOD |
| B | 128-191 | N.N.H.H | Large sites, usually subnetted, were hard to get |
| C | 192-223 | N.N.N.H | Easy to get, often obtained in sets |
| D | 224-239 | – | Multicast addresses, not permanently assigned |
| E | 240-254 | – | Experimental addresses |

a. The values 0 and 255 are special and are not used as the first byte of regular IP addresses. 127 is reserved for the loopback address.

## Subnetting and netmasks

It is rare for a single physical network to have more than a hundred computers attached to it. Therefore, class A and class B addresses (which allow for 16,777,214 and 65,534 hosts per network, respectively) are really quite silly and wasteful. For example, the 126 class A networks use up half of the available address space.

Most sites that have these addresses use a refinement of the addressing scheme called subnetting, in which part of the host portion of an address is "borrowed" to extend the network portion. For example, the four bytes of a class B address would normally be interpreted as N.N.H.H. If subnetting is used to assign the third byte to the network number rather than the host number, the address would be interpreted as N.N.N.H. This use of subnetting turns a single class B network address into 256 distinct class-C-like networks, each capable of supporting 254 hosts.

See page 300 for more information about **ifconfig**.

This reassignment is effected by using the **ifconfig** command to associate an explicit "subnet mask" with a network interface. Each bit of the netmask that corresponds to the network portion of an IP address is set to 1, and host bits are set to 0. For example, the netmask for the N.N.N.H configuration would be 255.255.255.0 in decimal or 0xFFFFFF00 in hex. **ifconfig** normally uses the inherent class of an address to figure out which bits are part of the network. When you set an explicit mask, you simply override this behavior.

The division between network part and host part need not fall on a byte boundary. However, the network bits must be contiguous and must appear at the high order end of the address. Configurations such as N.N.H.N were once allowed but were not common; they are no longer permitted.

Netmasks that do not end at a byte boundary can be annoying to decode and are often written as /XX, where XX is the number of bits in the network portion of the address. For example, the network address 128.138.243.0/26 refers to the first of four networks whose first bytes are 128.138.243. The other three networks have 64, 128, and 192 as their fourth bytes. The netmask associated with these networks is 255.255.255.192 or 0xFFFFFFC0; in binary, it's 26 ones followed by 6 zeros. Exhibit C shows the relationships among these numbers in a bit more detail.

**Exhibit C    Subnet mask base conversion**

| IP address | 128 | . | 138 | . | 243 | . | 0 |
|---|---|---|---|---|---|---|---|
| Decimal netmask | 255 | . | 255 | . | 255 | . | 192 |
| Hex netmask | f f | . | f f | . | f f | . | c 0 |
| Binary netmask | 1111 1111 | . | 1111 1111 | . | 1111 1111 | . | 1100 0000 |

A /26 network has 6 bits left (32 − 26 = 6) to number hosts. $2^6$ is 64, so the network has 64 potential host addresses. However, it can only accommodate 62 actual hosts, because the all-0 and all-1 host addresses are reserved (they are the network and broadcast addresses, respectively).

It's confusing to do all this bit twiddling in your head, but some tricks can make it simpler. The number of hosts per network and the value of the last byte in the netmask always add up to 256:

> last netmask byte = 256 − net size

For example, 256 − 64 = 192, which is the final byte of the netmask in the preceding example. Another arithmetic fact is that the last byte of an actual network address (as opposed to a netmask) must be evenly divisible by the number of hosts per network. We see this fact in action in the current example, where the last bytes are 0, 64, 128, and 192—all evenly divisible by 64.

In our example, the extra two bits of network address obtained by subnetting can take on the values 00, 01, 10, and 11. The 128.138.243.0/24 network has thus been divided into four /26 networks:

- 128.138.243.0/26        (0 in decimal is **00**000000 in binary)
- 128.138.243.64/26       (64 in decimal is **01**000000 in binary)
- 128.138.243.128/26      (128 in decimal is **10**000000 in binary)
- 128.138.243.192/26      (192 in decimal is **11**000000 in binary)

TCP/IP

The boldfaced bits of the last byte of each address are the bits that belong to the network portion of that byte.

Given an IP address (say, 128.138.243.100), we cannot tell without the associated netmask what the network address and broadcast address will be. Table 13.4 shows the possibilities for /16 (the default for a class B address), /24 (a sensible value), and /26 (a realistic value if address space is tight).

**Table 13.4   Example IP address decodings**

| IP address | Netmask | Network | Broadcast |
|---|---|---|---|
| 128.138.243.100/16 | 255.255.0.0 | 128.138.0.0 | 128.138.255.255 |
| 128.138.243.100/24 | 255.255.255.0 | 128.138.243.0 | 128.138.243.255 |
| 128.138.243.100/26 | 255.255.255.192 | 128.138.243.64 | 128.138.243.127 |

Keith Owens has written a wonderful little Perl script called **ipcalc.pl** that helps with binary/hex/mask arithmetic. It's available from ftp.ocs.com.au and requires Perl 5. **ipcalc** displays everything you might need to know about a network address and its netmask, broadcast address, hosts, etc. We've even found a version of **ipcalc** that was ported to the Palm Pilot; see www.ajw.com/ipcalc.htm.

Here's some sample **ipcalc** output, munged a bit to help with formatting:

```
% ipcalc.pl 128.138.243.100/26
IP address     128 . 138 . 243 . 100 / 26     128.138.243.100/26
Mask bits  11111111 11111111 11111111 11000000
Mask bytes   255 . 255 . 255 . 192             255.255.255.192
Address    10000000 10001010 11110011 01100100
Network      128 . 138 . 243 . 64              128.138.243.64
Broadcast    128 . 138 . 243 . 127             128.138.243.127
First Host    128 . 138 . 243 . 65             128.138.243.65
Last Host     128 . 138 . 243 . 126            128.138.243.126
Total Hosts       62
PTR               100.243.138.128.in-addr.arpa
IP Address (hex)  808AF364
```

The output provides both easy-to-understand versions of the addresses and "cut and paste" versions. Cool.

Red Hat includes a program, also called **ipcalc**, that performs similar calculations. Its syntax is a bit different.

The original RFC on IP subnetting (RFC950) did not permit the use of the first or last subnets (all 0s and all 1s). In our example with the /26 networks, this rule would eliminate half of the subnets: the 0 subnet and the 192 subnet. Everyone ignored the RFC except Novell and Cisco. (Though in recent versions of Cisco's IOS operating system—12.0 and later—subnet 0 is available by default.)

The RFC is wrong, although its intentions were fine. Subnet 0 was disallowed because it was thought that confusion might arise if a subnet address was indistinguishable from an unsubnetted network address. The fear proved groundless, however, and all-0/all-1 subnets are in common use today. It is the host portion that should not be all 0s or all 1s.

The network address and broadcast address steal two hosts from each network, so the smallest meaningful network would have four possible hosts: two real hosts—usually at either end of a point-to-point link—and the network and broadcast addresses. To have four values for hosts requires two bits in the host portion, so such a network would be a /30 network with netmask 255.255.255.252 or 0xFFFFFFFC.

Although the hosts on a network may agree that they are using subnetted addresses, the rest of the world doesn't know about this and continues to treat addresses according to their implicit class.[5] Rather than advertising every subnet to the outside world, in our 128.138.243.100 example you would only need to advertise a single class B network. Once a packet arrived within the subnetted area, its destination address would be reinterpreted with local netmasks, the real target network "discovered," and the packet routed to its exact destination.

### The IP address crisis

The Internet community realized in about 1992 that there were three fundamental problems with the original address allocation scheme. First, we were going to run out of class B addresses—the most desirable ones for moderately large organizations—by mid-1995. At the same time, the routing tables of Internet backbone sites were growing so large that they would not fit in the memory of available routers. And finally, IP addresses were being allocated on a first-come, first-served basis with no locality of reference; that is, numerically adjacent addresses could be within the same organization or on different continents. Imagine the confusion that would result if phone numbers or zip codes were assigned in this haphazard fashion.

To solve the problem, two solutions were advanced in tandem: one for the immediate future and one for the long term. Classless Inter-Domain Routing (CIDR), the short-term solution, is a different way of managing the existing four-byte address space that uses the available addresses more efficiently and allows routing tables to be simplified by taking numerical adjacencies into account. We discuss CIDR in more detail in the next section.

The long-term solution, IPv6, is a revision of the IP protocol that expands the address space to 16 bytes and incorporates several other lessons learned from the use of IP over the last 25 years. It removes several features of IP that experience has shown to be of little value, making the protocol potentially faster and easier to implement. It also integrates security and authentication into the basic protocol and eliminates fragmentation at intermediate routers. 16-byte addressing gives $2^{128}$ possible ad-

TCP/IP

---

5. Another lie in the name of a simple, as yet incomplete description; see the discussion of Classless Inter-Domain Routing (CIDR) on page 276 for the real scoop.

dresses: that's 665,570,793,348,866,943,898,599 addresses per square meter of the Earth's surface. IPv6 addresses were extended to 16 bytes after calculations showed a remote chance that 8 address bytes would not be enough. It has been suggested that the committee making the decision had rusty math skills and thought that 16 bytes would make twice as many addresses as 8 bytes did.

As of 2000, IPv6 is still in the process of being standardized, but CIDR has been fully deployed. CIDR is supported and used by the Internet backbone and by the major manufacturers of routing equipment. NAT, a scheme for reusing IP addresses that's covered on page 279, also played a large role in reducing the demand for IP addresses.

The complexity of IPv6, the efficiency of CIDR and NAT, and the inertia of an Internet that already works pretty well all combine to suggest that it may be a long time before we move to IPv6, if indeed we ever do. Such a move will likely be driven by countries such as Japan or China that cannot get the IPv4 address space they think they need or a new killer application that requires IPv6. A good candidate for such an application might be a new generation of cell phones and other wireless devices that embed a telephone number in an IPv6 address. Voice-over-IP systems would also benefit from a closer correspondence between phone numbers and IPv6 addresses.

Some additional details on IPv6 addressing are given on page 281.

### CIDR: Classless Inter-Domain Routing

CIDR, defined in RFC1519, eliminates the class system that formerly determined the network portion of an IP address. Like subnetting, of which it is a direct extension, it relies on an explicit netmask to define the boundary between the network and host parts of an address. But unlike subnetting, it allows, for purposes of routing, the network portion to be made *smaller* than would be implied by an address's implicit class. Using a shorter netmask has the effect of aggregating several networks. Hence, CIDR is sometimes referred to as supernetting.

With CIDR, several class C networks can be allocated to a site without requiring the Internet to have separate routing table entries for each one. The site could also be allocated a subspace of a class A or B address. For example, suppose a site has been given a block of 32 class C addresses numbered 192.144.0.0 through 192.144.31.0 (in CIDR notation, 192.144.0.0/21). Internally, the site could use them as

- 1 network of length /21, 2,046 hosts,[6] netmask 255.255.224.0
- 32 networks of length /24, 254 hosts each, netmask 255.255.255.0
- 64 networks of length /25, 126 hosts each, netmask 255.255.255.128
- 128 networks of length /26, 62 hosts each, netmask 255.255.255.192

and so on. It's also possible to mix and match regions of different subnet lengths, as long as all the pieces fit together without overlaps. This is called variable length sub-

---

6. The original Ethernet on RG-11 coaxial cable allowed at most 1,024 hosts on a single network, probably because of the maximum length of a cable and the separation required between hosts. This limit might still be lurking in code today, so this arrangement would not be practical for the real world.

netting. For example, an ISP with the 192.144.0.0/21 allocation could define some /30 networks for PPP dial-up customers, some /24s for large customers, and some /27s for smaller folks.

When you mix and match like this, all the hosts on a particular network must be configured with the same netmask. You cannot tell one host on the network that it is a /24 and another host on that same network that it is a /25.

The beauty and value of CIDR is that from the perspective of the Internet, it's not necessary to have 256, 128, or even 32 routing table entries for these addresses. They all refer to the same organization, and the packets all need to go to the same place. A single routing entry for the address 192.144.0.0/21 suffices.

With the advent of CIDR, system administrators have gotten good at binary and hex arithmetic, or have discovered that the UNIX utility **bc** can do math in any base, using the **ibase** and **obase** directives.[7] You can use Table 13.5 as a cheat sheet.

**Table 13.5    Network configurations for various lengths of netmask**

| Length[a] | Host bits | Hosts/net[b] | Dec. netmask | Hex netmask |
|---|---|---|---|---|
| /20 | 12 | 4094 | 255.255.240.0 | 0xFFFFF000 |
| /21 | 11 | 2046 | 255.255.248.0 | 0xFFFFF800 |
| /22 | 10 | 1022 | 255.255.252.0 | 0xFFFFFC00 |
| /23 | 9 | 510 | 255.255.254.0 | 0xFFFFFE00 |
| /24 | 8 | 254 | 255.255.255.0 | 0xFFFFFF00 |
| /25 | 7 | 126 | 255.255.255.128 | 0xFFFFFF80 |
| /26 | 6 | 62 | 255.255.255.192 | 0xFFFFFFC0 |
| /27 | 5 | 30 | 255.255.255.224 | 0xFFFFFFE0 |
| /28 | 4 | 14 | 255.255.255.240 | 0xFFFFFFF0 |
| /29 | 3 | 6 | 255.255.255.248 | 0xFFFFFFF8 |
| /30 | 2 | 2 | 255.255.255.252 | 0xFFFFFFFC |

a. The network length + the number of host bits is always 32, since we are dividing up the fixed-size "pie" of a 32-bit IP address.

b. Mathy folks will notice that the number of hosts per net is $2^{\#hostbits} - 2$; the −2 reflects the fact that the all-0 and all-1 host addresses are special.

When CIDR was introduced in 1993, the backbone tables contained approximately 20,000 routes. Despite the exponential growth of the Internet since that time, the size of the routing tables had grown to only 80,000 routes by the summer of 2000. This modest growth in routing entries is due to extensive aggregation of both old and new address allocations.[8]

7. But be careful not to back yourself into a corner… This puzzle is left as an exercise for the reader.

8. When we started writing this chapter in the summer of 1999, the number of routes in the backbone table was 60,000. Now, less than a year later, it is 80,000—that's more than 25% growth per year. Current routing hardware and algorithms can sustain a few percent growth per year, but not 25%. See www.telstra.net/ops/bgptable.html for more information.

TCP/IP

There is still an unaggregated region of the address space, called the 192 swamp (and smaller swamps in the 199 and 205 ranges), consisting of early class C addresses whose owners cannot aggregate them and do not want to turn them in and then have to renumber. The United States is particularly bad in this regard. Europe and Asia, which started a bit later, learned from our mistakes and did a much better job of allocating addresses. Sites with an unaggregated 192 network should turn it back into the American Registry for Internet Numbers (ARIN) and get a new block from their ISP. Unfortunately, the cost of renumbering (in IPv4 space at least) precludes most sites from doing this.

Although CIDR was only intended as an interim solution, it has proved to be strong enough to handle the Internet's growth problems for the foreseeable future. In fact, CIDR has worked so well that it is unclear if we really need a new IP protocol. An enormous amount of engineering work has gone into the IPv6 specification and prototype implementations of IPv6. It would be a shame to waste this work, but wholesale deployment of IPv6 will probably require either a new killer application written only for IPv6, a yuppie toy that uses IPv6 addressing, or a decision by Microsoft to obsolete IPv4.

### Address allocation

In the early days of the Internet, individual sites applied to the Internet Network Information Center (InterNIC) for address space. ARIN has now replaced the InterNIC in the Americas.[9] Only ISPs who allocate significant amounts of address space per year are eligible to apply to ARIN for IP address space. All other sites must apply to their ISP.

Only network numbers are formally assigned; sites must define their own host numbers to form complete IP addresses. You can subdivide the address space given to you however you like.

Administratively, ICANN (the Internet Corporation for Assigned Names and Numbers) has delegated blocks of addresses to three regional Internet registries, and these regional authorities are responsible for doling out subblocks to ISPs within their regions (see Table 13.6). These ISPs in turn divide up their blocks and hand out pieces to individual clients. Only large ISPs should ever have to deal directly with one of the ICANN-sponsored address registries.

**Table 13.6   Regional IP address registries**

| Name | Web address | Region covered |
|------|-------------|----------------|
| ARIN | www.arin.net | North and South America, sub-Saharan Africa |
| APNIC | www.apnic.net | Asia/Pacific region |
| RIPE | www.ripe.net | Europe and surrounding areas |

9. A new registry is being created for Latin America, but it won't be operational for a while.

The delegation from ICANN to ARIN, RIPE, and APNIC and then on to national or regional ISPs has allowed for further aggregation in the backbone routing tables. ISP customers who have been allocated address space within the ISP's block do not need individual routing entries on the backbone. A single entry for the aggregated block that points to the ISP suffices.

Originally, address space was not very fairly allocated. The U.S. government reserved about half the address space for itself and gave relatively small blocks to Europe and Asia. But Europe and Asia managed their address space much more wisely than we did in the United States. The address space map at

http://www.caida.org/outreach/learn/ipv4space

illustrates this fact quite effectively, showing the IP address space as a whole, the portions that have been allocated, the portions that are routed (and therefore reachable), and the addresses for which traffic has been observed at a couple of major exchange points in the United States.

### Private addresses and NAT

Another temporary solution to address space depletion is the use of private IP address spaces, described in RFC1918. In the CIDR era, sites normally obtain their IP addresses from their Internet service provider. If a site wants to change ISPs, it may be held for ransom by the cost of renumbering its networks. The ISP gave it the address space as long as it was a customer. If the site now wants to choose a different ISP, it will have to convince the old ISP to let it have the addresses and also convince the new ISP to make the routing work correctly to the new location with the old addresses. Typically, ISPs don't want to bother with these issues and will require customers to renumber.

One alternative to using ISP-assigned addresses is to use private addresses that are never shown to your ISP. RFC1918 sets aside one class A network, 16 class B networks, and 256 class C networks that will never be globally allocated and can be used internally by any site. The catch is that packets bearing those addresses must never be allowed to sneak out onto the Internet. You should filter them at your border router just to make sure. If some packets slip by, you should track down the misconfigurations that allowed them to escape.

Table 13.7 shows the network numbers reserved for private addressing. (The "CIDR range" column shows the range for each class in the more compact CIDR notation; it does not add any additional information.)

**Table 13.7    IP addresses reserved for private use**

| IP class | From | To | CIDR range |
|----------|------|------|-----------|
| Class A | 10.0.0.0 | 10.255.255.255 | 10.0.0.0/8 |
| Class B | 172.16.0.0 | 172.31.255.255 | 172.16.0.0/12 |
| Class C | 192.168.0.0 | 192.168.255.255 | 192.168.0.0/16 |

Sites can choose from this set the size of network that best fits their organization.

To allow hosts that use these private addresses to talk to the Internet, the site's border router runs a system called NAT (Network Address Translation). NAT intercepts packets addressed with these internal-only addresses and rewrites their source addresses, using a real external IP address and perhaps a different source port number. It also maintains a table of the mappings it has made between internal and external address/source-port pairs so that the translation can be performed in reverse when answering packets arrive from the Internet.

NAT's use of port number mapping allows several conversations to be multiplexed onto the same IP address so that a single external address can be shared by many internal hosts. In some cases, a site can get by with only one "real" IP address.

A site that uses NAT must still request address space from its ISP, but most of the addresses thus obtained are used for NAT mappings and are not assigned to individual hosts. If the site later wants to choose another ISP, only the border router and its NAT configuration need to change, not the configurations of the individual hosts.

Several router vendors implement NAT, including Cisco. It is also possible to have a UNIX box perform the NAT function, although we do not recommend this implementation for real companies. Both Red Hat and FreeBSD can do it.[10] See the vendor-specific sections later in this chapter for details. For some reason, Linux calls NAT "IP masquerading."

An incorrect NAT configuration can let private-address-space packets escape onto the Internet. The packets will get to their destinations, but answering packets won't be able to get back. CAIDA,[11] an organization that measures everything in sight about the backbone networks, finds that 0.1% to 0.2% of the packets on the backbone have either private addresses or bad checksums.

This sounds like a tiny percentage, and it is, but it represents about 20,000 packets every 10 minutes on a busy circuit at MAE-West (one of the major public exchanges at which different ISPs meet to exchange traffic). See www.caida.org for other interesting statistics and network measurement tools.

One disadvantage of NAT (or perhaps it's an advantage) is that an arbitrary host on the Internet cannot connect directly to your site's internal machines. Some implementations (e.g., Cisco PIX) let you configure "tunnels" that support direct connections for particular hosts.

Another problem is that some applications embed IP addresses in the data portion of packets; these applications are foiled or confused by NAT. Examples include some

---

10. Strictly speaking, Red Hat does not support NAT, but rather PAT (port address translation). It uses the IP address of the machine doing the translation as the only "external" address and uses the source port number as a basis for multiplexing connections.

11. CAIDA, pronounced "kay duh," is the Cooperative Association for Internet Data Analysis at the San Diego Supercomputer Center on the UCSD campus (www.caida.org).

routing protocols, streaming programs such as RealVideo and SHOUTcast, some FTP commands such as PORT and PASV, ICQ instant messaging, and many games.

NAT hides interior structure. This secrecy feels like a security win, but the security folks say NAT doesn't really help for security and certainly does not replace the need for a firewall. It also foils any attempt to measure the size or topology of the Internet.

### IPv6 addressing

An IPv6 address is 128 bits long. These long addresses were originally intended to solve the problem of IP address exhaustion. Now that they're here, however, they are being exploited to help with issues of routing, mobility, and locality of reference.

IP addresses have never been geographically clustered in the way that phone numbers or zip codes are. Now, with the proposed segmentation of the IPv6 address space, they will at least cluster to ISPs. The boundary between the network portion and the host portion of an IPv6 address is fixed at /64; the boundary between public topology and a site's local topology is fixed at /48. Table 13.8 shows the various parts of an IPv6 address.

**Table 13.8    The parts of an IPv6 address**

| Complete IPv6 address (128 bits) | | | |
|---|---|---|---|
| | **ISP prefix** | **Subnet** | **Host identifier** |
| | 45 bits | 16 bits | 64 bits |

⌐ **Address type**  3 bits

| Bits | Acronym | Translation |
|---|---|---|
| 1-3 | FP | Format prefix; the type of address, e.g., unicast |
| 4-16 | TLA ID | Top-level aggregation ID, like backbone ISP |
| 17-24 | RES | Reserved for future use |
| 25-48 | NLA ID | Next-level aggregation ID, e.g., regional ISPs and site ID |
| 49-64 | SLA ID | Site-level aggregation ID, like local subnet |
| 65-128 | INTERFACE ID | Interface identifier (MAC address plus padding) |

Of these pieces, only the SLA ID and the INTERFACE ID belong to the host and its site. The other parts are provided by the upstream ISP. The SLA specifies a local subnet. The 64-bit interface ID identifies the host network interface. It typically contains the 48-bit MAC address with the hex digits 0xFFFE in the middle. A special bit in the MAC address (bit 6 of the first byte, numbering bits from the left, starting at 0) called the universal/local bit must be complemented (see RFC2373). This scheme allows hosts to be automatically numbered, which is a nice feature for the sysadmin since only the subnet needs to be managed.

In IPv6, the MAC address is seen at the IP layer, which has both good and bad implications. The brand and model of interface card are encoded in the first half of the MAC address, so hackers with code for a particular architecture will be helped along. The visibility of this information has also worried some privacy advocates. The IPv6 folks have responded by pointing out that sites are not actually required to use MAC addresses; they're free to use whatever they want for the host address. A scheme to include a random token in the local part of the address has also been proposed. Too many bits to play with!

On the other hand, assigning IPv6 addresses should be easier than assigning IPv4 addresses since you need only keep track of the subnet address. The hosts can configure themselves—or at least, that's the theory.

The format prefix identifies the type of IPv6 address: unicast, multicast, or anycast. Unicast addresses set FP to 001 (binary). The TLA and NLA IDs identify your top-level IP backbone carrier and the local ISPs up the chain to your backbone provider.

Most vendors have IPv6 stacks either in development or already deployed. Table 13.9 shows the IPv6 readiness of some common OS and router vendors. (Switches don't really care about IPv6 because they don't make routing decisions and don't look inside the IP header.)

**Table 13.9   IPv6 readiness for some common vendors**

| System | IPv6? | Comments |
|--------|-------|----------|
| Solaris | yes | Solaris 8 and later |
| HP-UX | yes | Developers kit shipped with HP-UX 11.00 |
| Red Hat | yes | IPv6 is in the Linux kernel, versions 2.2 and later |
| FreeBSD | yes | FreeBSD 4.0 and later[a] |
| Windows 2K | kind of | Research version available (including source code) |
| Cisco | yes | Implemented in the slow path (CPU)[b] |
| Juniper | no | – |
| Bay | yes | Shipping since 1997 |

a. FreeBSD 3.4 does not ship with IPv6, but third-party implementations from INRIA, KAME, and the U.S. Naval Research Lab run on FreeBSD.
b. Will probably move to the fast path if customers demand it

To see the full scoop on IPv6 implementation status, check

> http://playground.sun.com/pub/ipng/html/ipng-implementations.html

More than 30 host implementations and 10 router implementations are listed.

The address registries have just begun allocating IPv6 address space. At the moment, ARIN will only allocate space to large ISPs who plan to implement an IPv6 network within 12 months. These ISPs can then allocate subspaces to their customers.

Here are some useful sources of IPv6 information:

- www.6bone.net – the IPv6 testbed; uses tunnels to bypass IPv4 routers
- www.6ren.net – a world-wide IPv6 research and education network
- www.ipv6.org – FAQs and technical information
- www.ipv6forum.com – marketing folks and IPv6 propaganda

One major advantage of IPv6 is that it solves the renumbering issue. In the IPv4 world, ISPs allocate address space to customers, but the addresses are not portable; when customers leave an ISP, they must return their addresses and renumber with addresses from their new ISP. With IPv6, the new ISP gives you an address prefix that you simply prepend to the local parts of your addresses, probably at your border router. This scheme is similar to that of NAT for IPv4 addressing, but without any of NAT's little problems.

## 13.5  ROUTING

Routing is the process of directing a packet through the maze of networks that stand between its source and its destination. In the TCP/IP system, it is similar to asking for directions in an unfamiliar country. The first person you talk to might point you toward the right city. Once you were a bit closer to your destination, the next person might be able to tell you how to get to the right street. Eventually, you get close enough that someone can identify the building you're looking for.

TCP/IP routing information takes the form of rules ("routes") such as, "To reach network A, send packets through machine C." There can also be a default route that tells what to do with packets bound for a network to which there is no explicit route.

Routing information is stored in a table in the kernel. Each table entry has several parameters, including a netmask for each listed network (once optional but now required if the default netmask is not correct). To route a packet to a particular address, the kernel picks the most specific of the matching routes (that is, the one with the longest netmask). If the kernel finds no relevant route and no default route, then it returns a "network unreachable" ICMP error to the sender.

The word "routing" is commonly used to mean two distinct things:

- Looking up a network address in the routing table to forward a packet toward its destination

- Building the routing table in the first place

In this section we examine the forwarding function and look at how routes can be manually added to or deleted from the routing table. We defer the more complicated topic of routing protocols that build and maintain the routing table until Chapter 14.

### Routing tables

You can examine a machine's routing table with **netstat -r** on all systems and also with the **route get** command on BSD-based systems. We discuss **netstat** in more

TCP/IP

detail starting on page 631, but here is a short example to give you a better idea of what routes look like. This host has two network interfaces: 132.236.227.93 (eth0) on the 132.236.227.0/24 net and 132.236.212.1 (eth1) on the 132.236.212.0/26 net.

```
% netstat -r -n
Kernel IP routing table
Destination      Mask               Gateway          Fl    MSS   If
132.236.227.0    255.255.255.0      132.236.227.93   U     1500  eth0
default          0.0.0.0            132.236.227.1    UG    1500  eth0
132.236.212.0    255.255.255.192    132.236.212.1    U     1500  eth1
132.236.220.64   255.255.255.192    132.236.212.6    UG    1500  eth1
127.0.0.1        255.255.255.255    127.0.0.1        U     3584  lo0
```

The destination field is usually a network address; the gateway must be a host address. For example, the fourth route says that to reach the network 132.236.220.64/26, packets must be sent to the gateway 132.236.212.6 via interface eth1. The second entry is a default route; packets not explicitly addressed to any of the three networks listed (or to the machine itself) will be sent to the default gateway host, 132.236.227.1. Hosts can route packets only to gateway machines that are directly attached to their same network.

See page 302 for more information about the **route** command.

Routing tables can be configured statically, dynamically, or with a combination of the two approaches. A static route is one that you enter explicitly with the **route** command. Static routes should stay in the routing table as long as the system is up; they are often set up at boot time from one of the system startup scripts. For example, the Red Hat commands

```
# route add -net 132.236.220.64 netmask 255.255.255.192 132.236.212.6
# route add default 132.236.227.1
```

would add the fourth and second routes displayed by **netstat -r -n** above. (The first and third routes in that display were added by **ifconfig** when the eth0 and eth1 interfaces were configured.)

The final route is also added at boot time. It configures a pseudo-device called the loopback interface. The loopback prevents packets sent from the host to itself from going out on the network; instead, they are transferred directly from the network output queue to the network input queue inside the kernel.

In a stable local network, static routing is an efficient solution. It is easy to manage and reliable. However, it requires that the system administrator know the topology of the network accurately at boot time and that the topology not change often.

Most machines on a local area network have only one way to get out to the rest of the network, and so the routing problem is easy. A default route added at boot time suffices to point toward the way out.

For more complicated network topologies, dynamic routing is required. Dynamic routing is typically performed by a daemon process that maintains and modifies the routing table. Routing daemons on different hosts communicate to discover the topology of the network and to figure out how to reach distant destinations. Several routing daemons are available. In Chapter 14, we describe the standard UNIX daemon, **routed** ("route dee"), and a more full featured daemon called **gated** ("gate dee") as well as the routing protocols they speak.

### ICMP redirects

Although IP generally does not concern itself with the management of routing information, it does define a small damage control feature called an ICMP redirect. When a router forwards a packet to a machine on the same network from which the packet was originally received, something is clearly wrong. Since the sender, the router, and the next-hop router are all on the same network, the packet could have been forwarded in one hop rather than two. The router can conclude that the sender's routing tables are inaccurate or incomplete.

In this situation, the router can notify the sender of its problem with an ICMP redirect packet. In effect, a redirect says, "You should not be sending packets for host *xxx* to me; you should send them to host *yyy* instead." The ICMP protocol allows redirects to be sent for both individual host addresses and entire networks. However, many implementations generate only host redirects.

Upon receiving a redirect, a naive sender updates its routing table so that future packets bound for that destination will take the more direct path. In the early days of multicasting, a few systems generated ICMP routing redirects in response to multicast packets. Modern systems do not have this problem.

The standard ICMP scenario contains no authentication step. Your router receives a redirect that claims to be from another, well-respected router and directs you to send traffic elsewhere. Should you listen? Paying attention to redirects actually creates something of a security problem. Redirects are generally ignored by Linux and BSD-based kernels and by Cisco routers. It's not a good idea to let untrusted hosts modify your routing tables.

## 13.6  ARP: THE ADDRESS RESOLUTION PROTOCOL

Even though IP packets are usually thought of in terms of IP addresses, hardware addresses must be used to actually transport data across a network's link layer.[12] ARP, the Address Resolution Protocol, discovers the hardware address associated with a particular IP address. It can be used on any kind of network that supports broadcasting but is most commonly described in terms of Ethernet.

If host A wants to send a packet to host B on the same Ethernet, it uses ARP to discover B's hardware address. When B is not on the same network as A, host A uses ARP to find the hardware address of the next-hop router to which a packet destined for B should be sent. Since ARP uses broadcast packets, which cannot cross net-

TCP/IP

---

12. Except on point-to-point links, on which the identity of the destination is sometimes implicit.

works,[13] it can only be used to find the hardware addresses of machines connected directly to the sending host's local network.

Every machine maintains a table in memory called the ARP cache, which contains the results of recent ARP queries. Under normal circumstances, many of the addresses a host needs are discovered soon after booting, so ARP does not account for a lot of network traffic.

ARP functions by broadcasting[14] a packet of the form, "Does anyone know the hardware address for 128.138.116.4?" The machine being searched for recognizes its own IP address and sends back a reply, "Yes, that's the IP address assigned to one of my network interfaces, and the corresponding Ethernet address is 8:0:20:0:fb:6a."

The original query includes the IP and Ethernet addresses of the requestor so that the machine being sought can reply without issuing an ARP query of its own. Thus, the two machines learn each other's ARP mappings with only one exchange of packets. Other machines that overhear the requestor's initial broadcast can record its address mapping, too. This passive inspection of ARP traffic is sometimes called snooping.

Most systems include a command called **arp** that examines and manipulates the kernel's ARP cache. **arp** is typically used to add or delete an entry; it can also flush the table or show it. On most systems, **arp -a** displays the contents of the **arp** cache— with a different format on each system, of course …

Here are examples of **arp -a** output from Solaris and Red Hat:

```
solaris% /usr/sbin/arp -a
Net to Media Table
Device  IP Address    Mask                 Flags  Phys Addr
-------- ------------- -------------------  ------ ---------------------
hme0    titania       255.255.255.255             00:50:da:6b:b5:90
hme0    earth         255.255.255.255             00:50:da:12:4e:e5
hme0    pluto         255.255.255.255             00:50:da:12:4e:19
```

```
redhat% /sbin/arp -a
xor.com (192.108.21.1) at 08:00:20:77:5E:A0 [ether] on eth0
earth.xor.com (192.108.21.180) at 00:50:DA:12:4E:E5 [ether] on eth0
lollipop.xor.com (192.108.21.48) at 08:00:20:79:4F:49 [ether] on eth0
```

The **arp** command is generally useful only for debugging and for situations that involve special hardware. Some devices are not smart enough to speak the ARP protocol (for example, network-attached printers or special-purpose graphics displays). To support such devices, you might need to configure another machine to proxy-ARP for your crippled hardware. That's normally done with the **arp** command as well.

If two hosts on a network are using the same IP address, one will have the right ARP table entry and one will be wrong. You can use the **arp** command to track down the offending machine.

---

13. Routers can often be configured to flood broadcast packets to other networks; don't do this.

14. ARP uses the underlying link layer's broadcasting conventions, not IP broadcasting.

Sometimes, hardware addresses need to be translated into IP addresses. A lot of handicapped hardware (e.g., diskless workstations, network computers, printers) needs to perform this translation at boot time. Instead of having an IP address hardwired into a configuration file, a machine can query a central server to discover its own address. The near-obsolete RARP protocol (Reverse ARP) extends ARP to cover reverse translations.

Unlike ARP, RARP requires a central server process to be installed on each network. RARP is not self-configuring; you must supply an explicit mapping between Ethernet addresses and IP addresses. On most systems that support RARP, the server is called **rarpd** and configuration data is drawn from **/etc/ethers** and **/etc/hosts**.

RARP has been largely superseded, first by BOOTP and now by DHCP.

## 13.7  DHCP: THE DYNAMIC HOST CONFIGURATION PROTOCOL

*DHCP is defined in RFCs 2131 and 2132.*

UNIX hosts have always required manual configuration to be added to a network. When you plug a Mac or PC into a network, it just works. Why can't UNIX do that? The Dynamic Host Configuration Protocol (DHCP) brings this reasonable expectation several steps closer to reality.

The protocol enables a DHCP client to "lease" a variety of network and administrative parameters from a central server that is authorized to distribute them. The leasing paradigm is particularly convenient for PCs that are turned off when not in use and for ISPs that have intermittent dial-up customers.

Leasable parameters include

- IP addresses and netmasks
- Gateways (default routes)
- DNS name servers
- Syslog hosts
- WINS servers, X font servers, proxy servers, NTP servers
- TFTP servers (for loading a boot image)

and dozens more (see RFC2132). Real-world use of the more exotic parameters is rare, however. In many cases, a DHCP server supplies only basic networking parameters such as IP addresses, netmasks, default gateways, and name servers.

Clients must report back to the DHCP server periodically to renew their leases. If a lease is not renewed, it eventually expires. The DHCP server is then free to assign the address (or whatever was being leased) to a different client. The lease period is configurable, but it's usually quite long (hours or days).

DHCP can save a formerly hapless sysadmin a lot of time and suffering. Once the server is up and running, clients can use it to obtain their network configuration automatically at boot time. No fuss, no mess.

### DHCP software

Table 13.10 shows the DHCP software that is shipped with our four example systems.

**Table 13.10   DHCP software on our example systems**

| System | DHCP client | DHCP server |
|--------|-------------|-------------|
| Solaris | **/sbin/dhcpagent** | **/usr/lib/inet/in.dhcpd**[a] |
| HP-UX | built in, also **auto_params** | **bootpd** |
| Red Hat | **/usr/sbin/dhcpcd** and **/sbin/pump** | **/usr/sbin/dhcpd** from ISC |
| FreeBSD | **/sbin/dhclient** | **/usr/ports/net/isc-dhcp2** |

a. **dhcpconfig** is a shell script that helps you configure Solaris's DHCP server.

ISC, the Internet Software Consortium, has built a reference implementation of the DHCP protocol. The server, client, and relay agent are available from ftp.isc.org. The ISC server also speaks the BOOTP protocol, which is similar in concept to DHCP but less sophisticated.

We recommend the ISC package over all the vendor-specific implementations. In a typical heterogeneous network environment, administration can be greatly simplified by standardizing on a single implementation. The ISC software provides a reliable, open source solution that builds without incident on most versions of UNIX. As of this writing, the pending release of version 3.0 promises many new useful configuration options, including conditional behavior, separate address pools, and more.

DHCP clients must initiate a conversation with the DHCP server by using the generic all-1s broadcast address because they don't yet know their subnet masks and therefore cannot use the subnet broadcast address. Unfortunately, some kernels (HP-UX and Linux) use only the subnet broadcast address. This problem can prevent the client and server from ever connecting and exchanging information. ISC's documentation includes workarounds that address this situation. Mixed environments are still a bit iffy for DHCP services, though; test carefully after you install a new server or a new type of client.

ISC's DHCP server speaks the DNS dynamic update protocol. Not only does the server give your host its IP address and other networking parameters, but it also updates the DNS database with the correct hostname-to-IP-address mapping. See page 459 for more information about dynamic DNS updates.

We briefly discuss the DHCP protocol, then explain how to set up the ISC server that implements it. We defer a discussion of DHCP client configuration issues until the vendor-specific sections later in this chapter.

### How DHCP works

DHCP is a backward-compatible extension of BOOTP, a protocol that was originally devised to enable diskless UNIX workstations to boot. BOOTP supplies clients with their IP address, netmask, default gateway, and TFTP booting information. DHCP generalizes the parameters that can be supplied and adds the "lease" concept.

A DHCP client begins its interaction with a DHCP server by sending a "Help! Who am I?" DHCPDISCOVER[15] message. Since it knows neither its own nor the server's IP address, it sends the message to the broadcast address 255.255.255.255, with a source address of 0.0.0.0. The DISCOVER message can contain hints from the client, such as information about the client's hardware architecture or a specific address the client wants to request.

The DISCOVER message is usually received by a DHCP server attached to the same subnet. However, DHCP servers on different subnets can also receive the message via a proxy called a "relay agent."

Servers respond with an OFFER message containing a suggested address and other basic parameters. The client receives the OFFER message(s)—possibly from multiple servers—and accepts one of the offers by sending a REQUEST message back to the offering server. Normally, the server responds with an ACK acknowledgment and allocates the address.

The ACK message can include any number of configurable parameters; it also specifies the duration of the address lease. The server can respond to a faulty REQUEST with a NAK (negative acknowledgment), indicating that the client should restart its discovery process.

Before using an address, the client checks it out with ARP. If the address appears to already be in use, the client complains to the server with a DECLINE message and restarts negotiations.

When the client's lease nears expiration, it should renew the lease by sending another REQUEST message if it intends to continue using the allocated address. Should a client decide to terminate its lease, it does so with a RELEASE message.

The server is obliged to keep track of the addresses it has handed out, and this information must persist across reboots. Clients are supposed to keep their lease state across reboots too, although many do not. The goal is to maximize stability in network configuration.

Incidentally, DHCP is normally not used to configure dial-up PPP interfaces. PPP's own PPPCP (PPP Control Protocol) typically fills that role.

### ISC's DHCP server

ISC's DHCP server is available from ftp.isc.org or www.isc.org. The details that follow are for version 2 of the package. The 3.0 release is imminent, so be sure to check the version you actually download against these instructions.

---

15. Each of the DHCP protocol message types begins with "DHCP." We'll leave out the DHCP from now on to make the text easier to read.

Unpack the **tar.gz** file and **cd** to the distribution directory. You should see subdirectories for the server, the client, and the relay agent, along with a directory of shared code. Run **./configure** followed by **make** and **make install** to build and install each of the pieces.

To configure the DHCP server, **dhcpd**, you need to edit the sample **dhcpd.conf** file from the **server** directory and install it in **/etc/dhcpd.conf**.[16] You must also create an empty lease database file called **/var/db/dhcp.leases**. Make sure that **dhcpd** can write to this file. To set up the **dhcpd.conf** file, you need the following information:

- The subnets for which **dhcpd** should manage IP addresses, and the ranges of addresses to dole out

- The initial and maximum lease durations, in seconds

- Configurations for BOOTP clients if you have any (they have static IP addresses and must have their MAC-level hardware address listed as well)

- Any other options the server should pass to DHCP clients: netmask, default route, DNS domain, name servers, etc.

The **dhcpd** man page gives an overview of the configuration process. The exact syntax of the config file is covered in the **dhcpd.conf** man page. Both are located in the distribution's **server** subdirectory.

**dhcpd** should be started automatically at boot time. You may find it helpful to make the startup of the daemon conditional on the existence of **/etc/dhcpd.conf**.

Here's a sample **dhcpd.conf** file from a Linux box with two interfaces, one internal and one that connects to the Internet. This machine performs NAT translation for the internal network and leases out a range of 10 IP addresses on this network as well. The **dhcpd.conf** file contains a dummy entry for the external interface (required) and a host entry for one particular machine that needs a fixed address.

```
# dhcpd.conf
#
# global options
option domain-name "synack.net";
option domain-name-servers gw.synack.net;
option subnet-mask 255.255.255.0;
default-lease-time 600;
max-lease-time 7200;

subnet 192.168.1.0 netmask 255.255.255.0 {
    range 192.168.1.51 192.168.1.60;
    option broadcast-address 192.168.1.255;
    option routers gw.synack.net;
}
```

---

16. Be careful: the **dhcpd.conf** file format is a bit fragile. Leave out a semicolon, and you'll receive an obscure, unhelpful error message.

```
subnet 209.180.251.0 netmask 255.255.255.0 {
}

host gandalf {
    hardware ethernet 08:00:07:12:34:56;
    fixed-address gandalf.synack.net;
}
```

*See Chapter 16 for more information about DNS.*

Addresses assigned by DHCP might potentially be in conflict with the contents of the DNS database. Sites often assign a generic name to each dynamically leased address (e.g., dhcp1.synack.net) and allow the names of individual machines to "float" along with their IP addresses. If you are running a recent version of BIND that supports dynamic updates, you can also configure **dhcpd** to update the DNS database as it hands out addresses. The dynamic update solution is more complicated, but it has the advantage of preserving each machine's hostname.

**dhcpd** records each lease transaction in the file **dhcp.leases**. It also periodically backs up this file by renaming it to **dhcpd.leases~** and recreating the **dhcp.leases** file from its in-memory database. If **dhcpd** were to crash during this operation, you might end up with only a **dhcp.leases~** file. In that case, **dhcpd** will refuse to start, and you will have to rename the file before restarting it. *Do not* just create an empty **dhcp.leases** file, or chaos will ensue as clients end up with duplicate addresses.

## 13.8  PPP: THE POINT-TO-POINT PROTOCOL

PPP, the Point-to-Point Protocol, is a serial line encapsulation protocol that specifies how IP packets must be encoded for transmission on a slow (and often unreliable) serial line. Serial lines simply transmit streams of bits and have no concept of the beginning or end of a packet. The PPP device driver takes care of encoding and decoding packets on the serial line; it adds a link-level header and markers that separate packets.

PPP is sometimes used with the newer home technologies such as DSL and cable modems, but this fact is usually hidden from you as an administrator. Encapsulation is typically performed by the interface device, and the traffic is bridged to Ethernet. You just see an Ethernet connection.

Designed by committee, PPP is the "everything *and* the kitchen sink" encapsulation protocol. It was inspired by the SLIP (Serial Line IP) and CSLIP (compressed SLIP) protocols designed by Rick Adams and Van Jacobson, respectively. PPP differs from these systems in that it allows the transmission of multiple protocols over a single link. It is specified in RFC1331.

PPP has three main components:

- A method for encapsulating datagrams over serial links

- A Link Control Protocol (LCP) for establishing, configuring, and testing the data link connection

TCP/IP

- A family of Network Control Protocols (NCPs) for establishing and configuring different network-layer protocols

These components, complete with state tables that rival the best finite-state automata final exams, are explained in detail in the RFC; we don't discuss them in detail.

PPP is shipped with each of our example systems. Table 13.11 shows the locations of the relevant commands and config files. We have not attempted to show any correspondence between particular config files and the commands that refer to them.

**Table 13.11   PPP-related commands and config files by system**

| System | Commands[a] | Config files |
|--------|-------------|--------------|
| Solaris | /usr/sbin/aspppd<br>/usr/sbin/aspppls | /etc/asppp.cf<br>/etc/uucp/Systems<br>/etc/uucp/Devices<br>/etc/uucp/Dialers<br>/etc/uucp/Auth |
| HP-UX | /usr/bin/pppd<br>/etc/ppp/Autostart | /etc/ppp/Systems<br>/etc/ppp/Filter<br>/etc/ppp/Devices<br>/etc/ppp/Dialers<br>/etc/ppp/Auth<br>/etc/ppp/Keys |
| Red Hat | /usr/sbin/pppd<br>/usr/sbin/chat | /etc/ppp/options<br>/etc/ppp/ppp.conf<br>/etc/ppp/allow |
| FreeBSD | /usr/sbin/pppd<br>/usr/bin/chat | /etc/ppp/options<br>/etc/ppp/options.ttyserver<br>/etc/ppp/chat.ttyserver |

a. The commands and config files have no particular correspondence; they are independent lists.

### Addressing PPP performance issues

PPP provides all the functionality of Ethernet, but at *much* slower speeds. Normal office LANs operate at 10 Mb/s or 100 Mb/s—that's 10,000-100,000 Kb/s. A dial-up connection operates at about 28-56 Kb/s.[17] To put these numbers in perspective, it takes about 5 minutes to transfer a one-megabyte file across a PPP line. The speed is OK for email or web browsing with images turned off, but glitzy web sites will drive you crazy. To improve interactive performance, you can set the MTU of the point-to-point quite low. It usually defaults to 512 bytes; try 128 if you are doing a lot of interactive work.

---

17. PPP is normally used at speeds over 19,200 bps. Technically, it can be used on slower links, but it becomes insufferably slow.

*See Chapter 17 for
more information
about NFS.*
Running NFS over a PPP link can be painfully slow. You should consider it only if you
have the ability to run NFS over TCP instead of UDP. On some systems (e.g., Solaris),
NFS mounts use TCP by default.

The X Windows protocol uses TCP, so it's possible to run X applications over a PPP
link. Programs like **xterm** work fine, but avoid applications that use fancy fonts or
bitmapped graphics.

### Connecting to a network with PPP

To connect a host to a network with PPP, you must satisfy three prerequisites:

- Your host's kernel must be able to send IP packets across a serial line as
  specified by the PPP protocol standard.

- You must have a user-level program that allows you to establish and maintain PPP connections.

- There must be a host on the other end of the serial line that understands
  the protocol you are using.

### Making your host speak PPP

*See page 300 for
more information
about **ifconfig**.*
To establish a PPP connection, your host must be capable of sending and receiving
PPP packets. On UNIX systems, PPP is generally implemented as a kernel module
that places network packets in the serial device output queue, and vice versa. This
module usually pretends to be just another network interface, so it can be manipulated with standard configuration tools such as **ifconfig**.

### Controlling PPP links

The exact sequence of events involved in establishing a PPP connection depends on
your OS and on the type of server you are dialing into. Connections can be initiated
either manually or dynamically.

To establish a PPP connection manually, you run a command that dials a modem,
logs in to a remote host, and starts the remote PPP protocol engine. If this procedure
succeeds, the serial port is then configured as a network interface. This option normally leaves the link up for a long time, which makes it best suited for a phone line
dedicated to IP connectivity.

In a dynamic configuration, a daemon watches your serial "network" interfaces to
see when traffic has been queued for them. When someone tries to send a packet,
the daemon automatically dials a modem to establish the connection, transmits the
packet, and if the line goes back to being idle, disconnects the line after a reasonable
amount of time. Dynamic dial-up is often used if a phone line carries both voice and
data traffic or if the connection involves long distance or connect-time charges.

Software to implement both of these connection schemes is included with most versions of PPP.

TCP/IP

### Finding a host to talk to

If you're setting up a link between two sites within your own company or, perhaps, between home and work, you can simply install the PPP software on both ends. However, if your intent is to use PPP to obtain an Internet connection, you'll probably need to deal with a commercial ISP. Most ISPs offer dial-up PPP service to the public at a reasonable cost.

### Assigning an address

*See page 298 for more information about assigning IP addresses.*

Just as you must assign an IP address to a new host on your Ethernet, you need to assign an IP address to each PPP interface. There are a number of ways to assign addresses to these links (including assigning no addresses at all). We discuss only the simplest method here.

Think of a PPP link as a network of its own. That is, a network of exactly two hosts, often called a "point-to-point" network. You need to assign a network number to the link just as you would assign a network number to a new Ethernet segment, using whatever rules are in effect at your site. You can pick any two host addresses on that network and assign one to each end of the link. Follow other local customs, such as subnetting standards, as well. Each host then becomes a "gateway" to the point-to-point network as far as the rest of the world is concerned.

DHCP can also be used to assign the IP address at the end of a PPP link. ISPs typically offer home service that uses DHCP and business service that costs more but includes static addresses.

### Routing

*See Chapter 14 for more information about routing.*

Since PPP requires the remote server to act as an IP router, you need to be concerned with IP routing just as you would on a "real" gateway, such as a machine that connects two Ethernets. The purpose of routing is to direct packets through gateways so that they can reach their ultimate destinations. Routing can be configured in several different ways.

A run-of-the-mill PPP client host should have a default route that forwards packets to the PPP server. Likewise, the server needs to be known to the other hosts on its network as the gateway to the leaf machine.

Most PPP packages handle these routing chores automatically.

### Ensuring security

*See Chapter 21 for more information about security.*

Security issues arise whenever you add a host to a network. Since a host connected via PPP is a bona fide member of the network, you need to treat it as such: verify that the system has no accounts without passwords or with insecure passwords, that all appropriate vendor security fixes have been installed, and so on. See the *Security issues* section on the next page for some specifics on network security.

### Using terminal servers

You may find that once you begin offering PPP connections to home users, you have more requests than you have serial ports. A number of terminal servers offer PPP capability, and recent ones also have integrated modems. Our favorite is the Lucent Portmaster 3. The Cisco Access Server AS5x00 series is also popular. These products provide a convenient and easily maintainable source of serial ports complete with PPP software already installed. They allow you to establish a dial-in "pool" of modems that offer PPP service to off-site users.

### Using chat scripts

Many PPP implementations use a "chat script" to talk to the modem and also to log in to the remote machine and start up a PPP server. The idea of a chat script originated with the UUCP store-and-forward system of days gone by. It consists of a sequence of strings to send and strings to expect in return, with a limited form of conditional statement that can express concepts such as "expect the string 'Login', but if you don't get it, send a carriage return and wait for it again."

Most PPP implementations come with sample chat scripts that you can adapt to your own environment. You'll need to edit the scripts to set parameters such as the telephone number to call and the command to run after a successful login. Most chat scripts contain a cleartext password; set the permissions accordingly.

## 13.9  SECURITY ISSUES

We address the topic of security in a chapter of its own (Chapter 21), but several security issues relevant to IP networking merit discussion here. In this section, we briefly look at a few networking features that have acquired a reputation for causing security problems and recommend ways to minimize their impact. The details of our example vendors' default behavior on these issues (and appropriate methods for changing them) are covered later in this chapter.

### IP forwarding

If a UNIX box has IP forwarding enabled, it can act as a router. Unless your system has multiple network interfaces and is actually supposed to function as a router, it's advisable to turn this feature off. Hosts that forward packets can sometimes be coerced into compromising security by making external packets appear to have come from inside your network. This subterfuge can help naughty packets evade network scanners and packet filters.

### ICMP redirects

ICMP redirects can be used maliciously to reroute traffic and mess with your routing tables. Most operating systems listen to them and follow their instructions by default. It would be bad if all your traffic were rerouted to a competitor's network for few hours, especially while backups were running! We recommend that you configure your routers (and hosts acting as routers) to ignore and perhaps log ICMP redirects.

TCP/IP

### Source routing

IP's source routing mechanism lets you specify an explicit series of gateways for a packet to transit on the way to its destination. Source routing bypasses the next-hop routing algorithm that's normally run at each gateway to determine how a packet should be forwarded.

Source routing was part of the original IP specification; it was intended primarily to facilitate testing. It can create security problems because packets are often filtered according to their origin. If someone can cleverly route a packet so as to make it appear to have originated within your own network instead of the Internet, it might slip through your firewall. We recommend that you neither accept nor forward source-routed packets.

### Broadcast pings and other forms of directed broadcast

Ping packets addressed to a network's broadcast address (instead of to a particular host address) will typically be delivered to every host on the network. Such packets have been used in denial of service attacks; for example, the so-called smurf attacks. Most hosts have a way to disable broadcast pings—that is, they can be configured not to respond to or forward them. Your Internet router can also filter out broadcast pings before they reach your internal network. It's a good idea to use both host and firewall-level security measures if you can.

Broadcast pings are a form of "directed broadcast," in that they are packets sent to the broadcast address of a distant network. The default handling of such packets has been gradually changing. For example, versions of Cisco's IOS through 11.x forwarded directed broadcast packets by default, but IOS releases since 12.0 do not. It is usually possible to convince your TCP/IP stack to ignore broadcast packets that come from afar, but since this behavior must be set on each interface, this can be a nontrivial task at a large site.

### UNIX-based firewalls

Red Hat and FreeBSD include packet filtering (aka "firewall") software in their kernels and basic software distributions. Although we describe this software in the vendor-specific sections for each OS (pages 326 and 333), we don't really recommend using a workstation as a firewall. The security of UNIX hosts (especially as shipped by our friendly vendors) is weak, and NT's security is even worse. We suggest that you buy a dedicated hardware solution to use as a firewall. Even a sophisticated software solution such as Checkpoint's Firewall-1 product (which runs on a Solaris host) is not as good as a piece of dedicated hardware such as Cisco's PIX—and it's almost the same price!

A more thorough discussion of firewall-related issues begins on page 675.

### Virtual private networks

Many organizations that have offices in several parts of the world would like to have all those locations connected to one big private network. Unfortunately, the cost of leasing a transoceanic or even transcountry data line can be prohibitive. Such organizations can actually use the Internet as if it were a private data line by establishing a series of secure, encrypted "tunnels" among their various locations. A "private" network that includes such tunnels is known as a virtual private network or VPN.

Some VPNs use the IPSEC protocol, which has recently been standardized by the IETF. Others use proprietary solutions that don't usually interoperate with each other. If you need VPN functionality, we suggest that you look at products like Cisco's 3660 router or the Watchguard Firebox, both of which can do tunneling and encryption. The Watchguard device uses PPP to a serial port for management. A sysadmin can dial into the box to configure it or to access the VPN for testing.

### IPSEC: secure IP

IPSEC is an IETF-approved, end-to-end authentication and encryption system. Its deployment has been hampered by the U.S. encryption laws, which prohibit the export of strong encryption software. Several non-U.S. software efforts have produced implementations.

None of the implementations address the issue of key distribution, which is an important prerequisite to the widespread deployment and use of IPSEC. Everyone hopes that DNS will somehow solve the problem. RFC2409 (which is on the standards track) defines an Internet Key Exchange (IKE) protocol, which is a sort of hybrid key exchange system.

In its current form, IPSEC encrypts the transport layer header, which includes the source and destination port numbers. Unfortunately, this scheme conflicts directly with the way that most firewalls work. A proposal to undo this feature is making its way through the IETF.

Table 13.12 shows the status of IPSEC implementations for our example systems.

**Table 13.12    IPSEC implementation status for various operating systems**

| System | Got it? | Comments |
| --- | --- | --- |
| Solaris | yes | In version 8 and later |
| HP-UX | yes | Praesidium IPSec/9000 ships with HP-UX 11.00 |
| Red Hat | not quite | Free S/WAN IPSEC will be in Red Hat soon[a] |
| FreeBSD | yes | KAME Project's IPSEC in version 4.0 and later |

a. It has been in SuSE Linux since 1999.

As might be expected, IPSEC reduces the performance of the networking stack.

To set up IPSEC between a pair of end hosts, you must create a Security Association Database (SAD) and a Security Policy Database (SPD). Use the **setkey** command together with the **add** and **spdadd** subcommands to create entries in these two databases. See www.kame.net for details.

TCP/IP

## 13.10  ADDITION OF MACHINES TO A NETWORK

Only a few steps are involved in adding a new machine to an existing local area network, but some vendors hide the files you must modify and generally make the chore difficult. Others provide a setup script that prompts for the networking parameters that are needed, which is fine until you need to undo something or move a machine.

The basic steps are:

- Assign an IP address and hostname
- Set up the new host to configure its network interfaces at boot time
- Set up a default route and perhaps fancier routing
- Point to a DNS name server, to allow access to the rest of the Internet

We first cover the general outline of these steps, then return to each vendor's special incantations in a series of vendor-specific sections.

Of course, you could add a debugging step to this sequence as well. After any change that might affect booting, you should always reboot to verify that the machine comes up correctly. Six months later when the power has failed and the machine refuses to boot, it's hard to remember what change you made that might have caused the problem. (You might also refer to Chapter 20, *Network Management and Debugging.*)

One fact worth mentioning is that some systems are smart enough to distinguish whether they are connected to a network or not. The boot sequence may be quite different in the networked and nonnetworked cases; a machine that works fine on its own can inexplicably hang at boot time when a network cable is plugged in, even if no configuration changes have been made.

The process of designing and installing a physical network is touched on in Chapter 15, *Network Hardware.* If you are dealing with an existing network and have a general idea of how it is set up, it may not be necessary for you to read too much more about the physical aspects of networking unless you plan to extend the existing network.

We describe the process of network configuration in terms of Ethernet; other technologies are essentially similar.

### Assigning hostnames and IP addresses

*See Chapter 16 for more information about DNS.*

Administrators have various theories about how the mapping from hostnames to IP addresses is best maintained at a local site: the **hosts** file, NIS or NIS+, the DNS system, or perhaps some combination of those sources. If multiple systems are used, there must also be a sensible plan for how they are to work together. The conflicting values are scalability and maintainability versus a system that is flexible enough to allow machines to boot when not all services are available (and flexible enough to handle the heterogeneity of your site).

The **/etc/hosts** file is the oldest and simplest way to map names to IP addresses. Each line starts with an IP address and continues with the various symbolic names by which that address is known. Here is a typical minimalist **/etc/hosts** file for the host lollipop:

```
127.0.0.1        localhost
192.108.21.48    lollipop.xor.com lollipop loghost
192.108.21.254   chimchim-gw.xor.com chimchim-gw
192.108.21.1     ns.xor.com ns
192.225.33.5     licenses.xor.com license-server
```

It is common to have localhost as the first entry in the **/etc/hosts** file; on some systems, it is even rumored to be necessary (FreeBSD, for example).

Because **/etc/hosts** contains only local mappings, most modern systems use it only for mappings that are needed at boot time. DNS is then consulted to find mappings for the rest of the local network and the rest of the world. Sometimes **/etc/hosts** is used to specify mappings that you do not want the rest of the world to know about and therefore do not publish in DNS.

**/etc/hosts** is important during the boot process because DNS is not yet available. It must contain at least the mapping for the host itself and for the loopback address. In addition, it should probably contain the mappings for the default gateway machine and a name server. Many sites put all of their really important hosts, servers, and gateways in the **/etc/hosts** file. Others put only the host itself and the loopback interface; still others add in all local hosts and their off-site backup name servers.

If your **/etc/hosts** file contains all your local data, it must be replicated on every machine that wants to use symbolic names. Various schemes allow a single version of the **hosts** file to be kept in a central location and distributed to or shared by other hosts at your site; see Chapter 18, *Sharing System Files*, for more information. DNS is really the "correct" way to manage the mapping. Chapter 16 describes DNS and BIND, its UNIX implementation, in detail.

The **hostname** command assigns a hostname to a machine. **hostname** is typically run at boot time from one of the startup scripts, which obtains the name to be assigned from a configuration file. Of course, each vendor names that configuration file differently. See the vendor-specific sections beginning on page 306 for information about your specific system. Most systems today assign a fully qualified name (that is, a name that includes both the hostname and the DNS domain name, such as anchor.cs.colorado.edu).

At a small site, you can easily dole out hostnames and IP addresses by hand. But when many networks and many different administrative groups are involved, it helps to have some central coordination. Colorado's home-grown **addhost** system is a set of distributed tools that solve several of the problems of host management. DHCP is another way to solve this problem, and LDAP would also work. **addhost** is pretty old and crufty, but it is still in use at several sites; if you don't find anything better, it's available from ftp.xor.com.

TCP/IP

### ifconfig: configure network interfaces

**ifconfig** enables or disables a network interface, sets its IP address and subnet mask, and sets various other options and parameters. It is usually run at boot time (with command-line parameters taken from config files), but it can also make changes on the fly. Be careful if you are making **ifconfig** changes and are logged in remotely; many a sysadmin has been locked out this way and had to drive in to fix things.

An **ifconfig** command most commonly has the form

> **ifconfig** *interface address options* ... **up**

For example:

> ifconfig en0 128.138.240.1 netmask 255.255.255.0 up

*interface* identifies the hardware interface to which the command applies. It is usually a two or three-character device name followed by a number. Some common names are ie0, le0, le1, ln0, en0, we0, qe0, hme0, eth0, and lan0; lo0 is the name of the loopback interface. The interface name is derived from the name of the device driver used to run it, and it usually corresponds to the chipset used by the interface (Intel Ethernet, Lance Ethernet, etc.).

**ifconfig** *interface* displays the current settings for *interface* without changing them. Many systems understand **-a** to mean "all interfaces," and **ifconfig -a** can be therefore be used to find out what interfaces are present on the system. If your system does not understand **ifconfig -a**, try **netstat -i** to find the interface names.

 Under Solaris, network interfaces must be "attached" with **ifconfig** *interface* **plumb** before they become configurable and visible to **netstat -i**.

The *address* parameter specifies the interface's IP address. Many versions of **ifconfig** also accept a hostname for the address parameter. We prefer to use the actual IP address; if **ifconfig** is given a hostname (or the output of the **hostname** command), the potential for boot-time problems is increased. If there's a problem resolving the hostname, the machine won't boot or it will boot into a state in which it cannot be accessed from the network, requiring you to physically go to the machine to debug the problem. DNS queries that cannot complete take a long while to time out, making it seem that the machine is hung.

The keyword **up** turns the interface on; **down** turns it off.

**ifconfig** understands many other options. We cover only the most common ones; as always, consult your man pages for the final word on your particular system. **ifconfig** options all have symbolic names. Listing the option selects it. Some options require an argument, which should be placed immediately after the option name. Some versions of **ifconfig** used to require an address family parameter, too. Today, that parameter is not required and defaults to **inet**.

The **netmask** option sets the subnet mask for the interface and is required if the network is not subnetted according to its address class (A, B, or C). The mask can be specified in dotted decimal notation or as a 4-byte hexadecimal number beginning with **0x**. In either case, bits set to 1 are part of the network number, and bits set to 0 are part of the host number.

The **broadcast** option specifies the IP broadcast address for the interface, expressed in either hex or dotted quad notation. The correct broadcast address is one in which the host part is set to all 1s, and most systems default to this value; they use the netmask and IP address to calculate the broadcast address.

On UNIX, you can set the broadcast address to any IP address that's valid for the network to which the host is attached. Some sites have chosen weird values for the broadcast address in the hope of avoiding certain types of denial of service attacks that are based on broadcast pings. We dislike this approach for several reasons.

First, it requires you to reset the broadcast address on every host on the local network, which can be a time-consuming chore on a large net. Second, it requires you to be absolutely sure that you reconfigure every host, or broadcast storms can result in which packets travel from machine to machine until their TTLs expire.

Broadcast storms occur because the same link-layer broadcast address must be used to transport packets no matter what the IP broadcast address has been set to. For example, suppose that machine X thinks the broadcast address is A1 and that machine Y thinks it is A2. If X sends a packet to address A1, Y will receive the packet (because the link-layer destination address is the broadcast address), will see that the packet is not for itself and also not for the broadcast address (because Y thinks the broadcast address is A2), and will then forward the packet back onto the net. If there are two machines in Y's state, the packet will circulate forever until it expires. Broadcast storms can erode your bandwidth, especially on a large switched net.

A better way to avoid problems with broadcast pings is to prevent your border routers from forwarding them and to tell individual hosts not to respond to them. See the vendor-specific sections starting on page 306 for instructions on how to implement these constraints on each of our example systems.

In the **ifconfig** example at the beginning of this section, the broadcast address is 128.138.240.255 because the network is a /24, as specified by the netmask value of 255.255.255.0.

Executing **ifconfig en0** shows the following output:

```
en0: flags=63<UP,BROADCAST,NOTRAILERS,RUNNING> inet 128.138.240.1
    netmask ffffff00 broadcast 128.138.240.255
```

Let's look at some complete examples.

```
# ifconfig lo0 127.0.0.1 up
```

This command configures the loopback interface, which doesn't usually require any options to be set. You should never need to change your system's default configuration for this interface. The implied netmask of 255.0.0.0 is correct and does not need to be manually overridden.

TCP/IP

```
# ifconfig en0 128.138.243.151 netmask 255.255.255.192
    broadcast 128.138.243.191 up
```

This is a typical example for an Ethernet interface. The IP and broadcast addresses are set to 128.138.243.151 and 128.138.243.191, respectively. The network is class B (you can tell from the first byte of the address), but it has been subnetted by an additional ten bits into a /26 network. 192 in the netmask is 11000000 in binary and so adds 2 extra bits to the 24 contained in the three 255 octets. The 191 in the broadcast address is 10111111 in binary, which sets all 6 host bits to 1s and indicates that this interface is part of the $3^{rd}$ network (10) in the group of 4 carved out of the $4^{th}$ octet.

Now that you know how to configure a network interface by hand, you need to figure out how the parameters to **ifconfig** are set when the machine boots, and you need to make sure that the new values are entered correctly. You normally do this by editing one or more configuration files; see the vendor-specific sections starting on page 306 for more information.

### route: configure static routes

The **route** command defines static routes, explicit routing table entries that never change (you hope), even if you run a routing daemon.[18] When you add a new machine to a local area network, you usually only need to specify a default route; see the next section for details. Be sure to read your system's man page for **route** as well. Syntax, flags, and arguments vary enormously among vendors.

This book's discussion of routing is split between this section and Chapter 14, *Routing*. Although most of the basic information about routing and the **route** command is here, you might find it helpful to read the first few sections of Chapter 14 if you need more information.

Routing is performed at the IP layer. When a packet bound for some other host arrives, the packet's destination IP address is compared with the routes in the kernel's routing table. If it matches or partially matches a route in the table, the packet is forwarded to the "next gateway" IP address associated with that route.

There are two special cases: First, a packet may be destined for some host on a directly connected network. In this case, the "next gateway" address in the routing table will be one of the local host's own interfaces, and the packet is sent directly to its destination. This type of route is added to the routing table for you by the **ifconfig** command when you configure an interface.

Second, there may be no route that matches the destination address. In this case, the default route is invoked if one exists. Otherwise, an ICMP "network unreachable" message is returned to the sender. Many local area networks have only one way out, and their default route points to it. On the Internet backbone, the routers do not have default routes—the buck stops there. If they do not have a routing entry for a destination, that destination cannot be reached.

---

18. However, some versions of **routed** will overwrite static routes.

Each **route** command adds or removes one route. The format is usually

> **route** [**-f**] *op* [*type*] *destination gateway* [*hop-count*]

The *op* argument should be **add** to add a route and **delete** to remove one. Some versions of **route** have other values that *op* can assume, such as **get**, **change**, **flush**, and **monitor**. *destination* can be a host address, a network address, or the keyword **default**. Some systems represent the default route by the network address 0.0.0.0.

The *gateway* is the machine to which packets should be forwarded. It *must* be on a directly connected network; forwarding can only be performed one hop at a time. Some versions let you specify an interface instead of (or along with) the *gateway*.

*hop-count* is the number of forwardings required to reach the destination. Some operating systems require the hop count, others allow it but ignore it, and others have made it obsolete and wrong to include. On operating systems that require a hop count, the value need not be exact, and it is often set to 1.

 FreeBSD has not only eliminated the *hop-count* variable but, if you inadvertently use it, it will be interpreted as the netmask. A netmask of 1 is not very useful!

The optional *type* argument supports host routes, which apply to a complete IP address (a specific host) rather than to a network address. The values **net** and **host** are accepted for the *type* parameter. If a *type* isn't specified, **route** checks the host part of the destination address to see if it's zero. If the host part is 0 or the address is a network defined in the **/etc/networks** file (if your system has one), then the route is assumed to be a normal network route.[19]

Since **route** cannot magically know which network numbers have been subnetted, you must frequently use the *type* field to install certain routes. For example, the address 128.138.243.0 refers to a subnetted class B network at our site, but to **route** it looks like a class B address of 128.138 with a host part of 243.0; you must specify the **net** option to deconfuse **route**. In general, it's good hygiene to provide an explicit *type* for all routes that involve subnets.

**route delete** *destination* removes a specific entry from the routing table. **route -f** removes (flushes) all routing entries from the table. If combined with an **add** command, **route -f** first flushes the table and then makes the requested change.

 Systems derived from late Berkeley releases use **route flush** instead of **route -f**. They also use **-net** and **-host** rather than **net** and **host**.

 Red Hat uses BSD's **-net** and **-host** convention but not **route flush**; in fact, Red Hat seems to provide no way at all to flush the routing table in one step.

To inspect existing routes, use the command **netstat -nr**. See page 631 for more information about **netstat**.

---

19. **/etc/networks** can be used to map names to network numbers much like the **/etc/hosts** file maps hostnames to complete IP addresses. Many commands that expect a network number can accept a network name if it is listed in the **/etc/networks** file (or in DNS, on some systems).

TCP/IP

### Default routes

A default route causes all packets whose destination network is not found in the kernel's routing table to be sent to the indicated gateway. To set a default route, simply add the following line to your startup files:

**route add default** *gateway-IP-address*

Rather than hardcoding an explicit IP address into the startup files, most vendors have their systems get the gateway IP address from a configuration file. The way that local routing information is integrated into the startup sequence is unfortunately different for each operating system. Table 13.13 summarizes the incantations necessary on our four example systems.

**Table 13.13    How to set the default route**

| System | File to change | Variable to change |
|--------|----------------|--------------------|
| Solaris | **/etc/defaultrouter** | – |
| HP-UX | **/etc/rc.config.d/netconf** | ROUTE_GATEWAY[0] |
| Red Hat | **/etc/sysconfig/network** | GATEWAY, GATEWAYDEV |
| FreeBSD | **/etc/rc.conf** | defaultrouter |

Where the Variable column lacks an entry, just put the IP address or hostname of the default gateway machine in the indicated file. If you use a hostname, it must be listed in the **/etc/hosts** file.

### Configuring DNS

To configure a machine as a DNS client, you only need to edit one or two files: all systems require **/etc/resolv.conf** to be modified, and some require you to modify a "service switch" file as well.

The **/etc/resolv.conf** file lists the DNS domains that should be searched to resolve names that are incomplete (that is, not fully qualified, such as anchor instead of anchor.cs.colorado.edu) and the IP addresses of the name servers to contact for name lookups. A sample is shown here; for more detail, see page 411.

```
search cs.colorado.edu colorado.edu
nameserver 128.138.242.1
nameserver 128.138.243.151
nameserver 192.108.21.1
```

**/etc/resolv.conf** should list the "closest" stable name server first because the server in the first position will be contacted first. You can have up to three nameserver entries. If possible, you should always have more than one. The timeout period seems quite long, so if the first name server does not respond, your users will notice.

You will sometimes see a domain line instead of a search line. Such a line indicates either an ancient **resolv.conf** file that has not been updated to use the search directive or an ancient resolver that doesn't understand search. domain and search are not equivalent; search is preferred.

*See Chapter 18 for more information about NIS and NIS+.*

Some systems do not use DNS by default, even if a properly configured **resolv.conf** file exists. These systems have a "service switch" file that determines which mechanisms will be used to resolve hostname-to-IP-address mappings. Prioritization of information sources is covered in more detail starting on page 523, but we mention the topic here as well, since it sometimes foils your attempts to configure a new machine.

The service switch file lets you specify the order in which DNS, NIS (or NIS+), and **/etc/hosts** should be consulted. In most cases, you can also rule out certain sources of data entirely. Your choice of order impacts the machine's ability to boot and the way that booting interacts with the contents of the **/etc/hosts** file.

If DNS is chosen as the first data source to consult, you may need to have a name server on the local network and have its hostname and IP address in the **hosts** file in order for everything to work at boot time.

Table 13.14 lists the location of the relevant config files and the default configuration for host lookups on each of our example systems.

**Table 13.14    Service switch files by system**

| System | Switch file | Default for hostname lookups |
|--------|-------------|------------------------------|
| Solaris | **/etc/nsswitch.conf** | nis [NOTFOUND=return] files |
| HP-UX | **/etc/nsswitch.conf** | dns [NOTFOUND=return] nis [NOTFOUND=return] files |
| Red Hat | **/etc/nsswitch.conf**[a] **/etc/host.conf** | db files nisplus dns hosts, bind |
| FreeBSD | **/etc/host.conf** | hosts, bind |

a. Most applications are linked against **libc6**, which uses BIND's resolver and **nsswitch.conf**. A few older applications are linked with **libc5**, which uses **host.conf**.

The default value under Solaris is actually determined by the options that were selected during the installation process. The entry to change is called hosts through Solaris 7; Solaris 8 and later add an ipnodes line that also refers to the hostname-to-IP-address mapping process.

The entries for both Solaris and HP-UX include the clause [NOTFOUND=return], which specifies what to do if a lookup should fail. If the service is running but the name is not found, this clause makes the lookup terminate (fail) immediately. The process continues to the next service listed only if the first is unavailable. Several other determinants can be part of a conditional phrase (SUCCESS, UNAVAIL, and TRYAGAIN), and two actions are defined (return and continue).

Solaris and HP-UX both provide some sample switch configurations in **/etc**; check for files called **nsswitch.***. The HP-UX default settings are in **nsswitch.hp_defaults**.

## 13.11  VENDOR-SPECIFIC NETWORK CONFIGURATION

On older systems, you configured the network by editing the startup script **/etc/rc** (or perhaps **/etc/rc.local**) and directly changing the **ifconfig** and **route** commands it contained. Modern systems are set up to minimize the number of modifications that are made to the actual startup scripts.

The newer scripts reuse configuration information from other system files or define their own configuration files. Although this separation of configuration and implementation is a good idea, every vendor does it differently, and it means that you sometimes have to go through a layer of indirection to get the proper arguments forwarded to **ifconfig** and **route**.

In general, we recommend using your vendor's standard system if possible. It's tempting to just "fix" things that get in your way, but UNIX is a delicate ecosystem, and it is vulnerable to unintended side effects, especially while booting.

Chapter 2 describes the succulent details of our example systems' booting procedures. In the next four sections, we simply summarize the chores that are related to configuring a network. Our example systems configure the loopback interface automatically; you should never need to modify that part of the configuration. Beyond that, each system is different.

UNIX vendors are serious sufferers of the "not invented here" syndrome. They mess with and rename configuration files all the time, never realizing (or caring?) that they are not the only ones who write code that depends on the format of these files. Table 13.15 lists the files you must touch to set a machine's hostname and IP address on our example systems.

Two files are common to all operating systems: **/etc/hosts** and **/etc/resolv.conf**; we listed these once at the beginning of the table instead of with each individual operating system. We also omitted the service switch files; see Table 13.14 on page 305 for a summary of those.

After changing one of these files, you may need to reboot or bring the network interface down and back up again for your change to take effect.

In the next four sections, we cover the details of network configuration for each of our supported operating systems. In particular, we cover:

- Basic configuration
- Examples
- DHCP client configuration
- Dynamic reconfiguration and tuning
- Security, firewalls, filtering, and NAT configuration
- PPP configuration
- Quirks

Not all of our operating systems need sections for each topic, although they all have a quirks section!

**Table 13.15    Network configuration files by system**

| System | File | Purpose |
|---|---|---|
| All | **/etc/hosts** | Hostname-to-IP mapping for local hosts |
| | **/etc/resolv.conf** | DNS domain and name servers |
| Solaris | **/etc/hostname.**_ifname_ | Network addresses per interface |
| | **/etc/dhcp.**_ifname_ | Requests DHCP configuration per interface |
| | **/etc/nodename** | Hostname |
| | **/etc/defaultrouter** | Default route |
| | **/etc/inet/netmasks** | Real version of subnet masks file |
| | **/etc/inet/hosts** | Real version of the **/etc/hosts** file |
| | **/etc/inet/ipnodes**[a] | Augments **/etc/hosts** in Solaris 8 and later |
| HP-UX | **/etc/rc.config.d/netconf** | All networking parameters |
| Red Hat | **/etc/sysconfig/network** | Hostname, default route, domain |
| | **network-scripts/Ifcfg-**_ifname_[b] | IP address, netmask, broadcast address |
| FreeBSD | **/etc/rc.conf** | All networking parameters |

a. In Solaris 8 and later, **/etc/inet/inodes** will replace **/etc/hosts**. It can contain both IPv4 addresses and IPv6 addresses. **/etc/hosts** will survive for a while for legacy reasons.

b. Relative to **/etc/sysconfig**

## 13.12  SOLARIS NETWORK CONFIGURATION

Solaris comes with a bounteous supply of startup scripts. At a recent trade show, we scored a tear-off calendar with sysadmin trivia questions on each day's page. The question for January 1 was to name all the files you had to touch to change the hostname and IP address of a machine running Solaris and a machine running SunOS. A quick peek at the answers showed six files for Solaris. This is modularization taken to bizarre extremes. That said, let's look at Solaris network configuration.

### Basic network configuration for Solaris

Solaris stashes some network configuration files in **/etc** and some in **/etc/inet**. Many are duplicated through the magic of symbolic links, with the actual files living in **/etc/inet** and the links in **/etc**.

_See page 530 for more information about NIS+._

To set the hostname, enter it into the file **/etc/nodename**. The change will take effect when the machine is rebooted. Some sites use just the short hostname; others use the fully qualified domain name. NIS+ may have trouble with fully qualified names in the **nodename** file.

_See page 523 for more information about the name service switch._

The **/etc/defaultdomain** file's name suggests that it might be used to specify the DNS domain, but it actually specifies the NIS or NIS+ domain name. The DNS domain is specified in **/etc/resolv.conf**.

Solaris uses **/etc/nsswitch.conf** to set the order in which **/etc/hosts**, NIS, NIS+, and DNS are consulted for hostname resolution. We recommend looking at the **hosts**

TCP/IP

file, then DNS for easy booting, but that contradicts Sun's recommendations. The line from **nsswitch.conf** would be:

```
hosts:    files  dns
```

Solaris configures the IP address of each network interface through a file called **/etc/hostname.***interface*, where *interface* is the usual name of the interface (e.g., le0, smc0, or hme0). These files can contain either a hostname that appears in the **hosts** file or an IP address. Older versions of Solaris used hostnames, but newer ones use IP addresses. The value in a **hostname.***interface* file is used as the *address* parameter to **ifconfig**, so it's safest to use an address, even though the configuration filename implies that a hostname is expected. Any special **ifconfig** options can also be put in the **hostname.***interface* file, but that is not commonly done. For interfaces with no corresponding **hostname** files, the startup scripts try to discover their IP addresses by using DHCP or RARP.[20]

As shipped, the Solaris startup files rely on using the **ifconfig** options **netmask +** and **broadcast +**; the pluses mean to look in **/etc/netmasks** for the netmask value and to figure out the broadcast address value from it. The **/etc/netmasks**[21] file lists network numbers and their corresponding netmask values. Any network that is subnetted differently from its inherent network class (A, B, or C) must be represented in the file. Here is an example of a **netmasks** file:

```
# CS Department network masks database
# Network       netmask
# =======       =======
#
128.138.0.0     255.255.255.192   # default for dept.
#
128.138.192.64  255.255.255.192   # drag
128.138.192.192 255.255.255.192   # csops
128.138.193.0   255.255.255.224   # bcrg
128.138.193.32  255.255.255.224   # database
128.138.198.0   255.255.255.0     # slip
...
```

The first line sets a default of /26 for the class B address 128.138.0.0, which is then overridden with specific masks that vary from the default. All networks are listed, even though many use the default value and could technically be left out. On the systems from which this example is taken, the **netmasks** file is centrally maintained and distributed to all hosts. No single host has interfaces on all these networks.

Interface configuration must be performed early in the boot process, before network information servers are started. Solaris redoes the **ifconfig**s several times after various services get started (on the theory that the extra services might provide more or better parameters to the **ifconfig** command).

20. Solaris network interfaces must be scoped out with **ifconfig plumb** to make them accessible. You might have to run this command by hand when performing manual configuration.

21. The **netmasks** man page is broken on Solaris 7; it is fixed in later versions.

To see the exact details, read the following startup scripts:

- **/etc/init.d/rootusr**
- **/etc/init.d/inetinit**
- **/etc/init.d/sysid.net**
- **/etc/init.d/inetsvc**

If the file **/etc/defaultrouter** exists, it is assumed to contain the identity (which again can be either a hostname or a numeric address) of the default gateway, and no further routing configuration is performed. As usual, a numeric address is preferable; using a name requires an **/etc/hosts** entry or a DNS server on the local network.

If no default router is specified, Solaris tries to run **routed** to build its routing tables. The number of network interfaces is counted, and if there is more than one interface or if the **/etc/gateways** file exists, **routed** is started in server mode and advertised by the router discovery daemon. If there is only one interface or if the **/etc/notrouter** file exists, **routed** is started in quiet mode. **routed** in any mode but quiet mode is evil—turn it off.[22]

### Configuration examples for Solaris

Here are some examples of the commands needed to bring up a Solaris interface and add a route to a default gateway.

```
# ifconfig hme0 plumb
# ifconfig hme0 192.108.21.48 netmask 255.255.255.0 up
# route add default 192.108.21.254
```

The following examples show how to see the status of network interfaces and routing tables. Commands prefaced with **sudo** must be run as root. The final example shows a feature of the Solaris and FreeBSD **route** commands that is not present on our other architectures: the **get** argument shows the next hop to a particular destination. We have taken some liberties to make the examples fit on the page.

```
% ifconfig -a
lo0: flags=849<UP,LOOPBACK,RUNNING,MULTICAST> mtu 8232 inet 127.0.0.1
    netmask ff000000
hme0:flags=863<UP,BROADCAST,NOTRAILERS,RUNNING,MULTICAST>
    mtu 1500 inet 192.108.21.48 netmask ffffff00 broadcast 192.108.21.255

% sudo ifconfig hme0
hme0:flags=863<UP,BROADCAST,NOTRAILERS,RUNNING,MULTICAST>
    mtu 1500 inet 192.108.21.48 netmask ffffff00 broadcast 192.108.21.255
    ether 8:0:20:79:4f:49
```

Notice that when run as root, **ifconfig** shows the hardware address, but when run as a user, it does not.

---

22. **routed** has no access controls and believes everything it hears. A host running **routed -q** listens but doesn't talk; without the **-q**, the host can advertise routes. A confused host can really mess up your network because every other **routed** will believe its advertisements.

```
% netstat -nr
Destination    Gateway          Flags Ref  Use  Interface
-------------  ---------------  ----- ---- ---  ---------
192.108.21.0   192.108.21.48      U    3   244  hme0
224.0.0.0      192.108.21.48      U    3     0  hme0
default        192.108.21.254     UG   0   459
127.0.0.1      127.0.0.1          UH   0   296  lo0

% sudo route get anchor.cs.colorado.edu
    route to: anchor.cs.Colorado.EDU
 destination: default
        mask: default
     gateway: xor-gw2
   interface: hme0
       flags: <UP,GATEWAY,DONE,STATIC>
 recvpipe  sendpipe  ssthr  rtt,msec  rttvar  hopct   mtu   expire
        0         0      0         0       0      0  1500        0
```

### DHCP configuration for Solaris

Solaris includes a DHCP client and wins the prize for the easiest and most sensible DHCP client configuration:

> ifconfig *interface* **dhcp**

It just works! It calls the **dhcpagent** program to get the parameters for the interface from DHCP and to configure the interface with them. You can include several options on the **ifconfig** command line to specify the interface as the primary one, set timeouts, increase lease times, or display the status of the interface. To manually unconfigure DHCP, just run

> ifconfig *interface* **drop**

This is all very nice, but you probably want DHCP to be automatically consulted at boot time. This behavior must be requested separately for each interface. To do so, create an **/etc/dhcp.**interface file to go with **/etc/hostname.**interface. If you like, the **dhcp.**interface file can contain additional command-line parameters to be passed to the **ifconfig** command.

The **hostname.**interface file must still exist in order for the interface to be plumbed; however, it can be left empty if you are using DHCP. If the **hostname.**interface file is not empty, the startup scripts will first statically configure the interface by using its contents and then later reconfigure the interface by using DHCP.

You can use the **dhcpinfo** command to see the parameters that have been supplied by the DHCP server. You can also look in the file **/etc/dhcp/**interface**.dhc**, which stores the current configuration for the specified interface.

**dhcpagent** manages the interface from DHCP's point of view. Among other tasks, it negotiates extensions to leases and cancels leases when they are no longer needed. If an interface that has been configured with DHCP is later reconfigured by hand, **dhcpagent** will discontinue management of that interface.

**dhcpagent** collects the leased values from the DHCP server (default route, domain, name servers, etc.), but it does not act on most of them directly. Instead, it writes the parameters out to the appropriate interface files in **/etc/dhcp**. From there, the various pieces of information are read in by the **/etc/rc.*** scripts and used as arguments to **route**, put into the **resolv.conf** file, etc., as appropriate for each.

*See Chapter 11 for more information about syslog.*

**dhcpagent** transmits errors to syslog with facility "daemon" and priority "error"; it also writes them to the file **/dev/console**. It discards lesser errors (warnings, informational messages, and so on) by default, unless you explicitly turn them on with the command-line flag -l*N*. If *N* is 1, warnings are logged; if *N* is higher, less important priorities are also logged. If you send **dhcpagent** a USR1 signal (with **kill**), it dumps the state of its leases.

You can check the files in **/etc/dhcp** to view the configuration of a particular interface. However, the mere fact that there is an *interface*.**dhc** file for an interface does not mean that **dhcpagent** is managing the interface—the lease may have expired.

### Dynamic reconfiguration and tuning for Solaris

Solaris's **ndd** command lets you reconfigure the device drivers on a running system. Perhaps "reconfigure" is too strong a word; each driver provides access to several parameters that can be examined and in some cases adjusted on the fly. It is often very useful to be able to peek at the values of particular parameters, and that's how we've most often used **ndd**. For example, **ndd** lets you determine whether a dual-speed Ethernet card is running at 10 Mb/s or 100 Mb/s or whether source-routed packets will be forwarded.

The syntax of Solaris's **ndd** is similar to that of HP-UX's **ndd**, but its documentation is much worse. The basic syntax from the man page is:

```
ndd [-set] device ? | variable [value]
```

If you give the argument **?** (which must be protected from most shells as **\?**), **ndd** returns the list of variables understood by the driver for the specified device. If you supply the name of a *variable*, **ndd** returns the value of that variable. If you use the -**set** flag and supply a *value*, the specified *variable* is set to the value you specify.

Unfortunately, the **ndd** man page neglects to tell you the possible names of devices, and it doesn't tell you that you must be root to run **ndd** on some devices (**ip** and **hme**, for example) and not on others (**tcp** and **udp**). **ndd** supplies a cryptic error message such as

```
"couldn't push module 'ip', No such device or address"
```

when you try to run it as a user but it requires you to be root.

Table 13.16 (page 312) lists the devices we were able to discover by playing with **ndd**.

Most modern Ethernet cards can work at either 10 Mb/s or 100 Mb/s. As our local nets have transitioned from shared 10 Mb/s to switched 100 Mb/s, we've often had occasion to ask at what speed a machine's network interface is currently running.

**Table 13.16    Devices you can probe with Solaris's ndd command**

| Device | Description | Variable names |
|---|---|---|
| **/dev/tcp** | TCP protocol variables | tcp_* |
| **/dev/udp** | UDP protocol variables | udp_* |
| **/dev/ip** | IP protocol variables | ip_* |
| **/dev/icmp** | ICMP protocol variables | icmp_* |
| **/dev/rawip** | Identical to **/dev/icmp** | icmp_* |
| **/dev/arp** | ARP protocol variables | arp_* |
| **/dev/hme** | hme Ethernet variables | no particular schema |

Here's a handy script by Todd Williams that uses **ndd** to determine the configuration of an Ethernet interface:

```
#!/bin/sh
['ndd /dev/hme link_status'-eq 1] && STATUS=UP || STATUS=DOWN
['ndd /dev/hme link_speed'-eq 1] && SPEED=100 || SPEED=10
['ndd /dev/hme link_mode'-eq 1] && MODE=FULL || MODE=HALF
echo "ethernet is ${STATUS}, running ${SPEED} Mbps ${MODE} duplex"
```

It produces output like this:

```
ethernet is UP, running 10 Mbps HALF duplex
```

which is an English translation of following variables:

- link_status = 1 if up, 0 if down
- link_speed = 1 if 100, 0 if 10
- link_mode = 1 if full duplex, 0 if half duplex

Another set of variables specifies the speed and duplexness if there are multiple interfaces. The following script turns off the interfaces' autonegotiation feature, sets the first interface to 10 Mb/s half duplex, and sets the second interface to 100 Mb/s full duplex:

```
#!/bin/sh
ndd -set /dev/hme instance          0
ndd -set /dev/hme adv_autoneg_cap   0
ndd -set /dev/hme adv_100fdx_cap    0
ndd -set /dev/hme adv_100hdx_cap    0
ndd -set /dev/hme adv_10fdx_cap     0
ndd -set /dev/hme adv_10hdx_cap     1

ndd -set /dev/hme instance          1
ndd -set /dev/hme adv_autoneg_cap   0
ndd -set /dev/hme adv_100fdx_cap    1
ndd -set /dev/hme adv_100hdx_cap    0
ndd -set /dev/hme adv_10fdx_cap     0
ndd -set /dev/hme adv_10hdx_cap     0
```

If you have a card with autonegotiation skills that isn't quite doing the right thing, you may need to turn it off and set the speed and duplex parameters by hand, as was done in this example.

If you have access to an HP-UX machine, run **ndd** there with the **-h** flag (for help) and it will give you device names, variable names, and the meanings of the variables. Many variable names are the same, so you can partially work around Sun's lousy **ndd** man page.

### Security, firewalls, filtering, and NAT for Solaris

Table 13.17 shows Solaris's default behavior with regard to various touchy network issues. For a brief description of the implications of these behaviors, see page 295. You can modify most of them with **ndd**.

**Table 13.17    Security-related network behaviors in Solaris**

| Feature | Default | ndd variable to change |
| --- | --- | --- |
| IP forwarding | off | Set ip_forwarding: 0 is off, 1 is on |
| ICMP redirects | obeys | You can't; you can only change the entries' TTL |
| Source routing | allowed | Set ip_forward_src_routed to 0 |
| Broadcast ping | allowed | Set ip_respond_to_echo_broadcast to 0<br>Set ip_forward_directed_broadcasts to 0 |

As our security chapter says, you should *not* use a UNIX box (or NT box) as a firewall or NAT gateway for your site; use a dedicated piece of hardware such as the Cisco PIX. Solaris makes it easier to follow that rule by not including any firewalling or IP filtering software in the basic distribution.

Solaris does provide a programming interface called **pfmod** that can be used to write packet filtering STREAMS modules. Sun also has a firewall package for Solaris that can be purchased separately.

Third-party software packages can provide both NAT and IP filtering for Solaris. Our favorite is the IPFilter suite, which not only does IP filtering and NAT, but also transparent port forwarding. It is free, open source, and advertised to work on either SPARC or Intel hardware. It's available from

http://cheops.anu.edu.au/~avalon/ip-filter.html

For details on configuring the IPFilter programs **ipf** and **ipnat**, see the FreeBSD section on page 333.

Checkpoint's commercial Firewall-1 offering runs on Solaris and provides functionality similar to that of IPFilter. It's quite pricey, however, and judging from the number of gripes we have heard about it from various web hosting sites, it might be one to research carefully before you spend lots of money.

TCP/IP

### PPP configuration for Solaris

The package that's integrated into Solaris is "asynchronous PPP," since it is designed to handle connections over standard serial lines, such as dial-up modems. It's an official part of Solaris, so you don't need to perform all the sticky steps of installing a kernel PPP module. You can verify that PPP is available with the command

```
# pkginfo | grep ppp
```

If PPP is installed, you should get a response such as

```
system  SUNWapppr PPP/IP Async PPP daemon config files
system  SUNWapppu PPP/IP Async PPP daemon, login service
system  SUNWpppk  PPP/IP and IPdialup Device Drivers
```

If PPP is not already installed, you'll need to install it as a Solaris package. See the manual page for **pkgadd** for more details. Table 13.18 lists the files that configure and manage Solaris's PPP software.

**Table 13.18   PPP-related files on Solaris**

| File | Purpose |
| --- | --- |
| /etc/init.d/asppp | Boot-time startup script for dial-up PPP |
| /usr/sbin/aspppd | Daemon that manages PPP links |
| /etc/asppp.cf | Config file that lists connections |
| /usr/sbin/aspppls | Login shell for dial-in connections |
| /var/adm/log/asppp.log | PPP activity log |
| /tmp/.asppp.fifo | Hook into **aspppd** for dial-in connections |

The Solaris man page for **aspppd** claims that its log file is **/etc/log/asppp.log**. This is a lie; a **grep** on the startup files and **strings** on the binary show that the log file is really in **/var/adm**, not **/etc**.

We were sure that UUCP was all but dead, but alas, Solaris's PPP uses the old UUCP config files to set up PPP servers and to manage dial-out modems. Sigh. To set up a PPP connection to a remote site, you should first add the modem and the site to the **Systems**, **Dialers**, and **Devices** files in the **/etc/uucp** directory. The details of this procedure were covered in the previous edition of this book, but they are not included in this one. If you have a copy of the second edition (red cover), you can refer to Chapter 30. Better yet, buy a terminal server and avoid all this mess.

Once the modem and remote site have been set up in the UUCP files (including a login script for the remote site in **/etc/uucp/Systems**), you must edit **/etc/asppp.cf** to configure the connection's IP address and associate it with a **Systems** entry.

The following example **/etc/asppp.cf** illustrates a link to "pphub" (192.225.32.1) from "myhost" (192.225.32.2).

```
# set IP addresses of the pseudo-interface
ifconfig ipdptp0 plumb 192.225.32.2 192.225.32.1 up

# dynamic dial-up parameters for pseudo-interface path
    interface ipdptp0
    peer_system_name ppphub  # Same as in Systems file
    inactivity_timeout 600      # time out if idle 10 minutes
```

Once this file is in place, you can start the PPP daemon manually with the command

```
# /etc/init.d/asppp start
```

This step should only be necessary when you first configure PPP. On subsequent reboots, the PPP daemon will be started by **init**. If all goes well (check for error messages in **/var/adm/log/asppp.log**), you should be able to reach the remote site with commands such as **ssh** and **ftp**.

### Networking quirks for Solaris

Solaris has two versions of the **ifconfig** command, one in **/sbin** and one in **/usr/sbin**. The **/sbin** version uses a fixed search order for name-to-IP-address lookups: it first consults **/etc/hosts**, and then DNS. The **/usr/sbin** version uses **/etc/nsswitch.conf** to determine the search order; this is the more normal behavior. **/sbin/ifconfig** is used at boot time in the expectation that the **/etc/hosts** file will have enough entries to get the interfaces up without recourse to DNS lookups.

The output of **ifconfig -a** is different when it is run as root than when it is run as a regular user, for both versions of **ifconfig**. When run as root, it shows the link-level Ethernet addresses in addition to the IP addresses and parameters.

Solaris lets you change the link-level (MAC) address of an interface with the **ifconfig** command and the address family **ether**. We consider this a bug, not a feature.

## 13.13  HP-UX NETWORK CONFIGURATION

HP-UX gets a gold star for easy network configuration. All configuration parameters are set in the file **/etc/rc.config.d/netconf**. The values in this file (and all the other files in the **rc.config.d** directory) are read into the environment at boot time and used by the **/sbin/rc** script as the machine boots. **netconf** is liberally scattered with comments that tell you just which variables must be set and what they mean.

### Basic network configuration for HP-UX

To assign a hostname to a machine and configure its first network interface, edit the **netconf** file and assign a value to the following variables:

```
HOSTNAME
INTERFACE_NAME[0]
IP_ADDRESS[0]
SUBNET_MASK[0]
```

TCP/IP

For example:

```
HOSTNAME=disaster
INTERFACE_NAME[0]=lan0
IP_ADDRESS[0]=192.108.21.99
SUBNET_MASK[0]=255.255.255.0
```

A second network interface would have subscript 1, and its existence would be indicated by the variable NET_CARDS being set to 2.

The **netconf** file also contains variables to configure static routes and start a routing daemon. To establish a default route, set the following variables:

```
ROUTE_DESTINATION[0]=default
ROUTE_MASK[0]=""
ROUTE_GATEWAY[0]=192.108.21.254
ROUTE_COUNT[0]=1
```

The ROUTE_MASK variable is needed for a network in which the netmask differed from the default for the class of addresses used. The ROUTE_COUNT variable should be 0 if the gateway is the local machine and 1 if it is remote. To add more static routes, just enter their parameters to a set of ROUTE_* variables with indexes [1], [2], etc. These arguments are passed directly to the route command. For example, the destination parameter can be the word **default** as above or **net** *netaddr* or **host** *hostaddr*.

HP-UX supplies **gated** but not **routed**; to use **gated**, set the variable GATED to 1 and GATED_ARGS to the arguments you want **gated** started with. See Chapter 14, *Routing*, for more details about **gated** configuration. The HP-UX man page on routing (**man routing**) contains a lot of good background information.

Many fields in the **netconf** file can contain either a hostname or an IP address. If a hostname is used, it *must* be defined in **/etc/hosts**. At boot time, HP-UX looks only at **/etc/hosts** and does not use any other name lookup mechanism. The machines in **/etc/hosts** should have their fully qualified domain names listed first, followed by their short names and any aliases.

HP uses the **lanscan** command to show information about the network interfaces on a machine. **ifconfig -a** does not work, but **ifconfig** *interface* does. Network interface names begin with either "lan" or "snap": lan for Ethernet link-layer encapsulation and snap for IEEE 802.3 encapsulation. The first interface is lan0, the second is lan1, and so on.

HP-UX has the same sort of "plumbing" concept that Solaris does, but interfaces are automatically plumbed when they are assigned an IP address by **ifconfig**.

SAM is HP's system administration tool, which is alleged to make UNIX system administration a breeze. It is a menu-based system and can be used to configure network interfaces, as well as to perform many other sysadmin chores.

### Configuration examples for HP-UX

To bring up an HP-UX network interface and add a default route by hand, you'd use commands such as the following:

```
# ifconfig lan0 192.108.21.99 netmask 0xffffff00
# route add default 192.108.21.254 1²³
```

HP's **lanscan** command lists the network interfaces in the system and the characteristics of the device driver that controls them. **lanscan -v** shows slightly more information. The examples below were munged to fit the page. The MAC entry with value ETHER implies that the network device name should be lan0, not snap0; **ifconfig** shows this to be true.

```
% lanscan
Hardware  Station   Crd  Hdw   Net-Int     NM   MAC    HP-DLPI  DLPI
Path      Address   In#  State NamePPA     ID   Type   Support  Mjr#
8/0/20/0  0x001...  0    UP    lan0 snap0  1    ETHER  Yes      130
```

```
% ifconfig lan0
lan0: flags=843<UP,BROADCAST,RUNNING,MULTICAST> inet 192.108.21.99
    netmask ffffff00 broadcast 192.108.21.255
```

```
% ifconfig snap0
ifconfig: no such interface
```

**netstat -i** shows network interface names, and **netstat -nr** displays routing tables:

```
% netstat -i
Name       Mtu   Network       Address            Ipkts  Opkts
lan0       1500  192.108.21.0  disaster.xor.com   6047   3648
lo0        4136  127.0.0.0     localhost.xor.com  231    231
```

```
% netstat -nr
Routing tables
Dest/Netmask      Gateway         Flags  Refs   Use   Int   Pmtu
127.0.0.1         127.0.0         UH     0      231   lo0   4136
192.108.21.99     192.108.21.99   UH     8            lan0  4136
192.108.21.0      192.108.21.99   U      2      0     lan0  1500
127.0.0.0         127.0.0.1       U      0      0     lo0   4136
default           192.108.21.254  UG     0      0     lan0  1500
```

The **lanadmin** command displays a summary of the network traffic that each interface has seen. It can also manipulate and monitor interfaces. It's a menu-based program with useful help lists to lead you to the information you want. Here is an example that displays the statistics for the lan0 interface:

```
% lanadmin
        LOCAL AREA NETWORK ONLINE ADMINISTRATION, Version 1.0
            Copyright 1994 Hewlett Packard Company.
                   All rights are reserved.
```

23. On HP-UX 11, the hop count field is not required; it defaults to 0 if not explicitly specified. Earlier versions required the count field to be present.

```
Test Selection mode.
      lan     = LAN Interface Administration
      menu    = Display this menu
      quit    = Terminate the Administration
      terse   = Do not display command menu
      verbose = Display command menu

Enter command: lan
LAN Interface test mode. LAN Interface PPA Number = 0
      clear    = Clear statistics registers
      display  = Display LAN Interface status/statistics
      end      = End LAN Interface Admin., go up 1 level
      menu     = Display this menu
      ppa      = PPA Number of the LAN Interface
      quit     = Terminate the Admin, return to shell
      reset    = Reset LAN Interface, execute selftest
      specific = Go to Driver specific menu

Enter command: display
                  LAN INTERFACE STATUS DISPLAY
                   Thu, Mar 2,2000  00:41:24
PPA Number                     = 0
Description                    = lan0 HP 10/100 TX Half-Duplex Hw Rev 0.
Type (value)                   = ethernet-csmacd(6)
MTU Size                       = 1500
Speed                          = 10
Station Address                = 0x108303e9e6
Administration Status (value)  = up(1)
Operation Status (value)       = up(1)
...
Inbound Unicast Packets        = 4204
Inbound Non-Unicast Packets    = 5594
...
Inbound Unknown Protocols      = 501
Outbound Octets                = 454903
Outbound Unicast Packets       = 3603
...
Deferred Transmissions         = 2
Late Collisions                = 0
Excessive Collisions           = 2
...
```

At the time this example was run, the box had been up for only 3 hours in the middle of the night (we were adding a disk and rebooting frequently), so the traffic loads are very low. In addition to the commands **lan** and **display**, for which the output is shown above, we also tried **clear** and **reset**, which clear the counters and reset the interface. But since we didn't run **lanadmin** as root, we were rebuffed.

### DHCP configuration for HP-UX

As with other network configuration parameters, you turn on the use of DHCP at boot time by setting variables in the **/etc/rc.config.d/netconf** file. In this case, the variable names start with DHCP_ENABLE; the index [0] refers to the first interface, [1] to the second interface, and so on. For example,

```
DHCP_ENABLE[0]=1
```

sets the first network interface to DHCP mode. It will get its IP address, netmask, and other networking parameters from the DHCP server on the local network. Setting the variable equal to 0 would disable DHCP; you'd have to assign a static address in the **netconf** file. If no DHCP_ENABLE clause is present, the variable defaults to 1.

The **/sbin/auto_parms** script does the real legwork of contacting the DHCP server. The program **dhcpdb2conf** enters the DHCP parameters secured by **auto_parms** into the **netconf** file, from which boot-time configuration information is taken.

On the server side, HP-UX provides a DHCP server in the form of **bootpd**, which also handles BOOTP requests. The program **dhcptools** dumps the DHCP parameters in **bootpd**'s database, checks the configuration files for syntax errors, reclaims unused addresses, and performs many other tasks. If you are having trouble, you will appreciate **dhcptools**' diagnostic dumps. The files are put in **/tmp** and have **dhcp** in their names.

DHCP can also be configured with SAM. Compatibility issues may arise when HP-UX clients are mixed with non-HP-UX servers, or vice versa.

### Dynamic reconfiguration and tuning for HP-UX

As in Solaris, you can use the **ndd** command to tune many different networking parameters (over 100 at last count). When used interactively, **ndd** tunes values on the fly. To change values permanently, enter them in the file **/etc/rc.config.d/nddconf**, which is read at boot time.

**ndd**'s -h (help) option is quite useful. With no arguments, it lists all the parameters you can tune. If you also specify a variable name, **ndd -h** describes what the variable does and shows its minimum, maximum, and default values. For example:

```
% ndd -h | grep source
ip_forward_src_routed -  Controls forwarding of source routed packets

% ndd -h ip_forward_src_routed
ip_forward_src_routed:
  Set to 1 to forward source-routed packets; set to 0 to
  disable forwarding. If disabled, an ICMP Destination
  Unreachable message is sent to the sender of source-
  routed packets needing to be forwarded. [0,1] Default: 1
```

**ndd**'s output shows that this version (11.00) of HP-UX allows forwarding of source-routed packets by default. (Let's hope that when a default value such as forwarding of source-routed packets is changed, the documentation in the **ndd** help database is changed as well.) To view and change the value of the ip_forward_src_routed variable, use **ndd**'s **-get** and **-set** options.

TCP/IP

```
% ndd -get /dev/ip ip_forward_src_routed
1
% sudo ndd -set /dev/ip ip_forward_src_routed 0
% ndd -get /dev/ip ip_forward_src_routed
0
```

To turn off source routing permanently, you could add the following lines to the **nddconf** file:

```
# turn off forwarding source routed packets
TRANSPORT_NAME[0]=ip
NDD_NAME[0]=ip_forward_src_routed
NDD_VALUE[0]=0
```

For the next variable that you wanted to change, you would add another copy of the same three lines with appropriate values and with subscript 1 instead of 0. Unfortunately, only 10 parameters can be set through **nddconf**.

### Security, firewalls, filtering, and NAT for HP-UX

Table 13.19 shows HP-UX's default behavior with regard to various touchy network issues. For a brief description of the implications of these behaviors, see page 295. You can modify most of them with **ndd**.

**Table 13.19    Security-related network behaviors in HP-UX**

| Feature | Default | ndd variable to change |
|---------|---------|------------------------|
| IP forwarding | dynamic[a] | Set ip_forwarding: 0 is off, 1 is on, and 2 is dynamic |
| ICMP redirects | obeys | Can't be changed |
| Source routing | allowed | Set ip_forward_src_routed to 0 |
| Broadcast ping | allowed | Set ip_forward_directed_broadcasts to 0 |

a. On with >1 network interface, off otherwise.

HP-UX does not include any firewalling or IP filtering software, except for network connections established with PPP. See the next section for specifics. NAT is not supported either. Darren Reed is porting his free IPFilter package to HP-UX; it should be ready by the end of 2000.

HP-UX's version of **inetd** has built-in TCP wrapper functionality that you configure in the file **/var/adm/inetd.sec**. See page 666 for details.

We recommend that you use a dedicated piece of hardware such as a Cisco PIX box as your packet filtering firewall; UNIX hosts are too insecure to be used in this role. If you wonder in exactly what ways HP has shipped you an insecure system, check

> http://people.hp.se/stevesk/bastion11.html

to see all the steps necessary to turn an HP-UX 11.00 host into a bastion host on an unprotected network. This document is an excellent description of all the creature comforts in HP-UX that must be turned off if the machine is to be secure on the open Internet. We wish we knew of a web site like this for our other example vendors.

### PPP configuration for HP-UX

HP ships Morning Star's PPP software, which makes use of **tun**, the HP-UX IP tunnel driver. HP-UX's PPP configuration is very similar to that of Solaris. Both systems use HoneyDanBer UUCP configuration as a model, with Sun just jamming it in and HP moving the files and describing them appropriately in their man pages.

Table 13.20 shows the HP-UX files. See the section on Solaris PPP configuration (page 314) for a more detailed description of the files and their format.

**Table 13.20    PPP-related files on HP-UX**

| File | Purpose |
| --- | --- |
| **/etc/ppp/Auth** | Configures peer names and authentication keys |
| **/etc/ppp/Devices** | Defines and describes physical devices (modems) |
| **/etc/ppp/Dialers** | Tells how to dial each of the system's modems |
| **/etc/ppp/Filter** | Controls autodialer; filters and logs packets |
| **/etc/ppp/Keys** | Holds keys for encrypting connections |
| **/etc/ppp/Systems** | Holds information about neighboring systems |
| **/etc/ppp/Autostart** | Starts **pppd** with appropriate arguments |
| **/usr/bin/pppd** | The PPP daemon |

Despite their quality, the man pages for these configuration files suffer from a bizarre and unaccountable lapse of naming: the name of each man page has **ppp.** prefixed to the name of the file it describes. For example, the command **man Systems** fails, but **man ppp.Systems** shows a nicely detailed description of the format of the **Systems** file, including several examples.

The **/etc/ppp** directory also contains sample files for each configuration file. Here is a snippet from the **Systems.ex** file; these lines were preceded by hundreds of lines of comments that seemed to include most of the **ppp.Systems** man page:

```
# Examples of entries that we use at Morning Star Technologies
#
#roughy Any ACU 19200-PEP 5551212 ogin:--ogin: Premora ssword: \qkjLJHIuD
#manatee Any ACU 38400 5552468 ogin:--ogin: Premora ssword: \qd7DW3KlZ
```

The directory **/etc/ppp/examples** contains some specifics regarding terminal servers from various manufacturers.

To run PPP on HP-UX, you must populate the UUCP files with information about your modems and the systems you want to talk to, including the remote login and password that are needed to connect to the terminal server at the other end of your phone line. You must then create and edit the **/etc/ppp/Autostart** script to start the **pppd** daemon with the appropriate arguments for your connection. The sample

TCP/IP

script **Autostart.ex** is well commented and includes examples. At boot time, one of the files in **/sbin/rc2.d** will call **Autostart** automatically.

### Networking quirks for HP-UX

HP-UX is testy about hostnames longer than 8 characters. You can use longer names, but you must specify a UUCP-style nodename in **/etc/rc.sysconfig.d/NODENAME** that is 8 characters or less.

## 13.14  NETWORK CONFIGURATION FOR RED HAT

Red Hat Linux keeps most network configuration files in the **/etc/sysconfig** and **/etc/sysconfig/network-scripts** directories. It supports DHCP, PPP, and IP filtering. The networking stack also includes support for SACKs—selective acknowledgments—which sometimes improve TCP performance on congested links.

### Basic network configuration for Red Hat

A Red Hat machine's hostname is set in the file **/etc/sysconfig/network**, which also contains lines that specify the machine's DNS domain and default gateway. For example, here is a **network** file for a host that has a single Ethernet interface and should not forward IP packets:

```
NETWORKING=yes
FORWARD_IPV4=false
HOSTNAME=redhat.xor.com
DOMAINNAME=xor.com
GATEWAY=192.108.21.254
GATEWAYDEV=eth0
```

When you set the hostname in the **network** file, you should also update the contents of the **/etc/hostname** file. The **hostname** file is currently only used for backward compatibility, however.

Interface-specific data is stored in **/etc/sysconfig/network-scripts/ifcfg-***ifname*, where *ifname* is the name of the network interface. These configuration files let you set the IP address, netmask, network, and broadcast address for each interface. They also include a line that specifies whether the interface should be configured "up" at boot time, which is useful on a laptop or mobile computer.

Typically, files for an Ethernet interface (eth0) and for the loopback interface (lo) are present. For example,

```
DEVICE=eth0
IPADDR=192.108.21.73
NETMASK=255.255.255.0
NETWORK=192.108.21.0
BROADCAST=192.108.21.255
ONBOOT=yes
```

and

```
DEVICE=lo
IPADDR=127.0.0.1
NETMASK=255.0.0.0
NETWORK=127.0.0.0
BROADCAST=127.255.255.255
ONBOOT=yes
```

are the **ifcfg-eth0** and **ifcfg-lo0** files for the machine redhat.xor.com described in the **network** file earlier in this section.

Red Hat provides a couple of handy scripts that facilitate interface management. **/sbin/ifup** and **/sbin/ifdown** take the name of a network interface as an argument and bring the specified interface up or down. After changing network information in any of the **/etc/sysconfig** directories, be sure to do **/sbin/ifdown** *ifname* followed by **/sbin/ifup** *ifname*. Better yet, reboot the system to be sure your changes don't cause some kind of subtle problem.

If you need to manage all the interfaces at once, the **/etc/rc.d/init.d/network** script takes the arguments **start**, **stop**, **restart**, and **status**. This script is invoked at boot time with the **start** argument.

The Red Hat startup scripts can also configure static routes. Any routes added to **/etc/sysconfig/static-routes** are entered into the routing table at boot time. The entries provide arguments to a **route add** command, although in mixed-up order:

```
eth0 net 130.225.204.48 netmask 255.255.255.248 gw 130.225.204.49
eth1 net 192.38.8.0 netmask 255.255.255.224 gw 192.38.8.129
```

The interface is specified first, followed by arguments to the **route** command: the route type (net or host), the target network, the netmask associated with that network, and finally, the next-hop gateway. The keyword gw is required. Current Linux kernels do not use the metric parameter to **route** but allow it to be entered and maintained in the routing table for routing daemons to use.

Red Hat 5.1 and later include a utility called **linuxconf**. This utility provides a simple interface for managing many system administration tasks, including most network-related configuration.

### Configuration examples for Red Hat

The following commands bring up a Red Hat network interface and add a default route. Notice that the keyword **up** on the **ifconfig** line is not required, but **gw** is required on the **route** line.

```
# ifconfig eth0 192.108.21.73 netmask 255.255.255.0
# route add default gw 192.108.21.254 eth0
```

By default, Red Hat's **ifconfig** gives lots of information, including hardware address, link encapsulation, and statistics.

TCP/IP

```
% /sbin/ifconfig
eth0      Link encap:Ethernet  HWaddr 00:C0:F0:1F:57:61
          inet addr:192.108.21.73  Bcast:192.108.21.255  Mask:255.255.255.0
          UP BROADCAST RUNNING MULTICAST  MTU:1500 Metric:1
          RX pkts:248725 errors:0 dropped:0 overruns:0 frame:0
          TX pkts:5219 errors:24 dropped:0 overruns:0 carrier:20
          collisions:1280 txqueuelen:100
          Interrupt:10 Base addr 0x6500
lo        Link encap:Local Loopback
          inet addr:127.0.0.1  Mask:255.0.0.0
          UP LOOPBACK RUNNING  MTU:3924  Metric:1
          RX packets:44 errors:0 dropped:0 overruns:0 frame:0
          TX packets:44 errors:0 dropped:0 overruns:0 carrier:0
          collisions:0 txqueuelen:0
```

The value for collisions on the Ethernet interface is 1,280, which as a percentage of output packets is 24.5%; this value is extremely high and indicates a loaded network that needs to be split into multiple subnets or migrated to a switched infrastructure.

As on most systems, **netstat -nr** dumps the kernel's routing table, and **netstat -i** shows information about network interfaces:

```
% netstat -nr
Kernel IP routing table
Destination    Gateway         Genmask          Flags  MSS  Window  irtt  Iface
192.108.21.73  0.0.0.0         255.255.255.255  UH       0  0          0  eth0
192.108.21.0   0.0.0.0         255.255.255.0    U        0  0          0  eth0
127.0.0.0      0.0.0.0         255.0.0.0        U        0  0          0  lo
0.0.0.0        192.108.21.254  0.0.0.0          UG       0  0          0  eth0
```

```
% netstat -i
Kernel Interface table
              ------------Receive-----------  ----------Transmit---------
Iface MTU Met     OK ERR DRP OVR     OK ERR DRP OVR    Flg
eth0  1500   0 251684   0   0   0   5710  24   0   0    BRU
lo    3924   0     44   0   0   0     44   0   0   0    LRU
```

The output of Red Hat's **netstat -i**, which we have cleaned up a bit to make it fit on the page, shows per-interface counts of normal packets, errors, dropped packets, and overruns in both the receive and transmit directions.

## DHCP configuration for Red Hat

Red Hat comes with a DHCP server, **dhcpd**, and two different DHCP clients: **pump**[24] and **dhcpcd**, an old DHCP client from CMU that is basically a hacked-up **bootpd**. We suggest that you ignore both of the supplied DHCP clients and install the client from the Internet Software Consortium at www.isc.org. In our experience, it is more reliable. Red Hat's DHCP server is from ISC, so it's something of a puzzlement as to why Red Hat didn't just use their client as well. Our coverage of ISC client configuration starts on page 332.

---

24. A pump, like a boot (as in BOOTP), is a type of footwear.

**pump** is Red Hat's default DHCP client. It is started at boot time when requested by one of the **/etc/sysconfig/network-scripts/ifcfg-***interface* script fragments. For example, to configure interface eth0 automatically with DHCP, you should edit the file **/etc/sysconfig/network-scripts/ifcfg-eth0**. Instead of setting the interface's IP address, netmask, and other parameters, you would include the line

```
BOOTPROTO=dhcp
```

If you need to manually start **pump** to manage eth0, run the command

```
# pump -i eth0
```

To stop **pump**'s management of eth0, use

```
# pump -r -i eth0
```

**dhcpcd**, the supplied alternative to **pump**, is essentially vestigial. Its use is deprecated, but Red Hat was perhaps afraid to break existing installations by removing it. **dhcpcd** is configured through files in the directory **/etc/dhcpc**.

### Dynamic reconfiguration and tuning for Red Hat

Linux has its own special way of tuning kernel and networking parameters. Instead of providing a command that reads and sets the parameters, Linux puts a representation of each variable that can be tuned into the **/proc** filesystem. The important networking variables are in **/proc/sys/net/ipv4**; here is an abridged listing:

```
% cd /proc/sys/net/ipv4; ls -F
conf/
icmp_destunreach_rate               icmp_echo_ignore_all
icmp_echo_ignore_broadcasts         icmp_echoreply_rate
icmp_ignore_bogus_error_responses   icmp_paramprob_rate
icmp_timeexceed_rate                igmp_max_memberships
ip_always_defrag                    ip_autoconfig
ip_default_ttl                      ip_dynaddr
ip_forward                          ip_local_port_range
ip_masq_debug                       ip_no_pmtu_disc
ipfrag_high_thresh                  ipfrag_low_thresh
ipfrag_time                         neigh/
route/                              tcp_fin_timeout
tcp_keepalive_probes                tcp_keepalive_time
tcp_max_ka_probes                   tcp_max_syn_backlog
tcp_retrans_collapse                tcp_retries1
tcp_retries2                        tcp_rfc1337
tcp_sack                            tcp_stdurg
tcp_syn_retries                     tcp_syncookies
tcp_timestamps                      tcp_window_scaling
```

Many of the variables with **rate** and **max** in their names are used to thwart denial of service attacks. The **conf** subdirectory contains variables that are set on a per-interface basis. It contains subdirectories **all** and **default** and a subdirectory for each interface (including the loopback). Each subdirectory contains the same set of files.

```
% ls -F
accept_redirects    accept_source_route    bootp_relay
forwarding          log_martians           mc_forwarding
proxy_arp           rp_filter              secure_redirects
send_redirects      shared_media
```

If you change something in the **all** subdirectory, your change applies to all interfaces. If you change the same variable in, say, the **eth0** subdirectory, only that interface will be affected. The **defaults** subdirectory contains the default values as shipped.

To see the value of a variable, use **cat**; to set it, use **echo** redirected to the proper filename. For example, the command

```
% cat icmp_echo_ignore_broadcasts
0
```

shows that this variable is currently set to 0, meaning that broadcast pings are not ignored. To set it to 1 (and thereby avoid falling prey to smurf-type denial of service attacks), run

```
% sudo csh -c "echo 1 > icmp_echo_ignore_broadcasts"[25]
```

You'll typically be logged in over the same network you are tweaking as you adjust these variables, so be careful! You can mess things up badly enough to require a reboot from the console to recover, which might be inconvenient if the system happens to be in Point Barrow, Alaska, and it's January. Test-tune these variables on your desktop system before you even think of attacking a production machine.

The document **/usr/src/linux/Documentation/proc.txt**, written by the SuSE Linux folks, is a nice primer on kernel tuning with **/proc**. It tells you what the variables really mean and sometimes provides suggested values.

### Security, firewalls, filters, and NAT for Red Hat

Table 13.21 shows Red Hat's default behavior with regard to various touchy network issues. For a brief description of the implications of these behaviors, see page 295.

**Table 13.21    Security-related network behaviors in Linux**

| Feature | Host | Gateway | Control file (in /proc/sys/net) |
|---------|------|---------|---------------------------------|
| IP forwarding | off | on | **ipv4/ip_forward** for the whole system<br>**ipv4/conf/**_interface_**/forwarding** per interface[a] |
| ICMP redirects | obeys | ignores | **ipv4/conf/**_interface_**/accept_redirects** |
| Source routing | ignores | obeys | **ipv4/conf/**_interface_**/accept_source_route** |
| Broadcast ping | answers | answers | **ipv4/ip_echo_ignore_broadcasts** |

a. The _interface_ can be either a specific interface name or **all**.

25. If you try this command in the form **sudo echo 1 > icmp_echo_ignore_broadcasts**, you'll just generate a "permission denied" message—your shell attempts to open the output file before it runs **sudo**. You want the **sudo** to apply to both the **echo** command and the redirection. Ergo, you must create a root subshell in which to execute the entire command.

To change any of these parameters permanently (or more accurately, to reset them every time the system boots), add the appropriate **echo** commands to a script that is run during the boot sequence.

Red Hat comes with some pretty reasonable IP filtering software. We normally don't recommend the use of UNIX (or NT) systems as firewalls because of their general insecurity. However, a UNIX firewall is better than nothing at all for a home site or a site with no budget for appropriate hardware (such as a Cisco PIX box), so we describe Red Hat's **ipchains** software in a bit more detail.

If you are set on using a Linux machine as a firewall, please at least make sure that it's up to date with respect to security upgrades and patches. Chapter 21, *Security*, reviews some of the many issues to consider when you are trying to make a machine as secure as possible. A firewall machine is an excellent place to put into practice all of that chapter's recommendations. (The section that starts on page 675 discusses packet-filtering firewalls in general. If you are not familiar with the basic concept of a firewall, it would probably be wise to read that section before continuing.)

**ipchains** uses the concept of an ordered "chain" of rules against which network packets are checked. Each rule has a "target" clause that determines the disposition of matching packets. As soon as a packet matches a rule, its fate is sealed and no more rules need be checked. For this reason, the rules in a chain generally run from most to least specific.

Three chains are defined by default: input, output, and forward. You can also define your own chains (for accounting, for example). Each packet handled by the kernel is submitted to exactly one of the default chains. The forward chain sees all packets that arrive on one interface and need to be forwarded on another. The input chain processes all packets that come in from the network and are bound for the local machine. The output chain sees only packets that originate on the local host. Each network interface has its own copy of these chains, so you are free to establish different handling criteria for different interfaces.

The common targets are ACCEPT, DENY, REJECT, MASQ, REDIRECT, and RETURN. When a rule results in an ACCEPT, matching packets are allowed to proceed on their way. DENY and REJECT both drop their packets. DENY is silent, and REJECT returns an ICMP error message.

*See page 279 for more information about NAT.*

MASQ is used for IP masquerading, which is the Linux jargon for NAT.[26] For masquerading to work, the variable FORWARD_IPV4 in the **network** file must be set to true and the kernel must be built with CONFIG_IP_MASQUERADE defined.

REDIRECT shunts packets to a proxy instead of letting them go on their merry way. Compile the kernel with CONFIG_IP_TRANSPARENT_PROXY defined in order to

---

26. Strictly speaking, Red Hat performs only a limited form of NAT which is more properly called PAT, for Port Address Translation. Instead of using a range of IP addresses as a true NAT implementation would, PAT multiplexes all connections onto a single address. This detail doesn't make much practical difference, so we will refer to the Red Hat implementation as NAT for the sake of consistency.

TCP/IP

use REDIRECT. You might use this feature to force all your site's web traffic to go through a web cache such as Squid, for example. RETURN terminates user-defined chains and is analogous to the return statement in a subroutine call.

A Red Hat firewall is usually implemented as a series of **ipchains** commands contained in an **rc.firewall** startup script. Individual **ipchains** commands usually take one of the following forms:

```
ipchains -F chain-name
ipchains -A chain-name -i interface -j target
```

The first form flushes all prior rules from the chain. The second form appends the current specification to the chain. The **-i** and **-j** parameters must be specified for each **ipchains** statement to be appended to the filter. **ipchains** can also take several other parameter clauses, shown in Table 13.22.

**Table 13.22    Command-line flags for ipchains**

| Clause | Meaning or possible values |
|---|---|
| **-p** proto | Matches by protocol: **tcp**, **udp**, or **icmp** |
| **-s** source-ip | Matches host or network source IP address (CIDR notation is OK) |
| **-d** dest-ip | Matches host or network destination address |
| **--sport** port# | Matches by source port (note the double dashes) |
| **--dport** port# | Matches by destination port (note the double dashes) |
| **--icmp-type** type | Matches by ICMP type code (note the double dashes) |
| **-l** | Logs the packet through syslog: facility "kernel", priority "info" |
| **-y** | Matches only new TCP connection requests, based on header flags |
| **!** | Negates a clause |

Below are some complete examples. We assume that the ppp0 interface goes to the Internet and that the eth0 interface goes to the internal network. This first set of rules accepts all packets from the internal interfaces and drops any packets that arrive on the ppp0 interface with source addresses in the private address space (NAT) ranges. Such packets should also probably be dropped in the output chain, since we wouldn't want to let them sneak out onto the Internet.

```
ipchains -A input -i lo -j ACCEPT
ipchains -A input -i eth0 -j ACCEPT
ipchains -A input -i ppp0 -s 192.168.0.0/16 -j DENY
ipchains -A input -i ppp0 -s 172.16.0.0/12 -j DENY
ipchains -A input -i ppp0 -s 10.0.0.0/8 -j DENY
```

To block TELNET access from the Internet (to port 23) but allow mail and SSH connections (to ports 25 and 22, respectively), we would use rules such as these:

```
ipchains -A input -i ppp0 -p tcp --dport 23 -j DENY
ipchains -A input -i ppp0 -p tcp --dport 25 -j ACCEPT
ipchains -A input -i ppp0 -p tcp --dport 22 -j ACCEPT
```

We end the input chain with a rule that forbids all packets not explicitly permitted. It might be interesting to see who is knocking on our door from the Internet, so we add a -l flag after DENY to log all the packets rejected by this rule.

```
ipchains -A input -i ppp0 -j DENY -l
```

Finally, we set up IP masquerading (aka NAT, aka PAT) to disguise the private address space used on the internal network 192.168.1.0/24:[27]

```
ipchains -A forward -i ppp0 -s 192.168.1.0/24 -d ! 192.168.1.0/24 -j MASQ
```

Here, we have specified in the matching criteria that the source address must be internal but the destination address must be external (the ! negates the sense of the test) in order for IP masquerading to occur. Internal traffic that happens to pass through this host is not affected.

Since Linux implements PAT rather than true NAT (see the footnote on page 327), it's not necessary to specify a range of external addresses to be used on the Internet. The Linux gateway uses its own IP address for all external traffic and uses port numbers to multiplex connections from multiple interior hosts.

Once you get used to its notation, **ipchains** seems like a reasonable way to describe firewall rules, but mixing NAT into the same mechanism seems messy. More examples of **ipchains** firewalls are available at www.wiley.com/compbooks/sonnenreich.

It is rumored that **ipchains** will go away in Linux kernels after 2.2 and be replaced by a new filtering mechanism.

### PPP configuration for Red Hat

Red Hat uses the same PPP implementation as FreeBSD (the kernel version, not the user version), and it is configured identically. Rather than repeat that description here, we refer you to the FreeBSD PPP configuration section beginning on page 337.

### Networking quirks for Red Hat

Unlike most kernels, Linux pays attention to the type-of-service (TOS) bits in IP packets and gives faster service to packets that are labeled as being interactive (low latency). Jammin'! Unfortunately, brain damage on the part of Microsoft necessitates that you turn off this perfectly reasonable behavior.

All packets originating on Windows 95, 98, NT, and 2000 are labeled as being interactive, no matter what their purpose. UNIX systems, on the other hand, usually do not mark any packets as being interactive. If your Linux gateway serves a mixed network of UNIX and Windows systems, the Windows packets will consistently get preferential treatment. The performance hit for UNIX can be quite noticeable.

You can turn off TOS-based packet sorting when you compile the Linux kernel. Just say no to the option "IP: use TOS value as routing key."

---

27. Why aren't such packets rejected by the previous rule? Because this rule is a part of the forward chain, whereas the "reject everything else" rule is part of the input chain.

TCP/IP

When IP masquerading (NAT) is enabled, it tells the kernel to reassemble packet fragments into a complete packet before forwarding them, even if the kernel must immediately refragment the packet to send it on its way. This reassembly can cost quite a few CPU cycles, but CPUs are fast enough now that it shouldn't really be an issue on modern machines.

Linux lets you change the MAC-level addresses of certain types of network interfaces. We consider this a bug. Don't do it.

## 13.15  NETWORK CONFIGURATION FOR FREEBSD

FreeBSD has all the latest goodies in its networking arsenal: two firewall packages (including NAT), two PPP implementations, support for T/TCP (a somewhat successful attempt to make web connections more efficient), and more.

You perform most FreeBSD network configuration by setting the values of variables in **/etc/rc.conf**. The system startup scripts also read **/etc/defaults/rc.conf**, which sets the defaults for most variables. You can also create an **/etc/rc.conf.local** file for host-specific parameters.

These three files are really just shell scripts that are executed to establish a context for the execution of other startup scripts. The format of their contents is the same, but they are three in number just to keep different classes of configuration data separate. The **/etc/defaults/rc.conf** file provides reasonable starting values for most parameters, the **/etc/rc.conf** file contains parameters that are local but perhaps common to several FreeBSD machines, and the **rc.conf.local** file holds settings that apply only to the local machine. For simplicity, we will assume in this section that you are using only the **rc.conf** file.

You should not modify the contents of **/etc/defaults/rc.conf**. However, it's often useful to look at this file because it contains a near-complete list of the variables you can set, along with comments that describe their functions.

The only noticeable differences between FreeBSD 3.4 and 4.0 from a sysadmin's point of view are that the default kernel contains many more network device drivers (13 total) and that IPv6 support is built in. Our **ifconfig** examples section includes both.

### Basic network configuration for FreeBSD

You should set the following variables in **rc.conf** to override the empty values set in **/etc/defaults/rc.conf**:

```
hostname="hostname"              # Set this!
ifconfig_xxx="inet IP-address"   # Network device config
defaultrouter="gateway"          # Set to default gateway
```

The variable network_interfaces is set to auto by default, which makes the system find its network interfaces at boot time. It can also be set to a list of interfaces on the machine. If you choose to go this route, don't forget to include the loopback interface.

Here's an example:

```
network_interfaces="lo0 xl0"
```

To establish static routes, use the static_routes variable:

```
static_routes="backlan 212"              # Set to static route list
route_backlan="-net 10.0.1.0 132.236.212.2"
route_212="-net 132.236.212.64 -netmask 255.255.255.192 132.236.212.6
```

The static_routes clause takes a space-separated list of route names. A route name is an arbitrary string that is used in a route_*name* clause to define the arguments that should be passed to the **route add** command.

Routing is completely disabled by default. To get reasonable behavior at most sites, you must either set a default route, set static routes, enable **routed**, or enable **gated**. (NIS is also disabled by default.)

### Configuration examples for FreeBSD

To manually configure an Ethernet interface and set a default route, you'd use commands such as these:

```
# ifconfig xl0 inet 192.108.21.11 netmask 0xffffff00
# route add default 192.108.21.254
```

The second of these commands is equivalent to the command

```
# route add -net 0.0.0.0 192.108.21.254
```

Unlike most versions of **route**, FreeBSD's **route** requires a dash in front of the route type (**-net** or **-host**), and it does not accept a hop count parameter.

The output of **ifconfig** and **netstat -nr** show the results of the commands above:

```
% ifconfig xl0
xl0: flags=8843<UP,BROADCAST,RUNNING,SIMPLEX,MULTICAST> mtu 1500
     inet 192.108.21.11 netmask 0xffffff00 broadcast 192.108.21.255
     ether 00:60:97:9b:69:9a
     media: 10baseT/UTP <half-duplex>
     supported media: autoselect 100baseTX <full-duplex> 100baseTX
        <half-duplex> 100baseTX 10baseT/UTP <full-duplex> 10baseT/UTP
        10baseT/UTP <half-duplex>
```

```
% netstat -nr
Routing tables
Internet:
```

| Destination | Gateway | Flags | Refs | Use | Netif | Exp |
|---|---|---|---|---|---|---|
| default | 192.108.21.254 | UGSc | 0 | 18 | xl0 | |
| 127.0.0.1 | 127.0.0.1 | UH | 0 | 3 | lo0 | |
| 192.108.21 | link#1 | UC | 0 | 0 | xl0 | |
| 192.108.21.1 | 8:0:20:77:5e:a0 | UHLW | 2 | 2586 | xl0 | 1160 |
| 192.108.21.246 | 0:30:f2:f:48:0 | UHLW | 0 | 0 | xl0 | 303 |
| 192.108.21.254 | 0:0:c:14:82:81 | UHLW | 1 | 0 | xl0 | 1126 |

TCP/IP

The flag values c and C in **netstat -nr**'s output specify that new host routes should be automatically generated and installed in the routing table as the local network route and default route are used. This feature caused the addition of the host routes shown in the last three lines of the routing table; note that they all have expiration times.

There are two reasons for this proliferation of routing table entries. The first reason is that for routes on the local network, the routing table is also the ARP table. These tables are normally separate, but 4.4BSD merged them and FreeBSD inherited that architecture. The second reason is that FreeBSD attempts to preserve the connection parameters for external hosts (such as the path MTU for TCP) by caching them in the routing table. Subsequent connections to the same host can then reuse the parameters without having to recalculate them. As entries time out, they are removed from the routing table.

The S in the default route indicates that it is a static route and therefore should not be removed by a routing protocol.

The following example is from a FreeBSD 4.0 machine that is running both IPv4 and IPv6. The standard **ifconfig** command can be used to configure the interface and to display its configuration, even for IPv6.

```
% ifconfig fxp1
fxp1:   flags=8943<UP,BROADCAST,RUNNING,SIMPLEX,MULTICAST> mtu 1500
        inet 135.197.1.116 netmask 0xffffff00 broadcast 135.197.1.255
        inet6 fe80::208:c7ff:fe89:4f03%fxp1 prefixlen 64 scopeid 0x2
        ether 00:08:c7:89:4f:03
        media: autoselect (100baseTX <full-duplex>) status:active
        supported media: autoselect 100baseTX <full-duplex> 100baseTX
           10baseT/UTP <full-duplex> 10baseT/UTP
```

### DHCP configuration for FreeBSD

FreeBSD ships ISC's DHCP client. Its use is configured in the **rc.conf** files. The default values set in **/etc/defaults/rc.conf** are

```
dhcp_program="/sbin/dhclient"  # Path to dhcp client
dhcp_flags=""                   # Flags to pass to client
```

These values are probably right and don't need to be changed unless you move the **dhclient** program or want to use a different one. To turn on DHCP for a particular interface, add a line such as the following to **/etc/rc.conf**:

```
ifconfig_interface="DHCP"        # DHCP on this interface
```

This configuration will start **dhclient** at boot time if the file **/etc/dhclient.conf** exists. **dhclient** takes care of getting the IP address for the interface, installing a default route, pointing to the right name server, etc.

**dhclient.conf** is a free-form text configuration file similar in appearance to that of BIND or the ISC DHCP server. There are way too many options and behavior parameters to be described here. Conveniently, the defaults are quite sensible, so an empty **/etc/dhclient.conf** file usually is sufficient for basic network autoconfiguration.

**dhclient** keeps its lease information in a file named **dhclient.leases** and its process ID in **/var/run/dhclient.pid**.

### Dynamic reconfiguration and tuning for FreeBSD

FreeBSD uses the **sysctl** command to get or set kernel variables. Hundreds of different variables are defined, of which about 65 are related to networking. The **sysctl**(3) man page lists the variables and their meanings.

**sysctl -A** displays the variables and their current values. Network-related variables all have "net" in their names, so the command **sysctl -A | grep net** limits the display to those variables.

To get the value of a specific variable, just name it on the **sysctl** command line. For example, you could use the following command to see if a host forwards IP packets:

```
% sysctl net.inet.ip.forwarding
net.inet.ip.forwarding: 1
```

The 1 means yes. To change a variable's value, use the **-w** flag and assign a new value with an equals sign (=):

```
% sudo sysctl -w net.inet.ip.forwarding=0
net.inet.ip.forwarding: 1 -> 0
```

We have just turned off IP forwarding.

### Security, firewalls, filters, and NAT for FreeBSD

Table 13.23 shows FreeBSD's behavior with regard to various security-related network issues. For a brief description of the implications of these behaviors, see page 295. The third column of Table 13.23 shows how to change each behavior; the listed variables should be set in **/etc/rc.conf**, *not* set with **sysctl**.

**Table 13.23    Security-related network behaviors in FreeBSD**

| Feature | Default | rc.conf variable to change |
|---|---|---|
| IP forwarding | off | gateway_enable |
| ICMP redirects | accepts | icmp_drop_redirect[a] |
| Source routing | ignores | forward_sourceroute and accept_sourceroute |
| Broadcast ping | ignores | icmp_bmcastecho |

a. Also icmp_log_redirect to log them.

It's not a good idea to use a UNIX or NT box as a network firewall, especially at a corporate site that has important data on-line. A dedicated hardware solution such as Cisco's PIX is a far more secure and reliable solution. That said, UNIX firewall software is probably OK for a home machine that is assiduously kept up to date with all the latest security patches. In the following pages, we take a quick look at the two firewall software packages that are provided with FreeBSD: **ipfw** and Darren Reed's IPFilter package.

TCP/IP

**ipfw** includes support for "dummynet", a nice feature that lets you play with your Internet traffic by setting bandwidth and queue length limits and by simulating delays and losses. Dummynet was originally designed as a testing tool for TCP congestion control, but it turned out to be useful in a variety of other contexts. It has recently been used for tasks such as limiting the bandwidth consumed by one customer on a DSL line and limiting the bandwidth consumed by web or FTP traffic so that interactive traffic remains speedy. A slow home link with a popular set of web or FTP data might "pipe" packets to dummynet to keep them from flooding the link. See the **dummynet** man page for details on its integration with **ipfw**.

**ipfw** is easy to use and has a syntax similar to that of Cisco's access lists. To implement NAT with **ipfw**, use the **natd** program in **/sbin**.

As when configuring **ipchains** on Linux, you run the **ipfw** command once to establish each filtering rule. A complete **ipfw** configuration takes the form of a shell script that runs a series of **ipfw** commands. We include a partial **ipfw** configuration below to illustrate the command's syntax, but we provide no detailed coverage.

You can compare the example below to the IPFilter examples on page 335 to get a feel for each system. In this example, de0 is the external interface and ed1 is the internal interface. The third parameter of each line identifies the rule number; rules are processed in numeric order, from smallest to largest. The ordering is important because the first rule that matches determines what action will be taken.

```
# freebsd ipfw file
# First flush any old rules laying around
ipfw -f flush
# Allow everything from the dhcp server and gw.syanck.net
ipfw add 500 allow ip from 128.138.129.136 to any
ipfw add 510 allow ip from 209.180.251.58 to any
# Allow ssh in and out
ipfw add 600 allow tcp from any to any 22 in via de0
ipfw add 605 allow tcp from any 22 to any in via de0
# Weird hack to allow arp packets over the bridge
ipfw add 1000 allow udp from 0.0.0.0 2054 to 0.0.0.0
```

Other rules let DNS traffic in and out, support web browsing to the outside, let DHCP through, and allow UDP for **traceroute** and Quake (it's a student's machine). Everything from the local network is allowed out. Folks hammering on his DNS server with queries for nonexistent hosts are blacklisted, and everything else from the outside world is blocked.

We cover Darren Reed's IPFilter programs in more detail than **ipfw** because they are compatible with many other versions of UNIX. The IPFilter package includes **ipf** for configuring a firewall, **ipfstat** for printing out the filtering rules that have been installed, and **ipnat** for implementing NAT. It's available from

http://coombs.anu.edu.au/~avalon/ip-filter.html

To use IPFilter, make sure that your kernel has been compiled with the clauses

```
option IPFILTER
option IPFILTER_LOG
```

The IPFilter package makes a clear distinction between packet filtering chores and NAT, rather than smushing them together as Red Hat's **ipchains** does.

The **ipf**(1) and **ipf**(5) man pages document the details of IPFilter's filtering language and give plenty of examples.

**ipf** reads a file (**/etc/ipf.rules**, by default) of rules of the form

```
action in|out [quick] condition …
```

where the *action* can be

- pass to accept the packet
- block to drop the packet
- log to log the packet through syslog, or
- count to tally the packets that match.

The block action can also specify that a TCP reset or a particular ICMP error message should be returned to the sender.

The modifier quick causes an action to be performed as soon as the conditions are fulfilled; it's the default for count and log. Normally, the rules are applied in turn and no action is taken until all rules have been tried. If multiple rules match a packet, *the last one to match determines the action that is taken.*

This behavior is the exact opposite of that of **ipchains** and **ipfw**, but in all of these systems the order of rules determines the actual functionality of the firewall. The Linux order is faster—match and go—whereas under FreeBSD, all rules are read and applied before the action is taken. The **ipf** paradigm makes it easy to implement conservative firewalls. If you make your first rule deny everything, you can then add additional rules to enable particular types of traffic.

Table 13.24 on the next page shows some of the possible conditions that can appear in an **ipf** rule. The conditions shown here are really just the tip of the iceberg. Consult the **ipf** man page for the messy details.

Let's reimplement the filter specification on page 328 using **ipf** instead of **ipchains**. As before, we assume that interface ppp0 is the connection to the Internet and that interface eth0 is our internal Ethernet. To allow all local traffic and discard private addresses coming in from the outside world, we'd use the following rules:

```
pass in on eth0 all
pass in on lo all
block in quick on ppp0 from 192.168.0.0/16 to any
block in quick on ppp0 from 172.16.0.0/12 to any
block in quick on ppp0 from 10.0.0.0/8 to any
```

TCP/IP

**Table 13.24   ipf conditions**

| Condition | Meaning or possible values |
|---|---|
| on *interface* | Applies the rule to the specified interface |
| proto *protocol* | Selects packet according to protocol: tcp, udp, or icmp |
| from *source-ip* | Filters based on source: host, network, or any |
| to *dest-ip* | Filters based on destination: host, network, or any |
| port = *port#* | Ports can be specified by name (from **/etc/services**) or number; the = sign can be any arithmetic operator (=, <, >, <=, >=, etc.) |
| flags *flag-spec* | Filters based on the TCP header flags bits |
| icmp-type *number* | Filters based on ICMP type and code |
| keep state | Retains details about the flow of a session; normally used to treat established TCP sessions differently from new sessions |

To block TELNET but allow mail and SSH, the rules would be:

```
block in proto tcp from any to any port = 23
pass in on ppp0 proto tcp from any to any port = 25
pass in on ppp0 proto tcp from any to any port = 22
```

The rules for mail and SSH should also include the flags and keep state clauses to guard against hijacking of TCP sessions. See the firewalls section starting on page 675 and the **ipf**(5) man page for more detail on what rules to include and how to format them. If you have access to an OpenBSD system, check out **/usr/share/ipf**. It contains many example files for both **ipf** and **ipnat**.

To make NAT work, we must tell the kernel what addresses to map from, what addresses to map to, and what port range to use to extend the address space. See page 279 for a general discussion of NAT and the mechanisms it uses to bridge from private to public address space.

The syntax of **ipf** rules is just about right for NAT, so the NAT rules should look familiar. Beware the following whammo: like **ipf** rules, **ipnat** rules are ordered. However, they have opposite precedence. Just to keep you on your toes, the *first* matching rule is selected, not the last.

Here are some examples of **ipnat** rules (these would go in the **ipnat.rules** file):

```
map ppp0 192.168.1.0/24 -> 128.138.198.0/26 portmap tcp/udp 20000:65000
map ppp0 192.168.1.0/24 -> 128.138.198.0/26
```

We have again assumed that ppp0 is our interface to the Internet and that our internal network is numbered with the private address space range. These rules map addresses from a /24 network into addresses from a /26 network. Since a /26 network can accommodate only one-quarter of the hosts that a /24 network can, it's potentially possible to run out of target addresses in this configuration. But the portmap clause extends the address range by allowing each address to be used with 45,000 different source ports.

The first rule above covers all TCP and UDP traffic but does not affect ICMP; ICMP does not use the concept of a port. The second rule catches ICMP messages and tries to get them routed back to the right host. If the kernel can't unambiguously determine who should receive a particular ICMP message, it sends the packet out as a broadcast; any machines that receive it out of context should just drop it.

On a home machine, you might be assigned just a single real IP address by your ISP or your ISP's DHCP server. If you're given a static address assignment, just give the target network in the map line a /32 designation and a large enough port range to accommodate the needs of all your local hosts. If you get a different dynamic address each time you connect, use the notation 0/32 in the map line; it will make **ipnat** read the address directly from the network interface. For example, here is a line you might use for a single, dynamically assigned address:

```
map ppp0 192.168.1.0/24 -> 0/32 portmap tcp/udp 20000:65000
```

You should start packet filtering, NAT, and logging at boot time. The commands are:

```
# ipf -E -Fa -f /etc/ipf.rules
# ipnat -CF -f /etc/ipnat.rules
# ipmon -D -s
```

The flags to **ipf** enable the filter, flush existing rules in all streams, and read new rules from **/etc/ipf.rules**. Likewise for **ipnat**, we delete all old rules first and then load new rules from the **/etc/ipnat.rules** file. **ipmon** runs as a daemon, monitoring packets that are logged via **ipf** to the pseudo-device **/dev/ipl** and sending them on to syslog.

By default, FreeBSD assumes that the **ipfw** filtering system will be used, not **ipf**. You must invent some new variables in the **rc.conf** file to turn on **ipf** filtering and create corresponding **sh** lines in the **rc.network** startup file. Use the **ipfw** startup lines as a model. You can configure NAT just by setting the values of the natd_* **rc.conf** variables. We have illustrated the NAT startup but leave the **rc.network** hacking for **ipf** as an exercise for the reader.

```
natd_program="/usr/sbin/ipnat"
natd_enable="YES"
natd_interface="xxx"            # device name or IP address
natd_flags="-f /etc/ipnat.rules"   # + any flags you want
```

Be mindful of the order in which things are done at startup time. If you are really paranoid, you'll want to have filtering in place before you configure any network interfaces. IPFilter's NAT implementation depends on **ipf**, so be sure to enable both if you want to use NAT.

### PPP configuration for FreeBSD

FreeBSD supports two PPP implementations, one inside the kernel and one in user space that uses the IP tunnel device driver. The user-level package is called **ppp** and uses the configuration file **/etc/ppp/ppp.conf**. It's a bit slower than the kernel implementation but has many more features. See the man pages for details—we do not cover the user-level **ppp** as thoroughly as we do the kernel-level implementation.

User-level **ppp** requires that the kernel be configured to include the pseudo-device "tun" and that devices **/dev/tun0**, **/dev/tun1**, etc. exist. The system is configured in the **ppp.conf** file; a sample lives in the **/etc/ppp** directory and includes an example of every option and feature you might ever want to try. A couple of companion files keep things safe. **ppp.deny** lists logins that should never use **ppp**, such as root and bin. **ppp.shells** lists the paths to all valid shells; **ppp** denies access to users whose shell is not listed.

A default entry in **ppp.conf** sets parameters such as the baud rate, the device file for the modem, the logging options, and the dialing sequence. It is followed by entries for each site that you might want to connect to with PPP, for example:

```
allow user local-user-name-here
netblazer800:
    set phone phone-number-here
    set login "ABORT NO\\sCARRIER TIMEOUT 5 ogin:--ogin: login word: passwd"
    set timeout 120
    delete ALL
    add default HISADDR
```

In this example, we specify the user that's allowed to use **ppp** (so it doesn't have to run as root), the phone number to call, and the login chat script (including login name and password). The last two lines delete any existing routes and add a default route to the PPP server (your ISP, presumably).

The kernel-level PPP package uses a daemon called **pppd**. Like the user-level implementation, it keeps configuration files in **/etc/ppp**. The main configuration files are called **options** and **ppp.deny**. These are usually supplemented by local files for the terminal server at the other end of the connection; for example, **options.netblazer** for device-specific options and **chat.netblazer** for login information. FreeBSD supplies sample configuration files for several PPP scenarios in **/usr/share/examples**.

**ppp.deny** is a list of users who should never use PPP; for example, the user "bin".

The configuration files below bring up a PPP connection from Evi's home machine to the University of Colorado. The first file sets global options for **pppd**, the second sets the specific options used to connect to the ancient Netblazer terminal server that the CS department uses for PPP accounts, and the final file is the chat script that performs the actual login.

### /etc/ppp/options

```
# Global PPP options
lock                     # Always lock the device you're using
asyncmap 0x00000000      # By default, don't escape anything
crtscts                  # Use hardware flow control
modem                    # Use modem control lines
defaultroute             # Add default route thru the ppp int.
mru 552                  # MRU/MTU 512 (data) + 40 (header)
mtu 552
```

### /etc/ppp/options.netblazer

```
# Options file for dedicated ppp connection
128.138.198.47:128.138.243.167  # Local:Remote ip addrs
netmask 255.255.255.0           # The 128.138 net is subnetted
/dev/cuaa2                       # Use the third serial port
57600                           # Baud rate
#persist                        # Keep trying even after failure
#holdoff 5                      # Wait 5 seconds between dial attempts
connect "/usr/bin/chat -v -f /etc/ppp/chat.netblazer"
disconnect "/etc/ppp/hangup"   # Try to hangup nicely
```

### /etc/ppp/chat.netblazer

```
ABORT BUSY ABORT 'NO CARRIER'
TIMEOUT 5 OK-''-'' ATZ OK-+++ATHZ-OK ATDTphone#_goes_here
TIMEOUT 60 CONNECT ''
TIMEOUT 10 ogin:--ogin: Pevi
ssword: password_was_here
'Packet mode enabled'
```

You can usually adapt an existing chat script to your environment without worrying too much about exactly how it works. Here, the first line sets up some general conditions on which the script should abort, the second line initializes the modem and dials the phone, and the remaining lines wait for a connection and enter the appropriate username and password.

PPP logins at our site are just usernames with a P in front of them. This convention makes it easy to remember to whom a particular PPP machine belongs.

To start **pppd** with these configuration files, we'd run the command

    % **sudo pppd file /etc/ppp/options.netblazer**

You can feed options to **pppd** on the command line, in the file **/etc/ppp/options**, in **~/.ppprc**, and in **/etc/ppp/options.***terminal-server*. Whew!

To take the PPP connection down, just kill the **pppd** daemon:

    % **sudo kill `cat /var/run/ppp0.pid`**

If your machine is portable and sometimes uses Ethernet instead of PPP, there will most likely be a default route through the Ethernet interface before **pppd** starts up. Unfortunately, **pppd** is too polite to rip out that route and install its own, which is the behavior you'd actually want. To fix the problem, remove the existing default route before you start **pppd**. We suggest that you write yourself a little **ppp.up** script that removes the default route automatically.

Here's what the PPP interface configuration and routing table look like after the PPP connection is brought up:

    % **ifconfig ppp0**
    ppp0: flags=8051<UP,POINTOPOINT,RUNNING,MULTICAST> mtu 552
    inet 128.138.198.47 --> 128.138.243.167 netmask 0xffffff00

TCP/IP

```
% netstat -nr
Routing tables
Internet:
Destination       Gateway          Flags   Refs  Use    Netif   Expire
default           128.138.243.167  UGSc    3     0      ppp0
127.0.0.1         127.0.0.1        UH      0     0      lo0
128.138.243.167   128.138.198.47   UH      4     0      ppp0
```

You can obtain statistics about the PPP connection and the packets it has transferred with the **pppstats** command:

```
% pppstats
        IN  PACK COMP UNC ERR  |   OUT  PACK COMP UNC NON-VJ
  1647029  5101 4596 157   0  | 203582  5051 4566 210    275
```

The COMP column counts packets that use TCP header compression, and the UNC column counts those that don't. See RFC1144 for details.

### Networking quirks for FreeBSD

FreeBSD's **route** command does not accept a hop count parameter, but if you forget and put one on the command line, **route** will interpret it as a netmask. A netmask of 1—which becomes 0.0.0.1 in netmask land—will make any route totally useless, including the default route.

## 13.16 RECOMMENDED READING

STEVENS, W. RICHARD. *TCP/IP Illustrated, Volume One: The Protocols.* Reading, MA: Addison-Wesley. 1994.

WRIGHT, GARY R., AND STEVENS, W. RICHARD. *TCP/IP Illustrated, Volume Two: The Implementation.* Reading, MA: Addison-Wesley. 1995.

These two books are an excellent and thorough guide to the TCP/IP protocol stack. A bit dated, but still solid.

STEVENS, W. RICHARD. *UNIX Network Programming.* Prentice Hall. 1990.

STEVENS, W. RICHARD. *UNIX Network Programming, Volume 1: Networking APIs— Sockets and XTI.* Upper Saddle River, NJ: Prentice Hall. 1997.

STEVENS, W. RICHARD. *UNIX Network Programming, Volume 2: Interprocess Communications.* Upper Saddle River, NJ: Prentice Hall. 1998.

These books are the student's bibles in networking classes that involve programming. If you need only the Berkeley sockets interface, the original edition is a fine reference. If you need the STREAMS interface too, then the second edition, which became too large to bind in one volume, is a good bet. All three are clearly written in typical Rich Stevens style.

TANENBAUM, ANDREW. *Computer Networks, 3rd Edition.* Upper Saddle River, NJ: Prentice Hall. 1996.

This was the first networking text, and it is still a classic. It contains a very thorough description of all the nitty-gritty details going on at the physical and link layers of the protocol stack. Earlier editions were kind of stuck on the ISO protocols, but the latest edition has been updated to cover the modern Internet.

SALUS, PETER H. *Casting the Net, From ARPANET to INTERNET and Beyond.* Reading, MA: Addison-Wesley. 1995.

This is a lovely history of the ARPANET as it grew into the Internet, written by a historian who has been hanging out with UNIX people long enough to sound like one of them!

COMER, DOUGLAS. *Internetworking with TCP/IP Volume 1: Principles, Protocols, and Architectures, 4th Edition.* Upper Saddle River, NJ: Prentice Hall. 2000.

The Comer books were for a long time the standard reference for the TCP/IP protocols. This new edition has descriptions of modern networking technologies as well as the TCP/IP protocol suite. It is designed as an undergraduate textbook and is a good source of background material.

HEDRICK, CHARLES. "Introduction to the Internet Protocols." Rutgers University.

This document is a gentle introduction to TCP/IP. It does not seem to have a permanent home, but it is widely distributed on the web; search for it.

HUNT, CRAIG. *TCP/IP Network Administration, Second Edition.* Sebastopol, CA: O'Reilly & Associates. 1998.

Like other books in the nutshell series, this book is directed at administrators of UNIX systems. Half the book is about TCP/IP, and the rest deals with higher-level UNIX facilities such as email and remote login.

SONNENREICH, WES, AND TOM YATES. *Building Linux and OpenBSD Firewalls.* New York, NY: J.W. Wiley. 2000.

This is an awesome little book: it's easy to read, has good examples, shows a good sense of humor, and is just generally excellent. Our only gripe with this book is that it argues against the use of **sudo** for root access, claiming that it's too hard to use and not worth the trouble. We strongly disagree.

www.netscan.org maintains a list of "smurf" attack amplifiers (systems that respond to broadcast ICMP). You can type in your network's IP address to verify that it's OK, provided that you subnet on byte boundaries. If your network is on this list, disable directed broadcast as described in the TCP chapter to become a nicer netizen.

An excellent collection of documents about the history of the Internet and its various technologies can be found at www.isoc.org/internet/history.

TCP/IP

# 14 *Routing*

Chapter 13 provided a short introduction to IP packet forwarding. In this chapter, we examine the forwarding process in more detail and investigate several network protocols that allow routers to discover efficient routes automatically. Routing protocols not only lessen the day-to-day administrative burden of maintaining routing information, but they also allow network traffic to be redirected quickly if a router or network should fail.

It's important to distinguish between the process of actually forwarding IP packets and the management of the routing table that drives this process, both of which are commonly called "routing." Packet forwarding is simple, whereas route computation is tricky; consequently, the second meaning is used more often in practice. This chapter describes only unicast routing; multicast routing involves an array of very different problems and is beyond the scope of this book.

Conventional wisdom says that IP routing is exceptionally difficult, understood only by a few long-haired hippies that live in the steam tunnels under the Lawrence Berkeley Laboratories campus in Kalifornia. In reality, this is not the case, as long as you understand the basic premise that IP routing is "next hop" routing. At any given point, you only need to determine the *next* host or router in a packet's journey to its final destination. This is a different approach from that of many legacy protocols which determine the exact path a packet will travel before it leaves its originating host, a scheme known as source routing.[1]

---

1. It is also possible to source-route IP packets, but this is almost never done. The feature is not widely supported because of security considerations.

## 14.1  PACKET FORWARDING: A CLOSER LOOK

Before we jump into the management of routing tables, let's take a more detailed look at how the tables are used. Consider the network shown in Exhibit A.

**Exhibit A   Example network**

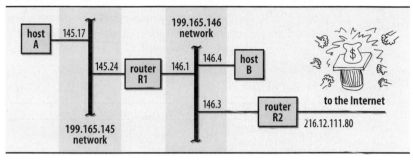

Router R1 connects the two Ethernets, and router R2 connects one of the nets to the outside world. (For now, we'll assume that R1 and R2 are UNIX computers rather than dedicated routers.) Let's look at some routing tables and some specific packet forwarding scenarios. First, host A's routing table:

```
A% netstat -rn
Routing tables
Destination      Gateway         Flags  Refs  Use       If
127.0.0.1        127.0.0.1       UH     6     563131    lo0
199.165.145.0    199.165.145.17  U      5     2845294   le0
default          199.165.145.24  UG     2     168589    le0
```

*See page 300 for more information about **ifconfig**.*

Host A has the simplest routing configuration of the four machines. The first two routes describe the machine's own network interfaces in standard routing terms. These entries exist so that forwarding to directly connected networks need not be handled as a special case. le0 is host A's Ethernet interface,[2] and lo0 is the loopback interface, a virtual network interface emulated in software. Entries such as these are normally added automatically by **ifconfig** when a network interface is configured.

As indicated by the H flag, the loopback route is a "host route" to one particular IP address rather than an entire network. This route could also be configured as a network route, but since 127.0.0.1 is the only IP address that will ever exist on the loopback network, it doesn't really matter how it's defined. The only changes you'd see in the routing table would be 127.0.0.0 in the destination column instead of 127.0.0.1 and no H in the Flags column.

*See the discussion of netmasks starting on page 272.*

There is no substantive difference between a host route and a network route. They are treated exactly the same when the kernel goes to look up addresses in the routing table; only the length of the implicit mask is different.

---

2. Interface names such as le0 will vary, depending on your exact OS and hardware platform.

The default route on host A forwards all packets not addressed to the loopback address or to the 199.165.145 network to the router R1, whose address on this network is 199.165.145.24. The G flag indicates that this route goes to a gateway, not to one of A's local interfaces. Gateways can be only one hop away.

See page 269 for more information about Ethernet vs. IP addressing.

Suppose a process on A sends a packet to B, whose address is 199.165.146.4. The IP implementation looks for a route to the target network, 199.165.146, but none of the routes match. The default route is invoked and the packet is forwarded to R1. Exhibit B shows the packet that actually goes out on the Ethernet (the addresses in the Ethernet header are the MAC addresses of A's and R1's interfaces on the 145 net).

**Exhibit B    Ethernet packet**

| Ethernet header | IP header | UDP header and data |
|---|---|---|
| From: A<br>To: R1<br>Type: IP | From: 199.165.145.17<br>To: 199.165.146.4<br>Type: UDP | 110010101101010111010101101101101<br>0111011011011101010001010010001010<br>010111110110101010100111010000 |

```
                                               UDP PACKET
                                    IP PACKET
                    ETHERNET FRAME
```

The Ethernet destination hardware address is that of router R1, but the IP packet hidden within the Ethernet frame does not mention R1 at all. When R1 inspects the packet it has received, it will see from the IP destination address that it is not the ultimate destination of the packet. It will then use its own routing table to forward the packet to host B without rewriting the IP header, so that it still shows the packet coming from A.

Here's the routing table for host R1:

```
R1% netstat -rn
Routing tables
Destination     Gateway         Flags   Refs   Use      If
127.0.0.1       127.0.0.1       UH      10     10233    lo0
199.165.146.0   199.165.146.1   U       15     4529     le1
199.165.145.0   199.165.145.24  U       0      121      le0
default         199.165.146.3   UG      4      168589   le1
```

This table is similar to that of host A, except that there are two physical network interfaces. The default route in this case points to R2, since that's the gateway through which the Internet can be reached. Packets bound for either of the 199.165 networks can be delivered directly.

Like host A, host B has only one real network interface. However, B needs an additional route to function correctly because it has direct connections to two different routers. Traffic for the 199.165.145 net must travel via R1, while other traffic should go out to the Internet via R2.

```
B% netstat -rn
Routing tables
Destination     Gateway         Flags  Refs  Use      If
127.0.0.1       127.0.0.1       UH     2     1543     lo0
199.165.146.0   199.165.146.4   U      15    4529     le0
199.165.145.0   199.165.146.1   UG     0     121      le0
default         199.165.146.3   UG     4     168589   le0
```

*See page 285 for an explanation of ICMP redirects.*

It is possible to configure host B with initial knowledge of only one gateway, thus relying on the help of ICMP redirects to eliminate extra hops. For example, one possible initial configuration for host B is:

```
B% netstat -rn
Routing tables
Destination     Gateway         Flags  Refs  Use      If
127.0.0.1       127.0.0.1       UH     2     1543     lo0
199.165.146.0   199.165.116.4   U      15    4529     le0
default         199.165.146.3   UG     4     168589   le0
```

If B then sends a packet to host A (199.165.145.17), no route will match and the packet will be forwarded to R2 for delivery. R2 (which, being a router, presumably has complete information about the network) will send the packet on to R1. Since R1 and B are on the same network, R2 will also send an ICMP redirect notice to B, and B will enter a host route for A into its routing table:

```
199.165.145.17 199.165.146.1    UGHD 0     1         le0
```

This route will send all future traffic for A directly through R1. However, it does not affect routing for other hosts on A's network, all of which will have to be routed by separate redirects from R2.

Some sites have chosen ICMP redirects as their primary routing "protocol," thinking that this approach is very dynamic. Unfortunately, once the kernel learns a route from a redirect, either the route must be manually deleted or the machine must be rebooted if that information changes. Because of this problem and several other disadvantages of redirects (increased network load, increased load on R2, routing table clutter, dependence on extra servers), we don't recommend the use of redirects for configurations such as this. In a properly configured network, redirects should never appear in the routing table.

## 14.2  ROUTING DAEMONS AND ROUTING PROTOCOLS

In simple networks such as the one shown in Exhibit A, it is perfectly reasonable to configure routing by hand. At some point, however, networks become too complicated to be managed this way (possibly due to their growth rate). Instead of having to explicitly tell every computer on every network how to reach every other computer and network, it would be nice if the computers could just put their heads together and figure it all out. This is the job of routing protocols and the daemons that implement them.

Routing protocols have a major advantage over static routing systems in that they can react and adapt to changing network conditions. If a link goes down, the routing daemons can quickly discover and propagate alternate routes to the networks that link served, if any exist.

Routing daemons collect information from three sources: configuration files, the existing routing tables, and routing daemons on other systems. This information is merged to compute an optimal set of routes, and the new routes are then fed back into the system routing table (and possibly fed to other systems through a routing protocol). Because network conditions change over time, routing daemons must periodically check in with each other to reassure themselves that their routing information is still current.

The exact way that routes are computed depends on the routing protocol. Two types of protocols are in common use: distance-vector protocols and link-state protocols.

### Distance-vector protocols

Distance-vector (aka "gossipy") protocols are based on the general idea, "If router X is five hops away from network Y, and I'm adjacent to router X, then I must be six hops away from network Y." You announce how far you think you are from the networks you know about. If your neighbors don't know of a better way to get to each network, they mark you as being the best gateway. If they already know a shorter route, they ignore your advertisement.[3] Over time, everyone's routing tables are supposed to converge to a steady state.

This is really a very elegant idea. If it worked as advertised, routing would be relatively simple. Unfortunately, this type of algorithm does not deal well with changes in topology. In some cases, infinite loops (e.g., router X receives information from router Y and sends it on to router Z, which sends it back to router Y) can prevent routes from converging at all. Real-world distance-vector protocols must avoid such problems by introducing complex heuristics or by enforcing arbitrary restrictions such as the RIP (Routing Information Protocol) notion that any network more than 15 hops away is unreachable.

Even in nonpathological cases, it can take many update cycles for all routers to reach a steady state. Therefore, to guarantee that routing will not jam for an extended period, the cycle time must be made short, and for this reason distance-vector protocols as a class tend to be talkative. For example, RIP requires that routers broadcast

---

3. Actually, it is not quite this simple, since there are provisions for handling changes in topology that may lengthen existing routes. Some DV protocols such as EIGRP maintain information about multiple possible routes so that they always have a fallback plan. The exact details are not important.

all of their routing information every 30 seconds. IGRP and EIGRP send updates every 90 seconds.

On the other hand, BGP, the Border Gateway Protocol, transmits the entire table once and then transmits changes as they occur. This optimization substantially reduces the potential for "chatty" (and mostly unnecessary) traffic.

Table 14.1 lists the distance-vector protocols that are in common use today.

**Table 14.1    Common distance-vector routing protocols**

| Nym | Long name | Application |
| --- | --- | --- |
| RIP | Routing Information Protocol | Internal LANs |
| IGRP | Interior Gateway Routing Protocol | Small WANs |
| EIGRP | Enhanced Interior Gateway Routing Protocol | WANs, corporate LANs |
| BGP | Border Gateway Protocol | Internet backbone routing |

### Link-state protocols

Link-state protocols distribute information in a relatively unprocessed form. The records traded among routers are of the form "Router X is adjacent to router Y, and the link is up." A complete set of such records forms a connectivity map of the network from which each router can compute its own routing table. The primary advantage that link-state protocols offer over distance-vector protocols is the ability to quickly converge on an operational routing solution after a catastrophe occurs. The tradeoff is that maintaining a complete "map" of the network at each node requires memory and CPU power that would not be needed by a distance-vector routing system.

Because the communications among routers in a link-state protocol are not part of the actual route-computation algorithm, they can be implemented in such a way that transmission loops do not occur. Updates to the topology database propagate across the network efficiently, at a lower cost in network bandwidth and CPU time.

Link-state protocols tend to be more complicated than distance-vector protocols, but this can be explained in part by the fact that link-state protocols make it easier to implement advanced features such as type-of-service routing and multiple routes to the same destination. Neither of these features is supported on stock UNIX systems; you must use dedicated routers to benefit from them.

The common link-state protocols are shown in Table 14.2.

**Table 14.2    Common link-state routing protocols**

| Nym | Long name | Application |
| --- | --- | --- |
| OSPF | Open Shortest Path First | Internal LANs, small WANs |
| IS-IS | Intermediate System to Intermediate System | Insane asylums |

Routing

## Cost metrics

In order for a routing protocol to determine which path to a network is shortest, it has to define what is meant by "shortest".[4] Is it the path involving the fewest number of hops? The path with the lowest latency? The largest minimal intermediate bandwidth? The lowest financial cost?

For routing purposes, the quality of a link is represented by a number called the cost metric. By adding together the costs of each link in a path, a path cost can be computed. In the simplest systems, every link has a cost of 1, leading to hop counts as a path metric. But any of the considerations mentioned above can be converted to a numeric cost metric.

Networking mavens have labored long and hard to make the definition of cost metrics flexible, and some modern protocols even allow different metrics to be used for different kinds of network traffic. Nevertheless, in 99% of cases, all this hard work can be safely ignored. The default metrics for most systems work just fine.

You may encounter situations in which the actual shortest path to a destination may not be a good default route for political reasons. To handle these cases, you can artificially boost the cost of the critical links to make them seem less appealing. Leave the rest of the routing configuration alone.

## Interior and exterior protocols

An "autonomous system" is a group of networks under the administrative and political control of a single entity. The definition is vague; real-world autonomous systems can be as large as a worldwide corporate network or as small as a building or a single academic department. It all depends on how you want to manage routing. The general tendency is to make autonomous systems as large as possible. This convention simplifies administration and makes routing as efficient as possible.

Routing within an autonomous system is somewhat different from routing between autonomous systems. Protocols for routing among ASs ("exterior" protocols) must often handle routes for many networks, and they must deal gracefully with the fact that neighboring routers are under other people's control. Exterior protocols do not reveal the topology inside an autonomous system, so in a sense they can be thought of as a second level of routing hierarchy that deals with collections of nets rather than individual hosts or cables.

In practice, small to medium sites rarely need to run an exterior protocol unless they are connected to more than one ISP. With multiple ISPs, the easy division of networks into local and Internet domains collapses, and routers must decide which route to the Internet is best for any particular address. (However, that is not to say that *every* router must know this information. Most hosts can stay stupid and route their default packets through an internal gateway that is better informed.)

---

4. Fortunately, it does not have to define what the meaning of "is" is.

While exterior protocols are not so different from their interior counterparts, this chapter concentrates on the interior protocols and the daemons that support them. If your site must use an external protocol as well, see the recommended reading list on page 371 for some suggested references.

## 14.3 PROTOCOLS ON PARADE

Several interior routing protocols are in common use. In this section, we introduce the major players and summarize their main advantages and weaknesses.

### RIP: Routing Information Protocol

RIP, defined in RFC1058, is an old Xerox protocol that has been adapted for IP networks. It is the protocol used by **routed**. RIP is a simple distance-vector protocol that uses hop counts as a cost metric. Because RIP was designed in an era when a single computer cost hundreds of thousands of dollars and networks were relatively small, RIP considers any host fifteen or more hops away to be unreachable. Therefore, large local networks that have more than fifteen routers along any single path cannot use the RIP protocol.

Although RIP is a resource hog because of its profligate use of broadcasting, it does a good job when a network is changing often or when the topology of remote networks is not known. However, it can be slow to stabilize after a link goes down.

RIP is widely implemented on non-UNIX platforms. A variety of common devices from printers to SNMP-manageable network components can listen to RIP advertisements to learn about possible gateways. In addition, almost all versions of UNIX provide **routed**, so RIP is a de facto lowest common denominator routing protocol. Often, RIP is used for LAN routing and a more featureful protocol is used for wide-area connectivity.

### RIP-2: Routing Information Protocol, version 2

*See page 276 for information about classless addressing, aka CIDR.*

RIP-2 is a mild revision of RIP that adds support for a few features that were missing from the original protocol. The most important change is that RIP-2 distributes netmasks along with next-hop addresses, so it provides better support for subnetted networks and CIDR. A vague gesture towards increasing the security of RIP was also included, but the definition of a specific authentication system has been left for future development.

Many sites use **routed** in its **-q** ("quiet") mode, in which it manages the routing table and listens for routing updates on the network but does not broadcast any information of its own. At these sites, the actual route computations are usually performed with a more efficient protocol such as OSPF (see below). The computed routes are converted to RIP updates for consumption by nonrouter machines. **routed** is lightweight (in **-q** mode) and universally supported, so most machines can enjoy the benefits of dynamic routing without any special configuration.

Routing

RIP-2 provides several features that seem targeted for this multiprotocol environment. "Next hop" updates allow broadcasters to advertise routes for which they are not the actual gateway, and "route tags" allow externally discovered routes to be propagated through RIP.

RIP-2 can be run in a compatibility mode that preserves most of the new features of RIP-2 without entirely abandoning vanilla RIP receivers. In most respects, RIP-2 is identical to RIP and should be preferred over RIP if it is supported by the systems you are using.

### OSPF: Open Shortest Path First

OSPF is defined in RFC2328. It's a link-state protocol. "Shortest path first" refers to the mathematical algorithm used to calculate routes; "open" is used in the sense of "nonproprietary."

OSPF was the first link-state routing protocol to be broadly used, and it is still the most popular. Its widespread adoption was spurred in large part by its support in **gated**, a popular multiprotocol routing daemon of which we will have more to say later. Unfortunately, the protocol itself is very complex and hence only worthwhile at sites of significant size (where routing protocol behavior really makes a difference).

The OSPF protocol specification does not mandate any particular cost metric. **gated**'s implementation uses hop counts by default, as does Cisco's. Cisco routers can also be configured to use network bandwidth as a cost metric.

OSPF is an industrial-strength protocol that works well for large, complicated topologies. It offers several advantages over RIP, including the ability to manage several paths to a single destination and the ability to partition the network into sections ("areas") that share only high-level routing information.

### IGRP and EIGRP: Interior Gateway Routing Protocol

IGRP and its souped-up successor EIGRP are proprietary routing protocols that run only on Cisco routers. IGRP was created to address some of the shortcomings of RIP before robust standards like OSPF existed. EIGRP is configured similarly to IGRP, though it is actually quite different in its underlying protocol design. IGRP only handles route announcements using traditional IP address class boundaries, whereas EIGRP understands arbitrary CIDR netmasks.

Both IGRP and EIGRP are distance-vector protocols, but they are designed to avoid the looping and convergence problems found in other DV systems. EIGRP in particular is widely regarded as the paragon of distance-vector routing. For most purposes, EIGRP and OSPF are equally functional.

In our opinion, it is best to stick with an established, nonproprietary, and multiply implemented routing protocol such as OSPF. More people are using and working on OSPF than EIGRP, and several implementations are available.

### IS-IS: the ISO "standard"

IS-IS, the Intra-Domain Intermediate System to Intermediate System Routeing Protocol, is the International Organization for Standardization's answer to OSPF. It was originally designed to manage "routeing" for the OSI network protocols and was later extended to handle IP routing.

Both IS-IS and OSPF were developed in the early 90s at a time when ISO protocols were politically in vogue. Early attention from the IETF helped to lend IS-IS a veneer of legitimacy for IP, but it seems to be falling farther and farther behind OSPF in popularity. Today, IS-IS use is rare. The protocol itself is mired with lots of ISO baggage and generally should be avoided.

### MOSPF, DVMRP, and PIM: multicast routing protocols

MOSPF (Multicast OSPF), DVMRP (Distance Vector Multicast Routing Protocol), and PIM (Protocol Independent Multicast) are protocols designed to support IP multicasting, a technology that is not yet widely deployed. You can find pointers to more information about these protocols at www.mbone.com.

### Router Discovery Protocol

Router Discovery Protocol uses ICMP messages sent to the IP multicast address 224.0.0.1 to announce and learn about other routers on a network. Unfortunately, not all routers currently make these announcements, and not all hosts listen to them. The hope is that someday this protocol will become more popular.

## 14.4  ROUTED: RIP YOURSELF A NEW HOLE

You may not be rich. You may not be good looking. But you'll always have **routed**. **routed** was for a long time the standard UNIX routing daemon, and it's still supplied with most every version of UNIX.[5]

**routed** speaks only RIP. Some **routed**s support RIP-2 and some don't. If you need RIP-2 and your **routed** doesn't support it, you can always use **gated** as a RIP-2 daemon instead. It's just a bit more complicated, especially if you have to install it yourself. (You only really need RIP-2 if you have subnets with different mask lengths.)

**routed** can be run in server mode (**-s**) or in quiet mode (**-q**). Both modes listen for broadcasts, but only servers distribute their own information. Generally, only machines with multiple interfaces should be servers. If neither **-s** nor **-q** is specified, **routed** is supposed to run in quiet mode with one interface and in server mode with more. But on many systems, this feature is broken.[6]

*See page 302 for more about route.* **routed** adds its discovered routes to the kernel's routing table. Routes must be reheard at least every four minutes or they will be removed. However, **routed** knows

---

5. A few versions of UNIX (e.g., HP-UX) have adopted **gated**.

6. **routed** has a reputation for misbehavior on many systems. One of our reviewers went so far as to say, "**routed** is simply not to be trusted."

which routes it has added and will not remove static routes that were installed with the **route** command.

**routed -t** can be used to debug routing. This option makes **routed** run in the foreground and print out all packets it sends or receives.

**routed** normally discovers routing information dynamically and does not require configuration. However, if your site contains gateways to the Internet or to other autonomous systems, you may have to take some additional steps to make these links work with **routed**.

If you have only a single outbound gateway, you can advertise it as a global default route by running its **routed** with the **-g** flag. This is analogous to setting the default route on a single machine, except that it is propagated throughout your network.

**routed** also supports a configuration file, **/etc/gateways**, which was designed to provide static information about gateways to "preload" into the **routed** routing table. In modern times, if you find yourself needing this functionality, you should really be running **gated** instead**.**

## 14.5   GATED: A BETTER ROUTING DAEMON

*gated can be obtained from www.gated.org.*

**gated** is a generic routing framework that allows many different routing protocols to be used simultaneously. **gated** provides pinpoint control over advertised routes, broadcast addresses, trust policies, and metrics. It can share routes among several protocols, allowing routing gateways to be constructed between areas that have standardized on different routing systems. **gated** also has one of the nicest administrative interfaces and configuration file designs of any UNIX administrative software.

Many people have contributed to the development of **gated**. Work was originally coordinated by Cornell University. **gated** started out as freely distributable software, but in 1992 it was privatized and turned over to the Merit GateD Consortium. Current versions of **gated** are available only to Consortium members. Membership (ten categories! four product lines! but wait! you also get…) is open to everyone, but it requires the execution of a license agreement, and it's expensive for nonacademic users.

Although the definition of "academic and research use" is quite broad, we recommend steering clear of the bureaucratic quagmire in which **gated** has become mired. Version 3 was the last **gated** to be unencumbered with red tape, and it works just fine. Version 3.5.10 was the current release (of version 3) as of this writing, and that's the version we describe below.

**gated** supports RIP (both versions), OSPF, and IS-IS for interior routing and also the exterior protocols EGP and BGP. An older protocol called HELLO is supported for historical reasons.

Table 14.3 shows the support for **routed** and **gated** that exists on stock copies of our example systems. The current **gated** will compile on almost any common system, so it's easy to upgrade.

**Table 14.3    Vendor-supplied routing daemons**

| System | routed? | gated? |
|--------|---------|--------|
| Solaris | Yes | No |
| HP-UX | No | 3.5 Beta 3 |
| Red Hat | Yes | 3.5.10 |
| FreeBSD | Yes[a] | 3.5.11 |

a. **routed** on FreeBSD also speaks RDP.

### gated startup and control

**gated** is normally started at boot time with no arguments. The correct way to do this is system dependent; see the notes starting on page 366 or Chapter 2, *Booting and Shutting Down*, for more information.

**gated** takes its operating instructions from a single configuration file. The config file is normally **/etc/gated.conf**, but this can be changed with a command-line flag. Once running, **gated** can be manipulated with the **gdc** command, which is installed along with it. Most uses of **gdc** take the form

> gdc *command*

The most common **gdc** commands are shown below:

**interface**   signals **gated** to recheck the kernel's list of active network interfaces. **gated** does this periodically on its own, but if you have just changed an interface's configuration, you may want to force an immediate update.

**reconfig**   makes **gated** reread its configuration file.

**checkconf**   parses the configuration file and checks it for syntax errors, but does not tell **gated** to load it.

**toggletrace**   starts or stops logging.

**stop**   terminates **gated**: gracefully if possible, forcibly if not.

**start**   spawns a new **gated** if one is not already running.

**restart**   kills and restarts **gated**. Equivalent to **stop** followed by **start**.

### Tracing

**gated** can be run with debugging (called "tracing") turned on, causing its actions to be archived to a log file. **gated**'s tracing features are very useful when you are first setting up the config file; they also provide a history of routing updates.

Depending on which tracing options have been enabled, the log file may grow quickly and should be restarted or truncated periodically. **gdc toggletrace** will completely close the log file, allowing you to rename or truncate it. A second **gdc toggletrace** turns logging back on.

Routing

Trace options can be specified in the configuration file or on the **gated** command line (preceded by -**t** for options, nothing for the log file name). In the config file, different options can be specified for each protocol; on the command line, they are global. The most useful options are listed below.

|  |  |
|---:|---|
| **all** | turns on all tracing options. |
| **normal** | traces normal events. Abnormal events are always traced. |
| **policy** | traces the way that administratively configured policy statements affect the distribution of routes. |
| **route** | traces routing table changes. |
| **general** | turns on both **normal** and **route**. |

An even more detailed level of tracing dumps individual network packets to the log file. However, packet tracing can only be enabled in the config file, not on the command line.

### The gated configuration file

Unlike many UNIX administrative systems, **gated** has reasonable default behavior. Hundreds of options are supported, but simple networks should need only a few lines of configuration. As you read this rest of this chapter and the **gated** documentation, keep in mind that most features will not apply to you.

The following sections provide a quick look at the most mainstream **gated** configuration options. Because of the way **gated**'s configuration file works, it's necessary to show syntax outlines for many of the options. We've pruned these outlines so that they contain only the parts we want to talk about. If you find yourself thinking that there really ought to be an XYZ option available somewhere, there probably is; we just haven't shown it. Refer to the **gated** documentation for complete coverage.

**gated** comes with an explanation of the format of its configuration file, but the documentation won't do much to educate you about advanced routing issues. You may need to refer to one of the sources listed on page 371 to really understand the function and purpose of each option.

**gated**'s configuration file consists of a series of statements separated by semicolons. Tokens are separated by whitespace, which may include newlines. Curly braces are sometimes used for grouping, but only in specific contexts.

There are several classes of statement. Statements of each type must appear together in the configuration file, and the sections must appear in the following order:

- Options and definitions (including declarations of network interfaces)
- Configuration of individual protocols
- Static routes
- Import, export, and aggregation controls

It's fine for a section to be empty.

Tracing options can appear anywhere. If they appear within curly braces, they apply only within the context of the option or protocol being configured. The options are specified with a **traceoptions** statement:

> **traceoptions** [ *"log"* [ **replace** ] [ **size** *size*[**k**|**m**] **files** *num* ] ] *trace_options*
>     [ **except** *trace_options* ] ;

The *log* is the filename into which tracing output is stored. If **replace** is specified, the log will be truncated and restarted whenever **gated** restarts; the default is to append. The **size** parameter specifies the maximum size of the log file in kilo or megabytes. When the log gets too big, it will be restarted and the old log renamed *log*.**1**, *log*.**2**, etc., up to the number of files specified by the **files** clause. If you specify **size**, you must also specify **files**.

The possible *trace_options* are those specified above (some additional minor options not listed here are also supported).

Here's an example that creates the file **/usr/local/etc/gated.log** and rotates 1MB files up to 3 deep, with all possible tracing options turned on:

```
traceoptions "/usr/local/etc/gated.log" replace size 1m files 3 all;
```

### Option configuration statements

The most common options are:

> **options** [ **nosend** ] [ **noresolv** ] [ **syslog** [ **upto** ] *log_level* ] ;

The arguments have the following meanings:

**nosend**   prevents **gated** from sending any packets. This argument is useful for debugging, since **gated** can be asked to process information from other routers without interfering with the actual routing of the network.

**noresolv**   prevents **gated** from attempting to use DNS to translate hostnames to IP addresses. DNS queries can fail if not enough routing information is available to process them, leading to a chicken-and-egg deadlock. We recommend against using hostnames in any network configuration context, and this option can be used to help enforce that policy.

*See Chapter 11 for more information about syslog.*

**syslog**   controls how much information is logged via syslog. This option is meaningless if your site does not use syslog. The valid *log_levels* are listed in the **syslogmask** man page. The default is **syslog upto info**.

Example:

```
options noresolv;
```

## Network interface definitions

The properties of network interfaces are set with an **interfaces** statement, which has the following format:

```
interfaces {
    options [strictinterfaces] ;
    define address [broadcast addr] | [pointtopoint addr]
    interface iflst [preference prf] [passive] [simplex] ;
    [netmask mask] [multicast] ;
} ;
```

There may be multiple **options**, **interface**, or **define** statements—or none. This is generally true for all clauses throughout the **gated** configuration file.

The **strictinterfaces** option makes it illegal to refer to an interface in the configuration file that cannot be found by the kernel at startup time and that has not been listed in a **define** statement. This is always an error, but without **strictinterfaces** turned on, it is not fatal.

*See page 291 for more information about point-to-point links.*

The **define** statement describes a network interface that may or may not be present at startup. It's mostly used for dial-up links or for other interfaces that might "appear" at a later time. Another good example is a PCMCIA Ethernet card that might be inserted in a slot sometime down the road.

An **interface** statement (repeated here for clarity)

```
interface iflst [preference prf] [passive] [simplex] ;
```

sets the options for a particular interface or set of interfaces. *iflst* can be an interface name such as **de0** or **le1**, a name wild card such as **de** or **le** (matching all instances of that type of interface), a hostname or IP address (indicating the interface to which that address is bound), or the literal string **all**.

If an interface is **passive**, routes through it will be maintained even if it does not appear to be properly connected. If it's **simplex**, the interface cannot receive its own broadcast packets. **gated** can normally figure this out for itself, but on some systems you may need to say so explicitly.

The **preference** field requires a more elaborate explanation. Since routing protocols work in different ways and use different cost metrics to determine the "shortest" paths, there's no guarantee that any two protocols will agree about which routes are best. When the results computed by different protocols are incompatible, an administrative policy must be used to decide which routes are propagated to the kernel's routing table and exported to other routers.

To implement this policy, **gated** associates a numeric preference value with each route. When two routes conflict, the one with the lowest preference is the winner of the routing beauty contest.

Preference values can originate from a variety of sources. Every routing protocol has an intrinsic preference value. Preference values can also be assigned to network interfaces and to remote gateways. Since most routes have a protocol of origin *and* a network interface *and* a remote gateway, there may be several candidate preference values. **gated** assigns the most specific of these values. In other words, the path with the lowest numeric preference value (as determined by any of the preference metrics for the path) is the chosen path.

Normally, routes to directly connected networks have a preference value of 0. If it is necessary to prefer one interface over another, you can use **preference** clauses to prioritize them. Some of the other default preference values used by **gated** are shown in Table 14.4.

**Table 14.4**    **Default route preference values**

| Source of routing information | Preference |
|---|---|
| Routes to directly connected networks | 0 |
| Routes learned via OSPF | 10 |
| ICMP redirects | 30 |
| Externally defined static routes | 40 |
| Static routes defined in **gated.conf** | 60 |
| Routes learned from RIP | 100 |
| Routes across point-to-point interfaces | 110 |
| Routes through interfaces that are down | 120 |

The following example sets the interface le0 to be passive, meaning that it will not be used to advertise any routing information:

```
interfaces {
     interface le0 passive;
};
```

### Other miscellaneous definitions

Several other global parameters can be set in the definitions section.

> **routerid** *host* ;

The **routerid** statement sets the router identification number, which is used by the BGP and OSPF protocols. It should be listed in the form of an IP address, and it defaults to the address of the machine's first physical interface. This value is important to the protocols that use it, and other routers may need to refer to it explicitly in their configuration files.

```
martians {
     host host [allow] ;
     network [allow] [exact | refines] ;
     network mask mask [allow] [exact | refines] ;
     network masklen number [allow] [exact | refines] ;
     default [allow] ;
} ;
```

Martian routes are routes to destinations that you would prefer to ignore. There may be misconfigured routers on your network that are broadcasting routes to bogus destinations, or you may simply want to exclude certain destinations from the routing table. Any route to a destination listed in a **martians** statement is simply ignored by **gated**.

Each routing destination has an address and a mask associated with it. The various flavors of specification are all just different ways of providing an address/mask pair against which these can be matched.

A network number with a **mask** or **masklen** specifies the two values explicitly. If no mask is supplied, the mask implied by the address's intrinsic class is used.

**exact** and **refines** request different flavors of address matching. Actually, there are three. With neither keyword, the mask of the destination is ignored. As long as the portion of the destination address covered by the rule's mask matches the rule's address, the destination is considered a martian.

If **exact** is specified, the destination's address and mask must both match the rule's values exactly in order for the destination to be martian. An exact match selects a network, but not its subnets or supernets.

If **refines** is specified, the destination's mask must be longer than the rule's. If it is longer, then the addresses are compared normally (using the rule's mask only). This has the effect of selecting a network's subnets without selecting the network itself.

The entries

```
host host ;
default ;
```

are equivalent to

```
host mask 255.255.255.255 exact ;
0.0.0.0 mask 0.0.0.0 exact ;
```

The **allow** keyword can be used to reenable certain addresses disabled by a previous, broader specification. For example:

```
martians {
     128.138.0.0 mask 255.255.0.0 ;
     128.138.145.0 mask 255.255.255.0 allow ;
} ;
```

This configuration rejects all information about the class B network 128.138. However, routes to the 128.138.145 subnet are accepted. The most specific rule always has precedence.

### Protocol configuration for RIP

Both versions of the RIP protocol are configured with a **rip** statement.

```
rip yes | no | on | off [ {
    broadcast ;
    nobroadcast ;
    preference pref ;
    defaultmetric metric ;
    interface interface_list
        [noripin | ripin] [noripout | ripout]
        [version 1]|[version 2 [multicast|broadcast]] ;
    trustedgateways gateway_list ;
    sourcegateways gateway_list ;
    traceoptions [packets | request | response [detail]] ;
} ] ;
```

**yes** and **no** are synonymous with **on** and **off**. RIP is enabled by default, so you must include the line

```
rip no ;
```

if you don't want to run RIP at all. The **broadcast** and **nobroadcast** options are similar to the **-s** and **-q** flags of **routed**: **broadcast** forces RIP updates to be sent out even if the host does not appear to be on more than one network. **nobroadcast** prevents RIP from sending out any updates.

The **defaultmetric** clause assigns the cost *metric* to routes learned through other protocols when they are rebroadcast through RIP. This is a very crude form of translation, but there isn't really an elegant solution. By default, this value is set at 16—unreachable—so that other protocol's routes will never go out over RIP. If you want to redistribute these routes, a good value to use is 10.

Per-interface options are set with the same type of interface specification found in the **interfaces** statement earlier in the configuration file. **ripin** accepts RIP updates on an interface, and **noripin** rejects them. **ripout** and **noripout** are essentially interface-specific versions of **broadcast** and **nobroadcast**. **noripout** is the default on point-to-point links such as dial-ups.

The **version** statement tells whether to run RIP-1 or RIP-2 on the specified interfaces. The default when running RIP-2 is to multicast updates rather than broadcast them, which prevents RIP-1 routers from seeing them. You can specify **broadcast** to force broadcasting to occur.

By default, **gated** will listen to RIP updates from anyone who sends them. If a list of **trustedgateways** is present, however, **gated** will only pay attention to the listed hosts. A *gateway_list* is just a series of IP addresses separated by whitespace.

**sourcegateways** are hosts to which RIP updates should be sent directly, rather than via broadcasting. This feature can be used to reach hosts on different networks or to target routers on a network that does not support broadcasting (or on which broadcasting has been disabled).

**traceoptions** are specified as described on page 355. Any options included here will apply only to RIP. The RIP-specific packet-tracing options **request**, **response**, and

Routing

**packets** log requests received, outgoing responses, and all packets, respectively. Packets are normally summarized. If **detail** is specified, a more detailed dump of each packet is included in the log.

An actual RIP configuration clause appears in section 1 of the complete **gated.conf** config file example on page 365.

### Some preliminary background on OSPF

Before launching into the gory details of OSPF configuration (which are in truth not really so gory), we need to talk a bit about two more features of OSPF: routing areas and designated routers.

*Routing areas*

At a large site, it may not be necessary or desirable to distribute a complete set of link states from one corner of the network to another. To cut down on the amount of up-date traffic, OSPF allows individual networks to be grouped into "areas." Link-state information (i.e., information about the network's physical topology) is propagated only within an area; information about the area is distributed to the outside world in the form of routing summaries.

Every network is a member of exactly one area, and areas can include more than one network. Routers are considered to be members of all the areas on which they have network interfaces. A router that belongs to more than one area is called an area-border router and is responsible for translating link-state records into sum-mary records.

A routing summary is really just a collection of routes: "Router X can send packets to network Y in 3 hops," where X is an area-border router. The routers outside an area combine the declared summary cost with the computed cost to the area-border router to determine a total path cost to the network.

This scheme might sound like a distance-vector routing protocol in disguise, but there are two important differences. First, summaries are propagated exactly as they came from the area-border router that originated them. A router may compute that if it is two hops away from X and X is 3 hops from Y, then it must be 5 hops away from Y. However, it will never reveal the result of this calculation to another router. It will just pass along the original summary route.[7]

The second difference from a distance-vector protocol is that the OSPF scheme does not attempt to deal with arbitrary network topologies. OSPF requires that all routing areas be logically adjacent to a central backbone area known as area 0 (though they may be adjacent to each other as well). Route summaries can travel only from a leaf area to the backbone, and vice versa, not directly between leaf areas.[8] This simple two-level hierarchy forestalls the possibility of loops.

---

7. This is true only within an area. If the summary record crosses into an adjacent area, the area-border router that forwards it will restate the information relative to itself.

If your real-world network architecture does not match OSPF's two-layer model, all is not lost. You can still represent it as a two-layer hierarchy by using an OSPF concept called "virtual links." Unfortunately, a discussion of virtual links is beyond the scope of this book.

### Designated routers

In theory, link-state protocols distribute routing information in the form of records that describe connectivity among routers; for example, "Router A is adjacent to router B, and the cost of the link is 1." If there were 6 routers on a network, 30 different link-state advertisements would potentially need to be propagated, because each router was adjacent to 5 other routers. Even worse, the routers would all have to treat each other as neighbors and make sure that their databases were synchronized.

OSPF reduces the amount of information that is propagated by appointing one of the routers on a network to be the *designated router*.[9] The designated router listens to link-state advertisements from all the other routers and then sends out a digest of what it has learned.

The routers on a network cooperate to elect a designated router based on a per-router priority value that is set administratively. Routers with a priority of 0 are ineligible to be the designated router. Among the remaining routers, the one with the highest priority is declared the winner. If there is a tie, a router is selected pseudo-randomly.

A backup designated router is also selected in the same way. Each router on the network maintains an ongoing relationship with both the designated router and the designated router's backup. If the designated router should fail, the backup immediately steps in to assume control and a new backup is elected.

Designated routers handle a bit more protocol traffic than their peers, so they should be selected accordingly.

### Protocol configuration for OSPF

In **gated.conf**, you configure OSPF options with the **ospf** statement:

```
ospf yes | no | on | off [ {
    defaults {
        router-prio ;
    } ;
    traceoptions trace_options ;
    backbone | (area area) {
        networks {
            network [exact | refines] [restrict] ;
            network mask mask [exact | refines] [restrict] ;
```

8. OK, this statement isn't entirely true. There are a few special area types, such as the "Not So Stubby Area" (NSSA) that may bridge routing information between leaves, but each route learned in this fashion is specially tagged so that it doesn't accidentally create a loop.

9. Actually, "broadcast domain" would be a better term than "network" here. There is also a mechanism defined to support the concept of a designated router on a nonbroadcast (but multiaccess) network.

Routing

```
            network masklen num [exact | refines] [restrict] ;
            host host [exact | refines] [restrict] ;
        } ;
        stubhosts {
            host cost cost ;
        } ;
        interface interface_list [cost cost] {
            enable | disable ;
            priority priority ;
        } ;
    } ;
} ] ;
```

This statement is less complicated than it looks. **on**, **off**, **yes**, and **no** have the obvious meanings; the default is not to run OSPF.

In the **defaults** section, **router-prio** specifies a default router priority (to be used when electing a designated router) of 1 on all interfaces. This value may be overridden on specific interfaces if desired. The default priority is 0, which makes **gated** ineligible to become any network's designated router.

The definition of each area begins with either the **backbone** or the **area** keyword. There must be one area or backbone statement for each area of which the router is a member. The backbone is defined as area 0 in the OSPF protocol specification, but **gated** requires you to use the **backbone** keyword instead of **area 0**.

The *area* may be given as a decimal number or as a four-byte number in IP address format (e.g., 128.138.45.2). The area number is never interpreted as an IP address by **gated**, but the dotted quad format is supported in case you want to label areas with the IP addresses of principal routers or servers.

The list of **networks** defines the networks that compose the area. It is only necessary to enumerate networks in the configuration files of area-border routers. The specification of addresses and masks is done exactly as for **martians**, as described on page 357, except that there is no **allow** keyword. Networks marked with the **restrict** option are not included in route summaries; they are "secret" networks that are reachable only within the area.

**stubhosts** are directly attached hosts that should be advertised as being reachable via this router with the specified *cost* (1 is usually fine). This feature is used primarily to support links to hosts that are connected via PPP or SLIP.

Finally, the **interface** list specifies the *cost* to the attached networks (usually 1, the default), and the *priority* of this **gated** for becoming the designated router. If an interface is set to **disable**, then no OSPF conversations will take place over this interface.

A real example of an OSPF configuration clause appears in section 2 of the complete **gated.conf** configuration file on page 365.

### Protocol configuration for ICMP redirects

**gated** lets you exert some administrative control over the handling of routes learned through ICMP redirects (see page 285 for an explanation of what these are).

```
redirect yes | no | on | off [ {
     preference preference ;
     interface interface_list [noredirects] | [redirects] ;
     trustedgateways gateway_list ;
     traceoptions trace_options ;
} ] ;
```

These options should all be familiar by now. **preference** sets the route preference for redirect-derived routes in general (the default is 30, which is fairly good). The options **redirects** and **noredirects** enable and disable acceptance of redirects per network interface, and **trustedgateways** enables them only when sent by specific routers. There are no redirect-specific tracing options.

On some systems, the kernel acts on ICMP redirects without allowing **gated** to intervene and enforce its own handling policy. On these systems, **gated** checks to see if the kernel accepted a redirect and will manually remove the redirect from the routing table if it is not wanted.

### Static routes

Static routes are configured with a **static** statement:

```
static {
     dest gateway gateway_list [interface interface_list] [preference preference]
          [retain] [reject] [blackhole] [noinstall] ;
} ;
```

The *dest* can be specified with any of the usual suspects:

```
host host
default
network
network mask mask
network masklen length
```

The *gateway_list* is the set of routers through which this destination can be reached. While there may in theory be more than one gateway, most kernels do not support multipath routing.

If the designated gateway is not on a directly connected network (via one of the interfaces specified in the optional *interface_list*), the route will be ignored.

The route preference defaults to 60, which allows it to be superseded by OSPF-computed routes or by ICMP redirects.

If a route is marked with **retain**, it will be left in the kernel's routing table when **gated** exits. Normally, **gated** cleans up after itself and leaves only interface and preexisting routes. Conversely, the **noinstall** option causes the route not to be installed in the local routing table, but only made available for propagation to other routers. This option is useful on routers that act as "route servers," meaning that they don't actually route traffic but rather coordinate routing information for the network infrastructure (they may have access to an alternate "management traffic only" network that carries their packets).

Routes marked with the **blackhole** and **reject** tags prevent forwarding from occurring on systems that support these features. With **reject**, an ICMP error is returned to the sender; with **blackhole**, the packets just mysteriously disappear without a trace, kind of like Evi's email.

A static route example appears in section 3 of the complete **gated.conf** configuration file example on page 366.

### Exported routes

Once **gated** has computed the routes it likes, it defaults to putting them in the kernel's forwarding table. For most applications, this is all that's necessary. Sometimes, however, it's desirable to configure **gated** to act as a kind of translator, accepting information from one protocol and distributing it out another. This is done in the configuration file with an **export** clause:

```
export proto protocol
    [interface interface_list | gateway gateway_list]
    restrict ;
```

or

```
export proto protocol
    [interface interface_list | gateway gateway_list]
    [metric metric] {
        export_list ;
    } ;
```

In this case, *protocol* is the routing protocol that will be advertising the translated information, and *export_list* is what to translate as specified by listing a **proto** clause for each dataset to be translated. Here's a sample *export_list*:

```
proto static {
    ALL metric 1;
} ;
```

This snippet translates all static routes and inserts them into the exported list with a metric of 1.

### A complete gated configuration example

The configuration on the next page is for an environment in which both RIP and OSPF are in use. The configuration is for the area-border router shown in Exhibit C (also on the next page).

**Exhibit C    Network topology for our sample gated configuration**

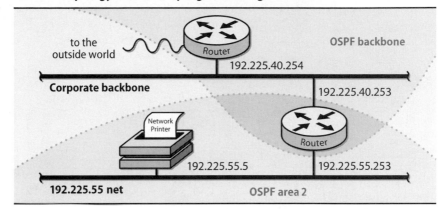

The upstream network (the corporate backbone) has standardized on OSPF, but the downstream LAN has devices (a few network printers) that can only listen to RIP. In this environment, **gated** is used to rebroadcast the OSPF routes via RIP. This is a good configuration for a corporate or campus environment because it lets PCs and network appliances learn information via RIP, yet uses a more sensible protocol to communicate on the backbone among groups, floors, and buildings.

The contents of the configuration file are as follows:

*Section 1:*
```
rip yes {
     broadcast;
     defaultmetric 10;
     interface 192.225.40.253 noripout;
     interface 192.225.55.253 ripout;
};
```

*Section 2:*
```
ospf yes {
     area 0.0.0.2 {
          authtype none;
          networks {
               192.225.55.0 mask 255.255.255.0;
          };
          interface 192.225.55.253 cost 1 {
               priority 2;
          };
     };
     backbone {
          interface 192.225.40.253 {
               priority 2;
          };
     };
};
```

```
Section 3:     static {
                     default gateway 192.225.40.254 preference 140 retain;
               };

Section 4:     export proto rip {
                     proto ospf {
                         ALL metric 1;
                     };
                     proto direct {
                         ALL metric 1;
                     };
                     proto static {
                         ALL metric 1;
                     } ;
               };

Section 5:     export proto ospf {
                     proto direct {
                         ALL metric 1;
                     };
               };
```

In section 1, **gated** is instructed to speak the RIP protocol. It listens for RIP broadcasts from other routers on both interfaces but sends out RIP packets of its own only on the 192.225.55.253 interface. This restriction serves to eliminate undesirable broadcast traffic on the corporate backbone.

Section 2 enables OSPF. The 192.225.40.253 interface is in area 0, the backbone area. It will send out OSPF HELLO messages to other routers on this network to discover who its neighbors are. 192.225.55.253 is in area 2. (There may or may not be other downstream routers that want to share information via OSPF.)

Currently, there is only one way out of this network to the outside world. Hence, for good measure, section 3 includes a static default route to the Internet gateway on the 192.225.40.0 network.

In sections 4 and 5, we tell **gated** what routes to advertise via RIP and OSPF, respectively. We want the RIP advertisements to include any directly connected networks, the static default route, and any routes learned via OSPF. We want the OSPF advertisements to include any directly connected networks (such as the 192.225.55.0 network). Since we are an interior router, we do not want to announce a default route.

## 14.6  VENDOR SPECIFICS

 **gated** is not shipped with the Solaris distribution. **routed** is turned on in chatty mode if the host has two or more (real) network interfaces *and* does not use DHCP. If either of these conditions is not met, **routed** is turned on in quiet (**-q**) mode if a default route is not set (in **/etc/defaultrouter**) *and* the Router Discovery Protocol (the **in.rdisc** daemon) isn't in use. Whew.

**gated** is started if GATED=1 is asserted in **/etc/rc.config.d/netconf**. **routed** is not shipped with the HP-UX distribution.

 On Red Hat systems, **gated** is started if the file **/etc/gated.conf** exists. **routed** is disabled by default; to enable it, rename the startup file **/etc/rc.d/rc3.d/K55routed** to **S55routed** (you can also do this with the graphical interface, **control-panel**).

 FreeBSD starts **routed** at boot time if router_enable is set to YES and router is set to routed in **rc.conf**. In order for a FreeBSD box to perform packet forwarding among interfaces, gateway_enable must also be set to YES in **rc.conf**. You can install **gated** from the **/usr/ports/gated** directory.

## 14.7 ROUTING STRATEGY SELECTION CRITERIA

There are essentially four levels of complexity at which the routing for a network can be managed:

- No routing
- Static routes only
- Mostly static routes, but clients listen for RIP updates
- Dynamic routing everywhere

The topology of the overall network has a dramatic effect on each individual segment's routing requirements. Different nets may need very different levels of routing support. The following rules of thumb can help you choose a strategy:

- A stand-alone network requires no routing.

- If there is only one way out of a network, clients (nongateway machines) on that network should have a static default route to the lone gateway. No other configuration is necessary, except on the gateway itself.

- A gateway with a small number of networks on one side and a gateway to "the world" on the other side can have explicit static routes pointing to the former and a default route to the latter. However, dynamic routing is advisable if there is more than one routing choice on both sides.

- If you use RIP and are concerned about the network and system load this entails, avoid using **routed** in active mode—it broadcasts everything it knows (correct or not) at short intervals. **gated** allows you to specify what routes may be sent out ("advertised"), thus reducing the flood of routing information. **gated** can also send RIP updates to particular gateways rather than broadcasting them everywhere.

- To have clients listen passively for routing updates without sending out their own information, use **routed -q**. Clients can also listen passively with **gated**, but **gated** has a larger footprint.

- Many people will tell you that RIP is a horrible, terrible protocol and that **routed** is the spawn of Satan. It isn't necessarily so. If it works for you and

Routing

you are happy with the performance, go ahead and use it. You get no points for spending time on an overengineered routing strategy.

- If RIP is not your primary routing protocol, you can have **gated** broadcast its routing information as RIP purely for the benefit of passive clients.

- **routed** listens to everyone and believes everything it hears. **gated** gives you more control over updates. Even if your site uses RIP, you may want to manage the exchange of routing data with **gated** and run **routed** only on client machines.

- Use dynamic routing at points where networks cross political or administrative boundaries.

- On dynamically routed networks that contain loops or redundant paths, use OSPF if possible.

- Routers connected to the Internet backbone that have a choice of upstream paths must use BGP. Most routers connected to the Internet have only one upstream path, and therefore a simple static route is sufficient.

A good routing strategy for a medium-sized site with a relatively stable local structure and a connection to someone else's net is to use a combination of static and dynamic routing. Machines within the local structure that do not have a gateway to external networks can use static routing, forwarding all unknown packets to a default machine that understands the outside world and does dynamic routing.

A network that is too complicated to be managed with this scheme should rely on dynamic routing. Default static routes can still be used on leaf networks, but machines on networks with more than one router should run **routed** in passive mode. All machines with more than one network interface should run **gated** in active mode and broadcast routes with RIP.

## 14.8 CISCO ROUTERS

Routers made by Cisco Systems, Inc., are the de facto standard for Internet routing today. Having captured over 70% of the router market, Cisco's products are well known, and staff that know how to operate them are relatively easy to find. Before Cisco, UNIX boxes with multiple network interfaces were often used as routers. Today, dedicated routers are the favored gear to put in datacom closets and above ceiling tiles where network cables come together. They're cheaper, faster, and more secure than their UNIX counterparts.

Most of Cisco's router products run an operating system called Cisco IOS, which is proprietary and unrelated to UNIX. Its command set is rather large; the full documentation set fills up about 4.5 feet of shelf space. We could never fully cover Cisco IOS here, but knowing a few basics can get you a long way.

IOS defines two levels of access (user and privileged), both of which are password-protected. By default, you can simply **telnet** to a Cisco router to enter user mode.[10] You'll be prompted for the user-level access password:

```
% telnet xor-gw.xor.com
Connected to xor-gw.xor.com.
Escape character is '^]'.

User Access Verification
Password:
```

Upon entering the correct password, you will receive a prompt from Cisco's EXEC command interpreter:

```
xor-gw.xor.com>
```

At this prompt, you can enter commands such as **show interfaces** to see the router's network interfaces or **show ?** to get help about the other things you can see.

To enter privileged mode, type **enable** and enter the privileged password when it is requested. Once you have reached the privileged level, your prompt will end in a #:

```
xor-gw.xor.com#
```

BE CAREFUL—you can do anything from this prompt, including erasing the router's configuration information and its operating system. When in doubt, consult Cisco's manuals or one of the comprehensive books published by Cisco Press.

You can type **show running** to see the current running configuration of the router and **show config** to see the current nonvolatile configuration. Most of the time, these are the same. Here's a typical configuration:

```
xor-gw.xor.com# show running
Current configuration:
version 12.0
hostname xor-gw
enable secret xxxxxxxx
ip subnet-zero

interface Ethernet0
description XOR internal network
ip address 192.108.21.254 255.255.255.0
no ip directed-broadcast
interface Ethernet1
description XOR backbone network
ip address 192.225.33.254 255.255.255.0
no ip directed-broadcast

ip classless
line con 0
transport input none
```

10. A variety of access methods can be configured. If your site already uses Cisco routers, contact your network administrator to find out which methods have been enabled.

```
line aux 0
transport input telnet
line vty 0 4
password xxxxxxxx
login

end
```

The router configuration can be modified in a variety of ways. Cisco offers graphical tools that run under some versions of UNIX and NT. Real network administrators never use these; the command prompt is always the "sure bet." It is also possible to **tftp** a config file to or from a router so that you can edit it in your favorite editor.[11]

To modify the configuration from the command prompt, type **config term**:

```
xor-gw.xor.com# config term
Enter configuration commands, one per line.  End with CNTL/Z.
xor-gw(config)#
```

You can then type new configuration commands exactly as you want them to appear in the **show running** output. For example, if we wanted to change the IP address of the Ethernet0 interface in the example above, we could enter

```
interface Ethernet0
ip address 192.225.40.253 255.255.255.0
```

When you've finished entering configuration commands, press <Control-Z> to return to the regular command prompt. If you're happy with the new configuration, enter **write mem** to save the configuration to nonvolatile memory.

Here are some tips for a successful Cisco router experience:

- Name the router with the **hostname** command. This precaution helps to prevent accidents caused by changing the configuration on the wrong router. The hostname will always appear in the command prompt.

- Always keep a backup router configuration on hand. You can write a short **expect** script that **tftp**s the running configuration over to a UNIX box every night for safekeeping.

- Control access to the router command line by putting access lists on the router's VTYs (VTYs are like PTYs on a UNIX box). This precaution prevents unwanted parties from trying to break into your router.

- Control the traffic flowing among your networks (and possibly to the outside world) with access lists on each interface. See *Packet-filtering firewalls* on page 675 for more information about how to set up access lists.

- Keep routers physically secure. It's easy to reset the privileged password if you have physical access to a Cisco box.

---

11. Hot tip: Microsoft Word isn't the best choice for this application.

## 14.9  RECOMMENDED READING

HUITEMA, CHRISTIAN. *Routing in the Internet, Second Edition.* Prentice Hall. 1999.

This book is a clear and well-written introduction to routing from the ground up. It covers most of the protocols in common use and also some advanced topics such as multicasting. Amazon.com customers who bought this book also bought the album *The Dirty Boogie* by The Brian Setzer Orchestra.

MOY, JOHN T. *OSPF: Anatomy of an Internet Routing Protocol.* Addison-Wesley. 1998.

A thorough exposition of OSPF by the author of the OSPF protocol standard and a big chunk of **gated**. Amazon.com customers who bought this book also bought the album *Stunt* by the Barenaked Ladies.

HALABI, BASSAM. *Internet Routing Architectures.* Cisco Press. 1997.

This book focuses on BGP, the most widely used exterior gateway protocol. Amazon.com customers who bought this book also bought the soundtrack to the movie *The Matrix*, featuring explicit lyrics.

There are many routing-related RFCs. The main ones are shown in Table 14.5.

**Table 14.5   Routing-related RFCs**

| RFC | Title | Authors |
| --- | --- | --- |
| 2328 | OSPF Version 2 | John T. Moy |
| 1058 | Routing Information Protocol | C. Hedrick |
| 2453 | RIP Version 2 | Gary Scott Malkin |
| 1256 | ICMP Router Discovery Messages | Stephen E. Deering |
| 1142 | OSI IS-IS Intra-domain Routing Protocol | David R. Oran |
| 1075 | Distance Vector Multicast Routing Protocol | D. Waitzman et al. |
| 1519 | CIDR: an Address Assignment and Aggregation Strategy | Vince Fuller et al. |
| 1771 | A Border Gateway Protocol 4 (BGP-4) | Yakov Rekhter et al. |

Routing

# 15 *Network Hardware*

Nothing is influencing our culture today more than the ability to move large amounts of data from one place to another very quickly. We now have world-wide connectivity at a level that only die-hard sci-fi fanatics could have dreamed of just a few years ago. Behind all of this craziness is fancy network hardware and—you guessed it—a whole bunch of stuff that originated in the deep, dark caves of UNIX.

Keeping up with all these fast-moving bits is the challenge. The speed and reliability of your network has a direct effect on your organization's productivity. A poorly designed network is a personal and professional embarrassment. It can also be very expensive to fix.

At least three major factors contribute to a successful installation:

- Development of a reasonable network design
- Selection of high-quality hardware
- Proper installation and documentation

The first sections of this chapter discuss the media that are commonly used for local area and wide area networking, including Ethernet, ATM, frame relay, and DSL. We then cover design issues you are likely to face on any network, be it new or old.

## 15.1 LAN, WAN, or MAN?

We're lucky, in a sense, that TCP/IP can be easily transported over a variety of media. In reality, however, the network hardware market is split into a variety of confusing classifications.

Networks that exist within a building or group of buildings are generally referred to as Local Area Networks or LANs. High-speed, low-cost connections prevail. Wide Area Networks—WANs—are networks in which the endpoints are geographically dispersed, perhaps separated by thousands of kilometers. In these networks, high speed usually comes at high cost, but there are virtually no bounds to the sites you can include on the network (Brugge, Belgium to Sitka, Alaska!). MAN is an up-and-coming term for Metropolitan Area Network, meaning a high-speed, medium-cost access medium used within a city or cluster of cities. In this chapter, we explore some of the technologies used to implement these beasts.

## 15.2  ETHERNET: THE COMMON LAN

Having captured over 80% of the world-wide LAN market, Ethernet can be found just about everywhere in its many forms. It started as Bob Metcalfe's Ph.D. thesis at MIT. Bob graduated and went to Xerox PARC; together with DEC and Intel, Xerox eventually developed Ethernet into a product. It was one of the first instances in which competing computer companies joined forces on a technical project.

Ethernet was originally specified at 3 Mb/s (mega*bits* per second), but it moved to 10 Mb/s almost immediately. It was developed on the Xerox Alto, which didn't have enough room on the circuit board for an external clock. The Ethernet interface had to use the Alto's clock, which meant that the network speed had to be 2.94 Mb/s. This was rounded up to 3 Mb/s. Metcalfe and other early developers who had worked on the architecture of the ARPANET objected to a roundoff error that exceeded the ARPANET's entire bandwidth, but marketing won out.

Ethernet weathered its early years in the 1980s, a time at which a variety of network operating systems, including UNIX, were also gaining basic networking skills and learning to play with each other. When Ethernet hit its mid-teenage years, it was ready to drive. In 1994, Ethernet caught attention as it was standardized at 100 Mb/s. Just after turning 19 years old in 1998, it was ready to fight a new war—at 1 Gb/s. Now an adult in its early 20s, Ethernet is headed for the new frontier of 10 Gb/s, having eclipsed all of its rivals.[1] Table 15.1 on the next page highlights the evolution of the various Ethernet standards.

### How Ethernet works

Ethernet can be described as a polite dinner party at which guests (computers) don't interrupt each other but rather wait for a lull in the conversation (no traffic on the network cable) before speaking. If two guests start to talk at once (a collision) they both stop, excuse themselves, wait a bit, and then one of them starts talking again.

The technical term for this scheme is CSMA/CD:

- Carrier Sense: you can tell whether anyone is talking.
- Multiple Access: everyone can talk.
- Collision Detection: you know when you interrupt someone else.

---

1. Current speculation predicts the widespread availability of terabit Ethernet by 2008!

**Table 15.1    The evolution of Ethernet**

| Year | Speed | Common name | IEEE# | Dist | Media |
|---|---|---|---|---|---|
| 1973 | 3 Mb/s | Xerox Ethernet | – | ? | Coax |
| 1980 | 10 Mb/s | Ethernet 1 | – | 500m | RG-11 coax |
| 1982 | 10 Mb/s | DIX Ethernet (Ethernet II) | – | 500m | RG-11 coax |
| 1985 | 10 Mb/s | 10Base5 ("Thicknet") | 802.3 | 500m | RG-11 coax |
| 1985 | 10 Mb/s | 10Base2 ("Thinnet") | 802.3 | 180m | RG-58 coax |
| 1989 | 10 Mb/s | 10BaseT | 802.3 | 100m | Category 3 UTP[a] copper |
| 1993 | 10 Mb/s | 10BaseF | 802.3 | 2km | MM[b] Fiber |
|  |  |  |  | 25km | SM Fiber |
| 1994 | 100 Mb/s | 100BaseTX ("100 meg") | 802.3u | 100m | Category 5 UTP copper |
| 1994 | 100 Mb/s | 100BaseFX | 802.3u | 2km | MM fiber |
|  |  |  |  | 20km | SM fiber |
| 1998 | 1 Gb/s | 1000BaseSX | 802.3z | 260m | 62.5-µm MM fiber |
|  |  |  |  | 550m | 50-µm MM fiber |
| 1998 | 1 Gb/s | 1000BaseLX | 802.3z | 440m | 62.5-µm MM fiber |
|  |  |  |  | 550m | 50-µm MM fiber |
|  |  |  |  | 3km | SM fiber |
| 1998 | 1 Gb/s | 1000BaseCX | 802.3z | 25m | Twinax |
| 1999 | 1 Gb/s | 1000BaseT ("Gigabit") | 802.3ab | 100m | Cat 5E and 6 UTP copper |

a. Unshielded twisted pair
b. Multimode and single-mode fiber

The actual delay upon collision detection is somewhat random. This convention avoids the scenario in which two hosts simultaneously transmit to the network, detect the collision, wait the same amount of time, and then start transmitting again, thus flooding the network with collisions. This was not always true!

**Exhibit A    A polite Ethernet dinner party**

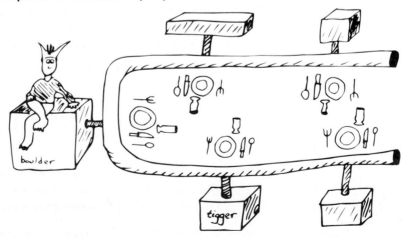

## Ethernet topology

The Ethernet topology is a branching bus with no loops; there is only one way for a packet to travel between any two hosts on the same network. Ethernet provides a mechanism to exchange three types of packets on a segment: unicast, multicast, and broadcast. Unicast packets are addressed to only one host. Multicast packets are addressed to a group of hosts. Broadcast packets are delivered to all hosts on a segment.

A "broadcast domain" is the set of hosts that receive packets destined for the hardware broadcast address, and there is exactly one broadcast domain for each logical Ethernet segment. Under the early Ethernet standards and media (such as 10Base5), physical segments and logical segments were exactly the same since all the packets traveled on one big cable, with host interfaces strapped onto the side of it.[2]

With the advent of modern switches, today's logical segments usually consist of many (possibly dozens or hundreds) physical segments to which only two devices are connected: the switch port and the host. The switches are responsible for escorting multicast and unicast packets to the physical segments on which the intended recipients reside; broadcast traffic is forwarded to all ports in a logical segment.

A single logical segment may consist of physical segments operating at different speeds (10 Mb/s, 100 Mb/s, or 1 Gb/s); hence switches must have buffering and timing capabilities in order to eliminate potential conflicts.

## Unshielded twisted pair

Unshielded twisted pair (UTP) is the preferred cable medium for Ethernet. It is based on a star topology and has several advantages over other media:

- It uses inexpensive, readily available copper wire. (Sometimes, existing phone wiring can be used.)

- UTP wire is much easier to install and debug than coax or fiber. Custom lengths are easily made.

- UTP uses RJ-45 connectors, which are cheap, reliable, and easy to install.

- The link to each machine is independent, so a hardware failure or cabling problem on one link is unlikely to affect other hosts on the network.

The general "shape" of a UTP network is illustrated in Exhibit B on the next page.

UTP wire suitable for use in modern LANs is commonly broken down into eight classifications. The performance rating system was first introduced by Anixter, a large cable supplier. Today, these classifications are known as Category 1 through Category 7, with a special Category 5E in the middle.

---

2. We're not kidding! Attaching a new computer involved boring a hole into the outer sheath of the cable with a special drill to reach the center conductor. A "vampire tap" which bit into the outer conductor was then clamped on with screws. This contraption was especially fun to try to get right in places like elevator shafts and steam tunnels.

**Exhibit B    A UTP installation**

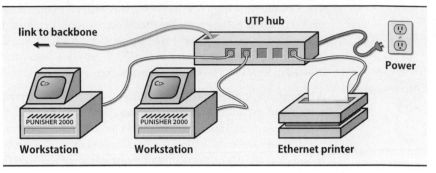

Category 1 and Category 2 cables are suitable only for voice applications (if that). Category 3 cable is as low as you can go for a LAN; it is the standard for 10 Mb/s 10BaseT. Category 4 cable is something of a orphan, not exactly suited for any particular application. It is occasionally used for 16 Mb/s UTP token ring or for fancy 10BaseT installations. Category 5 cable can support 100 Mb/s and is the most common standard currently in use for data cabling. Category 5E and Category 6 cabling support 1 Gb/s.

See page 386 for more information about wiring.

10BaseT connections require two pairs of Category 3 wire, and each link is limited to a length of 100 meters; 100BaseTX has the same length limitation but requires two pairs of Category 5 wire. Both PVC-coated and Teflon-coated wire are available. Your choice of jacketing should be based on the environment in which the cable will be installed. Enclosed areas that feed into the building's ventilation system ("return air plenums") typically require Teflon. PVC is less expensive and easier to work with.

RJ-45 connectors wired with pins 1, 2, 3, and 6 are used to make the connections. Although only two pairs of wire are needed for a working 10 Mb/s or 100 Mb/s connection, we recommend that when installing a new network you use four-pair Category 5E wire and connect all eight pins of the RJ-45 jack.

See page 93 for more information about the RS-232 standard.

For terminating the four-pair UTP cable at patch panels and RJ-45 wall jacks, we suggest that you use the TIA/EIA-568A RJ-45 wiring standard. This standard, which is compatible with other uses of RJ-45 (e.g., RS-232), is a convenient way to keep the wiring at both ends of the connection consistent, regardless of whether you can easily access the cable pairs themselves. The 568A standard is detailed in Table 15.2.

**Table 15.2    TIA/EIA-568A standard for wiring four-pair UTP to an RJ-45 jack**

| Pair | Colors | Wired to | Pair | Colors | Wired to |
|------|--------|----------|------|--------|----------|
| 1 | White/Blue | Pins 5/4 | 3 | White/Green | Pins 1/2 |
| 2 | White/Orange | Pins 3/6 | 4 | White/Brown | Pins 7/8 |

Existing building wiring may or may not be suitable for network use, depending on how and when it was installed. Many old buildings were retrofitted with new cable in the 1950s and 1960s. Unfortunately, this cable usually won't support even 10 Mb/s.

### Connecting and expanding Ethernets

Ethernets can be logically connected at several points in the seven-layer ISO network model. At layer 1, the physical layer, you can use either hardware connectors or repeaters (commonly called hubs in modern times). They transfer the signal directly, much like two tin cans connected by string.

At layer 2, the data link layer, switches are used. Switches transfer frames on the basis of the hardware source and destination addresses, much like delivering a message in a bottle by reading only the label on the outside of the bottle.

At layer 3, the network layer, routers are used. Routers transfer messages to the next hop according to the location of the final recipient, rather like looking at the message in a bottle to see who it's really addressed to.

#### Hubs and concentrators

Hubs (which are also referred to as concentrators) are active devices that connect physical segments in UTP Ethernet networks. They require external power. Acting as a repeater, a hub retimes and reconstitutes Ethernet frames but does not interpret them; it has no idea where packets are going or what protocol they are using.

The two farthest points on the network must never be more than 4 hubs apart. Ethernet versions 1 and 2 specified at most 2 hubs in series per network. The IEEE 802.3 standard extended the limit to 4 for 10 Mb/s Ethernets. 100 Mb/s Ethernets allow 2 repeaters, and 1000BaseT Ethernets allow only 1. Exhibit C shows both a legal and an illegal configuration for a 10 Mb/s network.

**Exhibit C    Count the hubs**

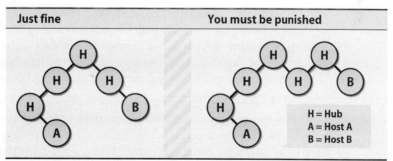

Hubs occasionally require attention from a system administrator, so they should not be kept in obscure or hard-to-reach locations. Power cycling usually allows them to recover from a wedged state.

*Switches*

Switches connect Ethernets at the data link layer (layer 2) of the ISO model. Their purpose is to join two different physical networks in a way that makes them seem like one big physical network. They do not require software, but rather receive, regenerate, and retransmit packets in hardware.[3] Most switches use a dynamic learning algorithm. They notice which source addresses come from one port and which come from another. Packets are forwarded between ports only when necessary. At first all packets are forwarded, but in a few seconds the switch has learned the locations of most hosts and can be more selective.

Since not all packets are forwarded between networks, each segment of cable is less saturated with traffic than it would be if all machines were on the same cable. Since most communication tends to be localized, the increase in apparent bandwidth can be dramatic. And since the logical model of the network is not affected by a switch, there are few administrative consequences to installing one.

Switches can sometimes become confused if your network contains loops because packets from a single host appear to be on two (or more) ports of the switch. A single Ethernet cannot have loops, but as you connect several Ethernets together with routers and switches, the topology can include multiple paths to a host. Some switches can handle this situation by holding alternate routes in reserve in case the primary route goes down. They perform a pruning operation on the network they see until the remaining sections present only one path to each node on the network. Some switches can also handle duplicate links between the same two networks and route traffic in a round robin fashion.

Switches keep getting smarter as more functionality is built into their firmware. Some can be used to monitor security on the network. They record any foreign Ethernet addresses they see, thereby detecting and reporting newly connected machines. Since they operate at the Ethernet layer, switches are protocol independent and can handle any mix of high-level packet types (for example, IP, AppleTalk, or NetBEUI).

Switches must scan every packet to determine if it should be forwarded. Their performance is usually measured by both the packet scanning rate and the packet forwarding rate. Many vendors do not mention packet sizes in the performance figures they quote; therefore, actual performance may be less than advertised. Switches are a good but slightly expensive way to connect Ethernets.

Although Ethernet switching hardware is getting faster all the time, it is still not a reasonable technology for connecting more than a hundred hosts in a single logical segment. Problems such as "broadcast storms" often plague large switched networks, since broadcast traffic must be forwarded to all ports in a switched segment. To solve this problem, you should use a router to isolate broadcast traffic between switched segments (thereby creating more than one logical Ethernet).

---

3. Because packets are regenerated and retimed, fully switched networks do not suffer from the "repeater count" limitations shown in Exhibit C.

Large sites can benefit from switches that can partition their ports (through software configuration) into subgroups called Virtual Local Area Networks or VLANs. A VLAN is a group of ports that belong to the same logical segment, as if the ports were connected to their own dedicated switch. Such partitioning increases the ability of the switch to isolate traffic, and that has salutary effects on both security and performance.

Traffic between VLANs is handled by a router, or in some cases, by a routing module or routing software layer within the switch. An extension of this system known as "VLAN trunking" (such as that provided by the IEEE 802.1Q protocol) allows physically separate switches to service ports on the same logical VLAN.

Choosing a switch can be difficult. The switch market is a very competitive segment of the computing industry, and it's plagued with marketing claims that aren't even partially true. When selecting a vendor to buy switches from, you should rely on independent evaluations ("bake offs" such as those that appear in magazine comparisons) rather than any data supplied by vendors themselves. In recent years, it has been common for one vendor to have the "best" product for a few months, but then completely destroy its performance or reliability when trying to make improvements, thus elevating another manufacturer to the top of the heap.

In all cases, make sure that the backplane speed of the switch is adequate—that's the number that really counts at the end of a very long day. A well-designed switch should have a backplane speed that exceeds the sum of the speeds of all its ports.

### Routers

Routers are dedicated computers-in-a-box that contain two or more network interfaces and direct traffic at layer 3 of the ISO protocol stack (the network layer). They shuttle packets to their final destinations based on the information in the TCP/IP protocol headers. In addition to simply moving the packets from one place to another, they may also perform other functions such as packet filtering (for security reasons), prioritization (for quality of service reasons), and big-picture network topology discovery. See all the gory details of how routing really works in Chapter 14.

Hardware interfaces of many different types (e.g., FDDI, Ethernet, and ATM) can be found on a single router. On the software side, some routers can also handle non-IP traffic such as IPX or AppleTalk. In these configurations, the router and its interfaces must be configured for each protocol you want it to handle.

Routers take one of two forms: fixed configuration and modular. Fixed configuration routers have specific network interfaces permanently installed at the factory. They are usually suitable for small, specialized applications. For example, a router with a T1 interface and an Ethernet interface might be a good choice to connect a small company to the Internet.

Modular routers have a slot or bus architecture to which interfaces can be added by the end user. While this approach is usually more expensive, it provides for greater flexibility down the road.

Depending on your reliability needs and expected traffic load, a dedicated router may or may not be cheaper than a UNIX system configured to act as a router. However, the dedicated router will usually provide superior performance and reliability. This is one area of network design in which it's usually advisable to spend the extra money up front in order to avoid headaches later.

## 15.3 FDDI: THE DISAPPOINTING AND EXPENSIVE LAN

At 10 Mb/s, the Ethernet of the 1980s didn't offer enough bandwidth for some networking needs, such as connecting workgroups via a corporate (or campus) backbone. In an effort to provide higher-bandwidth options, the ANSI X3T9.5 committee produced the Fiber Distributed Data Interface (FDDI) standard as an alternative to Ethernet.[4] Designed and marketed as a 100 Mb/s token ring, FDDI once looked like it would be the easy solution to many organizations' bandwidth needs.

Unfortunately, FDDI has been a disappointment in absolutely every way. In the early days of FDDI, the cost of FDDI interfaces often exceeded the cost of the workstations they were installed in (around $10,000 each) and performance was often worse than Ethernet (early DEC boards, for example). Interfaces are still expensive, but the performance is better. Modern interfaces yield around 80 Mb/s of throughput.

*See page 268 for more information about maximum transmission units (MTUs).*

For good performance, FDDI needs a much higher MTU than the default, which is tuned for Ethernet. An MTU value of 4,352 (set with **ifconfig**) is about right. Until the software used to move files around networks has been tuned for the speed and characteristics of FDDI, mere mortals will probably see performance numbers in the range of one-third to one-half the theoretical maximum.

The FDDI standard specifies a 100 Mb/s token-passing, dual ring, all-singing, all-dancing LAN using a fiber optic transmission medium, as shown in Exhibit D. The dual ring architecture provides for a primary ring that's used for data transmission and a secondary ring that's used as a backup in the event the ring is cut (either physically or electronically).

**Exhibit D    FDDI dual token ring**

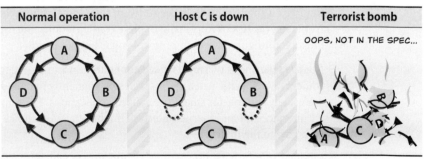

---

4. FDDI has also been accepted as an ISO standard.

Hosts can either be connected to both rings (they are then referred to as class A or "dual attached" hosts) or just to the primary ring (class B or "single-attached" hosts). Most commonly, backbone routers and concentrators are dual attached, and work-stations are single-attached, usually through a "concentrator," a sort of fiber hub.

One advantage of token ring systems is that access to the network is controlled by a deterministic protocol. There are no collisions, so the performance of the network does not degrade under high load, as it does with Ethernet. Many token ring systems can operate at 90% to 95% of their rated capacity when serving multiple clients.

For physical media, the FDDI standard suggests two types of fiber: single-mode and multimode. "Modes" are essentially bundles of light rays that enter the fiber at a par-ticular angle. Single-mode fiber allows exactly one frequency of light to travel its path and thus requires a laser as an emitting source.[5] Multimode fiber allows for multiple paths and is usually driven by less expensive and less dangerous LEDs. Single-mode fiber can be used over much longer distances than multimode. In practice, 62.5 μm multimode fiber is most commonly used for FDDI.

Several fiber connector standards are used with FDDI, and they vary from vendor to vendor. Regardless of what connectors you use, keep in mind that a clean fiber con-nection is essential for reliable operation. Although self-service fiber termination kits are available, we suggest that wherever possible you have a professional wiring firm install the ends on fiber segments.

## 15.4  ATM: THE PROMISED (BUT SORELY DEFEATED) LAN

ATM stands for Asynchronous Transfer Mode, but some folks insist on Another Technical Mistake. One datacomm industry spokesman describes it as "an attempt by the phone company to turn your networking problem into something they know how to tariff."

ATM is technically "special" because it promotes the philosophy that small, fixed-size packets (called "cells") are the most efficient way to implement gigabit networks. ATM also promises capabilities that haven't traditionally been promised by other me-dia, including bandwidth reservation and quality-of-service guarantees.

ATM was widely marketed as an all-in-one switched network medium that could be used for LAN, WAN, and MAN needs. In modern times, ATM is mostly dead, pre-served only in WAN environments where large telco corporations are still trying to leverage their misguided investments in ATM hardware.

On top of ATM's 53-byte cells, five ATM Adaptation Layers (AALs) are described for cell transport. The purpose of each adaptation layer is summarized in Table 15.3.

---

5. *Never look directly at the ends of dangling or cut fibers.* If they are laser driven, they can burn your eyes without your immediate knowledge.

**Table 15.3  ATM adaptation layers**

| AAL | Application |
|-----|-------------|
| 1 | Constant bit-rate applications, like voice (requires bounded delay) |
| 2 | Variable bit-rate applications requiring bounded delay |
| 3 | Connection-oriented data applications |
| 4 | Connectionless data applications |
| 5 | General data transport (especially IP traffic, replaces 3 and 4) |

It is unclear how AAL 2 would ever be used in real life. Currently, there is no defined standard for it. AALs 3 and 4 turned out to be very similar and were combined. A group of vendors that had to implement ATM were unhappy with AALs 3 and 4 because of their high overhead. They developed their own solution, the Simple and Efficient Adaptation Layer (SEAL), which soon became AAL 5.

## 15.5  FRAME RELAY: THE SACRIFICIAL WAN

Frame relay is a WAN technology that offers packet-switched data service, usually for a reasonable cost. Although the claim is not 100% accurate, frame relay is often said to be remarketed X.25, a scary packet-switched technology from the mid-1970s. Fortunately, it's in such widespread use that the equipment, software, and staff that support it have evolved to be robust and to perform well.

Traditionally, users who wished to connect to remote sites would purchase a dedicated circuit from the phone company, such as a 56 Kb/s DDS line or a T1 line. These are point-to-point data circuits that are connected 24 hours a day. Unfortunately, this type of connection is often expensive, as it requires that the phone company dedicate equipment and bandwidth to the link.

In contrast, frame relay is an "economy of scale" approach. The phone company creates a network (often referred to as a "cloud"[6]) that connects its central offices. Users such as yourself provide data for remote sites in small packets. The phone company switches the packets through the appropriate central offices, ultimately delivering them to their destinations. In this model, you and the phone company are gambling that at any given second, the total amount of traffic won't exceed the bandwidth of the network (a condition known euphemistically as "being oversubscribed").

A router encapsulates IP traffic over frame relay connections. Packets are switched over invisible "permanent virtual circuits" (PVCs), which allow your packets to travel only to the sites you've paid for them to reach. These PVCs provide some degree of privacy protection from the other sites connected to the frame relay network.

The biggest advantage of frame relay is that it is usually inexpensive. But in the world of "you get what you pay for," you may find that frame relay's performance is some-

---

6. Which is an all-too-appropriate name, since it's never quite clear what the weather forecast will be in a frame relay network. Stormy? Rainy? Sleet? Hail?

times poor. Frame relay connections have some packet switching overhead, and link speed may degrade during periods of heavy use.

## 15.6   ISDN: THE INDIGENOUS WAN

Integrated Services Digital Network (ISDN) is a phone company offering that takes many forms. In its most common and usable form, called Basic Rate Interface (BRI) ISDN, it is essentially an all-digital phone line that provides two dial-up 64 Kb/s "B" channels and a single 16 Kb/s signaling "D" channel. Each B channel can be used for either voice or data (a voice line can be carried on a single 64 Kb/s channel).

ISDN offers a relatively high-speed digital line at a reasonable cost ($30–$150 per month, depending on where you live). Devices called terminal adaptors convert the phone line into a more familiar interface such as RS-232. They are used (and priced) much like modems. Most adaptors can aggregate the two B channels, yielding a 128 Kb/s data channel.

ISDN can be used in place of normal dial-up networking and also as a wide-area technology that uses a router or bridge to connect remote sites across the line.

Although many U.S. phone companies have installed switches that are compatible with ISDN, they still haven't figured out how to market or support them.[7] Only in a few areas can you just call up the phone company and order an ISDN line. Some tips: make sure you deal with the branch of the phone company that handles business services, since that is how ISDN is usually classified. In many regions, you will have to argue your way past several waves of drones before you reach someone who has heard of ISDN before, even if the service really is available.

## 15.7   DSL: THE PEOPLE'S WAN

It's easy to move large amounts of data among businesses and other large data facilities. Carrier-provided technologies such as T1, T3, SONET, ATM, and frame relay provide relatively simple conduits for moving bits from place to place. However, these technologies are not realistic options for connecting individual houses and home offices. They cost too much, and the infrastructure they require is not universally available.

Digital Subscriber Line (DSL) uses ordinary copper telephone wire to transmit data at speeds of up to 7 Mb/s (although typical DSL connections yield between 256 Kb/s and 768 Kb/s). Since most homes already have existing telephone wiring, DSL is a viable way to provide the "last mile" of connectivity from the telephone company to the home. DSL connections are usually terminated in a box that acts as a TCP/IP router and provides an Ethernet connection to other devices within the home. DSL is typically both cheaper and faster than ISDN, so it is now the preferred technology for home users.

---

7. Hence the interpretation: It Still Does Nothing

Unlike regular POTS (Plain Old Telephone Service) and ISDN connections, which require you to "dial up" an endpoint, DSL is a dedicated network service that is always connected. This feature makes it even more attractive, because there is no setup or connection delay when a user wants to transfer data.

DSL comes in several forms, and as a result it's often referred to as xDSL, with the x representing a specific subtechnology such as A for asymmetric, S for symmetric, H for high speed, or RA for rate adaptive. The exact technology variants and data transfer speeds available in your area depend on the central office equipment that your telephone company or carrier has chosen to deploy.

The race for "last mile" connectivity to hundreds of millions of homes is a hot one. It's also highly politicized, well capitalized, and overpublicized. The DSL approach leverages the copper infrastructure that is common among the Incumbent Local Exchange Carriers (ILECs), who favored higher profit margins over investments in infrastructure as the networking revolution of the 1980s and 90s passed them by.

Cable television companies, which already have fiber infrastructure in most neighborhoods, are promoting their own "last mile" solutions, which yield similar (though asymmetric) high-bandwidth connections to the home. The cable modem industry has recently become enlightened about data standards and is currently promoting the Data Over Cable Service Interface Specification (DOCSIS) standard. This standard defines the technical specs for both the cable modems and the equipment used at the cable company, and it allows various brands of equipment to interoperate.

All in all, the fight between cable modem and DSL technologies largely boils down to "my marketing budget is bigger than yours."

## 15.8 WHERE IS THE NETWORK GOING?

When you look closely at the technologies described above, you'll see one thing in common: the simple, inexpensive ones are succeeding, whereas the complex and expensive ones are dying quickly. Where does this put us down the road?

Ethernet has pummeled its rivals because it is incredibly inexpensive. It's so simple to implement that today you can even buy microwave ovens with Ethernet interfaces. Ethernet has scaled well: in many organizations, 10 Mb/s Ethernet infrastructure from the early 1980s is still in production use, connected into 100 Mb/s and 1 Gb/s segments. 10 Gb/s Ethernet is already in development and should be widely available by 2004. We expect to see this trend continue, with faster and faster switching hardware to connect it all.

On the "connectivity to the home" front, DSL offers new life to the tired old Ma Bell copper plant. It's likely that advances in technology will soon increase the speed of DSL by up to tenfold, which will offer a whole new world of options to homes and home offices.

Another exciting area of development is wireless networking. Production-grade products are now becoming available at prices that are affordable. Unfortunately, with the recent advances in traditional wired network technology, the speeds of these networks seem a bit inadequate, usually ranging from 2 Mb/s to 11 Mb/s. Debugging a wireless network is also something of a black art, since a wide range of variables come into play when there are problems. In short, wireless is currently a neat toy for homes, small offices, conferences, or the beach, but it's not going to replace wired corporate backbones anytime soon.

What's great about all of these new developments is that regardless of the medium or its speed, TCP/IP is compatible with it.

## 15.9  NETWORK TESTING AND DEBUGGING

One major advantage of the large scale migration to Ethernet (and other UTP-based technologies) is the ease of network debugging. Since these networks can be analyzed link by link, hardware problems can often be isolated in seconds rather than days.

The key to debugging a network is to break it down into its component parts and test each piece until you've isolated the offending device or cable. The "idiot lights" on switches and hubs (such as "link status" and "packet traffic") often provide immediate clues to the source of the problem. Top-notch documentation of your wiring scheme is essential for making these indicator lights work in your favor.

As with most tasks, having the right tools for the job is a big part of being able to get the job done right and without delay. The market offers two major types of network debugging tools (although they are quickly growing together).

The first is the hand-held cable analyzer. This device can measure the electrical characteristics of a given cable, including its length (with a groovy technology called "time domain reflectrometry"). Usually, these analyzers can also point out simple faults such as a broken or miswired cable. Our favorite product for LAN cable analysis is the Fluke LanMeter. It's an all-in-one analyzer that can even perform IP pings across the network. High-end versions have their own web server that can show you historical statistics. For WAN (telco) circuits, the T-Berd line analyzer is the cat's meow. The T-Berd and its high-end LAN-testing companion, the FireBERD, are made by TTC (www.ttc.com). Be forewarned: all these products cost as much as a small house in most cities.

The second type of debugging tool is the network sniffer. This device disassembles network packets to look for protocol errors, misconfigurations, and general snafus. It usually requires a substantial amount of training and patience to use such a device effectively, and these days analysis at the network-packet level is rarely necessary. If you must do it, the Cadillac of network sniffers is made by Sniffer Technologies (www.sniffer.com).

## 15.10  BUILDING WIRING

Whether you're running gigabit Ethernet or just serial cables, we recommend that you use the highest possible quality of wire. It will increase the chances that you can still use the same wire ten years down the road. It's cheapest to wire an entire building at once rather than wiring it one connection at a time.

### UTP cabling options

Category 5E wire is relatively new and offers the best price vs. performance tradeoff in today's market. Its normal format is four pairs per sheath, which is just right for a variety of data connections from RS-232 to gigabit Ethernet.

Category 5E specifications require that the twist be maintained to within half an inch of the connection to the punchdown block. This implies that any wire with more than four pairs per sheath will have to be taped or secured to maintain the twist, since it feeds more than one connection.

You must use Category 5E termination parts in addition to Category 5E wire. We've had the best luck using parts manufactured by The Siemon Company of Watertown, Connecticut (www.siemon.com).

### Connections to offices

One connection per office is clearly not enough. But should you use two or four? We recommend four, for several reasons:

- They can be used for serial connections (modem, printer, etc.).
- They can be used with voice telephones.
- They can be used to accommodate visitors or demo machines.
- The cost of the materials is typically only 5%–10% of the total cost.
- Your best guess doubled is often a good estimate.
- It's much cheaper to do it once rather than adding wires later.

If you're in the process of wiring your entire building, you might consider installing a few outlets in the hallways, conference rooms, lunch rooms, and bathrooms. Networking is becoming pervasive.

### Wiring standards

Modern buildings often require a large and complex wiring infrastructure to support all of the various activities that take place inside. Walking into the average telecommunications closet is usually a shocking experience for the weak of stomach, as identically colored, unlabeled wires often cover the walls.

In an effort to increase traceability and standardize building wiring, the TIA/EIA-606 Administration Standard for the telecommunication infrastructure of commercial buildings was released in February, 1993. EIA-606 specifies requirements and guidelines for the identification and documentation of telecommunications infrastructure.

Items covered by EIA-606 include:

- Termination hardware
- Cables
- Cable pathways
- Equipment spaces
- Infrastructure color coding
- Symbols for standard components

In particular, it specifies standard colors to be used for wiring. The occult details are revealed in Table 15.4.

**Table 15.4    EIA-606 color chart**

| Termination type | Color | Code[a] | Comments |
|---|---|---|---|
| Demarcation point | Orange | 150C | Central office terminations |
| Network connections | Green | 353C | Also used for aux. circuit terminations |
| Common equipment[b] | Purple | 264C | Major switching/data eqpt. terminations |
| First-level backbone | White | – | Cable terminations |
| Second-level backbone | Gray | 422C | Cable terminations |
| Station | Blue | 291C | Horizontal cable terminations |
| Inter-building backbone | Brown | 465C | Campus cable terminations |
| Miscellaneous | Yellow | 101C | Maintenance, alarms, etc. |
| Key telephone systems | Red | 184C | – |

a. According to the Pantone Matching System®
b. PBXes, hosts, LANs, muxes, etc.

Pantone now sells software to map between the Pantone systems for ink-on-paper, textile dyes, and colored plastic. Hey, you could color-coordinate the wiring, the uniforms of the installers, and the wiring documentation! On second thought...

## 15.11  NETWORK DESIGN ISSUES

This section addresses the logical and physical design of the network. It's targeted at medium-sized installations. The ideas presented here will scale up to a few hundred hosts but are overkill for three machines and inadequate for thousands. We also assume that you have an adequate budget and are starting from scratch, which is probably only partially true.

Most of network design consists of the specification of:

- The types of media that will be used
- The topology and routing of cables
- The use of repeaters, bridges, and routers

Another key issue in network design is congestion control. For example, NFS taxes the network quite heavily, and so file serving on a backbone cable is undesirable.

The issues presented in the following sections are typical of those that must be considered in any network design.

### Network architecture vs. building architecture

The network architecture is usually more flexible than the building architecture, but the two must coexist. If you are lucky enough to be able to specify the network before the building is constructed, be lavish. For most of us, both the building and a facilities management department already exist and are somewhat rigid.

In existing buildings, the network must use the building architecture, not fight it. Modern buildings often contain utility raceways for data and telephone cables in addition to high-voltage electrical wiring and water or gas pipes. They often use drop ceilings, a boon to network installers. Many campuses and organizations have underground utility tunnels that facilitate network installation.

The integrity of fire walls[8] must be maintained; if you route a cable through a fire wall, the hole must be snug and filled in with a noncombustible substance. Respect return air plenums in your choice of cable. If you are caught violating fire codes, you may be fined and will be required to fix the problems you have created, even if that means tearing down the entire network and rebuilding it correctly.

Your network's logical design must fit into the physical constraints of the buildings it serves. As you specify the network, keep in mind that it is easy to draw a logically good solution and then find that it is physically difficult or impossible to implement.

### Existing networks

Computer networks are the focus of this discussion, but many organizations already have CATV networks and telephone networks capable of transmitting data. Often, these include fiber links. If your organization is ready to install a new telephone system, buy lots of extra fiber and have it installed at the same time.

We had that opportunity several years ago and asked the contractors if they would string some fiber for us. They said, "Sure, no charge," and were a bit miffed when we showed up with a truckload of fiber for them to install.

### Expansion

It is very difficult to predict needs ten years into the future, especially in the computer and networking fields. Therefore, it is important to design the network with expansion and increased bandwidth in mind. As cable is being installed, especially in out-of-the-way, hard-to-reach places, pull three to four times the number of pairs you actually need. Remember: the majority of installation cost is labor, not materials.

Even if you have no immediate plans to use fiber, it is wise to install some when wiring your building, especially if it is hard to install cables later. Run both multimode

---

8. This type of "fire wall" is a concrete, brick, or flame-retardant wall that prevents flames from spreading and burning down a building. While much different from a network security firewall, it's probably just as important.

and single-mode fiber; the kind you will need in the future is always the kind you didn't install.

### Congestion

A network is like a chain: only as good as its weakest or slowest link. The performance of Ethernet, like that of many other network architectures, degrades as the network gets loaded.

Diskless nodes, terminal concentrators, mismatched interfaces, and low-speed links can all lead to congestion. It is helpful to isolate local traffic by creating subnets and by using interconnection devices such as routers. Subnets can also be used to cordon off machines that are used for experimentation; it's difficult to run an experiment that involves several machines if there is no easy way to isolate those machines both physically and logically from the rest of the network.

### Maintenance and documentation

We have found that the maintainability of a network correlates highly with the quality of its documentation. Accurate, complete, up-to-date documentation is absolutely indispensable.

Cables should be labeled at all termination points and also every few feet so that they can easily be identified when discovered in a ceiling or wall.[9] It's a good idea to keep copies of local cable maps posted inside communications closets so that they can be updated on the spot when changes are made. Once every few weeks, someone should copy the changes down for entry into an electronic database.

Joints between major population centers in the form of repeaters, bridges, routers, or even connectors can facilitate debugging by allowing parts of the network to be isolated and debugged separately. It's also helpful to put joints between political and administrative domains.

## 15.12  MANAGEMENT ISSUES

If the network is to work correctly, some things need to be centralized, some distributed, and some local. Reasonable ground rules and "good citizen" guidelines need to be formulated and agreed on.

A typical environment includes:

- A backbone network among buildings
- Departmental subnets connected to the backbone
- Group subnets within a department
- Connections to the outside world (e.g., Internet or field offices)

Several facets of network design and implementation must have site-wide control, responsibility, maintenance, and financing. Networks with charge-back algorithms

---

9. Some cable manufacturers will prelabel spools of cable every few feet for you.

for each connection grow in very bizarre but predictable ways as departments try to minimize their own local costs. Prime targets for central control are:

- The network design, including the use of subnets, routers, switches, etc.
- The backbone cable itself, including the connections to it
- Host IP addresses, hostnames, and subdomain names
- Protocols, mostly to ensure that they interoperate
- Routing policy to the Internet

Domain names, IP addresses, and network names are in some sense already controlled centrally by authorities such as ARIN and ICANN. However, your site's use of these items must be coordinated locally as well.

A central authority has an overall view of the network: its design, capacity, and expected growth. It can afford to own monitoring equipment (and the staff to run it) and to keep the backbone network healthy. It can insist on correct network design, even when that means telling a department to buy a router and build a subnet to connect to the campus backbone network. Such a decision might be necessary so that a new connection does not adversely impact the existing network.

If a network serves many types of machines, operating systems, and protocols, it is almost essential to have a very smart router (e.g., Cisco) as a gateway between nets.

## 15.13  RECOMMENDED VENDORS

In the past 15+ years of installing networks around the world, we've gotten burned more than a few times by products that didn't quite meet specs or were misrepresented, overpriced, or otherwise failed to meet expectations. Below is a list of vendors in the United States that we still trust, recommend, and use ourselves today.

### Cables and connectors

AMP
P.O. Box 3608
Harrisburg, PA 17105
(800) 522-6752
www.amp.com

Anixter
4711 Golf Rd.
Skokie, IL 60076
(708) 677-2600
www.anixter.com

Belden Cable
P.O. Box 1980
Richmond, IN 47375
(319) 983-5200
www.belden.com

Lan-Tech
7808 Cherry Crk S. Dr. #209
Denver, CO 80231
(303) 695-9473
www.lantechinc.com

Newark Electronics
4801 N. Ravenswood Ave.
Chicago, IL 60640
(312) 784-5100
www.newark.com

The Siemon Company
76 Westbury Park Road
Watertown, CT 06795
(203) 274-2523
www.siemon.com

Krone
6950 S. Tucson Way
Englewood, CO 80112
(800) 992-9901
www.krone.com

Black Box Corporation
P.O. Box 12800
Pittsburgh, PA 15241
(412) 746-5500
www.blackbox.com

**Test equipment**

Wavetek
9045 Balboa Ave.
San Diego, CA 92123
(800) 854-2708
www.wavetek.com

The Siemon Company
76 Westbury Park Road
Watertown, CT 06795
(203) 274-2523
www.siemon.com

Fluke
P.O. Box 9090
Everett, WA 98206
(800) 323-5700
www.fluke.com

TTC
20400 Observation Drive
Germantown, Maryland 20876
(800) 638-2049
www.ttc.com

**Routers/switches**

Cisco Systems
PO Box 3075
1525 O'Brien Drive
Menlo Park, CA 94026-1435
(415) 326-1941
www.cisco.com

## 15.14  RECOMMENDED READING

GROTH, DAVID AND JIM MCBEE. *The Complete Guide to Network Wiring.* Sybex. 2000.

SEIFERT, RICH. *Gigabit Ethernet.* Reading, MA: Addison-Wesley. 1998.

ANSI/TIA/EIA-568-A, *Commercial Building Telecommunications Cabling Standard,* and ANSI/TIA/EIA-606, *Administration Standard for the Telecommunications Infrastructure of Commercial Buildings,* are the telecommunication industry's standards for building wiring. Unfortunately, they are not free. See www.tiaonline.org.

SPURGEON, CHARLES. "Guide to Ethernet."
http://wwwhost.ots.utexas.edu/ethernet/ethernet-home.html

# 16 *The Domain Name System*

Zillions of hosts are connected to the Internet. How do we keep track of them all when they belong to so many different countries, networks, and administrative groups? Two key pieces of infrastructure hold everything together: the Domain Name System (DNS), which keeps track of who the hosts are, and the Internet routing system, which keeps track of how they are connected.

This chapter is about the DNS portion of that system. Although DNS has come to serve several different purposes, its primary job is to map between hostnames and IP addresses. Users and user-level programs like to refer to machines by name, but low-level network software understands only numbers. DNS provides the glue that keeps everyone happy. It has also come to play an important role in the routing of email.

DNS is a distributed database. "Distributed" means that my site stores the data about its computers, your site stores the data about your computers, and somehow, our sites automatically cooperate and share data when one site needs to look up some of the other's data.

## 16.1 DNS FOR THE IMPATIENT: ADDING A NEW MACHINE

This chapter is almost a mini-book in itself. Before we dive into its mind-numbing depths, let's take a quick breather to answer the most common DNS question: How do you add a new host to a network that's already using DNS? The following recipe shows you how to do it by copying and modifying the existing records for a similar computer—templatehost.my.domain.

**Step 1:** Choose a hostname and IP address for the new machine in conjunction with local sysadmins or your upstream ISP (Internet service provider).

**Step 2:** Identify a similar machine on the same subnet. We'll use that machine's records as a model for our new ones.

**Step 3:** Log in to the master name server machine.

**Step 4:** Look through **/etc/named.conf** or **/etc/namedb/named.conf**:

- From the options statement, find the directory line that tells where zone data files are kept at your site (see page 418). The zone files contain the actual host and IP address data.

- From the zone statements, find the filenames for the forward zone file and for the reverse zone file of the network your new IP address is on (page 424).

**Step 5:** Go to the zone file directory and edit the forward zone file (using RCS and **sudo**, of course). Find the records for the template host you identified earlier. They'll look something like this:

```
templatehost      IN    A     128.138.243.100
                  IN    MX    10  mail-hub
                  IN    MX    20  templatehost
```

**Step 6:** Duplicate those records and change them appropriately for your new host. The zone file might be sorted by hostname; follow the existing convention. Also change the serial number in the SOA record at the beginning of the file (it's the first of the five numbers in the SOA record). The serial number should only increase; add 1 if your site uses an arbitrary serial number, or set the field to the current date if your site uses that convention.

**Step 7:** Edit the reverse zone file,[1] duplicate the record for the template host, and update it. It should look something like this:

```
100                  IN    PTR   templatehost.my.domain.
```

You must also update the serial number in the SOA record of the reverse zone file.

If your reverse zone file shows more than just the last byte of each host's IP address, you must enter the bytes in reverse order. For example, the record

```
100.243              IN    PTR   templatehost.my.domain.
```

corresponds to the IP address 128.138.243.100 (here, the reverse zone is relative to 138.128.in-addr.arpa rather than 243.138.128.in-addr.arpa).

**Step 8:** While still logged in to the master name server machine, run **ndc reload**.[2]

---

1. The reverse zone might be maintained elsewhere (e.g., at your ISP's site). If so, the reverse entry will have to be entered there.

2. Versions of Solaris prior to Solaris 8 did not include the **ndc** command, so unless your site installed **ndc** from the BIND distribution, you will have to send **named** a HUP signal to initiate a reload.

**Step 9:** Try to **ping** or **traceroute** to your new host's name, even if the new host has not been set up yet. A "host unknown" message means you goofed; "host not responding" means that everything is probably OK. You can also check the configuration with **dig**; see page 475.

## 16.2  THE HISTORY OF DNS

In the good old days, the mapping between hostnames and addresses was kept in a single text file that was managed centrally and distributed to all the hosts on the ARPANET. Hostnames were not hierarchical, and the procedure for naming a computer included verifying that no one else in the world had taken the name you wanted. Updates consumed a large portion of the ARPANET's bandwidth, and the file was constantly out of date.

It soon became clear that although a static host table was reasonable for a small network, it was inadequate for the large and growing ARPANET. DNS solves the problems of a static table by using two key concepts: hierarchical hostnames and distributed responsibility. DNS was formally specified by Paul Mockapetris in RFCs 882 and 883 (1983) and updated in RFCs 1034 and 1035 (1987). Paul also wrote an early non-UNIX implementation.

The original UNIX work was done by four graduate students at Berkeley (Douglas Terry, Mark Painter, David Riggle, and Songnian Zhou) in 1984. It was then picked up by Ralph Campbell of Berkeley's Computer Systems Research Group, who started gluing it into BSD. In 1985, Kevin Dunlap, a DEC engineer on loan to Berkeley, took over the project and produced BIND, the Berkeley Internet Name Domain system. Mike Karels, Phil Almquist, and Paul Vixie have maintained BIND over the years. It is shipped with most vendors' UNIX systems and is also available from www.isc.org.

ISC, the Internet Software Consortium, is a nonprofit organization that maintains several crucial pieces of Internet software, including BIND. Paul Vixie currently maintains the BIND 8 code tree on ISC's behalf with help from folks on the bind-workers mailing list. ISC is developing BIND 9 with funding from several vendors, government agencies, and other organizations.

ISC also provides various types of support for these products, including help with configuration and even custom programming. These services are a boon for sites that must have a support contract before they can use open source software. Several companies use service contracts as a way to contribute to the ISC—they buy expensive contracts but never call for help.

RFCs 1034 and 1035 are still considered the baseline specification for DNS, but more than 30 other RFCs have superseded and elaborated upon various aspects of the protocol and data records over the last decade (see the list at the end of this chapter). Currently, no single standard or RFC brings all the pieces together in one place. Historically, DNS has more or less been defined as "what BIND implements," though this is becoming less accurate as other DNS servers emerge.

Although DNS has been implemented on non-UNIX operating systems, this book discusses only BIND. Nortel ported BIND to Windows NT and contributed the port back to ISC; since then, BIND version 8.2 has been available for NT, too. Thanks to the standardization of the DNS protocol, UNIX and non-UNIX DNS implementations can interoperate and share data. Many sites run UNIX servers to provide DNS service to their Windows desktops; the combination works well.

## 16.3  WHO NEEDS DNS?

DNS defines:

- A hierarchical namespace for hosts and IP addresses
- A host table implemented as a distributed database
- A "resolver" – library routines that query this database
- Improved routing for email
- A mechanism for finding services on a network
- A protocol for exchanging naming information

To be full citizens of the Internet, sites need DNS. Maintaining a local **/etc/hosts** file with mappings for every host your users might ever want to contact is not feasible.

Each site maintains one or more pieces of the distributed database that makes up the world-wide DNS system. Your piece of the database consists of two or more text files that contain records for each of your hosts. Each record is a single line consisting of a name (usually a hostname), a record type, and some data values.

For example, the lines

```
forklift        IN   A     192.108.21.7
                IN   MX    10 chimchim.xor.com.
```

in the "forward" file, and

```
7               IN   PTR   forklift.xor.com.
```

in the "reverse" file associate "forklift.xor.com" with the IP address 192.108.21.7.

DNS is a client/server system. Servers ("name servers") load the data from your DNS files into memory and use it to answer queries both from internal clients and from clients and other servers out on the Internet. All of your hosts should be DNS clients, but relatively few need to be DNS servers.

If your organization is small (a few hosts on a single network), you can run a server on one host or ask your ISP to supply DNS service on your behalf. A medium-sized site with several subnets should run multiple DNS servers to reduce query latency and improve reliability. A very large site can divide its DNS domain into subdomains and run several servers for each subdomain.

## 16.4 What's new in DNS

Several significant changes have been made to DNS over the last few years. This section gives you the flavor of the major changes and a road map to the places where they are covered in more detail.

Both DNS and BIND are constantly being updated. DNS has new types of resource records, new protocol tweaks, and some new features. BIND has been redesigned and rewritten with support for multithreading and multiprocessor systems. Table 16.1 lists the major changes.

**Table 16.1   New features in DNS and BIND**

| Page | RFCs | Feature |
|------|------|---------|
| 448 | 2052 | SRV records for the location of services |
| 450 | – | A6 records for IPv6 addresses |
| 451 | 2672–3 | DNAME records for IPv6 address lookup redirection |
| 445 | 2317 | Classless in-addr delegation (the CNAME hack) |
| 451[a] | – | The ip6.arpa domain for reverse IPv6 mappings |
| –[a] | – | An IPv6-aware resolver |
| 410 | 2671 | EDNS0, protocol changes and extensions |
| 418 | 1996 | Asynchronous notification of zone changes |
| 459 | 2136 | Dynamic update (for sites that use DHCP) |
| 458 | 1995 | Incremental zone transfers |
| 464 | 2535–41 | DNSSEC, authentication and security for zone data |
| 462 | 2845 | TSIG/TKEY transaction signatures and keys |

a. Not covered in this book, or in the case of ip6.arpa, not covered in much detail

Some of these new features are enormous projects that the IETF has not yet finished standardizing. The working groups that are writing the standards have good writers but lack vigilant code warriors; some of the more recent specifications may be difficult or even impossible to implement. The current release of BIND (8.2.2-P5) includes some of the new features; the initial release of BIND 9 (9.0.0) includes almost all of them, but not necessarily in their final form.

*IPv6 is described in more detail in Chapter 13.*

Two massive new features, IPv6 support and DNSSEC, warrant a bit of commentary. IPv6 increases the length of IP addresses from 32 bits to 128 bits. If ever fully implemented, it will have an enormous impact on the Internet. BIND 9 supports the pieces of IPv6 that have been standardized so far, but it appears unlikely that IPv6 will be widely deployed during the lifetime of this book. Therefore, our coverage of BIND 9's IPv6 support is brief. There's enough in this chapter to give you the general flavor, but not enough to let you migrate your site to IPv6 and configure DNS for it.

The DNSSEC standard attempts to add authentication to the DNS database and its servers. It uses public key cryptography to verify the source and integrity of DNS data and uses DNS to distribute keys as well as host data.

Simpler authentication mechanisms have also been introduced, such as support for authentication through the use of a "shared secret." However, the shared secret must be distributed to each pair of servers that wants to perform mutual authentication. Although that's fine for a local site with a handful of servers, it doesn't scale to the level of the Internet. BIND 9 implements both the DNSSEC public key system and the TSIG (transaction signatures) shared secret system.

We expect to see some form of authentication used extensively in the next few years, starting with the root zones. Experiments have shown that some top-level zones (e.g., nl and de) can be signed in a few hours, but that to sign com with current (circa 2000) technology would take months. Since com is currently updated twice a day, signing that takes months won't work. Security attacks against the integrity of DNS will no doubt hasten the adoption of authentication measures.

## 16.5 THE DNS NAMESPACE

In the sections that follow, we first discuss the general anatomy of DNS (the specification) and then describe the configuration files used by BIND (the implementation). If you are familiar with DNS and want to get right to the meat of the chapter, skip ahead to *BIND client issues* on page 410 or *BIND server configuration* on page 414.

In the real world and elsewhere in this book, you will see the terms DNS and BIND used interchangeably. However, in this chapter we attempt (perhaps unsuccessfully) to preserve the distinction between them.

The DNS namespace is a tree of "domains." Each domain represents a distinct chunk of the namespace and is loosely managed by a single administrative entity. The root of the tree is called "." or dot, and beneath it are the top-level (or root-level) domains. The top-level domains have been relatively fixed in the past, but ICANN[3] has been considering the creation of some new ones.

One branch of the naming tree maps hostnames to IP addresses, and a second branch maps IP addresses back to hostnames. The former branch is called the "forward mapping," and the BIND data files associated with it are called "forward zone files." The address-to-hostname branch is the "reverse mapping," and its data files are called "reverse zone files."

For historical reasons, two sorts of top-level domain names are in current use. In the United States, top-level domains originally described organizational and political structure and were given three-letter names such as com and edu. Some of these domains (primarily com, org, and net) are used outside the United States as well; they are called the generic top-level domains or gTLDs for short.

Table 16.2 lists the most important gTLDs along with their original purposes. Once good names in the com domain became scarce, the registries began to offer names in org and net without regard to those domains' original restrictions.

---

3. ICANN is the Internet Corporation for Assigned Names and Numbers, the governing body of the Internet. See page 263 for more information about ICANN.

**Table 16.2   Generic top-level domains**

| Domain | What it's for | Domain | What it's for |
|--------|---------------|--------|--------------|
| com | Commercial companies | net | Network providers |
| edu | Educational institutions | org | Nonprofit organizations |
| gov | Government agencies | int | International organizations |
| mil | Military agencies | arpa | Anchor for IP address tree |

For most domains outside the United States, two-letter ISO country codes are used; they are called ccTLDs. Both the geographical and the organizational TLDs coexist within the same global namespace. Table 16.3 shows some common country codes.

**Table 16.3   Common country codes**

| Code | Country | Code | Country | Code | Country |
|------|---------|------|---------|------|---------|
| au | Australia | fi | Finland | hk | Hong Kong |
| ca | Canada | fr | France | ch | Switzerland |
| br | Brazil | jp | Japan | mx | Mexico |
| de | Germany | se | Sweden | hu | Hungary |

Some countries outside the United States build an organizational hierarchy with second-level domains. Naming conventions vary. For example, an academic institution might be an edu in the United States and an ac.jp in Japan.

The top-level domain "us" is also sometimes used in the United States, primarily with locality domains; for example, bvsd.k12.co.us, the Boulder Valley School District in Colorado. The "us" domain is never combined with an organizational domain—there is no "edu.us" (yet). The advantage of "us" domain names is that they are free or inexpensive to register; see www.nic.us for more details.

Domain mercenaries have in some cases bought an entire country's namespace. For example, the domain for Moldovia, "md", is now being marketed to doctors and residents of the state of Maryland (MD) in the United States. Another example is Tuvalu, for which the country code is "tv". The first such sale was Tonga ("to"), the most active is currently Niue ("nu"), and perhaps the most attractive is "tm" from Turkmenistan. These deals have sometimes been fair to the country with the desirable two-letter code and sometimes not.

Domain squatting is also widely practiced: folks register names they think will be requested in the future and then resell them to the businesses whose names they have snitched. Years ago, all the Colorado ski areas were registered to the same individual, who made quite a bit of money reselling them to individual ski areas as they became web-aware. The going rate for a good name in the com domain is between several thousand and a few million dollars—business.com sold recently for $3.5M. We were offered $50,000 for the name admin.com, which we obtained years ago when sysadmin.com had already been taken by /Sys/Admin magazine.

Domain names are case insensitive. "Colorado" is the same as "colorado", which is the same as "COLORADO" as far as DNS is concerned. Current DNS implementations must ignore case when making comparisons, but propagate case when it is supplied. In the past it was common to use capital letters for top-level domains and an initial capital for second-level domains. These days, fingers are weary from typing and all-lowercase is the norm.

Two new features of DNS collide with respect to case sensitivity: internationalization of names and DNSSEC security. Internationalized names require case to be significant and preserved, but DNSSEC maps all names to lower case before computing cryptographic signatures. It's likely that DNS will canonicalize names to lower case internally for its cryptographic computations but send the actual data with case preserved. Any international encoding will have to include canonicalization rules. With luck, the IETF standards folks will sort out these issues before either new feature is in widespread use.

An Internet host's fully qualified name is formed by appending its domain name to its hostname. For example, boulder.colorado.edu is the fully qualified name for the host boulder at the University of Colorado. Other sites can use the hostname boulder without colliding because the fully qualified names will be different.

Within the DNS system, fully qualified names are terminated by a dot, for example, "boulder.colorado.edu.". The lack of a final dot indicates a relative address. Depending on the context in which a relative address is used, additional components might be added. The final dot convention is generally hidden from everyday users of DNS. In fact, some systems (such as mail) will break if you supply the dot yourself.

It's common for a host to have more than one name. The host boulder.colorado.edu could also be known as www.colorado.edu or ftp.colorado.edu if we wanted to make its name reflect the services it provides. In fact, it's a good practice to make service hostnames such as www be "mobile," so that you can move servers from one machine to another without changing any machine's primary name.

When we were issued the name colorado.edu, we were guaranteed that colorado was unique within the edu domain. We have further divided that domain into subdomains along department lines. For example, the host anchor in the computer science department is called anchor.cs.colorado.edu on the Internet.

The creation of each new subdomain must be coordinated with the administrators of the domain above to guarantee uniqueness. Entries in the configuration files for the parent domain delegate authority for the namespace to the subdomain.

### Masters of their domains

Management of the top-level domains com, org, net, and edu was formerly coordinated by Network Solutions, Inc., under contract with the National Science Foundation. This monopoly situation has now changed, and other organizations are allowed to register domain names in those gTLDs. Other top-level domains, such as those for individual countries, are maintained by regional organizations.

There have been various proposals to allow private companies to operate their own top-level domains, and it is likely that additional top-level domains will be available in the near future. Consult www.icann.org for up-to-date information.

Most ISPs offer fee-based domain name registration services. They deal with the top-level domain authority on your behalf and configure their DNS servers to handle name lookups within your domain. Although you can reduce direct expenses by dealing directly with the registrars and running your own DNS servers, you will not necessarily save money. The disadvantage of relying on an ISP's servers is that you lose direct control over the administration of your domain.

*See page 276 for more information about CIDR.*

Even if you want to manage your own DNS services, you must still coordinate with your ISP. Most ISPs supply reverse DNS mappings for IP addresses within their CIDR blocks. If you take over DNS management of your addresses, make sure that your ISP disables its service for those addresses and delegates that responsibility to you.

A domain's forward and reverse mappings should be managed in the same place whenever possible. Some ISPs are happy to let you manage the forward files but are reluctant to relinquish control of the reverse mappings. Such split management can lead to synchronization problems. See page 445 for an elegant hack that makes delegation work even for tiny pieces of address space.

DNS domains should (must, in fact; see RFC1219) be served by at least two servers. One common arrangement is for a site to operate its own master server and to let the ISP's servers act as a backup. Once the system has been configured, the ISP's servers automatically download their configuration information from your master server. Changes made to the DNS configuration are reflected on the backup servers without any explicit work on the part of either site's administrator.

### Selecting a domain name

Certain names are taboo; for example, names that are already taken. Others that used to be off-limits have recently been allowed, such as combinations of top-level domains (edu.com[4]) and domains that contain a repeating component (x.x.com[5]).

Our advice in the second edition of this book was that names should be short and easy to type and that they should identify the organization that uses them. These days, the reality is that all the good, short names have been taken, at least in the com domain. It's tempting to blame this state of affairs on squatters, but in fact most of the good names are in actual use.

RFC1032 recommends that the names of second-level domains be no longer than 12 characters, but DNS actually allows up to 63 characters in each component and up to 255 characters in a complete name. The 12-character suggestion is often ignored, and there is no real reason to adhere to it other than to relieve the tedium of typing longer names.

---

4. However, names like edu.com break many versions of BIND.

5. Not all names with repeated components were illegal. For example, xinet.xinet.com was always a valid name. The domain part is xinet.com and the domain contains a host called xinet.

### Domain bloat

DNS was designed to map an organization's domain name to a name server for that organization. In that mode it needs to scale to the number of organizations in the world. Now that the Internet has become a conduit of mass culture, however, domain names are being applied to every product, movie, sporting event, English noun, etc. Domain names such as twinkies.com are not (directly) related to the company that makes the product; they're simply being used as advertisements. It's not clear that DNS can continue to scale in this way. The real problem here is that the DNS naming tree is an efficient data structure only when it has some hierarchy and is not totally flat. With each organization naming hundreds or thousands of products at the top level of the tree, hierarchy is doomed.

What we really need is a directory service that maps brand and marketing names to organizations, leaving DNS free to deal with IP addresses. The beginnings of this idea are implemented in most modern web browsers through a service provided by the RealNames Corporation. Unfortunately, RealNames is a proprietary monopoly; only organizations that subscribe and pay a fee can have their keywords listed in the database. Another possible solution is to enforce hierarchy in the system; for example, twinkies.hostess-foods.com. But this will never happen—we've already gone too far down the marketing-domain-name.com path.

Sony does things the right way from DNS's perspective—all of its products are subdomains of sony.com. It might take an extra click or two to find the products you want, but DNS appreciates the hierarchy.

### Registering a second-level domain name

To obtain a second-level domain name, you must apply to the authority for the appropriate top-level domain. ICANN is currently accrediting various agencies to be part of its shared registry project for registering names in the gTLDs. As of this writing, you have something like 25 choices of registrar, with about 80 others in various stages of the approval process. Check www.icann.org for the definitive list.

In Europe, contact the Council of European National Top-level Domain Registries at www.centr.org to identify your local registry and apply for a domain name. For the Asia-Pacific region, the appropriate body is the Asia-Pacific Network Information Center, www.apnic.net.

To complete the domain registration forms, you must identify a technical contact person, an administrative contact person, and at least two hosts that will be servers for your domain. You'll also have to choose a name that is not already taken.

### Creating your own subdomains

The procedure for creating a subdomain is similar to that for creating a second-level domain, except that the central authority is now local (or more accurately, within your own organization). Specifically, the steps are as follows.

- Choose a name that is unique in the local context.
- Identify two or more hosts to be servers for your new domain.
- Coordinate with the administrator of the parent domain.

Parent domains should check to be sure that a child domain's name servers are up and running before performing the delegation. If the servers are not working, a "lame delegation" results, and you might receive nasty email asking you to clean up your DNS act. Page 478 covers lame delegations in more detail.

## 16.6  THE BIND SOFTWARE

BIND, the Berkeley Internet Name Domain system, is an open source software package from ISC that implements the DNS protocol and provides name service on UNIX systems (and now, on Windows NT).

### Versions of BIND

There have been three main flavors of BIND: BIND 4, BIND 8, and BIND 9. BIND 4 has been around since the late 1980s (roughly corresponding to the release of RFCs 1034 and 1035). BIND 8 was released in 1997, and BIND 9 in mid-2000. There is no BIND 5, 6, or 7; BIND 8 was such a significant update that the authors felt it merited a version number twice as big as the old one.[6] Well, not really … BIND 8 was released with 4.4BSD, for which all version numbers were raised to 8. **sendmail** also skipped a few numbers and went to version 8 at the same time.

BIND 8 incorporated numerous technical advances that improved efficiency, robustness, and security. BIND 9 raises the ante even further with multiprocessor support, thread-safe operation, real security (public key cryptography), IPv6 support, incremental zone transfers, and a host of other features. A new data structure (at least, new to BIND), the red-black tree, stores zone data in memory. BIND 9 is a complete redesign and reimplementation. It isolates the OS-specific parts of the code, making it easier to port BIND to non-UNIX systems. The internals of BIND 9 are significantly different, but its configuration procedure remains the same.

BIND 4 is only maintained with respect to security patches, and it will soon be discontinued. It is expected that a year or two after BIND 9 is stable and in common use, BIND 8 will be discontinued as well. We were tempted to cover only BIND 9 in this book, but since V9's configuration language is a superset of V8's and since we don't yet have much operational experience with V9, we cover both.

Many sites postpone upgrading because they are hesitant to mess with working code. If you are still using BIND 4, the Perl script **named-bootconf.pl** that ships with the V8 and V9 distributions can convert a V4 configuration file to its V8 or V9 equivalent. The actual database of DNS records does not need to change. A configuration file converted from version 4 will not use any of the new BIND 8 and BIND 9 features, but it should provide a good starting point for you to expand upon.

---

6. Who says marketing and engineering can't get along?

**Finding out what version you have**

It often doesn't seem to occur to vendors to document which version of an external software package they have included with their systems, so you might have to do some sleuthing to find out exactly what software you are dealing with. In the case of BIND, you can sometimes determine the version number with a sneaky query from **dig**, a command that comes with BIND. The command

> **dig @***server* **version.bind txt chaos**

returns the version number unless someone has decided to withhold that information by changing it in the config file. For example, the command works on vix.com:

```
% dig @bb.rc.vix.com version.bind txt chaos
VERSION.BIND.  0S CHAOS TXT "8.2.3-T4B"
```

but not on cs.colorado.edu:

```
% dig @mroe.cs.colorado.edu version.bind txt chaos
VERSION.BIND.  0S CHAOS TXT "wouldn't you like to know..."
```

Some sites configure BIND to conceal its version number on the theory that this provides some degree of "security through obscurity." We don't really endorse this practice, but it might help fend off some of the script kiddies. See page 417 for a more detailed discussion of this topic.

*See Chapter 11 for more information about syslog.*

You can also usually tell what BIND version you have by inspecting the log files in **/var/log** or its equivalent on your system. The BIND server daemon, **named**, logs its version number to syslog (facility "daemon") as it starts up. **grep** for lines like these:

```
Dec 13 16:32:27 disaster named[2399]: starting.  named 4.9.7 Wed Sep  2 09:39:
    12 GMT 1998 PHNE_14618
Dec 13 16:35:13 suod named[9325]: starting.  named 8.2.2-P3 Wed Nov 10 17:
    27:59 MST 1999  millert@haxrus /nfs/depot/src/cs/Bind/bind-8.2.2-
    P3/obj/sun4+SunOS4/bin/named
```

The first line is from HP-UX 11.00 as it is shipped, and the second is from a SunOS machine as we maintain it locally. The last line lies a bit since patch 4 for BIND 8.2.2 didn't increment the patch level. It is really 8.2.2-P4.

If **named** is installed but your system does not normally start it at boot time, just run it by hand as root with no arguments. **named** will log its version number, realize that it has no configuration file, and exit.

Table 16.4 on the next page shows the versions of BIND that are included with our example systems. Versions less than 8.2.2-P3 have known security problems.

 Red Hat has been known to freeze version numbers, then install patches, thus putting themselves out of sync with the rest of the community. Ergo, their 8.2 might be OK, although it violates the 8.2.2-P3 warning above. Red Hat's internal version numbers are included in the names of package files and sometimes have an internal bug fix number or patch number appended. For example, **bind-8.2-7.arch.rpm** is Red Hat's version 7 of isc.org's version 8.2. Confusing.

**Table 16.4    Versions of BIND on our example systems**

| System | OS version | BIND version |
|--------|-----------|--------------|
| Solaris | 7 or 8 | 8.1.2 |
| HP-UX | 11.00 | 4.9.7 |
| Red Hat Linux | 6.1 | 8.2 |
| | 6.2 | 8.2.2-P5 |
| FreeBSD | 3.4 or 4.0 | 8.2.2-P5 |

## Components of BIND

The BIND system has three components:

- A daemon called **named** that answers queries
- Library routines that resolve host queries by contacting the servers of the DNS distributed database
- Command-line interfaces to DNS: **nslookup**, **dig**, and **host**

In DNS parlance, a daemon like **named** (or the machine on which it runs) is called a "name server," and the client code that contacts it is called a "resolver." We briefly discuss the function of each component below but postpone the actual configuration of BIND until page 410.

### named: the BIND name server

**named** answers queries about hostnames and IP addresses. If **named** doesn't know the answer to a query, it asks other servers and caches their responses. **named** also performs "zone transfers" to copy data among the servers of a domain. (A "zone" is a domain minus its subdomains. Name servers deal with zones, but "domain" is often used where "zone" is really meant.)

Name servers can operate in several different modes. The distinctions among them fall along several axes, so the final categorization is often not very tidy. To make things even more confusing, a single server can play different roles with respect to different zones. Table 16.5 lists some of the adjectives used to describe name servers. Indented entries are loosely classified under their unindented headings.

These categorizations are based on a name server's source of data (authoritative, caching, master, slave), on the type of data saved (stub), on the query path (forwarders), on the type of answers handed out (recursive, nonrecursive), and finally, on the visibility of the server (distribution). The next few sections provide some additional details on the most important of these distinctions; the other distinctions are described elsewhere in this chapter.

### Authoritative and caching-only servers

Master, slave, and caching-only servers are distinguished by two characteristics: where the data comes from and whether the server is authoritative for the domain.

**Table 16.5    A name server taxonomy**

| Type of server | Description |
| --- | --- |
| authoritative | An official representative of a zone |
|    master | The primary repository of a zone's data; gets data from a disk file |
|    slave | Copies its data from the master |
|    stub | Similar to a slave, but copies only name server data (not host data) |
|    distribution | A server that's visible[a] only inside a domain; (aka "stealth server") |
| nonauthoritative[b] | Answers a query from cache; doesn't know if the data is still valid |
|    caching | Caches data from previous queries; usually has no local zones |
|    forwarder | Performs queries on behalf of many clients; builds a large cache |
| recursive | Queries on your behalf until it returns either an answer or an error |
| nonrecursive | Refers you to another server if it can't answer a query |

a. A distribution server can be visible to anyone who knows its IP address.
b. Strictly speaking, "nonauthoritative" is an attribute of a DNS query response, not a server.

Each zone has one master name server. The master server keeps the official copy of the zone's data on disk. The system administrator changes the zone's data by editing the master server's data files.

*See page 458 for more information about zone transfers.*

A slave server gets its data from the master server through a "zone transfer" operation. A zone can have several slave name servers and *must* have at least one. A stub server is a special kind of slave that loads only the NS (name server) records from the master. See page 456 for an explanation of why you might want this behavior. It's fine for the same machine to be both a master server for your zones and a slave server for other zones. Such cooperation usually makes for good DNS neighbors.

A caching-only name server loads the addresses of the servers for the root domain from a startup file and accumulates the rest of its data by caching answers to the queries it resolves. A caching-only name server has no data of its own and is not authoritative for any zone. See *A university department* on page 431 for an example of a caching-only configuration.

An authoritative answer from a name server is "guaranteed" to be accurate; a nonauthoritative answer might be out of date. However, a very high percentage of nonauthoritative answers are perfectly correct. Master and slave servers are authoritative for their own zones, but not for information they have cached about other domains. Truth be told, even authoritative answers can be inaccurate if a sysadmin changes the master server's data and forgets to update the serial number of its data or run **ndc reload** (or if the changes have not yet propagated to slave servers).

The master server should be located on a machine that is stable, does not have many users, is relatively secure, and perhaps is on an uninterruptible power supply. There should be at least two slaves, one of which is off-site. On-site slaves should live on different networks and different power circuits. When name service stops, all normal network access stops, too.

A domain's zone data normally includes the identities of the name servers of all of its subdomains. This name server chaining enables DNS clients to walk down the domain tree to look up any host on the Internet. If a parent domain does not mention certain name servers of a subdomain, those servers become "internal" servers and are not accessible from the outside world.

Although they are not authoritative, caching-only servers can reduce the latency seen by your users and the amount of DNS traffic on your internal networks. Consider putting a caching-only server on each subnet. At most sites, desktop machines typically go through a caching server to resolve queries about hosts on the Internet.

In BIND 4 and BIND 8, it wasn't a good idea to use a single name server as an authoritative server for some zones and as a caching server for others. Each **named** ran with a single in-memory database, and cross-contamination could occur if memory was tight and cached data mixed with authoritative data. BIND 9 has eliminated this problem, so mix away.

### Recursive and nonrecursive servers

Name servers are either recursive or nonrecursive. If a nonrecursive server has the answer to a query cached from a previous transaction or is authoritative for the domain to which the query pertains, it provides an appropriate response. Otherwise, instead of returning a real answer, it returns a referral to the authoritative servers of another domain that are more likely to know the answer. A client of a nonrecursive server must be prepared to accept and act on referrals.

Although nonrecursive servers may seem lazy, they usually have good reason not to take on extra work. Root servers and top-level domain servers are all nonrecursive, but at 10,000 queries per second we can excuse them for cutting corners.

A recursive server returns only real answers or error messages. It follows referrals itself, relieving the client of this responsibility. The basic procedure for resolving a query is essentially the same; the only difference is that the name server takes care of handling referrals rather than passing them back to the client.

The resolver libraries that come with most versions of UNIX do not understand referrals; they expect the local name server to be recursive.

One side effect of having a name server follow referrals is that its cache acquires information about intermediate domains. On a local network this caching is often the behavior you want, since it allows subsequent lookups from any host on the network to benefit from the name server's previous work. On the other hand, the server for a high-level domain such as com or edu should not save up information requested by a host several domains below it.

Early versions of BIND required source code changes and recompilation to modify a server's recursiveness. This option then moved to a command-line flag (**-r**), and it is now a parameter in the configuration file. A server can even be configured to be recursive for its own clients and nonrecursive for outsiders.

Name servers generate referrals hierarchically. For example, if a server can't supply an address for the host lair.cs.colorado.edu, it refers to the servers for cs.colorado.edu, colorado.edu, edu, or the root domain. A referral must include addresses for the servers of the referred-to domain, so the choice is not arbitrary; the server must refer to a domain for which it already knows the servers.

The longest known domain is generally returned. If the address of lair was not known but the name servers for cs.colorado.edu were known, then those servers' address would be returned. If cs.colorado.edu was unknown but colorado.edu was known, then the addresses of name servers for colorado.edu would be returned, and so on.

Name servers preload their caches from a "hints" file that lists the servers for the root domain. Some referral can always be made, even if it's just "Go ask a root server."

### The resolver library

Clients look up hostname mappings by calling the **gethostbyname** family of library routines. The original implementation of **gethostbyname** looked up names in the **/etc/hosts** file. For host mappings to be provided by DNS, these routines must use the resolver library, which knows how to locate and communicate with name servers. All modern versions of UNIX have integrated the resolver into the standard libraries.

Most systems' implementations of **gethostbyname** can draw upon information from several different sources: flat files (such as **/etc/hosts**), DNS, and perhaps a local administrative database system such as NIS or NIS+. Some systems allow for detailed administrative control over which sources are searched and in what order. See *Prioritizing sources of administrative information* on page 523 for specifics. The vendor-specific sections of this chapter present bite-sized treatments of this topic as it pertains to host lookups; they start on page 481.

### Shell interfaces to DNS

The BIND software distribution includes the **dig** and **nslookup** commands, both of which provide a command-line interface for executing DNS queries. They are useful as debugging aids and as tools for extracting information from DNS. Although the commands are similar in function, they are somewhat different in design. See page 475 for more information.

## 16.7  HOW DNS WORKS

Each host that uses DNS is either a client of the system or simultaneously a client and a server. If you do not plan to run any DNS servers, it's not essential that you read the next few sections (skip ahead to *Resolver configuration on page 411*). However, they will help you develop a more solid understanding of the architecture of DNS.

### Delegation

All name servers know about the root servers. The root servers in turn know about com, org, edu, fi, de, and other top-level domains. Farther down the chain, edu knows about colorado.edu, com knows about admin.com, and so on. Each zone can delegate authority over its subdomains to other servers.

Let's inspect a real example. Suppose we want to look up the address for the machine vangogh.cs.berkeley.edu from the machine lair.cs.colorado.edu. The host lair asks its local name server, ns.cs.colorado.edu, to figure out the answer. Exhibit A illustrates the subsequent events. We used relative names to reduce clutter and to make the labels more readable. The numbers on the arrows between servers show the order of events, and a letter indicates the type of transaction (query, referral, or answer). We assume that none of the required information was cached before the query, except for the names and IP addresses of the servers of the root domain.

**Exhibit A   DNS query process**

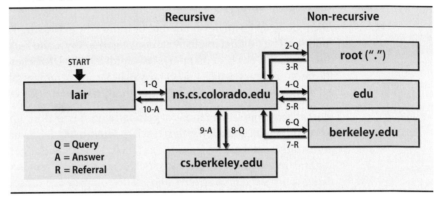

The local name server doesn't know the address; furthermore, it doesn't know anything about cs.berkeley.edu or berkeley.edu or even edu. It does know some servers for the root domain, however, and since it is a recursive server, it queries a root server about vangogh.cs.berkeley.edu.

Root servers used to contain data for both the root zones and for the gTLDs, but these days the gTLDs have their own servers. In answer to our root-server query about vangogh.cs.berkeley.edu, we receive a referral to the servers for the edu domain.

The local name server then sends its query to an edu server (asking, as always, about vangogh.cs.berkeley.edu) and gets back a referral to the servers for berkeley.edu. It then repeats the query in the berkeley.edu domain. If the Berkeley server is not recursive and doesn't have the answer cached, it returns a referral to cs.berkeley.edu. The cs.berkeley.edu server is authoritative for the requested information and returns vangogh's address.

When the dust settles, ns.cs.colorado.edu has cached vangogh's address. It has also cached lists of servers for edu, berkeley.edu, and cs.berkeley.edu.

**named** queries use the UDP protocol and port 53. Responses come back via UDP unless they are longer than 512 bytes, in which case they use TCP. Zone transfers between servers always use TCP.

## Caching and efficiency

Caching increases the efficiency of lookups: a cached answer is almost free and is usually correct, because mappings change infrequently. Most queries are for local hosts and can be resolved quickly. Users also inadvertently help with efficiency because they repeat many queries.

For a long time, caching was only applied to positive answers. If a host's name or address could not be found, that fact was not saved. A scheme for negative DNS caching was described in RFC1034, but it was incomplete and was not implemented in most versions of BIND. In 1998, RFC2308 defined an updated scheme for negative caching. This scheme was implemented in BIND 8.2 as an optional feature; it is mandatory in BIND 9.

One measurement at the RIPE root server in Europe showed that 60% of DNS queries were for nonexistent data (many queries were for 127.in-addr.arpa or for Microsoft services as hostnames). Caching this information further down the DNS tree should dramatically reduce the load on the root servers.

Negative caching saves answers of the following types:

- No host or domain matches the name queried.
- The type of data requested does not exist for this host.
- The server to ask is not responding.
- The server is unreachable because of network problems.

The first two types of negative data are cached for 1–3 hours, and the other types are cached for 5 minutes. Nonauthoritative answers *may* be cached; authoritative negative answers *must* be cached.

**named** often receives multiple DNS records in response to a query. For example, a query for the name servers of the root domain would receive a response that listed all 13 root servers. Which one should your server query?

When **named** must choose among several remote servers, all of which are authoritative for a domain, it first determines the network round trip time (RTT) to each server. It then sorts the servers into "buckets" according to their RTTs and selects a server from the fastest bucket. Servers within a bucket are treated as equals and are used in a round robin fashion.

You can achieve a primitive but effective form of load balancing by assigning a single hostname to several IP addresses (which in reality are different machines):

```
www          IN   A    192.168.0.1
             IN   A    192.168.0.2
             IN   A    192.168.0.3
```

Busy web servers such as Yahoo or AltaVista are not really a single machine. They're just a single name in DNS. A name server that has multiple records for the same name and record type returns all of them to the client, but in round robin order. For example, round robin order for the A records above would be 1, 2, 3 for the first query, 2, 3, 1 for the next, 3, 1, 2 for the third, and so on.

### The extended DNS protocol

The original DNS protocol definition dates from the late 1980s and uses both UDP and TCP. UDP is typically used for queries and responses, and TCP for zone transfers between master servers and slave servers. Unfortunately, the maximum packet size that's guaranteed to work in all UDP implementations is 512 bytes, which is much too small for some of the new DNS security features that must include digital signatures in each packet.

The 512-byte constraint also affects the number and names of the root servers. To make all root server data fit in a 512-byte UDP packet, the number of root servers is limited to 13, and each server is named with a single letter of the alphabet.

Many resolvers issue a UDP query first; then, if they receive a truncated response, they reissue the query over TCP. This procedure gets around the 512-byte limit, but it is inefficient. You might think that DNS should just bail on UDP and use TCP all the time, but TCP connections are much more expensive. A UDP name server exchange can be as short as two packets, one query and one response. A TCP exchange involves at least seven packets: a three-way handshake to initiate the conversation, a query, a response, and a final handshake to close the connection.

In the mid-1990s, the DNS protocol was amended to include incremental zone transfers (like a **diff** between old and new zone files, inspired by Larry Wall's **patch** program), asynchronous notifications (to tell slaves when the master's data files have been updated), and dynamic updates (for DHCP hosts). These changes added features but did not really address the fundamental transport problem.

In the late 1990s, EDNS0 (Extended DNS, version 0) addressed some of the shortcomings of the DNS protocol in today's Internet. It lets speakers advertise their reassembly buffer size, supported options, and protocol versions spoken. If the receiving name server responds with an error message, the sender drops back to the original DNS protocol. BIND 9 implements EDNS0 in both the server and the resolver.

## 16.8  BIND CLIENT ISSUES

*See Chapter 18 for more information about distributing files on a network.*

Before we dive into the configuration of BIND, let's outline the chores that are associated with using BIND on the Internet. Table 16.6 summarizes what must be done, for whom, and how often. An entry in the "How often" column that includes the word "distribute" means that you do it once per subnet or architecture and then copy the result to the appropriate hosts with a tool like **rdist** or **rsync**.

**Table 16.6    BIND installation and maintenance chores**

| Chore | For | How often |
|---|---|---|
| Obtain domain name | Site | Once |
| Choose name servers | Site | Once or more |
| Obtain BIND distribution | Site | Once, but keep current |
| Configure resolver | Client | Once and distribute |
| Configure efficient resolver | Client | Each subnet and distribute |
| Configure services switch | Client | Each architecture and distribute |
| Start **named** at boot time | Server | Each name server |
| Set up **named** config file | Server | Each type of server |
| Configure hints file | Server | Once[a] and distribute to servers |
| Configure zone files | Master | Once |
| Update zone files | Master | As needed |
| Review log files | Log host | At least weekly |
| Educate users | All hosts | Continuously |

a. But must be redone if the root servers change

Since each host on the network must be a BIND client, we begin our detailed discussion with client-side chores.

### Resolver configuration[7]

Each host on the network has a file called **/etc/resolv.conf** that lists the DNS servers the host should query. If your host gets its IP address and network parameters from a DHCP server, the **/etc/resolv.conf** file should be set up for you automatically. Otherwise, you must edit it by hand. The format is:

```
search domainname …
nameserver ipaddr
```

Up to three name servers can be listed. Here's a complete example:

```
search cs.colorado.edu colorado.edu ee.colorado.edu
nameserver 128.138.243.151    ; ns
nameserver 128.138.204.4      ; piper
nameserver 128.138.240.1      ; anchor
```

Comments were never defined for the **resolv.conf** file. They are somewhat supported in that anything that is not recognized is ignored. It's safe to put comments at the end of nameserver lines because the parser just looks for an IP address and ignores the rest of the line. Because the search line can contain multiple arguments, comments there could cause problems.

---

7. Many hosts have a "switch" file that specifies what sources of data should be used to implement name lookups. DNS will not be used on some systems (e.g., Solaris 7 and earlier) unless dns is added to the switch file; see the vendor-specific sections starting on page 481 for details.

The search line lists the domains to query if a hostname is not fully qualified. If a user issues the command **ssh foo**, for example, the resolver completes the name with the first domain in the search list (in the **resolv.conf** above, cs.colorado.edu) and looks for foo.cs.colorado.edu. If no such name can be found, the resolver also tries foo.colorado.edu and foo.ee.colorado.edu.

Users in our cs subdomain can use simple hostnames for any local host, but users in the parent domain must use *hostname*.cs to reach a host in the subdomain. If you create new subdomains, you will also have to reconfigure (educate) your users.

A search directive in the **resolv.conf** files of machines in the parent domain could allow simple hostnames to be used in both directions:

```
search colorado.edu. cs.colorado.edu. ee.colorado.edu.
```

Of course, this configuration assumes that hostnames are unique across the three domains. A search directive can specify up to eight domains.

The servers listed in **resolv.conf** must be recursive (since the resolver does not understand referrals), and they should each have a cache. If you are using BIND 4 or BIND 8, the servers should not be authoritative for any zones. Their caches can grow quite large, and since versions 4 and 8 do not manage the cache properly, it can take over the entire memory of the machine. If you must mix cached and authoritative data, see the listen-on configuration option for a way to do it safely by running two separate servers on the same machine that listen to different ports.

The servers in nameserver lines are contacted in order; as long as the first one continues to answer queries, the others will be ignored. If a problem occurs, the query times out and the next name server is tried. Each server is tried in turn, up to four times. The timeout interval increases with every failure.

Most resolvers allow a maximum of three name servers to be listed. If more are provided, they are silently ignored. If a host is itself a name server, it should be listed first in its own **resolv.conf** file.

Earlier versions of BIND used the domain directive in **resolv.conf** instead of the search directive. It specified a single domain to add to names that were not fully qualified. We recommend replacing domain directives with search directives. The two directives are mutually exclusive, so only one should be present. If you have an older resolver and include both directives in the **resolv.conf** file, the last one listed is used.

The default behavior of today's resolvers is a real hodgepodge. Some resolvers are more aggressive with default values than others. Some assume the local machine is a DNS server if no name servers are listed. Some deconstruct a local (fully qualified) hostname to come up with a search list. Some can operate with no **/etc/resolv.conf** file at all. Don't count on any of these misfeatures. Just configure **resolv.conf** normally for each of your hosts.

DNS queries arriving from the outside world will come to your authoritative name servers. It's a good idea to provide separate servers for resolving queries from inside your domain. Your internal servers should be caching-only and recursive. A large site should have several name servers running throughout the site and should customize the **resolv.conf** file to spread the load among the servers, minimize network traffic, and reduce the vulnerability of machines to a single point of failure. If name service is broken, your whole site grinds to a halt.

Forwarders are also a good way for a local site to optimize name service. Local name servers point to a forwarder that makes all the external queries for your site and builds a very rich cache. This configuration minimizes the external bandwidth used for name service and allows all local machines to share one large cache. Forwarders are covered in the configuration section starting on page 421.

Exhibit B illustrates the design recommended in the previous paragraphs. It shows a two-level forwarding hierarchy, which is overkill for small sites. Adjust the balance between servers that handle outgoing queries and servers that handle incoming queries so that neither group is too loaded. Also note the use of the off-site slave server, which is highly recommended if you can get an ISP or local university to fill this role.

**Exhibit B    DNS server architecture**

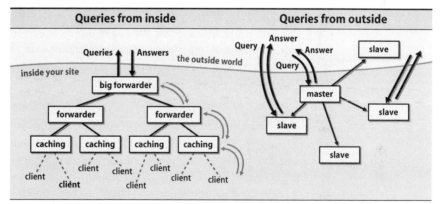

### Resolver testing

On some systems, all you have to do to start using DNS is add a nameserver line to **/etc/resolv.conf**. On others, you must explicitly tell the system to use DNS instead of the **/etc/hosts** file or NIS in the system switch file (often called **/etc/nsswitch.conf**). Comments about using BIND on each of our example systems begin on page 481. For a more general discussion of prioritizing sources of administrative data, see page 523.

After configuring **/etc/resolv.conf** (and assuming that your local network connection is up and running correctly), you should be able to refer to other machines by name rather than by IP address. If you try to reach another local machine and the command just hangs, try referring to the machine by its address. If that works, then your DNS configuration is the problem. Verify that the name server IP addresses in **/etc/resolv.conf** are correct and that the servers you point to allow queries from your network (see page 422).

### Impact on the rest of the system

The change from static host tables to DNS creates some potential dependencies in booting and configuration that you need to protect against.

As a host boots, references to hostnames in the **/etc/rc\*** or **init.d** startup files might be unresolvable if they are encountered before the network is up. The commands in the startup files will unsuccessfully try to contact DNS. Thanks to the resolver's robustness, they will try multiple times on multiple servers, increasing their timeout period with each attempt. A couple of minutes later, the command needing the hostname will finally fail.

To fix the problem, use only literal IP addresses in the early stages of the boot process. Or, if your system supports the simultaneous use of both DNS and **/etc/hosts** by way of a switch file, you can install a **hosts** file that contains the server addresses needed at boot time. Be sure the **hosts** file is checked before DNS so you don't have to wait for DNS to time out.

*See Chapter 17 for more information about NFS.*

Now that your host is using DNS, fully qualified domain names are required in several places. One is the **/etc/exports** file, which controls NFS file sharing on some systems. The clauses that list the hosts allowed to mount a filesystem must contain the fully qualified names of those hosts. On some systems, each **exports** line is limited to 1,024 characters; when hostnames change from anchor to anchor.cs.colorado.edu, this limit comes awfully early.

## 16.9  BIND SERVER CONFIGURATION

In this section, we assume that your political chores have been completed. That is, we assume that you have a domain name (possibly a subdomain), have coordinated with the DNS administrator of the parent domain, and have been delegated your address space in the in-addr.arpa reverse tree. You have chosen your master name server and a couple of secondaries, and you have installed BIND.

### Hardware requirements

BIND is a memory hog. Its database is kept in memory, so as the cache grows, so does the **named** process. Some of the new features of BIND 9 are also CPU intensive, most notably DNSSEC and IPv6. To help reduce this burden, BIND 9 is multithreaded and can make full use of multiprocessor systems. BIND 9 also contains configuration options that control **named**'s use of resources.

The best way to determine if a name server machine has enough memory is to run it for a while and watch the size of the **named** process. It takes a week or two to converge on a stable size at which old cache records are expiring at about the same rate that new ones are being inserted.

### named startup

**named** is started at boot time and runs continuously. For example, to start **named** from the scripts on a Solaris system:

```
if [ -f /usr/sbin/in.named -a -f /etc/named.conf ]; then
    /usr/sbin/in.named; echo -n ' named' > /dev/console
fi
```

Recent versions of BIND come with a command-line interface to **named** called **ndc** or **rndc**, depending on the version of BIND. The usage is just

```
# ndc command
```

Some useful commands are **start**, **stop**, **restart**, and **status**, which have the obvious meanings. **ndc** is described in the BIND debugging section that starts on page 473.

*See page 823 for more information about **inetd**.*

**named** uses syslog, and therefore **syslogd** should be started before **named**. Do not use **inetd** to manage **named**; it will restart **named** every time it's needed, slowing response times and preventing any useful cache from being developed.

### Configuration files

The complete configuration for **named** consists of the config file, the hints file, and, for master servers, the zone data files that contain address mappings for each host. **named**'s config file has its own format; all the other files are collections of individual DNS data records that are formatted according to the DNS specification. We discuss the config file in the next two sections. The format of DNS data records is described beginning on page 436.

**named**'s configuration file specifies the role (master, slave, or stub) of this host relative to each zone and the way in which it should get its copy of the resource records that make up the local part of the database. It's also the place where options are specified—both global options related to the operation of **named** itself and server or zone-specific options that affect only specific venues.

The format of **named**'s configuration file changed completely between BIND 4 and BIND 8, with the newer format resembling that of **gated.conf**. The name of the config file also changed: in BIND 4, it was **/etc/named.boot**, and in BIND 8 and 9 it is **/etc/named.conf**. The format of cache files and data files remains the same.

We describe the BIND 8/9 config file and skip BIND 4, hoping to encourage folks to beat on their vendors to upgrade or just do it themselves. As with any software, older versions of BIND may contain security vulnerabilities that have been patched in the current versions.

**named.conf** consists of a series of statements, each terminated by a semicolon. Tokens are separated by whitespace, which can include newlines. Curly braces are sometimes used for grouping, but only in specific contexts. The format is quite fragile—a missing semicolon can wreak havoc.

Comments can appear anywhere that whitespace is appropriate. C, C++, and shell-style comments are all understood:

```
/* This is a comment and can span lines. */
// Everything to the end of the line is a comment.
# Everything to the end of the line is a comment.
```

Each statement begins with a keyword that identifies the type of statement. There can be more than one instance of each type of statement, except for options and logging. Statements and parts of statements can also be left out, invoking default behavior for the missing items. Table 16.7 shows the statements included in BIND 9.

**Table 16.7    Statement types used in named.conf**

| Statement | Function |
|---|---|
| include | Interpolates a file (e.g., trusted keys readable only by **named**) |
| options | Sets global name server configuration options and defaults |
| server | Specifies per-server options |
| key | Defines authentication information |
| acl | Defines access control lists |
| zone | Defines a zone of resource records |
| trusted-keys | Uses preconfigured keys |
| controls | Defines channels used to control the name server with **ndc** |
| logging | Specifies logging categories and their destinations |
| view | Defines a view of the namespace (BIND 9 only) |

Before describing these statements and the way they are used to configure **named**, we need to describe a data structure that is used in many of the statements: the address match list. An address match list is a generalization of an IP address that can include:

- An IP address (e.g., 199.165.145.4)
- An IP network specified with a CIDR netmask (e.g., 199.165/16)
- The name of a previously defined access control list (see page 422)
- A cryptographic authentication key
- The ! character to negate things

Address match lists are used as parameters to many statements and options. Some examples:

```
{ ! 1.2.3.13; 1.2.3/24; };
{ 128.138/16; 198.11.16/24; 204.228.69/24; 127.0.0.1; };
```

The first of these lists excludes the host 1.2.3.13 but allows the rest of the 1.2.3/24 network; the second defines the networks assigned to the University of Colorado. The braces and final semicolon are not really part of the address match list, but are part of the enclosing statement that uses it.

When an IP address or network is compared to a match list, the list is searched in order until a match is found. This "first match" algorithm makes the ordering of entries important. For example, the first address match list above would not have the desired effect if the two entries were reversed, because 1.2.3.13 would succeed in matching 1.2.3/24 and the negated entry would never be encountered.

Now, on to the statements! Some are short and sweet; others almost warrant a chapter unto themselves.

### The include statement

To break up or better organize a large configuration, you can put different portions of the configuration in separate files. Subsidiary files are brought into **named.conf** with an include statement:

```
include "path";
```

If the *path* is relative, then it is interpreted relative to the directory specified in the directory option (next page). A common use of the include statement is to bring in cryptographic keys that should not be world-readable. Rather than closing read access to the whole **named.conf** file, keys are kept in files with restricted permissions that only **named** can read. Those files are then included into the **named.conf** file.

### The options statement

The options statement specifies global options, some of which may later be overridden for particular zones or servers. The general format is:

```
options {
    option;
    option;
    ...
};
```

If no options statement is present in **named.conf**, then default values are used.

BIND 8 had about 30 options, and BIND 9 has over 50. For a complete list, refer to the BIND documentation or to O'Reilly's *DNS and BIND* by Paul Albitz and Cricket Liu (the third edition covers BIND 8, and the fourth will include BIND 9). We have biased our coverage of these options and discuss only the ones whose use we recommend. (We also asked the BIND developers for their suggestions on which options to cover, and took their advice.) The default values are listed in square brackets beside each option.

```
version "string";                        [real version number of the server]
```

There are two schools of thought on the issue of hiding the version number. Some sites believe that their servers will be more vulnerable to attack if hackers can tell what version they are running. Others think that hiding the version information is counterproductive because hackers will try their luck anyway and most newly discovered bugs are present in all versions of the software.

We recommend that you not reset the version string in spite of the fact that our site does (we lost the security-through-obscurity argument with the sysadmin group). It is very handy to be able to query your name servers and find out what version they are running (for example, if you want to know if your vendor is shipping a current release, or if you need to verify that you have in fact upgraded all your servers to the latest revision).

```
directory "path";                          [directory where the server was started]
```

The directory statement causes **named** to **cd** to the specified directory. Wherever relative pathnames appear in **named**'s configuration files, they are interpreted relative to this directory. The *path* should be an absolute path. Any output files (debugging, statistics, etc.) are also written in this directory.

We recommend putting all BIND-related configuration files (other than **named.conf** and **resolv.conf**) in a subdirectory beneath **/var** (or wherever you keep your configuration files for other programs). We use **/var/named**.

```
notify yes | no;                  [yes]
also-notify servers_ipaddrs;      [empty]
```

If notify is set to yes and this **named** is the master server for one or more zones, **named** automatically notifies those zones' slave servers whenever the corresponding zone database changes. The slave servers can then rendezvous with the master to update their copies of the zone data. The notify option can be used as both a global option and as a zone-specific option. It makes the zone files converge much more quickly after you make changes.

*See page 456 for more information about stub zones.*

**named** normally figures out which machines are slave servers of a zone by looking at that zone's NS records. If also-notify is specified, a set of additional servers that are not advertised with NS records can also be notified. This tweak is sometimes necessary when your site has internal servers. Don't also-notify stub servers; they are only interested in the zone's NS records and can wait for the regular update cycle.

BIND 4 servers do not understand notification messages. They log an error and wait for the refresh interval prescribed in the zone data (see page 438) to expire before updating themselves. The localhost reverse zone is also a good place to turn notification off.

```
recursion yes | no;                        [yes]
allow-recursion { address_match_list };    [all hosts]
```

The recursion option specifies whether **named** queries other name servers on behalf of clients, as described on page 406. It's fairly unusual to configure a name server with recursion off. However, you might want to allow recursion for your own clients but not for outside queries.

Recursion can be controlled at a finer granularity with the allow-recursion option and an address list that includes the hosts and networks on whose behalf you are willing to perform recursive queries.

```
use-id-pool yes | no;                    [no (V8 only)]
```

In BIND V8, this option causes **named** to keep track of outstanding query IDs so that it doesn't issue duplicates and so that the sequence of IDs it issues can be more random. It helps prevent DNS spoofing. If you turn it on, expect **named** to use a bit more memory. The feature is worth the extra memory cost, however; we recommend that you use this option. In BIND 9, the use-id-pool option is gone and **named** always manages its query IDs this way.

```
maintain-ixfr-base yes | no;        [no, V8 only]
```

Incremental zone transfers (see RFC1995) allow servers to send out "patches" to a zone when it changes instead of resending the entire zone. For a zone like com, this incrementality is very important. The current release of BIND 8 allows incremental zone transfers for any zone that does dynamic updates; it keeps a transaction log file if maintain-ixfr-base is set to yes. BIND 9 always maintains a log. *Zone transfers* on page 458 covers incremental zone transfers in more detail.

```
check-names { master|slave|response action }      [see text]
```

BIND has included code to check the validity of hostnames since version 8—not in the sense of "Does this host exist?" but in the sense of "Does this hostname actually follow the rules specified in the RFCs for hostnames?" A surprising number of them don't. A name is valid if it contains only letters, numbers, and dashes and is no longer than 64 characters per component (including the dot) and 256 characters overall. The rules for names and the distinction between the host portion and the domain portion are subjects of current debate. Internationalization of the DNS system and support for non-ASCII character sets might change all the naming rules.

You can specify the check-names behavior globally and also individually for each zone; a zone specification overrides the global values. You can apply the option to master servers, to slave servers, or to the answers returned in response to queries. Each type has three possible action values:

- ignore  – do no checking
- warn    – log bad names, but continue processing
- fail    – log and reject bad names

The default for the master is to fail, since errors on the master are likely to be typos or noncompliant names that the sysadmin should fix. A site should not knowingly propagate noncompliant names. The default for slave servers is to warn, and the default for responses is to ignore. The default values are just right; you should not need to change them.

check-names logging data is a prime candidate for tuning with the infinitely flexible logging system that is covered beginning on page 469.

```
transfer-format one-answer | many-answers;     [see text]
```

This option affects the way that DNS data records (described starting on page 436) are replicated from master servers to their slaves. The actual transmission of data

records used to take place one record at a time, which is a recipe for sloth and inefficiency. An option to combine many records into one packet (many-answers) was
added in BIND 8.1; it is the default in BIND 9. Use this option only if all the servers
with which you share zone data are running at least 8.1, since BIND 4 servers do not
understand it. If you have a mixed environment, you can specify a transfer format
in individual server statements to override the global option. Your mix of servers
will dictate whether you choose many-answers globally and override it for specific
servers, or vice versa.

```
transfers-in number;              [10]
transfers-out number;             [10 (V9 only)]
transfers-per-ns number;          [2]
transfer-source IP-address;       [system-dependent]
serial-queries number;            [4 (V8 only)]
```

A large site—one that serves a very large zone (such as com, which currently is over
two gigabytes), or one that serves thousands of zones—may need to tune some of
these zone transfer options.

The transfers-in and transfers-out options limit the number of inbound or outbound zone transfers that can happen concurrently. The transfers-per-ns option
sets the maximum number of inbound zone transfers that can be running concurrently from the same remote server. Large sites may need to increase transfers-in or
transfers-out; be careful that you don't run out of file descriptors for the **named**
process. transfers-per-ns should probably not be changed; it controls how many resources the master server is willing to devote to us. It should only be increased if all
remote master servers are willing to handle more than two simultaneous zone transfers. Changing it on a per-server basis with the transfers clause of the server statement is a better way to fine-tune the convergence of slave zones.

The transfer-source option lets you specify the IP address of the interface you want
to use for incoming transfers. It must match the address specified in the master's
allow-transfer statement.

In BIND 8 you can limit the number of simultaneous inquiries for the serial number
of a zone with the serial-queries option. Each such inquiry keeps state on the local
server; if thousands of queries are being received, this limit can help the server maintain its sanity. The default value is four, which is way too low for a big site; raise it to
several hundred or even a thousand. In BIND 9 this parameter is currently ignored;
it will be replaced by a query rate in the future.

As with any parameter that you change drastically, you should watch things carefully
after changing one of these throttle values to be sure the machine is not thrashing.
The log files are your friends.

```
files number;                          [unlimited]
```

The files option sets the maximum number of files the server is allowed to have open
concurrently. The default value, unlimited, is not possible on some operating sys-

tems; in such cases, you can use the files directive to inform **named** of the operating system limit. If you don't specify files explicitly and the operating system does not allow an unlimited number of open files, **named** uses the **sysconf** library routine to determine the limit and the **setrlimit** system call to try to increase it.

```
listen-on port ip_port address_match_list;          [53 all]
query-source address ip_addr port ip_port;          [random]
```

The listen-on option specifies the network interfaces and ports on which **named** listens for queries. The query-source option specifies the interface and port that **named** uses to query other name servers. The values of these options default to the standard **named** behavior: listening on port 53 on all interfaces and using a random, high-numbered UDP port and any interface for queries.

*See page 691 for more information about virtual interfaces.*

The listen-on option lets you run multiple name servers on one host. For example, you might want to do this because it's best not to configure a BIND 4 or BIND 8 server to be both authoritative and caching—those versions of **named** keep all their data in one giant database. **named** can run out of memory, and the data can become corrupted. To avoid this risk, you can run two separate **named** processes: one as an authoritative server and the other as a caching server that uses the listen-on statement and a different virtual IP address. The authoritative and caching servers can interact just as if they ran on separate machines. Put only the caching server's IP address in the **resolv.conf** file.

If your site has a firewall, you can use the query-source option to give external DNS queries a specific, recognizable profile. You typically set **named** to use port 53 as the source port so that the firewall can recognize outbound DNS traffic as trustworthy packets from one of your name servers.

```
forwarders { in_addr; in_addr; ... };               [empty list]
forward only | first;                               [first]
```

Instead of having every name server perform its own external queries, you can designate one or more servers as *forwarders*. A run-of-the-mill server can review its cache and the records for which it is authoritative, and if it doesn't find the answer it's looking for, it can then send the query on to a forwarder host. That way, the forwarders build up caches that benefit the entire site. Forwarders reduce the load on your network, limit CPU and memory use on weaker servers, increase performance for users, and reduce your reliance on external Internet connectivity. Many sites designate their more powerful and memory-rich servers as forwarders.

A medium-sized site can construct a very efficient DNS system with a series of caching servers that point to just one or two forwarders. Large sites may need a hierarchy of forwarders. The example on page 431 uses a two-level forwarding scheme.

The forwarders option lists the IP addresses of the servers you want to use as forwarders. They are queried in turn. The use of a forwarder circumvents the normal DNS procedure of starting at a root server and following the chain of referrals. Be careful not to create forwarding loops.

A forward only server caches values and queries forwarders, but it never queries anyone else. If the forwarders do not respond, queries will fail. A forward first server prefers to deal with forwarders but will process queries directly if need be.

Since the forwarders option has no default value, forwarding does not occur unless it has been specifically configured. You can turn on forwarding either globally or within individual zone statements.

```
allow-query { address_match_list };      [all hosts]
allow-transfer { address_match_list };   [all hosts]
blackhole { address_match_list };        [empty]
```

These options let you specify which hosts (or networks) can query your name server and request block transfers of your zone data. The blackhole address list identifies servers that you never want to talk to; **named** will not accept queries from these servers and will not ask them for answers.

```
sortlist { address_match_list };         [should die, don't use]
```

We mention this option only to warn you away from it. The sortlist option should go away and die. Its purpose was to help along primitive resolvers that don't sort record sets properly. It lets you specify the order that multiple answers are returned and works against current BINDs' internal smarts.

Other BIND options that meddle with the order of things are the rrset-order statement, which specifies whether to return multiple answers in cyclic (round robin), fixed, or random order, and the topology statement, which tries to second-guess BIND's system for selecting remote servers to query. In most cases there is no need to use these statements, either.

### The acl statement

An access control list is just a named address match list:

```
acl acl_name {
    address_match_list
};
```

You can use an access control list anywhere that an address match list is called for.

An acl must be a top-level statement in **named.conf**, so don't try sneaking it in amid your other option declarations. **named.conf** is read in a single pass, so access control lists must be defined before they are used. Four lists are predefined: any, localnets, localhost, and none, matching all hosts, all hosts on the local network, the machine itself, and nothing, respectively. The networks included in localnets are determined by the interfaces on the machine modulo their netmasks.

### The server statement

**named** can potentially talk to many servers, not all of which are running the latest version of BIND, and not all of which are even nominally sane. The server statement tells **named** about the characteristics of its remote peers.

```
server ip_addr {
    bogus yes | no;                                    [no]
    provide-ixfr yes | no;                             [yes (V9 only)]
    request-ixfr yes | no;                             [yes (V9 only)]
    support-ixfr yes | no;                             [no (V8 only)]
    transfers number;                                  [2 (V9 only)]
    transfer-format one-answer | many-answers;        [V8: one, V9: many]
    keys { key-id; key-id; ... };
};
```

You can use a server statement to override the values of server-related configuration options. Just list the ones for which you want nondefault behavior.

If you mark a server as being bogus, **named** won't send any queries its way. This directive should generally be reserved for servers that really are bogus.

The ixfr clauses changed between V8 and V9, though both sets are similar. V8 has support-ixfr, and V9 has provide-ixfr and request-ixfr. The server statements in the config file of a server running V8 can set support-ixfr to yes if the remote server understands incremental zone transfers. A V9 server acting as master for a zone will do incremental zone transfers if provide-ixfr is set to yes. Likewise, a V9 server acting as a slave will request incremental zone transfers from the master if request-ixfr is set to yes.

The transfers clause limits the number of concurrent inbound zone transfers from the remote server. It is a server-specific version of transfers-in, but because it applies to only one server, it acts like a per-server override of the transfers-per-ns option. The name is different to preserve compatibility with BIND 8.

The transfer-format clauses are the server-specific forms of the options discussed on page 419. Use transfer-format if you talk to both BIND 8/9 and BIND 4 servers.

The keys clause identifies a key ID that has been previously defined in a key statement for use with TSIG transaction signatures (see page 462). Any requests sent to the remote server are signed with this key. Requests originating at the remote server are not required to be signed, but if they are, the signature will be verified.

### The logging statement

**named** is the current holder of the "most configurable logging system on Earth" award. Syslog put the prioritization of log messages into the programmer's hands and the disposition of those messages into the sysadmin's hands. But for a given priority, the sysadmin had no way to say, "I care about this message but not about that message." BIND 8 added categories that classify log messages by type, and channels that broaden the choices for the disposition of messages. Categories are determined by the programmer, and channels by the sysadmin.

Since the issue of logging is somewhat tangential (especially given the amount of explanation required), we discuss it in the debugging section later in this chapter. It starts on page 469.

## The zone statement

zone statements are the heart of the **named.conf** file. They tell **named** about the zones for which it is authoritative and set the options that are appropriate for managing each zone. A zone statement is also used to preload the root server hints (the names and addresses of the root servers, which bootstrap the DNS lookup process).

The exact format of a zone statement varies depending on the role that **named** is to play with respect to that zone (for example, master server or slave server). We examine each possibility in turn. Many of the global options covered earlier can become part of a zone statement and override the previously defined values. We have not repeated those options here except to mention certain ones that are frequently used.

*Configuring the master server for a zone*

Here is the format you need for a zone of which this **named** is the master server:

```
zone "domain_name" {
    type master;
    file "path";
    allow-query { address_match_list };       [all]
    allow-transfer { address_match_list };    [all]
    allow-update { address_match_list };      [none]
    ixfr-base "path";                         [domain_name.ixfr (V8 only)]
};
```

The *domain_name* in a zone specification must always be in double quotes.

The zone's data is kept on disk in a human-readable (and human-editable) file. Since there is no default for the filename, you must provide a file statement when declaring a master zone. A zone file is just a collection of DNS resource records; the format is described beginning on page 436.

The access control options are not required, but it's a good idea to use them. If dynamic updates are used for this zone, the allow-update clause must be present with an address match list that limits the hosts from which updates can occur. Dynamic updates apply only to master zones; the allow-update clause cannot be used for a slave zone (in BIND 9). Be sure that this clause includes just your local DHCP servers and not the whole Internet.[8]

If incremental zone transfers are to be used with this zone, BIND 8 keeps a transaction log in a file called *domain_name*.**ixfr** in **named**'s home directory. If you want to change the name, use the ixfr-base clause to specify a new filename. This file is maintained by **named** and needs no attention from you.

In BIND 9, the transaction log is used for both dynamic updates and IXFR. Its name ends with **.jnl** and is not configurable. Both dynamic updates and incremental zone transfers are relatively new features of BIND. They are discussed in more detail starting on page 458.

---

8. You also need ingress filtering at your firewall; see page 675. Better yet, use TSIG for authentication.

With all these zone-specific options (and several more we have not covered), the configuration is starting to sound complicated. However, a master zone declaration consisting of nothing but a pathname to the zone file is perfectly reasonable. In BIND 4, that's all you could specify. Here is an example from the BIND documentation that we have modified slightly:

```
zone "example.com" {
    type master;
    file "forward/example.com";
    allow-query { any; };
    allow-transfer { my-slaves; };
}
```

my-slaves is an access control list that was previously defined.

### Configuring a slave server for a zone

The zone statement for a slave is very similar to that of a master:

```
zone "domain_name" {
    type slave | stub;
    file "path";
    ixfr-base "path";                             [V8 only]
    masters { ip_addr; ip_addr;     };            [no default]
    allow-query { address_match_list };           [all]
    allow-transfer { address_match_list };        [all]
};
```

Slave servers normally maintain a complete copy of their zone's database. However, if the type is set to stub instead of slave, only NS (name server) records are transferred. Stub zones allow the **named**s for the parent zone to automatically discover which machines provide DNS service for their delegated child zones, just in case the administrator of the child zone is not conscientious about informing the parent of changes. The parent needs this information to make appropriate referrals or recursive queries. We revisit this topic in greater detail on page 455.

The file statement specifies a local file in which the replicated database can be stored. Each time the server fetches a new copy of the zone, it saves the data in this file. If the server crashes and reboots, the file can then be reloaded from the local disk without being transferred across the network.

You shouldn't edit this cache file, since it's maintained by **named**. However, it can be interesting to look at if you suspect you have made an error in the master server's data file. The slave's disk file shows you how **named** has interpreted the original zone data; relative names and origin directives have all been expanded. If you see a name in the data file that looks like one of these

128.138.243.151.cs.colorado.edu.
anchor.cs.colorado.edu.cs.colorado.edu.

you can be pretty sure that you forgot a trailing dot somewhere.

The masters statement lists the IP addresses of one or more machines from which the zone database can be obtained. We have said that only one machine can be the master for a zone, so why is it possible to list more than one address? Two reasons.

First, the master machine might have more than one network interface, and therefore more than one IP address. It's possible for one interface to become unreachable (due to network or routing problems) while others are still accessible. Therefore, it's a good practice to list all of the master server's topologically distinct addresses.

Second, **named** really doesn't care where the zone data comes from. It can pull the database just as easily from a slave server as from the master. You could use this feature to allow a well-connected slave server to serve as a sort of backup master, since the IP addresses will be tried in order until a working server is found. In theory, you can also set up a hierarchy of servers, with one master serving several second-level servers, which in turn serve many third-level servers.

We suggest that you list only bona fide master server addresses on the masters line.

### Setting up the root hints

Another form of zone statement points **named** toward a file from which it can prime (preload) its cache with the names and addresses of the root name servers:

```
zone "." {
    type hint;
    file "path";
};
```

The "hints" are a set of DNS records that list servers for the root domain ("."). They're needed to give **named** a place to start searching for information about other sites' domains. Without them, **named** would only know about the domains it actually serves and their subdomains.

The hints file is often called **root.cache**; it contains the response you would get if you queried a root server for the name server records in the domain ".". We discuss how to set up a proper hints file starting on page 479.

BIND 9 has root server hints compiled into its code, so no configuration of the root zone is really needed. If you provide a hints file, however, BIND 9 will use it. We recommend that you do supply explicit hints; politics have entered the DNS arena, making root name servers and their IP addresses more volatile.

### Setting up a forwarding zone

A zone of type forward overrides **named**'s global forwarding settings (described on page 421) for a particular domain:

```
zone "domain_name" {
    type forward;
    forward only | first;
    forwarders { ip_addr; ip_addr; ... };
};
```

You might use a forward zone if your organization had a strategic working relationship with some other group or company and you wanted to funnel traffic directly to that company's name servers, bypassing the standard query path. You could use such an arrangement to access name servers that were invisible to the outside world.

### The key statement

The key statement defines a named encryption key to be used for authentication with a particular server. Background information about BIND's support for cryptographic authentication is given in the *Security issues* section starting on page 460. Here, we just touch briefly on the mechanics of the process.

To build a key, you specify both the cryptographic algorithm that you want to use and a "shared secret," represented as a base-64-encoded string:

```
key key-id {
    algorithm string;
    secret string;
};
```

As with access control lists, the *key-id* must be defined earlier in the **named.conf** file than it is first used. To associate the key with a particular server, just include *key-id* in the keys clause of that server's server statement. The key is used both to verify requests from that server and to sign the responses to those requests.

### The trusted-keys statement

The trusted-keys statement is for DNSSEC security, specified in RFC2065. Each entry is a 5-tuple that identifies the domain name, flags, protocol, algorithm, and key that are needed to talk securely to a name server for that domain. The format is:

```
trusted-keys {
    domain flags protocol algorithm key;
    domain flags protocol algorithm key;
    ...
}
```

Each line represents the trusted key for a particular domain. The *flags*, *protocol*, and *algorithm* are nonnegative integers. The *key* is a base-64 encoded string.

The trusted-keys construct is intended to be used when a zone is signed but its parent zone is not, so you cannot be sure that the public key for the zone that you get from DNS is really kosher. Entering a trusted key with a trusted-keys statement (using out-of-band methods) ensures that you really have the appropriate key for the domain in question.

DNSSEC is covered in more detail starting on page 464.

### The controls statement

The controls statement specifies how **ndc** controls a running **named** process. **ndc** can start and stop **named**, dump its state, put it in debug mode, etc. **ndc** is a network program, and without proper configuration it might let anyone on the Internet mess around with your name server. The syntax is:

```
controls {
    inet ip_addr port port# allow { address_match_list | key ... };
    unix permission owner group;                              [0600 0 0]
}
```

Allowing your name server to be accessed at the listed *ip_addr* and *port* sounds both handy and dangerous. Best might be to just leave the inet line out and access your name server only through the UNIX domain socket and the unix keyword. Another alternative is to control access with an authentication key. Slightly riskier would be to configure the *address_match_list* to accept connections only from 127.0.0.1 and to block that address from the outside world at your firewall. Limiting the inet line to localhost implies that you trust all local users to not mess with your name server; any user could **telnet** to the control port and type "stop"—quite an effective denial of service attack on the host. The default is to omit the inet clause.

**ndc** can also contact **named** through a UNIX domain socket called **/var/run/ndc**. The unix configuration line sets the permissions and ownerships on that socket and hence restricts access to it. The *permission* parameter should be an octal number that represents the desired mode of the socket; the *owner* and *group* parameters are the UID and GID of the owner of the socket. The defaults are read and write permission only for root.

### The view statement

Views are a new feature of BIND 9 that let you show your internal machines a different view of the DNS naming hierarchy than that seen by the outside world. For example, you might reveal all of a zone's hosts to internal users but restrict the external view to a few well-known servers. Or, you might expose the same set of hosts in both views but supply additional (or different) records to internal users.

This type of configuration (sometimes called "split DNS") seems to be increasingly popular. In the past, you implemented it by setting up separate servers for the internal and external versions of reality. Local clients pointed at distribution servers that dished out the internal version of the zone, while the parent zone's NS records pointed at servers that held the external version. BIND 9's view statement simplifies the configuration by putting both sets of data inside the same copy of **named**. **named** uses address match lists to figure out which clients should see which data.

The view statement packages up an access list that controls who sees the view, some options that apply to all the zones in the view, and finally, the zones themselves. The syntax is:

```
view view-name {
    match-clients { address_match_list } ;
    view_option; ...
    zone_statement; ...
} ;
```

The match-clients clause controls who can see the view. Views are processed in order, so put the most restrictive views first. Zones in different views can have the same names. Views are an all-or-nothing proposition; if you use them, all zone statements in your **named.conf** file must appear in the context of a view.

Here is an example from the BIND 9 documentation that mimics the split DNS scheme described above. The two views define the same zone, but with different data.

```
view "internal" {
    match-clients { our_nets; };      // only internal networks
    recursion yes;                    // internal clients only
    zone "example.com" {              // complete view of zone
        type master;
        file "example-internal.db";
    };
};

view "external" {
    match-clients { any; };           // allow all queries
    recursion no;                     // but no recursion
    zone "example.com" {              // only "public" hosts
        type master;
        file "example-external.db";
    }
};
```

If the order of the views were reversed, no one would ever see the internal view. Internal hosts would match the any value in the match-clients clause of the external view before they reached the internal view.

## 16.10  BIND CONFIGURATION EXAMPLES

Now that we have explored the wonders of **named.conf**, let's look at some complete examples. In the following sections, we show three sample configurations:

- A student's home Linux box
- A university department that uses a three-level forwarding hierarchy
- A company that does web hosting and serves about 2,000 zones

### A home Linux box

Rob Braun, a student, has a Linux box at home that provides DNS name service for his domain, synack.net, and for the domains of a couple of friends. He is running BIND 8.2.2-P5. His **named.conf** file is below. We have added a few comments to the ends of lines.

Rob's configuration is pretty straightforward. The options are mostly the defaults: a recursive server, files in the usual places, queries and transfers OK, a one-answer transfer format, speaking on port 53, etc. Some control is exercised over the configuration of individual zones. For example, the synack.net zone allows transfers to only one host, and it does not allow dynamic updates.

This name server is the master server for two domains: synack.net and xinetd.org. It's also a slave server for two friends' domains: teich.net and rmtai.com. As might be expected in a computer science student's configuration, the logging section is not the default. It includes mild debugging and curiosity channels modeled after the sample config file shipped with BIND.

```
/* named.conf file, gw.synack.net */

options {
    directory "/var/named";
    pid-file "/var/named/named.pid";
};

zone "synack.net" {
    type master;
    file "synack.forw";
    allow-transfer { 198.11.19.15; };
};

zone "xinetd.org" {
    type master;
    file "xinetd.forw";
    allow-transfer { 198.11.19.15; };
};

zone "1.168.192.in-addr.arpa" {
    type master;                     // reverse, for private addresses
    file "named.rev";
};

zone "." {
    type hint;
    file "cache.db";
};

zone "teich.net" {
    type slave;
    file "teich.net.sec";
    masters { 216.103.220.218; };
};

zone "rmtai.com" {
    type slave;
    file "rmtai.com.sec";
    masters { 216.103.220.218; };
};

// Define three logging channels (important syslog messages,
// moderate debugging, and loading zone messages) and
// then map categories to them.

logging {
    channel syslog_errors {
        syslog local1;
```

```
        severity error;
    };
    channel moderate_debug {
        severity debug 3;        // level 3 debugging
        file "foo";              // to file foo
        print-time yes;          // timestamp log entries
        print-category yes;      // print category name
        print-severity yes;      // print severity level
    };
    channel no_info_messages {
        syslog local2;
        severity notice;
    };

    category parser {
        syslog_errors;
        default_syslog;
    };
    category lame-servers { null; };      // don't log these
    category load { no_info_messages; };
    category default {
        default_syslog;
        moderate_debug;
    };
};    // end of logging clause
```

This configuration has no reverse localhost zone; localhost must be mapped in the **/etc/hosts** file.

## A university department

The computer science department at the University of Colorado uses caching servers on each subnet; the caching servers forward to a list of slave servers. The slaves themselves forward to a master server that contacts the Internet on their behalf. Each forwarding server is configured to forward first. Below, we show all three configurations: the caching-only servers, the slave servers, and the master. All of the servers are running BIND 8.

The caching-only configuration is appropriate for a subnet that wants a local server but doesn't want to soil its hands with data files. We need only set up the **named.conf** file and the hints file and start **named** at boot time. In the config file there are no real local zones, only the root server hints and the reverse localhost zone.

```
// bind 8.2 conf file - caching server

// Global options
options {
    directory "/var/named";
    named-xfer "/usr/local/sbin/named-xfer";    // bind 8 only
    // build a rich cache on our master and official slaves
    forwarders {
        128.138.243.151;    // mroe
```

```
            128.138.243.140;   // anchor
            128.138.243.137;   // moet
            128.138.243.138;   // vulture
            128.138.236.20;    // piper
      };
      forward first;
      query-source address * port 53;
};

// Logging, syslog to local3, no lame servers
logging {
      channel syslog_info {
            syslog local3;
            severity info;
      };
      category lame-servers { null; };
      category default { syslog_info; };
};

// Root servers cache
zone "." {
      type hint;
      file "named.cache";
};

// Master server for localhost reverse zone
zone "0.0.127.in-addr.arpa" {
      type master;
      file "localhost";
      notify no;
};
```

The config file for slave servers includes the cs.colorado.edu forward zone and several reverse zones that we have cut down to one or two for illustration. In this example, the reverse zones are not subdivided on a byte boundary (they are mostly /26s), but because all four subnets are controlled by the same administrative authority, they are kept in the same file and the CNAME hack described on page 445 is not necessary.

```
// bind 8.2 conf file - slave server

options {
      directory "/var/named";
      named-xfer "/usr/local/sbin/named-xfer";   // bind 8 only
      forwarders { 128.138.243.151; };            // master
      forward first;
      query-source address * port 53;
      allow-transfer { none; };
};

// Logging, root server hints, and localhost reverse zone are the
// same as for a caching server, so they're not shown here.

// Slave zones
```

```
zone "cs.colorado.edu" {
    type slave;
    file "forward/cs.colorado.edu";
    masters { 128.138.243.151; };
};

zone "250.138.128.in-addr.arpa" {
    type slave;
    file "reverse/250.138.128";
    masters { 128.138.243.151; };
};

zone "245.138.128.in-addr.arpa" {
    type slave;
    file "reverse/245.138.128";
    masters { 128.138.243.151; };
};

// ... many, many reverse slave zones omitted
```

The next configuration is for the server that is both the master for cs.colorado.edu and the forwarder through which all local queries flow. This setup builds a nice cache but breaks the don't-mix-authoritative-and-caching-servers rule.

This configuration sets a preference for local servers with a topology statement. Several servers are not listed in the parent domain's delegations; these are notified of changes with an also-notify clause.

The master server keeps its DNS database in several files. Reverse-mapping zones are organized by subnet number. Each subnet (in our case, the third octet of a class B address) has its own file. This organization is not strictly necessary, but it keeps the files to a manageable size and makes it easy to update them. However, it does presuppose either that subnets are divided on a byte boundary or that if subnets are further subdivided, each piece remains under our administrative control.

If a single file were used for all reverse mappings, the records could be organized by network and the $ORIGIN directive could be used at the beginning of each section to reset the identity of the default domain. See page 453.

```
# bind 8.x conf file - master server for cs.colorado.edu
# $Id: named.conf,v 1.28 2000/01/12 00:20:34 root Exp $

acl CUnets {
    128.138/16; 198.11.16/24; 204.228.69/24; 127.0.0.1;
};

# Global options
options {
    directory "/var/named";
    named-xfer "/usr/local/sbin/named-xfer"; # BIND 8 only
    notify yes;
    also-notify {
        128.138.192.205;   # suod
```

```
              128.138.244.9;      # riker
              128.138.243.70;     # squid
              128.138.241.12;     # goober
              128.138.244.100;    # av-server
              128.138.202.19;     # nago
      };
      query-source address * port 53;
      topology { localhost; localnets; CUnets; };
};

# Logging, root hints, and localhost zone are the same and are not shown

# CS
zone "cs.colorado.edu" {
      type master;
      file "forward/cs.colorado.edu";
};

# CS reverse records (128.138.X.X)
zone "250.138.128.in-addr.arpa" {
      type master;
      file "reverse/250.138.128";
};
zone "245.138.128.in-addr.arpa" {
      type master;
      file "reverse/245.138.128";
};

# ... many, many reverse zones omitted

# Slaves
zone "colorado.edu" {  # colorado.edu top level
      type slave;
      file "secondary/colorado.edu";
      allow-transfer { none; };
      masters { 128.138.240.1; };
};
zone "openbsd.org" {   # openbsd project
      type slave;
      file "secondary/openbsd.org";
      masters { 199.45.131.58; };
};
zone "233.in-addr.arpa" {# experimental multicast addresses
      type slave;
      file "secondary/233.in-addr.arpa";
      masters { 128.223.32.35; };
};

# lots more zones omitted
```

### A web hosting company

Our next example is from a company that does web design and web hosting; they run DNS services for their clients. The master server deals with almost 2,000 zones, about half as master and half as slave. Most of the zones are not large (typically 10–30K, with the largest being 160K), but there are a lot of them. The server is a SPARC 20 running SunOS 4.1.3 and BIND 8.2.2-P5. It has two network interfaces and about 512MB of memory.

Here, we show only a few snippets from the master configuration file. No slave configurations are shown; they're the same as the master configurations except for the zone type and a masters line that indicates where to get the zone data. The root server hint zone and the localhost reverse mapping zone have been deleted; they are the same as in previous examples.

With so many zones, many of them loaded from off-site servers, the log files are full of "zone expired" and "not authoritative for zone" messages. The remote sites have often not kept their secondary DNS provider up to date on changes.

```
// XOR master server

options {
        directory "/var/domain";
        query-source address 192.225.33.1 port 53;
        also-notify 192.108.21.2;
};

// XOR, internal, forward zones

zone "xor.com" {
        type master;
        file "xor.com";
};
zone "creative.xor.com" {
        type master;
        file "creative.xor.com";
};
//  ... more internal zones deleted

// XOR, reverse zones

zone "21.108.192.in-addr.arpa" {
        type master;
        file "xor.rev";
};
zone "2.168.192.in-addr.arpa" {  // hidden backlan for backups
        type master;
        file "backlan-2.rev";
};
// ... many reverse zones deleted

// Customer forward zones

// =========================================================
// Boulder Community Hospital        setup:01/21/2000
//=========================================================
```

```
zone "boulderhospital.com" {
    type master;
    file "boulderhospital.com";
};
zone "boulderhospital.org" {
    type master;
    file "boulderhospital.com";
};

// Another 1750 or so zones were deleted from this example.
// Most were product names, not organization names.
```

## 16.11  THE DNS DATABASE

A domain's DNS database is a set of text files maintained by the system administrator on the domain's master name server. These text files are often called zone files. They contain two types of entries: parser commands (things like $ORIGIN and $TTL) and "resource records," or RRs as they are sometimes called. Only the resource records are really part of the database; the parser commands just provide some shorthand ways to enter records.

We start this section by describing the DNS resource records, which are defined in RFCs 882, 1035, 1183, 2065, 2181, 2308, and 2535. We defer discussion of the parser commands until page 453.

### Resource records

Each zone of the DNS hierarchy has a set of resource records associated with it (the set might be empty). The basic format of a resource record is

[name] [ttl] [class] type data

Fields are separated by whitespace (tabs or spaces) and can contain the special characters shown in Table 16.8.

**Table 16.8   Special characters used in RRs**

| Character | Meaning |
|:---:|:---|
| ; | Introduces a comment |
| @ | The current domain name |
| ( ) | Allows data to span lines |
| * | Wild card[a] (*name* field only) |

a. See page 444 for some cautionary statements.

The *name* field identifies the entity (usually a host or domain) that the record describes. If several consecutive records refer to the same entity, the name can be left out after the first record. The name field must begin in column one if it is present.

A name can be either relative or absolute. Absolute names end with a dot and are complete. Internally, the software deals only with absolute names; it appends the current domain and a dot to any name that does not already end in a dot. This feature allows names to be shorter, but it also invites mistakes.

For example, in the cs.colorado.edu domain, the name "anchor" would be interpreted as "anchor.cs.colorado.edu.". If the name were entered as "anchor.cs.colorado.edu", the lack of a final dot would still imply a relative name, and the default domain would be appended, resulting in the name "anchor.cs.colorado.edu.cs.colorado.edu.". This is a very common mistake.

The *ttl* (time to live) field specifies the length of time, in seconds, that the data item can be cached and still be considered valid. It is often omitted, except in the root server hints file. It defaults to the value set by the $TTL directive at the top of the data file for the zone. In BIND 9, the $TTL directive is required. If there is no $TTL directive in BIND 8, the *ttl* defaults to a per-zone value set in the zone's SOA record.

*See Chapter 18 for more information about NIS.*

Increasing the value of the *ttl* parameter to about a week reduces network traffic and DNS load substantially. However, once records have been cached outside your local network, you cannot force them to be discarded. If you plan a massive renumbering, set the $TTL value low so that stale records that have been cached elsewhere on the Internet expire quickly.

The *class* specifies the network type. Three values are recognized: IN for the Internet, CH for ChaosNet, and HS for Hesiod. ChaosNet is a nearly obsolete network protocol formerly used by Symbolics Lisp machines. Hesiod is a database service built on top of BIND. The default value for the class is IN. It is often specified explicitly in zone data files even though it is the default. Today only one piece of data is normally tucked away in the Chaos class: the version number of the running **named**, which can be extracted with **dig** as shown on page 403.

Many different types of DNS records are defined, but fewer than 10 are in common use; IPv6 adds a few more. We divide the resource records into four groups:

- Zone records – identify domains and their name servers
- Basic records – map names to addresses and route mail
- Security records – add authentication and signatures to zone files
- Optional records – provide extra information about hosts or domains

The contents of the *data* field depend on the record type. Table 16.9 on the next page lists the various record types.

A few additional record types are obsolete, experimental, or not widely used. See the BIND documentation for a complete list.

The order of resource records is almost arbitrary. The SOA record for a zone should be first. The subsequent records can be in any order, but NS records usually come right after the SOA. The records for each host are usually kept together. It's a common practice to sort by the *name* field.

**Table 16.9   DNS record types**

| | Type | Name | Function |
|---|---|---|---|
| **Zone** | SOA | Start Of Authority | Defines a DNS zone of authority |
| | NS | Name Server | Identifies zone servers, delegates subdomains |
| **Basic** | A | IPv4 Address | Name-to-address translation |
| | AAAA | Original IPv6 Address | Now obsolete, DO NOT USE |
| | A6 | IPv6 Address | Name-to-IPv6-address translation (V9 only) |
| | PTR | Pointer | Address-to-name translation |
| | DNAME | Redirection | Redirection for reverse IPv6 lookups (V9 only) |
| | MX | Mail Exchanger | Controls email routing |
| **Security** | KEY | Public Key | Public key for a DNS name |
| | NXT | Next | Used with DNSSEC for negative answers |
| | SIG | Signature | Signed, authenticated zone |
| **Optional** | CNAME | Canonical Name | Nicknames or aliases for a host |
| | LOC | Location | Geographic location and extent[a] |
| | RP | Responsible Person | Specifies per-host contact info |
| | SRV | Services | Gives locations of well-known services |
| | TXT | Text | Comments or untyped information |

a. The LOC record is not well supported in NT (querying for LOC records crashes NT servers).

As we describe each type of resource record in detail, we inspect some sample records from cs.colorado.edu's data files. The default domain is "cs.colorado.edu." throughout, so a host specified as "anchor" really means "anchor.cs.colorado.edu.".

### The SOA record

An SOA record marks the beginning of a zone, a group of resource records located at the same place within the DNS namespace. This node of the DNS tree is also called a delegation point or zone cut. As we discuss in greater detail on page 442, the data for a DNS domain usually includes at least two zones: one for translating hostnames to IP addresses, and others that map in the reverse direction. The DNS tree has a forward branch organized by name and a reverse branch organized by IP address.

Each zone has exactly one SOA record. The zone continues until another SOA is encountered. The SOA record includes the name of the zone, a technical contact, and various timeout values. An example:

```
; Start of authority record for cs.colorado.edu

@            IN   SOA  ns.cs.colorado.edu. admin.cs.colorado.edu. (
                    1999121501  ; Serial
                    21600       ; Refresh,   6 hours
                    1800        ; Retry,     30 minutes
                    1209600     ; Expire,    2 weeks
                    432000 )    ; Minimum,   5 days
```

Here, the *name* field contains the symbol @, which is shorthand for the name of the current zone. In this example, "cs.colorado.edu." could have been used instead. The value of @ is the domain name specified in the zone statement in the **named.conf** file; it can be changed from within the zone file with the $ORIGIN parser directive (see page 453).

This example has no *ttl* field. The class is IN for Internet, the type is SOA, and the remaining items form the *data* field.

"ns.cs.colorado.edu." is the zone's master name server.

"admin.cs.colorado.edu." is the email address of the technical contact in the format *"user.host."* rather than the standard *user@host*. Just replace that first dot with an @ and remove the final dot if you need to send mail to a domain's administrator. Sites often use an alias such as admin or hostmaster in place of an actual login name.

The parentheses continue the SOA record over several lines. Their placement is not arbitrary in BIND 4 or 8—we tried to shorten the first line by splitting it before the contact address, but then **named** failed to recognize the SOA record. In some implementations, parentheses are only recognized in SOA and TXT records. BIND 9 has a better parser and parentheses can be used anywhere.

The first numeric parameter is the serial number of the zone's configuration data. The serial number is used by slave servers to determine when to get fresh data. It can be any 32-bit integer and should be incremented every time the data file for the zone is changed. Many sites encode the file's modification date in the serial number. For example, 2000123101 would be the first change to the zone on December 31, 2000.

Serial numbers need not be continuous, but they must increase monotonically. If by accident you set a really large value on the master server and that value is transferred to the slaves, then correcting the serial number on the master will not work. The slaves request new data only if the master's serial number is larger than theirs.

There are three ways to fix this problem. BIND 4.9 and BIND 8 include a hack that lets you set the serial number to zero for one refresh interval and then restart the numbering. The zero always causes a reload, so don't forget to set it to a real value after each of the slaves has reloaded the zone with serial number 0. A sneaky but more tedious way to fix the problem is to change the serial number on the master, kill the slave servers, remove the slaves' backup data files so they are forced to reload from the master, and restart the slaves. A third way to fix the problem is to exploit properties of the sequence space in which the serial numbers live. This procedure involves adding a large value to the serial number, letting all the slave servers transfer the data, and then setting the serial number to just what you want. This weird arithmetic, with explicit examples, is covered in detail in the O'Reilly DNS book; RFC1982 describes the sequence space.

It is a common mistake to change the data files but forget to update the serial number. **named** will punish you by failing to propagate your changes to slave servers.

The next four entries in the SOA record are timeout values, in seconds, that control how long data can be cached at various points throughout the world-wide DNS database. These values represent a tradeoff between efficiency (it's cheaper to use an old value than to fetch a new one) and accuracy (new values are more accurate).

The first is the *refresh* timeout, which specifies how often slave servers should check with the master to see if the serial number of the zone's configuration has changed. Whenever the zone changes, slaves must update their copy of the zone's data. Common values for this timeout range from one to six hours (3,600 to 21,600 seconds).

Instead of just waiting passively for slave servers to time out, BIND servers now notify their slaves every time a zone changes, unless the notify parameter is specifically turned off in the configuration file. Slaves that understand the notification act immediately to refresh themselves.

If a slave server tries to check the master's serial number but the master does not respond, the slave tries again after the *retry* timeout period has elapsed. Our experience suggests that 20–60 minutes (1,200–3,600 seconds) is a good value.

If a master server is down for a long time, slaves will try to refresh their data many times but always fail. Each slave should eventually decide that the master is never coming back and that its data is surely out of date. The *expire* parameter determines how long the slaves will continue to serve the domain's data authoritatively in the absence of a master. The system should be able to survive if the master server is down for a week, so this parameter should have a longish value. We recommend a week to a month.

Prior to BIND 8.2, the *minimum* parameter set the default time to live for resource records. It was included with each record and used to expire the cached records on nonauthoritative servers. As of BIND 8.2, the meaning of the *minimum* parameter in the SOA record has changed. It now sets the time to live for negative answers that are cached. The default for positive answers (i.e., actual records) is specified at the top of the zone file with the $TTL directive. Experience suggests values between a few hours and several days for $TTL and an hour or two for the *minimum*. *minimum* cannot be more than three hours.

The $TTL, *expire*, and *minimum* parameters eventually force everyone that uses DNS to discard old data values. The design of DNS relied on the fact that host data was relatively stable and did not change often. However, DHCP and mobile hosts have changed the rules. BIND is desperately trying to cope by providing the dynamic update and incremental zone transfer mechanisms described starting on page 458. For more information about TTLs and a concept called TTL harmonization, see page 454.

### NS records

NS (name server) records identify the servers that are authoritative for a zone (that is, all the master and slave servers) and delegate subdomains to other organizations. NS records usually follow the SOA record.

The format is

*zone [ttl]* IN NS *hostname*

For example:

```
cs.colorado.edu.    IN   NS    ns.cs.colorado.edu.
cs.colorado.edu.    IN   NS    anchor.cs.colorado.edu.
cs.colorado.edu.    IN   NS    ns.cs.utah.edu.
```

Since the zone name is the same as the *name* field of the SOA record that precedes these NS records, it can be left blank. Thus, the lines

```
                    IN   NS    ns.cs.colorado.edu.
                    IN   NS    anchor.cs.colorado.edu.
                    IN   NS    ns.cs.utah.edu.
```

immediately following the SOA record for cs.colorado.edu would be equivalent.

Every authoritative name server for cs.colorado.edu should be listed both in the zone file for cs.colorado.edu and also in the file for the parent zone, colorado.edu. Caching-only servers cannot be authoritative; do not list them. No parameter in the NS records specifies whether a server is a master or a slave. That information is specified in the **named.conf** file.

**named** uses a zone's NS records to identify slave servers when it wants to send out notifications of changes to the zone. Those same NS records inside the parent zone (colorado.edu) define the cs subdomain and delegate authority for it to the computer science department's name servers. If the list of name servers in the parent zone is not kept up to date with those in the zone itself, any new servers that are added become stealth servers and are not used to answer queries from the outside world. This situation happens sometimes through design and sometimes through forgetfulness.

*See page 455 for more information about delegation.*

A quick look at our own delegations revealed a major server for colorado.edu that the edu domain knew nothing about. Do as we say and not as we do: check your delegations with **nslookup** or **dig** to be sure they specify an appropriate set of servers.

### A records

A (address) records are the heart of the DNS database. They provide the mapping from hostnames to IP addresses that was formerly specified in the **/etc/hosts** file. A host must have one A record for each of its network interfaces. The format is

*hostname [ttl]* IN A *ipaddr*

For example:

```
anchor        IN   A     128.138.243.100
```

A machine with multiple network interfaces can use a single hostname associated with all interfaces or have separate hostnames for each interface.

### PTR records

PTR (pointer) records perform the reverse mapping from IP addresses to hostnames. As with A records, a host must have one for each network interface. Before we describe PTR records, however, we need to digress and talk about a special top-level domain called in-addr.arpa.

Fully qualified hostnames can be viewed as a notation in which the "most significant part" is on the right. For example, in the name anchor.cs.colorado.edu, anchor is in cs, cs is in colorado, and colorado is in edu. IP addresses, on the other hand, have the "most significant part" on the left. In the address 128.138.243.100, host 100 is on subnet 243, which is part of network 128.138.

The in-addr.arpa domain was created to allow one set of software modules and one naming tree to map from IP addresses to hostnames as well as from hostnames to IP addresses. Domains under in-addr.arpa are named like IP addresses with their bytes reversed. For example, the zone for our 243 subnet is 243.138.128.in-addr.arpa.

The general format of a PTR record is

   *addr* [ttl] IN PTR *hostname*

For example, the PTR record in the 243.138.128.in-addr.arpa zone that corresponds to anchor's A record above is

   100          IN   PTR   anchor.cs.colorado.edu.

The name 100 does not end in a dot and therefore is relative. But relative to what? Not "cs.colorado.edu.". For this sample record to be accurate, the default domain has to be "243.138.128.in-addr.arpa.".

You can set the domain by putting the PTR records for each subnet in their own file, as in this example. The default domain associated with the file is set in **named**'s configuration file. Another way to do reverse mappings is to include records such as

   100.243      IN   PTR   anchor.cs.colorado.edu.

with a default domain of 138.128.in-addr.arpa. Some sites put all reverse records in the same file and use $ORIGIN directives to specify the subnet. Note that the hostname anchor.cs.colorado.edu must end with a dot to prevent 138.128.in-addr.arpa from being appended to its name.

Since cs.colorado.edu and 243.138.128.in-addr.arpa are different regions of the DNS namespace, they constitute two separate zones. Each zone must have its own SOA record and RRs. In addition to defining an in-addr.arpa zone for each real network, you also need a zone that takes care of the loopback network, 127.0.0.0.

This all works fine if the subnets are on byte boundaries. But how do you handle the reverse mappings for a subnet such as 128.138.243.0/26? An elegant hack defined in RFC2317 exploits CNAME resource records to accomplish this feat; see page 445.

The reverse mappings provided by PTR records are used by any program that authenticates inbound network traffic. For example, **sshd** may allow remote logins without a password if the machine of origin is listed, by name, in a user's ~/.**shosts** file. When the destination host receives a connection request, it knows the source machine only by IP address. It uses DNS to convert the IP address to a hostname, which is then compared to the appropriate file. **netstat**, **tcpd**, **sendmail**, **sshd**, X Windows, **syslogd**, **fingerd**, **ftpd**, and **rlogind** all do reverse mappings to get hostnames from IP addresses.

It is important that A records match their corresponding PTR records. Mismatched and missing PTR records cause authentication failures that can slow your system to a crawl. This problem is annoying in itself; it can also facilitate denial of service attacks against any application that requires the reverse mapping to match the A or A6 resource records.

## MX records

*See Chapter 19 for more information about email.*

The mail system uses mail exchanger records to route mail more efficiently. An MX record preempts the destination of a message, in most cases directing it to a mail hub at the recipient's site rather than the recipient's own workstation.

The format of an MX record is

*name* [*ttl*] IN MX *preference host* ...

Two examples are shown below, one for a host that receives its own mail unless it is down, and one for a host that can't receive mail at all:

```
piper       IN   MX    10 piper
            IN   MX    20 mailhub
            IN   MX    50 boulder.colorado.edu.
xterm1      IN   MX    10 mailhub
            IN   MX    20 anchor
            IN   MX    50 boulder.colorado.edu.
```

Hosts with low preference values are tried first: 0 is the most desirable, and 65,535 is as bad as it gets. In this example, mail addressed to bob@xterm1 would be sent to mailhub if it were accessible, to anchor as a second choice, and if both mailhub and anchor were down, to boulder. Note that boulder's name must be fully qualified since it is not a member of the default domain (here, "cs.colorado.edu.").

The list of preferences and hosts can all be on the same line, but separate lines are easier to read. Leave numeric "space" between preference values so you don't have to renumber if you need to squeeze in a new destination.

MX records are useful in many situations:

- When you have a central mail hub
- When the destination host is down
- When the destination isn't reachable from the Internet
- When the destination host doesn't speak SMTP
- When the local sysadmin knows where mail should be sent better than your correspondents do

In the first of these situations, mail is routed to the mail hub, the machine where most users read mail. In the second case, mail is routed to a nearby host and forwarded when the destination comes back up.

Hosts that are not directly on the Internet can't have A records, but they can have MX records. **sendmail** can't connect directly to the destination, but it can get the mail closer by connecting to one of the destination's MX hosts. The MX hosts presumably have a direct connection to the destination or know how to reach it (behind a firewall or with the UUCP protocol, perhaps).

The final reason to use MX records is that the local sysadmins probably know the mail architecture much better than your correspondents. They need to have the final say on how your site channels its mail stream.

*Every host should have MX records.* For minor hosts, one or two alternates is enough. A major host should have several records. For example, the following set of records might be appropriate for a site at which each host sends and receives its own mail:

- One for the host itself, as first choice
- A departmental mail hub as second choice
- A central mail hub for the domain or parent domain as a backup

The domain itself should have an MX record to a mail hub machine so that mail to *user@domain* will work. Of course, this configuration does require that user names be unique across all machines in the domain. For example, to be able to send mail to evi@cs.colorado.edu, we need a machine called cs, MX records in cs.colorado.edu, or perhaps both.

```
cs          IN   MX   10 mailhub.cs.colorado.edu.
            IN   MX   20 anchor.cs.colorado.edu.
            IN   MX   50 boulder.colorado.edu.
```

A machine that accepts mail for another host must list that other host in its **sendmail** configuration files; see page 578 for a discussion of **sendmail**'s use_cw_file feature and the file **local-host-names**.

Wild card MX records are also sometimes seen in the DNS database:

```
*           IN   MX   10 mailhub.cs.colorado.edu.
```

At first glance, this record seems like it would save lots of typing and add a default MX record for all hosts. But wild card records don't quite work as you might expect. They match anything in the *name* field of a resource record that is *not* already listed as an explicit name in another resource record.

Thus, you *cannot* use a star to set a default value for all your hosts. But perversely, you can use it to set a default value for names that are not your hosts. This setup causes lots of mail to be sent to your hub only to be rejected because the hostname matching the star really does not belong to your domain. Ergo, avoid wild card MX records.

### CNAME records

CNAME records assign additional names to a host. These nicknames are commonly used either to associate a function with a host or to shorten a long hostname. The real name is sometimes called the canonical name (hence, "CNAME").

Some examples:

```
ftp            IN   CNAME   anchor
kb             IN   CNAME   kibblesnbits
```

The format of a CNAME record is

*nickname* [ttl] IN CNAME *hostname*

When the DNS software encounters a CNAME record, it stops its query for the nickname and switches to the real name. If a host has a CNAME record, other records (A, MX, NS, etc.) for that host must refer to its real name, not its nickname. For example, the lines

```
colo-gw        IN   A       128.138.243.25
moogie         IN   CNAME   colo-gw
www            IN   CNAME   moogie
```

are OK. But assigning an address or mail priority (with an A or MX record) to either www or moogie in this example would be wrong.

CNAME records can nest eight deep in BIND. That is, a CNAME record can point to another CNAME, and that CNAME can point to a third CNAME, and so on, up to seven times; the eighth target must be the real A record.

Some sites use CNAME records in a weak attempt at load balancing. They map the public name of their web server to several different machines:

```
www            IN   CNAME   web1
www            IN   CNAME   web2
www            IN   CNAME   web3
```

This use of CNAME records is nonstandard. In fact, it is illegal. An option in BIND 8 allowed you to use this against-the-spec mechanism. BIND 9 is pickier, so it's really not a good idea to use multiple CNAMES. A better way to achieve the same result is to have multiple A records for the web server that point to different machines.

### The CNAME hack

*See page 276 for more information about CIDR.*

CNAMEs are also used to torture the existing semantics of DNS into supporting reverse zones for networks that are not subnetted on a byte boundary. Before CIDR addressing was commonplace, most subnet assignments were on byte boundaries or within the same organization, and the reverse delegations were easy to manage. For example, if the class B network 128.138 was subnetted into a set of class C-like networks, each subnet would make a tidy package for the in-addr.arpa domain. The reverse zone for the 243 subnet would be 243.138.128.in-addr.arpa.

DNS

But what happens if the 243 subnet is further divided into, say, four pieces as a /26 network? If all four pieces are assigned to the same organization, there is actually no problem. The four subnets can still share a single file that contains all their PTR records. However, if the 243 subnet is assigned to an ISP that wants to delegate each /26 network to a different customer, a more complicated solution is necessary. The ISP must either maintain the reverse records on behalf of each client, or it must find a way to take the third octet of the IP address (243 in this case) and divide it into four different pieces that can be delegated independently.

When an administrative boundary falls in the middle of a byte, you have to be sneaky. You must also work closely with the domain above or below you. The trick is this: for each possible host address in the natural in-addr.arpa zone, add a CNAME that deflects the lookup to a zone controlled by the owner of the appropriate subnet. This scheme makes for messy zone files on the parent, but it does let you delegate authority to the actual users of each subnet.

Here is the scheme in gory detail. The parent organization (in our case, the ISP) creates CNAME records for each possible IP address with an extra fake component (dot-separated chunk) that represents the subnet. For example, in the /26 scenario just described, the first quarter of the addresses would have a "0-63" component, the second quarter would have a "64-127" component, and so on. Here's what it looks like:

```
$ORIGIN 243.138.128.in-addr.arpa.
1               IN   CNAME   1.0-63
2               IN   CNAME   2.0-63
...
63              IN   CNAME   63.0-63
64              IN   CNAME   64.64-127
65              IN   CNAME   65.64-127
...
```

To delegate the 0-63 piece of the reverse zone to the customer that has been assigned that subnet, we'd add the following NS records:

```
0-63            IN   NS      ns1.customer1.com.
0-63            IN   NS      ns2.customer1.com.
...
```

customer1.com's site would have a zone file that contained the reverse mappings for the 0-63.243.138.128.in-addr.arpa zone. For example:

```
1               IN   PTR     host1.customer1.com.
2               IN   PTR     host2.customer1.com.
...
```

By adding this extra component, we create a new "cut" at which to perform delegation. When someone looks up the reverse mapping for 128.138.243.1, for example, the CNAME record at 1.243.138.128.in-addr.arpa refocuses their search to the name 1.0-63.243.138.128.in-addr.arpa, and that name is controlled by the customer.

The customer's files are clean; it's only the ISP that must deal with an inelegant configuration mess. But things can get even more complicated. Customer1 could itself be an ISP that wants to further subdivide its addresses. But that's OK: BIND supports CNAME chains up to 8 links long, and since a byte has only eight bits, we can never run out. CNAME chains are discouraged but not forbidden in the RFCs; they do slow down name resolution since each link in a CNAME chain causes the link to be followed and a new query for the target to be initiated.

This whole scheme is a blatant misuse of the CNAME record, but it's so powerful and useful that a variant of it has become the official standard for the handling of IPv6 reverse zones. See the information about DNAME records on page 451 for more information.

Very early in the life of the CNAME hack, the $GENERATE command (see page 453) was added to **named**'s repertoire to facilitate the creation of resource records in the parent zone. For example, to produce the records for the first subnet, the following lines suffice:

```
$ORIGIN 243.138.128.in-addr.arpa.
$GENERATE 0-63 $ CNAME $.0-63
0-63           NS  ns1.customer1.com.
0-63           NS  ns2.customer1.com.
```

The $ in the $GENERATE command iterates from 0 to 63 and creates 64 different CNAME records. The other three /26 networks would be handled similarly.

The CNAME hack works fine for BIND 8 and 9. Some older BIND 4 resolvers don't expect to get a CNAME when they query for a PTR record, so they fail. Yet another good reason to upgrade, perhaps.

### LOC records

*LOC records are defined in RFC1819.*

A LOC record describes the geographic location and, optionally, the physical size (diameter) of a DNS object. LOC records currently have no effect on the technical operation of the Internet, and no standard software looks for them. However, a number of interesting potential uses for the information have been suggested, including route tracing and optimization, automated mapping, and network research.

The format is:

*name [ttl] IN LOC lat lon [alt [size [hp [vp]]]]*

The latitude and longitude are given as space-separated degrees, minutes, and seconds followed by N, S, E, or W. Seconds can be omitted; if they are, minutes can also be omitted.

The other fields are all specified in centimeters (no suffix) or meters (m). *alt* is the object's altitude, *size* is the diameter of the object's bounding sphere, *hp* is the horizontal precision of the measurement, and *vp* is the vertical precision. The default size is one meter, and the default horizontal and vertical precisions are 10 meters and 10 kilometers, respectively.

Here is an example for caida.org in San Diego, California:

```
caida.org.     IN   LOC   32 53 01 N 117 14 25 W 107m 30m 18m 15m
```

Many of the graphical visualization tools written by CAIDA (the Cooperative Association for Internet Data Analysis) require latitude and longitude data, and sites are encouraged to include it in their DNS. However, if you are paranoid and run a high-visibility server or ISP, you may not want the general public to know the exact location of your machines. In such situations, we recommend that you use inexact values. They are still of value to the network research folks but offer some anonymity.

Another noteworthy feature of LOC records is that they appear to crash NT 4.0's name server; take precautions.

## SRV records

A SRV record specifies the location of services within a domain. For example, the SRV record allows you to query a remote domain directly and ask for the name of its FTP server. Until now, you mostly had to guess. To contact the FTP server for a remote domain, you had to hope that the remote sysadmins had followed the current custom and added a CNAME for "ftp" to their server's DNS records.

SRV records make more sense than CNAMEs for this application and are certainly a better way for sysadmins to move services around and control their use. However, they must be explicitly sought and parsed by clients, so it will be a while before their effects are really felt.

SRV records resemble generalized MX records with fields that let the local DNS administrator steer and load-balance connections from the outside world. The format is

```
service.proto.name [ttl] IN SRV pri wt port target
```

where *service* is a service defined in the IANA assigned numbers database (see page 270 or www.iana.org/numbers.htm), *proto* is either tcp or udp, *name* is the domain to which the SRV record refers, *pri* is an MX-style priority, *wt* is a weight used for load balancing among several servers, *port* is the port on which the service runs, and *target* is the hostname of the server that provides this service. The A record of the target is usually returned automatically with the answer to a SRV query. A value of 0 for the *wt* parameter means that no special load balancing should be done. A value of "." for the target means that the service is not run at this site.

Here is an example, snitched from RFC2052 (where SRV is defined) and adapted for the cs.colorado.edu domain:

```
ftp.tcp          SRV  0  0  21  ftp-server.cs.colorado.edu.

; don't allow finger anymore (target = .)
finger.tcp       SRV  0  0  79  .

; 1/4 of the connections to old box, 3/4 to the new one
ssh.tcp          SRV  0  1  22  old-slow-box.cs.colorado.edu.
                 SRV  0  3  22  new-fast-box.cs.colorado.edu.
```

```
; main server on port 80, backup on new box, port 8000
http.tcp            SRV   0   0  80  www-server.cs.colorado.edu.
                    SRV  10   0 8000 new-fast-box.cs.colorado.edu.

; so both http://www.cs.colo... and http://cs.colo... work
http.tcp.www        SRV   0   0  80  www-server.cs.colorado.edu.
                    SRV  10   0 8000 new-fast-box.cs.colorado.edu.

; block all other services (target = .)
*.tcp               SRV   0   0   0  .
*.udp               SRV   0   0   0  .
```

This example illustrates the use of both the weight parameter (for SSH) and the priority parameter (HTTP). Both SSH servers will be used, with the work being split between them. The backup HTTP server will only be used when the principal server is unavailable. The **finger** service is not included, nor are other services that are not explicitly mentioned. The fact that the **finger** daemon does not appear in DNS does not mean that it is not running, just that you can't locate the server through DNS.

WKS (well-known services) was an earlier service-related DNS record that did not catch on. Instead of pointing you to the host that provided a particular service for a domain, it listed the services provided by a particular host. WKS seems sort of useless and was also deemed a security risk. It was not widely adopted.

Microsoft uses standard SRV records in Windows 2000 but inserts them into the DNS system in an undocumented, incompatible way. We are shocked, shocked.

### TXT records

A TXT record adds arbitrary text to a host's DNS records. For example, we have a TXT record that identifies our site:

```
IN                  TXT  "University of CO, Boulder Campus, CS Dept"
```

This record directly follows the SOA and NS records for the "cs.colorado.edu." zone and so inherits the *name* field from them.

TXT records are also used in conjunction with the RP record, which allows you to specify the person responsible for a host in more detail than the contact email address encoded in the SOA record of the zone.

The format of a TXT record is

```
name [ttl] IN TXT info ...
```

All *info* items must be quoted. You can use a single quoted string or multiple strings that are individually quoted. Be sure the quotes are balanced—a missing quote will wreak havoc with your DNS data because all the records between the missing quote and the next occurrence of a quote will mysteriously disappear.

TXT records have no intrinsic order. If you use several of them to add a paragraph of information to your DNS, they may all be scrambled by the time **named** and UDP are done with them.

## IPv6 resource records

*See Chapter 13 for a*
*more detailed discus-*
*sion of IPv6.*

IPv6 is a new version of the IP protocol. It has spent nearly 10 years in the specification process and still isn't done. IPv6 was originally motivated by a perceived need for more IP network addresses. However, the stopgap solutions to this problem—CIDR, NAT, and stricter control of addresses—have been so successful that a mass migration to IPv6 is unlikely to happen any time soon. Unless someone comes up with a new killer app that runs only on IPv6 (or some future version of Microsoft Windows defaults to it), sysadmins are unlikely to have to deal with IPv6 for a few more years. Some folks feel that the next generation of cell phones, which may have IP addresses, might just tip the scales in favor of IPv6.

Even though we don't expect to see IPv6 deployed anytime soon, we think it's worthwhile to describe the impact of 128-bit IP addresses on the DNS system. Both the address records and the pointer records have to change, but those changes are relatively simple compared to the task of supporting one of IPv6's totally new concepts: shared ownership of addresses.

The host interface to which an IPv6 address corresponds owns some of the address bits but not all of them. Other bits are delegated to the site's upstream ISPs in an attempt to make renumbering and changing ISPs an easy task. This design adds a lot of complexity. After looking at all the hoops that DNS has had to jump through to support the standards, we wonder if the standards' authors have written any code lately. Probably not.

The IPv6 equivalent of DNS A records were originally called AAAA records, because IPv6 addresses were four times longer than IPv4 addresses. As the split-control scheme for IPv6 addresses evolved, the IETF standardized on two new record types: A6 records for name-to-address mappings and DNAME records for delegating portions of an address to different organizations. DNAMEs were inspired by the CNAME hack (see page 445), which allows delegation on bit boundaries. A6 records specify an address, but with the possibility that some of the high-order prefix bits must be obtained from another source.

Since we don't expect IPv6 to be widely deployed before the next revision of this book, we defer detailed descriptions of the IPv6 lookup mechanisms until they have been better defined by the IETF and we have some operational experience with them. In the meantime, the following sections outline the gist of the new plan. You can skip ahead to *Commands in zone files* on page 453 if you'd rather not read about IPv6.

## A6 records

The format of an A6 record is

    *hostname* [*ttl*] IN A6 *#-bits-deferred ipaddr referral*

For example:

    anchor      IN   A6    0   3ffe:8050:201:9:a00:20ff:fe81:2b32 .
    anchor      IN   A6    48  ::9:a00:20ff:fe81:2b32 prefix.myisp.net.

These two records specify the same IPv6 address for the host anchor; one is fully specified with no prefix bits deferred, and the other has 48 prefix bits deferred to the host prefix.myisp.net. Note the dot as the referral parameter in the first form of the A6 record; it indicates that no further referral is needed.

Forward name lookups might have to talk to many name servers up the A6 chain to assemble a complete 128-bit address. For example, with the second line above, the next level up could defer 47 bits, the next level could defer 46 bits, and so on. 48 queries might be needed to get the full answer. Add to that number the DNSSEC queries needed to verify each piece of the address, and you have a 100-fold increase in DNS traffic to resolve one name. Design by committee is not always simple and efficient.

Those 48 potential levels will in practice be more like 2 or 3, but the concept may present interesting avenues for denial of service attacks. For more complete (and less prejudiced) documentation, see the BIND 9 **doc** directory.

### DNAME records

DNS's scheme for performing reverse IPv6 address lookups uses both traditional PTR records and records of a new, IPv6-specific type, DNAME. PTR records resolve the local bits of an IPv6 address to a particular hostname, and DNAME records determine which parts of the rest of the address are delegated to which organizations.

In IPv4, reverse mappings live in the in-addr.arpa domain and forward mappings live in the other branches of the domain tree (under com or edu, for example). In IPv6, the reverse mapping information is a bit more scattered. Some of it lives under the ip6.arpa domain and the rest is stored among the forward domains.

The components of names in the in-addr.arpa hierarchy represent the bytes of an IP address. For IPv6, DNS generalizes this scheme and allows name components to represent arbitrary sections of an address. Address sections can be any number of bits wide (for values of "any number" between 1 and 128) and are known as bitstrings.

Bitstrings are represented with a peculiar syntax known as a bitstring label. Let's look at an example. All IPv6 unicast addresses begin with the three bits 001. To express this prefix in the language of bitstrings, we start with the binary number 001 and pad it out to a multiple of four bits: 0010. This computation give us the hex digit 2; the digit has three valid bits and one discard bit. The final bitstring is:

    \[x2/3]

The backslash, square brackets, and x delimit every bitstring. The important parts are a series of hex digits (just one in this case, 2) and the length qualifier, /3. The length qualifier, which tells how many of the bits represented by the hex digits are really valid, is optional. If omitted, the bitstring defaults to its natural length as determined by the number of hex digits (here, 4 bits).

Even if your bitstrings end at a hex-digit boundary, it's a good idea to include the length qualifier. Otherwise, the readers of your DNS files will go blind from counting long strings of tiny little hex digits.

The leftmost bits of a hex string are the significant ones. Extra bits used to pad out the rightmost hex digit are simply discarded. Pad bits must be 0s.

Because all unicast IPv6 addresses share the same 001 prefix, the effective top-level domain for IPv6 reverse mappings is \[x2/3].ip6.arpa.

Here is a more complete example. The lines below show three different representations of the same address: the first undivided, the second divided into three pieces (3/45/80), and the third divided into four pieces (3/13/32/80).[9] As address chunks get shifted around, their hex representations change completely—it's still the same bits underneath, however. **bc** is your friend for bit twiddling.

```
\[x3ffe8050020100090a0020fffe812b32/128].ip6.arpa.
\[x00090a0020fffe812b32/80].\[xfff402801008/45].\[x2/3].ip6.arpa.
\[x00090a0020fffe812b32/80].\[x80500201/32].\[xfff0/13].\[x2/3].ip6.arpa
```

As with IPv4 in-addr.arpa zones, individual numbers read from left to right and components (dot-separated chunks) read from right to left. The first component on the second and third lines above is the local part of the address. It represents the low-order 80 bits of the address and consists of the hex digits 00090a0020fffe812b32. Here are the same three lines again with the local part of the address boldfaced:

```
\[x3ffe80500201**00090a0020fffe812b32**/128].ip6.arpa.
\[x**00090a0020fffe812b32**/80].\[xfff402801008/45].\[x2/3].ip6.arpa.
\[x**00090a0020fffe812b32**/80].\[x80500201/32].\[xfff0/13].\[x2/3].ip6.arpa
```

The /3 in the second line says that the first three of the four bits in the hex digit 2 are valid parts of the address. The /45 in the second line means that the first 45 of the 48 bits present in the hex string fff402801008 are valid in the middle piece of the address. Aren't all these fragments going to be easy to type into your DNS files without making mistakes? Geez.

DNAME records delegate address chunks to other name servers. Their format is:

```
bitstring-label [ttl] IN DNAME domain-delegated-to
```

The idea is that different organizations can control the different pieces of an address or address prefix. You control the local 80 bits, your ISP controls a chunk, your ISP's ISP controls a chunk, and so on. The excerpts below demonstrate the delegation that DNAME records can do. We use the address above in its four-pieces incarnation, in which the delegation path is from the root to my-isp to my-domain.

In this example, the $ORIGIN statements identify the context of each record. These excerpts are from the zone files at three different sites: the root of the ip6.arpa tree, my-isp.net, and my-domain.com—they do not represent a consistent configuration for a single site.

---

9. While poking around at the level of bits, it's easy to lose sight of the fact that IPv6 addresses have some internal structure of their own. See page 281 for a discussion of the boundaries and meanings of the regions into which an IPv6 address is conventionally divided.

The root of the ip6.arpa tree, \[x2/3].ip6.arpa, delegates a particular 13-bit address to my-isp.net by entering the following lines into its zone file:

```
; delegate prefix to my-isp.net
$ORIGIN \[x2/3].ip6.arpa.
\[xfff0/13]        IN  DNAME  ip6.my-isp.net.
```

These records create a sort of nickname for \[xfff0/13].\[x2/3].ip6.arpa that points to the string "ip6.my-isp.net.". The ISP in turn delegates a 32-bit segment of address space to my-domain.com by including these lines in its ip6.my-isp.net zone file:

```
; delegate prefix to my-domain.com
$ORIGIN ip6.my-isp.net.
\[x80500201/32] IN  DNAME  ip6.my-domain.com.
```

This line forms a name, "\[x80500201/32].ip6.my-isp.net.", which when expanded from the previous DNAME record becomes the 48-bit prefix of the IPv6 address. Those 48 bits are nicknamed ip6.my-domain.com.

In the zone files for ip6.my-domain.com, the rest of the address is mapped with a PTR record:

```
$ORIGIN ip6.my-domain.com.
\[x00090a0020fffe812b32/80]   IN  PTR   host.my-domain.com.
```

We suggest that you not bother with the DNAME delegations if you have only one ISP and are not multihomed. Just list the whole 128-bit address in both forward and reverse zones. You still get some bits from your upstream ISP, but you can put them in your own zone files as long as your ISP tells you when it changes the prefix.

IPv6 is still young, at least from the deployment point of view. The registries are just starting to assign addresses, and the process will become smoother with experience. The local part of the IPv6 address never needs to change, and that's great—no renumbering. But at many organizations, upstream ISPs don't change frequently either, and so putting the ISP's bits into your own data files seems like a good thing. A quick Perl script could change the prefix of all your addresses if you ever switched ISPs.

### Commands in zone files

Now that we have looked at all the basic resource records, let's look at the commands that can be embedded in a zone file to modify the records that follow them. There are four:

```
$ORIGIN domain-name
$INCLUDE filename
$TTL default-ttl
$GENERATE lots-of-args
```

Commands *must* start in the first column and be on a line by themselves.

As **named** reads a zone file, it adds the default domain (or "origin") to any names that are not already fully qualified. The origin is initially set to the domain name specified in the corresponding zone statement in **named.conf**. However, you can set the origin by hand within a zone file by using the $ORIGIN directive.

The use of relative names where fully qualified names are expected saves lots of typing and makes zone files much easier to read. For example, the reverse records for a subnetted class B site might all be in one zone file, with $ORIGIN statements setting the context for each subnet. A statement such as

    $ORIGIN 243.138.128.in-addr.arpa

could precede the records for the 243 subnet.

Many sites use the $INCLUDE directive in their zone database files to separate overhead records from data records, to separate logical pieces of a zone file, or to keep cryptographic keys in a file with restricted permissions. The syntax of the $INCLUDE directive is

    $INCLUDE *filename*

The specified file is read into the database at the point of the $INCLUDE directive.

The $TTL directive sets a default value for the time-to-live field of the records that follow it. Previously, the only way to set the default was in the SOA record (described on page 438). BIND 8 likes to have a $TTL at the beginning of zone files; BIND 9 requires it and refuses to load zone files that do not set a default $TTL.

BIND 9 enforces a concept known as TTL harmonization; it forces all records in an RRset (that is, all records of the same type that pertain to a single node) to have the same TTL. The value that's actually used is that of the first resource record for the node/type pair.

$GENERATE, a relatively new BIND 8 construct, provides a simple way to generate a series of similar records. It serves mostly to help with generating RFC2317-style classless in-addr.arpa mappings (the CNAME hack for reverse zone files), for cases in which the boundaries of administrative authority do not match the boundaries of bytes in an IP address.

The format of the $GENERATE directive is

    $GENERATE *start-stop/[step] lhs type rhs [comment]*

and the generated lines are of the form

    *lhs type rhs*

The *start* and *stop* fields specify the range of values for a single numeric iterator. One line is generated for each value in the interval. The iterator value is incorporated into *lhs* and *rhs* with the $ character. If you also specify a *step*, the iteration is by *step*-size increments. *type* is the record type. Currently, only CNAME, PTR, and NS are supported, and only in BIND 8. BIND 9 might support this construct in later releases. See page 447 for an example.

## The localhost zone

The address 127.0.0.1 refers to a host itself and should always be mapped to the name "localhost.*localdomain*.", for example, localhost.cs.colorado.edu. Some sites map the address to just plain "localhost." as though it were part of the root domain; this configuration is incorrect.

If you forget to configure the localhost zone, your site may end up querying the root servers for localhost information. The root servers are currently receiving so many of these queries that the operators are considering adding a generic mapping between localhost and 127.0.0.1 at the root level.

See page 480 for an example of a complete and correct localhost configuration.

## Glue records: links between zones

Each zone stands alone with its own set of data files, name servers, and clients. But zones need to be connected together to form a coherent hierarchy: cs.colorado.edu is a part of colorado.edu, and we need some DNS linkage between them.

Since DNS referrals occur only from parent domains to child domains, it is not necessary for a name server to know anything about the domains (or more accurately, zones) above it in the DNS hierarchy. However, the servers of a parent domain must know the IP addresses of the name servers for all of its subdomains. In fact, *only* the name servers known to the parent zone can be returned as referrals in response to external queries.

In DNS terms, the parent zone needs to contain the NS records for each delegated zone. Since NS records are written in terms of hostnames rather than IP addresses, the parent server must also have a way to resolve the hostnames, either by making a normal DNS query (if this does not create a dependency loop) or by having copies of the appropriate A records.

There are two ways to meet this requirement: by including the necessary records or by using stub zones.

With the first method, you can simply include the necessary NS and A records in the parent zone. For example, the colorado.edu zone file could contain these records:

```
; subdomain information

cs          IN   NS   ns.cs.colorado.edu.
            IN   NS   piper.cs.colorado.edu.
            IN   NS   ns.xor.com.
ee          IN   NS   ns.ee.colorado.edu.
            IN   NS   ns.cs.colorado.edu.

; glue records

ns.cs       IN   A    128.138.243.151
piper.cs    IN   A    128.138.204.4
ns.ee       IN   A    128.138.200.1
```

The "foreign" A records are called glue records because they don't really belong in this zone. They're only reproduced here to connect the new domain to the Internet naming tree. Missing or incorrect glue records will leave part of your namespace inaccessible, and users trying to reach it will get "host unknown" errors.

It is a common error to include glue records for hostnames that don't need them. For example, ns.xor.com in the example above can be resolved with a normal DNS query. An A record would initially just be unnecessary, but it could later become downright misleading if ns.xor.com's address were to change. The rule of thumb is to include A records only for hosts that are within the current domain or any of its subdomains. Current versions of BIND ignore unnecessary glue records and log their presence as an error.

The scheme just described is the standard way of connecting zones, but it requires the child to keep in touch with the parent and tell the parent about any changes or additions to its name server fleet. Since parent and child zones are often run by different sites, updates are often a tedious manual task that requires coordination across administrative boundaries. A corollary is that in the real world, this type of configuration is often out of date.

The second way to maintain links is to use stub zones. Stub zones are fully supported in BIND 8, but were also available in BIND 4 (though documented as being experimental). A stub zone is essentially the same thing as a slave zone, but it includes only the zone's NS records.

Stub zones work fine in BIND 8, which mixes different zones' data in memory, but they don't work as well with BIND 9. In BIND 9, the stub zones must be configured identically on both the master and slave servers of the parent, something that is in itself hard to keep consistent. Your best bet is to just keep in touch with your parent domain and to verify its configuration at least a couple of times a year.

You can use the **dig** command to see which of your servers your parent domain is currently advertising. First run

>     **dig** *parent-domain* **ns**

to determine the name servers for your parent domain. Pick one and run

>     **dig** *@name-server.parent-domain child-domain* **ns**

to see your list of public name servers.

One situation in which stub zones are very useful is when your internal addressing uses the RFC1918 private address space and you need to keep the RFC1918 delegations in sync. The BIND 8 distribution contains an example in **src/conf/recursive**.

A couple of stub zone subtleties are worth mentioning:

- Stub zones are not authoritative copies of the zone's data, and stub servers should not be listed among the zone's NS records.

- Since stub servers are not listed in NS records, they are not notified automatically when the zone's data changes. To update stub servers, you can either add an also-notify clause to the configuration of the master servers, or you can simply wait for the zone to be updated at the end of the refresh interval specified in the zone's SOA record. The timeout option should work just fine in most cases, though it can potentially result in transitory lame delegations (see page 478).

- Theoretically, it's no use for **named** to have copies of a zone's NS records if it cannot also obtain the matching A records. However, **named** can bootstrap itself by using the master's IP address, which is given in **named.conf**.

- Why limit yourself to NS records? Why not just be a secondary server for the subdomains? This works, too. However, if every server of the parent domain is also a server of a child domain, then no referrals will ever be made to downstream servers. The parent domain's servers will be providing all the DNS service for the subdomain. Perhaps this is what you want, and perhaps not.

## 16.12  UPDATING ZONE FILES

When you make a change to a domain (such as adding or deleting a host), the data files on the master server must be updated. You must also increment the serial number in the SOA record for the zone and then run **ndc reload** to signal **named** to pick up the changes. You can also kill and restart **named** (**ndc restart**), but this operation causes cached data from other domains to be discarded.

Earlier versions of BIND used signals and the UNIX **kill** command to control **named**, but just as the developers started running out of signal numbers, **ndc** came along and fixed it all. Most of the historical signal stuff in BIND (except for the HUP signal to reread the configuration file and the TERM signal to die) is likely to go away in future releases, so we recommend sticking with **ndc**.

The updated zone data is propagated to slave servers right away because the notify option is on by default. If you have inadvertently turned this option off, your slave servers do not pick up the changes until after *refresh* seconds, as set in the zone's SOA record (typically one to six hours later). If you want a more timely update when the notify option is turned off, **ndc reload** on a slave causes it to check with the master, see that the data has changed, and request a zone transfer.

Don't forget to modify both the forward and reverse zones when you change a hostname or IP address. Forgetting the reverse files leaves sneaky errors: some commands work and some won't.

Changing the data files but forgetting to change the serial number makes the changes take effect on the master server (after a reload) but not on the slaves.

It is improper to edit data files belonging to slave servers. These files are maintained by **named**; sysadmins should not meddle with them. It's fine to look at the data files as long as you don't make changes. They can often reveal hidden errors in the zone files. For example, a pesky missing dot that's easy to overlook in the master's config files can result in obviously bogus entries such as

```
foo.cs.colorado.edu.cs.colorado.edu
```

appearing in the data file of a slave.

BIND allows zone changes to be made through a programmatic API, as specified in RFC2136. This feature, called dynamic update, is necessary for autoconfiguration protocols like DHCP. The dynamic update mechanism is described on page 459.

### Zone transfers

DNS servers are synchronized through a mechanism called a zone transfer. The original DNS specification (and BIND 4) required all zone data to be transferred at once. Incremental updates were eventually defined in RFC1995 and implemented in BIND 8.2. Original and incremental-style zone transfers are sometimes referred to as AXFR and IXFR, respectively. Once configured, they're supposed to be equivalent.

A slave that wants to refresh its data requests a zone transfer from the master server and makes a backup copy of the zone data on disk. If the data on the master has not changed, as determined by a comparison of the serial numbers (not the actual data), no update occurs and the backup files are just touched (that is, their modification time is set to the current time).

Zone transfers use the TCP protocol on port 53 and log information through syslog with the tag "named-xfer." IXFR as specified by the IETF can use either TCP or UDP, but BIND has only implemented it over TCP.

Both the sending and receiving server remain available to answer queries during a zone transfer. Only after the transfer is complete does the slave begin to use the new data. BIND 8 actually calls a separate **named-xfer** program to perform the transfer, but BIND 9's **named** handles the transfers directly. Therefore, the named-xfer option that specified the path to the **named-xfer** program is no longer part of the configuration language for BIND 9.

When zones are huge (like com) or dynamically updated (see the next section), changes are typically small relative to the size of the entire zone. With IXFR, only the changes are sent (unless they are larger than the complete zone, in which case a regular AXFR transfer is done). The IXFR mechanism is like the **patch** program in that it applies differences to an old database to bring it into sync with a new database.

In BIND 8, you enable IXFR by telling **named** to keep a transaction log in the global options section and then turning it on in the server statements for any servers that use it. The relevant configuration lines are:

```
maintain-ixfr-base true ;        # in options section
use-ixfr true ;                  # in server statement
```

If you want to change the default names for the transaction log and temporary file used by IXFR, do it in the zone statements with:

```
ixfr-base "filename" ;          # in zone statements
ixfr-tmp-file "filename" ;      # in zone statements
```

In BIND 9, IXFR is the default for any zones configured for dynamic update, and **named** keeps a transaction log whenever possible. The options provide-ixfr and request-ixfr can be set in the server statements for individual peers. provide-ixfr enables or disables IXFR service for zones for which this server is the master. The request-ixfr option requests IXFRs for zones for which this server is a slave.

```
provide-ixfr yes ;              # in server statement
request-ixfr yes ;              # in server statement
```

BIND cannot cope with a zone being both dynamically updated and edited by hand. BIND 9 provides outgoing IXFR for changes that resulted from dynamic updates or from incoming IXFRs, but not for changes that resulted from edits to the master zone files. This feature will likely be added in a later release.

A lot of work has gone into the IXFR mechanism to ensure that a server crash during an update does not leave the zones with trashed data. An IXFR request to a server that does not support it automatically falls back to the standard AXFR zone transfer.

### Dynamic updates

The DNS system is built on the premise that name-to-address mappings are relatively stable and do not change frequently. However, a site that uses DHCP to dynamically assign IP addresses as machines boot and join the network breaks this rule constantly. There are two classical solutions: add generic entries to the DNS database or continually edit the DNS files. For many sites, neither solution is satisfactory.

The first solution should be familiar to anyone who has used a dial-up ISP. The DNS configuration looks something like this:

```
dhcp-host1.domain.    IN   A    192.168.0.1
dhcp-host2.domain.    IN   A    192.168.0.2
```

Although this is a simple solution, it means that hostnames are permanently associated with particular IP addresses and that computers therefore change hostnames whenever they receive a new IP address. Hostname-based logging or security measures become very difficult in this environment.

The dynamic update feature in recent versions of BIND provides an alternative solution. It allows the DHCP daemon to notify BIND of the address assignments it makes, thus updating the contents of the DNS database on the fly. A shell interface is also provided for making dynamic updates by hand.

Dynamic updates can add, delete, or modify resource records. The granularity at which dynamic updates are regulated is the zone. It's a bit scary to allow dynamic updates to your site's entire DNS database, so many sites create a subdomain (perhaps dhcp.*site*) and allow dynamic updates only within that subdomain.

Dynamic updates to a zone are enabled in **named.conf** with an allow-update clause. Once a zone has been dynamically updated, you cannot edit it by hand without first stopping BIND so that the current copy of the database can be written out to disk. You can then edit the zone file by hand and restart **named**. Of course, the original formatting of the zone file will be destroyed (the file will look like those maintained by **named** for slave servers).

Incremental zone transfers are the default for zones that use dynamic updates, but IXFR cannot handle changes that are made to the zone by editing the master file by hand, even when you stop **named**, edit the zone file, and restart.

## 16.13 SECURITY ISSUES

DNS started out as an inherently open system, but it has steadily grown more and more secure—or at least, securable. By default, anyone on the Internet can investigate your domain with individual queries from tools like **dig**, **host**, or **nslookup**. In some cases, they can dump your entire DNS database.

To address such vulnerabilities, BIND now supports various types of access control based on host and network addresses or on cryptographic authentication. Table 16.10 summarizes the security features that are configured in **named.conf**. The Page column shows where in this chapter to look for more information.

**Table 16.10    Security features in named.conf**

| Feature | Statements | Page | What it specifies |
|---------|-----------|------|-------------------|
| allow-query | options, zone | 422 | Who can query a zone or server |
| allow-transfer | options, zone | 422 | Who can request zone transfers |
| allow-update | zone | 424 | Who can make dynamic updates |
| blackhole | options | 422 | Which servers to completely ignore |
| bogus | server | 423 | Which servers should never be queried |
| acl | various | 422 | Access control lists |

**named** can run in a **chroot**ed environment under a nonprivileged UID, thus removing any possibility of rootly running-amok. It can use transaction signatures to control dynamic updates, and of course, it also supports the whole DNSSEC hairball. These topics are taken up in the next few sections.

### Access control lists revisited

ACLs are named address match lists that can appear as arguments to statements such as allow-query, allow-transfer, and blackhole. ACLs can help with two major DNS security issues: spoofing and denial of service attacks. Their basic syntax was described on page 422.

Every site should at least have one ACL for bogus addresses and one ACL for local addresses. For example:

```
acl bogusnets {           // ACL for bogus networks
     0.0.0.0/8 ;          // default, wild card addresses
     169.254.0.0/16 ;     // link-local delegated addresses[10]
     192.0.2.0/24 ;       // sample addresses, like example.com
     224.0.0.0/3 ;        // multicast address space
     10.0.0.0/8 ;         // private address space (RFC1918)[11]
     172.16.0.0/12 ;      // private address space (RFC1918)
     192.168.0.0/16 ;     // private address space (RFC1918)
} ;

acl cunets {              // ACL for University of Colorado networks
     128.138.0.0/16 ;     // main campus network
     198.11.16/24 ;
     204.228.69/24 ;
};
```

In the global options section of your config file, you could then include

```
allow-recursion { cunets; } ;
blackhole { bogusnets; } ;
```

It's also a good idea to restrict zone transfers to legitimate slave servers. An ACL makes things nice and tidy.

```
acl ourslaves {
     128.138.242.1 ;      // anchor
     ...
} ;

acl measurements {
     128.9.160.157 ;      // bill manning's measurements
     198.32.4.0/24 ;      // bill manning's measurements
     192.5.5.0/24 ;       // mark lottors's measurements
} ;
```

The actual restriction is implemented with a line such as:

```
allow-transfer { ourslaves; measurements; } ;
```

Transfers are limited to our own slave servers and to the machines of two Internet measurement projects that walk the reverse DNS tree to determine the size of the Internet and the percentage of misconfigured servers. Limiting transfers in this way makes it impossible for other sites to dump your entire database with **nslookup**, **dig**, or **host**.

---

10. The link-local address is used by Macs and PCs that have been told to use IP but cannot find a DHCP server. These machines just assign themselves an address on the 169.254.0.0/16 network. Addresses in this range should be aggressively filtered so that they never escape from the local wire. Cable and DSL modems are starting to use this address range as well.

11. Don't make private addresses bogus if you use them and are configuring your internal DNS servers!

For example:

```
% nslookup
Default Server: server-name
Address: server-IP-address

> ls cs.colorado.edu.
[server name]
*** Can't list domain cs.colorado.edu: Unspecified error
```

You should still protect your network at a lower level through router access control lists and normal security hygiene on each host. If those measures are not possible, you can refuse DNS packets except to a gateway machine that you monitor closely.

### Confining named

To confine the damage that someone could do if they compromised your server, you can run **named** in a **chroot**ed environment and/or run it as a nonprivileged user. The -**t** flag specifies the directory to **chroot** to, and the -**u** and -**g** flags specify the UID and GID under which to run. BIND 9 supports the -**u** flag, but not the -**g** flag. For example, the commands

```
# named -u 53 -g 53 -t /var/named    /* BIND 8 */
# named -u 53 -t /var/named          /* BIND 9 */
```

would start **named** with UID 53, GID 53 (in BIND 8 only), and a root directory of **/var/named**.

The **chroot** directory cannot be an empty directory since it must contain all the files that **named** normally requires in order to run: **/dev/null**, shared libraries, the zone files, **named.conf**, etc. If you can compile **named** to statically link its libraries, you don't have to figure out which library files to copy to **/var/named**.

If hackers compromise your **named**, they can potentially gain access to the system as whatever user **named** runs as. If this user is root and you do not use a **chroot**ed environment, such a breach can be quite destructive. Many sites don't bother to use the -**u**, -**g**, and -**t** flags, but they must then be faster to upgrade than the hackers are to attack when a new vulnerability is announced.

### Secure server-to-server communication with TSIG and TKEY

While DNSSEC (covered in the next section) was being specified, the IETF developed a simpler mechanism called TSIG (RFC2845) to allow secure communication among servers through the use of transaction signatures. Access control based on transaction signatures is more secure than access control based on IP source addresses.

Transaction signatures use a symmetric encryption scheme. That is, the encryption key is the same as the decryption key. This single key is called a shared-secret key. You must use a different key for each pair of servers that want to communicate securely. TSIG is much less expensive computationally than public key cryptography, but it is only appropriate for a local network on which the number of pairs of communicating servers is small. It does not scale to the global Internet.

TSIG signatures sign DNS queries and responses to queries. They are used only between servers, not between servers and resolvers. TSIG signatures are checked at the time a packet is received and are then discarded; they are not cached and do not become part of the DNS data. Although the TSIG specification allows multiple encryption methods, BIND implements only one, the HMAC-MD5 algorithm.

BIND's **dnssec-keygen**[12] utility generates a key for a pair of servers. For example, to generate a shared-secret key for two servers, *serv1* and *serv2*, use

```
# dnssec-keygen -H 128 -h -n serv1-serv2
```

to create a 128-bit key and store it in the file **K***serv1-serv2***+157+00000.private**. The file contains the string "Key:" followed by a base-64 encoding of the actual key.

The generated key is really just a long random number. You could generate the key manually by writing down an ASCII string of the right length and pretending that it's a base-64 encoding of something or by using **mmencode** to encode a random string. The way you create the key is not important; it just has to exist on both machines.

*scp is part of the SSH suite. See page 672 for details.*

Copy the key to both *serv1* and *serv2* with **scp**, or cut and paste it. *Do not* use **telnet** or **ftp** to copy the key; even internal networks may not be secure. The key must be included in both machines' **named.conf** files. Since **named.conf** is usually world-readable and keys should not be, put the key in a separate file that is included into **named.conf**. For example, you could put the snippet

```
key serv1-serv2 {
    algorithm hmac-md5 ;
    secret "shared-key-you-generated" ;
} ;
```

in the file **serv1-serv2.key**. The file should have mode 600 and its owner should be **named**'s UID. In the **named.conf** file, you'd add the line

```
include "serv1-serv2.key"
```

near the top.

This part of the configuration simply defines the keys. To make them actually be used to sign and verify updates, each server needs to identify the other with a keys clause. For example, you might add the lines

```
server serv2's-IP-address {
    keys { serv1-serv2 ; } ;
} ;
```

to serv1's **named.conf** file and

```
server serv1's-IP-address {
    keys { serv1-serv2 ; } ;
} ;
```

---

12. This command is called **dnskeygen** in BIND 8.

to serv2's **named.conf** file. Any allow-query, allow-transfer, and allow-update clauses in the zone statement for the zone should also refer to the key. For example:

```
allow-transfer { key serv1-serv2 ;} ;
```

When you first start using transaction signatures, run **named** at debug level 1 (see page 473 for information about running **named** in debug mode) for a while to see any error messages that are generated. Older versions of BIND do not understand signed messages and complain about them, sometimes to the point of refusing to load the zone.

TKEY is a BIND 9 mechanism that allows two hosts to generate a shared secret key automatically without phone calls or secure copies to distribute the key. It uses an algorithm called the Diffie-Hellman key exchange in which each side makes up a random number, does some math on it, and sends the result to the other side. Each side then mathematically combines its own number with the transmission it received to arrive at the same key. An eavesdropper might overhear the transmission but will be unable to reverse the math.[13]

## DNSSEC

DNSSEC is a set of DNS extensions that authenticate the origin of zone data and verify its integrity by using public key cryptography. That is, the extensions permit DNS clients to ask the questions, "Did this DNS data really come from the zone's owner?" and "Is this really the data sent by that owner?"

DNSSEC provides three distinct services: key distribution by means of KEY resource records stored in the zone files, origin verification for servers and data, and verification of the integrity of zone data. DNSSEC relies upon a cascading chain of trust: the root servers provide validation information for the top-level domains, the top-level domains provide validation information for the second-level domains, and so on.

Public key cryptosystems use two keys: one to encrypt (sign) and a different one to decrypt (verify). Publishers sign their data with a secret "private" key. Anyone can verify the validity of a signature with a matching "public" key that is widely distributed. If a public key correctly decrypts a zone file, then the zone must have been encrypted with the corresponding private key. The trick is to make sure that the public keys you use for verification are authentic. Public key systems allow one entity to sign the public key of another, thus vouching for the legitimacy of the key; hence the term "chain of trust."

The data in a DNS zone is too voluminous to be encrypted with public key cryptography—the encryption would be too slow. Instead, since the data is not secret, a secure hash (e.g., an MD5 checksum) is run on the data and the results of the hash are signed (encrypted) by the zone's private key. The results of the hash are like a fingerprint of the data, and the signed fingerprint is called a digital signature.

---

13. The math involved is called the discrete log problem and relies on the fact that for modular arithmetic taking powers is easy but taking logs to undo the powers is close to impossible.

Digital signatures are usually appended to the data they authenticate. To verify the signature, you decrypt it with the public key of the signer, run the data through the same secure hash algorithm, and compare the computed hash value with the decrypted hash value. If they match, you have authenticated the signer and verified the integrity of the data.

In the DNSSEC system, each zone has its own public and private keys. The private key signs each RRset (that is, each set of records of the same type for the same host). The public key verifies the signatures and is included in the zone's data in the form of a KEY resource record.

Parent zones sign their child zones' public keys. **named** verifies the authenticity of a child zone's KEY record by checking it against the parent zone's signature. To verify the authenticity of the parent zone's key, **named** can check the parent's parent, and so on back to the root. The public key for the root zone is included in the root hints file.

Several steps are required to create and use signed zones. First, you generate a key pair for the zone. For example, in BIND 9,

```
# dnssec-keygen -a DSA -b 768 -n ZONE mydomain.com.
```

or in BIND 8,

```
# dnskeygen -D768 -z -n mydomain.com.
```

Table 16.11 shows the meanings of the arguments to these commands.

**Table 16.11    Decoding guide for dnssec-keygen and dnskeygen arguments**

| Argument | Meaning |
|---|---|
| For **dnssec-keygen** | |
| **-a DSA** | Uses the DSA algorithm |
| **-b 768** | Creates a 768-bit key pair |
| **-n ZONE mydomain.com.** | Creates keys for a zone named mydomain.com |
| For **dnskeygen** | |
| **-D768** | Uses the DSA algorithm, with a 768-bit key |
| **-z** | Creates a zone key |
| **-n mydomain.com.** | Creates keys for a zone named mydomain.com |

**dnssec-keygen** and **dnskeygen** return the following output:

```
alg = 003
key identifier = 12345
flags = 16641
```

They also create files containing the public and private keys:

**Kmydomain.com.+003+12345.key**          # public
**Kmydomain.com.+003+12345.private**       # private key

The public key is typically $INCLUDEd into the zone file. It can go anywhere after the SOA record, but is usually the next record after SOA.

DNSSEC requires a chain of trust, so a zone's public key must be signed by its parent to be verifiably valid. BIND 8 had no mechanism to get a parent zone to sign a child zone's key other than out-of-band cooperation among administrators. BIND 9 provides a program called **dnssec-makekeyset** to help with this process.

**dnssec-makekeyset** bundles the keys you want signed (there may be more than just the zone key), a TTL for the resulting key set, and a signature validity period, then sends the bundle to the parent for signing. For example, the command

```
# dnssec-makekeyset -t 3600 -s now -e now+864000
    Kmydomain.com.+003+12345
```

bundles the public zone key that you just generated with a TTL of 3,600 seconds (one hour) and requests that the parent's signature be valid for 10 days starting from now. **dnssec-makekeyset** creates a single output file, **mydomain.com.keyset**. You must then send the file to the parent zone for signing. It contains the public key and signatures generated by the zone keys themselves so that the parent can verify the child's public key.

In BIND 9, the parent zone uses the **dnssec-signkey** program to sign the bundled set of keys:

```
# dnssec-signkey mydomain.com.keyset Kcom.+003+56789
```

This command produces a file called **mydomain.com.signedkey**, which the parent (com) sends back to the child (mydomain.com) to be included in the zone files for mydomain.com. In BIND 8, the parent uses the **dnssigner** command.

Once you have obtained the parent's signature, you are ready to sign the zone's actual data. The signing operation takes a normal zone data file as input and adds SIG and NXT records immediately after every set of resource records. The SIG records are the actual signatures, and the NXT records support signing of negative answers.

In BIND 8, you use the **dnssigner** program in the **contrib** directory of the distribution to sign a zone; in BIND9, you use the **dnssec-signzone** command. For example, the commands

```
# dnssigner -or mydomain.com -zi db.mydomain -zo
    db.mydomain.signed -k1 mydomain.com dsa 12345 -st    # BIND 8
# dnssec-signzone -o mydomain.com db.mydomain           # BIND 9
```

read the zone file **db.mydomain** and produce a signed version of the zone file called **db.mydomain.signed**. The BIND 8 command shows several statistics about the signing operation (requested by the **-st** parameter). In particular, it shows how long it took to sign the zone and shows what records were added or deleted. It can take a long time to sign a zone.

A SIG record contains a wealth of information:

- The type of record set being signed
- The signature algorithm used (in our case, it's 3, the DSA algorithm)
- The TTL of the record set that was signed
- The time the signature expires (as *yyyymmddhhssss*)
- The time the record set was signed (also *yyyymmddhhssss*)
- The key identifier (in our case 12345)
- The signer's name (mydomain.com.)
- And finally, the digital signature itself

To use the signed zone, change the file parameter in the **named.conf** zone statement for mydomain.com to point at **db.mydomain.signed** instead of **db.mydomain**. In BIND 8, you must also include a pubkey statement in the zone statement; BIND 8 verifies the zone data as it loads and so must know the key beforehand. BIND 9 does not perform this verification. It gets the public key from the KEY record in the zone data and does not need any other configuration. Whew! That's it.

Digital signatures are fine for positive answers like "Here is the IP address for the host anchor.cs.colorado.edu, along with a signature to prove that it really came from cs.colorado.edu and that the data is valid." But what about negative answers like "No such host?" Such negative responses typically do not return any signable records.

In DNSSEC, this problem is handled by NXT records that list the next record in the zone in a canonical sorted order.[14] If the next record after anchor in cs.colorado.edu was awesome.cs.colorado.edu and a query for anthill.cs.colorado.edu arrived, the response would be a signed NXT record such as

```
anchor.cs.colorado.edu.   IN   NXT awesome.cs.colorado.edu A MX NXT
```

This record says that the name immediately after anchor in the cs.colorado.edu zone is awesome, and that anchor has at least one A record, MX record, and NXT record. The last NXT record in a zone wraps around to the first host in the zone. For example, the NXT record for zamboni.cs.colorado.edu would point back to the first record, that of cs.colorado.edu itself:

```
zamboni.cs.colorado.edu.  IN   NXT cs.colorado.edu A MX NXT
```

NXT records are also returned if the host exists but the record type queried for does not exist. For example, if the query was for a LOC record for anchor, anchor's same NXT record would be returned and would show only A, MX, and NXT records.

The material in this section describes DNSSEC as of BIND v9.0.0 (July, 2000). Judging from the significant changes that occurred during the beta cycle, this information may not be correct for long. As always, consult your manuals, the documentation that

---

14. The ordering is sort of alphabetical, but with names higher up the DNS tree coming first. For example, in the cs.colorado.edu zone, cs.colorado.edu comes before any host.cs.colorado.edu. Within a level of the hierarchy, the ordering is alphabetical.

comes with BIND, and the O'Reilly DNS book for the exact details. That said, lets look at some potential problems with the current DNSSEC design.

DNSSEC is at odds with the notions of caching and forwarders. DNSSEC assumes that queries contact the root zone first and then follow referrals down the domain chain to get an answer. Each signed zone signs its children's keys, and the chain of trust is unbroken and verifiable. When you use a forwarder, however, the initial query is diverted from the root zone and sent to your forwarding server for processing. A caching server that is querying through a forwarder will recheck signatures, so responses are guaranteed to be secure. But, for the query to succeed, the forwarder must be capable of returning all the SIGs and KEYs needed for the signature checking. Non-DNSSEC servers don't know to do this, and the RFCs ignore the whole issue of forwarding.

BIND 9 implements some extra features beyond those required by RFC2535 so that a BIND 9 caching server can use DNSSEC through a BIND 9 forwarder. If you are using forwarders and want to use DNSSEC, you might have to run BIND 9 throughout your site.

Unfortunately, those busy sites that use forwarders and caching are probably the sites most interested in DNSSEC. Alas, the standards writers didn't quite think through all of the implications for the other parts of the DNS system.

DNSSEC also relies on the existence of a public key infrastructure that isn't quite a reality yet. There is no smooth way to get the parent to sign a child's keys; we cannot send mail to the hostmaster@com and get signed keys back. In the next few years we should start to see DNSSEC deployed, probably beginning with signed versions of the root zones. Sysadmins need to keep an eye on DNSSEC development, but it's too early (Summer, 2000) to really worry about DNSSEC for now.

Transaction signatures (TSIG/TKEY) use less CPU time and network bandwidth than does public key authentication, but they guarantee only that you know where your responses came from, not that the responses are correct. A combination of a TSIG relationship with a server known to do full DNSSEC might provide a reasonable degree of security. It is not possible to have a TSIG relationship with every server you might ever want to talk to, since TSIG relationships must be manually configured.

### Microsoft bad, UNIX good

Windows 2000 uses SRV resource records to discover everything: name servers, printers, filesystems, and so forth. They have followed the IETF specs in their implementation of SRV records, but the way that they insert the records into DNS by using a secure dynamic update is nonstandard. Microsoft uses a variation of transaction signatures called GSS-TSIG that is also based on a shared secret. The shared secret is obtained through Kerberos from the Kerberos KDC (Key Distribution Center). At the moment, Microsoft's implementation is not compatible with the open source version of Kerberos 5. (Hmm... Embrace, extend, exterminate.)

If you want to run Win2K and use SRV records, you'll have to nuke your existing Kerberos realm and run a Win2K Kerberos server on your networks. For some sites with a rich Kerberos infrastructure, this problem is a showstopper. Perhaps Microsoft will document their extensions.

About a week after Win2K was released, the query load on the DNS root servers increased significantly. A bit of digging revealed that misconfigured Win2K boxes were trying to dynamically update the root or top-level zones. The number of UDP queries to the A root server more than doubled as a result. To make matters worse, when their update requests were refused, the Win2K boxes opened a TCP connection to request a KEY record and attempt an authenticated dynamic update. A root server does not have time for the zillions of TCP connection requests that resulted. This situation is still being sorted out as we go to press, with root server operators pointing fingers at Microsoft and Microsoft saying "No, no, not us!"

## 16.14  TESTING AND DEBUGGING

**named** provides several built-in debugging aids, foremost among which is its voluptuously configurable logging. You can specify debug levels on the command line or set them with **ndc**. You can also instruct **named** to dump its operating statistics to a file and verify name lookups with **dig** or **nslookup**.

### Logging

*See Chapter 11 for more information about syslog.*

**named**'s logging facilities are flexible enough to make your hair stand on end. BIND 4 used syslog to report error messages and anomalies. BIND 8 generalizes the concepts of syslog by adding another layer of indirection and support for logging directly to files. Before we dive in, let's take a look at the mini-glossary of BIND logging terms shown in Table 16.12.

**Table 16.12    A BIND logging lexicon**

| Term | What it means |
| --- | --- |
| channel | A place where messages can go: syslog, a file, or **/dev/null** |
| category | A class of messages that **named** can generate; for example, messages about dynamic updates or messages about answering queries |
| module | The name of the source module that generates a message (BIND 9 only) |
| facility | A syslog facility name. DNS does not have its own specific facility, but you have your pick of all the standard ones. |
| severity | The "badness" of an error message; what syslog refers to as a priority |

You configure BIND logging with a logging statement in **named.conf**. You first define channels, the possible destinations for messages. You then tell various categories of message to go to particular channels.

When a message is generated, it is assigned a category, a module (in BIND 9), and a severity at its point of origin. It is then distributed to all the channels associated with its category and module. Each channel has a severity filter that tells what severity level a message must have in order to get through. Channels that lead to syslog are also filtered according to the rules in **/etc/syslog.conf**.

Here's the outline of a logging statement:

```
logging {
      channel_def;
      channel_def;
      ...
      category category_name {
            channel_name;
            channel_name;
            ...
      };
};
```

A *channel_def* looks slightly different depending upon whether the channel is a file channel or a syslog channel. You must choose file or syslog for each channel; a channel can't be both at the same time.

```
channel channel_name {

      file path [versions numvers | unlimited] [size sizespec];
      syslog facility;

      severity severity;
      print-category yes | no;
      print-severity yes | no;
      print-time yes | no;
};
```

For a file, *numvers* tells how many backup versions of a file to keep, and *sizespec* specifies how large the file should be allowed to grow (examples: 2048, 100k, 20m, 15g, unlimited, default).

*See page 212 for a list of syslog facility names.* In the syslog case, *facility* specifies what facility name is used to log the message. It can be any standard facility. In practice, only daemon and local0 through local7 are reasonable choices.

The rest of the statements in a *channel_def* are optional. *severity* can have the values (in descending order) critical, error, warning, notice, info, or debug (with an optional numeric level, e.g., severity debug 3). The value dynamic is also recognized and matches the server's current debug level.

The various print options add or suppress message prefixes. Syslog prepends the time and reporting host to each message logged, but not the severity or the category. In BIND 9, the source filename (module) that generated the message is also available as a print option. It makes sense to enable print-time only for file channels; syslog records the time on its own.

The four channels listed in Table 16.13 are predefined by default. The default channels should be fine for most installations.

**Table 16.13    Predefined logging channels in BIND**

| Channel name | What it does |
|---|---|
| default_syslog | Sends severity info and higher to syslog with facility daemon |
| default_debug | Logs to file **named.run**, severity set to dynamic |
| default_stderr | Sends messages to standard error of **named**, severity info |
| null | Discards all messages |

Table 16.14 on the next page shows the current list of message categories for BIND 8 and 9. BIND 9's categories are not yet fully defined. When the Vers column shows "8/9?", the category exists in BIND 8 but not yet in BIND 9.

See the BIND 8 source file **include/dns/confcommon.h** for a definitive list. The file **log.h** in that same directory has a list of module names. For BIND 9, the relevant files are **lib/dns/include/dns/log.h** and **bin/named/include/named/log.h**.

The default logging configuration for BIND 8 is

```
logging {
    category default { default_syslog; default_debug; };
    category panic { default_syslog; default_stderr; };
    category eventlib { default_debug; };
    category packet { default_debug; };
};
```

and for BIND 9 it is

```
logging {
    category default { default_syslog; default_debug; };
};
```

You should watch the log files when you make major changes to BIND, and perhaps increase the logging level. Then, reconfigure to preserve only serious messages once **named** is stable. Some common log messages are listed below:

- *Lame server.* If you get this message about one of your own zones, you have configured something incorrectly. The message is relatively harmless if it's about some zone out on the Internet; it's someone else's problem.

- *Bad referral.* This message indicates a miscommunication among a zone's name servers.

- *Not authoritative for.* A slave server is unable to get authoritative data for a zone. Perhaps it's pointing to the wrong master, or perhaps the master had trouble loading the zone in question.

- *Rejected zone.* **named** rejected a zone file because it contained errors.

**Table 16.14  BIND logging categories**

| Category | Vers | What it includes |
|---|---|---|
| default | 8/9 | Categories with no explicit channel assignments[a] |
| general | 9 | Unclassified messages |
| config | 8/9 | Configuration file parsing and processing |
| parser | 8 | Low-level configuration file processing |
| queries/client | 8/9 | A short log message for every query the server receives (!) |
| dnssec | 9 | DNSSEC messages |
| lame-servers | 8/9? | Servers that are supposed to be serving a zone, but aren't[b] |
| statistics | 8/9? | Name server aggregate statistics |
| panic | 8/9? | Fatal errors (duplicated onto this category) |
| update | 8/9 | Messages about dynamic updates |
| ncache | 8/9? | Messages about negative caching |
| xfer-in | 8/9 | Zone transfers that the server is receiving |
| xfer-out | 8/9 | Zone transfers that the server is sending |
| db/database | 8/9 | Messages about database operations |
| eventlib | 8 | Debugging info from the event system[c] |
| packet | 8/9? | Dumps of packets received and sent[c] |
| notify | 8/9 | Messages about the "zone changed" notification protocol |
| cname | 8/9? | Messages of the form "… points to a CNAME" |
| security | 8/9 | Approved/unapproved requests |
| os | 8/9? | Operating system problems |
| insist | 8/9? | Internal consistency check failures |
| maintenance | 8/9? | Periodic maintenance events |
| load | 8/9? | Zone loading messages |
| response-checks | 8/9? | Commentary on malformed or invalid response packets |
| resolver | 9 | DNS resolution, e.g., recursive lookups for clients |
| network | 9 | Network operations |

a. The default category is also the catchall category for unclassified messages in BIND 8.
b. Either the parent zone or the child zone could be at fault; it's impossible to tell without investigating.
c. Must be a single file channel

- *No NS RRs found.* A zone file did not have NS records after the SOA record. It could be that the records are missing, or it could be they don't start with a tab or other whitespace. In the latter case, the records are not attached to the zone of the SOA record and are therefore misinterpreted.

- *No default TTL set.* The preferred way to set the default TTL is with a $TTL clause at the top of the zone file. This error message indicates that the $TTL is missing. In BIND 8 it defaults to the value of the *minimum* parameter from the SOA record.[15] In BIND 9, the $TTL is required; **named** refuses to load zone files that do not specify a $TTL.

15. The meaning of *minimum* changed in BIND 8.2 from the default TTL for all records to the default TTL for negative caching.

- *No root name server for class*. Your server is having trouble finding the root name servers. Check your hints file and the server's Internet connectivity.

- *Address already in use*. The port on which **named** wants to run is already being used by another process, probably another copy of **named**. If you don't see another **named** around, it might have crashed and left an **ndc** control socket open that you'll have to track down and remove.[16]

You can find a nice table of BIND error messages at

> http://www.acmebw.com/askmrdns/bind-messages.htm.

## Debug levels

**named** debug levels are indicated by integers from 0 to 11. The higher the number, the more verbose the output. Level 0 turns debugging off. Levels 1 and 2 are fine for debugging your configuration and database. Levels beyond about 4 are appropriate for the maintainers of the code.

You invoke debugging on the **named** command line with the **-d** flag. For example,

```
# named -d2
```

would start **named** at debug level 2. By default, debugging information is written to the file **named.run**, the location of which is OS dependent. See the tables in the vendor specifics section starting on page 481 for the exact locations. The **named.run** file grows very fast, so don't go out for a beer while debugging or you will have bigger problems when you return.

You can also turn on debugging while **named** is running with **ndc trace**, which increments the debug level by 1. **ndc notrace** turns debugging off completely. You can also enable debugging by defining a logging channel that includes a severity specification such as

```
severity debug 3
```

which sends all debugging messages up to level 3 to that particular channel. Other lines in the channel definition specify the destination of those debugging messages. The higher the severity level, the more information is logged.

Watching the logs or the debugging output illustrates how often DNS data is misconfigured. That pesky little dot at the end of names (or rather, the lack thereof) accounts for an alarming amount of DNS traffic. Theoretically, the dot is required at the end of each fully qualified domain name.

## Debugging with ndc

The **ndc** command (called **rndc** in BIND 9) is a useful tool for manipulating **named**. Table 16.15 shows some of the options it accepts. Commands that produce files put them in the directory specified as **named**'s home in **named.conf**.

16. On a gTLD server, this message probably means that com is still loading. :-)

**Table 16.15   Useful ndc debugging commands**

| Command | Function |
|---------|----------|
| **help** | Lists the available **ndc** commands |
| **status** | Displays current status of the running **named** |
| **trace** | Increments the debug level by 1 |
| **notrace** | Turns off debugging |
| **dumpdb** | Dumps DNS database to **named_dump.db** |
| **stats** | Dumps statistics to **named.stats** |
| **reload** | Reloads **named.conf** and zone files |
| **reload** *zone* | Reloads only the specified *zone* |
| **restart** | Restarts **named**, flushing the cache |
| **querylog** | Toggles tracing of incoming queries |

**ndc reload** is analogous to sending **named** a HUP signal; it makes **named** reread its configuration file and reload zone files. The **ndc reload** *zone* command is handy, especially on a busy server, when only one zone has changed and you don't want to reload all zones.

**ndc dumpdb** makes **named** dump its database to **named_dump.db**. The dump file is big and includes not only local data but also any cached data that the name server has accumulated. A recent dump of the database cache on our primary colorado.edu name server was over 16MB, but the zone data loaded was less than 200K. Lots of caching there.

Recent versions of **named** keep query statistics, which you can access with **ndc stats**. On command, **named** writes the stats to the file **named.stats**. A sample stats file from the cs.colorado.edu master server (which has been up for 43 days) is shown below. This information is normally printed in one long column, but we compressed it a bit by deleting entries for obsolete or unused resource record types. We also reformatted the lower section; it's normally one long line of values.

```
+++ Statistics Dump +++ Wed Feb  2 15:07:18 2000

180465      time since boot (secs)
52669       time since reset (secs)
0           Unknown query types
475460      A queries
3           NS queries
194         CNAME queries
15686       SOA queries
138816      PTR queries
76244       MX queries
130939      TXT queries
1           LOC queries
171         SRV queries
42          AXFR queries
124587      ANY queries
```

```
++ Name Server Statistics ++
```

| RR | RNXD | RFwdR | RDupR | RFail | RFErr | RErr | RAXFR | RLame |
|---|---|---|---|---|---|---|---|---|
| 320252 | 23620 | 249826 | 1013 | 3532 | 0 | 903 | 42 | 10339 |

| ROpts | SSysQ | SAns | SFwdQ | SDupQ | SErr | RQ | RIQ | RFwdQ |
|---|---|---|---|---|---|---|---|---|
| 0 | 55547 | 652973 | 265736 | 291448 | 0 | 963690 | 0 | 0 |

| RDupQ | RTCP | SFwdR | SFail | SFErr | SNaAns | SNXD |
|---|---|---|---|---|---|---|
| 47876 | 1605 | 249826 | 18 | 0 | 162533 | 190644 |

The cryptic data at the end counts things like the number of duplicate queries, duplicate responses, and lame delegations seen by this server. The initial letter in the abbreviations stands for received (R) or sent (S); the final letter indicates query (Q) or response (R). The real meaning of these headings is documented in the code, where a brief comment identifies each abbreviation—see the file **ns_stats.c** beneath the **src/bin/named** directory in the BIND 8 distribution. A less painful way to decode these abbreviations is to read the statistics section in the O'Reilly DNS book. Statistics have not yet been implemented in BIND 9, so we can't point you to the correct source code file. You should be able to find it in your current distribution with **grep** or **find**.

Any query that results in an error is logged, counted in one or more statistics buckets, and dropped. The category Unknown query types includes any query for a resource record type that the server does not recognize. As new record types are standardized, they show up in this column until the name servers have been upgraded to include the new record types. The ANY bucket is not a real resource record type; it counts queries that ask for any and all information a server might have about a particular name. The Dup entries in the bottom half of the output represent duplicate queries or responses. Duplicates normally occur when a query times out before its answer has been received; the querier then resubmits the query.

In BIND 8, **ndc stats** also produces memory statistics in the file **named.memstats** if deallocate-on-exit is set. BIND 9 memory statistics can be accessed only through **named**'s debug mode.

### Debugging with nslookup, dig, and host

*nslookup and dig are included in the BIND release.*

Three tools can be used from the shell to query the DNS database: **nslookup**, **dig**, and host. **nslookup** is the oldest of these tools and has always been distributed with BIND. **dig**, the domain information groper, was originally written by Steve Hotz and was rewritten for BIND 9 by Michael Sawyer. It is shipped with BIND as well. **host**, by Eric Wassenaar, is another open source tool; it features user-friendly output and functions to check the syntax of your zone files. We discuss each of these tools but prefer **dig** over **nslookup**; we like **host**, too. You might sometimes get different results from these tools because of the different resolver libraries that they use; **dig** and **host** use BIND's resolver, and **nslookup** has its own.

**nslookup** is a user-level command that queries the DNS database. It expects fully qualified names ending in a dot and appends the default domain if you forget the dot.

For local names, this behavior is often what you want. Table 16.16 gives a short list of **nslookup** commands.

**Table 16.16  Commands understood by nslookup**

| Command | Function |
| --- | --- |
| *name* | Prints info about the host or domain *name* |
| **help** or **?** | Shows a complete list of commands |
| **exit** | Quits |
| **server** *host* | Sets the default server, using the current server |
| **lserver** *host* | Sets the default server, using the initial server |
| **set type**=*xxx* | Sets the record types to query for[a] |
| **set debug** | Turns on debugging |
| **set d2** | Turns on lots of debugging |
| **ls** *domain* | Lists all host/address mappings |

a. **any** is a good value that means "all record types."

**dig** provides the same rough functionality as **nslookup**, but it has more sensible defaults, provides more information, and has a nicer user interface (especially when compared to older versions of **nslookup**).

For example, to ask for anchor's MX records, use

    % dig anchor.cs.colorado.edu. mx

The command

    % dig @ns1.berkeley.edu vangogh.berkeley.edu. any

obtains vangogh's complete records from a berkeley.edu server, and

    % dig -x 128.32.33.5

performs a reverse query for vangogh. Here is a complete example that uses both **nslookup** and **dig** to query for the same data:

```
% nslookup
Default Server:  bb.rc.vix.com
Address:  204.152.187.11
> set type=any
> amazon.com.
Server:  bb.rc.vix.com
Address:  204.152.187.11
Non-authoritative answer:
amazon.com          nameserver = AUTH00.NS.UU.NET
amazon.com          nameserver = NS2.PNAP.NET
amazon.com          nameserver = NS1.PNAP.NET
amazon.com          nameserver = NS-1.amazon.com
amazon.com          preference = 10, mail exchanger = service-4.amazon.com
amazon.com          preference = 10, mail exchanger = service-5.amazon.com
```

```
amazon.com                internet address = 208.216.182.15
Authoritative answers can be found from:
amazon.com                nameserver = AUTH00.NS.UU.NET
amazon.com                nameserver = NS2.PNAP.NET
amazon.com                nameserver = NS1.PNAP.NET
amazon.com                nameserver = NS-1.amazon.com
AUTH00.NS.UU.NET          internet address = 198.6.1.65
NS2.PNAP.NET              internet address = 206.253.194.97
NS1.PNAP.NET              internet address = 206.253.194.65
NS-1.amazon.com           internet address = 209.191.164.20
service-4.amazon.com internet address = 209.191.164.50
service-5.amazon.com internet address = 209.191.164.51
```

**nslookup** returns four NS records, two MX records, and an A record. It also provides the IP addresses of the name servers and MX hosts.

```
% dig amazon.com. any
; <<>> DiG 8.3 <<>> amazon.com any
;; res options: init recurs defnam dnsrch
;; got answer:
;; ->>HEADER<<- opcode: QUERY, status: NOERROR, id: 4
;; flags: qr rd ra; QUERY: 1, ANSWER: 7, AUTHORITY: 4, ADDITIONAL: 6
;; QUERY SECTION:
;;       amazon.com, type = ANY, class = IN
;; ANSWER SECTION:
amazon.com.               1h27m11s  IN  NS   AUTH00.NS.UU.NET.
amazon.com.               1h27m11s  IN  NS   NS2.PNAP.NET.
amazon.com.               1h27m11s  IN  NS   NS1.PNAP.NET.
amazon.com.               1h27m11s  IN  NS   NS-1.amazon.com.
amazon.com.               59m22s    IN  MX   10 service-4.amazon.com.
amazon.com.               59m22s    IN  MX   10 service-5.amazon.com.
amazon.com.               1h59m29s  IN  A    208.216.182.15
;; AUTHORITY SECTION:
amazon.com.               1h27m11s  IN  NS   AUTH00.NS.UU.NET.
amazon.com.               1h27m11s  IN  NS   NS2.PNAP.NET.
amazon.com.               1h27m11s  IN  NS   NS1.PNAP.NET.
amazon.com.               1h27m11s  IN  NS   NS-1.amazon.com.
;; ADDITIONAL SECTION:
AUTH00.NS.UU.NET.         13h11m20s IN  A    198.6.1.65
NS2.PNAP.NET.             20h51m44s IN  A    206.253.194.97
NS1.PNAP.NET.             20h51m44s IN  A    206.253.194.65
NS-1.amazon.com.          59m22s    IN  A    209.191.164.20
service-4.amazon.com.     59m22s    IN  A    209.191.164.50
service-5.amazon.com.     59m22s    IN  A    209.191.164.51
;; Total query time: 7 msec
;; FROM: bb.rc.vix.com to SERVER: default -- 204.152.187.11
;; WHEN: Sun Jul  2 12:45:59 2000
;; MSG SIZE  sent: 28  rcvd: 338
```

**dig** is verbose. Its output includes not only the same domain information but also the number of queries sent and the answers' round trip time. The output is formatted correctly to be used in a zone file, which is particularly handy when you are querying for the root servers for your hints file.

**host** provides terse-but-friendly output by default, but it can be made more verbose with the **-v** option (although not as verbose as **dig**). It expects the domain you are querying to end in a dot. If you look up a relative name, **host** first tries appending the domains in your **resolv.conf** file; if none of them work, it simply appends the dot.

```
% host amazon.com.
amazon.com has address 208.216.182.15
amazon.com mail is handled (pri=10) by service-4.amazon.com
amazon.com mail is handled (pri=10) by service-5.amazon.com
```

When testing a new configuration, be sure that you look up data for both local and remote hosts. If you can access a host by IP address but not by name, DNS is probably the culprit.

### Lame delegations

When you apply for a domain name, you are asking for a part of the DNS naming tree to be delegated to your primary name server and your DNS administrator. If you never use the domain or you change the name servers without updating the parent domain's glue records, a "lame delegation" results.

The effects of a lame delegation can be very bad. If a user tries to contact a host in your lame domain, your name server will refuse the query. DNS will retry the query several hundred times, pummeling both your master server and the root servers. In one log file that was 3.5MB (at level info) after almost a week, over one-third of the entries were lame delegations. Of those, 16% involved queries to the root servers, presumably for nonexistent domains. One persistent user queried the root servers for tokyotopless.net hundreds of times. Sigh. Here is an example:

```
Jan 29 05:34:52 ipn.caida.org named[223]: Lame server on 'www.games.net' (in
    'GAMES.net'?): [207.82.198.150].53 'NS2.EXODUS.net'
```

Here's how we'd track down the problem with **dig**; we truncated some of **dig**'s verbose output:

```
% dig www.games.net.
;; ...
;; QUESTIONS:
;;      www.games.net, type = A, class = IN
;; ANSWERS:
www.games.net.      3600    A    209.1.23.92
;; AUTHORITY RECORDS:
games.net.          3600    NS   ns.exodus.net.
games.net.          3600    NS   ns2.exodus.net.
games.net.          3600    NS   ns.pcworld.com.
;; ADDITIONAL RECORDS: ...
```

The first query at the local server returns the address record for www.games.net and a list of authoritative servers.

The server at ns.exodus.net worked fine when we queried it (not shown), but ns2.exodus.net is another story:

```
% dig @ns2.exodus.net www.games.net.
;; QUESTIONS:
;;        www.games.net, type = A, class = IN
;; AUTHORITY RECORDS:
net.                 244362 NS   F.GTLD-SERVERS.net.
net.                 244362 NS   J.GTLD-SERVERS.net.
net.                 244362 NS   K.GTLD-SERVERS.net.
net.                 244362 NS   A.GTLD-SERVERS.net.
;; ...
```

ns2 is listed as an authoritative server for the domain, but it returns no records and refers us to the servers for the net top-level domain. Therefore, we can conclude that ns2.exodus.net is configured incorrectly.

## 16.15  LOOSE ENDS

This section includes a few loose ends and examples that should have come earlier in the chapter, but for which we just couldn't find the right place. We collect them here, in no particular order

### The hints file

The hints file primes **named**'s cache with information about the servers of the root domain. Putting the root servers in the cache bootstraps the lookup process for all other names. If you don't provide a hints file, BIND 9 uses a list of root servers hard-wired into its code and will be able to load the root zone anyway. All earlier versions of BIND require a hints file. (If you supply a hints file for BIND 9, it overrides the hardwired hints.)

The root name servers change from time to time, but it's easier to track them down than it used to be because they are all assigned hostnames in the root-servers.net domain. Use the sample file below for reference only.

If you already have access to a system with a running name server, you can have **dig** contact a root name server and generate the hints file for you. The master server is currently a.root-servers.net, but any of the root servers will do:

```
% dig @f.root-servers.net . ns > root.cache
```

Mind the dot. If f.root-servers.net is not responding, you can run the query without specifying a particular server:

```
% dig . ns > root.cache
```

The output will be similar; however, you will be obtaining the list of root servers from the cache of a local name server, not from an authoritative source. That should be just fine. Even if you have not rebooted or restarted your name server for a year or two, it has been refreshing its root server records periodically as their TTLs expire. When

**named** starts, it reloads the hints from one of the root servers. Ergo, you'll be fine as long as your hints file contains at least one valid reachable root server.

Here's what the cache file looks like:

```
cs.colorado.edu.   IN   NS   anchor.cs.colorado.edu.
cs.colorado.edu.   IN   NS   ns.cs.utah.edu.

; <<>> DiG 8.2 <<>> @f.root-servers.net . ns
; Lots of detailed dig info formatted as comments here...

.                       1d1h42m  IN  NS  E.ROOT-SERVERS.NET.
.                       1d1h42m  IN  NS  D.ROOT-SERVERS.NET.
.                       1d1h42m  IN  NS  A.ROOT-SERVERS.NET.
.                       1d1h42m  IN  NS  H.ROOT-SERVERS.NET.
...
E.ROOT-SERVERS.NET.  2d1h42m  IN  A   192.203.230.10
D.ROOT-SERVERS.NET.  2d1h42m  IN  A   128.8.10.90
A.ROOT-SERVERS.NET.  2d1h42m  IN  A   198.41.0.4
H.ROOT-SERVERS.NET.  2d1h42m  IN  A   128.63.2.53
...
```

Note the dots that begin the first set of records; they are not fly specks but rather they define the domain (the root) to which the NS records apply. Some versions of **dig** show the TTL in seconds instead of days, minutes, and seconds.

A current hints file can also be obtained by anonymous FTP from rs.internic.net[17] in the file domain/named.root. Comments in this version of the root hints file show the old names of the root servers, which hint at their historic locations. This file is also mirrored at ftp://ftp.nic.mil/domain/named.root.

### Localhost configuration

The forward mapping for the name localhost or localhost.*domain* is done in the forward zone file for the domain. Each server is usually the master for its own reverse localhost domain, however. Here is a sample zone file:

```
@          IN   SOA  cs.colorado.edu. hostmaster.cs.colorado.edu. (
                     1996110801  ; Serial number
                     3600        ; Refresh
                     900         ; Retry
                     3600000     ; Expire
                     14400 )     ; Minimum
           IN   NS   cs.colorado.edu.
1          IN   PTR  localhost.cs.colorado.edu.
```

The reverse mapping for the localhost address (127.0.0.1) never changes, so the timeouts can be large. Note the serial number, which encodes the date; the file was last changed in 1996. Also note that only the master name server is listed for the localhost domain. The meaning of @ here is "0.0.127.in-addr.arpa.".

---

17. The identity of this host may soon change, since Network Solutions will not be running the primary root name server much longer.

Be sure that you reverse-map 127.0.0.1 to "localhost.*domain*." not just "localhost.". The root servers receive many queries for "localhost." and may end up defining an Internet-wide 0.0.127.in-addr.arpa entry.

### Host management tools

DNS database files often span local administrative and political domains. In many cases, tight central control is unfeasible. This situation presents a common administration problem: How do you manage critical (but fragile) data files that many untrained people may need to edit at random times? It would also be nice if the physics department could not change the engineering department's records, and vice versa.

If a political domain contains several hosts and has an administrative staff, then a subdomain is a good way to distribute control. But for a small department with only a few hosts, a subdomain is not necessary.

*addhost is available from ftp.xor.com.*

This data is a good candidate for an LDAP database that holds organization-wide host data, and for tools that build individual departments' zone files. We use an ancient, crufty, home-grown tool called **addhost**, but we intend to change to LDAP as soon as we can assign it as a student project.

### DNS for systems not on the Internet

*See page 675 for more information about firewalls.*

If you are not part of the Internet but want to use DNS, you can declare your primary name server to be authoritative for the root domain. This configuration might be appropriate for either a small company that is not yet on the Internet or for an organization that hides its local structure behind a firewall.

In this setup, your hints file should point to local name servers, not to the root servers of the Internet. You should still get a registered domain name and legitimate IP addresses, or perhaps use the RFC1918 private addresses described on page 279.

## 16.16  Vendor Specifics

This section describes the atrocities committed on ISC's freely distributed BIND code by our helpful vendors. We include pointers to the configuration files, the release of BIND on which each vendor's software is based, and information about how to integrate BIND with other sources of administrative data such as flat files or NIS.

A more complete discussion of this last topic is presented in Chapter 18. In particular, refer to the material beginning on page 523.

### Specifics for Solaris

Both Solaris 7 and 8 currently ship with BIND 8.1.2. Solaris uses a service order file called **/etc/nsswitch.conf** to specify how BIND, NIS, NIS+, and the **/etc/hosts** file interact. Modifying the hosts line in that file to

```
hosts:  files dns
```

causes name resolution to try **/etc/hosts** first and then try DNS. Putting crucial servers and routers in the **/etc/hosts** file eases the chicken-and-egg problems that sometimes occur at boot time before name service is available.

The Sun manual recommends that you run your NIS servers in DNS forwarding mode, in which they forward queries that cannot be answered from the local database to a DNS server. Thus, the vendor-recommended configuration is

```
hosts:  nis [NOTFOUND=return] files
```

We disagree. A local NIS server is no faster than a local DNS server and the data must be in DNS in order for the outside world to access your site anyway. Even if your site uses NIS, it's best to keep the two systems separate.

Table 16.17 summarizes the BIND filenames and locations for Solaris.

**Table 16.17   BIND files in Solaris**

| File | Directory | Description |
|------|-----------|-------------|
| **resolv.conf** | **/etc** | Resolver library configuration file |
| **in.named** | **/usr/sbin** | Name server daemon |
| **named-xfer** | **/usr/sbin** | Zone transfer code |
| **named.conf** | **/etc** | Configuration file for name server |
| **named.pid** | **/etc** | Process ID of the running **in.named** |
| **named.run** | *directory*[a] | Output from debug mode |
| **named.stats** | *directory*[a] | Statistics output |
| **named_dump.db** | *directory*[a] | Dump of the entire database |
| **named-bootconf** | **/usr/sbin** | Converts BIND 4 configs to BIND 8 format |

a. The directory specified in **/etc/named.conf** as the home for BIND files

The Solaris man page for **in.named** contains several lies. It mentions dumping the statistics with the IOT signal, which the Solaris **kill** command doesn't support; it has been replaced with the ABRT signal. However, even ABRT does not dump the statistics—it kills **named** dead. We found by reading the source code that it's the ILL signal that dumps the statistics file.

The man page also says that the database is dumped into the file **nameddump.db**, but that's wrong too. The correct filename is **named_dump.db**. The switch from BIND 4 to BIND 8 may not have included a careful rewrite of the man page (perhaps not even by the BIND folks).

### Specifics for HP-UX

HP-UX 11.00's BIND is based on BIND 4.9.7. It uses the same **nsswitch.conf** system that Solaris does. The raw system ships with several sample files in the **/etc** directory, but none named **nsswitch.conf**. (Try **ls /etc/nssw*** to see your options.)

To create an **nsswitch.conf** file, read the man page to see what configuration you want to implement and then steal the right bits from the samples provided. One of the samples is **/etc/nsswitch.hp_defaults**, which shows the behavior you'll get if the **nsswitch.conf** file does not exist or if it contains a syntax error. With respect to host lookups, it is the following:

```
hosts:  dns [NOTFOUND=return] nis [NOTFOUND=return] files
```

This configuration uses DNS first, but if DNS is unavailable or not configured, the lookup next tries NIS and then the **/etc/hosts** file. If DNS is available but is unable to find the name in question, the lookup returns with a "host unknown" error.

To be sure that DNS and booting do not conflict, we recommend a configuration more like this:

```
hosts:  files [NOTFOUND=continue] dns
```

If you use NIS, put it between files and DNS, again with continue as the action to take when an error occurs. It's important to be able to configure the network in the boot sequence without looking up hostnames in NIS or DNS; putting files first ensures that there won't be problems, as does using IP addresses instead of names in the startup files.

Table 16.18 summarizes the important filenames and locations for HP-UX.

**Table 16.18    BIND files in HP-UX**

| File | Directory | Description |
| --- | --- | --- |
| **resolv.conf** | **/etc** | Resolver library configuration file |
| **named** | **/usr/sbin** | Name server daemon |
| **named-xfer** | **/usr/sbin** | Zone transfer code |
| **named.boot** | **/etc** | Configuration file for name server |
| **named.pid** | **/var/run** | Process ID of the running **named** |
| **named.run** | **/var/tmp** | Output from debug mode |
| **named.stats** | **/var/tmp** | Statistics output |
| **named_dump.db** | **/var/tmp** | Dump of the entire database |

HP-UX has well-commented sample files for just about everything in the directory **/usr/newconfig**, but nothing for name service. Earlier versions of HP-UX (pre-11.00) put sample **named.conf** files, zone files, and **resolv.conf** files in **/etc/newconfig**. The **/usr/newconfig** directory seems to be a generalization of **/etc/newconfig**, but the switch to a better, more complete set of samples somehow overlooked the BIND files. Let's hope they come back when HP-UX switches to BIND 8 or BIND 9.

HP-UX provides some tools to help you transition from the flat hosts file to DNS resource records. The command **hosts_to_named** converts from **/etc/hosts** format to DNS resource record format. **sig_named** can be used to send signals to **named**; it is just a friendly front end to **kill** with arguments similar to those of **ndc**.

### Specifics for Red Hat Linux

Red Hat Linux 6.1 ships BIND 8.2 with the files in the standard spots; see Table 16.19. If you are running Red Hat 6.2, check the table in the FreeBSD section, as it too uses 8.2.2-P5. Red Hat uses the Solaris-style switch file, **/etc/nsswitch.conf**, to prioritize the various sources of naming information. (The man page is filed under **nsswitch** rather than **nsswitch.conf**.)

**Table 16.19   BIND files in Red Hat Linux**

| File | Directory | Description |
|------|-----------|-------------|
| resolv.conf | /etc | Resolver library configuration file |
| named | /usr/sbin | Name server daemon |
| named-xfer | /usr/sbin | Zone transfer code |
| named.conf | /etc | Configuration file for name server |
| named.pid | /var/run | Process ID of the running **named** |
| named.run | directory[a] | Output from debug mode |
| named.stats | directory[a] | Statistics output |
| named.memstats | directory[a] | Memory usage statistics |
| named_dump.db | directory[a] | Dump of the entire database |

a. The directory specified in **/etc/named.conf** as the home for BIND files

Without an **nsswitch.conf** file, Red Hat defaults to the following scheme for hosts:

```
hosts:  dns [!UNAVAIL=return] files
```

The !UNAVAIL clause, which the man page says is the default, seems wrong. It's also contradicted by the sample file that is shipped with Red Hat, where the hosts line is:

```
hosts:  db files nisplus dns
```

We recommend promoting DNS and using the configuration

```
hosts:  files dns
```

Red Hat has some sample configuration files, but they're just in **/etc** instead of a special directory. The comments are pretty good. **named.conf** has no man page.

### Specifics for FreeBSD

FreeBSD 3.4 and 4.0 include BIND 8.2.2-P5. A service-order file called **/etc/host.conf** controls the order of services for host lookups only. The possible sources of host information are listed on separate lines in the order you want them to be consulted:

```
# First try the /etc/hosts file
hosts
# Now try the name server next.
bind
# If you have YP/NIS configured, uncomment the next line
# nis
```

If the **host.conf** file does not exist, DNS is consulted first. If that fails, **/etc/hosts** is consulted. FreeBSD has moved **named.conf** from the **/etc** directory to **/etc/namedb**. Table 16.20 summarizes the relevant filenames and locations.

**Table 16.20    BIND files in FreeBSD**

| File | Directory | Description |
|---|---|---|
| **resolv.conf** | **/etc** | Resolver library configuration file |
| **named** | **/usr/sbin** | Name server daemon |
| **named-xfer** | **/usr/libexec** | Zone transfer code |
| **named.conf** | **/etc/namedb** | Configuration file for name server |
| **named.pid** | **/var/run** | Process ID of the running **named** |
| **named.run** | *directory*[a] | Output from debug mode |
| **named.stats** | *directory*[a] | Statistics output |
| **named.memstats** | *directory*[a] | Memory usage statistics |
| **named_dump.db** | *directory*[a] | Dump of the entire database |
| Zone files | **/etc/namedb** | Default location for zone files |

a. The directory specified in **/etc/namedb/named.conf** as the home for BIND files.

**/etc/namedb** contains some sample files: a root cache file (**named.root**), a prototype for the localhost reverse zone file (**PROTO.localhost.rev**), and a shell script called **make-localhost** that prompts for your domain name and then makes a correct reverse localhost zone file from the prototype.

The **named-bootconf** Perl script in **/usr/sbin** converts from BIND 4's **named.boot** to BIND 8's **named.conf** startup file.

In our opinion, moving **named.conf** out of **/etc** should be a punishable offense; we suggest that you link it so that both names work. In looking at the comments at the bottom of the sample **named.conf** file, we guessed that FreeBSD originally intended to run **named** in a **chroot**ed environment. However, the default configuration does not actually do this. See the named_* variables in **/etc/defaults/rc.conf** for more information.

FreeBSD's **named** man page is wrong about certain paths, such as those of the statistics file and the dump database. It's probably wrong in the distribution from isc.org, since Solaris and FreeBSD both have the same errors.

## 16.17  RECOMMENDED READING

DNS and BIND are described by a variety of sources, including the documentation that comes with the distribution, chapters in several books on Internet topics, an entire book in the O'Reilly Nutshell series, and various on-line resources.

## Mailing lists and newsgroups

The following mailing lists are associated with BIND:

- bind-users – mail bind-users-request@isc.org to join
- bind-announce – mail bind-announce-request@isc.org
- namedroppers – mail namedroppers-request@internic.net
- bind-workers – mail bind-workers-request@isc.org (for code warriors)

Send bug reports to bind-bugs@isc.org or bind9-bugs@isc.org.

## Books and other documentation

THE NOMINUM BIND DEVELOPMENT TEAM. *BINDv9 Administrator Reference Manual.* Available in the BIND distribution (**doc/arm**) from www.isc.org.

This document outlines the administration and management of BIND 9. An earlier document, the *Bind Operations Guide,* or BOG as it is called, describes in detail the operation and configuration of BIND 4. The BOG is included in BIND distributions up through version 8.

ALBITZ, PAUL, AND CRICKET LIU. *DNS and BIND, Third Edition.* Sebastopol, CA: O'Reilly, 1998.

This popular and well-respected book about BIND includes coverage of BIND 8, and we hear that the fourth edition is coming soon and will include BIND 9.

## On-line resources

The FAQ for comp.sys.tcp-ip.domains includes a lot of BIND information, mostly about BIND 4. It's maintained by Chris Peckham and is available from

> http://www.intac.com/~cdp/cptd-faq

The DNS Resources Directory, www.dns.net/dnsrd, is a useful collection of resources and pointers to resources maintained by András Salamon.

## The RFCs

The RFCs that define the DNS system are available from www.rfc-editor.org. Early and evolving ideas appear first in the Internet-Drafts series and later move into the RFC series. A selected subset of the RFCs, including those that have caused BIND 9 to be such a major undertaking, are listed below.

*The original, definitive standards*

- 1034 – Domain Names: Concepts and Facilities
- 1035 – Domain Names: Implementation and Specification.

*Proposed standards*

- 1995 – Incremental Zone Transfer in DNS
- 1996 – A Mechanism for Prompt Notification of Zone Changes
- 2136 – Dynamic Updates in the Domain Name System

- 2181 – Clarifications to the DNS Specification
- 2308 – Negative Caching of DNS Queries

*Newer standards-track RFCs*

- 2535 – Domain Name System Security Extensions
- 2671 – Extension Mechanisms for DNS (EDNS0)
- 2672 – Non-Terminal DNS Name Redirection (DNAME)
- 2673 – Binary Labels in the Domain Name System

*Miscellaneous RFCs*

- 1535 – A Security Problem … with Widely Deployed DNS Software
- 1536 – Common DNS Implementation Errors and Suggested Fixes
- 1982 – Serial Number Arithmetic
- 2536–2541 – Various DNSSEC RFCs

*Resource record types*

- 1183 – New DNS RR Definitions: AFSDB, RP, X25, ISDN, RT
- 1706 – DNS NSAP Resource Records
- 1876 – A Means for Expressing Location Information in DNS
- 2052 – A DNS RR for Specifying the Location of Services (SRV)
- 2168 – Resolution of Uniform Resource Identifiers using DNS
- 2230 – Key Exchange Delegation Record for the DNS

*DNS and the Internet*

- 1101 – DNS Encoding of Network Names and Other Types
- 1123 – Requirements for Internet Hosts: Application and Support
- 1591 – Domain Name System Structure and Delegation
- 2317 – Classless in-addr.arpa Delegation

*DNS operations*

- 1537 – Common DNS Data File Configuration Errors
- 1912 – Common DNS Operational and Configuration Errors
- 2182 – Selection and Operation of Secondary DNS Servers
- 2219 – Use of DNS Aliases for Network Services

*Other DNS-related RFCs*

- 1464 – Using DNS to Store Arbitrary String Attributes
- 1713 – Tools for DNS debugging
- 1794 – DNS Support for Load Balancing
- 2240 – A Legal Basis for Domain Name Allocation
- 2345 – Domain Names and Company Name Retrieval
- 2352 – A Convention for Using Legal Names as Domain Names

DNS

# 17 *The Network File System*

The Network File System, commonly known as NFS, allows you to share filesystems among computers. NFS is almost transparent to users and is "stateless," meaning that no information is lost when an NFS server crashes. Clients can simply wait until the server returns and then continue as if nothing had happened.

NFS was introduced by Sun Microsystems in 1985. It was originally implemented as a surrogate filesystem for diskless clients, but the protocol proved to be well designed and very useful as a general file-sharing solution. In fact, it's difficult to remember what life was like before NFS. All UNIX vendors provide a version of NFS; many use code licensed from Sun.

## 17.1 GENERAL INFORMATION ABOUT NFS

NFS consists of a number of components, including a mounting protocol and mount server, daemons that coordinate basic file service, and several diagnostic utilities. A portion of both the server-side and client-side software resides in the kernel. However, these parts of NFS need no configuration and are largely transparent from an administrator's point of view.

### NFS protocol versions

The NFS protocol has been remarkably stable over time. The original public release of NFS was version 2. In the early 1990s, a collection of changes was integrated into the protocol to produce version 3, which increases performance and provides better support for large files.

Since NFS version 2 clients cannot assume that a write operation is complete until they receive an acknowledgment from the server, version 2 servers must commit each modified block to disk before replying, to avoid discrepancies in the event of a crash. This constraint introduces a significant delay in NFS writes, since modified blocks would normally be written only to the in-memory UNIX buffer cache.

NFS version 3 eliminates this bottleneck with a coherency scheme that makes writes safely asynchronous. It also updates several other aspects of the protocol that were found to have caused performance problems. The net result is that NFS version 3 is quite a bit faster than version 2.

Version 3 software is always capable of interoperating with version 2, although it simply falls back to using the earlier protocol.

**Choice of transport**

NFS runs on top of Sun's RPC (Remote Procedure Call) protocol, which defines a system-independent way for processes to communicate over a network. One advantageous side effect of this architecture is that it's possible to use either UDP or TCP as the underlying transport protocol.

NFS originally used UDP because that was what performed best on the LANs and computers of the 1980s. Although NFS does its own packet sequence reassembly and error checking, UDP and NFS both lack the congestion control algorithms that are essential for good performance on a large IP network.

To remedy these potential problems, most systems now allow you to use TCP as the transport for NFS instead of UDP. This option was first explored as a way to help NFS work through routers and over the Internet. However, the current consensus seems to be that TCP is usually the best option for local NFS traffic as well. Over time, most of the original reasons for preferring UDP over TCP have evaporated in the warm light of fast CPUs and cheap memory.

Servers that support TCP will generally accept connections on either transport, so the choice between TCP and UDP is made by the client. Most clients default to UDP; Solaris uses TCP.

TCP support was officially integrated into the NFS protocol specification in version 3. However, there are version 2 implementations out there that support TCP (such as Red Hat) and version 3 implementations that don't (such as HP-UX).

Table 17.1 shows the support for TCP and NFS version 3 on our example systems. The Default column shows whether the client software defaults to using TCP or UDP.

**WebNFS**

In 1996, Sun launched an effort to promote the use of NFS on the Internet in a slightly tweaked form called WebNFS. A superset of the standard NFS version 3 protocol, WebNFS does away with (or more accurately, makes optional) several of the prefatory transactions that traditional NFS clients must go through before accessing a filesys-

**Table 17.1    Advanced NFS feature support by OS**

| System | NFSv3? | TCP? | Default |
|--------|--------|------|---------|
| Solaris | Yes | Yes | TCP |
| HP-UX | Yes | No | UDP |
| Red Hat | No | Yes[a] | UDP |
| FreeBSD | Yes | Yes | UDP |

a. TCP is supported on the client side only.

tem. It's not intended to replace traditional NFS, but rather to support applets running within web browsers. Unless your organization is involved in writing such applets, WebNFS will probably not be of much interest to you.

As of this writing, all of our example operating systems except HP-UX provide server-side support for WebNFS. You can find out more at www.sun.com/webnfs.

### File locking

File locking (as provided by the **flock** and/or **lockf** systems calls) has been a sore point on UNIX systems for a long time. On local filesystems, it has been known to work less than perfectly. In the context of NFS, the ground is shakier still. By design, NFS servers are stateless: they have no idea which machines are using any given file. However, this information is needed to implement locking. What to do?

The traditional answer has been to implement file locking separately from NFS. Most systems provide two daemons, **lockd** and **statd**, that try to make a go of it. Unfortunately, the task is difficult for a variety of subtle reasons, and NFS file locking has generally tended to be flaky.

### Disk quotas

Access to remote disk quota information can be provided by a similar out-of-band server, **rquotad**. An NFS server will enforce disk quotas, but users cannot view their quota information unless **rquotad** is running on the remote server. We consider disk quotas to be largely obsolete, so we won't discuss **rquotad** any further.

### Global UIDs and GIDs

*See Chapter 6 for more information about UIDs and GIDs.*

UNIX identifies users and groups by number. If machine X shares files with machine Y, then UID 644 had better refer to the same user on both systems or a serious security or privacy problem could result.

Some NFS servers have been hacked to provide a way to map remote UIDs and GIDs to local ones, but this feature is not part of the NFS protocol and it can't be relied upon to work among multiple OSes. We recommend that you manage UIDs the old-fashioned way: by making sure that they always map to the same users on all machines that share files. To forestall administrative headaches, it's best if UIDs and GIDs are unique across your entire site.

NFS servers need not allow remote users to log in. In fact, remote users do not even need to have entries in the **/etc/passwd** file unless the server uses an unusual option such as Red Hat's map_nis facility.

### Root access and the nobody account

While users should generally be given identical privileges wherever they go, it's traditional to prevent root from running rampant on NFS-mounted filesystems. By default, NFS servers intercept incoming requests made on behalf of UID 0 and change them to look as if they came from some other user. The root account is therefore not entirely shut out, but it is limited to the abilities of a normal user.

On most systems, a placeholder account named "nobody" is defined specifically to be the "user" that a remote root masquerades as on an NFS server. Its UID varies and is not important; it is often -2 or -2's two's-complement equivalent, 65,534. The important thing is that the UID not be shared with any real user. On Solaris and HP-UX, access will be denied altogether if root is mapped to UID -1.

The intent behind these precautions is good, but their ultimate value is not as great as it might seem. Root on an NFS client can **su** to whatever UID it wants, so user files are never really protected. System logins such as "bin" and "sys" aren't UID-mapped,[1] so any files they own (a large percentage of the system files) are vulnerable to attack. The only real effect of UID mapping is to prevent access to files that are owned by root and not readable or writable by the world.

### Cookies and stateless mounting

A client must explicitly mount an NFS filesystem before using it, just as it must mount a filesystem stored on a local disk. However, because NFS is stateless, the server does not keep track of which clients have mounted each filesystem. Instead, the server simply discloses a secret "cookie" at the conclusion of a successful mount negotiation. The cookie identifies the mounted directory to the NFS server and so provides a way for the client to access its contents.

Unmounting and remounting a filesystem on the server normally changes its cookie. As a special case, cookies persist across a reboot so a server that crashes can return to its previous state. But don't try to boot single-user, play with filesystems, then boot again; this procedure will revoke cookies and make clients unable to access the filesystems they have mounted until they either reboot or remount.

Once a client has a magic cookie, it uses the RPC protocol to make requests for filesystem operations such as creating a file or reading a data block. Because NFS is stateless, the server doesn't care what requests the client has or hasn't made before. In particular, the client is responsible for making sure that the server acknowledges write requests before it deletes its own copy of the data to be written.

---

1. Actually, Red Hat does allow you to UID-map accounts other than root; see page 497. Be careful that you don't break standard software such as **sendmail** with such a mapping.

### Naming conventions for shared filesystems

It is easier to manage NFS if you have a standard naming scheme. Names that include the server (such as **/anchor/tools** for a filesystem that lives on anchor) are useful, since they allow users to translate announcements such as "anchor will be down all day Saturday for an upgrade" into "I won't be able to use **/anchor/tools/TeX** on Saturday to finish my thesis, so I should go skiing instead."

Unfortunately, this scheme requires the directory **/anchor** to exist in the root directory of all client machines. If a client gets filesystems from several other hosts, the root can get cluttered. Consider providing a deeper hierarchy (e.g., **/home/anchor**, **/home/rastadon**, etc.). We recommend implementing such a scheme with one of the automounter daemons described starting on page 504.

### Security and NFS

NFS provides a convenient way to access files on a network, and thus it has great potential to cause security problems. In many ways, NFS is a poster child for everything that is or ever has been wrong with UNIX security.

The NFS protocol was originally designed with essentially no concern for security. Later, the underlying RPC protocol was revised to allow the use of pluggable authentication modules. However, the new specification stopped short of actually specifying or recommending any particular security mechanism.

*See page 670 for more information about Kerberos.*

Several contenders stepped up to the plate: Sun, which hoarked out an enormous public-key-based hairball that other vendors generally ignored, and Kerberos, which extended its standard authentication to RPC. Both of these schemes help to ensure that remote users really are who they say they are. However, neither actually encrypts data on the network, so you're still at the mercy of anyone running a packet sniffer.

If your site is already using Sun's public key system or Kerberos, by all means use it for NFS. You bought the cow; you might as well drink the milk. If not, the NFS situation doesn't provide much impetus for installing such a system. Although a paranoid site might find both systems worth investigating, in reality both systems offer only a minimal increase in security over good common sense. For the average site, tight control over shared filesystems is adequate protection from unwanted access.

The greatest risk is presented by on-site machines that are legally allowed to mount a filesystem. If anyone that you don't fully trust has root access on a client host, don't export any filesystems to that host.

*See page 675 for more information about firewalls.*

If your site has installed a network firewall, it's a good idea to block access to TCP and UDP ports 2049, which are used by NFS.[2] You should also block access to the SunRPC **portmap** daemon, which normally listens on TCP and UDP ports 111. It's implicit in these precautions but perhaps worth saying explicitly that NFS filesystems should not be exported to nonlocal machines (WebNFS excepted).

---

2. You'll have to unblock TCP port 2049 if your site provides WebNFS service, however. *Do not* unblock this port for any machine that contains sensitive data!

## 17.2  SERVER-SIDE NFS

A server is usually said to "export" a directory when it makes the directory available for use by other machines. Solaris uses the word "share" instead. For clarity, we'll use "export" throughout this chapter.

The process used by clients to mount a filesystem (that is, to learn its secret cookie) is completely separate from the process used to access files. The operations use separate protocols, and the requests are served by different daemons: **mountd** for mount requests and **nfsd** for actual file service. On some systems, these daemons are called **rpc.nfsd** and **rpc.mountd** as a reminder that they rely on SunRPC as an underlying protocol (and hence require **portmap** to be running; see page 826).

On an NFS server, both **mountd** and **nfsd** should start when the system boots, and both should remain running as long as the system is up. Most systems start them for you automatically; the system startup scripts check to see if you have any exports configured and run the daemons if you do.

**mountd** and **nfsd** share a single access control database that tells which filesystems should be exported and which clients may mount them. The operative copy of this database is usually kept in a binary file (called **xtab** on most systems, **sharetab** on Solaris) somewhere within the root filesystem; a copy may also be stashed within the kernel.

Since **xtab** and **sharetab** aren't human-readable, you use a helper command to add and modify entries. On most systems this command is **exportfs**; Solaris uses **share**. To remove entries from the exports table, use **exportfs -u** or **unshare**.

Maintaining a binary file by hand is not much fun, so most systems assume (correctly) that you would rather maintain a text file that enumerates all of the system's exported directories and their access settings. The system can then consult this text file at boot time to automatically construct the **xtab** or **sharetab** file.

On most systems, **/etc/exports** is the canonical, human-readable list of exported directories. Its contents are read by **exportfs -a**. Under Solaris, the canonical list is **/etc/dfs/dfstab**, which is really just a script containing a series of **share** commands. (The **shareall** command greps the NFS-related commands out of **dfstab** and runs them. Since NFS is the only file-sharing system in common use, **shareall** is equivalent to **sh /etc/dfs/dfstab**.)

 FreeBSD is unusual in that its **mountd** consults **/etc/exports** directly; there is no binary **xtab** file or **exportfs** command. After editing the **exports** file, you must send **mountd** a HUP signal to tell it to reread the file's contents:

```
# kill -HUP `cat /var/run/mountd.pid`
```

Table 17.2 summarizes the last few paragraphs. It tells you what file to edit when you want to export a new filesystem and what to do once you've finished editing to make your changes take effect.

**Table 17.2    Where to set up exported directories**

| System | Exports info in | What to do after changing it |
|---|---|---|
| Solaris | /etc/dfs/dfstab | Run shareall. |
| HP-UX | /etc/exports | Run /usr/sbin/exportfs -a. |
| Red Hat | /etc/exports | Run /usr/sbin/exportfs -a. |
| FreeBSD | /etc/exports | Send a HUP signal to mountd. |

NFS deals with the logical layer of the filesystem. Any directory can be exported; it doesn't have to be a mount point or the root of a physical filesystem. However, for security reasons, NFS does pay attention to the boundaries between filesystems and does require each device to be exported separately. For example, on a machine that has a **/users** partition, the root directory can be exported without exporting **/users**.

Clients are usually allowed to mount subdirectories of an exported directory if they wish, although the protocol does not require this feature. For example, if a server exports **/chimchim/users**, a client could mount only **/chimchim/users/joe** and ignore the rest of the **users** directory. Most systems don't let you export subdirectories of an exported directory with different options, although Red Hat is an exception.

### The share command and dfstab file (Solaris)

**/etc/dfs/dfstab** executes the **share** command once for each exported filesystem. For example, on a server that shares **/chimchim/users** with hosts band and moon (with band allowed root access) and shares **/usr/share/man** with chimchim and rastadon, the **/etc/dfs/dfstab** file would contain the following commands:

```
share -F nfs -o rw=band.xor.com:moon.xor.com,root=band.xor.com
    /chimchim/users
share -F nfs -o rw=chimchim.xor.com:rastadon.xor.com /usr/share/man
```

After editing **/etc/dfs/dfstab**, remember to run **shareall** to make your changes take effect. Note that since **shareall** simply runs the commands in the **dfstab** file, it will not unshare filesystems that you remove. Table 17.3 lists the most common options.

**Table 17.3    Options for the share command (Solaris)**

| Option | Description |
|---|---|
| **ro** | Exports read-only to the entire world (not recommended) |
| **ro=**_list_ | Exports read-only with access only by listed hosts |
| **rw** | Exports read-write to the entire world (not recommended) |
| **rw=**_list_ | Exports read-write with access only by listed hosts |
| **root=**_list_ | Lists hosts permitted to access this filesystem as root. Otherwise, root access from a client is equivalent to access by "nobody" (usually UID -2). |
| **anon=**_uid_ | Specifies the UID to which root is remapped; the default is "nobody" |
| **nosub** | Forbids clients to mount subdirectories of the exported directory |
| **nosuid** | Prevents setuid and setgid files from being created via NFS |

Wherever a *list* is called for in a **share** option, it should consist of a colon-separated group of the items shown in Table 17.4, all of which are ways of specifying hosts or groups of hosts.

**Table 17.4   Client specifications for the share command**

| Type | Syntax | Meaning |
|------|--------|---------|
| Hostname | *hostname* | Individual hosts (must be fully qualified if you use DNS) |
| Netgroup | *groupname* | NIS netgroups; see page 522 for details |
| DNS domains | *.xxx.yyy* | Any host within the domain |
| IP networks | *@netname* | Network names as defined in **/etc/networks**[a] |

a. CIDR-style specifications are also accepted; for example, **@128.138.92.128/25**.

The note in Table 17.4 regarding hostnames bears repeating: if your site uses DNS, individual hostnames *must* be fully qualified or they will be ignored.

You can put a dash in front of an item to explicitly disallow it. The list is examined from left to right during each lookup until a matching item is found, so negations should precede the more general items that they modify. For example, the line

```
share -F nfs -o rw=-@128.138.243/24:.cs.colorado.edu /users
```

exports **/users** read-write to all hosts in the cs.colorado.edu DNS domain except for hosts on the 128.138.243 network.

It's possible to export a directory read-only to some clients and read-write to others: just include both the **rw=** and **ro=** options.

The **share**(1M) man page documents a few basic NFS options. For a complete list, refer to the **share_nfs**(1M) man page.

### The exportfs command and the exports file (HP-UX, Red Hat, FreeBSD)

The **exports** file consists of a list of exported directories in the leftmost column, followed by lists of associated options and attributes. For example, the HP-UX **exports**

```
/chimchim/users    -access=band:moon,root=band
/usr/share/man     -access=xorasaurus:rastadon:moon,ro
```

permit **/chimchim/users** to be mounted by the machines band and moon, and allow root access to the filesystem from band.[3] In addition, they let **/usr/share/man** be mounted by xorasaurus, rastadon, and moon.

Filesystems that are listed in the **exports** file without a specific set of hosts are usually mountable by *all* machines. This is a sizable security hole.

Some NFS implementations limit lines in the **exports** file to 1,024 characters. That limit can come awfully fast, especially when you're using fully qualified domain

---

3. Root access is also allowed from chimchim, the real owner of the filesystem.

names. Netgroups and network masks can help to keep line lengths manageable on the machines that support them.

The exact options and syntax used in the **exports** file vary greatly by system, though there is a certain thematic similarity. The following sections describe the formats for HP-UX, Red Hat Linux, and FreeBSD; as always, be sure to check the man page.

### Exports under HP-UX

HP-UX has the most "classic" **exports** format of our four example systems. The permissible options (shown in Table 17.5) are actually quite similar to those understood by the Solaris **share** command. However, there are some subtle differences. For example, the option

```
rw=anchor.cs.colorado.edu:moet.cs.colorado.edu
```

on Solaris means to export the directory read-write with access only by the listed hosts. Under HP-UX, this option allows the entire world to mount the directory read-only. Gotcha! Under HP-UX, you must use the access clause to restrict mounting to a specified list of clients:

```
rw,access=anchor.cs.colorado.edu:moet.cs.colorado.edu
```

Read-write exporting is the default, so the rw clause could actually be eliminated. It doesn't hurt to say it explicitly, however.

Each line in an HP-UX **exports** file should consist of a directory path, whitespace, and then a dash followed by a comma-separated list of options. See the lines on the previous page for some simple examples.

In Table 17.5, a *list* consists of a colon-separated series of hostnames and netgroup names. (See page 522 for more information about netgroups.)

Remember to run **exportfs -a** after changing the **/etc/exports** file.

### Table 17.5    Common export options for HP-UX

| Option | Description |
| --- | --- |
| access=list | Lists the hosts that can mount the filesystem. |
| ro | Exports read-only; no clients may write on the filesystem. |
| rw | Exports for reading and writing (the default). |
| rw=list | Exports read-mostly. *list* enumerates the hosts allowed to mount for writing; all others must mount read-only. |
| root=list | Lists hosts that can access the filesystem as root. Without this option, root access from a client is equivalent to access by the user nobody. |
| anon=n | Specifies the UID to which remote roots are mapped. Defaults to -2 (nobody). Setting this value to -1 denies root access entirely. |
| async | Processes all write requests asynchronously. This option improves write performance but raises the possibility of data loss in the event of a crash. |

*Exports under Red Hat Linux*

In Red Hat's **exports** file, the clients that may access a given filesystem are presented in a whitespace-separated list. Each client is followed immediately by a parenthesized list of comma-separated options. Lines can be continued with a backslash.

Here's what the format looks like:

```
/chimchim/users     band(rw,no_root_squash) moon(rw)
/usr/share/man      *.cs.colorado.edu(ro)
```

There is no way to list multiple clients for a single set of options, although certain types of "client" refer to multiple hosts. Table 17.6 lists the four types of client specifications that can appear in a Red Hat **exports** file.[4]

**Table 17.6    Client specifications under Red Hat**

| Type | Syntax | Meaning |
|---|---|---|
| Hostname | *hostname* | Individual hosts |
| Netgroup | *@groupname* | NIS netgroups; see page 522 for details |
| Wild cards | * and ? | FQDNs[a] with wild cards. "*" will not match a dot. |
| IP networks | *ipaddr/mask* | CIDR-style specifications (e.g., 128.138.92.128/25) |

a. Fully qualified domain names

Table 17.7 describes the most common export options understood by Red Hat.

**Table 17.7    Common export options for Red Hat**

| Option | Description |
|---|---|
| ro | Exports read-only. |
| rw | Exports for reading and writing (the default). |
| rw=*list* | Exports read-mostly. *list* enumerates the hosts allowed to mount for writing; all others must mount read-only. |
| root_squash | Maps ("squashes") UID 0 and GID 0 to the values specified by anonuid and anongid.[a] This is the default. |
| no_root_squash | Allows normal access by root. Dangerous. |
| all_squash | Maps all UIDs and GIDs to their anonymous versions. Useful for supporting PCs and untrusted single-user hosts. |
| anonuid=xxx | Specifies the UID that remote roots should be squashed to. |
| anongid=xxx | Specifies the GID that remote roots should be squashed to. |
| secure | Requires remote access to originate at a privileged port. |
| insecure | Allows remote access from any port. |
| noaccess | Prevents access to this dir and its subdirs (used with nested exports). |

a. Unlike most operating systems, Red Hat allows UIDs other than root to be collapsed. Look up the squash_uids and all_squash options for more details.

4. Well, actually there is a fifth, =public, that's used with WebNFS.

Red Hat's NFS software has the unusual feature of allowing subdirectories of exported directories to be exported with different options. The noaccess option is provided to "unexport" subdirectories that you would rather not share. For example, the configuration

```
/users      *.xor.com(rw)
/users/evi  (noaccess)
```

allows hosts in the xor.com domain to access all of **/users** except for **/users/evi**. The lack of a client name on the second line means that the option applies to all hosts; it's perhaps somewhat more secure this way.

Red Hat provides a rich set of facilities for mapping between remote and local UIDs. While we don't advise using them at a heterogeneous site, an all-Linux shop might find them useful. See the **exports**(5) man page for more information.

Red Hat's **mountd** can be run out of **inetd** rather than run continuously. This configuration allows supplemental access control to be performed by Wietse Venema's TCP wrapper program, **tcpd**. See page 666 for more information.

Red Hat's NFS implementation does not currently support NFS 3, although it is expected to do so in the near future. Clients that default to version 3 must be told explicitly to mount using version 2 or cryptic errors will ensue.

*Exports under FreeBSD*

In yet a third similar but different take on the **exports** file, FreeBSD entries consist of a whitespace-separated list of directories, a whitespace-separated group of options (all of which start with a dash), and then a series of client specifications separated by whitespace. Here's a short example:

```
/chimchim/users   -maproot=root band
/chimchim/users   moon
/usr/share/man    -ro -mapall=daemon xorasaurus rastadon moon
```

The FreeBSD philosophy is unusual in that directories can appear on more than one line. Each line defines one set of options and the clients to which those options apply. If different option sets apply to different clients, there must be more than one entry for the directory.

Table 17.8 describes the most common export options. Unlike most implementations, FreeBSD does not permit clients to mount subdirectories of exported filesystems unless this is explicitly allowed with the -alldirs option. Why this is considered a feature must remain forever a mystery; it does not appear to enhance security.

Clients in FreeBSD can be specified as hostnames or netgroup names, or they can be network numbers specified with the following syntax:

```
-network netaddr -mask mask
```

**Table 17.8   Common export options for FreeBSD**

| Option | Description |
| --- | --- |
| -ro | Exports read-only. The default is to export read-write. |
| -maproot=*user* | Maps root to the specified *user*, which may be a UID or a name. The default is nobody, -2. To allow root access, use -maproot=root. |
| -mapall=*user* | Maps all UIDs to the specified *user*. Useful for supporting PCs and untrusted single-user hosts. |
| -alldirs | Allows any subdirectory to be mounted. The default is to allow only mounts of the listed directory. |
| -webnfs | Export as a WebNFS directory: read-only access to everyone with all UIDs mapped to nobody. |

The documentation sometimes shows an = between -network or -mask and its argument, but either notation seems to work equally well. Both the network and the mask are specified in the traditional dotted notation. For example:

```
/chimchim/users   -ro -network 128.138.243.0 -mask 255.255.255.0
```

A network and mask specification can't appear on the same line with hosts and netgroups. If you would like to use both, include multiple lines for the same directory.

Remember to send **mountd** a HUP signal to tell it to reread **/etc/exports** after you have finished making changes. Unfortunately, this convention does not give **mountd** any opportunity to provide you with error messages if you have botched the configuration. You will have to check the system logs; **mountd** submits error messages via syslog under the "daemon" facility.

### nfsd: serve files

Once a client's mount request has been validated by **mountd**, it can request various filesystem operations. These requests are handled on the server side by **nfsd**, the NFS operations daemon.[5] **nfsd** need not be run on an NFS client machine unless the client exports filesystems of its own.

**nfsd** takes a numeric argument that specifies the number of copies of itself that it should fork. Selecting the appropriate number of **nfsd**s is important and is unfortunately something of a black art. If the number is too low or too high, NFS performance can suffer.

The performance of older systems could degrade quite a bit as a result of having too many **nfsd**s because the kernel would wake up all the idle **nfsd**s in response to each incoming request. Current systems are better about this, and it's OK to err a bit on the side of generosity.

---

5. In reality, **nfsd** is usually a very simple program that makes a nonreturning system call to NFS server code embedded in the kernel.

In the past, the maximum number of **nfsd**s was closely tied to the number of process contexts supported by your computer's CPU chip. These days many implementations share a single context among all copies of **nfsd**, so that number is no longer a reliable guide. A more reasonable metric is the number of hard disks being served; when NFS activity is heavy, disk bandwidth will be the limiting factor in the NFS pipeline. There's no reason to run more than a few **nfsd**s per spindle.

Generally speaking, 4 **nfsd**s is adequate for a server that is used infrequently and is few enough that performance problems can't really arise. On a production server, somewhere between 12 and 20 is a good number. If you notice the load average (as reported by **uptime**) rising as you add **nfsd**s, you've gone too far; back off a bit from that threshold.

On a loaded NFS server with a lot of UDP clients, UDP sockets can overflow if requests arrive while all **nfsd** "piers" are already in use. You can monitor the number of overflows with **netstat -s**. Add more **nfsd**s until UDP socket overflows drop to zero. Overflows indicate a severe undersupply of server daemons, so you should probably add a few more than this metric would indicate.

On many systems, you must tweak one of the **/etc/rc\*** files or one of the **rc** files run by **init** to set the number of **nfsd**s. Other systems provide a more elegant way to set this value.

Under Solaris, **nfsd** should be started with the **-a** option to enable service via both TCP and UDP. This is the default.

Under HP-UX, you can set the number of **nfsd**s by setting the NUM_NFSD variable in **/etc/rc.config.d/nfsconf** to the value you want.

Under FreeBSD, **nfsd** should be given the **-t** and **-u** flags to request both TCP and UDP service. The FreeBSD version of **nfsd** also requires that the **nfsd** count be preceded by the **-n** flag (for example, **nfsd -t -u -n 8**). The command-line arguments with which **nfsd** is started come from the variable nfs_server_flags in **/etc/rc.conf** (or **/etc/defaults/rc.conf** if you don't set it yourself; the default is "**-u -t -n 4**"). You must also set the nfs_server_enable variable to "YES" to start the NFS daemons.

## 17.3 CLIENT-SIDE NFS

**mount** understands the notation

> hostname:directory

to mean the path *directory* interpreted by the host *hostname*.

The **mount** command and its associated NFS extensions represent the most significant concerns to a system administrator of an NFS client. On most systems, the optional but highly recommended daemon **biod** (block I/O daemon, sometimes called **nfsiod**) provides performance enhancements.

### biod and nfsiod: provide client-side caching

**biod/nfsiod** performs basic read-ahead and write-behind filesystem block caching. Both NFSv2 and NFSv3 mounts can benefit from this daemon. We suggest that you run it on NFS clients that provide it, but that is not strictly required. The presence or absence of the caching daemon does not affect administration.

Like **nfsd**, **biod** takes as its argument the number of copies of itself to start. On a garden-variety machine, 4 or 8 copies should be plenty. If both **nfsd** and **biod** run on the same machine, it may be wise to split the "optimal" number of slots between them. This will depend on how your system is used; you'll have to experiment.

 Under FreeBSD, **nfsiod** needs a **-n** flag on the command line in front of the number of copies to run.

### Mounting remote filesystems

*See page 504 for more information about automount and amd.* You can use the **mount** command to establish temporary network mounts, but you should list mounts that are part of a system's permanent configuration in **/etc/fstab** (**/etc/vfstab** in Solaris) so that they are mounted automatically at boot time. Alternatively, mounts can be handled by an automatic mounting service such as **automount** or **amd**; see *Automatic mounting* on page 504.

The following **fstab** entries mount the filesystems **/beast/users** and **/usr/man** from the hosts beast and chimchim:

```
# filesystem         mountpoint     fstype   flags            dump fsck
beast:/beast/users   /beast/users   nfs      rw,bg,intr,hard   0    0
chimchim:/usr/man    /usr/man       nfs      ro,bg,intr,soft   0    0
```

 The Solaris **/etc/vfstab** file is slightly different in format, but NFS options are listed similarly. The available options are largely the same as those on other systems.

*See page 133 for more information about the fstab file.* When you add entries to **fstab/vfstab**, be sure to create the mount point directories with **mkdir**. You can make your changes take effect immediately by running **mount -a -F nfs** on Solaris or HP-UX; use **-t** instead of **-F** on Red Hat or FreeBSD.

The flags field of **/etc/fstab** specifies options for NFS mounts. Common flags are listed in Table 17.9 on the next page.

Filesystems mounted hard can cause processes to hang when their servers go down. This behavior is particularly bothersome when the processes in question are standard daemons. In general, the use of the soft and intr options will reduce the number of NFS-related headaches. However, these options can have their own undesirable side effects, such as aborting a 20-hour simulation after it has run for 18 hours just because of a transient network glitch.[6] **amd**, discussed starting on page 509, also provides some remedies for mounting ailments.

---

6. Jeff Forys, one of our technical reviewers, remarked, "Most mounts should use hard, intr, and bg, because these options best preserve NFS's original design goals (reliability and statelessness). soft is an abomination, an ugly Satanic hack! If the user wants to interrupt, cool. Otherwise, wait for the server and all will eventually be well again with no data lost."

NFS

**Table 17.9  NFS mount flags**

| Flag | Systems[a] | Description |
|---|---|---|
| rw | SHRF[b] | Mounts the filesystem read-write (must be exported R/W) |
| ro | SHRF[b] | Mounts the filesystem read-only |
| bg | SHRF | If the mount fails (server doesn't respond), keeps trying it in the background and continues with other mount requests |
| hard | SHR[c] | If a server goes down, causes operations that try to access it to block until the server comes back up |
| soft | SHRF | If a server goes down, causes operations that try to access it to fail and return an error. This is useful to avoid processes "hanging" on inessential mounts. |
| intr | SHRF | Allows users to interrupt blocked operations (and make them return an error) |
| nointr | SHRF[b] | Does not allow user interrupts |
| retrans=n | SHRF[d] | Specifies the number of times to repeat a request before returning an error on a soft-mounted filesystem |
| timeo=n | SHRF[d] | Sets the timeout period (in tenths of a second) for requests |
| rsize=n | SHRF[d] | Sets the read buffer size to n bytes |
| wsize=n | SHRF[d] | Sets the write buffer size to n bytes |
| vers=n | SH | Selects NFS protocol version 2 or 3 (normally automatic) |
| nfsv3, nfsv2 | F | Selects NFS protocol version 2 or 3 (normally automatic) |
| proto=prot | S | Selects transport; possible values are tcp and udp |
| tcp | RF | Selects transport via TCP. UDP is the default. |

a. S = Solaris, H = HP-UX, R = Red Hat Linux, F = FreeBSD
b. This option does not appear in the FreeBSD man pages, but it does work.
c. FreeBSD does not permit this option to be listed explicitly, but it is the default behavior.
d. FreeBSD calls these options by different names: retrans is -x, timeo is -t, rsize is -r, and wsize is -w.

The read and write buffer sizes apply to both UDP and TCP mounts, but the optimal values differ. Because you can trust TCP to transfer data efficiently, the values should be higher; Solaris defaults to 32K. For UDP, a good value when server and client are on the same network is 8K. Some systems default to significantly smaller values than these (Red Hat defaults to 1K).

NFS partitions can be unmounted with the **umount** command.

### Secure port restrictions

NFS clients are free to use any TCP or UDP port they like when connecting to an NFS server. However, some servers may insist that requests come from a privileged port (a port numbered lower than 1,024). Others allow this behavior to be set as an option. In the world of PCs and desktop UNIX boxes, the use of privileged ports provides little actual security.

Most NFS clients adopt the traditional (and still recommended) approach of defaulting to a privileged port, which averts the potential for conflict.

## 17.4  NFSSTAT: DUMP **NFS** STATISTICS

Most systems provide a command called **nfsstat** that can display various statistics kept by the NFS system. **nfsstat -s** displays statistics for NFS server processes, and **nfsstat -c** shows information related to client-side operations. For example:

```
chimchim% nfsstat -c

Client rpc:
calls    badcalls   retrans   badxid   timeout   wait   newcred   timers
64235    1595       0         3        1592      0      0         886

Client nfs:
calls    badcalls   nclget    nclsleep
62613    3          62643     0
null     getattr    setattr   readlink   lookup   root   read
0%       34%        0%        21%        30%      0%     2%
write    wrcache    create    remove     rename   link   symlink
3%       0%         0%        0%         0%       0%     0%
mkdir    readdir    rmdir     fsstat
0%       6%         0%        0%
```

This example is from a relatively healthy NFS client. If more than 3% of calls time out, it's likely that there is a problem with your NFS server or network. You can usually discover the cause by checking the badxid field. If badxid is near 0 with timeouts greater than 3%, packets to and from the server are getting lost on the network. You may be able to solve this problem by lowering the rsize and wsize mount parameters (read and write block sizes). If badxid is nearly as high as timeout, then the server is responding, but too slowly. Either replace the server or increase the timeo mount parameter.

Running **nfsstat** occasionally and becoming familiar with its output will help you discover NFS problems before your users do.

## 17.5  DEDICATED **NFS** FILE SERVERS

Fast, reliable file service is one of the most important elements of any production computing environment. While you can certainly roll your own file server from a UNIX workstation and a handful of off-the-shelf hard disks, this is often not the most performant or easiest-to-administer solution (though it is often the cheapest).

Dedicated NFS file servers have been around for more than a decade. They offer a host of potential advantages over the homebrew approach:

- They are optimized for file service and typically provide the best possible NFS performance.

- As storage requirements grow, they can scale smoothly to support terabytes of storage and hundreds of users.

- They are more reliable than UNIX boxes thanks to their simplified software, redundant hardware, and use of disk mirroring.

- They usually provide file service for both UNIX and Windows clients. Some even contain integral web and FTP servers.

- They are often easier to administer than UNIX file servers.

- They often provide backup and checkpoint facilities that are superior to those found on vanilla UNIX systems.

Of the current offerings, our favorites are those made by Network Appliance, Inc. (www.netapp.com). Their servers run the gamut from very small to very large, and their pricing is OK. Auspex and EMC are players in the high-end server market. They make good products, but be prepared for sticker shock and build up your tolerance for marketing buzzwords.[7]

## 17.6 AUTOMATIC MOUNTING

Mounting filesystems one at a time by listing them in **/etc/fstab** or **/etc/vfstab** introduces a number of problems in large networks. First, maintaining **/etc/fstab** on a few hundred machines can be tedious. Each one may be slightly different and thus require individual attention.

Second, if filesystems are mounted from many different hosts, chaos ensues when one of those servers crashes. Every command that **stat**s the mount points will hang.

Third, when an important server crashes, it may cripple users by making important partitions like **/usr/share/man** unavailable. In this situation, it's best if a copy of the partition can be mounted temporarily from a backup server.

An automount daemon mounts filesystems when they are referenced and unmounts them when they are no longer needed. This procedure minimizes the number of active mount points and is mostly transparent to users. With most automounters, it is also possible to supply a list of "replicated" (identical) filesystems so that the network can continue to function when a primary server becomes unavailable.

To implement this behind-the-scenes mounting and unmounting, the automounter mounts a virtual filesystem driver on the directories you've designated as locations for automatic mounting to occur. In the past, the automounter did this by posing as an NFS server, but this scheme suffers from several significant limitations and is rarely found on contemporary systems. These days, a kernel-resident filesystem driver called autofs is used.

Instead of mirroring an actual filesystem, an automounter "makes up" a filesystem hierarchy according to the specifications you list in its configuration file. When a user references a directory within the automounter's virtual filesystem, the automounter intercepts the reference and mounts the actual filesystem the user is trying to reach. On systems that support autofs, the NFS filesystem is simply mounted

---

7. Speaking of buzzwords, one of the main ones you'll hear in this context is "network attached storage," also known as NAS. It's just a fancy way of saying "file service."

within the autofs filesystem in normal UNIX fashion. Other systems may require mounting to occur in a separate directory that is then pointed to by symbolic links.

The idea of an automounter originally comes from Sun. Sun's implementation is called **automount** and is shipped with most Sun-derived NFS clients. Red Hat supplies an **automount** designed to mimic Sun's, though it is an independent implementation of the concept.

Prior to the autofs era, **automount** was plagued with bugs and design flaws and could not reliably be used on production systems. Current implementations are generally much better, though reviews are still somewhat mixed. Many people use it extensively with no problems; others still experience occasional hangs. Reliability no doubt varies by system and implementation.

**amd**, originally written by Jan-Simon Pendry of Imperial College in London, is the product of a doctoral thesis that expanded upon Sun's original idea. **amd** corrected many of the problems in the original **automount**. It also had the advantage of being free and installable on a wide variety of UNIX systems.

**automount** configuration is relatively simple and concise. **amd** is more complicated and more powerful, and it includes some features that are largely experimental. You might want to check out **amd**'s feature list and see if there's anything that you can't live without.

The second edition of this book vigorously recommended **amd** over **automount**. Since **automount** did not actually work, the choice was easy.[8] However, in the context of a working, autofs-based **automount**, there isn't really a compelling argument to be made in favor of either automounter. In general, the simplicity of **automount** and the fact that it's preinstalled on many systems make it a good default. Try it and see if it works for you.

## 17.7  AUTOMOUNT: THE ORIGINAL AUTOMOUNTER

Both Solaris and HP-UX provide a current **automount**. Red Hat has an **automount** clone with some minor variations in configuration syntax. See the Red Hat information on page 509 for specifics.

**automount** understands three different kinds of configuration files (called "maps"): direct maps, indirect maps, and master maps.[9] Direct and indirect maps provide information about filesystems that are to be automounted. A master map lists direct and indirect maps that **automount** should pay attention to. Only one master map can be active at once; the default master map is kept in **/etc/auto_master**.

When run, **automount** reads its configuration files, sets up any necessary autofs mounts, and exits. References to automounted filesystems are actually handled (via

---

8. If your system supports only the older NFS-based **automount**, we'd still suggest giving it a wide berth.

9. A direct map can also be managed as an NIS database, but don't try this at home.

autofs) by a separate daemon, **automountd**. **automountd** normally does its work silently and does not need additional configuration.

If you change the master map or one of the direct maps that it references, you must rerun **automount** to pick up the changes. With the **-v** option, **automount** will show you the adjustments it's making to its configuration.

**automount** accepts a **-t** argument that tells how long (in seconds) an automounted filesystem may remain unused before being unmounted. The default is 5 minutes. Since an NFS mount whose server has crashed can cause programs that touch it to hang, it's good hygiene to clean up automounts that are no longer in use; don't raise the timeout too much.[10]

### Indirect maps

Indirect maps automount several filesystems underneath a common directory. The path of the directory is specified in the master map, not in the indirect map itself. For example, an indirect map for filesystems that get mounted under **/chimchim** might look like this:

```
users    chimchim:/chimchim/users
devel    -soft,proto=udp chimchim:/chimchim/devel
info     -ro chimchim:/chimchim/info
```

The first column names the subdirectory where each automount should be installed, and subsequent items list the mount options and source path of the filesystem. This example (perhaps stored in **/etc/auto.chim**) tells **automount** that it can mount the directories **/chimchim/users**, **/chimchim/devel**, and **/chimchim/info** from host chimchim, with **info** being mounted read-only and **devel** being mounted via UDP (this example is from a Solaris system, so TCP is the default).

In this configuration the paths on chimchim and the local host will be identical, but this correspondence is not required.

### Direct maps

Direct maps list filesystems that do not share a common prefix, such as **/usr/src** and **/cs/tools**. A direct map (e.g., **/etc/auto.direct**) that described both of these filesystems to **automount** might look something like this:

```
/usr/src    chimchim:/usr/src
/cs/tools   -ro anchor:/cs/tools
```

Because they do not share a common parent directory, these automounts must each be implemented with a separate autofs mount. This configuration requires slightly more overhead, but it has the added advantage that the mount point and directory structure are always accessible by commands such as **ls**. Using **ls** on a directory full of indirect mounts can often be confusing to users because **automount** doesn't

---

10. The other side of this issue is the fact that it takes a certain amount of time to mount a filesystem. System response will be faster and smoother if filesystems aren't being continually remounted.

show the subdirectories until their contents have been accessed (**ls** doesn't look inside the automounted directories, so it does not cause them to be mounted).

### Master maps

A master map lists the direct and indirect maps that **automount** should pay attention to. For each indirect map, it also specifies the root directory used by the mounts defined in the map.

A master map that made use of the direct and indirect maps shown in the previous examples would look something like this:

```
# Directory    Map
/chimchim      /etc/auto.chim  -proto=tcp
/-             /etc/auto.direct
```

The first column is a local directory name for an indirect map, or the special token /- for a direct map. The second column identifies the file in which the map is stored. You can have several maps of each type. When you specify mount options at the end of a line, they set the defaults for all mounts within the map.

 On most systems, default options set on a master map entry do not "blend" with options specified in the direct or indirect map to which it points. If a map entry has its own list of options, the defaults are completely ignored. Red Hat merges the two sets, however. If the same option is specified in both places, the map entry's value overrides the default.

The master map can usually be replaced or augmented by a version shared via NIS or NIS+. See your documentation for details.

### Executable maps

If an indirect map file is executable, it's assumed to be a script that dynamically generates automounting information. Instead of reading the map as a text file, the automounter will execute it with an argument (called the "key") that indicates which subdirectory a user has attempted to access. The script is responsible for printing out an appropriate indirect map entry; if the specified key is not valid, the script can simply exit without printing anything.

This feature is very powerful and makes up for many of the potential deficiencies in **automounter**'s rather strange configuration system. In effect, it allows you to easily define a site-wide automount configuration file in a format of your own choice. You can write a simple Perl script to decode the global configuration on each machine.

Since automount scripts run dynamically as needed, it's unnecessary to distribute the master configuration file after every change or to convert it preemptively to the **automounter** format; in fact, the global configuration file can have a permanent home on an NFS server.

### Replicated filesystems using automount

In some cases, a read-only filesystem such as **/usr/man** may be identical on several different servers. In this case, you can tell **automount** about several potential sources for the filesystem. It will choose a server based on its own idea of which ones are closest given network numbers, NFS protocol versions, and response times from an initial query.

Although it is not required by **automount**, replicated mounts should represent read-only filesystems such as **/usr/man** or **/usr/local/X11**. There's no way for **automount** to synchronize writes across a set of servers, and so replicated read-write filesystems are of little practical use.

Replicated filesystems should be truly identical. Otherwise, users will become agitated when a filesystem is replaced, and they may act in unpredictable ways.

Under Solaris, **automount** can smoothly switch from one server of a replicated mount to another when problems occur. This feature is only supposed to work properly for read-only mounts, but rumor has it that read-write mounts are handled more reasonably than the documentation would suggest. References to files that have been opened for writing will still hang when **automount** switches servers, however, which is yet another reason why replicated read-write mounts are perhaps not so useful.

Although **automount** can pick servers according to its own criteria of efficiency and locality, you can assign explicit priorities if you like. The priorities are small integers, with larger numbers indicating lower priority. The default priority is 0, most eligible.

An **auto.direct** file that defines **/usr/man** and **/cs/tools** as replicated filesystems might look like this:

```
/usr/man    -ro chimchim:/usr/share/man band(1):/usr/man
/cs/tools   -ro anchor,band:/cs/tools
```

Note that server names can be listed together if the source path on each is the same. The (1) after band in the first line sets that server's priority with respect to **/usr/man**.

### Automatic automounts

Instead of listing every possible mount in a direct or indirect map, it's possible to tell **automount** a little about your filesystem naming conventions and let it figure things out for itself. The key piece of glue that makes this work is the fact that it is possible to query the **mountd** running on a remote server to find out what filesystems the server exports.

There are several ways to configure "automatic automounts," the simplest of which is the -hosts mount type. If you list -hosts as a map name in your master map file, **automount** will map remote hosts' exports into the specified automount directory:

```
/net    -hosts -nosuid,soft
```

For example, if chimchim exports **/usr/share/man**, that directory could then be reached via the automounter at the path **/net/chimchim/usr/share/man**.

The implementation of -hosts does not enumerate all possible hosts from which filesystems can be mounted; that would be impossible. Instead, it waits for individual subdirectory names to be referenced, then runs off and mounts the exported filesystems from the requested host.

A similar but finer-grained effect can be achieved with the * and & wildcards in an indirect map file. Also, a number of macros available for use in maps expand to the current hostname, architecture type, and so on. See the **automount**(1M) man page for details.

### Specifics for Red Hat Linux

Red Hat's **automount** is an independent implementation, and it has diverged a bit from Sun's. The changes mostly have to do with the naming of commands and files.

First, in Red Hat, **automount** is the daemon that actually mounts and unmounts remote filesystems. It fills the same niche as the **automountd** daemon in Sun's system and generally does not need to be run by hand.

The command that you use to make your changes to the master map take effect— **automount**, in Sun-land—is **/etc/rc.d/init.d/autofs** under Red Hat. The **autofs** command takes the arguments **stop**, **start**, **reload**, and **status**; **reload**, of course, is what you'd generally want to do after making changes.

The default master map file is **/etc/auto.master**. Its format and the format of indirect maps are as described previously. The documentation can be hard to find, however. The master map format is described in **auto.master**(5) and the indirect map format in **autofs**(5); be careful, or you'll get **autofs**(8), which documents the syntax of the **autofs** command. (As one of the man pages says, "The documentation leaves a lot to be desired.")

Red Hat does not support direct maps.

## 17.8  AMD: A MORE SOPHISTICATED AUTOMOUNTER

**amd** is an elaborate riff on the automounter concept. It became something of an orphan when its original author stopped maintaining it. It's now kept up by Erez Zadok at Columbia University as a component of the **am-utils** package. The current URL is

> http://www.cs.columbia.edu/~ezk/am-utils

**amd** offers the following advantages over **automount**:

- **amd** sends "keep alive" queries to remote servers at regular intervals and maintains a list of servers that are accessible. **amd** will mount, unmount, and replace filesystems based on this information. If a server crashes, future filesystem accesses return an "operation would block" error rather than hanging.

- **amd** contains no proprietary source code and has been ported to over 20 versions of UNIX.

- **amd** offers support for a number of mount types, such as the "union" mount, that are not supported by **automount**.

- The **amd** distribution includes a query-and-manipulation tool, **amq**, that lets you monitor **amd**'s status and send it hints and commands (such as forced unmount requests).

- **amd**'s map syntax is more generic than **automount**'s. You can create a single file for all hosts at your site and distribute it with **rdist** or **rsync**.

- **amd** is based on the concept that each server has one or more filesystems, with each filesystem containing one or more volumes (a coherent set of files). This makes the handling of subdirectories more straightforward than with **automount**.

- **amd** won't eat all the popcorn or send you out to get Milk Duds.

### amd maps

The **amd** map format is extremely flexible and allows the same configuration file to be used on many machines. Map entries can contain conditionals that activate them only in specific contexts (e.g., on a specific host or type of machine). Conditionals use built-in "selector variables" that are filled in with various pieces of information about the environment in which **amd** is running. The most commonly used selector variables are listed in Table 17.10.

**Table 17.10   amd selector variables**

| Variable | Description |
|----------|-------------|
| arch | Architecture of the current machine |
| autodir | Default directory under which to mount filesystems |
| byte | CPU byte sex (big-endian or little-endian) |
| cluster | Name of local cluster of machines, defaults to domain |
| domain | Local NIS domain name |
| host | Local hostname |
| hostd | Hostname concatenated with local DNS domain name |
| karch | Kernel architecture (defaults to value of arch selector) |
| key | Volume name being resolved |
| map | Name of mount map being used |
| network | Matches network name or number of any net interface |
| os | Operating system |
| osver | Operating system version |

The entry for a mount point can describe several different things that might be mounted there. For example, the following map file tells **amd** about two filesystems, **/usr/man** and **/cs/tools**. Each filesystem has one set of options that controls mounting on the machine where the filesystem actually lives and another that mounts the filesystem over the network.

```
/default     opts:=rw,soft,timeo=10,retrans=5

usr/man      host==chimchim;type:=ufs;dev:=/dev/sd1f \
             host!=chimchim;rhost=chimchim;rfs:=/${key};\
             type=nfs;fs:=${autodir}/${key}
cs/tools     host==anchor;type:=ufs;dev:=/dev/sd3c \
             host!=anchor;rhost=anchor;rfs:=/${key};\
             type=nfs;fs:=${autodir}/${key}
```

Elements of the form name:=value define various attributes of the mount. For example, the first line sets the default mount options to "rw,soft,timeo=10,retrans=5". Elements of the form name==value or name!=value are conditionals; subsequent elements are only used if the conditional evaluates to true. Notations like ${autodir} and ${key} insert the value of the appropriate variable.

The /default clause specifies defaults that apply to all map entries unless they are explicitly overridden. Table 17.11 describes the various options.

**Table 17.11    amd map options**

| Option | Description |
| --- | --- |
| rhost | Remote host on which the volume lives |
| rfs | Remote filesystem name |
| type | Type of mount, usually nfs or ufs (local disk) |
| fs | Local mount point |
| opts | Mount options |
| addopts | Options to be added to the default options |
| remopts | Options to use if server is nonlocal (e.g., smaller read/write sizes) |

### Starting amd

A running copy of **amd** manages one virtual filesystem directory beneath which all of its automounting action occurs. The name of the virtual directory and the map file that tells what to mount within it are specified on the command line.

**amd** can be started with a script such as this:

```
#!/bin/csh -f
cd /usr/local/etc/amd
exec /usr/local/bin/amd -x fatal,error,user -r -l syslog -a /tmp_mnt
    /amd amd.master.map >& /dev/console
```

The options used in this script are described in Table 17.12.

**Table 17.12    amd command-line options**

| Option | Description |
|---|---|
| **-x** | Sets run-time logging options |
| **-r** | "Adopts" existing mounts |
| **-l** | Specifies log file or **syslog** for error messages |
| **-a** | Specifies alternate location for mount points[a] |
| **/amd** | Sets the virtual (automount) directory |
| **amd.master.map** | Specifies the map file containing the mount options |

a. The default is **/a**.

When a user references one of the filesystems defined in **amd**'s map file, **amd** mounts the filesystem and monitors subsequent use of the mount. After it has been inactive for a period of time (usually 5-15 minutes), **amd** unmounts the filesystem until it is referenced again.

Use the **amq** command to see the status of mounts.

### Stopping amd

**amd** needs to be stopped gracefully so that it has a chance to untangle itself from the filesystem structure. Sending **amd** a SIGTERM is the polite way to ask it to leave.

## 17.9   RECOMMENDED READING

CALLAGHAN, BRENT. *NFS Illustrated*. Addison-Wesley. 1999.

PENDRY, JAN-SIMON, AND NICK WILLIAMS. "AMD: The 4.4BSD Automounter Reference Manual." 4.4BSD System Manager's Manual, Usenix and O'Reilly. 1994.

STERN, HAL. *Managing NFS and NIS*. Sebastopol: O'Reilly & Associates, 1992.

Table 17.13 lists the various RFCs for the NFS protocol and its extensions.

**Table 17.13    NFS-related RFCs**

| RFC | Title | Author | Date |
|---|---|---|---|
| 1094 | Network File System Protocol Specification | Sun Microsystems | Mar 1989 |
| 1813 | NFS Version 3 Protocol Specification | B. Callaghan et al. | Jun 1995 |
| 2054 | WebNFS Client Specification | B. Callaghan | Oct 1996 |
| 2055 | WebNFS Server Specification | B. Callaghan | Oct 1996 |
| 2224 | NFS URL Scheme | B. Callaghan | Oct 1997 |
| 2623 | NFS Version 2 and Version 3 Security Issues | M. Eisler | Jun 1999 |
| 2624 | NFS Version 4 Design Considerations | S. Shepler | Jun 1999 |

# 18 *Sharing System Files*

A properly functioning system depends on tens, perhaps hundreds, of configuration files all containing the right pieces of information. When you multiply the number of configuration files on a host by the number of hosts on a network, the result can be thousands of files—too many to manage by hand.

In the real world, machines are often similar from an administrative point of view. Instead of editing text files on each machine, it's more efficient to combine machines into groups that share configuration information. You can combine machines in several different ways.

The simplest way is to keep a master copy of each configuration file in one place and distribute it to members of the group whenever it changes. This solution has the advantages of being simple and working on every UNIX system.

Another approach is to eliminate text files altogether and have each machine obtain its configuration information from a central server. This is more complicated than copying files, but it solves some other problems as well. For example, clients can't miss updates, even if they are down when a change is made. It may also be faster to obtain information from a server than from a file, depending on the speed of the local disk and the amount of caching performed by the server. On the other hand, the entire network can hang when the central server goes down.

Several attempts have been made to develop administrative databases for large networks, and they are all interesting systems. However, none of the current products seems exactly right in its approach. Some are simple but not secure and not scalable. Others are functional but unwieldy. Some look promising but are not yet fully baked.

All the systems seem to have limitations that can prevent you from setting up the network the way you want to.

In this chapter we'll first discuss some basic techniques for keeping files synchronized on a network. We'll then talk about two widely used administrative database systems (NIS and NIS+) and one relatively new system that may become commonly used over the next few years (LDAP).

## 18.1 WHAT TO SHARE

Of the many configuration files on a UNIX system, only a subset can be usefully shared among machines. The most commonly shared files are listed in Table 18.1.

**Table 18.1    System files that are commonly shared**

| Filename | Function |
|---|---|
| /etc/passwd | User account information database |
| /etc/shadow[a] | Shadow password file |
| /etc/group | UNIX group definitions |
| /etc/hosts | Maps between hostnames and IP addresses |
| /etc/networks[a] | Associates text names with IP network numbers |
| /etc/services | Lists port numbers for well-known network services |
| /etc/protocols | Maps text names to protocol numbers |
| /etc/ethers[a] | Maps between hostnames and Ethernet addresses |
| /etc/mail/aliases | Electronic mail aliases |
| /etc/rpc | Lists ID numbers for RPC services |
| /etc/netgroup[a] | Defines collections of hosts, users, and networks |
| /etc/printcap | Printer information database |
| /etc/termcap | Terminal type information database |

a. Not used on all systems.

Most server-based systems are set up to work with only these and perhaps a few additional files. You can sometimes distribute additional files of your own choosing, but since the system software won't automatically make use of them, that feature is most useful for sharing local files.

The files in Table 18.1 are usually accessed through routines in the standard C library. For example, the **/etc/passwd** file is searched with the **getpwuid**, **getpwnam**, and **getpwent** routines. These routines take care of opening, reading, and parsing the **passwd** file so that user-level programs don't have to do it themselves.

Since few programs access these configuration files directly, it is relatively easy to convert a system to use a network database. Once the library routines are patched, most client programs become automatically "upgraded." Even software that you obtain from the public domain and from third-party vendors should work correctly with an updated library.

## 18.2  COPYING FILES AROUND

We use brute-force file copying to maintain the University of Colorado's Engineering network. It is not an elegant solution, but it works on every kind of machine and is easy to set up and maintain. It's also a reliable system because it minimizes the interdependencies among machines.

It's often assumed in manuals and in UNIX culture that you will use a system such as NIS or NIS+ if one is available. But if your needs aren't complex, you don't need a complex solution. Sometimes the dumbest, most straightforward solution is best.

Our site consists of several connected but independent fiefdoms. Only a little bit of administrative data is shared everywhere. In our distribution scheme, each fiefdom has one or two servers that store master copies of its system files. This is the sort of environment in which file copying works well, since the task is simply to pump the data around, not to tailor it for particular machines or networks.

File copying systems can use either a "push" model or a "pull" model. With "push," the master server periodically distributes the freshest files to each client, whether the client wants them or not. Files may be pushed explicitly whenever a change is made or may simply be distributed on a regular schedule (perhaps with some files being transferred more often than others).

The push model has the advantage of keeping the distribution system centralized on one machine. Files, lists of clients, update scripts, and timetables are all stored in one place, making the scheme easy to control. One disadvantage is that each client must allow the master to modify its system files, creating a security hazard.

In a pull system, each client is responsible for updating itself from the server. This is a less centralized way of distributing files, but it is also more adaptable and more secure. A pull system is especially attractive when data is shared across administrative boundaries because the master and client machines need not be run by the same political faction.

### rdist: push files

The **rdist** command is the easiest way to distribute files from a central server. It has something of the flavor of **make**: you use a text editor to create a specification of the files to be distributed, and then you use **rdist** to bring reality into line with your specification. **rdist** copies files only when they are out of date, so you can write your specification as if all files were to be copied and let **rdist** optimize out unnecessary work.

**rdist** preserves the owner, group, mode, and modification time of files. When **rdist** updates an existing file, it first deletes the old version before installing the new. This feature makes **rdist** suitable for transferring executables that might be in use during the update.[1]

---

1. Though the old version disappears from the filesystem namespace, it continues to exist until all references have been released. You must also be aware of this effect when managing log files. See page 206 for more information.

Unfortunately, **rdist** has some security issues. It runs on top of **rsh** and relies on **rsh**-style authentication to gain access to remote systems. Under this scheme, root access is permitted from any host listed in a target system's **/.rhosts** file. This scheme was acceptable on the relatively open and isolated networks of the past, but it's really too dangerous to use in the context of the modern Internet. If one host is broken into, the security of all hosts that trust it is automatically compromised.

Since you are distributing administrative files such as **/etc/passwd**, it's pretty much a given that root access on the master server can be parlayed into root access on clients. That's not the problem. The problem is that by running **rlogind** (the server for **rsh** and also **rlogin** and **rcp**), client machines leave themselves open to other types of attack.

Our general advice is not to run **rlogind** at all. If you are determined to use **rdist**, you should at least use Wietse Venema's TCP wrappers package to restrict which hosts may contact each client's **rlogind**. The TCP wrappers package is available from ftp.porcupine.org; more information is given on page 666.

It's possible to run **rdist** as a user other than root, but **rlogind** must still run on each remote host. In addition, this configuration requires that software run on each client to pick up the copied-over files and install them in their final destinations, which can only be done as root. Even with these changes, it would still be easy for a nonroot intruder to submit a falsified **/etc/passwd** file to the remote systems. Therefore, we do not feel that nonroot **rdist** offers much additional security.

 Red Hat and FreeBSD's **rdist**s allows **rsh** to be substituted with any other command that understands the same syntax. In practice, this means **ssh**, which offers two main advantages. First, **ssh** can use public key cryptography to verify the identity of the master host. Second, **ssh** encrypts the entire **rdist** conversation, preventing network eavesdroppers from obtaining copies of your system files. The disadvantage is that you must run the remote **ssh** servers in a mode that does not require a password, which is a less secure mode than we would normally recommend. See page 672 for more information about **sshd** and its authentication modes.

Now that we've belabored the perils of **rdist**, let's look at how it actually works. Like **make**, **rdist** looks for a control file (**Distfile** or **distfile**) in the current directory. **rdist -f** *distfile* explicitly specifies the control file's pathname. Within the **Distfile**, tabs, spaces, and newlines are used interchangeably as separators. Comments are introduced with a pound sign (#).

The meat of a **Distfile** consists of statements of the form

> *label: pathnames -> destinations commands*

The *label* field associates a name with the statement. From the shell, you can run **rdist** *label* to distribute only the files described in a particular statement.

The *pathnames* and *destinations* are lists of files to be copied and hosts to copy them to, respectively. If there is more than one entry in a list, it must be surrounded with parentheses and the elements must be separated with whitespace. The *pathnames* can include shell-style globbing characters (e.g., **/usr/man/man[123]** or **/usr/lib/***). The notation ~*user* is also acceptable, but it is evaluated separately on the source and destination machines.

By default, **rdist** copies the files and directories listed in *pathnames* to the equivalent paths on each destination machine. You can modify this behavior by supplying a sequence of commands. Terminate each command with a semicolon.

The following commands are understood:

```
install options [destdir];
notify namelist;
except pathlist;
except_pat patternlist;
special [pathlist] string;
```

The install command sets options that affect the way **rdist** copies files. Options typically control the treatment of symbolic links, the correctness of **rdist**'s difference-checking algorithm, and the way that deletions are handled. Options are specified differently on different systems and are not explained here in detail; check your man pages for more information.

The name "install" is somewhat misleading, since files are copied whether or not an install command is present. Options are specified as they would be on the **rdist** command line, but when included in the **Distfile** they apply to only one set of files.

The optional *destdir* specifies an installation directory on the destination hosts. By default, **rdist** uses the original pathnames.

The notify command takes a list of email addresses as its argument. **rdist** sends mail to these addresses whenever a file is updated. Any addresses that do not contain an at sign (@) are suffixed with the name of the destination host. For example, **rdist** would expand "pete" to "pete@anchor" when reporting a list of files updated on host anchor.

The except and except_pat commands remove pathnames from the list of files to be copied. Arguments to except are matched literally, and those of except_pat are interpreted as regular expressions. These exception commands are useful because **rdist**, like **make**, allows macros to be defined at the beginning of its control file. You might want to use a similar list of files for several statements, specifying only the additions and deletions for each host.

The special command executes an **sh** command (the *string* argument, which should be quoted) on each remote host. If a *pathlist* is present, **rdist** executes the command once after copying each of the specified files. Without a *pathlist*, **rdist** executes the command after every file. There is unfortunately no way to execute a command after all files have been copied.

Here's a simple example of a **Distfile**:

```
SYS_FILES = (/etc/passwd /etc/group /etc/mail/aliases)
GET_ALL   = (chimchim lollipop barkadon)
GET_SOME = (whammo spiff)

all: ${SYS_FILES} -> ${GET_ALL}
    notify barb;
    special /etc/mail/aliases "/usr/bin/newaliases";

some: ${SYS_FILES} -> ${GET_SOME}
    except /etc/mail/aliases;
    notify eddie@spiff;
```

*See page 557 for more information about **newaliases**.*

This configuration replicates the three listed system files on chimchim, lollipop, and barkadon and sends mail to barb@*destination* describing any updates or errors that occur. After **/etc/mail/aliases** is copied, **rdist** runs **newaliases** on each destination. Only two files are copied to whammo and spiff. **newaliases** is not run, and a report is mailed to eddie@spiff.

### rsync: push files more securely

*rsync is available from rsync.samba.org.*

**rsync**, written by Andrew Tridgell and Paul Mackerras, is similar in spirit to **rdist** but with a somewhat different focus. It does not use a control file. It's more like a souped-up version of **rcp** that is scrupulous about preserving links, modification times, and permissions. **rsync** is more network-efficient than **rdist** because it looks inside of individual files and attempts to transmit only the differences between versions.

From our perspective, the main advantage of **rsync** is the fact that receiving machines can run the remote side as a server process out of **inetd**. The server (actually just a different mode of **rsync**, which must be installed on both the master and the clients) is quite configurable: it can restrict remote access to a set of given directories and can require the master to prove its identity with a password. Since no **rsh** access is necessary, you can set up **rsync** to distribute system files without making too many security compromises. (However, if you prefer to use **rsh** or **ssh** instead of an **inetd**-based server process, **rsync** lets you do that too.)

Since **rsync** uses no configuration file on the sending side, it must be run repeatedly to transfer a set of files to multiple hosts. For example, the command

```
# rsync -gopt --password-file=/etc/rsync.pwd /etc/passwd lollipop::/etc
```

transfers the **/etc/passwd** file to the machine lollipop. The **-gopt** options preserve the permissions, ownerships, and modification times of the file. The double colon in **lollipop::/etc** makes **rsync** contact the remote **rsync** directly on port 873 instead of using **rsh**. The password stored in **/etc/rsync.pwd** authenticates the connection.[2]

---

2. Although the password is not sent in plaintext across the network, the transferred files are not encrypted. If you use **ssh** as the transport (**rsync -gopt -e ssh /etc/passwd /etc/shadow lollipop:/etc** – note the single colon), the connection will be encrypted, but **sshd** will have to be configured not to require a password. Name your poison!

Several steps are necessary to set up an **rsync** server on each client machine (that is, each machine that is receiving files. From **rsync**'s perspective, these "clients" are really more like servers):

- Add the **rsync** port number to **/etc/services**.
- Add the server (**rsync --daemon**) to **/etc/inetd.conf**.
- Store authentication passwords in **/etc/rsyncd.secrets**.
- Configure the server in **/etc/rsyncd.conf**.

The **services** and **inetd.conf** entries are straightforward:

```
rsync          873/tcp
```

for **services** and

```
rsync stream tcp nowait root   /local/bin/rsync rsyncd --daemon
```

for **inetd.conf**. If you use the TCP wrappers package, you may want to configure it to block access from all hosts except the one that will be distributing your system files. Host rejection can also be specified in **rsynd.conf**, but it never hurts to erect multiple barriers.

The **rsyncd.secrets** file should contain a single entry:

```
root:password
```

The *password* used for **rsync** should be different from the actual root password. Because the password is shown in plaintext, the **rsyncd.secrets** file must be readable only by root.

Finally, set up an **/etc/rsynd.conf** file to tell the **rsync** server (the receiver) how to behave. A reasonable configuration looks something like this:

```
[sysfiles]
path = /etc
secrets file = /etc/rsyncd.secrets
hosts allow = distribution_master_hostname
```

Many other options can be set, but the defaults are reasonable. This configuration will limit operations to the **/etc** directory and will allow access only by the listed host.

**rsync** is included with Red Hat. The source code (common to all systems) can be downloaded from the web at rsync.samba.org.

### expect: pull files

There are several ways to implement a pulling system. One way that we like, and which happens to be useful for other tasks, is to make system files available via FTP from a central server and to use **expect** to retrieve and install them. See page 696 for more information about FTP.

**expect** is a set of extensions to John Ousterhout's Tcl (Tool Command Language) that allows you to write control scripts for interactive programs. It was written by Don Libes at NIST. **expect** is different from a normal scripting language (such as that provided by most shells) in that it provides for incremental control of subprocesses. The output produced by each operation can be examined to determine what input should be sent next. **expect** is also immune to the unfriendly maneuvers a program may attempt because it thinks it is manipulating a real terminal.

Tcl is itself a complete scripting language. Technically, **expect** scripts are just Tcl scripts that happen to use the extra commands defined by the **expect** extensions. However, you don't need to know much Tcl to write simple **expect** scripts.

Tcl is syntactically simple. Most commands are invoked like shell commands in that you simply separate the command and its arguments by spaces. Curly braces group elements into single Tcl "words" and extend statements over multiple lines. The command separator is a semicolon, but it is optional at the end of lines and before closing curly braces.

The fundamental **expect** commands are:

- spawn – start up a subprocess to control
- send – feed input to a subprocess
- expect – take action depending on a subprocess's output

A fourth command, interact, can also be useful if you want **expect** to do part of a task and then turn control over to you.

Before discussing the individual commands, let's look at a simple example. This script **ftp**s the **/etc/passwd** file from the machine *netserver*:

```
spawn /usr/bin/ftp netserver
while 1 { expect {
    "Name*: "   {send "netclient\r"}
    "Password:" {send "netclientpassword\r"}
    "ftp> "     {break}
    "failed"    {send_user "Can't log in.\r"; exit 1}
    timeout     {send_user "Timeout problem.\r"; exit 2}
}}
send "lcd /etc\r"
expect "ftp> " {send "cd pub/sysfiles\r"}
expect "ftp> " {send "get passwd\r"}
expect "ftp> " {send "quit\r"; send_user "\r"}
exit 0
```

The general flow of control should be apparent. The script first starts the command **ftp** *netserver* and then waits to be prompted for a name and password inside a while loop (a generic Tcl construct). After arriving at the main "ftp>" prompt, the while loop exits and a simple series of commands is spoon-fed to **ftp**. The script waits for each command to complete before sending the next; this is not strictly necessary, but it makes for tidy output.

Two kinds of problems are handled within the initial login loop. First, the check for the string "failed" traps the case in which the remote host rejects the given name and password, causing **ftp** to print "Login failed." The timeout clause detects cases in

Sharing System Files

which nothing interesting happens for ten seconds, perhaps because *netserver* is down. Either condition causes the script to print an error message and exit.

This script assumes that no errors can happen after a successful login; in the real world, you'd probably want to add more embellishments. In this example, the same error handling is applied to several exchanges through the use of a while loop. There are some special versions of the expect command that are designed to solve this problem in a less kludgey way.

The send command places a string on the subprocess's standard input. You must explicitly include a carriage return (entered as "\r") if you want one. A string without spaces or special characters need not be quoted. The send_user command is similar to the send command, except that the text is sent to the script's standard output rather than to the slave process.

The expect command accepts a series of *pattern/action* pairs. If the pairs span multiple lines, as in the example above, they should be enclosed in curly braces. Actions should generally be enclosed in curly braces as well.

Each *pattern* is something to watch for in the command's output; when a string is seen, its corresponding *action* is triggered. Patterns are normally matched using unanchored shell-style globbing, but regular expressions are also available. Actions for the special strings timeout and eof are triggered after a (settable) period of inactivity and at the end of the input stream, respectively.

The source code for **expect** can be downloaded from the web at expect.nist.gov.

## 18.3  NIS: THE NETWORK INFORMATION SERVICE

NIS, released by Sun in the 1980s, was the first "prime time" administrative database. It was originally called the Sun Yellow Pages, but eventually had to be renamed for legal reasons. NIS commands still begin with the letters **yp**, so it's hard to forget the original name. Many vendors have licensed Sun's code, making NIS the most widely supported file sharing system.

Sun released a new administrative database system called NIS+ in the early 90s. Despite their similar names, NIS and NIS+ do not really have much to do with each other. NIS+ is considerably more complex than NIS, and it has not enjoyed the same degree of popular support. More information about NIS+ is given on page 530; Table 18.2 shows the current state of support for NIS and NIS+ on our example systems.

**Table 18.2    Support for NIS and NIS+**

| System | Supports NIS? | Supports NIS+? |
|--------|---------------|----------------|
| Solaris | Yes | Yes |
| HP-UX | Yes | Yes |
| Red Hat | Yes | No |
| FreeBSD | Yes | No |

The unit of sharing in NIS is the record, not the file. A record usually corresponds to one line in a config file. A master server maintains the authoritative copies of system files, which are kept in their original locations and formats and are edited with a text editor just as before. A server process makes the contents of the files available over the network. A server and its clients constitute an NIS "domain".[3]

Data files are preprocessed into database files by a hashing library (usually **ndbm** or the GNU equivalent, **gdbm**); this procedure improves the efficiency of lookups. After editing files on the master server, you tell NIS to convert them to their hashed format, using either **make** or a script called **ypmake**, depending on your system.

The common hashing libraries allow only one key to be associated with each entry, so a system file may have to be translated into several NIS "maps." For example, the **/etc/passwd** file is translated into two different maps called **passwd.byname** and **passwd.byuid**. One is used to look up entries by username, and the other to look up entries by UID. Either map can be used to enumerate the entries in the **passwd** file. However, since hashing libraries do not preserve the order of records, there is no way to reconstruct an exact duplicate of the original file (unless it was sorted).

NIS allows you to replicate the network maps on a set of slave servers. Providing more than one server helps to relieve load on the master and keep clients functioning even when some servers become unavailable. Whenever a file is changed on the master server, the corresponding NIS map must be pushed out to the slaves so that all servers provide the same data. Clients do not distinguish between the master server and the slaves.

In the traditional NIS implementation, you must place at least one NIS server on every physical network. Clients use IP broadcasting to locate servers, and broadcast packets are not forwarded by routers and gateways. The **ypset** command can be used to point a client at a particular server; however, at the first hint of trouble, the client will attempt to locate a new server by using broadcasting. Unless there is a server on the client's network, this sequence of events may cause the client to hang.

Solaris and Red Hat Linux both let you reliably circumvent the traditional broadcast method of locating NIS servers. See page 529 for instructions.

### Netgroups

NIS introduced a popular abstraction known as netgroups. Netgroups name sets of users, machines, and nets for easy reference in other system files. They are defined in **/etc/netgroup** and are also shared as an NIS map.

The format of a **netgroup** entry is

*groupname list-of-members*

---

3. Do not confuse NIS domains with DNS domains. They are completely separate and have nothing to do with one another.

Members are separated by whitespace. A member is either a netgroup name or a triplet of the form

(*hostname, username, nisdomainname*)

Any empty field in a triplet is a wild card; thus the entry (boulder,,) refers to all users in all domains on the host boulder (or to the host boulder itself, depending on the context in which the netgroup is used). A dash in a field indicates negation, so the entry (boulder,-,) refers to the machine boulder and no users. Netgroup definitions can nest.

Here's a simple example of an **/etc/netgroup** file:

```
bobcats        (snake,,) (headrest,,)
servers        (anchor,,) (moet,,) (piper,,) (kirk,,)
anchorclients  (xx,,) (watneys,,) (molson,,)
beers          (anchor,,) (anchor-gateway,,) anchorclients
allhosts       beers bobcats servers
```

These netgroups are all defined in terms of hosts; that's typical for real-world use.

*See Chapter 17 for more information about NFS.*

Netgroups can be used in several system files that define permissions. The most common application these days is for configuring NFS exports. Netgroups can be mentioned in the **/etc/exports** file or in **share** commands (under Solaris) to specify groups of hosts that are allowed to mount each filesystem. This feature is very handy when you are exporting to a lot of hosts, particularly on systems that require fully qualified domain names and that limit lines in the **exports** file to 1,024 characters.

Netgroups are a nice idea. They simplify system files, making them more understandable. They also add a layer of indirection that permits the status of a user or machine to be changed in one file rather than fifteen.

### Prioritizing sources of administrative information

Most systems allow configuration information to be distributed in several ways. Every system understands flat files; most also understand NIS and know how to use DNS to look up hostnames and Internet addresses. Since there may be several potential sources for a given piece of information, vendors usually provide a way for you to specify sources that are to be checked and the order in which the checks are made.

In the original NIS implementation, some configuration files (the **/etc/passwd** and **/etc/group** files in particular) had to be configured to "invite in" the contents of the corresponding NIS maps. The invitation was extended by including special incantations in the files themselves. A lone "+" at the beginning of a line would include the entire NIS map, "+@*netgroup*" would include only entries relevant to a given netgroup, and "+*name*" would include a single entry.

This approach was never very well liked, and in most systems it has been superseded by a central config file, **/etc/nsswitch.conf**, that allows an explicit search path to be specified for each type of administrative information. A typical **nsswitch.conf** file looks something like the following example.

```
passwd:  files nis
hosts:   files dns
group:   files
...
```

Each line configures one type of information (usually, one flat-file equivalent). The potential sources are nis, nisplus, files, dns, and compat; they refer to NIS, NIS+, vanilla flat files (ignoring tokens such as "+"), DNS, and NISified flat files (honoring "+"), respectively. DNS is only a valid data source for host information.

Sources are tried from left to right until one of them produces an answer for the query. In the example above, the **gethostbyname** routine would first check the **/etc/hosts** file, and if the host was not listed there, would then check DNS. Queries about UNIX groups, on the other hand, would check only the **/etc/group** file.

If necessary, you may define the "failure" of a source more specifically by putting bracketed expressions after it. For example, the line

```
hosts:   dns [NOTFOUND=return] nisplus
```

causes DNS to be used exclusively if it is available; a negative response from the name server makes queries return immediately (with a failure code) without checking NIS+. However, NIS+ will be used if no name server is available. The various types of failures are shown in Table 18.3; each may be set to return or continue, indicating whether the query should be aborted or forwarded to the next source.

**Table 18.3   Failure modes recognized in /etc/nsswitch.conf**

| Condition | Meaning |
| --- | --- |
| UNAVAIL | The source doesn't exist or is down. |
| NOTFOUND | The source exists, but couldn't answer the query. |
| TRYAGAIN | The source exists but is busy. |
| SUCCESS | The source was able to answer the query. |

Several suggested **nsswitch.conf** configurations are often provided in the **/etc** directory. Check to see if one of these is appropriate for your site (**ls /etc/nss\***) before rolling your own.

 FreeBSD does not yet support a centralized switch file. The priority of data sources for host lookups can be set in the **/etc/host.conf** file, which is self-documenting. NIS tokens must appear in the **passwd** and **group** files to import remote maps; see the section 5 man pages for **passwd** and **group** for more information.

### Advantages and disadvantages of NIS

One nice feature of NIS is that it can be understood by mere mortals. NIS is analogous to copying files around; in most cases, it's unnecessary for administrators to be aware of NIS's internal data formats. Administration is performed with the same old flat files, and only one or two new procedures need to be learned.

Since there is no way to link NIS domains, NIS is not suitable for managing a large network of machines unless a single configuration is to be applied to every machine. You can divide a large network into several NIS domains, but each domain must be administered separately.

*See Chapter 9 for more information about **cron**.*

If a slave server is down or inaccessible when a map is changed, the slave's copy will not be updated. Slaves must periodically poll the master to be sure that they have the most recent version of every map. Although basic tools for polling are provided with NIS, you must implement the polling scheme you want by using **cron**. Even so, there is the possibility that two different versions of a map will be served simultaneously for a while, with clients randomly seeing one or the other.

NIS is not secure. Any host on a network can claim to serve a particular domain, thus feeding bogus administrative data to NIS clients. And anyone can read your NIS maps, perhaps feeding the encrypted passwords to a cracking program to look for poorly protected accounts.

Some NIS servers attempt to increase password security by denying access to the shadow password map from unprivileged ports. While well-intentioned, this is a very weak form of protection. If you are concerned about security, you should not use NIS.

### How NIS works

NIS's data files (and often some of its commands) are stored in one directory, usually **/var/yp**. Hereafter, we refer to this as "the NIS directory." Each NIS map is stored in a hashed format in a subdirectory of the NIS directory named for the NIS domain. The exact name and number of the map files depends on the hashing library being used. For example, in the domain "cssuns", the **ndbm** files for the **/etc/passwd** maps might be

```
/var/yp/cssuns/passwd.byname.dir
/var/yp/cssuns/passwd.byname.pag
/var/yp/cssuns/passwd.byuid.dir
/var/yp/cssuns/passwd.byuid.pag
```

Remember that a separate map is required for each field by which the file can be searched. The **passwd** file is searchable by both name and uid, so two maps (four files, in the **ndbm** case) are derived from it.

The **makedbm** command generates NIS maps from flat files. However, you need never invoke this command directly. On most systems, a **Makefile** in the NIS directory generates all the common NIS maps. After you modify a system file, you **cd** to the NIS directory and run **make**. **make** checks the modification time of each file against the modification times of the maps derived from it and runs **makedbm** for each map that needs to be rebuilt.

 On HP-UX systems, a command called **ypmake** is used instead of make.

Maps are copied from the master server to the slave servers by the **ypxfr** command. **ypxfr** is a "pull" command; it must be run on each slave server to make that server import the map. Slaves usually execute **ypxfr** every so often just to verify that they have the most recent maps; you can use **cron** to control how often this is done.

The default implementation of map copying is somewhat inefficient, and most systems provide a daemon called **ypxfrd** that can be run on the master server to respond in a speedier fashion to **ypxfr** requests. **ypxfrd** sidesteps the normal NIS protocol and simply hands out copies of the map files. Unfortunately, map files are stored with different database formats and byte ordering on different systems, so the use of **ypxfrd** introduces some potential incompatibilities.

**yppush** is a "push" command that's used on the master server. It actually does not transfer any data but rather instructs each slave to execute a **ypxfr**. **yppush** is used by the **Makefile** in the NIS directory to ensure that newly updated maps are propagated to slaves.

There is a special map called **ypservers** which does not correspond to any flat file. This map contains a list of all the servers of the domain. It's constructed automatically when the domain is set up with **ypinit** (see *Configuring NIS servers* on page 528). Its contents are examined whenever the master server needs to distribute maps to slaves.

After initial configuration, the only active components of the NIS system are the **ypserv** and **ypbind** daemons. **ypserv** runs only on servers (both master and slave); it accepts queries from clients and answers them by looking up information in the hashed map files.

**ypbind** runs on every machine in the NIS domain, including servers. The C library contacts the local **ypbind** daemon whenever it needs to answer an administrative query (provided that **/etc/nsswitch.conf** says to do so). **ypbind** locates a **ypserv** in the appropriate domain and returns its identity to the C library, which then contacts the server directly. The query mechanism is illustrated in Exhibit A.

**Exhibit A    NIS query procedure**

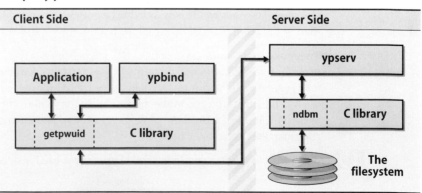

Once **ypbind** locates a server, it continues to rely on that server for all queries until the server goes down or some other communication problem occurs. A **ypbind** on a server machine does not give itself preferential treatment, so servers don't necessarily bind to themselves.

In some circumstances (for example, when all servers but one are simultaneously rebooted), clients can fixate on one server and refuse to let go even after other servers become available. This situation can slow response time considerably.

NIS includes a number of minor commands that examine maps, find out which version of a map each server is using, and control the binding between clients and servers. A complete list of NIS commands and daemons is given in Table 18.4.

**Table 18.4    NIS commands and daemons**

| Program | Description |
|---|---|
| ypserv | NIS server daemon, started at boot time |
| ypbind | NIS client daemon, started at boot time |
| domainname | Sets the NIS domain a machine is in (run at boot time) |
| ypxfr | Downloads current version of a map from master server |
| ypxfrd | Serves requests from **ypxfr** (runs on master server) |
| yppush | Makes slave servers update their versions of a map |
| makedbm | Builds a hashed map from a flat file |
| ypmake[a] | Rebuilds hashed maps from flat files that have changed |
| ypinit | Configures a host as a master or slave server |
| ypset | Makes **ypbind** connect to a particular server |
| ypwhich | Finds out which server the current host is using |
| yppoll | Finds out what version of a map a server is using |
| ypcat | Prints the values contained in an NIS map |
| ypmatch | Prints map entries for a specified key |
| yppasswd | Changes a password on the NIS master server |
| ypchfn | Changes GECOS information on the NIS master server |
| ypchsh | Changes a login shell on NIS master server |
| yppasswdd | Server for **yppasswd**, **ypchsh**, and **ypchfn** |
| ypupdated[a] | Server for updating NIS maps (managed by **inetd**) |

a. Not used or supported on all systems.

### Setting up an NIS domain

NIS must be initialized on the master server, on the slave servers, and on each client. You do this in two steps. First, run **ypinit** on each server. Second, on every machine in the domain, set the domain name from one of the system startup files and configure **/etc/nsswitch.conf** to import NIS data.

*Configuring NIS servers*

**ypinit** initializes both the master and slave servers for a domain. On the master, you use the following commands:[4]

```
# cd /var/yp          /* The NIS directory, wherever it is */
# domainname foo      /* Name the new domain. */
# ypinit -m           /* Initialize as master server. */
# ypserv              /* Start the NIS server. */
```

The **-m** flag tells **ypinit** that it's configuring a master server; it will prompt you to enter a list of slave servers. Once the master is up and running, you should prime each slave server by running **ypinit** with the **-s** (slave) flag:

```
# cd /var/yp
# ypinit -s master    /* Argument is  master's hostname. */
# ypserv
```

**ypinit -s** makes a local copy of the master's current data; the presence of the domain's data files is enough to let **ypserv** know that it should serve the domain.

*See Chapter 9 for more information about* ***cron***.

On each slave, you should set up crontab entries to pull fresh copies of all maps from the master. The command **ypxfr** *map*, where *map* is a name such as **passwd.byuid**, will transfer the specified map from the master server. You must run the command once for each map. Maps tend to change at different rates, and if network bandwidth is precious, you may want to transfer some maps more often than others. In most circumstances, transferring all the maps once or twice a day (perhaps late at night) is good enough. The following script transfers every map:

```
#!/bin/csh -f
set mydomain = `/usr/bin/domainname`
cd /var/yp/$mydomain   # the NIS directory
foreach map (`/bin/ls`)
    /usr/lib/yp/ypxfr $map
end
```

Some systems provide prefabricated scripts called **ypxfr_1perday**, **ypxfr_2perday**, and **ypxfr_1perhour** that transfer NIS maps at various frequencies.

Many systems that support NIS check at boot time to see if the current host is an NIS server, and if so, they automatically start the **ypserv** daemon. On others, you must turn on **ypserv** explicitly. See the vendor specifics section for details.

If you want users to be able to change their passwords with **yppasswd**, you must run the **yppasswdd** daemon on the master NIS server.

*Configuring NIS clients*

After setting up servers, you must inform each client machine that it is a member of the new domain. The servers of a domain are generally clients as well.

---

4. NIS commands such as **ypinit** and **ypserv** are often hidden away in nonstandard directories. Check the man pages to find the location on your particular system.

*See Chapter 2 for more information about the system startup scripts.*

The **domainname** command sets a machine's NIS domain. It's usually run at boot time from one of the startup scripts. The exact contortions necessary to configure this vary by system; system-specific details are given below.

Each client must have at least a minimal private version of the **passwd**, **group**, and **hosts** files. **passwd** and **group** are needed to allow root to log in when no NIS server is available. They should contain the standard system accounts and groups: root, bin, daemon, wheel, etc. The **hosts** file must be present to answer boot-time queries that occur before NIS is up and running.

### Vendor specifics

Under Solaris, the NIS domain name should be put in the file **/etc/defaultdomain**. The **/etc/init.d/inetinit** script checks this file at startup, and if it exists, calls the **domainname** command with its contents as the only argument. Later in the startup process, the **ypstart** script notices that the domain name has been set and starts **ypbind** and **ypserv** as appropriate. **yppasswd** and **ypxfrd** are also started automatically on the master server.

To prevent **ypbind** from broadcasting to find NIS servers, run **ypinit -c** on each NIS client machine and enter the names of the servers you would like that client to use. You must kill and restart **ypbind** on the client without the **-broadcast** option (or reboot) to make the change take effect. The server names must appear in **/etc/hosts** so that they can be resolved before NIS is running.

---

NIS configuration information is kept in **/etc/rc.config.d/namesvrs** on HP-UX systems. On clients, set the NIS_DOMAIN variable to the NIS domain name and set NIS_CLIENT to 1. On servers, you should also set either NIS_MASTER_SERVER or NIS_SLAVE_SERVER to 1, but not both. **yppasswdd** and **ypxfrd** are automatically started on NIS master servers.

---

Under Red Hat, you set the NIS domain name in **/etc/sysconfig/network** by setting the variable NISDOMAIN. **ypbind**, **ypserv**, and **yppasswdd** are enabled and disabled with **chkconfig**; for example,

```
# chkconfig ypbind on
```

You can force Red Hat's **ypbind** to use a particular NIS server (rather than letting it forage via broadcasting) by putting the following line in **/etc/yp.conf**:

```
ypserver hostname
```

This should be the only line in the **/etc/yp.conf** file. The specified *hostname* must be listed in **/etc/hosts**.

---

On FreeBSD systems, you specify the NIS domain name in **/etc/rc.conf** by setting the nisdomainname variable. For example:

```
nisdomainname="cssuns"
```

The **ypbind**, **ypserv**, and **yppasswdd** daemons are started by setting the variables nis_client_enable, nis_server_enable, and nis_yppasswdd_enable to YES.

**/etc/passwd** and **/etc/group** must contain the magic cookie "+" if they are to use NIS as an information source; see page 523.

## 18.4 NIS+: SON OF NIS

NIS+, aka "NIS on steroids whose face nobody is Ever Going to Kick Sand in Again," was designed to correct the deficiencies of NIS and introduce deficiencies of its own. It handles large networks of machines. It has security features built in. It permits multiple domains to be administered from anywhere on a network. It transfers updates efficiently. It's a distributed database *and* a dessert topping; it sings, it dances, it leaps capital T in a single bound.

Although NIS+ servers can serve data to NIS clients (at some security expense), NIS+ is a different system that shares no code with NIS. It is supported by some big-ticket OS vendors (such as HP), but its complexity has prevented it from diffusing onto any of the free versions of UNIX.

NIS+ is a good example of what Frederick P. Brooks, Jr. calls "the second system effect" in his classic book on software engineering, *The Mythical Man-Month*. It attempts to build on the success of its progenitor while avoiding all of the mistakes and pitfalls of the previous design. It devotes substantial effort to the system's formal architecture. In theory it should be perfect. In practice it's somewhat clunky, over-engineered, and adrift from everyday reality. We've been told that even Sun does not use NIS+ internally.

There are several significant differences between NIS and NIS+:

- NIS+ domains are arranged in a site-wide hierarchy patterned after the one used by DNS. As with NIS, each domain includes various kinds of administrative information. You can subdivide domains to delegate administrative authority. Each machine belongs to a single domain, but domains can refer to each other's contents, allowing individual machines to obtain information from several domains.

- NIS+ is more database-like than NIS and allows maps (now called "tables") to be searched by any field. This feature removes the need to maintain several maps for each system file; NIS+ equates each file with a single table.

- NIS+ doesn't use flat files as NIS does. Although you can transfer data from a UNIX file (or an NIS map) into NIS+, NIS+ is then considered the authoritative source for the information. NIS+ won't automatically refresh itself if you later change the file. To make changes, you use a command that directly edits the information in NIS+'s tables.

- NIS+ is much better than NIS at maintaining slave servers (called "replicas" in NIS+). Only incremental changes are transferred, and a nifty logging scheme accommodates replicas that come in and out of contact with the master server. The master is also able to transfer its entire NIS+ database to a replica if it decides that the replica is too far out of date to be updated incrementally.

- NIS+ is built on top of Sun's Secure RPC system, which allows authentication based on public key encryption as well as the traditional "I claim to be Fred" style of nonauthentication. NIS+ servers can be configured to require encrypted credentials or, for the more convenience-minded, to obey the usual UNIX conventions.

  Like a file, every NIS+ object (table, column, or entry) has an owner and a group owner. Permissions on objects are set separately for the owner, the group, and the world. A special "nobody" category is applied to those who cannot supply credentials, such as NIS clients. Both users and machines can be Secure RPC "principals" (entities capable of supplying credentials). When you access NIS+ as root, your machine's credentials are used instead of root's user credentials.

From a client's perspective, NIS+ looks much the same as any other administrative database system. Most data is accessed through the same library routines as always, and the complex world of domains, tables, permissions, and search paths is in the end rendered down to an analog of the original UNIX flat files.

NIS+ has nothing to do with DNS, but it borrows DNS's naming scheme. DNS and NIS+ use names that are the inverse of filesystem paths; as you read from left to right, you go up (toward the root) in the hierarchy.

For example, cs.colorado.edu is a subdomain of colorado.edu. A machine in that domain might be named anchor.cs.colorado.edu.

By convention, the root of your NIS+ hierarchy is named the same as your site's top-level DNS domain. If your DNS domain is xor.com, then xor.com would also be your NIS+ root domain, and marketing.xor.com might be the NIS+ subdomain for your marketing department. Since DNS and NIS+ do not interact, you risk nothing but your sanity by using the same names for both.

Technically, NIS+ doesn't understand or enforce the idea of domains; it simply provides a generic way of creating NIS+ directories in a hierarchy, inserting various tables in those directories, and binding portions of the hierarchy to different master servers. But by convention, an NIS+ "domain" is a directory that contains subdirectories called org_dir and groups_dir. The domain's administrative data is put in tables inside org_dir, and the credentials for the domain's NIS+ principals are defined in groups_dir. Theoretically, a groups_dir or org_dir directory could have other subdirectories, but this isn't normally done.

For example, org_dir.marketing.xor.com would be the name of the directory containing system tables for the marketing.xor.com domain. Syntactically, tables are referred to as if they were directories: the string hosts.org_dir.marketing.xor.com refers to the

NIS+ equivalent of the **/etc/hosts** file for this domain. To refer to a specific entry within a table, a different syntax (not described here) is used.

Our judgement regarding NIS+ is that it should generally be avoided if possible. It works, but so do some much simpler alternatives. While it's not worth going to great lengths to avoid, neither is there a very compelling case to be made for adopting it.

## 18.5 LDAP: THE LIGHTWEIGHT DIRECTORY ACCESS PROTOCOL

UNIX sites need a good way to distribute their administrative configuration data; however, the problem is really more general than that. What about nonadministrative data such as telephone and email directories? What about information that you want to share with the outside world? What everyone really needs is a generalized directory service.

A directory service is just a database, but one that makes a few assumptions. Any data set that has characteristics matching the assumptions is a candidate for inclusion. The basic assumptions are as follows:

- Data objects are relatively small.
- The database will be widely replicated and cached.
- The information is attribute based.
- Data are read often but written infrequently.
- Searching is a common operation.

The current IETF standards-track system designed to fill this role is the Lightweight Directory Access Protocol (LDAP). The LDAP specifications don't really speak to the database itself, just the way that it's accessed via a network. But because they specify how the data is schematized and how searches are performed, they imply a fairly specific data model as well.

The history of LDAP could not possibly be more sordid. The story begins with the OSI networking system, a cradle-to-grave network protocol suite that was misguidedly adopted as an international standard in the mid-1980s. The OSI system as a whole proved to be a big flop, but several of its component protocols have enjoyed a macabre afterlife in mutant forms adapted to life in the TCP/IP world. The network management protocol CMIP is one of these, as is LDAP.

LDAP was originally designed as a simple gateway protocol that would allow TCP/IP clients to talk to the X.500 directory servers that ran on OSI systems. Over time, it became apparent both that X.500 was going to die out and that UNIX really needed a standard directory of some sort. These factors have led to LDAP being developed as a full-fledged directory system in its own right (and perhaps to its no longer being quite so deserving of the L).

At this point (in the year 2000), we are still somewhere in the middle of the development process. The most widely implemented version of LDAP, version 2, lacks many features that will be needed to get LDAP to the same level of functionality and reliability as, say, DNS. Even version 3 of the protocol, which is not yet standardized, appears to have some substantial gaps. Outside of a few specific domains (Internet phone books, **sendmail** alias configuration, some calendaring applications), real-world experience with LDAP has been limited.

Unfortunately, LDAP has become chum for an industry-wide feeding frenzy of sorts, with everybody and their dog pledging undying support for the protocol. Like Java technology in the mid-1990s, the swirling waters have thrown off a lot of press releases but relatively little actual software. We will just have to wait and see if a beautiful Venus eventually rises from the waves.

Our sense of LDAP is that it may or may not develop further in the direction of helping sysadmins. LDAP hasn't really found its niche yet. We advise a policy of "watchful waiting" for now.

### LDAP documentation and specifications

Currently, the best introduction to LDAP is a booklet called *Understanding LDAP* written by Heinz Johner et al. for IBM's International Technical Support Organization. It's available for download as an Acrobat file from www.redbooks.ibm.com. The parts about the C language programming API can be ignored; all the rest is useful information for system administrators. And don't say IBM never did anything for you.

The LDAP-related RFCs are many and varied. Some of the high points are listed in Table 18.5. Most of the listed RFCs have version 2 equivalents that are not shown. As this table suggests, most LDAP objects and transactions can be represented in plain-text, which is one of the protocol's nicer features. It's easy to generate queries from a script or to set up gateways to other protocols, such as HTTP.

**Table 18.5    LDAP-related RFCs**

| RFC | Title |
| --- | --- |
| 1777 | Lightweight Directory Access Protocol (v2) |
| 2251 | Lightweight Directory Access Protocol (v3) |
| 2252 | LDAPv3: Attribute Syntax Definitions |
| 2253 | LDAPv3: UTF-8 String Representation of Distinguished Names |
| 2254 | The String Representation of LDAP Search Filters |
| 2255 | The LDAP URL Format |
| 2256 | A Summary of the X.500 User Schema for Use with LDAPv3 |
| 2307 | An Approach for Using LDAP as a Network Information Service |

RFC2307 suggests ways of mapping traditional UNIX data sets such as the **passwd** and **group** files into the LDAP namespace. This RFC is still classified as "experimental," which suggests, perhaps, how far we have yet to go before LDAP will really be a viable replacement for systems such as NIS.

## Hands-on LDAP

*See page 560 for more information about using LDAP with sendmail.*

LDAP has been implemented by the University of Michigan, by Netscape, and by others. The best source today is the OpenLDAP group at www.openldap.org, which took over and enhanced the University of Michigan code base. As of mid-2000, there is still very little documentation for setting up OpenLDAP. The "quick start" guide on the web will get you up and running, but the documentation does not provide any information on how to customize or debug the package.

In the OpenLDAP distribution, **slapd** is the standard server daemon and **slarpd** handles replication, sort of like an NIS slave server. This scheme adds hierarchy to the server network independently of whether the data is truly hierarchical. When version 3 of the LDAP protocol is fully deployed, we will have true hierarchy in both the data and the infrastructure.

If you want to use LDAP to distribute configuration information (which we do not yet recommend), there are currently two ways to do it. The first option is to use an LDAP-to-NIS gateway product called **ypldapd** sold by PADL Software. This daemon grabs user, group, and host information out of LDAP and poses as an NIS server, spoon-feeding the data to your innocent NIS clients. Unfortunately, it's rather expensive to license, even for nonprofit organizations. See www.padl.com for more information.

The other option is to integrate LDAP support into your C library so that LDAP can be listed in the **/etc/nsswitch.conf** file like any other data source. PADL provides a freeware package called **nss_ldap** that will allow you to do this, although as with any change to standard libraries, the degree of meddling required is above average. There is also a **pam_ldap** package that allows you to use LDAP with pluggable authentication modules.

# *19* *Electronic Mail*

When we first tackled the job of updating this chapter for the third edition of this book, we thought it would be pretty easy. Not much has changed in 5 years: a couple of security patches, some new spam control features, and the obsolescence of IDA **sendmail**. But we were wrong.

Electronic mail was important then, but now it is absolutely essential to both business and personal communication. Many of the recent changes in **sendmail** respond to the scaling and flexibility issues faced by ISPs with millions of email-hungry customers. Spam has inspired additional changes and increasingly stringent enforcement of the existing rules. The IETF has been busy issuing new email-related RFCs. And hackers have been busy beating on any system that trusts user-supplied content to be reasonable and follow the rules. Both email and the web fall into this category.

Email has introduced some interesting social behavior. It seems to be less formal than paper, and people therefore tend to say more directly what they mean and feel. It is also somehow less personal and more removed than voice contact, so rage and frustration sometimes emerge. Email flame wars result, in which two people fire off messages they would never speak aloud or write on paper to each other.

For example, one of our users was easily upset and had a habit of abusing the administrators regularly. The only defense seemed to be to save his messages and send them back to him a few weeks later when he had cooled down. He was appalled at the things he had committed to print.

Another social aspect of email that has become prevalent in the last few years is unsolicited commercial email, colloquially called spam, the junk mail of the Internet.

Sending email on the Internet is cheap—much cheaper than buying postage stamps. The sender is typically billed a flat rate, so it costs the same to send one message as to send 25 million. But to the ISP who must provide enough bandwidth to handle the influx of spam—estimated to be as much as 30% of the incoming mail at America Online—spam is certainly not free. Attempts to control spam through laws and the courts have so far had minimal success. Technical solutions in the form of mail filters have been more effective. We cover the current state of the art in spam fighting starting on page 595.

The sheer bulk of this chapter—almost 100 pages—attests to the complexity of email systems. The chapter contains both background information and details of software configuration, in roughly that order.

We tried to divide this chapter into four smaller ones (on mail systems, **sendmail** configuration, spam, and Postfix), but that left it confusing, full of chicken-and-egg problems, and, we think, less useful. Instead, we offer the annotated table of contents shown in Table 19.1.

**Table 19.1   A road map for this chapter**

|  | Section | Page | Contents |
|---|---|---|---|
| **Background** | 1 | 537 | Mail systems and their various pieces |
| | 2 | 541 | Addressing, address syntax, mail headers |
| | 3 | 546 | Philosophy, client/server design, mail homes |
| | 4 | 550 | Aliases, mail routing, mailing list software, LDAP |
| **sendmail configuration** | 5 | 562 | **sendmail**: installing it, starting it, the mail queue |
| | 6 | 570 | Introduction to configuring **sendmail** |
| | 7 | 573 | Basic **sendmail** configuration primitives |
| | 8 | 577 | Fancier **sendmail** configuration primitives |
| | 9 | 588 | Examples: home machine, company, virtual hosting site |
| | 10 | 595 | Spam |
| | 11 | 607 | Security |
| | 12 | 614 | Statistics, testing, and debugging |
| **Other** | 13 | 618 | Postfix, an alternative to **sendmail** (simpler, not as flexible) |
| | 14 | 623 | Additional sources of information |

This organization makes the flow a bit smoother when the chapter is read straight through, but it sometimes separates the items relevant to a particular email-related task. The postmaster for a medium-sized organization might need to read the entire chapter, but a sysadmin setting up PC email support for a typical business client surely does not.

Table 19.2 provides a navigation guide for several common sysadmin chores.

**Table 19.2    An index of chores**

| Chore | Sections |
|---|---|
| Upgrading **sendmail** | 5, 6 |
| Configuring **sendmail** for the first time | 3, 6, 7, 8, 9, 12 |
| Designing a mail system for a site | 3, 4, 6, 7, 8, 9, 11 |
| Fighting spam | 10 |
| Auditing security | 11 |
| Setting up a PC to get mail | 1, 3 |
| Setting up a mailing list | 4 |
| Performance tuning | 3, 8 |
| Virtual hosting | 8, 9 |

Most of this chapter deals with the configuration of **sendmail**, the UNIX program that parses and routes electronic mail. **sendmail** was originally written by Eric Allman at the University of California, Berkeley. There have been three major versions: version 5, IDA, and version 8. Version 9 is looming on the horizon. Version 5 and IDA are no longer in common use; version 8 has replaced them. In this chapter we cover version 8 (8.11, to be precise) and look ahead to the features that are expected in version 9.

**sendmail** is being developed commercially by Sendmail, Inc., which also maintains a free, open source version. The commercial versions feature a graphical configuration user interface and performance enhancements that are not yet included in the open source version.

**sendmail** is still going strong, but several new open source mail transport agents have emerged over the last few years, most notably Postfix by Wietse Venema of TCP wrappers fame. We discuss Postfix briefly starting on page 618. The other alternatives are mentioned only in passing.

## 19.1  MAIL SYSTEMS

In theory, a mail system consists of four distinct components:

- A "mail user agent" (MUA) that lets users read and compose mail
- A "mail transport agent" (MTA) that routes messages among machines
- A "delivery agent" that places messages in a local message store[1]
- An optional "access agent" that connects the user agent to the message store (e.g., IMAP or POP)

Some sites also use a mail submission agent that speaks SMTP (the mail transport protocol) and does some of the work of the transport agent. Exhibit A shows the relationship of these components.

---

1. The receiving users' mailboxes or, sometimes, a database.

Electronic Mail

**Exhibit A**   **Mail system components**

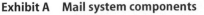

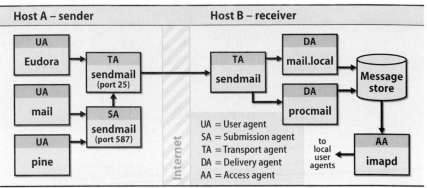

### User agents

Email users employ a user agent to read and compose messages. Email messages originally consisted only of text, but a standard known as Multipurpose Internet Mail Extensions (MIME) is now used to encode text formats and attachments (including many viruses) into email. It is supported by most user agents. Since it does not affect the addressing or transport of mail, we do not discuss it further in this chapter.[2]

One chore of user agents is to make sure that any text embedded in the contents of a mail message that might be misunderstood by the mail system gets protected. An example is the string "From " that is used as a record separator between messages.

**/bin/mail** was the original user agent. Several alternatives now exist. The popular user agents are listed below, along with their original sources.

- **/bin/mail** from the original UNIX
- **/usr/ucb/mail** from BSD[3]
- **mh** and **nmh** ("new **mh**") based on software from the Rand Corporation, plus the **exmh** front end by Brent Welch of Scriptics
- **pine** by from the University of Washington, www.washington.edu/pine
- **elm** by David Taylor, now maintained by the Elm Development Group and Kari Hurrta, available from ftp.virginia.edu
- **mutt** by Michael Elkins, available from ftp.mutt.org
- **rmail** and **VM**, mail user agents that are part of **emacs** and **XEmacs**
- Communicator from Netscape Communications, for a variety of platforms
- Eudora from Qualcomm for Macs or PCs running Windows
- Outlook Express from Microsoft,[4] also for Windows

---

2. Some feel that the primary effect of the MIME standard has been to convert the Internet's open email format into a morass of proprietary subformats. The dust is still settling.

3. **/usr/ucb/mail** is sometimes called **/bin/mailx** or **/bin/Mail** on systems derived from System V.

4. Outlook Express is a free, slightly crippled mail reader from Microsoft that has no relationship to the commercial product Microsoft Outlook.

Some user agents support a system-wide configuration file that sets defaults for all users. Individual users can override these defaults by setting up a personal configuration file in their home directories. User agents from the Windows and Mac worlds are configured from the application's UI, although most also support some form of global or automatic configuration for use at large sites.

Table 19.3 shows the features of the various user agents and the locations of their startup files. The locations and even the names of the global configuration files are sometimes vendor-specific; many are in **/etc**.

**Table 19.3    User agent features and configuration files**

| User agent | Sys. prefs | User prefs | MIME | POP | IMAP | SMTP |
|------------|------------|------------|------|-----|------|------|
| **bin/mail** | – | – | | | | |
| **ucb/mail** | **Mail.rc** | **.mailrc** | | | | |
| **\*mh** | – | .mh_profile<br>.maildelivery | ✔ | ✔ | | ✔ |
| **pine** | **pine.conf** | **.pinerc** | ✔ | ✔ | ✔ | ✔ [a] |
| **elm** | **lib/elm.rc** | **.elm/elmrc** | ✔ | ✔ [b] | ✔ [b] | |
| **mutt** | **Muttrc** | **.muttrc** | ✔ | ✔ | ✔ | |
| Netscape | – | – | ✔ | ✔ | ✔ | ✔ |
| Eudora | – | – | ✔ | ✔ | ✔ | ✔ |
| Outlook Express | – | – | ✔ | ✔ | ✔ | ✔ |

a. **pine** calls **sendmail** by default, but it can also speak SMTP.

b. Not supported in the standard release, but a patch is available.

The SMTP column refers to the way the user agent conveys mail to the transport agent or mail submission agent. A check means that the user agent opens a network connection directly to the transport or submission agent. No check means that the user agent executes the transport or submission agent as a subcommand.

### Transport agents

A transport agent must accept mail from a user agent, understand the recipients' addresses, and somehow get the mail to the correct hosts for delivery. Most transport agents also act as message submission agents for the initial injection of new messages into the mail system. Transport agents speak the Simple Mail Transport Protocol (SMTP) defined in RFC821 or the Extended SMTP protocol (ESMTP) defined in RFCs 1869, 1870, 1891, and 1985.

Several transport agents are available for UNIX (PMDF, Postfix, **smail**, **qmail**, **exim**, and **zmailer**, among others), but **sendmail** is the most comprehensive, most flexible, and most widely used (75% at last estimate).

### Delivery agents

A delivery agent accepts mail from a transport agent and actually delivers it to the appropriate local recipients. Mail can be delivered to a person, to a mailing list, to a file, or even to a program.

Each type of recipient may require a different agent. **/bin/mail** is the delivery agent for local users. **/bin/sh** is the original delivery agent for mail going to a file or to a program. Recent versions of **sendmail** ship with safer local delivery agents called **mail.local** and **smrsh** (pronounced "smursh"). **procmail** from www.procmail.org can also be used as a local delivery agent; see page 587.

 **mail.local** should not be used on systems such as HP-UX that deliver mail to users' mailboxes by exploiting **chown**'s ability to give away files to other users. Older Solaris systems should not use **mail.local** either, but its use is supported as of Solaris 7.

### Message stores

As email grew from servicing the computer science department at a university to servicing sites such as America Online with millions of subscribers, the UNIX file-system became inadequate as a message store. Searching a directory that contains a million mailboxes is prohibitively expensive.

The message store is the spot on the local machine where email is stored. It used to be the directory **/var/spool/mail** or **/var/mail**, with mail being stored in files named after users' login names. That's still the standard message store, but ISPs with thousands or millions of email clients are looking to other technologies for the message store (databases, usually).

On systems that use the standard **/var/spool/mail** or **/var/mail** store, the mail directory is created during the installation of the operating system. It should have permissions set to mode 775, with group owner mail.

### Access agents

Programs such as **imapd** and **spop** are access agents for PC, Mac, or UNIX users whose mail is delivered to a UNIX server and then downloaded with the Internet Message Access Protocol (IMAP) or the Post Office Protocol (POP), respectively. IMAP and POP are covered starting on page 549.

### Mail submission agents

Another newcomer to the mail arena that was necessitated by high volume sites is the mail submission agent. The transport agent at a busy mail hub spends lots of time doing preprocessing of mail messages: ensuring that all hostnames are fully qualified, modifying headers inherited from lame MUAs, logging errors, rewriting headers, and so forth. RFC2476 introduced the idea of splitting the mail submission agent (MSA) from the mail transport agent (MTA) to spread out the workload and maximize performance.

The idea is to use the MSA, which runs on a different port, as a sort of "receptionist" for new messages injected into the mail system by local user agents. The MSA does all the prep work and error checking that must be done before a message can be sent out by the transport agent. It's a bit like inserting a sanity checker between the MUA and the MTA.

In particular, the MSA ensures that all hostnames are fully qualified; it verifies that local hostnames are legitimate before adding the local domain portion. The MSA also fixes message headers if they are missing or nonconformant. Often, the MSA adds a From or Date header or adjusts the Message-Id header. One final chore that an MSA can do is to rewrite the sender's address from a login name to a preferred external form such as *First_Last*.

To make this scheme work, user agents must be configured to connect to the MSA on port 587 instead of to port 25, which is the traditional port for mail. If your user agents cannot be taught to use port 587, you can still run an MSA on port 25, but on a different server from your MTA. You must also configure your transport agent so that it doesn't duplicate the work done by the MSA. Duplicate processing won't affect the correctness of mail handling, but it does represent useless extra work.

**sendmail** can act as an MSA as well as an MTA. As of **sendmail** 8.10, the MSA service is turned on by default. This configuration is set up with the nocanonify feature and DAEMON_OPTIONS; see pages 579 and 588 for details. When **sendmail** is acting as both an MTA and an MSA, it provides each service on a different network port: port 25 for MTA service and port 587 (by default) for MSA service.

## 19.2  THE ANATOMY OF A MAIL MESSAGE

A mail message has three distinct parts that we must understand before we get embroiled in **sendmail** configuration:

- The envelope
- The headers
- The body of the message

The envelope determines where the message will be delivered or, if the message can't be delivered, to whom it should be returned. These addresses generally agree with the From and To lines of the header, although they are supplied separately to the MSA. The envelope is invisible to users; it's used internally by **sendmail** to figure out where to send the message.

The headers are a collection of property/value pairs formatted according to RFC822. They record a variety of information about the message, such as the date and time at which it was sent and the transport agents through which it passed on its journey. The headers are a bona fide part of the mail message, although user agents often hide some of the less interesting ones when displaying messages for the user.

The body of the message is the actual content to be sent. It must consist of plain text, although that text often represents a mail-safe encoding of various binary content.

As we get into the configuration section, we sometimes speak of the envelope sender and recipients and sometimes speak of the header sender and recipients. We try to specify which addresses we are referring to if it's not clear from the context.

## Mail addressing

Local addressing is simple because a user's login name is a unique identifier. But when an addressee does not have an account on the local machine, addressing and delivery are a bit more complicated.

There are basically two kinds of email addresses: route based (relative) and location independent (absolute). Route-based addressing requires the sender to know the intermediate machines through which a message should travel to reach its destination. Location-independent addressing simply identifies the final destination. UUCP, an early store-and-forward networking scheme that ran over phone lines and modems, used route-based addresses. Internet addresses are (usually) location independent.

The general form of Internet mail address is

*user@host.domain*

*See Chapter 16 for more information about DNS.*

where the @ separates the username from the host specification. Mail is delivered to *user*'s mailbox on the machine *host.domain*. By *domain* we simply mean the host's normal DNS domain. For example, in the address evi@boulder.colorado.edu, evi is the *user*, boulder is the *host*, and colorado.edu is the *domain*.

Other types of address have been used in the past. In particular, there have been several different forms of route-based addressing. We won't describe them here in detail, since they are largely obsolete, but Table 19.4 shows a few quick examples along with their equivalent present-day forms.

**Table 19.4    Examples of obsolete, route-based address types**

| Address type | Example address | Modern form |
|---|---|---|
| UUCP | mcvax!uunet!ucbvax!hao!boulder!lair!evi | evi@lair |
| Route-based | <@site1,@site2,…,@siteN:user@final-site> | user@final.site |
| "Percent hack" | user%host1%host2@host3 | user@host1 |

Much of the complexity of **sendmail** configuration stems from the early requirement to handle such addresses. Each of these forms of addressing relies on relaying, and thanks to spammers, sites are slowly turning relaying off. The percent hack (last line in Table 19.4) is a favorite tool of spammers who are trying to hide their identity or to relay mail through your machines. If you need to deal with any of these address forms, see the **sendmail** documentation or the O'Reilly **sendmail** book for help.

### Reading mail headers

Every mail message starts with several lines called headers that contain information about the message. Each header begins with a keyword such as To, From, or Subject, followed by a colon and the contents of the header. The format of the standard headers is defined in RFC822; however, custom headers are allowed, too. Any header beginning with "X-" is be ignored by the mail system but propagated along with the message. Ergo, you can add a header such as X-Joke-of-the-Day to your email messages without interfering with the mail system's ability to route them.

Some headers are added by the user agent and some by the transport agent. Several headers trace the path of a message through the mail system. Many user agents hide these "uninteresting" headers from you, but there is usually an option to make the agent reveal them all. Reading headers is becoming an important skill as we are bombarded with spam and must sometimes try to trace a message back to its source. Here is the header block from a simple message:

```
From evi Wed Jan 19 19:01:11 2000
Received: (from evi@localhost) by xor.com (8.9.3/8.9.3) id TAA17820; Wed, 19
    Jan 2000 19:01:11 -0700 (MST)
Date: Wed, 19 Jan 2000 19:01:11 -0700 (MST)
From: Evi Nemeth <Evi.Nemeth@xor.com>
Message-Id: <200001200201.TAA17820@xor.com>
To: trent@xor.com
Subject: xor.mc
Cc: evi@xor.com
Status: R

------ body of the message was here ---
```

This message stayed completely on the local machine; the sender was evi and the recipient was trent. The first From line was added by **mail.local**, which was the local delivery agent in this case. The Status header was added by Evi's mail reader, and the other headers were added by **sendmail**, the mail transport agent. Each machine that touches a message adds a Received header.

The headers on a mail message tell a lot about where the message has been, how long it stayed there, and when it was finally delivered to its destination. Below is a more complete dissection of a mail message sent across the Internet. It is interspersed with comments that describe the purpose of the various headers and identify the programs that added them. The line numbers at the left are for reference in the following discussion and are not part of the message. Some lines have been folded to allow the example to fit the page.

```
1: From eric@knecht.sendmail.org
```

Line 1 was added by **/bin/mail** or **mail.local** during final delivery to separate this message from others in the recipient user's mailbox. Some mail readers recognize message boundaries by looking for a blank line followed by the characters "From "; note the trailing space. This line does not exist until the message is delivered, and it is distinct from the From header line. Many mail readers don't display this line, so you may not see it at all.

> 2: Return-Path: eric@knecht.sendmail.org

> 3: Received: from anchor.cs.Colorado.EDU (root@anchor.cs.colorado.edu [128.138.242.1]) by columbine.cs.colorado.edu (8.9.3/8.9.2) with ESMTP id HAA21741 for <evi@rupertsberg.cs.colorado.edu>; Fri, 1 Oct 1999 07:04:25 -0700 (MST)

> 4: Received: from mroe.cs.colorado.edu (mroe.cs.colorado.edu [128.138.243.151]) by anchor.cs.colorado.edu (8.9.3/8.9.2) with ESMTP id HAA26176 for <evi@anchor.cs.colorado.edu> Fri, 1 Oct 1999 07:04:24 -0700 (MST)

> 5: Received: from knecht.sendmail.org (knecht.sendmail.org [209.31.233.160]) by mroe.cs.colorado.edu (8.9.3/8.9.2) with ESMTP id HAA09899 for <evi@anchor.cs.colorado.edu>; Fri, 1 Oct 1999 07:04:23 -700 (MST)

> 6: Received: from knecht.sendmail.org (localhost [127.0.0.1]) by knecht.sendmail.org (8.9.3/8.9.3) with ESMTP id GAA18984; Fri 1 Oct 1999 06:04:02 -800 (PST)

Line 2 specifies a return path, which may be a different address from that shown on the From line later in the mail header. Error messages should be sent to the address in the Return-Path header line; it contains the envelope sender address.

Lines 3–6 document the passage of the message through various systems en route to the user's mailbox. Each machine that handles a mail message adds a Received line to the message's header. New lines are added at the top, so in reading them you are tracing the message from the recipient back to the sender. If the message you are looking at is a piece of spam, the only Received line you can really believe is the one generated by your local machine.

Each Received line includes the name of the sending machine, the name of the receiving machine, the version of **sendmail** (or whatever transport agent was used) on the receiving machine, the message's unique identifier while on the receiving machine, the recipient (if there is only one), the date and time, and finally, the offset from Universal Coordinated Time (UTC, previously called GMT for Greenwich Mean Time) for the local time zone. This data is collected from **sendmail**'s internal macro variables. In the next few paragraphs, we trace the message from the sender to the recipient (backwards, from the point of view of header lines).

*See page 443 for more information about MX records.*

Line 6 shows that the message went from knecht's localhost interface (which Eric's particular mail user agent, **exmh**, chose for its initial connection) to knecht's external interface via the kernel loopback pseudo-device. Line 5 documents the fact that knecht then sent the message to mroe.cs.colorado.edu, even though the message was addressed to evi@anchor.cs.colorado.edu (see header line 9). A quick check with **nslookup** or **dig** shows that the host anchor has an MX record that points to mroe, causing the delivery to be diverted. Line 5 illustrates the difference between the envelope address (evi@mroe.cs.colorado.edu) and the recipient address in the headers (evi@anchor.cs.colorado.edu).

The machine mroe was running **sendmail** version 8.9.3, and it identified the message with queue ID HAA09899 while it was there. The message was then forwarded to anchor.cs.colorado.edu as addressed (line 4), and immediately forwarded again to evi@rupertsberg.cs.colorado.edu (line 3) because of aliasing, a mail handling feature that is described in detail starting on page 550.

Aliases play an important role in the flow of mail. An alias maps a username to something else, for example, to the same user at a different machine, to a group of users, or even to an alternate spelling of the user's name. You cannot determine why the message was diverted by examining only the example headers. As with MX records, you must seek external sources of information.

Received lines 5 and 4 include the "for <evi@anchor.cs.colorado.edu>" phrase, which identifies how the mail was addressed when it arrived at the local site. This information is very helpful if you are trying to unsubscribe from a mailing list that requires you to either send the unsubscribe message from the same host that you subscribed from (sometimes years earlier) or to know that address and use it as a parameter in your unsubscribe message.

The final Received line (line 3) shows "for <evi@rupertsberg.cs.colorado.edu>"; the value of **sendmail**'s destination address macro has been changed by the alias lookup on the machine anchor. But instead of going to rupertsberg.cs.colorado.edu, the message is actually delivered to the machine columbine. A quick look at the DNS records shows that rupertsberg has MX records that point to columbine, something that should have been changed when rupertsberg was upgraded to a spiffy new PC, but was probably forgotten.

The machine columbine, which was running **sendmail** V8.9.3, delivered the message (which had queue ID HAA21741 locally) to Evi's mailbox.

```
7: Message-Id: <199910011404.GAA18984@knecht.sendmail.org
```

Line 7 contains the message ID, which is different from a queue ID and is unique within the world-wide mail system. It is added to the message when it's initially submitted to the mail system.

```
 8: X-Mailer: exmh version 2.0.2 2/24/98
 9: To: Evi Nemeth <evi@anchor.cs.colorado.edu>
10: From: Eric Allman <eric@sendmail.com>
11: Cc: eric@sendmail.com
12: Subject: Re: hi
13: Date: Fri, 1 Oct 1999 06:04:02 -800
```

Line 8 identifies Eric's mail user agent as **exmh**. In fact, **exmh** itself added this line to the header. Notice that it begins with an X, making it an unofficial header. When mail was first specified, it was not envisioned that there would be more than one user agent, so no standard header was included.

Lines 9–13 are standard. Although a Subject header is not required, most user agents include it. The To line contains the address of the primary recipient or recipients. The

Date line shows the date and time at which the message was sent. In this case, the send time matches the dates in the Received lines pretty closely, even though each was measured with a different clock.

The Received lines are usually added by the transport agent (unless they are forged), and the other headers are added by the user agent. Some user agents are lame and do not add proper headers; in this case, **sendmail** steps in to add the missing headers.

The first Received line that is added (usually on the sending machine, when the mail is transferred to the outgoing interface) sometimes includes an "ident" clause that gives the sender's login name. It should be the same as the name on the From line, but it won't be if the From line is forged. In our example, Eric's machine knecht was not running the daemon that implements this feature (**identd**), so there is no clause that lists the sender's login name.

Exhibit B illustrates this message's journey through the mail system. It shows what actions were taken, where they happened, and what programs performed them.

**Exhibit B    A message from Eric**

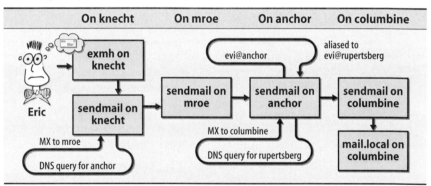

As you can see, **sendmail** is the workhorse in this process. It handles the message from the time it leaves **exmh** in Berkeley until it arrives on columbine for delivery.

See *Spam examples* on page 604 for more practice reading headers.

## 19.3  MAIL PHILOSOPHY

The mail philosophy we outline in this chapter is almost mandatory for keeping the administration of medium and large sites manageable. However, it is also appropriate for small sites. The main concepts that lead to easy administration are:

- Servers for incoming and outgoing mail; or for really large sites, a hierarchy
- A mail home for each user at a physical site
- IMAP or POP[5] to integrate PCs, Macs, and remote clients

5.  IMAP is preferred over POP these days.

*See page 443 for more information about MX records.*

We discuss each of these key issues below and then give a few examples. Other subsystems must cooperate with the design of your mail system as well: DNS MX records must be set correctly, Internet firewalls must let mail in and out, the message store machine(s) must be identified, and so on.

Mail servers have three functions:

- To accept outgoing mail from user agents and inject it into the mail system
- To receive incoming mail from the outside world
- To deliver mail to end users' desktops with IMAP or POP

At a small site, the servers that implement these functions might all be the same machine wearing different hats. At larger sites, they should be separate machines. It is much easier to configure your network firewall rules if incoming mail arrives at only one machine and outgoing mail appears to originate at only one machine.

Some sites use a proxy to receive mail from the outside world. The proxy doesn't really process mail; it just accepts and spools it. A separate process then forwards the spooled mail to **sendmail** for transport and processing. **smtpd** and **smtpfwdd** from www.obtuse.com are examples of such proxies for **sendmail**; **smtpd** can also filter incoming mail with access lists. Both are open source products.

### Using mail servers

Pick stable, reliable machines to use as your mail servers. Here, we outline a mail system design that seems to scale well and is relatively easy to manage and secure. It centralizes the handling of both incoming and outgoing mail on servers dedicated to those purposes. Exhibit C illustrates one form of this system.

**Exhibit C    Mail system architecture**

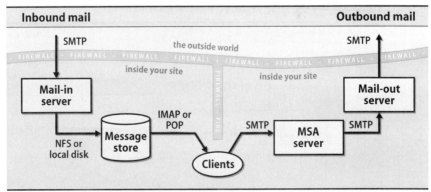

The mail system depicted in Exhibit C has a single point of exposure to the outside world: the mail server that receives messages from the Internet. That server can be carefully monitored, can be upgraded with security patches, and can run the latest version of **sendmail** with spam filters for incoming mail.

Electronic Mail

The server that handles outgoing mail must also be well maintained. It can include spam filters of its own to verify that no local user is contributing to the spam problem. If your site has concerns about the leakage of proprietary information, establishing a single server through which all outgoing mail must pass makes it easier to implement or enforce content policies. If your site manages large mailing lists, the outgoing mail server can be configured to take advantage of some of **sendmail**'s performance-oriented features.

Both the incoming and outgoing mail servers can be replicated if your mail load requires it. Don't pass any mail directly between the incoming servers and the outgoing servers, however; they should be separated from each other by an internal firewall.

ISPs who are designing a mail system for customers should add another server that acts as the target of customers' backup MX records and handles mailing lists. This machine has to accept mail and relay it back out, but it must be heavily filtered to make sure that it only relays the mail of actual customers. It, too, should be separated from the incoming and outgoing mail servers by a firewall.

*See page 515 for a discussion of file distribution issues.*

Garden-variety UNIX hosts can be given a minimal **sendmail** configuration that forwards outgoing mail to the server for processing. They do not need to accept mail from the Internet. Some sites may want to relax this funneling model a bit and allow arbitrary UNIX hosts to send mail directly to the Internet. In either case, nonserver machines can all share the same **sendmail** configuration. You might want to distribute the configuration with a tool such as **rdist** or **rsync**.

Sites that use software such as Microsoft Exchange and Lotus Notes but are not comfortable directly exposing these applications to the Internet can use a design modeled on that shown in Exhibit D.

**Exhibit D    Mail system architecture diagram #2**

Whatever design you choose, make sure that your **sendmail** configuration, your DNS MX records, and your firewall rules are all implementing the same policy with respect to mail.

### Using mail homes

It is convenient for users to receive and keep their mail on a single machine, even if they want to access that mail from several different systems. Mail homes can be enforced through the **aliases** file, the maildrop field of the user database, or even an LDAP database (see page 560). Remote access to each user's mailbox can be provided by IMAP or POP.

The aliasing scheme we use lets the alias files be the same on all machines within an administrative domain. This uniformity is a big win from the administrator's point of view. (We assume that login names and UIDs are unique across all machines, a policy we recommend highly.)

Some sites centralize mail by exporting **/var/spool/mail** over NFS. Locking problems with NFS files can cause users to lose mail or to have their spool files garbled. Finger pointing among NFS, **sendmail**, and the delivery agents with regard to proper locking does not help the poor user whose mailbox has been corrupted (however, **sendmail** is always innocent, since it never actually delivers mail).

Some NFS implementations (such as those on dedicated NFS file servers) include a lock manager that works correctly. Most implementations either do not support locking or support it improperly. Some sites just ignore the locking problem and hope for the best, and others require users to read mail on the file server.

Our best advice is just not to use an NFS-shared **/var/spool/mail**.

### Using IMAP or POP

IMAP and POP are protocols that download email to a user's desktop machine when it joins the network. It is the ideal way to manage mail, especially for hosts that are not always connected, either because they are turned off when not in use or because they are at home and share the phone line with teenagers.

IMAP, the Internet Message Access Protocol from the University of Washington, is our favorite of these tools. It delivers your mail one message at a time rather that all at once, which is much kinder to the network (especially on a slow link) and better for someone traveling from location to location. It is especially nice for dealing with the giant Microsoft attachments that some folks like to send: you can browse the headers of your mail messages and not download the attachments until you are ready to deal with them. IMAP manages mail folders among multiple sites, for example, between your mail server and your PC. Mail that stays on the UNIX server can be part of the normal backup schedule. www.imap.org contains lots of information about IMAP and a list of available implementations.

POP, the Post Office Protocol, is similar but assumes a model in which all the mail is downloaded from the server to the PC. It can be either deleted from the server (in which case it might not be backed up) or saved on the server (in which case your mail spool file grows larger and larger). The "whole mailbox at a time" paradigm is hard on the network and less flexible for the user. It can be really slow on dial-up lines if you are a pack rat and have a large mail spool file. Mail ends up getting scattered around with POP. A reasonable implementation of POP is available from Qualcomm at www.eudora.com/qpopper.

The IMAP server software is available from www.washington.edu/imap. No configuration is needed except to put the proper IMAP entries in the **/etc/services** and **/etc/inetd.conf** files and to make sure that your firewall (if any) doesn't prevent it from working. IMAP has been guilty of security problems in the past; see the CERT advisories and be sure to get the latest version.

## 19.4  MAIL ALIASES

Aliases allow mail to be rerouted either by the system administrator or by individual users.[6] They can define mailing lists, forward mail among machines, or allow users to be referred to by more than one name. Alias processing is recursive, so it's legal for an alias to point to other destinations that are themselves aliases.

**sendmail** supports several aliasing mechanisms: LDAP (the Lightweight Directory Access Protocol), NIS and NIS+ from Sun, NetInfo from NeXT/Apple, mail routing databases, and various alias files that users and system administrators can set up.

*See page 560 for more information about LDAP.*
If you want to use the mail homes concept, we recommend that you implement it by storing your aliases in an LDAP server. The alternatives have several disadvantages. Flat alias files usually must be maintained by root. Their database representation must be rebuilt with every change, and they must be replicated on every mail-delivering machine. Some sites that have lots of virtual domains maintain separate alias file fragments for each domain and merge them with a script to form the actual alias file.

LDAP alone does not work for mailing lists aliases; these are better handled with the standard aliasing mechanisms.

**sendmail** uses an LDAP server much like it uses the DNS name server. It calls on the DNS server to resolve names into IP addresses so that messages can be sent. It calls on the LDAP server to look up aliases to reroute messages to the right place. In both cases, the lookups have moved from flat files (**/etc/hosts** and **/etc/aliases**) to databases, with servers managing the queries.

We cover LDAP in more detail in three places in this chapter, and we also mention it in Chapter 18, *Sharing System Files*. We introduce and explain LDAP on page 560. Then, we describe LDAP's interaction with **sendmail** and with **sendmail**'s configuration file on page 582, and our first example, on page 590, uses LDAP to do aliasing and virtual hosting.

Before diving into LDAP, however, we first describe the traditional aliasing mechanisms. Aliases can be defined in the following three places (unfortunately, with three different syntaxes).

---

6. Technically, aliases are configured only by sysadmins. The user's control of mail routing by use of a **.forward** file is not really aliasing, but we have lumped them together here.

- In a user agent's configuration file (by the sending user)
- In the system-wide **/etc/mail/aliases** file (by the sysadmin)
- In a user's forwarding file, **~/.forward** (by the receiving user)

The user agent looks for aliases in the user's config files and expands them before injecting the message into the mail system. The transport agent, **sendmail**, looks for aliases in the global **aliases** file and then in the system's or recipients' forwarding files. Aliasing is applied only to messages that **sendmail** considers to be local.

Here are some examples of aliases in the **aliases** file format:

```
nemeth: evi
evi: evi@mailhub
authors: evi,garth,scott,trent
```

The first line says that mail sent to "nemeth" should be delivered to the user evi on the local machine. The second line says that all mail to evi should be delivered on the machine mailhub, and the third line says that mail addressed to "authors" should be delivered to the users evi, garth, scott, and trent. Recursion is supported, so mail sent to "nemeth" actually ends up going to "evi@mailhub".

*See Chapter 18 for more information about NIS.* Global aliases are defined in **/etc/mail/aliases** (which used to be **/usr/lib/aliases** or **/etc/aliases** on some systems). The path to the **aliases** file is specified in **sendmail**'s configuration file. Sites may have multiple **aliases** files, and they can also use alternate mechanisms such as NIS or database files.

The format of an entry in the **aliases** file is

```
local-name: recipient1,recipient2,…
```

where *local-name* is the original address to be matched against incoming messages and the recipient list contains either recipient addresses or the names of other aliases. Indented lines are considered continuations of the preceding lines.

From mail's point of view, the **aliases** file supersedes **/etc/passwd**, so the entry

```
david: david@somewhere-else.edu
```

would prevent the local user david from ever getting any mail. Therefore, administrators and **adduser** tools should check both the **passwd** file and the **aliases** file when selecting new user names.

The **/etc/mail/aliases** file should always contain an alias named "postmaster" that forwards mail to whoever maintains the mail system. An alias for automatic messages from **sendmail** must also be present; it's usually called Mailer-Daemon and is often aliased to postmaster.

You should redirect root's mail to your site administrators or to someone who logs in every day. The bin, sys, daemon, nobody, and hostmaster accounts (and any other pseudo-user accounts you set up) should also have aliases that forward mail to a human. The file **sendmail/aliases** in the distribution is a good template for the system-wide aliases that should be included. It also includes security suggestions and an example of how some common user requests are routed at Berkeley.

**sendmail** detects loops that would cause mail to be forwarded back and forth forever by counting the number of Received lines in a message's header and returning it to the sender when the count reaches a preset limit (usually 25).[7] Each visit to a new machine is called a "hop" in **sendmail** jargon; returning a message to the sender is known as "bouncing" it. The previous sentence, properly jargonized, would be, "Mail bounces after 25 hops."[8]

In addition to lists of users, aliases can refer to:

- A file containing a list of addresses
- A file to which messages should be appended
- A command to which messages should be given as input

Since the sender of a message totally determines its content, these delivery targets were often abused by hackers. **sendmail** has gotten very fussy about the ownership and permissions on such files and commands. To override **sendmail**'s paranoia, you must set one of the DontBlameSendmail options, so named to discourage you from doing it. Unfortunately, the error messages that **sendmail** produces when it encounters unsafe permissions or ownerships are not always clear.

### Getting mailing lists from files

The :include: directive is a great way to let users manage their own mailing lists. It allows the members of an alias to be taken from an external file rather than listed directly in the **aliases** file. The file can also be changed locally without requiring intervention by the system administrator who is responsible for the global **aliases** file.

When setting up the list, the sysadmin must enter the alias into the global **aliases** file, create the included file, and **chown** the included file to the user maintaining the mailing list. For example, the **aliases** file might contain

```
sabook: :include:/usr/local/mail/usah.readers
```

The file **usah.readers** should be on a local filesystem, not an NFS-mounted filesystem,[9] and should be writable only by its owner. To be really complete, we should also include aliases for the mailing list's owner so that errors (bounces) are sent to the owner of the list and not to the sender of a message addressed to the list:

```
owner-sabook: evi
```

See page 557 for more about mailing lists and their interaction with the **aliases** file.

---

7. The default hop limit is 25, but you can change it in the config file.

8. We have been inconsistent with terminology in this chapter, sometimes calling a returned message a "bounce" and sometimes calling it an "error." They both mean the same thing: a message that is undeliverable and so is being returned, usually to the sender.

9. If the NFS filesystem is mounted "hard" and NFS fails, **sendmail** will block, with several file handles open and several waiting processes. You may eventually run out of process IDs or file handles and have to reboot the machine to clear things.

## Mailing to files

If the target of an alias is an absolute pathname (double-quoted if it includes special characters), messages are appended to the specified file. The file must already exist. For example:

```
complaints: /dev/null
```

It's useful to be able to send mail to files and programs, but this feature introduces security concerns and is therefore restricted. This syntax is only valid in the **aliases** file and in a user's **.forward** file (or in a file that's interpolated into one of these files with :include:). A filename is not understood as a normal address, so mail addressed to /etc/passwd@host.domain will bounce.

LDAP databases cannot refer to a file as an email destination. Some user agents allow you to mail to a local file (such as an outbox folder), but that copy of the message is simply saved by the user agent and is never really sent through the mail system.

If the destination file is referenced from the **aliases** file, it must be world-writable, setuid but not executable, or owned by **sendmail**'s default user. The identity of the default user is set with the DefaultUser option. It is normally mailnull, daemon, or UID 1, GID 1.

If the file is referenced in a **.forward** file, it must be owned and writable by the original message recipient, who must be a valid user with an entry in the **/etc/passwd** file and a valid shell that's listed in **/etc/shells**. For files owned by root, use mode 4644 or 4600, setuid but not executable.

## Mailing to programs

An alias can also route mail to the standard input of a program. This behavior is specified with a line such as

```
autoftp: "|/usr/local/bin/ftpserver"
```

It's even easier to create security holes with this feature than with mailing to a file, so once again it is only permitted in **aliases**, **.forward**, or :include: files. In the **aliases** file, the program runs as **sendmail**'s default user; otherwise, the program runs as the owner of the **.forward** or :include: file. That user must be listed in the **/etc/passwd** file with a valid shell (in **/etc/shells**).

The target program uses **sendmail**'s queue directory as its working directory, which some shells object to. If you try this approach and it doesn't work, look in the documentation for the mailer D= flag to see how to fix it.

Mailing to programs is a major potential security hole. To be safe, don't use **/bin/sh** as your program mailer; use **sendmail**'s restricted shell, **smrsh**, instead. See *Security and sendmail* on page 607 for more information about **smrsh**.

## Examples of aliases

Here are some typical aliases that a system administrator might use.

```
# Required aliases10

postmaster: trouble, evi
postmistress: postmaster
MAILER-DAEMON: postmaster
hostmaster: trent
abuse: postmaster
webmaster: trouble, trent
root: trouble, trent
usenet: newsmaster

# include for local trouble alias
trouble: :include:/usr/local/mail/trouble.alias
troubletrap: "/usr/local/mail/logs/troublemail"
tmr: troubletrap,:include:/usr/local/mail/tmr.alias

# sysadmin conveniences
diary: "/usr/local/admin/diary"
info: "|/usr/local/bin/sendinfo"

# class aliases that change every semester
sa-class: real-sa-class@nag
real-sa-class: :include:/usr/local/adm/sa-class.list
```

In this example, we would like users from all over campus to be able to send mail to a single alias "trouble" whenever problems occur. Problem reports should always be routed to an appropriate group of local system administrators. In particular, we'd like to set up the mail aliases so that

- Trouble mail always goes to an appropriate group.
- A single version of the aliases file is used on all hosts.
- Individual admin groups control their own distribution lists.
- A copy of all trouble mail goes to a local log file for each group.

The configuration above satisfies these goals by taking the definition of the trouble alias from a file on each machine. Mail sent to the addresses trouble@anchor and trouble@boulder would end up in different places even though anchor and boulder use the same **/etc/mail/aliases** file.

Trouble mail is usually handled on one particular machine in each locale. For example, the **trouble.alias** file on a slave machine could contain the address

trouble@*master*

to make trouble mail go to the appropriate master machine.

When a trouble message is resolved, it is sent to the alias "tmr", which stands for "trouble mail readers." The tmr alias archives the message to the troubletrap alias and also sends it to a list of users taken from a file on the master machine. Adding novice administrators to the tmr list is a great way to let them see the support ques-

10. A white lie. Only postmaster and MAILER-DAEMON are really required (by the RFCs), but it is conventional to include hostmaster, abuse, and webmaster as well.

tions that arise, the administrators' replies, and also the proper sycophantic tone that should be used with users (i.e., customers).

This mechanism is just the tip of the iceberg of a complete trouble ticket tracking system called **queuemh**, which is based on the **mh** user agent.

The sa-class alias has two levels so that the data file containing the list of students only needs to be maintained on a single machine, nag. The sabook alias example earlier should really have this same type of indirection so that the include file does not need to be replicated.

The "diary" alias is a nice convenience and works well as a documentation extraction technique for squirrelly student sysadmins who bristle at documenting what they do. Sysadmins can easily memorialize important events in the life of the machine (OS upgrades, hardware changes, crashes, etc.) by sending mail to the diary file. Don't put the file on a filesystem that contains your log files; that would allow hackers to fill up the filesystem and prevent syslog from writing log entries (thus covering their tracks).

### Mail forwarding

The **aliases** file is a system-wide config file that should be maintained by an administrator. If users want to reroute their own mail (and your site doesn't use POP or IMAP to access mail), they can do so by creating **.forward** files in their home directories. Formerly, **sendmail** always looked in a user's home directory for a **.forward** file, but now the ForwardPath variable must be set to enable this behavior. It's convenient to use a **.forward** file when a user wants to receive mail on a particular host or when someone leaves your site and wants to have mail forwarded to a new location.

A **.forward** file consists of a list of comma-separated addresses on a single line or several entries on separate lines. For example,

```
evi@ipn.caida.org
evi@xor.com
```

or

```
\mcbryan, "/home/mcbryan/archive", mcbryan@f1supi1.gmd.de
```

In the first example, mail for evi is not delivered on the local machine, but is instead forwarded to the machine ipn at CAIDA in San Diego and to xor.com. The second entry is from a user who does not trust mail systems and wants his mail replicated in three places: the regular mail spool on the local machine, a permanent archive of all incoming mail, and a temporary address in Germany where he is traveling at the moment. The backslash before his username says to deliver mail locally no matter what the aliases or forward files might say.

For temporary changes in mail routing, use of a **.forward** file is preferable to use of the global **aliases** file. The overhead (computer time and people time) required to change the system-wide aliases is quite high.

A user's **.forward** file must be owned by the user and must not be group or world-writable. If **sendmail** thinks the directory path to the **.forward** file is safe (i.e., the permissions from the root all the way down are OK), it can be a link; otherwise, it cannot be a link. **sendmail** ignores forwarding files on which the permissions look suspicious; the permissions on the parent directory must also be safe (writable only by the user who owns the files).

Naturally, **sendmail** must be able to access a user's home directory on the machine where mail is delivered to determine whether it contains a **.forward** file. Permanent changes of address should be put in the **/etc/mail/aliases** file because a user's home directory and files will eventually be removed.

**sendmail** has a nifty feature, FEATURE(`redirect'), that helps with the management of permanent email changes. If an alias points to user@newsite.REDIRECT, mail will be returned to the sender with a notification of the new address. The message is not forwarded to the new address, so the sender must update his address book and re-send the message.

You can configure **sendmail** to support a central directory for **.forward** files, but users do not expect this configuration. The location of **.forward** files is controlled by the ForwardPath option, which usually points to that central directory and then to the user's home directory. The **generic.m4** domain file illustrated on page 594 contains an example of a central location for **.forward** files.

An entry in the global **aliases** file takes precedence over an entry in a **.forward** file. Since these files are maintained by different people, users must be careful not to inadvertently create mail loops. If a user on a network has a mail home (and therefore an entry in the global **aliases** file), that user cannot use a **.forward** file to reroute mail to another machine that shares the same aliases. For example, at the University of Colorado, where we use a site-wide **aliases** file, an entry such as

    evi: evi@boulder

and a **.forward** file on the machine boulder containing

    evi@anchor.cs

would create a loop. Mail addressed to evi would be forwarded to boulder, where the **.forward** file would cause it to be sent to anchor in the cs subdomain. The **aliases** file on anchor would cause it to be forwarded back to boulder, and so on. After 25 hops, the mail would be returned to the sender.

Notifying a user of a mail loop is challenging if your primary mode of communication is email. Mail to \user[11] delivers the message on the local machine, regardless of what the system-wide **aliases** file or the user's **.forward** file might say. If the local machine is where the user expects to read mail, fine; otherwise, send mail to the postmaster to report the loop or pick up the phone!

---

11. You may have to use two or more backslashes to get one of them past the shell and into **sendmail**.

### The hashed alias database

Since entries in the **aliases** file are in no particular order, it would be inefficient for **sendmail** to search this file directly. Instead, a hashed version is constructed with either the Berkeley DB database system or the **ndbm** database system that is standard on most versions of UNIX. This hashing significantly speeds alias lookups, especially when the file gets big.

The files derived from **/etc/mail/aliases** are called **aliases.db** for DB and **aliases.dir** and **aliases.pag**, for **ndbm**. The **dir** file is an index for the **pag** file, in which the data actually resides. Every time you change the **aliases** file, you must rebuild the hashed database with the **newaliases** command. **newaliases** is really just **sendmail** in disguise with command-line flags (**-bi**) that tell it to rebuild the database. Save the error output if you run **newaliases** automatically—you might have introduced formatting errors.

*See Chapter 18 for more information about NIS.*

When you compile **sendmail**, you should include database library support for the **dbm/ndbm** routines, the new Berkeley DB routines, or both. If both are included and **sendmail** needs to create a database file but the type is not specified, it uses DB. If you are using NIS, **sendmail** *creates* both but *uses* only the DB version.

The DB library, written and maintained by Keith Bostic and Margo Seltzer, is available at www.sleepycat.com. It is much better (faster access, smaller database files) than the **ndbm** system. DB is open source and free unless you ship it in a proprietary product; then, you need a license.

### Mailing lists and list wrangling software

A mailing list is a giant alias that sends a copy of each message posted to it to each person who has joined the list. It's like a Usenet newsgroup that is delivered by email. Some mailing lists have thousands of recipients.

Mailing lists are usually specified in the **aliases** file but maintained in an external file. Some standard naming conventions are understood by **sendmail** and most mailing list software. Experienced users have come to rely on them as well. The conventions are illustrated by the following aliases:

```
mylist: :include:/etc/mail/include/mylist
owner-mylist: mylist-request
mylist-request: evi
owner-owner: postmaster
```

In this example, mylist is the name of the mailing list. The members are read from the file **/etc/mail/include/mylist**. Bounces from mailing to the list are sent to its owner, evi, as are requests to join the list. The indirection from "owner" to "request" to evi is useful because the owner's address (in this case, mylist-request) becomes the Return-Path address on each message sent to the list. mylist-request is a bit better than the actual maintainer for this field. Errors in messages to the owner-mylist alias (evi, really) would be sent to owner-owner.

The case when a message is undeliverable is called a bounce. The case when the error message sent about the bounce cannot be delivered is a double bounce. So in our example, double bounces are sent to owner-owner or postmaster.

If you use a site-wide aliases file, you need to add an extra level of indirection pointing mylist to myreallist@master, so that the data file containing the list of members only needs to exist in one place.

Several software packages automate the maintenance of mailing lists. They typically allow users to add and remove themselves from the list, obtain information about the list, and obtain files through email. A few of the popular mailing list managers (and their download sources) are

- Majordomo, from www.greatcircle.com
- Mailman, the GNU mailing list processor, from www.list.org
- ListProc, from www.cren.net
- SmartList, from ftp.informatik.rwth.aachen.de
- LISTSERV Lite, from www.lsoft.com[12]

A good FAQ by Norm Aleks on mailing list software is available from rtfm.mit.edu via FTP (look under comp.answers/mail/list-admin). Unfortunately, the FAQ is no longer maintained and so might be a bit out of date. However, it still includes useful information to help you choose the best mailing list software for your needs.

In general, SmartList is small and simple, ListProc is large and complex, and the others are in between. They differ in their philosophies of list maintenance, with some leaning toward sysadmins as administrators (ListProc) and others leaning toward users as maintainers (Majordomo, Mailman, SmartList, LISTSERV Lite). Majordomo and LISTSERV Lite support remote administration; the list maintainer does not even need to have a login on the machine where the list is located because all transactions take place through email. Most of the list packages allow information posted to the list to be assembled into digests, some automatically (ListProc, Mailman, and LIST-SERV Lite) and some through manual configuration (SmartList and Majordomo).

Majordomo is our favorite list manager, but we hear that some sites are switching to Mailman. ListProc and LISTSERV Lite are proprietary: the first expensive, the other binary-only and crippled. We have not tried SmartList, but we like **procmail**, on which it depends.

We describe each of these packages briefly below. For more detail, see the documentation with each package or the O'Reilly book *Managing Mailing Lists* by Alan Schwartz and Paula Ferguson.

### Majordomo

Majordomo is a Perl/C package available from www.greatcircle.com. It was originally written by Brent Chapman, was souped up by John Rouillard, and is now maintained

---

12.  LISTSERV Lite is a free version of the commercial package LISTSERV.

by Chan Wilson. Development of Majordomo has ceased; Majordomo 2 is a total re-write but is still in beta test, so we describe only the original Majordomo.

*See page 608 for more information about trusted users.*

Majordomo runs as an unprivileged user, typically with username majordom and default group daemon. If your system supports long user names (> 8 characters), you can use majordomo as the login name. The user must be one that **sendmail** recognizes as "trusted" and so must be mentioned in your **sendmail** configuration, usually in a confTRUSTED_USERS declaration.

Majordomo is configured through the **majordomo.cf** file, which consists of valid Perl commands that initialize variables, define the directories where things are or where they should be put, specify the lists to be supported, and configure the handling of bounced mail. A helper program, **config-test**, will test your configuration file for missing variables or bad syntax.

Majordomo requires special aliases to be installed in **sendmail**'s **aliases** file. The cleanest way to integrate these aliases is to create a separate alias file used just for Majordomo (recent versions of **sendmail** support multiple alias files). The file contains a set of aliases for Majordomo itself and a set for each mailing list that it manages. The distribution contains a sample aliases file, **majordomo.aliases**.

The most common user question about mailing lists is, "How do I unsubscribe?" For lists managed by Majordomo, the answer for listname@host is to send mail to the address majordomo@host with the words "unsubscribe listname" or "unsubscribe listname email-address" in the body of the message (not on the subject line).

With the first form, you need to send the unsubscribe message from the same host that you used when you subscribed to the list; in the second form, that host is part of the email address. See page 545 for hints on how to glean this information from the mail headers so that you can unsubscribe properly, even if you have forgotten which machine you used when you joined the list. Some mailing lists also accept mail to listname-request@host with just the word "unsubscribe" in the body.

Never, ever send an unsubscribe message to the list itself. If you do, your message announces to all the recipients of the list that you don't know what you're doing.

### Mailman

Mailman, a fairly recent addition to the mailing list software fleet (version 1.0 released in July, 1999), is available from www.list.org or the GNU archives. It was originally written by John Viega and is currently being developed in collaboration with Ken Manheimer, and Barry Warsaw. Like Majordomo, Mailman is primarily written in a scripting language with C wrappers, but in this case the language is Python (available from www.python.org).

Mailman was inspired by its authors' use of Majordomo and their frustration with bounce errors, tricky configuration of advanced features such as digests and moderated lists, and performance difficulties with bulk mailings. Mailman provides a script that imports Majordomo lists. It also has some ability to detect and control spam.

Mailman's big claim to fame is its web interface, which makes it easy for the moderator or postmaster to manage a list and also easy for users to subscribe, unsubscribe, and configure their options.

*ListProc*

ListProc is an old-timer in mailing list management software. It was written in 1991 by Anastasios Kotsikonas and maintained until about 1994. It then lay idle for a few years but has recently been resurrected with a new beta release in 1998. It used to be available from the computer science department at Boston University for free, but with slightly strange licensing rules. Now it is available from www.cren.net for a hefty licensing fee ($2,000 per copy, even for universities). Forget ListProc and go with one of the free, open source packages.

*SmartList*

SmartList was originally written by Stephen R. van den Berg, who is also the author of the **procmail** package. SmartList is available from ftp.informatik.rwth-aachen.de or www.mindwell.com/smartlist. It uses **procmail**, so you will need to download both **procmail.tar.gz** and **SmartList.tar.gz**.

SmartList is small and simple. It's a combination of C code, **procmail** rules, and shell scripts. Bounces, the maintenance headache of mailing lists, are automatically dealt with by the software. Users are automatically removed from a list after a certain number of bounces to their address. SmartList requires a login entry in the **passwd** file ("smart" or perhaps "list") that is a trusted user in **sendmail**'s configuration file.

The installation includes **led**, a lock wrapper for editing that tries to protect SmartList against being left with an incoherent, partially edited configuration file.

*LISTSERV Lite*

LISTSERV Lite by Eric Thomas is a crippled version of LISTSERV, the commercial product from L-Soft International, Inc. Some of the features of the real version are missing, and the software is limited to managing 10 mailing lists of up to 500 people. LISTSERV Lite needs to run as the pseudo-user listserv, which must own its files. It also likes to have a listserv group. LISTSERV Lite provides a web interface both for subscribing to a list and for maintaining it.

The distribution is available from www.lsoft.com. Source code is not distributed, but precompiled binaries and stubs for many versions of UNIX and Linux are provided. If you already are familiar with LISTSERV and have lists that use it, you might be able to justify running a binary-only, crippled list manager. If you're starting from scratch, choose one of the open source, unrestricted alternatives mentioned above.

## LDAP: the Lightweight Directory Access Protocol

LDAP is a protocol that provides access to a generic administrative directory service. It has been around for a few years, but it has just recently started to become popular.

Administrators have discovered that LDAP is good for almost everything:

- **sendmail** configuration: aliases, virtual domains, and mail homes
- User management: login names, passwords, hosts (e.g., Stanford University)
- Administrative config files (e.g., SuSE Linux)
- As a replacement for NIS
- As a calendar server
- For use with Pluggable Authentication Modules (PAM)

It's envisioned that LDAP will eventually become a global directory system used for many different purposes.

LDAP grew out of the ISO protocols and the X.500 mail system. That heritage immediately suggests complex, bloated, verbose, bad, etc., but the L in LDAP is supposed to take care of all that. Protocol versions 1 and 2 have been standardized. Version 3 is close. Fortunately, all versions are backward compatible. Versions 1 and 2 are not hierarchical, but version 3 is.

Mail aliases are a particularly good match for LDAP, especially now that **sendmail** supports LDAP internally. **sendmail** can query the LDAP server for alias lookups instead of doing them directly. LDAP can also manage mail routing and virtual domains. LDAP support must be compiled into the **sendmail** binary.

If you are looking for an LDAP implementation, we recommend the server produced by the OpenLDAP group at www.openldap.org. This group took over and enhanced the code of an earlier server that was developed at the University of Michigan. For a bit more information about LDAP-related software, see page 534.

LDAP database entries resemble a termcap entry with longer variable names. The attributes (variable names) in the LDAP database are not yet fully standardized, and this fact can result in incompatibilities among different implementations.

The attributes on the first line of a database entry are defined by the LDAP configuration file. The examples in this section assume that the LDAP server daemon (**slapd**, in the OpenLDAP case) was configured with a root distinguished name (rootdn) of:

```
"cn=root, dc=synack, dc=net"
```

The dc attribute appears twice because the domain component values cannot contain a dot; to express the domain synack.net, two entries are necessary. Further attributes, or variable names, can be whatever you want. They are case insensitive. **sendmail** (whose code looks for specific attribute names and assigns them predetermined interpretations), the LDAP server, and the builder of the LDAP database must all cooperate and use the same naming conventions.

Some possible attributes that can appear on the first line of a database entry (the database keys) are dn for a domain name, dc for a domain component, o for an organization name, c for a country name, and uid for a unique ID (e.g., a login name).

**sendmail** recognizes the following data tags:

```
mailLocalAddress
mailRoutingAddress
mailHost
```

Here is an example of a **slapd ldap.conf** file

```
# LDAP Defaults, ldap.conf file, should be world-readable.
#
BASE    dc=synack, dc=net
HOST    gw.synack.net
PORT    389
```

that supports database entries of the form

```
dn: uid=jon, dc=synack, dc=net
objectClass: inetLocalMailRecipient
mailLocalAddress: jon@synack.net
mailRoutingAddress: stabilej@cs.colorado.edu
uid:jon
```

The incoming recipient is matched against the mailLocalAddress field. If it matches, the mail is redirected to the mailRoutingAddress. The objectClass line has to be there—it comes from the draft RFC that defines the interaction of LDAP and mail systems. On the host gw.synack.net, this database entry corresponds to the alias:

```
jon: stabilej@cs.colorado.edu
```

A bit long-winded, isn't it? These database entries could replace the typical entries in the **aliases** file for defining a mail home for each user. However, the **aliases** file is still the best way to define mailing lists (with the :include: directive). Mailing list software typically pipes the message to a wrapper script and resends it. An LDAP query can return a local address that handles the mailing list (by way of the **aliases** file), but it cannot directly call a program.

See page 582 for information about configuring **sendmail** to use LDAP and page 590 for an example that uses LDAP to implement aliases and virtual hosting.

## 19.5   SENDMAIL: RINGMASTER OF THE ELECTRONIC MAIL CIRCUS

**sendmail** is the most complex and complete mail transport system in common use. It was written by Eric Allman while he was a student at Berkeley. Eric had recently taken a computer science course in which he used production systems, so he decided to tackle the mail delivery problem with a similar approach. At the time, he thought he was attacking a fly with a sledgehammer and was intending to move to a simpler technique once he understood the problem better.

As it turned out, **sendmail**'s generality allowed Eric to keep up with the fast-paced world of email standards. Several important standards were just taking form and were often changing every week. He came to realize that the fly was in fact an elephant and that his sledgehammer was just barely adequate.

**sendmail** can adapt to the whims of standards-makers thanks in part to the flexibility of its configuration file, which allows **sendmail** to meet the needs of a diverse community of users. The rest of this chapter is primarily devoted to the understanding and construction of this configuration file, the infamous **sendmail.cf**.

**sendmail** is a transport agent, a program that interfaces between user agents and delivery agents. It speaks the SMTP protocol and delivers messages to peers on remote machines via the Internet. **sendmail**'s list of chores includes:

- Controlling messages as they leave the user's keyboard
- Understanding the recipients' addresses
- Choosing an appropriate delivery or transport agent
- Rewriting addresses to a form understood by the delivery agent
- Reformatting headers as required
- Passing the transformed message to the delivery agent

**sendmail** also generates error messages and returns messages to the sender if they are undeliverable.

### The history of sendmail

**sendmail** V5 was written by Eric Allman in 1983. One branch was enhanced by Lennart Lövstrand at the University of Linköping in Sweden in 1987 and called IDA **sendmail**.[13] It was maintained by Neil Rickert and Paul Pomes. Another branch, King James Sendmail, was developed by Paul Vixie at DECWRL during 1989–1993. It was based on IDA **sendmail** but had a far greater emphasis on throughput and performance for commercial sites. IDA and KJS pioneered several of the features that are now included in **sendmail** V8, Eric's major rewrite of 1993.

As of this writing, most vendors' implementations of **sendmail** are derived from V8. They are typically a release or two behind the master version from Sendmail, Inc., however. Vendors often customize a particular version of **sendmail** and are then reluctant to upgrade their base system to include current revisions. See Table 19.5 for information about the versions of **sendmail** that are shipped with various systems.

We base our discussion of **sendmail** on V8.11 and totally ignore both V5 and IDA, which are obsolete. V8 uses the **m4** macro processor to allow easy configuration of the standard cases. This "config lite" is all that most sites need.

Unfortunately, if your configuration has a problem, you may have to base your debugging on an understanding of the raw config file, which we've heard described as unapproachable, daunting, picky, cryptic, onerous, infamous, boring, sadistic, confusing, tedious, ridiculous, obfuscated, and twisted. We have replaced the 22-page config file section from the second edition with a reference to the O'Reilly **sendmail** book by Bryan Costales and Eric Allman or the *Sendmail Installation and Operations Guide* that's included with the **sendmail** distribution.

---

13. Lennart was a student in the computer science department, which in Swedish is the Institutionen för Datavetenskap; hence the name IDA.

### Vendor-supplied versions of sendmail

*gcc is available from*
*www.gnu.org.*
Table 19.5 lists the version of **sendmail** shipped with each of our example systems. It also shows where our friendly vendors have stashed the **sendmail** binary and its configuration file, **sendmail.cf**. We have listed sendmail.org as a vendor so that you can match their defaults if you replace your vendor's version.

**Table 19.5    Vendors' versions of sendmail (circa 2000)**

| System | Code | Config | Binary dir | Config dir |
|--------|------|--------|-----------|-----------|
| sendmail.org | 8.11.0 | 8.11.0 | – | /etc/mail |
| Solaris 7 | 8.9.3[a] | 8.9.1 | /usr/lib | /etc/mail |
| HP-UX 11.00 | 8.8.6 | 8.8.6 | /usr/sbin | /etc/mail |
| Red Hat Linux 6.2 | 8.9.3 | 8.9.3 | /usr/sbin | /etc |
| FreeBSD 4.0 | 8.9.3 | 8.9.3 | /usr/sbin | /etc |

a. Sunified

New releases of **sendmail** are sometimes issued to address security problems; we suggest that you check the release notes from www.sendmail.org and upgrade if you have missed any security-related patches. You'll need a C compiler and the **m4** macro preprocessor (both of which are usually included in standard UNIX releases).

Sometimes it's difficult to determine the actual **sendmail** base release, but if the vendor hasn't meddled too much, you can run

```
# /usr/sbin/sendmail -d0.1 -bt < /dev/null
```

to make **sendmail** disclose its version, the options that were compiled into it, and who it thinks it is after reading the config file. The -**d** flag sets a debug level (see page 615 for more info on debugging levels in **sendmail**), the -**bt** flag puts **sendmail** into address test mode, and the redirect from **/dev/null** gives it no addresses to test. Here is some sample output:

```
Version 8.9.3
 Compiled with: MAP_REGEX LOG MATCHGECOS MIME7TO8 MIME8TO7
    NAMED_BIND NDBM NETINET NETUNIX NEWDB NIS NISPLUS QUEUE
    SCANF SMTP USERDB XDEBUG
=============== SYSTEM IDENTITY (after readcf) ===============
    (short domain name) $w = katroo
 (canonical domain name) $j = katroo.Sendmail.COM
      (subdomain name) $m = Sendmail.COM
          (node name) $k = katroo.Sendmail.COM
=============================================================
```

**sendmail** should always use DNS MX (mail exchanger) records and will do so if compiled with the NAMED_BIND option (as in the preceding example).

## sendmail installation

This section briefly describes the installation process; refer to the installation notes in the **sendmail** distribution for the gory details and for issues related to particular architectures or operating systems. If you are replacing your vendor's version of **sendmail**, some of the configuration chores (such as installing help files) may already have been done for you.

The players:

- The **sendmail** binary, usually installed in **/usr/sbin** or **/usr/lib**. It runs setuid to root (mode 4755)

- The configuration file, **/etc/mail/sendmail.cf**, installed by the sysadmin

- The mail queue directory, **/var/spool/mqueue** (mode 700, owned by root), created manually by the sysadmin

- Various links to **sendmail** (**newaliases**, **mailq**, **hoststat**, etc.)

- **sendmail**'s safer local delivery agents, **smrsh** and **mail.local**, usually installed in **/usr/libexec**

You can download the latest version of **sendmail** from www.sendmail.org. To compile and install the package, run the **Build** script and then **Build install**.

Before you start compiling, however, you must decide on a database format and a strategy for interfacing **sendmail** with administrative databases such as NIS, NIS+, NetInfo, or even Hesiod. For on-disk databases, we recommend the Berkeley DB package specified in the **Makefile** as NEWDB. Don't edit the **Makefile**, though; create your own **site.config.m4** file to make customizations and set options. For example, if you intend to use LDAP, create a **site.config.m4** file that contains:

```
define(`confMAPDEF', `-DLDAPMAP')
define(`confLIBS', `-lldap -llber')
```

And then compile **sendmail** with

```
# sh ./Build -c -f site.config.m4
```

**sendmail** should not normally be set up to be controlled by **inetd** and so it must be explicitly started in the **rc** files at boot time. A typical sequence is

```
if [-f /usr/sbin/sendmail -a -f /etc/mail/sendmail.cf];
then
    (cd /var/spool/mqueue; rm -f [tTx]f*)
    /usr/sbin/sendmail -bd -q30m &
    echo -n ' sendmail' > /dev/console
fi
```

*See page 585 for more information about the nullclient feature.*

which checks for the **sendmail** binary and its configuration file and then starts the program in daemon mode. If your machine is not a mail server but still wants to run **sendmail**, you would configure it as a "nullclient" and would not run **sendmail** in daemon mode (no **-bd** flag); it therefore would not accept direct connections from the Internet.

This **sh** fragment should be added to the **/etc/rc** file on a Berkeley-based system or to **/etc/init.d/sendmail** on a System V system. If you like, you can use the fancier script in the installation guide, which tries to clean up previously interrupted queue runs.

This script assumes a single queue directory. If you have multiple queues, your script will be more complicated. See page 568 for more information about multiple queues.

Historically, **sendmail**'s supporting files have wandered around the filesystem to glamorous destinations such as **/usr/lib**, **/etc**, **/usr/ucblib**, and **/usr/share**. With the 8.10 release of **sendmail**, all files are expected to be kept beneath the **/etc/mail** directory.[14] Let's hope that vendors take the hint and leave them together in one consistent place.

### The switch file

*The service switch is covered in more detail in Chapter 18.*

Many operating systems have a configuration file called the service switch that enumerates the methods that can be used to satisfy various standard queries such as lookups of hosts and users. The service switch also determines the order in which resolution methods are tried when more than one of them is listed for a given type of query.

The operation of the service switch is normally transparent to other software, but **sendmail** likes to exert fine-grained control over its lookups and so on Solaris it reads the switch file directly. On other versions of UNIX, it uses its own personal switch configuration.

Two fields in the service switch that impact the mail system are aliases and hosts. The possible values for the hosts service are dns, nis, nisplus, and files. Support for all the mechanisms you use (except files) must be compiled into the **sendmail** binary before the service can be used.

The default location of the **sendmail** service switch is **/etc/mail/service.switch**, and its default contents are:

```
aliases    files nisplus nis      # if compiled with nis/nis+
hosts      dns nisplus nis files
```

If dns is listed in the hosts entry, **sendmail** will look up MX records in DNS, even if NIS is listed first.

### Modes of operation

You can run **sendmail** in several modes, selected with the **-b** flag. **-b** stands for "be" or "become" and is always used with another flag that determines the role **sendmail** will play. Table 19.6 lists the legal values.

---

14. Well, it's not quite totally true yet that all files are kept under **/etc/mail**. The **sendmail.pid** file and sometimes the statistics file are still kept elsewhere.

**Table 19.6    Command-line flags for sendmail's major modes**

| Flag | Meaning |
|------|---------|
| **-bd** | Run in daemon mode, listening for connections on port 25 |
| **-bD** | Run in daemon mode, but in the foreground rather than the background[a] |
| **-bh** | View recent connection info (same as **hoststat**) |
| **-bH** | Purge disk copy of outdated connection info (same as **purgestat**) |
| **-bi** | Initialize hashed aliases (same as **newaliases**) |
| **-bp** | Print mail queue (same as **mailq**) |
| **-bt** | Enter address test mode |
| **-bv** | Verify mail addresses only; don't send mail |
| **-bs** | Enter SMTP server mode (on standard input, not port 25) |

a. This mode is used for debugging, so that you can see error and debugging messages.

If you expect incoming mail to arrive over the network, run **sendmail** in daemon mode (**-bd**). In this mode, **sendmail** listens on network port 25 and waits for work.[15] When you run **sendmail** in daemon mode, you will usually specify the **-q** flag. It sets the interval at which **sendmail** processes the mail queue; for example, -q30m or -q1h to run the queue every thirty minutes or every hour.

**sendmail** normally tries to deliver messages immediately, saving them in the queue only momentarily to guarantee reliability. But if your host is too busy or the destination machine is unreachable, **sendmail** queues the message and tries to send it again later. **sendmail** forks a child process every time it processes the queue, so don't set the queue processing time too short. RFC1123 recommends at least 30 minutes between runs. **sendmail** does locking, so multiple, simultaneous queue runs are safe.

**sendmail** reads its configuration file, **sendmail.cf**, only when it starts up. Therefore, you must either kill and restart **sendmail** or send it a HUP signal when you change the config file. **sendmail** creates a **sendmail.pid** file that contains its process ID and the command that started it. You should start **sendmail** with an absolute path because it re**exec**s itself on receipt of the HUP signal. The **sendmail.pid** file allows the process to be HUPed with:

```
# kill -HUP `head -1 sendmail.pid`
```

The location of the PID file used to be a compile-time parameter, but it can now be set in the **.mc** config file with the confPID_FILE option:

```
define(confPID_FILE, `/var/run/sendmail.pid')
```

The default value is OS dependent but is usually **/var/run/sendmail.pid** for BSD systems and **/etc/mail/sendmail.pid** for others.

15. The ports that **sendmail** listens on are determined by DAEMON_OPTIONS; port 25 is the default.

### The mail queue

Mail messages are stored in the queue directory when the machine is too busy to deliver them immediately or when a destination machine is unavailable. The queue directory is usually **/var/spool/mqueue** and usually has owner root and mode 700.[16] All messages go into the queue briefly as they come in from the user agent.

**sendmail** allows you to have more than one mail queue. If the **mqueue** directory contained subdirectories **q1**, **q2**, and **q3** and you specified the queue directory to be **/var/spool/mqueue/q***, then all three queues would be used. **sendmail**'s ability to handle multiple queues helps performance under high load.[17]

When a message is queued, it is saved in pieces in several different files. Each filename has a two-letter prefix that identifies the piece; then, a random ID built from **sendmail**'s process ID. This ID is not fixed because **sendmail** is constantly forking and each copy gets a new process ID. Table 19.7 shows the six possible pieces.

**Table 19.7  Prefixes for files in the mail queue**

| Prefix | File contents |
|--------|---------------|
| **qf** | The header of the message and control file |
| **df** | The body of the message |
| **tf** | A temporary version of the **qf** file while the **qf** file is being updated |
| **Tf** | Signifies that 32 or more failed locking attempts have occurred |
| **Qf** | Signifies that the message bounced and could not be returned |
| **xf** | Temporary transcript file of error messages from mailers |

If subdirectories **qf**, **df**, or **xf** exist in a queue directory, then those pieces of the message are put in the proper subdirectory. The **qf** file contains not only the message header but also the envelope addresses, the date at which the message should be returned as undeliverable, the message's priority in the queue, and the reason the message is in the queue. Each line begins with a single-letter code that identifies the rest of the line.

Each message that is queued must have a **qf** and **df** file. All the other prefixes are used by **sendmail** during attempted delivery. When a machine crashes and reboots, the startup sequence for **sendmail** should delete the **tf**, **xf**, and **Tf** files from each queue directory. The sysadmin responsible for mail should check occasionally for **Qf** files in case local configuration is causing the bounces.

The mail queue provides several opportunities for things to go wrong. For example, the filesystem can fill up (avoid putting **/var/spool/mqueue** and **/var/spool/news**

16. If the recipient of a mail message is a **csh** script, the spool directory must have mode 711 or the D= mailer clause must specify a directory with (at least) execute permission in which the script can be run.

17. UNIX directories are an efficient storage mechanism if they do not contain too many files. If you have a busy mail server with lots of mailing lists that get out of date, the queue directory can easily get so large that it is inefficient to deal with.

on the same partition), the queue can become clogged, and orphaned mail messages can get stuck in the queue.

**sendmail** has a configuration option (confMIN_FREE_BLOCKS) to help manage disk space. When the filesystem that contains the mail queue gets too full, mail is rejected with a "try again later" error until more space has been made available. This option leaves a bit of slop space so mail starts being rejected before the filesystem is totally full and everything wedges.

*See page 443 for more information about DNS MX records.*
If a major mail hub goes down, its MX backup sites can become overloaded with thousands of messages.[18] **sendmail** can fork too many copies of itself and thrash a machine to death. To handle a temporarily clogged queue, you need to move the clog aside, continue processing new mail as usual, and run a separate copy of **sendmail** on the clogged queue after things quiet down.

For example, with a single queue directory:

```
# kill `head -1 sendmail.pid`
# mv mqueue cloggedqueue   /* To another FS if necessary */
# mkdir mqueue             /* Set owner/perms, too */
# chown root mqueue
# chmod 700 mqueue
# /usr/sbin/sendmail -bd -q1h &
```

When things settle down, run **sendmail** with the following flags:

```
# /usr/sbin/sendmail -oQ/var/spool/cloggedqueue -q
```

These flags point **sendmail** at the clogged queue directory and specify that **sendmail** should process it immediately. Repeat this command until the queue empties.

For giant clogs, consider sorting messages into different queues by the last digit of their message IDs, as shown in the following script:

```
#!/bin/csh -f
foreach suffix (0 1 2 3 4 5 6 7 8 9)
    mkdir clog${suffix}
    mv ?f*${suffix} clog${suffix}
    sendmail -oQclog${suffix}
end
```

The point of separating messages into different queues is just to reduce the overhead of the linear directory search. Ten mini-queues will run faster than one big queue because **sendmail** is almost always I/O bound and not CPU bound.

The point at which the queue becomes clogged depends on the site and the hardware on which **sendmail** is running. Your system and the mail hub for aol.com, which pro-

---

18. A few years ago, Sun Microsystems decided to change its mail routing from direct-to-workstation addresses to division-wide gateways. The queue lengths on these gateways became so long that mail to the employee across the hall took more than a day to arrive. Unclogging these queues required hardware upgrades of all the gateway machines on a very tight schedule.

cesses millions of messages a day, will have different definitions of a clogged queue. See page 614 for information about measuring your traffic levels.

## 19.6  SENDMAIL CONFIGURATION

**sendmail**'s actions are controlled by a single configuration file, **sendmail.cf**, which is kept in **/etc/mail** (it was formerly found in **/etc** or **/usr/lib**). We call it the config file for short. It determines **sendmail**'s

- Choice of delivery agents
- Address rewriting rules
- Mail header formats
- Options
- Security precautions
- Spam resistance

The raw config file format was designed to be easy to parse. This focus has made it a bit lacking in warm, user-friendly features. Maintenance of the config file is the most significant administrative chore related to electronic mail and scares the pejeebers out of even seasoned sysadmins.

Every version of **sendmail** uses a config file, but modern versions make the configuration process easier through the use of **m4** macros, which disguise much of the underlying complexity. It might be said that the raw config file is at the level of assembly language, whereas **m4** configuration is more at the level of Perl.[19]

When the **m4** macros were first introduced, it was hoped that they would handle 80%–90% of cases. In fact, the coverage rate turned out to be much higher, probably closer to 98%. In this book, we cover only the **m4**-based "config lite." You need delve into the low-level config file only if you are debugging a thorny problem or growing your mail site in bizarre ways.

Three key pieces of documentation arc the O'Reilly book *sendmail* by Bryan Costales and Eric Allman, the paper *Sendmail Installation and Operations Guide* by Eric Allman (included in the **doc/op** directory of the distribution), and the **README** file (in the **cf** directory). We often refer to *sendmail* as a source for more information and refer to it as "the **sendmail** book." Likewise, we refer to the installation paper as "the installation guide" and the README file as **cf/README**.

### Using the m4 preprocessor

We first describe a few **m4** features, then show how to build a configuration file from an **m4** master file, and finally describe some of the important prepackaged **m4** macros that come with the **sendmail** distribution.

---

19.  The **sendmail** config language is "Turing complete," which means that it can be used to write any possible computer program. Readers who have experienced the raw config file will realize what a frightening concept this is...

We conclude this section with example configurations for three distinct sites:

- A computer science student's home Linux box
- A medium-sized company that knows how to configure **sendmail** properly
- A site that does lots of web hosting

**m4** was originally intended as a front end for programming languages that would let the user write more readable (or perhaps more cryptic) programs. **m4** is powerful enough to be useful in many input transformation situations, and it works nicely for **sendmail** configuration files.

**m4** macros have the form

```
name(arg1, arg2, ..., argn)
```

There should be no space between the name and the opening parenthesis. Left and right single quotes are used to quote strings as arguments. **m4**'s quoting conventions are different from those of other languages you may have used, since the left and right quotes are different characters.[20] Quotes nest, too. With today's compiler building tools, one wonders how **m4** survived with such a rigid and exotic syntax.

**m4** has some built-in macros, and users can also define their own. Table 19.8 lists the most common built-in macros used in **sendmail** configuration.

**Table 19.8    m4 macros commonly used with sendmail**

| Macro | Function |
|-------|----------|
| define | Defines a macro named *arg1* with value *arg2* |
| undefine | Discards a previous definition of macro named *arg1* |
| include | Includes (interpolates) the file named *arg1* |
| dnl | Discards characters up to and including the next newline |
| divert | Manages output streams |

Some sites add a dnl macro to the end of every line to keep the translated **.cf** file tidy; without dnl, **m4** adds extra blank lines to the configuration file. These blank lines don't affect **sendmail**'s behavior, but they make the config file hard to read. We have omitted the dnls from our examples.

**sendmail** requires a version of **m4** that is newer than the original UNIX version 7 code from Bell Labs. Most **m4**'s shipped today are OK; if in doubt, get GNU's version.

**m4** does not really honor comments in files. A comment such as:

```
# And then define the ...
```

would not do what you expect because define is an **m4** keyword and would be expanded. Instead, use the m4 dnl keyword (for "delete to newline"). For example,

---

20. The quote characters can actually be changed with the changequote macro, but it's better not to tamper with the syntax. You'll just confuse the next person that maintains the file.

```
dnl # And then define the ...
```

would work. You must include a space between the dnl and the comment itself.

### The sendmail configuration pieces

The **sendmail** distribution includes a **cf** subdirectory that contains all the pieces necessary for **m4** configuration: a **README** file and several subdirectories, listed in Table 19.9.

**Table 19.9   Configuration subdirectories**

| Directory | Contents |
|-----------|----------|
| **cf** | Sample **mc** (master configuration) files |
| **domain** | Sample **m4** files for various domains at Berkeley |
| **feature** | Fragments that implement various features |
| **hack** | Special features of dubious value or implementation |
| **m4** | The basic config file and other core files |
| **ostype** | OS-dependent file locations and quirks |
| **mailer** | **m4** files that describe common mailers (delivery agents) |
| **sh** | Shell scripts used by **m4** |

The **cf/cf** directory contains examples of **.mc** files. In fact, it contains so many examples that yours will get lost in the clutter. We recommend that you move the **cf** directory aside to **cf.examples** and create a new **cf** directory for your own local **.mc** files. If you do this, copy the **Makefile** and **Build** script over to your new directory so the instructions in the **README** file still work. It's best to also copy all the configuration **.mc** files to a central location rather than leaving them inside the **sendmail** distribution. The **Build** script has paths that will have to be changed if you try to build a **.cf** file from a **.mc** file and are not in the distribution hierarchy.

### Building a configuration file from a sample .mc file

Before we dive into pages and pages of details about the various configuration macros, features, and options, we will put the cart before the horse and create a "no frills" configuration to illustrate the process. Our example is for a leaf node, foo.com, and the master configuration file is called **foo.mc**.

We'll put **foo.mc** in our shiny new **cf** directory. The translated (by **m4**) configuration file will be **foo.cf** in the same directory and we'll ultimately install it as **sendmail.cf** in **/etc/mail**.

Some boilerplate should go in each new **.mc** file:

```
divert(-1)
#### basic .mc file for foo.com
divert(0)
VERSIONID(`$Id$')
```

If you want to put comments at the start of your file, the first line has to be a divert statement, which throws away any spurious garbage on the **m4** output streams. The #-style comments come next, followed by another divert. A VERSIONID line (here, in RCS format) completes the boilerplate. It is described in detail in the next section.

In many cases, specifying an OSTYPE (see page 574) to bring in operating-system-dependent paths or parameters and also a set of MAILERs (see page 576) will complete the configuration:

```
OSTYPE(`linux')
define(`confCOPY_ERRORS_TO', `postmaster')
MAILER(`local')
MAILER(`smtp')
```

Here, we also set an option (confCOPY_ERRORS_TO) that sends a copy of the headers of any bounced mail to the local postmaster. This notification allows the postmaster to intervene when the problem is at the local site.

To build the real configuration file, just run the **Build** command you copied over to the new **cf** directory:

```
# ./Build foo.cf
```

Finally, install **foo.cf** in the right spot—normally **/etc/mail/sendmail.cf**, but some vendors move it. Favorite vendor hiding places are **/etc** and **/usr/lib**.

A larger site can create a separate **m4** file to hold site-wide defaults in the **cf/domain** directory; individual hosts can then include the contents of this file. Not every host needs a separate config file, but each group of hosts that are similar (same architecture and same role: server, client, etc.) will probably need its own configuration.

Even with **sendmail**'s easy new configuration system, you still have to make several configuration decisions for your site. As you read about the features described below, think about how they might fit into your site's organization. A small site will probably have only a hub node and leaf nodes and thus will need only two versions of the config file. A larger site may need separate hubs for incoming and outgoing mail and, perhaps, a separate POP/IMAP server.

Whatever the complexity of your site and whatever face it shows to the outside world (exposed, behind a firewall, or on a virtual private network, for example), it's likely that the **cf** directory contains some appropriate ready-made configuration snippets just waiting to be customized and put to work.

## 19.7  BASIC SENDMAIL CONFIGURATION PRIMITIVES

**sendmail** configuration commands are case sensitive. By convention, the names of predefined macros are all caps (e.g., OSTYPE), **m4** commands are all lower case (e.g., define), and configurable variable names start with a lowercase conf and end with an all-caps variable name (e.g., confCOPY_ERRORS_TO). Macros usually (all except VERSIONID) refer to an **m4** file called ***../*macroname*/arg1*.m4**. For example, the macro OSTYPE('linux') causes ***../ostype/linux.m4** to be included.

In this section we cover the basic configuration commands and leave the fancier features for later.

### The VERSIONID macro

You should maintain your config files with CVS, RCS or SCCS, not only so that you can back out to an earlier config version if that should be necessary but also so that you can identify the versions of the **m4** files that go into making up the config file. Use the VERSIONID macro to automatically embed version information. The syntax for CVS/RCS is

```
VERSIONID(`$Id$')
```

and for SCCS it's

```
VERSIONID(`%W% (ident) %G%')
```

The actual version information will be filled in by RCS or SCCS as you check in the file. It will appear in the final **sendmail.cf** file as a comment. This information can also be useful if you forget where you put the **sendmail** distribution; often, the location of files is dictated by available disk space and not by filesystem design logic.

In the SCCS form, %W% expands to the filename and version, and %G% expands to the last modification time. Replace *ident* with a string that identifies your site.

### The OSTYPE macro

Files in the **ostype** directory are named for the operating system whose default values they contain. An OSTYPE file packages up a variety of vendor-specific information, such as the expected locations of mail-related files, paths to commands that **sendmail** needs, flags to mailer programs, etc.

By convention, OS-specific information is interpolated into the config file with the OSTYPE macro.[21] Every config file must include an OSTYPE macro near the top, typically just after VERSIONID.

OSTYPE files do their work primarily by defining other **m4** variables. For example,

```
define(`ALIAS_FILE', `/usr/lib/aliases')
```

specifies the location of the system-wide aliases file. You can override the default values for your OS later in the **.mc** file if you wish, but don't change the distributed OSTYPE file unless it's actually wrong, in which case you should submit a bug report too. Some sites want a consistent location for the aliases file across platforms and so redefine its location in their DOMAIN file.

---

21. So where is the OSTYPE macro itself defined? In a file in the **cf/m4** directory that is magically prepended to your config file when you run the **Build** script.

The **README** file in the **cf** directory lists all the variables that can be defined in an OSTYPE file. Some of the important ones are shown in Table 19.10, along with several that you may want to configure for spam abatement (but which are undefined by default). The default values are what you get if your OSTYPE file doesn't specify something else.

**Table 19.10    Default values of some variables set in OSTYPE files**

| Variable | Default value |
|---|---|
| ALIAS_FILE | **/etc/mail/aliases** |
| HELP_FILE | **/etc/mail/helpfile** |
| STATUS_FILE | **/etc/mail/statistics** |
| QUEUE_DIR | **/var/spool/mqueue** |
| LOCAL_MAILER_PATH | **/bin/mail** |
| LOCAL_SHELL_PATH | **/bin/sh** |
| LOCAL_MAILER_MAX | undefined |
| LOCAL_MAILER_MAXMSGS | undefined |
| SMTP_MAILER_MAX | undefined |
| SMTP_MAILER_MAXMSGS | undefined |

*See Chapter 18 for more information about NIS.*

**sendmail** supports the use of multiple alias files and NIS maps, both to allow the simultaneous use of files and NIS and to facilitate the division of aliases between global and local files. For example,

        define(`ALIAS_FILE', ``/etc/aliases,nis:mail.aliases'')

would search the file **/etc/aliases** first, and if that failed, would then try the NIS map called mail.aliases.

If you install **sendmail** on a new OS release or architecture, be sure to create a corresponding OSTYPE file and give it to sendmail.org so that it can be included in the next release. Just model your new file after those already there and check it against the table of defaults in the **cf/README** file. If the value of a variable on your new system is the same as the default value, you don't need to include an entry for it (but it doesn't hurt to protect yourself in case the default changes).

Table 19.11 shows the OSTYPE files for our four reference platforms.

**Table 19.11    OSTYPE files for common systems**

| System | File | Usage |
|---|---|---|
| Solaris | **solaris2.m4** | OSTYPE(`solaris2') |
| HP-UX | **hpux11.m4** | OSTYPE(`hpux11') |
| Red Hat | **linux.m4** | OSTYPE(`linux') |
| FreeBSD | **bsd4.4.m4** | OSTYPE(`bsd4.4') |

### The DOMAIN macro

The DOMAIN directive allows site-wide generic information to be specified in one place (**cf/domain/***filename***.m4**) and then referred to in each host's individual config file with

    DOMAIN(`filename')

The filename is usually chosen to describe your site. For example, our file for the computer science department is called **cs.m4** and appears in our **.mc** files as:

    DOMAIN(`cs')

Like OSTYPE, DOMAIN is really just a nice way of doing an include. But it makes the structure of the config file clearer and provides a hook for future tweaks. It is most useful when you centralize and build all your site's **.cf** files from **.mc** files kept in a single location.

Small sites do not usually need a domain file, but larger sites often use them for references to relay machines, site-wide masquerading or privacy options, and references to tables for mailers, virtual domains, and spam databases.

The generic DOMAIN file included with the distribution shows the types of entries that are usually put in site-wide domain files. Its contents are shown on page 594.

### The MAILER macro

You must include a MAILER macro for every delivery agent you want to enable. You'll find a complete list of supported mailers in the directory **cf/mailers** in the **sendmail** distribution. Currently, the options are local, smtp, fax, usenet, procmail, qpage, cyrus, pop, phquery, and uucp. Some examples:

    MAILER(`local')
    MAILER(`smtp')

The first line includes the local and prog mailers. The second line includes smtp, csmtp, dsmtp, smtp8, and relay.

If you plan to tune any mailer-related macros (such as USENET_MAILER_ARGS or FAX_MAILER_PATH), be sure that the lines that set these parameters *precede* the line that invokes the mailer itself; otherwise, the old values will be used. For this reason, MAILER declarations usually come toward the bottom of the config file.

The pop mailer interfaces to the **spop** program that is part of the MH mail handler package and implements the Post Office Protocol defined in RFC1460. It's used by PCs and Macs that need to access mail on a UNIX host. The cyrus mailer is for use with CMU's IMAP server.

MAILER(`uucp') includes several flavors of UUCP mailers.

The usenet mailer provides an email interface to Usenet news. To use it, verify the values of the USENET_MAILER_* macros in the OSTYPE file for your architecture.

Send mail to *newsgroup*.USENET to post an article. Some sites add a mailer argument that identifies the local organization.

For example,

```
-o "Organization: University of Colorado"
```

added to the USENET_MAILER_ARGS line would add an Organization header to each news article. Unfortunately, Usenet is a spammer's heaven. You will have even bigger spam problems if you use the usenet mailer; we recommend that you don't.

*HylaFAX is available from ftp.sgi.com.*

The fax mailer integrates Sam Leffler's HylaFAX package into the mail system. Mailing to *user@destination*.fax sends the body of the message as a fax document. The *destination* is typically a phone number. To allow symbolic names as destinations (rather than just phone numbers), use a keyed database file or the **/etc/remote** and **/etc/phones** files.

*ghostscript is available from www.gnu.org.*

You must glue HylaFAX and **sendmail** together by installing a script from the Hyla-FAX distribution in **/usr/local/bin**. If necessary, you must also change the value of the macro FAX_MAILER_PATH. Human intervention is still needed to deliver incoming faxes from the spool area to a user's mailbox. You can convert fax documents to PostScript (with HylaFAX) and view them with the GNU package **ghostscript**.

The qpage mailer interfaces to QuickPage software to deliver email to your pager. See www.qpage.org for more information about QuickPage.

The previous macros VERSIONID, OSTYPE, DOMAIN, and MAILER are all you need to build a basic *hostname*.**mc** file.

## 19.8   FANCIER SENDMAIL CONFIGURATION PRIMITIVES

In the next sections, we describe a few more macros and some of the most common FEATUREs used to modify **sendmail**'s default behavior. We also discuss some policy issues in the context of **sendmail** configuration: hiding information by use of masquerading and virtual domains, security, privacy, and spam.

### The FEATURE macro

With the FEATURE macro you can enable several common options by including **m4** files from the **feature** directory. In the discussion below, we intermix our presentation of FEATUREs and some of **sendmail**'s other macros, as they are occasionally intertwined. When **m4** configuration was first added to **sendmail**, describing the FEATURE macro became a big section of our mail chapter. Now, so many features have been added that FEATURE almost needs its own chapter. The syntax is:

```
FEATURE(keyword, arg, arg, ...)
```

where *keyword* corresponds to a file *keyword*.**m4** in the **cf/feature** directory and the *args* are passed to it. See the directory itself or the **cf/README** file for a definitive list of features. A few commonly used ones are described below.

### The use_cw_file feature

The **sendmail** internal class w (hence the name **cw**) contains the names of all local hosts for which this host accepts and delivers mail. A client machine might include its hostname, its nicknames, and localhost in this class. If the host being configured is your mail hub, then the w class should also include any local hosts and virtual domains for which you accept email.

The use_cw_file feature defines class w from the file **/etc/mail/local-host-names** (which used to be called **sendmail.cw**; the exact filename is configurable with the confCW_FILE option, discussed later). Without this feature, **sendmail** accepts only mail addressed to the machine on which it is running. Since **sendmail** reads the **.cw** file only when it starts, you must send a HUP signal to **sendmail** if you change the **.cw** file to make the change take effect.

```
FEATURE(`use_cw_file')
```

invokes the feature and uses **local-host-names**;

```
FEATURE(`use_cw_file', `other-filename')
```

lets you choose the filename.

### The redirect feature

When people leave your organization, you usually either forward their mail or let mail to them bounce back to the sender with an error. The redirect feature provides support for a more elegant way of bouncing mail. If Joe Smith has graduated from oldsite.edu to newsite.com, then enabling redirect with

```
FEATURE(`redirect')
```

and adding the line

```
smithj: joe@newsite.com.REDIRECT
```

to the aliases file causes mail to smithj to be returned to the sender with an error message which suggests that the sender try the address joe@newsite.com instead. The message itself is not automatically forwarded.

### The always_add_domain feature

This feature makes **sendmail** add the local hostname to destination addresses that are not fully qualified. For example, suppose a message from lynda@cs.colorado.edu to barb@netrack.net also copies the local user evi. Without always_add_domain, the mail that barb receives will show "evi" on the Cc header line. If she responds to all recipients, her response will go to "evi", which might not be a valid account at netrack.com or might be a different person. With always_add_domain turned on, evi's address is mapped to evi@cs.colorado.edu before it leaves lynda's machine.

It is also appropriate to use always_add_domain when you share spool directories among machines that do not share an alias file or that do not have the same **passwd** file (incidentally, you probably shouldn't do such sharing). Mail to an alias or user that is not known everywhere would be fully qualified on the originating machine and therefore replyable.

Another selling point for this feature is that unqualified names are often rejected as spam. We recommend that you always use it.

If you are using MASQUERADE_AS (see page 583), always_add_domain adds the name of the host you are masquerading as, not the local hostname. This convention can cause problems if the **aliases** file or **passwd** file on the local host is not a subset of the equivalent file on the MASQUERADE_AS host.

### The nocanonify feature

This feature postpones the DNS lookups that are necessary to send a message. For example, at a site with a master mail hub and client machines that forward all their mail through the master, the clients might use

```
FEATURE(`nocanonify')
```

to avoid doing the DNS lookups locally. Our second example (page 591) uses this scheme. It can also be used in the MSA/MTA scheme that might be used at a very large mail site. In this scenario, the MSA does all the DNS lookups and the master machine running the MTA specifies nocanonify.

### Tables and databases

**sendmail** has several FEATUREs that use a construct called a "table" to figure out where mail should be routed. A table is a text file of routing, aliasing, access, or other information that is converted to a database format externally with the **makemap** command and then used as an internal database for **sendmail**'s various lookups. The use of a centralized IMAP or POP server relieves **sendmail** of the chore of chasing down users and obsoletes some of the tables discussed below.

Two database libraries are supported: the **dbm/ndbm** library that is standard with most versions of UNIX, and Berkeley DB, a more extensible library that supports multiple storage schemes. Your choice of database libraries must be specified at compile time. We recommend DB if you can install it; it's faster than **dbm** and creates smaller files.

Three database map types are available:

* dbm   – uses an extensible hashing algorithm (**dbm/ndbm**)
* hash  – uses a standard hashing scheme (DB)
* btree – uses a B-tree data structure (DB)

For most table applications in **sendmail**, the hash database type—the default—is the best. Use the **makemap** command to build the database file from a text file; you specify the database type and the output file base name. The text version of the database should appear on **makemap**'s standard input, for example:

```
# makemap hash /etc/mail/access < /etc/mail/access
```

At first glance this command looks like a mistake that would cause the input file to be overwritten by an empty output file. However, **makemap** tacks on an appropriate suffix, so the actual output file is **/etc/mail/access.db** and in fact there is no conflict. Each time the text file is changed, the database file must be rebuilt with **makemap** (but **sendmail** need not be HUPed).

The longest possible match is used for database keys, so the order of entries in the input text file is not significant. FEATUREs that expect a database file as a parameter default to hash as the database type and **/etc/mail/**tablename**.db** as the filename for the database. To override this behavior, either specify the desired type to both the **makemap** command and the FEATURE or reset the default by defining a different value for the variable DATABASE_MAP_TYPE, for example:

```
define(`DATABASE_MAP_TYPE', `dbm')
```

To use your new **access.db** database, you'd add the following line to your **.mc** file:

```
FEATURE(`access_db', `hash /etc/mail/access')
```

Since this line uses the default type and naming scheme, you could just write

```
FEATURE(`access_db')
```

You can specify the database filename either with or without the suffix (**.db**); without is preferred.

Don't forget to rebuild the database file with **makemap** every time you change the text file, or your changes will not take effect.

We cover the mailertable, genericstable, and virtusertable FEATUREs in the next few sections. The access_db is covered later in the spam section. The user_db is not covered at all, since it is not in widespread use today.

### The mailertable feature

The mailertable feature redirects mail addressed to a particular host or domain to an alternate destination via a particular mailer. It is applied as the mail goes out from a site. It only looks at the host portion of the address, not the user portion. The envelope address is not rewritten, so the mail continues to be addressed to the same user but is sent to a different host via a different mailer. mailertable was originally designed to deal with other mail systems such as UUCP, DECnet, and BITNET, but since these systems are no longer in common use, many sites no longer need constructs like mailertable.

An entry in the mailertable has the form:

```
old_domain        mailer:user@new_domain
```

A leading dot in front of the key on the left side is a wild card that means any host in that domain. Only host and domain names are allowed as mailertable keys; usernames are not allowed. The *user@new_domain* value on the right side can be null, in which case the mail headers are not changed. The *mailer* value must be the name of a mailer defined in a MAILER clause; see page 576.

To use a mailertable, include the following line in your **.mc** file.

```
FEATURE(`mailertable')
```

### The genericstable feature

The genericstable feature ("generics table," not "generic stable") is like aliasing for outgoing mail. For example, it can map trent@xor.com to trent.hein@xor.com on outbound mail. It is the headers that are rewritten, not the envelope. Mail delivery is not affected, only replies.

Several mechanisms can be used to map hostnames, but the genericstable is the only one that includes both the username and the hostname in the mapping key. The masquerade_envelope and allmasquerade features discussed later in this section can also apply to addresses in the genericstable.

To use the genericstable, ensure your domain is in the generics class. To put a domain in the generics class, you can either list it in the GENERICS_DOMAIN macro or put it in the file specified by the GENERICS_DOMAIN_FILE macro.

For example, to use the genericstable with the defaults for the database, add

```
GENERICS_DOMAIN_FILE(`/etc/mail/local-host-names')
FEATURE(`genericstable')
```

to your **.mc** configuration file. In this example, any host you accept mail for is included. Enabling the genericstable feature slows down **sendmail** slightly because every sender address must be looked up.

### The virtusertable feature

The virtual user table supports domain aliasing for incoming mail. This feature allows multiple virtual domains to be hosted on one machine and is very common at web hosting sites.

The key field of the table contains either an email addresses (*user@host.domain*) or a domain specification (*@domain*). The value field is a local email address, an external email address, or a *mailer:address* specification. If the key is a domain, the value can either pass the user field along as the variable %1 or route the mail to a different user. Additional information is passed along as %2.

Let's look at some examples (we have added the comments):

```
info@foo.com    foo-info                # route to a local user
info@bar.com    bar-info                # another local user
joe@bar.com     error:No such user      # to return an error
@baz.org        jane@elsewhere.com      # all mail to jane
@baz.org        %1@elsewhere.com        # to the same user
```

All the host keys on the left side of the data mappings must be in the **cw** file (or the new VirtHost class); otherwise, **sendmail** tries to find the host on the Internet and to deliver the mail there. If DNS points **sendmail** back to this server, you get a "local configuration error" message in bounces. Unfortunately, **sendmail** cannot tell that the error message for this instance should be "virtusertable key not in cw file."

Several pieces are actually involved here:

- DNS MX records must exist so that mail is routed to the right host in the first place, then

- **cw** entries must be present or VIRTUSER_DOMAIN specified (or equivalently, VIRTUSER_DOMAIN_FILE) to allow the local machine to accept the mail, and finally

- the virtual user table must tell **sendmail** what to do with the mail.

The feature is invoked with:

```
FEATURE(`virtusertable')
```

The examples starting on page 588 use virtusertable to implement virtual hosting.

### The ldap_routing feature

As a final chunk floating in this cesspool of aliasing, rewriting, and falsification, we have LDAP, the Lightweight Directory Access Protocol. LDAP (see page 560 for general information) can be used as a substitute for the virtusertable with respect to routing email and accepting mail for virtual domains. It can also manage aliases, except for mailing lists.

To use LDAP in this way, you must include several statements in your config file, and you must have built **sendmail** to include LDAP support. In your **.mc** file you need the lines

```
FEATURE(`ldap_routing')
LDAPROUTE_DOMAIN(`my_domain')
define(`confLDAP_DEFAULT_SPEC', `-h server -b searchbase')
```

to tell **sendmail** that you want to use an LDAP database for routing incoming mail addressed to the specified domain. The LDAP_DEFAULT_SPEC option identifies the LDAP server and database search base name.

In the following example, the search base is o=sendmail.com, c=US. If you run LDAP on a different port (not 389), add -p ldap_port# to the LDAP_DEFAULT_SPEC.

**sendmail** uses the values of two tags in the LDAP database:

- mailLocalAddress for the addressee on incoming mail
- mailRoutingAddress for the alias to send it to

**sendmail** also supports the tag mailHost, which if present routes mail to the highest-priority MX record for the specified host with the mailRoutingAddress as recipient.

For example, the LDAP entry (for a server configured with a root distinguished name of cn=root, o=sendmail.com, c=US)

```
dn: uid=eric, o=sendmail.com, c=US
objectClass: inetLocalMailRecipient
mailLocalAddress: eric@sendmail.org
mailRoutingAddress: eric@eng.sendmail.com
```

would cause mail addressed to eric@sendmail.org (which DNS MX records caused to be delivered to sendmail.com) to be sent to eric@eng.sendmail.com. If the entry also contained the line

```
mailHost: mailserver.sendmail.com
```

then mail to eric@sendmail.org would be addressed to eric@eng.sendmail.com and sent to the host with the best MX record for mailserver.

LDAP database entries support a wild card entry, *@domain*, that reroutes mail addressed to anyone at the specified domain (as was done in the virtusertable).

### Masquerading and the MASQUERADE_AS macro

The MASQUERADE_AS macro allows you to specify a single identity that other machines hide behind. All mail appears to emanate from the designated machine or domain. The sender's address is rewritten to be *user@masquerading-name* instead of *user@original-host.domain*. Of course, those masqueraded addresses must be valid so that people can reply to the mail.

This configuration permits all users at a site to use a generic email address. For example, if all hosts at xor.com masquerade behind the domain xor.com, then mail from *user@host*.xor.com will be stamped as being from *user@*xor.com with no mention of the actual hostname from which the user sent the mail. The machine that represents xor.com must know how to deliver all users' mail, even mail for users that do not have a login on the incoming mail server. Naturally, login names must be unique across the whole domain.

Some users and addresses (such as root, postmaster, hostmaster, trouble, operations, Mailer-Daemon, etc.) should be exempted from this behavior. They can be explicitly excluded with the EXPOSED_USER macro. For example, the sequence

```
MASQUERADE_AS(`xor.com')
EXPOSED_USER(`root')
EXPOSED_USER(`Mailer-Daemon')
```

would stamp mail as coming from user@xor.com unless it was sent by root or the mail system; in these cases, the mail would carry the name of the originating host.

There are several extensions to the basic MASQUERADE_AS macro, both through other macros and through FEATUREs:

- The MASQUERADE_DOMAIN macro
- The MASQUERADE_DOMAIN_FILE macro

- The MASQUERADE_EXCEPTION macro
- The limited_masquerade FEATURE
- The allmasquerade FEATURE
- The masquerade_envelope FEATURE
- The masquerade_entire_domain FEATURE

We recommend using the MASQUERADE_AS macro described above along with the allmasquerade and masquerade_envelope features. The limited_masquerade feature modifies the behavior of MASQUERADE_DOMAIN and is useful for virtual hosting environments. MASQUERADE_DOMAIN lets you list domains that you want to masquerade; the list is preloaded from the w class that is typically defined with the use_cw_file feature and lists the hosts in your domain. limited_masquerade does not preinitialize the list with class w. All those domains will be hidden by the domain you are masquerading as.

The allmasquerade feature extends masquerading to the recipients of the message (as opposed to just the sender), and the masquerade_envelope feature extends it to the envelope as well as to the header addresses.[22] With these two extensions, all addresses are hidden in a consistent fashion. The limited_masquerade feature extends masquerading to a specified list of other domains.

If you want to use other masquerading techniques, you can read about their behavior in the **cf/README** file or in the **sendmail** book. Read carefully; some of the masquerading primitives can hide too much.

### The MAIL_HUB and SMART_HOST macros

Masquerading makes all mail appear to come from a single host or domain by rewriting the headers and, optionally, the envelope. Some sites may want all mail to really come from (or go to) a single machine. You can achieve this configuration with the macros MAIL_HUB for incoming mail and SMART_HOST for outgoing mail.

If you want to route all incoming mail to a central server for delivery, set MAIL_HUB to the value *mailer:host*, where *mailer* is the agent to use to reach the designated *host*. If no delivery agent is specified, relay is used. For example:

```
define(`MAIL_HUB', `smtp:mailhub.cs.colorado.edu')
```

The SMART_HOST designation causes a host to deliver local mail but to punt external mail to SMART_HOST. This feature is useful for machines behind a firewall that cannot use DNS directly. Its syntax parallels that of MAIL_HUB; the default delivery agent is again relay. For example:

```
define(`SMART_HOST', `smtp:mailhub.cs.colorado.edu')
```

---

22. The header addresses are the To, From, Cc, and Bcc addresses that appear in the header of a message. The envelope addresses are the addresses to which the mail is actually delivered. The envelope addresses are originally built from the header addresses by the user agent, but they are processed separately by **sendmail**. Many of **sendmail**'s masquerading and redirection features would be impossible to implement if the distinction between header and envelope addresses was not maintained.

In these examples, the same machine acts as the server for both incoming and outgoing mail. A larger site might split these into separate machines.

### Masquerading and routing

With all these features and macros ready and waiting to massage your email addresses, we thought it might be nice to try to compare the various mechanisms in terms of whether they change the headers, the envelope, or the delivery of a message, whether they apply to incoming or outgoing messages, sender or recipient addresses, etc. If the page were double or triple width, we might have succeeded in really illustrating the differences among the various constructs.

Instead, we give you just a hint; you will have to look up the details in the **sendmail** documentation to get all the nuances of the different variations.

Entries in Table 19.12 that are all capital letters are **m4** macros; lowercase entries are the names of features that are invoked with the FEATURE macro. Indented items depend on the items above; for example, a feature that modifies the MASQUERADE_AS behavior does nothing unless MASQUERADE_AS has been turned on. In the table, the feature would be indented to indicate this dependency. Masquerading affects the header addresses on outgoing mail and whether a message can be replied to; routing affects the actual delivery of the mail.

**Table 19.12  Comparison of masquerading and routing features**

| | Construct | Dir | Affects[a] | Which piece |
|---|---|---|---|---|
| Masquerading | MASQUERADE_AS | out | SH | host.domain |
| | allmasquerade | out | RH | host.domain |
| | MASQUERADE_DOMAIN[_FILE] | out | SH | host.domain |
| | masquerade_entire_domain | out | SH | host.sub.domain |
| | limited_masquerade | out | SH | host.domain |
| | masquerade_envelope | out | SE[b] | host.domain |
| | genericstable | out | SH | user@host.domain |
| Routing | mailertable | out | MAD | host.domain |
| | virtusertable | in | RD | user@host.domain |
| | ldap | in | RD | user@host.domain |
| | mailhub | in | RD | host.domain |
| | smarthost | out | RD | host.domain |

a. S = sender, R = recipient, D = delivery, H = header, E = envelope, M = mailer, A = address
b. Once envelope rewriting has been enabled with the masquerade_envelope feature, all other masquerading constructs rewrite not only the header but the envelope as well.

### The nullclient feature

This feature is used for a host that should never receive mail directly and that sends all its outgoing mail to a central server. The **.mc** file for such a host has only two lines.

```
OSTYPE(`ostype')
FEATURE(`nullclient', `mail_server')
```

The nullclient feature overrides many other features. All mail, without exception, is delivered to *mail_server* for processing.[23] Note that the server must allow the client to relay through it if users regularly originate mail on the client and don't use a separate server for outgoing mail. Recent versions of **sendmail** have relaying turned off by default. See the spam section (page 595) for details on how to control relaying. A nullclient configuration masquerades as *mail_server*, so you might want to include an EXPOSED_USER clause for root.

The client that uses the nullclient feature must have an associated MX record that points to the server. It must also be included in the server's **cw** file, which is usually **/etc/mail/local-host-names**. These settings let the server accept mail for the client.

A host with a nullclient configuration should not accept incoming mail. If it did, it would just forward the mail to the server anyway. Start **sendmail** without the **-bd** flag so that it doesn't listen for SMTP connections on port 25. Leave the **-q30m** flag on the command line so that if *mail_server* goes down, the client can queue outgoing mail and try to send it to *mail_server* later.

nullclient is appropriate for leaf nodes at sites that have a central mail machine. At larger sites, consider the mail load on the hub machine. You may want to separate the incoming and outgoing servers or adopt a hierarchical approach.

### The local_lmtp and smrsh features

**/bin/mail** is getting pretty tired as UNIX's local mailer. If the local_lmtp feature is specified, then its argument is a local mailer capable of speaking LMTP, the Local Mail Transport Protocol (see RFC2033). The default is **mail.local** in the **sendmail** distribution, which is usually installed in **/usr/libexec/mail.local**. Actually, you can specify the installation directory with the confEBINDIR option.

**smrsh** is a restricted shell provided with the **sendmail** distribution as a replacement for the traditional program mailer, **/bin/sh**. It improves the ability of the local system administrator to control what commands can be run by email. Only programs that are in the **smrsh** binaries directory, **/usr/adm/sm.bin** (configurable when **smrsh** is being compiled), can be run. **smrsh** also checks for suspicious characters (such as output redirection symbols) in a command and aborts the delivery if any are found.

We recommend that you install both **smrsh** and **mail.local** and that you turn on the features that use them:

```
FEATURE(`local_lmtp', `/usr/libexec/mail.local')
FEATURE(`smrsh', `/usr/libexec/smrsh')
```

See page 610 for a more detailed discussion of **smrsh**.

---

23. If you configure a client this way and then test the configuration with **sendmail -bt**, the client will appear to locally deliver local mail. The reason is that the nullclient directive is processed later, in ruleset 5 of the raw config file.

### The local_procmail feature

You can use Stephen van den Berg's **procmail** as your local mailer by enabling the local_procmail feature. It takes a single argument: the path to the **procmail** binary.

**procmail** can do fancier things for the user than plain **/bin/mail** or **mail.local**. In addition to delivering mail to users' mailboxes, it can sort messages into folders, save them in files, run programs, and filter spam. **procmail** is not distributed with **sendmail**; get it from www.procmail.org if it is not installed by your vendor. You can also use other mail processing programs with this feature just by lying to **sendmail** and saying that you are just showing it the local copy of **procmail**:

```
FEATURE(`local_procmail', `/usr/local/bin/mymailer')
```

### The LOCAL_* macros

If you really need to get your hands dirty and write some exotic new rules to deal with special local situations, you use a set of macros prefaced by LOCAL_. The section on spam, later in this chapter, has some examples of this low-level construct.

### Configuration options

Config file options and macros (the O and D commands in the raw config language) can be set with the define **m4** command. A complete list of options accessible as **m4** variables and their default values is given in the **cf/README** file. The default values are OK for most sites.

Some examples:

```
define(`confTO_QUEUERETURN', `7d')
define(`confTO_QUEUEWARN', `4h')
define(`confPRIVACY_FLAGS', `noexpn')
```

The queue return option determines how long a message will remain in the mail queue if it cannot be delivered. The queue warn option determines how long it will sit before the sender is notified that there might problems with delivery. The first two lines set these to 7 days and 4 hours, respectively.

*See page 610 for more information about privacy options.* The next line sets the privacy flags to disallow the SMTP EXPN (expand address) command. The confPRIVACY_FLAGS option takes a comma-separated list of values. Some versions of **m4** require two sets of quotes to protect the commas:

```
define(`confPRIVACY_FLAGS', ``noexpn, novrfy'')
```

The default values for most options are about right for a typical small to medium-sized site that is not too paranoid about security or too concerned with performance. With the defaults, you may become a spam target; you must adjust several options to be a good citizen relative to spam. If your mail hub machine is very busy and services lots of mailing lists, you may need to tweak some of the performance values.

Table 19.13 lists some options that you might need to adjust (about 15% of the almost 150 configuration options), along with their default values. To save space, the option names are shown without their conf prefix; for example, the FALLBACK_MX option is really named confFALLBACK_MX. We divided the table into subsections that identify the kind of issue the variable addresses: generic, resources, performance, security and spam abatement, and miscellaneous. Some options clearly fit in more than one category, but we listed them only once.

Use the HOST_STATUS_DIRECTORY option when a busy host has to handle lots of failed mail deliveries. This option directs **sendmail** to keep a file for each host to which delivery has failed in the status directory and causes **sendmail** to use that status information to prioritize the hosts when the queue is run again. This status information effectively implements negative caching and allows information to be shared across queue runs. It's a big performance win on busy servers. Here is an example that uses the directory **/etc/mail/.hoststat** (create the directory first):

```
define(`confHOST_STATUS_DIRECTORY', `.hoststat')
```

The FALLBACK_MX option is also a performance win. It forwards all undeliverable mail to a local server that can handle the bogons, freeing the regular mail server to deliver the mail with good addresses. This feature is very useful for a site with large mailing lists that invariably contain addresses that are temporarily or permanently undeliverable. For example,

```
define(`confFALLBACK_MX', `mailbackup.xor.com')
```

would forward all messages that fail on their first delivery attempt to the central server mailbackup.xor.com for further processing.

Some daemon options that affect performance are invoked with a slightly different syntax. For example, to make **sendmail** act as both an MSA (mail submission agent) and an MTA (mail transport agent), use

```
DAEMON_OPTIONS(`Port=25,Name=MTA')
DAEMON_OPTIONS(`Port=587,Name=MSA,M=E')
```

This is the default configuration starting with version 8.10.

## 19.9  CONFIGURATION FILE EXAMPLES

We haven't really finished with all the configuration options (a spam section and a security section are coming up), but it's time to look at some example configuration files. This order may be a bit like putting the cart before the horse, but it seems to work the best of the arrangements that we've tried. The essential configuration feature that we have not yet covered is the access database, which is used primarily to filter and control spam. It's covered starting on page 599.

In documenting the config files in use at various sites, we invariably run into some cruft left over from bygone days that is either wrong or not needed. We have cleaned up these inconsistencies, spelling errors, etc., before using the config files as examples, so they are not shown here exactly as they appeared on the original servers. Nevertheless, they reflect real-world configurations.

**Table 19.13    Basic configuration options**

| | Option name | Description and (default value) |
|---|---|---|
| **Generic** | CW_FILE | Hosts you accept mail for and treat as local (**/etc/mail/local-host-names**) |
| | COPY_ERRORS_TO | Addresses to Cc on error messages (none) |
| | DOUBLE_BOUNCE_ADDRESS | Catches a lot of spam; some sites use **/dev/null**, but that can hide serious problems (postmaster) |
| **Resources** | MIN_FREE_BLOCKS | Minimum filesystem space to accept mail (100) |
| | MAX_MESSAGE_SIZE | Max size in bytes of a single message (infinite) |
| | TO_*lots_o_stuff* | Timeouts for all kinds of things (various) |
| | TO_IDENT | Timeout for ident queries to check sender's identity; if 0, ident checks are not done (5s) |
| | MAX_DAEMON_CHILDREN | Max number of child processes[a] (no limit) |
| **Performance** | MCI_CACHE_SIZE | Number of open TCP connections cached (2) |
| | MCI_CACHE_TIMEOUT | Time to keep cached connections open (5m) |
| | HOST_STATUS_DIRECTORY | See the explanation in the text (no default) |
| | FALLBACK_MX | Local host to forward delivery failures to; centralizes difficult deliveries (no default) |
| | QUEUE_LA | Load average at which mail should be queued instead of delivered immediately (8 * #CPUs) |
| | REFUSE_LA | Load avg. at which to refuse mail (12 * #CPUs) |
| | MIN_QUEUE_AGE | Minimum time jobs must stay in queue; makes a busy machine handle the queue better (0) |
| | DONT_INIT_GROUPS | Turn on if your mail server has a large group file managed by NIS (false) |
| **Security/spam** | TRUSTED_USERS | For mailing list software owners; allows forging of the From line (root, daemon) |
| | PRIVACY_FLAGS | Limits info given out by SMTP (authwarnings) |
| | MAX_HEADERS_LENGTH | Max size (bytes) of a mail header; can prevent user agent buffer overflow attacks (no limit) |
| | MAX_MIME_HEADER_LENGTH | Also protects against UA overflows (no limit) |
| | CONNECTION_RATE_THROTTLE | Slows DOS attacks by limiting the rate at which mail connections are accepted (no limit) |
| | MAX_RCPTS_PER_MESSAGE | Slows spam delivery; defers extra recipients and sends a temporary error msg (infinite) |
| | DONT_BLAME_SENDMAIL | Overrides **sendmail**'s security and file checking; don't change casually! (safe) |
| | AUTH_MECHANISMS | List of SMTP authentication mechanisms for the Cyrus SASL library (empty) |
| | DEF_AUTH_INFO | File with auth info for outgoing mail (undefined) |
| **Misc** | LDAP_DEFAULT_SPEC | Map spec for LDAP database, including the host and port the server is running on (undefined) |

a. More specifically, the maximum number of child processes that can run at once. When the limit is reached, **sendmail** refuses connections. This option can prevent (or create) denial of service (DOS) attacks.

### A computer science student's home machine

Our first example is a student, Rob Braun, who has a Linux box (gw.synack.net) at home and does virtual hosting for a few friends' domains: xinetd.org, teich.net, and cubecast.com.

He also hosts his own domain, synack.net. Rob maps all incoming mail to the correct person with LDAP. He uses the virtusertable to handle the virtual hosting mappings, and the genericstable to handle outgoing mail. Of the many table types that affect outgoing mail, genericstable is the only one that can rewrite the username as well as the destination host.

Rob's genericstable file (which he actually calls **outmap**) contains:

```
bbraun        rob@synack.net
stabilej      jon@synack.net
teich         oren@teich.net
```

Rob uses the DNS Realtime Blackhole List (dnsbl) for spam control. He also uses masquerading features to stamp any outgoing mail that is not already rewritten by the genericstable as coming from user@synack.net instead of user@gw.synack.net. Here is the complete **gw.mc** file:

```
divert(0)
VERSIONID(`@(#)synack.net.mc 8.7 (Berkeley)5/19/1998')
OSTYPE(linux)
DOMAIN(generic)
FEATURE(dnsbl)
FEATURE(virtusertable, `/etc/mail/inmap')
FEATURE(genericstable, `/etc/mail/outmap')
GENERICS_DOMAIN_FILE(`/etc/mail/local-host-names')
MASQUERADE_AS(synack.net)
FEATURE(`masquerade_envelope')
FEATURE(`ldap_routing')
LDAPROUTE_DOMAIN(`synack.net')
define(`confLDAP_DEFAULT_SPEC', `-h gw.synack.net -b dc=synack,dc=net')
MAILER(local)
MAILER(smtp)
```

The **/etc/mail/local-host-names** file contains the hosts and domains for which this host accepts mail (it used to be called **sendmail.cw**). The use_cw_file feature that would invoke it is hidden in the generic domain file; see page 594 for a listing of its contents. Relaying is turned off by default because the file **/etc/mail/relay-domains** is normally empty. Here, that file contains the domains that are virtually hosted by gw.synack.net. The LDAP database is configured with an **ldap.conf** file that sets the LDAP root distinguished name, server host, and port:

```
BASE dc=synack, dc=net
HOST gw.synack.net
PORT 389
```

The LDAP database is then built from a text file with entries such as:

```
dn: uid=rob, dc=synack, dc=net
objectClass: inetLocalMailRecipient
mailLocalAddress: rob@synack.net
mailRoutingAddress: bbraun@synack.net
uid:rob

dn: uid=webmaster, dc=synack, dc=net
objectClass: inetLocalMailRecipient
mailLocalAddress: webmaster@synack.net
mailRoutingAddress: bbraun@synack.net
uid:webmaster

dn: uid=teich, dc=synack, dc=net
objectClass: inetLocalMailRecipient
mailLocalAddress: teich@synack.net
mailRoutingAddress: oren@teich.net
uid:teich

dn: uid=xinetd, dc=synack, dc=net
objectClass: inetLocalMailRecipient
mailLocalAddress: xinetd@synack.net
mailRoutingAddress: xinetd
uid:xinetd
```

The first three entries map the login names rob, webmaster, and oren to their aliases. The fourth is a mailing list that maps to a local alias and is handled from there by Majordomo by means of these entries in the **/etc/mail/aliases** file:

```
xinetd: "|/usr/local/majordomo/wrapper resend -l test xinetd-list"
xinetd-list: :include:/usr/local/majordomo/lists/xinetd
xinetd-owner: bbraun
owner-xinetd: bbraun
xinetd-request: bbraun
xinetd-approval: bbraun
```

We have shown several supporting files and sample contents for this example. Our next examples keep closer to the point of illustrating how **sendmail** configuration works and do not show peripheral files.

Keep in mind that in any **sendmail** example, DNS MX records play a crucial role and need to agree with the assumptions made by your configuration.

### A small but sendmail-clueful company

As our next example, we look at the config files for a small but very **sendmail**-savvy company, Sendmail, Inc. Their mail design includes a master mail host that serves as both the mail hub for incoming mail and the smart host for outgoing mail. We look at the clients' configuration first, then inspect the more complicated master machine.

In all of the examples, we have modified the originals slightly, leaving out the copyright notices, adding occasional comments, and removing the **m4** dnl directive at the ends of lines. If you use any of our examples as a model for your **.mc** file, be sure to remove the comments from the ends of lines.

### Client machines at sendmail.com

The **smi-client.mc** file for client machines is quite simple. It uses the master machine smtp.sendmail.com, which is really just an alias (a DNS CNAME) to the machine katroo.sendmail.com. Using a CNAME is a good idea; it's easy to change when you want to move your master mail machine.

Note that the date on this file is October 1998. **sendmail** has been upgraded many times since then, but the configuration file did not need to change.

```
divert(-1)
#####  This file contains definitions for a Sendmail,
#####  Inc. client machine's version 8.9.3 .mc file.
divert(0)
VERSIONID(`@(#)smi-client.mc 1.0 (Sendmail) 10/14/98')
OSTYPE(`bsd4.4')
FEATURE(`nocanonify')
undefine(`ALIAS_FILE')
define(`MAIL_HUB', `smtp.sendmail.com')
define(`SMART_HOST', `smtp.sendmail.com')
define(`confFORWARD_PATH', `')
MAILER(`local')
MAILER(`smtp')
```

The MAIL_HUB and SMART_HOST lines direct incoming and outgoing mail to the host smtp.sendmail.com. MX records in DNS should cooperate and list that host with higher priority (lower number in MX record) than the individual client machines. The path for **.forward** files is set to null, and the alias file is also set to null; all alias expansion occurs on the master machine. The nocanonify feature is specified here to save time, since DNS lookups are done on the master anyway.

### Master machine at sendmail.com

The master machine at sendmail.com may be one of the most attacked **sendmail** installations around. It must deal with spam as best it can, be secure to all the twisty mailer attacks that people come up with, and protect the machines behind it. Here is its configuration file:

```
divert(-1)
#####  smi-master, katroo.mc, version 8.9.3
divert(0)
VERSIONID(`@(#)katroo.mc     2.1 (sendmail) 10/19/98')
OSTYPE(`solaris2')
DOMAIN(`generic')
MASQUERADE_AS(`sendmail.com')
MASQUERADE_DOMAIN(`sendmail.com')
undefine(`BITNET_RELAY')
undefine(`UUCP_RELAY')
define(`confCHECK_ALIASES', `True')
```

```
define(`confCOPY_ERRORS_TO', `Postmaster')
define(`confEBINDIR', `/usr/lib')
define(`confERROR_MODE', `m')
define(`confHOST_STATUS_DIRECTORY', `.hoststat')
define(`confNO_RCPT_ACTION', `add-to-undisclosed')
define(`confPRIVACY_FLAGS', `authwarnings,needmailhelo,noexpn,novrfy')
define(`confTRUSTED_USERS', `majordomo')
define(`confMAX_DAEMON_CHILDREN', `30')
FEATURE(`allmasquerade')
FEATURE(`masquerade_entire_domain')
FEATURE(`masquerade_envelope')
FEATURE(`always_add_domain')
FEATURE(`local_lmtp')
define(`LOCAL_MAILER_FLAGS', `SXfmnz9PE')
FEATURE(`mailertable', `hash /etc/mail/mailertable')
FEATURE(`virtusertable', `hash /etc/mail/virtusertable')
MAILER(`local')
MAILER(`smtp')

LOCAL_CONFIG
`######  Regular expression to reject:'
`#     * numeric-only localparts from aol.com and msn.com'
`#     * localparts starting with a digit from juno.com'
Kcheckaddress regex -a@MATCH
   ^([0-9]+<@(aol|msn)\.com|[0-9][^<]*<@juno\.com)\.?>
`######  Names that won't be allowed in a To: line'
C{RejectToLocalparts}      friend you
C{RejectToDomains}            public.com

LOCAL_RULESETS
HTo: $>CheckTo
SCheckTo
R$={RejectToLocalparts}@$*  $#error $: "553 Header error"
R$*@$={RejectToDomains}   $#error $: "553 Header error"

HMessage-Id: $>CheckMessageId
SCheckMessageId
R< $+ @ $+ >     $@ OK
R$*              $#error $: "553 Header error"

LOCAL_RULESETS
SLocal_check_mail
`# check address against various regex checks'
R$*              $: $>Parse0 $>3 $1
R$+              $: $(checkaddress $1 $)
R@MATCH          $#error $: "553 Header error"
```

The LOCAL_CONFIG rules at the end of the config file do header checking for various viruses and known spammers. We have left this section in, without describing it in detail, for those of you who grew up on the raw config file and can easily read it and adapt it to your own site.

Clients have no spam control in their config files because all mail coming into the site comes through the mail hub and the spam is winnowed there. Some of the features and other constructs in this example are not covered in our configuration section, but you can find documentation on them in the **cf/README** file.

The **generic.m4** domain file referenced by **katroo.mc** is distributed with **sendmail** as an example and contains the following lines:

```
divert(-1)
`######## generic.m4 from domain directory'
divert(0)
VERSIONID(`$Id: generic.m4,v 8.15 1999/04/04 00:51:09 ca Exp $')
define(`confFORWARD_PATH', `$z/.forward.$w+$h:$z/.forward+$h:
     $z/.forward.$w:$z/.forward')
define(`confMAX_HEADERS_LENGTH', `32768')
FEATURE(`redirect')
FEATURE(`use_cw_file')
EXPOSED_USER(`root')
```

The confFORWARD_PATH line above was wrapped to fit the page; it's a single line.

### Another master/client example

XOR Inc. is a medium-sized company with a single master mail machine. Although XOR's overall mail design is similar to that of sendmail.com, it's implemented with slightly different configuration primitives.

Here is the client configuration:

```
divert(-1)
##### xor-client.mc, all clients to relay to xor.com
divert(0)
VERSIONID(`@(#)tcpproto.mc8.5 (Berkeley) 3/23/96')
OSTYPE(`bsdi')
define(`confPRIVACY_FLAGS', `noexpn')
FEATURE(`nullclient', `xor.com')
```

This configuration is pretty minimal. Even local mail is forwarded to xor.com, the machine specified in the nullclient feature. No mailers are specified.

Below is the master configuration that goes with this client setup. XOR does a lot of web hosting and accepts and manages mail for many virtual domains. Our first example, the student machine, managed three virtual domains with LDAP and the genericstable. XOR manages about 1,000 virtual domains with the virtusertable. It uses the genericstable for mapping login names to *first.last* for outgoing mail. It implements aliases with the standard **aliases** file, which is 3,000 lines long and contains many mailing lists, some with several thousand recipients (and one with over 100,000). All this on a slightly tired, old SunOS sun4m box.

The aliases file should really be cleaned up, and client aliases separated from employee aliases. All the employee aliases point to an IMAP server, and users use IMAP to access their mail.

Note that the divert statements and comments that are usually present at the beginning of a **.mc** file are missing. They are only necessary if you use shell-style (#) comments at the beginning of your config file.

This site is running sendmail 8.9.3 and uses some of the old (pre-8.10) constructs for configuration lines. Its mail load has caused many of the performance parameters to be set quite a bit higher than their default values.

```
VERSIONID(`@(#)xor.mc3.0 (trent) 3/29/99')
OSTYPE(`sunos4.1')

define(`confPRIVACY_FLAGS', `noexpn,novrfy')
define(`confMESSAGE_TIMEOUT',`5d/72h')
define(`LOCAL_MAILER_PATH', `/usr/bin/mail.local')

dnl ##### increase values for performance and heavy load
define(`confMCI_CACHE_SIZE', `16')
define(`confMCI_CACHE_TIMEOUT', `10m')
define(`confCHECK_ALIASES', `False')
define(`confDOMAIN_NAME', `xor.com')
define(`confMAX_MESSAGE_SIZE', `5000000')
define(`confDAEMON_OPTIONS',`Port=NNN')
define(`confQUEUE_LA', 25)
define(`confREFUSE_LA', 30)

FEATURE(always_add_domain)
FEATURE(use_cw_file)
FEATURE(virtusertable)
GENERICS_DOMAIN(`xor.com')
FEATURE(genericstable)
FEATURE(`masquerade_envelope')
FEATURE(`redirect')
FEATURE(`access_db', `hash -o /etc/mail/access')

MAILER(local)
MAILER(smtp)

LOCAL_RULESETS
###### Spam and virus checking rules removed; see page 593
```

As you can see from the diversity of these examples, there is no single right way to set up your configuration file. **sendmail** contains many constructs for routing mail and munging headers. To some degree, the ones you choose depend on personal preference or on whatever the person from whom you copied the file did.

## 19.10  SPAM-RELATED FEATURES IN SENDMAIL

Spam is the jargon word for junk mail, also known as unsolicited commercial email. It has become a serious problem, primarily because the sender (at least in the United States) does not pay by the byte, but rather pays a flat rate for connectivity. Or if they do pay per byte, they send a single message with many thousands of recipients and relay it through another machine. The other machine pays the big per-byte cost and the spammer only pays for one copy. In many countries, end users pay per byte received and get pretty angry at having to pay to receive spam.

Spam seems to be primarily a U.S. problem. The U.S. marketing culture has found a gold mine and continues to exploit it.

ISPs in the United States are starting to feel the effects of spam as their support lines have to deal with more and more instances of spam abuse originating from their customers. One ISP in Colorado with about 150 downstream T1 customers (many of them ISPs) needs a half-time person just to deal with spam complaints.

From the marketing folks' point of view, spam works well. Response rates are high, costs are low, and delivery is instantaneous. A list of 30 million email addresses only costs about $40.

Many spammers try to appear innocent by suggesting that you answer their email with a message that says "remove" if you want to be removed from their mailing list. Although they may remove you, you have just verified for them that they have a valid, current email address; this fact can land you on other lists. Spammers also like to mess with their mail headers in an attempt to disguise who the mail is from and on which machine it originated.

Folks that sell email addresses to spammers have recently started to use a form of dictionary attack to ferret out unknown addresses. Starting with a list of common last names, the scanning software adds different first initials in hopes of hitting on a valid email address. To check the addresses, the software connects to the mail servers at, say, 50 large ISPs and does a VRFY on each of zillions of addresses.

This probing has a huge impact on your mail server and its ability to deliver your customers' legitimate mail. **sendmail** can deal with this situation through the use of the PrivacyOption goaway which is covered starting on page 610. But the smarter spam software is very robust; if VRFY is blocked, they try EXPN, and if both are blocked they try RCPT. They can try millions of addresses that way and never send a single message—it sure keeps your mail server busy, though.

**sendmail** has added some very nice features to help with spam control and also to help with the occasional mail-borne computer virus. Unfortunately, most ISPs must pass along all mail, so these features may be too draconian for customer policy (or then again, maybe they aren't). However, the features can be used to great effect at the end user's site.

There are four types of spam control features:

- Rules that control relaying, which is the use of your mail server by one off-site user to send mail to another off-site user. Spammers often use relaying in an attempt to mask the true source of their mail and therefore avoid detection by their ISPs. It also lets them use *your* cycles and save their own. That's the killer.

- The access database, which allows mail to be filtered by address, rather like a firewall for email.

- Blacklists containing open relays and known spam-friendly sites that **sendmail** can check against.

- Header checking, the beginnings of a powerful feature that we may see in **sendmail** version 9. It allows arbitrary scanning of messages and lets you reject any messages that match a particular profile.

We describe these new features here and then look at a couple of pieces of spam we received today to see how we might have tuned our mail system to recognize and reject them automatically.

### Relaying

**sendmail** and other mail transport agents accept incoming mail, look at the headers and envelope addresses, decide where the mail should go, and then pass it along to an appropriate destination. That destination can be local, or it can be another transport agent further along in the delivery chain. When an incoming message has no local recipients, the transport agent that handles it is said to be acting as a relay.

Prior to **sendmail** version 8.9, promiscuous relaying (also called open relaying) was on by default. **sendmail** would accept any message presented to it on port 25 and try its best to make the delivery. It was the neighborly Internet thing to do.

Unfortunately, spammers started to abuse relaying; they exploited it to disguise their identities and, more importantly, to use your bandwidth and cycles instead of their own. It is now considered very bad to configure your mail server as an open relay.

It makes sense to worry about not only your own relaying policy, but also that of other sites. After all, any mail you receive from an open relay is probably spam. Paul Vixie, an avid spam-hater, and the Open Relay Behavior-modification System (ORBS) project have both collected databases of IP addresses that run open relays. **sendmail** can easily be configured to use those databases as a blacklist and to reject any mail that arrives from one of those addresses. The ORBS folks provide an automatic way to get yourself removed from their list if you fix your open relay, so being blacklisted is an easily remediable condition.

One site estimated that between one-third and one-half of all mail servers are configured as open relays today (Spring, 2000). ORBS statistics show a minimum of 15%.

Starting with **sendmail** 8.9, relaying is turned off by default. Only hosts tagged with RELAY in the access database (see page 599) or listed in **/etc/mail/relay-domains** are allowed to submit mail for relaying. The proportion of open relays should fall over the next few years as a result of this change in default behavior, along with increasing public awareness and the help of ORBS' proactive screening.

So, promiscuous relaying is bad. At the same time, some types of relaying are useful and legitimate. How can you tell which messages to relay and which to reject? Relaying is actually necessary in only two situations:

- *When the transport agent acts as a gateway for hosts that are not reachable any other way*; for example, UUCP hosts, hosts that are not always turned on (PPP hosts, Windows PCs), and virtual hosts. In this situation, all the recipients for which you want to relay lie within the same domain.

- *When the transport agent is the outgoing mail server for other, not-so-smart hosts*. In this case, all the senders' hostnames or IP address are local.

Any other situation that appears to require relaying is probably just an indication of bad design. You can obviate the first use of relaying (above) by eliminating UUCP (it's almost dead anyway) and designating a centralized server to receive mail (with POP or IMAP used for client access). The second case should always be allowed, but only for your own hosts. It's better to check IP addresses than hostnames because the hostnames are easy to fake.

Although **sendmail** comes with relaying turned off by default, several features have been added to turn it back on, either fully or in a limited and controlled way. These features are listed below for completeness, but our recommendation is that you be careful about opening things up too much. Most sites do not need any of the really dangerous features in the second list. The access_db feature, covered in the next section, is the safest way to allow limited relaying.

- FEATURE(`relay_entire_domain`) – allows relaying for just your domain
- RELAY_DOMAIN(`domain, ...`) – adds more domains to be relayed
- RELAY_DOMAIN_FILE(`filename`) – same, but takes domain list from a file
- FEATURE(`relay_hosts_only`) – affects RELAY_DOMAIN, accessdb

You will need to make an exception if you use the SMART_HOST or MAIL_HUB designations to route mail through a particular mail server machine. That server will have to be set up to relay mail from local hosts. It should be configured with:

    FEATURE(`relay_entire_domain`)

Sites that also do virtual hosting may need RELAY_DOMAIN as well, to allow relaying for their virtual names, although

    FEATURE(`use_cw_file`)

effectively opens relays for those domains or hosts.

There are a few other possibilities, but they are fraught with problems:

- FEATURE('promiscuous_relay') – allows all relaying; don't use
- FEATURE('relay_based_on_MX') – relays for anyone that MXes to you
- FEATURE('loose_relay_check') – allows "percent hack" addressing
- FEATURE('relay_local_from') – relays based on the From address

The promiscuous_relay feature allows relaying from any site to any other site. Using it is a one-way ticket to Paul Vixie's black hole lists. **Do not** use this feature.

The relay_based_on_MX feature is bad because you do not control what sites are allowed to point their MX records at you. Typically, the only hosts that have an MX record pointing to your mail server are your own, but nothing prevents other sites from changing their MX records to point to you. Spammers do not usually have the ability to change MX records, but shady sites certainly could.

The loose_relay_check feature allows the "% hack" form of addressing that spammers love to use.

The relay_local_from feature trusts the sender address on the envelope of the message and relays messages that appear to be from a local address. Of course, both the envelope and the headers of mail messages are trivial to forge, and spammers are forging experts.

If you consider turning on relaying in some form, consult the **sendmail** documentation in **cf/README** to be sure you don't inadvertently become a friend of spammers. When you are done, have one of the relay checking sites verify that you did not inadvertently create an open relay—try orbs.org or abuse.net.

There are mismatched configurations in which your host might be convinced to relay weird addresses that misuse the UUCP addressing syntax. Just to be sure, if you have no UUCP (or BITNET or DECnet) connectivity, you can use

```
FEATURE(`nouucp', `reject')
undefine(`UUCP_RELAY')
undefine(`BITNET_RELAY')
undefine(`DECNET_RELAY')
```

to forestall this possibility. A good spot for these lines is in your DOMAIN file.

Another relay that is often defined in the DOMAIN file is the LUSER_RELAY for local users who do not exist. A site with **sendmail** misconfigured sometimes leaks unqualified local user names (usually on the Cc line) out to the Internet. Someone trying to reply to the mail will be addressing their reply to an apparent local user who does not exist. This relay is often called the "loser relay" and is directed to the error mailer with an entry such as

```
define(`LUSER_RELAY', `error:No such user')
```

## The access database

**sendmail** includes support for an access database that you can use to build a mail-specific firewall for your site. It checks mail coming in from the outside world and rejects it if it comes from specific users or domains. You can also use the access database to specify which domains a machine is willing to relay for.

The access database is enabled with the line

```
FEATURE(`access_db', `type filename')
```

If *type* and *filename* are not specified, the database defaults to type hash built from the file **/etc/mail/access**. As always, create the database with **makemap**:

```
# makemap hash /etc/mail/access < /etc/mail/access
```

The key field of the access file can contain email addresses, user names, domain names, or network numbers. For example:

```
cyberspammer.com          550 Spam not accepted
okguy@cyberspammer.com    OK
badguy@aol.com            REJECT
sendmail.org              RELAY
128.32                    RELAY
170.201.180.16            REJECT
hotlivesex@               550 Spam not accepted
friend@                   550 You are not my friend!
```

The value part must contain one of the items shown in Table 19.14.

**Table 19.14    Things that can appear in the value field of the access database**

| Value | What it does |
| --- | --- |
| OK | Accepts mail and delivers it normally |
| RELAY | Accepts the mail as addressed and relays it to its destination; enables per-host relaying |
| REJECT | Rejects the mail with a generic error message |
| DISCARD | Silently discards the message |
| *xxx message* | Returns an error; *xxx* must be an RFC821 numeric code[a] |
| ERROR:*xxx message* | Same as above, but clearly marked as an error message |
| ERROR:*x.x.x message* | *x.x.x* must be an RFC1893-compliant delivery status notification (a generalization of the 550 error code) |

a. For example, 550 is the single-error code.

This database file would allow messages from okguy at cyberspammer.com but would reject all other mail from cyberspammer.com with the indicated error message. Mail from either sendmail.org or 128.32.0.0/16 (UC Berkeley's network) would be relayed. Mail from badguy at AOL and from hotlivesex or friend at any domain would also be rejected.

IPv6 addresses in their colon-separated form can be used on the left-hand side as well. The @ after the usernames hotlivesex and friend is required to differentiate them from domain names.

550 is an RFC821 error code. The RFC1893 error codes (or "delivery status notification messages," as they are called) are more extensive. First digit 4 indicates a temporary error; 5 means a permanent error. We've listed a few in Table 19.15.

**Table 19.15    RFC1893 delivery status codes**

| Temporary | Permanent | Meaning |
|-----------|-----------|---------|
| 4.2.1 | 5.2.1 | Mailbox is disabled |
| 4.2.2 | 5.2.2 | Mailbox is full |
| 4.2.3 | 5.2.3 | Message is too long |
| 4.2.4 | 5.2.4 | List expansion problem |
| 4.3.1 | 5.3.1 | Mail system is full |
| 4.4.4 | 5.4.4 | Unable to route |
| 4.4.5 | 5.4.5 | Mail congestion |

For even finer control, the key field (left side) can contain the tags Connect, To, and From to control the way in which the filter is applied. Connect refers to connection information such as client address or client name. To and From refer to the envelope addresses, not the headers. These tags provide finer control over relaying and can be used to override other restrictions.

If one of these tags is used, the lookup is tried first with the tag info and then without, to maintain backward compatibility with older access databases.

Here are some examples:

```
From:spammer@some.domain  REJECT
To:friend.domain          RELAY
Connect:friend.domain     OK
```

Mail from spammer@some.domain would be blocked, but you could still send mail to that address, even if it was blacklisted. Mail will be relayed to friend.domain, but not from it (assuming that relaying has been disabled elsewhere). Connections to friend.domain would be allowed even if it was in one of the DNS-based rejection lists.

Many sites use an access database to control spam. Our incoming master mail machine in the computer science department at the University of Colorado rejects mail from over 500 known spammers identified by addresses, domains, or IP networks.

### Blacklisting users or sites

If you have local users or hosts that you want to block mail to, use

```
FEATURE(`blacklist_recipients')
```

which supports the following types of entries in your access file:

```
nobody@                   550 Mailbox disabled for this user
printer.mydomain.edu      550 This host does not accept mail
user@host.mydomain.edu    550 Mailbox disabled for this user
```

These lines block incoming mail to user nobody on any host, to host printer, and to a particular user's address on one machine.

To include the black hole lists from Paul Vixie's MAPS (Mail Abuse Prevention System; see maps.vix.com) project—or any other DNS-style blocking list—use the dnsbl feature:

```
FEATURE(`dnsbl')
```

*See Chapter 16 for more information about DNS.*

This feature causes **sendmail** to reject mail from any site whose IP address is in the Realtime Blackhole List of known spammers maintained by MAPS. Other lists catalog known dial-up spammers and sites that run open relays.

These blacklists are distributed through a clever tweak of the DNS system; hence the name dnsbl. For example, a special DNS resource record of the form

```
IP-address.rbl.maps.vix.com  in  a  127.0.0.2
```

put into the DNS database of the rbl.maps.vix.com domain would block mail from that host if the dnsbl feature was enabled (because **sendmail** would check explicitly to see if such a record existed). The *IP-address* in this example is a host address in its dotted quad form with the order of the octets reversed.

You can include the dnsbl feature several times to check different lists of abusers: just add a second argument to specify the blacklist name server and a third argument with the error message that you would like returned. If the third argument is omitted, a fixed error message from the DNS database containing the records is returned. Here are examples of three lists: rbl (the default), the dul list of dial-up users, and the rss list of open relays.

```
FEATURE(`dsnbl', `rbl.maps.vix.com', `Rejected - see www.mail-abuse.org/rbl/')
FEATURE(`dsnbl', `dul.maps.vix.com', `Dialup - see www.mail-abuse.org/dul/')
FEATURE(`dsnbl', `relays.mail-abuse.org', `Relay - see www.mail-abuse.org/rss/')
```

### Header checking

Header checking is a powerful spam-fighting mechanism that makes use of the low-level **sendmail** configuration file syntax, which we do not cover in this edition of *UNIX System Administration Handbook*. By using header checking, **sendmail** can look for patterns in headers (e.g., "To: friend@public.com") and reject messages before they are delivered to your users' mailboxes.

Header checking can also be used to recognize viruses carried by email provided that they have a distinctive header line. For example, the Melissa virus of 1999 contained the subject line "Important Message From …". Within hours of the Melissa virus being released and recognized, sendmail.com posted a local ruleset to identify it and discard it. When the fingerprint of a virus is distinctive and easy to express in **sendmail** rules, sendmail.com typically posts a fix for it (at both the sendmail.com and sendmail.org web sites) very quickly.

For a representative sample of filtering rules for spam and viruses, see the **sendmail** configuration for Eric Allman's home machine, knecht. This configuration is included in the **sendmail** distribution as **cf/cf/knecht.mc**. Steal the spam-filtering rules and add them to the end of your **.mc** file.

In looking at various examples, we have seen header checking rules for

- Mail addressed to any user in the domain public.com
- Mail addressed to "friend" or "you"
- Mail with the X-Spanska header, which indicates the Happy99 worm
- Mail with subject "Important Message From …" (the Melissa virus)
- Mail with subject "all.net and Fred Cohen …" (the Papa virus)
- Mail with subject "ILOVEYOU" (the iloveyou virus and variants)
- Mail with numeric usernames from aol.com and msn.com
- Mail with usernames beginning with a number from juno.com

All of the header checking rules go under LOCAL_CONFIG and LOCAL_RULESETS statements at the end of the **.mc** configuration file. With the help of **m4**'s divert command, **sendmail** just knows where to put them in the raw config file.

To some degree, any spam abatement that you implement blocks some spammers but raises the bar for the remaining ones. Use the error mailer with a "user unknown" error message instead of the discard mailer, because many spammers clean up their lists. Clean lists are more valuable, so you might get removed from some if you can intercept the spam, filter it, and respond with an error message.

### Handling spam

Fighting spam can be a difficult and frustrating job. Past a certain point, it's also quite futile. Don't be seduced into chasing down individual spammers, even though lots will get through your anti-spam shields. Time spent analyzing spam headers and fretting about spammers is wasted time. Yes, it's fighting the good fight, but time spent on these issues will probably not reduce the amount of spam coming into your site.

You can nail stationary spammers pretty quickly by ratting them out to their ISP, but hit-and-run spammers that use an ISP account once and then abandon it are hard to hold accountable. If they advertise a web site, then the web site is responsible; if it's a telephone number or postal address, it's harder to identify the perpetrator, but not impossible. Many mobile spammers seem essentially immune from punishment.

The various black hole lists have been somewhat effective at blocking spam and have reduced the number of open relays dramatically. Being blacklisted can seriously impact business, so some ISPs and companies are careful to police their users. Our main recommendation regarding spam is that you use the preventive measures and publicly maintained blacklists that are available.

Advise your users to simply delete the spam they receive. Many spam messages contain instructions on how recipients can be removed from the mailing list. If you follow those instructions, the spammers may remove you from the current list, but they immediately add you to several other lists with the annotation "reaches a real human who reads the message." Your email address is then worth even more.

If you'd like to take a seat on the spam-fighting bandwagon, some web sites can help. Two awesome sites are maps.vix.com and www.abuse.net. www.spamrecycle.com

asks that you email them your spam; they forward it to your state representative, who might choose to do something politically at the state level. This site also has a nice set of guidelines for protecting yourself against spam. The site analyzes the spam and uses it to help improve anti-spam filters. Three other web sites of note are orbs.org, spamcop.net, and cauce.org. orbs.org has the most effective open relay databases. SpamCop has tools that help parse mail headers and determine the real sender. The cauce.org site has good information on spam laws.

### Spam examples

Though we don't recommend analyzing spam as a matter of course, it is sometimes useful to know how to do it. For example, you may be called upon to explain why the CEO of your company received a solicitation for pornography (and to verify that it did not come from a company employee!).

In the next few pages we analyze the headers from some recent spam. These examples illustrate how hard it is to determine the actual sender and how easy it is to fake mail headers. First, some key points:

- Received headers should chain together from the top of a message to the bottom of the message.

- Any Received headers below the Date header are fake.

- Take note of any Received headers in which the two hostnames don't match. The mail is probably being relayed through the first host (the parenthesized host is the real origin).

- A Received header with an old date is probably forged.

- The host part of the From header should agree with the last Received header.

- The Message-Id header's domain should match the From header's domain.

- Check to see if the Received headers show that the message was relayed through an unrelated host.

- Check all listed hosts to be sure they exist in DNS.

Our first example is a message selling a CD of 10,000,000 email addresses for future spammers. The spam CD was interesting—it guaranteed no duplicate addresses and no "poison" addresses (presumably, addresses that automatically submit the sender to one of the black hole lists).

We numbered the lines of the header to facilitate the commentary; the numbers are not really there.

```
1: From mrktnet77@kayak.msk.ru Thu Nov  4 22:10:48 1999
2: Received: from gaia.es ([195.55.166.66]) by xor.com (8.9.3/8.9.3) with ESMTP
      id WAA26343 for <evi@xor.com>; Thu, 4 Nov 1999 22:10:42 -0700 (MST)
3: From: mrktnet77@kayak.msk.ru
```

```
4: Received: from default by gaia.es (8.8.8+Sun/SMI-SVR4) id GAA03907; Fri, 5
      Nov 1999 06:31:10 -0100 (Etc/GMT)
5: Date: Fri, 5 Nov 1999 06:31:10 -0100 (Etc/GMT)
6: Received: from login_011556.wgukas.com (mail.wgukas.com [233.214.241.87])
      by (8.8.5/8.7.3) with SMTP id XAA01510 for fraklin321@thaxghklo.um.de;
      Thu, 4 November 1999 00:21:59 -0700 (EDT)
7: To: mrktnet77@kayak.msk.ru
8: Subject: Just Released!  Millions CD Vol. 6A
9: Comments: Authenticated Sender is <user11556@wgukas.com>
10:Message-Id: 02202108722648597456@sa_ghklo.um.de

/* Several pages of marketeering removed here */
**************************************************
Do not reply to this message -
To be removed from future mailings:
mailto:greg1148@usa.net?Subject=Remove
**************************************************
```

Line 1 was added by **/bin/mail** during local delivery. The domain msk.ru exists, but host kayak.msk.ru does not. Line 2 is a valid Received line—it's the only Received line whose accuracy is guaranteed, because it was added by our own host (in this case, xor.com). Line 3 is a From header added by **sendmail** along the way because the message did not originally have one.

Line 4 is a valid Received line from an unsuspecting scapegoat host (gaia.es) running sendmail 8.8, under which relaying is allowed by default (and which Sun shipped that way). Line 6 is a fake Received line. It's below the Date line and so must have been put there before the first **sendmail** process got the message. Plus, the format is wrong and 233.214.241.87 has no reverse DNS entry.

Line 7, the To line, is bogus. The recipients' addresses were on the envelope only.

Line 9 purports to identify the authenticated sender, which is sometimes a clue to a message's provenance. This one implies that the sender is from wgukas.com, but that domain does not exist. This line was actually added by a PC mail user agent and so it could well be forged.

Line 10 implies that the sending machine was actually sa_ghklo.um.de, but it has the wrong format (missing angle brackets, < >) and so is probably forged.

It's impossible to tell where this message came from. It was relayed through gaia.es, probably without their permission. They are not yet in the maps.vix.com black hole list, but may end up there soon. greg1148 could be the spammer himself, or he could be a user who complained about previous spam. In the latter case, greg1148 assumes the victim role in this message and may receive hundreds or thousands of angry messages from folks asking to be removed from the list.

The body of the message required you to call or fax your order to an 800 number. It is typical to have all the information needed to respond to the spammer and buy his product in the actual body of the message. Note that the address on the From line is the same as the address on the To line; both are probably forged.

Another piece of spam from this same day offered to make you rich if you faxed them a check for $40 by November 15, after which the price went up to $195. Are faxed copies of a check legal tender? Or are they just interested in obtaining your bank account routing number and your signature so they can print their own checks? Protect your identity.

```
1: From jimdelno@apexmail.com Thu Nov 11 10:31:41 1999
2: Received: from saturn.globalcon.com (saturn.globalcon.com [209.5.99.8]) by
       xor.com (8.9.3/8.9.3) with ESMTP id KAA15479; Thu, 11 Nov 1999
       10:31:30 -0700 (MST)
3: Received: from hamilton ([168.191.61.20]) by saturn.globalcon.com
       (Post.Office MTA v3.1.2 release (PO205-101c) ID# 0-35881U1500L100S0)
       with SMTP id AAA148; Thu, 11 Nov 1999 12:33:24 -0500
4: Date: Thu, 11 Nov 1999 02:39:57 +0000
5: Subject: Free Information On "Debt Reduction!"
6: Message-Id: <yjsul.lnmqgaasnjymgqaac@hamilton>
7: From: F.Pepper@pmail.net
8: To: benfranklin@onehundred.net
```

Line 2 is a valid Received header. Line 3 is also valid, but **traceroute**s from xor.com, the destination, to hamilton (168.191.61.20) and saturn.globalcon.com (209.5.99.8) show that those two sites have nothing to do with each other. 168.191.61.20 is on Sprint's dial-up network, and judging from the time zone indication, it might be in Europe. 209.5.99.8 is a company in Ontario, Canada. saturn.globalcon.com is probably an open relay. They are not running **sendmail**, but rather version 3.1.2 of the Post.Office mail transport agent from software.com.

On line 4, the date added by the sender's user agent is about 2:00 a.m. in Europe, 2 hours before it was received on the machine satrun.globalcon.com. Perhaps the recipient list was very long and took 2 hours to process. Or perhaps the message was composed off-line on the spammer's PC and then submitted to the Internet at a later time. The time zone indication (if it isn't forged) is 5 hours different—the same as the difference between Europe and the East coast of the United States.

On line 6, the host portion of the Message-Id should be a fully qualified domain name, not just the local part "hamilton". The host hamilton is probably misconfigured, because the unqualified name also appears on line 3. The portion of the Message-Id to the left of the @ sign typically consists of numbers. In this case it contains random letters, which indicates that the line might be forged.

Line 8 is clearly forged. The actual recipients' addresses were only on the envelope of the message and do not appear anywhere in the headers.

This message might actually be from F.Pepper@pmail.net. The hostname pmail.net resolves to a valid IP address, and **whois** says pmail.net is a British telecom company. Among the twenty or so spam messages we examined for this section, this one alone might have contained enough information to make up a reasonable complaint (to the hostmaster indicated in DNS for the IP address in line 3 of the header). Never complain directly to the spammer or the spammer's domain.

SpamCop is a software package that parses mail headers and identifies which lines are real, which are probably forged, and which are totally bogus. It provides users who submit spam messages via email or the web (spamcop.net) with a blow-by-blow description of the headers and tells which pieces check out and which don't. This site also makes it easy to submit a spam complaint. The complaint includes all the relevant information that you gleaned from parsing your headers. SpamCop was implemented by Julian Haight.

We ran SpamCop on our first spam example above, which tried to sell us a CD full of address lists. It determined that the gaia.es Received line was OK, but that the domain wgukas.com was fake. It then determined that gaia.es did not have the IP address the mail said it did and that the real culprit was probably at a site called ttd.net. Clearly, SpamCop's analysis was much better than ours, and it only took a few seconds.

Here's a small snippet of a SpamCop analysis for some fresher spam:

```
Received: from sun1.cskwam.mil.pl (cskwam.mil.pl) [148.81.119.2] by
    mail1.es.net with smtp (Exim 1.81 #2) id 126BHL-000494-00, Sat, 6 May
    2000 13:34:23 -0700
Possible spammer: 148.81.119.2
"nslookup cskwam.mil.pl" (checking ip) [show] ip not found; cskwam.mil.pl
    discarded as fake.
"dig cskwam.mil.pl mx" (digging for Mail eXchanger) [show] "nslookup
    cskwam.mil.pl" (checking ip) [show] cskwam.mil.pl not 148.81.119.2,
    discarded as fake.
"nslookup sun1.cskwam.mil.pl" (checking ip) [show] ip = 148.81.119.2
Taking name from IP...
"nslookup 148.81.119.2" (getting name) [show] 148.81.119.2 =
    sun1.cskwam.mil.pl
"nslookup sun1.cskwam.mil.pl" (checking ip) [show] ip = 148.81.119.2
"nslookup 2.119.81.148.rbl.maps.vix.com." (checking ip) [show] not found
"nslookup 2.119.81.148.relays.orbs.org." (checking ip) [show] ip = 127.0.0.2
blocked by ORBS
Chain test:mail1.es.net =? mail1.es.net
Chain verified mail1.es.net = mail1.es.net
148.81.119.2 has already been sent to ORBS
Received line accepted
```

Each of the [show] words are links on SpamCop's web page. They show you the actual command that was executed and its output.

## 19.11 SECURITY AND SENDMAIL

With the explosive growth of the Internet, programs such as **sendmail** that accept arbitrary user-supplied input and deliver it to local users, files, or shells have frequently provided an avenue of attack for hackers. **sendmail**, along with DNS and even IP, is flirting with authentication and encryption as a built-in solution to some of these fundamental security issues.

Recent softening of the export laws of the United States regarding encryption has allowed **sendmail** to be shipped with built-in hooks for encryption. Versions 8.11 and later support both SMTP authentication and encryption with SSL, the Secure Socket Layer, which is also called TLS for Transport Layer Security. **sendmail** uses the term TLS in this context and has implemented it as an extension, STARTTLS, to the SMTP protocol. TLS brought with it six new configuration options for certificate files and key files. New actions for access database matches can require that authentication must have succeeded.

In this section, we describe the evolution of **sendmail**'s permissions model, ownerships, and privacy protection. We then briefly discuss SASL, the Simple Authentication and Security Layer, and its use with **sendmail**.

**sendmail** has gradually tightened up its security over time, and it is now very picky about file permissions before it believes the contents of, say, a **.forward** or **aliases** file. Although this tightening of security has generally been welcome, it's sometimes necessary to relax the tough new policies. To this end, **sendmail** has introduced the DontBlameSendmail option, so named in hopes that the name will suggest to sysadmins that what they are doing is considered unsafe.

This option has many possible values. The default is safe. For a complete list of values, see **sendmail/conf.c**; they are not listed in the second edition of the O'Reilly **sendmail** book, but will surely be in the third. Or, just leave the option set to safe.

### Ownerships

Three user accounts are important in the **sendmail** universe: the DefaultUser, the TrustedUser, and the RunAsUser.

By default, all of **sendmail**'s mailers run as the DefaultUser unless the mailer's flags specify otherwise. If a user "mailnull" or "sendmail" exists in the **/etc/passwd** file, DefaultUser will be that. Otherwise, it defaults to UID 1 and GID 1, which is usually "daemon". We recommend the use of the "mailnull" account. Add it to **/etc/passwd** with a star as the password, no valid shell, no home directory, and a default group of "nogroup". The mailnull account should not own any files.

**sendmail**'s TrustedUser can own maps and alias files. The TrustedUser is allowed to start the daemon or rebuild the **aliases** file. The TrustedUser is different from the **sendmail** class called TRUSTED_USERS, which determines who can rewrite the From line of messages.[24]

The RunAsUser is the UID that **sendmail** runs under after opening its socket connection to port 25. Ports numbered less than 1,024 can only be opened by the superuser; therefore, **sendmail** must initially run as root. However, after performing this operation, **sendmail** can switch to a different UID. Such a switch reduces the risk of damage or access if **sendmail** is tricked into doing something bad.

---

24. The TRUSTED_USERS feature is typically used to support mailing list software. For example, if you use Majordomo, you must add the "majordom" user to the TRUSTED_USERS class. The users root and daemon are the default members of the class.

By default, **sendmail** does not switch identities and continues to run as root. If you change the RunAsUser to something other than root, you must change several other things as well. The RunAsUser must own the mail queue, be able to read all maps and include files, be able to write logs, be able to run programs, etc. Expect to spend a few hours finding all the file and directory ownerships that must be changed.

### Permissions

File and directory permissions are very important to **sendmail** security. Use the settings listed in Table 19.16 to be safe.

**Table 19.16    Owner and permissions for sendmail-related directories**

| Path | Owner | Mode | What it contains |
|------|-------|------|------------------|
| **/var/spool/mqueue** | RunAsUser | 700 | Mail queue directory |
| **/, /var, /var/spool** | root | 755 | Path to **mqueue** |
| **/etc/mail/*** | TrustedUser | 644 | Maps, the config file, aliases |
| **/etc/mail** | TrustedUser | 755 | Parent directory for maps |
| **/etc** | root | 755 | Path to **mail** directory |

**sendmail** will not read files that have lax permissions (for example, files that are group or world-writable or that live in group or world-writable directories). Some of **sendmail**'s rigor with regard to ownerships and permissions was motivated by operating systems that allow users to give their files away with **chown** (those derived from System V, mostly).[25]

In particular, **sendmail** is *very* picky about the complete path to any alias file or forward file. This pickiness sometimes clashes with the way sites like to manage Majordomo mailing list aliases. If the Majordomo list is in **/usr/local**, for example, the entire path must be trusted; no component can have group write permission. This constraint makes it more difficult for the list owner to manage the alias file. To see where you stand with respect to **sendmail**'s ideas about permissions, run

```
# sendmail -v -bi
```

The -**bi** flag initializes the alias database and warns you of inappropriate permissions.

**sendmail** will no longer read a **.forward** file that has a link count greater than 1 if the directory path to it is unsafe (has lax permissions). This rule bit Evi recently when her **.forward** file, which was typically a hard link to either **.forward.to.boulder** or **.forward.to.sandiego**, silently failed to forward her mail from a small site at which she did not receive much mail. It was months before she realized and understood that "I never got your mail" was her fault and not a valid excuse anymore.

You can turn off many of the restrictive file access policies mentioned above with the DontBlameSendmail option.

---

25. The promiscuous version of **chown** has led to numerous security problems over the years. We consider it a design flaw. Some systems allow you to disable it; do so if you can.

## Safe mail to files and programs

We recommend that you use **smrsh** instead of **/bin/sh** as your program mailer and that you use **mail.local** instead of **/bin/mail** as your local mailer. See page 586 for more information. Both helper programs are included in the **sendmail** distribution. To incorporate them into your configuration, add the lines

```
FEATURE(`smrsh', `path-to-smrsh')
FEATURE(`lmtp', `path-to-mail.local')
```

to your **.mc** file. If you omit the explicit paths, they default to **/usr/libexec/smrsh** and **/usr/libexec/mail.local**.

**smrsh** will only execute the programs contained in one directory, **/usr/adm/sm.bin** by default.[26] **smrsh** ignores user-specified paths and tries to find any requested commands in its own known-safe directory. **smrsh** also blocks the use of certain shell metacharacters such as "<", the input redirection symbol. Symbolic links are allowed in **sm.bin**, so you don't need to make duplicate copies of the programs you allow.

Here are some example shell commands and their possible **smrsh** interpretations:

| | |
|---|---|
| **vacation eric** | executes /usr/adm/sm.bin/vacation eric |
| **cat /etc/passwd** | rejected, cat not in sm.bin |
| **vacation eric < /etc/passwd** | rejected, no < allowed |

**sendmail**'s SafeFileEnvironment option controls where files can be written when email is redirected to a file by an **aliases** or **.forward** file. It causes **sendmail** to execute a **chroot** system call, making the root of the filesystem no longer **/** but rather **/safe**, or whatever path you specified in the SafeFileEnvironment option. An alias that directed mail into the **/etc/passwd** file, for example, would really be written to **/safe/etc/passwd**.

The SafeFileEnvironment option also protects device files, directories, and other special files by allowing writes only to regular files. Besides increasing security, this option helps to ameliorate the effects of user mistakes. Some sites set the option to **/home** to allow access to home directories while keeping system files off-limits.

Mailers can also be run in a **chroot**ed directory. This option must be specified in the mailer definition at the moment, but it should soon be configurable via **m4**.

## Privacy options

**sendmail** also has privacy options that control

- What external folks can determine about your site from SMTP
- What you require of the host on the other end of an SMTP connection
- Whether your users can see or run the mail queue

Table 19.17 lists the possible values for the privacy options as of this writing; see the file **sendmail/conf.c** in the distribution for current information.

---

26. Don't put programs such as **procmail** that can spawn a shell in **sm.bin**. Instead, specify **procmail** as the local mailer. It's not secure, but if that's what your users need...

**Table 19.17**   **Values of the PrivacyOption variable**

| Value | Meaning |
|---|---|
| public | Does no privacy/security checking |
| needmailhelo | Requires SMTP HELO (identifies remote host) |
| noexpn | Does not allow the SMTP EXPN command |
| novrfy | Does not allow the SMTP VRFY command |
| needexpnhelo | Does not expand addresses (EXPN) without a HELO |
| needvrfyhelo | Does not verify addresses (VRFY) without a HELO |
| noverb[a] | Does not allow verbose mode for EXPN |
| restrictmailq | Allows only **mqueue** directory's group to see the queue |
| restrictqrun | Allows only **mqueue** directory's owner to run the queue |
| noetrn[b] | Does not allow asynchronous queue runs |
| authwarnings | Adds Authentication-Warning header (this is the default) |
| noreceipts | Turns off DSN (Delivery Status Notification) for return receipts |
| nobodyreturn | Does not return message body in a DSN |
| goaway | Disables all SMTP status queries (EXPN, VRFY, etc.) |

a. Verbose mode follows **.forward** files when an EXPN command is given and provides more information about a user's mail-whereabouts. Use noverb or, better yet, noexpn on any machine exposed to the outside world.

b. ETRN is an ESMTP command designed for use by dial-up hosts. It requests that the queue be run just for messages to that host.

We recommend conservatism; use

```
define(`confPRIVACY_OPTIONS', ``goaway, authwarnings, restrictmailq,
   restrictqrun'')
```

in your **.mc** file. The default value for the privacy options is authwarnings; the line above would reset that value. Notice the double sets of quotes; some versions of **m4** require them to protect the commas in the list of privacy option values.

### Running a chrooted sendmail (for the truly paranoid)

If you are worried about the access that **sendmail** has to your filesystem, you can start it in a **chroot**ed jail. Make a minimal filesystem in your jail, including things like **/dev/null**, **/etc** essentials (**passwd**, **group**, **resolv.conf**, **sendmail.cf**, any map files, **mail/\***), the shared libraries that **sendmail** needs, the **sendmail** binary, the mail queue directory, and any log files. You will probably have to fiddle with the list to get it just right. Use the **chroot** command to start a jailed **sendmail**. For example:

```
# chroot /jail /usr/sbin/sendmail -bd -q30m
```

### Denial of service attacks

Denial of service attacks are impossible to prevent because there is no a priori way to determine that a message is an attack rather than a valid piece of email. Attackers can try various nasty things, including flooding the SMTP port with bogus connections, filling disk partitions with giant messages, clogging outgoing connections, and mail bombing. **sendmail** has some configuration parameters that can help slow down or limit the impact of a denial of service attack, but these parameters can also interfere with legitimate mail.

The MaxDaemonChildren option limits the number of **sendmail** processes. It prevents the system from being overwhelmed with **sendmail** work, but it also allows an attacker to shut down SMTP service very easily. The MaxMessageSize option can help prevent the mail queue directory from filling, but if you set it too low, legitimate mail will bounce. (You might mention your limit to users so that they aren't surprised when their mail bounces. We recommend a fairly high limit anyway, as some legitimate mail is huge.) The ConnectionRateThrottle option, which limits the number of connections per second that are permitted, can slow things down a bit. And finally, setting MaxRcptsPerMessage, which controls the maximum number of recipients allowed on a single message, might help.

In spite of all these knobs to turn to protect your mail system, someone mail bombing you will still interfere with legitimate mail. Mail bombing can be quite nasty.

The University of Colorado provides an email account for each student (25,000), with **pine** as the default mail reader. A student with a new job at a local computer store was convinced to give a copy of the password file to his employer. The company then sent an advertisement to everyone in the password file, in batches of about 1,000 recipients at a time (which made for a very long To line).

**pine** had been compiled with the default reply mode set to reply to all recipients as well as the sender. Many students replied with questions such as, "Why did you send me this junk?", and of course it went to everyone else on the To line. The result was total denial of service on the server—for email or any other use. **sendmail** took over all the CPU cycles, the mail queue was enormous, and all useful work ground to a halt. The only solution was to take the machine off-line, go into every user's mail spool, and remove the offending messages.

### Forgeries

Forging email has in the past been trivial. **sendmail** 8.10 includes SMTP authentication that verifies the identity of the sending machine. Prior to 8.10, any user could forge mail to appear as though it came from your domain. Even in 8.10, checking must be turned on with the AuthMechanisms option.

Likewise, it is possible to impersonate any user in mail messages. Be careful if mail messages are your organization's authorization vehicle for things like keys, access cards, and money. You should warn administrative users of this fact and suggest that if they see suspicious mail that appears to come from a person in authority, they should verify the validity of the message. This is doubly true if the message asks that unreasonable privileges be given to an unusual person. Mail authorizing a grand master key for an undergraduate student might be suspect!

The authwarnings privacy option flags local attempts at forgery by adding an Authentication-Warning header to outgoing mail that appears to be forged. However, many user agents hide this header by default.

If forged mail is coming from a machine that you control, you can actually do quite a bit to thwart it. You can use the **identd** daemon to verify a sender's real login name. **sendmail** does a callback to the sending host to ask the **identd** running there for the login name of the user sending the mail. If **identd** is not running on the remote host, **sendmail** learns nothing. If the remote machine is a single-user workstation, its owner could configure **identd** to return a bogus answer. But if the remote host is a multiuser machine such as that found at many university computing centers, **identd** returns the user's real login name for **sendmail** to put in the message's header.

Many sites do not run **identd**; it's often blocked by firewalls. **identd** is only really useful within a site, since machines you don't control can lie. At a large site with somewhat irresponsible users (e.g., a university), it's great.

Several years ago, when we were first experimenting with **identd**, a student at our site became frustrated with the members of his senior project team. He tried to send mail to his teammates as his instructor, telling them he knew that they were not pulling their weight and that they should work harder. Unfortunately, he made a syntax error and the message bounced to the instructor. **sendmail**'s use of the IDENT protocol told us who he was. **sendmail** included the following lines in the bounced message:

    The original message was received at Wed, 9 Mar 1994 14:51 -0700 from
        student@benji.Colorado.EDU [128.138.126.10]

But the headers of the message itself told a different story:

    From: instructor@cs.Colorado.EDU

Moral: avoid syntax errors when sneaking around. Our policy on forging mail caused the student's login to be disabled for the rest of the semester, which actually accomplished exactly what the student wanted. He was unable to work on the project and his partners had to pick up the slack.

### Message privacy

*See page 671 for more information about PGP.*

Message privacy basically does not exist unless you use an external encryption package such as Pretty Good Privacy (PGP) or Transport Layer Security (TLS). By default, all mail is sent unencrypted. Tell your users that they must do their own encryption if they want their mail to be private.

Efforts are underway to extend SMTP to include both authentication and encryption, but such efforts have in the past been hampered by the U.S. government's export policies. End-to-end encryption requires support from mail user agents as well as from **sendmail**.

Two other systems enhance the privacy of email: S/MIME and PGP. Both are documented in the RFC series, with S/MIME on the standards track. We prefer PGP; it's more widely available and was designed by an excellent cryptographer, Phil Zimmermann, whom we trust. These emerging standards offer a basis for email confidentiality, authentication, message integrity assurance, and nonrepudiation of origin.

### SASL: the Simple Authentication and Security Layer

**sendmail** 8.10 and later support the SMTP authentication defined in RFC2554. It's based on SASL, the Simple Authentication and Security Layer.

SASL is a generic authentication mechanism that can be integrated into a variety of protocols. **sendmail** and Cyrus's **imapd** use it (so far). The SASL framework (it's a library) has two fundamental concepts: an authorization identifier and an authentication identifier. It can map these to permissions on files, UNIX passwords, Kerberos tickets, etc. SASL contains both an authentication part and an encryption part, but because of U.S. export laws, **sendmail** only used the authentication part through version 8.10. Because U.S. export regulations were relaxed in early 2000, the encryption portion that was originally slated to be in the commercial **sendmail** product has become available in version 8.11 to everyone.

To use SASL with **sendmail**, get Cyrus SASL from

>    ftp://ftp.andrew.cmu.edu/pub/cyrus-mail

and install it. The configuration and installation instructions are a bit cryptic; we suggest you check out a web page created by Claus Assmann of Sendmail, Inc. on using SASL with **sendmail**. It's at

>    http://www.sendmail.org/~ca/email/auth.html

The new encryption part of the puzzle is standardized in RFC2487 and is implemented in **sendmail** as an extension to SMTP called STARTTLS. TLS is the same as the Secure Socket Layer protocol used by secure web sites. Unfortunately, **sendmail** version 8.11 is still in beta, and we have not yet had any experience with TLS.

## 19.12   SENDMAIL STATISTICS, TESTING, AND DEBUGGING

**sendmail** can collect statistics on the number and size of messages it has handled. The data can be displayed with the **mailstats** command and is organized by mailer. **sendmail**'s confSTATUS_FILE option in the OSTYPE file specifies the name of the file in which statistics should be kept. The existence of the specified file turns on the accounting function.

*See page 205 for help with rotating and restarting log files.*

The default location for the statistics file is **/etc/mail/statistics**, but some vendors put it in **/var/log/sendmail.st** or **/usr/lib/sendmail.st**. The totals are cumulative since the creation of the statistics file. If you want periodic statistics, you can rotate and reinitialize the file from **cron**.

To make the following example fit the page, we omitted the first column (which numbers the mailers) and the seventh column (discards, because there were none).

```
Statistics from Wed Nov 17 00:56:30 1999
 msgsfr  bytes_from  msgsto  bytes_to  msgsrej   Mailer
      0         0K     2015     5314K        0   prog
      0         0K        2        4K        0   *file*
   5399     37455K       20       20K       18   local
  42449    383837K    72885   450631K     4207   esmtp
=========================================================
  47848    421292K    74922   455969K     4225
```

Six values are shown: messages and kilobytes received (msgsfr, bytes_from), messages and kilobytes sent (msgsto, bytes_to), messages rejected (msgsrej), and messages discarded (msgsdis). These values include both local and relayed mail.

### Testing and debugging

**m4**-based configurations are to some extent pretested. You probably won't need to do low level debugging if you use them. One thing the debugging flags cannot test is your design. While researching this chapter, we found errors in several of the configuration files and designs that we examined. The errors ranged from invoking a feature without the prerequisite macro (e.g., using masquerade_envelope without having turned on masquerading with MASQUERADE_AS) to total conflict between the design of the **sendmail** configuration and the firewall that controlled whether mail was allowed in and under what conditions.

You cannot design a mail system in a vacuum. You must be synchronized with (or at least not in conflict with) your DNS MX records and your firewall policy.

**sendmail** provides one of the richest sets of debugging aids known to UNIX, with debug flags that are not simple Booleans or even integers but are two-dimensional quantities $x.y$, where $x$ chooses the topic and $y$ chooses the amount of information to display. A value of 0 gives no debugging and 127 wastes many trees if you print the output. Topics range from 0 to 99; currently, 68 are defined.

The file **sendmail/TRACEFLAGS** in the distribution lists the values in use and the files and functions in which they are used. All debugging support is at the level of the raw config file.

If **sendmail** is invoked with a **-d**$x.y$ flag, debugging output comes to the screen (standard error). Table 19.18 on the next page shows several important values of $x$ and some Eric-suggested values for $y$.

*checksendmail is available from www.harker.com.*

Gene Kim and Rob Kolstad have written a Perl script called **checksendmail** that invokes **sendmail** in address test mode on a file of test addresses that you supply. It compares the results to those expected. This script lets you test new versions of the configuration file against a test suite of your site's typical addresses to be sure you haven't inadvertently broken anything that used to work.

### Verbose delivery

Many user agents that invoke **sendmail** on the command line accept a **-v** flag, which is passed to **sendmail** and makes it display the steps taken to deliver the message.

**Table 19.18    Debugging topics**

| Topic | Meaning and suggestions |
|---|---|
| 0 | Shows compile flags and system identity (try y = 1 or 10) |
| 8 | Shows DNS name resolution (try y = 7) |
| 11 | Traces delivery (shows mailer invocations) |
| 12 | Shows local-to-remote name translation |
| 17 | Lists MX hosts |
| 21 | Traces rewriting rules (use y = 2 or y = 12 for more detail) |
| 27 | Shows aliasing and forwarding (try y = 4) |
| 44 | Shows file open attempts in case things are failing (y = 4) |
| 60 | Shows database map lookups |

The example below uses **/usr/bin/mailx**, which is the same as **/usr/ucb/mail** on some systems. The words in bold were typed as input to the user agent, and the rest is **sendmail**'s verbose output.

```
anchor 53% mail -v evi@xor.com
Subject: just testing, please ignore
hi
.
Cc:
evi@xor.com... Connecting to xor.com. via esmtp...
220 xor.com ESMTP Sendmail 8.9.3/8.9.3; Fri, 26 Nov 1999 17:42:57 -0700 (MST)
>>> EHLO anchor.cs.colorado.edu
250-xor.com Hello anchor.cs.Colorado.EDU [128.138.242.1], pleased to meet you
250-8BITMIME
250-SIZE 5000000
250-DSN
250-ONEX
250-ETRN
250-XUSR
250 HELP
>>> MAIL From:<evi@anchor.cs.colorado.edu> SIZE=57
250 <evi@anchor.cs.colorado.edu>... Sender ok
>>> RCPT To:<evi@xor.com>
250 <evi@xor.com>... Recipient ok
>>> DATA
354 Enter mail, end with "." on a line by itself
>>> .
250 RAA00511 Message accepted for delivery
evi@xor.com... Sent (RAA00511 Message accepted for delivery)
Closing connection to xor.com.
>>> QUIT
221 xor.com closing connection
```

The **sendmail** on anchor connected to the **sendmail** on xor.com. Each machine used the ESMTP protocol to negotiate the exchange of the message.

### Talking in SMTP

You can make direct use of SMTP when debugging the mail system. To initiate an SMTP session, **telnet** to TCP port 25. By default, this is the port on which **sendmail** listens when run in daemon (**-bd**) mode. Table 19.19 shows some SMTP commands.

**Table 19.19    SMTP commands**

| Command | Function |
|---|---|
| HELO *hostname* | Identifies the connecting host if speaking SMTP |
| EHLO *hostname* | Identifies the connecting host if speaking ESMTP |
| MAIL From: *revpath* | Initiates a mail transaction (envelope sender) |
| RCPT To: *fwdpuath*[a] | Identifies envelope recipients |
| VRFY *address* | Verifies that *address* is valid (deliverable) |
| EXPN *address* | Shows expansion of aliases and **.forward** mappings |
| DATA | Begins the message body[b] |
| QUIT | Ends the exchange and closes the connection |
| RSET | Resets the state of the connection |
| HELP | Prints a summary of SMTP commands |

a. There can be multiple RCPT commands for a message.
b. The body is terminated by entering a dot on its own line.

The whole language has only 14 commands, so it is quite easy to learn and use. It is not case sensitive. The specification for SMTP can be found in RFC821 (also, see RFC1123). RFCs 1869, 1870, 1891, and 1985 extend SMTP to ESMTP.

Most transport agents, including **sendmail**, speak both SMTP and ESMTP; **smap** is the lone exception these days. ESMTP speakers start the conversation with the EHLO command instead of HELO. If the process at the other end understands and responds with an OK, then the participants negotiate supported extensions and arrive at a lowest common denominator for the exchange. If an error is returned, then the ESMTP speaker falls back to SMTP.

### Logging

*See Chapter 11 for more information about syslog.*

**sendmail** uses syslog to log error and status messages with syslog facility "mail" and levels "debug" through "crit"; messages are tagged with the string "sendmail."

The confLOG_LEVEL option, specified on the command line or in the config file, determines the severity level that **sendmail** uses as a threshold for logging. High values of the log level imply low severity levels and cause more info to be logged.

Recall that a message logged to syslog at a particular level is reported to that level and all those above it. The **/etc/syslog.conf** file determines the eventual destination of each message. Table 19.20 gives an approximate mapping between log levels and syslog severity levels.

**Table 19.20    sendmail log levels vs. syslog levels**

| L | Levels | L | Levels |
|---|--------|---|--------|
| 0 | No logging | 4 | notice |
| 1 | alert or crit | 5–10 | info |
| 2 | crit | >=11 | debug |
| 3 | err or warning | | |

## 19.13    THE POSTFIX MAIL SYSTEM

The Postfix project started when Wietse Venema spent a sabbatical year at IBM's T. J. Watson Research Center. It is an alternative to **sendmail** that tries to be fast, easy to administer, and (hopefully) secure. It is a direct competitor to **qmail** by Dan Bernstein. Postfix's design goals included an open source distribution policy, speedy performance, robustness, flexibility, and security.

The most important things about Postfix are probably, first, that it works almost out of the box (the simplest config files are only one or two lines long), and second, that it leverages regular expression maps, especially with the PCRE (Perl Compatible Regular Expression) library to filter mail effectively. Very powerful, but the complicated regular expressions remind you of **sendmail**'s raw config file syntax. Postfix is compatible with **sendmail** in the sense that Postfix **aliases** and **.forward** files have the same format and semantics as those of **sendmail**.

Postfix speaks ESMTP and has limited support for UUCP. Virtual domains and spam filtering are both supported. Postfix does not use an address rewriting language as **sendmail** does; instead, it relies on table lookups from flat files, DB, **dbm**, LDAP, NIS, or NetInfo.

### Postfix architecture

Postfix comprises several small, cooperating processes that send network messages, receive messages, deliver mail locally, etc. Communication among the processes is performed through UNIX domain sockets or FIFOs. This architecture is quite different from that of **sendmail**, wherein a single large process does everything.

Postfix uses four different mail queues:

- Maildrop  – where the user agent puts outgoing messages
- Incoming  – for mail that is arriving
- Active      – an in-memory queue of mail being processed for delivery
- Deferred  – mail for which delivery has failed in the past

A queue manager process moves messages among queues. It uses a round robin strategy that balances between the incoming and deferred queues to determine what goes into the active queue. Messages in the active queue are sorted by destination before processing, so if several messages are bound to the same destination, they can be transferred over a single TCP connection.

In order not to overwhelm a receiving host, especially after it has been down, Postfix uses a slow start algorithm to control how fast it tries to deliver mail. Deferred messages are given a try-again time stamp that exponentially backs off so as not to waste resources on undeliverable messages. A status cache of unreachable destinations avoids unnecessary delivery attempts (similar to **sendmail**'s host status option; see page 588).

Security is implemented at several levels. Most of the Postfix daemons can run in a **chroot**ed environment. The daemons are separate programs with no parent/child relationship. None of them are setuid. Memory for strings and buffers is dynamically allocated, and long lines are broken and reassembled for delivery to prevent buffer overrun issues. The mail drop queue is world-writable (but not world-readable), so Postfix does not need to trust user agents.

A world-writable directory opens opportunities for a malicious local user to mess around, but Postfix averts most problems by using a special file format for queue files. It does not try to process invalid files. Optionally, the mail drop directory can be set to be only group-writable if the **postdrop** program is setgid; this feature was added under pressure from Dan Bernstein's bashing on the bugtraq mailing list.

At the center of the Postfix system are the master daemon that starts the other daemons and the **master.cf** file that sets limits and controls. The default values set in **master.cf** are right for all but very slow or very fast machines or networks; in general, no tweaking is necessary. Another configuration file, **main.cf**, does message routing, rewriting, and filtering. **main.cf** corresponds loosely to the **sendmail.cf** file; the **master.cf** file does not have an analog in **sendmail** since **sendmail** consists of a single daemon process.

Several command-line utilities allow users to interact with the mail system:

- **postfix** – starts and stops the mail system (must be run as root)
- **postalias** – makes the **newaliases** command work
- **postcat** – prints the contents of queue files
- **postconf** – displays and edits the mail configuration file, **main.cf**
- **postdrop** – adds messages to the maildrop queue
- **postkick**, **postlock**, **postlog** – provide locking and logging for shell scripts
- **postmap** – builds database tables, like the UNIX **makemap** command
- **postsuper** – manages the queues (run at startup)

### Configuring Postfix

About 100 parameters can be specified in the **mail.cf** file. Most have sensible defaults. The language looks a bit like a series of Bourne shell assignment statements. In the examples below, we have sometimes annotated the configuration statements with a comment that identifies the **sendmail** equivalent. These comments at the end of configuration lines are not part of the configuration statements; remove the comments if you want to use the statements in your own configuration.

Electronic Mail

First, let's define a few variables that will be used later. The myhostname variable defaults to the machine's hostname. If it's not fully qualified, set it manually before using it:

```
myhostname = host.xxx.yyy
```

The mydomain variable defaults to the parent domain of $myhostname, which Postfix calculates by stripping off the host portion. If this algorithm won't give the right result, define the domain yourself:

```
mydomain = local.domain
```

Both myhostname and mydomain can specify virtual identities.

The mynetworks variable specifies all the networks to which the machine is connected, including the loopback network. For example:

```
mynetworks = 128.138.243.64/26, 127.0.0.0/8
```

Postfix understands CIDR notation for the netmask length. The inet_interfaces variable specifies the interfaces that Postfix should listen on (by default, all active interfaces). You need to specify a value for this variable if you use virtual domains.

For the simplest configuration case, you need configure only three variables:

- myorigin – what domain to use in outgoing mail
- mydestination – what domains to receive mail for
- notify_classes – what types of trouble to report to the postmaster

The variable myorigin determines what domain to use for outgoing mail. Use one of the following:

```
myorigin = $myhostname
myorigin = $mydomain          # like sendmail masquerading
```

The variable mydestination determines the domains for which we will accept incoming mail; it plays the role of **sendmail**'s use_cw_file feature. The value assigned to mydestination can be a list of hostnames, a domain, a filename, or a lookup table specification. Here are some examples:

```
mydestination = $myhostname localhost.$mydomain
mydestination = $myhostname localhost.$mydomain $mydomain
mydestination = /etc/mail/local-host-names
```

The notify_classes clause determines which problems are brought to the attention of the postmaster. Several classes can result in so much mail that it doesn't get read. The default is

```
notify_classes = resource, software
```

which limits the errors to host machine problems and Postfix software problems. Table 19.21 shows the possible classes.

**Table 19.21    Values that can be included in notify_classes**

| Class | What it sends mail about |
|---|---|
| bounce | Undeliverable messages (header only) |
| 2bounce | Double bounces (when the bounce message also bounces) |
| delay | Messages delayed in the queue (header only) |
| policy | Spam rejections (includes SMTP transcript) |
| protocol | Protocol errors (includes SMTP transcript) |
| resource | Resource problems (e.g., queue write fails, filesystem full) |
| software | Internal Postfix "this can't happen" errors |

Postfix has options for controlling the resources used by the mail system, both rate controls and resource controls.

Postfix can also do limited address rewriting; for example, it can

- Map login names to first.last style addresses
- Trim source route addresses
- Convert UUCP addresses to domain style
- Undo the %-hack
- Add a local domain to produce fully qualified names

Masquerading is supported but not in as many variations as **sendmail** allows. Virtual address mapping is done by table lookups, as it is in **sendmail**. Redirects are implemented with the relocated users table (relocated_maps variable). Aliases and **.forward** files are supported and look just like **sendmail**'s. Even the luser_relay (pronounced "loser relay") for handling "user unknown" messages is supported.

Relaying is turned off by default, but the exact default behavior is a bit different from that of **sendmail**. **sendmail** does no relaying at all by default; Postfix relays for your own domains, subdomains, and class A, B, or C networks.

### Spam control

Postfix uses regular expressions, database tables, and the MAPS project's black hole lists to filter out spam. Table 19.22 shows some of Postfix's spam-related variables.

**Table 19.22    Variables that affect Postfix's spam filtering**

| Variable | Meaning |
|---|---|
| header_checks | Filters on headers |
| smtpd_client_restrictions | Filters on client connections, black hole lists, etc. |
| smtpd_sender_restrictions | Filters on sender addresses |
| smtpd_recipient_restrictions | Filters on recipient addresses |
| smtpd_helo_required | Requires SMTP HELO with hostname identified |
| smtpd_helo_restrictions | Requires reverse DNS lookup |
| smtpd_etrn_restrictions | Lists hosts allowed to request queue runs |

Electronic Mail

If a message matches a table lookup and the table value is REJECT, then the message is rejected with an appropriate error message. For the Perl hackers among our readers, here is an example of a regular expression used in one site's spam filters:

```
/^friend@.*$/              550 Stick this in your pipe $0
```

If you really had a user named "friend" at your domain, you could exclude that user from the friendly error message with:

```
/^friend@(?!mysite.com).*$/ 550 Stick this in your pipe $0
```

To use the MAPS projects black hole lists, add the following to your **main.cf** file:

```
maps_rbl_domains =
    rbl.maps.vix.com
    dul.maps.vix.com
    relays.mail-abuse.org

smtpd_client_restrictions = reject_maps_rbl
```

### Postfix examples

Since our experience with Postfix is much more limited than our experience with **sendmail**, we asked Wietse for some examples. The **conf** directory of the Postfix distribution also contains several examples.

In a Postfix mail hub/client environment, all systems send mail as *user@domain*. All systems receive mail for *user@hostname*; the hub receives mail for *user@domain*, too.

On the clients, **/etc/postfix/main.cf** contains:

```
myorigin = $mydomain
```

On the mail hub, **/etc/postfix/main.cf** looks like this:

```
myorigin = $mydomain
mydestination = $myhostname, localhost.$mydomain, $mydomain
```

To modify this configuration so that the workstation receives no mail from the network and relays everything through a mail hub, you must change both the **main.cf** configuration file and the **master.cf** daemon configuration file.

Client **/etc/postfix/main.cf**:

```
myorigin = $mydomain
relayhost = $mydomain
```

On the clients, comment out the SMTP server line in **/etc/postfix/master.cf**:

```
#smtp   inet n   -   n   -   -   smtpd
```

If you export the mail queue over NFS to clients, the clients need only the Postfix mail posting agent and zero-length **main.cf** and **master.cf** files.

Here's an example where mail comes in and out to individual hosts, but messages in BITNET or UUCP format are forwarded to the master.

The hub's configuration is:

```
myorigin = $mydomain
mydestination = $myhostname,localhost.$mydomain,$mydomain
transport_maps = hash:/etc/postfix/transport
```

The clients use:

```
myorigin = $mydomain
transport_maps = hash:/etc/postfix/transport
```

On both the master machine and the clients, **/etc/postfix/transport** should contain:

```
.bitnet     smtp:master
.uucp       smtp:master
```

## 19.14  RECOMMENDED READING

COSTALES, BRYAN and ERIC ALLMAN. *sendmail, 2nd Edition.* Sebastopol, CA: O'Reilly, 1997.

This book is the definitive tome—1,000 pages' worth. It includes a tutorial as well as a very complete reference section. The book reads well in the open-to-a-random-page mode, which we consider an important feature for a reference book. It has a good index too. The third edition is being worked on and will be out in 2000.

AVOLIO, FREDERICK M. AND PAUL A. VIXIE. *Sendmail Theory and Practice.* Digital Press, 1995.

Avolio and Vixie address the "why and how" of **sendmail**, whereas the Costales/Allman book talks more about the "what." This 250-pager takes a high-level approach.

CLAYTON, RICHARD. "Good Practice for Combating Unsolicited Bulk Email." RIPE/Demon Internet. 2000. http://www.ripe.net/ripe/docs/ripe-206.html

This document is aimed at ISPs. It has lots of policy information and some good links to technical subjects.

SCHWARTZ, ALAN, AND PAULA FERGUSON. *Managing Mailing Lists.* O'Reilly, 1998.

This book is a good reference on mailing lists.

The man page for **sendmail** describes its command-line arguments. See *Sendmail: An Internetwork Mail Router,* by Eric Allman, for an overview.

Installation instructions and a good description of the configuration file are covered in *Sendmail Installation and Operation Guide*, which can be found in the **doc/op** subdirectory of the **sendmail** distribution. This document is quite complete, and in conjunction with the **README** file in the **cf** directory, it gives a good nuts-and-bolts view of the **sendmail** system.

RFC822 describes the syntax of messages and addresses in a networked mail system, and RFC1123 describes host requirements. These are, in a sense, the functional specifications to which **sendmail** was built.

RFC821 defines the Simple Mail Transport Protocol (SMTP), and RFCs 1869, 1870, 1891, and 1985 extend it to ESMTP.

RFC974 describes MX records in the Domain Name System and their relationship to mail routing.

Other mail-related RFCs include:

- RFCs 1891–1894 – Delivery status notifications (bounce messages)
- RFC1985 – Remote queueing
- RFC2033 – LMTP, the Local Mail Transport Protocol
- RFC2034 – SMTP error codes
- RFC2045 – MIME extensions
- RFC2476 – MSA, Mail Submission Agent specifications
- RFC2487 – Secure SMTP over TLS
- RFC2554 – SMTP authentication

Postfix documentation and information can be found at www.porcupine.org.

# 20 *Network Management and Debugging*

Because networks increase the number of interdependencies among machines, they tend to magnify problems. As the saying goes, "Networking is when you can't get any work done because of the failure of a machine you have never even heard of."

Network management is the art and science of keeping a network healthy. It generally includes the following tasks:

- Fault detection for networks, gateways, and critical servers
- Schemes for notifying an administrator of problems
- General monitoring, to balance load and plan expansion
- Documentation and visualization of the network
- Administration of network devices from a central site

On a single Ethernet, it is generally not worthwhile to establish formal procedures for network management. Just test the network thoroughly after installation, and check it occasionally to be sure that its load is not excessive. When it breaks, fix it.

As your network grows, management procedures should become more automated. On a network consisting of several different subnets joined with switches or routers, you may want to start automating management tasks with shell scripts and simple programs. If you have a WAN or a complex local network, you should consider installing a dedicated network management station with special software.

In some cases, your organization's reliability needs will dictate the sophistication of your network management system. A problem with the network can bring all work to a standstill. If your site cannot tolerate downtime, it may well be worthwhile to obtain and install a high-end enterprise network management system.

Unfortunately, even the best network management system cannot prevent all failures. It is critical to have a well-documented network and a high-quality staff available to handle the inevitable collapses.

## 20.1 TROUBLESHOOTING A NETWORK

Several good tools are available for debugging a network at the TCP/IP layer. Most give low-level information, so you must understand the main ideas of TCP/IP and routing in order to use the debugging tools.

On the other hand, network issues can also stem from problems with higher-level protocols such as DNS, NFS, and HTTP. You might want to read through Chapter 13, *TCP/IP Networking*, and Chapter 14, *Routing*, before tackling this chapter.

In this section, we start with some general troubleshooting strategy. We then cover several essential tools, including **ping**, **traceroute**, **netstat**, **tcpdump**, and **snoop**. We don't discuss the **arp** command in this chapter, though it, too, is a useful debugging tool—see page 286 for more information.

When your network is broken, chances are that you'll be in quite a rush to repair it. Stop right there! It's important to take a moment and consider how to approach the problem before jumping into action. The biggest mistake you can make is to introduce poorly planned changes into an already failing network.

Before you attack your network, consider these principles:

- Make one change at a time, and test each change to make sure that it had the effect you intended.

- Document the situation as it was before you got involved, and document every change you make along the way.

- Start at one "end" of a system or network and work through the system's critical components until you reach the problem. For example, you might start by looking at the network configuration on a client, work your way up to the physical connections, investigate the network hardware, and finally, check the server's physical connections and software configuration.

- Communicate regularly. Most network problems involve or affect lots of different people: users, ISPs, system administrators, telco engineers, network administrators, etc. Clear, consistent communication will prevent you from hindering each other's efforts to solve the problem.

- Work as a team. Years of experience show that people make fewer stupid mistakes if they have a peer helping out.

- Use the layers of the network to negotiate the problem. Start at the "top" or "bottom" and work your way through the protocol stack.

This last point deserves a bit more discussion. As described on page 265, the architecture of TCP/IP defines several layers of abstraction at which components of the network can function. For example, HTTP depends on TCP, TCP depends on IP, IP depends on the Ethernet protocol, and the Ethernet protocol depends on the integrity of the network cable. You can dramatically reduce the amount of time spent debugging a problem if you first figure out which layer is misbehaving.

Ask yourself questions like these as you work up (or down) the stack:

- Do you have physical connectivity and a link light?
- Is your interface configured properly?
- Is DNS configured properly?[1]
- Do your ARP tables show other hosts?
- Can you ping the localhost address (127.0.0.1)?
- Can you ping other local hosts by IP address?
- Can you ping other local hosts by hostname?
- Can you ping hosts on another network?
- Do high-level commands like **telnet** and **ssh** work?

Once you've identified where the problem lies, take a step back and consider the effect your subsequent tests and prospective fixes will have on other services and hosts.

## 20.2  PING: CHECK TO SEE IF A HOST IS ALIVE

The **ping** command is embarrassingly simple, but in many situations it is all you need. It sends an ICMP ECHO_REQUEST packet to a target host and waits to see if the host answers back. Despite its simplicity, **ping** is one of the workhorses of network debugging.

You can use **ping** to check the status of individual hosts and to test segments of the network. Routing tables, physical networks, and gateways are all involved in processing a ping, so the network must be more or less working for **ping** to succeed. If **ping** doesn't work, you can be pretty sure that nothing more sophisticated will work either. However, this rule does not apply to networks that block ICMP echo requests with a firewall. Make sure that a firewall isn't interfering with your debugging before you conclude that the target host is ignoring a **ping**. You might consider disabling a meddlesome firewall for a short period of time to facilitate debugging.

Every vendor provides a **ping**. Most versions of **ping** run in an infinite loop unless a packet count argument is given. Under Solaris, **ping -s** provides the extended output that other versions use by default. Once you've had your fill of pinging, type the interrupt character (usually <Control-C>) to get out.

Here's an example:

```
% ping beast
```

---

1. If your machine hangs at boot time, boots very slowly, or hangs on inbound **telnet** connections, DNS should be a prime suspect.

```
PING beast (10.1.1.46): 56 data bytes
64 bytes from 10.1.1.46: icmp_seq=0 ttl=255 time=0.808 ms
64 bytes from 10.1.1.46: icmp_seq=1 ttl=255 time=0.400 ms
64 bytes from 10.1.1.46: icmp_seq=2 ttl=255 time=0.390 ms
^C
--- beast ping statistics ---
3 packets transmitted, 3 packets received, 0% packet loss
round-trip min/avg/max/stddev = 0.390/0.533/0.808/0.195 ms
```

The output for beast shows the host's IP address, the ICMP sequence number of each response packet, and the round trip travel time. The most obvious thing that the output above tells you is that the server beast is alive and connected to the network.

On a healthy network, **ping** can allow you to determine if a host is down. Conversely, when a remote host is known to be up and in good working order, **ping** can give you useful information about the health of the network. Ping packets are routed by the usual IP mechanisms, and a successful round trip means that all networks and gateways lying between the source and destination are working correctly, at least to a first approximation.

The ICMP sequence number is a particularly valuable piece of information. Discontinuities in the sequence indicate dropped packets. Despite the fact that IP does not guarantee the delivery of packets, a healthy network should drop very few of them. Lost-packet problems are important to track down because they tend to be masked by higher-level protocols. The network may appear to function correctly, but it will be much slower than it ought to be, not only because of the retransmitted packets but also because of the protocol overhead needed to detect and manage them.

To track down the cause of disappearing packets, first run **traceroute** (see the next section) to discover the route that packets are taking to the target host. Then ping the intermediate gateways in sequence to discover which link is dropping packets. To pin down the problem, you need to send a statistically significant number of packets. The network fault will generally lie on the link between the last gateway that you can ping without significant loss of packets and the gateway beyond it.

The round trip time reported by **ping** gives you insight into the overall performance of a path through a network. Moderate variations in round trip time do not usually indicate problems. Packets may occasionally be delayed by tens or hundreds of milliseconds for no apparent reason; that's just the way IP and UNIX work. You should expect to see a fairly consistent round trip time for the majority of packets, with occasional lapses. Many of today's routers implement rate-limited responses to ICMP packets, which means that a router may delay responding to your ping if it is already dealing with a lot of ICMP traffic.

The **ping** program allows you to send echo request packets of any size. By using a packet larger than the MTU of the network (1,500 bytes for Ethernet), you can force fragmentation to take place. This practice will help you to identify media errors or other low-level issues such as problems with a congested ATM network.

Under Solaris and HP-UX, you simply add the desired packet size to the end of the **ping** command:

% **ping cuinfo.cornell.edu 1500**

Red Hat Linux and FreeBSD require you to specify the desired size in bytes with the **-s** flag. Because excessively large packets can cause network problems, FreeBSD restricts the use of this option to root:[2]

# **ping -s 1500 cuinfo.cornell.edu**

Use the **ping** command with the following caveats in mind. First, it is hard to distinguish the failure of a network from the failure of a server with only the **ping** command. A failed ping just tells you that *something* is wrong.

Second, a ping does not guarantee much about the target machine's state. Echo request packets are handled within the IP protocol stack and do not require a server process to be running on the probed host. A response guarantees only that a machine is powered on and has not experienced a kernel panic. You'll need higher-level methods to verify the availability of individual services such as HTTP and DNS.

## 20.3  TRACEROUTE: TRACE IP PACKETS

**traceroute**, written by Van Jacobson, lets you discover the sequence of gateways that an IP packet travels through to reach its destination. Almost all modern operating systems come with some version of **traceroute**.

The syntax is simply

**traceroute** *hostname*

There are a variety of options, most of which are not important in daily use. As usual, the *hostname* can be specified either symbolically or numerically. The output is simply a list of hosts, starting with the first gateway and ending at the destination.

For example, a **traceroute** from the host jaguar to the host drevil produces the following output:

```
% traceroute drevil
traceroute to drevil (192.225.55.137), 30 hops max, 38 byte packets
 1  xor-gw2 (192.108.21.254)  0.840 ms  0.693 ms  0.671 ms
 2  xor-gw4 (192.225.56.10)  4.642 ms  4.582 ms  4.674 ms
 3  drevil (192.225.55.137)  7.959 ms  5.949 ms  5.908 ms
```

From this output we can tell that jaguar is exactly three hops away from drevil, and we can see which gateways are involved in the connection. The round trip time for each gateway is also shown—three samples for each hop are measured and displayed. A typical **traceroute** between Internet hosts can include ten or twenty hops.

2. The 1998 Ping of Death attack that could crash both UNIX and Windows systems was executed simply by transmission of an overly large ping packet. When the fragmented packet was reassembled, it filled the default memory buffer and crashed the machine.

Network Management

**traceroute** works by setting the time-to-live (TTL, actually "hop count to live") field of an outbound packet to an artificially low number. As packets arrive at a gateway, their TTL is decreased. When a gateway decreases the TTL to 0, it discards the packet and sends an ICMP "time exceeded" message back to the originating host.

*See page 442 for more information about reverse DNS lookups.*

The first few **traceroute** packets have their TTL set to 1. The first gateway to see such a packet (xor-gw2 in this case) determines that the TTL has been exceeded and notifies jaguar of the dropped packet by sending back an ICMP message. The sender's IP address in the header of the error packet identifies the gateway; **traceroute** looks up this address in DNS to find the gateway's hostname.

To identify the second-hop gateway, a second round of packets with TTL fields set to 2 are sent out. The first gateway routes the packets and decreases their TTL by 1. At the second gateway, the packets are then dropped and ICMP error messages generated as before. This process continues until the TTL is equal to the number of hops to the destination host and the packets reach their destination successfully.

Most routers send their ICMP messages from the interface "closest" to your host. If you run **traceroute** backwards from the destination host, you will probably see different IP addresses being used to identify the same set of routers.

Since **traceroute** sends three packets for each value of the TTL field, you may sometimes observe an interesting artifact. If an intervening gateway multiplexes traffic across several routes, the packets might be returned by different hosts; in this case, **traceroute** simply prints them all.

Let's look at a more interesting example from a host at colorado.edu to xor.com:

```
rupertsberg% traceroute xor.com
traceroute: Warning: xor.com has multiple addresses; using 192.225.33.1
traceroute to xor.com (192.225.33.1), 30 hops max, 40 byte packets
  1  cs-gw3-faculty.cs.colorado.edu (128.138.236.3)  1.362 ms  2.144 ms  2.76 ms
  2  cs-gw-dmz.cs.colorado.edu (128.138.243.193)  2.720 ms  4.378 ms  5.052 ms
  3  engr-cs.Colorado.EDU (128.138.80.141)  5.587 ms  2.454 ms  2.773 ms
  4  hut-engr.Colorado.EDU (128.138.80.201)  2.743 ms  5.643 ms  2.772 ms
  5  cuatm-gw.Colorado.EDU (128.138.80.2)  5.587 ms  2.784 ms  2.777 ms
  6  204.131.62.6 (204.131.62.6)  5.585 ms  3.464 ms  2.761 ms
  7  border-from-BRAN.coop.net (199.45.134.81)  5.593 ms  6.433 ms  5.521 ms
  8  core-gw-eth-2-5.coop.net (199.45.137.14)  53.806 ms  *  19.202 ms
  9  xor.com (192.225.33.1)  16.838 ms  15.972 ms  11.204 ms
```

This output shows that packets must traverse five of our internal gateways before leaving the colorado.edu network (cs-gw3-faculty to cuatm-gw). The next-hop gateway on the BRAN network (204.131.62.6) doesn't have a name in DNS. After two hops in coop.net, we arrive at xor.com.

At hop 8, we see a star in place of one of the round trip times. This notation indicates that no response (error packet) was received in response to the probe. In this case, the cause is probably congestion, but that is not the only possibility. **traceroute** relies on low-priority ICMP packets, which many routers are smart enough to drop in preference to "real" traffic. A few stars shouldn't send you into a panic.

If you see stars in all of the round trip time fields for a given gateway, no "time exceeded" messages are arriving from that machine. Perhaps the gateway is simply down. Sometimes, a gateway will be configured to silently discard packets with expired TTLs. In this case, you will still be able to see through the silent host to the gateways beyond. Another possibility is that the gateway's error packets are slow to return and that **traceroute** has stopped waiting for them by the time they arrive.

Some firewalls block ICMP "time exceeded" messages entirely. If there's one of these firewalls along the path, you won't get information about any of the gateways beyond it. However, you can still determine the total number of hops to the destination because the probe packets will eventually get all the way there. Also, some firewalls may block the outbound UDP datagrams that **traceroute** sends to trigger the ICMP responses. This problem causes **traceroute** to report no useful information at all.

A slow link does not necessarily indicate a malfunction. Some physical networks have a naturally high latency. Sluggishness can also be a sign of congestion on the receiving network, especially if the network uses a CSMA/CD technology that makes repeated attempts to transmit a packet (Ethernet is one example). Inconsistent round trip times would support such a hypothesis, since collisions increase the randomness of the network's behavior.

Sometimes, you may see the notation !N instead of a star or round trip time. It indicates that the current gateway sent back a "network unreachable" error, meaning that it doesn't know how to route your packet. Other possibilities include !H for "host unreachable" and !P for "protocol unreachable." A gateway that gives you any of these error messages will usually be the last hop you can get to. That host usually has a routing problem (possibly caused by a broken link): either its static routes are wrong or dynamic protocols have failed to propagate a usable route to the destination.

If **traceroute** doesn't seem to be working for you (or is working incredibly slowly), it may be timing out while trying to resolve the hostnames of gateways by using DNS. If DNS is broken on the host you are tracing from, use **traceroute -n** to request numeric output. This option prevents the use of DNS; it may be the only way to get **traceroute** to function on a crippled network.

## 20.4  NETSTAT: GET TONS O' NETWORK STATISTICS

**netstat** provides a wealth of information about the state of your computer's networking software, including interface statistics, routing information, and connection tables. There isn't really a unifying theme to the different sets of output, except for the fact that they all relate to the network. Every system provides **netstat**, but since the command is kind of a "kitchen sink," different systems understand somewhat different options.

Here, we discuss the four most common uses of **netstat**:

- Monitoring the status of network connections
- Inspecting interface configuration information
- Examining the routing table
- Getting operational statistics for various network protocols

## Monitoring the status of network connections

With no arguments, **netstat** displays the status of active TCP and UDP ports. Inactive ("listening") servers waiting for connections aren't normally shown; they can be seen with **netstat -a**.[3] The output looks like this:

```
% netstat -a
Active Internet connections (including servers)
Proto   Recv-Q  Send-Q  Local Address   Foreign Address    (state)
tcp4    0       0       *.6013          *.*                LISTEN
tcp46   0       0       *.6013          *.*                LISTEN
tcp4    0       0       nimi.ssh        xor.com.4105       ESTABLISHED
tcp4    0       20      nimi.ssh        xor.com.1612       ESTABLISHED
tcp4    0       0       *.13500         *.*                LISTEN
tcp4    0       0       nimi.ssh        135.197.2.114.883  ESTABLISHED
tcp4    0       0       nimi.1599       xor.com.telnet     ESTABLISHED
tcp4    0       0       *.ssh           *.*                LISTEN
tcp46   0       0       *.ssh           *.*                LISTEN
tcp4    0       0       nimi.ssh        135.197.2.114.776  ESTABLISHED
tcp4    0       0       *.cvsup         *.*                LISTEN
udp4    0       0       *.syslog        *.*
udp4    0       0       *.ntalk         *.*
...
```

The preceding example was run on the host nimi. It shows several inbound SSH connections, an outbound **telnet** connection, and a bunch of ports listening for other connections. Also of note are the lines showing the protocol as tcp46, which are services running on IPv6.

Addresses are shown as *hostname.service*, where the *service* is a port number. For well-known services, **netstat** shows the port symbolically, using the mapping defined in **/etc/services**. You can obtain numeric addresses with the **-n** option. Remember, if your DNS is broken, **netstat** will be painful to use without the **-n** flag.

Send-Q and Recv-Q show the sizes of the send and receive queues for the connection on the local host; the queue sizes on the other end of a TCP connection might be different. They should tend toward 0 and at least not be consistently nonzero. Of course, if you are running **netstat** over a network terminal, the send queue for your connection will probably never be 0.

The connection state has meaning only for TCP; UDP is a connectionless protocol. The most common states you'll see are ESTABLISHED for currently active connec-

---

3. Connections for "UNIX domain sockets" are also shown, but since they aren't related to networking, we do not discuss them here.

tions, LISTEN for servers waiting for connections (not normally shown without **-a**), and TIME_WAIT for connections in the process of closing.

This display is primarily useful for debugging higher-level problems once you have determined that basic networking facilities are working correctly. It lets you verify that servers are set up correctly and facilitates the diagnosis of certain types of miscommunication, particularly with TCP. For example, a connection that stays in state SYN_SENT identifies a process that is trying to contact a nonexistent or inaccessible network server.

*See Chapter 12 for more information about kernel tuning.*

If **netstat** shows a lot of connections in the SYN_WAIT condition, your host is probably unable to handle the number of connections being requested. This inadequacy may be due to kernel tuning limitations or even to malicious flooding.

### Inspecting interface configuration information

**netstat -i** shows the status of network interfaces. For example, here is output from **netstat -i** on the Solaris machine evolve:

```
% netstat -i
Name  Mtu   Net/Dest    Ipkts  Ierrs  Opkts   Oerrs  Collis
lo0   8232  loopback    11650  0      11650   0      0
hme0  1500  evolve      16438  0      18356   0      110
hme1  1500  evolve-bl   94852  7      379410  13     487
```

This host has two network interfaces: one for regular traffic and a "backlan" connection called evolve-bl. Ipkts and Opkts report the number of packets that have been received and transmitted on each interface since the machine was booted. Ierrs and Oerrs show the number of input and output errors; many different types of errors are counted in these buckets, and it is normal for a few to show up.

Errors should be less than 1% of the associated packets. If your error rate is high, compare the rates of several neighboring machines. A large number of errors on a single machine suggests a problem with that machine's interface or connection. An error rate that is high everywhere most likely indicates a media problem.

Collisions indicate a loaded network; errors often indicate cabling problems. Although a collision is a type of error, it is counted separately by **netstat**. The Collis column gives the number of collisions that were experienced while packets were being sent.[4] Use this number to calculate the percentage of output packets (Opkts) that result in collisions. In the example above, the collision rate on interface hme0 is about 0.6% and the collision rate on interface hme1 is 1.3%. On a properly functioning network, collisions should be less than 5% of output packets, and anything over 15% indicates serious congestion problems.

**netstat** can also monitor a specific interface in real time, although the flags to request this behavior are different on each version of UNIX. The following commands give

---

4. This field has meaning only on broadcast-based networks such as Ethernet.

Network Management

interface statistics at one-second intervals. The output that is shown is adapted from a FreeBSD system.

```
solaris% netstat -i 1
hp-ux% netstat 1
redhat% netstat -i -c
freebsd% netstat 1
```

| input | (Total) | | output | | |
|---|---|---|---|---|---|
| packets | errs | packets | errs | colls |
| 13971549 | 1216 | 14757869 | 16 | 1431629 |
| 512 | 0 | 99 | 1 | 27 |
| 464 | 1 | 94 | 0 | 40 |
| 516 | 0 | 101 | 0 | 26 |
| 452 | 1 | 87 | 0 | 14 |
| 336 | 0 | 71 | 0 | 19 |

...

In this example, the collision rate is running at 20%–30%. The network is probably very slow and possibly even unusable.

**netstat**'s continuous mode is especially useful for tracking down the source of errors. **netstat -i** can alert you to the existence of problems, but it can't tell you whether the errors came from a continuous, low-level problem or from a brief but catastrophic event. Observing the network over time under a variety of load conditions will give you a much better impression of what's going on. Try running **ping** with a large ping packet size while you watch the output of **netstat**.

### Examining the routing table

**netstat -r** displays the kernel's routing table. Here is a sample from a Solaris machine with two network interfaces:

```
% netstat -r -n
Routing Table:
Destination     Gateway            Flags  Ref    Use    Interface
192.225.44.0    192.225.44.88      U      3     1841    hme0
192.168.3.0     192.168.3.12       U      2     1317    hme1
10.0.0.0        192.168.3.252      UG     0        4    hme1
default         192.225.44.254     UG     0    91668
127.0.0.1       127.0.0.1          UH     0      543    lo0
...
```

Destinations and gateways can be displayed either as hostnames or as IP addresses; the **-n** flag requests numeric output.

*See page 283 for more information about the routing table.*

The Flags characterize the route: U means up (active), G is a gateway, and H is a host route. The D flag (not shown) indicates a route resulting from an ICMP redirect. G and H together indicate a host route that passes through an intermediate gateway. The remaining fields give statistics on the route: the current number of TCP connections using the route, the number of packets sent, and the interface used. Remember that this output varies slightly among operating systems.

Use this form of **netstat** to check on the health of your machine's routing table. It's particularly important to verify that the system has a default route and that it is correct. On some systems, the default route is represented by an all-0 destination address (0.0.0.0); on others, the word "default" appears instead.

### Viewing operational statistics for various network protocols

**netstat -s** dumps the contents of counters that are scattered throughout the network code. The output has separate sections for IP, ICMP, TCP, and UDP. Below are pieces of **netstat -s** output from a gateway machine; they have been edited to show only the tastiest pieces of information.

```
ip:
    2313683 total packets received
    0 bad header checksums
    1642600 packets for this host
    25743 packets sent from this host
    0 output packets dropped due to no bufs, etc.
```

The absence of checksum errors indicates a clean hardware connection. It is important to check that packets are not getting dropped because of lack of memory (bufs in this example, but often referred to as "mbufs").[5]

```
icmp:
    57 calls to icmp_error
    Output histogram:
        echo reply: 157
        destination unreachable: 57
    Input histogram:
        echo reply: 6
        destination unreachable: 4
        echo: 157
        time exceeded: 14
    157 message responses generated
```

The number of echo requests, responses generated, and echo replies all match. Note that "destination unreachable" messages can still be generated even when all packets are apparently forwardable. Bad packets can eventually reach a gateway that rejects them, and error messages are then sent back along the gateway chain.

```
tcp:
    25087 packets sent
    25499 packets received
    31 connection requests
    30 connection accepts
    56 connections established (including accepts)
    64 connections closed (including 13 drops)
    4 embryonic connections dropped
```

---

5. To get more details about memory usage by network services on Solaris and FreeBSD, try using the **-m** flag with **netstat**.

It's a good idea to develop a feel for the normal ranges of these statistics so that you can recognize pathological states.

## 20.5 PACKET SNIFFERS

**tcpdump**, **snoop**, and **nettl** belong to a class of tools known as packet sniffers. They listen to the traffic on a network and record or print packets that meet certain criteria specified by the user. For example, all packets sent to or from a particular host or TCP packets related to one particular network connection could be inspected.

Packet sniffers are useful both for solving problems you know about and for discovering entirely new problems. It's a good idea to take an occasional sniff of your network to make sure the traffic is in order.

Since packet sniffers need to be able to intercept traffic that the local machine would not normally receive (or at least, pay attention to), the underlying network hardware must allow access to every packet. Broadcast technologies such as Ethernet work fine, as do some types of token ring network on which the sender of a packet removes it from the ring after it has made a complete circuit.

*See page 377 for more information about network switches.* Since packet sniffers need to see as much of the raw network traffic as possible, they can be thwarted by network switches, which by design try to limit the propagation of "unnecessary" packets. However, it can still be informative to try out a sniffer on a switched network. You may discover problems related to broadcast or multicast packets. Depending on your switch vendor, you may be surprised at how much traffic you can see.

In addition to having potential access to all network packets, the interface hardware must provide a way to actually transport those packets up to the software layer. Packet addresses are normally checked in hardware, and only broadcast/multicast packets and those addressed to the local host are relayed to the kernel. In "promiscuous mode," an interface lets the kernel read all packets on the network, even the ones intended for other hosts.

Packet sniffers understand many of the packet formats used by standard UNIX daemons, and they can often print out packets in a human-readable form. This capability makes it easier to track the flow of a conversation between two programs. Some sniffers print the ASCII contents of a packet in addition to the packet header, which can be useful for investigating high-layer protocols. Since some of these protocols send information (and even passwords) across the network as cleartext, you must exercise caution to avoid invading the privacy of your users.

Each of our example operating systems comes with a packet sniffer. The sniffer must read data from a raw network device, so it must run as root. Although the root limitation serves to decrease the chance that normal users will listen in on your network traffic, it is really not much of a barrier. Some sites choose to remove the sniffers from most hosts to reduce the chance of abuse. If nothing else, you should check your systems' interfaces to be sure they are not running in promiscuous mode without your knowledge or consent.

### snoop: Solaris's packet sniffer

Solaris includes a packet sniffer called **snoop**. It takes arguments on the command line that specify how to behave and what packets to collect. **snoop** can filter packets based on host, protocol, packet type, and port number, among other things.

With no arguments, **snoop** collects packets from the first interface it finds, which is usually also the first interface listed by **netstat -i** (excluding the loopback). To specify a particular interface, use the **-d** *device* flag, where *device* is the name of the interface as reported by **netstat -i** (often hme0 for the first Ethernet interface). Using the **-V** flag gives you a little more information, and the **-v** flag gives you several lines of detail on each packet.

**snoop**'s command-line language is quite sophisticated, and it is well documented in the **snoop** man page. Expressions can be created with primitives such as **host**, **port**, **tcp**, **udp**, and **ip**. Simple expressions can be combined with primitives such as **and**, **or**, and **not**. Let's look at a couple of examples.

Below is the output of a **snoop** session that might be useful for debugging mail between the hosts evolve and xor.com. We overspecified the filters to **snoop** to give a better example:

```
# snoop host chimchim and host evolve and tcp port 25
evolve.xor.com -> xor.com SMTP C
     xor.com -> evolve.xor.com SMTP R 220 xor.com ESMTP Se
evolve.xor.com  > xor.com SMTP C
evolve.xor.com -> xor.com SMTP C EHLO evolve.xor.com\r
     xor.com -> evolve.xor.com R 250- xor.com Hello ev
evolve.xor.com -> xor.com SMTP C MAIL FROM: <root@evol
     xor.com -> evolve.xor.com SMTP R
     xor.com -> evolve.xor.com SMTP R 250 <root@evolve.xor
evolve.xor.com -> xor.com SMTP C RCPT TO:<ned@xor.com>
     xor.com -> evolve.xor.com SMTP R 250 <ned@xor.com>...
evolve.xor.com -> xor.com SMTP C DATA\r\n
     xor.com -> evolve.xor.com SMTP R 354 Enter mail, end
```

You should read the command and arguments above like this: "Capture all packets between the hosts chimchim and evolve which involve TCP port 25."

This example shows one line for each packet that was collected. The packet's source is written first, and the destination appears in the second column. The remainder of the line contains information from the highest layer of the packet, such as protocol, port, and the first few bytes of the packet's data (we cut out a few columns from this example to save space).

If you **telnet** to a host and run **snoop** there, you must filter out the traffic from your **telnet** session. Otherwise, output to your terminal will get caught in loop as it is displayed on the virtual terminal, sent across the **telnet** session, and captured again. To ignore all traffic to or from the host evolve, you would use a command such as:

```
# snoop not host evolve
```

If we were investigating a failing DNS server named mrhat, we might use the following command line:

```
# snoop host mrhat | grep DNS
```

This command incorporates a **grep** to further limit the packets that are displayed.

### nettl: HP-UX's packet sniffer

HP-UX is bundled with a sick joke of a packet sniffer called **nettl**.[6] **nettl** is actually very powerful and can keep up with a fast network, but configuring it is such a hassle that it is rarely useful for short-term network debugging. If you plan on doing network debugging from an HP-UX host, we recommend that you install **tcpdump**.

**nettl** is part of HP-UX's Network Tracing and Logging package. By default, **nettl** logging is started at boot time. Unless you want to use **nettl** to collect data indefinitely, it is wise to disable it until you need it. Edit the **/etc/rc.config.d/nettl** file and set the NETTL variable to 0.

**nettl** reads its configuration information from **/etc/nettlgen.conf**.

### tcpdump: king of sniffers

**tcpdump**, yet another amazing network tool by Van Jacobson, is distributed with Red Hat Linux and FreeBSD. It is also available in source form for HP-UX, Solaris, and most other operating systems. **tcpdump** behaves much like **snoop** and has long been the industry-standard sniffer.

By default, **tcpdump** tunes in on the first network interface that it comes across. If it chooses the wrong interface, you can force an interface with the **-i** flag. If DNS is broken or you just don't want **tcpdump** doing name lookups, use the **-n** option. This option is important because slow DNS service can cause the filter to start dropping packets before they can be dealt with by **tcpdump**. The **-v** flag increases the information you see about packets, and **-vv** gives you even more data. Finally, **tcpdump** can store packets to a file with the **-w** flag and can read them back in with the **-r** flag.

For example, the following output comes from the machine jaguar.xor.com. The filter specification **host jaguar** limits the display of packets to those that directly involve the machine jaguar, either as source or as destination.

```
# tcpdump host jaguar
13:40:23 jaguar.xor.com.1697 > xor.com.domain: A? cs.colorado.edu.
13:40:23 xor.com.domain > jaguar.xor.com.1697: A mroe.cs.colorado.edu
13:40:23 jaguar.xor.com.1698 > xor.com.domain: PTR? 5.96.138.128.in-addr.arpa.
13:40:23 xor.com.domain > jaguar.xor.com.1698: PTR mroe.cs.colorado.edu.
```

6. Score one for truth in command naming: "nettle, vt.: to irritate; vex," *American Heritage Dictionary of the English Language, Third Edition.*

The first packet shows jaguar sending a DNS lookup request about cs.colorado.edu to xor.com. The response is the actual name of the machine for which that name is an alias, which is mroe.cs.colorado.edu. The third packet is a reverse lookup of mroe's IP address, and the fourth packet contains the expected response.

The **tcpdump** man page contains several good examples of advanced filtering along with a complete listing of primitives.

## 20.6  NETWORK MANAGEMENT PROTOCOLS

Networks have grown rapidly in size and value over the last decade, and along with that growth has come the need for an efficient way to manage them. Commercial vendors and standards organizations have approached this challenge in many different ways. The most significant developments have been the introduction of several standard device management protocols and a glut of high-level products that exploit those protocols.

Network management protocols provide a standard way of probing a device to discover its configuration, health, and network connections. In addition, they allow some of this information to be modified so that network management can be standardized across different kinds of machinery and performed from a central location.

The most common management protocol used with TCP/IP is the Simple Network Management Protocol, SNMP. Despite its name, SNMP is actually quite complex. It defines a hierarchical namespace of management data and a way to read and write the data at each node. It also defines a way for managed entities ("agents") to send event notification messages ("traps") to management stations. The protocol itself is simple; most of SNMP's complexity lies above the protocol layer in the conventions for constructing the namespace and the conventions for formatting data items within a node. SNMP is widely supported.

Several other standards are floating around out there. Many of them originate from the Distributed Management Task Force (DMTF), which is responsible for concepts such as WBEM (Web-Based Enterprise Management), DMI (Desktop Management Interface), and the CIM (Conceptual Interface Model). Some of these concepts, particularly DMI, have been embraced by several major vendors and may become a useful complement to (or even a replacement for) SNMP. For now, however, the vast majority of network management takes place over SNMP.

Since SNMP is only an abstract protocol, you need both a server program ("agent") and a client ("manager") to make use of it. (Perhaps counterintuitively, the server side of SNMP represents the thing being managed, and the client side is the manager.) Clients range from simple command-line utilities to dedicated management stations that graphically display networks and faults in eye-popping color.

Dedicated network management stations are the primary reason for the existence of management protocols. Most products let you build a topographic model of the network as well as a logical model; the two are presented together on-screen, along with a continuous indication of the status of each component.

Just as a chart can reveal the hidden meaning in a page of numbers, a network management station can summarize the state of a large network in a way that's easily accepted by a human brain. This kind of executive summary is almost impossible to get any other way.

A major advantage of management-by-protocol is that it promotes all kinds of network hardware onto a level playing field. UNIX systems are all basically similar, but routers, switches, and other low-level components are not. With SNMP, they all speak a common language and can be probed, reset, and configured from a central location. It's nice to have one consistent interface to all the network's hardware.

## 20.7  SNMP: THE SIMPLE NETWORK MANAGEMENT PROTOCOL

When SNMP first became widely used in the early 1990s, it started a mini gold rush. Hundreds of companies have come out with SNMP management packages. Also, many hardware and software vendors ship an SNMP agent as part of their product.

Before we dive into the gritty details of SNMP, we should note that the terminology associated with it is some of the most wretched technobabble to be found in the UNIX arena. The standard names for SNMP concepts and objects will actively lead you away from an understanding of what's going on. The people responsible for this state of affairs should have their keyboards smashed.

### SNMP organization

SNMP data is arranged in a standardized hierarchy. This enforced organization allows the data space to remain both universal and extensible, at least in theory. Large portions are set aside for future expansion, and vendor-specific additions are localized to prevent conflicts. The naming hierarchy is made up of "Management Information Bases" (MIBs), structured text files that describe the data accessible via SNMP. MIBs contain descriptions of specific data variables, which are referred to with names known as object identifiers or OIDs.

Translated into English, this means that SNMP defines a hierarchical namespace of variables whose values are tied to "interesting" parameters of the system.

The basic data types that an SNMP variable can contain are integer, string, and null. These can be combined into sequences of the basic types, and a sequence can be instantiated repeatedly to form a table. Most implementations support a variety of other data types as well.

The SNMP hierarchy is very much like a filesystem. However, a dot is used as the separator character, and each node is given a number rather than a name. By convention, nodes are also given text names for ease of reference, but this naming is really just a high-level convenience and not a feature of the hierarchy (it is similar in principle to the mapping of hostnames to IP addresses).

For example, the OID that refers to the uptime of the system is 1.3.6.1.2.1.1.3. This OID is also known by the human readable name

> iso.org.dod.internet.mgmt.mib-2.system.sysUpTime

The top levels of the SNMP hierarchy are political artifacts and generally do not contain useful data. In fact, useful data can currently be found only beneath the OID iso.org.dod.internet.mgmt (numerically, 1.3.6.1.2).

The basic SNMP MIB for TCP/IP (MIB-I) defines access to common management data: information about the system, its interfaces, address translation, and protocol operations (IP, ICMP, TCP, UDP, and others). A later and more complete reworking of this MIB (called MIB-II) is defined in RFC1213. Most vendors that provide an SNMP server support MIB-II. Table 20.1 presents a sampling of nodes from the MIB-II namespace.

**Table 20.1    Selected OIDs from MIB-II**

| OID[a] | Type | Contents |
|---|---|---|
| system.sysDescr | string | System info: vendor, model, OS type, etc. |
| system.sysLocation | string | Physical location of the machine |
| system.sysContact | string | Contact info for the machine's owner |
| system.sysName | string | System name, usually the full DNS name |
| interfaces.ifNumber | int | Number of network interfaces present |
| interfaces.ifTable | table | Table of infobits about each interface |
| ip.ipForwarding | int | 1 if system is a gateway, otherwise 2 |
| ip.ipAddrTable | table | Table of IP addressing data (masks, etc.) |
| ip.ipRouteTable | table | The system's routing table |
| icmp.icmpInRedirects | int | Number of ICMP redirects received |
| icmp.icmpInEchos | int | Number of pings received |
| tcp.tcpConnTable | table | Table of current TCP connections |
| udp.udpTable | table | Table of UDP sockets with servers listening |

a. Relative to iso.org.dod.internet.mgmt.mib-2.

In addition to the basic MIB, there are MIBs for various kinds of hardware interfaces and protocols. There are MIBs for individual vendors and MIBs for particular hardware products. A MIB for you, a MIB for me, catch that MIB behind the tree.

A MIB is only a convention about the naming of management data. It must be backed up with agent-side code that maps between the SNMP namespace and the device's actual state to be useful. Code for the basic MIB (now MIB-II) comes with most UNIX SNMP agents. Some agents are extensible to include supplemental MIBs, and some are not.

### SNMP protocol operations

There are only four basic SNMP operations: get, get-next, set, and trap.

Get and set are the basic operations for reading and writing data to a node identified by a specific OID. Get-next is used to step through a MIB hierarchy, as well as to read the contents of tables.

A trap is an unsolicited, asynchronous notification from server (agent) to client (manager) that reports the occurrence of an interesting event or condition. Several standard traps are defined, including "I've just come up" notifications, traps that report the failure or recovery of a network link, and traps for various routing and authentication problems. Many other not-so-standard traps are in common use, including some that simply watch the values of other SNMP variables and fire off a message when a specified range is exceeded. The mechanism by which the destinations of trap messages are specified depends on the implementation of the agent.

Since SNMP messages can potentially modify configuration information, some security mechanism is needed. The simplest version of SNMP security is based on the concept of an SNMP "community name," which is really just a horribly obfuscated way of saying "password." There's usually one community name for read-only access and another that allows writing.

Version 3 of the SNMP standard introduced access control methods with higher security. Although support for these schemes is still somewhat limited in production network hardware, it is reasonable to expect this situation to change soon.

### RMON: remote monitoring MIB

The RMON MIB permits the collection of generic network performance data (that is, data not tied to any one particular device). Network sniffers or "probes" can be deployed around the network to gather information about utilization and performance. Once a useful amount of data has been collected, statistics and interesting information about the data can be shipped back to a central management station for analysis and presentation. Many probes have a packet capture buffer and can provide a sort of remote **tcpdump** facility.

RMON is defined in RFC1757, which became a draft standard in 1995. The MIB is broken up into nine "RMON groups." Each group contains a different set of network statistics. If you have a large network with many WAN connections, you should consider buying probes to reduce the SNMP traffic across your WAN links. Once you have access to statistical summaries from the RMON probes, there's usually no need to gather raw data remotely. Many switches and routers support RMON and will store at least some network statistics.

## 20.8  SNMP AGENTS

Many OS and network hardware vendors ship their products with SNMP agents that can run right out of the box. The read-only community string is usually set to "public," and the write community string is occasionally set to "private" or "secret". We recently saw a list of dozens of vendors that follow this practice. Although it can be handy for system administrators, it is equally useful for hackers. If you decide to enable SNMP, be sure to configure your agents to use hard-to-guess community strings for both write *and* read access.

Solaris and HP-UX are shipped with decent SNMP agents. FreeBSD includes UCD SNMP in the **/usr/ports/net/ucd-snmp** directory. Red Hat Linux has no SNMP support in its standard distribution.

In the following sections we first describe the Solaris and HP-UX agents. We then talk a bit about the UCD SNMP package, which we recommend for systems that do not come with their own agent.

### SNMP on Solaris

Solaris comes with respectable management support. In addition to a rather comprehensive SNMP agent, it also provides DMI support.

The main SNMP agent is **/usr/lib/snmp/snmpdx**, which reads its configuration from the file **/etc/snmp/conf/snmpd.conf**. In this file, you can specify the values of many MIB variables and also set the agent's general configuration. For example, you can set the system description string (sysdescr), the trap host or hosts (trap), and the community strings (read-community, write-community). After you modify this file, kill and restart **snmpdx** to force your changes to take effect.

**snmpdx** also reads security information from **/etc/snmp/conf/snmpdx.acl**. In this file, you can list the IP addresses of hosts that should be allowed access to the local SNMP agent. Each set of hosts can have its own read and write community names. These features can dramatically increase the security of SNMP; unfortunately, all restrictions are turned off by default.

An off-the-shelf Solaris installation boots with two DMI-related processes. The first of these is **/usr/lib/dmi/dmispd**, which answers DMI queries directly. The second is **/usr/lib/dmi/snmpXdmid**, which translates SNMP requests into DMI requests and passes them on to **dmispd**. Once **dmispd** responds, **snmpXdmid** passes the responses back to the SNMP server, **snmpdx**. SNMP/DMI translations are defined by files in the **/var/dmi/map** directory. Only two variable translations are defined by default, so unless you are planning on adding more, you should really have no reason to run **snmpXdmid**.

If you don't have DMI management software or don't plan on using it, you can prevent both DMI processes from starting at boot time by renaming **/etc/rc3.d/S77dmi** to **/etc/rc3.d/s77dmi**. If you just want to disable **snmpXdmid**, you should rename its configuration file from **snmpXdmid.conf** to **snmpXdmid.conf.orig**.

### SNMP on HP-UX

One of HP's most successful software ventures is an enterprise network management tool called HP OpenView. Since HP is a leader in the network management space, it shouldn't be much of a surprise that HP-UX ships with an SNMP agent. Instead of providing a single, monolithic agent, HP's system employs a number of specialized subagents. This design allows HP to add subagents for new hardware or software without changing the overall system.

The master agent is **/usr/sbin/snmpdm**, but it should never be run directly. Use the shell script **/usr/sbin/snmpd** instead. In addition to starting **snmpdm**, the **snmpd** script starts the subagents that are responsible for gathering data.

The agent reads its configuration from **/etc/SnmpAgent.d/snmpd.conf**. Configuration information can also be specified on the **snmpd** command line.

Only five keywords can be used within **snmpd.conf**. They're illustrated in the following example:

```
# SNMP configuration for disaster.xor.com
get-community-name: ro-community
set-community-name: D8j4kL.2nG
trap-dest: jaguar.xor.com
trap-dest: ov.xor.com
location: First floor lab machine room
contact: root@disaster.xor.com
```

The get-community-name and set-community-name keywords set the SNMP community strings (aka passwords) that a client must provide to read and write data values. There can be more than one instance of each. However, access control cannot be subdivided: any name listed in any set-community-name statement is valid for any supported operation.

The trap-dest keyword specifies the name or IP address of an SNMP client that is to receive trap notifications. There can be several trap destinations—all traps are sent to all destinations.

The location and contact keywords set the values of the MIB-II sysLocation and sysContact OIDs.

You can control the amount of logging that **snmpd** generates with the **-m** flag:

```
snmpd -m logmask
```

The *logmask* should be a bitwise OR of your choice of the option flags in Table 20.2.

**Table 20.2    Option flag values for HP-UX snmpd**

| Flag | Meaning | Flag | Meaning |
|------|---------|------|---------|
| 0 | Disable logging | 8 | Log SNMP transactions |
| 1 | Log authentication failures | 16 | Log added objects |
| 2 | Log errors | 32 | Dump all packets in hex |
| 4 | Log configuration requests | 64 | Log trace messages |

Unfortunately, HP's SNMP agent does not use syslog. You can specify the location of its log file with **-l** *log*; the default is **/var/adm/snmpd.log**.

### The UCD SNMP agent

When SNMP was first standardized, Carnegie Mellon University and MIT both produced implementations. CMU's implementation was more complete and quickly became the de facto standard for UNIX systems. When active development at CMU died down, researchers at UC Davis took over the software.

The UCD distribution is now the authoritative free SNMP implementation for UNIX. We recommend it highly for systems with no SNMP implementation of their own. It includes an SNMP agent, some command-line tools, and even a library for developing SNMP-aware applications. We discuss the agent in some detail here and take a look at the command-line tools later in the chapter. The latest version is available from the web at ucd-snmp.ucdavis.edu.

As in other implementations, the agent collects information about the local host and serves it to SNMP managers across the network. The default installation includes MIBs for network interface, memory, disk, process, and CPU statistics. The agent is easily extensible since it can execute an arbitrary UNIX command and return the command's output as an SNMP response. You can use this feature to monitor almost anything on your system with SNMP.

By default, the agent is installed as **/usr/sbin/snmpd**. It is usually started at boot time and reads its configuration information from files in the **/etc/snmp** directory. The most important of these files is **snmpd.conf**, which contains most of the configuration information and comes shipped with a bunch of sample data collection methods enabled. Although the intention of the UCD authors seems to have been for users to edit only the **snmpd.local.conf** file, you must edit the **snmpd.conf** file at least once to disable any default data collection methods that you do not plan to use.

The UCD SNMP **configure** script lets you specify a default log file and a couple of other local settings. You can use **snmpd -l** to specify an alternate log file or **-s** to direct log messages to syslog. Table 20.3 shows a list of **snmpd**'s most important flags. We recommend that you always use the **-a** flag. For debugging, you should use the **-V**, **-d**, or **-D** flags, each of which gives progressively more information.

**Table 20.3    Useful flags for UCD's snmpd**

| Flag | Function |
|------|----------|
| **-l** *logfile* | Logs information to *logfile* |
| **-a** | Logs the addresses of all SNMP connections |
| **-d** | Logs the contents of every SNMP packet |
| **-V** | Enables verbose logging |
| **-D** | Logs debugging information (lots of it) |
| **-h** | Displays all arguments to **snmpd** |
| **-H** | Displays all configuration file directives |
| **-A** | Appends to the log file instead of overwriting it |
| **-s** | Logs to syslog (uses the daemon facility) |

It's worth mentioning that many useful SNMP-related Perl modules are available. Look on CPAN[7] for the latest information if you are interested in writing your own network management scripts.

## 20.9  NETWORK MANAGEMENT APPLICATIONS

We begin this section by exploring the simplest SNMP management tools: the commands provided with the UCD SNMP package. These commands are useful for familiarizing yourself with SNMP, and they're also great for one-off checks of specific OIDs. Next, we look at MRTG, a program that generates historical graphs of SNMP values, and NOCOL, an event-based monitoring system. We conclude with some recommendations of what to look for when purchasing a commercial system.

### The UCD SNMP tools

Even if your system comes with its own SNMP server, you may still want to compile and install the seven client-side tools, listed in Table 20.4, from the UC Davis package.

**Table 20.4  Command-line tools in the UCD SNMP package**

| Command | Function |
| --- | --- |
| snmpget | Gets the value of an SNMP variable from an agent |
| snmpgetnext | Gets the next variable in sequence |
| snmpset | Sets an SNMP variable on an agent |
| snmptable | Gets a table of SNMP variables |
| snmptranslate | Searches for and describes OIDs in the MIB hierarchy |
| snmptrap | Generates a trap alert |
| snmpwalk | Traverses a MIB starting at a particular OID |

In addition to their value on the command line, these programs are tremendously handy in simple scripts. It is often helpful to have **snmpget** save interesting data values to a text file every few minutes. (Use **cron** to implement the scheduling; see Chapter 9, *Periodic Processes*.)

**snmpwalk** is another useful tool. Starting at a specified OID (or at the beginning of the MIB, by default), this command repeatedly makes "get next" calls to an agent. This behavior results in a complete list of available OIDs and their associated values. Here's a sample **snmpwalk** of the host jaguar ("public" is the community string):

```
% snmpwalk jaguar public
system.sysDescr.0 = Linux jaguar 2.2.12-20 #1 Mon Sep 27 10:40:35 EDT 1999
system.sysUpTime.0 = Timeticks: (88516617) 10 days, 5:52:46.17
system.sysName.0 = jaguar
```

---

7. CPAN, the Comprehensive Perl Archive Network, is an amazing collection of useful Perl modules. Check it out at www.cpan.org.

```
system.sysLocation.0 = Second Floor Machine Room
interfaces.ifNumber.0 = 2
interfaces.ifTable.ifEntry.ifIndex.1 = 1
interfaces.ifTable.ifEntry.ifIndex.2 = 2
interfaces.ifTable.ifEntry.ifDescr.1 = "lo0" Hex: 6C 6F 30
interfaces.ifTable.ifEntry.ifDescr.2 = "eth0" Hex: 65 74 68 30
interfaces.ifTable.ifEntry.ifType.1 = softwareLoopback(24)
interfaces.ifTable.ifEntry.ifType.2 = ethernet-csmacd(6)
interfaces.ifTable.ifEntry.ifMtu.1 = 3924
interfaces.ifTable.ifEntry.ifMtu.2 = 1500
interfaces.ifTable.ifEntry.ifInOctets.1 = 12590602
interfaces.ifTable.ifEntry.ifInOctets.2 = 2287718531
interfaces.ifTable.ifEntry.ifInUcastPkts.1 = 75576
interfaces.ifTable.ifEntry.ifInUcastPkts.2 = 79730602
interfaces.ifTable.ifEntry.ifInErrors.1 = 0
interfaces.ifTable.ifEntry.ifInErrors.2 = 218
interfaces.ifTable.ifEntry.ifOutOctets.1 = 12591593
interfaces.ifTable.ifEntry.ifOutOctets.2 = 3374588125
...
```

In this example, we see some general information about the system, followed by statistics about the host's network interfaces, lo0 and eth0. Depending on the MIBs supported by the agent you are managing, a complete dump can run to hundreds of lines.

### MRTG: the Multi-Router Traffic Grapher

MRTG, written by Tobi Oetiker at ETH in Zurich, collects SNMP data over time and then graphs it. It's written mostly in Perl. MRTG is invaluable for analyzing the historical use of your system and network resources.

MRTG runs regularly from **cron** and can collect data from any SNMP source. Each time the program runs, new data is stored and new graph images are created.

MRTG is free and offers several attractive features. First, it maintains a zero-maintenance, statically-sized database; the software stores only enough data to create the necessary graphs. For example, MRTG could store one sample every minute for a day, one sample every hour for a week, and one sample every week for a year. This consolidation scheme lets you maintain important historical information without having to store unimportant details or to consume your time with database administration.

Second, MRTG can record and graph any SNMP variable. You're free to collect whatever data you want. When combined with the UCD SNMP agent, MRTG can provide a historical perspective on almost any system or network resource.

Exhibit A on the next page shows some examples of the graphs created by MRTG. These graphs show the traffic on a network interface over periods of a day and a week.

The future of MRTG lies in a new package, RRDtool, by the same author. RRDtool is similar in concept to MRTG, but with improved data consolidation and graphing features. Unlike MRTG, RRDtool does not offer any data collection methods of its own. Instead, a separate piece of software must collect the data.

**Exhibit A    Examples of MRTG graphs**

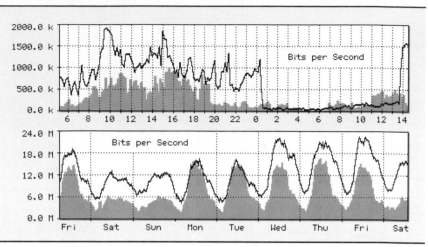

Currently, Jeff Allen's Cricket tool is the best choice for this role. Cricket is not limited to collecting SNMP data; it can pull in data from almost any network source. Since it is written in Perl, it's easy to add new data sources.

Tobi Oetiker's home page at ee-staff.ethz.ch/~oetiker provides links to the current versions of MRTG, RRDtool, and Cricket.

### NOCOL: Network Operation Center On-Line

NOCOL is an event-driven management tool that's currently maintained by Vikas Aggarwal. Although it will not help you determine how much your bandwidth utilization has increased over the last month, it will page you when your web server goes down. Actually, NOCOL can be configured to page (or email) your operations staff after many kinds of events.

The distribution includes monitor programs that supervise a variety of common points of failure. You can whip up new monitors in Perl, or even in C if you are feeling ambitious. For notification methods, the distribution can send email, generate web reports, view status with a **curses** interface, and use a dial-up modem to page you. As with monitor programs, it's easy to roll your own.

If you cannot afford a commercial network management tool, we suggest giving strong consideration to NOCOL. The software works very well for networks of less than 100 hosts and devices. You can read more at www.netplex-tech.com.

### Commercial management platforms

Hundreds of companies sell network management software, and new competitors enter the market every week. Instead of recommending the hottest products of the moment (which may no longer exist by the time this book is printed), we'll try to identify the features you should look for in a network management system.

**Data gathering flexibility:** It's important for management tools to be able to collect data from sources other than SNMP. Many packages include the ability to gather data from almost any network service. For example, some packages can make SQL database queries, check DNS records, and connect to web servers.

**User interface quality:** Expensive systems often offer a custom GUI or a web interface. The most well-marketed packages today all tout the ability to understand XML templates for data presentation. Although the UI often seems like just more marketing hype, it is important to have an interface that relays information clearly, simply, and comprehensibly.

**Value:** Some management packages come at a stiff price. HP's OpenView is both one of the most expensive and one of the most widely adopted network management systems. For many corporations, there is a definite value in being able to say that your site is managed by a high-end commercial system. If that isn't so important to your organization, you should look at the other end of the spectrum for free tools like MRTG and NOCOL.

**Automated discovery:** Many systems offer the ability to "discover" your network. Through a combination of broadcast pings, SNMP requests, ARP table lookups, and DNS queries, they are able to identify all your local hosts and devices. All the discovery implementations we have seen work pretty well, but none are very accurate on a complex (or heavily firewalled) network.

**Reporting features:** Many products can send alert email, activate pagers, and automatically generate tickets for popular trouble-tracking systems. Make sure that the platform you choose allows for flexible reporting; who knows what electronic devices you will be dealing with in a few years?

**Configuration management:** Some vendors step far beyond monitoring and alerting. They offer the ability to manage actual host and device configurations. For example, CiscoWorks provides an interface that lets you change a router's configuration in addition to monitoring its state with SNMP. Because device configuration information allows for a deeper analysis of network problems, we predict that many packages will develop along these lines in the future.

## 20.10 RECOMMENDED READING

CISCO ONLINE. *Internetworking Technology Overview: SNMP.* http://www.cisco.com/univercd/cc/td/doc/cisintwk/ito_doc/snmp.htm.

HUNT, CRAIG, AND GIGI ESTABROOK. *TCP/IP Network Administration, Second Edition*. Sebastopol: O'Reilly & Associates. 1998.

STALLINGS, WILLIAM. *Snmp, Snmpv2, Snmpv3, and Rmon 1 and 2, Third Edition*. Reading, MA: Addison-Wesley. 1999.

You may find the following RFCs to be useful as well. Instead of citing the actual titles of the RFCs, we have described their contents. The actual titles are an unhelpful jumble of buzzwords and SNMP jargon.

- RFC1155 – Characteristics of the SNMP data space (data types, etc.)
- RFC1156 – MIB-I definitions (description of the actual OIDs)
- RFC1157 – Simple Network Management Protocol
- RFC1213 – MIB-II definitions (OIDs)
- RFCs 1901-1910 – SNMPv2
- RFC2011 – SNMPv2 MIB for IP
- RFC2012 – SNMPv2 MIB for TCP
- RFC2013 – SNMPv2 MIB for UDP
- RFC2021 – RMON Version 2 using SMIv2
- RFC2570 – Introduction to SNMPv3

# 21 *Security*

UNIX was not designed with security in mind, and for that reason no UNIX system can be made truly secure. Throughout history, UNIX systems have regularly been broken into, beaten, brutalized, corrupted, commandeered, compromised, and illegally **fsck**ed. The Internet has made things even worse.

There are some steps you can take to make your system somewhat more resistant to attack. Even so, several fundamental flaws in the UNIX model ensure that you will never reach security nirvana:

- UNIX is optimized for convenience and doesn't make security easy or natural. UNIX was designed by researchers, for researchers, and its philosophy stresses easy manipulation of data in a networked, multiuser environment.

- UNIX security is effectively binary: you are either a powerless user, or you're root. UNIX facilities such as setuid execution tend to confer total power all at once. Slight lapses in security can compromise entire systems.

- Most administrative functions are implemented outside the kernel, where they can be inspected and tampered with. Hackers have broad access to the system.

The first edition of this book was published just months after the 1988 "Internet Worm" gained national attention after catching a large number of sites (including ours) off guard. At the time, it seemed that Robert Morris, Jr., the worm's author, had unleashed an inexcusable plague on the neighborly Internet community.

In reality, the worm caused little actual damage and increased security awareness on the Internet more than any other event to date. Once again, we were painfully reminded that good fences make good neighbors. A number of excellent tools for use by system administrators (as well as a formal organization for handling incidents of this nature) came into being as a result.

Many known security holes in UNIX will never be fixed, and others have been fixed by some vendors but not by all. In addition, many sites are a release or two behind, either because localization is too troublesome or because they do not subscribe to their vendor's software maintenance plan. When a vendor fixes a security hole, the window of opportunity for hackers does not disappear overnight.

It might seem that UNIX security should gradually improve over time as security problems are discovered and corrected, but unfortunately this does not seem to be the case. System software is growing ever more complicated, hackers are becoming better and better organized, and computers are connecting more and more intimately on the Internet. Security is an ongoing battle that can never really be won.

Remember, too, that

$$\text{Security} = \frac{1}{(1.072)(\text{Convenience})}$$

The more secure your system, the more miserable you and your users will tend to be.

## 21.1 SEVEN COMMON-SENSE RULES OF SECURITY

Effective system security has its roots in common sense and is a lot like dealing with an infestation of mice in your house. Here are seven rules you might use:

- Don't leave things that are likely to be interesting to mice lying on the kitchen table overnight. Cheese and peanut butter are excellent mouse getters.

- Plug the holes that mice are using to get into the house. If they can't get in, they won't bother you.

- Don't provide places within the house for mice to build nests. Piles of dirty clothes on the floor make good nests.

- Set traps along walls where you often see mice out of the corner of your eye.

- Check the traps daily to rebait them and to dispose of squashed mice. Full traps don't catch mice, and they smell.

- Avoid using commercial bait-and-kill poisons to deal with the situation. These can leave you with dead mice in your walls or kill your dog. Traditional snap traps are best.

- Get a cat!

You can use these same seven rules (well, slightly modified) to secure your UNIX systems. Here's how you might rewrite them:

- Don't put files on your system that are likely to be interesting to hackers or to nosy employees. Trade secrets, personnel files, payroll data, election results, etc., must be handled carefully if they're on-line. Securing such information cryptographically will provide a far higher degree of security than simply trying to prevent unauthorized users from accessing the files that contain it.

  Your site's security policy should specify how sensitive information is handled. See Chapter 27, *Policy and Politics*, and RFC2196 (the *Site Security Handbook*) for some suggestions.

- Plug holes that hackers can use to gain access to your system. Monitor the security bulletins from your vendor and the security mailing lists discussed in this chapter to learn about patches as they become available. Turn off unnecessary services.

- Don't provide places for hackers to build nests on your system. Hackers often break into one system and then use it as a base of operations to get into others. World-writable anonymous FTP directories, group accounts, and accounts with poorly chosen passwords all encourage nesting activity.

- Set traps to detect intrusions and attempted intrusions. Tools such as **tripwire**, **tcpd**, and **crack** (described starting on page 663) will help keep you abreast of potential problems.

- Monitor the reports generated by these security tools. A minor problem that is ignored in one report may grow into a catastrophe by the time the next report is sent.

- Teach yourself about UNIX system security. Any number of high-priced security consultants will happily come to your site and instill terror in you and your management about the insecurity of your systems. They'll explain that for only $250K they can make your site secure.

  Unfortunately, their solutions will often leave you with dead mice in your walls and kill your users' productivity. Traditional know-how and common sense are the most important parts of a site security plan.

- Prowl around looking for unusual activity. Investigate anything that seems unusual, such as odd log messages or changes in the activity of an account (more activity, activity at strange hours, or perhaps activity while the owner is on vacation).

## 21.2  HOW SECURITY IS COMPROMISED

The sections below discuss some common UNIX security problems and their standard countermeasures. But before we leap into the details, we should take a more general look at how real-world security problems tend to occur. Most security lapses stem from one of the following types of problems:

- **Unreliable wetware:** The human users (and administrators) of a computer system are often the weakest links in the chain of security. For example, America Online used to be notorious for being infested by hackers who posed as AOL employees. The hackers sent email to potential victims asking them to send back their passwords as part of a "system test" or "to verify your account." Unsophisticated users often didn't (and still don't) know any better than to comply.

  There are countless variations on this ploy. As an administrator, part of your job includes teaching users about proper security hygiene. Many users are still very new to the Internet, and they often have no idea how many scams and freaks are afoot. Tell them how to select and defend good passwords, how to protect their work, and how not to talk to strangers. Make sure your instructions cover non-email communication, too; a telephone can be a hacker's best friend.

- **Software bugs:** Over the years, countless security-sapping bugs have been discovered in UNIX software (including software from third parties, both commercial and free). By exploiting subtle programming errors or context dependencies, hackers have been able to manipulate UNIX into doing whatever they want. What can you as an administrator do to prevent this? Very little, at least until a bug has been identified, fixed by the vendor, and addressed in a patch. Keeping up with patches and security bulletins is an important part of most administrators' jobs.

- **Open doors:** Many pieces of software can be configured securely or not-so-securely. Unfortunately, not-so-securely is often the default. Hackers frequently gain access by exploiting software features that would be considered helpful and convenient in less treacherous circumstances: accounts without passwords, disks shared with the world, and remote logins equivalenced among machines, to name a few. One of the most important parts of securing a system is just making sure that you haven't inadvertently put out a welcome mat for hackers.

Problems in the last of these categories are the easiest to find and fix, although there are potentially a lot of them and it's not always obvious what to check for. Most of the effort that has been put into security-checking tools over the last ten years has been directed at codifying the many ways in which UNIX systems can be inadvertently left open to intruders. Programs such as COPS[1] (discussed starting on page 667) help to make the auditing process rapid and automatic.

---

1. A number of commercial security auditing tools, such as Axent's Enterprise Security Manager, are also available. See www.axent.com for more information about Axent products.

## 21.3  SECURITY PROBLEMS IN THE /ETC/PASSWD FILE

*See page 76 for more information about the* ***passwd*** *file.*

The contents of **/etc/passwd** (and on some systems, **/etc/shadow**) determine who can log in and what they can do once they get inside. This file is the system's first line of defense against intruders. It must be scrupulously maintained and free of errors, security hazards, and historical baggage.

 On FreeBSD systems, the **/etc/passwd** file is derived from **/etc/master.passwd** and should not be edited directly. It's probably a good idea to check both **master.passwd** and **passwd** for security problems, however. See page 81 for more information about the **master.passwd** file.

### Password checking and selection

It is important to continually verify (preferably daily) that every login has a password. Entries in the **/etc/passwd** file that describe pseudo-users such as "daemon" who own files but never log in should have a star (*) in the encrypted password field. The star will not match any password and will thus prevent use of the account.

Several specialized software packages exist to check **/etc/passwd** for security problems, but the command[2]

```
perl -F: -ane 'print if not $F[1];' /etc/passwd
```

suffices just as well for finding null passwords. A script that performs this check and mails you the results can be run out of **cron**. You can add extra security by writing a script that **diff**s the **passwd** file against a version from the previous day and emails any differences to you. You can then verify that any modifications are legitimate.

**/etc/passwd** and **/etc/group** must be readable by the world but writable only by root. If your system has an **/etc/shadow** file, it should be neither readable nor writable by the world. The FreeBSD **/etc/master.passwd** file should be readable and writable only by root.

UNIX allows users to choose their own passwords, and although this is a great convenience, it leads to many security problems. When you give users their logins, you should also provide them with instructions for choosing a good password. Tell them not to use their name or initials, the name of a child or spouse, or any word that can be found in a dictionary. Passwords derived from personal data such as telephone numbers or addresses are also easily broken.

Passwords should be at least eight characters long and should include numbers, punctuation, or changes in case. Nonsense words, combinations of simple words, or the first letters of words in a memorable phrase make the best passwords. Of course, "memorable" is good but "traditional" is risky. Make up your own phrase. The comments in the section *Choosing a root password* on page 39 are equally applicable to user passwords.

---

2. This command requires Perl 5 or higher.

On many systems, only the first eight characters of a password are significant. More can be entered, but characters beyond the first eight will be silently ignored. See page 78 for details.

Passwords are normally changed with the **passwd** command. Various replacements for the standard **passwd** command force users to select better passwords. We recommend a version of the venerable **npasswd** package maintained by Clyde Hoover at the University of Texas. It's available from

> http://www.utexas.edu/cc/unix/software/npasswd

Solaris includes a version of **passwd** that forces users to adhere to certain common-sense rules, like not using their login names as passwords. You can customize the rules for the construction of passwords in the file **/etc/default/passwd**.

Red Hat's authentication model is based on pluggable authentication modules, also known as PAM. As a result, **passwd** under Red Hat uses a PAM ruleset to validate passwords. You can configure its rules in the file **/etc/pam.d/passwd**. Learn more about PAM at http://parc.power.net/morgan/Linux-PAM/index.html.

### Shadow passwords

*See page 666 for more information about password guessing.*

Traditionally, each line in **/etc/passwd** consists of seven fields. The second field contains a string that represents the user's encrypted password. Since **/etc/passwd** must be world-readable for commands like **ls** to work, the encrypted password string is available to all users on the system. Evildoers can encrypt selected dictionaries or words and compare the results with the strings in **/etc/passwd**. If the encrypted strings match, a password has been found.

How much of a threat is this? In the 80s, there was at least one way to decrypt passwords posthaste,[3] but run-of-the-mill hackers had to be content with using the **crypt** library routine[4] to encrypt dictionary words for comparison. A "fast" machine in the 80s could do a few hundred encryptions per second. In 1998, John Gilmore of the Electronic Frontier Foundation and cryptographer Paul Kocher cracked a 56-bit DES key in 56 hours, using a brute force search. Recent proposals suggest that a $1 million special-purpose computer could crack any 56-bit DES key in just a few hours.

These results are frightening, and they suggest that user access to encrypted password strings really ought to be restricted. A common way to impose restrictions is to put passwords in a separate file that is readable only by root, leaving the rest of **/etc/passwd** intact. The file that contains the actual password information is then called the shadow password file (often, it is **/etc/shadow**). Most UNIX vendors support shadow passwords, as do all of our example systems.

---

3. Evi Nemeth broke the Diffie-Hellman key exchange often used with DES in 1984, using a HEP super-computer. Although DES is thought to be mathematically secure, the short key lengths in common use offer relatively little security.

4. Don't confuse the **crypt** library routine with the **crypt** command, which uses a different and less secure encryption scheme.

*(hp)* HP-UX requires you to install its optional "trusted system" package to get shadow passwords. The package includes a number of additional security enhancements, but it adds considerable complexity to the administration of users and passwords.

### Group logins and shared logins

Any login that is used by more than one person is bad news. Group logins (such as "guest" or "demo") are sure terrain for hackers to homestead. Don't allow them at your site.

*See page 780 for some additional comments on shared logins.*

Likewise, don't allow users to share logins with family or friends. If little Johnny needs a login to work on his science project, give him one with that stated purpose. It's much easier to take away Johnny's login when he abuses it than to get rid of Dad and his account, especially at government sites.

At most sites, "root" is a group login. Dangerous! We recommend using the **sudo** program to control access to rootly powers. See page 41.

### Password aging

Most systems that have shadow passwords also allow you to compel users to change their passwords periodically, a facility known as password aging. This may seem like a good idea at first glance, but it has several problems. Users often become resentful at having to change their passwords, and since they don't want to forget the new password, they choose something simple that is easy to type and remember. Many users switch between two passwords each time they are forced to change, defeating the purpose of password aging.

*See page 41 for more information about **sudo**.*

Nevertheless, passwords should be changed regularly, especially the root password. A root password should roll easily off the fingers so that it can be typed quickly and cannot be guessed by someone watching the movement of fingers on the keyboard. At our site most people use **sudo** rather than the real root password, but we select the root password carefully all the same.

### User shells

Do not use a script as the shell for an unrestricted (passwordless) login. Password-less logins should be used only as a facility for running small, noninteractive utilities such as **date**, **sync**, or **lpq**.

### Rootly entries

The only distinguishing feature of the root login is its UID of zero. Since there can be more than one entry in the **/etc/passwd** file that uses this UID, there can be more than one way to log in as root.

A common way for hackers to install a back door once they have obtained a root shell is to edit new root logins into **/etc/passwd**. Programs like **who** and **w** refer to the name stored in **/etc/utmp** rather than the UID that owns the login shell, so they cannot expose hackers that appear to be innocent users but are really logged in as UID 0.

The defense against this subterfuge is a mini-script similar to the one used for finding logins without passwords:[5]

```
perl -F: -ane 'print if not $F[2];' /etc/passwd
```

This script prints out any lines in the **passwd** file that have null or 0 UIDs. You could easily adapt it to find entries with suspicious groups or UIDs that are the same as those of key people within your organization.

You should also check for **passwd** entries that have no username or that have punctuation as a username. These entries may seem nonsensical, but they will often allow a hacker to log in.

## 21.4  SETUID PROGRAMS

Programs that run setuid, especially ones that run setuid to root, are prone to security problems. The setuid commands distributed with UNIX are theoretically secure; however, security holes have been discovered in the past and will undoubtedly be discovered in the future.

The surest way to minimize the number of setuid *problems* is to minimize the number of setuid programs. Think twice before installing a software package that needs to run setuid, and avoid using the setuid facility in your own home-grown software.

Setuid shell scripts are especially apt to cause security problems. Under at least one common shell, they are automatically and entirely insecure. Shells tend to be highly customizable, which makes them relatively easy to trick. Although a shell spawned to execute a script doesn't necessarily read the user's shell configuration files, it can be influenced by the user's environment, by the contents of the current directory, or by the manner in which the script is invoked.

There's no rule that says setuid programs must run as root. If all you need to do is restrict access to a particular file or database, you can add a pseudo-user to the **passwd** file whose only reason for existence is to own the restricted resources. Follow the normal pseudo-user conventions: use a low UID, put a star in the password field, and make the pseudo-users's home directory be **/dev/null**.

Most systems allow setuid and setgid execution to be disabled on individual filesystems through use of the **-o nosuid** option to **mount**. It's a good idea to use this option on filesystems that contain users' home directories or that are mounted from less trustworthy administrative domains.

It's useful to scan your disks periodically to look for new setuid programs. A hacker who has breached the security of your system will sometimes create a private setuid shell or utility to facilitate repeat visits. Some of the tools discussed starting on page 663 will locate such files, but you can do just as well with **find**. For example,

---

5.  This command requires Perl 5 or higher.

```
/usr/bin/find / -user root -perm -4000 -print |
    /bin/mail -s "Setuid root files" netadmin
```

will mail a list of all setuid root files to the "netadmin" user.

## 21.5   IMPORTANT FILE PERMISSIONS

Many files on a UNIX system must have particular permissions to avoid security problems. Some vendors ship software with permissions set for their own "friendly" development environment. These permissions may not be appropriate for you.

On some systems, the device file **/dev/kmem** allows access to the kernel's own virtual address space. It is used by programs such as **ps** that need to look at kernel data structures. This file should only be readable by the owner and group, never by the world. Programs that need to access this file should be setgid to the group that owns the file, usually "kmem".

In the past, a few vendors have carelessly distributed systems with **/dev/kmem** publicly readable. This is a major security problem because a competent programmer can then look for things like unencrypted passwords in the kernel data structures and buffers. If your system has **/dev/kmem** publicly readable, change that immediately. If the change causes any programs to stop working, make those programs setgid to the group that owns **/dev/kmem**.

Check also the permissions on **/dev/drum** and **/dev/mem** if your system has them. These files provide unfettered access to the system's swap space and physical memory, and they are potentially just as dangerous as **/dev/kmem**.

**/etc/passwd** and **/etc/group** should not be world-writable. They should have owner root and mode 644. The group should be set to some system group, usually daemon. The **passwd** command runs setuid to root so that users can change their passwords without having write permission on **/etc/passwd**.

*See page 696 for information about setting up a secure FTP server.*
Directories that are accessible through anonymous FTP should not be publicly writable. Such directories create a nest for hackers to distribute illegally copied software and other sensitive files. If you manage an FTP archive that allows submissions, be sure to screen the submissions directory regularly.

Setting up anonymous FTP usually involves copying a skeleton password file into **~ftp/etc/passwd** so that **ls** will work correctly. Make sure to remove the encrypted password strings.

Device files for hard disk partitions are another potential source of problems. Having read or write permission on a disk device file is essentially the same as having read or write permission on every file in the filesystem it represents. Only root should have both read and write permission. The group owner is sometimes given read permission to facilitate backups, but there should be no permissions for the world.

## 21.6  MISCELLANEOUS SECURITY ISSUES

The sections below present some miscellaneous security-related topics. Most are either features that are useful to you as an administrator or misfeatures that can provide nesting material for hackers if not kept in check.

### Remote event logging

*See Chapter 11 for more information about syslog.*

The syslog facility allows log information for both the kernel and user processes to be forwarded to a file, a list of users, or another host on your network. Consider setting up a secure host that acts as a central logging machine and prints out security violations (the auth facility) on an old line printer. This precaution prevents hackers from covering their tracks by rewriting or erasing log files.

### Secure terminals

Some systems can be configured to restrict root logins to specific "secure" terminals. It's a good idea to disable root logins on channels such as dial-up modems. Often, network pseudo-terminals are also set to disallow root logins.

The secure channels are usually specified as a list of TTY devices or as a keyword in a configuration file. On Solaris, the file is **/etc/default/login**.[6] On HP-UX and Red Hat Linux, the file is **/etc/securetty**, and on FreeBSD it is **/etc/ttys**.

### /etc/hosts.equiv and ~/.rhosts

The **hosts.equiv** and ~/.**rhosts** files define hosts as being administratively "equivalent" to one another, allowing users to log in (via **rlogin**) and copy files (via **rcp**) between machines without typing their passwords.[7] Use of this facility was once common during the party days of UNIX, but everyone eventually woke up with a nasty headache and realized that it wasn't such a good idea.

We recommend that **rshd** and **rlogind**, the server processes that read .**rhosts** and **hosts.equiv**, be disabled. On most systems, this is done by simply commenting them out of **/etc/inetd.conf**. Once the server daemons have been disabled, the host will no longer be reachable by **rlogin**, **rsh**, or **rcp**. However, the functionality of these commands can be replaced with higher-security equivalents such as SSH; see page 672.

For basic remote logins, you can use **telnet** to continue to access a system on which **rlogin** has been disabled. But be aware that **telnet** transmits your password over the network without encryption.

Some of the replacements for **rlogin** (including SSH!) pay attention to .**rhosts** and **/etc/hosts.equiv** if they are not configured properly. For added safety, you can create the **/etc/hosts.equiv** file and a ~/.**rhosts** file for each user (including root) as an unwritable, zero-length file. It's easier to assess what the state of a file was at 3:00 a.m.

---

6. The file **/etc/default/su** is also relevant.

7. These files are also used by the printing software on some systems to authorize remote printer access. See Chapter 23, *Printing*, for details.

if it exists and is untouched than to assess the state of a nonexistent file. This distinction can be crucial when you are tracking intruders and their attempts to compromise your system.

### rexd, rexecd, and tftpd

Sun's **rexd** (which is also found on other systems, including HP-UX) is a poorly secured remote command execution server. It is generally shipped disabled (in the **/etc/inetd.conf** file) and should be left that way. **rexd** is not used by any standard system software.

**rexecd** is yet another remote command execution daemon. It is the server for the **rexec** library routine. Requests sent to **rexecd** include a plaintext password, so anyone listening on the network can learn passwords and gain access to the target system. This daemon should be disabled.

**tftpd** is a server for the Trivial File Transfer Protocol, an easy-to-implement protocol that's sometimes used to download firmware or boot code into network devices. Because it allows machines on the network to request files from your hard disk, it's a potential security hole. It's best left disabled if you are not using it.

### fingerd

**finger** is a UNIX command that prints a short report about a particular user:

```
% finger evi
Login name: evi                In real life: Evi Nemeth
Directory: /beast/users3/evi   Shell: /bin/tcsh
On since Jan 22 07:07:55 on ttyp3 from xor-train4.xor.com
50 minutes Idle Time
Mail last read Sat Jan 22 07:08:57 2000
No Plan.
```

Without an argument, **finger** prints a summary of all logged-in users.

When supported by the **fingerd** daemon on a remote host, **finger** can also be run in the form **finger** *user@host* or just **finger** *@host*. Unfortunately, the information returned is potentially useful to hackers, so we recommend that **fingerd** be disabled in **/etc/inetd.conf**.[8]

### Security and NIS

*See Chapter 18 for more information about NIS.*

Other than the title of this section, these words should never be used together. The Network Information Service (NIS, formerly the Yellow Pages) is a Sun database distribution tool that many sites use to maintain and distribute files such as **/etc/group**, **/etc/passwd**, and **/etc/hosts**. Unfortunately, its very nature of "easy information access" makes it tasty hacker bait. A later replacement for NIS called NIS+ makes a feeble attempt to address the security problems of NIS. You'd be safer not to run either form of NIS at your site.

---

8. It's also worth noting that a number of security-related bugs have been discovered in **fingerd** over the years, which is unusual for such a simple program.

*expect is available from expect.nist.gov.*

A more secure and reliable way to distribute these files is to create a login such as "netadmin" and to place the most recent copies of these files in ~**netadmin**. You can then run a script out of **cron** on each client machine to **scp**, sanity check, and install the files. See page 672 for more information about SSH, of which **scp** is a part.

### Security and NFS

See page 492 for more information about NFS security. You can use **showmount -e** to see which filesystems are being exported and to whom. Every exported filesystem should have an access list, and all hostnames should be fully qualified.

### Security and sendmail

*See Chapter 19 for more information about **sendmail**.*

**sendmail** is a massive network system, a large part of which runs as root. As a result, it has often been subject to the attacks of hackers, and numerous vulnerabilities have been exposed over time. Make sure that you're running the most up-to-date version of **sendmail** on all your systems. Since security problems are one of the most likely issues to spark new software releases, it's probable that all versions of **sendmail** but the most current have them. You can find out what's known about the security of your current release at www.sendmail.org.

### Security and backups

*See Chapter 10 for more information about backups.*

Regular system backups are an essential part of any site security plan. Make sure that all partitions are regularly dumped to tape and that you store some backups off-site. If a significant security incident occurs, you'll have an uncontaminated checkpoint to restore.

Backups can also be a security hazard. Since anyone can read the contents of a tape once it's mounted on a drive, you must keep all backup tapes under lock and key.

### Trojan horses

Trojan horses are programs that aren't what they seem to be. An example of a Trojan horse was a program called **turkey** that was distributed on Usenet a long time ago. The program said it would draw a picture of a turkey on your terminal screen, but it actually deleted files from your home directory.

Given the number of security-related escapades the UNIX community has seen over the last few decades, it is remarkable how few Trojan horse incidents there have been. In fact, we are not aware of a single documented instance of a program that

- Had some useful purpose,
- Was not distributed as part of an operating system,
- Was supplied in source code form, and
- Was widely available

that contained intentionally malicious code or that intentionally circumvented system security. Don't misunderstand us: we're sure it must have happened. But the risk to the average administrator is very low.

Credit for this state of affairs is due largely to the comity of the Internet. Obvious security problems tend to be discovered quickly and widely discussed. Malicious packages don't stay available for very long on well-known Internet servers.

You can be certain that any software that has been discovered to be malicious will be widely discussed on Usenet. If you want to do a quick check before installing something, search the archives at www.deja.com for the name of the software package.

## 21.7 SECURITY POWER TOOLS

Some of the nest-avoidance chores mentioned in the previous sections can be automated with freely available tools. Here are a few of the tools you'll want to look at.

### nmap: scan network ports

**nmap** is a network port scanner. Its main function is to check a set of target hosts to see which TCP and UDP ports have servers listening on them.[9] Since most network services are associated with "well-known" port numbers, this information tells you quite a lot about the software a machine is running.

Running **nmap** is a great way to find out what a system looks like to someone who is trying to break in. For example, here's a report from a run-of-the-mill, relatively unsecured machine:

```
% nmap -sT host1.uexample.com
Starting nmap V. 2.12 by Fyodor (fyodor@dhp.com, www.insecure.org/nmap/)
Interesting ports on host1.uexample.com (10.10.2.1):

Port    State    Protocol    Service
7       open     tcp         echo
9       open     tcp         discard
13      open     tcp         daytime
19      open     tcp         chargen
21      open     tcp         ftp
23      open     tcp         telnet
25      open     tcp         smtp
...
513     open     tcp         login

Nmap run completed -- 1 IP address (1 host up) scanned in 1 second
```

The **-sT** argument asks **nmap** to try and connect to each TCP port on the target host in the normal way.[10] Once a connection has been established, **nmap** immediately disconnects, which is impolite but not harmful to a properly written network server.

---

9. As described in Chapter 13, a port is a numbered communication channel. An IP address identifies an entire machine, and an IP address + port number identifies a specific server or network conversation on that machine.

10. Actually, only the privileged ports (those with port numbers under 1,024) and the well-known ports are checked by default. Use the **-p** option to explicitly specify the range of ports to scan.

From the example above, we can see that host1.uexample.com is running several servers that have historically been associated with security problems: **ftpd** (ftp), **rlogind** (login), and probably **sendmail** (smtp). Several potential lines of attack have been made clear.

The state column in **nmap**'s output shows "open" for ports with servers, "unfiltered" for ports without servers, and "filtered" for ports that cannot be probed because of an intervening firewall. Unfiltered ports are the typical case and are normally not shown unless there are relatively few of them. For example, here's a dump from a more secure commercial web server, www.aexample.com:

```
% nmap -sT www.aexample.com
Starting nmap V. 2.12 by Fyodor (fyodor@dhp.com, www.insecure.org/nmap/)
(Not showing ports in state: filtered)

Port    State        Protocol    Service
53      unfiltered   tcp         domain
80      open         tcp         http
179     unfiltered   tcp         bgp
443     open         tcp         https

Nmap run completed -- 1 IP address (1 host up) scanned in 122 seconds
```

In this case, it's clear that the host is set up to handle web traffic only. A firewall blocks access to other ports. DNS and BGP traffic is allowed through, but no servers are running to receive it. Ideally, the firewall at this site should block traffic to all unused services (such as BGP and DNS in this case), so that these ports cannot be hijacked for other purposes.

In addition to straightforward TCP and UDP probes, **nmap** also has a repertoire of sneaky ways to probe ports without initiating an actual connection. In most cases, these probes send packets that look like they come from the middle of a TCP conversation (rather than the beginning) and wait for diagnostic packets to be sent back. The stealth probes may be effective at getting past a firewall or at avoiding detection by a network security monitor on the lookout for port scanners. If your site uses a firewall (see *Firewalls* on page 675), it's a good idea to probe it with these alternate scanning modes to see what they turn up.

**nmap** has the magical and useful ability to guess what OS a remote system is running by looking at the particulars of its implementation of TCP/IP. The **-O** option turns on this behavior. For example:

```
% nmap -O disaster mrhat lollipop
Starting nmap V. 2.12 by Fyodor (fyodor@dhp.com, www.insecure.org/nmap/)

Interesting ports on disaster.xor.com (192.108.21.99):
...
Remote operating system guess: HP-UX 11.00

Interesting ports on mrhat.xor.com (192.108.21.2):
...
Remote operating system guess: BSDI 4.0
```

```
Interesting ports on lollipop.xor.com (192.108.21.48):
...
Remote operating system guess: Solaris 2.6 - 2.7

Nmap run completed -- 3 IP addresses (3 hosts up) scanned in 5 seconds
```

This feature can be very useful for taking an inventory of a local network. Unfortunately, it is also very useful to hackers, who can base their attacks on known weaknesses of the target OS.

### SAINT: check networked systems for vulnerabilities

SAINT is an updated version of SATAN, a network security checker released in 1995 amid much hand-wringing about how it would bring about the end of the world. The original SATAN was written by Dan Farmer and Wietse Venema; SAINT is now maintained by World Wide Digital Security, Inc., from whose web site it can be downloaded (www.wwdsi.com). It's free.

Like **nmap**, SAINT probes computers on a network to find out what servers they are running. But unlike **nmap**, SAINT knows quite a lot about the actual UNIX server programs and their historical vulnerabilities. It looks for common misconfigurations that degrade security, and it also checks for the presence of known bugs.

Because a SAINT report essentially provides instructions for breaking into a system, a small but vocal minority of system administrators feel that you would be wise to run SAINT—or a similar program such as Nessus, below—on your systems before the hackers do.

SAINT's user interface is entirely web based, and it requires that a web browser be installed on the machine on which it runs. Fortunately, SAINT makes good use of HTML and can present its results in a variety of well-designed formats. SAINT does not require that **nmap** be installed but will use **nmap** if it is available. SAINT also claims to make use of the utilities supplied with Samba for checking Windows hosts if they have been installed. See www.samba.org or Chapter 26, *Cooperating with Windows*, for more information about Samba.

### Nessus: next generation network scanner

Renaud Deraison is developing a package called Nessus that promises to provide many of the same features as SAINT, but in a more architecturally clean and more easily extensible way. It's available from www.nessus.org.

We took a look at an early (pre-1.0) release of Nessus and found that it wasn't quite ready for prime time. Although it's not clear how good the final package will be or whether it will ultimately catch on, we think it's worth mentioning because of its modular design, which makes it easy for third parties to add new security checks. If the user community begins to write and collect script databases for Nessus, it could stay current for a long time without constant updates from the original developers.

### crack: find insecure passwords

Since some vendors still distribute systems that leave encrypted passwords in plain view, naughty hackers can easily compare them with an encrypted dictionary. One way to head off this attack is to make the comparison yourself and force users to change passwords that you have broken. **crack** is a sophisticated tool by Alec D. E. Muffett that implements several common password-guessing techniques.

Even if you use a shadow password file to hide encrypted passwords from public view, it's still wise to verify that your users' passwords are **crack**-resistant. Knowledge of a user's password can be useful because people tend to use the same password over and over again. A single password might provide access to another system, decrypt files stored in a user's home directory, and allow access to financial accounts on the web. (Needless to say, it's not very security-smart to reuse a password this way. But nobody wants to remember ten different passwords.)

As of this writing, the current version of **crack** is 5.0a. It's available from ftp.cert.org. Since **crack**'s output contains the passwords it has broken, you should carefully protect it and delete it as soon as you are done with it.

### tcpd: protect Internet services

**tcpd**, often referred to as the "TCP wrappers" package, allows you to log connections to TCP services such as **telnetd**, **ftpd**, and **fingerd**. In addition, it allows you to restrict which systems can connect to these services. Both of these features can be very handy when you are tracking or controlling unwanted guests. **tcpd** was written by Wietse Venema and is available from ftp.porcupine.org. It comes standard with Red Hat and FreeBSD (in **/usr/ports/security/tcp_wrapper**).

*See page 823 for more information about inetd.*

**tcpd** is easy to install and doesn't require modifications to existing network programs. It piggybacks on top of **inetd**; you simply modify your **/etc/inetd.conf** file to execute **tcpd** instead of the actual network server program. **tcpd** then performs any necessary logging and security checks before executing the server. For example, if your **/etc/inetd.conf** originally contained the line

```
telnet stream tcp    nowait root   /usr/sbin/in.telnetd   in.telnetd
```

you could change this to

```
telnet stream tcp    nowait root   /usr/sbin/tcpd        in.telnetd
```

The resulting log file (configured in **/etc/syslog.conf**) would look something like:

```
Nov 12 08:52:43 chimchim in.telnetd[25880]: connect from tintin.Colorado.EDU
Nov 12 19:19:44 chimchim in.telnetd[15520]: connect from catbelly.com
Nov 12 23:48:45 chimchim in.telnetd[19332]: connect from atdt.xor.com
Nov 13 20:14:57 chimchim in.telnetd[2362]: connect from 130.13.13.11
```

*Built-in TCP wrappers for HP-UX*

HP-UX includes a version of **inetd** that has some similar security features built in. It's configured in the file **/usr/adm/inetd.sec**. Entries in this file have the form *service* allow|deny *hostname|address hostname|address* ...

The *service* must be listed in either **/etc/services** or **/etc/rpc**. Any *hostname*s you use should be fully qualified (e.g., moomin.xor.com).

Wild cards and ranges are also understood. For example, "192.108.21.*" refers to all hosts on the listed class C network, and "192.108.21.1-50" refers to the first 50 hosts on that network.

Comments are designated by a pound sign (#), but they must occur on a line by themselves. Multiple lines for the same service are not permitted; only the last one survives. If a service is not listed, anyone may connect to it.

The following lines allow remote logins from only two networks and deny access to the spray daemon from two specific hosts:

```
login    allow   192.108.21.*   192.225.33.*
sprayd   deny    192.108.21.5   freddy.xor.com
```

HP-UX's **inetd** does not log connections by default, but if invoked with the -l flag, it logs connections to syslog using facility "daemon" and priority "info". Service denials (based on your **inetd.sec** criteria) are logged at priority "notice".

### COPS: audit system security

The Computer Oracle and Password System, COPS, is a set of programs, originally written by Dan Farmer, that monitor several aspects of UNIX security. You can run COPS every night out of **cron** to search through the filesystem for problems.

By standardizing and streamlining a variety of simple checks, COPS can save you many hours of manual labor. Although it is no longer under active development, COPS is a classic tool that identifies many classic security problems. Run it before one of your users does.

COPS warns you of potential problems by sending email; it makes no attempt to fix the problems it has discovered. A list of the items monitored includes

- File, directory, and device permissions and modes
- The contents of **/etc/passwd** and **/etc/group**
- The contents of system startup and crontab files
- The writability of users' home directories

Once you install COPS, you will receive a nightly security report similar to this one:

```
ATTENTION:
Security Report from host raja.xor.com

Warning!  Root does not own the following file(s): /etc
Warning!  "." (or current directory) is in root's path!
Warning!  /var/spool/mail is _World_ writable!
Warning!  /etc/utmp is _World_ writable!
Warning!  User randy's home directory /home/staff/randy is mode 0777!
Warning!  Password file, line 8, no password:
```

```
runmailq::33:10:,,,:/home/staff/runmailq:/bin/csh
Warning! /usr/bin/uudecode creates setuid files!
Warning!  Password Problem: Guessed: beth shell: /bin/csh
```

COPS includes the Kuang expert system, which attempts to intuit devious ways that regular users could attempt to become root. More information about COPS is available from www.cerias.purdue.edu.

### tripwire: monitor changes to system files

**tripwire**, written by Gene Kim and Gene Spafford of Purdue, monitors the permissions and checksums of important system files so that you can easily detect files that have been replaced, corrupted, or tampered with. For example, **tripwire** makes it easy to determine that an intruder has replaced your copy of **/bin/login** with one that records passwords in a clandestine file.

**tripwire** checks files against a database that records their characteristics and checksums at the time the database was built. The general idea is to make a baseline database from a trusted state of the system and then regularly **diff** the filesystem against that historical database. Files that are expected to change (such as **/etc/utmp**) can be marked in **tripwire**'s configuration file so that they do not generate warnings. When the configuration of the system is changed or new software is installed, the database should be rebuilt so that real problems do not disappear among a flood of spurious **tripwire** warnings.

If possible, **tripwire's** database and config file should be mounted from a secure server that exports it read-only. This configuration makes it harder for hackers to cover their tracks and remain undetected.

**tripwire** should be set up to mail you a nightly report. A typical **tripwire** report looks like this:

```
# tripwire
Tripwire(tm) ASR (Academic Source Release) 1.3.1
File Integrity Assessment Software
(c) 1992, Purdue Research Foundation, (c) 1997, 1999 Tripwire
Security Systems, Inc. All Rights Reserved. Use Restricted to
Authorized Licensees.
### Phase 1:   Reading configuration file
### Phase 2:   Generating file list
### Phase 3:   Creating file information database
### Phase 4:   Searching for inconsistencies
###
###                 Total files scanned:   20344
###                        Files added:       0
###                      Files deleted:       0
###                      Files changed:       1
###
###                 Total file violations:     1
###
changed: -rwxr-xr-x root       262184 Jan 22 12:04:42 2000 /bin/tcsh
```

```
### Phase 5:   Generating observed/expected pairs for changed files
###
### Attr          Observed (what it is)      Expected (what it should be)
### ===           ==================         ========================
/bin/tcsh
     st_ctime:     Sat Jan 22 12:04:42 2000   Fri May 14 05:11:41 1999
```

In this example, **tripwire** reports that the inode change time of **/bin/tcsh** is different from what it was when the database was generated. This may be an indication that a wily hacker has replaced the vendor's version of **/bin/tcsh** with one that contains a surprise waiting to be found the next time the shell is executed by root. Comparing the checksum of the executable with the version on the distribution tape (use the **siggen** utility that comes with **tripwire** to do this) can confirm or deny this as potential hacker droppings. Since some hackers are wily enough to rig the checksums on modified files, **tripwire** uses two different checksum methods.

**tripwire** is a bit unusual in that it started out as free software but was later privatized and turned into a commercial product. However, it's not really possible to unrelease something that was formerly free. Tripwire, Inc., has graciously continued to make the free version available and has even released commercial-quality documentation and updates for it. It's available from their web site, www.tripwiresecurity.com.

### Forensic tools

One up-and-coming security power tool (tool *kit*, actually) is The Coroner's Toolkit (TCT) from Dan Farmer and Wietse Venema. TCT is a collection of utilities that help to analyze the system after a security breach has occurred. It's known to work on Solaris, Red Hat, and FreeBSD systems, but not on HP-UX (yet).

TCT helps you to identify both *what* happened and *how* it happened. In some cases, it will even recover data that was destroyed during the break-in. One particularly interesting utility is **mactime**, a program that tracks the modification, access, and change times for all files on the system. Although **mactime** wasn't ready for public consumption at press time, it should be available from www.fish.com/security by the time you read this.

## 21.8  CRYPTOGRAPHIC SECURITY TOOLS

Most of the UNIX protocols in common use date from a time before the deployment of the Internet and before the invention of modern cryptography. Security was simply not a factor in the design of many protocols; in others, security concerns were waved away with the transmission of a plaintext password or with a vague check to see if packets originated from a trusted host or port.

These protocols now find themselves operating in the shark-infested waters of large corporate LANs and the Internet, where, it must be assumed, all traffic is open to inspection. Not only that, but there is little to prevent anyone from actively interfering in network conversations. How can you be sure who you're really talking to?

Cryptography provides a solution to many of these problems. It has been possible for a long time to scramble messages so that an eavesdropper cannot decipher them, but this is just the beginning of the wonders of cryptography. Developments such as public key cryptography and secure hashing have allowed the design of cryptosystems that meet almost any conceivable need.[11]

Unfortunately, these mathematical developments have largely failed to translate into secure, usable software that is widely embraced and understood. The developers of cryptographic software systems tend to be very interested in provable correctness and absolute security and not so interested in whether a system makes practical sense for the real world. Most current software tends to be rather overengineered, and it's perhaps not surprising that users run away screaming when given half a chance. Today, the cryptography-using population consists largely of hobbyists interested in cryptography, black-helicopter conspiracy theorists, and those who have no choice because of administrative policy.

We may or may not see a saner approach to cryptography developing over the next few years. In the meantime, the following sections discuss some current offerings.

### Kerberos: a unified approach to network security

The Kerberos system, designed at MIT, attempts to address some of the issues of network security in a consistent and extensible way. Kerberos is an authentication system, a facility that "guarantees" that users and services are in fact who they claim to be. It does not provide any additional security or encryption beyond that.

Kerberos uses DES to construct nested sets of credentials called "tickets." Tickets are passed around the network to certify your identity and to provide you with access to network services. Each Kerberos site must maintain at least one physically secure machine (called the authentication server) to run the Kerberos daemon. This daemon issues tickets to users or services that request authentication based on credentials they provide, such as passwords.

In essence, Kerberos improves upon traditional UNIX password security in only two ways: it never transmits unencrypted passwords on the network, and it relieves users from having to type passwords repeatedly, making password protection of network services somewhat more palatable.

Kerberos has been around for a long time, and many vendors support it in their standard releases. Systems with "Kerberos stubs" come ready to work with Kerberos if you have already set up an authentication server. But just as buying a cable-ready television doesn't get you HBO, you must still obtain a copy of Kerberos from an outside source if you are starting from scratch (look on web.mit.edu/kerberos).

---

11. Two excellent resources for those interested in cryptography are "RSA Labs' Frequently Asked Questions about Today's Cryptography" at www.rsasecurity.com/rsalabs/faq and the sci.crypt FAQ available by FTP from rtfm.mit.edu.

Among our example systems, Solaris and HP-UX include Kerberos stubs, and Free-BSD provides the entire Kerberos system. Cisco's routers provide some support as well, although it has been buggy in the past. Microsoft has announced extensive support for Kerberos in Windows 2000, but it remains to be seen exactly how they plan to use it and how compliant their implementation will be.

The Kerberos community boasts one of the most lucid and enjoyable documents ever written about a cryptosystem, Bill Bryant's "Designing an Authentication System: a Dialogue in Four Scenes." It's required reading for anyone interested in cryptography and is available at

> http://web.mit.edu/kerberos/www/dialogue.html

There's also a good FAQ:

> http://www.nrl.navy.mil/CCS/people/kenh/kerberos-faq.html

Kerberos offers a better network security model than the "ignoring network security entirely" model. However, it is neither perfectly secure nor painless to install and run. It does not supersede any of the other security measures described in this chapter. In our opinion, most sites are better off without it. Good system hygiene and a focused cryptographic solution for remote logins such as SSH or SRP (see pages 672–674) should provide a more than-adequate level of security for your users.

### PGP: Pretty Good Privacy

Philip Zimmermann's PGP package provides a tool chest of bread-and-butter cryptographic utilities focused primarily on email security. It can be used to encrypt data, to generate signatures, and to verify the origin of files and messages.

Attempts to regulate or stop the distribution of PGP have given it a rather checkered history. It now exists in several versions, including a set of commercial products from Network Associates (www.nai.com). A governmentally vetted version of PGP is a available for use in the United States, and an international version with somewhat stronger and more varied encryption is available from www.pgpi.org. The international archive sites do not seem to screen out U.S. addresses, so American users must be very careful not to accidentally go to www.pgpi.org and download the full-featured version of PGP.

PGP is the most popular cryptographic software in common use. Unfortunately, the UNIX version is nuts-and-bolts enough that you have to understand a fair amount of cryptographic background in order to use it. Fortunately (?), PGP comes with an 88-page treatise on cryptography that can help to set the stage. While you may find PGP useful in your own work, we don't recommend that you support it for users, as it has been known to spark many puzzled questions. We have found the Windows version of PGP to be considerably easier to use than the UNIX **pgp** command with its 38 different operating modes.

Software packages on the Internet are often distributed with a PGP signature file that purports to guarantee the origin and purity of the software. Unfortunately, it is difficult for people who are not die-hard PGP users to validate these signatures—not because the validation process is complicated, but because true PGP security can only come from having collected a personal library of public keys from people whose identities you have directly verified. Downloading a single public key along with a signature file and software distribution is approximately as secure as downloading the distribution alone.

### SSH: the secure shell

The SSH system, written by Tatu Ylönen, is a secure replacement for **rlogin**, **rcp**, and **telnet**. It uses cryptographic authentication to confirm a user's identity and encrypts all communications between the two hosts. The protocol has been well studied and is being standardized by the IETF.

Like **tripwire**, SSH has morphed from being a freely distributed open source project (SSH1) to being a commercial product (SSH2). As with **tripwire**, the free version of the software is still widely available. The wire protocol has changed, however, and the two versions are not compatible. Although SSH2 is available for download for noncommercial purposes, the license terms are quite restrictive. We recommend sticking with SSH1, which works fine.

The original release of SSH1 is available from ftp.cs.hut.fi/pub/ssh. However, this version does not appear to be under active development anymore. The OpenBSD group has picked up the source code and provided some maintenance and restructuring of the SSH1 code base, while leaving the administration and behavior largely alone. Their version is called OpenSSH and has a web page at www.openssh.com. We'd recommend the OpenSSH version over the original, but the process you must use to obtain the source code is currently so tortuous that we hardly think it's worth the bother. Perhaps this will change in the future.

We should mention in any case that the legal status of SSH is somewhat ambiguous in the United States because it uses an encryption system (RSA) that is patented. However, the patent is due to expire in September, 2000.

The main components of SSH are a server daemon, **sshd**, and two user-level commands: **ssh** for remote logins and **scp** for copying files. Other components are an **ssh-keygen** command that generates public key pairs and a couple of utilities that help to support secure X Windows.

**sshd** can authenticate user logins in several different ways. It's up to you as the administrator to decide which of these methods are acceptable:

- **Method A:** If the name of the remote host that the user is logging in from is listed in **~/.rhosts**, **~/.shosts**, **/etc/hosts.equiv**, or **/etc/shosts.equiv**, then the user is logged in automatically without a password check. This scheme mirrors that of the old **rlogin** daemon and in our opinion is not acceptable for normal use.

- **Method B:** As a refinement of method A, **sshd** can also use public key cryptography to verify the identity of the remote host. For that to happen, the remote host's public key (generated at install time) must be listed in the local host's **/etc/ssh_known_hosts** file or the user's **~/.ssh/known_hosts** file. If the remote host can prove that it knows the corresponding private key (normally stored in **/etc/ssh_host_key**, a world-unreadable file), then the user is logged in without being asked for a password. Method B is more restrictive than method A, but we think it's still not quite secure enough. If the security of the originating host is compromised, the local site will be compromised as well.

- **Method C: sshd** can use public key cryptography to establish the user's identity. At login time, the user must have access to a copy of his or her private key file and must supply a password to decrypt it. This method is the most secure, but it's somewhat annoying to set up. It also means that you cannot log in when traveling unless you bring a copy of your private key file with you (perhaps on your laptop).

- **Method D:** Finally, **sshd** can simply allow the user to enter his or her normal login password. This makes **ssh** behave very much like **telnet**, except that the password and session are both encrypted. The main drawbacks of this method are that system login passwords are relatively weak (often limited to 8 significant characters) and that there are ready-made tools (like **crack**) designed to break them. However, this method is probably the best choice for normal use.

Authentication policy is set in the **/etc/sshd_config** file. You will see at once that this file has been filled up with configuration garbage for you, but most of it can be safely ignored. The options relevant to authentication are shown in Table 21.1.

**Table 21.1    Authentication-related options in /etc/sshd_config**

| Option | Meth[a] | Dflt | Meaning when turned on |
|---|---|---|---|
| RhostsAuthentication | A | no | Allows login via **~/.shosts**, **/etc/shosts.equiv**, etc. |
| RhostsRSAAuthentication | B | yes | Allows **~/.shosts** et al., but also requires host key |
| IgnoreRhosts | A,B | no | Ignores the **~/.rhosts** and **hosts.equiv** files[b] |
| IgnoreRootRhosts | A,B | no[c] | Prevents **rhosts/shosts** authentication for root |
| RSAAuthentication | C | yes | Allows per-user public key crypto authentication |
| PasswordAuthentication | D | yes | Allows use of normal login password |

a. The authentication methods to which this variable is relevant.

b. But continues to honor **~/.shosts** and **shosts.equiv**.

c. Defaults to the value of IgnoreRhosts.

Our suggested configuration, which allows methods C and D but not methods A or B, is as follows.

```
RhostsAuthentication no
RhostsRSAAuthentication no
RSAAuthentication yes
PasswordAuthentication yes
```

### SRP: Secure Remote Password

The SRP protocol from Thomas Wu at Stanford provides a simple, fast, exportable, patent-free, and highly secure way to verify passwords over a public network. SRP has been less widely adopted than SSH, but it appears to be a more elegant protocol. The software is administratively simpler, and the protocol is easier to adapt to existing services. Rather than switching over to a new set of commands, as SSH requires, users can continue to use **telnet** and **ftp** in the same way they always did. The only difference is that network communications will now be transparently secured. In the specific cases of **telnet** and **ftp**, the SRP-ized clients and servers are backward compatible with their standard counterparts. Secure authentication and encryption are used only when both parties support it.

Unfortunately, the standard DES encryption used by UNIX does not have the mathematical properties necessary to support SRP, and user passwords for SRP must therefore be stored outside the **/etc/passwd** file. The current SRP package (available on the web from srp.stanford.edu) defines a sort of shadow password file, **/etc/tpasswd**, that contains the SRP version of each user's password. A replacement for the standard **passwd** command keeps the passwords in both files synchronized.

### OPIE: One-time Passwords in Everything

One of the problems with systems such as SSH and SRP is that both ends of a connection must support a special protocol to secure the connection. This is normally not a problem, but users can sometimes find themselves stranded. SSH clients are not available for all operating systems, and users may occasionally want to log in through other people's computers when on the road.

The one-time password (OTP) standard defined in RFC1938 takes a somewhat different approach to password security: instead of encrypting passwords, you just make sure that they only work once. Plaintext passwords can then be entered over the net with impunity, since it does not matter if anyone overhears them. Users typically print out a series of one-time passwords to carry around with them. Unlike regular passwords, one-time passwords are generated on your behalf; you don't get to select them.

OPIE is the most commonly used OTP system today. It's an offshoot of an earlier system called S/Key from Bellcore (now Telcordia Technologies) that was further developed at the U.S. Naval Research Laboratories. OPIE's main features are OTP-compatible versions of **telnetd** and **ftpd** and utilities for generating and administering password lists. It's available from www.inner.net/pub/opie.

It's important to note that OTP systems address only the issue of password snooping. They cannot and do not encrypt the actual content of a conversation. Someone listening in on your **telnet** session might not be able to obtain a usable password, but they could certainly find out a lot about your account. Any passwords you typed after logging in (to **sudo**, for example) would be completely exposed.[12]

Given the growing availability of systems such as SSH, there is less and less need for OPIE. If you don't really need it, don't use it—it's troublesome to install and maintain, and the procedures that users must follow are somewhat confusing.

## 21.9 FIREWALLS

In addition to protecting individual machines, you can also implement security precautions at the network level. The basic tool of network security is the "firewall." There are three main categories of firewalls: packet-filtering, service proxy, and stateful inspection.

### Packet-filtering firewalls

A packet-filtering firewall limits the types of traffic that can pass through your Internet gateway (or through an internal gateway that separates domains within your organization) based on information in the packet header. It's much like driving your car through a customs checkpoint at an international border crossing. You specify which destination addresses, port numbers, and protocol types are acceptable, and the gateway simply discards (and in some cases, logs) packets that don't meet the profile.

Packet filtering is supported by dedicated routers such as those made by Cisco. It may also be available in software, depending on the machine you're using as a gateway and its configuration. In general, packet-filtering firewalls offer a significant increase in security with little cost in performance or complexity.

Both Red Hat and FreeBSD include packet filtering software (see pages 326 and 333 for more information). It's also possible to buy commercial software to perform this function. These packages all have entertainment value, and they can provide a reasonably secure firewall for a home or small office. However, you should refer to the comments at the beginning of this chapter before you consider a UNIX system as a production-grade corporate firewall.[13] This is one case in which you should really spend the money for a dedicated network appliance, such as Cisco's PIX firewall.

### How services are filtered

Most well-known services are associated with a network port in the **/etc/services** file or its vendor-specific equivalent. The daemons that provide these services bind to the appropriate ports and wait for connections from remote sites.[14] Most of the well-known service ports are "privileged," meaning that their port numbers are in

---

12. In particular, users should not try to obtain a list of more OTP passwords after having logged in with OTP; the passwords will all be transmitted without protection.

13. We assume you already know not to consider something like Windows as a firewall platform. Does the name "Windows" evoke images of security? Silly rabbit, Windows is for desktops.

14. In many cases, **inetd** does the actual waiting on their behalf. See page 823 for more information.

the range 1 to 1,023. These ports can only be used by a process running as root. Port numbers 1,024 and higher are referred to as nonprivileged ports.

Service-specific filtering is based on the assumption that the client (the machine that initiates a TCP or UDP conversation) will use a nonprivileged port to contact a privileged port on the server. For example, if you wanted to allow only inbound SMTP connections to a machine with the address 192.108.21.200, you would install a filter that allowed TCP packets destined for that address at port 25 and permitted outbound TCP packets from that address to anywhere.[15] The exact way that such a filter would be installed depends on the kind of router you are using.

*See page 696 for more information about setting up an **ftp** server.*

Some services, such as FTP, add a twist to the puzzle. The FTP protocol actually uses two TCP connections when transferring a file: one for commands and the other for data. The client initiates the command connection, and the server initiates the data connection. Ergo, if you want to use FTP to retrieve files from the Internet, you must permit inbound access to all nonprivileged TCP ports, since you have no idea what port might be used to form an incoming data connection.

This tweak largely defeats the purpose of packet filtering, since some notoriously insecure services (for example, X11 at port 6000) naturally bind to nonprivileged ports. This configuration also creates an opportunity for curious users within your organization to start their own services (such as a **telnet** server at a nonstandard and nonprivileged port) that they and/or their friends can access from the Internet.

The most secure way to use a packet filter is to start with a configuration that allows nothing but inbound SMTP. You can then liberalize the filter bit by bit as you discover useful things that don't work.

Some extremely security-conscious sites use two-stage filtering. In this scheme, one filter is a gateway to the Internet, and a second filter lies between the outer gateway and the rest of the local network. The idea is to leave the outer gateway relatively open and to make the inner gateway very conservative. If the machine in the middle is administratively separate from the rest of the network, it can provide a variety of services on the Internet with reduced risk.

A reasonable approach to the FTP dilemma is to allow FTP to the outside world only from this single, isolated host. Users can also log in to the FTP machine when they need to perform other network operations that are forbidden from the inner net. Since replicating all user accounts on the FTP "server" would defeat the goal of administrative separation, you may wish to create FTP accounts by request only. Naturally, the FTP host should run a full complement of security-checking tools.

### Service proxy firewalls

Service proxies intercept connections to and from the outside world and establish new connections to services inside your network, acting as a sort of shuttle or chaperone between the two worlds. It's much like driving to the border of your country,

---

15. Port 25 is the SMTP port as defined in **/etc/services**.

walking across the border, and renting a sanitized, freshly washed car on the other side of the border to continue your journey.

Because of their design, service proxy firewalls are much less flexible (and much slower) than pure packet filters. Your proxy must have a module that decodes and conveys each protocol you want to let through the firewall. In the early 1990s this was relatively easy because there were only a few protocols in common use. Today, internauts might use several dozen protocols in an hour of web surfing. As a result, service proxies are relatively unpopular in organizations that use the Internet as a primary medium of communication.

### Stateful inspection firewalls

The theory behind stateful inspection firewalls is that if you could carefully listen to and understand all the conversations (in all the languages) that were taking place in a crowded airport, you could make sure that someone wasn't planning to bomb a plane later that day. Stateful inspection firewalls are designed to inspect the traffic that flows through them and compare the actual network activity to what "should" be happening. For example, if the packets exchanged in an FTP command sequence name a port to be used later for a data connection, the firewall should expect a data connection to occur only on that port. Attempts by the remote site to connect to other ports are presumably bogus and should be dropped.

Unfortunately, reality usually kills the cat here. It's no more realistic to keep track of the "state" of the network connections of thousands of hosts using hundreds of protocols than it is to listen to every conversation in every language in a crowded airport. Someday, as processor and memory capacity increase, it may eventually be feasible.

So what are vendors really selling when they claim to provide stateful inspection? Their products either monitor a very limited number of connections or protocols, or they search for a particular set of "bad" situations. Not that there's anything wrong with that; there is clearly some benefit to be obtained from any technology that can detect traffic anomalies. In this particular case, however, it's important to remember that the claims are *mostly* marketing hype.

### Firewalls: how safe are they?

A firewall should not be your primary means of defense against intruders. It's only appropriate as a supplemental security measure. The use of firewalls often provides a false sense of security. If it lulls you into relaxing other safeguards, it will have had a *negative* effect on the security of your site.

Every host within your organization should be individually secured and regularly monitored with tools such as **crack**, **tcpd**, **nmap**, COPS, and **tripwire**. Otherwise, you are simply building a structure that has a hard crunchy outside and a soft chewy center. On the Internet, it doesn't take many licks to get to the center of that bonbon.

Ideally, local users should be able to connect to any Internet service they want, but machines on the Internet should only be able to connect to a limited set of local services. For example, you may want to allow FTP access to a local archive server and allow SMTP (email) connections to your mail server.

If you want to maximize the value of your Internet connection, we recommend that you emphasize convenience and accessibility when deciding how to set up your network. At the end of the day, it's the system administrator's vigilance that makes a network secure, not a fancy piece of firewall hardware.

## 21.10  SOURCES OF SECURITY INFORMATION

Half the battle of keeping your system secure consists of staying abreast of security-related developments in the world at large. If your site is broken into, it probably won't be through the use of a novel technique. More likely, the chink in your armor will have been widely discussed on security-related newsgroups and mailing lists.

### CERT: a registered service mark of Carnegie Mellon University

In response to the uproar over the 1988 Internet worm, the Defense Advanced Research Projects Agency (DARPA) formed an organization called CERT, the Computer Emergency Response Team, to act as a clearing house for computer security information. CERT is still the best-known point of contact for security information, though it seems to have grown rather sluggish and bureaucratic of late. CERT also now insists that the name CERT does not stand for anything and is merely "a registered service mark of Carnegie Mellon University."

Although CERT's charter includes some degree of problem solving, in reality CERT lacks the ability to investigate problems or discipline offenders, and so it is really little more than a repository for vendor security patches and security tool announcements. These patches and announcements are called "CERT advisories." New advisories are posted to www.cert.org, emailed to the cert-advisory mailing list, and submitted to the newsgroup comp.security.announce. To subscribe, see

> http://www.cert.org/contact_cert/certmaillist.html.

### SecurityFocus.com and the BugTraq mailing list

SecurityFocus.com is a site that specializes in security-related news and information. The news includes current articles on general issues and on specific problems; there's also an extensive technical library of useful papers, nicely sorted by topic.

SecurityFocus's archive of security tools includes software for a variety of operating systems, along with blurbs and user ratings. It is the most comprehensive and detailed source of tools that we are aware of.

The BugTraq list is a moderated forum for the discussion of security vulnerabilities and their fixes. To subscribe, send email to listserv@securityfocus.com with the following message body:

> SUBSCRIBE BUGTRAQ *lastname, firstname*

Traffic on this list can be fairly heavy, however. A database of BugTraq vulnerability reports is also available from the web site.

### SANS: the System Administration, Networking, and Security Institute

SANS is a professional organization that sponsors security-related conferences and training programs, as well as publishing a variety of security information. Their web site, www.sans.org, is a useful resource that occupies something of a middle ground between SecurityFocus and CERT: neither as frenetic as the former nor as stodgy as the latter.

SANS offers several weekly and monthly email bulletins that you can sign up for on their web site. The weekly NewsBites are nourishing, but the monthly summaries contain a lot of boilerplate. Neither is a great source of late-breaking security news.

### Vendor-specific security resources

Because security problems have the potential to generate a lot of bad publicity, vendors are often eager to help customers keep their systems secure. Most large vendors have an official mailing list to which security-related bulletins are posted, and many maintain a web site about security issues as well. It's common for security-related software patches to be distributed for free, even by vendors that normally charge for software support.

There are also security portals on the web, such as www.securityfocus.com, that contain vendor-specific information and links to the latest official vendor dogma.

To subscribe to Sun's security bulletin, send email to security-alert@sun.com; include the line "subscribe cws *your-address*" in the body of the message. Software patches and an archive of historical security bulletins are available on the web at sunsolve.sun.com.

HP's offerings can be accessed through its support sites: us-support.external.hp.com for the Americas and Asia, and europe-support.external.hp.com for Europe. The security-related goodies have been carefully hidden. To find them, enter the maintenance/support area and select the option to search the technical knowledge base (you will need to register if you have not already done so). An option at the bottom of that page will take you to the security bulletins, and from there you can access security patches as well. To have security bulletins sent to you, return to the maintenance/support main page and choose the "support information digests" option. Unfortunately, there does not appear to be any way to subscribe directly by email.

A list of Red Hat security advisories can be found at www.redhat.com/support/errata. As of this writing, no official security mailing list is sponsored by Red Hat. However, there are a variety of Linux security resources on the net; most of the information applies directly to Red Hat.

Information about FreeBSD security can be found at www.freebsd.org/security. FreeBSD maintains a formal list of advisories as well as some informal mailing lists and archives. All of this activity is overseen by the FreeBSD "security officer," which is actually a team of dedicated professionals.

Security information about Cisco products is distributed in the form of field notices, a list of which can be found at www.cisco.com/warp/public/770. To subscribe to Cisco's security mailing list, send mail to majordomo@cisco.com with the line "subscribe cust-security-announce" in the message body.

### Other mailing lists and web sites

The contacts listed above are just a few of the many security resources available on the net. The second edition of this book listed quite a few more, but given the volume of info that's now available and the rapidity with which resources come and go, we thought it would be more helpful to point you toward some meta-resources.

One good starting point is the X-Force web site (xforce.iss.net) at Internet Security Systems, which maintains a variety of useful FAQs. One of these is a current list of security-related mailing lists. The vendor and security patch FAQs provide useful contact information for a variety of vendors.

www.yahoo.com has an extensive list of security links; be sure to look under the general "computers and Internet" security section, as the UNIX-specific section is somewhat anemic. Another good source of links on the subject of network security can be found at www.about.com.

## 21.11  WHAT TO DO WHEN YOUR SITE HAS BEEN ATTACKED

The key to handling an attack is simple: Don't panic. It's very likely that by the time you discover the intrusion, most of the damage has already been done. In fact, it has probably been going on for weeks or months. The chance that you've discovered a break-in that just happened an hour ago is slim to none.

In that light, the wise owl says to take a deep breath and begin developing a carefully thought out strategy for dealing with the break-in. You need to avoid tipping off the intruder by announcing the break-in or performing any other activity that would seem abnormal to someone who may have been watching your site's operations for many weeks. Hint: performing a system backup is usually a good idea at this point and (hopefully!) will appear to be a normal activity to the intruder.[16]

This is also a good time to remind yourself that some studies have shown that 60% of security incidents involve an insider. Be very careful who you discuss the incident with until you're sure you have all the facts.

Here's a quick 9-step plan that may assist you in your time of crisis:

**Step 1: Don't panic.** In many cases, a problem isn't noticed until hours or days after it took place. Another few hours or days won't affect the outcome. The difference

---

16. If system backups are not a "normal" activity at your site, you have much bigger problems than the security intrusion.

between a panicky response and a rational response will. Many recovery situations are exacerbated by the destruction of important log, state, and tracking information during an initial panic.

**Step 2: Decide on an appropriate level of response.** No one benefits from an over-hyped security incident. Proceed calmly. Identify the staff and resources that must participate and leave others to assist with the post-mortem after it's all over.

**Step 3: Hoard all available tracking information.** Check accounting files and logs. Try to determine where the original breach occurred. Perform a backup of all your systems. Make sure that you physically write-protect backup tapes if you put them in a drive to read them.

**Step 4: Assess your degree of exposure.** Determine what crucial information (if any) has "left" the company, and devise an appropriate mitigation strategy. Determine the level of future risk.

**Step 5: Pull the plug.** If necessary and appropriate, disconnect compromised machines from the network. Close known holes and stop the bleeding. The Compromise FAQ from ISS provides some good technical suggestions on what to actually do with the systems that were broken into. It can be found at

> http://xforce.iss.net/library/faqs/compromise.php3

**Step 6: Devise a recovery plan.** With a creative colleague, draw up a recovery plan on nearby whiteboard. This procedure is most effective when performed away from a keyboard. Focus on putting out the fire and minimizing the damage. Avoid assessing blame or creating excitement. In your plan, don't forget to address the psychological fallout your user community may experience.

**Step 7: Communicate the recovery plan.** Educate users and management about the effects of the break-in, the potential for future problems, and your preliminary recovery strategy. Be open and honest. Security incidents are part of life in a modern networked environment. They are not a reflection on your ability as a system administrator or on anything else worth being embarrassed about. Openly admitting that you have a problem is 90% of the battle, as long as you can demonstrate that you have a plan to remedy the situation.

**Step 8: Implement the recovery plan.** You know your systems and networks better than anyone. Follow your plan and your instincts. Speak with a colleague at a similar institution (preferably one who knows you well) to keep yourself on the right track.

**Step 9: Report the incident to authorities.** If the incident involved outside parties, you should report the matter to CERT. They can be reached by fax at (412) 268-6989 or by email at cert@cert.org. Provide as much information as you can.

A standard form is available from www.cert.org to help jog your memory. Here are some of the more useful pieces of information you might provide.

- The names, hardware types, and OS versions of the compromised machines
- The list of patches that had been applied at the time of the incident
- A list of accounts that are known to have been compromised
- The names and IP addresses of any remote hosts that were involved
- Contact information if you know it for the administrators of remote sites
- Relevant log entries or audit information

If you believe that a previously undocumented software problem may have been involved, you should report the incident to your vendor as well.

## 21.12  RECOMMENDED READING

BRYANT, WILLIAM. "Designing an Authentication System: a Dialogue in Four Scenes." web.mit.edu/kerberos/www/dialogue.html

CERT COORDINATION CENTER. "Intruder Detection Checklist." www.cert.org/tech_tips/intruder_detection_checklist.html

CERT COORDINATION CENTER. "UNIX Configuration Guidelines." www.cert.org/tech_tips/unix_configuration_guidelines.html

CHESWICK, WILLIAM R., AND STEVEN M. BELLOVIN. *Firewalls and Internet Security, Second Edition.* Reading, MA; Addison-Wesley. 2000.

CURTIN, MATT, AND MARCUS RANUM. "Internet Firewalls: Frequently Asked Questions." www.interhack.net/pubs/fwfaq

FARMER, DAN, AND WIETSE VENEMA. "Improving the Security of Your Site by Breaking Into it." 1993. www.fish.com/security

FRASER, B., EDITOR. *RFC2196: Site Security Handbook.* www.rfc-editor.org.

GARFINKEL, SIMSON, and GENE SPAFFORD. *Practical UNIX and Internet Security.* Sebastopol: O'Reilly & Associates. 1996.

KERBY, FRED, ET AL. "SANS Intrusion Detection and Response FAQ." SANS. www.sans.org/newlook/resources/IDFAQ/ID_FAQ.htm

MANN, SCOTT, AND ELLEN L. MITCHELL. *Linux System Security: The Administrator's Guide to Open Source Security Tools.* Upper Saddle River, NJ: Prentice Hall PTR. 2000.

MORRIS, ROBERT, AND KEN THOMPSON. "Password Security: A Case History." Communications of the ACM, 22 (11): 594-597, November 1979. Reprinted in *UNIX System Manager's Manual,* 4.3 Berkeley Software Distribution. University of California, Berkeley. April 1986.

PICHNARCZYK, KARYN, STEVE WEEBER, AND RICHARD FEINGOLD. "UNIX Incident Guide: How to Detect an Intrusion." Computer Incident Advisory Capability, U.S. Department of Energy. 1994. http://ciac.llnl.gov/ciac/documents

RITCHIE, DENNIS M. "On the Security of UNIX." May 1975. Reprinted in *UNIX System Manager's Manual*, 4.3 Berkeley Software Distribution. University of California, Berkeley. April 1986.

SCHNEIER, BRUCE. *Applied Cryptography: Protocols, Algorithms, and Source Code in C.* New York, NY: Wiley, 1995.

THOMPSON, KEN. "Reflections on Trusting Trust." in *ACM Turing Award Lectures: The First Twenty Years 1966-1985*. Reading, MA: ACM Press (Addison-Wesley). 1987.

ZIMMERMANN, PHILIP R. *The Official PGP User's Guide*. Cambridge: MIT Press, 1995.

Security

# 22 Web Hosting and Internet Servers

The last few years have been a wild ride in computing. UNIX was the amino acid-laden tidal pool that gave rise to modern client/server computing and the Internet itself. In the 1980s, UNIX established a reputation for providing a high-performance, production-quality networked environment on a variety of hardware platforms. When the World Wide Web appeared on the scene as the ultimate distributed client/server application in the early 1990s, UNIX was there as its ready-made platform, and a new era was born.

Today, there are a variety of Internet-centric services that you might want to "host," either at your site or at one of the many colocation outsourcing providers.[1] In this chapter, we address the three most common services: the web, FTP, and news.

## 22.1 WEB HOSTING

In the early 1990s, UNIX was (literally) the only choice for serving content to the web. As the web's popularity grew, an increasing number of parties—ranging from advertising agencies to zoos—developed an interest in having their own presence on the net. However, UNIX was a foreign culture to many of these folks.

Seizing the opportunity, companies large and small jumped into the ring with their own server solutions. In many cases, these solutions involved substantial reengineering of operating systems that, unlike UNIX, were not built from the ground up with true preemptive multitasking in mind. Nevertheless, a new industry segment known

---

1. The more modern term for a hosting provider is an Application Service Provider or ASP.

as "web hosting" or "Internet hosting" was born around the task of serving content to the web. Web hosting servers not only deliver raw web (HTML) pages but also provide supporting services such as FTP, SSL, and streaming audio or video.

These days we have a variety of web hosting platforms to choose from, and a number of specialized web servers have been developed to meet the needs of specific market channels. Microsoft's once and future flagship product, Windows, has been widely marketed as a web hosting platform. But for folks looking for extreme reliability, maintainability, security, and performance, UNIX is still way ahead of the pack in the web hosting game.

The industry press has published countless articles that ask the question "Which web hosting platform is best?", usually positioning Windows and UNIX at opposite corners of the ring. Although some of this brouhaha is akin to the "Less filling!" "Tastes great!" battle, there are concrete reasons why UNIX is usually a better choice for production sites.

The foremost advantages of UNIX are its maintainability and performance. UNIX was designed from the start as a multiuser, interactive operating system. On a UNIX box, one administrator can maintain a database while another looks at I/O performance and a third maintains the web server. Under Windows, the person in control of the console (either physically or remotely, using a tool such as PC-Anywhere) is the only one who can perform critical administration tasks. As for performance, a good administrator can tune UNIX to perform two to three times faster than Windows on identical hardware.

## 22.2  WEB HOSTING BASICS

Hosting a web site isn't substantially different from providing any other network service. The foundation of the World Wide Web is the Hyper-Text Transfer Protocol (HTTP), a simple TCP-based protocol that's used to format, transmit, and link documents containing a variety of media types, including text, pictures, sound, animation, and video. HTTP behaves much like the other client/server protocols used on the Internet, for example, SMTP (for email) and FTP (for file transfer).

A web server is simply a system that's configured to answer HTTP requests. To convert your generic UNIX system into a web hosting platform, you need to install a daemon that listens for connections on TCP port 80 (the HTTP standard), accepts requests for documents, and transmits them to the requesting user.

Web browsers such as Netscape and Internet Explorer contact remote web servers and make requests on behalf of users. The documents thus obtained can contain hypertext pointers (links) to other documents, which may or may not live on the server that the user originally contacted. Since the HTTP protocol standard is well defined, clients running on any operating system or architecture can connect to any HTTP server. This platform independence, along with HTTP's ability to transparently pass a user from one server to another, have helped to spark its amazing success.

There is life beyond straight HTTP, however. Many enhanced protocols have now been defined for providing everything from encryption to streaming video. These additional services are often managed by separate daemons, even if they are provided by the same physical server. For example, one of the most popular enhanced services is Secure HTTP, aka HTTPS. It's handled by a daemon that understands the Secure Socket Layer (SSL) protocol and listens for requests on TCP port 443. You may need to obtain additional daemons from a third-party supplier if your UNIX vendor does not provide everything you need as part of the base operating system.

### Uniform resource locators

A uniform resource locator (URL) is a pointer to an object or service on the Internet. It describes how to access an object by means of five basic components:

- Protocol or application
- Hostname
- TCP/IP port (optional)
- Directory (optional)
- Filename (case sensitive; often ends in ".htm" or ".html")

Exhibit A illustrates a typical URL and its components.

**Exhibit A    Parts of a URL**

**WHERE**
*The file is on the machine www.apache.org in the directory /foundation.*

### http://www.apache.org/foundation/FAQ.html

**HOW**
*Hyper-Text Transfer Protocol*

**WHAT**
*The file I want is FAQ.html.*

Table 22.1 shows the protocols that are commonly used in URLs.

**Table 22.1    URL protocols**

| Proto | What it does | Example |
|-------|--------------|---------|
| http | Accesses a remote file via HTTP | http://admin.com/index.html |
| https | Accesses a remote file via HTTP/SSL | https://admin.com/order.shtml |
| ftp | Accesses a remote file via FTP | ftp://ftp.xor.com/adduser.tar.gz |
| mailto | Sends email to a designated address | mailto:sa-book@admin.com |
| news | Accesses Usenet newsgroups | news:alt.cooking |
| telnet | Logs in to a remote computer | telnet://spot.acme.com |
| ldap | Accesses LDAP directory services | ldap://ldap.bigfoot.com:389/cn=Herb |
| file | Accesses a local file (no Internet) | file://etc/syslog.conf |

## How HTTP works

HTTP is the protocol that makes the World Wide Web really work, and to the amazement of many, it is an extremely basic, stateless, client/server protocol. In the HTTP paradigm, the initiator of a connection is always the client (usually a browser). The client asks the server for the "contents" of a specific URL. The server responds with either a spurt of data or with some type of error message. In HTTP versions 0.9 and 1.0, the connection is then closed; in HTTP 1.1, the client can go on to request another object.

Because HTTP is so simple, you can easily make yourself into a crude web browser by using **telnet**. Since the standard port for HTTP service is port 80, just **telnet** directly to that port on your web server of choice. Once you're connected, you can issue HTTP commands. The most common command is **GET**, which requests the contents of a document. Usually, **GET /** is what you want, since it requests the root document (usually, the home page) of whatever server you've connected to. HTTP is case sensitive, so make sure you type commands in capital letters.

```
% telnet localhost 80
Trying 127.0.0.1...
Connected to localhost.xor.com.
Escape character is '^]'.
GET /
<contents of your index.html file appear here>
Connection closed by foreign host.
```

## CGI scripting: generating content on the fly

In addition to serving up static documents, an HTTP server can provide the user with content that has been created on the fly. For example, if you wanted to provide the current time and temperature to users visiting your web site, you might have the HTTP server execute a script to obtain this information. This amaze-the-natives trick is normally accomplished with the Common Gateway Interface, or CGI.

CGI is not a programming language, but rather a specification that allows an HTTP server to exchange information with other programs. Most often, CGI scripts are Perl or C programs that have been written specifically to interface with an HTTP server. But really, almost any programming language that can perform real-time I/O is acceptable. Just think of all those lonely FORTRAN programmers that can now reapply their skills to the Internet!

For the most part, CGI scripts are the concern of web developers and programmers. Unfortunately, in one important area CGI scripting collides with the job of the system administrator: security. Because CGI scripts have access to files, network connections, and other methods of moving data from one place to another, their execution can potentially affect the security of the machine on which the HTTP server is running. Ultimately, a CGI script gives anyone in the world the ability to run a program (the CGI script) on your server. Therefore, CGI scripts need to be just as secure as any other network-accessible program.

For a good source of information on the secure handling of CGI scripts, see the file www.w3.org/Security/Faq/www-security-faq.html.

### Load balancing

It's difficult to predict how many hits (requests for a single object, such as a text file or image) or page views (requests for all the objects on a single viewable page) a single server will be able to handle. The exact capacity of a server depends on the operating system it is running, the extent of system tuning, the system's hardware architecture (including subsystems) and the construction of the site (for instance, is it purely static HTML pages, or are there database calls and numeric calculations to be made?). Only direct benchmarking and measurement of your actual site running on your actual hardware can answer the "how many hits?" question. Sometimes, people who have built similar sites on similar hardware may be able to give you a wild-ass guess that will be useful for planning purposes. In no case should you believe the numbers quoted by UNIX system suppliers.

That said, instead of single-server hit counts, a better parameter to focus on is scalability. Make sure that you and your web design team have a plan that allows you to spread the load of a heavily trafficked site across multiple servers. The easiest way to spread the traffic is to use commercial third-party load balancing hardware, such as Cisco's Local Director product or the Alteon ACEswitch. These products distribute the work as specified by a variety of administrator-configurable parameters such as individual server response time and availability. Load balancing adds both performance and redundancy to your network—don't leave home without it.

## 22.3  HTTP SERVER INSTALLATION

Installing a web server is easy! Web services rank far below email and DNS in complexity and difficulty of administration. You'll be raking in the IPO bucks in no time.

### Choosing a server

Most UNIX vendors do not include an HTTP server as part of their operating system distribution (although both FreeBSD and Red Hat include the Apache HTTP server). Thus, you will probably need to spend some time deciding which server is best for your application and your platform. Fortunately, several very good servers are available. The most popular ones are produced by Netscape and the Apache Group.[2]

You can find a useful comparison of all the currently available HTTP servers at the site webcompare.internet.com. Here are some of the factors you may want to consider in making your selection:

- Robustness
- Performance
- Timeliness of updates and bug fixes

2. The Apache group was formed by several people who provided patch files for NCSA **httpd**, a popular web server in the "early days," circa 1993. The end result was "a patchy" server. Giddit?

- Availability of source code
- Cost
- Access control and security
- Ability to act as a proxy
- Ability to handle encryption

Over the last few years, Apache has been commonly regarded as the overall front-runner in terms of performance and number of operating systems supported. For these reasons, we've chosen it as our example server in this chapter. Other servers are essentially similar.

### Compiling and installing Apache

The Apache HTTP server is "free to a good home," and full source code is available from the Apache Group site at www.apache.org. The first thing to do is contact this site and download the latest version of the server.

Once you have downloaded the server, execute the **configure** script that is included with the distribution. This script automatically detects the type of system that you use and sets up the appropriate makefiles. You need to specify where in your directory tree the Apache server should live with the --**prefix** option. For example:

```
% ./configure --prefix=/usr/local/apache/
```

Some of Apache's features can be included in or removed from the server by invoking the -**enable-module**= and -**disable-module**= options to **configure**. Although the default set of modules is reasonable, you may also want to enable the modules shown in Table 22.2.

**Table 22.2   Useful Apache modules that are not enabled by default**

| Module | Function |
|--------|----------|
| auth_dbm | Uses a DBM database to manage user/group access (recommended)[a] |
| auth_db | Uses a DB database to manage user/group access (recommended)[a] |
| usertrack | Enables click-trail tracking of browsers that support "cookie" technology |
| rewrite | Rewrites URLs using regular expressions |
| expires | Lets you attach expiration dates to documents |
| proxy | Uses Apache as a proxy server (more on this later) |

a. We recommend that you use one of these modules, but there's no need to enable both.

Likewise, you may want to disable the modules listed in Table 22.3. For security and performance, it's a good idea to disable modules that you know you will not be using.

For a complete list of standard modules, see the **src/Configuration** file in your Apache distribution or http://www.apache.org/docs/mod/index.html.

When **configure** has finished executing, run **make** and then run **make install** to actually compile and install the appropriate files.

Web Hosting

**Table 22.3   Apache modules we suggest removing**

| Module | Function |
|--------|----------|
| asis | Allows designated file types to be sent without HTTP headers |
| autoindex | Indexes directories that don't have a default HTML file (e.g., **index.html**) |
| env | Lets you set special environment variables for CGI scripts |
| include | Allows server-side includes, an obsolete on-the-fly content creation scheme |
| userdir | Allows users to have their own HTML directories |

On FreeBSD systems, Apache is one of the additional software packages that can be installed from **/usr/ports** (see page 808 for more information about the **/usr/ports** mechanism). To install Apache, **cd** to **/usr/ports/www/apache13** and type **make**.

### Configuring Apache

Now that you've installed the server, you'll need to configure it for your application. All configuration files are kept in the **conf** directory (e.g., **/usr/local/apache/conf**). You will need to examine and customize three different configuration files to meet your site's needs: **httpd.conf**, **srm.conf**, and **access.conf**.

**httpd.conf** specifies how the Apache daemon (**httpd**) interacts with your system. In this file, you can set the TCP port on which the HTTP server listens for queries (usually port 80, though you can choose another—and yes, you can run multiple HTTP servers on different ports on a single machine), the location of log files, and various network and performance parameters. **httpd.conf** is also the file in which you can configure **httpd** to respond to virtual interface connections; see page 694 for details.

Resources that the server needs to access are controlled in the **srm.conf** file. This file includes the all-important DocumentRoot definition, which defines the root of the directory tree in which servable documents are located. The file also addresses issues such as the handling of "special" URLs like http://www.xor.com/~steve.

You manage security concerns through the **access.conf** file. This file contains directives that control access on a per-file or per-directory basis. These permissions prevent access to sensitive files via **httpd**, whether from the outside world or from inside your site.

You should specify at least two access controls: one that covers the entire document directory and one that applies only to the **cgi-bin** directory. Only the designated **cgi-bin** directory should allow script execution. That way, individual users cannot create security holes—accidental or otherwise—with their own scripts. Use the option ExecCGI in **srm.conf** to enable this restriction.

### Running Apache

You can start **httpd** by hand or from your machine's **rc** scripts. The latter is preferable, since this configuration will ensure that the web server restarts whenever the machine reboots. To start the server by hand, you would type something like

```
% /usr/local/apache/apachectl start
```

If you want **httpd** to start automatically at boot time, insert the following command in the **localrc()** function of your **rc** files, or insert it in **/etc/rc.local** if you use a separate local script:

```
if [ -x /usr/local/apache/httpd ]; then
    /usr/local/apache/apachectl start
    echo -n ' www_server'
fi
```

## 22.4  VIRTUAL INTERFACES

In the early days, a UNIX machine typically acted as the server for a single web site (e.g., www.acme.com). As the web's popularity grew, everybody wanted to have their own web site, and overnight, thousands of companies became web hosting providers.

Providers quickly realized that they could achieve significant economies of scale if they were able to host more than one site on a single server. This trick would allow www.acme.com, www.ajax,com, www.xor.com, and many other sites to be transparently served by the same hardware. In response to this business need, virtual interfaces were born.

Virtual interfaces allow a daemon to identify connections based not only on the destination port number (e.g., port 80 for HTTP) but also on the connection's destination IP address. Today, virtual interfaces are in widespread use and have proved to be useful for other applications besides web hosting.

The idea is simple: a single UNIX machine responds on the network to more IP addresses than it has physical network interfaces. Each of the resulting "virtual" network interfaces can be associated with a corresponding domain name that users on the Internet might want to connect to. This feature allows a single UNIX machine to serve literally hundreds of web sites. (By comparison, a competing Intel-centric operating system supports virtual interfaces but can only be practically used to host about a dozen sites. Of course, we could never name names.)

The HTTP 1.1 protocol defines a form of virtual-interface-like functionality (officially called "non-IP virtual interfaces") that eliminates the need to assign unique IP addresses to web servers or to configure a special interface at the OS level. This approach conserves IP addresses and is useful for some sites, especially sites at which a single server is home to hundreds or thousands of home pages (such as universities). However, the scheme isn't very practical for commercial sites; it reduces scalability (you must change the IP address of the site to move it to a different server) and may also have a negative impact on security (if you filter access to a site at your firewall based on IP addresses). It appears that true virtual interfaces will be around for a while.

Web Hosting

### Configuring virtual interfaces

Setting up a virtual interface involves two steps. First, you must create the virtual interface at the TCP/IP level. The exact way you do this depends on your version of UNIX; the next few sections provide instructions for each of our example systems. Second, you must tell the Apache server about the virtual interfaces you have installed. We cover this second step starting on page 694.

*Solaris virtual interfaces*

Solaris supports virtual interfaces (aka "secondary interfaces") through the concept of a physical interface and a logical unit. For example, if hme0 was the name of a physical interface, hme0:1, hme0:2, and so on would be the names of the corresponding virtual interfaces. By default, each physical interface can have up to 256 virtual identities attached to it. If you need to change this limit, use **ndd** to change the parameter ip_addrs_per_if (see page 311 for details on using **ndd**).

To configure a virtual interface, just use **ifconfig** on one of the virtual names. (The underlying physical interface must already have been "plumbed.") In most cases, you'll want to set up the system so that the **ifconfig**s for virtual interfaces happen automatically at boot time.

Here is an example in which a Solaris machine has an address in private address space on an internal virtual private network (VPN) and an external address for the Internet, both associated with the same physical interface, hme0. To have these interfaces configured automatically at boot time, the administrator has set up two different hostname files: **/etc/hostname.hme0** and **/etc/hostname.hme0:1**:

```
% ls -l /etc/host*
-rw-r--r--  1 root   10 Nov  4 10:19  /etc/hostname.hme0
-rw-r--r--  1 root   16 Dec 21 19:34  /etc/hostname.hme0:1
```

Hostname files can contain either hostnames from the **/etc/hosts** file or IP addresses. In this case, the administrator has used one of each:

```
% cat /etc/hostname.hme0
overkill
% cat /etc/hostname.hme0:1
206.0.1.133
% grep overkill /etc/hosts
10.1.2.9   overkill overkill.domain
```

At boot time, both of these addresses are automatically configured (along with the loopback address, which we omitted from the output shown below):

```
% ifconfig -a
hme0: flags=863<UP,BROADCAST,NOTRAILERS,RUNNING,MULTICAST> mtu
     1500 inet 10.1.2.9 netmask ffffff00 broadcast 10.1.2.255
hme0:1: flags=863<UP,BROADCAST,NOTRAILERS,RUNNING,MULTICAST> mtu
     1500 inet 206.0.1.133 netmask ffffff80 broadcast 206.0.1.255
```

### HP-UX virtual interfaces

HP-UX versions 11.00 and later support virtual or "secondary" interfaces through a naming convention much like that of Solaris. If lan0 is the name of a physical network interface, lan0:1 is the first virtual interface associated with it. The ":1" is called an IP index number. Each interface (real or virtual) can be configured with its own IP address, netmask, and options by the **ifconfig** command.

HP-UX 10.20 has the beginnings of virtual interfaces, but you have to install a patch. The patch adds the **ifalias** command, which configures the virtual interfaces.

### Red Hat virtual interfaces

Red Hat virtual interfaces are named with the same *interface:instance* notation used by Solaris and HP-UX. For example, if your Ethernet interface is eth0, then the virtual interfaces associated with it would be eth0:0, eth0:1, and so on. All interfaces are configured with the **ifconfig** command. For example, the command

```
# ifconfig eth0:0 128.138.243.150 netmask 255.255.255.192 up
```

configures the interface eth0:0 and assigns it an address on the 128.138.243.128/26 network. To make virtual address assignments permanent, you must make files for them in the **/etc/sysconfig/network-scripts** directory.

For example, the file **ifcfg-eth0:0** corresponding to the **ifconfig** command shown above would contain

```
DEVICE=eth0:0
IPADDR=128.138.243.150
NETMASK=255.255.255.192
NETWORK=128.138.243.128
BROADCAST=128.138.243.191
ONBOOT=yes
```

### FreeBSD virtual interfaces

FreeBSD supports virtual interfaces ("IP aliases") with the **ifconfig** option **alias**. For example, the following command binds an additional IP address to the xl0 interface:

```
# ifconfig xl0 inet 192.168.0.1 netmask 255.255.255.255 alias
```

To see the full configuration of the interface, we can run **ifconfig** again:

```
% ifconfig xl0
xl0: flags=8843<UP,BCAST,RUNNING,SIMPLEX,MCAST> mtu 1500
inet 192.108.21.9 netmask 0xffffff00 bcast 192.108.21.255
inet 192.168.0.1  netmask 0xffffffff bcast 192.168.0.1
  ether 00:60:97:9b:69:9a
  media: 10baseT/UTP <half-duplex>
  supported media: autoselect 100baseTX <full-duplex>
    100baseTX <half-duplex> 100baseTX 10baseT/UTP <full-
    duplex> 10baseT/UTP 10baseT/UTP <half-duplex>
```

Note the two different IP addresses listed in the second and third lines of output.

Web Hosting

To delete a virtual interface, just use **ifconfig** with the keyword **delete**. For example:

```
# ifconfig xl0 inet 192.168.0.1 delete
```

To configure virtual interfaces at boot time, add lines such as these to the **rc.conf** file:

```
ifconfig_xl0_alias0="inet 192.168.0.1 netmask 255.255.255.255"
ifconfig_xl0_alias1="..."
```

The numbering must start at alias0 and must be contiguous.

### Telling Apache about a virtual interface

In addition to creating the virtual interfaces with **ifconfig**, you need to tell Apache what documents to serve when a client tries to connect to each interface. You do this with a VirtualHost clause in the **httpd.conf** file, one VirtualHost clause for each virtual interface that you've configured. Here's an example:

```
<VirtualHost 192.225.33.37>
ServerAdmin webmaster@www.company.com
DocumentRoot /usr/local/apache/htdocs/company
ServerName www.company.com
ErrorLog logs/www.company.com-error_log
TransferLog logs/www.company.com-access_log
</VirtualHost>
```

When a client connects to the virtual host 192.225.33.37, it will be served documents from the directory **/usr/local/apache/htdocs/company**, which should be unique to this site.

## 22.5  CACHING AND PROXY SERVERS

The Internet and the information on it are growing exponentially. Ergo, the bandwidth and computing resources required to support it are growing exponentially as well. How can this state of affairs continue?

The only way to deal with this growth is to use replication. Whether it's on a national, regional, or site level, Internet content needs to be more readily available from a closer source as the Internet grows. It just doesn't make sense to transmit the same popular web page from Australia across a very expensive link to North America millions of times each day. There should be a way to store this information once it's been sent across the link once. Fortunately, there is.

One answer is the freely available Squid Internet Object Cache.[3] This package is both a caching and a proxy server that runs under UNIX and supports several protocols, including HTTP, FTP, Gopher, and SSL.

Here's how it works. Client web browsers (such as Netscape and Internet Explorer) contact the Squid server to request an object from the Internet. The Squid server then makes a request on the client's behalf (or provides the object from its cache, as dis-

---

3. Why "Squid"? According to the FAQ, "all the good names were taken."

cussed in the following paragraph) and returns the result to the client. Proxy servers of this type are often used to enhance security or filter content.

In a proxy-based system, only one machine needs to have direct access to the Internet through the organization's firewall. At organizations such as K-12 schools, a proxy server can also filter content so that inappropriate material doesn't fall into the wrong hands. Many commercial and freely available proxy servers (some based on Squid, some not) are available today.

Proxy service is nice, but it's the caching features of Squid that are really worth getting excited about. Squid not only caches information from local user requests, but it also allows a hierarchy of Squid servers to be constructed. Groups of Squid servers use the Internet Cache Protocol (ICP) to communicate information about what's in their caches.

This feature allows administrators to build a system in which local users contact an on site caching server to obtain content from the Internet. If another user at that site has already requested the same content, a copy can be returned at LAN speed (usually, 10 or 100 Mb/s). If the local Squid server doesn't have it, perhaps it contacts the regional caching server. As in the local case, if anyone in the region has requested the object, it is served immediately. If not, perhaps the caching server for the country or continent can be contacted, and so on. Users perceive a performance improvement, so they are happy.

For many, Squid offers economic benefits. Because users tend to share web discoveries, significant duplication of external web requests can occur at a reasonably-sized site. One study has shown that running a caching server can reduce external bandwidth requirements by up to 40%. This extra efficiency can be a big win at sites that pay for usage by the minute or the megabyte.

### Setting up Squid

Squid is easy to install and configure and runs on most modern UNIX architectures. Since Squid needs space to store its cache, you should run it on a dedicated machine that has a lot of free memory and disk space. A reasonable configuration would be a machine with 256 MB of RAM and 20 GB of disk space.

You can download a fresh copy of Squid from squid.nlanr.net. After unpacking the distribution, you run the **configure** script at the top of the tree. This script assumes that you wish to install the package in **/usr/local/squid**. If you prefer some other location, use the **--prefix=***dir* option to **configure**.

After **configure** has completed, run **make all** and then **make install**. Next, localize the configuration file, **/usr/local/squid/etc/squid.conf**. See the **QUICKSTART** file in the distribution directory for a list of the changes you must make to the sample **squid.conf** file.

You must also run **/usr/local/squid/bin/squid -z** by hand to build and zero out the directory structure in which cached web pages will be stored. Finally, you can start the server by hand with the **/usr/local/squid/bin/RunCache** script; you will eventually want to call this script from your system's **rc** files so that they start the Squid server when the machine boots.

To test Squid, configure your desktop web browser to use the Squid server as a proxy. This option is usually found in browser's preferences panel.

## 22.6  ANONYMOUS **FTP** SERVER SETUP

FTP is one of the oldest and most basic services on the Internet, yet it continues to be widely used today. Although FTP has a variety of internal uses at a site, the most common use on the Internet is "anonymous FTP," which lets users that do not have accounts at your site download files you have made available.

FTP is useful for distributing bug fixes, software, document drafts, and the like. Its main advantage over HTTP (for this purpose) is that it allows users to inspect the tree of available materials for themselves and to see the sizes and modification dates of files. You don't need to write any HTML to point to new files—just drop them into the target zone and you're done.

To enable anonymous FTP, you create an account for the fake user "ftp", configure its home directory, and set up the FTP server daemon, **ftpd**. Because of the public nature of anonymous FTP, it is important to configure it correctly so that sensitive files are not accidentally made available to the whole world.

*See page 823 for more information about **inetd**.*

**ftpd** is managed by **inetd** and therefore must have an entry in the **/etc/inetd.conf** and **/etc/services** files. When an FTP users logs in anonymously, **ftpd** executes a **chroot** system call to make files outside of the ~**ftp** directory invisible and inaccessible. The enhanced security provided by this precaution is important because **ftpd** must run setuid to root to manipulate privileged socket ports.

To allow anonymous **ftp** from your site, take the following steps:

- Add the user "ftp" to your regular password file.
- Create subdirectories **bin**, **etc**, and **pub** beneath ~**ftp**.
- Copy the **ls** program to the ~**ftp/bin** directory.
- Copy **/etc/passwd** and **/etc/group** to ~**ftp/etc**.
- Edit the **passwd** and **group** files as described below.
- Replace all passwords in ~**ftp/etc/passwd** with stars.
- Set the proper permissions on files and directories under ~**ftp**.

No one needs to log in to the ftp account, so use a star as ftp's password. It's also a good idea to specify **/bin/false** as ftp's login shell.

Since an anonymous **ftp** session runs **chroot**ed to ~**ftp**, the subdirectories **bin** and **etc** must provide a copy of all the commands and configuration information needed by **ftpd**. After the **chroot**, ~**ftp/bin** and ~**ftp/etc** will masquerade as **/bin** and **/etc**.

In most cases, **ftpd** uses only the **ls** command and skeletal copies of **/etc/passwd** and **/etc/group** from ~**ftp/etc**.

*See page 655 for more information about password security.*
The **passwd** file under ~**ftp** should only contain the users root, daemon, and ftp. You must replace the passwords with stars, since this copy of the **passwd** file will be available to people who use your **ftp** server. Even if the passwords are encrypted, there is still a risk involved in allowing other people to discover them.[4]

For added security, make ~**ftp/bin/ls** execute-only by setting its mode to 111. This tweak prevents clients from copying away the binary and studying it for weaknesses.

Put the files you want to make available in ~**ftp/pub**.

If your system uses shared libraries and your **ls** command is not statically linked, you may need to copy or hard-link extra files into ~**ftp** to provide a proper execution environment, since the files that contain the shared libraries aren't normally accessible after a **chroot**.

Permissions on the various files and directories are quite important. We recommend that permissions be set as shown in Table 22.4.

**Table 22.4    Recommended permissions under ~ftp**

| File/Dir | Owner | Mode | File/Dir | Owner | Mode |
|----------|-------|------|----------|-------|------|
| ~ftp | root | 555 | ~ftp/etc/passwd | root | 444 |
| ~ftp/bin | root | 555 | ~ftp/etc/group | root | 444 |
| ~ftp/bin/ls | root | 111 | ~ftp/pub | root | 755 |
| ~ftp/etc | root | 555 | | | |

Solaris requires **ls** to be put in ~**ftp/usr/bin**; ~**ftp/bin** should be a symbolic link to **usr/bin** (*not* a symbolic link to ~**ftp/usr/bin** because the path will be unresolvable after a **chroot** has occurred). Solaris is a shared library system, and many extra files must be installed under ~**ftp** to get **ls** to work. Refer to the **ftpd** manual page for instructions. Be sure to put a copy of **/etc/netconfig** in ~**ftp/etc**.

Since HP-UX uses **/etc/logingroup** instead of **/etc/group**, you must put a copy of the **logingroup** file in the ~**ftp/etc** directory.

Both FreeBSD and Red Hat use shared libraries, but everything you need is automatically installed in ~**ftp** during the OS installation process. In fact, anonymous FTP is turned on by default. Although the default configuration makes anonymous FTP setup easy, it does pose a risk to the unsuspecting system administrator who is unaware of its presence. Remove the ftp user from the **passwd** file if you do not wish to provide anonymous FTP service.

---

4. On some systems, you must run **mkpasswd passwd** after modifying the password file.

**Web Hosting**

## 22.7  USENET NEWS

Usenet news is a software system that originated in the 1970s to distribute short messages ("articles") to sites around the world. It is not really a type of network, but rather a set of protocols, file formats, and affiliations among sites. Usenet is made up of a large number of "newsgroups," which are similar to the message boards hosted by some web sites and on-line services. These days, Usenet has in many ways been supplanted by the World Wide Web. Many ISPs don't even bother to offer it as a service anymore, and new users often don't discover it.

Usenet uses a "flood fill" method of delivery. There is no central site from which content originates.[5] Instead, when a user creates ("posts") a new article, it is sent to the news server of the ISP for that user. The ISP's server offers the article to the other sites with which it exchanges articles. Each time an article reaches a new server, that server offers it to any other servers with which it has a peer relationship. A path list in the article helps to prevent servers from offering articles to a sites through which they have already passed.

At the time of this writing, a full Usenet feed with no filtering (spam or article size) contains new articles in excess of 100 GB/day. The daily volume has increased five-fold in just the past year and a half, but the article count has only increased by 50% over the same period.

The bulk of Usenet traffic consists of music and video files in MPEG format and pirated software (often referred to as "warez"). In the past, most of the volume consisted of pornographic pictures. Whether or not this is progress is subject to debate, but either way, Usenet has earned the well-deserved moniker "gigabytes of copyright violations."

With article sizes limited to 1MB and with spam and misspelled group name[6] filtering, the daily traffic volume goes down to a more manageable 35 GB/day. This is still a staggering amount of data and, in general, only large ISPs have the resources (bandwidth and disk storage) or desire to handle it.[7] Several alternate schemes have been devised to deliver news to sites that lack the resources to handle a full feed.

### Usenet news feeds

The simplest way to obtain a news feed is to retain the services of a company, such as www.supernews.com or www.giganews.com, that specializes in hosting Usenet. In general, you just point your users' browsers to the outsourcing provider's news server. This option takes news administration completely off your plate.

---

5. This is a little white lie. Due to the huge volume of news today, most well-connected sites get a feed from at least one of the major network providers (Sprint, WorldCom, AT&T, etc.). These large sites act as de facto distribution points and virtually guarantee the efficient propagation of articles.

6. It is amazing how many different ways "binaries" can be misspelled.

7. The bulk of the news (~97%) is in the "alt" hierarchy, mostly in the "alt.binaries" groups (92%).

Another option, if your upstream service provider offers it, is to get a "pull" feed. With a pull feed, your server fetches articles from another server only on demand. It also caches articles locally so that popular articles do not have to be refetched.

The advantages of using a pull feed over outsourcing news to a third party are that articles are transmitted from the remote server only once (saving bandwidth) and that since the server is local to your organization, access may feel "faster" to your users. The chief disadvantage of a demand-based pull feed is the delay between the time at which the remote server gets an article and the time at which your local server receives it. Also, if your users read a group infrequently, articles may expire on the remote server before they can be transferred to the local server.

To work around these limitations, some pull servers track the groups that users read and prefetch articles for those groups as they arrive. Unfortunately, this scheme can lead to a very large number of groups being tracked, defeating the purpose of a pull feed in the first place.

A third option is a hybrid approach in which the server receives a normal feed that includes the article headers but not the bodies.[8] Since the headers are relatively small, this plan does not consume much bandwidth or disk space. Only when a user asks to read an article is it pulled from the upstream server. Because the headers are pre-loaded onto the local system, the server can quickly present the user with the subject lines and other information for all available articles.

### Usenet software

If you want to provide news services in-house rather than pay for an outsourced provider, you will need to find an upstream feed, install software to manage the article tree on your system, and dedicate system administration time to manage and maintain the system.[9] Before making any elaborate plans, first ask whether your ISP offers an upstream feed. Even if your ISP is willing to consider providing a feed, you may have to pay extra to receive it.

Next, you will have to track down a news management software package. Table 22.5 lists the popular packages and their fortes.

**Table 22.5    Usenet software**

| Name | Free? | Feed types | More information |
|------|-------|-----------|------------------|
| INN | yes | Traditional, supports readers | www.isc.org |
| Diablo | yes | Traditional, pull, hybrid | www.openusenet.org |
| Dnews | no | Traditional, pull, supports readers | netwinsite.com |
| Cyclone | no | Traditional only | www.bcandid.com |
| Typhoon/Breeze | no | Supports readers only | www.bcandid.com |

8. Header information includes the author, subject, date, message ID, and threading data.

9. News can require a substantial amount of administration time, possibly as high as .25 to .75 FTEs for a site that receives a full traditional feed. Outsourcing usually looks a lot more attractive in this case.

Web Hosting

### Whither Usenet news?

It's hard to say where Usenet is headed. The percentage of Internet users who post articles has decreased dramatically since the advent of the Web, but at the same time the overall volume of news has increased many times over. Some old timers claim that the signal-to-noise ratio on Usenet today is so low that the system should be abandoned. Meanwhile, new Ph.D. candidates are rushing to write their theses on what a wonderful world-wide community Usenet fosters. As the saying goes, one person's trash is another person's treasure.

# SECTION THREE
## BUNCH O' STUFF

# 23 *Printing*

When we wrote the first edition of this book, the most common printers were ASCII line printers. Laser printers were new, expensive, and rare. High-resolution output devices required custom driver software and formatting programs.

By the time the second edition was published, line printers had practically become antiques. Numerous standards had been established for page description and printing languages. Laser printers had permeated the market and were widely used.

Today, as we prepare this third edition for publication, laser printers often connect to an Ethernet network instead of a serial or parallel port. They have largely lost the low-end market to inkjet printers.

With all of these changes in technology, you might expect that the UNIX printing systems would have changed dramatically. Unfortunately, they have not. The old line printer spooling systems have been hacked and overloaded in an attempt to support the new technology.

All major vendors use some mutation of the vanilla BSD spooling system (**lpd**, **lpc**, **lpr** and friends), the System V spooling system (**lpsched**, **lpadmin**, **lp** et al.), or a combination of both. Of our reference operating systems, Red Hat and FreeBSD fall into the BSD category, whereas Solaris and HP-UX are descendents of System V.

To determine which printing system you have, check to see which spooler is present (**lpd** for BSD and **lpsched** for SysV) rather than looking at the queuing commands. Many vendors provide queueing commands that mimic those of the other system. For example, HP-UX provides **lpr**, but its printing system is based on SysV.

We start with brief descriptions of printing terminology and the BSD and System V systems, then provide specifics on configuring printers for each of our reference systems. We then discuss LPRng, an alternative to the traditional printing systems. Finally, we conclude with a brief guide to printer debugging, a discussion of common printing software, and some general printing hints.

## 23.1 MINI-GLOSSARY OF PRINTING TERMS

Although an overview of current printing technology is beyond the scope of this book, we will try to give you enough information to respond when someone begins haranguing you in printer jargon.

*spooler*    A spooler is a piece of software that receives print jobs, stores them, prioritizes them, and sends them out sequentially to a printer. A user-level command submits jobs to the spooler for printing. A spooler is often called a print server. Some printers have their own internal spoolers.

*dpi*    Many modern printers are bitmap devices, meaning that the actual output is composed of rows of tiny dots. A printer's *dpi* is the number of dots per inch that it can print. Generally speaking, the higher the dpi, the better the print quality. A printer's resolution is sometimes asymmetrical; a notation such as "300 x 600 dpi" indicates a horizontal resolution of 300 dpi and a vertical resolution of 600 dpi.

*PDL*    Most printers accept input in one or more "page description languages" that specify the images to be placed on the page in an abstract way. PDL descriptions are more efficient to transmit than raw images, and they are easier for applications to generate. They also have the benefit of being device and resolution-independent. The best-known PDLs are PostScript and PCL.

*bitmap*    Sometimes you need to print images that are not easily described in a PDL. In these cases, you use a bitmap, which is a set of data that specifies which dots are filled in and which are not (or what color each dot is, in the case of a color or grayscale image).

As with PDLs, there are several competing formats for storing bitmaps. Every PDL supports at least one format. Since bitmaps are usually very large, they are often compressed. Common bitmap formats include JPEG, PNG, TIFF, and GIF.

*RIP*    A Raster Image Processor (RIP) is a system that accepts documents in one or more PDLs and converts them to a bitmap format appropriate for a particular output device. PDL-to-bitmap conversion is often done by a RIP within the printer.

*filters*    Filters are programs that modify print jobs en route from the spooler to the printer. Filters translate file formats, do accounting, and often handle communications with the printer. Filters are usually not necessary with simple text printers, but they are essential for sending jobs to printers that require nonstandard PDLs. Some PostScript printers can deal with unfiltered input, but the majority prefer specially filtered print jobs. In the SysV universe, filters are called *interfaces*. See pages 716 and 726 for more information about filters and interfaces.

*PostScript*    PostScript is by far the most common PDL found on UNIX systems. It was originally developed by Adobe Systems, and most PostScript printers use an interpreter licensed from Adobe. Almost all page layout programs can generate PostScript.

PostScript is actually a full-fledged programming language. You can read PostScript programs with a text editor or **more**. The programs contain a multitude of parentheses, curly braces, and slashes and often start with the characters %!PS. Although these starting characters are not required by the language itself, some versions of the UNIX printing software look for them when attempting to classify print jobs.

*PCL*    Printer Command Language is HP's alternative to PostScript. It's found almost exclusively on HP printers and is quite common in the PC world. UNIX applications usually cannot generate PCL, so they require a filter to convert other formats.

## 23.2  TYPES OF PRINTERS

UNIX lets you spool jobs to almost any type of printer. At the most basic level, printers are classified by their connection interface (network, serial, parallel) and by the type of data they understand (text, PostScript, PCL, or something else entirely).

Many of the "el cheapo" printers used on Windows systems (known collectively as WinPrinters) cannot be used with UNIX. These printers have very little built-in intelligence and cannot understand any PDL. Some of the information necessary to communicate with these printers is hidden in proprietary driver code. Such secrecy frustrates efforts to develop UNIX support for these devices.

### Serial and parallel printers

Serial printers require a mess of extra configuration. For basic information about serial ports, see Chapter 7, *Serial Devices*. The spooler software needs to know the appropriate values for the baud rate and other serial options so that it can communicate properly with the printer. Refer to your printing system's on-line man pages for information on how to specify these details.

Printing

Only PCs commonly provide a parallel port. Parallel ports are faster than standard serial ports, and fortunately for sysadmins, fewer options need be configured. Although the standard has not aged gracefully, it does provide us with ports that require relatively little tinkering. Under Red Hat Linux, the first (and usually only) parallel port is **/dev/parport0**; FreeBSD uses **/dev/lpt0**.

A faster and better serial technology called the Universal Serial Bus (USB) is just making its way into the UNIX world. USB has become wildly popular under Windows, but UNIX support has taken a while to arrive. At the time of this writing, the latest stable releases of FreeBSD and Linux are finally starting to offer USB support.

### Network printers

Some printers contain full-fledged network interfaces, which allow them to sit directly on a network and accept jobs through one or more network or printing protocols. Data can be sent to network-attached printers much more quickly than it can be sent to printers on serial or parallel ports.

Because any computer on the network can potentially spool directly to the network printer, contention issues arise. There is often a lack of administrative control.

To simplify administration, you should try to set up your network so that a few hosts control all of your printers. Other machines should simply transmit jobs to these print server machines. This setup can save you work because you will not have to keep a close eye on the printing system on every machine. In addition, you will have relatively few configurations to investigate when a printing problem occurs.

Many network laser printers include an **lpd** server that runs inside the printer. This feature allows UNIX clients to spool files to the printer in exactly the same manner they would spool files to a BSD server. Since all of our reference operating systems can spool to an **lpd** server, we like these printers a lot.

Older network printers required that print jobs be sent to TCP port 9100. This configuration is difficult to support with the BSD and SysV printing systems, but it's easy with LPRng. If you have this kind of printer, we strongly recommend that you read about LPRng starting on page 735.

### Life without PostScript

PostScript printers are naturally supported by UNIX printing systems, and configuration of these printers is relatively easy. Unfortunately, non-PostScript printers such as inkjets and some cheap laser printers are more difficult to deal with.

*See page 740 for more information about **ghostscript**.*

To print to a non-PostScript printer, you often need special software to convert the print job into the printer's preferred PDL. Some vendors can provide the appropriate UNIX software—usually for a price. The alternative is to use the free package **ghostscript**, which can convert from PostScript to the custom PDLs of hundreds of printers. You will need to specify a printing filter to properly invoke **ghostscript** on the fly. The **ghostscript** documentation contains examples. LPRng can make this task easier, too.

## 23.3  BSD PRINTING

BSD's printing system was designed specifically for use with line printers. Fortunately, efficient design has allowed the system to scale to support most of today's printers and PDLs. The network portion of the BSD printing system also extends well to large, heterogeneous networks and permits many computers to share printers. The **lpd** print spooler has become such a de facto standard that it has found its way inside many network printers.

Among our example systems, Red Hat and FreeBSD use the BSD system as the basis of their printing software.

### An overview of the printing process

Under BSD, access to printers is controlled by the **lpd** daemon, which usually lives in **/usr/sbin** and is normally started at boot time. **lpd** is responsible for accepting print jobs from users or other (remote) **lpd**s, processing them, and sending them on to an actual printer. To accomplish these last three steps, **lpd** reads printer configuration information from **/etc/printcap**, the system's printer information database.

Users invoke the **lpr** program to submit their print jobs to **lpd**. These two processes communicate through the UNIX socket **/dev/printer**.

When determining what printer to send the job to, **lpr** first looks at the command line. If a **-P***printer* argument is passed to **lpr**, *printer* becomes the destination. Otherwise, **lpr** checks the environment to see if the PRINTER variable is defined, and if so, **lpr** uses the variable's value. If all else fails, the job is submitted to the system-wide default printer, which is the printer named lp, or if there is no lp, to the first entry in the **/etc/printcap** file. Almost all printing-related commands, including **lpq** and **lprm**, understand the PRINTER environment variable and the **-P** argument.

As soon as **lpr** knows where the current job is headed, it looks up the printer in the **/etc/printcap** file. This file tells **lpr** into which directory print jobs for that printer should be placed. This "spool directory" is often **/var/spool/lpd/***printername*.

**lpr** creates two files in the spool directory for each job. The first file's name consists of the letters **cf** (control file) followed by a number that identifies the job.[1] This file contains reference and handling information for the job, such as the identity of the user who submitted it. The numeric portion of the filename allows space for only three digits, so the printing system becomes confused if more than 999 jobs are queued. The second file's name begins with **df** (data file) followed by the same number. This file contains the actual data to be printed. After the file has been spooled, **lpr** notifies the **lpd** daemon of the job's existence.

When **lpd** receives this notification, it consults the **printcap** file to determine if the destination is local or remote. If the printer is connected locally, **lpd** checks to be

---

1. The **cf** file is actually called **tf** ("temporary file") while **lpr** is in the process of accepting a job. After the file has been written, **lpr** changes the file's name from **tf***xxx* to **cf***xxx*.

sure a printing daemon is running on the appropriate printer's queue and creates one (by forking a copy of itself) if necessary.

If the requested printer is connected to a different machine, **lpd** opens a connection to the remote machine's **lpd** and transfers both the data and the control file. **lpd** then deletes the local copies of these files.

Scheduling for print jobs is done on a first-in, first-out basis, but the system administrator can modify the printing agenda by using **lpc** on individual jobs. Unfortunately, there is no way to permanently instruct the printing system to give preferential treatment to jobs spooled by a particular user or machine.

When the job is ready to print, **lpd** creates a series of UNIX pipes between the spool file and the printing hardware through which the data to be printed is transported. In the middle of this channel **lpd** installs a filter process that can review and edit the contents of the data stream before it reaches the printer.

Filter processes can perform various transformations on the data or do nothing at all. Their chief purposes are to provide formatting and to support any device-specific protocols that may be required for dealing with a particular printer. A printer's default filter is specified in **/etc/printcap**, but the default filter can be overridden on the **lpr** command line.

### Controlling the printing environment

For day-to-day maintenance of the printing system, you need only three commands: **lpq**, **lprm**, and **lpc**. **lpq** examines the queue of jobs waiting to be printed on a particular printer. **lprm** deletes one or more of these jobs, erasing their stored data files and removing any references to them from within the printing system. Both of these commands are available to users, and both work transparently across a network.

**lpc** lets you make a number of changes to the printing environment, such as disabling printers and reordering print queues. Although some of its functions are available to users, **lpc** is primarily an administrative tool. Table 23.1 shows some other commands and daemons associated with the BSD print system.

**Table 23.1   BSD printing commands**

| Command | Location | Function |
|---------|----------|----------|
| lpq | /usr/bin | Shows print queue contents and status |
| lpr | /usr/bin | Queues jobs for printing |
| lprm | /usr/bin | Cancels a queued or printing job |
| lpc | /usr/sbin | Controls a printer or queue |
| lpd | /usr/sbin | Schedules and prints jobs |
| lptest | /usr/bin | Generates an ASCII test pattern |
| lpunlock | /usr/bin | Unlocks stuck printers (Red Hat only) |
| printtool | /usr/bin | Configures the printing system (Red Hat only) |
| lptcontrol | /usr/sbin | Configures the parallel port for printing (FreeBSD only) |

## lpd: the BSD print spooler

When **lpd** first starts, it reads the **/etc/printcap** file, in which the system's printers are defined. It then starts printing any jobs that are waiting in the spool directory and starts listening for new print requests.

If you start **lpd** with the -l flag, it logs print requests through syslog under the "lpr" facility. Without the -l flag, **lpd** logs only printing system errors.

*See page 660 for more information about the* **hosts.equiv** *file.*

Access control is defined for each host; the BSD printing system cannot support access control for specific remote users.[2] Only hosts whose names appear in the files **/etc/hosts.equiv** or **/etc/hosts.lpd** are allowed to spool print jobs. Remember that adding a hostname to **/etc/hosts.equiv** indicates complete trust of that host. We recommend that you stick to the **/etc/hosts.lpd** file for printer access control. If you require a finer-grained security model, consider switching to LPRng.

## lpr: submit print jobs

**lpr** is the only program on a BSD system that can queue files for printing. Other programs that cause files to be printed (for example, **enscript** and **netscape**) must do so by calling **lpr**.

Several useful options can be specified as arguments to **lpr**. The -#*num* flag produces *num* copies, and the -**h** flag suppresses the header page. Reminiscent of the days of slow printers, the -**m** flag requests that email be sent to the owner when the print job is complete.

For example, to print two copies of a file named **thesis** to a printer called **howler-lw**, you could type

```
% lpr -Phowler-lw -#2 thesis
```

## lpq: view the printing queue

**lpq** is normally used with just a -**P** option to select a printer, although the -**l** flag is available to produce more detailed output. Output from **lpq** looks like this:

```
% lpq
anchor-lw is ready and printing
Rank    Owner    Job  Files            Total Size
active  garth    314  domain.2x1.ps    298778 bytes
1st     kingery  286  standard input   17691 bytes
2nd     evi      12   appendices       828 bytes
3rd     garth    13   proc             43229 bytes
4th     scott    14   periodic         16676 bytes
5th     garth    16   standard input   489 bytes
```

The first column tells you the order in which the jobs will be printed. This information is rather superfluous because the output lines are always in order, with the ac-

---

2. Actually, it is possible for printing filters to do this kind of authentication. But because most systems use a variety of filters, maintaining uniform access control among them is impractical.

tive job on top and the last job to be printed on the bottom. If the first job is listed as 1st rather than active, no printing daemon is running on the printer.

The second column tells you which user spooled each job. The third column gives the job identification number for each job; this number is important to know if you intend to manipulate the job later with **lprm** or **lpc**. The fourth column shows the filenames that were listed on the **lpr** command line used to spool the job. If the data came in via a pipe (as the first and fifth jobs did above), the entry in this column will be standard input. The fifth and final column tells you the size of the job. This number is the size of the job before it is sent to the filter program and gives no information about how many pages a job will be or how long it will take to print.

### lprm: remove print jobs

The most common form of **lprm** is **lprm** *jobid*, where *jobid* is the job identification number reported by **lpq**. **lprm** *user* removes all jobs belonging to *user*. **lprm** without arguments removes the active job. **lprm** - removes all the jobs you submitted; if you are root, it removes every job in the queue. No ordinary user can remove another user's jobs, but the superuser can remove any job.

Perversely, **lprm** fails silently but produces output on success. If you don't see output that looks like

```
dfA621xinet dequeued
cfA621xinet dequeued
```

after running **lprm**, it means you did not invoke the command correctly.

The printing system maintains a notion of the origin of a job as well as the user who spooled it, and **lprm**'s matching process takes both into account. Thus garth@sigi is not equivalent to garth@boulder, and neither can remove the other's jobs.

Trying to **lprm** the active job can cause problems on some printers. The filter process for the job is not properly notified of the termination, causing the whole system to come to a grinding halt with the filter process holding an exclusive lock on the printer's port and preventing other processes from using the printer.

The only way to fix this situation is to use **ps** to identify the filter processes and kill them off by hand. **lpc** is not of use in this situation. Rebooting the system will always cure a hung printer, but this is a drastic measure. Before you resort to a reboot, kill and restart the master copy of **lpd** and manually remove jobs from the spool directory with the **rm** command.

### lpc: make administrative changes

The **lpc** command can perform the following functions:

- Enable or disable queuing for a particular printer
- Enable or disable printing on a particular printer
- Remove all jobs from a printer's queue
- Move a job to the top of a printer's queue

- Start, stop, or restart the **lpd** daemon
- Get printer status information

When the printing system is running smoothly, **lpc** works just fine. But as soon as a filter gets stuck or some other minor problem appears, **lpc** wigs out completely. And it lies: it sometimes claims to have fixed everything when in reality, it has done nothing at all. You may have to fix things up by hand or even power-cycle your equipment when printing gets badly snarled.

**lpc** cannot be used across a network; you must log into the machine that owns the printer you want to manipulate. **lpc** is normally used interactively, although you can also invoke it in a one-shot mode by putting one of the interactive commands on **lpc**'s command line. Once you have activated **lpc**, the various commands described below are available:

> **help** [*command*]

**help** without arguments shows you a short list of all available **lpc** commands. With an argument, it shows a one-line description of a particular command.

> **enable** *printer*
> **disable** *printer*

These commands enable or disable spooling of jobs to the named printer. Users who attempt to queue files are politely informed that spooling has been disabled. Jobs that are already in the queue are not affected. You perform this operation by simply setting or clearing group execute permission on **/var/spool/lpd/***printer***/lock**.

> **start** *printer*
> **stop** *printer*

**start** enables and **stop** disables printing on the named printer. Print jobs can still be spooled when a printer has been stopped, but they will not be printed until printing is restarted. **start** and **stop** operate by setting or clearing owner execute permission on **/var/spool/lpd/***printer***/lock**. They also start and kill the appropriate daemons for the printer. **stop** allows the active job to complete before disabling printing.

> **abort** *printer*

**abort** is just like **stop**, but it doesn't allow the active job to complete. When printing is reenabled, this job will be printed again.

> **down** *printer message*
> **up** *printer*

These commands affect both spooling and printing. Use them when a printer is really broken or has to be taken off-line for an extended period. The *message* parameter supplied to **down** can be as long as you like (on one line) and need not be quoted; it will be put in the printer's **/var/spool/lpd/***printer***/status** file and shown to users who run **lpq**. You'll normally want to use this feature to register a short explanation of why the printer is unavailable and when it will be back in service. The **up** command reverses the effect of a **down**.

**clean** *printer*

This command removes all jobs from the printer's queue, including the active job. Because the printing daemon for the queue will still hold references to the files of the current job, UNIX will not really delete them and the current job will complete.

**topq** *printer jobid*
**topq** *printer username*

The first form moves the specified job to the top of the printer's queue. The second form promotes all jobs belonging to *username*.

**restart** *printer*

The **restart** command restarts a printing daemon that has mysteriously died. You'll know that the daemon is dead when **lpq** tells you "no daemon present." Although you might think **restart** would have the same effect as a **stop** followed by a **start**, it does not; **restart** will fail to restart a printer that still has a filter running.

**status** *printer*

The **status** command shows you four things about a printer: whether spooling is enabled, whether printing is enabled, the number of entries in the queue, and the status of the daemon for that printer. If no entries are in the queue, you'll see something like this:

```
lpc> status cer
cer:
queuing is enabled
printing is enabled
no entries
no daemon present
```

The fact that no daemon is present is not a cause for concern; printer-specific daemons go away after the queue is empty and aren't restarted by the master copy of **lpd** until another job is spooled.

## The /etc/printcap file

**/etc/printcap** is the BSD printing system's master database. It contains information necessary for printing to local and remote printers. A printer must be described in the **printcap** file before jobs can be submitted to it.

**/etc/printcap** uses the same format as **/etc/termcap** and **/etc/remote**. The first item in each entry is a list of names for the printer, separated by vertical bars. The names are followed by a number of configuration settings separated by colons. Configuration options are of the form xx, xx=*string*, or xx#*number*, where xx is the two-character name of a parameter and *string* and *number* are values to be assigned to it. When no value is assigned, the variable is Boolean and its presence indicates "true."

The null statement is acceptable, so you can place two colons side by side. It is helpful to begin and end each line with a colon to make subsequent modifications easier.

Comments in **/etc/printcap** start with a pound sign (#). Entries can span several lines if intermediate lines are terminated with a backslash. Continuation lines are, by convention, indented.

The syntax of the **printcap** file is illustrated in the following example, which defines a remote printer attached to the machine anchor:

```
# HP LaserJet 5M remote printcap. CS Department.

anchor-lj|cer|1-56|LaserJet 5M in cer lab:\
     :lp=/var/spool/lpd/anchor-lj/.null:\
     :sd=/var/spool/lpd/anchor-lj:\
     :lf=/var/adm/lpd-errs:\
     :rw:mx#0:rm=anchor:rp=anchor-lj:
```

From the first line, we can see that "cer", "anchor-lj", "1-56" and "LaserJet 5M in cer lab" are all equivalent names for the same printer. These names are the printer's given name, a well-known abreviation, the room number of the printer's location, and a full description. Although you can give your printers as many names as you like, you should include at least three forms of the primary name:

- Short name – three or four characters, easy to type (e.g., "cer")
- Full name – hostname and type of printer (e.g., "anchor-lw")
- Descriptive name – other information (e.g., "LaserJet 5M in cer lab")

The second two lines in our example contain configuration settings for device name (lp), spool directory (sd), and error log file (lf). The last line specifies a read-write connection with the printer (rw), the maximum file size (mx, unlimited in this case), the remote machine name (rm), and the remote printer name (rp).

Jobs submitted to the printing system without a specific destination are routed to the first printer that has "lp" as one of its aliases. You should not use lp as a printer's primary name; that makes it difficult to change the default printer. If no printer has the name lp, the first printer in the **printcap** file is the system-wide default printer.

### printcap variables

The flexibility of the **printcap** file is largely responsible for the BSD printing system's adaptability. The details are documented in the **printcap** man page, so we discuss only the most common variables here. They're shown in Table 23.2 on the next page.

All **printcap** entries should include at least a specification of the spool directory (sd), the error log file (lf), and the printing device (lp). If you have a modern printer, you should specify that the printer be opened for reading and writing (rw) so that the printer can send error and status messages back to the host.

### sd: spool directory

Each printer should have its own spool directory. All spool directories should be in the same parent directory (usually **/var/spool/lpd**) and should have the same name as the full name of the printer they serve (anchor-lw in the preceding example). A

**Table 23.2   Commonly used printcap variables**

| Name | Type | Meaning | Example |
|------|------|---------|---------|
| sd | string | Spool directory | sd=/var/spool/lpd/howler-lw |
| lf | string | Error log file | lf=/var/log/lpr |
| lp | string | Device name | lp=/dev/lp0 |
| af | string | Accounting file | af=/usr/adm/lpr.acct |
| rm | string | Remote machine name | rm=beast.xor.com |
| rp | string | Remote printer name | rp=howler-lw |
| of | string | Output filter | of=/usr/libexec/lpr/lpf |
| if | string | Input filter | if=/usr/sbin/stylascii |
| mx | number | Maximum file size | mx#0 |
| sh | bool | Suppress headers | sh |

spool directory is needed even if the printer being described lives on a different machine; spooled files are stored locally until they can be transmitted to the remote system for printing.

When you install a new printer, you must create its spool directory by hand. Permissions should be 775, with both owner and group daemon.

The spool directory for a printer also contains two status files: **status** and **lock**. The **status** file contains a one-line description of the printer's state. This information is maintained by **lpd** and viewed with the **lpq** command. The **lock** file prevents multiple invocations of **lpd** from becoming active on a single queue and holds information about the active job. The permissions on the **lock** file are manipulated by **lpc** to control spooling and printing on the printer.

### lf: error log file

*See Chapter 11 for more information about log files.*

Errors generated by print filters are logged to the file named in this variable. One error log can be shared by all printers, and it can be placed anywhere you like. When a log entry is made, the name of the offending printer will be included. Even remote printers should have log files, just in case of a communication problem with the remote machine.

Keep in mind that **lpd** sends error messages to syslog. Some filters send their error messages to syslog as well, leaving nothing in their **printcap**-specified log file. Check both of these locations when problems arise.

### lp: device name

The device name for a printer must be specified if the printer is local. This name is usually the file in the **/dev** directory that represents the port to which the printer is attached. If the **printcap** entry addresses a network printer (that is, a printer on your LAN, not just a "remote" UNIX printer; see page 706), the lp variable should be a pointer to a dummy file. (We like to use **/var/spool/lpd/***printer***/.null** for our dummy files.) This variable does not have to be defined for remote printers, but if it is, the file must exist.

**lpd** uses an advisory lock on the lp file to determine if the printer is in use. Even if the printer is really accessed through a network connection, you should provide a value for the lp variable. Specify a unique file that already exists on a local disk.

### rw: device open mode

If a printer can send status information back to the host through its device file, the Boolean variable (rw) should be specified to request that the device be opened for both reading and writing. Read-write mode is useful for accounting and status reporting, and some filters require it.

### af: accounting file

Even if you don't intend to charge for printer use, printer accounting can give you a good feel for how your printing resources are being consumed. We recommend that you enable accounting for all shared printers. You do that simply by specifying an accounting file. The file need only be specified and present on the machine to which the printer is physically connected, since accounting records are not written until a job is actually printed.

For a summary of accounting information, use the **pac** command. By convention, printer accounting data files are usually called **/var/adm/***printer***-acct**. They list the number of pages printed for each job (usually a lie), the hostnames where the jobs originated, and the usernames of the jobs' owners.

It is the responsibility of the printer's input filter to generate accounting records. On PostScript printers, unless the filter actually queries the printer for its page count before and after the job, the page counts are extremely suspect.

### mx: file size limits

The mx variable sets a limit on the amount of data that can be spooled at one time. File sizes are meaningless for printers other than line printers, however. Small PostScript or PCL files could print hundreds of pages of garbage. This disconnect between file size and page length is particularly evident when students try to print the compiled binary versions of their programming assignments.

On some systems, mx defaults to some value other than 0 (no limit), and an explicit mx#0 entry is necessary to allow large jobs. Note that mx is a numeric field, so the entry mx=0 is incorrect.

If you really need to control how many pages people can print, you will need to use custom filters or switch to LPRng.

### rm and rp: remote access information

In most situations, you will want to access a printer from more than one machine on the network. Even if the printer is a network device, you should pick a single machine to be responsible for communicating with it. All other machines should forward jobs to the designated handler. This setup allows **lpd** to take care of queuing the jobs in order rather than having several machines constantly squabbling over control of the printer. It also gives you a single place to look when printing is not working.

Remote machines (machines that are not directly connected to the printer) have a simple **printcap** entry that tells where to send the job, as in the example on page 733. The rm variable specifies the machine to which jobs should be sent, and the rp variable gives the name of the printer on that machine. The details of remote printing are described in the OS-specific sections starting on page 729.

The fact that **printcap** entries are different for local and remote printers necessitates a bit of subterfuge on the part of the system administrator if one **printcap** file is to be shared among several machines. The fix is to make the local and remote names for a printer distinct; for example, howler-lw-local and howler-lw. This configuration makes howler-lw a "remote" printer even on the machine where it actually lives, but that's perfectly OK. You will have to refer to howler-lw-local if you want to use the **lpc** command, however.

### *of, if, nf: printing filters*

Filters serve a number of purposes. The default printing filter (usually **/usr/lib/lpf**) fixes up various nonprinting sequences and writes out an accounting record, if appropriate. Unfortunately, filters are not standardized. Any of several filter packages could do the same job, but each vendor tends to have unique filters.

If you have a character-only printer, you don't really need to be concerned with filters. If you have a laser printer, typesetter, or plotter, the necessary filters will usually be provided with the printer's software. If you need to configure a printer for which you have no software, you will have to read through the details of the rest of this section. Otherwise, skip ahead and live in blissful ignorance.

Filters are usually just shell scripts that call a series of translation programs. The filter program must accept the print job on standard input, translate the job to a format appropriate for the device, and send the result to standard output.

If the user does not specify a filter when executing **lpr**, either the if (input filter) or the of (output filter) will be used. The names are deceptive—both actually send data to a printer.

If the **printcap** entry lists an input filter but does not specify an output filter, the device will be opened once for each job. The filter will be expected to send one job to the printer and then exit.

Conversely, if an output filter is specified without an input filter, **lpd** will open the device once and call the filter program once, sending all the jobs in the queue in a big clump. This convention is OK for devices that take a long time to connect to; however, such devices are rare.

If both an input filter and an output filter are specified, the banner page will be sent to the output filter (and the output filter will be called even if banners are turned off). The input filter will be called to process the rest of the job. This combination of options is really too confusing for mere mortals. Avoid it. Use LPRng if you have complex filtering requirements.

If you have to write new filters, stick to using input filters, as they are easier to debug.

Input filters are called with numerous arguments, which vary among implementations. The most interesting are the username, host of origin, and accounting file name. If you want to do accounting for the printer, the input filter must generate the accounting records and append them to the accounting file. If you want to restrict access to a printer (for example, to deny printing to the user "guest"), the input filter must also take care of that since **lpd** has no built-in way to prevent individual users from printing.

To clarify the uses of filters, let's look at a simple example of an input (if) filter. The example is for a PostScript printer connected to a serial line on the local machine:

```
#!/bin/csh -f
/usr/local/bin/textps $* | /usr/local/bin/psreverse
```

Because the printer is serially connected, **lpd** takes care of opening the device with the correct modes, as specified in **/etc/printcap**. The first program called is **textps**, which looks at the input and decides if it is PostScript (which our printer expects), and if not, converts it to PostScript. **textps** gets all the filter arguments that were passed (the $*) and is expected to generate accounting records from that information. The second program, **psreverse**, reverses the order of the pages so that they come out in a proper stack.

### printcap variables for serial devices

The next few **printcap** variables are useful only for local serial printers. If you are setting up a network printer, skip the rest of this section. Otherwise, open your manual, look up your printer's communication specifications, and read on.

You control three types of communication settings through **printcap**: the baud rate, the "flag" bits, and the "local mode" bits.

*br: baud rate*

If your printer is connected to a serial port, you will need a br entry. A serial printer is like any other piece of hardware: for correct operation, it and its host computer must agree on a common set of communication parameters such as speed, parity, and flow control. Configuration of a printer is much like the configuration of a terminal. See Chapter 7 for general information about serial devices and cabling.

The baud rate is the speed at which communication occurs (in bits per second) and is a simple integer. Since it is a numeric value, you use the pound sign (#) to set it. For example, br#9600 sets the baud rate to 9,600 bps.

### fc and fs: flag bits

Mucking with the flag bits is usually only necessary if you are trying to set up an old impact printer such as a Teletype. Like local mode bits (below), flag bits are integers, but each bit within the number modifies the behavior of the port in its own special way. Setting up these parameters correctly requires that you look up the meaning of each bit in the **tty** man page (section 4, *not* section 1) and add up the values for the bits you want to set or clear. Settings need only be specified on the machine to which the printer is connected.

You can assign two variables when adjusting the flag bits: fc and fs. fc (flag clear) specifies the bits that should be turned off, and fs (flag set) specifies the ones that should be turned on. Bits assigned to neither variable assume default values. It is meaningless to both set a bit and clear it.

The **tty** man page explains the meaning of each flag bit in detail. As long as you know the communication settings of your printer, setting the flag bits properly is trivial.

### xc and xs: local mode bits

The local mode bits are useful only for serial line printers. The xc and xs variables clear and set individual mode bits in much the same way that fc and fs clear and set flags bits. The difference between the two sets of bits is that local mode bits configure the serial driver, whereas the flag bits configure the actual communication link. Most of the mode bits are intended for use on interactive video terminals and so are not relevant to printer configuration.

### printcap extensions

A nice feature of the **lpr/lpd** system is that it does not mind if you supply values for nonstandard **printcap** variables. Often, when a particular printer needs more configuration information than the base system defines, you can put extra variables in **printcap** for the printer's filters to use.

For example, the output filter for a network printer might need to know the network name of the device. The **printcap** entry for the printer might contain an entry such as

```
:nn=laser.colorado.edu:\
```

The use of **printcap** extensions allows all of the configuration information for a printer to be stored in one convenient place. If you see variables in the **printcap** file that are not discussed in the **printcap** manual page, check the documentation for the printer filters for the meanings of the variables.

Our site has taken advantage of this feature to document the physical location of each printer. Our printers have entries such as

```
:lo=Room 423, Engineering building:\
```

We have scripts that monitor paper and toner levels in the printers send mail to support staff with instructions such as "take more paper to room 423 in the Engineering building" when necessary. For more information about monitoring network devices, see Chapter 20, *Network Management and Debugging*.

### Printing to something besides a printer

We recently saw an instance of "creative misuse" by Sean McCreary in which the BSD printing system was used to spool MP3 music to a software jukebox. If nothing else, this is a great testimonial to the flexibility of the printing system.

The printcap entry looked something like this:

```
mp3-local:\
     :sd=/var/spool/lpd/mp3-local:\
     :lf=/var/log/lpd-errs:\
     :if=/usr/local/lib/mp3-play:\
     :lp=/dev/null:\
     :mx#0:
```

The actual MP3 player, **amp**, does not read from stdin by default, so a one-line script, called **mp3-play**, interfaced it to the printing system:

```
#!/bin/sh
exec /usr/local/bin/amp -
```

## 23.4  SYSTEM V PRINTING

Unfortunately, the System V printing software was not designed with network printing in mind, and it has not scaled well. Most vendors that use it have made numerous changes, some that add useful functionality, and some that are purely gratuitous.

Among our example systems, Solaris and HP-UX use the SysV software. However, both have modified it significantly. Below, we discuss the standard system with many vendor-specific notes.

### Overview

A user who wants to print something must either use the **lp** command or a command that invokes **lp** indirectly. **lp** places input in a file in the spool directory appropriate for its final destination. The **lpsched** daemon determines when and where a particular file should be printed, then executes an interface program that formats the data and outputs it to the correct printer. Table 23.3 on the next page briefly describes the commands in the SysV printing system.

### Destinations and classes

Each destination has a name that consists of up to 14 alphanumeric characters and underscores. In addition to being named, a destination can belong to zero or more *classes*. As in BSD printing, a destination does not have to be a printer, although in practice it usually is. For example, a destination could be an ordinary text file that needs to be appended to by many users. The printing system could be used to avoid a situation in which two people attempt to add to the file at the same time.

Printing

**Table 23.3    System V printing commands**

| | Command | Location | Function |
|---|---|---|---|
| **Generic commands** | accept | /usr/sbin | Accepts jobs into the queue |
| | cancel | /bin | Removes jobs from the queue |
| | disable | /bin | Disables printing of jobs from the queue |
| | enable | /bin | Enables printing of jobs from the queue |
| | lp | /bin | Queues jobs for printing |
| | lpadmin | /usr/sbin | Configures the printing system |
| | lpmove | /usr/sbin | Moves jobs between queues |
| | lpsched | /usr/lib/ | Schedules and prints jobs |
| | lpshut | /usr/sbin | Stops printing services |
| | lpstat | /bin | Reports the status of printing services |
| | reject | /usr/sbin | Stops acceptance of jobs into the queue |
| **Solaris** | lpfilter | /usr/sbin | Controls print filters |
| | lpforms | /usr/sbin | Controls the use of preprinted forms |
| | lpusers | /usr/sbin | Controls queue priorities |
| | lpget | /bin | Reads configuration settings |
| | lpset | /bin | Modifies configuration settings |
| **HP-UX** | lpalt | /bin | Modifies jobs in the queue |
| | lpr | /bin | Provides support for BSD printing |
| | lpana | /usr/sbin | Analyzes performance logs |
| | lpfence | /usr/sbin | Sets the minimum job priority for a printer |

A class is a group of destinations that all serve the same purpose in some way. For example, if a site had two printers in the same room, they could be placed in a class. Likewise, two printers with similar features (such as color, resolution, duplex, or speed) might be grouped into a class. **lpsched** would direct output for that class to whichever printer became available first. Class names have the same restrictions as destination names.

In the rest of this chapter we use the words "printer" and "destination" interchangeably to refer to destinations, even though a destination is not necessarily a printer.

### A brief description of lp

**lp** is a user-level command that queues data for printing. **lp** makes a copy of the data to be printed (which can come either from named files or from **lp**'s standard input) and places it in a file or set of files in the spool directory. Under HP-UX, the spool directory for a destination is **/var/spool/lp/request/**dest where dest is the name by which **lp** knows the printer or class of printers. Solaris uses the pluralized version, **/var/spool/lp/requests/**dest.

The spool file(s) are named xxxn, where n is a job identification number assigned by **lp** and xxx varies from system to system. This filename identifies the job both to the user and internally to the printing system. We refer to this name as the job identification or jobid, for short.

If the **-d** *destination* option is specified to **lp**, the input is queued for output to the specified *destination*, where *destination* is either a printer or a class. If the **-d** option is not used, **lp** uses the contents of the LPDEST environment variable as the name of the output destination. If this environment variable is not set, **lp** queues the data for output to the default destination if one exists or rejects the request if there is no default destination. (The default destination is set with **lpadmin -d**.)

In Solaris, if no default device is specified with **lpadmin -d**, then **lp** searches the **~/.printers** file, the **/etc/printers.conf** file, and finally, the Federated Naming Service[3] for a default destination.

### lpsched and lpshut: start and stop printing

The **lpsched** daemon sends the files placed in the spool directory by **lp** to an appropriate device as soon as one is available. **lpsched** keeps a log of each file it processes and any errors that occur. In Solaris, the default log file is **/var/lp/logs/lpsched**.

When the HP-UX **lpsched** is started (usually at boot time), it moves its default log file from **/var/adm/lp/log** to **/var/adm/lp/oldlog** and starts a new log file.

A log file looks something like this:

```
***** LP LOG: Jul  6 12:05 *****
pr1-107     garth    pr1    Jul 6    12:10
pr-112      scott    pr1    Jul 6    12:22
pr-117      evi      pr2    Jul 6    12:22
pr1-118     garth    pr1    Jul 6    12:25
pr1-119     garth    pr1    Jul 6    13:38
pr-132      evi      pr1    Jul 6    13:42
```

The first column is the jobid of each job. The second column is the user who requested the job. The third column is the actual printer the job was sent to, and the last column is the time at which the job was queued.

On the HP-UX system in this example, there are two printers: pr1 and pr2, both of which are in the class pr. The user garth always specified the specific printer pr1, so that's where his jobs were always sent. The users scott and evi, on the other hand, specified the class pr, so their jobs were sent to the first available printer in that class.

To stop **lpsched** for any reason, run **lpshut** as root or as the user lp. When **lpsched** is not running, no jobs will actually be printed, though **lp** can still queue jobs for printing. Jobs that are being printed when the daemon is stopped will be reprinted in their entirety when the daemon is restarted. To restart the daemon, run **lpsched**.

---

3. Yes, the Federated Naming Service. It's the Solaris scheme for managing naming services such as **/etc/hosts**, DNS, NIS, NIS+, and LDAP. Try not to be intimidated by this acronym; individual services behave in fairly standard ways.

Printing

**lpsched** creates the file **/var/spool/lp/SCHEDLOCK** to indicate that it is running. If you try to start another copy of **lpsched**, it will notice that this file exists and refuse to run. If you stop **lpsched** by any means other than **lpshut**, you must remove the **SCHEDLOCK** file by hand before you can restart **lpsched**.

### lpadmin: configure the printing environment

The **lpadmin** command tells the printing system about your printer configuration. It names printers, creates classes, and specifies the default printer. All the **lpadmin** command really does is create and modify a collection of text files that are found in the **/var/spool/lp** directory.

Despite the fact you can read these configuration files, they are a good place to practice the old adage "Look but don't touch." You should not try to edit them directly because they are very format sensitive and break easily.

 The Solaris **lpadmin** tries to use a **printcap**-like file to make things easier to configure. But in fact, the Solaris system just spreads the configuration information out into two additional locations: **/etc/printers.conf** and **/etc/lp**.

Solaris wants **lpsched** to be running during most administrative commands. On the other hand, under HP-UX, most **lpadmin** commands will not work when **lpsched** is running, so **lpsched** must be stopped with **lpshut** before **lpadmin** is used. There appears to be no method to this madness.

Before the printing system can output jobs to a particular printer, it must be told that the printer exists. To add a new printer, execute

```
# /usr/sbin/lpadmin -pprinter -vdevice { -eprinter | -mmodel | -iinterface }
     [ -cclass ... ] [{ -l | -h }]
```

where *printer* is the name of the new printer (both internally in the queuing system and at the level of user commands) and *device* is the file with which the printer is associated. *device* is usually a special file in **/dev**, but it can be any file.

The flags **-e**, **-m**, or **-i** tell the queuing system which printer interface program to use. The interface program is responsible for actually formatting jobs before they are sent to the printer. System V interface programs are analogous to BSD filters. The section *Interface programs* on page 726 goes into more detail.

The interface program can be specified in three ways:

-e*printer*    In this case, *printer* is the name of an existing printer. This method of specifying the interface program is useful if you are adding a printer that is exactly like an existing one. The **lpadmin** command makes a copy of the interface program with the new destination's name.

-m*model*    With this option, *model* is a type of device for which your system has an interface program. To determine which models your system supports, look in **/var/spool/lp/model**.

When a model file is specified, **lpadmin** makes a copy of the file **/var/spool/lp/model/***model* to be used exclusively by that destination.

-**i***interface*   With the -**i** option, *interface* is the full pathname of a program that is to be used as the interface script. Most versions of **lpadmin** make a copy of the interface program, so if you want to change the program after you have run **lpadmin**, you must change the destination-specific copy and not your original.

HP-UX lets you specify programs that return status information and cancel printer jobs. These programs are specified like interface scripts, but different option prefixes are used (-**ocm** and -**osm** for cancel and status scripts, respectively).

**lpadmin** also accepts the following additional options:

-**p***printer*   tells **lpadmin** which *printer* or printers are being referred to. Combine this flag with other options to modify a printer.

-**c***class*   where *class* is the name of a class in which the printer should be included. Any number of classes can be specified for a given printer. If you specify a nonexistent class, it will be created. The class name is limited to 14 characters.

-**x***printer*   removes *printer* from the print system. If *printer* is the only member of a class, then that class is also removed. Neither a printer nor a class can be removed if it has jobs queued for output. If queued jobs are keeping you from removing a printer, use the **reject** command to stop new jobs from being spooled. Then, use the **lpmove** and **cancel** commands to remove the existing jobs. If **lpadmin -x** still won't remove the printer, follow the advice on page 727.

-**r***class*   removes a printer from *class*. The -**r** flag does not remove the printer; it just removes it from the class. If the specified printer is the only member of *class*, the class is removed.

**lp** will not accept requests for a new printer until it is told to do so with the **accept** command. See page 725.

When the flags to a command could refer to multiple objects, you can use a quoted, comma-separated list of destinations in place of a single object. For example,

```
# /usr/sbin/lpadmin -p"howler-lw,ralphie-lw" -ceng-printers
```

would put the printers howler-lw and ralphie-lw in the eng-printers class. The other printing commands accept multiple printers when it makes sense (and sometimes even when it does not). Table 23.4 summarizes the flags understood by **lpadmin**.

Here are some examples of **lpadmin** commands, with explanations of what they do:

```
# /usr/sbin/lpadmin -phowler-lw -v/dev/tty06 -mPostScript -cpr
```

**Table 23.4   lpadmin flags**

| Flag | Function |
|------|----------|
| **-p***printer* | Specifies the printer to which other options apply |
| **-d***dest* | Makes *dest* the system default destination |
| **-x***dest* | Removes *dest* from the printing system |
| **-c***class* | Adds the printer to *class* |
| **-r***class* | Removes the printer from *class* |
| **-e***dest* | Copies another printer's interface program |
| **-i***interface* | Makes *interface* the interface program for the printer |
| **-m***model* | Makes the printer use the interface program for *model* |
| **-h** | Signifies that the printer is hardwired |
| **-l** | Signifies that the printer is a login terminal[a] |
| **-v***file* | Specifies the full path of printer device file |
| **-D**"*desc*" | Sets the printer description string to *desc* |

a. Printing is disabled by default on printers marked with **lpadmin -l**.

This command tells the printing system that a printer to be called howler-lw is connected to **/dev/tty06**, that the printer should be in the class pr, and that the interface program for PostScript printers should be used. Note that **lpadmin** takes care of creating the spool directory with the right permissions. The command

    # /usr/sbin/lpadmin  -dpr

sets the system default destination to class (or printer) pr.

    # /usr/sbin/lpadmin -phowler-lw -D"LaserJet named howler"[4]

sets the description of howler-lw.

    # /usr/sbin/lpadmin -phowler-lw -rpr -cfast

removes printer howler-lw from class pr and adds it to class fast.

    # /usr/sbin/lpadmin -xhowler-lw

removes howler-lw completely. This command also removes the class the printer was in if the printer was the only member of that class.

Several more examples of **lpadmin** command lines are shown in the Solaris and HP-UX sections starting on page 729.

### lpstat: get status information

**lpstat** shows the status of the printing system. If executed without any arguments, it gives the status of all jobs that belong to the user who executed it. With a **-p** argument, **lpstat** gives information on the status of a particular printer. For example,

---

4. The convention of naming printers with a "-lw" ending is a historical remnant from the original Apple LaserWriter. You might consider developing your own naming system.

```
% lpstat -phowler-lw
howler-lw is now printing pr-125. enabled since Jul 4 12:25
```

shows the status of printer howler-lw. To determine the status of the **lpsched** daemon, run **lpstat -r**. For example,

```
% lpstat -r
scheduler is running
```

shows that everything is OK.

Table 23.5 lists the flags for **lpstat**.

**Table 23.5    lpstat flags**

| Flag | Function |
|------|----------|
| **-r** | Shows the status of the **lpsched** daemon |
| **-d** | Shows the default destination |
| **-c***class* | Lists the members of *class* |
| **-o***arg* | Shows the status of output requests for *arg*[a] |
| **-u***user* | Shows the status of jobs submitted by *user* |
| **-p***printer* | Shows the status of *printer* |
| **-v***printer* | Lists the output device associated with *printer* |
| **-a***dest* | Shows the acceptance status of *dest* |
| **-s** | Shows a summary of status information |
| **-t** | Shows all status information |

a. *arg* can be a printer, a class, or a jobid, but unfortunately not a user.

### cancel: remove print jobs

**cancel** removes from the queue the jobs that are queued or being printed. You can invoke **cancel** with either a job number (determined with **lpstat**) or with a printer name. If you specify a printer, then the job currently being printed is canceled.

For example, **cancel 576** would cancel job 576, and **cancel howler-lw** would cancel the job currently printing on howler-lw. The **cancel** command is usually owned by the pseudo-user lp with group bin and mode 6775 so that anyone can use it to cancel jobs that are obviously bogus. If someone who did not send a job cancels it, mail is sent to the job's owner. If users abuse this privilege, set the mode of the command so that it does not run setuid.

### accept and reject: control spooling

If a printer will be unavailable for a long time (for example, because of a hardware failure), spooling to that device should be disabled so that users who are unaware of the situation do not fill up the queue. Disable spooling with the **reject** command. For example, the following command would cause **lp** to reject requests for howler-lw:

```
# /usr/sbin/reject -r"howler-lw will be down until Tuesday" howler-lw
```

The **-r** flag is optional, but it is a nice way to tell users the reason why the printer is rejecting requests. When someone tries to print a file, **lp** displays your message:

```
% /usr/bin/lp -dhowler-lw myfile
lp: cannot accept requests for destination "howler-lw"
   -- howler-lw will be down until Tuesday
```

**accept** *printer* tells **lp** to begin accepting requests for *printer*. You must run **accept** once for each new printer added with **lpadmin** because new printers are configured to reject requests by default. You can give **accept** and **reject** a class name instead of a destination name to enable or disable spooling for an entire class.

### enable and disable: control printing

The **disable** command tells **lpsched** to stop sending jobs to a particular printer. Unlike **reject**, **disable** does not stop **lp** from queuing jobs for the printer. However, queued jobs will not be output until the printer is reenabled with **enable**. **disable** does not normally abort printing of the current job, but the **-c** option requests this behavior. Like **reject**, **disable** supports a **-r** flag that allows you to explain why a printer is disabled.

For example, the command

```
# /bin/disable -r"Being cleaned, back in 5 minutes" howler-lw
```

disables printing on howler-lw. To restart printing, type:

```
# /bin/enable howler-lw
```

### lpmove: transfer jobs

It's sometimes necessary to move jobs queued for one printer or class to another printer. You accomplish this feat with **lpmove**, which you run with a list of jobids and the name of a new printer. For example, the command

```
# /usr/sbin/lpmove howler-lw-324 howler-lw-325 anchor-lw
```

would move the jobs numbered 324 and 325 from the queue for howler-lw to the queue for anchor-lw. You can also give **lpmove** a printer or class as a source. For example, the command

```
# /usr/sbin/lpmove howler-lw anchor-lw
```

moves all jobs queued for howler-lw to the queue for anchor-lw. When **lpmove** is used in this way, it has the side effect of executing a **reject** on the printer of origin. In the preceding example, **lp** would no longer accept requests for howler-lw.

 By design, the HP-UX version of **lpmove** cannot be used when **lpsched** is running. Run **lpshut** first.

### Interface programs

An interface program must take information from a file that **lpsched** specifies, format it, and send the formatted data to its standard output. The interface program is also responsible for setting the correct modes on its output device and for generating headers and trailers if they are desired. Interface programs are usually shell scripts, but they can be executable binaries, too.

**lpsched** calls interface programs with the following arguments:

*jobid user title copies options file [file ...]*

Where:

- *jobid* is the job identification that is assigned by **lp**
- *user* is the user to whom the job belongs
- *title* is an optional title supplied by the user
- *copies* is the number of copies to print
- *options* are user-supplied options
- The *files* are full pathnames of files to be printed

All of the arguments are supplied each time the interface program is executed, but some of them may be null strings. The interface program gets its standard input from **/dev/null**, and both standard output and standard error are directed to the destination device as specified by **lpadmin -v**.

Unlike the BSD system, which uses different interface programs for different file formats, SysV requires interface programs to handle all the kinds of data that the printer can accept (and to fail nicely if unrecognizable input is received). For this reason, interface programs are usually just shell scripts that process their arguments and call other programs to do the real work of formatting.

Essentially, the interface script is responsible for the entire output stage of the printing system. Although the use of interface scripts makes customization easy, it also leads to different printers behaving in very different ways.

Interfaces are almost essential if you are planning on printing to anything other than a generic text or PostScript printer. Today, almost all printers use them. Inkjet printers absolutely require an interface to translate the print job to their format of choice.

An interface program should exit with a 0 on successful completion and with an integer in the range 1 to 127 if an error is encountered. If a job fails, the interface script should attempt to reprint it. If a serious error occurs, the interface program should **disable** (see page 726) the printer. If you are having erratic printing problems, you can probably find the cause somewhere in the interface script.

### What to do when the lp system is completely hosed

Sometimes, attempts to configure and unconfigure printers leave the **lp** system hopelessly confused. The config files that hold printer information are complicated and neurotic. One stray character can completely whack out an entire printer.

If you somehow create a printer that is confusing the system, the best solution is to remove the destination completely and start over. Sometimes, the system can be so confused that even removing the printer is hard.

Printing

The following brute-force technique will often rescue you from this sort of situation. Here, we try to remove the printer hoser. Don't use this exact sequence unless your equivalent of hoser is a single printer (not a class).

```
# lpshut
# lpadmin -xhoser
# find /usr/spool/lp -name hoser -exec rm -rf {} \;
# lpsched
# lpstat -t
```

The first two commands turn off the spooler and attempt to remove the printer according to the USDA-approved method. If the system is confused, **lpadmin -x** may fail. The **find** command removes all interface programs and spool directories for the printer. **lpsched** restarts the spooler, and **lpstat** should show you that there are no more references to hoser within the printing system.

## 23.5  ADDING A PRINTER

In this section we discuss vendor-specific printer configuration details. For each operating system, we investigate:

- Setting up a local serial or parallel printer
- Printing to a network **lpd** print server
- Accepting **lpd** print jobs from the network

You'll note that we only discuss network printing from a BSD-ish perspective. That's because there is no such thing as System V remote printing; SysV-based systems that want to enable remote printing have adopted parts of the BSD protocol.

In the discussions that follow, we assume that the printer hardware has already been physically connected to a host or the network. See Chapter 7, *Serial Devices*, for information about connecting serial printers, and Chapter 15, *Network Hardware*, for general information about connecting devices to a network.

*See page 287 for more information about DHCP.*

Network printers require a bit of extra configuration. In particular, they have to be assigned an IP address. That's usually accomplished by one of two methods.

First, most modern printers support the ability to boot across the network from a BOOTP or DHCP server. This method works well in environments with many homogeneous printers.

Alternatively, all network printers allow you to set their IP address from the console. Sometimes the "console" is a serial port, but often it's just a scheme for using buttons on the front of the printer. After your printer is on the network and you can ping it, make sure to secure it as discussed on page 742.

To make the following sections more fluid, we talk about a consistent set of hardware. The server beast is a generic **lpd** spooler attached to a PostScript laser printer named howler-lw.

### Adding printers to Solaris

With Solaris 2.6, Sun introduced yet another printing system. The best way to administer printing under Solaris is to use the Solstice Printer Manager available in the Solstice AdminSuite. If your site has not purchased this product, the Admintool (found at **/usr/bin/admintool**) is a good second choice. For those of you who want a better understanding of the printing system, we discuss the gory details here.

Solaris provides several nonstandard printing commands. **lpfilter** views and adds new interface programs to the system.[5]

The **lpset** and **lpget** commands facilitate the editing and review of printer configuration information. **lpset** provides basically the same functionality as **lpadmin**, but it has the unique characteristic of working on both system-wide and personal configuration files.

The **lpusers** command manages a slightly enhanced prioritization and access control system, and **lpforms** provides a system for standardizing page presentation across a group of users. Neither of these commands is particularly exciting and we do not discuss them further.

Solaris provides the BSD printing commands as part of the "SunOS/BSD Compatibility Package," which is included by default in Solaris distributions. Ergo, you can use **lpd** for all network printing between your Solaris hosts if you so choose.

Solaris printer configuration information is stored in a **printcap**-like file that's called **/etc/printers.conf**. Additional information is stored in the **/etc/lp** directory, and printer-specific information in **/etc/lp/printers/**_printername_. Users can customize their printing environment with an optional **~/.printers** file, which allows them to set defaults for printers and aliases for print commands. Errors from the spooler **lpsched** are logged by default to **/var/lp/logs/lpsched**.

Unlike commands in the traditional SysV printing family, Solaris's print commands accept a space between option flags and their values (e.g., **lpstat -p anchor-lw** instead of **lpstat -panchor-lw**). However, they seem to accept the older format as well. It's probably best to stick with the documented (spaceful) syntax.

Solaris requires you to specify what types of input your device can handle. With this information the printing system determines whether a printer will be able to handle a given print job. The interface programs reject input that is not of one of the correct types, so if you do not specify a type, your printer is useless. Use **lpadmin -I** to set this value. **-I PostScript,simple** works well for PostScript printers. For line printers that can understand only text, use **-I simple**.

You must also specify the type of printer; use the **-T** flag of **lpadmin**. The printing system needs the type specification to determine how to initialize and communicate with the printer. Some filters also depend on this value being properly set. A printer's

---

5. Why a SysV-based printing system like Solaris uses the term _filters_ instead of _interfaces_ escapes us.

type can be any value listed in the **terminfo** database in **/usr/share/lib**. Look for an entry that matches your printer. A generic PostScript printer can use the PS type:

```
# lpadmin -p howler-lw -T PS
```

Solaris stores new interface programs in **/etc/lp/interfaces**, although no filters are provided there with a fresh installation. For a listing of all the interface programs available on your machine, run the **lpfilter** command:

```
# lpfilter -f all -l
```

*Setting up a local serial printer under Solaris*

First, connect your serial printer and determine the device with which it is associated. Common Solaris serial devices are **/dev/term/a** and **/dev/term/b**. The device needs to be owned by the user lp, and the permissions must be set so that only the user lp can read or write to the device:

```
# chown lp /dev/term/a
# chmod 600 /dev/term/a
```

Next, configure the printer with **lpadmin**. You must specify the printer name, the device, the printer type (PostScript or simple text), and the content types the printer can handle. Your **lpadmin** command should look something like this:

```
# lpadmin -p printername -v /dev/term/a -T printertype -I contenttype
    -D "description"
```

Tell the spooler to start accepting print jobs and tell the printer to start printing them:

```
# enable printername
# accept printername
```

Finally, check that the printer installation was successful with the **lpstat** command:

```
# lpstat -p printername
```

*Printing from Solaris to a BSD print server*

To allow spooling from Solaris to a remote **lpd** server (either one running on another host or one inside a network printer), use the Solaris-specific **-s** flag to **lpadmin**. This flag lets you specify a remote printer as *server!printer*. Your shell will probably require you to escape the exclamation mark with a backslash, so the actual command will look like this:

```
# lpadmin -p howler-lw -s beast\!howler-lw -I PostScript,simple -T PS
    -D "howler-lw via beast"
```

If the printer is to have the same name on the server and the local machine, you can omit the *!printer* part of the command ("**\!howler-lw**" in this case).

Once the remote printer has been defined, start it up as usual:

```
# enable howler-lw
# accept howler-lw
```

Finally, test the new printer.

```
# lp -phowler-lw /etc/motd
# lpstat -phowler-lw
```

If you have a network printer that doesn't support **lpd**, it probably expects output to be shoveled to it through a raw TCP connection. Solaris supports this configuration with the **netstandard** interface program. **netstandard** delivers the print job across the network, so the local device specified with the -**v** flag can be set to /**dev/null**.

The **lpadmin -o** flag is passes options to **netstandard**. For example, the following command creates a new PostScript printer called dinger-lw for a network printer that accepts raw PostScript on TCP port 9100:

```
# lpadmin -p dinger-lw -v /dev/null -I PostScript -T PS -m netstandard
    -o protocol=tcp -o dest=dinger-lw:9100 -o timeout=15
```

The **netstandard** interface also supports sending jobs to a BSD **lpd** server through the notation **lpadmin -o protocol=bsd**. You will probably not have to use this feature, however, since **lpadmin -s** provides the same functionality.

### Making Solaris accept network print jobs from BSD

Solaris includes a daemon called **in.lpd** that runs from **inetd** by default. This server understands the **lpd** protocol and can seamlessly spool jobs from **lpr** clients to local or network printers. **in.lpd** reads its configuration from /**etc/printers.conf**, so no configuration beyond **lpadmin** is necessary. If you do not intend to provide printing services to **lpd** clients, comment out the **in.lpd** line in /**etc/inetd.conf**.

### Adding printers to HP-UX

In addition to a full implementation of the conventional SysV commands, HP-UX offers several unique client commands and a feature-rich server. HP-UX doesn't like administrative changes to be made while **lpsched** is running.

The **lpana** command analyzes the performance of the print spooler. This tool provides enough information to actually be useful for optimization of your print spooler system; it includes statistics such as the average wait time of jobs in the queue and the average printing time of a job. To record the accounting data needed by **lpana**, run the **lpsched** daemon with the -**a** flag.

The **lpfence** command defines a minimum priority that incoming jobs must have in order to be printed. The fence is set for a printer, whereas job priority is set for a job. **lpfence** can only be run when **lpsched** isn't running.

Jobs that have been spooled but have not started printing can be altered with the **lpalt** command. **lpalt** lets you change most of the **lp** options, saving the user from having to cancel and respool jobs that require adjustment.

As in Solaris, the HP-UX version of **lpadmin** supports the -**o** flag to pass parameters to an interface program. The -**o** flag is a nice feature, since it means that the sysadmin is not forced to edit scripts or recompile interface programs just to change their options. See page 731 for an example.

## Setting up a local serial printer under HP-UX

Suppose we have connected our HP LaserJet 4M to the serial port associated with **/dev/ttyp2**. Before running **lpadmin**, we must stop all printing services:

```
# /usr/sbin/lpshut
```

An interface model already exists for printing to HP LaserJet 4 printers in the **/usr/lib/lp/model** directory, so we'll use **lpadmin -m** to configure the printer:

```
# /usr/sbin/lpadmin -phowler-lw -mlaserjet4 -v/dev/ttyp2
```

Finally, we'll start accepting jobs into the spool, enable the printer, and restart the spooler daemon:

```
# /usr/lib/accept howler-lw
# /bin/enable howler-lw
# /usr/sbin/lpsched
```

## Printing from HP-UX to a BSD print server

HP-UX provides an interface script called **rmodel** that can send jobs to a remote **lpd**. **rmodel** options are set with **lpadmin -o**. For example, the following commands make the printer howler-lw on the machine beast available to local users:

```
# /usr/sbin/lpshut
# /usr/sbin/lpadmin -phowler-lw -v/dev/null -mrmodel -ormbeast
    -orphowler-lw -ob3
# /usr/lib/accept howler-lw
# /bin/enable howler-lw
# /usr/sbin/lpsched
```

The **rmodel** interface accepts the arguments **orm**, **orp**, and **ob** to specify the remote machine, the remote printer, and the use of BSD-style, three-digit sequence numbers.

The **rmodel** interface actually calls **rlp** to send the job to the remote **lpd** server. Unfortunately, the **rlp** and **rcancel** and **rlpstat** commands are intended only for use by other parts of the printing system; they should never be invoked directly by users. If this limitation frustrates you, consider the **rlpr** package described on page 740.

## Making HP-UX accept network print jobs from BSD

The HP-UX remote printing spooler, **rlpdaemon**, accepts jobs from **lpr/lpd** systems. **rlpdaemon** is usually run from **inetd**, but a host that receives a large number of print jobs should start it at boot time. **rlpdaemon** accepts jobs from any hosts listed in **/etc/hosts.equiv** or **/usr/spool/lp/.rhosts**.

## Adding printers to Red Hat Linux

Red Hat's printing system is a fairly vanilla implementation of the BSD standard. Some of Red Hat's tools are very useful, especially the graphical **printtool**, which automates editing of the **/etc/printcap** file, and the **lpunlock** script, which rescues locked print servers. The beloved **printtool** holds your hand in configuring a variety of printers, including local, remote **lpd**, SMB (Windows), and NetWare (NCP) printers. Be forewarned that **printtool** requires the format of the **/etc/printcap** file to be very precise; if you edit the file by hand, you may not be able to open it in **printtool** anymore.

Red Hat is notorious for supporting a relatively limited collection of printers. The main reason is that Red Hat Linux uses the GNU version of **ghostscript**, which supports far fewer printers than the popular Aladdin Enterprises version. The free but quasi-commercial Aladdin **ghostscript**, used in many other distributions, can rasterize images for many different non-PostScript printers. If you find that your printer is not supported by Red Hat's default engine, consider installing the Aladdin version of **ghostscript** from www.aladdin.com.

### Setting up a local printer under Red Hat

Red Hat uses the RHS print filters package, which is difficult to configure without **printtool**. An entry without filters looks like this:

```
howler-lw|howl|laserjet:\
    :sd=/var/spool/lpd/howler-lw:\
    :mx#0:\
    :lp=/dev/parport0:\
    :sh:
```

The above entry defines three names for the printer, specifies a spool directory and port device, eliminates maximum job sizes, and suppresses print headers.

We can tell from the device file that this is a parallel printer. Serial printers are configured similarly. The device would probably be **/dev/ttyS0** (or **S1** for your second serial port) instead of **/dev/parport0**, and the filters would be different. Additionally, you would have to specify serial options such as baud rate. Look up relevant settings in the on-line man pages for **printcap**.

### Printing from Red Hat to a network print server

As with all BSD printing systems, new printers need an **/etc/printcap** entry on the client machine. For our LaserJet, we'd add something like this:

```
howler-lw|lp|8-6|"LaserJet 5M, called howler-lw on beast":
    :lp=/var/spool/lpd/howler-lw/.null:\
    :rm=beast:rp=howler-lw:\
    :sd=/var/spool/lpd/howler-lw:mx#0:
```

We would then create the spool directory and the **.null** file on the client:

```
# mkdir /var/spool/lpd/howler-lw
# touch /var/spool/lpd/howler-lw/.null
# chown -R daemon /var/spool/lpd/howler-lw
# chgrp -R daemon /var/spool/lpd/howler-lw
# chmod 775 /var/spool/lpd/howler-lw
```

If the **lpd** server is a real machine (and not just a smart printer), make sure you can print jobs from that machine before configuring network clients. To test printing from the client, use a sequence of commands similar to the following:

```
# lpc start howler-lw
# lpr -Phowler-lw /etc/motd
# lpq -Phowler-lw
```

*Making Red Hat accept network print jobs*

Before you try to spool jobs from across the network, make sure you can print locally. Then, add to your **/etc/hosts.lpd** file the clients from which you want to accept jobs.

## Adding printers to FreeBSD

The default FreeBSD **/etc/printcap** file comes with some prebuilt examples of local and network printer configuration that you can refer to when adding your own printers. The **printcap** examples in the Red Hat section also work with the FreeBSD printing system (though the filters mentioned there are not included with FreeBSD).

By default, printing services on FreeBSD are disabled. To turn them on, change NO in the following line to YES in the **/etc/rc.conf** file:

```
lpd_enable="NO"        # Run the line printer daemon.
```

None of FreeBSD's printing commands (except perhaps **lptcontrol**) should surprise you. **lptcontrol** lets you configure your parallel port to use any of several different modes, such as interrupt-driven, polled, extended, and standard. To set your first parallel port (**/dev/lpt0**) to run in interrupt-driven mode, use **lptcontrol** as follows:

```
# lptcontrol -i -u 0
```

**lptcontrol** only changes the current state of the parallel port. If you want the port configured a certain way each time you boot, put the appropriate **lptcontrol** command in one of the system startup scripts.

Several useful printing examples and scripts are included in the FreeBSD handbook. It is on-line at www.freebsd.org.

*Setting up a local printer under FreeBSD*

The first parallel port on a FreeBSD machine is **/dev/lpt0**. The first serial port is usually **/dev/ttyd0**. Aside from the difference in device names, **printcap** configuration of local serial or parallel printers is almost identical to that in Red Hat (see page 733).

The FreeBSD distribution includes a relatively simple text filter, **/usr/libexec/lpr/lpf**, that does basic formatting, such as fixing carriage returns and indents, as well as converting from text to PostScript format.

*Network printing configuration under FreeBSD*

FreeBSD handles remote printers much like Red Hat, although the filters are different. Making local printers available to the network is also done similarly.

## 23.6  LPRng

LPRng is a relatively new print spooler that is based on the BSD system. Currently maintained by Patrick Powell at AStArt Technologies, LPRng is a successful attempt to merge the best features of the Berkeley and SysV printing schemes.

LPRng replaces your current printing system with compatible but improved commands. All the common BSD commands are available. The most important SysV commands are also supported and are implemented as links to their BSD counterparts. For example, the **lp** command is a link to **lpr** and **cancel** is a link to **lprm**. The commands check to see how they were invoked and behave accordingly.

One of the most significant problems with the BSD printing system is the need for most of the printing software to run as root. In addition to having **lpr** clients run setuid to root, **lpd** filters also run as root. Because filters are often shell scripts, this is a frightening prospect.

LPRng solves the problem by allowing clients to run as normal users. In cases in which LPRng doesn't have to interact with non-LPRng clients, even the printing daemon can run as a nonroot user. The package also adds lots of new security checking that is lacking in most BSD systems.

One of the more useful features of LPRng is its ability to produce verbose diagnostics and error messages. Instead of silently failing or returning a cryptic message, programs in this package give descriptive and helpful explanations of what went wrong.[6]

Although **lpd** supports access control through the **/etc/hosts.lpd** file, no authentication is available. LPRng support Kerberos 5, SSL, and PGP authentication methods.

Finally, LPRng offers some great queue management features, most of which come from SysV. LPRng includes dynamic redirection of print queues, support for multiple printers on one queue, and even load balancing across several printers.

With all these advantages, why would you *not* want to start using LPRng? In small environments with few users and fewer printers, the BSD and System V print systems both work well. If you don't plan on adding lots of new printers or if the features and added security of LPRng do not interest you, installing and configuring LPRng is probably not worth the effort.

At a minimum, consider installing LPRng on your print server. This simple step will buy you much of the security and functionality of a network-wide deployment with very little hassle.

### The LPRng commands

LPRng's version of **lpr** maintains backward compatibility with most other **lpr** implementations. The only exception is the **-s** flag, which is silently ignored by LPRng's **lpr**. This flag was originally used to create a symbolic link to the file to be printed instead of making a new copy, which was useful for printing large files.

---

6. Perhaps the UNIX standards committee was on vacation the day that LPRng came up for review…

The LPRng version of **lpr** provides a wealth of new functionality. Particularly useful are the verbose flag (-**V**) and the debugging flag (-**D5** for the most detail).

LPRng commands let you specify a printer's host and port in addition to its name. This feature allows users to print to remote printers that are not defined in the local **printcap** file.

To specify the host to which a printer is attached, append *@hostname* to the printer's name. A port is specified by further appending %*port*. For example:

```
% lpr -Phowler-lw@beast%8552 filename
```

This method of specifying a printer works for the LPRng versions of **lpr**, **lpq**, **lprm**, and **lpc**, which means that print clients often don't need a **printcap** file at all.

If a printer isn't specified on the command line, the value of the PRINTER environment variable is used. If the PRINTER environment variable is not set, the first entry of the **/etc/printcap** file is used. If no **printcap** file exists, the default printer specified in the **lpd.conf** file is used.

LPRng builds several new features into **lpq**. Several alternative output formats are available with the short (-**s**), long (-**l**), and verbose long (-**L**) flags. These options can be useful with scripts that depend on the output of **lpq**. The command now accepts a flag to make periodic repeated queries (-**t** *seconds*). Finally, the debugging flag described above is supported. With the flag -**D5**, the command output will include detailed status messages from local and remote printers and print spoolers.

Perhaps the greatest addition to LPRng's **lpc** is its ability to prioritize queue entries based on something more useful than the order in which they were submitted. The rules for queuing priority can be made complex enough to accommodate almost any desired policy. Unlike the traditional **lpc**, LPRng's **lpc** can be run across a network.

LPRng's **lprm** allows job removal based on any of several criteria. In the traditional system, the jobid or username was required. With LPRng, jobs can also be removed from a spool by a regular expression that is matched against the jobid.

### Obtaining and installing LPRng

The current LPRng distribution is available from www.astart.com. The documentation that comes with it should get you through the installation. A FAQ at the web site provides detailed installation and configuration instructions.

One of the coolest features of LPRng is its ability to operate with a minimum of setuid binaries. To compile LPRng in this manner, use the --**disable-setuid** option to **configure** when first setting up the compilation environment:

```
# ./configure --disable-setuid
```

However, if you want **lpd** to listen on its standard port, 515, it will need to run as root. You will have to fix the **lpd** permissions by hand:

```
# chmod 4755 /usr/local/sbin/lpd
```

As of LPRng version 3.6.12, the default **Makefile** doesn't work with the Solaris 2.7 version of **make**. To get LPRng to compile correctly, include in your path a directory that contains the GNU **make** before the directory that contains the default Solaris **make** (**/usr/ccs/bin**).

### /etc/lpd.conf: configure lpd

The LPRng **lpd** server is highly configurable through the **/etc/lpd.conf** file. In fact, as of this writing 185 different parameters can be set in this file. Most of the parameters set directory and operating system defaults. Also provided is a mechanism by which you provide default values for unspecified **/etc/printcap** variables.

The best way to create an **lpd.conf** file for your site is to copy the **lpd.conf** file in the root of the LPRng distribution. This file contains an option-by-option description with examples. If you do not have time to wade through this long list of options, refer to the on-line man page for **lpd.conf**, which contains explanations of all the settings and even an example.

### /etc/lpd.perms: configure access control

With **/etc/lpd.perms**, you can establish very complex printing policies. Rules for controlling print access are applied to print jobs in the order in which they appear in the **lpd.perms** file.

Rules are made up of two parts. The first part is simply an ACCEPT or REJECT token that determines whether the specified operation will be allowed. It's followed by a series of clauses that specify which people, hosts, printers, or operations the rule should apply to.

For example, the following line tells the printing system that the user evi on the remote host beast can print jobs, spool jobs, remove jobs, and check the status of jobs on the printer howler-lw.

```
ACCEPT SERVICE=P,R,M,Q REMOTEHOST=beast REMOTEUSER=evi
    PRINTER=howler-lw
```

The one-letter codes in the SERVICE clause determine which operations the rule is referring to. Table 23.6 shows the values it can contain.

**Table 23.6    SERVICE codes in /etc/lpd.perms**

| Code | Action | What it refers to |
| --- | --- | --- |
| P | Print | Printing a job from a queue |
| C | Control | Using **lpc** (lets secretaries unjam the printer) |
| R | Spool | Submitting jobs to the spool queue with **lpr** |
| M | Remove | Removing jobs from the queue with **lprm** |
| Q | Status | Obtaining status information with **lpq** |
| X | Connect | Connecting to **lpd** |

Printing

The best way to set up your site's **lpd.perms** file is to copy the example from the root of your LPRng distribution. This file describes the ACCEPT and REJECT lines in detail and includes several enlightening examples. All possible configuration flags are described in this file.

### Setting up the printcap file

The most important thing to remember about the LPRng **printcap** file is that it is completely backward compatible with the traditional BSD **printcap** file. That is, all traditional **printcap** files are also valid LPRng **printcap** files.

However, LPRng provides many new **printcap** features as well. Lines can be continued simply by indentation instead of an appended backslash. Variable names are no longer limited to two characters. Several macros are available to help simplify configuration. Entries can be targeted at particular hosts.

Probably the coolest configuration tool LPRng brings us is the **checkpc** program. Installed as **/usr/local/bin/checkpc** by default, this program checks the validity and consistency of the **printcap** file. It warns of missing spool directories, missing files, and incorrect permissions. If you run **checkpc** with the -**f** flag, it attempts to fix simple problems (such as making a directory or changing the permissions of a file). Running **checkpc** with the -**D5** flag produces verbose diagnostics.

### Filters

In addition to providing BSD filter functionality, LPRng allows filters to be applied to jobs that are sent to remote printers. This feature allows customized data formatting for a host instead of for a printer.

The output filter (of) and input filter (if) printcap variables act a little differently in LPRng. The output filter under traditional BSD **lpr** is applied to both the document and the banner. Under LPRng, the output filter is used only for the banner. The LPRng input filter is used only for printing text. Filters for other file types are specified with tags named $xf$, where $x$ is a one-letter type abbreviation. You can completely disable filters for a job by adding **/direct** to the **lpr** command line.

Included in LPRng are the **lpbanner**, **pclbanner**, and **psbanner** commands. These commands create text, PCL, and PostScript banners, respectively. Each accepts command-line arguments that specify the banner name, login name, and job title.

LPRng comes with one particularly useful filter, **ifhp**, which prints to a tremendous variety of printers. Although it was designed primarily to support HP printers, it can handle most printers out of the box. Printers that are not supported internally can usually be made to work without too much hassle.

### Accounting

In the days of line printers, accounting was a simple task. You could get an accurate page count for any job simply by counting lines. However, this method fails completely on PostScript and other types of files.

The only accurate way to account for the number of pages used for a job is to actually count those pages as they leave the printer. Fortunately, many modern printers keep a counter of the number of pages they have printed over their lifetime. By checking this counter before and after a print job, the printer driver can determine the true page count.

One method for implementing this concept is actually included with LPRng. The script is located in the LPRng distribution at **./UTILS/accounting.pl**. Read the comments at the beginning of this script for an idea of how to call it correctly from the **printcap** file.

## 23.7  DEBUGGING PRINTING PROBLEMS

Network **lpd** print jobs are delivered on TCP port 515. Unless you want to be printing jobs for strangers, your firewall should block all traffic to this port from the Internet. To test your connectivity to a remote **lpd** server, **telnet** from the client to port 515 of the server. If you can establish a connection, you can at least verify that the network is working and that **lpd** is running on the server.

If you have problems debugging a remote printer connection, you need to look in six (yes, six) places to track down the problem:

- The system log file (as specified in **/etc/syslog.conf**) on the machine hosting the printer, for messages about permission problems

- The system log files on the sending machine, for name resolution and permission problems

- The print daemon log file on the printing machine, for messages about bad device names, incorrect formats, etc. (as specified in **/etc/syslog.conf** for the lpr syslog facility)

- The print daemon log file on the sending machine, for missing filters, unknown printers, missing directories, etc.

- The printer log file on the printing machine, for errors in transmitting the job (as specified by the lf variable in the **/etc/printcap** file)

- The printer log file on the sending machine, for errors about preprocessing or queuing the job

When debugging remote printers, always keep in mind that there must be a queue for the job on the requesting machine, a way to decide where to send the job, and a method of sending the job to the remote machine. On the printing machine, there must be a place to queue the job, sufficient permissions to allow the job to be printed, and a way to output to the device.

Before you start tracking down a network printing problem, make sure you can print from the machine that actually hosts the printer. You may not have a network problem at all.

## 23.8  COMMON PRINTING SOFTWARE

Although BSD and System V both provide adequate systems for queuing, monitoring, and outputting print jobs, neither of them provides much of the format translation necessary to drive modern printers. Most vendors have at least one set of tools that sits on top of the printing system to provide these features. Sometimes these tools are included in the OS, but more often they are extra-cost add-ons. Third-party and freely distributed packages are also in wide use.

Our purpose in this section is not to tell you everything you need to know about these packages but just to let you know about the functionality they advertise.

### rlpr

If you're not willing to take the leap to LPRng but would still like a better way to print to remote printers, then **rlpr** is probably for you. This free package contains replacements for the BSD client commands (**lpr**, **lpq**, and **lprm**). The replacements are compatible with the originals, but they also provide new functionality and security and are more reliable.

The **rlpr** commands send print jobs directly to a variety of network printers without going through a local **lpd**. Local printing services are entirely bypassed, so users can send data to new printers and print servers without help from a sysadmin. The **rlpr** home page is truffula.com/rlpr. The software works on most UNIX platforms.

### ghostscript

**ghostscript** is a freely distributed PostScript interpreter that enables you to view PostScript files on your screen. If you need to drive some sort of raster output device and you don't want to spend the money for a commercial driver, use **ghostscript** as a starting point for building your own driver. Be forewarned that building a driver is a very complicated process. Several different versions of **ghostscript** are available; see www.ghostscript.com for information about the differences among them.

### mpage

**mpage** is a text-to-PostScript converter that places multiple logical pages on a single physical page. This trick is a great tree saver when you are printing things like source code for which you don't need big type and large margins.

### enscript

Adobe originally developed a product called **enscript** to convert text files to PostScript for printing. This software, or something like it, makes text output look nice on PostScript printers. **enscript** provides page formatting features such as fancy page headers and "two up" printing (two pages printed at half-size on one sheet).

Although the Adobe version of this program is no longer maintained, a good alternative exists. GNU **enscript** is a free, open source version of **enscript** that is completely backward compatible with Adobe's version. GNU **enscript** offers a wealth of new features including language-sensitive highlighting, support for various paper sizes, PostScript font downloading, and user-defined headers.

You can download the GNU **enscript** from the web at people.ssh.fi/mtr/genscript. Since most of the work on this project is done in Finland by Markku Rossi, the default paper type is A4. A4 paper is slightly longer than letter, just enough to cut off vital slivers of your documents such as headers, footers, or page numbers. To Americanize GNU **enscript**, run the **configure** command with the following argument when you are first installing it:

```
# ./configure --with-media=Letter
```

The paper type can also be set on the **enscript** command line. If you forget to change the media type and use **enscript** to print to a high-end printer that knows what kinds of paper it has loaded, the printer may refuse to print at all.

## 23.9  PRINTER PHILOSOPHY

The main things to expect when dealing with printers are troubles and frustrations. If all else fails, just be glad it's not MS-DOS.

### Use printer accounting

You should enable printer accounting even if you don't plan to charge for printer use. The overhead is very slight and you get to see exactly who is using the printer. Printer accounting also gives good information about the various sources of print jobs, which is good information to know when you are locating new printers.

### Use banner pages only when necessary

The printing system can preface each job with a page showing the title of the job and the user who submitted it. This banner page can be helpful on printers used by many different people, but it's a waste of time and paper in most office situations. If you don't need banner pages, suppress them by setting the Boolean **printcap** variable sh on BSD systems, or just don't have your interface script generate them on SysV.

### Provide recycling bins

All kinds of computer paper are recyclable. You can use the boxes that paper comes in as recycling bins. Post a sign asking that no foreign material (such as staples, paper clips, and newspaper) be discarded there.

### Provide previewers

Users will often print a document, find a small error in the formatting, and end up reprinting the whole job. This waste of paper can easily be avoided with software that allows users to see how the printed output will look on their screens.

Previewing is built into many modern WYSIWYG editors, but if your users are addicted to an older typesetting system, you will need to provide some other way to preview documents.

Printing

For random PostScript documents, you can use **ghostscript**; for **roff**, pipe the output of **psroff** into **ghostview**; for TeX, try **xdvi**. After you have provided the necessary previewers, train your users to use them. A good use of accounting records is to check for cases in which the same document has been printed repeatedly.

### Buy cheap printers

Printer technology is mature. You don't need to spend a lot of money for great output and reliable mechanics.

Don't splurge on an expensive "workgroup" printer unless you really need it. There's no difference in the output, and a medium-grade "personal" printer can often be just as fast and just as reliable, not to mention tens of pounds lighter. A 10-page-a-minute printer can serve about five full-time writers. In most cases, you'd be better off buying five $500 printers for a group of 25 writers than one $2,500 printer.

In general, never buy a printer (or a hard disk, or memory) from a computer manufacturer. Their printers are usually just rebranded commodity printers at twice the price. The best bet is to invest in PostScript printers manufactured for the PC and Macintosh markets. We have had particularly good luck with HP and Lexmark laser printers. They are superior products that can spool network **lpd** print jobs, and they work pretty well with the generic UNIX PostScript drivers.

### Keep extra toner cartridges on hand

Laser printers occasionally need their toner cartridges replaced. Buy replacements before you need them. Areas of faded type are a sign that the printer is running out of toner. Before you replace a cartridge, remove it from the printer and gently rock it to redistribute the remaining toner particles. You can often get another hundred pages out of a cartridge this way. Streaks and unexpected spots probably mean you should clean your printer.

Rather than replacing cartridges with new ones, you can often get them refilled by a third party. Good shops will clean the cartridge and replace the imaging drum in addition to adding more toner. This service is expensive, but it's cheaper than buying new cartridges. We have had mixed experiences with refurbished cartridges; their quality and life span can vary wildly. Some refurbished cartridges seem to last only half as long as new cartridges. Figuring out an optimal toner management plan is an excellent hobby project for the statistically minded sysadmin.

Printer manufacturers make a big chunk of their money on ink and special papers. Recently, a few greedy vendors have started building cartridges so that they cannot be refilled. Before you buy a particular printer, check the web to make sure that cartridge refilling services are available for that model.

### Secure your printer

Most newer network printers support some form of remote management. Remote management is nice for sysadmins because it allows for convenient configuration without a lot of walking. Some common ways to remotely access a printer include **telnet**, HTTP, and SNMP. Through the remote interface, you can set the printer's IP address, default gateway, syslog server, SNMP community name, protocol options, and most importantly, password.

By default, most remotely administrable printers are unprotected and must have a password assigned as part of the installation process. For example, to set a password on a new HP JetDirect printer with the "JetDirect Telnet Client," first set IP information on the printer, using the buttons on the printer. Then, **telnet** to the printer:

```
% telnet howler-lw
> passwd
Enter Password[16 character max.; 0 to disable]: > junk#bond
Password set to : newpass
```

# *24* *Maintenance and Environment*

Over the years, UNIX has served as the underlying operating system for a wide range of hardware platforms. Once upon a time, dozens of programmers shared a single system, such as the now-famous VAX. In that era, a tremendous amount of effort went into maintaining equipment and providing a nurturing environment for it. Seasoned UNIX system administrators often knew as much about ethylene glycol cooling systems as they did about UNIX account management.

The 90s brought an influx of desktop workstations and a move away from "big iron" computing platforms. For a while, it appeared that the days of the central machine room might be numbered. Recently, the client/server computing paradigm has resulted in an increased dependence on server platforms running an operating system that provides flexibility, reliability, security, and performance. UNIX has moved in to fill that marketplace, and as a result, herds of UNIX servers have moved into those once-abandoned machine rooms (though in many cases, the machine rooms themselves have been downsized). Providing a healthy, well-maintained environment for these servers is as important as ever.

This chapter offers some hints on handling and maintaining hardware, as well as on giving it a good home. Some of these suggestions will most likely void your manufacturers' warranties. *Follow our advice at your own risk.*

## 24.1 MAINTENANCE BASICS

Hardware maintenance was traditionally something that was covered by an expensive annual maintenance contract. While such contracts are still readily available, today it is often possible to use the "fly by the seat of your pants" approach to hardware maintenance. Maintenance contract rates are typically 10%–12% of a component's list price per year. If you can afford such a contract from the manufacturer or a reputable third-party vendor, by all means use it. If not, you can soon develop a sense of the ways in which machines fail and create a maintenance plan of your own.

*See page 812 for more information about retiring hardware.*

If you keep a log book, a quick glance at the records for the last six to twelve months will give you an idea of your failure rates. It's a good idea to keep a careful record of failures and replacements so that you can accurately evaluate the different maintenance options available to you. Some parts fail more often than anticipated by the manufacturer, so contracts are sometimes not only convenient but also financially advantageous. But remember, there comes a time when all hardware should be replaced, not maintained. Know your hardware and let it go gracefully when its time has finally come. You might even consider donating outdated equipment to your local university or school. For them, equipment is rarely too old to be useful.

Desktop workstations usually contain wave-soldered motherboards with no user-serviceable parts inside. These are cheap and very reliable. However, when something does go wrong, often you must replace the whole motherboard.

The best maintenance scheme is probably the "selective warranty" strategy. Disk drive manufacturers offer warranties up to five years long, and some memory modules even come with a lifetime guarantee. Many workstations have at least a year of warranty. When purchasing new equipment, shop around for the best warranty—it will save you money in the long run.

## 24.2  Maintenance contracts

Several major companies offer hardware maintenance on computer equipment that they do not manufacture. These vendors are often anxious to displace the manufacturer and get their foot in the door, so to speak. You can sometimes negotiate very attractive maintenance contracts by playing a manufacturer against a third-party provider. If possible, get references on all potential maintenance vendors, preferably from people you know and trust.

It is rare for any maintenance provider to diagnose problems beyond the board level. Old joke: "How many customer engineers does it take to fix a flat tire? Four—one to replace each wheel." It is not unusual for a customer engineer to simply swap boards until the system starts working again.

A typical maintenance call involves several steps; policies vary.

### On-site maintenance

If you have an on-site maintenance contract, a service technician will bring spare parts directly to your machine. Guaranteed response time varies between 4 and 24 hours; it's usually spelled out in the contract. Response times during business hours may be shorter than at other times of the week.

### Board swap maintenance

A board swap program requires you and your staff to diagnose problems, perhaps with the help of hotline personnel at the manufacturer's site. After diagnosis, you call a maintenance number, describe the problem, and order the necessary replacement board. It is usually shipped immediately and arrives the next day. You then install the board, get the hardware back up and happy, and return the old board in the same box in which the new board arrived.

The manufacturer will often want to assign a "return merchandise authorization" (RMA) number to the transaction. Be sure to write that number on the shipping documents when you return the bad board.

### Warranties

The length of the manufacturer's warranty should play a significant role in your computation of a machine's lifetime cost of ownership. Three months' warranty is standard for computers, but warranties of a year or more are not uncommon.

In a university environment, it seems to be easier to get federal funding for capital equipment than for support personnel or maintenance. We have occasionally paid for an "extended warranty" option on new hardware (which could also be described as prepaid maintenance) to convert equipment dollars to maintenance dollars.

If you order a computer system from several vendors, the parts will not necessarily arrive at the same time. The warranty period should not start until all the equipment is there and the system has been installed. Most vendors are cooperative about delaying the beginning of the warranty period (for a month or two). With many pieces of hardware, the biggest maintenance and reliability problems occur quite soon after installation. Hardware failures that occur within a day or two of installation are referred to as "infant mortality."

## 24.3 BOARD-HANDLING LORE

These days, you rarely need to get into the guts of a system to install or remove circuit boards. PC-based systems are perhaps an exception, as they seem to require at least four or five add-on boards to reach workstation standards (SCSI, sound, video, network, memory... Hmm, what's on that motherboard anyway?).

Circuit boards should be handled gently, not dropped, not have coffee spilled on them, not have books piled on them, etc. Most customer engineers (those friendly repair people that come with your maintenance contract) are ten times rougher on boards than seems reasonable.

### Static electricity

Electronic parts are sensitive to static electricity. To handle boards safely, you must ground yourself before and during installation. A ground strap worn on the wrist and attached to a special mat that you kneel on (most computers require you to show proper respect!) will isolate you properly.

Remember that you need to worry about static when you first open the package containing a printed circuit board and anytime the electronic component is handled—not just when you perform an installation. Be especially careful if the office where you receive your mail (and where you might be tempted to open your packages) is carpeted; carpet generates more static electricity than does a hard floor.

One way to reduce static on carpeted floors is to purchase a spray bottle at your local Wal-Mart and fill it with one part Downy fabric softener to 10 parts water. Spray this on the carpet (but not on computing equipment) once every month to keep static levels low. This procedure also leaves your office area with that all-important April-fresh scent.

### Reseating boards

You can fix many hardware problems by simply powering down the equipment, reseating its interface cards (SCSI, Ethernet, etc.) and powering it back up. To reseat a card, pull it out from its "seat" (usually a high-density connector) and then reinstall it. If this works temporarily but the same problem comes back a week or a month later, the electrical contact between the card and the motherboard is probably poor.

If the card uses an edge connector, take it all the way out and clean the contacts with a pencil eraser. Don't use an eraser that is old and hard. If your eraser doesn't work well erasing pencil marks from paper, it won't work well on electrical contacts either. Try to keep your fingers off the contacts. Just "erase" them with the pencil (a mild abrasive), brush off the eraser droppings, and reinstall the card.

Some motherboards (especially those of the PC variety) still have socketed ICs, although this is increasingly rare. Over time, the connections in the sockets deteriorate, mostly because of vibrations from fans. You can press firmly on the top of the chips with your thumb (after you've donned a grounding strap, of course) to tuck them in.

## 24.4 MONITORS

The monitor is often the least reliable component of modern computer systems. Many monitors have brightness and convergence adjustments that are accessible only from the circuit board. Unfortunately, monitors often use internal charges of tens of thousands of volts that can persist long after the power has been disconnected. Because of the risk of electric shock, we recommend that you always have your monitors adjusted by a qualified technician. *Do not attempt the job yourself.*

## 24.5 MEMORY MODULES

Most of today's hardware accepts memory in the form of SIMMs (Single Inline Memory Modules) or DIMMs (Dual Inline Memory Modules) rather than individual chips. These modules range in size from 256K to 512MB, all on one little card.

If you need to add memory to a workstation or server, you can usually order it from a third-party vendor and install it yourself. Don't buy memory from workstation vendors; they will soak you 'til you're good and soggy.[1] When adding memory, think big. The price of memory is continually decreasing, but so is the standard allotment of expansion slots on a typical motherboard.

If you install your own memory, keep these two rules in mind:

- Memory is more sensitive than anything else to static electricity. Make sure you're well grounded before opening a baggie full of memory.

- The connector that's used to attach the module to the motherboard varies from machine to machine. Most usually snap in easily enough, but you need a special tool to remove them once they've been installed. It's always tempting to use a ballpoint pen or a paper clip to release the fasteners, but this approach often ends up damaging the connector.

Memory modules are frequently a candidate for the pencil eraser cleaning technology described earlier in this chapter.

## 24.6 PREVENTIVE MAINTENANCE

Some pieces of hardware have filters that must be regularly cleaned or changed. Clogged filters impede the flow of air and may result in overheating, a major cause of equipment failure. It's important to keep the air vents on all equipment open and unobstructed. It is not uncommon to find books or newspapers lying on top of a computer's vents; in these cases, we recommend repeatedly punching the perpetrator in the shoulder until it really starts to hurt.

Anything with moving parts may need regular lubrication, cleaning, and belt maintenance. Old line printers are prime candidates, as are old tape drives and disk drives (but all disks made within the last five years or so are totally sealed and maintenance free). Listen for squeaks from your older equipment and pamper it accordingly.

On server systems, the part that most frequently fails is the fan and power supply module—especially on PCs, where it is often a single field-replaceable unit (FRU). Periodically check your servers to make sure their main fans are spinning fast and strong. If not, you must usually replace the entire power supply assembly—otherwise, you run the risk of overheating your equipment. *Do not* try to lubricate the fan itself; this procedure might postpone the inevitable breakdown, but it could also accelerate the problem or cause damage to other components.

A computer in a dusty environment will burn out components much more frequently than one whose environment is relatively clean. Dust clogs filters, dries out lubrication, jams moving parts (fans), and coats components with a layer of dusty "insulation" that reduces their ability to dissipate heat. All of these effects tend to increase operating temperatures. Check and clean dust filters regularly. You may also need to give your systems' innards an occasional housecleaning in bad environments. (Any environment that features carpeting is likely to be bad.)

---

1. That is, unless memory is part of a package deal; some of these deals are OK.

Vacuuming is the best way to remove dust, but be sure to keep the motor at least five feet from system components and disks to minimize magnetic field interference. Your machine room should be vacuumed regularly, but make sure this task is performed by people who have been trained to respect proper distances and not harm equipment (office janitorial staff are usually not acceptable candidates for this task).

Tape drives usually require regular cleaning as well. You clean most cassette-type drives by inserting a special cleaning cassette. Other formats may need manual cleaning with Q-Tips and denatured alcohol.

## 24.7 Environment

Just like humans, computers work better and longer if they're happy in their environment. Although they don't care much about having a window with a view, you do need to pay attention to other aspects of their home.

### Temperature

The ideal operating temperature for computer equipment is 64° to 68°F (17° to 20°C), with about 45% humidity. Unfortunately, this temperature does not coincide with the ideal operating temperature of a computer user. Ambient temperatures above 80°F (27°C) in the computer room imply about 120°F (49°C) inside machines. Commercial-grade chips have an operational range up to about 120°F, at which point they stop working; beyond about 160°F (71°C), they break.

### Humidity

The ideal humidity for most computer hardware is in the range of 40% to 60%. If the humidity is too low, static electricity becomes a problem. If it is too high, condensation can form on the boards, causing shorting and oxidation.

### Office cooling

These days, many computers live in people's offices and must survive on building air conditioning (often turned off at night and on weekends) and overcome an healthy dose of papers and books on cooling vents. When you put a computer in an office, keep in mind that it will steal air conditioning that is intended for humans. Heating, Ventilation, and Air Conditioning (HVAC) engineers are notoriously bad at estimating the actual cooling load for an office with a computer in it. If you are in a role where you can influence cooling capacity, a good rule of thumb is that each human in the room produces 300 BTUH worth of heat, whereas your average office PC produces about 1,100 BTUH. Don't let the engineers forget to add in solar load for any windows that receive direct sunlight.

### Machine room cooling

If you are "lucky" enough to be moving your herd of UNIX servers into one of those fancy raised-floor machine rooms built in the 1980s that has enough capacity to cool all of your equipment *and* the state of Oklahoma, then your biggest concern will likely be to find some remedial education in primitive cooling system maintenance. For the rest of us, correctly sizing a cooling system is what makes the difference in the long term. A well-cooled machine room is a happy machine room.

We have found that it's a good idea to double-check the cooling load estimates provided by the HVAC folks, especially when installing a system for a machine room. You'll definitely need an HVAC engineer to help you with calculations for the cooling load that your roof, walls, and windows (don't forget solar load) contribute to your environment. HVAC engineers usually have a lot of experience with those components and should be able to give you an accurate estimate. The part you need to check up on is the internal heat load for your machine room.

You will need to determine the heat load contributed by the following components:

- Roof, walls, and windows (see your HVAC engineer for this estimate)
- Electronic gear
- Light fixtures
- Operators (people)

*Electronic gear*

You can estimate the heat load produced by your servers (and other electronic gear) by determining their power consumption. Direct measurement power consumption is by far the best method to obtain this information. Your friendly neighborhood electrician can often help you with this. Alternatively, most equipment is labeled with its maximum power consumption in watts, though typical consumption tends to be less than the maximum. You can convert this figure to the standard heat unit, BTUH, by multiplying by 3.412 BTUH/watt. For example, if we wanted to build a machine room that would house 25 servers rated at 450 watts each, the calculation would be:

$$\left(25 \text{ servers}\right) \left(\frac{450 \text{ watts}}{\text{server}}\right) \left(\frac{3.412 \text{ BTUH}}{\text{watt}}\right) = 38{,}385 \text{ BTUH}$$

*Light fixtures*

As with electronic gear, you can estimate light fixture heat load based on power consumption. Typical office light fixtures contain four 40-watt fluorescent tubes. If your new machine room had six of these fixtures, the calculation would be:

$$\left(6 \text{ fixtures}\right) \left(\frac{160 \text{ watts}}{\text{fixture}}\right) \left(\frac{3.412 \text{ BTUH}}{\text{watt}}\right) = 3{,}276 \text{ BTUH}$$

*Operators*

At one time or another, humans will need to enter the machine room to service something. Allow 300 BTUH for each occupant. If you want to allow for four humans in the machine room at the same time:

$$\left(4 \text{ humans}\right) \left(\frac{300 \text{ BTUH}}{\text{human}}\right) = 1{,}200 \text{ BTUH}$$

*Total heat load*

Once you have calculated the heat load for each component, add them up to determine your total heat load. For our example, we will assume that our HVAC engineer estimated the load from the roof, walls, and windows to be 20,000 BTUH.

| | |
|---:|:---|
| 20,000 | BTUH for roof, walls, and windows |
| 38,385 | BTUH for servers and other electronic gear |
| 3,276 | BTUH for light fixtures |
| 1,200 | BTUH for operators |
| 62,861 | BTUH total |

Cooling system capacity is typically expressed in tons. You can convert BTUH to tons by dividing by 12,000 BTUH/ton. You should also allow at least a 50% slop factor to account for errors and future growth:

$$\left(62{,}681 \text{ BTUH}\right) \left(\frac{1 \text{ ton}}{12{,}000 \text{ BTUH}}\right) \left(1.5\right) = 7.86 \text{ tons of cooling required}$$

See how your estimate matches up with the one provided by your HVAC folks.

**Temperature monitoring**

If you are supporting a mission-critical computing environment, it's a good idea to monitor the temperature (and other environmental factors, such as noise and power) in the machine room even when you are not there. It can be very disappointing to arrive on Monday morning and find a pool of melted plastic on your machine room floor. Fortunately, automated machine room monitors can watch the goods while you are away. We use and recommend the Phonetics Sensaphone product family. These inexpensive boxes monitor environmental variables such as temperature, noise, and power and telephone you (or your pager) when a problem is detected. You can reach Phonetics in Aston, PA at (610) 558-2700 or visit them on the web at www.sensaphone.com.

## 24.8  POWER

Computer hardware would like to see nice, stable, clean power. In a machine room, this means a power conditioner, an expensive box that filters out spikes and can be adjusted to provide the correct voltage levels and phases. In offices, surge protectors placed between machines and the wall help to insulate hardware from power spikes.

You might want to consider putting your servers and network infrastructure equipment on an Uninterruptible Power Supply (UPS). Good UPSs have an RS-232 interface that can be attached to the machine to which they supply power. This allows the UPS to warn the computer that the power has failed and that it should shut itself down cleanly before the batteries run out. We've had fantastic luck with UPSs manufactured by BEST Power Technology. They're not the least expensive, but they are very nice products.

Maintenance

*See page 33 for more information about shutdown procedures.*

One study has estimated that 13% of the electrical power consumed in the United States is used to run computers. Traditionally, UNIX boxes were based on hardware and software that expected the power to be on 24 hours a day. These days, only servers and network devices really need to be up all the time. Desktop machines can be powered down at night if there is an easy way for users to turn them off (and you trust your users to do it correctly).

At the very least, ask users to turn off monitors and laser printers when they go home; these are the biggest power hogs. When buying new equipment, look for an Energy Star certification. It signifies that an item complies with EPA guidelines for energy-efficient operation. For example, Energy Star monitors must be able to automatically shut off their displays after a certain period of inactivity.

### Remote power control

You may occasionally find yourself in a situation in which you have to regularly power-cycle[2] a UNIX server because of a kernel or hardware glitch. Or perhaps you have non-UNIX servers in your machine room that are more prone to this type of problem. In either case, you may want to consider installing a system that will allow you to power-cycle problem servers by remote control.

One inexpensive and popular solution is the X-10 power control system, which includes a box that will answer a phone line and will power-cycle machines based on touch-tone codes. The basic X-10 product line is described and sold on-line at the site www.x10.com. If you're really serious about this approach, be sure to check out what's available at www.smarthome.com, which primarily focuses on home automation but includes higher-quality X10-compatible gear.

A more deluxe (and expensive) solution is manufactured by American Power Conversion (APC). Their MasterSwitch product is similar to a power strip, except that it can be controlled by a web browser through its built-in Ethernet port. You can reach APC at (401) 789-0204 or on the web at www.apcc.com.

## 24.9  RACKS

Much to the dismay of the folks on Wall Street who once viewed raised floors as a corporate status symbol akin to owning a Lamborghini, the days of the true raised-floor machine room are over. Have you ever tried to trace a cable that runs under the floor of one of these behemoths? Our experience is that while it looks nice through glass, "raised floor" is a synonym for "rat's nest." If you *must* put in a raised floor, use it to hide electrical power feeds and *nothing else*.

If your goal is to operate your computing equipment in a professional manner, a dedicated machine room for server-class machines is essential. A server room not only provides a cozy, temperature-controlled environment for your machines but also addresses their physical security needs.

---

2. Power-cycling is the process of turning a machine off, waiting 30 to 60 seconds for the capacitors to drain, and then turning the machine back on again.

In a dedicated machine room, storing equipment in racks (as opposed to, say, setting it on tables or on the floor) is the only maintainable, professional choice. Today, the best storage schemes use racks that are interconnected with an overhead track system for routing cables. This approach provides that irresistible high-tech feel without sacrificing organization or maintainability.

The best overhead track system is manufactured by Chatsworth Products (Chatsworth, CA, (818) 882-8595). Using standard 19" single-rail telco racks, you can construct homes for both shelf-mounted and rack-mounted servers. Two back-to-back 19" telco racks make a high-tech-looking "traditional" rack (for cases in which you need to attach rack hardware both in front of and in back of equipment). Chatsworth provides the racks, cable races, and cable management doodads, as well as all the hardware necessary to mount them in your building. Since the cables lie in visible tracks, they are easy to trace, and you will naturally be motivated to keep them tidy.

## 24.10  TOOLS

A well-outfitted system administrator is an effective system administrator. Having a dedicated tool box is an important key to minimizing downtime in the event of an emergency. Table 24.1 lists some items you should probably keep in your tool box, or at least within easy reach.

**Table 24.1    A system administrator's tool box**

| General tools | |
| --- | --- |
| Phillips-head screwdrivers: #0, #1, and #2 | Tweezers |
| Slot-head screwdrivers: 1/8", 3/16", and 5/16" | Scissors |
| Electrician's knife or Swiss army knife | Socket wrench kit |
| Pliers, both flat-needlenose and regular | Small flashlight or penlight |
| Teensy tiny jeweler's screwdrivers | Hex wrench kit |
| Ball-peen hammer, 4oz. | Torx wrench kit |
| **Computer-related specialty items** | |
| Wire stripper (with an integrated wire cutter) | Fluke network analyzer |
| Cable ties (and their Velcro cousins) | IC chip extractor |
| Spare Category 5 RJ-45 crossover cables | RJ-45 end crimper |
| Spare RJ-45 connectors (solid core and stranded) | SCSI terminators |
| Digital multimeter (DMM) | Breakout box |
| Static grounding strap | |
| **Miscellaneous** | |
| List of emergency maintenance contacts[a] | Q-Tips |
| Home phone and pager #s of on-call support staff | Electrical tape |
| First-aid kit | Dentist's mirror |
| Six-pack of good beer | Cellular telephone |

a. And maintenance contract numbers if applicable.

# 25 *Performance Analysis*

Performance is one of the most visible characteristics of any system, and it's often high on the list of complaints from users. Many users are convinced that their computers could run twice as fast if only the administrator knew how to properly tune the system to release its vast, untapped potential. In reality, this is almost never true.

One common fantasy involves tweaking the kernel variables that control the paging system and the buffer pools. Once upon a time, there were situations in which this was necessary and prudent. These days, it is usually a bad idea. The most likely result is that you will *reduce* your system's overall performance and not even be aware of what you've done, all the while congratulating yourself on being such a clever kernel hacker.

Modern kernels are pretuned to achieve reasonable (though admittedly, not optimal) performance under a variety of load conditions. If you try to optimize the system based on one particular measure of performance, the chances are high that you will distort the system's behavior relative to other performance metrics and load conditions. It seems easy to get results, but the gains are usually illusory.

In particular, take everything you read on the web with a tablespoon of salt. In the area of system performance, you will see superficially convincing arguments on all sorts of topics. However, most of the proponents of these theories do not have the knowledge, discipline, and time required to design valid experiments. Popular support means absolutely nothing; for every hare-brained proposal, you can expect to see a Greek chorus of, "I increased the size of my buffer cache by a factor of ten just like Joe said, and my system feels MUCH, MUCH faster!!!" Right.

System performance is not entirely out of your control. It's just that the road to good performance is not paved with magic fixes and romantic kernel patches. The basic rules are these:

- Don't overload your systems or your network. UNIX gives each process an illusion of infinite resources. But once 100% of the system's resources are in use, UNIX has to work very hard to maintain that illusion, delaying processes and often consuming a sizable fraction of the resources itself.

- Collect and review *historical* information about your system. If it was performing fine a week ago, an examination of the aspects of the system that have recently changed is likely to lead you to a smoking gun. Keep regular baselines in your hip pocket to pull out in an emergency.

This chapter focuses on the performance of systems that are used as servers. Desktop systems typically do not experience the same types of performance issues that servers do, and the answer to the question of how to improve performance on a desktop machine is almost always "Upgrade the hardware." Users like this answer, because it means they get fancy new systems on their desk more often.

## 25.1  WHAT YOU CAN DO TO IMPROVE PERFORMANCE

Here are some specific things can you do to improve performance:

- You can make sure that the system has enough memory. As we will see below, memory size has a major influence on performance. Memory is so inexpensive these days that you can usually afford to load every performance-sensitive machine to the gills.

- You can correct problems of usage, both those caused by users (too many jobs run at once, inefficient programming practices, jobs run at excessive priority, and large jobs run at inappropriate times of day) and those caused by the system (quotas, CPU accounting, unwanted daemons).

- For cases in which you are using UNIX as a web server or some other type of network application server, you may want to spread traffic among a number of systems with a commercial load balancing appliance, such as Cisco's Local Director or Alteon Networks' ACEswitch.[1] These boxes make several physical servers appear to be one logical server to the outside world. They balance the load according one of several user-selectable algorithms such as "most responsive server" or "round robin."

  These load balancers also provide useful redundancy should a server go down. They're really quite necessary if your site must handle unexpected traffic spikes.

---

1. www.cisco.com and www.alteonwebsystems.com

- You can organize the system's hard disks and filesystems so that load is evenly balanced, maximizing I/O throughput. For specific applications such as databases, you can use a fancy multidisk technology such as RAID to optimize data transfers. Consult with your database vendor for recommendations.

  It's important to note that different types of applications and databases respond differently to being spread across multiple disks. RAID comes in many forms, and you will need to put effort into determining which form (if any) is appropriate for your particular application.

- You can monitor your network to be sure that it is not saturated with traffic and that the error rate is low. Networks can be supervised with the **netstat** command, described on page 631. See also Chapter 20, *Network Management and Debugging*.

- You can configure the kernel to eliminate unwanted drivers and options and to use tables of an appropriate size. These topics are covered in Chapter 12, *Drivers and the Kernel*.

- You can identify situations in which the system is fundamentally inadequate to satisfy the demands being made of it.

These steps are listed in rough order of effectiveness. Adding memory and balancing traffic across multiple servers can make a huge difference in performance. You might see some improvement from organizing the system's disks correctly and from correcting network problems. The other factors may not make any difference at all.

## 25.2 Factors that affect performance

Perceived performance is determined by the efficiency with which the system's resources are allocated and shared. The exact definition of a "resource" is rather vague. It can include such items as cached contexts on the CPU chip and entries in the address table of the memory controller. However, to a first approximation, only the following four resources have much effect on performance:

- CPU time
- Memory
- Hard disk I/O bandwidth
- Network I/O bandwidth

All processes consume a portion of the system's resources. If resources are still left after active processes have taken what they want, the system's performance is about as good as it can be.

If there are not enough resources to go around, processes must take turns. A process that does not have immediate access to the resources it needs must wait around doing nothing. The amount of time spent waiting is one of the basic measures of performance degradation.

CPU time is one of the easiest resources to measure. A constant amount of processing power is always available. In theory, that amount is 100% of the CPU cycles, but overhead and various inefficiencies make the real-life number more like 95%. A process that's using more than 90% of the CPU is entirely CPU-bound and is consuming most of the system's available computing power.

Many people assume that the speed of the CPU is the most important factor affecting a system's overall performance. Given infinite amounts of all other resources or certain types of applications (e.g., numerical simulations), a faster CPU *will* make a dramatic difference. But in the everyday world, CPU speed is relatively unimportant.

The most common performance bottleneck on UNIX systems is actually disk bandwidth. Because hard disks are mechanical systems, it takes many milliseconds to locate a disk block, fetch its contents, and wake up the process that's waiting for it. Delays of this magnitude overshadow every other source of performance degradation. Each disk access causes a stall worth millions of CPU instructions.

Because UNIX provides virtual memory, disk bandwidth and memory are directly related. On a loaded system with a limited amount of RAM, you often have to write a page to disk to obtain a fresh page of virtual memory. Unfortunately, this means that using memory is often just as expensive as using the disk. Swapping and paging caused by bloated software is performance enemy #1 on most workstations.

Network bandwidth resembles disk bandwidth in many ways, due to the latencies involved. However, networks are atypical in that they involve entire communities rather than individual computers. They are also susceptible to hardware problems and overloaded servers.

## 25.3   SYSTEM PERFORMANCE CHECKUP

Most performance analysis tools tell you what's going on at a particular point in time. However, the number and character of loads will probably change throughout the day. Be sure to gather a cross-section of data before taking action. The best information on system performance often becomes clear only after a long period (a month or more) of data collection.

### Analyzing CPU usage

You will probably want to gather three kinds of CPU data: overall utilization, load averages, and per-process CPU consumption. Overall utilization can help identify systems on which the CPU's speed itself is the bottleneck. Load averages give you an impression of overall system performance. Per-process CPU consumption data can identify specific processes that are hogging resources.

You can obtain summary information with the **vmstat** command on most systems and also with **sar -u** on Solaris and HP-UX. Both commands take two arguments: the number of seconds to monitor the system for each line of output and the number of reports to provide. For example,

```
% sar -u 5 5
13:33:40    %usr    %sys    %wio    %idle
13:33:45    4       58      27      11
13:33:50    7       83      9       0
13:33:55    9       77      13      0
13:34:00    2       25      3       71
13:34:05    0       0       0       100

Average     4       49      10      36
```

**sar -u** reports the percentage of the CPU's time that was spent running user code (%usr), running kernel code (%sys), and idling. Idle time is charged to the %wio category if there are processes blocked on high-speed I/O (disk, usually) and to the %idle column if not.

**vmstat** prints a variety of information, with the CPU-related columns at the end:

```
% vmstat 5 5
procs               page                    faults        cpu
r b w   re mf pi po fr de sr in     sy   cs    us sy id
0 0 0    0  0  0  0  0  0  0  4     22   19     2  1 97
1 0 0   67  2  0  0  0  0  0 26    751   52    53 47  0
0 0 0   96  0  0  0  0  0  0 39   1330   42    22 71  7
0 0 0   16  0  0  0  0  0  0 84   1626   99     7 74 19
0 0 0    1  0  0  0  0  0  0 11    216   20     1 11 88
```

Some columns have been removed from this example. We will defer discussion of the paging-related columns until later in this chapter.

User, system, and idle time are shown in the us, sy, and id columns. CPU numbers that are heavy on user time generally indicate computation, and high system numbers indicate that processes are making a lot of system calls or performing I/O. (**vmstat** shows the number of system calls per second in the sy column under faults.) A rule of thumb that has served us well over the years and that applies to most systems is that the system should spend approximately 50% of its nonidle time in user space and 50% in system space; the overall idle percentage should be nonzero. The cs column shows context switches per interval, the number of times that the kernel changed which process was running. An extremely high cs value typically indicates a misbehaving or misconfigured hardware device.

Long-term averages of the CPU statistics allow you to determine whether there is fundamentally enough CPU power to go around. If the CPU usually spends part of its time in the idle state, there are cycles to spare. Upgrading to a faster CPU won't do much to improve the overall throughput of the system, though it may speed up individual operations.

As you can see from these examples, the CPU generally flip-flops back and forth between full-on use and complete idleness. Therefore, it's important to observe these numbers as an average over time. The smaller the monitoring interval, the less consistent the results.

On a workstation with only one user, the CPU generally spends 99% of its time idle. Then, when you go to scroll one of the windows on your bitmap display, the CPU is floored for a few seconds. In this situation, information about long-term average CPU usage is not meaningful.

The second CPU statistic that's useful for characterizing the burden on your system is the "load average," the average number of runnable processes. In general, the load average includes processes waiting for disk and network I/O, so it is not a pure measure of CPU use. However, it does give you a good idea of how many pieces the CPU pie is being divided into. The load average is obtained with the **uptime** command:

```
% uptime
2:07pm up 4:02, 5 users, load average: 0.95, 0.38, 0.31
```

Three values are given, corresponding on most systems to the 5, 10, and 15-minute averages. In general, the higher the load average, the more important the system's aggregate performance becomes. If there is only one runnable process, that process will usually be bound by a single resource (commonly disk bandwidth or CPU). The peak demand for that one resource becomes the determining factor in performance.

When more processes share the system, loads may or may not be more evenly distributed. If the processes on the system all consume a mixture of CPU, disk, and memory, the performance of the system is less likely to be dominated by constraints on a single resource. In this situation, it becomes most important to look at average measures of consumption such as total CPU utilization.

*See page 47 for more information about priorities.*

Modern systems do not deal well with load averages over about 6.0. A load average of this magnitude is a hint that you should start to look for ways to artificially spread the load, such as asking users to run long processes at night or using **nice** to set process priorities.

The system load average is an excellent metric to track as part of a system baseline. If you know your system's load average on a normal day and it is in that same range on a bad day, this is a hint that you should look elsewhere for performance problems (such as the network). A load average above the expected norm suggests that you should look at the processes running on the UNIX system itself.

Another way to view CPU usage is to run the **ps** command with arguments that let you see how much of the CPU each process is using (-**elf** for HP-UX and Solaris, -**aux** for Red Hat and FreeBSD). More likely than not, on a busy system, at least 70% of the CPU will be consumed by one or two processes. (Remember that **ps** consumes some CPU itself.) Deferring the execution of the CPU hogs or reducing their priority will make the CPU more available to other processes.

*See page 57 for more information about **top**.*

An excellent alternative to **ps** is a program called **top**. **top** presents about the same information as **ps**, but in a "live" format that lets you watch the status of the system change over time.[2]

---

2. **top** itself can be quite a CPU hog, so be judicious in your use of it.

### How UNIX manages memory

UNIX manages memory in units called pages that are usually 4K or larger. They are sometimes called "page clusters" if they are bigger than the page size that's directly supported by the CPU or memory controller. Disk blocks are usually smaller than memory pages (1K or 512 bytes), so the kernel has to associate several disk blocks with each page that's written out.

UNIX tries to manage the system's memory so that pages that have been recently accessed are kept in memory and less active pages are paged out. This is known as an LRU system since the least recently used pages are the ones that get rotated to disk. It's not actually possible for the kernel to keep track of all page references, so most versions of UNIX use a statistical technique known as the clock algorithm to manage memory. It is much cheaper than a true LRU system, but it produces similar results.

The kernel maintains a free list of pages that are eligible to be paged out. When memory is low, pages are placed on the free list seemingly at random. (Actually, there is a defined order, so the "clock" hand points to every page equally often.) As a page is placed on the free list, its address mapping is unwired from the memory controller so that the next time a process attempts to access it, a fault is generated.

If a "freed" page is referenced before being paged out (an event called a soft fault), the kernel takes it off the free list and rewires its address mapping. The page is then safe until the next pass of the page-freeing clock. On average, infrequently referenced pages don't get rescued; their contents are eventually written out to disk and they are then recycled.[3]

Demand for memory varies, so the kernel can run the page-freeing clock at different speeds. If there is plenty of memory, the clock does not run at all, thus sparing the system the overhead of processing soft page faults. When the demand for memory is extreme, the clock runs at high speed and pages must be rescued in a shorter amount of time to avoid being paged out.

The virtual memory (VM) system depends on the lag between the time when a page is placed on the free list and the time when it's actually paged out to sort active pages from inactive pages. Therefore, it has to predict future paging activity in order to select an appropriate speed for the paging clock. If the clock runs too slowly, there might not be enough pages on the free list to satisfy demand. If too fast, the kernel spends excessive time processing soft page faults.

Since the paging algorithm is predictive, there is not necessarily a one-to-one correspondence between page-out events and page allocations by running processes. The goal of the system is to keep enough free memory handy that processes don't have to actually wait for a page-out each time they make a new allocation.

Swapping is handled somewhat differently from paging. It's also done predictively, but on the basis of accurate per-process records rather than statistical estimates. If

---

3. It is not always necessary to save the contents of a page that's being recycled. Text pages and other pages that can be retrieved from their original sources are simply discarded.

memory is scarce and a process is known to have been idle for a long time (tens of seconds), it makes sense to write out all its pages at once rather than waiting for the paging algorithm to collect them.

It is a very bad sign if the kernel forcibly swaps out runnable processes. This is called thrashing or desperation swapping, and it indicates an extreme memory shortage. In this situation, it's likely that a substantial portion of the system's resources are being devoted to memory housekeeping rather than to useful work.

A similar VM pathology can occur when two large processes compete for the CPU. When the first process gets to run, it brings in a group of its own pages, forcing out some of the second process's pages. Then the second process runs and reinstates its own pages at the expense of the first process. Neither process gets much work done.

Even processes running at a low CPU priority can be sneaky page thieves. For example, suppose you're running a simulation at very low priority (high nice value) on your workstation, while at the same time reading mail in a terminal window. As you pause to read a message, your CPU use falls to zero and the simulation is allowed to run. It brings in all of its pages, forcing out your shell, your window server, your mail reader, and your terminal emulator. When you type **n** to go on to the next message, there is a delay as a large chunk of the system's memory is turned over. In real life, a high nice value is no guarantee that a process won't cause performance problems.

## Analyzing memory usage

On a workstation, your best memory analysis tools are your ears. The amount of paging activity is generally proportional to the amount of crunching you hear from the disk. On most disks, the seeking of the heads is what you actually hear, but the correspondence is good enough to give you a general idea of what's going on.

There are basically two numbers that quantify memory activity: the total amount of active virtual memory and the paging rate. The first number tells you the total demand for memory, and the second suggests the proportion of that memory that is actively used. The goal is to reduce activity or increase memory until paging remains at an acceptable level. Occasional paging is inevitable, so don't worry about trying to eliminate it completely.

The amount of swap space currently in use can be determined with the command **swap -l** under Solaris, **swapinfo** under HP-UX, **swapon -s** on Red Hat, and **pstat -s** on FreeBSD. **sar -r** can also be used on Solaris systems (as always, with arguments to specify the monitoring interval), but for some reason it gives results that are not entirely consistent with **swap -l**.

```
% swap -l
swapfile            dev  swapl  blocks  free
/dev/dsk/c0t0d0s1   32,1    16  164400  162960

% sar -r 5
17:58:52  freemem  freeswap
17:58:57    361     179616
```

```
% pstat -s
Device          1K-blocks  Used     Avail  Capacity  Type
/dev/wd0s1b        70784      0     70656       0%   Interleaved
/dev/da0b        1048920      0   1048792       0%   Interleaved
Total            1119448      0   1119448       0%
```

**pstat** shows the swap sizes in kilobytes; **swap -l** and **sar -r** use 512-byte disk blocks. The sizes quoted by these programs do not include the contents of core memory, so you must compute the total amount of virtual memory yourself:

```
VM = size of real memory + amount of swap space used
```

On most systems, paging statistics are obtained with **vmstat**:

```
% vmstat 5 5
procs      memory              page                 disk            faults
r b w   swap    free   re mf pi po fr de sr   s0 s6 s4 --   in   sy  cs
0 0 0 338216 10384    0  3  1  0  0  0  0    0  0  0  0  132  101  58
0 0 0 341784 11064    0 26  1  1  1  0  0    0  0  1  0  150  215 100
0 0 0 351752 12968    1 69  0  9  9  0  0    0  0  2  0  173  358 156
0 0 0 360240 14520    0 30  6  0  0  0  0    0  0  1  0  138  176  71
1 0 0 366648 15712    0 73  0  8  4  0  0    0  0 36  0  390  474 237
```

CPU information has been removed from this example. Under the procs heading is shown the number of processes that are immediately runnable, blocked on I/O, and runnable but swapped. If the value in the w column is ever nonzero, it is likely that the system's memory is pitifully inadequate relative to the current load.

The swap column gives the number of available kilobytes of virtual memory. The free column tells the number of kilobytes on the system's free list; values lower than 3% of the system's total memory generally indicate problems.

The next seven columns give information about paging activity. All columns represent average values per second. Their meanings are:

- re  – the number of pages reclaimed (rescued from the free list)
- mf – the number of minor faults (minor meaning "small # of pages")
- pi  – the number of kilobytes paged in
- po – the number of kilobytes paged out
- fr  – the number of kilobytes placed on the free list
- de – the number of kilobytes of "predicted short-term memory shortfall"
- sr  – the number of number of pages scanned by the clock algorithm

The de column is the best indicator of serious memory problems. If it often jumps above 100, the machine is starved for memory. Unfortunately, some versions of **vmstat** don't show this number.

**vmstat -S** shows statistics for swapping rather than paging.

The apparent inconsistencies among the memory-related columns are for the most part illusory. Some columns count pages, others count kilobytes. The clock algorithm is not responsible for all frees because some pages may be voluntarily released by processes. All values are rounded averages. Furthermore, some are averages of scalar quantities and others are average deltas. For example, you can't compute the next value of free from the current free and paging information because the paging events that determine the next average value of free have not yet occurred.

A page-in does not necessarily represent a page being recovered from the swap area. It could be executable code being paged in from a filesystem or could be a copy-on-write page being duplicated, both of which are normal occurrences that do not necessarily indicate a shortage of memory. On the other hand, page-outs always represent data being forcibly ejected by the kernel.

If your system has a constant stream of page-outs, you need more memory. But if paging happens only occasionally and does not produce annoying hiccups or user complaints, you can ignore it. If your system falls somewhere in the middle, further analysis should depend on whether you are trying to optimize for interactive performance (e.g., a workstation) or to configure a machine with many simultaneous users (e.g., a compute server).

If half the operations are page-outs, you can figure that every 50 page-outs cause about one second of latency. If 75 page-outs must occur to let you scroll a window, you will wait for about 1.5 seconds. A rule of thumb used by interface researchers is that an average user perceives the system to be "slow" when response times are longer than seven-tenths of a second.

## Analyzing disk I/O

Most systems allow disk throughput to be monitored with the **iostat** command. Like **vmstat**, it takes optional arguments to specify an interval in seconds and a repetition count, and its first line of output is a summary since boot. Like **vmstat**, it also tells you how the CPU's time is being spent.

```
% iostat 5 5
        tty          sd0              sd1             nfs1          cpu
tin  tout  kps tps serv  kps tps serv  kps tps serv   us sy wt id
 0     1    5   1   18   14   2   20    0   0   0     0  0  0  99
 0    39    0   0    0    2   0   14    0   0   0     0  0  0 100
 2    26    3   0   13    8   1   21    0   0   0     0  0  0 100
 3   119    0   0    0   19   2   13    0   0   0     0  1  1  98
 1    16    5   1   19    0   0    0    0   0   0     0  0  0 100
```

Columns are divided into topics (in this case, five: tty, sd0, sd1, nfs1, and cpu), with the data for each topic presented in the fields beneath it. **iostat** output tends to be somewhat different on every system. (This output is from Solaris.)

The tty topic presents data concerning terminals and pseudo-terminals. This information is basically uninteresting, although it might be useful for characterizing the throughput of a modem. The tin and tout columns give the average total number of characters input and output per second by all of the system's terminals.

Each hard disk has columns kps, tps, and serv, indicating kilobytes transferred per second, total transfers per second, and average "service times" (seek times, essentially) in milliseconds. One transfer request can include several sectors, so the ratio between kps and tps tells you whether there are a few large transfers or lots of small ones. Large transfers are more efficient. Calculation of seek times seems to work only on specific drives and sometimes gives bizarre values (the values in this example are reasonable).

Some systems support **iostat -D**, which gives the percentage utilization of each disk.

```
% iostat -D 5 5
          sd1               sd2               sd3               sd5
rps wps  util  rps wps  util  rps wps  util  rps wps  util
  0   0   1.3    0   0   0.3    0   0   0.5    1   1   4.2
  9   8  41.1    1   0   1.8    1   0   2.4    6   8  34.8
 11   4  48.4    0   1   2.0    0   0   0.0    3  11  32.6
  8   0  15.6    0   0   0.0    0   0   0.0    3   0   9.2
  0   0   0.0    0   0   0.0    0   0   0.0    0   0   0.0
```

Here, volumes are quoted in reads and writes per second.

The cost of seeking is the most important factor affecting disk drive performance. To a first approximation, the rotational speed of the disk and the speed of the bus it's connected to have relatively little impact. Modern disks can transfer dozens of megabytes of data per second if they are read from contiguous sectors, but they can only perform about 100 to 300 seeks per second. If you transfer one sector per seek, you can easily realize less than 5% of the drive's peak throughput.

Seeks are more expensive when they make the heads travel a long distance. If you have a disk with several filesystem partitions and files are read from each partition in a random order, the heads will have to travel back and forth a long way to switch between partitions. On the other hand, files within a partition will be relatively local to one another. When partitioning a new disk, you may want to consider the performance implications and put files that are accessed together in the same filesystem.

To really achieve maximum disk performance, you should put filesystems that are used together on different disks. Although it depends on the bus architecture and device drivers, most computers can manage multiple disks independently, dramatically increasing throughput. For example, web server data and web server logs can profitably be put on different disks.

If you have a lot of disks, you may be able to boost performance even further by installing more than one disk controller or SCSI bus. The effectiveness of this technique will depend on the architecture of your system. Check your hardware documentation or consult your vendor.

It's especially important to split the swap area among several disks if possible, since paging tends to slow down the entire system. All systems support this configuration through the use of the **swapon** command, the **swap** command, or a kernel configuration option (see Chapter 8). Many systems can use both dedicated swap partitions and swap files on a formatted filesystem. Dedicated partitions are more efficient; do not use swap files if you have a choice.

Some systems also allow you to set up **/tmp** as a "memory based filesystem," which is essentially the same thing as a PC RAM disk. A special driver poses as a disk but actually stores data in memory. Using a RAM disk may reduce the average amount of memory available for general use, but it makes the reading and writing of temporary files blindingly fast. It's generally a good deal. For more information, see the man page for **tmpfs** on Solaris, the man page for **ram** on Red Hat, or the man page for **mfs** on FreeBSD.

Some software degrades the system's performance by delaying basic operations. Two examples are disk quotas and CPU accounting. Quotas require a disk usage summary to be updated as files are written and deleted. CPU accounting writes a data record to an accounting file whenever a process completes. Disk caching helps to soften the impact of these features, but they may still have a noticeable effect on performance and should not be enabled unless you really use them.

### Virtual Adrian

Solaris administrators can leave the driving to Adrian—Adrian Cockcroft, that is. Adrian is a performance expert employed by Sun who distributes his own analysis and tuning tools. His SymbEL tool kit (known as SE) is an interpreted language designed for building performance tools and utilities. The tool kit includes the "Virtual Adrian" ruleset, which is said to embody Adrian's many years of Solaris performance tuning experience. Although it's not officially supported by Sun, you can download the tool kit from Sun's web site at

> http://www.sun.com/sun-on-net/performance/se3

### procinfo: display Red Hat performance data

Red Hat's **procinfo** command provides a nice summary of system performance information, much like that of **vmstat** but in a more understandable form. The information it provides about PC interrupts is especially useful. If you have a spare terminal or window and can spare the CPU cycles, you can run **procinfo -f** to show updates every 5 seconds.

```
% procinfo
Linux 2.2.5-15 (root@porky.devel.redhat.com) (gcc egcs-2.91.66) #1 [redhat]

Memory:    Total    Used     Free   Shared   Buffers   Cached
Mem:       30756   23908     6848     9084     12496     3968
Swap:     133016     224   132792

Bootup: Tue May  2 12:26:13 2000    Load average: 0.08 0.02 0.01 1/26 16173

user   :       0:08:15.35    0.0%  page in  :  774301  disk 1: 229922r 109442w
nice   :       0:00:00.00    0.0%  page out :  177675
system :       0:10:46.41    0.0%  swap in  :     183
idle   : 30d  2:06:40.89  100.0%  swap out :      60
uptime : 30d  2:25:42.64          context  : 7221865
```

```
irq  0 : 260074265 timer      irq 10 :  3032801  eth0
irq  1 : 8          keyboard   irq 13 :  1        fpu
irq  2 : 0          cascade [4] irq 14 : 1905415  ide0
irq  6 : 3                     irq 15 :  5        ide1
irq  8 : 2          rtc
```

### pstat: print random FreeBSD statistics

Another useful tool available on FreeBSD systems is the **pstat** command. It dumps the contents of various kernel tables in an almost human-readable form. There is no unifying theme to the information **pstat** can display—it is just a gopher for tidbits maintained by the kernel. Here are some of the reports it can produce:

- A dump of the inode table (**-i**)
- A dump of the text table (**-x**)
- A dump of the process table, gorier than **ps** (**-P**)
- A dump of the open file table (**-f**)
- Status information for all terminals (**-t**)
- Information about a particular process (**-u**)
- Information about swap space usage (**-s**)
- Information about how full the kernel's tables are (**-T**)

**pstat -T** is useful for determining the optimal value of the maxusers variable when you are configuring the kernel. Unfortunately, **pstat -T** only shows you a small fraction of the things that are affected by maxusers, so you must still allow a generous margin of safety in your configuration. See Chapter 12, *Drivers and the Kernel*, for more information.

## 25.4  HELP! MY SYSTEM JUST GOT REALLY SLOW!

In previous sections, we've talked mostly about issues that relate to the average performance of a system. Solutions to these long-term concerns generally take the form of configuration adjustments or upgrades.

However, you will find that even properly configured systems are sometimes more sluggish than usual. Luckily, transient problems are often easy to diagnose. Ninety percent of the time, they are caused by a greedy process that is simply consuming so much CPU power or disk bandwidth that other processes have been stalled.

You can often tell which resource is being hogged without even running a diagnostic command. If the system feels "sticky" or you hear the disk going crazy, the problem is most likely a disk bandwidth or memory shortfall.[4] If the system feels "sluggish" (everything takes a long time, and applications can't be "warmed up"), the problem may be CPU.

The first step in diagnosis is to run **ps** or **top** to look for obvious runaway processes. Any process that's using more than 50% of the CPU is likely to be at fault. If no single

---

4. That is, it takes a long time to switch between applications, but performance is acceptable when an application is repeating a simple task.

process is getting an inordinate share of the CPU, check to see how many processes are getting at least 10%. If there are more than two or three (don't count **ps** itself), the load average is likely to be quite high. This is, in itself, a cause of poor performance. Check the load average with **uptime**, and use **vmstat** or **sar -u** to check whether the CPU is ever idle.

If no CPU contention is evident, check to see how much paging is going on with **vmstat** or **sar -g**. All disk activity is interesting: a lot of page-outs may indicate contention for memory, while disk traffic in the absence of paging may mean that a process is monopolizing the disk by constantly reading or writing files.

There's no direct way to tie disk operations to processes, but **ps** can narrow down the possible suspects for you. Any process that is generating disk traffic must be using some amount of CPU time. You can usually make an educated guess about which of the active processes is the true culprit.[5] Use **kill -STOP** to test your theory.

Suppose you do find that a particular process is at fault—what should you do? Usually, nothing. Some operations just require a lot of resources and are bound to slow down the system. It doesn't necessarily mean that they're illegitimate. It is usually acceptable to **renice** an obtrusive process that is CPU-bound. But be sure to ask the owner to use the **nice** command in the future.

Processes that are disk or memory hogs can't be dealt with so easily. **renice** generally will not help. You do have the option of killing or stopping a process, but we recommend against this if the situation does not constitute an emergency. As with CPU pigs, you can use the low-tech solution of asking the owner to run the process later.

Some systems allow a process's consumption of physical memory to be restricted with the **setrlimit** system call. This facility is available in the C shell with the built-in **limit** command. For example, the command

```
% limit memoryuse 32m
```

causes all subsequent commands that the user runs to have their use of physical memory limited to 32 megabytes. This feature is roughly equivalent to **renice** for memory-bound processes. You might tactfully suggest that repeat offenders put such a line in their **.cshrc** files.

If a runaway process doesn't seem to be the source of poor performance, there are two other possible causes to investigate. The first is an overloaded network. Many programs are so intimately bound up with the network that it's hard to tell where system performance ends and network performance begins. See Chapter 20 for more information about the tools used to monitor networks.

Some network overloading problems are hard to diagnose because they come and go very quickly. For example, if every machine on the network runs a network-related

---

5. A large virtual address space or resident set used to be a suspicious sign, but shared libraries have made these numbers less useful. Most versions of **ps** are not very smart about separating system-wide shared library overhead from the address spaces of individual processes. Many processes wrongly appear to have megabytes of active memory.

program out of **cron** at a particular time each day, there will often be a brief but dramatic glitch. Every machine on the net will hang for five seconds, and then the problem will disappear as quickly as it came.

Server-related delays are another possible cause of performance crises. UNIX systems are constantly consulting remote servers for NFS, NIS, DNS, and any of a dozen other facilities. If a server is dead or some other problem makes it expensive to communicate with, the effects can ripple back through client systems.

For example, on a busy system, some process may use the **gethostent** library routine every few seconds or so. If a DNS glitch makes this routine take two seconds to complete, you will likely perceive a difference in overall performance.

## 25.5 RECOMMENDED READING

COCKCROFT, ADRIAN AND RICHARD PETTIT. *Sun Performance and Tuning: Java and the Internet.* Upper Saddle River, NJ: Prentice Hall. 1998.

LOUKIDES, MIKE. *System Performance Tuning.* Sebastopol: O'Reilly. 1991.

# 26 *Cooperating with Windows*

windows    System administrator    Microsoft

It's a fact of life that Windows is not going away. We can't ignore it. We must peacefully coexist with it. One way to look at the situation is that UNIX has brought TCP/IP and the Internet to the table, while Windows has brought millions of users. The challenge for system administrators is to host the resulting Satanic banquet.

Fortunately, modern tools can significantly reduce the chance of PC-to-UNIX transplant rejection. It really is the case that both platforms have their strengths and that they can be made to work together. Windows is a popular and featureful desktop platform, capable of bridging the gap between the user and the network cable coming out of the wall. UNIX, on the other hand, is a rock solid, scalable infrastructure platform.

This chapter addresses a variety of topics faced by administrators in this postmodern, PCs-and-UNIX-living-together world.

## 26.1 FILE AND PRINT SHARING

Perhaps the most powerful level of PC/UNIX integration is achieved by sharing directories that live on a UNIX host (or a dedicated UNIX-like file server) with desktop PCs that run Windows.[1] The shared directories can be made to appear transparently under Windows, either as drives or as an extension to the regular Windows network file tree. Either NFS or CIFS can be used to implement this functionality.

---

1. You can also mount PC-resident filesystems under Linux, but this arrangement is somewhat unstable.

### NFS: the Network File System

*See Chapter 17 for more information about NFS.*

NFS was designed to share files among UNIX hosts, on which the file locking and security paradigms are significantly different from those of Windows. Although a variety of products that mount NFS-shared directories on Windows clients are available, their use should be aggressively avoided, both because of the paradigm mismatch and because CIFS just works better.

### CIFS: the Common Internet File System

CIFS is based on protocols that were formerly referred to as Server Message Block or SMB. SMB was an extension that Microsoft added to DOS in its early days to allow disk I/O to be redirected to a system known as NetBIOS (Network Basic Input/Output System). Designed by IBM and Sytec, NetBIOS was a crude interface between the network and an application.

In the modern world, SMB packets are carried in an extension of NetBIOS known as NBT, NetBIOS over TCP. While this all sounds very convoluted, the result is that these protocols have become widespread and are available on platforms ranging from MVS and VMS to our friends UNIX and Windows. Everybody dance now.

### Samba: CIFS for UNIX

Samba is an enormously popular software package available under the GNU public license that implements CIFS on UNIX hosts. It was originally created by Andrew Tridgell, an Australian, who reverse engineered the SMB protocol from another system and published the resulting code in 1992.

Today, Samba is well supported and actively under development to expand its functionality. It provides a stable, industrial-strength mechanism for integrating Windows machines into a UNIX network. The real beauty of it is that you only need to install one package on the UNIX machine; no additional software is needed on the Windows side.[2]

CIFS provides five basic services:

- File sharing
- Network printing
- Authentication and authorization
- Name resolution
- Service announcement (file server and printer "browsing")

Most of Samba's functionality is implemented by two daemons: **smbd** and **nmbd**. **smbd** implements file and print services, as well as authentication and authorization. **nmbd** provides the other major CIFS components, name resolution and service announcement.

Unlike NFS, which is deeply intertwined with the kernel, Samba requires no kernel modifications and runs entirely as a user process. It binds to the sockets used for

---

2. Provided that the PC has already been configured for "Microsoft networking."

NBT requests and waits for a client to request access to a resource. Once the request has been made and authenticated, **smbd** forks an instance of itself that runs as the user who is making the requests. As a result, all normal UNIX file access permissions (including group permissions) are obeyed. The only special functionality that **smbd** adds on top of this is a file locking service that provides client PCs with the locking semantics they are accustomed to.

### Installing and configuring Samba

Samba is currently shipped with both Red Hat and FreeBSD (in **/usr/ports**), but you'll need to download and install it for Solaris or HP-UX. It's available on the web from www.samba.org.

On all systems, you'll need to edit the **smb.conf** file to tell Samba how it should behave. In this file, you can specify the directories and printers that should be shared, their access rights, and Samba's general operational parameters. All of the options are documented in the **smb.conf** man page, which you'll definitely need to consult when integrating Samba into a network on which Microsoft file sharing is already in use.

It's important to be aware of the security implications of sharing files or resources across a network. Samba allows fine-grained control over security, but it only works if you actually use it. For a typical site, you need to do two things to ensure a basic level of security:

- In the **smb.conf** file, the hosts allow clause controls which clients may access the resources shared by Samba. Make sure that it contains only the IP addresses (or address ranges) that it should.

- You *must* block access from the Internet to the CIFS TCP ports using a packet-filtering firewall. These are TCP ports 137 through 139. More information on how to do this is given on page 675.

Here's a complete **smb.conf** example for a simple network:

```
[global]

# workgroup = NT-Domain-Name or Workgroup-Name

  workgroup = MYGROUP

# List the hosts that may access Samba-shared objects.
# Here, only hosts on two class C nets are allowed.

  hosts allow = 192.168.1. 192.168.2.

# Automatically load your printer list from a file.³

  printcap name = /etc/printcap
  load printers = yes
```

---

3. Printers must already be set up on the UNIX host. Not all flavors of UNIX use **printcap**, but Samba can adapt to whatever system is in use in your environment. See Chapter 23 for more details.

```
# Use a separate log file for each machine, and limit size to 50K.

  log file = /var/log/samba/log.%m
  max log size = 50

# Set the security mode. Most people will want user-level security. See
# security_level.txt in the Samba doc for details.

  security = user

# You may wish to use password encryption. Please read ENCRYPTION.txt,
# Win95.txt and WinNT.txt in the Samba documentation. Do not enable this
# option unless you have read those documents.

; encrypt passwords = yes
; smb passwd file = /etc/smbpasswd

# Most people will find that this option gives better performance. See
# speed.txt and the manual pages for details.

  socket options = TCP_NODELAY

# Share home directories. For instance, ~trent under UNIX will appear
# as the share "trent" in the PC browser.

[homes]
  comment = Home Directories
  browseable = no
  writable = yes

# Share all printers.

[printers]
  comment = All Printers
  path = /var/spool/samba
  browseable = no
  guest ok = no
  writable = no
  printable = yes

# Share a specific directory.

[devel]
  comment = Staff Development Shared Directory
  path = /devel/shared
  public = no
  writable = yes
  printable = no
  create mask = 0765
```

As you can see from the comments, this **smb.conf** file is set up so that when users log in to their PCs, their home directories and the **/devel/shared** directory are both available. They can also print to all the printers that the server knows about.

### Debugging Samba

Samba usually runs without requiring much attention. However, if you do have a problem, you can consult two primary sources of debugging information: the per-client log files and the **smbstatus** command.

The location of log files is specified in the **smb.conf** file, and in that directory you will find a file for each client that has attempted a connection. **smbd** grooms these files so that they do not exceed their specified maximum sizes.

These following log entries show successful connections:

```
01/19/2000 17:38:01 pan (192.225.55.154) connect to service trent as user trent
    (uid=8164,gid=10) (pid 16625)
01/19/2000 17:40:30 pan (192.225.55.154) connect to service silver-lw as user
    trent (uid=8164,gid=10) (pid 16625)
01/19/2000 17:43:51 pan (192.225.55.154) closed connection to service silver-lw
01/19/2000 17:43:51 pan (192.225.55.154) closed connection to service trent
```

**smbstatus** enables you to examine currently active connections and open files. This information can be especially useful when you are tracking down locking problems ("Which user has file **xyz** open read-write exclusive?"). The first section of output lists the resources that a user has connected to. The second part lists any active file locks, and the third part displays **smbd**'s resource usage.[4]

```
Samba version 2.0.5
Service uid    gid    pid     machine
-----------------------------------------------
info    trent  staff  22545   pan
trent   trent  staff  22545   pan

Locked files:
Pid    DenyMode    R/W    Oplock           Name
-----------------------------------------------------------------------
22545  DENY_NONE   RDWR   EXCLUSIVE+BATCH  /home/trent/res alloc 2.xls

Share mode memory usage (bytes):
    1048336(99%) free + 168(0%) used + 72(0%) overhead = 1048576(100%) total
```

You can force a lock to be released by killing the **smbd** that "owns" the lock; the PID for each lock is shown in the output of **smbstatus**. Don't tell your users you know how to do this, and be aware that breaking locks can lead to corrupted files. Sometimes you gotta do what you gotta do.

## 26.2  SECURE TERMINAL EMULATION WITH SSH

Some users may find themselves wanting to leave Windows behind and head for the snow-covered slopes of a good C shell or Korn shell. Of course, the easiest way to accomplish this is to use the **telnet** program that Microsoft ships with Windows. Unfortunately, it lacks a few creature comforts such as direct cut and paste. Also,

---

4. **smbstatus** output contains some very long lines; we have condensed it here for clarity.

like any implementation of the TELNET protocol, it has no concept of security. (But hey, who needs a command line, anyway?) Fortunately, there are a variety of terminal emulators available for Windows that are significantly more well-endowed than Microsoft's **telnet**.

*See page 672 for more information about SSH.*

Our favorite terminal emulator is SecureCRT from VanDyke Technologies, Inc. This inexpensive commercial product combines the secure login and data transfer capabilities of SSH with a robust terminal emulator. It provides 56 to 256-bit ciphers for data encryption and can also provide port forwarding for other applications, such as mail. Learn more about SecureCRT at www.vandyke.com.

Another commercial emulator is the Windows SSH client produced by F-Secure Corporation. Information about their products is available at www.fsecure.com.

If you're looking for a free emulator, we suggest using TeraTerm with the TTSSH plug-in. You can find TeraTerm at

> http://hp.vector.co.jp/authors/VA002416/teraterm.html

The plug-in lives at

> http://www.zip.com.au/~roca/ttssh.html

Together, these provide a very reasonable and secure environment.

## 26.3  X WINDOWS EMULATORS

X Windows is a windowing system that is in no way related to the Windows operating systems from Microsoft. X Windows was developed at MIT in the 1980s and has been adopted by most UNIX workstation manufacturers as their distributed windowing environment (sometimes, with substantial modifications). Never fear, X emulators are here.

X Windows emulators work by implementing the X11 protocol on a Windows PC. The server provides a conduit between client applications (such as the **xterm** terminal emulator) and the Windows desktop. Once the X11 server has been started on the PC, clients can be run from the UNIX environment and displayed on the PC desktop. For those of you who lived through the early 1990s, this basically turns your PC into an X terminal on steroids. X applications displayed in this fashion can coexist with other Windows applications on the desktop. With some emulators, it is also possible to use a window manager from the UNIX environment.

There are dozens of X emulators out there. The two that we have been impressed by are Hummingbird's eXceed (www.hummingbird.com) and Frontier Technologies' SuperX (www.frontiertech.com). SuperX is what Trent actually runs every day. It makes cutting and pasting between X applications and Windows applications work correctly, and its font mapping is particularly easy.

## 26.4  PC MAIL CLIENTS

The first thing users want to do at their PCs is check email. Providing a stable email environment is essential to most organizations; fortunately, this is one area where PCs on desktops and central UNIX servers really shine together.

PC mail clients such as Microsoft Outlook, Netscape Messenger, and Qualcomm's Eudora are packed with groovy features and far outshine the UNIX mail readers of yore. They let users exchange regular email, encrypted email, email with attachments, and email with specially formatted or even colored text. These are essential tools of the Internet world—long gone are the days of **/usr/ucb/mail** and other text-only mail tools.

*See page 549 for more information about IMAP and POP.*

Organizations need to be able to provide reliable mail service to hundreds or sometimes thousands of users. That's where UNIX comes in. UNIX provides a scalable, secure, and configurable environment for the receipt and transmission of email on the Internet. Messages can be stored on a UNIX server and accessed by PC mail clients via protocols such as IMAP and POP. This is the best of all worlds. (UNIX also has the advantage of not being susceptible to Windows viruses.)

Another advantage of this approach, especially when you are using IMAP, is that mail is stored on the server. If the PC crashes and burns, the user's mail folders are not lost. IMAP also allows users to access their mail from a variety of locations, such as from home or a from a kiosk when on the road.

## 26.5  PC BACKUPS

*See Chapter 10 for general information about backups.*

Backing up the data on desktop PCs can be a formidable problem, especially now that typical desktop storage capacity exceeds 20GB. There are a number of approaches to this problem, including industrial-strength network backup tools from vendors such as IBM and Seagate. Of course, there's always the handy local tape drive approach. If you have the money and the patience, this is an area where commercial products really are head and shoulders above the rest.

But what about the rest of us? It is possible to back up a PC's drive (all or part) to a UNIX server with the **smbtar** utility included in the Samba package. Unfortunately, this approach is very high maintenance and hence we don't recommend it.

The best solution here seems to be *not* to back up PCs. Sites that get away without PC backups have carefully educated their users that all important files must be stored on a shared network drive. The individual PCs can then be configured identically (in terms of installed applications, desktop configuration, etc.) throughout the organization.[5] If one PC fails, another can be swapped in with just a few minutes of work. Crazy? Maybe. Resource smart? Yes!

_____

5. Two products that can help with this process are Symantec's Norton Ghost and PowerQuest's Drive Image Pro. A standard disk image file can be kept on the network or written to a rescue CD-R.

Cooperating with Windows

## 26.6 DUAL BOOTING

Thank goodness for geeks. It may have occurred to you to "make the most of your life" by harnessing the power of more than one operating system on your PC. Fortunately, it is possible to "dual boot," meaning that you can choose one of several operating systems at boot time. Linux and Windows are a popular combo, especially among folks, like programmers, who must switch rapidly between environments. In some cases, it's even possible to share the same filesystems among the installed OSes. Read all about setting up a dual boot configuration page 20.

## 26.7 RUNNING WINDOWS APPLICATIONS UNDER UNIX

Many versions of UNIX can run Windows applications... kind of. It's done in a variety of ways, but they all generally boil down to creating a "virtual machine environment" that, to the application, looks like good ol' Windows. These virtual environments are typically a bit fragile, and they tend to work well only for mainstream apps.

 Two notable packages for Red Hat let you run Windows software directly in the Linux environment. The commercial product VMware (www.vmware.com) turns your entire PC into a virtual machine with the ability to run multiple operating systems at once. Wine (www.winehq.com) provides a Windows API in the Linux environment, allowing you to run applications that don't access any drivers.[6] At the time of this writing, however, Wine is advertised by its creators as "not for regular use, try it if you'll help fix bugs."

 Three packages for Solaris are worth considering. The most entertaining is SunPC, a product sold by Sun that provides an Intel-compatible processor on an SBus card to interpret the PC instructions. Third-party applications for Solaris include SoftWindows from FWB Software (www.fwb.com), a true Windows emulator, and NTRIGUE from Citrix (www.citrix.com), which needs a separate Intel system running NT to support it (it lets users run Windows-based applications on their Java desktops).

 Sun has graciously released StarOffice, a Microsoft Office-like package for Solaris and Linux, free of charge. It includes basic business tools such as a spreadsheet, a word processor, and a simple database application. These tools can read and write files generated by Microsoft Word and Microsoft Excel. See

> http://www.sun.com/products/staroffice

for more information.

## 26.8 PC HARDWARE TIPS

One of the really great things about PC hardware is that it's usually inexpensive. Unfortunately, PC hardware doesn't come to us from an alien planet where the motto is "You pay less, you get more!" Instead, as with most things here on Earth, you get what

---

6. Wine is also available for FreeBSD.

you pay for. But there are some gotchas to watch out for, even when you're paying for the extra-nice gear.

First of all, if you're planning to run an operating system other than Windows on a PC, make sure you check to see what hardware devices are supported. Device manufacturers typically provide Windows drivers for all their fancy new widgets, but those won't do you much good under UNIX. Some vendors have gotten a clue and are at least distributing drivers for Linux now.

Second, keep in mind that performance is based on a variety of factors. These days, processor clock rate is not the limiting factor. It's usually I/O performance that will bring your system to a crawl first. Choose PC hardware that supports the latest and greatest high-performance bus and transfer rates. Pay special attention when buying devices such as disk controllers; make sure that they're designed for true multiuser operating systems and can process more than one "command" simultaneously.

Another gotcha is inexpensive modems that require software on the host computer to do some signal processing. Since it's unlikely that the necessary software will ever be ported to UNIX, you'll need to choose modems that do all their own thinking.

Finally, be aware that prepackaged systems from places like CompUSA are usually designed and optimized to run the operating system that is installed at the factory, right down to special chips on the motherboard. These machines are usually not the best candidates to reinstall with some UNIX variant and use to host your startup .com web site. Consider purchasing production-quality PC hardware from shops that specialize in PC hardware for UNIX, such as Telenet Systems (www.tesys.com) and A2Z Computers (www.a2zcomp.com). These vendors supply industrial-strength hardware with redundant power supplies, extra fans, etc., and will guarantee their systems to work with some versions of UNIX.

# 27 *Policy and Politics*

This chapter covers some nontechnical topics that are often included in a system administrator's repertoire. In addition to discussing various issues of law and policy, we talk about some of the interpersonal aspects of system administration and the political intrigues that occur at UNIX sites.

UNIX and computer networks are both quite young—a mere 25 years old—yet they are a microcosm of social issues that have existed for thousands of years. In many cases, the legal and social institutions of the real world have been slow to adapt to the implications of new technology.

The Internet is well on its way to replacing or at least greatly altering several large pieces of economic infrastructure: the publishing industry, the telecommunications industry, the entertainment industry, the postal service, and middlemen of every stripe and color—travel agents, book sellers, music retailers, stockbrokers, and on and on. In many of these contexts, our technological and financial capabilities seem to have leaped far ahead of the policy infrastructure that's needed to support them.

For example, well-defined laws and conventions exist regarding the privacy, use, and misuse of paper mail. But what about email? Is it private, or does the owner of the disk on which it is stored have a right to read it? If a computer forwards a message, is the computer's owner liable when the message turns out to be libelous or obscene?

The lines regarding intellectual property seem to be getting fuzzier and fuzzier. It's well established that you can let someone listen to your new CD or even loan that CD to a friend. And it's fine to transfer the music to your computer and listen to it that way. But what if you want to play the CD over the Internet from work? What if you let your friend listen that way, too? What if only one of you listens at a time?

Applications such as Napster (napster.com) have pushed this concept of sharing music via the Internet to extremes. Napster turns every user's digital music collection into an Internet server. From a computer science point of view, Napster is an interesting system—it's probably the largest distributed client/server application in existence. As might be expected, however, it has raised a lot of hackles.

Napster hit college campuses in the fall of 1999 and instantly doubled many sites' Internet service bills. Some ISPs threatened to cancel service to customers who used it. The music industry has sued Napster for violation of copyright laws. As of this writing, the situation has snowballed into a kind of Gordian lawsuit involving many different parties. Somehow, we doubt that the resolution of this situation will shed much light on the general issues that it raises.

As might be expected given the uncertainty surrounding these issues, many sites (not to mention governments) lack a well-defined policy for dealing with them.

## 27.1  POLICY AND PROCEDURE

While researching this chapter, we talked to bigshots in the system administration world, in computer security, in the standards community, and in computer law. We were surprised that they all mentioned "signed, written policy" as being essential to a healthy organization.

Policies and procedures should be written down, approved by management, and checked by lawyers. It's preferable that this preparation be completed *before* the documents need to be used to deal with a thorny problem. Several different policy documents should exist:

- Administrative service policies
- Rights and responsibilities of users
- Policies regarding sysadmins (users with special privileges)
- Guest account policy

Procedures in the form of checklists or recipes can be used to codify existing practice. They are useful both for new sysadmins and for old hands. Several benefits of standard procedures are:

- The chores are always done in the same way.
- Checklists reduce the likelihood of errors or forgotten steps.
- It's faster for the sysadmin to work from a recipe.
- The changes are self-documenting.
- Written procedures provide a measurable standard of correctness.

Today, UNIX is replacing the big mainframes of the past and performing mission-critical functions in the corporate world. In these big UNIX shops, checklists, often called "run books," serve as the documentation for common tasks. They're usually kept on-line and also in the form of printed manuals. The sysadmins that write and maintain the run books are often a layer away from the support crew that uses them, but such organization and standardization pays off in the long run.

Here are some common tasks for which you might want to set up procedures:

- Adding a host
- Adding a user
- Localizing a machine
- Setting up TCP wrappers on a machine
- Setting up backups for a new machine
- Securing a new machine
- Restarting a complicated piece of software
- Reviving a web site that is not responding or not serving any data
- Unjamming and restarting a printer
- Upgrading the operating system
- Installing a software package
- Installing software from the net
- Upgrading critical software (**sendmail**, **gcc**, **named**, etc.)
- Backing up and restoring files
- Performing emergency shutdowns (all hosts, all but important hosts, etc.)

Many issues sit squarely between policy and procedure. For example:

- Who can have an account?
- What happens when they leave?

The resolutions of such issues need to be written down so that you can stay consistent and avoid falling prey to the well-known, four-year-old's ploy of "Mommy said no, let's go ask Daddy!" Often, the "if" portion is the policy and the "how" portion is the procedure.

Some policy decisions will be dictated by the software you are running or by the policies of external groups, such as ISPs. Some policies are mandatory if the privacy of your users' data is to be protected. We call these topics "nonnegotiable policy."

In particular, we believe that Internet addresses, hostnames, UIDs, GIDs, and usernames should all be managed on a site-wide basis. Some sites (multinational corporations, for example) are clearly too large to implement this policy, but if you can swing it, site-wide management makes things a lot simpler. Tools that facilitate the management of hosts and user accounts across administrative domains are available from the net. Our crufty old versions, **addhost** and **adduser**, are not sterling examples of the genre, but they're still in use and are available from ftp.xor.com if you can't find anything better.

We strongly believe that logins should *never* be shared. It is a lot easier to enforce this policy if the temptation to share is removed. We used to maintain a guest machine with a liberal account creation policy as an easy alternative to clandestine sharing, but now with free email accounts available from several sources (AOL, Hotmail, Yahoo, et al.) and public terminals everywhere (libraries, Internet cafes, etc.) we no longer find this service to be necessary.

Other important policy issues that may have a larger scope than just your local sysadmin group are:

- Handling of security break-ins
- Filesystem export controls
- Password selection criteria
- Removal of logins for cause
- Copyrighted material (MP3s and DVDs, for example)
- Software piracy

Maintaining good channels of communication among administrative groups at a large site can prevent problems and help to develop trust and cooperation. Consider throwing a party as a communication vehicle. Some sysadmin groups use an IRC-like MUD or MOO as a communication vehicle. It can get very chatty, but if used properly can make your organization run more smoothly, especially if some staff work off-site or from home.

### Security policies

What do you want to protect? Your data? Your hardware? Your ability to recover quickly after a disaster? You must consider several tradeoffs when designing a security policy for your site:

- Services offered vs. security provided (more services = less secure)
- Ease of use and convenience vs. security (security = 1/convenience)
- Cost of security vs. risk (cost) of loss

RFC2196, the *Site Security Handbook*, is a 75-page document written in 1997 by a subgroup of the Internet Engineering Task Force (IETF). It advises sysadmins on various security issues, user policies, and procedures. It does not include a recipe for securing an Internet site, but it does contain some valuable information. The last 15 pages are a wonderful collection of both on-line and published references.

RFC2196 suggests that your policy documents include the following points:

- *Purchasing guidelines* for hardware and software. It can be a big win to involve sysadmins in the procurement process because they often know about hardware quirks, software limitations, and support issues that are not advertised by the vendors' marketing teams.

- A *privacy policy* that sets expectations regarding the monitoring of users' email and keystrokes and policies for dealing with user files.

- An *access policy*: who can have access, what they can do with their access, what hardware and software they can install, etc. This document should include the same warnings about authorized use and line monitoring that are included in the privacy policy.

- An *accountability policy* that spells out the responsibilities of both users and sysadmins.

- An *authentication policy* that sets guidelines for passwords and remote access.

- An *availability policy* that describes when the system is supposed to be up, lists scheduled maintenance times, gives instructions for reporting problems, and sets expectations regarding response times.

- A *maintenance policy* that includes rules about outsourcing and specifies procedures for giving access to third-party maintenance personnel.

Noticeably missing from the RFC2196 list is an authorization policy that specifies who can authorize new accounts and extended privileges. The original *Site Security Handbook*, RFC1244, contained lists of concrete issues rather than types of policies, which might be a bit more useful from the sysadmin's point of view. The newer RFC includes recommendations for each type of service a machine might run and describes the problems of the services and potential solutions.

Whatever policies you adopt, they must be explicit, written down, understood, and signed by all users and sysadmins. Enforcement must be consistent, even when users are customers who are paying for computing services. Failure to apply policies uniformly weakens their legal and perceived validity.

### User policy agreements

At the University of Colorado's computer science department, user policy is delivered in the form of an initial shell that prints the policy and requires users to agree to and "sign" it before they can get a real shell and use their accounts. This scheme saves time and hassle, but check with *your own* lawyers before implementing it at your site.

Here are some explicit issues that should be addressed in a user policy agreement:

- Sharing accounts with friends and relatives
- Running password crackers[1] on the local **passwd** file
- Running password crackers on other sites' **passwd** files
- Disrupting service
- Breaking into other accounts
- Misusing or forging electronic mail
- Looking at other users' files (if readable? writable? invited?)
- Posting to Usenet (never? with a disclaimer? any time?)
- Importing software from the net (never? always? if the user checks?)
- Using system resources (printers, disk space, modems, CPU)
- Copying licensed software
- Allowing others to copy licensed software
- Copying copyrighted material (music, movies, etc.)
- Conducting illegal activities (fraud, libel, etc.)
- Engaging in activities illegal in some states but not in others (e.g., porn)

---

1. For example, **crack**, which is a program for guessing passwords. See page 666 for more information.

Two sample policy agreements are included on our web site, www.admin.com. One is aimed at undergraduate students in a laboratory where a login is a privilege and not a right. It is the more militant of the two. The other document is for faculty, staff, and graduate students.

As an example of a short and simple policy agreement, we here include the agreement that the computer science department at the University of Melbourne requires students to sign in order to use the university's computers:

*I, the undersigned, HEREBY DECLARE that I will abide by the rules set out below:*

- *I will use the Department's computing and network facilities solely for academic purposes directly related to my study of Computer Science subjects.*

- *I understand that the Department grants computer accounts for the exclusive use of the recipient. Therefore, I will not authorise or facilitate the use of my account or files by any other person, nor will I divulge my password to any other person.*

- *I will not access, or attempt to gain access to any computer, computer account, network or files without proper and explicit authorisation. Such access is illegal under State and Federal laws, and is contrary to University regulations. I will inform the Computer Science Office immediately should I become aware that such access has taken place.*

- *I understand that some software and data that reside on file systems that I may access are protected by copyright and other laws, and also by licenses and other contractual agreements; therefore, I will not breach these restrictions.*

- *I will not use University facilities for obtaining, making, running or distributing unauthorised copies of software.*

- *I will undertake to keep confidential any disclosure to me by the University of software (including methods or concepts used therein) licensed to the University for use on its computers and I hereby indemnify and hold harmless the University against claims of any nature arising from any disclosure on my part to another of the said software in breach of this undertaking.*

- *I undertake to maintain the highest standard of honesty and personal integrity in relation to my usage of the Department's computing and network facilities. I further warrant that I will avoid any actions in relation to my usage of the Department's computing or network facilities that may bring any disrepute upon the Department or the University.*

*I understand that I am bound by Regulation 8.1.R7 of the University of Melbourne (set out in the Student Diary), which also governs and regulates my use of University computing and network facilities.*

*I understand that acting in breach of any of the principles set out above will incur severe penalties including failure in an assignment or a subject, the suspension or withdrawal of access to University computing facilities, suspension or expulsion from the University, imposition of fines, and/or legal action taken under the Crimes (Computer) Act 1988.*[2]

Take special note of the weasel words about honesty, personal integrity, and not bringing the University into disrepute. Vague requirements such as these give you some room for later maneuvering and help to cover any specifics that may have been inadvertently left out of the policy. Although their true legal weight is probably negligible, it's a good idea to include such requirements in your policy agreements.

### Sysadmin policy agreements

A policy document for sysadmins (and others with special status) must set guidelines for using root privileges and for honoring users' privacy. It is hard to respond to a user's complaint that mail is broken without looking at messages that have bounced. But a copy of the headers is often sufficient to characterize and fix the problem.

*See page 41 for more information about **sudo**.*

If your site uses a tool such as **sudo** for root access, it is essential that your sysadmins use good passwords and not share their logins with *anyone*. Consider running **crack** on sysadmins' passwords regularly. It's also essential that they not execute **sudo tcsh** (token use of **sudo**) because that defeats **sudo**'s logging feature.

For some sysadmins, the urge to show off rootly powers overcomes common sense. Gently suggest other career alternatives.

At some sites, having the root password is a status symbol, perhaps more valuable than a key to the executive washroom. Often, the people that have the password are engineers that don't need it or should not have it. One site we know offered all engineers the root password, but stipulated that any takers would have to wear a beeper and help others when necessary. Requests plummeted.

Another technique that we have used with good success is to seal the root password in an envelope and hide it in a spot known to the sysadmin staff. Sysadmins generally use **sudo** to do their work; if they actually need the root password for some reason, they open the envelope. The root password is then changed and a new envelope is stashed. It's not difficult to steam open an envelope, but only sysadmins have physical access to the hiding place, and we trust our staff to respect the system.

### Policy and procedures for emergency situations

Decide ahead of time who will be in charge in the event of a security incident. Set up a chain of command and keep the names and phone numbers of the principals offline. It may be that the best person to put in charge is a sysadmin from the trenches, not the IT director (who is usually a poor choice for this role).

We are accustomed to using the network to communicate and to access documents. However, these facilities may be unavailable or compromised after an incident. Store

---

2. Keep in mind that this is an Australian law, although similar computer and software-related legislation has been passed in the United States. See page 787.

all the relevant contacts and procedures off-line. Know where to get recent dump tapes and what **restore** command to use without looking at **/etc/dumpdates**. Avoid talking to the media, especially if the incident is unfolding in real time.

Web site hijacking is the latest craze in security break-ins. For the sysadmin at a web hosting company, a hijacking can be a serious event. Phone calls stream in from the customer, from the media, from the company VIPs who just saw the news of the hijacking on CNN. Who will take the calls? What should that person say? Who is in charge? What role does each person play? If you are in a high-visibility business, it's definitely worth thinking through this type of scenario, coming up with some pre-planned answers, and perhaps even having a practice session to work out the details.

Procedures for dealing with a security break-in are outlined in Chapter 21, *Security*, starting on page 680.

### Disaster planning

Planning for a disaster is best accomplished before the disaster hits. An unfortunate disaster fact is that most disasters occur on managers' laptops, and from the sysadmin's point of view, they can yell the loudest. In this section we look at various kinds of disasters, the data you need to gracefully recover, and the important elements of a disaster plan.

There are several kinds of disasters:

- Security breaches (of which 60% originate from within the organization)

- Environmental problems: power spikes and outages, cooling failures, floods, hurricanes, earthquakes, meteors, alien invasions

- Human error: deleted or damaged files and databases, lost configuration information (Does your mirroring system respond so quickly that an error propagates everywhere before you realize what's happened?)

- Spontaneous hardware meltdowns: dead servers, fried hard disks, malfunctioning networks

In all of these situations, you will need access to both on-line and off-line copies of essential information. The on-line copies should be kept on an independent machine if possible, one that has a fairly rich complement of tools, has key sysadmins' environments, runs its own name server, has a complete local **/etc/hosts** file, has no file sharing dependencies, has a printer attached, etc. Here's a list of handy data to keep on the backup machine and in printed form;

- An outline of the disaster procedure: people to call, when to call, what to say
- Service contract phone numbers and customer numbers
- Key local phone numbers: staff, police, fire, boss, employment agency
- Data on hardware and software configurations: partition tables, PC hardware settings, IRQs, DMAs, and the like
- Backup tapes[3] and the backup schedule that produced them

- Network maps
- Software serial numbers, licensing data, and passwords
- Vendor contact info for that emergency disk you need immediately

An important but sometimes unspoken assumption made in most disaster plans is that administration staff will be available to deal with the situation. Unfortunately, people get sick, graduate, go on vacation, and leave for other jobs. It's worth considering what you'd do if you needed extra emergency help. (Not having enough sysadmins around can sometimes constitute an emergency in its own right if your systems are fragile or your users unsophisticated.)

You might try forming a sort of NATO pact with a local consulting company or university that has shareable system administration talent. Of course, you must be willing to share back when your buddies have a problem. Most importantly, don't operate close to the wire in your daily routine. Hire enough system administrators and don't expect them to work 12-hour days.

Test your disaster recovery plan before you need to use it. If you amassed a lot of Y2K supplies, some items (such as flashlights) may still be useful for more generic disasters. We found a really neat kind of flashlight that plugs into a wall socket. While the power is on, it stays at full charge. When the power goes out, it lights up so you can find it in the dark.

Test your generators and UPSs. Verify that everything you care about is plugged into a UPS, that the UPS batteries are healthy, and that the failover mechanism works. To test an individual UPS, just unplug it from the wall. To make sure that your critical equipment is properly UPSified, you may have to throw the circuit breakers and make sure your emergency configuration is really as functional as you had planned.

Most power hits are of short duration, but plan for two hours of battery life so that you have time to shut down machines properly in the event of a longer outage. Some UPSs have a serial port or Ethernet interface that you can use to initiate a graceful shutdown of noncritical machines after 5 minutes (configurable) of power outage.

Take advantage of power outages to do any 5-minute upgrades that you already have planned, such as adding a disk to a server. You're down anyway, so people expect to be inconvenienced. In some shops, an extra 5 minutes during a power outage is easier to accept than a scheduled downtime with a week's notice. If you have old machines that you think are not in use anymore, leave them turned off until someone complains. It might not be until weeks later—or never—that the "missing" machine is noticed.

*See page 749 for more information about environment issues.*
Cooling systems often have a notification system that can call you if the temperature gets too high. Tune the value of "too high" so that you have time to get in after the cooling system pages you before machines start to fry; we use 76 degrees instead of 90. Keep a mechanical or battery operated thermometer in the machine room—losing power means that you lose all those nifty electronic indicators that normally tell you the temperature.

---

3. Backups can be subpoenaed; you might want to expire some backup images.

A large U.S. government lab recently built a fancy new machine room and filled it with a 256-node Alpha cluster for running large scientific models. Everything was plugged into a UPS, and all the facilities were state of the art. Unfortunately, a minor power outage brought the center down for four hours. Why? The PC that controlled the HVAC (air conditioner) was not on the UPS. It failed and messed up the air conditioning system. Test carefully.

### Miscellaneous tidbits

ISPs are merging and being acquired at a fantastic rate. These mergers have demolished many companies' carefully laid plans for maintaining redundant connections to the Internet. A post-merger ISP will often consolidate circuits that belonged to the independent companies. Customers that formerly had independent paths to the Internet may then have both connections running through a single conduit and once again be at the mercy of a single backhoe fiber cut.

When CNN or Slashdot announces that your web site is down, the same effect that makes highway traffic slow down to look at an accident at the side of the road causes your Internet traffic to increase enormously, often to the point of breaking whatever it was that you just fixed. If your web site cannot handle an increase in traffic of 25% or more, consider having your load balancing software route excess connections to a server that presents a single page that says "Sorry, we are too busy to handle your request right now."

*See page 668 for more information about **tripwire**.*

Use **tripwire** to keep abreast of what your sysadmins are doing, especially if different groups are responsible for different aspects of the same machine. Oracle database patches and OS patches can conflict with each other without either group realizing that they should ask what the other group has been up to. **tripwire** snooping is also useful if you are a sysadmin service organization and you find yourself having to clean up after a customer's somewhat clueless in-house sysadmin. It can clearly identify what has changed and when, making it easier to respond if the local sysadmin tries to blame you for his mistakes.

## 27.2  LEGAL ISSUES

The U.S. federal government and several states have laws regarding computer crime. At the federal level, there are two from the early 1990s and two more recent ones:

- The Federal Communications Privacy Act
- The Computer Fraud and Abuse Act
- The No Electronic Theft Act
- The Digital Millennium Copyright Act

As we start the new millennium, the big issues are the liability of sysadmins, network operators, and web hosting sites; strong cryptography for electronic commerce; copyright issues; and privacy issues.

### Liability

System administrators are generally not held liable for content stored by users on the machines for which they are responsible. ISPs typically have an appropriate use policy (AUP) that they require anyone connecting to them to "flow down" to their customers. Such AUPs assign responsibility for users' actions to the users themselves, not to the ISP or the ISP's upstream provider. These policies have been used to attempt to control spam (unsolicited commercial email) and to protect ISPs in cases where customers stored child pornography in their accounts. Check the laws in your area; your mileage may vary.

A good example, but one that is too long to include here, is the AUP at www.mibh.net. It includes the usual lawyerish words about illegal actions, intellectual property violations, and appropriate use. It also includes a specific list of prohibited activities as well as enforcement policies, procedures for registering complaints, and a statement regarding liability.

### Encryption

The need for encryption in electronic commerce and communication is clear. However, encryption is against the law in some countries. Law enforcement agencies do not want citizens to be able to store data that they (the police) cannot decrypt.

In the United States, the laws regarding encryption are changing. In the past, it was illegal to export any form of strong encryption technology. Companies had to create two versions of software that incorporated encryption: one for sale in the domestic market and a crippled version for export. The patent absurdity of this policy (the rest of the world has had cryptographic technology for a very long time) and the needs of electronic commerce eventually motivated the government to change its stance. Although the export restrictions are not yet completely gone, the situation in the United States is better than it used to be.

Another side effect of the former U.S. laws is that many encryption-related software development projects are based in other countries. The IETF has done standards work in the area of end-to-end secure communications at the protocol level—the IPSEC effort—and vendors are beginning to ship systems that include it. The authentication part is typically bundled, but the encryption part is often installed separately. This architecture preserves flexibility for countries in which encryption cannot be used.

### Copyright

The music and movie industries have noticed with some consternation that home computers are capable of playing music from CDs and viewing movies on DVD. It's kind of an opportunity for them and kind of a threat, particularly with the prospect of widespread Napsterization drawing ever closer.

The DVD format uses an encryption key to scramble the contents of a disk by a technique called CSS, the Content Scrambling System. The idea was to limit the ability to play DVDs to licensed and approved players. Consumer DVD players include the appropriate decoding key, as do the software players that come with most DVD computer drives.

A student from Norway and two as-yet-unidentified European hackers reverse-engineered the CSS encryption process and posted a program called DeCSS to the web. The program did not bypass the DVD encryption scheme; it simply used the decryption key from a legitimate Windows player to decode the DVD data stream and save it to disk.

The Norwegian student is now under criminal indictment in Norway, and the Motion Picture Association of American and the DVD Copy Control Association have both filed lawsuits against numerous distributors of the DeCSS software. The lawsuits allege that the defendants were engaged not in theft of copyrighted materials, but in the distribution of trade secrets and "circumvention of copy protection," which was made illegal in the United States by the Digital Millennium Copyright Act of 1998.

These legal cases offer up a steaming smorgasbord of some of the murkiest issues in computer law, so they're being watched with great interest by Electronic Frontier Foundation and computer law types. See the most excellent Openlaw DVD/DeCSS FAQ maintained by Rob Warren at www.cssfaq.org for more opinions and details.

CyberPatrol makes Internet filtering software that religious groups are promoting to parents, schools, and libraries to protect children from objectionable content. A Canadian and a Swede wrote a tool called **cphack** that enabled them to decrypt the software's blocking list to see exactly which web sites were being blocked, how high the error rate was, and what nonobvious agendas might be present. They reported, for example, that anyone who criticized the software was blocked in all categories.

Mattel, which owns CyberPatrol, sued the authors of the tool, claiming that the CyberPatrol license forbids reverse engineering. Mattel obtained a preliminary injunction against the distribution of the software, but unfortunately the case never came to trial; it was settled just before the trial was scheduled to start. The authors of the tool sold it to Mattel for $1 and agreed to a consent decree. It seemed that the authors had caved in (lawyers' bills aside!), but looking closely, it appears that Mattel is now attempting to assert ownership of a tool that was originally released under the GNU Public License.

Mattel hoped to use its newly acquired intellectual property rights to prevent **cphack** from being copied on the Internet (as if that would ever work). But because **cphack**'s authors released it under the GPL, unlimited distribution of the original program is permitted even if Mattel owns the copyright. Once a piece of software is publicly released under liberal terms such as those of the GPL, it can't be "unreleased."

## Privacy

Privacy has always been difficult to safeguard, but with the rise of the Internet it's in more danger than ever. During a recent incident at the University of Michigan, for example, the medical records of patients in the University of Michigan health care system were inadvertently published on the Internet. The data was freely available for months until a student noticed the oversight.

Another big privacy scandal, this one intentional, has involved DoubleClick.net, an advertising agency that provides many of the banner ads shown on web pages. DoubleClick promised for years that users in their system were never tracked or identified. Recently, however, they purchased a company that does data mining and began gathering data from each user that visited a web page containing a DoubleClick ad. The furor that ensued caused DoubleClick to withdraw the project for now and to hire two high-powered lawyers into "privacy" positions to find a way for DoubleClick to legally stalk the users who are subjected to their ads.

DoubleClick is small potatoes compared to a new threat to privacy from the combination of our ISPs and a company called Predictive Networks. According to the PRIVACY Forum Digest, Predictive, with help from ISPs, plans to collect the URLs you visit, the keywords you type into search engines, and other information by watching your work on the web. From this data, they will build a digital "signature" of you and use that profile to target Internet content and ads just to you.

Predictive says that your information is "anonymous" and that you can trust everyone involved: Predictive's employees, the ISPs' employees, the advertisers, the content providers—everyone. You can request a copy of your digital signature, but you might have to pay for it. You can also opt out of this "service," but your Internet connectivity through that ISP might cost more or be rescinded. As of this writing, Predictive's web site (www.predictivenetworks.com) still has no privacy policy and not much hard information about what they really do. The PRIVACY Forum Digest article (V09, #13, www.vortex.com) includes more details on their plans and on their position with respect to Internet users' privacy.

### Policy enforcement

Log files may prove to you beyond a shadow of a doubt that person X did bad thing Y, but to a court it is all just hearsay evidence. Protect yourself with written policies. Log files sometimes include timestamps, which are useful but not necessarily admissible as evidence unless your computer is running the Network Time Protocol (NTP) to keep its clock synced with reality.

You may need a security policy in order to prosecute someone for misuse. It should include a statement such as this: *Unauthorized use of University computing systems may involve not only transgression of University policy but also a violation of state and federal laws. Unauthorized use is a crime and may involve criminal and civil penalties; it will be prosecuted to the full extent of the law.*

We advise you to put a warning in **/etc/motd** (the message of the day file) that advises users of your snooping policy. Ours reads:

```
Your keyboard input may be monitored in the event of a real or
perceived security incident.
```

Some connections do not see the message of the day; for example, **ftp** sessions and **rsh**ed copies of **xterm**. Users can also suppress the message by creating a file called **.hushlogin** in their home directories. You may want to ensure that users see the notification at least once by including it in the startup files you give to new users.

Be sure to specify that users indicate acknowledgment of your written policy by using their accounts. Explain where users can get additional copies of policy documents and post key documents on an appropriate bulletin board. Also include the specific penalty for noncompliance (deletion of the account, etc.).

Suppose something naughty is posted to news or the web from your site. If you are CompuServe (now part of AOL), this is a problem. In a case called *Cubby v. CompuServe*, something libelous was posted. The judge ruled that CompuServe was not guilty, but found the moderator of the newsgroup to which it was posted negligent. The more you try to control information, the more liable you become.

This principle is beautifully illustrated by the story of a Texas business founded by an enterprising computer science student of ours, Cheeser. He wrote Perl scripts to mine the Usenet news groups, collect naughty pictures, and build a subscription web site based on that content. He charged $12/month to subscribers and was raking in money hand over fist.

Cheeser tried to be a responsible pornographer and did not subscribe to newsgroups known to carry child pornography. He also monitored several newsgroups that were on the edge, sometimes with illegal content, sometimes not. This minimal oversight and his choice of a conservative county in Texas in which to locate his business were his downfall.

Acting on an anonymous tip (perhaps from a competitor), the local police confiscated his computers. Sure enough, they found an instance of child pornography that had been posted to one of the "safer" newsgroups. The criminal case never went to trial, but during the plea bargaining it became clear that the judge thought Cheeser was guilty—not because he had created the content, but because he was not a good enough censor. The implication was that if Cheeser had done no censoring at all, he would have been legally OK. Never censor your porn.

*See page 698 for more information about Usenet news.* If your site provides news to its users, you may be safest if your site subscribes to all the newsgroups. Do not censor postings or base your pruning of the newsgroup hierarchy on content. However, a technical reason for pruning (such as a lack of disk space) is probably OK. If you must prune, do it high in the tree. Removing all of alt is easier to justify than removing alt.sex.fetish.feet but not alt.sex.bestiality.hamsters.

This principle also applies to other interactions with the outside world. From a legal standpoint, the more you monitor your users' use of the Internet, the more you may be liable for their actions or postings. If you are aware of an illegal or actionable activity, you have a legal duty to investigate it and to report your findings to Big Brother.

For this reason, some sites limit the data that they log, the length of time for which log files are kept, and the amount of log file history kept on backup tapes. Some software packages (e.g., the Squid web cache) help with the implementation of this policy by including levels of logging that help the sysadmin debug problems but do not violate users' privacy.

System administrators should be familiar with all relevant corporate or university policies and should make sure the policies are followed. Unenforced or inconsistent policies are worse than none, from both a practical and legal point of view.

### Software licenses

Many sites have paid for K copies of a software package and have N copies in daily use, where K << N. Getting caught in this situation could be damaging to the company, probably more damaging than the cost of those N-minus-K other licenses. Other sites have received a demo copy of an expensive software package and hacked it (reset the date on the machine, found the license key, etc.) to make it continue working after the expiration of the demo period. How do you as a sysadmin deal with requests to violate license agreements and make copies of software on unlicensed machines? What do you do when you find that machines for which you are responsible are running pirated software? What about shareware that was never paid for?

It's a very tough call. Management will often not back you up in your requests that unlicensed copies of software be either removed or paid for. Often, it is a sysadmin who signs the agreement to remove the demo copies after a certain date, but a manager who makes the decision not to remove them.

Even if the jobs is the best one you've ever had, your personal and professional integrity are on the line. Fortunately, in today's job market, quality sysadmins are in high demand and your job search will be short. We are aware of several cases in which a sysadmin's immediate manager would not deal with the situation and told the sysadmin not to rock the boat. The sysadmin then wrote a memo to the boss asking to correct the situation and documenting the number of copies of the software that were licensed and the number that were in use. The admin quoted a few phrases from the license agreement and cc'ed the president of the company and his boss' managers. In one case this procedure worked and the sysadmin's manager was let go. In another case, the sysadmin quit when even higher management refused to do the right thing.

### Spam: unsolicited commercial email

Advertisers, marketing folks, and con artists have flocked to the Internet in droves to take advantage of "free" email communication. The cost of junk mailing an ad to thousands of people is tiny compared to the cost of sending traditional paper mail, and the response rate is apparently better. This scenario creates two big losers: consumers, who have to wade through mounds of spam every day, and ISPs, who pay for the traffic on their networks.

We won't go into the technical details of spam tracing and spam fighting in detail here. That subject is covered more thoroughly in Chapter 19, *Electronic Mail*, starting on page 595. However, we will mention a few of the legal aspects.

The United States has laws, mostly at the state level, that have been used to successfully prosecute the senders of spam. In at least one case, the senders were required to pay for each piece of mail sent because the spam interfered with a business's normal operations. Unfortunately, most recipients of spam just delete it and don't bother to try to track down the spammer and retaliate.

ISPs do try to keep spammers from using their facilities, not only because of the bandwidth they use but also because the spam typically violates the appropriate use policy of their upstream provider and thus puts them in jeopardy of losing their own network connection.

You can find a useful page of links to spam-related resources and legislation at

> http://www.elsop.com/wrc/nospam.htm

## 27.3 SYSADMIN SURVEYS

In 1992, Rob Kolstad and Jeff Polk surveyed attendees at LISA (USENIX's Large Installation System Administration conference, which denies that it's only for large sites) to determine how much time they spent on sysadmin chores and what level of support was required to maintain a site. Since then, SAGE, the System Administrators' Guild associated with the USENIX association, has performed several similar surveys, usually focusing on salary information. In 1999, SANS, the System Administration, Networking, and Security Institute, also did a salary survey. The results of these surveys are excerpted in the next sections.

### SAGE salary survey

At the LISA conference in the late fall of 1999, SAGE administered a sysadmin salary profile survey. The full report is available from www.usenix.org/sage. SAGE members can download an Acrobat file by supplying their membership number and password; others must register and are then emailed the file. SAGE does not sell your address but might send you information about their conferences and publications. (Actually, you can opt out of their spam when you register.)

Here are some interesting data points from the 1999 results, which incorporated responses from 2,300 system administrators who attended the conference or filled out the survey form on the web. Most of the respondents were full-time sysadmins who considered system administration their primary line of work. About 80% were from the United States; the remainder were from 48 different countries.

- The median salary was over $60,000 in the United States. The 90th percentile of earnings was almost $90,000.

- Over 86% received raises in 1999, ranging from 8% for those staying in the same job to 23% for those changing jobs and employers.

- Over 70% of organizations cannot find enough sysadmins—the hunt is on.

- Bonuses are not yet common for sysadmins, nor is overtime pay.

- Salaried sysadmins work 47.0[4] hours per week, on average.

- The most common operating systems were (in order): Solaris, Windows NT, Linux, Windows 95 and 98, HP-UX, SunOS, AIX, IRIX, MacOS, True 64 UNIX, and FreeBSD.

- Administration of NT and BSD systems was correlated with lower salaries.

- Education does not correlate strongly with salary. A BS degree was only worth an additional $6K over a high school degree.

- Years of experience did correlate strongly with salary; the most common value was 5 years of experience.

- Over a third of the sysadmins had been at their current job less than a year.

- Over 80% of respondents expected to still be sysadmins in 5 years. This is a nice change; system administration used to be the bottom of the barrel job that you did while waiting to be promoted to software developer. But some folks *like* getting more context switches in a day than a developer gets in a year.

- Less than 13% of the sysadmins were women.

- Almost 50% of the sysadmins were between 25 and 35 years old, with less that 1% below 20 or above 55.

- The most bothersome and problematic parts of the sysadmin's job were (in order of popularity): dealing with management, work load and hours, and office politics and bureaucracy.

When reviewing the survey form, most system administrators realized that they really did not know exactly how they spent their day. Most sites felt understaffed. It doesn't take too many whiny users for an insufficient user-to-sysadmin ratio to become oppressive.

### SANS salary survey

The SANS survey for 1999 was administered over the web; about 11,000 people participated. The respondents were categorized as system administrators, network administrators, security administrators, database administrators, security consultants, or security auditors.

Many of the questions matched those of the SAGE survey, but direct comparisons are difficult because of the wider range of participants. Another difficulty in direct comparison is that SAGE used median statistics and SANS used averages. The SANS data presented histograms for some items, and in those cases we have converted to median statistics so a more accurate comparison with the SAGE data can be made.

Of those completing the survey, 84% were from the United States, with about 50% labeling themselves as system administrators and another 24% as network adminis-

---

4. The number for the 1992 survey was 47.5 hours per week, although that survey disregarded responses greater than 70 hours/week on the theory that those numbers were not sustainable.

trators. The other categories were much smaller percentages. Here are some of the more interesting results:

- The OS type mix was quite different: 63% NT, followed by Solaris at 14%, Novell NetWare at 6%, and everything else below 3%. Linux was the primary operating system for only 2.1% of those completing the survey.

- The peak of the experience curve was at 3–4 years, instead of 5 as for the LISA/SAGE crowd.

- The median salary was in the low 50s for NT admins and mid 60s for UNIX admins. Gender cost female NT admins $2K and female UNIX admins $4K (normalized to similar education and experience levels). 12% of the respondents were women.

- A BS degree was worth $5K to an NT admin and $8K to a UNIX admin; a master's degree added another $5K–$8K.

- Novice, junior, and senior administrators received salaries that increased with expertise, but there was some compression on the top end.

- The average work week was 46.8 hours, with NT and UNIX admins reporting almost identical values.

## 27.4  SCOPE OF SERVICE

The services provided by an administrative support group must be clearly defined, or users' expectations will not match reality. Here are some issues to consider:

- Response time
- Service during weekends and off-hours
- House calls (support for machines at home)
- Weird (one of a kind) hardware
- Ancient hardware
- Supported operating systems
- Standard configurations
- Special-purpose software
- Janitorial chores (cleaning screens and keyboards)

In addition to knowing what services are provided, users must also know about the priority scheme used to manage the work queue. Priority schemes always have wiggle room, but try to design one that covers most situations with few or no exceptions. Some priority-related variables are:

- The number of users affected
- The importance of the affected users
- The loudness of the affected users (squeaky wheels)
- Importance of the deadline (late homework vs. research grant proposal that partially funds the sysadmin group)

Policy and Politics

Our support group for faculty, staff, and graduate students has developed a set of documents that delineates their services, priority scheme, and contact mechanisms. This group of customers contains several levels of importance and squeakiness. The policy documents have been used for a few years with good, but not perfect, results. Copies are available from www.admin.com.

## 27.5  TROUBLE-REPORTING SYSTEMS

Our trouble-reporting system uses an email alias called "trouble." At one time we were bombarded with trouble reports that were either incomplete or incomprehensible. We wrote a script that asked the user specific questions, such as

- On what host does the problem occur?
- Is the problem repeatable?
- How important is it that the problem be fixed immediately?

The user rebellion started about an hour later, and within a day we had backed the system out. Its only value seemed to be that with the furor over the script, many users actually read the questions it was asking and the quality of our free-form trouble reports improved.

Another site dealt with this problem by sending out a message that explained what information is important in a trouble report and showed examples of useless reports. When a useless report was received, it was answered with an apology ("Sorry, I don't have enough information to…") and a copy of the explanatory message. The users caught on quickly.

You need to use some sort of trouble ticketing system or problems will either receive five answers (the easy ones) or no answers (the hard ones). The system should log resolved trouble messages and perhaps send a copy of the resolution to novice sysadmins and trainees. The log files become a useful source of data to mine during preparation of management reports (especially when you need to justify more administrative staff), and the copies to new sysadmins let them familiarize themselves with your site's most common problems and their solutions. They also demonstrate the appropriate tone to use in messages to users.

We used a home-grown trouble ticketing system called **queuemh** or **troubmh** for years. Our current favorite is **wreq** (www.math.duke.edu/~yu/wreq). **wreq** is based on **req** from the University of Maryland, to which it adds extra functionality and a web interface. It has almost as many features as the commercial offering Remedy, but is easier to configure and use and easier to fit into your budget (free!).

**wreq**'s graphs of tickets submitted, resolved, and rotting are especially useful for both sysadmins and management. They can help you detect long-term trends. **wreq**'s main disadvantage is its poor (ever-so-close to nonexistent, really) documentation.

## 27.6  MANAGING MANAGEMENT

It's essential for your managers to respect and support you. Management support for tough security policies is sometimes the hardest to get. Tightening security invariably means inconveniencing users, and the users usually outweigh you both in number and in whining ability. Make sure that any security change that impacts users (changing from **telnet** to **ssh**, converting from passwords to RSA keys, etc.) is announced well in advance, is well documented, and is well supported at changeover time. Documentation should be easy to understand and should provide cookbook-type recipes for dealing with the new system. Allow for extra staffing hours when you first cut over to the new system so that you can deal with the panicked users who didn't read their email or the **motd**.

Upper management often has no idea what system administrators do. Keeping a diary for a week that records what you do and how long it takes will surprise even you. This kind of documentation is essential when you campaign for additional staff or equipment. It can also be a source of power in day-to-day political squabbles. It may be wise to keep good records even in the absence of a particular goal.

Managers, especially nontechnical managers, are often way off in their estimates of the difficulty of a task or the amount of time it will take to complete. This is especially true of troubleshooting tasks.

Try to set expectations realistically. Double or triple your time estimates for large or crucial tasks. If an upgrade is done in two days instead of three, most users will thank you instead of cursing you as they might have if your estimate had been one day.

It is sometimes hard for a sysadmin to get a written policy put in place. In that case, document existing practices and policy. For example, "We have 8 licenses for Excel and 47 copies installed." Ask for money to buy more copies. If this fails, write a memo documenting the problem with a copy to upper management. Fortunately, good system administrators are in demand, so your job search should be short.

## 27.7  HIRING, FIRING, AND TRAINING

There are two approaches to building a staff of system administrators:

- Hire experienced people.
- Grow your own.

Experienced people usually come up to speed faster, but you always want them to unlearn certain things. To do their job, they need root access. But you do not know them and may not be willing to put your company's data in their hands immediately.

It takes quite a bit of time and effort to train a sysadmin, and production networks are not an ideal training ground. But given the right person (smart, interested, curious, careful, etc.), the end result is often better.

Policy and Politics

We have developed two evaluation tools for experienced applicants. We used to call them "tests," but have found that some institutions are not allowed to test applicants. We no longer test; we evaluate and assess.

The first not-a-test, a written evaluation, asks applicants to rate their experience and knowledge of various system and networking tasks. The scale of familiarity is 0 to 4:

- Never heard of it (0)
- Heard of it, never did it (1)
- Have done it, could do it with supervision (2)
- Could do it without supervision (3)
- Know it well, could teach someone else to do it (4)

Embedded among the questions are several ringers. For example, in the hardware section is a question about RS-232 connectors followed by one about "MX connectors."[5] These bogus questions let you measure the BS factor in an applicant's answers. A 3 on the MX connectors would be suspect. After the not-a-test, you might ask innocently, "So, what do *you* use MX connectors for?"

The second evaluation is designed for use during a telephone interview. Questions are set up to elicit quick answers from applicants who know their stuff. We score +1 for a right answer, 0 for an "I don't know," and -1 for obvious BS or typing **man xxx** in the background.

These two schemes have been quite good metrics for us. The percentage of bogus questions we use is determined by our state hiring folks; one or two questions aren't enough. Keep in mind that these assessments do not address some of the most important issues regarding a prospective sysadmin:

- Will they get along with other members of the team?
- How is their user interface?
- Will they take direction?
- Are they on a growth curve with a positive slope?

A personal interview might answer some of these questions. A telephone conversation with references usually tells you more. Listen very carefully; many people do not like to say anything bad about a former employee or coworker, so they find clever ways to tell you (if you are listening carefully) that a potential employee has problems. Be very suspicious if the applicant does not include recent employers as references.

If you make a hiring mistake, fire early. You may miss a few late bloomers, but keeping people who are not pulling their own weight will alienate your other staff members as they take up the slack and clean up after the losers. In many organizations it is very hard to fire someone, especially after the initial evaluation period is over. Make sure that initial evaluations are taken seriously. Later, you may have to collect data showing incompetence, give formal warnings, set performance goals, and so on.

---

5. MX refers to a mail exchanger record in DNS, not to a serial connector.

The evaluation assessments we use are on-line at www.admin.com. Can you find all the bogus questions?

### Attitude adjustment

System administrators often forget that they are service providers and that users are their customers. Many sysadmins secretly hold the opinion that the systems are theirs to play with and that users are a regrettable nuisance.

Sysadmins today are respected, treated as skilled professionals, and paid well. In the past they have been looked upon as electronic janitors several castes below developers and engineers. But their leverage (fix the compiler for one engineer and it's fixed for many more) has changed their status in most organizations. They still secretly have their clueless user awards and other types of harmless fun, but they are much more respected than they were 10 years ago. Managers would do well to ask the sysadmin staff their opinion of intended promotees; a user's interaction with the sysadmin staff is often very revealing of that user's creativity, independence, and problem-solving abilities.

Some of the qualities of a good system administrator are contradictory. A sysadmin must be brash enough to try innovative solutions when stuck on a problem but must also be careful enough not to try anything truly destructive. Interpersonal skills and problem-solving skills are both important, yet they seem to lie on orthogonal axes among many of the sysadmins we have known. One of our reviewers suggested that a "personable sysadmin" was an oxymoron.

Microsoft's "adminless" systems will never replace sysadmins—someone still has to hit <Return> or click OK and take the blame!

### Operator wars

New sysadmins often become the victims of what we call "operator wars," in which more experienced users alias **ls** to **logout** in the novices' environments, send them mail bombs, and generally harass them and their inexperience. Sysadmins who forget to log out are especially tempting victims.

This phenomenon is more prevalent at universities than at commercial sites, but it probably happens everywhere to some degree. Although it seems fun, it can easily be carried too far and should be strictly discouraged. There are enough real whammos for a new sysadmin without adding more, even in jest.

### Iterative refinement

A sysadmin will often think that a problem has been fixed, only to receive several more trouble reports as the task slowly gets done completely and correctly. This process can occur because the user who first reported the problem did not describe it clearly or suggested the wrong solution. Equally often, it can happen because the sysadmin did not test the solution carefully.

Some common complaints include:

- Man pages and documentation not installed for new software
- Software not installed everywhere
- Software that turns out to be owned by the sysadmin or installed with permissions that are wrong.

Testing is boring, but a busy sysadmin can cut productivity in half by skipping it. Every trouble report costs time and effort, both for users and for the sysadmin. The job is not done until all operational glitches have surfaced and been taken care of.

A common problem is that a user reports that "X doesn't work on machine Y" and the sysadmin goes to machine Y and tries command X and it works fine. The trouble report answer comes back "works for me" with a bit of an attitude attached. If the sysadmin actually tried the command as the user who submitted the report (for example, executing **sudo su** - *username* in front of the command), he might nail the exact problem on the first try. The "-" argument to **su** causes the resulting shell to use the environment of the user you are **su**ing to. Ergo, you can really reproduce the environment that was reported not to be working.

Users can become upset when a problem is not completely solved on the first attempt. Try to set their expectations appropriately. It is often useful to get the user who reported a problem to work with you in solving it, especially if the problem relates to an unfamiliar software package. You will obtain additional information and the user will be less likely to think of your relationship as adversarial.

## 27.8  WAR STORIES AND ETHICS

Why ethics? A sysadmin's job involves a significant level of trust, from respecting users' privacy to protecting the company's trade secrets. Trust relationships go both downstream with your users and upstream with management. Without that trust, it's very hard for a sysadmins to do their jobs well. Your personal and professional integrity are priceless; protect them as you earn the trust of your users, your peers, and your managers.

This section contains war stories that illustrate some ethical dilemmas a system administrator may face. Some of the stories are our own, and others have been harvested from external sources, perhaps $N^{th}$-hand and perhaps not entirely in their most accurate forms.

### Boss's mistake #1

A department chair incorrectly sent personnel data to the entire faculty instead of to the executive committee for which it was intended. He asked a student sysadmin who was working that weekend to edit faculty members' mailboxes and remove the message. Should the student do it? Should he refuse? Should he look at the message and decide for himself if it was really serious enough to warrant an invasion of privacy?

In this instance, the sysadmin did do as he was asked, but he demanded that the chairman send mail to the faculty members explaining what had happened. He also stipulated that there be a witness to watch him trim mailboxes and verify that he did not browse around while editing. This was a good solution and one that both the sysadmin and the chairman felt comfortable with.

### Boss's mistake #2

A new secretary at a large computer manufacturer in the midwest was new to UNIX and email. At the end of her first week, she sent her boss a message about how nice the job was and how everyone had been very helpful. Her command line was something like:

```
% mail boss I like my new job, everyone is so helpful, thank you. Working
    here for you will be really fun ...
```

The boss read the mail and responded with a jokingly rude and sexist remark about the size of her breasts. Other folks responded about the need to put a carriage return between the name of the recipient and the message itself. It seems "everyone" was an alias for all employees.

A few hours later, the head sysadmin (who by that time had seen both the secretary's message and the boss's response) got a call from the boss. The boss explained that he had made a mistake (**R** instead of **r**, perhaps) and needed copies of the message removed from everyone's mailbox—with "everyone" being several thousand employees. Needless to say, the sysadmin refused. A moral decision was unnecessary: removing a message from thousands of mailboxes spread all around the world is an impossible task.

### Dan, your new name is Lester

This story comes from a medium-sized company in the United States. They have thousands of employees and several locations. The commercial email program that they use has a name lookup feature that resolves the names of email recipients as you type them on the To line.

A new director of human resources, whose last name was something like Smith-Foo, was frantic because sensitive email that was supposed to be going to her was being received by a sales person named Foo Jones. It seems that the people (yes, there were more than one) sending her these messages would just type Foo on the To line and not check to see to whom the name resolved. All of this started happening during a time at which the company was being reorganized and people were being laid off. Most of the sensitive messages contained information regarding the layoffs.

The resulting political fallout had many managers scrambling to "fix" the "problem." Meetings were held and experts were consulted. One manager even promised to rename Foo Jones to something else in the company's databases. Just when the sysadmins thought that no one had any concept of reality, the IT manager stepped in and declared it a user-training issue. Finally, the users who sent email to the wrong person were trained to actually *look* to see where their messages were going before pushing the send button.

### Which ones to fire

A novice sysadmin and an operator trainee discovered how to break into the Computing Center's student computers. These hosts were run by a different group that was somewhat looked down on for being too conservative. The rookies wanted to leave a back door. As they were about to edit the **/etc/passwd** file, a senior sysadmin advised them to use **vipw** instead of **vi**. The novices never used the back door, but the senior sysadmin did and was caught. Who should be fired?

Our answer would be either all three, or just the senior sysadmin, who should have stopped the break-in when he became aware of it instead of aiding and abetting the installation of a back door. However, in this case the senior sysadmin was deemed too valuable to lose; the two rookies were fired instead.

We view this as a very bad management decision. If the limits of behavior are set by an employee's value rather than by a written policy that is consistently enforced, the company is vulnerable to litigation (to say nothing of disgruntled employees with assault rifles).

### Horndog Joe

Joe, a new sysadmin at a major computer manufacturer, was infatuated with the receptionist and asked her out for a date. She always went out with newcomers once, to show them around and welcome them to the area. Joe asked her out again but she refused. A week or so later, she mentioned to one of the senior sysadmins that the machine always told her she had new mail even when she didn't. Hmmm. The senior sysadmin checked log files and found that Joe was reading the receptionist's mail. What should he do?

- Fire Joe?
- Give him a strong talking to?
- Give him a mild talking to?
- Nothing?

The right answer is actually a question: Is there a written policy that says, "Don't read other peoples' email?" The answer was no. Management opted for a strong talking to.

A few weeks later, it happened again. This time it seemed to be a different person reading the mail, Tom. The senior sysadmin called Tom into his office and confronted him with the evidence. But Tom was at a basketball game when the log files showed that the access had occurred.

Upon further investigation and after backtracking through several machines, the sysadmin discovered that Joe was the true culprit once again. Half an hour later, Joe was fired and the contents of his desk were on the curb.

A policy that allows for one warning is a license to steal until caught.

### Wedding invitations

A sysadmin who was getting married and hadn't finished all the preparations for the wedding gave his best man (a sysadmin from another site) the key to his office and the root password to his workstation. The friend was to go into work and make last-minute place cards for the tables at the reception. This incident violated lots of local policies and was noticed by other sysadmins because the common practice was to use the **sudo** command instead of logging in as root or using **su**.

The root password was the same on all machines, so the visitor had actually been given the password and physical access to the entire site. But no damage was done.

The circumstances seemed special, but written policy was violated. The employee was a valuable member of the staff. What to do? He was somewhat reluctantly fired with cause; he fought it and lost.

### Pornographic GIF images

A student's high school buddy came down to visit the computer lab during the summer. The student showed his friend how to view GIF files and showed him the location of a few "interesting" ones. He installed the friend at the last workstation at the back of the room and then worked on his homework. When they were done, they left.

Some time later (days, probably) the dean of engineering, accompanied by the basketball coach, was showing a promising recruit from Texas (a woman) around the campus. The dean had a key to the labs and so instead of entering as the students do, with an access card, he entered at the back of the lab with his key.

The first workstation they saw was the one on which the friend had viewed GIFs. And thanks to the magic of screen savers, when the mouse was moved, a sexually explicit photograph appeared on the screen. Needless to say, the dean and the basketball coach were furious; the student thought it was no big deal. The dean demanded that all GIFs be removed from university-owned computers and that the student who left it on the screen be expelled from school.

Our policy agreement, which the student had signed, said that you should not display pictures on your screen that would offend other people. The end result was that the student lost his login for a semester. The policy agreement was reviewed by the lawyers (who upheld the computer science department's side, not the dean's), and the whole incident was handled within the department. We apologized to the recruit.

### Migrating data

A small Colorado business used a local service firm for hardware and software support. One evening, their system administrator was swapping out a disk on which the bearings were going bad. The service firm had supplied not only the replacement disk but also a large scratch disk so that the transfer could be made without going to tape and back again. The sysadmin installed the replacement disk and the scratch disk and rebooted.

He was surprised when the workstation booted from the replacement disk and complained that the clock was 297 days off. Should he wipe the disk immediately? Should he look at the data? Should he just return the disk to the service provider? His first instinct was to wipe the disk without looking at it, but after some reflection it seemed better to check and see whose data it was so that the service provider could determine how it had slipped out with data on it.

A quick scan of the **passwd** file showed that the disk had previously belonged to this very same company. It contained not only the root partition with encrypted passwords, but also the company's development databases and new products. In short, a large part of the assets of the company, a bit out of date, had arrived from the service provider on a replacement disk. When asked, the service provider admitted that the way they tested disks was to copy data from one to another, regardless of what data happened to be on the source disk.

This incident illustrates a problem that is obvious with hindsight and also hard to fix. Whose responsibility is the data on a broken disk? It cannot always be wiped before being returned for repair. Service providers (and probably more importantly, peripheral resellers) do not necessarily see your data as valuable; they see only a broken or breaking disk.

As sysadmins, we are used to protecting our backup tapes. Broken disks are taken for granted, and they shouldn't be. Whenever possible, a disk with valuable data should be wiped (a low-level format and verify should do it) before being returned for repair or trade-in. If it's too broken to reformat, make sure your service provider knows that it contains sensitive data that you would like deleted. Consider putting statements about your data in the contract with a repair service provider.

It is probably worthwhile to ask your service providers about their policy regarding customers' data. When they admit that they don't have one, act very surprised and shocked.

High security U.S. government sites (defense installations, especially) are sometimes forbidden to let any computer equipment off-site, ever. If it breaks, they have to buy a new one. It may sound paranoid, but as this story illustrates, it is not without basis. (The policy even applies to components such as CPU boards that wouldn't normally retain data.)

### Bill must die!

A student left himself logged in on a machine in the computer science undergraduate lab when he went to his TA's office to pick up a document. While he was gone, someone typed in a mail message to president@whitehouse.gov that made death threats against then-President Clinton. The Secret Service called the next morning.

The student was a foreigner who had served in his country's militia as an encryption expert. He had also neglected to mention to the local system administrators that he received an acknowledgment from the White House for mail he had not sent. Things did not look good.

The system administrators spent the weekend collecting log files and card access records to determine what had happened. Luckily, the log files provided enough circumstantial evidence to convince the Secret Service that the student had probably been the victim of a prank.

The student's command history file (~/**.history**, which included timestamps) verified that he was a regular user of **pine**. But the offending message had been sent with **mail**, with a sizable period of inactivity before and after the event. Most users cling tenaciously to a single user agent for reading and writing mail, so the discrepancy was highly suggestive of a compromised account.

As it turns out, threatening the president of the United States is a felony. Even though the foreign student was exonerated, the Secret Service investigation continued. The event occurred a second time. It was again a forgery, but the log files gave us enough information to identify who we thought was sending the messages. We were never told by the Secret Service if they pursued the person whose name we gave to them.

We now recommend that students use **xlock**[6] when they leave their terminals unattended. We have modified **xlock** to log the user out after a period of inactivity so that students can't hoard the good machines in the lab.

## 27.9  LOCALIZATION AND UPGRADES

Each site's localization and upgrade scenarios are different. There is no one right way—the size of your site and the scope of the required upgrade dictate the appropriate policies and procedures. This section should really be a whole chapter of its own, but we are going to cheat and just look at some systems for managing software localization and some common-sense guidelines for upgrades. Finally, we'll present a list of what we consider to be essential third-party (open source) software.

### Managing software across systems

*See page 515 for hints on distributing files.*

The management of your local software and vendor patches can become very complex as the size and diversity of your site increase. A number of tools are available to help, both commercial configuration management systems and cleverly applied standbys such as **rdist**, **rsync**, and **make**.

A site usually has several different combinations of hardware architectures and operating systems. In most cases, one machine's configuration is similar to that of other machines of the same type and software release, with some individual customizations sprinkled on top. At a small site you can organize your localizations poorly and not even notice, but at a large site, you need to be able to do the work once and somehow distribute it to all systems that need it.

Policy and Politics

---

6.  **xlock** is a locking screen saver program for the X Windows system that requires you to type your password or the root password to unlock the screen.

There are two fundamental issues:

- The organization of the directory hierarchy of software being maintained
- The distribution mechanism for getting software from the prototype machine onto other hosts

See page 504 for more information about automounters.

Some sites use the **automounter** or **amd** to hide the real location of software packages from users and present a consistent view (directory path) to everyone. Others have a central repository and consistent directory tree for each architecture. Throwing everything in **/usr/local/bin** does not work; programs from different packages often present naming conflicts.

Two packages developed by sysadmins to cope with this complexity and reduce manual labor are **cfengine** and SEPP. **cfengine**, by Mark Burgess at Oslo College in Norway, is a high-level language for describing machine configurations. It puts all the config data in one spot. **cfengine** does **diff**s and then synchronizes client systems to the master. **cfengine** is distributed by the GNU project and runs on each of our four example systems. It's available from www.iu.hioslo.no/cfengine.

SEPP, by Tobi Oetiker of the Swiss Federal Institute of Technology (ETH), is a packaging system for installing and sharing software. SEPP is also distributed under the GNU GPL and is available from www.ee.ethz.ch/sepp. You can obtain more details on both of these packages from the references at the end of the chapter.

Many vendors provide a way to automate and standardize the installation of operating system or add-on software. We do not cover them here, but Table 27.1 provides pointers to additional information.

**Table 27.1   Software installation tools by vendor**

| System | Program | More info |
|---|---|---|
| Solaris | JumpStart | See the *Solaris Advanced Installation Guide* at docs.sun.com |
| HP-UX | SD-UX | Software distributor, comes standard with HP-UX 11.X |
|  | SD-OV | Souped up SD-UX that uses OpenView and costs extra |
| Red Hat | Kickstart | See the *Red Hat Installation Guide* at www.redhat.com |
|  | RPM | The Red Hat Package Manager, **man rpm** |
| FreeBSD | **ports** directory | Uses **make** and **pkg_{add**, **create**, **delete**, **info}** |

### Upgrades

Upgrading is painful and disruptive, but it is often necessary. Don't put off the upgrade too long, especially if you need it because you underestimated the number of hits on your web server by a few orders of magnitude. Find a balance; you don't want to apply every upgrade that your vendor supplies, because each upgrade usually breaks something. On the other hand, the longer you wait between upgrades, the more things you will have to fix manually.

Upgrades of the operating system or of major software packages should first be installed on the sysadmin's desk. Test new releases for a period of weeks or months before moving them to the production environment. Invite your developers to try the new system out on your desktop so that they can make sure the tools they use are installed and working. Test each commercial application to make sure that licensing issues have been addressed.

The most important rule of upgrading is to be sure you have a complete, readable backup of the existing system before you begin the upgrade. It's also good to have a backout plan if the upgrade should fail. Backing out is easiest if you have a hot spare machine running the old code and data, or at least a spare disk with the old system on it. We have been burned[7] before, so we offer these additional guidelines:

- Be very careful with version x.0, from any vendor.

- Read the mailing lists for your vendor's products to learn from the experience of the bleeding-edge crowd and to hear of any major pitfalls.

- Announce triple the downtime you expect the upgrade to take.

- Have a backout plan and know how long it will take to execute it.

- Have a schedule and a drop-dead time at which you will back out the upgrade and try again another day. Stick to your schedule.

The following story from a large telecom company illustrates some typical problems (and one way to let management know how long and hard you have worked). The site was planning an upgrade that required both an OS upgrade and a major upgrade to a particular application. After reviewing the software involved and doing some research on the net, the sysadmins indicated that three days were required to perform the upgrade. They were given from 7:00 p.m. Friday until 6:00 a.m. Monday.

The initial upgrade attempt had to be cancelled when the sysadmins learned that the OS vendor no longer recommended the use of the CD set they had; it was too buggy. A good set of CDs arrived and they began. Unfortunately, the new application and the new OS interfered with each other, turning what was typically a few hours of work into a three-day fiasco. After about 60 hours of almost nonstop work, they finally had the OS installed. Management, including one vice president, was pleased that the upgrade was completed—but also quite tired, as they had requested status calls every 3–4 hours throughout the entire three-day process.

In hindsight, this is an example of an upgrade that probably should not have been performed until there was experience in the community (or at least on the sysadmins' desks) with the new version of the application running on the new version of the OS. It's always a bad idea to have a production box be your first example of an OS/application pair.

---

7. Years ago, a major upgrade from Sun changed the formatting of the disks, and thanks to a bug in the **format** program, we could not back out the upgrade. We have not installed the first version of a major release since that experience.

### Useful third-party software

Our list of useful software has a few entries that we consider so important that we would call them mandatory for all machines. Some of the other items may be necessary or useful only on selected machines. However, the price of disk space these days almost makes it easier to install everything everywhere and maintain the consistency of the local software tree. Table 27.2 shows our list of must-haves.

**Table 27.2    Essential third-party software packages**

| Package | Description and comments |
|---|---|
| **ssh** | Secure shell – uses cryptography, doesn't reveal passwords |
| **sudo** | Replaces **su** and adds control and logging |
| **sendmail** | Mail transport program – get the latest release (for security reasons) |
| **traceroute**[a] | Shows network routes – you need it to debug networking problems |
| **tcpdump** | Network sniffer – for analyzing net traffic and debugging problems |
| **nmap** | Network port scanner – for monitoring system and network security |
| **tcsh/bash** | Good shells – **tcsh** is a good default, always nice to have a usable shell |
| **gzip**[a] | GNU zip compressor – needed to unpack downloads |
| **netscape** | Web browser – gotta have it |
| **tcpd** | TCP wrappers – logs and controls incoming connections to servers |
| RCS[a]/SCCS/CVS | Revision control systems – useful for both sysadmins and users |
| Perl | Scripting language – get Perl 5; good for sysadmins and web CGI |

a. These programs are shipped with each of our example systems, but they are not necessarily installed by default on all of them. They may not be included in other vendors' basic installations either.

Table 27.3 shows our picks of nice-but-not-essential programs; we've divided the table into a sysadmin section and a general user section.

All of the programs listed in Tables 27.2 and 27.3 are free. Most of them are available on the web, but a few are still distributed only through FTP. Use a search engine to locate them, or see if a pointer is given in this book (check the index to see if a command is discussed elsewhere).

The Red Hat Linux archives contain a lot of third-party software bundled as RPM (Red Hat Package Manager) distribution files. You can use the **rpm** command to manage and install them; it's just like the **pkgadd** program in Solaris. Red Hat packages are far more convenient than most software's native compilation and installation procedures; always check to see if there's an RPM version of a command available before going off to find the original.

FreeBSD's **/usr/ports** directory contains a makefile that knows how to fetch and build several thousand different software packages. If you go to **/usr/ports** and type **make** *package-name*, the system will look in its makefile for the original location of the software, download it from the Internet, then compile and install it. It's a very slick system. It does need to be updated regularly, however, since both the contents

**Table 27.3    Useful third-party software packages**

| | Package | Description and comments |
|---|---|---|
| **Tools for system administrators** | **gcc** | C/C++ compiler – a high-quality compiler from GNU |
| | BIND | Name service tools – get current version (for security reasons)[a] |
| | **tripwire** | File status checker – detects changes to system files |
| | COPS | Security tool – checks system for weaknesses |
| | **crack** | Password cracker – attempts to guess users' passwords |
| | **npasswd** | **passwd** replacement – forces users to choose good passwords |
| | **sniffit/ethereal** | More network sniffers – for debugging network problems |
| | **xntpd** | Time daemon – keeps machines' clocks correct and synced |
| | Samba | Windows SMB – shares files/printers with Windows systems |
| | Apache | Web server |
| | Squid | Web proxy and caching software |
| | LPRng | Printing software – replaces **lpr/lpd**, has many improvements |
| | **imapd/procmail** | Mail tools – for accessing and filtering email |
| **Tools for users** | Acrobat Reader | Displays PDF files, a nice (free) tool from Adobe |
| | **xv/gimp** | Manipulate binary image formats under X Windows |
| | **xfig** | X11 drawing program – kind of like MacDraw for UNIX |
| | PGP | Pretty Good Privacy – signs, verifies, and encrypts messages |
| | **nvi/vim** | **vi**-like text editors – recommended for sysadmins |
| | **emacs** | Text editor/operating system – good for power users |
| | **pico** | Text editor – very nice choice for beginners |
| | **enscript/mpage** | Printing utilities – pretty printer and N-up formatter |
| | **pine/mh/exmh** | Mail readers – **pine** for beginners, **mh**/**exmh** for lots of mail |
| | **glimpse** | Indexing tool – indexes your files and performs fast searches |
| | **gs/gv/ghostview** | Tools for previewing and printing PostScript documents |

a. The BIND package includes **dig** and **nslookup**.

and the locations of packages can change over time. See the *FreeBSD Handbook* at www.freebsd.org/handbook for instructions.

## 27.10  LOCAL DOCUMENTATION

Documentation is often pushed down in the priority queue in favor of "real work." It's quite easy to defer documentation because at the moment you should be writing it, you remember how to do the task in question and have no need for a cheat sheet. Any administration group that includes students probably has serious documentation problems.

Local documentation serves many purposes. Have you ever walked into a machine room needing to reboot one server, only to face racks and racks of hardware, all alike, all different, and all unlabeled? Or had to install a piece of hardware that you've handled before, but all you can remember about the chore was that it was hard to figure out? Or gone through hours of localizing a new machine to fit your environment, only to realize that you have forgotten a couple of crucial steps?

Local documentation should be kept in a well-defined spot, perhaps **/usr/local/doc**. Some documentation is most appropriate as a paper booklet or as a sign taped to a piece of hardware.

All system consoles should bear printed instructions that list the hostname, boot instructions, architecture, and any special key sequence that's needed to reboot the machine (<L1-A>, <Control-Alt-Delete>, etc.). The hostname should be readable from across the room. The special key sequence may seem a bit silly, but many servers' monitors are snitched and replaced with an aging terminal when someone else's monitor dies. Finding the <L1> key on a VT100 can be a challenge. Be sure to keep a copy of the information on all these little sticky labels in your central records or inventory data.

Also tape the hostname to other pieces of hardware that are associated with each machine: disk drives, modems, printers, tape drives, etc. If the host is an important citizen (for example, a major server or a crucial router), include the location of its circuit breaker. If a floppy disk or flash memory card is required for bootstrapping, point to its location. Major file servers should have information about disk device names, partition tables, mount points, and the locations of backup superblocks ready to hand. Tape the information to the disk drives themselves or store it in a well-known location in the machine room.

Tape drives should be labeled with the device files and commands needed to access them. It's also a good idea to list the type of tapes the drive requires, the nearest place to buy them, and even the approximate price.

Printers should be labeled with their names, brief printing instructions, and the hosts that they depend on. Printers often come with network interfaces and are full citizens of the network, but they may depend on a UNIX host for spooling and configuration.

Network wiring must be scrupulously documented. Label all cables, identify patch panels and wall outlets, and mark network devices. Always make it easy for your wiring technician to keep the documentation up to date; keep a pencil and forms hanging on the wall of the wiring closet so that it's painless to note that a cable moved from one device to another. Later, you should transfer this data to on-line storage.

A **diary** file associated with each machine that documents major events in its life (upgrades, hardware repairs, major software installations, and crashes, for example) provides a central place to review the history and status of a machine. You can point an email alias at the file so that the diary can be carbon-copied on mail sent among sysadmins. This is perhaps the most painless and least organized way of keeping records, but its simplicity makes it easier to enforce.

It's a good idea to prepare a printed document that you can give to new users. It should document local customs, procedures for reporting problems, the names and locations of printers, your backup and downtime schedules, and so on. This type of document can save an enormous amount of sysadmin or user services time. You should also make the information available on the web. A printed document is more likely to be read by new users, but a web page is easier to refer to at the time questions arise. Do both.

In addition to documenting your local computing environment, you may want to prepare some introductory material about UNIX. Such material is essential in a university environment where the user community is transient and often UNIX-illiterate. We have printed one-page crib sheets about the **vi** editor, email, Usenet news, logging in and out, the X Windows environment, and the use of man pages.

## 27.11  PROCUREMENT

At many sites, the system administration team and the purchasing team are totally separate. This is bad.

Sysadmins need to know about any new hardware that's being ordered in order to verify that it fits the current infrastructure and can be supported. They also need to be able to influence the specifications that go into purchase requests. Sysadmins can often provide good information about the competence of vendors (especially third-party resellers) and the reliability of certain types of equipment.

A system administrator's participation is especially valuable in organizations that by default must buy from the lowest bidder (for example, government institutions and state universities). Most purchasing systems allow you to specify evaluation criteria. Be sure to include escape clauses such as "must be compatible with existing environment" or "must be able to run XYZ software package well."

The incremental impact of an additional workstation is not fixed. Is it the 60th of that architecture or the first? Does it have enough local disk for the system files? Does it have enough memory to run today's bloated applications? Is there a spare network port to plug it into? Will it be in an area of the building that is accessible to the network? Is it a completely new OS?

Questions like these tend to emphasize a more fundamental question: Do you stay stagnant and buy equipment from your current vendor, or do you try the latest whizzy toy from a startup that might shake the world or might be out of business in a year? The nature of your organization may answer this one. It's not a simple yes or no; you must often make a complex tradeoff between the latest and greatest equipment and the machines that you are comfortable with and understand.

If you are allowed to negotiate with vendors (officially or otherwise) you can often do much better than your purchasing department. Don't be shy about quoting prices from other vendors for comparable equipment or inflating the size of expected purchases for the coming year. After all, the sales people have inflated the value of their product. Being able to get an order out fast is useful at a bean counting boundary such as the end of a fiscal quarter or year. When you submit orders in the last week of a company's accounting period, you can often obtain a sizable additional discount just to make a department's quota look better. Another bargain time is just before or just after new models are introduced; vendors want to reduce their inventory of the older products. This kind of vendor bashing is common at universities and may or may not be appropriate at companies and government institutions. But it is fun.

## 27.12 DECOMMISSIONING HARDWARE

Retiring a computer is often a painful ordeal. Stubborn users won't let go; weaning requires them to learn a new system or convert to new applications. Some sites convince themselves that they cannot afford a new system and force the staff to support the old one and keep it running. This conservatism usually ends up costing more than the new system would have. An aging SunOS box is impossible to upgrade to newer hardware and so is dog slow for today's porky applications. Yet its user community is likely to be adamant about the impossibility of turning it off.

A related problem at universities involves donations from businesses that would like to get a tax deduction. Often, the right answer is, "No thanks, we don't need 2,000 nine-track tapes and racks to put them in." One university in Budapest was given an IBM mainframe several years ago. Instead of saying no and buying fast PCs, they dedicated their whole budget to shipping and electrical wiring the first year and maintenance in following years. Status just isn't worth it. On the other hand, many universities establish strong relationships with their local computer industry and get lots of valuable hardware donated—it's just last year's model. Just know when to say "No, thanks."

Every time hardware performance increases, software drags it back down, usually by getting bigger and more complex. For example, Windows 95 and 98 survived with 32MB of memory; Windows 2000 is rumored to run poorly unless you have more than 128MB. Yikes, talk about bloat. Old hardware slows down if new software is installed, sometimes to the point of becoming unusable.

Because users and management are often reluctant to scrap obsolete equipment, you will sometimes have to take the initiative. Financial information is the most persuasive evidence. If you can demonstrate on paper that the cost of maintaining old equipment exceeds the cost of replacement, you will remove many of the intellectual objections to upgrading.

You can ease the transition between systems by keeping both systems on-line. Leave the old system powered on, but step down the level of support that your administrative group provides. You can also discontinue hardware maintenance on the old machine, allowing it to limp along until it dies of its own accord. You can dangle various incentives in front of users to lure them onto the new system: better performance, next-generation software, better support, larger user community, etc.

Even a very old machine can find use as a print server or guest machine. If your organization is run for profit, it may be advantageous to donate older equipment to a university or school ("Hello? How would you like to have 2,000 nine-track tapes, with racks to put them in?"). Barring that, you may have to think of creative disposal methods. A Pyramid P90X that we had decommissioned found itself the primary piece of debris attached to our head sysadmin's car when he got married. Quite effective. Another use of old hardware we have seen was during the CU's annual Engineering egg drop contest, in which a raw egg is packaged so as not to break when dropped from an eighth-story window.

Smaller surplus computer gear is auctioned off to students by our local chapter of the Association for Computing Machinery, the computer science professional society. Students are not allowed to bid money; they bid points instead, with one point being worth two hours of their labor. They must donate the labor to the labs or to freshman classes in their area of study. Our CS faculty are used to this now, but faculty in other areas are often surprised to have students show up and say that they owe 10 hours of helping first year students or helping in labs. Such a system requires a good auctioneer; we are lucky to be able to entice Rob Kolstad of LISA quiz show fame to come up and be our auctioneer.

## 27.13  SOFTWARE PATENTS

Software patents continue to dog the computer industry. Although they do not have much to do with system administration, we're sneaking in a short diatribe anyway.

In the beginning, the patent office ruled that you could not patent a mathematical theorem. Then the theorem became an algorithm, and it still could not be patented. Then the algorithm was implemented in hardware, and that could certainly be patented. Firmware, maybe. Software, still no. But patents can be appealed, and one of the lower courts liked software patents. Against its will, the patent office started issuing them, in some cases for applications that were filed 10 to 15 years earlier.

Unfortunately, the patent office has historically had scant comprehension of the state of the art in software and has issued many inappropriate (some would say, stupid) patents. Five different patents exist for the Lempel-Ziv data compression algorithm. That algorithm was published in a mathematical journal and was implemented and distributed in Berkeley UNIX. The concept of an include file is patented. The concept of a cursor is patented. Subtraction was patented as a measure to fix software that was not Y2K compliant. The process of copying an image from memory to an on-screen window is patented, as is the use of the XOR operation to handle overlapping windows. Several data encryption standards are patented. The concept of embedding advertising material in a user interface is patented. Most recently, British Telecom has claimed to own a patent—which they say they intend to enforce—on hypertext links.

In the second edition of this book, we griped about software patents and the U.S. Patent and Trademark Office's naivete with respect to software. These issues are still of great concern five years later, but in the United States an even bigger evil has emerged: the business practice patent. Patents have been issued for mundane activities such as pulling up a customer's account from a computer database when the customer dials in to a help desk. Amazon.com has obtained a business practice patent on "1-click technology"; they obtained an injunction requiring Barnes and Noble to make their customers perform at least two mouse clicks to purchase books.[8]

The patent office is attempting to clean up its act, but the damage seems to have already been done in many cases. A major milestone was the 1994 recall of a patent belonging to Compton's New Media which involved retrieval systems for data stored on CD-ROM. Some analysts considered it broad enough to cover 80% of all existing CD-ROM products, although that is probably an exaggeration. In the end, each of 41 claims was invalidated through an expensive and time-consuming campaign on the part of software vendors to demonstrate the existence of prior art.

The discovery of prior art is the real weakness in the patent office's process. Patent applications are kept secret, and with very little software expertise in the patent office, it is difficult for them to know which applications really represent new technology. Lawsuits will eventually decide, and the lawyers will be the winners.

Check out the Electronic Frontier Foundation's archives at www.eff.org for more specifics. A good source of breaking news is slashdot.org's patent area.

## 27.14 Organizations, conferences, and other resources

Several UNIX support groups—both general and vendor-specific—exist to help you network with other people that are using the same software. Table 27.4 presents a brief list of organizations. Plenty of national and regional groups exist that are not listed in this table. Many of these organizations would probably take exception to our use of the word UNIX and insist that they are "open systems" folks.

**Table 27.4   UNIX organizations**

| Name | URL | What it is |
|------|-----|-----------|
| USENIX | www.usenix.org | UNIX users group, quite technical |
| SAGE | www.sage.org | The System Administrators' Guild associated with USENIX; holds the LISA conference each year |
| SANS | www.sans.org | Runs sysadmin and security conferences; less technical than SAGE, with a focus on tutorials |
| EUROPEN | www.europen.org | Used to be the United Nations of national user groups, but now largely defunct; remnants remain in NLUUG, DUUG, UKUUG, and others |
| AUUG | www.auug.org.au | Australian UNIX Users Group, covers both technical and managerial aspects of computing |
| SAGE-AU | www.sage-au.org.au | Australian SAGE, holds yearly conferences in Oz |
| JUS | www.jus.org | Japan UNIX Society; seems to be inactive |

Each organization holds conferences on UNIX-related topics; most are broader than just UNIX and include tracks and/or events for Windows NT, too. USENIX holds one

---

8. Perhaps DoubleClick.net could beat them to the punch by patenting double-clicking…

general conference and several specialized (smaller) conferences or workshops each year. The big event for sysadmins is the USENIX LISA (Large Installation System Administration) conference every fall. USENIX, EUROPEN, and AUUG have substantial trade shows associated with their conferences.

The premier trade show for the networking industry is Interop; its tutorial series is also of high quality and is not UNIX-specific. Interop used to be an annual event that was eagerly awaited by techies and vendors alike. Interops now happens several times a year—a traveling network circus, so to speak. The salaries of tutorial speakers have been cut in half, but the quality of the tutorials seems to have survived.

### SAGE: the System Administrators' Guild

SAGE, USENIX's System Administrators' Guild, is the first international organization for system administrators. It promotes system administration as a profession by sponsoring conferences and informal programs. See www.sage.org for all the details.

SAGE is currently exploring the issue of certification. They plan to develop a certification process for system administrators that would include both a written exam and a practicum. It would be more similar to the Cisco CCIE certification (very comprehensive in both theory and application) than to the Microsoft MCSE certification (less thorough, multiple choice exam only).

Since system administration is a broad field that spans many technical areas and many different vendors' systems, SAGE is planning to establish multiple certifications. There will probably be a core competency certificate along with supplemental certificates for specialized topics or individual vendors' systems. It all sounds very similar to the merit badge system used by the Boy Scouts in the United States. A Boy Scout gets a merit badge in wood carving; a sysadmin might get a merit badge in DNS after passing the DNS certification exam. The details of the SAGE program have not been fully worked out, and they will surely have changed by the time you read this. See www.usenix.org/sage for up-to-date information.

Another SAGE activity that's under development is a mentoring program in which senior sysadmins can mentor folks who are trying to enter the profession and improve their skills. Mentors would typically work one-on-one with their trainees once or twice a week. A more formal educational activity involves the members of the SAGE community who teach university classes in system administration; this group exchanges and shares assignments and teaching ideas via the sysadm-education mailing list. To subscribe, send mail to majordomo@maillist.peak.org and include "subscribe sysadm-education" in the body of your message.

The USENIX and SAGE newsletter *;login:* is produced by both organizations; it contains administrative news, tips, reviews, and announcements of interest to sysadmins. SAGE has also produced a series of short, focused booklets that are available for a small fee ($5 for members; ~$10 for nonmembers). New booklets are free if you are a SAGE member when they're first published. Here is the current list.

Policy and Politics

- *Job Descriptions for System Administrators*, edited by Tina Darmohray
- *A Guide to Developing Computing Policy Documents*, edited by Barbara Dijker
- *System Security: A Management Perspective*, by David Oppenheimer et al.
- *Educating and Training System Administrators: A Survey*, by David Kuncicky and Bruce Wynn
- *Hiring System Administrators*, by Gretchen Philips
- *A System Administrator's Guide to Site Audits*, by Geoff Halprin
- *System and Network Administration for Higher Reliability*, by John Sellens
- *The Role of Postmaster*, by Rose Chalup[9]

The last three of these are being published this year (2000), and several more are planned: *Effective Customer Support*, *Monitoring Techniques and Practices*, and *The Role of Web Master*.

SAGE, together with USENIX, its parent organization, puts on the LISA conference each fall and sometimes a network administration conference in the spring. The LISA conference is the biggest, best, most technical, and most focused of the conferences aimed at system and network administrators. It's held each fall and typically includes three days of tutorials and three days of technical sessions, invited talks, and help sessions. Occasionally, one-day workshops on special topics run in parallel. For information, send mail to conference@usenix.org or see www.usenix.org.

In addition to the original SAGE, several national and regional groups have been formed to help sysadmins interact more regularly with their peers. As of this writing, the national groups are SAGE-AU in Australia; SAGE-WISE in Wales, Ireland, Scotland, and England; and SAGE-PT in Portugal. Contact information for the regional groups can be found at the www.usenix.org/sage/locals.

### Mailing lists and web resources

Numerous mailing lists are available to sysadmins of specific systems.

For the Sun Managers list, send mail to majordomo@sunmanagers.ececs.uc.edu; include "subscribe sun-managers" in the body of the message. Archives back to 1991 are available from www.latech.edu/sunman.html; the relevant Usenet news groups are comp.sys.sun.admin and comp.unix.solaris.

There was at one time a list called hpux-admin, but it seems to have died some time in 1998. A replacement (sort of) is available from www.egroups.com.

Consult www.redhat.com/mailing-lists for Linux-related mailing lists; you can subscribe via the web. The lists are called linux-*xxx*, but none of the possible values of *xxx* are directly targeted to sysadmins.

Check www.freebsd.org/handbook/eresources.html for resources related to FreeBSD. You can subscribe to any of the lists by mailing majordomo@freebsd.org and saying "subscribe *xxx*". Unfortunately, none of the lists seem directly targeted to sysadmin

---

9. The title of this document might change; it's not due out until late 2000.

issues, but the freebsd-questions, freebsd-stable, and freebsd-security lists often have sysadmin content.

Sysadmins have plenty of web resources to choose from. The SAGE web pages have a list of helpful links. Table 27.5 shows a few of our favorites:

**Table 27.5    Useful web resources for system administrators**

| Site | Contents |
|------|----------|
| freshmeat.com | A huge collection of Linux software |
| www.ugu.com | Unix Guru Universe, lots of stuff for sysadmins |
| www.stokely.com | Good collection of links to sysadmin necessities |
| www.tucows.com | Windows and Mac software, filtered for quality |
| slashdot.org | News for nerds, geeky |
| securityfocus.com | Security info, huge searchable vulnerability database |
| google.com | Fast, intelligent searches, especially good for technical stuff |
| www.oreilly.com | Books, a little commercial but has other good stuff too |

### Printed resources

The best resources for UNIX administrators in the printed realm are the O'Reilly series of books. The series began with *UNIX in a Nutshell* over 20 years ago and now includes a separate volume on just about every important UNIX subsystem and command. It also includes books on the Internet, Windows NT, and other non-UNIX topics. All are typically reasonably priced, timely, and focused. Tim O'Reilly has become quite interested in the open source movement and runs a yearly conference on this topic as well as conferences on Perl, Java, and TCL/Tk. See www.oreilly.com for more information.

## 27.15  STANDARDS

The standardization process helps us in some cases (modems from different manufacturers can talk to each other) and hurts us in others (OSI protocols, millions of dollars down the drain). Standards committees should codify and formalize existing practice, not invent.

Standards are intended to level the playing field and make it possible for customers to buy compatible products from competing vendors. Some of the parties involved in the standardization process really do just want to codify existing practice. Others have a more political purpose: to delay a competitor or to reduce the amount of work required to bring their own company's products into conformance.

Government organizations are often the biggest procurers of standards-based systems and applications. The use of standards allows them to buy competitively without favoring a particular brand. However, some cynics have called standards a nonmonetary trade barrier—companies slow down the standards process until their products catch up.

There are several standards bodies, both formal and informal. Each has different rules for membership, voting, and clout. From a system or network administrator's perspective, the most important bodies are POSIX (Portable Operating System Interfaces, pronounced pahz-icks) and the IETF (the Internet Engineering Task Force, described on page 263). Summaries of emerging standards are posted to the newsgroups comp.std.unix and comp.org.usenix and published in the USENIX publication *;login:*.

POSIX, an offshoot of the IEEE, has engaged itself for the last several years in defining a general standard for UNIX. Has this had any effect on commercially available versions of UNIX? Yes! The Open Group, which licenses the UNIX trademark, bases its UNIX specification on POSIX. Every system that calls itself UNIX supports the POSIX interfaces. Some could argue that everything is more complicated now that vendors support both POSIX and their own original interfaces, but that assertion is largely untrue. Few domains have both a POSIX interface and an alternative proprietary interface. Unfortunately, POSIX does not have much to say about what goes on at the layers of the OS where sysadmins live and play.

*See page 735 for more information about LPRng.*

Three areas of system administration have been considered for standardization by POSIX: software installation, user administration, and print management. Print management got hopelessly embroiled in politics and was withdrawn; they started with MIT's Palladium printing system, which even MIT no longer uses. Efforts are underway to try again with either LPRng or the Internet Printing Protocol (IPP) standard from the IETF.

POSIX documents are not available on-line (and the current versions may never be), but you can buy a printed version from the IEEE Computer Society. POSIX.1 and POSIX.2 (also known as ISO 9945-1 and 9945-2) define the POSIX versions of the UNIX system calls and commands, respectively. These standards are currently being revised jointly by ISO, the IEEE, and The Open Group with a target completion date of late 2001 or early 2002. When complete, the same standard will be used by all three organizations. The completed version will supposedly be freely available on the web.

The Open Group (formerly known as X/Open) produced a superset of the POSIX standard called the Single UNIX Specification, SUS. This process started with a survey of all the systems and applications the members could get their hands on. It identified 1,170 different interfaces (commands, shell utilities, system calls, and the like) that were commonly used. Thus, the project was known for a while as Spec 1170.

The UNIX trademark originally belonged to AT&T Bell Labs. It went from there to UNIX Systems Laboratories (a subsidiary of AT&T), then on to Novell, and then to SCO. SCO gave The Open Group royalty-free licensing rights. If your product meets the Single UNIX Specification and you have sufficient money, then you can call your product UNIX. Test suites and accredited test laboratories handle the certification. The document that defines the Single UNIX Specification is for sale, of course, but it can also be found beneath www.opengroup.org/publications.

Attendance at most standards meetings has been declining for the last few years, although not at the IETF. Some standards organizations (most, in fact) receive a large portion of their income from selling copies of the standards documents, not for $20 (paper and reproduction costs) but for closer to $300. Nearly all standards are written by volunteers who are not paid by the standards body for their work.

A consortium called the Austin Group (because their first meeting was in Austin, Texas) that consists of standards folks from IEEE, ISO, and The Open Group maintains a web site containing the working documents for various standards. Interested users are encouraged to go to the site, download the drafts, and participate in the standards process. The web site does require you to register, but they won't spam you or charge for copies of working documents. The site is www.opengroup.org/austin.

USENIX funds a person to be an institutional representative to several standards bodies. They do this not necessarily to shape the direction that a standard may be taking, but rather to inform the UNIX community of the status of standards work and to derail bogus standards as they start to emerge. The standards representative collects input from many sources, the most notable of which are the snitches.

A snitch is a technical person who attends a particular session and writes a report "from the inside." These snitch reports become the basis for the summary reports in the *;login:* magazine. They have also been used, even by those attending, to understand what the standard is proposing and what's wrong with it (or even what's right with it!). If you are active in the standards process and are technically competent, consider volunteering to be a snitch in your area of expertise. The snitch dinners are reported to be very fine.

## 27.16  SAMPLE DOCUMENTS

Several of the policy or procedure documents referred to in this chapter are available from www.admin.com. Table 27.6 lists the docs and their corresponding contents.

**Table 27.6    Policy and procedure documents at www.admin.com**

| Document | Contents |
| --- | --- |
| **ugrad.policy** | Undergraduate lab user policy agreement |
| **grad.policy** | Faculty and graduate student user policy agreement |
| **sysadmin.policy** | Sysadmin policy agreement |
| **services** | CSOPS services, policies, and priorities |
| **hiring.quiz1** | "Rate your experience" quiz |
| **hiring.quiz2** | Administrative knowledge quiz |
| **localization** | Localization checklist |
| **amanda** | Checklist for client backups with Amanda |
| **tcp-wrappers** | Checklist for installing TCP wrappers |

Policy and Politics

## 27.17  RECOMMENDED READING

BURGESS, MARK. "Cfengine: a site configuration engine." USENIX Computing Systems, Vol 8, No 3. 1995.

BURGESS, MARK. "Computer Immunology." LISA 1998 proceedings.

OETIKER, TOBIAS. "SEPP – Software Installation and Sharing System." LISA 1998 proceedings.

SAN DIEGO SUPERCOMPUTER CENTER. Local policies, standards, and procedures. http://security.sdsc.edu/help/SGs.shtml

M.I.B.H., INC. "Acceptable Use Policy." http://www.mibh.net/mibh-aup.html

M.I.B.H. was acquired by Metromedia Fiber Network, but its AUP is still available on-line and is a good example of a fairly militant policy.

EATON, DAVID W. "comp.software.config-mgmt FAQ, part 3." http://www.iac.honeywell.com/Pub/Tech/CM/PMTools.html

This FAQ contains a summary of trouble ticketing systems, including many commercial ones we had never heard of. It seems to be well maintained but didn't contain any of our favorites.

HARROW, JEFFREY R., AND COMPAQ COMPUTER CORPORATION. *The Rapidly Changing Face of Computing* (periodical). http://www.compaq.com/rcfoc

This regularly updated site contains some interesting articles about technology-related issues. It's a combination of news and editorial content.

# 28 *Daemons*

Although UNIX provides a versatile and generic multitasking environment, the kernel itself lacks the vivid personality and functionality that folks look for when choosing an operating system to be their lifelong companion. Fortunately, UNIX systems come bundled with a rich set of daemons that provide much-needed vitality and flair. The system administrator can also add many additional daemons, whether downloaded, supplied by a vendor, or written by a user.

A daemon is a background process that performs a specific function or system-related task. In keeping with the UNIX philosophy of modularity, daemons are programs rather than parts of the kernel. Many daemons start at boot time and continue to run as long as the system is up. Other daemons are started when needed and run only as long as they are useful.

"Daemon" was first used as a computer term by Mick Bailey, a British gentleman who was working on the CTSS programming staff at MIT during the early 1960s.[1] Mick quoted the Oxford English Dictionary in support of both the meaning and the spelling of the word. The words "daemon" and "demon" both come from the same root, but "daemon" is an older form and its meaning is somewhat different. A daemon is an attendant spirit that influences one's character or personality. Daemons are not minions of evil *or* good; they're creatures of independent thought and will. Daemons made their way from CTSS to Multics to UNIX, where they are so popular that they need a superdaemon (**inetd**) to manage them.

---

1. This bit of history comes from Jerry Saltzer at MIT, via Dennis Ritchie.

This chapter presents a brief overview of the most common UNIX daemons. Not all of the daemons listed here are supplied with all versions of UNIX, and not every daemon supplied with some version of UNIX is listed here. Besides making you more aware of how UNIX works, a knowledge of what all the various daemons do will make you look really smart when one of your users asks, "What does **xntpd** do?"

Before **inetd** was written, all daemons started at boot time and ran continuously (or more accurately, they blocked waiting for work to do). Over time, more and more daemons were added to the system. The daemon population became so large that it began to cause performance problems. In response, the Berkeley gurus developed **inetd**, a daemon that is responsible for starting other daemons as they are needed. **inetd** was so successful that all major versions of UNIX now include it and most new daemons run under its control.

There are many daemons that system administrators should be intimately familiar with, either because they require a lot of administration or because they play a large role in the day-to-day operation of the system. Some daemons that are described here in one or two lines have an entire chapter devoted to them elsewhere in this book. We provide cross-references where appropriate.

We start this chapter by introducing a couple of very important system daemons (**init** and **cron**) and then move on to a discussion of **inetd**. Finally, we briefly describe most of the daemons a system administrator is likely to wrestle with on our four example systems.

## 28.1  INIT: THE PRIMORDIAL PROCESS

**init** is the first process to run after the system boots, and in many ways it is the most important daemon. It always has a PID of 1 and is an ancestor of all user processes and all but a few system processes.

At startup, **init** either places the system in single-user mode or spawns a shell to read the system's startup files. When you boot the system into single-user mode, **init** reads the startup files after you terminate the single-user shell, usually by typing **exit** or <Control-D>.

*See Chapter 7 for more information about TTYs.*

After processing the startup files, **init** consults a configuration file (**/etc/inittab** on most systems, **/etc/ttys** on FreeBSD) to determine on which physical ports it should expect users to log in. It opens these ports and spawns a **getty** process on each one.[2] If a port cannot be opened, **init** periodically issues complaints on the system console until the port either becomes openable or is removed from the list of active ports.

On older machines, the management of terminal ports was a mainstay of system administration. These days, terminals are something of a relic. Most login sessions are established over the network through daemons such as **rlogind**, **telnetd**, and **sshd** (discussed later in this chapter).

---

2.  Solaris is an exception to this behavior. See page 109 for the sordid details.

In addition to its terminal management duties, **init** also has the ghoulish task of exorcising undead zombie processes that would otherwise accumulate on the system. **init**'s role in this process is described on page 48.

You can shut down the system by sending **init** a signal—usually SIGTERM—that makes it take the system to single-user mode. This is the last step in most shutdown scripts. **init** is so essential to the operation of the system that the system will automatically reboot if **init** ever dies.

On most modern systems, **init** defines several "run levels" that determine what set of system resources should be enabled. There are usually seven or eight levels: 0 to 6, plus "s" for single-user mode. The characteristics of each run level are defined in the **/etc/inittab** file.

*See page 107 for more information about the inittab file.*
**init** is usually passed its initial run level as an argument from the boot loader. If "s" is specified, **init** enters single-user mode. Otherwise, it scans **/etc/inittab** for entries that apply to the requested run level and executes their corresponding commands.

The **telinit** command changes **init**'s run level once the system is up. For example, **telinit 4** forces **init** to go to run level 4. **telinit**'s most useful argument is **-q**, which causes **init** to reread the **/etc/inittab** file.

Many systems implement an additional layer of abstraction on top of the basic run level mechanism provided by **init**. These systems keep startup scripts in the directory **/etc/init.d**, from where they are linked into run-level-specific directories called **/etc/rcX.d**. Bringing **init** to a new run level causes the appropriate scripts to be executed with the arguments **start** or **stop**. This facility allows startup and shutdown to be handled in an orderly manner. A more detailed description of this mechanism is given starting on page 25.

On FreeBSD systems, you can tell **init** to reread its control file by sending it a hangup signal (SIGHUP). Since **init**'s PID is always 1, you can simply run **kill -HUP 1**. Don't forget the **-HUP**, or you will bring your system to a grinding halt.

## 28.2    CRON: SCHEDULE COMMANDS

The **cron** daemon is responsible for running commands at preset times. It accepts schedule files ("crontabs") from both users and administrators.

**cron** is frequently employed for administrative purposes, including management of accounting and log files and daily cleanup of the filesystem. In fact, **cron** is so important to system administrators that we have devoted an entire chapter to it. That chapter, *Periodic Processes*, begins on page 157.

## 28.3    INETD: MANAGE DAEMONS

**inetd** is a daemon that manages other daemons. It starts up its client daemons when there is work for them to do and allows them to die gracefully once their tasks have been completed.

**inetd** only works with daemons that provide services over the network. To find out when someone is trying to access one of its clients, **inetd** attaches itself to the network ports that would normally be managed by the quiescent daemons. When a connection occurs, **inetd** starts up the appropriate daemon and connects its standard I/O channels to the network port. Daemons must be written with this convention in mind to be compatible with **inetd**.

Some daemons (such as those associated with NIS and NFS) rely on a further layer of indirection known as the Remote Procedure Call (RPC) system. RPC was originally designed and implemented by Sun as a way of promoting the sharing of information in a heterogeneous networked environment. Port assignments for daemons that use RPC are managed by the **portmap** daemon (also known as **rpcbind** on some systems), which is discussed later in this chapter.

Many daemons can be used in either the traditional way (in which they are started once and continue to run until the system shuts down) or with **inetd**. Daemons discussed in this chapter are marked with an ⓣ if they are **inetd**-compatible.

### Configuring inetd

**inetd** consults a config file (usually **/etc/inetd.conf**) to determine which network ports it should listen to. The format is the same on all platforms. Here's a sample:

```
ftp         stream  tcp       nowait  root   /usr/sbin/ftpd ftpd
telnet      stream  tcp       nowait  root   /usr/sbin/telnetd telnetd
shell       stream  tcp       nowait  root   /usr/sbin/rshd rshd
finger      stream  tcp       nowait  guest  /usr/sbin/fingerd fingerd
bootp       dgram   udp       wait    root   /usr/sbin/bootpd bootp -f
pop-2       stream  tcp       nowait  root   /usr/sbin/popper popper
pop-3       stream  tcp       nowait  root   /usr/sbin/popper popper
mountd/1    stream  rpc/tcp   wait    root   /usr/sbin/mountd mountd
mountd/1    dgram   rpc/udp   wait    root   /usr/sbin/mountd mountd
...
```

The first column contains the service name. **inetd** maps service names to port numbers by consulting either the **/etc/services** file (for TCP and UDP services) or the **portmap** daemon (for RPC services). RPC services are identified by names of the form *name/num* and the designation rpc in column three. In the example above, the last two lines are RPC services.

The second column determines the type of socket that the service will use and is commonly stream or dgram. In general, stream is used with TCP (connection-oriented) services, and dgram is used with UDP.

The third column identifies the communication protocol used by the service. The allowable types are listed in the **protocols** file (usually in **/etc**). The protocol is almost always tcp or udp. RPC services prepend rpc/ to the protocol type, as with rpc/tcp and rpc/udp in the example above.

If the service being described can process multiple requests at one time (rather than processing one request and exiting), column four should be set to wait; this option prevents **inetd** from constantly forking new copies of the daemon. It is used with services that handle lots of small requests. If wait is not appropriate, put nowait here to make **inetd** fork a new copy of the daemon each time it receives a request.

The fifth column gives the username under which the daemon should run. If you do not trust a particular program or you know that it has security problems, you can run it as someone other than root to reduce your exposure. Of course, this technique works only for daemons that do not require rootly powers. In the example above, **fingerd** runs as the user "guest."

The remaining fields give the fully qualified pathname of the daemon and its command-line arguments. The first argument should always be the short name of the program. This requirement is not a peculiarity of **inetd** but a traditional UNIX convention that is normally hidden by the shell.

### The services file

After adding a new service to **inetd.conf**, you may also need to make an entry for it in the **services** file. This file is usually found in **/etc**. It is used by several standard library routines that map between service names and port numbers. For example, when you type the command

```
% telnet anchor smtp
```

**telnet** looks up the port number for the "smtp" service in the **services** file. Most systems ship with all the common services already configured; you need only edit the **services** file if you add something new.

The **services** file is used only for bona fide TCP/IP services; similar information for RPC services is stored in a separate configuration file, usually **/etc/rpc**.

Here are some selected lines from a **services** file (the original is about 70 lines long):

```
tcpmux     1/tcp                         # TCP port multiplexer
echo       7/tcp
echo       7/udp
...
smtp       25/tcp     mail
time       37/tcp     timserver
time       37/udp     timserver
rlp        39/udp     resource           # resource location
name       42/tcp                        # IEN 116
whois      43/tcp     nicname
...
```

The format of a line is

```
name       port/proto aliases           # comment
```

Services are generally listed in numerical order, although this order is not required. *name* is the symbolic name of the service (the name you use in the **inetd.conf** file).

The *port* is the port number at which the service normally listens; if the service is managed by **inetd**, it is the port that **inetd** will listen on.[3]

The *proto* indicates the protocol used by the service; in practice, it is always tcp or udp. If a service can use either UDP or TCP, a line for each must be included (as with the time service above). The *alias* field contains additional names for the service (for example, whois can also be looked up as nicname).

### Restarting inetd

*See Chapter 11 for more information about syslog.*

Changes to **/etc/inetd.conf** do not take effect until you tell **inetd** to reread it, which you do by sending **inetd** a hangup signal. After signalling, wait a minute and then check the log files for error messages related to your changes (**inetd** logs errors to syslog under the "daemon" facility). Test out any new services you have added to be sure they work correctly.

### Securing inetd

Because **inetd** is responsible for managing many common network-based services, it plays an important role in securing your system. It's important to verify that only services you need and trust have been enabled in **inetd.conf**. On a new system, you will almost certainly need to modify **inetd.conf** to disable services that are unnecessary or undesirable in your environment. A good rule of thumb is to enable only the services that you absolutely need and turn everything else off.

Even then, it's a good idea to supplement **inetd** with Wietse Venema's TCP wrappers package, which logs all connection attempts and restricts access to daemons, depending on who is attempting to connect to them. The package description starts on page 666.

HP-UX comes with a version of **inetd** that has TCP-wrapper-like features built in. It checks the file **/var/adm/inetd.sec** to determine who's allowed to connect to which services. If started with the **-l** flag, it also performs connection logging. For instructions on configuring HP's security features, see page 666.

### portmap/rpcbind: map RPC services to TCP and UDP ports

**portmap** (which is now called **rpcbind** on many systems—thanks, Sun!) maps RPC service numbers to the TCP/IP ports on which their servers are listening. When an RPC server starts up, it registers itself with **portmap/rpcbind**, listing the services it supports and the port at which it can be contacted. Clients query **portmap/rpcbind** to find out how to get in touch with an appropriate server.

This system allows a port to be mapped to a symbolic service name. It's basically another level of abstraction above the **services** file, albeit one that introduces additional complexity (and security issues) without solving any real-world problems.

---

3. Port numbers are not arbitrary. All machines must agree about which services go with which ports; otherwise, requests will constantly be directed to the wrong port. If you are creating a site-specific service, pick a high port number (in the thousands) that is not already listed in the **services** file.

Many RPC programs are actually started by way of **inetd**, thus providing not one but two full layers of indirection and deceit.

If **portmap/rpcbind** dies, all the services that rely on it (including **inetd** and NFS) must be restarted. In practical terms, this means that it's time to reboot the system. **portmap/rpcbind** must be started before **inetd** in order for **inetd** to handle RPC services correctly.

## 28.4 SYSTEM DAEMONS

A few system tasks, such as managing virtual memory and synchronizing the disk cache, are managed by daemons rather than by the kernel itself. The daemons that perform these functions cannot be manipulated by the system administrator and should generally be left alone.

### The paging daemon

The implementation of this daemon and its exact function vary widely across systems. It is named **pageout** on Solaris, **vhand** on HP-UX, **kpiod** under Red Hat, and **pagedaemon** under FreeBSD.

*See page 760 for more information about virtual memory.*

This daemon is part of the virtual memory system. When a page of virtual memory is accessed, the system's hardware consults a table to determine whether the page is currently in physical memory. If not, a fault occurs and the paging daemon is called to bring the page into memory from the swap area. If no physical pages are available, the paging daemon makes room by writing out some other page to the swap device and updating the appropriate page table entries.

### The swapping daemon

This daemon is called **swapper** on FreeBSD and HP-UX, and **kswapd** on Linux.

When many processes are running simultaneously, the system begins to spend a lot of time processing page faults because each process has a certain number of pages that it accesses regularly. This condition is called thrashing, and it can seriously degrade performance.

The swapping daemon monitors the number of page faults that occur in proportion to the number of memory references. If too many faults occur, the swapping daemon starts to move entire processes out to the swap space. Swapped processes are completely removed from physical memory and are prevented from running for a comparatively long time (seconds). The swapping daemon continues to eliminate processes until the page fault rate falls to an acceptable level.

Swapping was designed for an era in which physical memory was very expensive, and the need for it in today's computing landscape is questionable. Nevertheless, most systems still provide this capability.

Daemons

### The filesystem synchronization daemon

*See page 133 for more information about filesystem superblocks.*

The filesystem synchronization daemon executes the **sync** system call every 30 seconds. **sync** causes all "dirty" disk blocks to be written out, including filesystem superblocks, inode tables, and buffered data blocks.[4] This housekeeping minimizes the filesystem damage that can occur during a crash.

On most systems this daemon is called **update**, but HP-UX calls it **syncer** and Solaris calls it **fsflush**.

## 28.5 PRINTING DAEMONS

The BSD and System V printing systems each have their own family of daemons that provide printing-related services. In some cases the families have been hybridized, and in others both variants run on a single system.

### lpd: manage BSD-style printing

*See page 709 for more information about **lpd**.*

**lpd** is responsible for the BSD print spooling system. It accepts jobs from users and forks processes that perform the actual printing. **lpd** is also responsible for transferring print jobs to and from remote systems. **lpd** can sometimes hang and need to be manually restarted.

### lpsched: manage ATT printing

*See page 721 for more information about **lpsched**.*

**lpsched** is the ATT version of the line printer daemon. It receives print jobs from the **lp** program and queues them for printing. When an appropriate device becomes available, **lpsched** forks a process to manage the actual printing.

### rlpdaemon: print from BSD to HP-UX

**rlpdaemon** is an HP-UX daemon that allows HP's SysV-ish **lpsched** system to accept print requests from BSD-style systems. See page 732 for more information about **rlpdaemon**.

## 28.6 NFS DAEMONS

The following daemons are part of the NFS file sharing system. We give only a brief description of their functions here; Chapter 17 describes them in detail.

### nfsd: serve files

**nfsd** runs on file servers and handles requests from NFS clients. On some systems, this daemon is called **rpc.nfsd**.[5]

In most NFS implementations, **nfsd** is really just a part of the kernel that has been dressed up as a process for scheduling reasons. **nfsd** takes a single argument that

---

4. Actually, **sync** simply schedules these blocks to be written out; it doesn't guarantee that writing has completed by the time it returns.

5. The **rpc** prefix, when present, is just there to remind you that the daemon uses RPC.

specifies how many copies of itself to fork. Some voodoo is involved in picking the correct number of copies; see page 499 for specifics.

### mountd: respond to mount requests

**mountd** (which is called **rpc.mountd** on some systems) accepts filesystem mount requests from potential NFS clients. It verifies that each client has permission to mount the requested directories. **mountd** consults an export list to determine which applicants are legitimate.

### amd and automount: mount filesystems on demand

**amd** and **automount** are NFS automounters, daemons that wait until a process attempts to use a filesystem before they actually mount it. The automounters later unmount the filesystems if they have not been accessed in a specified period of time.

The use of automounters is very helpful in large environments where dozens or hundreds of filesystems are shared on the network. Automounters increase the stability of the network and reduce configuration complexity, since all systems on the network can share the same **amd** or **automountd** configuration. We cover the use of these daemons in detail, starting on page 504.

### lockd and statd: manage NFS locks

Although **lockd** and **statd** (aka **rpc.lockd** and **rpc.statd**) are two distinct daemons, they always run as a team. **lockd** maintains advisory locks (a la **flock** and **lockf**) on NFS files. **statd** allows processes to monitor the status of other machines that are running NFS. **lockd** uses **statd** to decide when to attempt to communicate with a remote machine.

### biod: cache NFS blocks

*See page 501 for more information about **biod**.*

**biod** (which is known as **nfsiod** on FreeBSD systems) caches read and write requests on some NFS clients. **biod** performs both read-ahead and write-behind buffering and greatly improves the performance of NFS.

## 28.7  NIS DAEMONS

Several daemons are associated with Sun's NIS and NIS+ administrative database systems. These systems are described in Chapter 18, *Sharing System Files*. Note that NIS and NIS+ are distinct and independent systems, despite their similar names. Although both packages originated at Sun, they are now used on many other vendors' systems as well.

### ypbind: locate NIS servers

The **ypbind** daemon runs on all NIS clients and servers. It finds an NIS server to which queries can be directed. **ypbind** does not actually process requests itself; it just tells client programs which server to use.

### ypserv: NIS server

**ypserv** runs on all NIS servers. **ypserv** accepts queries from clients and responds with the requested information. See page 527 for information on how to configure the machines that run **ypserv**.

### ypxfrd: transfer NIS databases

**ypxfrd** transfers NIS databases to slave servers in an efficient manner. A slave initiates a transfer with the **ypxfr** command. Whenever a database is changed on the master, it should immediately be pushed out to all the slaves so that the NIS servers remain consistent with one another.

### rpc.nisd: NIS+ server

*See Chapter 16 for more information about DNS.*

**rpc.nisd** is the NIS+ counterpart of **ypserv**. It runs on all NIS+ servers. If invoked with the -B option, **rpc.nisd** automatically forks **rpc.nisd_resolv**, which permits the use of DNS through NIS+.

## 28.8 INTERNET DAEMONS

We define "Internet daemons" very loosely to mean daemons that use Internet protocols to handle requests. Many Internet daemons actually spend the majority of their time servicing local requests.

### talkd: network chat service

Connection requests from the **talk** program are handled by **talkd**. When it receives a request, **talkd** negotiates with the other machine to set up a network connection between the two users who have executed **talk**.

**talk** comes in two flavors: the original (at port 517) and a newer one from 4.3BSD (**ntalk**, at port 518). **ntalk** is not backward compatible and will not accept connections from **talk** clients. Although 4.3BSD was released in 1986, many systems still use the "older" version of talk (15 years later!).

### comsat: notify users of new mail

**comsat** notifies users that new mail has arrived. When it receives an indication that a user has new mail and **/etc/utmp** shows that the user is logged on, **comsat** checks to see whether notifications have been enabled with **biff y**.[6] If so, **comsat** prints the beginning of the mail message on the user's terminal. In modern times, most users access their mail from a PC-based mail client by using IMAP or POP; **comsat** has nothing to do with that procedure.

### sendmail: transport electronic mail

**sendmail**'s tasks include accepting messages from users and remote sites, rewriting addresses, expanding aliases, and transferring mail across the Internet. **sendmail** is

---

6. The official explanation is that **biff** stands for "bark if from found." Biff was actually the name of Heidi Stettner's dog, who always barked when the mailman came.

an important and very complex daemon. Refer to Chapter 19, *Electronic Mail*, for the complete scoop.

### snmpd: provide remote network management service

**snmpd** responds to requests that use the Simple Network Management Protocol (SNMP) protocol. SNMP standardizes some common network management operations. See page 640 for more information about SNMP.

### rwhod: maintain remote user list

**rwhod** is a leftover from "the early days" (the 1980s) and maintains information about the users that are logged in to machines on the network. **rwhod** collects this information for the local machine and broadcasts it; when it receives information from other hosts, it verifies that the information is reasonable and then puts it in the file **/var/spool/rwho/whod.***hostname*, where *hostname* is the name of the host that sent the information. The programs **rwho** and **ruptime** refer to these files.

By default, **rwhod** broadcasts every three minutes, so the information reported by **rwho** and **ruptime** is only approximately correct. **rwhod** is very inefficient, so unless you have network bandwidth to burn and actually use the information, you should turn it off.

### ⓘ ftpd: file transfer server

*See page 696 for more information about **ftpd**.*

**ftpd** is the daemon that handles requests from **ftp**, the Internet file transfer program. Many sites disable it, either because it is a resource hog or because they are worried about security. **ftpd** can be set up to allow anyone to transfer files to and from your machine.

### ⓘ popper: basic mailbox server

The **popper** daemon implements the Post Office Protocol (POP). This protocol is commonly used by non-UNIX systems to receive electronic mail.

### ⓘ imapd: deluxe mailbox server

The **imapd** daemon implements the Internet Mail Access Protocol, IMAP, which is a more festive and featureful alternative to POP. It allows PC-based users (or UNIX users with IMAP-enabled mail readers) to access their email from a variety of locations, with mail folders being stored on the UNIX server. Check out www.imap.org for more information about IMAP.

### ⓘ rlogind: remote login server

**rlogind** is responsible for handling remote logins. When invoked by **inetd**, it tries to automatically authenticate the remote user by examining **/etc/hosts.equiv** and the user's **~/.rhosts** file. If automatic authentication is successful, the user is logged in directly. Otherwise, **rlogind** executes the **login** program to prompt the user for a password. Because of its cheap 'n' easy authentication, **rlogind** is something of a security hazard. See page 660 for more comments on this subject.

Daemons

### ⓘ telnetd: yet another remote login server

**telnetd** is very similar to **rlogind**, except that it uses the TELNET protocol. This protocol allows the two sides (client and server) to negotiate flow control and duplex settings, making it a better choice than **rlogind** for links that are slow or unreliable. Like **rlogin**, **telnet** transmits plaintext passwords across the network. Its use is therefore discouraged in modern networks. Many non-UNIX systems support **telnet**.

### ⓘ sshd: secure remote login server

**sshd** provides services that are similar to **rlogind**, but its sessions are transported (and authenticated) across an encrypted pipeline. A variety of encryption algorithms are available. Because of the harsh environment of the Internet today, you must allow shell access from the Internet *only* through a daemon such as this—*not* **rlogind** or **telnetd**. You can find more information about **sshd** starting on page 672.

### ⓘ rshd: remote command execution server

**rshd** handles remote command execution requests from **rsh**[7] and **rcmd**. The authentication process enforced by **rshd** is similar to that of **rlogind**, except that if automatic authentication does not work, **rshd** denies the request without allowing the user to supply a password. **rshd** is also the server for **rcp** (remote **cp**).

### ⓘ rexecd: yet another command execution server

**rexecd** is similar to **rshd**, except that it does not perform automatic authentication; all requests must be accompanied by a username and a password. This server was used by some early networking programs, but it is no longer in widespread use.

### ⓘ rpc.rexd: yet a third command execution server

**rexd** is the RPC remote execution daemon. It is not used much and is riddled with security holes. You should make sure that **rexd** is commented out of your **inetd** configuration file. **rexd** is used by the **on** command, which will stop working when you disable **rexd**.

### routed: maintain routing tables

**routed** maintains the routing information used by TCP/IP to send and forward packets on a network. **routed** deals only with dynamic routing; routes that are statically defined (that is, wired into the system's routing table with the **route** command) are never modified by **routed**. **routed** is relatively stupid and inefficient, and we recommend its use in only a few specific situations. See page 351 for a more detailed discussion of **routed**.

### gated: maintain complicated routing tables

**gated** understands several routing protocols, including RIP, the protocol used by **routed**. **gated** translates routing information among various protocols and is very

---

7. The **rsh** command is called **remsh** on HP-UX.

configurable. It can also be much kinder to your network than **routed**. See page 352 for more information about **gated**.

### named: DNS server

**named** is the most popular server for the Domain Name System. It maps hostnames into network addresses and performs many other feats and tricks, all using a distributed database maintained by **named**s everywhere. Chapter 16, *The Domain Name System*, describes the care and feeding of **named**.

### syslogd: process log messages

*See page 210 for more information about syslog.*

**syslogd** acts as a clearing house for status information and error messages produced by system software and daemons. Before **syslogd** was written, daemons either wrote their error messages directly to the system console or maintained their own private log files. Now they use the **syslog** library routine to transfer the messages to **syslogd**, which sorts them according to rules established by the system administrator.

### fingerd: look up users

**fingerd** provides information about the users that are logged in to the system. If asked, it can also provide a bit more detail about individual users. **fingerd** does not really do much work itself: it simply accepts lines of input and passes them on to the local **finger** program.

**finger** can return quite a bit of information about a user, including the user's login status, the contents of the user's GECOS field in **/etc/passwd**, and the contents of the user's ~**/.plan** and ~**/.project** files.

If you are connected to the Internet and are running **fingerd**, anyone in the world can obtain this information. **fingerd** has enabled some really neat services (such as the Internet white pages), but it has also enabled people to run a variety of scams, such as finding people to cold-call and prospecting for spammable addresses. Some sites have responded to this invasion by turning off **fingerd**, while others just restrict the amount of information it returns. If you choose to run **fingerd**, you should install a current version; a security hole in older **fingerd**s was exploited by the Internet worm.

### httpd: World Wide Web server

**httpd** lets your site become a web server. **httpd** can send text, pictures, and sound to its clients. See Chapter 22, *Web Hosting and Internet Servers*, for more information about serving up web pages.

## 28.9  TIME SYNCHRONIZATION DAEMONS

As computers have grown increasingly interdependent, it has become more and more important for them share a consistent idea of time. Synchronized clocks are essential for correlating log file entries in the event of a security breach, and they're also important for a variety of end-user applications, from joint development of software projects to the processing of financial transactions.

### timed: synchronize clocks

There are several different time synchronization systems, and more than one time daemon is named **timed**. Most systems use essentially the same scheme. One or more machines are designated as time masters. Their clocks are considered authoritative, and they negotiate with each other to agree on the "correct" time. Other machines are slaves; they periodically converse with a master to learn the time and then adjust their internal clocks.

The time between settings of a slave's clock is short enough that only slight adjustments are usually needed. Slaves use the **adjtime** system call (if it is available) to smooth the adjustment of the system's clock and prevent large time leaps backward or forward.[8] It is especially harmful to set the clock back suddenly; time should be a monotonically increasing function.

The notion of "correct" time is rather nebulously defined. Some systems poll the network to compute an average time, whereas others declare one master correct by fiat.

### xntpd: synchronize clocks even better

**xntpd** is a daemon that uses the Network Time Protocol defined in RFC1119 to synchronize a number of "peer" clocks to within milliseconds of each other. Servers are arranged in a hierarchal tree, each level of which is called a "stratum."

**xntpd** can access a number of reference time standards, such as those provided by WWV and GPS. As a result, **xntpd** provides a much more accurate way to set the clock on your UNIX machine than does **timed**; clocks are not only synchronized but are also accurate within a few milliseconds. You can obtain the current version of **xntp** by anonymous **ftp** from ftp.udel.edu.

## 28.10 BOOTING AND CONFIGURATION DAEMONS

In the 1980s, the UNIX world was swept by a wave of diskless workstation mania. These machines booted entirely over the network and performed all their disk operations through a remote filesystem technology such as NFS. As disk prices dropped and speeds increased, interest in diskless workstations quickly faded. They could come back into fashion at any moment, however, like the platform shoes of the 1970s. The two main remnants of the diskless era are a plethora of daemons designed to support diskless systems and the bizarre organization of most vendors' filesystems.

Although diskless workstations are not very common anymore, their booting protocols have been usurped by other devices. Most manageable network hubs and network printers boot using some combination of the services listed in this section.

---

8. **adjtime** biases the speed of the system's clock so that it gradually falls into correct alignment. When the system time matches the current objective time, the bias is cancelled and the clock runs normally.

### ⓣ bootpd: boot server

When a diskless client is powered on, it broadcasts a BOOTP request on the network. When **bootpd** hears such a request, it looks up the client's Ethernet address in the **/etc/bootptab** file. If it finds an appropriate entry, it responds by telling the client its (the client's) IP address and the file from which it should boot (usually obtained with the TFTP protocol). **bootpd** does not handle the actual transfer of the boot file.

### ⓣ tftpd: trivial file transfer server

**tftpd** implements a file transfer protocol similar to that of **ftpd**, but much, much simpler. Many diskless systems use TFTP to download their kernels from a server. **tftpd** does not perform authentication, but it is normally restricted to serving the files in a single directory (usually **/tftpboot**). Since anything placed in the TFTP directory is accessible to the entire network, it should contain only boot files and should not be publicly writable.

### rarpd: map Ethernet addresses to IP addresses

**rarpd** implements RARP, the Reverse Address Resolution Protocol. This mostly abandoned protocol allows diskless machines to determine their IP addresses at boot time. **rarpd** runs on a server; one copy is generally started at boot time for each network interface that needs RARP support. **rarpd** uses the **/etc/ethers** and **/etc/hosts** files to determine appropriate mappings, so there is no need for a separate configuration file. RARP is a subset of BOOTP, but your hardware will dictate which protocol you must use (possibly both).

### ⓣ bootparamd: advanced diskless life support

**bootparamd** uses the **/etc/bootparams** file to tell diskless clients where to find their filesystems. **bootparamd** service is often used by machines that get their IP addresses by using RARP and that use NFS to mount their filesystems.

### ⓣ dhcpd: dynamic address assignment

The Dynamic Host Configuration Protocol (DHCP) provides PCs, laptops, and other "mobile" platforms with information about their IP address, default gateway, and name server at boot time. **dhcpd** is the daemon that implements this service under UNIX. You can find more information about DCHP on page 287.

# *Colophon*

We produced the first edition of this book with the UNIX **troff** package. For the second edition, we used a Macintosh. We produced this third edition entirely on Microsoft Windows 95, 98, and 2000. Oh, such delight! We'll never touch UNIX again.

We used Adobe FrameMaker for layout, with Adobe Illustrator and Adobe Photoshop for graphics and illustrations. We also used Adobe Acrobat throughout the production process. It allowed us to distribute chapters and graphic files to many different people without worrying about fonts or application compatibility. We delivered the final manuscript as an Acrobat file, too.

Tyler Curtain drew the cartoons using pen and ink. We scanned them on a desktop scanner, cleaned them up in Photoshop, and converted them to PostScript artwork with Adobe Streamline.

The body text is Minion Multiple Master, designed by Robert Slimbach. Headings, tables, and illustrations are set in Myriad Multiple Master by Robert Slimbach and Carol Twombly.

The "code" font is PMN Caecilia, designed by Peter Matthias Noordzij. We searched for a long time for a fixed-width font that looked similar to Courier but lacked Courier's many typesetting problems. We couldn't find one. We finally settled on this proportional font and used tabs to line up columns of output. This approach works pretty well, but Caecilia is missing some of the characters needed for technical typesetting, and its italic version is noticeably slimmer than its roman.

The lack of good fonts for this application represents a sizable hole in an otherwise saturated and commodified typeface market. Type designers take note!

# Index

We have alphabetized files under their last components. And in most cases, *only* the last component is listed. For example, to find index entries relating to the **/etc/passwd** file, look under **passwd**. Our friendly vendors have forced our hand by hiding standard files in new and inventive directories on each system.

# M

# About the Authors

Evi Nemeth is a member of the computer science faculty at the University of Colorado and a part-time researcher at CAIDA, the Cooperative Association for Internet Data Analysis at the San Diego Supercomputer Center. She is about to get out of the UNIX and networking worlds and explore the real world on a sailboat.

evi@cs.colorado.edu

Garth Snyder has worked at NeXT and Sun and holds a degree in Electrical Engineering from Swarthmore College. He is currently a graduate student at the University of Rochester.

garth@cs.colorado.edu

Scott Seebass has worked on UNIX operating systems at a number of locations, including Interactive Systems and mt Xinu. He is currently the CEO of Xinet, a company that develops software for the prepress and premedia industries. Scott received degrees in Computer Science and Statistics from the University of California, Berkeley.

scott@xinet.com

Trent R. Hein is the Chief Technology Officer of XOR Inc., a full-service provider that builds and operates sophisticated eBusiness solutions for Fortune 1000 and dot-com companies. Trent has received a Lifetime Achievement Award from the USENIX Association for his work with UC Berkeley's CSRG, and he holds Cisco's highest technical certification.

trent@xor.com